CONTEMPORARY PLAYS

CONTEMPORARY PLAYS

EDITED BY
THOMAS H. DICKINSON
AND
JACK R. CRAWFORD

WILDSIDE PRESS

CONTEMPORARY PLAYS

Published in 2009 by Wildside Press.
www.wildsidepress.com

CONTENTS

INTRODUCTION v
PAOLO AND FRANCESCA, by Stephen Phillips 1
THE BOYSEY INHERITANCE,
    by Harley Granville-Barker 29
THE CASSILIS ENGAGEMENT, by St. John Hanikin 87
JOHN GLAYDE'S HONOUR, by Alfred Sutro 131
THE MOLLUSC, by Hubert Henry Davies 173
CHAINS, by Elizabeth Baker 209
KINDLING, by Charles Kenyon 245
HINDLE WAKES, by Stanley Houghton 289
RUTHERFORD AND SON, by Githa Sowerby. 329
THE UNCHASTENED WOMAN,
    by Louis Kaufman Anspacher 373
THE CIRCLE, by W. Somerset Maugham. 429
THE HAIRY APE, by Eugene O'Neill 469
MARY THE THIRD, by Rachel Crothers 497
ICEBOUND, by Owen Davis 539
THE ADDING MACHINE, by Elmer L. Rice 575
OLIVER CROMWELL, by John Drinkwater 607

    APPENDICES
  I.   AUTHORS AND PLAYS 639
 II.   NOTES ON THE PRODUCTION OF PLAYS 642
III.   BIBLIOGRPAHY 645
IV.   INDEX OF CHARACTERS 648

INTRODUCTION

THIS book contains sixteen plays from the contemporary drama of England and the United States. The period covered is from the year 1900 through 1923, comprehending approximately a quarter of a century of dramatic development. The publication of a group of plays in such a volume as this presents the reader with a chronological sequence of typical plays, thus offering a bird's-eye view of the period covered by the list. The editors advise those who use this book to add to the study of the plays in this volume the reading of the plays of George Bernard Shaw, Sir James Barrie, John Masefield, John Galsworthy, and of the Irish dramatists. Plays by this particular group of writers were omitted either for external causes or by editorial design. The student is further advised to supplement this survey of English and American plays by a study of the plays somewhat earlier in composition in *Chief Contemporary Dramatists, First and Second Series*. These volumes, taken together and supplemented by the reading indicated, contain ample and adequate materials for a school or college course in contemporary drama in English.

Some aspects of this collection of plays require comment. The first play in this book, Stephen Phillips's *Paolo and Francesca*, dates from the year 1900, although it was composed, at least in part, a year or so earlier; the last play, John Drinkwater's *Oliver Cromwell*, was produced in 1923. Six of the plays in this collection were written during the last eight years. The rapid movement of events in the theater, no less than certain other restrictions, precludes the issue at this time of a definitive selection of the chief plays written in English during the twentieth century. This fact is not one to be regretted. The variety of types and styles represented in this book is an illustration of the experimental period through which dramatic art is now passing, and a proof that the creative spirit of the contemporary stage is alive and vigorous.

The various types of plays reveal, however, certain tendencies in the present-day theater. When Stephen Phillips's plays were first produced, they were hailed by certain critics as a presage of the renascence of the poetic drama. This prophecy was, unfortunately, not fulfilled, in spite of the fact that Stephen Phillips's plays were successful in the theater. He had no immediate followers; he founded no school of poetic drama. Instead of being the first of a new race of dramatists, he was the last of the romantic dramatists of the Victorian age, and it is perhaps appropriate that the drama of the nineteenth century should come to an end in poetry that is delicate and musical.

The freedom to experiment and to express the spirit of revolt characteristic of the contemporary dramatists has been in part fostered by the age itself and in part made possible as dramatic expression by the growth and development of local, experimental theaters. A significant proportion of the plays published in this book had their origin in the provincial and experimental theaters. From such local theaters have come the plays of Drinkwater, Hankin, Houghton, Baker, and Sowerby, to mention only the dramatists here represented. If these theaters in America have hitherto sent forth only their Eugene O'Neill, the reason is to be found in the later rise of local theaters in America — a development delayed in part by the different conditions of our purely commercial theater. The evolution of an experimental theater in America required for its progress a reorganization and a reconstruction from the beginning. Such a development is now well under way. But it is a safe statement to make that no play of any importance has been written in England or America during the last fifteen years that does not carry in its greater freedom of structure and honesty of idea evidence of its indebtedness to the experimental reorganization of the theater.

INTRODUCTION

As between the drama of England and America since 1910 the advantage turns to the American stage. This is largely because the American playwright has accepted more freely his opportunities for experiment and the search for new forms. He has not feared entirely to reject the traditions of the "well-made" play; he has not hesitated to seek influence and inspiration from the revolutionary dramatists of the Continent. Generalizations are, of course, dangerous, but it is safe to say that the English playwright has clung rather more closely to the structural traditions of his art, while the American playwright has attempted to interpret our contemporary life in new forms of theatrical expression.

The plays in this volume reveal a tendency, characteristic of the modern theater, to use the medium of the stage for concrete inquiry into the realities of character and the mysteries of the human mind. Herein lies the explanation for the vogue of character comedy on the one hand and the search for a new form on the other. Comedy is undergoing a change from an artificial and conventionalized type of drama to one more flexible in which human character and motive are more directly revealed. It is yet too early to say what results will follow from those deeper thrusts into the motives of men's minds which the so-called expressionistic dramatists are beginning to make. Here are experiments, however, worth the making, provided they are made with honesty and sincerity of artistic purpose. Two plays of this type have been included in this volume: Eugene O'Neill's *The Hairy Ape* and Elmer Rice's *The Adding Machine*.

It is the policy of the editors to allow the plays in this collection to speak for themselves, leaving the task of interpretation to the reader. Such aids as matters of fact and bibliographical reference may give are provided in the Appendix.

. THE EDITORS

PAOLO AND FRANCESCA
A TRAGEDY IN FOUR ACTS
By STEPHEN PHILLIPS

O Lasso!
Quanti dolci pensier, quanto disto
Menò costoro al doloroso passo
                    DANTE

COPYRIGHT, 1897, 1905, BY DODD, MEAD & COMPANY, INC.

This play was commissioned by Mr. George Alexander, and accepted for production at the St. James's Theatre; meanwhile it is published by his consent, and he retains the entire acting rights

CHARACTERS

GIOVANNI MALATESTA ("LO SCIANCATO"), *Tyrant of Rimini*
PAOLO ("IL BELLO"), *Brother to Giovanni, and Captain of Mercenaries in the service of Florence*
VALENTINO, CORRADO, LUIGI, *Officers of Paolo's Company*
MARCO, *A soldier*
PULCI, *A drug-seller*
FRANCESCA DA RIMINI, *Bride of Giovanni, and daughter of Guido da Polenta, Tyrant of Ravenna*
LUCREZIA DEGL' ONESTI, *cousin to Giovanni*
COSTANZA, *kinswoman to Francesca*
TESSA, *daughter to Pulci*
NITA, *maid to Francesca*
ANGELA, *A blind and aged servant of the Malatesta*
MIRRA, *A peasant girl*

Guests, couriers, soldiers, customers of Pulci, servants, etc.

PAOLO AND FRANCESCA

ACT I

SCENE. — *A gloomy hall in the Malatesta Castle at Rimini, hung with weapons and instruments of the chase;* GUESTS *and* CITIZENS *assembled, with* SOLDIERS, HUNTSMEN, *and* RETAINERS; *hounds held in leash. As the scene opens, a trumpet is blown outside.*

[*Enter* GIOVANNI *hurriedly down a gallery to the hall, with papers in his hands. He pauses on the steps.*]

GIO. Peace to this house of Rimini henceforth!
Kinsmen, although the Ghibelline is fallen
And lies out on the plains of Trentola,
Still have we foes untrampled, wavering friends.
Therefore, on victory to set a seal,
To-day I take to wife Ravenna's child,
Daughter of great Polenta, our ally;
Between us an indissoluble bond.
Deep in affairs my brother I despatched,
My Paolo — who is indeed myself —
For scarcely have we breathed a separate thought —
To bring her on the road to Rimini.
[*A noise of falling chains is heard.*]
I hear them at the gates; the chains have fallen.

[*The doors at end of gallery are thrown open. Enter out of sunlight* PAOLO, *leading* FRANCESCA *by the hand, followed by* LADIES *and* SQUIRES. *Flowers are thrown over them.* FRANCESCA *bends low to* GIOVANNI, *who raises her up.*]

Rise up, Francesca, and unveil your face.
[*He kisses her on the forehead.*]
Kinsmen, and you that follow with my bride,
You see me beat with many blows, death-pale,
With gushing of much blood, and deaf with war —
You see me, and I languish for a calm.
I ask no great thing of the skies; I ask
Henceforth a quiet breathing, that this child,
Hither all dewy from her convent fetched,
Shall lead me gently down the slant of life.
Here then I sheathe my sword; and fierce must be
That quarrel where again I use the steel.
[*A murmur of approbation. He turns to* FRANCESCA.]
Tell me, Francesca; can you be content
To live the quiet life which I propose?
Where, though you miss the violent joys of youth,
Yet will I cherish you more carefully
Than might a younger lover of your years.
  FRANC. My lord, my father gave me to you: I
Am innocent as yet of this great life;
My only care to attend the holy bell,
To sing and to embroider curiously:
And as through glass I view the windy world.
Sweet is the stillness you ensure to me
Whose days have been so still: and yet I fear
To be found wanting in so great a house:
I lack experience in such governing.
So if at any time I seem to offend you,
Will you impute it to my youth! But I
Shall never fail in duty willingly.
  GIO. I like that coldness in you, my Francesca,
And to my cousin I will make you known.
Widowed and childless, she has ruled till now
This fort of soldiers, a rough hostelry,
Which henceforth is your home; since I remember

She was my friend: has often cooled a
    rashness,
Which I inherit: lean at first on her.
  Luc. Francesca, as your husband says,
    we two
Have long been friends; but friendship
    faints in love,
And since through inexperience you may
    err,
My place is near you; to advise and guide
Suits with my years.
  Costanza. O Lord of Rimini!
With sighs we leave her as we leave a child.
Be tender with her, even as God hath been!
She hath but wondered up at the white
    clouds;
Hath just spread out her hands to the
    warm sun;
Hath heard but gentle words and cloister
    sounds.   [Giovanni *bows to her.*]
  Gio. Friends, you will go with us to
    church; till then
Walk where you please — yet one word
    more — be sure
That, though I sheathe the sword, I am not
    tamed.
What I have snared, in that I set my teeth
And lose with agony; when hath the prey
Writhed from our mastiff-fangs?
  Luc. Giovanni, loose
Francesca's hands — the tears are in her
    eyes.
  Gio. Well, well, till church-time then.
    Paolo, stay!
      [*Exeunt* Lucrezia, Guests, *and*
       Retainers; Nita *and attendant*
       Ladies *remaining in the background.*
       Giovanni, Paolo, *and* Francesca
       come down.]
These delegates from Pesaro, Francesca,
Expect my swift decision on the tax.
Then will you think me negligent or cold
If to my brother I confide you still,
A moment — and no more?
                              [*Exit* Giovanni.]
  Franc. O, Paolo,
Who were they that have lived within
    these walls?
  Pao. Why do you ask?
  Franc. It is not sign nor sound;
Only it seemeth difficult to breathe,
It is as though I battled with this air.

  Pao. You are not sad?
  Franc. What is it to be sad?
Nothing hath grieved me yet but ancient
    woes,
Sea-perils, or some long-ago farewell,
Or the last sunset cry of wounded kings.
I have wept but on the pages of a book,
And I have longed for sorrow of my own.
  Pao. Come nothing nearer than such
    far-off tears
Or peril from the pages of a book;
And, therefore, sister, am I glad that you
Are wedded unto one so full of shelter.
Constant is he, and steel-true till the grave.
For me — to-night I must be gone.
  Franc. To-night!
Ah, Paolo, go not away so soon!
You brought me hither — leave me not at
    once,
Not now —
  Pao. Francesca!
  Franc. I am still a child.
I feel that to my husband I could go
Kiss him good-night, or sing him to his
    sleep,
And there an end.
  Pao. Sister, I would that I —
  Franc. Can we not play together a
    brief while?
Stay, then, a little! Soon I shall be used
To my grave place and duty — but not yet.
Stay, then, a little!
  Pao. Here my brother comes.

              [*Enter* Giovanni.]

  Gio. Stand either side of me — you
    whom I love.
I'd have you two as dear now to each other
As both of you to me. We are, Francesca,
A something more than brothers — fiercest
    friends;
Concordia was our mother named, and ours
Is but one heart, one honour, and one death.
Any that came between us I would kill.
  Franc. Sir, I will love him: is he not my
    brother?
      [Nita *advances, with attendant*
       Ladies.]
  Nita. My lady, it draws late.
  Gio. Go with her, child.
            [*Exeunt* Francesca, Nita *and*
             Ladies.]

Gio. [to Paolo]. You have set a new
    seal on an ancient love,
Bringing this bride.
    Pao. And having brought her, here
My office ends. I'll say farewell to-night.
    Gio. This very night!
    Pao. I'll go with you to church;
But from the after-feast I ask excuse.
    Gio. I do not understand.
    Pao. Brother, believe
I do not hasten thus without deep cause.
    Gio. Is there such haste indeed?
    Pao. Such haste indeed!
    Gio. [taking his hand]. Come, Paolo,
    we two have never held
A mystery between us — tell me out!
Harsh am I, but to you was ever gentle.
What is the special reason of your going?
    Pao. The troop for Florence which I
    mustered here
Should spur at daybreak.
    Gio. There is no such haste.
What are you holding from me?
    Pao. Ah, enough!
    Gio. What sudden face hath made this
    hall so dark?
Come, then, 'tis natural — walk to and
    fro
And tell me — ah! some lady you beheld
There at Ravenna in Francesca's train!
Was it not so?
    Pao. Urge me no more to words.
    Gio. What woman draws you thus away
    from me?
    Pao. No woman, brother, draws me
    from this house.
    Gio. You like not then my marriage! —
    but indeed,
No marriage can dissolve the bond between
    us.
Here you are free as ever in the house —
Once more, what is the reason of your
    going?
    Pao. Brother, 'tis nothing that hath
    chanced, but rather
That which may chance if here I am detained.
    Gio. Darker and yet more dark. Now
    speak it out.
    Pao. I cannot.
    Gio. Paolo, this is an ill
Beginning of my marriage, and I loathe
That you should put me off. We three, I
    thought —
We three together — tempt me not to rage!
And as your elder I command your stay,
Your presence both at church and at the
    feast.
You would affront Francesca publicly?
    Pao. Giovanni, 'tis enough, I stay. Forgive me.
    Gio. Brother, this is our first and last
    dispute.
Now leave me to these papers. [Paolo is
    going.] Paolo,
You go with me heart-whole into this
    marriage?
Give me your hand again!
    Pao. There is my hand.
        [Exit Paolo. Giovanni unfolds
        papers and reads.]
    Gio. "In Pesaro sedition! Andrea
    Sarti
Is urgent" —

[Enter Lucrezia. She touches him on the
    arm.]

    Luc. Pardon me — you sit alone.
While there is time, I have stolen in on you
To speak my dearest wishes for this
    marriage,
And in a manner, too, old friend, farewell.
    Gio. Farewell?
    Luc. And in a manner 'tis farewell.
    Gio. This marriage is political.
    Luc. No more?
    Gio. And yet since I have seen Francesca, I
Have fallen into a trance. It seems, indeed,
That I am bringing into this dark air
A pureness that shall purge these ancient
    halls.
    Luc. Watch, then, this pureness: fend it
    fearfully.
    Gio. I took her dreaming from her convent trees.
    Luc. And for that reason tremble at her
    more!
Old friend, remember that we two are
    passed
Into the grey of life: but O, beware
This child scarce yet awake upon the
    world!

Dread her first ecstasy, if one should come
That should appear to her half-opened
    eyes
Wonderful as a prince from fairyland
Or venturing through forests toward her
    face —
No — do not stride about the room —
    your limp
Is evident the more — come, sit by me
As you were wont to sit. Youth goes to-
    ward youth.
    Gio. What peril can be here? In Rim-
    ini?
    Luc. I have but said and say, "Youth
    goes toward youth,"
And she shall never prize, as I do still,
Your savage courage and deliberate force,
Even your mounded back and sullen gait.
    Gio. Lucrezia! this is that old bitter-
    ness.
    Luc. Bitterness — am I bitter? Strange,
    O strange!
How else? My husband dead and child-
    less left,
My thwarted woman-thoughts have in-
    ward turned,
And that vain milk like acid in me eats.
Have I not in my thought trained little feet
To venture, and taught little lips to move
Until they shaped the wonder of a word?
I am long practised. O those children,
    mine!
Mine, doubly mine: and yet I cannot
    touch them,
I cannot see them, hear them — Does
    great God
Expect I shall clasp air and kiss the wind
For ever? And the budding cometh on,
The burgeoning, the cruel flowering:
At night the quickening splash of rain, at
    dawn
That muffled call of babes how like to
    birds;
And I amid these sights and sounds must
    starve —
I, with so much to give, perish of thrift!
Omitted by His casual dew!
    Gio. Well, well,
You are spared much: children can wring
    the heart.
    Luc. Spared! to be spared what I was
    born to have!
I am a woman, and this very flesh
Demands its natural pangs, its rightful
    throes,
And I implore with vehemence these pains.
I know that children wound us, and sur-
    prise
Even to utter death, till we at last
Turn from a face to flowers: but this my
    heart
Was ready for these pangs, and had fore-
    seen.
O! but I grudge the mother her last look
Upon the coffined form — that pang is
    rich —
Envy the shivering cry when gravel falls.
And all these maiméd wants and thwarted
    thoughts,
Eternal yearning, answered by the wind,
Have dried in me belief and love and fear.
I am become a danger and a menace,
A wandering fire, a disappointed force,
A peril — do you hear, Giovanni? — O!
It is such souls as mine that go to swell
The childless cavern cry of the barren sea,
Or make that human ending to night-wind.
Why have I bared myself to you? — I know
    not,
Unless, indeed, this marriage — yes, this
    marriage —
Near now, is't not? — So near made me
    cry out.
Ah! she will bring a sound of pattering feet!
But now this message — and those papers. I
Must haste to see the banquet-table
    spread —
Your bride is yet so young.
                      [*Exit* Lucrezia.]
    Gio. [*reads*]. "Antonio
And Conti urge it is impolitic
To lay another load" — Youth goes
    toward youth! —
"On murmuring Pesaro" — in Rimini! —
"Foresee revolt." Here in the house all's
    safe.
[*Enter* Servant, *leading in blind* Angela.]
    Ser. My Lord, blind Angela entreats
    that she
Once more may touch you ere you go to
    church.
    Gio. Give me your hand, old nurse.
[*He kneels*.] Will you not bless me?

You will not? And your tears fall down
  on me?
ANG. My son, for are you not my very
  son?
I gave you milk: from me you sucked in
  life,
And still my breast is thrilling from your
  lips.
GIO. Well, well, then!
ANG. So that now my very flesh
Must quail at the approach of woe to you.
GIO. The drops stand on your forehead!
  What is this?
ANG. I never trembled for you till this
  hour.
GIO. What is it that you fear?
  [*He kisses her hand.*]
ANG. Now your lips touch
And I begin to feel more surely, child.
Ah! but a juice too pure hath now been
  poured
In a dark ancient wine: and the cup seethes.
GIO. Speak clearer to me.
ANG. Closer lay your head.
Ne'er in the battle have I feared for you.
What is the strange, soft thing which you
  have brought
Into our life?
GIO. Francesca, do you mean?
Why do you clutch my arm? What is't
  you see?
ANG. A kind of twilight struggles
  through my dark.
Be near me! Soon it seems that I shall
  know.
GIO. Upon what scene are those blind
  eyes so fixed?
ANG. A place of leaves: and ah! how still
  it is!
She sits alone amid great roses.
GIO. She?
ANG. Who is he that steals in upon your
  bride?
GIO. Angela!
ANG. And no sound in all the world!
GIO. What doth he there?
ANG. He reads out of a book.
There comes a murmuring as of far-off
  things.
Nearer he drew and kissed her on the lips.
GIO. His face, mother, his face?
ANG. 'Tis dark again.

GIO. His face? that I may know him
  when we meet.
ANG. His face was dim: a twilight
  struggles back.
I see two lying dead upon a bier —
Slain suddenly, and in each other's arms.
GIO. Are they those two that in the
  roses kissed?
ANG. Those two!
GIO. Then quickly tell me of him!
ANG. Ah!
Again 'tis dark. The twilight, as it
  seemed,
With difficulty came, and might not stay.
My son, art thou still here?
GIO. Why do your lips
Move fast and yet no words find out their
  way?
What are they vainly shaping?
ANG. Who hath now
Ta'en hold on me?
GIO. Speak, speak, then!
ANG. He shall be
Not far to seek: yet perilous to find.
Unwillingly he comes a wooing: she
Unwillingly is wooed: yet shall they woo.
His kiss was on her lips ere she was born.
GIO. Who used thy mouth then, and so
  strangely spoke?
O, this is folly! Yet it weighs me down.
  [*Trumpets are heard.*]
ANG. What is that sound?
GIO. My marriage trumpets!
ANG. Here
Still let me sit, and hear the folk pass by.
[*Enter from one side* KINSMEN *and* RETAIN-
  ERS, PAOLO *at their head.* GIOVANNI
  *joins him, putting his arm round his
  neck.*]
GIO. Paolo, shall we walk together still?
  [*Exit marriage procession of* KINS-
  MEN, *etc., led by* GIOVANNI *and*
  PAOLO. *Meanwhile enter from the
  other side* FRANCESCA, LUCREZIA,
  and attendant LADIES. FRANCESCA,
  *in passing, pauses and offers trinket
  to* ANGELA, *who shudders, letting it
  fall. Exeunt all but* ANGELA, *who
  remains staring before her.*]

CURTAIN

ACT II

Scene I. *A Hall in the Palace*

A week elapses between Acts I and II

[Giovanni *seated with papers;* Paolo, *in armour, pacing up and down.*]

Gio. You chafe to go?
Pao. I languish for the road,
The open road, and chime of mailéd feet.
Gio. And still I marvel at such anxious haste.
Pao. My troop is mustered now: six miles from hence
I take command for Florence.
Gio. Well, I'll urge
Your stay no more; yet I suspect no less.
Pao. What?
Gio. That no soldier-business lures you hence.
Pao. Brother, again!
Gio. I'll laugh at you no more.
   [*He rises and speaks slowly.*]
I have a deeper cause to wish your stay
Than when I urged it last.
Pao. A deeper cause?
Gio. I have been warned of peril to Francesca.
Pao. Peril!
Gio. Blind Angela in vision saw
One stealing in upon my wife to woo her.
Ah! you, too, start! I am not then the fool
I call myself to be so burdened down —
You too it touches.
Pao. 'Twas a moment's fear.
Gio. [*taking his hand*]. Such sympathy is ours so close are we,
That what I suffer you straightway must feel.
Pao. What manner, then, of man was he that wooed?
Gio. Ah, there! his face was dim. O, Paolo!
If but a moment I could see it clear,
Look in his eyes as into yours, and know.
Well, this is folly! — can be reasoned off —
And yet it troubles me. Now since I must
Surely be absent on affairs, I could
More easily Francesca leave behind
If you were by her side.
   Pao. If I?

Gio. And whom
Than my own brother could I better leave?
Pao. Ah, brother, such a charge I cannot well
Support. If this thing happened by some chance,
I in the house, you absent — 'tis a duty
I would not willingly take up.
Gio. See how
You cool to me.
Pao. Set me to any service;
Despatch me into peril — ask my life.
I'll give away my being and breath for you.
Giovanni, you doubt not, you cannot doubt,
My love?
Gio. I must not, else I should go mad,
So dear you are to me.
Pao. And he, this wooer,
If he should wrong Francesca any way
My dagger to his heart were swift as yours.
Gio. I know that well.

   [*Enter* Francesca.]

Francesca, whence come you?
Franc. From fostering garden flowers.
Gio. Paolo
Is set on going. I have urged, implored —
He has no answer, only he will go.

   [*Enter a* Servant *hurriedly.*]

Ser. A courier, sir, spurred out of Pesaro!
Gio. So I expected! I will come to him.
   [*Exit* Giovanni *hurriedly and* Servant.]
Franc. [*to* Paolo]. Will you not stay?
My husband wishes it —
My husband and your brother — so he speaks
Twice with each word.
Pao. My brother and myself
Have spoken of this, and yet you see I go.
Franc. If for his sake you will not stay, perhaps
Even for mine you will a little linger.
All here are kind to me, all grave and kind,
But O, I have a fluttering up toward joy,
Lightness and laughter, and a need of singing.
You are more near my age — you understand.

Where are you vulnerable, Paolo?
You are so cased in steel — is't here? or
    here?
Lay that sad armour by — that steel
    cuirass.
See then! I will unloose it with my hands.
I cannot loose it — there's some trick es-
    capes me.
  PAO. Francesca, think not I can lightly
    leave you
And go out from your face into the dark.
Ah! can you think it is not sweet to breathe
That delicate air and flowery sigh of you,
The stealing May and mystery of your
    spirit?
Am I not flesh and blood? — am I not
    young?
Is it easy, then, for youth to run from
    youth?
And yet from you I run. Or are we swift
To fly delight? — And yet from you I fly.
What shall I say?
  FRANC. Sweet are your words, but dark.
Is beauty to be dreaded, then, and shunned?
  PAO. How shall I tell you and sow in you
    thoughts
Which are not there as yet?
        [He moves to go.]
  FRANC. And you will go?
Will you not say farewell? Will you not
    kiss
My hand at least? Why do you tremble,
    then?
Is even the touch of me so full of peril?
  PAO. O! of immortal peril!
  FRANC. But how strange!
You dread this little hand? O, wonderful!
Your face is white, and yet you have killed
    men!
  PAO. Francesca!
  FRANC. Do you fear to look in my eyes,
You so ensteeled and clanging in your
    stride?
And you could crush my life out with your
    hand.
O, this new peril that I have about me!
  PAO. Child!
  FRANC. And this woe that comes from
    me to men!
And I can stay your going, can I not?
Look up! and with a smile I'll bind you
    fast.

  PAO. Sister, I suffer! now at last fare-
    well!
        [Exit PAOLO, tearing himself away.]
  FRANC. [running to a mirror]. Where is
    the glass? O, face unknown and
    strange!
Slight face, and yet the cause of woe to men!
        [Enter NITA.]
Nita, did any pass you on the stair?
  NITA. Lord Paolo came by me, all in
    steel.
  FRANC. Nita, he trembled to look up
    at me!
And when I nearer came all pale he grew.
And when I smiled he suffered, as it
    seemed;
And then I smiled again: for it was strange.
Is't wicked such sweet cruelty to use?
O! and that bluer blue — that greener
    green!
  NITA. My Lady, there's no help. And
    for my sake
Tall men have fought and lost bright blood
    for me.   [She looks in the glass.]
We cannot choose; our faces madden men!
  FRANC. And yet, Nita, and yet — can
    any tell
How sorrow first doth come? Is there a
    step,
A light step, or a dreamy drip of oars?
Is there a stirring of leaves, or ruffle of
    wings?
For it seems to me that softly, without
    hand,
Surely she touches me.
  NITA. O, such as you
Are from their birth uplifted above sorrow.
  FRANC. But am I? am I? Has he left
    the house?
How far, then, hath he gone by now —
    how far?
Surely 'tis natural to desire him back —
Most natural — is it not most natural?
    — Say!
And yet — my heart is wild —
  NITA. He is, my Lady,
Your husband's brother.
  FRANC. O, I had not thought!
I had not thought! I have sinned, and I
    am stained!   [She weeps.]
  NITA. Lady, you have done nothing.

[*Enter* GIOVANNI, *with* ATTENDANTS; LUCREZIA, *with* LADIES, *to whom she gives directions apart.* GIOVANNI *comes down to* FRANCESCA.]

GIO. Could you not
Prevail on him to stay? — he will return.
How beautiful you seem, Francesca, now,
As though new-risen with the bloom of dreams!
More difficult it grows to leave your side.
I, like a miser, run my fingers through
Your hair: yet tears are lately in your eyes!
What little grief perplexes you, my child?
 FRANC. I cannot tell, but suffer me to seek
The Lady Mother of the convent.
 GIO. Yet
You shall not stir alone. I have a fear.
[*To* ATTENDANTS.] Follow your mistress, and escort her back.
 [*Exit* FRANCESCA, NITA *and escort.* LUCREZIA *dismisses* LADIES *and comes down to* GIOVANNI.]
 GIO. [*looking after* FRANCESCA]. The peril, ah! the peril!
 LUC. What is this?
 GIO. Sit, then, and listen. You first sowed in me
The apprehension of Francesca's youth.
 LUC. O, I but said —
 GIO. Listen! That very hour
Blind Angela, that held me at her breast,
Whose very flesh anticipates my fate,
I found all shivering like a creature dumb.
She clutched my arm, and then, as from the touch,
There came a kind of twilight in her dark,
And in that twilight with blind eyes she saw
One stealing in upon my wife to woo her.
 LUC. Ah!
 GIO. In a place of leaves they sat and read.
Nearer he drew, and kissed her on the lips.
Again into her dark the twilight came,
And they two lay together on a bier,
Slain ere they knew, and in each other's arms.
These images have so enthralled my brain
I have lived since then in fever.
 LUC. But this shadow
That wooed Francesca, and then died with her,
Was nothing more discerned?
 GIO. The face was dim.
 LUC. But could she give no hint of form or voice?
 GIO. I cried — "How shall I know him?" — Then her lips,
After a frantic striving, shaped these words —
"Unwillingly he comes a wooing; she
Unwillingly is wooed: yet shall they woo."
 LUC. Unwillingly! This, as it seems, would point —
 GIO. [*starting to his feet*]. Ah! does the scent come to you? Set me on!
 LUC. [*slowly*]. To one who had dear reason not to woo —
To one who owed you much — some ancient friend!
 GIO. Fainter again! I know of no such man.
Hark back.
 LUC. Said she no more, then?
 GIO. "He shall be
Not far to seek, yet perilous to find!"
 [LUCREZIA *starts.*]
What, does the scent come stronger now? You start,
And your eyes glitter —
 LUC. [*going slowly to him and laying her hand on his shoulder*]. Let us hunt this trail!
And yet you will mislike whither it leads.
 GIO. Nothing can hold me now.
 LUC. "Not far to seek"
Points back to Rimini, this little town,
To one, perhaps, mad for Francesca's face,
That lurks about us.
 GIO. Wary now, yet swift!
 LUC. Here at our gates, or nearer still.
 GIO. Say, say!
 LUC. Perhaps, perhaps, within this very house.
 GIO. O barren restless woman, at what sight
Do you give cry at last?
 LUC. [*looking into his eyes*]. Are you still eager?
 GIO. I shut my eyes and I run into it.
 LUC. [*starting back*]. That crouch as of a beast about to spring!

I dare not, will not, speak till you are
    calm.
  Gio. I am calm [*bending his sword across
    his knee*]. This steel is true that I
    can bend it
Into a hoop!
  Luc. O, then, if it should be
One that had risen, eaten and drunk with
    you,
Whose hand was daily in your own!
  Gio. Is it? —
  Luc. Giovanni! who shall set a shore to
    love?
When hath it ever swerved from death, or
    when .
Hath it not burned away all barriers,
Even dearest ties of mother and of son,
Even of brothers? —
  Gio. [*seizing her arm*]. Is it Paolo?
  Luc. You stop the blood in my arm; re-
    lease your hold.
  Gio. [*slowly releasing her arm*]. Ah,
    gradual nature! let this thought
    come slow!
Accustom me by merciful degrees
To this idea, which henceforth is my home:
I am strong — yet cannot in one moment
    think it.
  Luc. [*softly*]. You speak as in a trance.
  Gio. Bring me not back!
Like one that walks in sleep, if suddenly
I wake, I die. [*With a cry.*] Paolo! Paolo!
  Luc. Giovanni!
  Gio. Paolo! ah, no, not there!
Not there, where only I was prone to love!
Beautiful wast thou in the battle, boy!
We came from the same womb, and we
    have slept
Together in the moonbeams! I have
    grown
So close to him, my very flesh doth tear!
Why, why, Lucrezia, I have lifted him
Over rough places — he was but a child,
A child that put his hand in mine! I reel —
My little Paolo!   [*He swoons off.*]
  Luc. Help, help! Ah, no!
I must not call — the foam is on his lips,
The veins outstand — and yet I have a
    joy,
A bitter joy! I'll lay his head down here.
    [*She raises his face, and looks into
    it.*]

Thou wast so rich — now thou art poor as
    I!
His eyes unclose! Master thyself!
  Gio. [*slowly opening his eyes*]. At last!
As to a soul new-come the murk of hell
Grows more accustomed, gradually light,
So I begin to see amid this gloom.
Let me explore the place and walk in it!
    [*He rises slowly to his feet.*]
We must live on, Lucrezia — we must still
Pace slowly on, and set our teeth until
Relief is sent.
  Luc. Can you stand now, Giovanni?
  Gio. You are my friend, my solitary
    friend!
  Luc. Am I not lone as you are, without
    ties?
Childless and husbandless, yet bitter-true!
  Gio. Be with me still — if Paolo it is!
Henceforward let no woman bear two sons.
Yet, wherefore should he go?
  Luc. He feared, perhaps.
  Gio. He too, then, feared — and went.
  Luc. Now he is gone,
There's breathing time at least.
  Gio. Can I not bind
Her beauty fast o'er which I 'gin to yearn?
Are there not drugs to charm the hearts of
    women?
  Luc. Put her to sleep, and so ensure her
    faith —
Yet, then, she'll dream.
  Gio. If Paolo it is!
  Luc. Lean upon me, Giovanni; you are
    weak.   [*Exeunt both, slowly.*]

Scene II. — *A Wayside Inn out of Rimini.*

*View of Rimini in distance, towers flushed
    with sunset.*

[*Enter* Marco *and other* Soldiers, Mirra
    and other Girls, *a* Sergeant.]

  A Soldier. What! Are we all to say
good-bye here, then?
  A Girl. We can come no further out of
Rimini.
  Another Soldier. We must all have a
kiss before we go.
  Another Girl. Ah! you are ready to
kiss us, and you are ready to go.
  Soldier. That is the soldier's life.

GIRL. To love and go away? Yes, we know you.

MAR. To love and go, and love again, to fight and love again, and go — a good life, too.

A GIRL. Listen to him! He tells us he will love some one else. Well, we have all had a merry time.

MAR. So we have; but the world is large. Little Mirra here is not the first or the last.
[*They laugh.*]

A SOLDIER. One last cup of wine all round.

MAR. Come, Mirra, we'll drink together out of this cup. Here's your health, sweetheart, and many other lovers to you.

A GIRL. Ah! he knows life is short. Isn't he a pretty fellow?

MAR. [*Sings.*]

O I love not, I, the long road and the march,
With the chink, chink, chinking, and the parch.
But I love the little town that springs in sight
At the falling of the day, with many a light.
    It is sweet! it is sweet —
      (Chorus)   Ha, ha! Ha, ha!

To clatter down the pebbly street,
When the taverns all are humming;
And the lads in front are drumming,
And the windows fill with girls,
All laughing, and all shaking down their curls.
      (Chorus)   Ha, ha! Ha, ha!

Then your armour's all unlaced,
And your arm is round a waist:
And she seems so much afraid,
You could swear she was a maid —

SERGEANT [*interrupting*]. Come, lads, give the girls the slip: your duty! We must start again.

MIR. [*clinging to* MARCO]. You will come back again, won't you, Marco?

MAR. May and may not, Mirra. Who can tell?

MIR. Because — because —

A GIRL. Look at her — she's crying! Why, he was only playing with you.

MIR. I know, I know.

A GIRL. And they say his play has ended in some earnest.

ANOTHER GIRL. Well, what then? Fools must go their own way.

MAR. Good-bye, girls: we have had a merry time.

GIRLS. Good-bye, good-bye!
[*All exeunt.*]

[*Enter* CORRADO, VALENTINO, LUIGI *and* PAOLO.]

COR. Here's an inn — the first since Rimini. Bring us some wine.

PAO. How straight the road is from here to Rimini! One can see the town at the end.

VAL. Yes, and your brother's castle. [*Enter* LANDLORD *with wine.*] Come, Lord Paolo, some wine. Why so dull?

PAO. It is that old wound pains me.

COR. [*drinking*]. Come, lad, out with it! Is it a debt or a wench? Let me talk with him. [*Goes over to* PAOLO.] I can advise you, Paolo. I have loved more, owed more, drunk more, and lived more. Confess to me!

LUI. Who would not to so easy a priest?

VAL. [*to* CORRADO]. Still staring down the road.

COR. [*whispering*]. I have it, then.

VAL. Corrado says that when a man sits down outside an inn and refuses wine, and stares back along the road he came, he is in love.

COR. Didn't you observe one of those girls as we passed them, crying? Shame, Paolo! and in your own town, too!

LUI. He doesn't hear us.

COR. Well, here's a health to her, whoever she is! Now, Paolo, let me speak to you. I have myself so often felt this — give me a word.

VAL. Pang!

COR. Pang — yes, pang!

LUI. So often?

COR. More times than I can count. Why, man, I have thriven on pangs. There was the landlord's wife at Ancona; there was the little black-eyed girl out of Florence. To look at me, you would scarcely suppose that I have left half the cities of Italy sighing behind me. I have suffered, and I have inflicted. There was —

LUI. O, Corrado! Not these old stories.

COR. Well, the fruit of all this! You must know that love is a thing physical.

It can be sweated out of a man by hard riding; it evaporates from the body like any humour.

VAL. Ha! ha!

COR. My advice is this — fill up, drink, and get to fighting quickly; and if, after a bottle or so, you have taken a girl on your knee in the twilight — Why Paolo! consider you have left behind you, perhaps, another soldier for your brother's wars. You have done a brotherly act, and —

PAO. [*rising*]. Corrado, we have been fast comrades, and I think you know me; but another word of this and there will be an end of talk between us — you understand?

COR. O! ho!

VAL. I tell you — you see, it is one of those serious matters, where the spirit is more concerned than the flesh. Come, Paolo, let us have it!

COR. Before he begins, I think it would be more fitting if we uncovered our heads, for the recitation is likely to be solemn.

LUI. Come, come, we must be going!

COR. God send us another inn soon.

[*Exeunt* CORRADO *and* VALENTINO.]

LUI. Give me your hand, Paolo — you know me. Tell me the trouble.

PAO. I cannot, Luigi.

LUI. Have you fallen out with your brother? You and he were such friends.

PAO. No.

LUI. Is it the young wife that he has married, and now he seems more cold to you? But this is natural at first. How can I help you?

PAO. No one can help me, Luigi.

LUI. Up, and lead us on, then!

PAO. I will catch you in a moment.

LUI. I am very sorry, Paolo.

[*Exit* LUIGI.]

PAO. I have fled from her; have refused the rose,
Although my brain was reeling at the scent.
I have come hither as through pains of death;
I have died, and I am gazing back at life.
Yet now it were so easy to return,
And run down the white road to Rimini!
And might I not return? [*He starts up and looks at the towers, red with sunset.*]
Those battlements
Are burning! they catch fire, those parapets!
And through the blaze doth her white face look out
Like one forgot, yet possible to save.
Might I not then return? Ah, no! no! no!
For I should tremble to be touched by her,
And dread the music of her mere goodnight.
Howe'er I sentinelled my bosom, yet
That moment would arrive when instantly
Our souls would flash together in one flame,
And I should pour this torrent in her ear
And suddenly catch her to my heart.

[*A drum is heard.*]

A drum!
O, there is still a world of men for a man!
I'll lose her face in flashing brands, her voice
In charging cries: I'll rush into the war!

[SOLDIERS *pass across the stage. Seeing* PAOLO, *they cheer and call him by name — then exeunt. He makes to follow, then stops.*]

I cannot go; thrilling from Rimini,
A tender voice makes all the trumpets mute.
I cannot go from her: may not return.
O God! what is Thy will upon me? Ah!
One path there is, a straight path to the dark.
There, in the ground, I can betray no more,
And there for ever am I pure and cold.
The means! No dagger blow, nor violence shown
Upon my body to distress her eyes.
Under some potion gently will I die;
And they that find me dead shall lay me down
Beautiful as a sleeper at her feet.

CURTAIN

ACT III

SCENE I. — *The shop of* PULCI, *late evening. The walls and ceiling are hung with skins, sharks' teeth, crucibles, wax figures, crystals, charms, etc. A counter, at which* TESSA *stands. As the scene opens figures are seen leaving the shop. Three* PEASANT GIRLS *and a* LADY'S MAID *remain.*

TESSA. I must ask you to choose quickly. It is past the hour for closing the shop.

FIRST GIRL. And will this syrup keep Antonio faithful?

TESSA. Two drops of this in anything he drinks, given every seven days, and he will have no eyes but for you.

FIRST GIRL. But will it keep his thoughts true while I am away?

TESSA. Wherever he may be his thoughts will be for you.

FIRST GIRL. Ah, but you don't know Antonio. He is so easily led off — any face if it is fresh — any fool with bright eyes.

TESSA. These drops will keep even Antonio faithful.

FIRST GIRL. I'll take it, then: it must be a wonderful syrup. [*Exit* FIRST GIRL.]

TESSA [*to* MAID]. And you?

MAID. I wondered how long I was to be made to wait for these common chattering wenches. I want another packet of that face-bloom for my mistress, and a darker shade. The other makes her appear hectic.

TESSA. This, then, has a darker tinge.

MAID. And you are to tell your father that the dye he sent withers her hair. He must add more oil.

TESSA. I will tell him. Good-night.

MAID. Good-night to you. [*Exit* MAID.]

SECOND GIRL [*holding out charm*]. What is this charm?

TESSA. It will ensure you against ague, fever, or infection, and not only this, but against peril of any kind. It is worn round the neck, and at the approach of danger it will tremble and give you a sign.

SECOND GIRL. O, I must have that. Will this money be enough to-day if I bring the rest next week?

TESSA. If the charm is not paid for soon it will lose its power. Take it, and remember. [*Exit* SECOND GIRL.] Now you — quickly, please — what do you want?

THIRD GIRL. I want a cure for love. Are they very expensive?

TESSA. We have some that will cure of love in a few hours; but these will cost you a great deal.

THIRD GIRL. It is terrible not to be able to sleep at nights.

TESSA. Here is one that will bring you back sleep, and cure you entirely in a few weeks — one that you could afford.

THIRD GIRL. I don't think I want to be cured entirely — and yet one never knows what one may come to when it grows late and there is music and dancing. It is hard to resist under the moon.

TESSA. Come, now — will you take it?

THIRD GIRL [*taking phial*]. I think I'll have it, and take it very slowly.

TESSA. There, then!

THIRD GIRL. There's money saved for six weeks. Ah, well!

[*Exit* THIRD GIRL. TESSA, *after barring up door, goes to glass.*]

TESSA. Now I can play for a while. [*She puts some bloom on her face.*] O, but this bloom is beautiful! And how it makes one's eyes sparkle! Now this red salve for the lips — that is just what I lacked. My lips are too pale — but now! Where is that pencil? Here. Shall I lengthen my eyebrows, curving them so? No: I will only deepen them. There, then! [*She walks up and down before a glass, then sits dejectedly.*] Yet what is the use of all this? I am never seen, may not stir into the streets. And I want to be seen, and hear music and —

PUL. [*entering down the stairs with a lighted brazier*]. Tessa!

TESSA. Yes, father.

PUL. Have I not forbidden you to touch these powders?

TESSA. Ah, but look at me, father. Am I always to stay shut up here, where no one comes but maids of fine ladies and girls from the shops?

PUL. My child, we must be patient a little longer. Listen! Soon we shall be rich, and then we will fly Rimini, and far from here we will have a palace — [*A knock.*] Tessa, go to your room instantly.

TESSA [*lingering*]. May I not stay and see who it is?

PUL. It is only some lady's-maid.

TESSA. No, father, I think it is a gentleman.

PUL. Quickly! Quickly!
[*Exit* TESSA. PULCI *puts out light and lights a lamp; he slowly unbars the door. Enter* GIOVANNI, *masked and cloaked.* PULCI *closes door after him.*]
PUL. Has no one seen you enter, sir?
GIO. No one.
PUL. Softly! What do you seek?
GIO. Some dreamy potion
That can enthral a woman's wandering heart
And all her thought subdue to me.
PUL. [*producing phial*]. This poured
In her night drink will woo her to your arms.
One amorous night at least it will procure.
GIO. One night! — what use of that?
Each day, each night
Must she be mine.
PUL. But one more drug I have —
[*Searches for another phial.*]
GIO. [*aside*]. I must beguile, it seems, my wedded wife,
And lure into my arms what is my own.
PUL. [*offering another phial*]. This, then, will purchase some infatuate days.
GIO. Some days!
PUL. No tincture longer holds the blood.
GIO. Here is a purse.
[*Throws purse of coins.*]
PUL. Ah! get you quickly gone.
[*As they approach the door a knock is heard.*]
See! I will slowly now unbar the door,
And whoso enters past him slip away
Into the night.
GIO. [*stops* PULCI]. I must not meet a stranger. [*Takes off mask.*]
Hither! look on my face.
PUL. [*falling on his knees*]. Mercy, great Lord!
Take not my life — this commerce after hours
Is for my child.
GIO. Hide me, and instantly.
PUL. [*hiding him behind the arras*]. Here, then. [*Another knock.*] And, sir, secrets of Rimini
And unsuspected movings of your subjects
You can o'erhear. I'll draw him on to speak —
Only stir not. [*Unbars door; enter* PAOLO.]
Warily, sir.
PAO. Old man —
GIO. Paolo's voice!
PAO. What is that sound? This business
Is for no other ear but yours.
PUL. If any stirred
It was my child preparing her for bed.
PAO. If any hear me, it were ill for him!
Old man, there is within this purse a calm
Decline for thee to death, and quiet hours.
Take it, and give me in exchange some drug
That can fetch down on us the eternal sleep,
Anticipating the slow mind of God.
PUL. Is this thing for thyself, or for another?
PAO. 'Tis for myself!
PUL. I will not sell to murder.
But unto any weary of their life
I sell a painless issue out of it.
Yet you are young!
PAO. Think you the old would die?
At any cost they would prolong the light.
'Tis we, in whose pure blood the fever takes
Newly inoculate with violent life,
'Tis we who are so mad to die.
PUL. 'Tis true
I would not lose a moment of the sun.
What hath so early ruined you?
PAO. Old sir,
I am on my death-bed, and to you confess,
Love, where to love is extreme treachery —
Love for another's wife.
PUL. Nothing so strange.
PAO. Yes, for she is my brother's wife — my sister.
GIO. [*aside*]. Thou hast said it!
PAO. O, I cannot near her bide
But infinite her lightest whisper grows.
There's peril in the rustling of her dress.
PUL. And are you, too, beloved?
PAO. She hath said no word,
But should I stay, she would catch fire from me.
PUL. Why, all's before you — yet you yield up breath.
PAO. I cannot go from her; I must not stay.
To die is left!
PUL. For such a drug the price —

Pao. Usher me to oblivion!
[*Shows purse with gold.*]
Pul. [*reaching down phial*]. This drunk off
Within an hour will terminate thy woe.
Pao. [*taking phial which* Pulci *hands him*]. Unbar the door! How the night rushes in! [*Exit* Paolo.]
Pul. [*to* Giovanni]. I'll follow him. If suddenly he drink
He must not fall and lie too near my door.
[*Exit* Pulci.]
Gio. [*coming from behind arras*]. All doubt at last is o'er! He hath said it out!
Almost I had my dagger in his heart!
Yet sooner than betray, he is gone to death.
[*Wildly.*] I cannot have thee die, my Paolo!
Perhaps even now he drinks: even now the phial
Touches his lips — ah, brother, dash it down!
How much, then, hast thou drunk? Not yet enough —
Not yet enough — I know — for death? Which way
Went he — I'll follow him. [*Rushes to door, then pauses.*] Yet, O my God!
It must be so! How else? He is so bound
To her, he cannot fly! — he must not stay!
He has gone out upon the only road.
And this is my relief! O dread relief!
Thus only am I pure of brother's blood!
I must be still while he goes out to die! —
And yet be still — while he who is most dear
Drinks poison — yet I must be very still!

[*Re-enter* Pulci.]

Pul. I watched till he was mingled with the night.
Gio. Tell me! Is he that's gone so sure to die?
Pul. Within an hour, so potent is the drug!
[*Fawning on* Gio.] You on more pleasant business came to me.
We who are older at such madness laugh.
Gio. I stifle here!
Pul. Tyrant of Rimini!
You will not kill me?

Gio. Till to-morrow night
I stay my hand. Which way went he — that fool?
Pul. Straight on; he never turned until I lost him. [*Exit* Giovanni.]
Tessa!
Tessa [*running in*]. Yes, father.
Pul. Now you have your wish;
To-morrow must we run from Rimini.
Tessa. To-morrow night the world then — the bright world!
[Pulci *pours the gold out on the counter.*]

Scene II. — *A lane outside the wall of the castle garden, postern door in the wall.*

[*Enter* Paolo.]

Pao. There is no other means: but ah, the pain!
Here is the garden where her lattice shines.
Perchance she looks toward me now, and makes
A music upon midnight with my name.
Perchance she leans into the air and sighs.
O! now is she attired in purest white,
Hanging above our heads 'twixt earth and heaven!
Life, life! I cannot leave thee, for she lives.
At least I must behold her before death;
And go straight from her face into the grave —
Straight from her touch at least into the ground.
Much is permitted to a man condemned.
I'll see her, hear her, touch her ere I die.
[*Exit* Paolo *through postern door into the gardens.*]

[*Enter two* Couriers *hastily with torches.*]

First Cour. Which way now?
Second Cour. Stay, I am out of breath.
First Cour. At such a moment, that Lord Malatesta cannot be found!
Second Cour. I must get my breath against this door. Have you the papers?
First Cour. Here. Lately married, yet out of his bed at this hour!
Second Cour. Ah, I wish I were back with —
First Cour. Hush! here is Carlo.

[*Enter* CARLO.]

Well, no sign of him?
CAR. None.
And I am aguish, and these night dews!
FIRST COUR. Stay!
CAR. What?
FIRST COUR. Listen! I tell you.
SECOND COUR. A step!
CAR. It is he, Lord Malatesta.

[*Enter* GIOVANNI, *slowly.*]

CAR. Great lord, we have pursued you up and down. Here's news that will not stay.
[*Gives him letter.*]
GIO. Hold the torch nearer. [*Reads.*] "Tyrant of Rimini! All Pesaro is risen against the tax laid on them. Our men are beaten behind the city walls — the city itself declares for Cosimo. We wait but for you; a noise of your coming — a sight of you — and the city will fall to us again. Linger not a moment. — ANDREA." Carlo, muster every man within call. Then to the palace — saddle my horse. Summon all in the house to follow you: rouse them from their beds; they must ride with me instantly. [*Exeunt* CARLO *and* COURIERS.

[*Enter running two* MESSENGERS *from other side.*]

A MESSENGER. Lord and tyrant of Rimini! We are come on you none too soon — we are ridden from the camp — our horses stand — there was no moment to write, but this by word of mouth: "Your garrison makes terms in that vacant room many are already gone over, and we fear for San Arcangelo and the whole province."
GIO. Get a cup of wine, both of you, and be prepared to ride with me within the half-hour. I'll fall like thunder on Pesaro, and catch San Arcangelo with the wind of it. [*Exit one* MESSENGER. GIOVANNI *to the other.*] Stay you, sir! and tell me more exactly as we hurry on. Where is Andrea now, then? There is a vantage-ground just out of Pesaro, and there —
[*Exeunt* GIOVANNI *and* MESSENGER.]

SCENE III. — *An Arbour in the Castle Gardens. Dawn beginning to break.*

[*Enter* FRANCESCA *with a book,* NITA *following with lamp.*]

FRANC. I cannot sleep, Nita; I will read here.
Is it dawn yet? [NITA *sets lamp down.*]
NITA. No, lady: yet I see
A flushing in the East.
FRANC. How still it is!
NITA. This is the stillest time of night or day.
FRANC. Know you why, Nita?
NITA. No, my lady.
FRANC. Now
Day in a breathless passion kisses night,
And neither speaks.
NITA. Shall I stay here?
FRANC. Ah, no!
Perhaps in the dawn silence I shall drowse.
If not, I'll read this legend to myself.
NITA. Is it a pretty tale?
FRANC. Pretty, ah no!
Nita; but beautiful and passing sad.
NITA. I love sad tales: though I am gay, I love
Sometimes to weep. But is it of our time?
FRANC. It is an ancient tale of two long dead.
NITA. O, 'tis a tale of love!
FRANC. Of love, indeed.
But, Nita, leave me to myself: I think
I would have no one stirring near me now.
[*Exit* NITA.]
The light begins, but he is far away.
[*She walks to and fro.*]
Better than tossing in that vacant room
Is this cool air and fragrance ere the dawn.
Where is the page which I had reached?
Ah, here!
Now let me melt into an ancient woe.
[*Begins to read.*]

[*Enter* PAOLO, *softly.*]

PAO. Francesca!
FRANC. Paolo! I thought you now
Gone into battle dim, far, far away.
PAO. And seems it strange that I should come, then?
FRANC. No,
It seems that it could not be otherwise.

Pao. I went indeed; but some few miles from hence
Turned, and could go no further. All this night
About the garden have I roamed and burned.
And now, at last, sleepless and without rest,
I steal to you.
   Franc. Sleepless and without rest!
   Pao. It seemed that I must see your face again,
Then nevermore; that I must hear your voice,
And then no more; that I must touch your hand,
Once. No one stirs within the house; no one
In all this world but you and I, Francesca.
We two have to each other moved all night.
   Franc. I moved not to you, Paolo.
   Pao. But night
Guided you on, and onward beckoned me.
What is that book you read? Now fades the last
Star to the East: a mystic breathing comes:
And all the leaves once quivered, and were still.
   Franc. It is the first, the faint stir of the dawn.
   Pao. So still it is that we might almost hear
The sigh of all the sleepers in the world.
   Franc. And all the rivers running to the sea.
   Pao. What is't you read?
   Franc. It is an ancient tale.
   Pao. Show it to me. Is it some drowsy page
That reading low I might persuade your eyes
At last to sleep?
   Franc. It is the history
Of two who fell in love long years ago;
And wrongly fell.
   Pao. How wrongly?
   Franc. Because she
Already was a wife, and he who loved
Was her own husband's dear familiar friend.
   Pao. Was it so long ago?
   Franc. So long ago.
   Pao. What were their famous and unlucky names?
   Franc. Men called him Launcelot, her Guenevere.
Here is the page where I had ceased to read.
   Pao. [taking book]. Their history is blotted with new tears.
   Franc. The tears are mine: I know not why I wept.
But these two were so glad in their wrong love:
It was their joy; it was their helpless joy.
   Pao. Shall I read on to you where you have paused?
   Franc. Here is the place: but read it low and sweet.
Put out the lamp!
            [Paolo puts out the lamp.]
   Pao. The glimmering page is clear.
[Reading.] "Now on that day it chanced that Launcelot,
Thinking to find the King, found Guenevere
Alone; and when he saw her whom he loved,
Whom he had met too late, yet loved the more;
Such was the tumult at his heart that he
Could speak not, for her husband was his friend,
His dear familiar friend: and they two held
No secret from each other until now;
But were like brothers born" — my voice breaks off.
Read you a little on.
   Franc. [reading]. "And Guenevere,
Turning, beheld him suddenly whom she
Loved in her thought, and even from that hour
When first she saw him; for by day, by night,
Though lying by her husband's side, did she
Weary for Launcelot, and knew full well
How ill that love, and yet that love how deep!"
I cannot see — the page is dim: read you.
   Pao. [reading]. "Now they two were alone, yet could not speak;
But heard the beating of each other's hearts.
He knew himself a traitor but to stay,
Yet could not stir: she pale and yet more pale

Grew till she could no more, but smiled on him.
Then when he saw that wished smile, he came
Near to her and still near, and trembled; then
Her lips all trembling kissed."
    FRANC. [*drooping towards him*]. Ah, Launcelot!
        [*He kisses her on the lips.*]

                CURTAIN

ACT IV

A Chamber in the Palace — late evening of the second day after GIOVANNI'S *departure.*

[GIOVANNI *discovered, stained as from hard riding.* CARLO *and* RETAINERS *attending him. Wine on table.*]

GIO. The Lady Lucrezia — is she in the house?
CAR. She is, sir.
GIO. Tell her that I am returned,
And ask some words with her. Well why, do you
Stand bursting with some news that you must tell?
What sudden thing has happened?
CAR. Nothing, sir.
GIO. Nothing? You then that huddle all together,
Like cattle against thunder — what hath chanced?
AN ATTENDANT. I know of nothing, sir.
SECOND ATTENDANT. Nor I.
THIRD ATTENDANT. Nor I.
GIO. Leave me and take my message!
        [*Exeunt* CARLO *and* ATTENDANTS.]
Lies he so
Quiet that none hath found him? They are driven
Out from the city and are fugitives.
Ne'er did I strike and hew as yesterday,
And that armed ghost of Paolo by me rode.
        [*He pours out wine and drinks.*]

        [*Enter* LUCREZIA.]

LUC. So soon returned, Giovanni?
GIO. A few hours'
Fast fighting ended it, Lucrezia.
What news at home?
LUC. O, Paolo is returned!
GIO. Paolo returned! What, from the grave?
LUC. The grave?
GIO. I left him dead, or going to his death.
LUC. What do you mean?
GIO. I heard from his own mouth
That he and she did for each other burn.
LUC. He told you?
GIO. No, not me: but yet I heard.
LUC. And you on the instant killed him?
GIO. No, he stole
Away to die: I thought him dead: 'twere better.
Now like a thief he creeps back to the house!
To her for whom I had begun to long
So late in life that now I may not cease
From longing!
LUC. Her that you must drug to kiss!
Will you not smell the potion in her sigh?
A few more drops, then what a mad caress!
GIO. He hath crept back like a thief into the house —
A thief — a liar — he feigned the will to die.
Lucrezia, when old Angela foretold,
I feared not him: when he was pointed at,
I doubted still: even after his own words,
Then, then had I forgiven him, for he
Went out as to a grave. But now I am changed —
I will be wary of this creeping thing.
O, I have no emotion now, no blood.
No longer I postpone or fight this doom:
I see that it must be, and I am grown
The accomplice and the instrument of Fate,
A blade! a knife! — no more.
LUC. He has been here
Since yestermorn.
GIO. Yet I'll be no assassin,
Or rashly kill: I have not seen them kiss.
I'll wait to find them in each other's arms,
And stab them there enfolded and entwined,
And so to all men justify my deed.
Yet how to find them where to kill is just?
LUC. Give out that this is no return, but merely

An intermission of the war: that you
Must ride back to the camp within the
   hour,
And for some days be absent: he and she
Will seize upon the dark and lucky hour
To be together: watch you round the house,
And suddenly take them in each other's
   arms.
   Gio. This plan commends itself to my
     cold heart.
   Luc. Here comes Francesca. Shall I
     stay, then?
   Gio. Stay!

         [*Enter* Francesca.]

   Franc. Sir, you have asked for me. I
did not know
You were so soon returned.
   Gio. Soldiers' returns
Are sudden and oft unexpected.
   Franc. Sir,
How pale you are! You are not wounded?
   Gio. No!
A scratch, perhaps. Give me some wine,
   Francesca,
For suddenly I must be gone again.
   Franc. I thought this broil was ended?
   Gio. No! not yet
Some days I may be absent, and can go
More lightly since I leave you not alone.
To Paolo I commend you, to my brother.
Loyal he is to me, loyal and true.
He has also a gaiety of mind
Which I have ever lacked: he is beside
More suited to your years, can sing and
   play,
And has the art long hours to entertain.
To him I leave you, and must go forthwith.
         [*He makes to go, then turns.*]
Come here, Francesca, kiss me — yet not so,
You put your lips up to me like a child.
   Franc. 'Tis not so long ago I was a
     child.   [*Seizing his arm.*]
O sir, is it wise, is it well to go away?
   Gio. What do you mean?
   Franc. I have a terror here.
   Gio. Can you not bear to part with me
     some hours?
   Franc. I dread to be alone: I fear the
     night
And yon great chamber, the resort of
     spirits.

I see men hunted on the air by hounds:
Thin faces of your house, with weary smiles,
The dead who frown I fear not: but I
   fear
The dead who smile! The very palace
   rocks,
Remembering at midnight, and I see
Women within these walls immured alive
Come starving to my bed and ask for food.
   Gio. Take some one then to sleep with
     you — Lucrezia,
Or little Nita else: lie not alone.
   Franc. [*still detaining him*]. Yet go
     not, sir.
   Gio. What is it that you fear?
   Franc. Sir, go not, go not!
   Gio. Child, I cannot stay
For fancies, and at once I'll say farewell
To both of you. I hear my courser fret.
         [*Exit* Giovanni.]
   Franc. [*looking after him, and turning
     slowly*]. Lucrezia, will you lie with
     me to-night?
   Luc. I will, Francesca, if you'll have it
     so.
   Franc. O, some one I can touch in the
     thick night! —
What sound is that?
   Luc. [*going to window*]. Your husband
     galloping
Away into the dark [*she looks from the
   window, then turns*]: now he is gone.
I left young Paolo pacing up and down;
         [*Looking steadfastly at her.*]
He seemed as faint for company as you.
Say, shall I call him in as I go out?
He will help waste the tardy time.
   Franc. [*quickly*]. No, no!
   Luc. Is there some little feud 'twixt you
     and him?
For when you meet words slowly come to
   you —
You scarce look in each other's eyes.
   Franc. No feud.
   Luc. Remember, when Giovanni mar-
     ried you
These two were to each other all in all;
And so excuse some natural jealousy
Of you from him.
   Franc. I think he means me well.
   Luc. Then shall I call him in?
   Franc. O, why so eager?

Where would all those about me drive me?
First
My husband earnestly to Paolo
Commends me; and now you must call him in.
[*Wildly.*] Where can I look for pity?
Lucrezia,
You have no children?
  Luc. None.
  Franc. Nor ever had?
  Luc. Nor ever had.
  Franc. But yet you are a woman.
I have no mother: let me be your child
To-night: I am so utterly alone!
Be gentle with me; or if not, at least
Let me go home; this world is difficult.
O, think of me as of a little child
That looks into your face, and asks your hand.
  [Lucrezia *softly touches* Francesca's *hair*.]
Why do you touch my head? Why do you weep?
I would not pain you.
  Luc. Ah, Francesca! You
Have touched me where my life is quivering most.
I have no child: and yet if I had borne one,
I could have wished her hair had been this colour.
  Franc. I am too suddenly cast in this whirl!
Too suddenly! I had but convent thoughts.
O woman, woman, take me to you and hold me!
  [*She throws herself into* Lucrezia's *arms*.]
  Luc. [*clasping* Francesca *to her*]. At last the long ice melts, and O relief
Of rain that rushes from me! Child, my child!
I clasp you close, close — do you fear me still?
Have you not heard love is more fierce than hate?
Roughly I grasp what I have hunted long.
You cannot know — how should you? — that you are
More, so much more, to me than just a child.
  Franc. I seem to understand a little.
  Luc. Close,

I hold you close: it was not all in vain,
The holy babble and pillow kissed all o'er!
O my embodied dream with eyes and hair!
Visible aspiration with soft hands;
Tangible vision! O, art thou alive,
Francesca, dost thou move and breathe?
Speak, speak!
Say human words out, lest thou vanish quite!
Your very flesh is of my sighs composed,
Your blood is crimson with my passioning!
And now I have conceived and have brought forth;
And I exult in front of the great sun:
And I laugh out with riches in my lap!
And you will deem me mad! but do not, Sweet:
I am not mad, only I am most happy.
I'll dry my tears — but O, if thou should'st die?
[*Aside*.] And ah, my God!
  Franc. Why did you start?
  Luc. [*aside*]. To stay him!
[*To* Francesca, *taking her hands*.] But I should be the shadow of a mother
If here I ceased. Francesca, I well know
That 'twixt bright Paolo and dark Giovanni
You stand — you hinted at some peril there.
I ask to know no more: but take these words —
Be not in company with Paolo
To-night. [*Aside*.] Giovanni must be found. My child,
I have some business on the moment, but
Within the hour I will return — [*Aside*.]
How find him?
And sleep with you — [*Aside*.] I'll search all secret places.
Kiss me. Remember, then! [*Aside*.] 'Tis not too late!
What meshes have I woven for what I love?
  [*Exit* Lucrezia.]

[*Enter* Nita *on the other side, with a lamp*.]

  Nita. Lady, shall I come in?
  Franc. Set the lamp here,
Nita, and take some sewing: I am alone
To-night, and you shall sit with me until
Lucrezia is returned. What lamp is that?

NITA. It is the same I set you in the
    arbour
That night you could not sleep.
FRANC. Yes, I remember.
NITA. Are you unhappy, mistress?
FRANC. I am lonely,
Nita, most lonely.
NITA. That were easily —
Pardon the saying, mistress — remedied.
FRANC. And how?
NITA. If I myself were married young,
Perhaps without my leave to some old
    man,
And found a younger gallant in the house,
I think I would not shun him.
FRANC. Well, say on.
NITA. No! And I think I would maintain some show
Of love to my grey husband: it is easy
To keep in humour an old man — a kiss,
A little look, a word will satisfy,
And I would have my pleasure.
FRANC. I have listened
So far to you: you do not understand.
O Nita, when we women sin, 'tis not
By art; it is not easy, it is not light;
It is an agony shot through with bliss:
We sway and rock and suffer ere we fall.
    [*She walks up and down.*]
NITA. I scarcely understand, my lady. I
Am ever gay, and this is a gay world;
And if we girls are prudent but a little,
'Tis easy to enjoy.   [*A knock.*]
FRANC. Who knocked, then? See!
NITA [*going to door and returning*]. It is
    Lord Paolo who asks for you.
FRANC. Tell him I cannot see him. Is
    he gone?
NITA. Yes, and so sad! He sighed so
    [*sighs*], and he went.
Shall I now call him back?
FRANC. No, no! Sit down.
[*Speaking quickly.*] Tell me some story,
    Nita.
NITA. Alas! I cannot:
Only the village talk I can repeat,
And how —
    FRANC. [*starting*]. Listen! What step
    is' that without?
A sad step, and it goeth to and fro.
Look out!
    NITA. It is Lord Paolo, my lady.

FRANC. [*quickly*]. Come from the window. [*Aside.*] O where tarries she,
This new-found mother? Tell me then
    this tale!
NITA. Lucía, my sister, has a lover
    whom
She thought so true: but he the other
    night —
FRANC. Listen again!
PAO. [*without*]. Francesca!
NITA. 'Tis his voice!
My lady, you are trembling!
FRANC. [*aside*]. Why did he
Speak? The sweet sound has floated to
    my brain.
PAO. Francesca!
FRANC. [*aside*]. Soft it comes out of the
    night.
Go to the window, Nita. What says he?
NITA. He does entreat he may come in
    to you
A moment. Shall I answer?
FRANC. [*walking to and fro and putting
    her hand to her heart*]. Let him
    come.
NITA. I will go tell him. [*Aside.*]
    They'll not want me: I
Can meet Bernardo now. [*Exit* NITA.]
FRANC. O voice too sweet!
And like the soul of midnight sending
    words!
Now all the world is at her failing hour,
And at her faintest: now the pulse is low!
Now the tide turns, and now the soul goes
    home!
And I to Paolo am fainting back!
A moment — but a moment — then no
    more!

    [*Enter* PAOLO.]

PAO. I am by music led into this room,
And beckoned sweetly: all the breezes die
Round me, and in immortal ecstasy
Toward thee I move: now am I free and
    gay —
Light as a dancer when the strings begin.
FRANC. What glow is on thy face, what
    sudden light?
PAO. It seems that I am proof against all
    perils.
FRANC. And yet I fear to see thy air so
    glad.

PAO. To-night all points of swords to me are dull.
FRANC. And still I dread the bravery of your words.
Kiss me, and leave me, Paolo, to-night.
PAO. What do you fear?
FRANC. One watches quietly.
PAO. Who?
FRANC. I know not: perhaps the quiet face
Of God: the eternal Listener is near.
PAO. I'll struggle now no more. Have I not fought
Against thee as a foe most terrible?
Parried the nimble thrust and thought of thee,
And from thy mortal sweetness fled away,
Yet evermore returned? Now all the bonds
Which held me I cast off — honour, esteem,
All ties, all friendships, peace, and life itself.
You only in this universe I want.
FRANC. You fill me with a glorious rashness. What!
Shall we two, then, take up our fate and smile?
PAO. Remember how when first we met we stood
Stung with immortal recollections.
O face immured beside a fairy sea,
That leaned down at dead midnight to be kissed!
O beauty folded up in forests old!
Thou wast the lovely quest of Arthur's knights —
FRANC. Thy armour glimmered in a gloom of green.
PAO. Did I not sing to thee in Babylon?
FRANC. Or did we set a sail in Carthage Bay?
PAO. Were thine eyes strange?
FRANC. Did I not know thy voice?
All ghostly grew the sun, unreal the air
Then when we kissed.
PAO. And in that kiss our souls
Together flashed, and now they are one flame,
Which nothing can put out, nothing divide.
FRANC. Kiss me again! I smile at what may chance.

PAO. Again, and yet again! and here and here.
Let me with kisses burn this body away,
That our two souls may dart together free.
I fret at intervention of the flesh,
And I would clasp you — you that but inhabit
This lovely house.
FRANC. Break open then the door,
And let my spirit out. Paolo, kill me!
Then kill thyself: to vengeance leave these weeds,
And let our souls together soar away.
PAO. [*recoiling*]. You are too beautiful for human blow.
[FRANCESCA *starts.*]
Why did you shiver and turn sudden cold?
FRANC. [*slowly*]. I felt a wind pass over me.
PAO. I too:
Colder than any summer night could give.
FRANC. A solitary wind: and it hath passed.
PAO. [*embracing her*]. Do you still fear?
FRANC. Ah, Paolo! if we
Should die to-night, then whither would our souls
Repair? There is a region which priests tell of
Where such as we are punished without end.
PAO. Were we together, what can punish us?
FRANC. Nothing! Ah, think not I can love you less —
Only I fear.
PAO. What can we fear, we two?
O God, Thou seest us Thy creatures bound
Together by that law which holds the stars
In palpitating cosmic passion bright;
By which the very sun enthrals the earth,
And all the waves of the world faint to the moon.
Even by such attraction we two rush
Together through the everlasting years.
Us, then, whose only pain can be to part,
How wilt Thou punish? For what ecstasy
Together to be blown about the globe!
What rapture in perpetual fire to burn
Together! — where we are is endless fire.
There centuries shall in a moment pass,
And all the cycles in one hour elapse!

Still, still together, even when faints Thy
  sun,
And past our souls Thy stars like ashes
  fall,
How wilt Thou punish us who cannot part?
  FRANC. I lie out on your arm and say
  your name —
"Paolo!" "Paolo!"
PAO. "Francesca!"
  [*They slowly pass through the curtains. A pause.*]

  [*Enter* NITA.]

NITA. Ah!
Where are my lady and Lord Paolo?
Gone out into the moonlight! It is well
For her to meet her lover when she choose:
And I must run in from Bernardo's arms.
Tis very late! I'll sit and end this sewing —
I cannot work. [*Walks up and down.*]
  Where can my mistress be?
  [NITA *touches abstractedly the strings of a mandolin.*]

  [LUCREZIA *enters hurriedly.*]

LUC. [*aside*]. O! he is subtly hidden —
  and where? — and where?
I have set that on which now I cannot stay.
Nita, you are alone! Where is your mistress?
NITA. I cannot tell, my lady.
LUC. Look in my eyes!
You left her?
Nita. But a moment.
LUC. And alone?
NITA. Lord Paolo —
LUC. [*seizing her arm*]. Ah!
NITA. My lady, hurt me not.
LUC. Stammer the truth out!
NITA. He came to the door —
LUC. No further?
NITA. And she sighed out, "Let him come."
LUC. And you left them together?
NITA. I went out —
LUC. Together then! Now, now!
  Quick, dry those tears
For we must use our wit.
NITA. And you, too, tremble!
LUC. And he — Lord Malatesta?
NITA. Know you not
He hath ridden off to the camp?

LUC. But might return!
NITA. [*trembling*]. O! but he must not!
LUC. Yet some accident —
NITA. There would be noise and stir at
  his return.
LUC. You have heard no sound? Remember fiercely! Nothing?
I do not mean of hooves, nor armour
  chink —
You have heard not even a step?
NITA. [*trembling*]. What mean you? —
  No.
LUC. Not even a soft step?
NITA. I am faint with fear.
  [*She staggers.*]
LUC. [*seizing her hand*]. Which way
  went they, these two?
NITA. I cannot tell.
LUC. This door is fast! — then through
  the curtains?
NITA. Yes.
LUC. They seem to tremble still! Come
  with me, quick!
NITA. I am faint.
LUC. Come with me.
  [*She drags her to the curtain.*]
Ah! whose hand is that?
  [GIOVANNI, *parting the curtains from the other side, comes slowly through.*]
NITA. O, sir! we had not thought you
  back so soon.
GIO. Where is your mistress?
NITA. Sir, I cannot tell.
GIO. Is it not time you dressed her all in
  white,
And combed out her long hair as for a sleep?
NITA. 'Tis past the hour.
GIO. You have a curl awry,
And falling o'er your eyebrow — bind it up.
NITA. I cannot, sir.
GIO. Well, leave us: when your mistress
Is ready, I will call for you.
  [*Exit* NITA. *There is a pause, in which* GIOVANNI *and* LUCREZIA *gaze at each other.*]
LUC. [*going slowly up to him*]. O, sir!
I would beseech of you -- [*She starts.*]
  Ah! Giovanni,
You have hurt your hand: there's blood
  upon it here.
  [*Takes his hand and looks at it.*]

Gio. 'Tis not my blood!
Luc. O, then —
Gio. "O, then!" is all.
[*As in a frenzy.*] And now their love that was so secret close
Shall be proclaimed. Tullio, Carlo, Biagi! —
They shall be married before all men. Nita!
Rouse up the house and bring in lights, lights, lights!
There shall be music, feasting, and dancing.
Wine shall be drunk. Candles, I say! More lights!
More marriage lights! Where tarry they the while,
The nuptial tapers? Rouse up all the house!
    [*All this while* SERVANTS *and others, half dressed, are continually rushing in with lights and torches. They stand whimpering.*]
    Gio. [*slowly*]. Carlo, go through the curtains, and pass in
To the great sleeping-chamber: you shall find
Two there together lying: place them, then,
Upon some litter and have them hither brought
With ceremony.
    [*Exeunt* CARLO *and Four* SERVANTS. GIOVANNI *paces to and fro.*]
The curse, the curse of Cain!
A restlessness has come into my blood,
And I begin to wander from this hour
Alone for evermore.
    Luc. [*rushing to him*]. Giovanni, say
Quickly some light thing, lest we both go mad!

Gio. Be still! A second wedding here begins,
And I would have all reverent and seemly:
For they were nobly born, and deep in love.
    [*Enter blind* ANGELA, *slowly.*]
    Ang. Will no one take my hand? Two lately dead
Rushed past me in the air. O! Are there not
Many within this room all standing still?
What are they all expecting?
    Gio. Lead her aside:
I hear the slow pace of advancing feet.
    [*Enter* SERVANTS *bearing in* PAOLO *and* FRANCESCA *dead upon a litter.*]
    Luc. Ah! ah! ah!
    Gio. Break not out in lamentation!
    [*A pause . . . The* SERVANTS *set down the litter.*]
    Luc. [*going to litter*]. I have borne one child, and she has died in youth!
    Gio. [*going to litter*]. Not easily have we three come to this —
We three who now are dead. Unwillingly
They loved, unwillingly I slew them. Now
I kiss them on the forehead quietly.
    [*He bends over the bodies and kisses them on the forehead. He is shaken.*]
    Luc. What ails you now?
    Gio. She takes away my strength.
I did not know the dead could have such hair.
Hide them. They look like children fast asleep!
    [*The bodies are reverently covered over.*]

CURTAIN

THE VOYSEY INHERITANCE
A PLAY, IN FIVE ACTS
By HARLEY GRANVILLE-BARKER

Mr. Granville-Barker does not supply a List of Persons for his plays. For convenience such a list for *The Voysey Inheritance* may be found in the notes on the play in the Appendix.

ENTERED AT THE LIBRARY OF CONGRESS, WASHINGTON, U.S.A.
ALL RIGHTS RESERVED.

Copyright, 1909, by Granville-Barker. Reprinted by permission of the publishers, Little, Brown & Company. "The Voysey Inheritance" must not be performed either by amateurs or professionals without written permission. For such permission, and for the "acting version" with full stage directions, apply to The Paget Dramatic Agency, 62 West 47th Street, New York.

THE VOYSEY INHERITANCE

1903-05

ACT I

The Office of Voysey and Son is in the best part of Lincoln's Inn. Its panelled rooms give out a sense of grandmotherly comfort and security, very grateful at first to the hesitating investor, the dubious litigant. MR. VOYSEY'S *own room into which he walks about twenty past ten of a morning radiates enterprise besides. There is polish on everything; on the windows, on the mahogany of the tidily packed writing-table that stands between them, on the brasswork of the fireplace in the other wall, on the glass of the firescreen which preserves only the pleasantness of a sparkling fire, even on* MR. VOYSEY'S *hat as he takes it off to place it on the little red curtained shelf behind the door.* MR. VOYSEY *is sixty or more and masterful; would obviously be master anywhere from his own home outwards, or wreck the situation in his attempt. Indeed there is a buccaneering air sometimes in the twist of his glance, not altogether suitable to a family solicitor. On this bright October morning,* PEACEY, *the head clerk, follows just too late to help him off with his coat, but in time to take it and hang it up with a quite unnecessary subservience.* MR. VOYSEY *is evidently not capable enough to like capable men about him.* PEACEY, *not quite removed from Nature, has made some attempts to acquire protective colouring. A very drunken client might mistake him for his master. His voice very easily became a toneless echo of* MR. VOYSEY'S; *later his features caught a line or two from that mirror of all the necessary virtues into which he was so constantly gazing; but how his clothes even when new contrive to look like old ones of* MR. VOYSEY'S *is a mystery, and to his tailor a most annoying one. And* PEACEY *is just a respectful number of years his master's junior. Relieved of his coat,* MR. VOYSEY *carries to his table the bunch of beautiful roses he is accustomed to bring to the office three times a week and places them for a moment only near the bowl of water there ready to receive them while he takes up his letters. These lie ready too, opened mostly, one or two private ones left closed and discreetly separate. By this time the usual salutations have passed,* PEACEY'S *"Good-morning, sir;"* MR. VOYSEY'S *"Morning, Peacey." Then as he gets to his letters* MR. VOYSEY *starts his day's work.*

MR. VOYSEY. Any news for me?
PEACEY. I hear bad accounts of Alguazils preferred, sir.
MR. VOYSEY. Oh ... who from?
PEACEY. Merrit and James's head clerk in the train this morning.
MR. VOYSEY. They looked all right on ... Give me the *Times*. [PEACEY *goes to the fireplace for the Times; it is warming there.* MR. VOYSEY *waves a letter, then places it on the table.*] Here, that's for you ... Gerrard's Cross business. Anything else?
PEACEY [*as he turns the Times to its Finance page*]. I've made the usual notes.
MR. VOYSEY. Thank'ee.
PEACEY. Young Benham isn't back yet.
MR. VOYSEY. Mr. Edward must do as he thinks fit about that. Alguazils, Alg — oh, yes.

[*He is running his eye down the columns.* PEACEY *leans over the letters.*]

PEACEY. This is from Mr. Leader about the codicil... You'll answer that?
MR. VOYSEY. Mr. Leader. Yes. Alguazils. Mr. Edward's here, I suppose.
PEACEY. No, sir.
MR. VOYSEY [*his eye twisting with some sharpness*]. What!
PEACEY [*almost alarmed*]. I beg pardon, sir.
MR. VOYSEY. Mr. Edward.
PEACEY. Oh, yes, sir, been in his room some time. I thought you said Headley; he's not due back till Thursday.
[MR. VOYSEY *discards the Times and sits to his desk and his letters.*]
MR. VOYSEY. Tell Mr. Edward I've come.
PEACEY. Yes, sir. Anything else?
MR. VOYSEY. Not for the moment. Cold morning, isn't it?
PEACEY. Quite surprising, sir.
MR. VOYSEY. We had a touch of frost down at Chislehurst.
PEACEY. So early!
MR. VOYSEY. I want it for the celery. All right, I'll call through about the rest of the letters.
[PEACEY *goes, having secured a letter or two, and* MR. VOYSEY *having sorted the rest (a proportion into the waste-paper basket) takes up the forgotten roses and starts setting them into a bowl with an artistic hand. Then his son* EDWARD *comes in.* MR. VOYSEY *gives him one glance and goes on arranging the roses but says cheerily.*]
MR. VOYSEY. Good-morning, my dear boy.
[EDWARD *has little of his father in him and that little is undermost. It is a refined face but self-consciousness takes the place in it of imagination, and in suppressing traits of brutality in his character it looks as if the young man had suppressed his sense of humour too. But whether or no, that would not be much in evidence now, for* EDWARD *is obviously going through some experience which is scaring him (there is no better word). He looks not to have slept for a night or two, and his standing there, clutching and unclutching the bundle of papers he carries, his eyes on his father, half appealingly but half accusingly too, his whole being altogether so unstrung and desperate, makes* MR. VOYSEY'S *uninterrupted arranging of the flowers seem very calculated indeed. At last the little tension of silence is broken.*]
EDWARD. Father...
MR. VOYSEY. Well?
EDWARD. I'm glad to see you.
[*This is a statement of fact. He doesn't know that the commonplace phrase sounds ridiculous at such a moment.*]
MR. VOYSEY. I see you've the papers there.
EDWARD. Yes.
MR. VOYSEY. You've been through them?
EDWARD. As you wished me...
MR. VOYSEY. Well? [EDWARD *doesn't answer. Reference to the papers seems to overwhelm him with shame.* MR. VOYSEY *goes on with cheerful impatience.*] Come, come, my dear boy, don't take it like this. You're puzzled and worried, of course. But why didn't you come down to me on Saturday night? I expected you... I told you to come. Then your mother was wondering why you weren't with us for dinner yesterday.
EDWARD. I went through all the papers twice. I wanted to make quite sure.
MR. VOYSEY. Sure of what? I told you to come to me.
EDWARD [*he is very near crying*]. Oh, father.
MR. VOYSEY. Now look here, Edward, I'm going to ring and dispose of these letters. Please pull yourself together.
[*He pushes the little button on his table.*]
EDWARD. I didn't leave my rooms all day yesterday.
MR. VOYSEY. A pleasant Sunday! You must learn, whatever the business may be, to leave it behind you at the Office. Why, life's not worth living else. [PEACEY *comes in to find* MR. VOYSEY *before the fire ostentatiously warming and rubbing his*

THE VOYSEY INHERITANCE

hands.] Oh, there isn't much else, Peacey. Tell Simmons that if he satisfies you about the details of this lease it'll be all right. Make a note for me of Mr. Grainger's address at Mentone. I shall have several things to dictate to Atkinson. I'll whistle for him.

PEACEY. Mr. Burnett... Burnett and Marks had just come in, Mr. Edward.

EDWARD [*without turning*]. It's only fresh instructions. Will you take them?

PEACEY. All right.

[PEACEY *goes, lifting his eyebrows at the queerness of* EDWARD'S *manner. This* MR. VOYSEY *sees, returning to his table with a little scowl.*]

MR. VOYSEY. Now sit down. I've given you a bad forty-eight hours, have I? Well, I've been anxious about you. Never mind, we'll thresh the thing out now. Go through the two accounts. Mrs. Murberry's first... how do you find it stands?

EDWARD [*his feelings choking him*]. I hoped you were playing off some joke on me.

MR. VOYSEY. Come now.

[EDWARD *separates the papers precisely and starts to detail them; his voice quite toneless. Now and then his father's sharp comments ring out in contrast.*]

EDWARD. We've got the lease of her present house, several agreements... and here's her will. Here's also a power of attorney expired some time over her securities and her property generally... it was made out for six months.

MR. VOYSEY. She was in South Africa.

EDWARD. Here's the Sheffield mortgage and the Henry Smith mortgage with Banker's receipts... her Banker's to us for the interest up to date... four and a half and five per cent. Then... Fretworthy Bonds. There's a note scribbled in your writing that they are at the Bank; but you don't say what Bank.

MR. VOYSEY. My own... Stukeley's.

EDWARD [*just dwelling on the words*]. Your own. I queried that. There's eight thousand five hundred in three and a half India stock. And there are her Banker's receipts for cheques on account of those dividends. I presume for those dividends.

MR. VOYSEY. Why not?

EDWARD [*gravely*]. Because then, father, there are her Banker's half yearly receipts for other sums amounting to an average of four hundred and twenty pounds a year. But I find no record of any capital to produce this.

MR. VOYSEY. Go on. What do you find?

EDWARD. Till about three years back there seems to have been eleven thousand in Queenslands which would produce — did produce exactly the same sum. But after January of that year I find no record of 'em.

MR. VOYSEY. In fact the Queenslands are missing, vanished?

EDWARD [*hardly uttering the word*]. Yes.

MR. VOYSEY. From which you conclude?

EDWARD. I supposed at first that you had not handed me all the papers.

MR. VOYSEY. Since Mrs. Murberry evidently still gets that four twenty a year, somehow; lucky woman.

EDWARD [*in agony*]. Oh!

MR. VOYSEY. Well, we'll return to the good lady later. Now let's take the other.

EDWARD. The Hatherley Trust.

MR. VOYSEY. Quite so.

EDWARD [*with one accusing glance*]. Trust.

MR. VOYSEY. Go on.

EDWARD. Father...

[*His grief comes uppermost again and* MR. VOYSEY *meets it kindly.*]

MR. VOYSEY. I know, my dear boy. I shall have lots to say to you. But let's get quietly through with these details first.

EDWARD [*bitterly now*]. Oh, this is simple enough. We're young Hatherley's only trustees till his coming of age in about five years' time. The property was eighteen thousand invested in Consols. Certain sums were to be allowed for his education; we seem to be paying them.

MR. VOYSEY. Regularly.

EDWARD. Quite. But where's the capital?

MR. VOYSEY. No record?

EDWARD. Yes... A note by you on a half sheet... Refer to the Bletchley Land Scheme.

MR. VOYSEY. That was ten years ago.

Haven't I credited him with the interest on his capital?

EDWARD. The balance ought to be reinvested. There's this (*a sheet of figures*) in your handwriting. You credit him with the Consol interest.

MR. VOYSEY. Quite so.

EDWARD. But I think I've heard you say that the Bletchley scheme paid seven and a half.

MR. VOYSEY. At one time. Have you also taken the trouble to calculate what will be due from us to the lad?

EDWARD. Yes... even on the Consol basis... capital and compound interest ... about twenty-six thousand pounds.

MR. VOYSEY. A respectable sum. In five years' time?

EDWARD. When he comes of age.

MR. VOYSEY. That gives us, say, four years and six months in which to think about it.

[EDWARD *waits, hopelessly, for his father to speak again; then says:*]

EDWARD. Thank you for showing me these, sir. Shall I put them back in your safe now?

MR. VOYSEY. Yes, you'd better. There's the key. [EDWARD *reaches for the bunch, his face hidden.*] Put them down. Your hand shakes... why, you might have been drinking... I'll put them away later. It's no use having hysterics, Edward. Look your trouble in the face.

[EDWARD'S *only answer is to go to the fire, as far from his father as the room allows. And there he leans on the mantelpiece, his shoulders heaving.*]

MR. VOYSEY. I'm sorry, my dear boy. I wouldn't tell you if I could help it.

EDWARD. I can't believe it. And that you should be telling me... such a thing.

MR. VOYSEY. Let yourself go... have your cry out, as the women say. It isn't pleasant, I know. It isn't pleasant to inflict it on you.

EDWARD. How I got through that outer office this morning, I don't know. I came early, but some of them were here. Peacey came into my room; he must have seen there was something up.

MR. VOYSEY. That's no matter.

EDWARD [*able to turn to his father again; won round by the kind voice*]. How long has it been going on? Why didn't you tell me before? Oh, I know you thought you'd pull through; but I'm your partner... I'm responsible too. Oh, I don't want to shirk that... don't think I mean to shirk that, father. Perhaps I ought to have discovered, but those affairs were always in your hands. I trusted... I beg your pardon. Oh, it's us... not you. Everyone has trusted us.

MR. VOYSEY [*calmly and kindly still*]. You don't seem to notice that I'm not breaking my heart like this.

EDWARD. What's the extent of the mischief? When did it begin? Father, what made you begin it?

MR. VOYSEY. I didn't begin it.

EDWARD. You didn't. Who then?

MR. VOYSEY. My father before me. [EDWARD *stares.*] That calms you a little.

EDWARD. I'm glad... my dear father! [*And he puts out his hand. Then just a doubt enters his mind.*] But I... it's amazing.

MR. VOYSEY [*shaking his head*]. My inheritance, Edward.

EDWARD. My dear father!

MR. VOYSEY. I had hoped it wasn't to be yours.

EDWARD. D'you mean to tell me that this sort of thing has been going on here for years? For more than thirty years!

MR. VOYSEY. Yes.

EDWARD. That's a little hard to understand just at first, sir.

MR. VOYSEY [*sententiously*]. We do what we must in this world, Edward; I have done what I had to do.

EDWARD [*his emotion well cooled by now*]. Perhaps I'd better just listen quietly while you explain.

MR. VOYSEY [*concentrating*]. You know that I'm heavily into Northern Electrics.

EDWARD. Yes.

MR. VOYSEY. But you don't know how heavily. When I got the tip the Municipalities were organising the purchase, I saw, of course, the stock must be up a hundred and forty-five — a hundred and fifty in no time. Now Leeds will keep up her silly quarrel with the other place... they won't apply for powers for another ten years. I bought at ninety-five. What are they to-day?

EDWARD. Seventy-two.

MR. VOYSEY. Seventy-one and a half. And in ten years I may be... I'm getting on for seventy, Edward. That's mainly why you've had to be told.

EDWARD. With whose money are you so heavily into Northern Electrics?

MR. VOYSEY. The firm's money.

EDWARD. Clients' money?

MR. VOYSEY. Yes.

EDWARD [coldly]. Well... I'm waiting for your explanation, sir.

MR. VOYSEY. You seem to have recovered pretty much.

EDWARD. No, sir, I'm trying to understand, that's all.

MR. VOYSEY [with a shrug]. Children always think the worst of their parents, I suppose. I did of mine. It's a pity.

EDWARD. Go on, sir, go on. Let me know the worst.

MR. VOYSEY. There's no immediate danger. I should think anyone could see that from the figures there. There's no real risk at all.

EDWARD. Is that the worst?

MR. VOYSEY [his anger rising]. Have you studied these two accounts or have you not?

EDWARD. Yes, sir.

MR. VOYSEY. Well, where's the deficiency in Mrs. Murberry's income... has she ever gone without a shilling? What has young Hatherley lost?

EDWARD. He stands to lose —

MR. VOYSEY. He stands to lose nothing if I'm spared for a little, and you will only bring a little common-sense to bear and try to understand the difficulties of my position.

EDWARD. Father, I'm not thinking ill of you... that is, I'm trying not to. But won't you explain how you're justified...?

MR. VOYSEY. In putting our affairs in order?

EDWARD. Are you doing that?

MR. VOYSEY. What else?

EDWARD [starting patiently to examine the matter]. How bad were things when you first came to control them?

MR. VOYSEY. Oh, I forget.

EDWARD. You can't forget.

MR. VOYSEY. Well... pretty bad.

EDWARD. Do you know how it was my grandfather began to —

MR. VOYSEY. Muddlement, muddlement! Fooled away hundreds and thousands on safe things... well, then, what was he to do? He'd no capital, no credit, and was in terror of his life. My dear Edward, if I hadn't found it out in time, he'd have confessed to the first man who came and asked for a balance sheet.

EDWARD. Well, what exact sum was he to the bad then?

MR. VOYSEY. I forget. Several thousands.

EDWARD. But surely it has not taken all these years to pay off —

MR. VOYSEY. Oh, hasn't it!

EDWARD [making his point]. Then how does it happen, sir, that such a comparatively recent trust as young Hatherley's has been broken into?

MR. VOYSEY. Well, what could be safer than to use that money? There's a Consol investment and not a sight wanted of either capital or interest for five years.

EDWARD [utterly beaten]. Father, are you mad?

MR. VOYSEY. On the contrary, when my clients' money is entirely under my control, I sometimes reinvest it. The difference between the income this money was bringing to them and the profits it then actually brings to me, I... I utilise in my endeavour to fill up the deficit in the firm's accounts... I use it to put things straight. Doesn't it follow that the more low-interest-bearing capital I can use the better... the less risky things I have to put it into. Most of young Hatherley's Consol capital... the Trust gives me full discretion... is now out on mortgage at four and a half and five... safe as safe can be.

EDWARD. But he should have the benefit.

MR. VOYSEY. He has the amount of his Consol interest.

EDWARD. Where are the mortgages? Are they in his name?

MR. VOYSEY. Some of them ... some of them. That really doesn't matter. With regard to Mrs. Murberry ... those Fretworthy Bonds at my bank ... I've raised five thousand on them. But I can release her Bonds to-morrow if she wants them.

EDWARD. Where's the five thousand?

MR. VOYSEY. I'm not sure ... it was paid into my own account. Yes, I do remember. Some of it went to complete a purchase ... that and two thousand more out of the Skipworth fund.

EDWARD. But, my dear father —

MR. VOYSEY. Well?

EDWARD [*summing it all up very simply*]. It's not right.

[MR. VOYSEY *considers his son for a moment with a pitying shake of the head.*]

MR. VOYSEY. Why? ... why is it so hard for a man to see beyond the letter of the law! Will you consider, Edward, the position in which I found myself at that moment? Was I to see my father ruined and disgraced without lifting a finger to help him? ... quite apart from the interest of our clients. I paid back to the man who would have lost most by my father's mistakes every penny of his money. And he never knew the danger he'd been in ... never passed an uneasy moment about it. It was I that lay awake. I have now somewhere a letter from that man to my father thanking him effusively for the way in which he'd conducted some matter. It comforted my poor father. Well, Edward, I stepped outside of the letter of the law to do that service. Was I right or wrong?

EDWARD. In the result, sir, right.

MR. VOYSEY. Judge me by the result. I took the risk of failure ... I should have suffered. I could have kept clear of the danger if I'd liked.

EDWARD. But that's all past. The thing that concerns me is what you are doing now.

MR. VOYSEY [*gently reproachful now*]. My boy, can't you trust me a little? It's all very well for you to come in at the end of the day and criticise. But I who have done the day's work know how that work had to be done. And here's our firm, prosperous, respected and without a stain on its honour. That's the main point, isn't it?

EDWARD [*quite irresponsive to this pathetic appeal*]. Very well, sir. Let's dismiss from our minds all prejudices about speaking the truth ... acting upon one's instructions, behaving as any honest firm of solicitors must behave ...

MR. VOYSEY. Nonsense, I tell no unnecessary lies. If a man of any business ability gives me definite instructions about his property, I follow them.

EDWARD. Father, no unnecessary lies!

MR. VOYSEY. Well, my friend, go and knock it into Mrs. Murberry's head, if you can, that four hundred and twenty pounds of her income hasn't, for the last eight years, come from the place she thinks it's come from, and see how happy you'll make her.

EDWARD. But is that four hundred and twenty a year as safe to come to her as it was before you meddled with the capital?

MR. VOYSEY. I see no reason why —

EDWARD. What's the security?

MR. VOYSEY [*putting his coping stone on the argument*]. My financial ability.

EDWARD [*really not knowing whether to laugh or cry*]. Why, one'd think you were satisfied with this state of things.

MR. VOYSEY. Edward, you really are most unsympathetic and unreasonable. I give all I have to the firm's work ... my brain ... my energies ... my whole life. I can't turn my abilities into hard cash at par ... I wish I could. Do you suppose that if I could establish everyone of these people with a separate and consistent bank balance to-morrow that I shouldn't do it?

EDWARD [*thankfully able to meet anger with anger*]. Do you mean to tell me that you couldn't somehow have put things right by this?

MR. VOYSEY. Somehow? How?

EDWARD. If thirty years of this sort of thing hasn't brought you hopelessly to grief ... during that time there must have been opportunities ...

MR. VOYSEY. Must there! Well, I hope that when I'm under ground, you may find them.

EDWARD. I!

Mr. Voysey. Put everything right with a stroke of your pen, if it's so easy!

Edward. I!

Mr. Voysey. You're my partner and my son; you'll inherit the business.

Edward [*realising at last that he has been led to the edge of this abyss*]. Oh no, father.

Mr. Voysey. Why else have I had to tell you all this?

Edward [*very simply*]. Father, I can't. I can't possibly. I don't think you've any right to ask me.

Mr. Voysey. Why not, pray?

Edward. It's perpetuating the dishonesty.

[Mr. Voysey *hardens at the unpleasant word.*]

Mr. Voysey. You don't believe that I've told you the truth.

Edward. I want to believe it.

Mr. Voysey. It's no proof ... my earning these twenty or thirty people their rightful incomes for the last — how many years?

Edward. Whether what you have done and are doing is wrong or right ... I can't meddle in it.

[*For the moment* Mr. Voysey *looks a little dangerous.*]

Mr. Voysey. Very well. Forget all I've said. Go back to your room. Get back to your own mean drudgery. My life work — my splendid life work — ruined! What does that matter?

Edward. Whatever did you expect of me?

Mr. Voysey [*making a feint at his papers*]. Oh, nothing, nothing. [*Then he slams them down with great effect.*] Here's a great edifice built up by years of labour and devotion and self-sacrifice ... a great arch you may call it ... a bridge which is to carry our firm to safety with honour. [*This variation of Disraeli passes unnoticed.*] My work! And now, as I near the end of my life, it still lacks the key-stone. Perhaps I am to die with my work just incomplete. Then is there nothing that a son might do? Do you think I shouldn't be proud of you, Edward ... that I shouldn't bless you from — wherever I may be, when you completed my life's work ... with perhaps just one kindly thought of your father?

[*In spite of this oratory, the situation is gradually impressing* Edward.]

Edward. What will happen if I ... if I desert you?

Mr. Voysey. I'll protect you as best I can.

Edward. I wasn't thinking of myself, sir.

Mr. Voysey [*with great nonchalance*]. Well, I shan't mind the exposure, you know. It won't make me blush in my coffin ... and you're not so quixotic, I hope, as to be thinking of the feelings of your brothers and sisters. Considering how simple it would have been for me to go to my grave in peace and quiet and let you discover the whole thing afterwards, the fact that I *didn't*, that I have taken thought for the future of all of you might perhaps have convinced you that I ... ! But there ... consult your own safety.

[Edward *has begun to pace the room; indecision growing upon him.*]

Edward. This is a queer thing to have to make up one's mind about, isn't it, father?

Mr. Voysey [*watching him closely and modulating his voice*]. My dear boy, I understand the shock to your feelings that this disclosure must have been.

Edward. Yes, I came this morning thinking that next week would see us in the dock together.

Mr. Voysey. And I suppose if I'd broken down and begged your pardon for my folly, you'd have done anything for me, gone to prison smiling, eh?

Edward. I suppose so.

Mr. Voysey. Yes, it's easy enough to forgive. I'm sorry I can't go in sackcloth and ashes to oblige you. [*Now he begins to rally his son; easy in his strength.*] My dear Edward, you've lived a quiet humdrum life up to now, with your poetry and your sociology and your agnosticism and your ethics of this and your ethics of that ... dear me, these are the sort of garden oats which young men seem to sow nowadays! ... and you've never before been brought face to face with any really vital question. Now don't make a fool of yourself just through inexperience. Try and give your mind without prejudice to the consideration of a very serious matter. I'm not angry at what you've said to me. I'm quite willing to forget it. And it's for your own sake and not for mine, Edward, that I do beg you to — to — to be a man and take a practical common-sense view of the position you find yourself in. It's not a pleasant position, I know, but it's unavoidable.

EDWARD. You should have told me before you took me into partnership.

[*Oddly enough it is this last flicker of rebellion which breaks down* MR. VOYSEY's *caution. Now he lets fly with a vengeance.*]

MR. VOYSEY. Should I be telling you at all if I could possibly help it? Don't I know that you're about as fit for the job as a babe unborn? Haven't I been worrying over that for these last three years? But I'm in a corner ... and am I to see my firm come to smash simply because of your scruples? If you're a son of mine you'll do as I tell you. Hadn't I the same choice to make? ... and it's a safer game for you now than it was for me then. D'you suppose I didn't have scruples? If you run away from this, Edward, you're a coward. My father was a coward and he suffered for it to the end of his days. I was sick-nurse to him here more than partner. Good Lord! ... of course it's pleasant and comfortable to keep within the law ... then the law will look after you. Otherwise you have to look pretty sharp after yourself. You have to cultivate your own sense of right and wrong; deal your own justice. But that makes a bigger man of you, let me tell you. How easily ... how easily could I have walked out of my father's office and left him to his fate; no one would have blamed me! But I didn't. I thought it my better duty to stay and ... yes, I say it with all reverence ... to take up my cross. Well, I've carried that cross pretty successfully. And what's more, it's made a happy man of me ... a better, **stronger** man than skulking about in shame and in fear of his life ever made of my poor dear father. [*Relieved at having let out the truth, but doubtful of his wisdom in doing so, he changes his tone.*] I don't want what I've been saying to influence you, Edward. You are a free agent ... and you must decide upon your own course of action. Now don't let's discuss the matter any more for the moment.

[EDWARD *looks at his father with clear eyes.*]

EDWARD. Don't forget to put these papers away.

[*He restores them to their bundles and hands them back: it is his only comment.* MR. VOYSEY *takes them and his meaning in silence.*]

MR. VOYSEY. Are you coming down to Chislehurst soon? We've got Hugh and his wife, and Booth and Emily, and Christopher for two or three days, till he goes back to school.

EDWARD. How is Chris?

MR. VOYSEY. All right again now ... grows more like his father. Booth's very proud of him. So am I.

EDWARD. I think I can't face them all just at present.

MR. VOYSEY. Nonsense.

EDWARD [*a little wave of emotion going through him*]. I feel as if this thing were written on my face. How I shall get through business I don't know!

MR. VOYSEY. You're weaker than I thought, Edward.

EDWARD [*a little ironically*]. A disappointment to you, father?

MR. VOYSEY. No, no.

EDWARD. You should have brought one of the others into the firm ... Trenchard or Booth.

MR. VOYSEY [*hardening*]. Trenchard! [*He dismisses that.*] Well, you're a better man than Booth. Edward, you mustn't imagine that the whole world is standing on its head merely because you've had an unpleasant piece of news. Come down to Chislehurst to-night ... well, say to-morrow night. It'll be good for you ... stop your brooding ... that's your worst vice, Edward. You'll find the household as if nothing had happened. Then you'll remember that nothing really has happened. And presently you'll get to see that nothing need happen, if you keep your head. I remember times, when things have seemed at their worst, what a relief it's been to me ... my romp with you all in the nursery just before your bedtime. Do you remember?

EDWARD. Yes. And cutting your head open once with that gun.

MR. VOYSEY [*in a full glow of fine feeling*]. And, my dear boy, if I knew that you were going to inform the next client you met of what I've just told you ...

EDWARD [*with a shudder*]. Oh, father!

MR. VOYSEY. ... And that I should find myself in prison to-morrow, I wouldn't wish a single thing I've ever done undone. I have never wilfully harmed man or woman. My life's been a happy one. Your dear mother has been spared to me. You're most of you good children and a credit to what I've done for you.

EDWARD [*the deadly humour of this too much for him*]. Father!

MR. VOYSEY. Run along now, run along. I must finish my letters and get into the City.

[*He might be scolding a schoolboy for some trifling fault.* EDWARD *turns to have a look at the keen, unembarrassed face.* MR. VOYSEY *smiles at him and proceeds to select from the bowl a rose for his buttonhole.*]

EDWARD. I'll think it over, sir.

MR. VOYSEY. Of course, you will. And don't brood, Edward, don't brood.

[*So* EDWARD *leaves him; and having fixed the rose to his satisfaction, he rings his table telephone and calls through it to the listening clerk.*]

Send Atkinson to me, please.

[*Then he gets up, keys in hand to lock away Mrs. Murberry's and the Hatherley Trust papers.*]

ACT II

The VOYSEY *dining-room at Chislehurst, when children and grandchildren are visiting, is dining-table and very little else. And at this moment in the evening when five or six men are sprawling back in their chairs, and the air is clouded with smoke, it is a very typical specimen of the middle-class English domestic temple; the daily sacrifice consummated, the acolytes dismissed, the women safely in the drawing-room, and the chief priests of it taking their surfeited ease round the dessert-piled altar. It has the usual red-papered walls (like a reflection, they are, of the underdone beef so much consumed within them), the usual varnished woodwork which is known as grained oak; there is the usual, hot, mahogany furniture; and, commanding point of the whole room, there is the usual black marble sarcophagus of a fireplace. Above this hangs one of the two or three oil paintings, which are all that break the red pattern of the walls, the portrait painted in* 1880 *of an undistinguished looking gentleman aged sixty; he is shown sitting in a more graceful attitude than it could ever have been comfortable for him to assume.* MR. VOYSEY'S *father it is, and the brass plate at the bottom of the frame tells us that the portrait was a presentation one. On the mantelpiece stands, of course, a clock; at either end a china vase filled with paper spills. And in front of the fire — since that is the post of vantage — stands at this moment* MAJOR BOOTH VOYSEY. *He is the second son, of the age that it is necessary for a Major to be, and of an appearance that many ordinary Majors in ordinary regiments are. He went into the army because he thought it would be like a schoolboy's idea of it; and, being there, he does his little all to keep it so. He stands astride, hands in pockets, coat-tails through his arms, cigar in mouth, moustache bristling. On either side of him sits at the table an old gentleman; the one is* MR. EVAN COLPUS, *the vicar of their parish, the other* MR. GEORGE BOOTH, *a friend of long standing, and the Major's godfather.* MR. COLPUS *is a harmless enough anachronism, except for the waste of four hundred pounds a year in which his stipend involves the community. Leaving most* of his parochial work to an energetic curate, he devotes his serious attention to the composition of two sermons a week. They deal with the difficulties of living the Christian life as experienced by people who have nothing else to do. Published in series from time to time, these form suitable presents for bedridden parishioners. MR. GEORGE BOOTH, on the contrary, is as gay an old gentleman as can be found in Chislehurst. An only son, his father left him at the age of twenty-five a fortune of a hundred thousand pounds (a plum, as he called it). At the same time he had the good sense to dispose of his father's business, into which he had been most unwillingly introduced five years earlier, for a like sum before he was able to depreciate its value. It was MR. VOYSEY's invaluable assistance in this transaction which first bound the two together in great friendship. Since that time MR. BOOTH has been bent on nothing but enjoying himself. He has even remained a bachelor with that object. Money has given him all he wants, therefore he loves and reverences money; while his imagination may be estimated by the fact that he has now reached the age of sixty-five, still possessing more of it than he knows what to do with. At the head of the table, meditatively cracking walnuts, sits MR. VOYSEY. He has his back there to the conservatory door — you know it is the conservatory door because there is a curtain to pull over it, and because half of it is frosted glass with a purple key pattern round the edge. On MR. VOYSEY's left is DENIS TREGONING, a nice enough young man. And at the other end of the table sits EDWARD, not smoking, not talking, hardly listening, very depressed. Behind him is the ordinary door of the room, which leads out into the dismal draughty hall. The Major's voice is like the sound of a cannon through the tobacco smoke.

MAJOR BOOTH VOYSEY. Of course I'm hot and strong for conscription...
MR. GEORGE BOOTH. My dear boy, the country'd never stand it. No Englishman —
MAJOR BOOTH VOYSEY [dropping the phrase heavily upon the poor old gentleman]. I beg your pardon. If we ... the Army ... say to the country ... upon our honour conscription is necessary for your safety ... what answer has the country? What? [He pauses defiantly.] There you are ... none!
TREGONING. Booth will imagine because one doesn't argue that one has nothing to say. You ask the country.
MAJOR BOOTH VOYSEY. Perhaps I will. Perhaps I'll chuck the Service and go into the House. [Then falling into the sing-song of a favorite phrase.] I'm not a conceited man ... but I believe that if I speak out upon a subject I understand and only upon that subject the House will listen ... and if others followed my example we should be a far more business-like and go-ahead community.

[He pauses for breath and MR. BOOTH seizes the opportunity.]

MR. GEORGE BOOTH. If you think the gentlemen of England will allow themselves to be herded with a lot of low fellers and made to carry guns —!
MAJOR BOOTH VOYSEY [obliterating him once more]. Just one moment. Have you thought of the physical improvement which conscription would bring about in the manhood of the country? What England wants is Chest! [He generously inflates his own.] Chest and Discipline. Never mind how it's obtained. Don't we suffer from a lack of it in our homes? The servant question now ...
MR. VOYSEY [with the crack of a nut]. Your godson talks a deal, don't he? You know, when our Major gets into a club, he gets on the committee ... gets on any committee to enquire into anything ... and then goes on at 'em just like this. Don't you, Booth?

[BOOTH knuckles under easily enough to his father's sarcasm.]

MAJOR BOOTH VOYSEY. Well, sir, people tell me I'm a useful man on committees.
MR. VOYSEY. I don't doubt it ... your voice must drown all discussion.

MAJOR BOOTH VOYSEY. You can't say I don't listen to you, sir.

MR. VOYSEY. I don't... and I'm not blaming you. But I must say I often think what a devil of a time the family will have with you when I'm gone. Fortunately for your poor mother, she's deaf.

MAJOR BOOTH VOYSEY. And wouldn't you wish me, sir, as eldest son... Trenchard not counting...

MR. VOYSEY [*with the crack of another nut*]. Trenchard not counting. By all means, bully them. Never mind whether you're right or wrong... bully them. I don't manage things that way myself, but I think it's your best chance... if there weren't other people present I might say your only chance, Booth.

MAJOR BOOTH VOYSEY [*with some discomfort*]. Ha! If I were a conceited man, sir, I could trust you to take it out of me.

MR. VOYSEY [*as he taps* MR. BOOTH *with the nut-crackers*]. Help yourself, George, and drink to your godson's health. Long may he keep his chest notes! Never heard him on parade, have you?

TREGONING. I notice military men must display themselves... that's why Booth acts as a firescreen. I believe that after mess that position is positively rushed.

MAJOR BOOTH VOYSEY [*cheering to find an opponent he can tackle*]. If you want a bit of fire, say so, you sucking Lord Chancellor. Because I mean to allow you to be my brother-in-law, you think you can be impertinent.

[*So* TREGONING *moves to the fire and that changes the conversation.*]

MR. VOYSEY. By the bye, Vicar, you were at Lady Mary's yesterday. Is she giving us anything towards that window?

MR. COLPUS. Five pounds more; she has promised me five pounds.

MR. VOYSEY. Then how will the debt stand?

MR. COLPUS. Thirty-three... no, thirty-two pounds.

MR. VOYSEY. We're a long time clearing it off.

MR. COLPUS [*gently querulous*]. Yes, now that the window is up, people don't seem so ready to contribute as they were.

TREGONING. We must mention that to Hugh!

MR. COLPUS [*tactful at once*]. Not that the work is not universally admired. I have heard Hugh's design praised by quite competent judges. But certainly I feel now it might have been wiser to have delayed the unveiling until the money was forthcoming.

TREGONING. Never deliver goods to the Church on credit.

MR. COLPUS. Eh?

[TREGONING *knows he is a little hard of hearing.*]

MR. VOYSEY. Well, as it was my wish that my son should do the design, I suppose in the end I shall have to send you a cheque.

MAJOR BOOTH VOYSEY. Anonymously.

MR. COLPUS. Oh, that would be —

MR. VOYSEY. No, why should I? Here, George Booth, you shall halve it with me.

MR. GEORGE BOOTH. I'm damned if I do.

MR. COLPUS [*proceeding, conveniently deaf*]. You remember that at the meeting we had of the parents and friends to decide on the positions of the names of the poor fellows and the regiments and coats of arms and so on... when Hugh said so violently that he disapproved of the war and made all those remarks about Randlords and Bibles and said he thought of putting in a figure of Britannia blushing for shame or something... I'm beginning to fear that may have created a bad impression.

MAJOR BOOTH VOYSEY. Why should they mind... what on earth does Hugh know about war? He couldn't tell a battery horse from a bandsman. I don't pretend to criticise art. I think the window'd be very pretty if it wasn't so broken up into bits.

MR. GEORGE BOOTH [*fortified by his "damned" and his last glass of port*]. These young men are so ready with their disapproval. When I was young, people weren't always questioning this and questioning that.

MAJOR BOOTH VOYSEY. Lack of discipline.

MR. GEORGE BOOTH [*hurrying on*]. The

way a man now even stops to think what he's eating and drinking. And in religious matters... Vicar, I put it to you... there's no uniformity at all.

MR. COLPUS. Ah... I try to keep myself free from the disturbing influences of modern thought.

MR. GEORGE BOOTH. You know, Edward, you're worse even than Hugh is.

EDWARD [*glancing up mildly at this sudden attack*]. What have I done, Mr. Booth?

MR. GEORGE BOOTH [*not the readiest of men*]. Well... aren't you another of those young men who go about the world making difficulties?

EDWARD. What sort of difficulties?

MR. GEORGE BOOTH [*triumphantly*]. Just so... I never can make out... Surely when you're young you can ask the advice of your elders and when you grow up you find Laws... lots of laws divine and human laid down for our guidance. [*Well in possession of the conversation he spreads his little self.*] I look back over a fairly long life and... perhaps I should say by Heaven's help... I find nothing that I can honestly reproach myself with. And yet I don't think I ever took more than five minutes to come to a decision upon any important point. One's private life is, I think, one's own affair... I should allow no one to pry into that. But as to worldly things... well, I have come into several sums of money and my capital is still intact... ask your father. [MR. VOYSEY *nods gravely.*] I've never robbed any man. I've never lied over anything that mattered. As a citizen I pay my taxes without grumbling very much. Yes, and I sent conscience money too upon one occasion. I consider that any man who takes the trouble can live the life of a gentleman.

[*And he finds that his cigar is out.*]

MAJOR BOOTH VOYSEY [*not to be outdone by this display of virtue*]. Well, I'm not a conceited man, but —

TREGONING. Are you sure, Booth?

MAJOR BOOTH VOYSEY. Shut up. I was going to say when my young cub of a brother-in-law-to-be interrupted me, that *Training,* for which we all have to be thankful to you, Sir, has much to do with it. [*Suddenly he pulls his trousers against his legs.*] I say, I'm scorching! D'you want another cigar, Denis?

TREGONING. No, thank you.

MAJOR BOOTH VOYSEY. I do.

[*And he glances round, but* TREGONING *sees a box on the table and reaches it. The* VICAR *gets up.*]

MR. COLPUS. M-m-m-must be taking my departure.

MR. VOYSEY. Already!

MAJOR BOOTH VOYSEY [*frowning upon the cigar box*]. No, not those. Where are the Ramon Allones? What on earth has Honor done with them?

MR. VOYSEY. Spare time for a chat with Mrs. Voysey before you go. She has ideas about a children's tea fight.

MR. COLPUS. Certainly I will.

MAJOR BOOTH VOYSEY [*scowling helplessly around*]. My goodness!... one can never find anything in this house.

MR. COLPUS. I won't say good-bye then.

[*He is sliding through the half-opened door when* ETHEL *meets him flinging it wide. She is the younger daughter, the baby of the family, but twenty-three now.*]

MR. VOYSEY. I say, it's cold again to-night! An ass of an architect who built this place... such a draught between these two doors.

[*He gets up to draw the curtain. When he turns* COLPUS *has disappeared, while* ETHEL *has been followed into the room by* ALICE MAITLAND, *who shuts the door after her.* MISS ALICE MAITLAND *is a young lady of any age to thirty. Nor need her appearance alter for the next fifteen years; since her nature is healthy and well-balanced. She possesses indeed the sort of athletic chastity which is a characteristic charm of Northern spinsterhood. It mayn't be a pretty face, but it has alertness and humour; and the resolute eyes and eyebrows are a more innocent edition of* MR. VOYSEY'S, *who is her uncle.* ETHEL *goes straight to her father (though her glance is on* DENIS *and* his on her) and chirps, birdlike, in her spoiled-child way.]

ETHEL. We think you've stayed in here quite long enough.

MR. VOYSEY. That's to say, Ethel thinks Denis has been kept out of her pocket much too long.

ETHEL. Ethel wants billiards . . . not proper billiards . . . snooker or something. Oh, Papa, what a dessert you've eaten. Greedy pig!

[ALICE *is standing behind* EDWARD, *considering his hair-parting apparently.*]

ALICE. Crack me a filbert, please, Edward . . . I had none.

EDWARD [*jumping up, rather formally, well-mannered*]. I beg your pardon, Alice. Won't you sit down?

ALICE. No.

MR. VOYSEY [*taking* ETHEL *on his knee*]. Come here, puss. Have you made up your mind yet what you want for a wedding present?

ETHEL [*rectifying a stray hair in his beard*]. After mature consideration, I decide on a cheque.

MR. VOYSEY. Do you!

ETHEL. Yes, I think that a cheque will give most scope to your generosity. If you desire to add any trimmings in the shape of a piano or a Turkey carpet you may . . . and Denis and I will be very grateful. But I think I'd let yourself go over a cheque.

MR. VOYSEY. You're a minx.

ETHEL. What is the use of having money if you don't spend it on me?

MAJOR BOOTH VOYSEY [*giving up the cigar search*]. Here, who's going to play?

MR. GEORGE BOOTH [*pathetically as he gets up*]. Well, if my wrist will hold out . . .

MAJOR BOOTH VOYSEY [*to* TREGONING]. No, don't you bother to look for 'them. [*He strides from the room, his voice echoing through the hall.*] Honor, where are those Ramon Allones?

ALICE [*calling after*]. She's in the drawing-room with Auntie and Mr. Colpus.

MR. VOYSEY. Now I should suggest that you and Denis go and take off the billiard-table cover. You'll find folding it up a very excellent amusement.

[*He illustrates his meaning with his table napkin and by putting together the tips of his forefingers, roguishly.*]

ETHEL. I am not going to blush. I do kiss Denis . . . occasionally . . . when he asks me.

MR. GEORGE BOOTH [*teasing her*]. You are blushing.

ETHEL. I am not. If you think we're ashamed of being in love, we're not, we're very proud of it. We will go and take off the billiard-table cover and fold it up . . . and then you can come in and play. Denis, my dear, come along solemnly and if you flinch I'll never forgive you. [*She marches off and reaches the door before her defiant dignity breaks down; then suddenly —*] Denis, I'll race you.

[*And she flashes out.* DENIS, *loyal, but with no histrionic instincts, follows her rather sheepishly.*]

DENIS. Ethel, I can't after dinner.

MR. VOYSEY. Women play that game better than men. A man shuffles through courtship with one eye on her relations.

[*The* MAJOR *comes stalking back, followed in a fearful flurry by his elder sister,* HONOR. *Poor* HONOR *(her female friends are apt to refer to her as "Poor HONOR") is a phenomenon common to most large families. From her earliest years she has been bottle-washer to her brothers. While they were expensively educated she was grudged schooling; her highest accomplishment was meant to be mending their clothes. Her fate is a curious survival of the intolerance of parents towards her sex until the vanity of their hunger for sons had been satisfied. In a less humane society she would have been exposed at birth. But if a very general though patronising affection, accompanied by no consideration at all, can bestow happiness,* HONOR *is not unhappy in her survival. At this moment, however, her life is a burden.*]

MAJOR BOOTH VOYSEY. Honor, they are not in the dining-room.

HONOR. But they must be! — Where else can they be?

[*She has a habit of accentuating one word in each sentence and often the wrong one.*]

MAJOR BOOTH VOYSEY. That's what you ought to know.

MR. VOYSEY [*as he moves towards the door*]. Well . . . will you have a game?

MR. GEORGE BOOTH. I'll play you fifty up, not more. I'm getting old.

MR. VOYSEY [*stopping at a dessert dish*]. Yes, these are good apples of Bearman's. I think six of my trees are spoilt this year.

HONOR. Here you are, Booth.

[*She triumphantly discovers the discarded box, at which the* MAJOR *becomes pathetic with indignation.*]

MAJOR BOOTH VOYSEY. Oh, Honor, don't be such a fool. These are what we've been smoking. I want the Ramon Allones.

HONOR. I don't know the difference.

MAJOR BOOTH VOYSEY. No, you don't, but you might learn.

MR. VOYSEY [*in a voice like the crack of a very fine whip*]. Booth.

MAJOR BOOTH VOYSEY [*subduedly*]. What is it, sir?

MR. VOYSEY. Look for your cigars yourself. Honor, go back to your reading or your sewing or whatever you were fiddling at, and fiddle in peace.

[MR. VOYSEY *departs, leaving the room rather hushed.* MR. BOOTH *has not waited for this parental display. Then* ALICE *insinuates a remark very softly.*]

ALICE. Have you looked in the Library?

MAJOR BOOTH VOYSEY [*relapsing to an injured mutter*]. Where's Emily?

HONOR. Upstairs with little Henry; he woke up and cried.

MAJOR BOOTH VOYSEY. Letting her wear herself to rags over the child . . . !

HONOR. Well, she won't let me go.

MAJOR BOOTH VOYSEY. Why don't you stop looking for those cigars?

HONOR. If you don't mind, I want a reel of blue silk now I'm here.

MAJOR BOOTH VOYSEY. I daresay they are in the Library. What a house!

[*He departs.*]

HONOR. Booth is so trying.

ALICE. Honor, why do you put up with it?

HONOR. Someone has to.

ALICE [*discreetly nibbling a nut, which* EDWARD *has cracked for her*]. I'm afraid I think Master Major Booth ought to have been taken in hand early . . . with a cane.

HONOR [*as she vaguely burrows into corners*]. Papa did. But it's never prevented him booming at us . . . oh, ever since he was a baby. Now he's flustered me so I simply can't think where this blue silk is.

ALICE. All the Pettifers desired to be remembered to you, Edward.

HONOR. I must do without it. [*But she goes on looking.*] I sometimes think, Alice, that we're a very difficult family . . . except perhaps Edward.

EDWARD. Why except me?

HONOR [*who has only excepted out of politeness to present company*]. And you were always difficult . . . to yourself. [*Then she starts to go, threading her way through the disarranged chairs.*] Mr. Colpus will shout so loud at Mother and she hates people to think she's so very deaf. I thought Mary Pettifer looking old. . . .

[*And she talks herself out of the room.*]

ALICE [*after her*]. She's getting old.

[*Now* ALICE *does sit down; as if she'd be glad of her tête-à-tête.*]

ALICE. I was glad not to spend August abroad for once. We drove into Cheltenham to a dance . . . carpet. I golfed a lot.

EDWARD. How long were you with them?

ALICE. Not a fortnight. It doesn't seem three months since I was here, does it?

EDWARD. I'm down so very little.

ALICE. I'm here a disgraceful deal.

EDWARD. You know they're always pleased.

ALICE. Well, being a homeless person! But what a cart-load to descend all at once . . . yesterday and to-day. The Major and Emily . . . Emily's not at all well. Hugh and Mrs. Hugh. And me. Are you staying?

EDWARD. No. I must get a word with my father . . .

ALICE. Edward, a business life is not healthy for you. You look more like half-baked pie-crust than usual.

THE VOYSEY INHERITANCE

EDWARD [*a little enviously*]. You're very well.

ALICE. I'm always well and nearly always happy.

[MAJOR BOOTH *returns. He has the right sort of cigar in his mouth and is considerably mollified.*]

ALICE. You found them?

MAJOR BOOTH VOYSEY. Of course, they were there. Thank you very much, Alice. Now I want a knife.

ALICE. I must give you a cigar-cutter for Christmas, Booth.

MAJOR BOOTH VOYSEY. Beastly things, I hate 'em, thank you. [*He eyes the dessert disparagingly.*] Nothing but silver ones. [EDWARD *hands him a carefully opened pocket-knife.*] Thank you, Edward. And I must take one of the candles. Something's gone wrong with the library ventilator and you never can see a thing in that room.

ALICE. Is Mrs. Hugh there?

MAJOR BOOTH VOYSEY. Writing letters. Things are neglected, Edward, unless one is constantly on the look out. The Pater only cares for his garden. I must speak seriously to Honor.

[*He has returned the knife, still open, and now having lit his cigar at the candle he carries this off.*]

ALICE. Honor has the patience of a ... of an old maid.

EDWARD. Yes, I suppose her mission in life isn't a very pleasant one. [*He gives her a nut, about the fifteenth.*] Here; 'scuse fingers.

ALICE. Thank you [*looking at him, with her head on one side and her face more humorous than ever*]. Edward, why have you given up proposing to me?

[*He starts, flushes; then won't be outdone in humour.*]

EDWARD. One can't go on proposing for ever.

ALICE [*reasonably*]. Why not? Have you seen anyone you like better?

EDWARD. No.

ALICE. Well ... I miss it.

EDWARD. What satisfaction did you find in refusing me?

ALICE [*as she weighs the matter*]. I find satisfaction in feeling that I'm wanted.

EDWARD. Without any intention of giving yourself ... throwing yourself away.

ALICE [*teasing his sudden earnestness*]. Ah, now you come from mere vanity to serious questions.

EDWARD. Mine was a very serious question to you.

ALICE. But, Edward, all questions are serious to you. I call you a perfect little pocket-guide to life ... all questions and answers; what to eat, drink, and avoid, what to believe and what to say ...

EDWARD [*sententiously*]. Well ... everything matters.

ALICE [*making a face*]. D'you plan out every detail of your life ... every step you take ... every mouthful?

EDWARD. That would be waste of thought. One must lay down principles.

ALICE. I prefer my plan, I always do what I know I want to do. Crack me another nut.

EDWARD. Haven't you had enough?

ALICE. I *know* I want one more. [*He cracks another, with a sigh which sounds ridiculous in that connection.*] I know it just as I knew I didn't want to marry you ... each time.

EDWARD. Oh, you didn't make a rule of saying no.

ALICE. As you proposed ... on principle? No, I always gave you a fair chance. I'll give you one now if you like. Courage, I might say yes ... all in a flash. Oh, you'd never get over it.

EDWARD. I think we won't run the risk.

ALICE. Edward, how rude you are. [*She eats her nut contentedly.*] There's nothing wrong, is there?

EDWARD. Nothing at all.

[*They are interrupted by the sudden appearance of* MRS. HUGH VOYSEY, *a brisk, bright little woman, in an evening gown, which she has bullied a cheap dressmaker into making look exceedingly smart.* BEATRICE *is as hard as nails and as clever as paint. But if she keeps her feelings buried pretty deep it is because they are precious to her; and if she is impatient with fools it is because her own brains have had to win her everything in the* world, so perhaps she does overvalue them a little. She speaks always with great decision and little effort.]

BEATRICE. I believe I could write important business letters upon an island in the middle of Fleet Street. But while Booth is poking at a ventilator with a billiard cue . . . no, I can't.

[She goes to the fireplace, waving her half-finished letter.]

ALICE [soothingly]. Didn't you expect Hugh back to dinner?

BEATRICE. Not specially . . . He went to rout out some things from his studio. He'll come back in a filthy mess.

ALICE. Ssh! Now if you listen . . . Booth doesn't enjoy making a fuss by himself . . . you'll hear him put up Honor.

[They listen. But what happens is that BOOTH appears at the door, billiard cue in hand, and says solemnly:]

MAJOR BOOTH VOYSEY. Edward, I wish you'd come and have a look at this ventilator, like a good fellow.

[Then he turns and goes again, obviously with the weight of an important matter on his shoulders. With the ghost of a smile EDWARD gets up and follows him.]

ALICE. If I belonged to this family I should hate Booth.

[With which comment she joins BEATRICE at the fireplace.]

BEATRICE. A good day's shopping?

ALICE. 'M. The baby bride and I bought clothes all the morning. Then we had lunch with Denis and bought furniture.

BEATRICE. Nice furniture?

ALICE. Very good and very new. They neither of them know what they want. [Then suddenly throwing up her chin and exclaiming.] When it's a question of money I can understand it . . . but if one can provide for oneself or is independent why get married! Especially having been brought up on the sheltered life principle . . . one may as well make the most of its advantages . . . one doesn't go falling in love all over the place as men seem to . . . most of them. Of course, with Ethel and Denis it's different. They've both been caught young. They're two little birds building their nest and it's all ideal. They'll soon forget they've ever been apart.

[Now HONOR flutters into the room, patient but wild-eyed.]

HONOR. Mother wants last week's Notes and Queries. Have you seen it?

BEATRICE [exasperated at the interruption]. No.

HONOR. It ought not to be in here. [So she proceeds to look for it.] She's having a long argument with Mr. Colpus over Oliver Cromwell's relations.

ALICE [her eyes twinkling]. I thought Auntie didn't approve of Oliver Cromwell.

HONOR. She doesn't, and she's trying to prove that he was a brewer or something. I suppose someone has taken it away.

[So she gives up the search and flutters out again.]

ALICE. This is a most unrestful house.

BEATRICE. I once thought of putting the Voyseys into a book of mine. Then I concluded they'd be as dull there as they are anywhere else.

ALICE. They're not duller than most people.

BEATRICE. But how very dull that is!

ALICE. They're a little noisier and perhaps not quite so well mannered. But I love them.

BEATRICE. I don't. I should have thought love was just what they couldn't inspire.

ALICE. Of course, Hugh is unlike any of the others.

BEATRICE. He has most of their bad points. But I don't love Hugh.

ALICE [her eyebrows up, though she smiles]. Beatrice, you shouldn't say so.

BEATRICE. Sounds affected, doesn't it? Never mind; when he dies I'll wear mourning . . . but not weeds; I bargained against that when we were engaged.

ALICE [her face growing a little thoughtful]. Beatrice, I'm going to ask questions. You were in love with Hugh when you married him?

BEATRICE. Well . . . I married him for his money . . .

ALICE. He hadn't much.

BEATRICE. I had none . . . and I wanted to write books. Yes, I loved him.

ALICE. And you thought you'd be happy?

BEATRICE [*considering carefully*]. No, I didn't. I hoped he'd be happy.

ALICE [*a little ironical*]. Did you think your writing books would make him so?

BEATRICE. My dear Alice, shouldn't a man ... or a woman feel it a very degrading thing to have their happiness depend upon somebody else?

ALICE [*after pausing to find her phrase*]. There's a joy of service. Is that very womanly of me?

BEATRICE [*ironical herself now*]. Ah, but you've four hundred a year.

ALICE. What has that to do with it?

BEATRICE [*putting her case very precisely*]. Fine feelings, my dear, are as much a luxury as clean gloves. Now, I've had to earn my own living; consequently there isn't one thing in my life that I have ever done quite genuinely for its own sake ... but always with an eye towards bread-and-butter, pandering to the people who were to give me that. I warned Hugh ... he took the risk.

ALICE. What risk?

BEATRICE. That one day I'd be able to get on without him.

ALICE. By the time he'd learnt how not to without you?

BEATRICE. Well, women must have the courage to be brutal.

[*The conservatory door opens and through it come* MR. VOYSEY *and* MR. BOOTH *in the midst of a discussion.*]

MR. VOYSEY. My dear man, stick to the shares and risk it.

MR. GEORGE BOOTH. No, of course, if you seriously advise me —

MR. VOYSEY. I never advise greedy children; I let 'em overeat 'emselves and take the consequences —

ALICE [*shaking a finger*]. Uncle Trench, you've been in the garden without a hat after playing billiards in that hot room.

MR. GEORGE BOOTH. We had to give up ... my wrist was bad. They've started pool.

BEATRICE. Is Booth going to play?

MR. VOYSEY. We left him instructing Ethel how to hold a cue.

BEATRICE. Ah! I can finish my letter.

[*Off she goes.* ALICE *is idly following with a little paper her hand has fallen on behind the clock.*]

MR. VOYSEY. Don't run away, my dear.

ALICE. I'm taking this to Auntie ... *Notes and Queries* ... she wants it.

MR. GEORGE BOOTH. Damn ... this gravel's stuck to my shoe.

MR. VOYSEY. That's a new-made path.

MR. GEORGE BOOTH. Now don't you think it's too early to have put in those plants?

MR. VOYSEY. No, we've had a frost or two already.

MR. GEORGE BOOTH. I should have kept the bed a good ten feet further from that tree.

MR. VOYSEY. Nonsense, the tree's to the north of it. This room's cold. Why don't they keep the fire up!

[*He proceeds to put coals on it.*]

MR. GEORGE BOOTH. You were too hot in that billiard room. You know, Voysey ... about those Alguazils?

MR. VOYSEY [*through the rattling of the coals*]. What?

MR. GEORGE BOOTH [*trying to pierce the din*]. Those Alguazils.

[MR. VOYSEY *with surprising inconsequence points a finger at the silk handkerchief across* MR. BOOTH'S *shirt front.*]

MR. VOYSEY. What d'you put your handkerchief there for?

MR. GEORGE BOOTH. Measure of precau — [*at that moment he sneezes*]. Damn it ... if you've given me a chill dragging me through your infernal garden ...

MR. VOYSEY [*slapping him on the back*]. You're an old crook.

MR. GEORGE BOOTH. Well, I'll be glad of this winter in Egypt. [*He returns to his subject.*] And if you think seriously, that I ought to sell out of the Alguazils before I go ... ? [*He looks with childlike enquiry at his friend, who is apparently yawning slightly.*] Why can't you take them in charge? ... and I'll give you a power of attorney ... or whatever it is ... and you can sell out if things look bad.

[*At this moment* PHŒBE, *the middle-aged parlour-maid comes in, tray in* hand. *Like an expert fisherman* MR. VOYSEY *once more lets loose the thread of the conversation.*]

MR. VOYSEY. D' you want to clear?

PHŒBE. It doesn't matter, sir.

MR. VOYSEY. No, go on . . . go on.

[*So* MARY, *the young housemaid, comes in as well, and the two start to clear the table. All of which fidgets poor* MR. BOOTH *considerably. He sits shrivelled up in the armchair by the fire; and now* MR. VOYSEY *attends to him.*]

MR. VOYSEY. What d'you want with high interest at all . . . you never spend half your income?

MR. GEORGE BOOTH. I like to feel that my money is doing some good in the world. Mines are very useful things and forty-two per cent is pleasing.

MR. VOYSEY. You're an old gambler.

MR. GEORGE BOOTH [*propitiatingly*]. Ah, but then I've you to advise me. I always do as you tell me in the end, now you can't deny that. . . .

MR. VOYSEY. The man who don't know must trust in the men who do!

[*He yawns again.*]

MR. GEORGE BOOTH [*modestly insisting*]. There's five thousand in Alguazils — what else could we put it into?

MR. VOYSEY. I can get you something at four and a half.

MR. GEORGE BOOTH. Oh, Lord . . . that's nothing.

MR. VOYSEY [*with a sudden serious friendliness*]. I wish, my dear George, you'd invest more on your own account. You know — what with one thing and the other — I've got control of practically all you have in the world. I might be playing old Harry with it for all you know.

MR. GEORGE BOOTH [*overflowing with confidence*]. My dear feller . . . if I'm satisfied! Ah, my friend, what'll happen to your firm when you depart this life! . . . not before my time, I hope, though.

MR. VOYSEY [*with a little frown*]. What d'ye mean?

MR. GEORGE BOOTH. Edward's no use.

MR. VOYSEY. I beg your pardon . . . very sound in business.

MR. GEORGE BOOTH. May be . . . but I tell you he's no use. Too many principles, as I told him just now. Men have confidence in a personality, not in principles. Where would you be without the confidence of your clients?

MR. VOYSEY [*candidly*]. True!

MR. GEORGE BOOTH. He'll never gain that.

MR. VOYSEY. I fear you dislike Edward.

MR. GEORGE BOOTH [*with pleasant frankness*]. Yes, I do.

MR. VOYSEY. That's a pity. That's a very great pity.

MR. GEORGE BOOTH [*with a flattering smile*]. He's not his father and never will be. What's the time?

MR. VOYSEY [*with inappropriate thoughtfulness*]. Twenty to ten.

MR. GEORGE BOOTH. I must be trotting.

MR. VOYSEY. It's early.

MR. GEORGE BOOTH. Oh, and I've not said a word to Mrs. Voysey . . .

[*As he goes to the door he meets* EDWARD, *who comes in apparently looking for his father; at any rate, catches his eye immediately, while* MR. BOOTH *obliviously continues.*]

MR. GEORGE BOOTH. Will you stroll round home with me?

MR. VOYSEY. I can't.

MR. GEORGE BOOTH [*mildly surprised at the short reply*]. Well, good-night. Good-night, Edward. [*He trots away.*]

MR. VOYSEY. Leave the rest of the table, Phœbe.

PHŒBE. Yes, sir.

MR. VOYSEY. You can come back in ten minutes.

[PHŒBE *and* MARY *depart and the door is closed. Alone with his son,* MR. VOYSEY *does not move; his face grows a little keener, that's all.*]

MR. VOYSEY. Well, Edward?

[EDWARD *starts to move restlessly about, like a cowed animal in a cage; silently for a moment or two. Then, when he speaks, his voice is toneless and he doesn't look at his father.*]

EDWARD. Would you mind, sir, dropping with me for the future all these protestations about putting the firm's affairs straight... about all your anxieties and sacrifices. I see now, of course... a cleverer man than I could have seen it yesterday... that for some time, ever since, I suppose, you recovered from the first shock and got used to the double-dealing, this hasn't been your object at all. You've used your clients' capital to produce your own income... to bring us up and endow us with. Booth's ten thousand pounds; what you are giving Ethel on her marriage ... It's odd it never struck me yesterday that my own pocket-money as a boy must have been quite simply withdrawn from some client's account. You've been very generous to us all, father. I suppose about half the sum you've spent on us first and last would have put things right.

MR. VOYSEY. No, it would not.

EDWARD [appealing for the truth]. Yes, yes... at some time or other!

MR. VOYSEY. Well, if there have been good times there have been bad times. At present the three hundred a year I'm to allow your sister is going to be rather a pull.

EDWARD. Three hundred a year... while you don't attempt to make a single client safe. Since it isn't lunacy, sir... I can only conclude that you enjoy such a position.

MR. VOYSEY. Safe? Three trusts — two of them big ones — have been wound up within this last eighteen months, and the accounts have been above suspicion. What's the object of all this rodomontade, Edward?

EDWARD. If I'm to remain in the firm, it had better be with a very clear understanding of things as they are.

MR. VOYSEY [firmly, not too anxiously]. Then you do remain?

EDWARD [in a very low voice]. I must remain.

MR. VOYSEY [quite gravely]. That's wise of you... I'm very glad. [And he is silent for a moment.] And now we needn't discuss the unpractical side of it any more.

EDWARD. But I want to make one condition. And I want some information.

MR. VOYSEY [his sudden cheerfulness relapsing again]. Well?

EDWARD. Of course no one has ever discovered... and no one suspects this state of things?

MR. VOYSEY. Peacey knows.

EDWARD. Peacey!

MR. VOYSEY. His father found out.

EDWARD. Oh. Does he draw hush money?

MR. VOYSEY [curling a little at the word]. It is my custom to make him a little present every Christmas. [He becomes benevolent.] I don't grudge the money... Peacey's a devoted fellow.

EDWARD. Certainly this should be a heavily taxed industry. [Then he smiles at his vision of the mild old clerk.] Peacey! There's another thing I want to ask, sir. Have you ever under stress of circumstances done worse than just make this temporary use of a client's capital? You boasted to me yesterday that no one had ever suffered in pocket in the end because of you. Is that absolutely true?

[MR. VOYSEY draws himself up, dignified and magniloquent.]

MR. VOYSEY. My dear Edward, for the future my mind is open to you; you can discover for yourself how matters stand to-day. But I decline to gratify your curiosity as to what is over and done with.

EDWARD [with entire comprehension]. Thank you, sir. The condition of my remaining is that we should really try as unobtrusively as you like and put things straight.

MR. VOYSEY [with a little polite shrug]. I've no doubt you'll prove an abler man of business than I.

EDWARD. We can begin by halving the salary I draw from the firm; that leaves me enough.

MR. VOYSEY. I see... Retrenchment and Reform.

EDWARD. And it seems to me that you can't give Ethel this five thousand pound dowry.

MR. VOYSEY [shortly, with one of the quick twists of his eye]. I have given my word to Denis...

EDWARD. Because the money isn't yours to give.

MR. VOYSEY [in an indignant crescendo]. I should not dream of depriving Ethel of what, as my daughter, she has every right to expect. I am surprised at your suggesting such a thing.

EDWARD [*pale and firm*]. I'm set on this, father.

MR. VOYSEY. Don't be such a fool, Edward. What would it look like ... suddenly to refuse without rhyme or reason? What would old Tregoning think?

EDWARD. Oh, can't you see it's my duty to prevent this?

MR. VOYSEY. You can prevent it by telling the nearest policeman. It is my duty to pay no more attention to these scruples of yours than a nurse pays to her child's tantrums. Understand, Edward, I don't want to force you to continue my partner. Come with me gladly or don't come at all.

EDWARD [*dully*]. It is my duty to be of what use I can to you, sir. Father, I want to save you if I can.

[*He flashes into this exclamation of almost broken-hearted affection.* MR. VOYSEY *looks at his son for a moment and his lip quivers. Then he steels himself.*]

MR. VOYSEY. Thank you! I have saved myself quite satisfactorily for the last thirty years, and you must please believe that by this time I know my own business best.

EDWARD [*hopelessly*]. Can't we find the money some other way? How do you manage now about your own income?

MR. VOYSEY. I have a bank balance and a cheque book, haven't I? I spend what I think well to spend. What's the use of earmarking this or that as my own? You say none of it is my own. I might say it's all my own. I think I've earned it.

EDWARD [*anger coming on him*]. That's what I can't forgive. If you'd lived poor ... if you'd really done all you could for your clients and not thought only of your own aggrandisement ... then, even though things were no better than they are now, I could have been proud of you. But, father, own the truth to me, at least ... that's my due from you, considering how I'm placed by all you've done. Didn't you simply seize this opportunity as a means to your own ends, to your own enriching?

MR. VOYSEY [*with a sledgehammer irony*]. Certainly. I sat that morning in my father's office, studying the helmet of the policeman in the street below, and thinking what a glorious path I had happened on to wealth and honour and renown. [*Then he begins to bully* EDWARD *in the kindliest way.*] My dear boy, you evidently haven't begun to grasp the A B C of my position. What has carried me to victory? The confidence of my clients. What has earned that confidence? A decent life, my integrity, my brains? No, my reputation for wealth ... that, and nothing else. Business now-a-days is run on the lines of the confidence trick. What makes old George Booth so glad to trust me with every penny he possesses? Not affection ... he's never cared for anything in his life but his collection of prints.

EDWARD [*stupefied, helpless*]. Is he involved?

MR. VOYSEY. Of course he's involved, and he's always after high interest too ... it's little one makes out of him. But there's a further question here, Edward. Should I have had confidence in myself, if I'd remained a poor man? No, I should not. You must either be the master of money or its servant. And if one is not opulent in one's daily life one loses that wonderful ... financier's touch. One must be confident oneself ... and I saw from the first that I must at any cost inspire confidence. My whole public and private life has tended to that. All my surroundings ... you and your brothers and sisters that I have brought into, and up, and put out in the world so worthily ... you in your turn inspire confidence.

EDWARD. Not our worth, not our abilities, nor our virtues, but the fact that we travel first class and take cabs when we want to.

MR. VOYSEY [*impatiently*]. Well, I haven't organised Society upon a basis of wealth.

EDWARD. I sat down yesterday to make a list of the people who are good enough to trust their money to us. It'll be a pretty long one ... and it's an interesting one, from George Booth with his big income to old Nursie with her savings which she brought you so proudly to invest. But you've let those be, at least.

MR. VOYSEY. I just... took the money...

EDWARD. Father!

MR. VOYSEY. Five hundred pounds. Not worth worrying about.

EDWARD. That's damnable.

MR. VOYSEY. Indeed. I give her seventy-five pounds a year for it. Would you like to take charge of that account, Edward? I'll give you five hundred to invest to-morrow.

[EDWARD, *hopelessly beaten, falls into an almost comic state of despair.*]

EDWARD. My dear father, putting every moral question aside... it's all very well your playing Robin Hood in this magnificent manner; but have you given a moment's thought to the sort of inheritance you'll be leaving me?

MR. VOYSEY [*pleased for the first time*]. Ah! That is a question you have every right to ask.

EDWARD. If you died to-morrow could we pay eight shillings in the pound... or seventeen... or five? Do you know?

MR. VOYSEY. And the answer is, that by your help I have every intention, when I die, of leaving a will behind me of property to you all running into six figures. D'you think I've given my life and my talents for a less result than that? I'm fond of you all... and I want you to be proud of me ... and I mean that the name of Voysey shall be carried high in the world by my children and grandchildren. Don't you be afraid, Edward. Ah, you lack experience, my boy... you're not full grown yet... your impulses are a bit chaotic. You emotionalise over your work, and you reason about your emotions. You must sort yourself. You must realise that money making is one thing, and religion another, and family life a third... and that if we apply our energies whole-heartedly to each of these in turn, and realise that different laws govern each, that there is a different end to be served, a different ideal to be striven for in each...

[*His coherence is saved by the sudden appearance of his wife, who comes round the door smiling benignly. Not in the least put out, in fact a little relieved, he greets her with an affectionate shout, for she is very deaf.*]

MR. VOYSEY. Hullo, mother!

MRS. VOYSEY. Oh, there you are, Trench. I've been deserted.

MR. VOYSEY. George Booth gone?

MRS. VOYSEY. Are you talking business? Perhaps you don't want me.

MR. VOYSEY. No, no... no business.

MRS. VOYSEY [*who has not looked for his answer*]. I suppose the others are in the billiard room.

MR. VOYSEY [*vociferously*]. We're not talking business, old lady.

EDWARD. I'll be off, sir.

MR. VOYSEY [*genial as usual*]. Why don't you stay? I'll come up with you in the morning.

EDWARD. No, thank you, sir.

MR. VOYSEY. Then I shall be up about noon to-morrow.

EDWARD. Good-night, mother.

[MRS. VOYSEY *places a plump kindly hand on his arm and looks up affectionately.*]

MRS. VOYSEY. You look tired.

EDWARD. No, I'm not.

MRS. VOYSEY. What did you say?

EDWARD [*too weary to repeat himself*]. Nothing, mother dear.

[*He kisses her cheek, while she kisses the air.*]

MR. VOYSEY. Good-night, my boy.

[*Then he goes.* MRS. VOYSEY *is carrying her Notes and Queries. This is a dear old lady, looking older too than probably she is. Placid describes her. She has had a life of little joys and cares, has never measured herself against the world, never even questioned the shape and size of the little corner of it in which she lives. She has loved an indulgent husband and borne eight children, six of them surviving, healthy. That is her history.*]

MRS. VOYSEY. George Booth went some time ago. He said he thought you'd taken a chill walking round the garden.

Mr. Voysey. I'm all right.
Mrs. Voysey. D'you think you have?
Mr. Voysey [in her ear]. No.
Mrs. Voysey. You should be careful, Trench. What did you put on?
Mr. Voysey. Nothing.
Mrs. Voysey. How very foolish! Let me feel your hand. You are quite feverish.
Mr. Voysey [affectionately]. You're a fuss-box, old lady.
Mrs. Voysey [coquetting with him]. Don't be rude, Trench.

[Honor *descends upon them. She is well into that nightly turmoil of putting everything and everybody to rights which always precedes her bedtime. She carries a shawl which she clasps round her mother's shoulders, her mind and gaze already on the next thing to be done.*]

Honor. Mother, you left your shawl in the drawing-room. Can they finish clearing?
Mr. Voysey [*arranging the folds of the shawl with real tenderness*]. Now who's careless! [Phœbe *comes into the room.*]
Honor. Phœbe, finish here and then you must bring in the tray for Mr. Hugh.
Mrs. Voysey [*having looked at the shawl, and* Honor, *and connected the matter in her mind*]. Thank you, Honor. You'd better look after your father; he's been walking round the garden without his cape.
Honor. Papa!
Mr. Voysey. Phœbe, you get that little kettle and boil it, and brew me some whiskey and water. I shall be all right.
Honor [*fluttering more than ever*]. I'll get it. Where's the whiskey? And Hugh coming back at ten o'clock with no dinner. No wonder his work goes wrong. Here it is! Papa, you do deserve to be ill.

[*Clasping the whiskey decanter, she is off again.* Mrs. Voysey *sits at the dinner table and adjusts her spectacles. She returns to* Notes and Queries, *one elbow firmly planted and her plump hand against her plump cheek. This is her favourite attitude; and she is apt, when reading, to soliloquise in her deaf woman's voice. At least, whether she considers it soliloquy or conversation is not easy to discover.* Mr. Voysey *stands with his back to the fire, grumbling and pulling faces.*]

Mrs. Voysey. This is a very perplexing correspondence about the Cromwell family. One can't deny the man had good blood in him . . . his grandfather Sir Henry, his uncle Sir Oliver . . .
Mr. Voysey. There's a pain in my back.
Mrs. Voysey. . . . and it's difficult to discover where the taint crept in.
Mr. Voysey. I believe I strained myself putting in all those strawberry plants.

[Mary, *the house parlourmaid, carries in a tray of warmed-up dinner for* Hugh *and plants it on the table.*]

Mrs. Voysey. Yes, but then how was it he came to disgrace himself so? I believe the family disappeared. Regicide is a root and branch curse. You must read this letter signed C. W. A. . . . it's quite interesting. There's a misprint in mine about the first umbrella maker . . . now where was it . . .

[*And so the dear lady will ramble on indefinitely.*]

ACT III

The dining-room looks very different in the white light of a July noon Moreover, on this particular day, it isn't even its normal self. There is a peculiar luncheon spread on the table. The embroidered cloth is placed cornerwise and on it are decanters of port and sherry; sandwiches, biscuits, and an uncut cake; two little piles of plates and one little pile of napkins. There are no table decorations, and indeed the whole room has been made as bare and as tidy as possible. Such preparations denote one of the recognised English festivities, and the appearance of Phœbe, *the maid, who has just completed them, the set solemnity of her face and the added touches of black to her dress and cap, suggest that this is probably a funeral. When* Mary *comes in, the fact that she has evidently*

MARY. Phœbe, they're coming back... and I forgot one of the blinds in the drawing-room.

PHŒBE. Well, pull it up quick and make yourself scarce. I'll open the door.

[MARY *got rid of*, PHŒBE *composes her face still more rigorously into the aspect of formal grief and with a touch to her apron as well goes to admit the funeral party. The first to enter are* MRS. VOYSEY *and* MR. BOOTH, *she on his arm; and the fact that she is in widow's weeds makes the occasion clear. The little old man leads his old friend very tenderly.*]

MR. GEORGE BOOTH. Will you come in here?

MRS. VOYSEY. Thank you.

[*With great solicitude he puts her in a chair; then takes her hand.*]

MR. GEORGE BOOTH. Now I'll intrude no longer.

MRS. VOYSEY. You'll take some lunch?

MR. GEORGE BOOTH. No.

MRS. VOYSEY. Not a glass of wine?

MR. GEORGE BOOTH. If there's anything I can do just send round.

MRS. VOYSEY. Thank you.

[*He reaches the door, only to be met by the* MAJOR *and his wife. He shakes hands with them both.*]

MR. GEORGE BOOTH. My dear Emily! My dear Booth!

[EMILY *is a homely, patient, pale little woman of about thirty-five. She looks smaller than usual in her heavy black dress and is meeker than usual on an occasion of this kind. The* MAJOR, *on the other hand, though his grief is most sincere, has an irresistible air of being responsible for, and indeed rather proud of, the whole affair.*]

BOOTH. I think it all went off as he would have wished.

MR. GEORGE BOOTH [*feeling that he is called on for praise*]. Great credit... great credit.

[*He makes another attempt to escape and is stopped this time by* TRENCHARD VOYSEY, *to whom he is extending a hand and beginning his formula. But* TRENCHARD *speaks first.*]

TRENCHARD. Have you the right time?

MR. GEORGE BOOTH [*taken aback and fumbling for his watch*]. I think so... I make it fourteen minutes to one. [*He seizes the occasion.*] Trenchard, as a very old and dear friend of your father's, you won't mind me saying how glad I was that you were present to-day. Death closes all. Indeed... it must be a great regret to you that you did not see him before... before...

TRENCHARD [*his cold eye freezing this little gush*]. I don't think he asked for me.

MR. GEORGE BOOTH [*stoppered*]. No? No! Well... well...

[*At this third attempt to depart he actually collides with someone in the doorway. It is* HUGH VOYSEY.]

MR. GEORGE BOOTH. My dear Hugh ... I won't intrude.

[*Quite determined to escape, he grasps his hand, gasps out his formula, and is off.* TRENCHARD *and* HUGH, *eldest and youngest son, are as unlike each other as it is possible for* VOYSEYS *to be, but that isn't very unlike.* TRENCHARD *has in excelsis the cocksure manner of the successful barrister;* HUGH *the rather sweet though querulous air of diffidence and scepticism belonging to the unsuccessful man of letters or artist. The self-respect of* TRENCHARD'S *appearance is immense, and he cultivates that air of concentration upon any trivial matter, or even upon nothing at all, which will some day make him an impressive figure upon the Bench.* HUGH *is always vague, searching Heaven or the corners of the room for inspiration, and even on this occasion his tie is abominably crooked. The inspissated gloom of this assembly, to which each member of the family as he arrives adds his share, is unbelievable. Instinct apparently leads them to reproduce as nearly as possible the ap-*

pearance and conduct of the corpse on which their minds are fixed. HUGH *is depressed partly at the inadequacy of his grief;* TRENCHARD *conscientiously preserves an air of the indifference which he feels;* BOOTH *stands statuesque at the mantelpiece; while* EMILY *is by* MRS. VOYSEY, *whose face in its quiet grief is nevertheless a mirror of many happy memories of her husband.*]

BOOTH. I wouldn't hang over her, Emily.

EMILY. No, of course not.

[*Apologetically, she sits by the table.*]

TRENCHARD. I hope your wife is well, Hugh?

HUGH. Thank you, Trench: I think so. Beatrice is in America . . . doing some work there.

TRENCHARD. Really!

[*There comes in a small, well-groomed, bullet-headed boy in Etons. This is the* MAJOR's *eldest son. Looking scared and solemn he goes straight to his mother.*]

EMILY. Now be very quiet, Christopher. . .

[*Then* DENIS TREGONING *appears.*]

TRENCHARD. Oh, Tregoning, did you bring Honor back?

DENIS. Yes.

BOOTH [*at the table*]. A glass of wine, mother.

MRS. VOYSEY. What?

[BOOTH *hardly knows how to turn his whisper decorously into enough of a shout for his mother to hear. But he manages it.*]

BOOTH. Have a glass of wine?

MRS. VOYSEY. Sherry, please.

[*While he pours it out with an air of its being medicine on this occasion and not wine at all,* EDWARD *comes quickly into the room, his face very set, his mind obviously on other matters than the funeral. No one speaks to him for the moment and he has time to observe them all.* TRENCHARD *is continuing his talk to* DENIS.]

TRENCHARD. Give my love to Ethel. Is she ill that —

TREGONING. Not exactly, but she couldn't very well be with us. I thought perhaps you might have heard. We're expecting . . .

[*He hesitates with the bashfulness of a young husband.* TRENCHARD *helps him out with a citizen's bow of respect for a citizen's duty.*]

TRENCHARD. Indeed. I congratulate you. I hope all will be well. Please give my best love to Ethel.

BOOTH [*in an awful voice*]. Lunch, Emily?

EMILY [*scared*]. I suppose so, Booth, thank you.

BOOTH. I think the boy had better run away and play . . . [*He checks himself on the word.*] Well, take a book and keep quiet; d'ye hear me, Christopher?

[CHRISTOPHER, *who looks incapable of a sound, gazes at his father with round eyes.* EMILY *whispers "Library" to him and adds a kiss in acknowledgement of his good behaviour. After a moment he slips out, thankfully.*]

EDWARD. How's Ethel, Denis?

TREGONING. A little smashed, of course, but no harm done . . . I hope.

[ALICE MAITLAND *comes in, brisk and businesslike; a little impatient of this universal cloud of mourning.*]

ALICE. Edward, Honor has gone to her room; I must take her some food and make her eat it. She's very upset.

EDWARD. Make her drink a glass of wine, and say it is necessary she should come down here. And d'you mind not coming back yourself, Alice?

ALICE [*her eyebrows up*]. Certainly, if you wish.

BOOTH [*overhearing*]. What's this? What's this?

[ALICE *gets her glass of wine and goes. The* MAJOR *is suddenly full of importance.*]

BOOTH. What is this, Edward?

EDWARD. I have something to say to you all.

BOOTH. What?

EDWARD. Well, Booth, you'll hear when I say it.

BOOTH. Is it business?... because I think this is scarcely the time for business.

EDWARD. Why?

BOOTH. Do you find it easy and reverent to descend from your natural grief to the consideration of money?... I do not.

[*He finds* TRENCHARD *at his elbow.*] I hope you are getting some lunch, Trenchard.

EDWARD. This is business and rather more than business, Booth. I choose now, because it is something I wish to say to the family, not write to each individually... and it will be difficult to get us all together again.

BOOTH [*determined at any rate to give his sanction*]. Well, Trenchard, as Edward is in the position of trustee — executor... I don't know your terms... I suppose...

TRENCHARD. I don't see what your objection is.

BOOTH [*with some superiority*]. Don't you? I should not have called myself a sentimental man, but...

EDWARD. You had better stay, Denis; you represent Ethel.

TREGONING [*who has not heard the beginning of this*]. Why?

[HONOR *has obediently come down from her room. She is pale and thin, shaken with grief and worn out besides; for needless to say the brunt of her father's illness, the brunt of everything has been on her. Six weeks' nursing, part of it hopeless, will exhaust anyone. Her handkerchief is to her eyes and every minute or two she cascades tears.* EDWARD *goes and affectionately puts his arm round her.*]

EDWARD. My dear Honor, I am sorry to be so... so merciless. There!... there!

[*He hands her into the room; then turns and once more surveys the family, who this time mostly return the compliment. Then he says shortly.*] I think you might all sit down. [*And then.*] Shut the door, Booth.

BOOTH. Shut the door!

[EDWARD *goes close to his mother and speaks very distinctly, very kindly.*]

EDWARD. Mother, we're all going to have a little necessary talk over matters ... now, because it's most convenient. I hope it won't... I hope you don't mind. Will you come to the table?

[MRS. VOYSEY *looks up as if understanding more than he says.*]

MRS. VOYSEY. Edward...

EDWARD. Yes, mother dear?

BOOTH [*commandingly*]. You'll sit here, mother, of course.

[*He places her in her accustomed chair at the foot of the table. One by one the others sit down,* EDWARD *apparently last. But then he discovers that* HUGH *has lost himself in a corner of the room and is gazing into vacancy.*]

EDWARD. Hugh, would you mind attending?

HUGH. What is it?

EDWARD. There's a chair.

[HUGH *takes it. Then for a minute — while* EDWARD *is trying to frame in coherent sentences what he must say to them — for a minute there is silence, broken only by* HONOR'S *sniffs, which culminate at last in a noisy little cascade of tears.*]

OOTH. Honor, control yourself.

[*And to emphasise his own perfect control he helps himself majestically to a glass of sherry. Then says:*]

BOOTH. Well, Edward?

EDWARD. I'll come straight to the point which concerns you. Our father's will gives certain sums to you all... the gross amount would be something over a hundred thousand pounds. There will be no money.

[*He can get no further than the bare statement, which is received only with varying looks of bewilderment, until* MRS. VOYSEY, *discovering nothing from their faces, breaks this second silence.*]

MRS. VOYSEY. I didn't hear.

HUGH [*in his mother's ear*]. Edward says there's no money.

TRENCHARD [*precisely*]. I think you said... "will be."

BOOTH [*in a tone of mitigated thunder*]. Why will there be no money?

EDWARD [*letting himself go*]. Because every penny by right belongs to the clients father spent his life in defrauding. I mean that in its worst sense ... swindling ... thieving. I have been in the swim of it, for the past year ... oh, you don't know the sink of iniquity. And now I must collect every penny, any money that you can give me; put the firm into bankruptcy; pay back all we can. I'll stand my trial ... it'll come to that with me ... and as soon as possible. [*He pauses, partly for breath, and glares at them all.*] Are none of you going to speak? Quite right, what is there to be said? [*Then, with a gentle afterthought.*] I'm sorry to hurt you, mother.

[*The VOYSEY family is simply buried deep by this avalanche of horror. MRS. VOYSEY, though, who has been watching EDWARD closely, says very calmly:*]

MRS. VOYSEY. I can't hear quite all you say, but I guess what it is. You don't hurt me, Edward ... I have known of this for a long time.

EDWARD [*with almost a cry*]. Oh, mother, did he know you knew?

MRS. VOYSEY. What do you say?

TRENCHARD [*collected and dry*]. I may as well tell you, Edward, I suspected everything wasn't right about the time of my last quarrel with my father. I took care not to pursue my suspicions. Was father aware that you knew, mother?

MRS. VOYSEY. We never discussed it. There was once a great danger, I believe ... when you were all younger ... of his being found out. But we never discussed it.

EDWARD [*swallowing a fresh bitterness*]. I'm glad it isn't such a shock to all of you.

HUGH [*alive to a dramatic aspect of the matter*]. My God ... before the earth has settled on his grave!

EDWARD. I thought it wrong to put off telling you.

[HONOR, *the word "swindling" having spelt itself out in her mind, at last gives way to a burst of piteous grief.*]

HONOR. Oh, poor papa! ... poor papa!

EDWARD [*comforting her kindly*]. Honor, we shall want your help and advice.

[*The MAJOR has recovered from the shock, to swell with importance. It being necessary to make an impression, he instinctively turns first to his wife.*]

BOOTH. I think, Emily, there was no need for you to have been present at this exposure, and that now you had better retire.

EMILY. Very well, Booth.

[*She gets up to go, conscious of her misdemeanour. But as she reaches the door, an awful thought strikes the MAJOR.*]

BOOTH. Good Heavens ... I hope the servants haven't been listening! See where they are, Emily ... and keep them away ... distract them. Open the door suddenly [*she does so, more or less, and there is no one behind it*]. That's all right.

[*Having watched his wife's departure, he turns with gravity to his brother.*]

BOOTH. I have said nothing as yet, Edward. I am thinking.

TRENCHARD [*a little impatient at this exhibition*]. That's the worst of these family practices ... a lot of money knocking around and no audit ever required. The wonder to me is to find an honest solicitor at all.

BOOTH. Really, Trenchard!

TRENCHARD. Well, do think of the temptation.

EDWARD. Why are one's clients such fools?

TRENCHARD. The world's getting more and more into the hands of its experts, and it certainly does require a particular sort of honesty.

EDWARD. Here were all these funds simply a lucky bag into which he dipped.

TRENCHARD. Did he keep no accounts of any sort?

EDWARD. Scraps of paper. Most of the original investments I can't even trace. The money doesn't exist.

BOOTH. Where's it gone?

EDWARD [*very directly*]. You've been living on it.

BOOTH. Good God!
TRENCHARD. What can you pay in the pound?
EDWARD. As we stand? ... six or seven shillings, I daresay. But we must do better than that.
[*To which there is no response.*]
BOOTH. All this is very dreadful. Does it mean beggary for the whole family?
EDWARD. Yes, it should.
TRENCHARD [*sharply*]. Nonsense.
EDWARD [*joining issue at once*]. What right have we to a thing we possess?
TRENCHARD. He didn't make you an allowance, Booth ... your capital's your own, isn't it?
BOOTH [*awkwardly placed between the two of them*]. Really ... I — I suppose so.
TRENCHARD. Then that's all right.
EDWARD [*vehemently*]. It was stolen money, most likely.
TRENCHARD. Ah, most likely. But Booth took it in good faith.
BOOTH. I should hope so.
EDWARD [*dwelling on the words*]. It's stolen money.
BOOTH [*bubbling with distress*]. I say, what ought I to do?
TRENCHARD. Do ... my dear Booth? Nothing.
EDWARD [*with great indignation*]. Trenchard, we owe reparation —
TRENCHARD [*readily*]. Quite so, but to whom? From which client or client's account was Booth's money taken? You say yourself you don't know. Very well, then!
EDWARD [*grieved*]. Trenchard!
TRENCHARD. No, my dear Edward. The law will take anything it has a right to and all it can get; you needn't be afraid. There's no obligation, legal or moral, for any of us to throw our pounds into the wreck that they may become pence.
EDWARD. That's just what he would have said.
TRENCHARD. It's what *I* say. But what about your own position ... can we get you clear?
EDWARD. That doesn't matter.
[BOOTH'S *head has been turning incessantly from one to the other and by this he is just a bristle of alarm.*]

BOOTH. But I say, you know, this is awful! Will this have to be made public?
TRENCHARD. No help for it.
[*The* MAJOR'S *jaw drops; he is speechless.* MRS. VOYSEY'S *dead voice steals in.*]
MRS. VOYSEY. What is all this?
TRENCHARD. Edward suggests that the family should beggar itself in order to pay back to every client to whom father owed a pound perhaps ten shillings instead of seven.
MRS. VOYSEY. He will find that my estate has been kept quite separate.
[EDWARD *hides his face in his hands.*]
TRENCHARD. I'm very glad to hear it, mother.
MRS. VOYSEY. When Mr. Barnes died, your father agreed to appointing another trustee.
TREGONING [*diffidently*]. I suppose, Edward, I'm involved?
EDWARD [*lifting his head quickly*]. Denis, I hope not. I didn't know that anything of yours —
TREGONING. Yes ... all I got under my aunt's will.
EDWARD. See how things are ... I've not found a trace of that yet. We'll hope for the best.
TREGONING [*setting his teeth*]. It can't be helped.
[MAJOR BOOTH *leans over the table and speaks in the loudest of whispers.*]
BOOTH. Let me advise you to say nothing of this to Ethel at such a critical time.
TREGONING. Thank you, Booth; naturally I shan't.
[HUGH, *by a series of contortions, has lately been giving evidence of a desire or intention to say something.*]
EDWARD. Well, what is it, Hugh?
HUGH. I have been wondering ... if he can hear this conversation.
[*Up to now it has all been meaningless to* HONOR, *in her nervous dilapidation, but this remark brings a fresh burst of tears.*]
HONOR. Oh, poor papa ... poor papa!
MRS. VOYSEY. I think I'll go to my room. I can't hear what any of you are saying. Edward can tell me afterwards.

EDWARD. Would you like to go too, Honor?

HONOR [through her sobs]. Yes, please, I would.

TREGONING. I'll get out, Edward. Whatever you think fit to do... Oh, well, I suppose there's only one thing to be done.

EDWARD. Only that.

TREGONING. I wish I were in a better position as to work, for Ethel's sake and — and the child's.

EDWARD. Shall I speak to Trenchard?

TREGONING. No... he knows I exist in a wig and gown. If I can be useful to him, he'll be useful to me, I daresay. Good-bye, Hugh. Good-bye, Booth.

[*By this time* MRS. VOYSEY *and* HONOR *have been got out of the room:* TREGONING *follows them. So the four brothers are left together.* HUGH *is vacant,* EDWARD *does not speak,* BOOTH *looks at* TRENCHARD, *who settles himself to acquire information.*]

TRENCHARD. How long have things been wrong?

EDWARD. He told me the trouble began in his father's time and that he'd been battling with it ever since.

TRENCHARD [smiling]. Oh, come now ... that's impossible.

EDWARD. I believed him! Now I look through the papers, such as they are, I can find only one irregularity that's more than ten years old, and that's only to do with old George Booth's business.

BOOTH. But the pater never touched his money... why, he was a personal friend.

EDWARD. Did you hear what Denis said?

TRENCHARD. Very curious his evolving that fiction about his father... I wonder why. I remember the old man. He was honest as the day.

EDWARD. To get my sympathy, I suppose.

TRENCHARD. I think one can trace the psychology of it deeper than that. It would give a finish to the situation... his handing on to you an inheritance he had received. You know every criminal has a touch of the artist in him.

HUGH [suddenly roused]. That's true.

TRENCHARD. What position did you take up when he told you?

EDWARD [shrugging]. You know what the pater was.

TRENCHARD. Well... what did you attempt to do?

EDWARD. I urged him at least to put some of the smaller people right. He said ... he said that would be penny wise and pound foolish. So I've done what I could myself... since he's been ill... Nothing to count...

TRENCHARD. With your own money?

EDWARD. The little I had. He kept tight hold to the end.

TRENCHARD. Can you prove that you did that?

EDWARD. I suppose I could.

TRENCHARD. It's a good point.

BOOTH [not to be quite left out]. Yes, I must say —

TRENCHARD. You ought to have written him a letter, and left the firm the moment you found out. Even then, legally...! But as he was your father... What was his object in telling you? He didn't think you'd take a hand?

EDWARD. I've thought of every reason ... and now I really believe it was that he might have someone to boast to of his financial exploits.

TRENCHARD [appreciatively]. I daresay.

BOOTH. Scarcely a thing to boast of!

TRENCHARD. Depends on the point of view.

EDWARD. Then, of course, he always protested that things would come right... that he'd clear the firm and have a hundred thousand to the good. Or that if he were not spared I might do it. But he must have known that was impossible.

TRENCHARD. But there's the gambler all over.

EDWARD. Drawing up this will!

TRENCHARD. Childish!

EDWARD. I'm the sole executor.

TRENCHARD. So I should think! Was I down for anything?

EDWARD. No.

TRENCHARD [without resentment]. How he did hate me!

EDWARD. You're safe from the results of his affection anyway.

TRENCHARD. What on earth made you stay in the firm once you knew?

[EDWARD *does not answer for a moment.*]

EDWARD. I thought I might prevent things from getting any worse. I think I did...

TRENCHARD. You knew the personal risk you were running?

EDWARD [*bowing his head*]. Yes.

[TRENCHARD, *the only one of the three who comprehends, looks at his brother for a moment with something that might almost be admiration. Then he stirs himself.*]

TRENCHARD. I must be off. Work waiting... end of term, you know.

BOOTH. Shall I walk to the station with you?

TRENCHARD. I'll spend a few minutes with mother. [*He says, at the door, very respectfully.*] You'll count on my professional assistance, please, Edward.

EDWARD [*simply*]. Thank you, Trenchard.

[*So* TRENCHARD *goes. And the* MAJOR, *who has been endeavouring to fathom his final attitude, then comments.*]

BOOTH. No heart, y'know! Great brain! If it hadn't been for that distressing quarrel he might have saved our poor father. Don't you think so, Edward?

EDWARD. Perhaps.

HUGH [*giving vent to his thoughts at last with something of a relish*]. The more I think this out, the more devilishly humorous it gets. Old Booth breaking down by the grave... Colpus reading the service...

EDWARD. Yes, the Vicar's badly hit.

HUGH. Oh, the Pater had managed his business for years.

BOOTH. Good God... how shall we ever look old Booth in the face again?

EDWARD. I don't worry about him; he can die quite comfortably enough on our six shillings in the pound. It's one or two of the smaller fry who will suffer.

BOOTH. Now, just explain to me... I didn't interrupt while Trenchard was talking... of what exactly did this defrauding consist?

EDWARD. Speculating with a client's capital... pocketing the gains... you cut the losses; and you keep paying the client his ordinary income.

BOOTH. So that he doesn't find it out?

EDWARD. Quite so.

BOOTH. In point of fact, he doesn't suffer?

EDWARD. He doesn't suffer till he finds it out.

BOOTH. And all that's wrong now is that some of their capital is missing.

EDWARD [*half amused, half amazed at this process of reasoning*]. Yes, that's all that's wrong.

BOOTH. What is the — ah — deficit?

[*The word rolls from his tongue.*]

EDWARD. Anything between two and three hundred thousand pounds.

BOOTH [*very impressed and not unfavourably*]. Dear me... this is a big affair!

HUGH [*following his own line of thought*]. Quite apart from the rights and wrongs of this, only a very able man could have kept a straight face to the world all these years, as the pater did.

BOOTH. I suppose he sometimes made money by these speculations.

EDWARD. Very often. His own expenditure was heavy, as you know.

BOOTH [*with gratitude for favours received*]. He was a very generous man.

HUGH. Did nobody ever suspect?

EDWARD. You see, Hugh, when there was any pressing danger... if a big trust had to be wound up... he'd make a great effort and put the accounts straight.

BOOTH. Then he did put some accounts straight?

EDWARD. Yes, when he couldn't help himself.

[BOOTH *looks very enquiring and then squares himself up to the subject.*]

BOOTH. Now look here, Edward. You told us that he told you that it was the object of his life to put these accounts straight. Then you laughed at that. Now you tell me that he did put some accounts straight.

EDWARD [*wearily*]. My dear Booth, you don't understand.

BOOTH. Well, let me understand... I am anxious to understand.

EDWARD. We can't pay ten shillings in the pound.

BOOTH. That's very dreadful. But do you know that there wasn't a time when we couldn't have paid five?

EDWARD [*acquiescent*]. Perhaps.

BOOTH. Very well, then! If it was true about his father and all that... and why shouldn't we believe him if we can? ... and he did effect an improvement, that's to his credit, isn't it? Let us at least be just, Edward.

EDWARD [*patiently polite*]. I am sorry if I seem unjust. But he has left me in a rather unfortunate position.

BOOTH. Yes, his death was a tragedy. It seems to me that if he had been spared he might have succeeded at length in this tremendous task and restored to us our family honour.

EDWARD. Yes, Booth, he spoke very feelingly of that.

BOOTH [*irony lost upon him*]. I can well believe it. And I can tell you that now ... I may be right or I may be wrong... I am feeling far less concerned about the clients' money than I am at the terrible blow to the Family which this exposure will strike. Money, after all, can to a certain extent be done without... but Honour —

[*This is too much for* EDWARD.]

EDWARD. Our honour! Does any one of you mean to give me a single penny towards undoing all the wrong that has been done?

BOOTH. I take Trenchard's word for it that that would be illegal.

EDWARD. Well... don't talk to me of honour.

BOOTH [*somewhat nettled at this outburst*]. I am speaking of the public exposure. Edward, can't that be prevented?

EDWARD [*with quick suspicion*]. How?

BOOTH. Well... how was it being prevented before he died — before we knew anything about it?

EDWARD [*appealing to the spirits that watch over him*]. Oh, listen to this! First Trenchard... and now you! You've the poison in your blood, every one of you. Who am I to talk? I daresay so have I.

BOOTH [*reprovingly*]. I am beginning to think that you have worked yourself into rather an hysterical state over this unhappy business.

EDWARD [*rating him*]. Perhaps you'd have been glad... glad if I'd held my tongue and gone on lying and cheating... and married and begotten a son to go on lying and cheating after me... and to pay you your interest in the lie and the cheat.

BOOTH [*with statesmanlike calm*]. Look here, Edward, this rhetoric is exceedingly out of place. The simple question before us is... What is the best course to pursue?

EDWARD. There is no question before us. There's only one course to pursue.

BOOTH [*crushingly*]. You will let me speak, please. In so far as our poor father was dishonest to his clients, I pray that he may be forgiven. In so far as he spent his life honestly endeavouring to right a wrong which he had found already committed... I forgive him. I admire him, Edward. And I feel it my duty to — er — reprobate most strongly the — er — gusto with which you have been holding him up in memory to us... ten minutes after we have stood round his grave... as a monster of wickedness. I think I may say I knew him as well as you... better. And ... thank God!... there was not between him and me this — this unhappy business to warp my judgment of him. [*He warms to his subject.*] Did you ever know a more charitable man... a larger-hearted? He was a faithful husband... and what a father to all of us, putting us out into the world and fully intending to leave us comfortably settled there. Further... as I see this matter, Edward... when as a young man he was told this terrible secret and entrusted with such a frightful task ... did he turn his back on it like a coward? No. He went through it heroically to the end of his life. And as he died I imagine there was no more torturing thought than that he had left his work unfinished. [*He is very satisfied with this peroration.*] And now if all these clients can be kept receiving their natural incomes and if father's plan could be carried out of gradually replacing the capital —

[EDWARD *at this raises his head and stares with horror.*]

EDWARD. You're asking me to carry on this ... Oh, you don't know what you're talking about!

[*The* MAJOR, *having talked himself back to a proper eminence, remains good-tempered.*]

BOOTH. Well, I'm not a conceited man ... but I do think that I can understand a simple financial problem when it has been explained to me.

EDWARD. You don't know the nerve ... the unscrupulous daring it requires to —

BOOTH. Of course, if you're going to argue round your own incompetence —

EDWARD [*very straight*]. D'you want your legacy?

BOOTH [*with dignity*]. In one moment I shall get very angry. Here am I doing my best to help you and your clients ... and there you sit imputing to me the most sordid motives. Do you suppose I should touch, or allow to be touched, the money which father has left us till every client's claim was satisfied?

EDWARD. My dear Booth, I know you mean well —

BOOTH. I'll come down to your office and work with you.

[*At this cheerful prospect even poor* EDWARD *can't help smiling.*]

EDWARD. I'm sure you would.

BOOTH [*feeling that it is a chance lost*]. If the pater had ever consulted me ...

[*At this point* TRENCHARD *looks round the door to say:*]

TRENCHARD. Are you coming, Booth?

BOOTH. Yes, certainly. I'll talk this over with Trenchard. [*As he gets up and automatically stiffens, he is reminded of the occasion and his voice drops.*] I say ... we've been speaking very loud. You must do nothing rash. I've no doubt he and I can devise something which will obviate ... and then I'm sure I shall convince you ... [*Glancing into the hall he apparently catches* TRENCHARD'S *impatient eye, for he departs abruptly, saying:*] All right, Trenchard, you've eight minutes.

[BOOTH'S *departure leaves* HUGH, *at any rate, really at his ease.*]

HUGH. This is an experience for you, Edward!

EDWARD [*bitterly*]. And I feared what the shock might be to you all! Booth has made a good recovery.

HUGH. You wouldn't have him miss such a chance of booming at us.

EDWARD. It's strange that people will believe you can do right by means which they know to be wrong.

HUGH [*taking great interest in this*]. Come, what do we know about right and wrong? Let's say legal and illegal. You're so down on the governor because he has trespassed against the etiquette of your own profession. But now he's dead ... and if there weren't the scandal to think of ... it's no use the rest of us pretending to feel him a criminal, because we don't. Which just shows that money ... and property —

[*At this point he becomes conscious that* ALICE MAITLAND *is standing behind him, her eyes fixed on his brother. So he interrupts himself to ask.*]

HUGH. D'you want to speak to Edward?

ALICE. Please, Hugh.

HUGH. I'll go.

[*He goes, a little martyr-like, to conclude the evolution of his theory in soliloquy; his usual fate.* ALICE *still looks at* EDWARD *with soft eyes, and he at her rather appealingly.*]

ALICE. Auntie has told me.

EDWARD. He was fond of you. Don't think worse of him than you can help.

ALICE. I'm thinking of you.

EDWARD. I may just escape.

ALICE. So Trenchard says.

EDWARD. My hands are clean, Alice.

ALICE [*her voice falling lovingly*]. I know that.

EDWARD. Mother's not very upset.

ALICE. She had expected a smash in his lifetime.

EDWARD. I'm glad that didn't happen.

ALICE. Yes. I've put Honor to bed. It

was a mercy to tell her just at this moment. She can grieve for his death and his disgrace at the same time ... and the one grief will soften the other, perhaps.

EDWARD. Oh, they're all shocked enough at the disgrace ... but will they open their purses to lessen the disgrace?

ALICE. Will it seem less disgraceful to have stolen ten thousand pounds than twenty?

EDWARD. I should think so.

ALICE. I should think so, but I wonder if that's the Law. If it isn't, Trenchard wouldn't consider the point. I'm sure Public Opinion doesn't say so ... and that's what Booth is considering.

EDWARD [with contempt]. Yes.

ALICE [ever so gently ironical]. Well, he's in the Army ... he's almost in Society ... and he has to get on in both; one mustn't blame him. Of course, if the money could have been given back with a flourish of trumpets ... ! But even then I doubt whether the advertisement would bring in what it cost.

EDWARD [very serious]. But when one thinks how the money was obtained!

ALICE. When one thinks how most money is obtained!

EDWARD. They've not *earned* it!

ALICE [her eyes humorous]. If they had they might have given it you and earned more. Did I ever tell you what my guardian said to me when I came of age?

EDWARD. I'm thankful your money's out of the mess.

ALICE. It wouldn't have been, but I was made to look after it myself ... much against my will. My guardian was a person of great character and no principles, the best and most lovable man I've ever met ... I'm sorry you never knew him, Edward ... and he said once to me ... You've no particular right to your money. You've not earned it or deserved it in any way. And don't be either surprised or annoyed when any enterprising person tries to get it from you. He has at least as much right to it as you have ... if he can use it better, perhaps he has more right. Shocking sentiments, aren't they? But perhaps that's why I've less patience with some of these clients than you have, Edward.

[EDWARD *shakes his head, treating these paradoxes as they deserve.*]

EDWARD. Alice ... one or two of them will be beggared.

ALICE [*sincerely*]. Yes, that is bad. What's to be done?

EDWARD. There's old nurse ... with her poor little savings gone!

ALICE. Surely that can be helped?

EDWARD. The Law's no respecter of persons ... that's its boast. Old Booth with more than he wants will keep enough and to spare. My old nurse, with just enough, may starve. But it'll be a relief to clear out this nest of lies, even though one suffers one's self. I've been ashamed to walk into that office, Alice ... I'll hold my head high in prison, though.

[*He shakes himself stiffly erect, his chin high.* ALICE *quizzes him.*]

ALICE. Edward, I'm afraid you're feeling heroic.

EDWARD. I!

ALICE. You looked quite like Booth for the moment. [*This effectually removes the starch.*] Please don't glory in your martyrdom. It would be very stupid to send you to prison and you must do your best to keep out. [*She goes on very practically.*] We were thinking if anything could be done for these people who'll be beggared.

EDWARD. It isn't that I'm not sorry for them all ...

ALICE. Of course not.

EDWARD. I suppose I was feeling heroic. I didn't mean to.

[*He has become a little like a child with her.*]

ALICE. It's the worst of acting on principle ... one is so apt to think more of one's attitude than of the use of what one is doing.

EDWARD. Fraud must be exposed.

ALICE. And people must be ruined ... !

EDWARD. What else is there to be done?

ALICE. Well ... have you thought?

EDWARD. There's nothing else to be done.

ALICE. No. When on principle there's nothing to be done I'm afraid I've no use for that principle.

[*He looks at her; she is smiling, it is*

true, but smiling quite gravely. ED-
WARD *is puzzled. Then the yeast of
her suggestion begins to work in his
mind slowly, perversely at first.*]
EDWARD. Unless you expect me to take
Booth's advice ... go on with the game
... as an honest cheat ... plunge, I suppose, just twice as wildly as my father did
on the chance that things might come
right ... which he never bothered his head
about. Booth offers to come to the office
and assist me.
ALICE. There's something attractive
about Booth at the right distance.
EDWARD. Oh ... give him the money
... send him to the City or Monte Carlo
.... he might bring it off. He's like my
father ... believes in himself.
ALICE. These credulous men!
EDWARD [*ignoring her little joke*]. But
don't think I've any talents that way,
principles or no. What have I done so far?
Sat in the shame of it for a year. I did take
a hand ... if you knew what it felt like ...
I managed to stop one affair going from
bad to worse.
ALICE. If that was the best you could do
wasn't it worth doing? Never mind your
feelings.
EDWARD. And that may cost me ... at
the best I'll be struck off ... one's liveli-
hood gone.
ALICE. The cost is your own affair.
[*She is watching him, stilly and
closely. Suddenly his face lights a
little and he turns to her.*]
EDWARD. I'll tell you what I could do.
ALICE. Yes.
EDWARD. It's just as irregular.
ALICE. That doesn't shock me ... I'm
lawless by birthright, being a woman.
EDWARD. There are four or five accounts
I believe I could get quite square. Mrs.
Travers ... well, she'd never starve, but
I'd like to see those two young Lyndhursts
safe. There's money to play with, Heaven
knows. It'd take a year or more to get it
right and cover the tracks. Cover the
tracks ... sounds well, doesn't it?
ALICE. Then you'd give yourself up as
you'd meant to do now?
EDWARD. Go bankrupt.

ALICE. It'd be worse for you then at the
trial?
EDWARD [*with a touch of another sort of
pride*]. You said that was my affair.
ALICE [*pain in her voice and eyes*]. Oh,
Edward!
EDWARD. Shall I do it?
ALICE [*turning away*]. Why must you
ask me?
EDWARD. If you've taken my principles
from me, give me advice in exchange.
ALICE [*after a moment*]. No ... you
must decide for yourself.
[*He jumps up and begins to pace
about, doubtful, distressed.*]
EDWARD. Ah, but ... it means still lying
and shuffling! And I'd sworn to be free of
that. And ... it wouldn't be easy. I'm
no good at that sort of devilment. I
should muddle it and fail.
ALICE. Would you?
[*He catches a look from her.*]
EDWARD. I might not.
ALICE. And do you need success for a
lure ... like a common man?
EDWARD. You want me to try?
[*For answer, she dares only put out
her hand, and he takes it.*]
ALICE. Oh, my dear ... cousin!
EDWARD [*excitedly*]. My people must
hold their tongues. I needn't have told
them.
ALICE. Don't tell them this! They
won't understand. *I* shall be jealous if you
tell them.
EDWARD [*looking at her as she at him*].
You'll have the right to be. If I bring it
off, the glory shall be yours.
ALICE. Thank you. I've always wanted
to have something useful to my credit ...
and I'd almost given up hoping.
[*Then suddenly his face changes,
his voice changes, and he grips the
hand he is holding so tightly as to
hurt her.*]
EDWARD. Ah, no, no, no, no, if my father's story were true ... perhaps he began
like this. Doing the right thing in the
wrong way ... then doing the wrong thing
... then bringing himself to what he was
... and so me to this. [*He flings away
from her.*] No, Alice, I won't ... I won't

do it. I daren't take that first step down. There's a worse risk than failure ... I might succeed.
[ALICE *stands very still, looking at him.*]
ALICE. Yes, that's the big risk. Well ... I'll take it. [*He turns to her, in wonder.*]
EDWARD. You?
ALICE. I'll risk your becoming a bad man. That's a big risk for me.
[*He understands, and is calmed and made happy.*]
EDWARD. Then there is no more to be said, is there?
ALICE. Not now. [*As she drops this gentle hint she hears something — the hall door opening.*] Here's Booth back again.
EDWARD [*with a really mischievous grin*]. He'll be so glad he's convinced me.
ALICE. I must go back to Honor, poor girl. I wonder she has a tear left.
[*She leaves him, briskly, brightly; leaves her cousin with his mouth set and a light in his eyes.*]

ACT IV

MR. VOYSEY'S *room at the office is* EDWARD'S *now. It has somehow lost that brilliancy which the old man's occupation seemed to give it. Perhaps it is only because this December morning is dull and depressing, but the fire isn't bright and the panels and windows don't shine as they did. There are no roses on the table either.* EDWARD, *walking in as his father did, hanging his hat and coat where his father's used to hang, is certainly the palest shadow of that other masterful presence. A depressed, drooping shadow too. This may be what* PEACEY *feels, if no more, for he looks very surly as he obeys the old routine of following his chief to this room on his arrival. Nor has* EDWARD *so much as a glance for his clerk. They exchange the formalest of greetings.* EDWARD *sits joylessly to his desk, on which the morning's pile of letters lies, unopened now.*

PEACEY. Good-morning, sir.

EDWARD. Good-morning, Peacey. Any notes for me?

PEACEY. Well, I've hardly been through the letters yet, sir.

EDWARD [*his eyebrows meeting*]. Oh ... and I'm half an hour late myself this morning.

PEACEY. I'm very sorry, sir.

EDWARD. If Mr. Bullen calls, you had better show him those papers I gave you. Write to Metcalfe as soon as possible; say I've seen Mr. Vickery myself this morning and the houses will not be proceeded with. Better show me the letter.

PEACEY. Very good, sir.

EDWARD. That's all, thank you.
[PEACEY *gets to the door, where he stops, looking not only surly, but nervous now.*]

PEACEY. May I speak to you a moment, sir?

EDWARD. Certainly.
[PEACEY, *after a moment, makes an effort, purses his mouth and begins.*]

PEACEY. Bills are beginning to come in upon me as is usual at this season, sir. My son's allowance at Cambridge is now rather a heavy item of my expenditure. I hope that the custom of the firm isn't to be neglected now that you are the head of it, Mr. Edward ... Two hundred your father always made it at Christmas ... in notes, if you please.
[*Towards the end of this,* EDWARD *begins to pay great attention. When he answers his voice is harsh.*]

EDWARD. Oh, to be sure ... your hush money.

PEACEY [*bridling*]. That's not a very pleasant word.

EDWARD. This is an unpleasant subject.

PEACEY. Well, it's not one I wish to discuss. Your father always gave me the notes in an envelope when he shook hands with me at Christmas.

EDWARD. Why notes now? Why not a rise in salary?

PEACEY. Mr. Voysey's custom, sir, from before my time ... my father ...

EDWARD. Yes. It's an hereditary pull you have over the firm, isn't it?

PEACEY. I remember my father only

saying to me when he retired ... been dead twenty-six years, Mr. Edward ... I have told the governor you know what I know; then Mr. Voysey saying ... I treat you as I did your father, Peacey. We'd never another word with him on the subject.

EDWARD. A decent arrangement ... and the cheapest, no doubt. Of the raising of salaries there might have been no end.

PEACEY. Mr. Edward, that's uncalled for. We have served you and yours most faithfully. I know my father would sooner have cut off his hand than do anything to embarrass the firm.

EDWARD. But business is business, Peacey. Surely he could have had a partnership for the asking.

PEACEY. Ah, that's another matter, sir.

EDWARD. Well ...

PEACEY. A matter of principle, if you'll excuse me. I must not be taken to approve of the firm's conduct. Nor did my dear father approve. And at anything like partnership he would have drawn the line.

EDWARD. I beg your pardon.

PEACEY. Well, that's all right, sir. Always a bit of friction in coming to an understanding about anything, isn't there, sir?

[*He is going when* EDWARD'S *question stops him.*]

EDWARD. Why didn't you speak about this last Christmas?

PEACEY. You were so upset at your father's death.

EDWARD. My father died the August before that.

PEACEY. Well ... truthfully, Mr. Edward?

EDWARD. As truthfully as you think suitable.

[*The irony of this is wasted on* PEACEY, *who becomes pleasantly candid.*]

PEACEY. Well, I'd always thought there must be a smash when your father died ... but it didn't come. I couldn't make you out. But then again by Christmas you seemed all on edge and I thought anything might happen. So I kept quiet and said nothing.

EDWARD. I see. Your son's at Cambridge?

PEACEY. Yes.

EDWARD. I wonder you didn't bring him into the firm.

PEACEY [*taking this very kind*]. Thank you. But I hope James may go to the bar. Our only son ... I didn't grudge him my small savings to help him wait for his chance ... ten years if need be.

EDWARD. I hope he'll make his mark before then. I'm glad to have had this talk with you, Peacey. I'm sorry you can't have the money you want.

[*He returns to his letters, a little steely-eyed.* PEACEY, *quite at his ease, makes for the door yet again, saying:*]

PEACEY. Oh, any time will do, sir.

EDWARD. You can't have it at all.

PEACEY [*brought up short*]. Can't I?

EDWARD [*very decidedly indeed*]. No ... I made up my mind about this eighteen months ago. My father had warned me, but since his death the trust business of the firm is not conducted as it used to be. We no longer make illicit profits out of our clients. There are none for you to share.

[*Having thus given the explanation he considers due, he goes on with his work. But* PEACEY *has flushed up.*]

PEACEY. Look here, Mr. Edward, I'm sorry we began this discussion. You'll give me my two hundred as usual, please, and we'll drop the subject.

EDWARD. You can drop the subject.

PEACEY [*his voice rising sharply*]. I want the money. I think it is not gentlemanly in you, Mr. Edward, to try like this and get out of paying it me. Your father would never have made such an excuse.

EDWARD [*flabbergasted*]. Do you think I'm lying to you?

PEACEY [*with a deprecating swallow*]. I've no wish to criticise your statements or your actions at all, sir. It was no concern of mine how your father treated his clients.

EDWARD. And now it's not to concern you how honest I am. You want your money just the same.

PEACEY. Well, don't be sarcastic ... a man does get used to a state of affairs whatever it may be.

EDWARD [*with considerable force*]. My

friend, if I drop sarcasm I shall have to tell you very candidly what I think of you.

PEACEY. That I'm a thief because I've taken money from a thief?

EDWARD. Worse than a thief. You're content that others should steal for you.

PEACEY. And who isn't?

[EDWARD *is really pleased with the aptness of this. He at once changes his tone, which, indeed, had become rather bullying.*]

EDWARD. What, my dear Peacey, you study sociology? Well, it's too big a question to discuss now. But I'm afraid the application of this bit of it is that I have for the moment, at some inconvenience to myself, ceased to receive stolen goods, so I am in a position to throw a stone at you. I have thrown it.

[PEACEY, *who would far sooner be bullied than talked to like this, turns very sulky.*]

PEACEY. Then I resign my position here.

EDWARD. Very well.

PEACEY. And I happen to think the secret's worth its price.

EDWARD. Perhaps someone will pay it you.

PEACEY [*feebly threatening*]. Don't presume upon it's not being worth my while to make use of what I know.

EDWARD [*not unkindly*]. My good Peacey, it happens to be the truth I told you just now. Well, how on earth do you suppose you can successfully blackmail a man who has so much to gain by exposure and so little to lose as I?

PEACEY [*peeving*]. I don't want to ruin you, sir, and I have a great regard for the firm . . . but you must see that I can't have my income reduced in this way without a struggle.

EDWARD [*with great cheerfulness*]. Very well, my friend, struggle away.

PEACEY [*his voice rising high and thin*]. Well, is it fair dealing on your part to dock the money suddenly like this? I have been counting on it most of the year, and I have been led into heavy expenses. Why couldn't you have warned me?

EDWARD. Yes, that's true, Peacey, it was stupid of me. I'm sorry.

[PEACEY *is a little comforted by this quite candid acknowledgement.*]

PEACEY. Things may get easier for you by and bye.

EDWARD. I hope so.

PEACEY. Will you reconsider the matter then?

[*At this gentle insinuation* EDWARD *looks up exasperated.*]

EDWARD. Then you don't believe what I told you?

PEACEY. Yes, I do.

EDWARD. But you think that the fascination of swindling one's clients will ultimately prove irresistible?

PEACEY. That's what your father found, I suppose you know.

[*This gives* EDWARD *such pause that he drops his masterful tone.*]

EDWARD. I didn't.

PEACEY. He got things as right as rain once.

EDWARD. Did he?

PEACEY. So my father told me. But he started again.

EDWARD. Are you sure of this?

PEACEY [*expanding pleasantly*]. Well, sir, I knew your father pretty well. When I first came into the firm, now, I simply hated him. He was that sour; so snappy with everyone . . . as if he had a grievance against the whole world.

EDWARD [*pensively*]. It seems he had in those days.

PEACEY. His dealings with his clients were no business of mine. I speak as I find. After a bit he was very kind to me, thoughtful and considerate. He got to be so pleasant and generous to everyone —

EDWARD. That you have great hopes of me yet?

PEACEY [*who has a simple mind*]. No, Mr. Edward, no. You're different from your father . . . one must make up one's mind to that. And you may believe me or not, but I should be very glad to know that the firm was solvent and going straight. I'm getting on in years myself now. I'm not much longer for the business, and there have been times when I have sincerely regretted my connection with it. If you'll let me say so, I think it's very noble of you to have undertaken the work you have. [*Then, as everything seems smooth again.*] And Mr. Edward, if you'll give me enough to cover this year's extra expense, I think I may promise you that I shan't expect money again.

EDWARD [*good-tempered, as he would speak to an importunate child*]. No, Peacey, no!

PEACEY [*fretful again*]. Well, sir, you make things very difficult for me.

EDWARD. Here's a letter from Mr. Cartwright which you might attend to. If he wants an appointment with me, don't make one till the New Year. His case can't come on before February.

PEACEY [*taking the letter*]. I show myself anxious to meet you in every way — [*He is handed another.*]

EDWARD. "Perceval Building Estate" ... that's yours too.

PEACEY [*putting them both down resolutely*]. But I refuse to be ignored. I must consider my whole position. I hope I may not be tempted to make use of the power I possess. But if I am driven to proceed to extremities ...

EDWARD [*breaking in upon this bunch of tags*]. My dear Peacey, don't talk nonsense ... you couldn't proceed to an extremity to save your life. You've taken this money irresponsibly for all these years. You'll find you're no longer capable even of such a responsible act as tripping up your neighbour.

[*This does completely upset the gentle blackmailer. He loses one grievance in another.*]

PEACEY. Really, Mr. Edward, I am a considerably older man than you, and I think that whatever our positions —

EDWARD. Don't let us argue, Peacey. You're quite at liberty to do whatever you think worth your while.

PEACEY. It's not the money, I can do without that, but these personalities —

EDWARD. I apologise for them. Don't forget the letters.

PEACEY. I will not, sir.

[*He takes them with great dignity and is leaving the room.*]

PEACEY. Here's Mr. Hugh waiting.
EDWARD. To see me? Ask him in.
PEACEY. Come in, Mr. Hugh, please.

[HUGH *comes in*, PEACEY *holding the door for him with a frigid politeness of which he is quite oblivious. At this final slight* PEACEY *goes out in dudgeon.*]

EDWARD. How are you, Hugh?
HUGH. Good Lord!

[*And he throws himself into the chair by the fire.* EDWARD, *quite used to this sort of thing, goes quietly on with his work, adding encouragingly after a moment:*]

EDWARD. How's Beatrice?
HUGH. She's very busy.

[*He studies his boots with the gloomiest expression. And, indeed, they are very dirty and his turned-up trousers are muddy at the edge. They are dark trousers and well cut, but he wears with them a loose coat and waistcoat of a peculiar light brown check. Add to this the roughest of overcoats and a very soft hat. Add also the fact that he doesn't shave well or regularly and that his hair wants cutting, and* HUGH'S *appearance this morning is described. As he is quite capable of sitting silently by the fire for a whole morning,* EDWARD *asks him at last:*]

EDWARD. What d'you want?

HUGH [*with vehemence*]. I want a machine gun planted in Regent Street ... and one in the Haymarket ... and one in Leicester Square and one in the Strand ... and a dozen in the City. An earthquake would be simpler. Or why not a nice clean tidal wave? It's no good preaching and patching up any longer, Edward. We must begin afresh. Don't you feel, even in your calmer moments, that this whole country is simply hideous? The other nations must look after themselves. I'm patriotic ... I only ask that we should be destroyed.

EDWARD. It has been promised.

HUGH. I'm sick of waiting. [*Then, as* EDWARD *says nothing:*] You say this is the cry of the weak man in despair! I wouldn't be anything but a weak man in this world. I wouldn't be a king, I wouldn't be rich ... I wouldn't be a Borough Councillor ... I should be so ashamed. I've walked here this morning from Hampstead. I started to curse because the streets were dirty. You'd think that an empire could keep its streets clean! But then I saw that the children were dirty too.

EDWARD. That's because of the streets.

HUGH. Yes, it's holiday time. Those that can cross a road safely are doing some work now ... earning some money. You'd think a governing race, grabbing responsibilities, might care for its children.

EDWARD. Come, we educate them now. And I don't think many work in holiday time.

HUGH [encouraged by contradiction]. Education! What's that? Joining the great conspiracy which we call our civilization. But one mustn't. One must stand aside and give the show away. By the bye, that's what I've come for.

EDWARD [pleasantly]. What? I thought you'd only come to talk.

HUGH. Take that money of mine for your clients. You ought to have had it when you asked for it. It has never belonged to me, in any real ... in any spiritual sense, so it has been just a clog to my life.

EDWARD [surprised]. My dear Hugh ... this is very generous of you.

HUGH. Not a bit. I only want to start fresh and free.

EDWARD [sitting back from his work]. Hugh, do you really think our money carries a curse with it?

HUGH [with great violence]. Think! I'm the proof of it! Look at me! I felt I must create or die. I said I'd be an artist. The governor gave me a hundred and fifty a year ... the rent of a studio and the price of a velvet coat he thought it; that was all he knew about art. But my respectable training got me engaged and married. Marriage in a studio puzzled the governor, so he guessed it at two hundred and fifty a year ... and looked for lay-figure babies, I suppose. Ha, ha! Well, I've learnt my job. I work in a sort of way, Edward, though you mightn't think it. Well, what have I really learnt ... about myself ... that's the only learning ... that there's nothing I can do or be but reflects our drawing-room at Chislehurst.

EDWARD [considering]. What do you earn in a year? I doubt if you can afford to give this up.

HUGH. Oh, Edward ... you clank the chain with the best of them. Afford! If I can't get free from these crippling advantages ... Unless I find out what I'm worth in myself ... whether I even exist or not? Am I only a pretence of a man animated by an income?

EDWARD. But you can't return to nature on the London pavements.

HUGH. No. Nor in England at all ... it's nothing but a big back garden. [Now he collects himself for a final outburst.] Is there no place on this earth where a man can prove his right to live by some other means than robbing his neighbour? Put me there naked and penniless. Put me to that test. If I can't answer it, then turn down your thumb ... O God ... and I won't complain.

[EDWARD waits till the effects of this explosion are over.]

EDWARD. And what does Beatrice say to your emigrating to the backwoods ... if that is exactly what you mean?

HUGH. Now that we're separating —

EDWARD [taken aback]. What?

HUGH. We mean to separate.

EDWARD. The first I've heard of it.

HUGH. Beatrice is making some money by her books, so it has become possible.

EDWARD [humorously]. Have you told anyone yet?

HUGH. We must now, I suppose.

EDWARD. Say nothing at home until after Christmas.

HUGH. They'll insist on discussing it solemnly. Ar-r-r. [Then he whistles.] Emily knows!

EDWARD [having considered]. I shan't take your money ... there's no need. All the good has been done that I wanted to do. No one will be quite beggared now. So why should you be?

HUGH [with clumsy affection]. We've

taken a fine lot of interest in your labours, haven't we, Hercules?

EDWARD. You hold your tongue about the office affairs, don't you? It's not through one of us it should come out, and I've told you more than Booth and the others

HUGH. When will you be quit of the beastly business?

EDWARD [becoming reserved and cold at once]. Some day.

HUGH. What do you gain by hanging on now?

EDWARD. Occupation.

HUGH. But, Edward, it must be an awfully wearying state of things. I suppose any moment a policeman may knock at the door . . . so to speak?

EDWARD [appreciating the figure of speech] Any moment. I take no precautions. I made up my mind that at least I wouldn't lower myself to that. And perhaps it's why the policeman doesn't come. At first I listened for him, day by day. Then I said to myself . . . next week. But a year has gone by and more. I've ceased expecting to hear the knock at all.

HUGH. But look here . . . is all this worth while, and have you the right to make a mean thing of your life like this?

EDWARD. Does my life matter?

HUGH. Well . . . of course!

EDWARD. It's so much easier to believe not. The world that you kick against is using me up. A little wantonly . . . a little needlessly, I do think. But let her. As I sit here now drudging honestly, I declare I begin to understand my father. But, no doubt, it's all I'm fit for . . . to nurse fools' money.

HUGH [responding at once to this vein]. Nonsense. We all want a lesson in values. We're never taught what is worth having and what isn't. Why should your real happiness be sacrificed to the sham happiness which people have invested in the firm? I've never believed that money was valuable. I remember once giving a crossing sweeper a sovereign. The sovereign was nothing. But the sensation I gave him was an intrinsically valuable thing.

[He is fearfully pleased with his essay in philosophy.]

EDWARD. And he could buy other sensations with the sovereign.

HUGH. But none like the first. You mean to stay here till something happens?

EDWARD. I do. This is what I'm brought to. No more good to be done. And I haven't the faith in myself to do wrong. And it's only your incurable optimist who has enterprise enough for suicide . . . even business suicide.

HUGH. Ah . . . I'm that. But I can't boast. Heaven knows when I shall really get out of it either. [Then the realities of life overwhelm him again.] Beatrice won't let me go until we're each certain of two hundred a year. And she's quite right . . . I should only get into debt You know that two fifty a year of mine is a hundred and eighty now.

EDWARD [mischievous]. Why would you invest sensationally?

HUGH [with great seriousness]. I put money into things which I knew ought to succeed . . .

[The telephone rings. EDWARD speaks through it.]

EDWARD. Certainly . . . bring him in. [Then to his brother, who sits on the table idly disarranging everything.] You'll have to go now, Hugh.

HUGH [shaking his head gloomily] You're one of the few people I can talk to, Edward.

EDWARD. I like listening.

HUGH [as much cheered as surprised]. Do you? I believe talking does stir up the world's atoms a bit.

[In comes old MR. GEORGE BOOTH, older, too, in looks than he was eighteen months back. Very dandyishly dressed, he still seems by no means so happy as his clothes might be making him.]

MR. BOOTH. 'Ullo, Hugh! I thought I should find you, Edward.

EDWARD [formally]. Good-morning, Mr. Booth.

HUGH [as he collects his hat, his coat, his various properties]. Well . . . Beatrice and I go down to Chislehurst to-morrow. I say . . . d'you know that old Nursie is furious with you about something?

EDWARD [*shortly*]. Yes, I know. Good-bye.

HUGH. How are you?

[*He launches this enquiry at* MR. BOOTH *with great suddenness just as he leaves the room. The old gentleman jumps; then jumps again at the slam of the door. And then he frowns at* EDWARD *in a frightened sort of way.*]

EDWARD. Will you come here ... or will you sit by the fire?

MR. BOOTH. This'll do. I shan't detain you long.

[*He takes the chair by the table and occupies the next minute or two carefully disposing of his hat and gloves.*]

EDWARD Are you feeling all right again?

MR. BOOTH. A bit dyspeptic. How are you?

EDWARD. Quite well, thanks.

MR. BOOTH. I'm glad ... I'm glad. [*He now proceeds to cough a little, hesitating painfully.*] I'm afraid this isn't very pleasant business I've come upon.

EDWARD. D'you want to go to Law with anyone?

MR. BOOTH. No ... oh, no. I'm getting too old to quarrel.

EDWARD. A pleasant symptom.

MR. BOOTH [*with a final effort*]. I mean to withdraw my securities from the custody of your firm ... [*and he adds apologetically*] with the usual notice, of course.

[*It would be difficult to describe what* EDWARD *feels at this moment. Perhaps something of the shock that the relief of death may be as an end to pain so long endured that it has been half forgotten. He answers very quietly, without a sign of emotion.*]

EDWARD. Thank you ... May one ask why?

MR. BOOTH [*relieved that the worst is over*]. Certainly ... certainly. I think you must know, Edward, I have never been able to feel that implicit confidence in your ability which I had in your father's. Well, it is hardly to be expected, is it?

EDWARD [*with a grim smile*]. No.

MR. BOOTH. I can say that without unduly depreciating you. Men like your father are few and far between. No doubt things go on here as they have always done, but ... since his death I have not been happy about my affairs.

EDWARD [*speaking as it is his duty to*]. I think you need be under no apprehension ...

MR. BOOTH. I daresay not. But for the first time in my long life to be worried about money affairs ... I don't like the feeling. The possession of money has always been a pleasure to me ... and for what are perhaps my last years I don't wish it to be otherwise. Remember you have practically my entire property unreservedly in your control.

EDWARD. Perhaps we can arrange to hand you over the reins to an extent which will ease your mind, and at the same time not ...

MR. BOOTH. I thought of that. I am very sorry to seem to be slighting your father's son. I have not moved in the matter for eighteen months. Really, one feels a little helpless ... and the transaction of business requires more energy than ... But I saw my doctor yesterday, Edward, and he told me ... well, it was a warning. And so I felt it my duty ... especially as I made up my mind to it some time ago. [*He comes to the end of this havering at last and adds:*] In point of fact, Edward, more than a year before your father died I had quite decided that I could never trust my affairs to you as I had to him.

[EDWARD *starts almost out of his chair; his face pale, his eyes black.*]

EDWARD. Did he know that?

MR. BOOTH [*resenting this new attitude*]. I think I never said it in so many words. But I fancy he guessed.

EDWARD [*as he relaxes and turns, almost shuddering, from the possibility of dreadful knowledge*]. Don't say so ... he never guessed. [*Then, with a sudden fresh impulse:*] I hope you won't do this, Mr. Booth.

MR. BOOTH. I have quite made up my mind.

EDWARD. Let me persuade you —

MR. BOOTH [*conciliatory*]. I shall make a point of telling the family that you are in no way to blame. And in the event of any personal legal difficulties I shall always be delighted to come to you. My idea is for the future to employ merely a financial agent —

EDWARD [*still quite unstrung really, and his nerves betraying him*]. Why didn't you tell my father . . . why didn't you?

MR. BOOTH. I did not choose to distress him by —

EDWARD [*pulling himself together; speaking half to himself*]. Well . . . well . . . this is one way out. And it's not my fault.

MR. BOOTH. You're making a fearful fuss about a very simple matter, Edward. The loss of one client, however important he may be . . . Why, this is one of the best family practices in London. I am surprised at your lack of dignity.

[EDWARD *yields smilingly to this assertiveness.*]

EDWARD. Yes . . . I have no dignity. Will you walk off with your papers now?

MR. BOOTH. What notice is usual?

EDWARD. To a good solicitor, five minutes. Ten to a poor one.

MR. BOOTH. You'll have to explain matters a bit to me.

[*Now* EDWARD *settles to his desk again; really with a certain grim enjoyment of the prospect.*]

EDWARD. I will. Mr. Booth, how much do you think you're worth?

MR. BOOTH [*easily*]. Do you know, I actually couldn't say offhand.

EDWARD. But you've a rough idea?

MR. BOOTH. To be sure.

EDWARD. You'll get not quite half that out of us.

MR. BOOTH [*precisely*]. I think I said I had made up my mind to withdraw the whole amount.

EDWARD. You should have made up your mind sooner.

MR. BOOTH. I don't in the least understand you, Edward.

EDWARD. The greater part of your capital doesn't exist.

MR. BOOTH [*with some irritation*]. Nonsense, it must exist. [*He scans* EDWARD'S *set face in vain.*] You mean that it won't be prudent to realise? You can hand over the securities. I don't want to reinvest simply because —

EDWARD. I can't hand over what I haven't got.

[*This sentence falls on the old man's ears like a knell.*]

MR. BOOTH. Is anything . . . *wrong?*

EDWARD [*grim and patient*]. How many more times am I to say that we have robbed you of half your property?

MR. BOOTH [*his senses failing him*]. Say that again.

EDWARD. It's quite true.

MR. BOOTH. My money . . . *gone?*

EDWARD. Yes.

MR. BOOTH [*clutching at a straw of anger*]. You've been the thief . . . you . . . you . . . ?

EDWARD. I wouldn't tell you if I could help it . . . my father.

[*That actually calls the old man back to something like dignity and self-possession. He thumps on* EDWARD'S *table furiously.*]

MR. BOOTH. I'll make you prove that.

[*And now* EDWARD *buries his face in his arms and just goes off into hysterics.*]

EDWARD. Oh, you've fired a mine!

MR. BOOTH [*scolding him well*]. Slandering your dead father . . . and lying to me, revenging yourself by frightening me . . . because I detest you.

EDWARD. Why . . . haven't I thanked you for putting an end to my troubles? I do . . . I promise you I do.

MR. BOOTH [*shouting, and his sudden courage failing as he shouts*]. Prove it . . . prove it to me! You don't frighten me so easily. One can't lose half of all one has and then be told of it in two minutes . . . sitting at a table.

[*His voice tails off to a piteous whimper.*]

EDWARD [*quietly now and kindly*]. If my father had told you in plain words, you'd have believed him.

MR. BOOTH [*bowing his head*]. Yes.

[EDWARD *looks at the poor old thing with great pity.*]

EDWARD. What on earth did you want to do this for? You need never have known . . . you could have died happy.

Settling with all those charities in your will would certainly have smashed us up. But proving your will is many years off yet, we'll hope.

MR. BOOTH [*pathetic and bewildered*]. I don't understand. No, I don't understand ... because your father ... But I *must* understand, Edward.

EDWARD. Don't shock yourself trying to understand my father, for you never will. Pull yourself together, Mr. Booth. After all, this isn't a vital matter to you. It's not even as if you had a family to consider ... like some of the others.

MR. BOOTH [*vaguely*]. What others?

EDWARD. Don't imagine your money has been specially selected for pilfering.

MR. BOOTH [*with solemn incredulity*]. One has read of this sort of thing but ... I thought people always got found out.

EDWARD [*brutally humorous*]. Well ... you've found us out.

MR. BOOTH [*rising to the full appreciation of his wrongs*]. Oh ... I've been foully cheated!

EDWARD [*patiently*]. I've told you so.

MR. BOOTH [*his voice breaks, he appeals pitifully*]. But by you, Edward ... say it's by you.

EDWARD [*unable to resist his quiet revenge*]. I've not the ability or the personality for such work, Mr. Booth ... nothing but principles, which forbid me even to lie to you.

[*The old gentleman draws a long breath and then speaks with great awe, blending into grief.*]

MR. BOOTH. I think your father is in Hell ... I'd have gone there myself to save him from it. I loved him very truly. How he could have had the heart! We were friends for nearly fifty years. Am I to think now he only cared for me to cheat me?

EDWARD [*venturing the comfort of an explanation*]. No ... he didn't value money quite as you do.

MR. BOOTH [*with sudden shrill logic*]. But he took it. What d'you mean by that?

[EDWARD *leans back in his chair and changes the tenor of their talk.*]

EDWARD. Well, you're master of the situation now. What are you going to do?

MR. BOOTH. To get my money back?

EDWARD. No, that's gone.

MR. BOOTH. Then give me what's left and —

EDWARD. Are you going to prosecute?

MR. BOOTH [*shifting uneasily in his chair*]. Oh, dear ... is that necessary? Can't somebody else do that? I thought the Law ... What'll happen if I don't?

EDWARD. What do you suppose I'm doing here still?

MR. BOOTH [*as if he were being asked a riddle*]. I don't know.

EDWARD [*earnestly*]. As soon as my father died, I began, of course, to try and put things straight ... doing as I thought best ... that is ... as best I could. Then I made up my accounts showing who has lost and who hasn't ... they can criticise those as they please and that's all done with. And now I've set myself to a duller sort of work. I throw penny after penny hardly earned into the half-filled pit of our deficit. But I've been doing that for what it's worth in the time that was left to me ... till this should happen. If you choose to let things alone — which won't hurt you, will it? — and hold your tongue, I can go on with the job till the next smash comes, and I'll beg that off, too, if I can. This is my duty, and it's my duty to ask you to let me go on with it. [*He searches* MR. BOOTH's *face and finds there only disbelief and fear. He bursts out.*] Oh, you might at least believe me. It can't hurt you to believe me.

MR. BOOTH. You must admit, Edward, it isn't easy to believe anything in this office ... just for the moment.

EDWARD [*bowing to the extreme reasonableness of this*]. I suppose not ... I can prove it to you. I'll take you through the books ... you won't understand them ... but I can boast of this much.

MR. BOOTH. I think I'd rather not. D'you think I ought to hold any further communication with you at all?

[*And at this he takes his hat.*]

EDWARD [*with a little explosion of contemptuous anger*]. Certainly not. Prosecute ... prosecute!

THE VOYSEY INHERITANCE

Mr. Booth [*with dignity*]. Don't lose your temper. You know it's my place to be angry with you.

Edward. But... [*then he is elaborately explanatory*] I shall be grateful if you'll prosecute.

Mr. Booth [*more puzzled than ever*]. There's something in this which I don't understand.

Edward [*with deliberate unconcern*]. Think it over.

Mr. Booth [*hesitating, fidgeting*]. Surely I oughtn't to have to make up my mind! There must be a right or a wrong thing to do. Edward, can't *you* tell me?

Edward. I'm prejudiced, you see.

Mr. Booth [*angrily*]. I believe you're simply trying to practise upon my goodness of heart. Certainly I ought to prosecute at once... Oughtn't I? [*Then at the nadir of helplessness.*] Can't I consult another solicitor?

Edward [*his chin in the air*]. You can write to the *Times* about it!

Mr. Booth [*shocked and grieved at his attitude*]. Edward, how can you be so cool and heartless?

Edward [*changing his tone*]. D'you think I shan't be glad to sleep at nights?

Mr. Booth. Perhaps you'll be put in prison?

Edward. I *am* in prison... a less pleasant one than Wormwood Scrubbs. But we're all prisoners, Mr. Booth.

Mr. Booth [*wagging his head*]. Yes, this is what comes of your philosophy. Why aren't you on your knees?

Edward. To *you?*

[*This was not what* Mr. Booth *meant, but as he gets up from his chair he feels all but mighty.*]

Mr. Booth. And why should you expect me to shrink from vindicating the law?

Edward [*shortly*]. I don't. I've explained you'll be doing me a kindness. When I'm wanted, you'll find me here at my desk. [*Then, as an afterthought:*] If you take long to decide... don't alter your behaviour to my family in the meantime. They know the main points of the business and —

Mr. Booth [*knocked right off his balance*]. Do they! Good God!... I'm invited to dinner the day after to-morrow... that's Christmas Eve. The hypocrites!

Edward [*unmoved*]. I shall be there... that will have given you two days. Will you tell me then?

Mr. Booth [*protesting violently*]. I can't go... I can't have dinner with them. I must be ill.

Edward [*with a half smile*]. I remember I went to dine at Chislehurst to tell my father of my decision.

Mr. Booth [*testily*]. What decision?

Edward. To remain in the firm when I first knew what was happening.

Mr. Booth [*interested*]. Was I there?

Edward. I daresay.

[Mr. Booth *stands there, hat, stick, and gloves in hand, shaken by this experience, helpless, at his wits' end. He falls into a sort of fretful reverie, speaking half to himself, but yet as if he hoped that* Edward, *who is wrapped in his own thoughts, would have the decency to answer, or at least listen, to what he is saying.*]

Mr. Booth. Yes, how often I dined with him! Oh, it was monstrous! [*His eyes fall on the clock.*] It's nearly lunch-time now. Do you know I still can hardly believe it all? I wish I hadn't found it out. If he hadn't died, I should never have found it out. I hate to have to be vindictive... it's not my nature. Indeed, I'm sure I'm more grieved than angry. But it isn't as if it were a small sum. And I don't see that one is called upon to forgive crimes... or why does the Law exist? I feel that this will go near to killing me. I'm too old to have such troubles... it isn't right. And now if I have to prosecute —

Edward [*at last throwing in a word*]. Well... you need not.

Mr. Booth [*thankful for the provocation*]. Don't you attempt to influence me, sir.

[*He turns to go.*]

Edward. And what's more, with the money you have left...

[Edward *follows him politely.*

Mr. Booth *flings the door open.*]

Mr. Booth. You'll make out a cheque for that at once, sir, and send it me.

EDWARD. You might...
MR. BOOTH [*clapping his hat on, stamping his stick*]. I shall do the right thing, sir, never fear.

[*So he marches off in fine style, having, he thinks, had the last word and all. But* EDWARD, *closing the door after him, mutters* ...]

EDWARD.... Save your soul!... I'm afraid I was going to say.

ACT V

Naturally it is the dining-room — consecrated as it is to the distinguishing orgy of the season — which bears the brunt of what an English household knows as Christmas decorations. They consist chiefly of the branches of holly (that unyielding tree), stuck cock-eyed behind the top edges of the pictures. The one picture conspicuously not decorated is that which now hangs over the fireplace, a portrait of MR. VOYSEY, *with its new gilt frame and its brassplate marking it also as a presentation.* HONOR, *hastily and at some bodily peril, pulled down the large bunch of mistletoe, which a callous housemaid had suspended above it, in time to obviate the shock to family feelings which such impropriety would cause. Otherwise the only difference between the dining-room's appearance at half-past nine on Christmas Eve and on any other evening in the year is that little piles of queer-shaped envelopes seem to be lying about, while there is quite a lot of tissue paper and string to be seen peeping from odd corners. The electric light is reduced to one bulb, but when the maid opens the door showing in* MR. GEORGE BOOTH *she switches on the rest.*

PHŒBE. This room is empty, sir. I'll tell Mr. Edward.

[*She leaves him to fidget towards the fireplace and back, not removing his comforter or his coat, scarcely turning down the collar, screwing his cap in his hands. In a very short time* EDWARD *comes in, shutting the door and taking stock of the visitor before he speaks.*]

EDWARD. Well?

MR. GEORGE BOOTH [*feebly*]. I hope my excuse for not coming to dinner was acceptable. I did have... I have a very bad headache.

EDWARD. I daresay they believed it.

MR. GEORGE BOOTH. I have come immediately to tell you my decision... perhaps this trouble will then be a little more off my mind.

EDWARD. What is it?

MR. GEORGE BOOTH. I couldn't think the matter out alone. I went this afternoon to talk it over with my old friend Colpus. [*At this news* EDWARD'S *eyebrows contract and then rise.*] What a terrible shock to him!

EDWARD. Oh, nearly three of his four thousand pounds are quite safe.

MR. GEORGE BOOTH. That you and your father... you, whom he baptised... should have robbed him! I never saw a man so utterly prostrate with grief. That it should have been your father! And his poor wife!... though she never got on with your father.

EDWARD [*with cheerful irony*]. Oh, Mrs. Colpus knows too, does she?

MR. GEORGE BOOTH. Of course he told Mrs. Colpus. This is an unfortunate time for the storm to break on him. What with Christmas Day and Sunday following so close they're as busy as can be. He has resolved that during this season of peace and good-will he must put the matter from him if he can. But once Christmas is over...!

[*He envisages the Christian old Vicar giving* EDWARD *a hell of a time then.*]

EDWARD [*coolly*]. So you mean to prosecute. If you don't, you've inflicted on the Colpuses a lot of unnecessary pain and a certain amount of loss by telling them.

MR. GEORGE BOOTH [*naïvely*]. I never thought of that. No, Edward, I have decided not to prosecute.

[EDWARD *hides his face for a moment.*]

EDWARD. And I've been hoping to escape! Well... it can't be helped.
[*And he sets his teeth.*]
MR. GEORGE BOOTH [*with touching solemnity*]. I think I could not bear to see the family I have loved brought to such disgrace. And I want to ask your pardon, Edward, for some of the hard thoughts I have had of you. I consider this effort of yours to restore to the firm the credit which your father lost a very striking one. You sacrifice your profits, I understand, to replacing the capital that has been misappropriated. Very proper... more than proper.
EDWARD. No. No. To pay interest on money that doesn't exist, but ought to... and the profits don't cover that or anything like it.
MR. GEORGE BOOTH. Patience... I shouldn't be surprised if you worked up the business very well.
EDWARD [*again laying the case before* MR. BOOTH, *leaning forward to him*]. Mr. Booth, you were fond of my father. You see the help you could give us, don't you?
MR. GEORGE BOOTH. By not prosecuting?
EDWARD [*earnestly*]. Beyond that. If you'd cut your losses... for the moment, and take only what's yours by right... why, that would relieve me of four thousand three hundred a year... and I could do so much with it. There are one or two bad cases still. One woman — I believe you know her — it's not that she's so poor ... and perhaps I'm not justified now in doing anything special... but she's got children... and if you'd help...
MR. GEORGE BOOTH. Stop, Edward... stop at once. If you attempt to confuse me I must take professional advice. Colpus and I have discussed this and quite made up our minds. And I've made a note or two. [*He produces a bit of paper and a pencil.* EDWARD *stiffens.*] May we understand that in straightening affairs you can show a proper preference for one client over another?
EDWARD [*pulled up, draws back in his chair*]. No... you had better not understand that.

MR. GEORGE BOOTH. Why can't you?
EDWARD. Well... suppose if I want to, I can?
MR. GEORGE BOOTH. Edward, do please be straightforward.
EDWARD. Why should I?
MR. GEORGE BOOTH. You certainly should. Do you mean to compare your father's ordinary business transactions — the hundreds of them — with his black treachery to... to the Vicar?
EDWARD. Or to you?
MR. GEORGE BOOTH. Or to me.
EDWARD. Besides that, holding your tongue should be worth something extra now, shouldn't it?
MR. GEORGE BOOTH. I don't want to argue. My own position morally — and otherwise — is a strong one... so Colpus impresses on me... and he has some head for business.
EDWARD. Well, what are your terms?
MR. GEORGE BOOTH. This is my note of them. [*He takes refuge in his slip of paper.*] I make these conditions, if you please, Edward, on the Vicar's behalf and my own. They are... [*now the pencil comes into play, ticking off each item*] that you at once return us the balance of any capital there is left...
EDWARD [*cold again*]. I am providing for that.
MR. GEORGE BOOTH. Good. That you should continue, of course, to pay us the usual interest upon the rest of our capital, which ought to exist and does not. And that you should, year by year, pay us back by degrees out of the earnings of the firm as much of that capital as you can afford. We will agree upon the sum... say a thousand a year. I doubt if you can ever restore us all we have lost, but do your best and I shan't complain. There, I think that is fair dealing!
[EDWARD *does not take his eyes off* MR. BOOTH *until the whole meaning of this proposition has settled in his brain. Then, without warning, he goes off into peals of laughter, much to the alarm of* MR. BOOTH, *who has never thought him over-sane.*]
EDWARD. How funny! How very funny!

Mr. George Booth. Edward, don't laugh.

Edward. I never heard anything quite so funny!

Mr. George Booth. Edward, stop laughing.

Edward. Oh, you Christian gentlemen!

Mr. George Booth. Don't be hysterical. The money's ours.

[Edward's *laughter gives way to the deepest anger of which he is capable.*]

Edward. I'm giving my soul and body to restoring you and the rest of you to your precious money bags... and you'll wring me dry. Won't you? Won't you?

Mr. George Booth. Now be reasonable. Argue the point quietly.

Edward. Go to the devil, sir.

[*And with that he turns away from the flabbergasted old gentleman.*]

Mr. George Booth. Don't be rude.

Edward [*his anger vanishing*]. I beg your pardon.

Mr. George Booth. You're just excited. If you take time to think of it, I'm reasonable.

Edward [*his sense of humour returning*]. Most. Most! [*There is a knock at the door.*] Come in. Come in.

[Honor *intrudes an apologetic head.*]

Honor. Am I interrupting business? I'm so sorry.

Edward [*crowing in a mirthless enjoyment of his joke*]. No! Business is over... quite over. Come in, Honor.

[Honor *puts on the table a market basket bulging with little paper parcels, and, oblivious of* Mr. Booth's *distracted face, tries to fix his attention.*]

Honor. I thought, dear Mr. Booth, perhaps you wouldn't mind carrying round this basket of things yourself. It's so very damp underfoot that I don't want to send one of the maids out to-night if I can possibly avoid it... and if one doesn't get Christmas presents the very first thing on Christmas morning quite half the pleasure in them is lost, don't you think?

Mr. George Booth. Yes... yes.

Honor [*fishing out the parcels one by one*]. This is a bell for Mrs. Williams... something she said she wanted so that you can ring for her, which saves the maids: cap and apron for Mary: cap and apron for Ellen: shawl for Davis when she goes out to the larder — all useful presents — and that's something for you, but you're not to look at it till the morning.

[*Having shaken each of these at the old gentleman, she proceeds to repack them. He is now trembling with anxiety to escape before any more of the family find him there.*]

Mr. George Booth. Thank you... thank you! I hope my lot has arrived. I left instructions...

Honor. Quite safely... and I have hidden them. Presents are put on the breakfast table to-morrow.

Edward [*with an inconsequence that still further alarms* Mr. Booth]. When we were all children our Christmas breakfast was mostly made off chocolates.

[*Before the basket is packed,* Mrs. Voysey *sails slowly into the room, as smiling and as deaf as ever.* Mr. Booth *does his best not to scowl at her.*]

Mrs. Voysey. Are you feeling better, George Booth?

Mr. George Booth. No. [*Then he elevates his voice with a show of politeness.*] No, thank you... I can't say I am.

Mrs. Voysey. You don't look better.

Mr. George Booth. I still have my headache. [*With a distracted shout.*] Headache.

Mrs. Voysey. Bilious, perhaps! I quite understood you didn't care to dine. But why not have taken your coat off? How foolish in this warm room!

Mr. George Booth. Thank you. I'm — er — just off.

[*He seizes the market basket. At that moment* Mrs. Hugh *appears.*]

Beatrice. Your shawl, mother.

[*And she clasps it round* Mrs. Voysey's *shoulders.*]

Mrs. Voysey. Thank you, Beatrice. I thought I had it on. [*Then to* Mr. Booth *who is now entangled in his comforter.*] A merry Christmas to you.

BEATRICE. Good-evening, Mr. Booth.
MR. GEORGE BOOTH. I beg your pardon. Good-evening, Mrs. Hugh.
HONOR [*with sudden inspiration, to the company in general.*] Why shouldn't I write in here ... now the table's cleared!
MR. GEORGE BOOTH [*sternly, now he is safe by the door*]. Will you see me out, Edward?
EDWARD. Yes.

[*He follows the old man and his basket, leaving the others to distribute themselves about the room. It is a custom of the female members of the* VOYSEY *family, especially about Christmas time, to return to the dining-room, when the table has been cleared, and occupy themselves in various ways which require space and untidiness. Sometimes as the evening wears on, they partake of cocoa, sometimes they abstain.* BEATRICE *has a little work-basket, containing a buttonless glove and such things, which she is rectifying.* HONOR'S *writing is done with the aid of an enormous blotting-book, which bulges with apparently a year's correspondence. She sheds its contents upon the end of the dining-table and spreads them abroad.* MRS. VOYSEY *settles to the fire, opens the Nineteenth Century and is instantly absorbed in it.*]

BEATRICE. Where's Emily?
HONOR [*mysteriously*]. Well, Beatrice, she's in the library talking to Booth.
BEATRICE. Talking to her husband; good Heavens! I know she has taken my scissors.
HONOR. I think she's telling him about you.
BEATRICE. What about me?
HONOR. You and Hugh.
BEATRICE [*with a little movement of annoyance*]. I suppose this is Hugh's fault. It was carefully arranged no one was to be told till after Christmas.
HONOR. Emily told me ... and Edward knows ... and mother knows ...
BEATRICE. I warned mother a year ago.
HONOR. Everyone seems to know but Booth ... so I thought he'd better be told.

I suggested one night so that he might have time to think over it ... but Emily said that'd wake Alfred. Besides she's nearly always asleep herself when he comes to bed.
BEATRICE. Why do they still have that baby in their room?
HONOR. Emily thinks it her duty.
[*At this moment* EMILY *comes in, looking rather trodden upon.* HONOR *concludes in the most audible of whispers:*]
HONOR. Don't say anything ... it's my fault.
BEATRICE [*fixing her with a severe forefinger*]. Emily ... have you taken my best scissors?
EMILY [*timidly*]. No, Beatrice.
HONOR [*who is diving into the recesses of the blotting-book*]. Oh, here they are! I must have taken them. I do apologise!
EMILY [*more timidly still*]. I'm afraid Booth's rather cross ... he's gone to look for Hugh.
BEATRICE [*with a shake of her head*]. Honor ... I've a good mind to make you do this sewing for me.
[*In comes the* MAJOR, *strepitant. He takes, so to speak, just time enough to train himself on* BEATRICE *and then fires.*]
BOOTH. Beatrice, what on earth is this Emily has been telling me?
BEATRICE [*with elaborate calm*]. Emily, what have you been telling Booth?
BOOTH. Please ... please do not prevaricate. Where is Hugh?
MRS. VOYSEY [*looking over her spectacles*]. What did you say, Booth?
BOOTH. I want Hugh, mother.
MRS. VOYSEY. I thought you were playing billiards together.
[EDWARD *strolls back from despatching* MR. BOOTH, *his face thoughtful.*]
BOOTH [*insistently*]. Edward, where is Hugh?
EDWARD [*with complete indifference*]. I don't know.
BOOTH [*in trumpet tones*]. Honor, will you oblige me by finding Hugh and saying I wish to speak to him, here, immediately?
[HONOR, *who has leapt at the sound*

of her name, flies from the room without a word.]

BEATRICE. I know quite well what you want to talk about, Booth. Discuss the matter by all means if it amuses you . . . but don't shout.

BOOTH. I use the voice Nature has gifted me with, Beatrice.

BEATRICE [*as she searches for a glove button*]. Certainly Nature did let herself go over your lungs.

BOOTH [*glaring round with indignation*]. This is a family matter, otherwise I should not feel it my duty to interfere . . . as I do. Any member of the family has a right to express an opinion. I want mother's. Mother, what do you think?

MRS. VOYSEY [*amicably*]. What about?

BOOTH. Hugh and Beatrice separating.

MRS. VOYSEY. They haven't separated.

BOOTH. But they mean to.

MRS. VOYSEY. Fiddle-de-dee!

BOOTH. I quite agree with you.

BEATRICE [*with a charming smile*]. Such reasoning would convert a stone.

BOOTH. Why have I not been told?

BEATRICE. You have just been told.

BOOTH [*thunderously*]. Before.

BEATRICE. The truth is, dear Booth, we're all so afraid of you.

BOOTH [*a little mollified*]. Ha . . . I should be glad to think that.

BEATRICE [*sweetly*]. Don't you?

BOOTH [*intensely serious*]. Beatrice, your callousness shocks me! That you can dream of deserting Hugh . . . a man of all others who requires constant care and attention.

BEATRICE. May I remark that the separation is as much Hugh's wish as mine?

BOOTH. I don't believe that.

BEATRICE [*her eyebrows up*]. Really!

BOOTH. I don't imply that you're lying. But you must know that it's Hugh's nature to wish to do anything that he thinks anybody wishes him to do. All my life I've had to stand up for him . . . and, by Jove, I'll continue to do so.

EDWARD [*from the depths of his armchair*]. If you'd taught him to stand up for himself —

[*The door is flung almost off its hinges by* HUGH *who then stands stamping and pale green with rage.*]

HUGH. Look here, Booth . . . I will not have you interfering with my private affairs. Is one never to be free from your bullying?

BOOTH. You ought to be grateful.

HUGH. Well, I'm not.

BOOTH. This is a family affair.

HUGH. It is not!

BOOTH [*at the top of his voice*]. If all you can do is to contradict me, you'd better listen to what I've got to say . . . quietly.

[HUGH, *quite shouted down, flings himself petulantly into a chair. A hush falls.*]

EMILY [*in a still small voice*]. Would you like me to go, Booth?

BOOTH [*severely*]. No, Emily. Unless anything has been going on which cannot be discussed before you . . . [*then more severely still*] and I hope that is not so.

HUGH [*muttering rebelliously*]. Oh, you have the mind of a . . . an official flunkey!

BOOTH. Why do you wish to separate?

HUGH. What's the use of telling you? You won't understand.

BEATRICE [*who sews on undisturbed*]. We don't get on well together.

BOOTH [*amazedly*]. Is that all?

HUGH [*snapping at him*]. Yes, that's all. Can you find a better reason?

BOOTH [*with brotherly contempt*]. I have given up expecting common-sense from you. But Beatrice — !

[*His tone implores her to be reasonable.*]

BEATRICE. It doesn't seem to me any sort of sense that people should live together for purposes of mutual irritation.

BOOTH [*protesting*]. My dear girl! . . . that sounds like a quotation from your last book.

BEATRICE. It isn't. I do think, Booth, you might read that book . . . for the honour of the Family.

BOOTH [*successfully side-tracked*]. I have bought it, Beatrice, and —

BEATRICE. That's the principal thing, of course —

BOOTH [*and discovering it*]. But do let us keep to the subject.

BEATRICE [*with flattering sincerity*]. Certainly, Booth. And there is hardly any subject that I wouldn't ask your advice about. But upon this . . . please let me know better. Hugh and I will be happier apart.

BOOTH [*obstinately*]. Why?

BEATRICE [*with resolute patience, having vented a little sigh*]. Hugh finds that my opinions distress him. And I have at last lost patience with Hugh.

MRS. VOYSEY [*who has been trying to follow this through her spectacles*]. What does Beatrice say?

BOOTH [*translating into a loud sing-song*]. That she wishes to leave her husband because she has lost patience!

MRS. VOYSEY [*with considerable acrimony*]. Then you must be a very ill-tempered woman. Hugh has a sweet nature.

HUGH [*shouting self-consciously*]. Nonsense, mother.

BEATRICE [*shouting good-humouredly*]. I quite agree with you, mother. [*She continues to her husband in an even just tone.*] You have a sweet nature, Hugh, and it is most difficult to get angry with you. I have been seven years working up to it. But now that I am angry, I shall never get pleased again.

[*The MAJOR returns to his subject, refreshed by a moment's repose.*]

BOOTH. How has he failed in his duty? Tell us. I'm not bigoted in his favour. I know your faults, Hugh.

[*He wags his head at HUGH, who writhes with irritation.*]

HUGH. Why can't you leave them alone . . . leave us alone?

BEATRICE. I'd state my case against Hugh, if I thought he'd retaliate.

HUGH [*desperately rounding on his brother*]. If I tell you, you won't understand. You understand nothing! Beatrice is angry with me because I won't prostitute my art to make money.

BOOTH [*glancing at his wife*]. Please don't use metaphors of that sort.

BEATRICE [*reasonably*]. Yes, I think Hugh ought to earn more money.

BOOTH [*quite pleased to be getting along at last*]. Well, why doesn't he?

HUGH. I don't want money.

BOOTH. You can't say you don't want money any more than you can say you don't want bread.

BEATRICE [*as she breaks off her cotton*]. It's when one has known what it is to be a little short of both . . .

[*Now the MAJOR spreads himself and begins to be very wise, while HUGH, to whom this is more intolerable than all, can only clutch his hair.*]

BOOTH. You know I never considered Art a very good profession for you, Hugh. And you won't even stick to one department of it. It's a profession that gets people into very bad habits, I consider. Couldn't you take up something else? You could still do those wood-cuts in your spare time to amuse yourself.

HUGH [*commenting on this with two deliberate shouts of simulated mirth*]. Ha! Ha!

BOOTH [*sublimely superior*]. Well, it wouldn't much matter if you didn't do them at all!

BEATRICE [*subtly*]. Booth, there speaks the true critic.

BOOTH [*deprecating any title to omniscience*]. Well, I don't pretend to know much about Art, but —

HUGH. It would matter to me. There speaks the artist.

BEATRICE. The arrogance of the artist!

HUGH. We have a right to be arrogant.

BEATRICE. Good workmen are humble.

HUGH. And look to their wages.

BEATRICE. Well, I'm only a workman.

[*With that she breaks the contact of this quiet deadly hopeless little quarrel by turning her head away. The MAJOR, who has given it most friendly attention, comments.*]

BOOTH. Of course! Quite so! I'm sure all that is a very interesting difference of opinion. But it's nothing to separate about.

[*MRS. VOYSEY leaves her armchair for her favorite station at the dining-table.*]

MRS. VOYSEY. Booth is the only one of you that I can hear at all distinctly. But if you two foolish young people think you want to separate ... try it. You'll soon come back to each other and be glad to. People can't fight against Nature for long. And marriage is a natural state ... once you're married.

BOOTH [*with intense approval*]. Quite right, mother.

MRS. VOYSEY. I know.

[*She resumes the Nineteenth Century. The* MAJOR, *to the despair of everybody, makes yet another start; trying oratory this time.*]

BOOTH. My own opinion is, Beatrice and Hugh, that you don't realise the meaning of the word "marriage." I don't call myself a religious man ... but dash it all, you were married in Church! ... And you then entered upon an awful compact! ... Surely ... as a woman, Beatrice ... the religious point of it ought to appeal to you. Good Lord, suppose everybody were to carry on like this! And have you considered, Beatrice, that ... whether you're right or whether you're wrong ... if you desert Hugh, you cut yourself off from the Family.

BEATRICE [*with the sweetest of smiles*]. That will distress me terribly.

BOOTH [*not doubting her for a moment*]. Of course.

[HUGH *flings up his head and finds relief at last in many words.*]

HUGH. I wish to Heaven I'd ever been able to cut myself off from the Family! Look at Trenchard.

BOOTH [*gobbling a little at this unexpected attack*]. I do not forgive Trenchard for quarrelling with and deserting our father.

HUGH. Trenchard quarrelled because that was his only way of escape.

BOOTH. Escape from what?

HUGH. From tyranny! ... from hypocrisy! ... from boredom! ... from his Happy English Home!

BEATRICE [*kindly*]. Hugh ... Hugh ... it's no use.

BOOTH [*attempting sarcasm*]. Speak so that mother can hear you!

[*But* HUGH *isn't to be stopped now.*]

HUGH. Why are we all dull, cubbish, uneducated ... that is hopelessly middle-class?

BOOTH [*taking this as very personal*]. Cubbish!

HUGH. ... Because it's the middle-class ideal that you should respect your parents ... live with them ... think with them ... grow like them. Natural affection and gratitude! That's what's expected, isn't it?

BOOTH [*not to be obliterated*]. Certainly.

HUGH. Keep your children ignorant of all that you don't know, penniless except for your good pleasure, dependent on you for permission to breathe freely ... and be sure that their gratitude will be most disinterested, and their affection very natural. If your father's a drunkard or poor, then perhaps you get free and can form an opinion of your own ... and can love him or hate him as he deserves. But our father and mother were models. They did their duty by us ... and taught us ours. Trenchard escaped, as I say. You took to the Army ... so, of course, you've never discovered how behind the times *you* are. [*The* MAJOR *is stupent.*] I tried to express myself in art ... and found there was nothing to express ... I'd been so well brought up. D'you blame me if I wander about in search of a soul of some sort? And Honor —

BOOTH [*disputing savagely*]. Honor is very happy at home. Everyone loves her.

HUGH [*with fierce sarcasm*]. Yes ... what do we call her? Mother's right hand! I wonder they bothered to give her a name. By the time little Ethel came they were tired of training children ...

[*His voice loses its sting; he doesn't complete this sentence.*]

BEATRICE. Poor little Ethel ...

BOOTH. Poor Ethel!

[*They speak as one speaks of the dead, and so the wrangling stops. Then* EDWARD *interposes quietly.*]

EDWARD. Ah, my dear Hugh ...

HUGH. I haven't spoken of your fate, Edward. That's too shameful.

EDWARD. Not at all. I sit at my desk daily as the servant of men whose ideal of life is to have a thousand a year ... or two thousand ... or three ...

BOOTH. Well?

EDWARD. That's all.

THE VOYSEY INHERITANCE

BOOTH. What's the point? One must live.
HUGH. And if Booth can be said to think, he honestly thinks that's living.
BOOTH. We will return, if you please, to the original subject of discussion. Hugh, this question of a separation —
[*Past all patience,* HUGH *jumps up and flings his chair back to its place.*]
HUGH. Beatrice and I mean to separate. And nothing you may say will prevent us. The only difficulty in the way is money. Can we command enough to live apart comfortably?
BOOTH. Well?
HUGH. Well . . . we can't.
BOOTH. Well?
HUGH. So we can't separate.
BOOTH [*speaking with bewilderment*]. Then what in Heaven's name have we been discussing it for?
HUGH. I haven't discussed it! I don't want to discuss it! Mind — can't you mind your own business? Now I'll go back to the billiard room and my book.
[*He is gone before the poor* MAJOR *can recover his lost breath.*]
BOOTH [*as he does recover it*]. I am not an impatient man . . . but really . . . [*And then words fail him.*]
BEATRICE [*commenting calmly*]. Hugh, I am told, was a spoilt child. They grow to hate their parents sooner than others. You taught him to cry for what he wanted. Now that he's older and doesn't get it, that makes him a wearisome companion.
BOOTH [*very sulky now*]. You married him with your eyes open, I suppose?
BEATRICE. How few women marry with their eyes open!
BOOTH. You have never made the best of Hugh.
BEATRICE. I have spared him that indignity.
BOOTH [*vindictively*]. I am very glad that you can't separate.
BEATRICE. As soon as I'm reasonably sure of earning an income I shall walk off from him. [*The* MAJOR *revives.*]
BOOTH. You will do nothing of the sort, Beatrice.
BEATRICE [*unruffled*]. How will you stop me, Booth?

BOOTH. I shall tell Hugh he must command you to stay.
BEATRICE [*with a little smile*]. I wonder would that still make a difference. It was one of the illusions of my girlhood that I should love a man who would master me.
BOOTH. Hugh must assert himself.
[*He begins to walk about, giving some indication of how it should be done.* BEATRICE'S *smile has vanished.*]
BEATRICE. Don't think I've enjoyed taking the lead in everything throughout my married life. But someone had to plan and scheme and be foreseeing . . . we weren't sparrows or lilies of the field . . . someone had to get up and do something, if not for money, at least for the honour of it. [*She becomes conscious of his strutting and smiles rather mischievously.*] Ah . . . if I'd married you, Booth!
[BOOTH'S *face grows beatific.*]
BOOTH. Well, I must own to thinking that I am a masterful man . . . that it's the duty of every man to be so. [*He adds forgivingly.*] Poor old Hugh!
BEATRICE [*unable to resist temptation*]. If I'd tried to leave you, Booth, you'd have whipped me . . . wouldn't you?
BOOTH [*ecstatically complacent*]. Ha . . . well . . . !
BEATRICE. Do say yes. Think how it'll frighten Emily.
[*The* MAJOR *strokes his moustache and is most friendly.*]
BOOTH. Hugh's been a worry to me all my life. And now as Head of the Family . . . Well, I suppose I'd better go and give the dear chap another talking to. I quite see your point of view, Beatrice.
BEATRICE. Why disturb him at his book?
[MAJOR BOOTH *leaves them, squaring his shoulders as becomes a lord of creation. The two sisters-in-law go on with their work silently for a moment; then* BEATRICE *adds:*]
BEATRICE. Do you find Booth difficult to manage, Emily?
EMILY [*putting down her knitting to consider the matter*]. No. It's best to allow him to talk himself out. When he's done that, he'll often come to me for advice. I

let him get his own way as much as possible ... or think he's getting it. Otherwise he becomes so depressed.

BEATRICE [*quietly amused*]. Edward shouldn't hear this. What has he to do with women's secrets?

EDWARD. I won't tell ... and I'm a bachelor.

EMILY [*solemnly as she takes up her knitting again*]. Do you really mean to leave Hugh?

BEATRICE [*slightly impatient*]. Emily, I've said so.

[*They are joined by* ALICE MAITLAND, *who comes in gaily.*]

ALICE. What's Booth shouting about in the billiard room?

EMILY [*pained*]. Oh ... on Christmas Eve, too!

BEATRICE. Don't you take any interest in my matrimonial affairs?

[MRS. VOYSEY *shuts up the Nineteenth Century and removes her spectacles.*]

MRS. VOYSEY. That's a very interesting article. The Chinese Empire must be in a shocking state! Is it ten o'clock yet?

EDWARD. Past.

MRS. VOYSEY [*as* EDWARD *is behind her*]. Can anyone see the clock?

ALICE. It's past ten, Auntie.

MRS. VOYSEY. Then I think I'll go to my room.

EMILY. Shall I come and look after you, mother?

MRS. VOYSEY. If you'd find Honor for me, Emily.

[EMILY *goes in search of the harmless necessary* HONOR *and* MRS. VOYSEY *begins her nightly chant of departure.*]

MRS. VOYSEY. Good-night, Alice. Good-night, Edward.

EDWARD. Good-night, mother.

MRS. VOYSEY [*with sudden severity*]. I'm not pleased with you, Beatrice.

BEATRICE. I'm sorry, mother.

[*But without waiting to be answered, the old lady has sailed out of the room.* BEATRICE, EDWARD, *and* ALICE *are attuned to each other enough to be able to talk with ease.*]

BEATRICE. Hugh is right about his family. It'll never make any new life for itself.

EDWARD. There are Booth's children.

BEATRICE. Poor little devils!

ALICE [*judicially*]. Emily is an excellent mother.

BEATRICE. Yes ... they'll grow up good men and women. And one will go into the Army and one into the Navy and one into the Church ... and perhaps one to the Devil and the Colonies. They'll serve their country and govern it and help to keep it like themselves ... dull and respectable ... hopelessly middle-class. [*She puts down her work now and elevates an oratorical fist.*] Genius and Poverty may exist in England, if they'll hide their heads. For show days we've our aristocracy. But never let us forget, gentlemen, that it is the plain solid middle-class man who has made us ... what we are.

EDWARD [*in sympathetic derision*]. Hear hear ... ! and cries of bravo!

BEATRICE. Now, that is out of my book ... the next one. [*She takes up her work again.*] You know, Edward ... however scandalous it was, your father left you a man's work to do.

EDWARD [*his face cloudy*]. An outlaw's!

BEATRICE [*whimsical after a moment*]. I mean that. At all events, you've not had to be your father's right arm ... or the instrument of justice ... or a representative of the people ... or anything second-hand of that sort, have you?

EDWARD [*with sudden excitement*]. Do you know what I found out the other day about [*he nods at the portrait*] ... him?

BEATRICE [*enquiring calmly*]. What?

EDWARD. He saved his firm once. That was true. A pretty capable piece of heroism. Then, fifteen years afterwards ... he started again.

BEATRICE [*greatly interested*]. Did he now?

EDWARD. It can't have been merely through weakness ...

BEATRICE [*with artistic enthusiasm*]. Of course not. He was a man of imagination and a great financier. He had to find scope for his abilities or die. He despised these

fat little clients living so snugly on their fattening little incomes... and put them and their money to the best use he could.
EDWARD [*shaking his head solemnly*]. Fine phrases for robbery.
[BEATRICE *turns her clever face to him and begins to follow up her subject keenly.*]
BEATRICE. But didn't Hugh tell me that your golden deed has been robbing your rich clients for the benefit of the poor ones?
ALICE [*who hasn't missed a word*]. That's true.
EDWARD [*gently*]. Well... we're all a bit in debt to the poor, aren't we?
BEATRICE. Quite so. And you don't possess and your father didn't possess that innate sense of the sacredness of property... [*she enjoys that phrase*] which mostly makes your merely honest man. Nor did the man possess it who picked my pocket last Friday week... nor does the taxgatherer... nor do I. And whether we can boast of our opinions depends on such a silly lot of prejudices and cowardices that —
EDWARD [*a little pained by as much of this as he takes to be serious*]. Why wouldn't he own the truth to me about himself?
BEATRICE. He was a bit of a genius. Perhaps he took care not to know it. Would you have understood?
EDWARD. Perhaps not. But I loved him.
[BEATRICE *looks again at the gentle, earnest face.*]
BEATRICE. Through it all?
EDWARD. Yes. And not from mere force of habit either.
BEATRICE [*with reverence in her voice now*]. That might silence a bench of judges. Well... well...
[*Her sewing finished, she stuffs the things into her basket, gets up in her abrupt, unconventional way and goes without another word. Her brain is busy with the Voysey Inheritance.* EDWARD *and* ALICE *are left in chairs by the fire, facing each other like an old domestic couple.*]
EDWARD. Stay and talk to me.
ALICE. I want to. Something has happened... since dinner.
EDWARD. Can you see that?

ALICE. What is it?
EDWARD [*with sudden exultation*]. The smash has come... and not by my fault. Old George Booth —
ALICE. Has he been here?
EDWARD. Can you imagine it? He got at the truth. I told him to take his money ... what there was of it... and prosecute. He won't prosecute, but he bargains to take the money... and then to bleed us, sovereign by sovereign, as I earn sovereign by sovereign with the sweat of my soul. I'll see him in his Christian Heaven first... the Jew!
ALICE [*keeping her head*]. You can't reason with him?
EDWARD. No. He thinks he has the whip hand, and the Vicar has been told... who has told his wife. She knows how not to keep a secret. It has come at last.
ALICE. So you're glad?
EDWARD. So thankful — my conscience is clear. I've done my best. [*Then, as usual with him, his fervour collapses.*] And oh, Alice... has it been worth doing?
ALICE [*encouragingly*]. Half a dozen poor devils pulled safe out of the fire.
EDWARD. But I'm wondering now if that won't be found out, or if I shan't just confess to the pious fraud when the time comes. Somehow I don't seem to have the conviction to carry any job through. A weak nature, my father said. He knew.
ALICE. You have a religious nature.
EDWARD [*surprised*]. Oh, no!
ALICE [*proceeding to explain*]. Which means, of course, that you don't cling to creeds and ceremonies. And the good things and the well-done jobs of this worldly world don't satisfy you... so you shirk contact with it all you can.
EDWARD [*his eyes far away*]. Yes. Do you never feel that there aren't enough windows in a house?
ALICE [*prosaically*]. In this weather... too many.
EDWARD. In my office then — I feel it when I'm at work — one is out of all hearing of all the music of the world. And when one does get back to Nature, instead of being curves to her roundness, one is all corners

ALICE [*smiling at him*]. And you love to think prettily, don't you... just as Hugh does. You do it quite well, too. [*Then, briskly:*] But, Edward, may I scold you?

EDWARD. For that?

ALICE. Why have you grown to be more of a sloven than ever lately? Yes, a spiritual sloven, I call it — deliberately letting yourself be unhappy.

EDWARD. Is happiness under one's control?

ALICE. My friend, you shouldn't neglect your happiness any more than you neglect to wash your face. I was desperate about you... so I came down to your office.

EDWARD. Yes, you did.

ALICE. But I found you master there, and I thanked God. Because with us, Edward, for these last eighteen months you've been more like a moral portent than a man — without a smile to throw to a friend... or an opinion upon any subject. Why did you throw up your boys' club? Why didn't you vote last November? — too out of keeping with your unhappy fate?

EDWARD [*contrite at this*]. I was wrong not to vote.

ALICE. You don't even eat properly.

[*With that she completes the accusation and* EDWARD *searches round for a defence.*]

EDWARD. But, Alice, it was always an effort to do all these things... and lately every effort has had to go to my work, hasn't it?

ALICE. Oh... if you only did them on principle... I retract... far better not do them at all.

EDWARD. Don't laugh at me.

ALICE. Edward, is there nothing you want from life... want for its own sake? That's the only test.

EDWARD. I daren't ask.

ALICE. Yes, you dare. It's all so long past that awful time when you were... more than a bit of a prig.

EDWARD [*with enough sense of humour to whisper back*]. Was I?

ALICE. I'm afraid so! He still stalks through my dreams sometimes... and I wake in a sweat. But I think he's nearly done with. [*Then her voice rises stirringly.*] Oh, don't you see what a blessing this cursed burden of disgrace and work was meant to be to you?

EDWARD [*without a smile now*]. But lately, Alice, I've hardly known myself. Sometimes I've lost my temper... I've been brutal.

ALICE. I knew it. I knew that would happen. It's your own wicked nature coming out at last. That's what we've been waiting for... that's what we want. That's you.

EDWARD [*still serious*]. I'm sorry for it.

ALICE. Oh, Edward, be a little proud of poor humanity... take your own share in it gladly. It so discourages the rest of us if you don't.

[*Suddenly he breaks down completely.*]

EDWARD. I can't let myself be glad and live. There's the future to think of, and I'm so afraid of that. I must pretend I don't care... even to myself... even to you.

ALICE [*her mocking at an end*]. What is it you fear most about the future... not just the obviously unpleasant things?

EDWARD. They'll put me in prison.

ALICE. Even then?

EDWARD. Who'll be the man who comes out?

ALICE. Yourself, and more than ever yourself.

EDWARD. No, no! I'm a coward. I can't stand alone, and after that I shall have to. I need affection... I need friends. I cling to people that I don't care for deeply... just for the comfort of it. I've no real home of my own. Every house that welcomes me now I like to think of as something of a home. And this disgrace in store will leave me... homeless.

[*There he sits shaken.* ALICE *waits a moment, not taking her eyes from him: then speaks.*]

ALICE. Edward, there's something else I want to scold you for. You've still given up proposing to me. Certainly that shows a lack of courage... and of perseverance. Or is it the loss of what I always considered a very laudable ambition?

[EDWARD *is hardly able to trust his ears. Then he looks into her face and his thankfulness frames itself into a single sentence.*]

EDWARD. Will you marry me?

ALICE. Yes, Edward.

[*For a minute he just holds his breath with happiness. But he shakes himself free of it, almost savagely.*]

EDWARD. No, no, no, we mustn't be stupid. I'm sorry I asked you that.

ALICE [*with serene strength*]. I'm glad that you want me. While I live ... where I am will be Home.

EDWARD [*struggling with himself*]. No, it's too late. And if you'd said Yes before I came into my inheritance ... perhaps I shouldn't have given myself to the work. So be glad that it's too late. I am.

ALICE [*happily*]. Marry you when you were only a well-principled prig! ... Thanks! I didn't want you ... and I don't believe you really wanted me. But now you do, and you must always take what you want.

EDWARD [*turning to her again*]. My dear, what have we to start life upon ... to build our house upon? Poverty ... and prison.

ALICE [*mischievous*]. Edward, you seem to think that all the money in the world was invested in your precious firm. I have four hundred a year of my own. At least let that tempt you.

[EDWARD *catches her in his arms with a momentary little burst of passion.*]

EDWARD. You're tempting me.

[*She did not resist, but nevertheless he breaks away from her, disappointed with himself. She goes on, quietly, serenely.*]

ALICE. Am I? Unworthily? Oh, my dear, don't be afraid of wanting me. Shall we be less than friends by being more? If I thought that, should I ever have let it come to this? But now you must ... look at me and make your choice ... to refuse me my work and happiness in life and to cripple your own nature ... or to take my hand.

[*She puts out her hand frankly, as a friend should. With only a second's thought he, happy too now, takes it as*

frankly. *Then she sits beside him and quite cheerfully changes the subject.*]

ALICE. Now, about old Mr. George Booth. What will he do?

EDWARD [*responsive though impatient*]. Nothing. I shall be before him.

ALICE. Can we bargain with him to keep the firm going somehow? ... for if we can, I'm afraid we must.

[*At this* EDWARD *makes a last attempt to abandon himself to his troubles.*]

EDWARD. No, no ... let it end here, it'll be so useless. They'll all be round in a day or two after their money like wasps after honey. And now they know I won't lift a finger in my own defence ... what sort of mercy will they have?

ALICE [*triumphantly completing her case*]. Edward, I have a faith by which I hope to live, not humbly, but defying the world to be my master. Dare to surrender yourself entirely, and you'll find them powerless against you. You see, you had something to hope or fear from Mr. Booth, for you hoped in your heart he'd end your trouble. But conquer that last little atom of fear which we call selfishness, and you'll find you are doing what you wish with selfish men. [*And she adds fervently:*] Yes, the man who is able, and cares deeply, and yet has nothing to hope or fear is all powerful ... even in little things.

EDWARD. But will nothing ever happen to set me free? Shall I never be able to rest for a moment ... turn round and say I've succeeded or I've failed?

ALICE. That's asking too much, and it isn't what matters ... one must have faith to go on.

EDWARD. Suppose they all meet and agree and syndicate themselves and keep me at it for life.

ALICE. Yes, I daresay they will, but what else could you wish for?

EDWARD. Than that dreary round!

ALICE. But the world must be put tidy. And it's the work which splendid criminals leave for poor commonplace people to do.

EDWARD [*with a little laugh*]. And I don't believe in Heaven either.

ALICE [*close to him*]. But there's to be our life. What's wrong with that?

EDWARD. My dear, when they put me in prison for swindling —

[*He makes the word sound its worst.*]

ALICE. I think they won't, for it wouldn't pay them. But if they are so stupid ... I must be very careful.

EDWARD. Of what?

ALICE. To avoid false pride. I shall be foolishly proud of you.

EDWARD. It's good to be praised sometimes ... by you.

ALICE. My heart praises you. Good-night.

EDWARD. Good-night.

[*She kisses his forehead. But he puts up his face like a child, so she bends down and for the first time their lips meet. Then she steps back from him, adding happily, with perhaps just a touch of shyness:*]

ALICE. Till to-morrow.

EDWARD [*echoing in gratitude the hope and promise in her voice*]. Till to-morrow.

[*She leaves him to sit there by the table for a few moments longer, looking into his future, streaked as it is to be with trouble and joy. As whose is not? From above ... from above the mantelpiece, that is to say ... the face of the late* MR. VOYSEY *seems to look down upon his son not unkindly, though with that curious buccaneering twist of the eyebrows which distinguished his countenance in life.*]

THE CASSILIS ENGAGEMENT
A COMEDY IN FOUR ACTS
By ST. JOHN HANKIN

COPYRIGHT, 1907, BY SAMUEL FRENCH
ALL RIGHTS RESERVED

The plays of St. John Hankin are published by Martin Secker, 5 John Street, Adelphi, London, in two volumes, price 25 /.

Permission to perform in America "The Cassilis Engagement" and other plays by the same author must be obtained from Messrs. Samuel French, Inc., 25 West 45th Street, New York City.

Caution: Professionals and Amateurs are hereby warned that The Cassilis Engagement, being fully protected under the copyright laws of the United States, is subject to a royalty, and anyone presenting the play without the consent of the author or his authorized agents will be liable to the penalties by law provided.

PERSONS OF THE COMEDY

MRS. CASSILIS.
THE COUNTESS OF REMENHAM.
LADY MARCHMONT, *Mrs. Cassilis's sister.*
MRS. HERRIES.
MRS. BORRIDGE.
LADY MABEL VENNING, *Lady Remenham's daughter.*
ETHEL BORRIDGE.
THE RECTOR
MAJOR WARRINGTON.
GEOFFREY CASSILIS.
WATSON, *Butler at Deynham.*
DORSET, *Mrs. Cassilis's maid.*
TWO FOOTMEN.

The Scene takes place at Deynham Abbey in Leicestershire.
ACT I. The Drawing-Room.
ACT II. The Lawn.
ACT III. The Smoking-Room off the Billiard-Room.
ACT IV. The Morning-Room.
One night elapses between Acts I and II.
One week between Acts II and III.
One night between Acts III and IV.

NOTE. The Leicestershire Cassilises pronounce their name as it is spelt

THE CASSILIS ENGAGEMENT

ACT

SCENE. — *The white drawing-room at Deynham Abbey, a very handsome room furnished in the Louis Seize style. There are big double doors at the back, and a large tea-table, with teacups, etc., on cloth, stands rather to the left of them. There is a large French window open on the left of the stage, with a sofa in front of it facing the view. On the opposite side of the room is the fireplace, but there is no fire as the month is August. Two or three arm-chairs stand near it. When the curtain rises the* RECTOR *is standing judicially on the hearthrug. He seems about to hum a tune, but thinks better of it.* MRS. HERRIES *is standing by the window. Presently she crosses to her husband, and sits in one of the arm-chairs. The* RECTOR *is a rubicund, humorous-looking man of fifty: his wife a prosperous-looking lady a few years younger.*

MRS. HERRIES. I wonder what can be keeping Mrs. Cassilis?

RECTOR [*back to fire*]. My dear, I told you we oughtn't to have called. On so sad an occasion —

MRS. HERRIES. My dear Hildebrand, it's just on these sad occasions that a visit is so consoling. One should always call after a birth, a funeral —

BUTLER [*showing in* LADY REMENHAM *and her daughter*]. I will tell Mrs. Cassilis you are here, my lady. She will be down in a moment.

LADY REMENHAM. Thank you. How do you do, Mrs. Herries? How do you do, Rector?

[LADY REMENHAM *goes towards fireplace and shakes hands. She is a dignified old lady of about sixty. Her normal expression is one of placid self-assurance, but to-day she has the air of disapproving of somebody or somebody.* MABEL *is a very pretty girl of two and twenty.* LADY REMENHAM *seats herself comfortably by* MRS. HERRIES. MABEL *goes over to window, where the* RECTOR *joins her.*]

MRS. HERRIES. How do you do, Lady Remenham?

RECTOR. How do you do, Mabel?

LADY REMENHAM. You've heard this dreadful news, haven't you?

[RECTOR *makes sympathetic gesture.*]

MRS. HERRIES. Yes. Poor Mrs. Cassilis.

LADY REMENHAM. Poor Adelaide, indeed! That unhappy boy! But there! How any mother can allow such a thing to happen passes my comprehension. To get engaged!

RECTOR [*nods sympathetically*]. Just so.

LADY REMENHAM. Engagements are such troublesome things. They sometimes even lead to marriage. But we'll hope it won't be as bad as that in this case. You've not heard who she is, I suppose?

MRS. HERRIES [*shaking her head mournfully*]. No.

LADY REMENHAM. Ah! Someone quite impossible, of course. Otherwise Adelaide would have told me in her letter.

MRS. HERRIES. I'm afraid so.

LADY REMENHAM [*irritably*]. It's really extremely wicked of Geoffrey. And so silly, too! — which is worse. A temporary infatuation I could understand, terminated by some small monetary payment. It would have been regrettable, of course, but young men are like that. And Adelaide could have stopped it out of his allowance. But an engagement! I am quite shocked at her.

MABEL [*at window, turning to her mother*]. Don't you think, mamma, we might leave Mrs. Cassilis to manage her son's affairs her own way?

LADY REMENHAM. She has *not* managed them. That's exactly what I complain of. I can't altogether acquit the Rector of some blame in the matter. He was Geoffrey's tutor for years. They used to say in *my* young days, "Train up a child in the way he should go — "

RECTOR [*attempting a mild jest*]. And when he's grown up, he'll give you a great deal of anxiety. So they did! So they did!

LADY REMENHAM [*severely*]. That is not the ending *I* remember.

RECTOR. That is the Revised Version.

[MRS. HERRIES *frowns. She feels this is not a moment for levity.*]

LADY REMENHAM. I dare say. They seem to alter everything nowadays. But, if so, I hardly see the use of education.

RECTOR [*obstinately cheerful*]. I have long been of that opinion, Lady Remenham.

[MRS. CASSILIS, *in a charming flutter of apologies, enters at this moment. She is a very pretty woman of forty, tall and graceful, and exquisitely dressed.*]

MRS. CASSILIS. You *must* forgive me, all of you. I had some letters to finish. [*General handshake. Kiss to* MABEL.] Dear Mabel. How do you do, Mrs. Herries?

RECTOR. How do you do, Mrs. Cassilis?

LADY REMENHAM. My dear Adelaide, *what* a charming gown! But you always do have the most delightful clothes. Where *do* you get them?

MRS. CASSILIS. Clarice made this.

[*Two footmen bring the tea-table down into the middle of the room. The* BUTLER, *who has brought in a teapot on a salver, places it on the table, and brings up a chair for* MRS. CASSILIS. *The footmen go out.*]

LADY REMENHAM. Clarice? The wretch! She always makes my things atrociously. If only I had your figure!

MRS. CASSILIS. Excuse me, dear. [*To* BUTLER.] The carriage has gone to the station to meet Lady Marchmont, Watson?

BUTLER. Yes, madam. It started five minutes ago. [*Exit* BUTLER.]

MRS. CASSILIS [*to* LADY REMENHAM]. I'm so glad you like it.

[*Goes to tea-table and seats herself.*]

LADY REMENHAM. Is Margaret coming to stay with you?

MRS. CASSILIS. Yes, for ten days.

LADY REMENHAM [*drawing chair up to table*]. And now will you please pour out my tea? I have come here to scold you, and I shall require several cups.

MRS. CASSILIS [*quite cheerful*]. To scold *me?* Won't you all bring up your chairs to the table? [*They all do so.*] Rector, where are you? [*To* LADY REMENHAM.] Cream?

LADY REMENHAM. Thank you. And a small lump.

MRS. CASSILIS. And why am I to be scolded?

LADY REMENHAM. You know quite well. [*Sternly.*] Adelaide, what is this I hear about Geoffrey's engagement?

MRS. CASSILIS [*not at all disturbed*]. Oh, that? Yes, Geoffrey has got engaged to a girl in London. Isn't it *romantic* of him! I know nothing whatever about her except that I believe she has no money, and Geoffrey is over head and ears in love with her.

MRS. HERRIES [*blandly*]. My dear Mrs. Cassilis, I should have thought *that* was quite enough!

MRS. CASSILIS. Rector, will you cut that cake? It's just by your hand.

LADY REMENHAM [*refusing to be diverted from the task of cross-examination*]. Where did he meet her?

MRS. CASSILIS. In an omnibus, I understand.

LADY REMENHAM [*scandalised*]. An omnibus!

MRS. CASSILIS. Yes. That was so *romantic,* too! One of the horses fell down, and she was frightened. They thought she was going to faint. Geoffrey got her out, took charge of her, discovered her address, and took her home. Wasn't it *clever* of him? Of course she asked him to come in.

He was introduced to her mother. And now they're engaged.
[*Gives cup to* RECTOR.]
LADY REMENHAM [*with awful dignity*]. And what is the name of this young person?
MRS. CASSILIS. Borridge.
LADY REMENHAM. Borridge! Mabel, my love, pray remember if ever you come home and inform me that you are engaged to a person of the name of Borridge I shall whip you. [*Puts down cup.*]
MABEL. Very well, mamma.
MRS. CASSILIS. Another cup?
LADY REMENHAM. Thank you. Rather less sugar, this time. [*Gives cup.*] I never could understand why you let Geoffrey be in London at all. Alone, too. Young men ought never to be allowed out alone at his age. They are so susceptible.
MABEL. Geoffrey has his profession, mamma.
MRS. CASSILIS. Geoffrey's at the Bar, you know.
LADY REMENHAM. The Bar! What business has Geoffrey to be at the Bar! Deynham has the best shooting in the Shires, and in the winter there's the hunting. What more does he want? It's disgraceful.
RECTOR [*another mild effort at humour*]. My dear Lady Remenham, you're sure you're not confusing the *Bar* with the *Dock?*
MRS. HERRIES. Hildebrand!
LADY REMENHAM [*impatiently*]. The Bar is a good enough profession, of course. But only for *very* younger sons. Geoffrey will have Deynham some day, and twelve thousand a year. I don't think Adelaide need have made a little attorney of him.
MRS. CASSILIS. Young men must do *something*, don't you think?
LADY REMENHAM [*briskly*]. Certainly not! It's this vulgar Radical notion that people ought to *do* things that is ruining English Society. What did Mr. Borridge *do*, by the way?
MRS. CASSILIS [*hesitates*]. He was a book-maker, I believe.
LADY REMENHAM [*triumphantly*]. There, you see! That's what comes of *doing* things!
MRS. CASSILIS [*slight shrug. Pouring herself out more tea, and still quite unruffled*]. Well, I'm afraid there's no use in discussing it. They're engaged, and Miss Borridge is coming down here.
MRS. HERRIES. Coming here!
LADY REMENHAM. Coming here!!!
MRS. CASSILIS. Yes. On a visit. With her mother.
LADY REMENHAM [*putting down her cup with a touch of solemnity*]. Adelaide, are you — excuse my asking the question — are you *quite* in your right mind?
MRS. CASSILIS [*laughing*]. I believe so.
LADY REMENHAM. You've noticed nothing? No dizziness about the head? No singing in the ears? [MRS. CASSILIS *shakes her head.*] And yet you ask this young woman to stay with you! *And* her mother! Neither of whom you know anything whatever about!
MRS. CASSILIS. Another cup?
[LADY REMENHAM *shakes her head irritably.*]
LADY REMENHAM. Is *Mr.* Borridge — Ugh! — coming, too?
MRS. CASSILIS. He is dead, I believe.
LADY REMENHAM. That, at least, is satisfactory.
MABEL. Mamma!
LADY REMENHAM. Mabel, I shall do my duty, whatever happens. [*Turning to* MRS. CASSILIS *again.*] And does Mrs. Borridge carry on the business? I think you said he was a *boot*-maker?
MABEL. *Book*-maker.
MRS. CASSILIS [*refusing to take offence*]. No. I believe he left her some small annuity.
LADY REMENHAM. Annuity? Ah, dies with her, of course?
MRS. CASSILIS. No doubt.
LADY REMENHAM [*gasps*]. Well, Adelaide, I never should have believed it of you. To ask these people to the house!
MRS. CASSILIS. Why shouldn't I ask them? Geoffrey tells me Ethel is charming.
LADY REMENHAM. Ethel?
MRS. CASSILIS. Miss Borridge.
LADY REMENHAM. Bah!

[*Enter* BUTLER, *showing in another visitor. This is* LADY MARCHMONT, MRS.

CASSILIS's *sister. She is a woman of about five-and-forty. She wears a light travelling-cloak. She is not unlike* MRS. CASSILIS *in appearance and manner, but is of a more delicate, fragile type.*]

BUTLER. Lady Marchmont.
MRS. CASSILIS [*rising*]. Ah, Margaret. How glad I am to see you. Some more tea, Watson.
LADY MARCHMONT [*kisses her*]. Not for me, please. No, really. My doctor won't *hear* of it. Hot water with a little milk is the most he allows me. How do you do, dear? [*Shaking hands with the others.*] How do you do? How do you do?
[BUTLER *goes out.*]
MRS. CASSILIS. How's the General?
LADY MARCHMONT. Very gouty. His temper this morning was atrocious, poor man.
LADY REMENHAM [*shakes her head*]. You bear it like a saint, dear.
LADY MARCHMONT [*philosophically, sitting in arm-chair after laying aside her cloak*]. Yes — I go away a good deal. He finds my absence very soothing. That's why I was so glad to accept Adelaide's invitation when she asked me.
MRS. CASSILIS. My dear, you'll be invaluable. I look to you to help me with my visitors.
LADY REMENHAM. Poor Margaret. But you always were so unselfish.
LADY MARCHMONT. Are they *very* — ?
LADY REMENHAM. *Very!!*
MRS. CASSILIS [*laughing*]. My dear, Lady Remenham knows nothing whatever about them.
LADY REMENHAM [*firmly*]. I know everything about them. The girl has no money. She has no position. She became engaged to Geoffrey without your knowledge. She has a perfectly dreadful mother. And her name is Borridge.
LADY MARCHMONT [*raising her brows*]. When are they coming?
MRS. CASSILIS. I expect them in half an hour. The carriage was to go straight back to the station to meet them.
LADY REMENHAM [*ruffling her feathers angrily*]. I hope Geoffrey is conscious of the folly and wickedness of his conduct.
LADY MARCHMONT. Where is he, dear?
MRS. CASSILIS. He's down here with me — and as happy as possible, I'm glad to say.
LADY REMENHAM. Extraordinary! But the young men of the present day *are* extraordinary. Young men nowadays seem always to be either irreclaimably vicious or deplorably silly. I prefer them vicious. They give less trouble. My poor brother Algernon — you remember Algernon, don't you, Rector? He was another of your pupils.
RECTOR [*sighs*]. Yes, I remember.
MRS. HERRIES. Major Warrington hasn't been down for quite a long time, has he?
LADY REMENHAM. No. We don't ask him to Milverton now. He comes to us in London, but in the country one has to be more particular. He really is dreadfully dissipated. Always running after some petticoat or other. Often more than one. But there is safety in numbers, don't you think?
RECTOR. Unquestionably.
LADY REMENHAM. Algernon always says he is by temperament a polygamist. I don't know what he means. However, I've no anxiety about *him*. *He never* gets engaged. He's far too *clever* for that. I wonder if he could help you out of this dreadful entanglement? In a case of this kind one should have the very best advice.
MRS. CASSILIS [*laughing*]. I shall be delighted to see Major Warrington — though not for the reason you suggest.
LADY REMENHAM. Well, I'll ask him down. Remenham won't like it. He disapproves of him so much. He gets quite virtuous about it. But that sort of moral indignation should never be allowed to get out of hand, should it? [RECTOR *nods.*] Besides, he's away just now. I'll write to Algernon directly I get back, and I'll bring him over to dinner one day next week. Say Thursday?
LADY MARCHMONT. Do, dear. I adore Major Warrington.
LADY REMENHAM. I dare say. [*Pre-

paring to go.] He isn't *your* brother. Meantime, I can ask him whether he knows anything against Mrs. Borridge. But he's sure to. He knows nearly all the detrimental people in London, especially if their daughters are in the least attractive.

MRS. CASSILIS [*smiling*]. You'll come *with* him on Thursday, won't you? And Mabel? [MABEL *rises.*]

LADY REMENHAM. Perhaps that will be best. Then I can keep my brother within bounds. Poor Algernon is apt to take too much champagne unless I am there to prevent him. And now, dear, I really must go. [*She and* MABEL *go up towards door.*] Good-bye.

MRS. CASSILIS. You won't stay to meet Mrs. Borridge?

LADY REMENHAM [*shudders*]. I think not. Thursday will be *quite* soon enough. Good-bye, Mrs. Herries. [*As they reach door,* GEOFFREY *opens it, and almost runs into her arms.*] Ah, *here* is the young man who is causing us all this distress.

GEOFFREY. I, Lady Remenham? [*Shakes hands.*] How do you do, Aunt Margaret? [*Shakes hands with others.*]

LADY REMENHAM [*shakes hands*]. You. What do you *mean* by getting engaged to someone we none of us know anything about?

MABEL. Mamma!

LADY REMENHAM. I consider your conduct perfectly heartless. Its foolishness needs no comment from me.

GEOFFREY. Really, Lady Remenham —

LADY REMENHAM. Tut, tut, sir. Don't "really" me. I'm ashamed of you. And now I'll be off before I quarrel with you. Come, Mabel.

[*Sweeps out, followed by* MABEL. GEOFFREY *opens door for them, takes them down to their carriage.*]

MRS. HERRIES. I think we ought to be going, too. Come, Hildebrand. [*Shakes hands.*] [MRS. CASSILIS *rings.*]

RECTOR. Good-bye, Mrs. Cassilis. Let's hope everything will turn out for the best.

MRS. HERRIES. It never does. Good-bye.

MRS. CASSILIS [*going towards door with* RECTOR]. Good-bye. [*Shakes hands warmly.*] And you'll both come and dine on Thursday, won't you? To-morrow week that is. Major Warrington will want to see his old tutor.

RECTOR. You're very good.

[*He and* MRS. HERRIES *go out.*]

MRS. CASSILIS [*returning to her sister*]. Dear Lady Remenham! What nonsense she talks!

LADY MARCHMONT. People who talk as much as that must talk a good deal of nonsense, mustn't they? Otherwise they have nothing to say.

[*Re-enter* GEOFFREY.]

GEOFFREY. Lady Remenham seems ruffled.

LADY MARCHMONT. About your engagement? I'm not surprised.

GEOFFREY. I don't see what it's got to do with her.

LADY MARCHMONT. You must make allowance for a mother's feelings, my dear Geoffrey.

GEOFFREY [*pats* MRS. CASSILIS's *hand, then goes to tea-table and helps himself to tea*]. Lady Remenham isn't my mother. She's my godmother.

LADY MARCHMONT. She's Mabel's mother.

MRS. CASSILIS. Sh! Margaret.

LADY MARCHMONT. My dear, there's no use making mysteries about things. Geoffrey was always supposed to be going to marry Mabel ever since they were children. He knows that.

GEOFFREY. That was only boy-and-girl talk.

LADY MARCHMONT. For you, perhaps.

GEOFFREY. And for her. Mabel never expected — [*Pause. He thinks.*]

LADY MARCHMONT. Did you ever ask her?

GEOFFREY. But I never supposed —

LADY MARCHMONT. I think you *should* have supposed. A boy should be very careful how he encourages a girl to think of him in that way.

GEOFFREY. But I'd no idea. Of course, I *like* Mabel. I like her awfully. We're like brother and sister. But beyond that — [*Pause.*] Mother, do *you* think I've behaved badly to Mabel?

Mrs. Cassilis [*gently*]. I think perhaps you've a little disappointed her.

Geoffrey [*peevishly*]. Why didn't somebody *tell* me? How was I to know?

Lady Marchmont. My dear boy, we couldn't be expected to know you were absolutely blind.

Mrs. Cassilis. Margaret, you're not to scold Geoffrey. I won't allow it.

Geoffrey. Mother, dear — you won't allow this to make any difference? With Ethel, I mean?

Mrs. Cassilis. Of course not, Geoff.
[*Lays hand on his.*]

Geoffrey [*earnestly*]. She's so fond of me. And I'm so fond of her. We were made for each other. I couldn't bear it if you were unkind to her.

Mrs. Cassilis. My dear Geoff, I'm sure Ethel is everything that is sweet and good, or my boy wouldn't love her. And I intend to fall in love with her myself directly I set eyes on her.

Geoffrey. Dear mother! [*Pats her hand affectionately. Pause; then thoughtfully.*] I'm afraid you'll find *her* mother rather trying — at first. She's not quite a lady, you know. . . . But she's very good-natured.

Mrs. Cassilis [*cheerfully*]. Well, well, we shall see. And now, run away, dear, and leave me to talk to Margaret, and I'll undertake that all symptoms of crossness shall have disappeared before our visitors arrive.

Geoffrey. All right, mother.
[*Kisses her and goes out.*]

Lady Marchmont [*looking after him reflectively*]. How you spoil that boy!

Mrs. Cassilis [*lightly*]. What else should I do with him? He's my only one. Mothers always spoil their sons, don't they? And quarrel with their daughters. More marriages are due to girls being unhappy at home than most people imagine.

Lady Marchmont. And yet Geoffrey wants to leave you, apparently.

Mrs. Cassilis [*smiling bravely; but her eyes have a suspicion of moisture in them*]. Evidently I didn't spoil him enough.

Lady Marchmont [*washing her hands of the whole affair*]. Well, I'm glad you're pleased with this engagement.

Mrs. Cassilis [*sudden change of manner. Her face loses its brightness, and she suddenly seems to look older*]. Pleased with it! Do you really believe that?

Lady Marchmont. Didn't you say so?

Mrs. Cassilis [*shrugs*]. To Lady Remenham and Mrs. Herries. Yes.

Lady Marchmont. And to Geoffrey.

Mrs. Cassilis. And Geoffrey too. [*Half to herself.*] Mothers can't always be straightforward with their sons, can they?

Lady Marchmont. Why not?

[*There is a pause while* Mrs. Cassilis *makes up her mind whether to answer this or not. Then she seems to decide to speak out. She moves nearer to her sister, and when she begins, her voice is very firm and matter-of-fact.*]

Mrs. Cassilis. My dear Margaret, what would *you* do if your son suddenly wrote to you that he had become engaged to a girl you knew nothing whatever about, a girl far beneath him in social rank?

Lady Marchmont [*firmly*]. I should have forbidden the engagement. Forbidden it absolutely.

Mrs. Cassilis. Without seeing the girl?

Lady Marchmont. Certainly. The mere fact of her accepting my son before I had ever set eyes on her would have been quite enough.

Mrs. Cassilis. But supposing your son were of age and independent?

Lady Marchmont [*impatiently*]. Geoffrey isn't independent.

Mrs. Cassilis. He has five hundred a year.

Lady Marchmont [*contemptuously*]. What's *that?*

Mrs. Cassilis. Besides, Geoffrey knows I should always be willing to help him.

Lady Marchmont. That's just it. He ought *not* to have known. You ought to have made it clear to him from the first that, if he married without your consent, he would never have a penny from you, either now or at your death. Deynham isn't entailed, fortunately.

Mrs. Cassilis. But, my dear, I couldn't *disinherit* Geoffrey! How could I?

Lady Marchmont [*shrugs*]. You could

have threatened to. And then the girl wouldn't have accepted him.

MRS. CASSILIS. I don't know. [*Thoughtfully.*] Five hundred a year may seem a considerable sum to her.

LADY MARCHMONT [*horrified*]. Is it as bad as that?

MRS. CASSILIS [*trying to smile*]. Besides, she may be really in love with him.

LADY MARCHMONT [*snappish*]. What *has* that to do with it?

MRS. CASSILIS. Young people. In love. They are seldom prudent, are they?

LADY MARCHMONT. Still, I should have forbidden the engagement.

MRS. CASSILIS. And then?

LADY MARCHMONT. What do you mean?

MRS. CASSILIS. If Geoffrey had defied me? Boys can be very obstinate.

LADY MARCHMONT. I should have refused ever to see him again.

MRS. CASSILIS. Ah, Margaret, I couldn't do that. Geoffrey is everything I have. He is my only son, my joy and my pride. I couldn't quarrel with him whatever happened. [LADY MARCHMONT *leans back with gesture of impatience.*] No, Margaret, my plan was the best.

LADY MARCHMONT. What *is* your plan?

MRS. CASSILIS [*quite practical*]. My plan is to give the thing a fair trial. Ask her down here. Ask her mother down here. And see what happens.

LADY MARCHMONT [*looking at her narrowly*]. Nothing else?

MRS. CASSILIS. Nothing else — at present.

LADY MARCHMONT. You could have done that without sanctioning the engagement.

MRS. CASSILIS. Yes. But love thrives on opposition. There's a fascination about a runaway match. It has romance. Whereas there's no romance at all about an ordinary wedding. It's only dull and rather vulgar. [*Wearily.*] And after all, the girl *may* be presentable.

LADY MARCHMONT. Borridge! [*Crisply.*] I'm not very sanguine about *that.*

MRS. CASSILIS. Anyhow, she's pretty, and Geoffrey loves her. That's all we know about her at present.

LADY MARCHMONT. Wretched boy. To think he should have allowed himself to be caught in this way! . . . Don't you think you might have asked the daughter *without* the mother?

MRS. CASSILIS. So Geoffrey suggested. He seemed rather nervous about having her here. She's rather a terrible person, I gather. But I said, as we were marrying into the family, we mustn't be unkind to her. [*With a slow smile.*] Poor boy, he rather blenched at that. I think he hadn't associated *Mrs.* Borridge with his matrimonial schemes. It's just as well he should do so at once, don't you think?

BUTLER. Mrs. and Miss Borridge.

[*Enter* MRS. BORRIDGE *and* ETHEL. *Both rise.* LADY MARCHMONT *turns sharp round to look at the newcomers.* MRS. CASSILIS *goes up to meet them with her sweetest smile. Nothing could be more hospitable than her manner or more gracious than her welcome. The change from the* MRS. CASSILIS *of a moment before, with the resolute set of the lips and the glitter in the eyes, to this gentle, caressing creature does the greatest credit to her powers of self-control.* LADY MARCHMONT *notices it, and is a little shocked.*]

MRS. CASSILIS. How do you do? How do you do, my dear? [*Kisses* ETHEL.] Tell Mr. Geoffrey, Watson. I hope you've not had a tiring journey, Mrs. Borridge? [*Exit* BUTLER.]

MRS. BORRIDGE. Not at all, Mrs. Cassilis. We 'ad — had — the compartment to ourselves, bein' first class. As I says to' my girlie, "They'll very likely send the carriage to meet us, and it looks better for the servants."

[MRS. BORRIDGE *comes down stage. She is a large, gross woman, rather overdressed in inexpensive materials. Too much colour in her hat and far too much in her cheeks. But a beaming, good-natured harridan for all that. As a landlady you would rather like her. She smiles nervously in* LADY MARCHMONT'S *direction, not sure whether she ought to say any-*

thing or wait to be introduced. Her daughter keeps by her side, watching to see she doesn't commit herself, and quite sure that she will. ETHEL *is pretty, but second-rate; she has the sense to dress simply, and therefore is less appallingly out of the picture than her far more amiable mother.*]

MRS. CASSILIS. Let me introduce you. Mrs. Borridge — Lady Marchmont, Miss Borridge. [LADY MARCHMONT *bows.*]

MRS. BORRIDGE [*extends gloved hand*]. How do you do, Lady Marchmont? Proud, I'm sure.

[LADY MARCHMONT *finds nothing to say, and for the moment there is a constrained pause. Then enter* GEOFFREY *hurriedly.*]

GEOFFREY [*with as much heartiness as he can muster, but it rings a little hollow*]. How do you do, Mrs. Borridge? Ethel, dear, how long have you been here? I didn't hear you come. [*Kisses her.*]

ETHEL. We've only just got here.

MRS. BORRIDGE [*subsiding into an armchair.*] Don't apologise, Geoffy. Your ma's been entertaining us most kind.

GEOFFREY [*with look of gratitude to* MRS. CASSILIS]. Dear mother.

MRS. BORRIDGE. Well, how *are* you, Geoffy? You *look* first-rate.

GEOFFREY. Oh, I'm all right.

MRS. BORRIDGE. And what a fine 'ouse — house — you've got! Quite a palace, I declare!

GEOFFREY. I'm glad you like it.

MRS. BORRIDGE. And it'll all be yours some day. Won't it?

ETHEL [*pulls her sleeve*]. Mother!

GEOFFREY. That's as my mother decides.

MRS. BORRIDGE. Then you're sure to 'ave it. I know what mothers are! And what a 'andsome room, too. Quite like the Metropole at Brighton.

[*Enter* MRS. CASSILIS'S *maid. She is in a perfectly plain black dress, and looks enormously more like a lady than* ETHEL.]

MAID. Can I have your keys, madam?

MRS. BORRIDGE [*surprised*]. My keys?

MAID. The keys of your trunks, madam.

MRS. BORRIDGE. Certainly not. Who ever 'eard of such a thing?

MAID. I thought you might wish me to unpack for you, madam.

MRS. BORRIDGE [*bristling*]. Oh. *Did* you? I don't want no strange girls ferriting in *my* boxes. [ETHEL *nudges her arm.*] What *is* it, Eth? Oh, very well. But I'm not going to let her, all the same. No, thank you.

MRS. CASSILIS [*quite self-possessed.* LADY MARCHMONT *nervously avoids her eye*]. Mrs. Borridge will unpack for herself, Dorset. [MAID *bows, and turns to go out.*] Wait a moment. [MAID *pauses at door.*] Would you like to take off your things at once, Mrs. Borridge? If so, Dorset shall show you your room. And I'll have some tea sent up to you there. You'll want it after your journey. [*Feels teapot.*] This is quite cold. What do you say, Ethel?

ETHEL. Thank you, Mrs. Cassilis. A cup of tea would be very nice.

MRS. CASSILIS. Show Mrs. Borridge her room, Dorset. [MRS. BORRIDGE *rises.*] And take her up some tea. Dinner will be at eight. You'll ring if there's anything you want, won't you?

MRS. BORRIDGE. Thank you, Mrs. Cassilis.

[MRS. BORRIDGE *waddles out, beaming. She feels that her first introduction to the houses of the great has gone off successfully.* GEOFFREY *holds the door open for them, and gives* ETHEL *a sly kiss in passing.* MRS. CASSILIS *makes no sign, but one can feel her shudder at the sound.* GEOFFREY *comes down to her a moment later, brimming with enthusiasm.*]

GEOFFREY. Well, mother, what do you think of her? Isn't she *sweet?*

MRS. CASSILIS [*gently*]. She's very pretty, Geoff. [*Lays hand on his.*]

GEOFFREY. And *good!* You don't know how *good* she is!

MRS. CASSILIS. So long as she's good to my boy, that's all I ask.

GEOFFREY. Dearest mother. [*Kisses her demonstratively.*] Now I'll go and dress.

[*Goes out quickly, with a boyish feeling that he has been rather too demonstrative for a true-born Englishman. There is a long pause, during which* LADY MARCHMONT *looks at her sister,* MRS. CASSILIS *at nothing. The latter is evidently in deep thought, and seems to have almost forgotten her sister's presence. At last* LADY MARCHMONT *speaks with the stern accent of "I told you so."*]

LADY MARCHMONT. And *that's* the girl your son is to marry.

MRS. CASSILIS. Marry her! Nonsense, my dear Margaret.

THE CURTAIN FALLS

ACT II

SCENE. — *The lawn at Deynham. Time, after breakfast the following morning. Under a tree stand two or three long wicker chairs, with bright red cushions. On the right stands the house, with windows open on to the terrace. A path on the left leads to the flower garden, and another on the same side to the strawberry beds. When the curtain rises,* MRS. CASSILIS *comes on the terrace, followed by* ETHEL, *and a little later by* MRS. BORRIDGE. *The last-named is flushed with food, and gorgeously arrayed in a green silk blouse. She is obviously in the best of spirits, and is generally terribly at ease in Zion.*

MRS. CASSILIS. Shall we come out on the lawn? It's such a perfect morning.

ETHEL. That *will* be jolly, Mrs. Cassilis. [*They come down.*] When I'm in the country, I shall always eat too much breakfast and then spend the morning on a long chair digesting it. So will mother.

MRS. BORRIDGE. How you go on, dearie!

MRS. CASSILIS. Try this chair then. [*Slightly moving long chair forward.*] Mrs. Borridge, what kind of chair do *you* like?

MRS. BORRIDGE. This'll do. I'm not particular. [*Subsides into another long chair.*] Am I showing my ankles, Eth?

ETHEL. Sh! mother! [*Giggles.*]

MRS. BORRIDGE. Well, I only asked, dearie.

MRS. CASSILIS. I wonder if you'd like a cushion for your head? Try this. [*Puts vivid red cushion behind* MRS. BORRIDGE'S *vivid green blouse. The effect is electrifying.*]

MRS. BORRIDGE. That's better. [MRS. CASSILIS *sinks negligently into wicker chair and puts up white lace parasol.*]

ETHEL [*sigh of content*]. I call this Heaven, Mrs. Cassilis.

MRS. CASSILIS. That's right, my dear. Are you fond of the country?

ETHEL. I don't know. I've never been there so far. Not to the real country, I mean. Mums and I have a week at Brighton now and then. And once we went for a month to Broadstairs after I had the measles. But that's not exactly country, is it?

MRS. CASSILIS. You're sure to like it. Geoffrey loves it. He's never so happy as when he's pottering about Deynham with his gun.

ETHEL. Doesn't he get tired of that?

MRS. CASSILIS. Oh, no. Besides he doesn't do that all the year round. He rides a great deal. We've very good hunting at Deynham. Are you fond of horses?

ETHEL. I can't bear them, Mrs. Cassilis.

MRS. BORRIDGE. When she was a little tot her father put 'er — her — on a pony and she fell off. It didn't hurt 'er, but the doctor said 'er nerve was shook. And now she can't bear 'orses.

MRS. CASSILIS. What a pity! I do hope you won't be dull while you're with us. Perhaps you're fond of walking?

ETHEL. Yes. I don't mind walking — for a little. If there's anything to walk *to*.

MRS. CASSILIS. We often walk up Milverton Hill on fine afternoons to see the view. It's the highest point about here.

ETHEL [*stifling a yawn*]. Is it, Mrs. Cassilis?

MRS. CASSILIS. And no doubt we shall find other things to amuse you. What *do* you like?

ETHEL. Oh, shops and theatres, and lunching at restaurants and dancing, and, oh, lots of things.

MRS. CASSILIS. I'm afraid we've no

shops nearer than Leicester, and that's twelve miles away. And we've no restaurants at all. But I dare say we could get up a dance for you.

ETHEL [*clapping her hands*]. That'll be sweet! I simply *love* dancing. And all the rest of the time I shall sit on the lawn and grow fat, like mummy. [*Protest from* MRS. BORRIDGE.] Oh, yes, I shall.

MRS. BORRIDGE. Ethel, don't be saucy.

ETHEL [*laughing*]. Mummy, if you scold me you'll have to go in. It's far too hot to be scolded.

MRS. BORRIDGE. Isn't she a spoilt girl, Mrs. Cassilis? What they taught you at that boarding-school, miss, *I* don't know. Not manners, *I* can see.

ETHEL [*ruffling her mother's wig*]. There! there! mums. Was 'em's cross?

MRS. BORRIDGE [*pettishly*]. Stop it, Ethel, stop it, I say. Whatever will Mrs. Cassilis think of you!

MRS. CASSILIS [*smiling sweetly*]. Don't scold her, Mrs. Borridge. It's so pleasant to see a little high spirits, isn't it?

MRS. BORRIDGE [*beaming*]. Well, if *you* don't mind, Mrs. Cassilis, *I* don't. But it's not the way girls were taught to behave in *my* young days.

ETHEL [*slight yawn*]. That was so long ago, mums!

MRS. CASSILIS [*rising*]. Well, I must go and see after my housekeeping. Can you entertain each other while I'm away for a little? My sister will be down soon, I hope. She had breakfast in her room. And Geoffrey will be back in half an hour. I asked him to ride over to Milverton for me with a note.

ETHEL. We shall be all right, Mrs. Cassilis. Mother'll go to sleep. She always does if you make her too comfortable. And then she'll snore, won't you, mums?

[MRS. CASSILIS *goes into the house, smiling bravely to the last.*]

MRS. BORRIDGE [*alarmed*]. Ethel, you shouldn't talk like that before Mrs. Cassilis. She won't like it.

ETHEL. Oh, yes, she will. And I'm going to make her like *me* awfully. What lovely clothes she has! I wish *you* had lovely clothes, mums.

MRS. BORRIDGE. What's the matter with my clothes, dearie? I 'ad on my best silk last night. And I bought this blouse special in the Grove only a week ago so as to do you credit.

ETHEL. I know. Still . . . Couldn't you have chosen something *quieter?*

MRS. BORRIDGE. Oh, no, dearie. I 'ate quiet things.

ETHEL. *H*ate, mother.

MRS. BORRIDGE. *H*ate then. Give me something *cheerful.*

ETHEL [*hopelessly*]. Very well, mummy.

MRS. BORRIDGE [*imploring*]. But do be careful what you say before Mrs. Cassilis. She's not used to girls being so free.

ETHEL. Oh, yes, she is, mums. All girls are like that nowadays. All girls that are ladies, I mean. They bet, and talk slang, and smoke cigarettes, and play bridge. I know all about that. I've read all about it in the "Ladies' Mail." One of them put ice down her young man's back at dinner, and when he broke off his engagement she only laughed.

MRS. BORRIDGE [*lamentably*]. Oh, dear, I do hope there won't be ice for dinner to-night.

ETHEL [*laughing*]. Poor mums, don't be anxious. I'll be *very* careful, I promise you.

MRS. BORRIDGE [*complaining*]. You're so 'eadstrong. And I' *do* want to see you married and respectable. I wasn't always respectable myself, and I know what it means for a girl. Your sister Nan, she's gay, she is. She 'adn't no ambition. An' look what she is now!

ETHEL [*looking round nervously*]. If Geoff were to hear of it!

MRS. BORRIDGE. 'E won't. Not 'e! I've seen to that.

ETHEL. These things always get known somehow.

MRS. BORRIDGE. Nan's changed 'er name. Calls 'erself Mrs. Seymour. An' she never comes to see us now. If she did, I'd show 'er the door fast enough. Disgracin' us like that!

ETHEL. Poor Nan!

MRS. BORRIDGE [*warmly*]. Don't you pity 'er. She don't deserve it. She

treated us like dirt. She's a bad 'un all through. I've done things myself as I didn't ought to 'ave done. But I've always *wanted* to be respectable. But it's not so easy when you've your living to make and no one to look to. [ETHEL *nods*.] Yes, I've 'ad my bad times, dearie. But I've pulled through them. And I *made* your father marry me. No one can deny that. It wasn't easy. An' I had to give him all my savings before 'e'd say "Yes." And then I wasn't 'appy till we'd been to church. But 'e did marry me in the end. An' then *you* was born, an' I says my girl shall be brought up respectable. She shall be a lady. And some day, when she's married an' ridin' in her carriage, she'll say, "It's all mother's doing."
[*Wipes her eyes in pensive melancholy.*]

ETHEL. How long *were* you married to father, mums?

MRS. BORRIDGE. Only eight years, dearie. Before that I was 'is 'ouse-keeper.

ETHEL. *H*is, mummy.

MRS. BORRIDGE. Very well, dearie. [*With quiet satisfaction.*] Father drank 'isself to death the year Ben Dor won the Derby. [*Shaking her head.*] He lost a pot o' money over that, and it preyed on 'is mind. So he took to the drink. If he 'adn't insured 'is life an' kep' the premiums paid, we should 'ave been in the 'ouse, that's where we should 'ave been, dearie.

ETHEL. Poor dad!

MRS. BORRIDGE. Yes. 'E 'ad 'is faults. But 'e was a kind-'earted man, was Joe Borridge. 'E died much respected. [*Cheering up.*] An' now you're engaged to a *real* gentleman! *That's* the sort for my Eth!

ETHEL. Oh! sh! mums.
[*Looking round nervously.*]

MRS. BORRIDGE. No one'll hear. And if they do, what's the harm? You've got 'is promise.

ETHEL. *H*is, mother.

MRS. BORRIDGE. You can hold 'im — — him — to it.

ETHEL [*nodding*]. Yes. Besides, Geoff's awfully in love with me. And I really rather like *him*, you know — in a way.

MRS. BORRIDGE. *I* know, dearie. Still, I'd get something from 'im on paper if I was you, something that'll 'old 'im. The men takes a bit of 'olding nowadays. They're that slippy! You get something that'll 'old 'em. That's what I always say to girls. Letters is best. Oh, the chances I've seen missed through not gettin' something on paper!

ETHEL [*confidently*]. You needn't worry, mummy. Geoff's all right.

MRS. BORRIDGE. I dare say. Still, I'd like something the lawyers can take hold of. Geoffy may get tired of *you*, dearie. Men are that changeable. *I* know them!

ETHEL [*viciously*]. He'd better not! I'd make him *pay* for it!

MRS. BORRIDGE. So you could, dearie, so long as you 'ad somethin' on paper. [ETHEL *shrugs impatiently*.] Well, if you won't, you won't. But if anythin' happens, don't say I didn't warn you, that's all. I wish Geoffy was a lord, like Lord Buckfastleigh.

ETHEL. *I* don't.

MRS. BORRIDGE. Well, not *just* like Buckfastleigh, per'aps. But still, a lord. You never did like Buckfastleigh.

ETHEL. That old beast!

MRS. BORRIDGE [*remonstrating*]. He's been a good friend to us, dearie. And he is an earl, whatever you may say.

ETHEL. Pah!

MRS. BORRIDGE. And he's rich. Richer than Geoffy. And he's awfully sweet on you, dearie. I believe he'd 'ave married you if 'is old woman 'ad turned up 'er toes last autumn. And he's seventy-three. He wouldn't 'ave lasted long.

ETHEL [*fiercely*]. I wouldn't marry him if he were twice as rich — and twice as old.

MRS. BORRIDGE [*placidly*]. I dare say you're right, dearie. He's a queer 'un is Buckfastleigh. But he offered to settle five thousand down if you'd go to Paris with 'im. Five thousand down on the nail. He wasn't what you'd call sober when he said it, but he meant it. I dare say he'd 'ave made it seven if you hadn't boxed 'is ears. [ETHEL *laughs*.] Wasn't I savage when you did that, dearie! But you was right as it turned out. For

Geoffy proposed next day. And now you'll be a real married woman. There's nothing like being married. It's so respectable. When you're married, you can look down on people. And that's what every woman wants. That's why I pinched and screwed and sent you to boarding-school. I said my girlie shall be a real lady. And she is.
[*Much moved at the reflection.*]
ETHEL. Is she, mums?
MRS. BORRIDGE. Of course, dearie. That's why she's 'ere. Deynham Abbey, *two* footmen in livery, fire in 'er bedroom, evenin' dress every night of 'er life. *Lady Marchmont invited to meet her!* Everythin' tip-top! And it's not a bit too good for my girl. It's what she was made for.
ETHEL [*thoughtfully*]. I wish Johnny Travers had had some money. Then I could have married him.
MRS. BORRIDGE. *Married* 'im — him! Married a auctioneer's clerk without twopence to bless 'isself. I should think not, indeed! Not likely!
ETHEL. Still, I was awfully gone on Johnny.
MRS. BORRIDGE [*decidedly*]. Nonsense, Eth. I should 'ope we can look 'igher than *that!*
ETHEL. Sh! mother. Here's Geoff.
[GEOFFREY, *in riding-breeches, comes out of the house.*]
GEOFFREY. Good-morning dear. [*Kisses* ETHEL.] I thought I should be back earlier, but I rode over to Milverton for the mater. [*To* MRS. BORRIDGE.] Good-morning.
MRS. BORRIDGE [*archly*]. You 'aven't no kisses to spare for *me*, 'ave you, Geoffy? Never mind. You keep 'em all for my girl. She's worth 'em.
GEOFFREY [*caressing her hand*]. Dear Ethel.
MRS. BORRIDGE. How well you look in those riding-togs, Geoffrey! Don't 'e, Eth?
[*Endeavouring to hoist herself out of her chair.*]
ETHEL [*smiling at him*]. Geoff always looks well in everything.
MRS. BORRIDGE. Well, I'll go indoors and leave you two to spoon. That's what you want, *I* know. I'll go and talk to your ma.
[*Waddles off into the house, beaming.*]
GEOFFREY [*picking rose and bringing it to* ETHEL]. A rose for the prettiest girl in England.
ETHEL. Oh, Geoff, do you think so?
GEOFFREY. Of course. The prettiest and the best. [*Takes her hand.*]
ETHEL. You do really love me, Geoff, don't you?
GEOFF. Do you doubt it? [*Kisses her.*]
ETHEL. No; you're much too good for me, you know.
GEOFFREY. Nonsense, darling.
ETHEL. It's the truth. You're a gentleman and rich and have fine friends. While mother and I are common as common.
GEOFFREY [*firmly*]. You're *not*.
ETHEL. Oh, yes, we are. Of course, I've been to school, and been taught things. But what's education? It can't alter how we're made, can it? And she and I are the same underneath.
GEOFFREY. Ethel, you're not to say such things, or to think them.
ETHEL. But they're true, Geoff.
GEOFFREY. They're *not*. [*Kisses her.*] Say they're not.
ETHEL [*shakes her head*]. No.
GEOFFREY. Say they're *not*. [*Kisses her.*] *Not!*
ETHEL. Very well. They're not.
GEOFFREY. That's right. [*Kiss.*] There's a reward.
ETHEL [*pulling herself away*]. I wonder if I did right to say "Yes" when you asked me, Geoff? Right for *you*, I mean.
GEOFFREY. Of course you did, darling. You love me, don't you?
ETHEL. But wouldn't it have been best for you if I'd said "No"? Then you'd have married Lady Somebody or other, with lots and lots of money, and lived happy ever afterwards.
GEOFFREY [*indignantly*]. I shouldn't.
ETHEL. Oh, yes, you would.
GEOFFREY. And what would *you* have done, pray?

ETHEL. Oh, I should have taken up with some one else, or perhaps married old Buckfastleigh when his wife died.
GEOFFREY. Ethel!
ETHEL. I should. I'm not the sort to go on moping for long. I should have been awfully down for a bit, and missed you every day. But by-and-by I should have cheered up and married some one else. I could have done it. I could!
GEOFFREY. And what about *me?*
ETHEL. Wouldn't you have been happier in the end, dear? I'm not the sort of wife you ought to have married. Some day I expect you'll come to hate me. [*Sighs.*] Heigho.
GEOFFREY. You know I shan't, dear.
ETHEL. But I did so want to marry a gentleman. Mother wanted it, too. [*Quite simply.*] So I said "Yes," you see.
GEOFFREY [*drawing her to him*]. Darling! [*Kisses her tenderly.*]
ETHEL. Geoff, what did *your* mother say when you told her we were engaged? Was she dreadfully down about it?
GEOFFREY. No.
ETHEL. On your honour?
GEOFFREY. On my honour. Mother never said a single word to me against it. Lady Marchmont scolded me a bit. She's my aunt, you see.
ETHEL. Old cat!
GEOFFREY. And so did Lady Remenham. She's my godmother. But mother stood up for us all through.
ETHEL [*sighs*]. I shall never get on with all your fine friends, Geoff.
GEOFFREY. You will. Any one who's as pretty as my Ethel can get on anywhere.
ETHEL. Yes, I *am* pretty, aren't I? I'm glad of that. It makes a difference, doesn't it?
GEOFFREY. Of course. In a week you'll have them all running after you.
ETHEL [*clapping her hands*]. Shall I, Geoff? Won't that be splendid! [*Kisses him.*] Oh, Geoff, I'm so happy. When shall we be married?
GEOFFREY. I'm afraid not till next year, dear. Next June, mother says.
ETHEL [*pouting*]. That's a *long* way off, Geoff.

GEOFFREY. Yes, but mother says you're to be here a *great* deal between now and then, almost all the time, in fact. So it won't be so bad, will it?
ETHEL. Why does your mother want it put off till then?
GEOFFREY. Something about the London season, she said. We shall be married in London, of course, because your mother's house is there.
ETHEL. Oh, yes, of course.
GEOFFREY. And, besides, mother says she never believes in very short engagements. She says girls sometimes don't quite know their own minds. I said I was sure *you* weren't like that. But she asked me to promise, so I did.
ETHEL. Well that's settled, then. [*Jumping up.*] And won't it be nice to be *married?* Really *married!* . . . And now I want to *do* something. I'm tired sitting still. What shall it be?
GEOFFREY [*with brilliant originality*]. We might go a walk up Milverton Hill. The view there's awfully fine. [*Looks at watch.*] But there's hardly time before lunch.
ETHEL. Besides, I should spoil my shoes. [*Puts out foot, the shoe of which is manifestly not intended for country walking.*]
GEOFFREY. Suppose we go to the strawberry bed and eat strawberries?
ETHEL. Oh, yes, that'll be splendid. I can be so deliciously greedy over strawberries. [*Puts her arm in his, and he leads her off to the strawberry beds. As they go off,* MRS. CASSILIS, LADY MARCHMONT, *and* MRS. BORRIDGE *come down from terrace.*]
MRS. CASSILIS. Going for a stroll, dears?
GEOFFREY. Only as far as the strawberry bed, mother, dear.
MRS. CASSILIS. Oughtn't dear Ethel to have a hat? The sun is very hot there.
ETHEL. I've got a parasol, Mrs. Cassilis. [*They disappear down the path.*]
MRS. BORRIDGE [*rallying her*]. You weren't down to breakfast, Lady Marchmont.
LADY MARCHMONT. No, I — had a headache.
MRS. CASSILIS. Poor Margaret.

MRS. BORRIDGE [*sympathetically*]. It's 'eadachy weather, isn't it?

[*Subsiding into a chair.* MRS. BORRIDGE *makes it a rule of life never to stand when she can sit.*]

LADY MARCHMONT. I suppose it is.

MRS. BORRIDGE. Or perhaps it was the oyster patties last night? I've often noticed after an oyster I come over quite queer. Specially if it isn't *quite* fresh.

LADY MARCHMONT. Indeed!

MRS. BORRIDGE. Yes. But crabs is worse. Crabs is simply poison to me.

LADY MARCHMONT [*faintly*]. How extraordinary.

MRS. BORRIDGE. They are, I do assure you. If I touch a crab, I'm that ill nobody would believe it.

MRS. CASSILIS. Well, Margaret, I expect you oughtn't to be talked to or it will make your head worse. You stay here quietly and rest while I take Mrs. Borridge for a stroll in the garden.

LADY MARCHMONT. Thank you. [*Closing her eyes.*] My head is a little bad still.

MRS. BORRIDGE [*confidentially*]. Try a drop of brandy, Lady Marchmont. My 'usband always said there's nothing like brandy if you're feeling poorly.

LADY MARCHMONT. Thank you. I think I'll just try what rest will do.

MRS. CASSILIS [*making* LADY MARCHMONT *comfortable*]. I expect that will be best. Put your head back, dear. Headaches are such trying things, aren't they, Mrs. Borridge? This way! And you're to keep quiet till luncheon, Margaret.

[LADY MARCHMONT *closes her eyes, with a sigh of relief. After a moment enter* BUTLER *from house, with* MRS. HERRIES.]

BUTLER. Mrs. Herries.

LADY MARCHMONT [*rises and goes up to meet her*]. How do you do? Mrs. Cassilis is in the garden, Watson. [*To* MRS. HERRIES.] She has just gone for a stroll with Mrs. Borridge.

MRS. HERRIES. Oh, pray don't disturb her. Pray don't. I can only stay for a moment. Literally a moment.

LADY MARCHMONT. But she would be so sorry to miss you. Will you let her know, Watson? She went that way.

[*Pointing to path along which* MRS. CASSILIS *went a moment before.*]

BUTLER. Yes, my lady.

LADY MARCHMONT. And how's the dear Rector? [*She and* MRS. HERRIES *sit.*] You've not brought him with you?

MRS. HERRIES. No. He was too busy. There is always so much to do in these *small* parishes, isn't there?

LADY MARCHMONT. Indeed?

MRS. HERRIES. Oh, yes. There's the garden — and the pigs. The Rector is devoted to his pigs, you know. And his roses.

LADY MARCHMONT. The Rector's roses are quite famous, aren't they?

[*But* MRS. HERRIES *has not come to Deynham to talk horticulture, but to inquire about a far more interesting subject. She looks round cautiously, and then, lowering her voice to an undertone, puts the important question.*]

MRS. HERRIES. And now tell me, dear Lady Marchmont, before Mrs. Cassilis comes back, what is she like?

LADY MARCHMONT. Really, dear Mrs. Herries, I think I must leave you to decide that for yourself.

MRS. HERRIES [*sighs*]. So bad as that! The Rector feared so. And the mother? [*No answer.*] Just so! What a pity. An *orphan* is so much easier to deal with.

LADY MARCHMONT [*laughing slightly*]. You may be glad to hear that Mr. Borridge *is* dead.

MRS. HERRIES. So Mrs. Cassilis said. How fortunate! How very fortunate!

[MRS. CASSILIS, *followed by* MRS. BORRIDGE, *return from their walk.* WATSON *brings up the rear.*]

MRS. HERRIES. Dear Mrs. Cassilis, how do you do? [*Sympathetically.*] *How* are you?

MRS. CASSILIS [*rather amused at* MRS. HERRIES's *elaborate bedside manner*]. Quite well, thanks. It's Margaret who is unwell.

MRS. HERRIES. Indeed! She didn't mention it.

LADY MARCHMONT [*hurriedly*]. I have a headache.

MRS. HERRIES. I'm so sorry.

MRS. CASSILIS [*sweetly*]. You have heard of my son's engagement, haven't you? Dear Ethel is with us now, I'm glad to say. Let me introduce you to her mother.

MRS. HERRIES. How do you do? [*Bows.*] What charming weather we're having, aren't we?

MRS. CASSILIS. You'll stay to luncheon now you are here, won't you?

[MRS. BORRIDGE *subsides into a chair.*]

MRS. HERRIES. I'm afraid I mustn't. I left the Rector at home. He will be expecting me.

MRS. CASSILIS. Why didn't you bring him with you?

MRS. HERRIES. So kind of you, dear Mrs. Cassilis. [*Nervously.*] But he hardly liked — How is *poor* Geoffrey?

MRS. CASSILIS [*cheerfully*]. He's very well. He's in the kitchen garden with Ethel. At the strawberry bed. You'll see them if you wait.

MRS. HERRIES [*hastily*]. I'm afraid I can't. In fact, I must run away at once. I only looked in in passing. It's nearly one o'clock, and the Rector always likes his luncheon at one. [*Shakes hands with gush of sympathic fervour.*] Good-bye, dear Mrs. Cassilis. Good-bye, Mrs. Borridge.

[*Bows.*]

MRS. BORRIDGE [*heartily*]. Good-bye, Mrs. — I didn't rightly catch your name.

MRS. HERRIES. Herries. Mrs. Herries.

[*Shakes hands nervously.*]

MRS. BORRIDGE. Good-bye, Mrs. 'Erries.

MRS. CASSILIS. And you're coming over to dine on Thursday? That's to-day week, you know. *And* the Rector, of course. You won't forget?

MRS. HERRIES. With pleasure. Good-bye, Lady Marchmont.

[*Looks at* MRS. BORRIDGE *who has turned away, then at* LADY MARCHMONT, *then goes off, much depressed, into the house. Pause.*]

MRS. BORRIDGE. I think I'll be going in, Mrs. Cassilis, just to put myself straight for dinner.

MRS. CASSILIS. Yes. Do. Luncheon will be ready in half an hour. [MRS. BORRIDGE *waddles off into the house complacently.* LADY MARCHMONT *sinks limply into chair, with a smothered groan.* MRS. CASSILIS *resumes her natural voice.*] How's your headache, Margaret? Better?

LADY MARCHMONT. Quite well. In fact, I never had a headache. That was a little deception on my part, dear, to excuse my absence from the breakfast table. Will you forgive me? [MRS. CASSILIS *nods without a smile. She looks perfectly wretched.* LADY MARCHMONT *makes a resolute effort to cheer her up by adopting a light tone, but it is obviously an effort.*] Breakfasts *are* rather a mistake, aren't they? So trying to the temper. And that awful woman! I felt a brute for deserting you. On the very first morning, too. But I didn't feel strong enough to face her again so soon. How *could* Geoffrey do it!

MRS. CASSILIS [*grimly*]. Geoffrey's not going to marry *Mrs.* Borridge.

LADY MARCHMONT. He's going to marry the daughter. And she'll grow like her mother ultimately. All girls do, poor things.

MRS. CASSILIS [*sighs*]. Poor Geoffrey. I suppose there's something wrong in the way we bring boys up. When they reach manhood, they seem quite unable to distinguish between the right sort of woman and — the other sort. A pretty face, and they're caught at once. It's only after they've lived for a few years in the world and got soiled and hardened — got what we call experience, in fact — that they even begin to understand the difference.

LADY MARCHMONT [*decidedly*]. You ought to have sent Geoffrey to a public school. His father ought to have insisted on it.

MRS. CASSILIS. Poor Charley died when Geoff was only twelve. And when I was left alone, I couldn't make up my mind to part with him. Besides, I hate the way public-schoolboys look on women.

LADY MARCHMONT. Still, it's a safeguard.

MRS. CASSILIS [*dismally*]. Perhaps it is.

[*Neither of the sisters speaks for a*

moment. Both are plunged in painful thought. Suddenly LADY MARCHMONT *looks up and catches sight of* MRS. CASSILIS'S *face, which looks drawn and miserable. She goes over to her with something like a cry.*]

LADY MARCHMONT. My dear Adelaide, don't look like that. You frighten me.

MRS. CASSILIS [*pulling herself together*]. What's the matter?

LADY MARCHMONT. Your face looked absolutely *grey!* Didn't you sleep last night?

MRS. CASSILIS. Not very much. [*Trying to smile.*] Has my hair gone grey, too?

LADY MARCHMONT. Of course not.

MRS. CASSILIS. I feared it might.

LADY MARCHMONT. You poor dear!

MRS. CASSILIS [*impulsively*]. I am pretty still, am I not, Margaret?

LADY MARCHMONT. My dear, you look perfectly sweet, as you always do. Only there *are* one or two little lines I hadn't noticed before. But your *hair's* lovely.

MRS. CASSILIS [*eagerly*]. I'm glad of that. I shall need all my looks now — for Geoffrey's sake.

LADY MARCHMONT [*puzzled*]. Geoffrey's?

MRS. CASSILIS. Looks mean so much to a man, don't they? And he has always admired me. Now I shall want him to admire me more than ever.

LADY MARCHMONT. Why, dear?

MRS. CASSILIS [*with cold intensity*]. Because I have a rival.

LADY MARCHMONT. This detestable girl?

MRS. CASSILIS [*nods*]. Yes.

LADY MARCHMONT. My dear Adelaide, isn't it too late now?

MRS. CASSILIS. Too late? Why, the time has scarcely begun. At present Geoffrey is over head and ears in love with her. While that goes on we can do nothing. [*With absolute conviction.*] But it won't last.

LADY MARCHMONT [*surprised at her confidence*]. Won't it?

MRS. CASSILIS. No. That kind of love never does. It dies because it is a thing of the senses only. It has no foundation in reason, in common tastes, common interests, common associations. So it dies. [*With a bitter smile.*] My place is by its deathbed.

LADY MARCHMONT [*with a slight shudder*]. That sounds rather ghoulish.

MRS. CASSILIS. It *is*.

LADY MARCHMONT [*more lightly*]. Are you going to do anything to hasten its demise?

MRS. CASSILIS [*quite practical*]. Oh, yes. In the first place, they're to stay here for a *long* visit. I want them to feel thoroughly at home. Vulgar people are so much more vulgar when they feel at home, aren't they.

LADY MARCHMONT. You can hardly expect any change in *that* direction from *Mrs.* Borridge.

MRS. CASSILIS [*a short, mirthless laugh*]. I suppose not. [*Practical again.*] Then I shall ask lots of people to meet them. Oh, *lots* of people. So that Geoffrey may have the benefit of the contrast. I've asked Mabel to stay, by the way — for a week — to help to entertain *dear* Ethel. When those two are together, it should open Geoffrey's eyes more than anything.

LADY MARCHMONT. Love is blind.

MRS. CASSILIS [*briskly*]. It sees a great deal better than it used to do, dear. Far better than it did when *we* were young people. [*Pause.*]

LADY MARCHMONT. Anything else?

MRS. CASSILIS. Not at the moment. [*A ghost of a smile.*] Yes, by the way. There's Major Warrington.

LADY MARCHMONT [*shocked*]. You're not really going to consult that dissipated wretch?

MRS. CASSILIS [*recklessly*]. I would consult the Witch of Endor if I thought she could help me — and if I knew her address. Oh, I am prepared to go any lengths. I wonder if he would elope with her for a consideration?

LADY MARCHMONT [*horrified*]. Adelaide, you wouldn't do that! It would be dreadful. Think of the scandal.

MRS. CASSILIS. My dear, if she would elope with Watson, I'd raise his wages. [*Rises.*]

LADY MARCHMONT. Adelaide!

MRS. CASSILIS [*defiantly*]. I *would.* Ah,

Margaret, you've no children. [*Her voice quivering and her eyes shining with intensity of emotion.*] You don't know how it feels to see your son wrecking his life and not be able to prevent it. I love my son better than anything else in the whole world. There is nothing I wouldn't do to save him. That is how mothers are made. That's what we're for.

LADY MARCHMONT [*slight shrug*]. Poor girl!

MRS. CASSILIS [*fiercely*]. You're *not* to pity her, Margaret. I forbid you. She tried to steal away my son.

LADY MARCHMONT. Still —

MRS. CASSILIS [*impatiently*]. Margaret, don't be sentimental. The girl's not in *love* with Geoffrey. Any one can see that. She's in love with his position and his money, the money he will have some day. She doesn't really care two straws for him. It was a trap, a trap from the beginning, and poor Geoff blundered into it.

LADY MARCHMONT. She couldn't *make* the omnibus horse fall down!

MRS. CASSILIS. No. That was chance. But after that she set herself to catch him, and her mother egged her on, no doubt, and taught her how to play her fish. And you pity her!

LADY MARCHMONT [*soothingly*]. I don't, really. At least, I did for a moment. But I suppose you're right.

MRS. CASSILIS [*vehemently*]. Of course I'm right. I'm Geoffrey's mother. Who should know if I don't? Mothers have eyes. If she really cared for him, I should know. I might try to blind myself, but I should *know*. But she doesn't. And she shan't marry him. She shan't!

LADY MARCHMONT. My dear, don't glare at me like that. *I'm* not trying to make the match.

MRS. CASSILIS. Was I glaring?

LADY MARCHMONT. You looked rather tigerish. [MRS. CASSILIS *gives short laugh. Pause.*] By the way, as she is *not* to be your daughter-in-law, is it necessary to be quite so affectionate to her all the time? It rather gets on my nerves.

MRS. CASSILIS. It is absolutely necessary. If there were any coolness between us, the girl would be on her guard, and Geoffrey would take her side. That would be fatal. Geoffrey must never know how I feel towards her. No! When this engagement is broken off, I shall kiss her affectionately at parting, and when the carriage comes round I shall shed tears.

LADY MARCHMONT [*wondering*]. Why?

MRS. CASSILIS. Because otherwise it would make a division between Geoffrey and me. And I couldn't bear that. I must keep his love whatever happens. And if I have to deceive him a little to keep it, isn't that what we women always have to do? In fact, I shall have to deceive everybody except you — Lady Remenham, Mrs. Herries, the whole county. If they once knew, they would be sure to talk. Lady Remenham never does anything else, does she? And later on, when the engagement was all over and done with, Geoffrey would get to hear of it, and he'd never forgive me.

LADY MARCHMONT. My dear, your unscrupulousness appals me. [MRS. CASSILIS *shrugs impatiently.*] Well, it's not very *nice*, you must admit.

MRS. CASSILIS [*exasperated*]. Nice! of course it's not *nice!* Good Heavens, Margaret, you don't suppose I *like* doing this sort of thing, do you? I do it because I must, because it's the only way to save Geoffrey. If Geoffrey married her he'd be miserable, and I won't have that. Of course it would be *pleasanter* to be perfectly straightforward, and tell the girl I detest her. But if I did she'd marry Geoff if only to spite me. So I must trap her as she has trapped him. It's not a *nice* game, but it's the only possible one. [*More calmly.*] Yes, I must be on the best of terms with Ethel. [*With a smile of real enjoyment at the thought.*] And *you* must make friends with that appalling mother.

LADY MARCHMONT [*firmly*]. No, Adelaide! I refuse!

MRS. CASSILIS [*crosses to her*]. You must. You *must!*
[*Takes her two hands and looks into her eyes.*]

LADY MARCHMONT [*giving way, hypnotised*]. Very well. I'll do my best. [MRS.

CASSILIS *drops her hands and turns away with a sigh of relief.*] But I shan't come down to breakfast! There are limits to my endurance. [*Plaintive.*] And I do so hate breakfasting in my room. The crumbs always get into my bed.

MRS. CASSILIS [*consoling her*]. Never mind. When we've won, you shall share the glory.

LADY MARCHMONT [*doubtfully*]. You are going to win?

MRS. CASSILIS [*nods*]. I am going to win. I've no doubt whatever about that. I've brains and she hasn't. And brains always tell in the end. Besides, she did something this morning which made me sure that I should win.

LADY MARCHMONT [*trying to get back her old lightness of tone*]. She didn't eat with her knife?

MRS. CASSILIS [*resolutely serious*]. No. She — yawned.

LADY MARCHMONT [*puzzled*]. Yawned?

MRS. CASSILIS. Yes. Three times. When I saw that, I knew that I should win.

LADY MARCHMONT [*peevish*]. My dear Adelaide, what *do* you mean?

MRS. CASSILIS. Girls like that can't endure boredom. They're used to excitement, the vulgar excitement of Bohemian life in London. Theatres, supper parties, plenty of fast society. She owned as much this morning. Well, down here she shall be dull, oh, how *dull!* I will see to that. The curate shall come to dinner. And old Lady Bellairs, with her tracts and her trumpet. I've arranged that it shall be a *long* engagement. She shall yawn to some purpose before it's over. And when she's bored, she'll get cross. You'll see. She'll begin to quarrel with her mother, and nag at Geoffrey — at every one, in fact, except me. *I* shall be too sweet to her for that! [*With a long look into her sister's eyes.*] And that will be the beginning of the end.

LADY MARCHMONT [*turning her eyes away with something like a shiver*]. Well, dear, I think your plan diabolical. [*Rising.*] But your courage is perfectly splendid, and I love you for it. [*Lays hand on her shoulder for a moment caressingly.*] And now I'll go in and get ready for lunch.

[LADY MARCHMONT *turns to go into house. As she does so, the* BUTLER *comes out, followed by* MABEL *in riding-habit.* MRS. CASSILIS'S *manner changes at once. The intense seriousness with which she has been talking to her sister disappears in an instant, and instead you have the charming hostess, without a care in the world, only thinking of welcoming her guest and making her comfortable. It is a triumph of pluck — and breeding.*]

BUTLER. Lady Mabel Venning.

MRS. CASSILIS [*rising*]. Ah, Mabel, dear, how are you. [*Kisses her.*] You've ridden over? But you're going to *stay* here, you know. Haven't you brought your things?

MABEL. Mamma is sending them after me. It was such a perfect morning for a ride. How do you do, Lady Marchmont?
[*Shaking hands.*]

MRS. CASSILIS. That's right. Watson, tell them to take Lady Mabel's horse round to the stables. She will keep it here while she is with us. [*To* MABEL.] Then you'll be able to ride every day with Geoffrey. [*To* LADY MARCHMONT.] Poor Ethel doesn't ride. Isn't it unfortunate?

LADY MARCHMONT. Very!

MRS. CASSILIS. She and Geoffrey are down at the strawberry bed spoiling their appetites for luncheon. Would you like to join them?

MABEL. I think not, thanks. It's rather hot, isn't it? I think I'd rather stay here with you.

MRS. CASSILIS. As you please, dear.
[*They sit.*]

MABEL. Oh, before I forget, mamma asked me to tell you she telegraphed to Uncle Algernon yesterday, and he's coming down next Wednesday. She had a letter from him this morning by the second post. It came just before I started. Such a funny letter. Mamma asked me to bring it to you to read.

MRS. CASSILIS [*taking letter, and reading it aloud to her sister*]. "My dear Julia, — I am at a loss to understand to what I owe the honour of an invitation to Milverton. I thought I had forfeited all claim to it for

ever. I can only suppose you have at last found an heiress to marry me. If this is so, I may as well say at once that unless she is both extremely rich and extremely pretty I shall decline to entèrtain her proposal. My experience is that that is a somewhat unusual combination. I will be with you next Wednesday. — Your affectionate brother, A. L. Warrington." [*Giving back letter.*] That's right, then. And now I think I'll just go down into the garden and tell Geoffrey you're here. [*Rises.*] No, don't come, too. You stay and entertain Margaret.
[*She goes off by the path leading to the strawberry beds.*]
LADY MARCHMONT. Dear Major Warrington. He always was the most delightfully witty, wicked creature. I'm so glad he's coming while I'm here. Adelaide must be sure and ask him over.
MABEL. Uncle Algernon is coming over to dine this day week — with mamma.
LADY MARCHMONT. To be sure; I remember.
[*Enter* GEOFFREY *quickly from garden.*]
GEOFFREY. Halloa, Mabel. How do you do? [*Shaking hands.*] I didn't know you were here.
MABEL. Mrs. Cassilis has just gone to tell you.
GEOFFREY. I know. She met us as we were coming back from eating strawberries. We've been perfect pigs. She and Ethel will be here in a moment. I ran on ahead.
LADY MARCHMONT [*rising*]. Well, it's close on lunch time. I shall go in and get ready.
[LADY MARCHMONT *goes off into the house, leaving the young people together. They begin to chatter at once with the easy familiarity of long acquaintance.*]
GEOFFREY. You rode over?
[*Sitting on the arm of her chair.*]
MABEL. Yes, on Basil. He really is the sweetest thing. I like him much better than Hector.
GEOFFREY. Poor old Hector. He's not so young as he was.
MABEL. No.
[GEOFFREY *suddenly remembers that there is something more important than horses which he has to say before* ETHEL *arrives. He hesitates for a moment, and then plunges into his subject.*]
GEOFFREY. Mabel... There's something I want to ask you.
MABEL. Is there?
GEOFFREY. Yes. But I don't know how to say it. [*Hesitates again.*]
MABEL [*smiling*]. Perhaps you'd better not try, then?
GEOFFREY. I must. I feel I ought. It's about something Aunt Margaret said yesterday.... [*Blushing a little.*] Mabel, did you ever... did I ever... did I ever do anything to make you think I... I was going to ask you to marry me?
[*Looking her bravely in the face.*]
MABEL [*turning her eyes away*]. No, Geoff.
GEOFFREY. Sure?
MABEL. Quite sure.
GEOFFREY. I'm glad.
MABEL [*looking up, surprised*]. Why, Geoff?
GEOFFREY. Because from what Aunt Margaret said I was afraid, without intending it, I'd ... I — hadn't been quite honourable.
MABEL [*gently*]. You have always been everything that is honourable, Geoff. And everything that is kind.
GEOFFREY [*relieved*]. Thank you, Mabel. You're a brick, you know. And we shall always be friends, shan't we?
MABEL. Always. [*Rises.*]
GEOFFREY. And you'll be friends with Ethel, too?
MABEL. If she'll let me.
GEOFFREY. Of course she'll let you. She's the dearest girl. She's ready to be friends with everybody. And she'll *love* you, I know. [*Stands up.*] You promise? [*Holds out hand.*]
MABEL [*takes it*]. I promise.

[MRS. CASSILIS *and* ETHEL *enter at this moment from garden.* MRS. CASSILIS *has her arm in* ETHEL'S, *and they make a picture of mutual trust and affection which would make* LADY MARCH-

MONT *scream. Luckily, she is safely in her rooms washing her hands.* MRS. CASSILIS *smiles sweetly at* MABEL *as she speaks, but does not relax her hold on her future daughter-in-law.*]

MRS. CASSILIS. Not gone in to get ready yet, Mabel?

MABEL. No. Lady Marchmont only went a minute ago.

MRS. CASSILIS [*to* ETHEL]. You've not met Mabel yet, have you? I must introduce you. Miss Borridge — Lady Mabel Venning. [*Sweetly.*] I want you two to be *great* friends! [*They shake hands.*] And now come in and get ready for luncheon.

[*They all move towards* house *as the curtain falls.*]

ACT III

SCENE.— *The smoking-room at Deynham. A week has elapsed since the last Act, and the time is after dinner. The room has two doors, one leading to the hall, the other communicating with the billiard-room. There is a fireplace on the left, in which a fire burns brightly. A writing-table occupies the centre of the stage. Further up is a grand piano. By its side a stand with music on it. Obviously a man's room from the substantial writing-table, with the cigar-box on it, and the leather-covered arm-chairs. "The Field" and "The Sportsman" lie on a sofa hard by. The room is lighted by lamps. The stage is empty when the curtain rises. Then* GEOFFREY *enters from hall. He crosses to the door of the billiard-room, opens it, and looks in. Then turns and speaks to* MAJOR WARRINGTON, *who has just entered from hall.* WARRINGTON *is a cheerful, rather dissipated-looking man of five-and-forty.*

GEOFFREY. It's all right, Warrington. They've lighted the lamps.

WARRINGTON [*strolling across towards fireplace*]. Good.

GEOFFREY [*at door of billiard-room*]. How many will you give me?

WARRINGTON. Oh, hang billiards. I'm not up to a game to-night. That was only an excuse to get away from the women. I believe that's why games were invented. But if you *could* get me a whisky-and-soda I should be your éternal debtor. Julia kept such an infernally strict watch on me all the evening that I never got more than a glass and a half of champagne. A fellow can't get along on *that*, can he?

GEOFFREY. I'll ring.

WARRINGTON. Do. There's a good fellow. [GEOFFREY *rings.*] Every man requires a certain amount of liquid per day. I've seen the statistics in *The Lancet*. But Julia never reads *The Lancet*. Women never do read anything, I believe.

GEOFFREY. Have another cigar?

WARRINGTON. Thanks. Don't mind if I do. [*Takes one and lights it.*] Aren't you going to?

GEOFFREY [*who looks seedy and out of spirits*]. No, thanks.

[*Enter* FOOTMAN, *with whisky-and-soda.*]

GEOFFREY. Whisky-and-soda, James.

FOOTMAN. Yes, sir. [*Puts it on small table and goes out.*]

WARRINGTON. Off your smoke?

GEOFFREY. Yes. [*Pouring whisky.*] Say when.

WARRINGTON. When. [*Takes soda.*] You're not going to have one?

GEOFFREY. No.

WARRINGTON. Off your drink?

GEOFFREY. Yes.

WARRINGTON. That's bad. What's the matter? [*Selects comfortable easy-chair and sits lazily.*]

GEOFFREY. Oh, nothing. I'm a bit out of sorts, I suppose.

WARRINGTON. How well your mother looks to-night, by the way! Jove, what a pretty woman she is!

GEOFFREY. Dear mother.

WARRINGTON [*sips whisky meditatively*]. How does she like this marriage of yours?

GEOFFREY [*off-hand*]. All right.

WARRINGTON. Ah. [*Nods.*] Bites on the bullet. No offence, my dear fellow. I like her pluck.

GEOFFREY [*exasperated*]. I assure you, you're mistaken. My mother's been kind-

ness itself over my engagement. She's never said a word against it from the first. I believe she's the only person in this infernal county who hasn't.
WARRINGTON. Except myself.
GEOFFREY. Except yourself. And *you* think me a thundering young fool.
WARRINGTON. Oh, no.
GEOFFREY. Oh, yes. I could see you looking curiously at me all through dinner — when you weren't eating — as if I were some strange beast. You think I'm a fool right enough.
WARRINGTON [*stretching himself luxuriously*]. Not at all. Miss Borridge is a very pretty girl, very bright, very amusin'. I sat next her at dinner, you know. Not quite the sort one *marries*, perhaps — as a rule —
GEOFFREY [*crossly*]. What do you mean?
WARRINGTON [*shrugs*]. Anyhow, *you're* going to marry her. So much the better for *her*. What amuses me is your bringing her old reprobate of a mother down here. The cheek of it quite takes away my breath.
GEOFFREY [*peevish*]. What's the matter with her mother? She's common, of course, and over-eats herself, but lots of people do that. And she's good-natured. That's more than some women are.
WARRINGTON [*looking thoughtfully at the end of his cigar*]. Still, she's scarcely the sort one introduces to one's *mother*, eh? But I'm old-fashioned, no doubt. There's no saying what you young fellows will do. Your code is peculiarly your own. [*Wanders across in quest of another whisky-and-soda.*]
GEOFFREY [*restively*]. Look here, Warrington, what do you mean?
WARRINGTON [*easily*]. Want to hit me in the eye, don't you? *I* know. Very natural feeling. Lots of people have it.
GEOFFREY [*sulkily*]. Why shouldn't I introduce her to my mother?
WARRINGTON. Well, she's a disreputable old woman, you know. She lived with Borridge for years before he married her. The other daughter's — [*Shrugs shoulders.*] And then to bring her down here and introduce her to Julia! Gad, I like your humour.

GEOFFREY [*much perturbed at his companion's news*]. Are you sure?
WARRINGTON [*nonchalantly*]. Sure? Why, it's common knowledge. Everybody knows old Borridge, and most people loathe her. I don't. I rather like her in a way. She's so splendidly vulgar. Flings her aitches about with reckless indifference. And I like her affection for that girl. She's really fond of *her*. So much the worse for you, by the way. You'll never be able to keep them apart.
GEOFFREY [*irritably*]. Why should I want to keep them apart?
WARRINGTON. Why should you —? [*Drinks.*] Oh, well, my dear chap, if *you're* satisfied —
GEOFFREY [*low voice*]. Her sister . . . ! Poor Ethel! Poor Ethel!
WARRINGTON [*with a good-natured effort to make the best of things*]. My dear chap, don't be so down in the mouth. There's no use fretting. I'd no idea you were so completely in the dark about all this, or I wouldn't have told you. Cheer up.
GEOFFREY [*huskily*]. I'm glad you told me.
WARRINGTON. To think you've been engaged all this time and never found it out! What amazing innocence! [*Chuckling.*] Ha! Ha! . . . Ha! Ha! Ha!
GEOFFREY. Don't. [*Sinks on to sofa with a groan.*]
WARRINGTON. Sorry, my dear boy. But it's so devilish amusing.
GEOFFREY. How blind I've been! How utterly blind!
WARRINGTON [*shrugs shoulders*]. Well, I rather like a chap who's a bit of an ass myself.
GEOFFREY. Poor mother!
WARRINGTON. Doesn't she know? Not about old Borridge? [GEOFFREY *shakes his head.*] She must! Women always do. They have an instinct about these things which is simply uncanny. It's often highly inconvenient, too, by the way. She probably says nothing on *your* account.
GEOFFREY [*dismally*]. Perhaps so. Or Ethel's. She's been wonderfully kind to Ethel ever since she came down. Perhaps that's the reason. [*Rises.*] After all, it's not Ethel's fault.

WARRINGTON. Of course not. [*Looks at him curiously, then, with an instinct of kindness, goes to him and lays hand on shoulder.*] Well, here's luck, my dear boy, and I won't say may you never repent it, but may you put off repenting it as long as possible. That's the best one can hope of most marriages.

GEOFFREY [*drily*]. Thanks!

WARRINGTON. Well, it's been an uncommon amusin' evening. Mrs. Herries's face has been a study for a lifetime. And as for Julia's — oh, outraged respectability! What a joy it is!

[*Further conversation is interrupted by the entrance of the other guests from the hall. These are* LADY REMENHAM, LADY MARCHMONT, MRS. HERRIES, MRS. BORRIDGE, ETHEL, *and* MABEL. *Last of all comes the* RECTOR, *with* MRS. CASSILIS. *They enter with a hum of conversation.*]

RECTOR [*to his hostess*]. Well, he's a disreputable poaching fellow. It's no more than he deserved.

MRS. CASSILIS. [*Nods dubiously.*] Still, I'm sorry for his wife.

MRS. HERRIES. I'll send down to her in the morning and see if she wants anything.

MRS. BORRIDGE [*beaming with good humour*]. So this is where you gentlemen have got to!

GEOFFREY. I brought Major Warrington to smoke a cigar.

LADY REMENHAM [*looking fixedly at whisky, then at* WARRINGTON]. Algernon!

WARRINGTON [*protesting*]. My dear Julia, I believe there is nothing unusual in a man's requiring *one* whisky-and-soda at this time in the evening.

LADY REMENHAM. I trust it has been only one.

[*Sits on sofa, where she is joined by* LADY MARCHMONT.]

WARRINGTON [*changing the subject*]. Whom have you been sending to jail for poaching now, Rector? No Justice's justice, I hope?

RECTOR. Old Murcatt. He's one of Mrs. Cassilis's tenants. A most unsatisfactory fellow. He was caught red-handed laying a snare in the Milverton woods. It was a clear case. [ETHEL *stifles a yawn.*]

ETHEL. I should have thought there was no great harm in that.

RECTOR. My dear young lady!

MRS. CASSILIS. Take care, Ethel, dear. An Englishman's hares are sacred.

MRS. BORRIDGE. How silly! I can't bear 'are myself.

[*Seats herself massively in armchair in front of piano. An awkward silence follows this insult to hares. As it threatens to grow oppressive, the* RECTOR *tries what can be done with partridges to bridge the gulf.*]

RECTOR. You'll have plenty of partridges this year, Mrs. Cassilis. We started five coveys as we drove here.

MRS. CASSILIS [*acknowledging his help with a smile*]. We generally have a good many.

[ETHEL, *stifling another yawn, strolls to piano, opens it, and strikes a note or two idly.*]

MABEL. You play, I know, Ethel. Won't you play something?

ETHEL [*sulkily*]. No.

[*Turns away, closing piano sharply. Another constrained silence.*]

MRS. HERRIES. I saw you out riding to-day, Mabel. I looked in at Dobson's cottage. Poor fellow, I'm afraid he's very ill.

MABEL. Yes. I was with Geoffrey. We had a long ride, all through Lower Milverton and Carbury to Mirstoke. It was delightful.

MRS. BORRIDGE [*to* MRS. HERRIES]. Your husband has a lot of that sort of thing to do down here, I suppose, Mrs. 'Erris?

MRS. HERRIES [*with frosty politeness*]. When people are ill they generally like a visit from a clergyman, don't they?

MRS. BORRIDGE [*bluntly*]. Well, there's no accounting for tastes. My 'usband, when he was ill, wouldn't 'ave a parson near 'im. Said it gave 'im the creeps.

[*Another silence that can be felt.* WARRINGTON's *shoulders quiver with delight, and he chokes hurriedly into a newspaper.*]

LADY MARCHMONT [*crossing to fire, with polite pretence that it is the physical, not the* social, atmosphere that is freezing her to the bone]. How sensible of you to have a fire, Adelaide.

MRS. CASSILIS [throwing her a grateful look]. It is pleasant, isn't it? These July evenings are often cold in the country.

[ETHEL stifles a prodigious yawn.]

GEOFFREY [going to her]. Tired, Ethel?

ETHEL [pettishly]. No.

[Glowers at him. He turns away with a slight shrug. There is yet another awkward pause.]

MRS. CASSILIS [rising nervously]. Won't somebody play billiards? Are the lamps lighted, Geoffrey?

GEOFFREY. Yes, mother.

MRS. CASSILIS. Or shall we play pyramids? Then we can all join in. [Persuasively.] You'll play, Mrs. Borridge, I'm sure?

MRS. BORRIDGE [beaming]. I'm on.

MRS. CASSILIS. You, Lady Remenham?

LADY REMENHAM. No, thanks. Mrs. Herries and I are going to stay by the fire and talk about the Rector's last sermon.

[The RECTOR raises hands in horror.]

MRS. CASSILIS. You, Margaret?

LADY MARCHMONT. No, really. I've never played pyramids in my life.

MRS. BORRIDGE [in high good humour]. Then it's 'igh time you began, Lady Marchmont. I'll teach you.

[MRS. CASSILIS looks entreaty. LADY MARCHMONT assents, smiling.]

LADY MARCHMONT. Very well. To please you, dear Mrs. Borridge!

[LADY MARCHMONT goes off to billiard-room, followed a moment later by MABEL.]

MRS. CASSILIS. You, Mabel? That's three. Ethel four.

ETHEL. No, thank you, Mrs. Cassilis. I won't play.

MRS. BORRIDGE. Why not, Eth? You're a nailer at pyramids.

ETHEL [pettishly]. Because I'd rather not, mother. [Turns away.]

MRS. BORRIDGE. All right, dearie. You needn't snap my nose off.

[Goes off to billiard-room with unruffled cheerfulness.]

MRS. CASSILIS. Geoffrey five. The Rector six.

RECTOR. Very well, if you won't play for money. I've no conscientious objections to playing for money, but whenever I do it I always lose. Which comes to the same thing. [Follows MRS. BORRIDGE off.]

MRS. CASSILIS. You, Major Warrington, of course?

WARRINGTON [laughing]. No, thanks. I shall stay here and flirt with Mrs. Herries.

MRS. CASSILIS. Very well. How many did I say? Six, wasn't it? And myself seven. Coming, Geoff?

GEOFFREY. All right, mother.

[GEOFFREY looks doubtfully at ETHEL for a moment, and even takes a step towards her, but she takes no notice of him. Baffled, he turns to his mother, who leads him off after the others. LADY REMENHAM settles herself comfortably in arm-chair above the fireplace. MRS. HERRIES takes another by her, and they begin to gossip contentedly. ETHEL looks sullenly in their direction. WARRINGTON makes a valiant effort to retrieve his glass from the mantelpiece, with a view to replenishing it with whisky.]

LADY REMENHAM. Now, Mrs. Herries, draw up that chair to the fire, and we'll talk scandal.

WARRINGTON [stretching out hand towards glass]. The Rector's sermon, Julia!

LADY REMENHAM. Algernon! [He stops dead. ETHEL seats herself in the arm-chair behind the writing-table, puts her elbows on the table, and glares into vacancy, looking rather like a handsome fury. Presently WARRINGTON joins her. She yawns with unaffected weariness. WARRINGTON looks at her with an amused smile.]

WARRINGTON. Bored, Miss Borridge?

ETHEL. I wonder.

WARRINGTON [draws up chair by her]. I don't. [She laughs.] Life isn't very lively down here till the shooting begins.

ETHEL [drumming with her fingers on table]. I don't shoot. So I'm afraid that won't help me much.

WARRINGTON. I remember. Nor ride, I think you told me?

ETHEL [yawns]. Nor ride.

WARRINGTON. Gad. I'm sorry for you.
ETHEL [looking curiously at him]. I believe you really are.
WARRINGTON. Of course I am.
ETHEL. I don't know about "of course." Except for Mrs. Cassilis — and poor Geoff — who doesn't count — I don't find much sympathy in *this* part of the country. Heigho! How they hate me!
WARRINGTON [protesting]. No, no.
ETHEL. Oh, yes, they do. Every one of them. From Watson, who pours out my claret at dinner, and would dearly love to poison it, to your sister, who is glaring at us at this moment.
[*As, indeed,* LADY REMENHAM *is doing with some intensity. She highly disapproves of her brother's attentions to* ETHEL, *but, as there is no very obvious method of stopping them, she says nothing. Presently she and* MRS. HERRIES *begin a game of bezique, and that for the time, at least, distracts her attention from her brother's depravity.*]
WARRINGTON [looking up and laughing]. Dear Julia. She never had any manners.
ETHEL. She's no worse than the rest. Mrs. Herries would do just the same if she dared. As for Mabel —!
WARRINGTON. Don't hit it off with Mabel?
ETHEL. Oh, we don't quarrel, if that's what you mean, or call one another names across the table. I wish we did. I could beat her at that. We're as civil as the Devil. [*He laughs.*] What *are* you laughing at?
WARRINGTON. Only at the picturesqueness of your language.
ETHEL [shrugs]. Yes, Mabel despises me, and I hate her.
WARRINGTON. Why?
ETHEL [wearily]. Because we're different, I suppose. She's everything I'm not. She's well-born and well-bred. Her father's an earl. Mine was a book-maker.
WARRINGTON. Is that all?
ETHEL [bitterly]. No. She's running after Geoffrey. [WARRINGTON *looks incredulous.*] She is!
WARRINGTON [raising eyebrows]. Jealous?
ETHEL. Yes. I am jealous. Little beast! [*Picks up flimsy paper-knife.*] I'd like to *kill* her.
[*Makes savage jab with knife. It promptly breaks.*]
WARRINGTON [taking pieces out of her hand]. Don't be violent.
[*Carries pieces blandly to fire.* ETHEL *stares straight in front of her. Meantime* LADY REMENHAM *has been conversing in an undertone with* MRS. HERRIES, *occasionally glancing over her shoulder at the other two. In the sudden hush which follows* WARRINGTON'S *movement towards the fireplace her voice suddenly becomes alarmingly audible.*]
LADY REMENHAM. Such a common little thing, too! And *I* don't even call her pretty.
MRS. HERRIES. It's curious how Mrs. Cassilis seems to have taken to her.
LADY REMENHAM. Yes. She even tolerates that awful mother. [*Irritably.*] What *is* it, Algernon?
WARRINGTON [blandly]. Only a little accident with a paper-knife.
[LADY REMENHAM *grunts.* WARRINGTON *returns to* ETHEL.]
MRS. HERRIES [lowering her voice discreetly]. For Geoffrey's sake, of course. She's so devoted to him.
LADY REMENHAM. It may be that. *I'm* inclined to think her mind has given way a little. I asked her about it last week.
[*The two ladies drop their voices again to a murmur, but* ETHEL *has heard the last remark or two, and looks like murder.*]
WARRINGTON [sitting by ETHEL *and resuming interrupted thread*]. You were going to tell me what makes you think Mabel is in love with Geoffrey.
ETHEL. Was I?
WARRINGTON. Weren't you?
ETHEL. Well, perhaps I will.
WARRINGTON. Go ahead.
ETHEL. She's staying here, and they're always together. They ride almost every morning. I can't ride, you know. And Geoffrey loves it.

WARRINGTON. You should take to it.
ETHEL. I did try one day. They were just starting when I suddenly said I'd like to go with them.
WARRINGTON [*starting*]. What did they say to that?
ETHEL. Oh, Mabel pretended to be as pleased as possible. She lent me an old habit, and Geoff said they'd let me have a horse that was as quiet as a lamb. Horrid kicking beast!
WARRINGTON. What horse was it?
ETHEL. It was called Jasmine, or some such name.
WARRINGTON. Mrs. Cassilis's mare? Why, my dear girl, she hasn't a kick in her.
ETHEL. Hasn't she! . . . Anyhow we started. So long as we walked it was all right, and I began to think I might actually get to like it. But soon we began to trot — and that was *awful*. I simply screamed. The beast stopped at once. But I went on screaming till they got me off.
WARRINGTON. What did Geoffrey say?
ETHEL. Nothing. But he looked terrible. Oh, how he despised me!
WARRINGTON. Poor girl.
ETHEL. They brought me back, walking all the way. And Geoff offered to give up riding in the mornings if I liked. [WARRINGTON *whistles*.] But, of course, I had to say no. So now they go out together every day, and often don't come back till lunch.
WARRINGTON. And what do *you* do?
ETHEL [*wearily*]. I sit at home and yawn and yawn. [*Does so.*] Mrs. Cassilis takes me out driving sometimes. She does what she can to amuse me. But of course she's busy in the mornings.
WARRINGTON. What does Mrs. Borridge do?
ETHEL. Lady Marchmont looks after her. I believe she gets a kind of pleasure in leading her on and watching her make a fool of herself. Old cat! And mother sees nothing. She's as pleased with herself as possible. She's actually made Lady Marchmont promise to come and stay with us in London!
WARRINGTON. Bravo, Mrs. Borridge!
ETHEL. So I sit here or in the drawing-room with a book or the newspaper and I'm bored! bored!
WARRINGTON. And Geoffrey?
ETHEL. He doesn't seem to notice. If I say anything to him about it, he just says I'm not *well!* He's very kind and tries to find things to amuse me, but it's a strain. And so it goes on day after day. Heigho! [*A short silence.*]
WARRINGTON. Well, my dear, I admire your courage.
ETHEL [*surprised*]. What do you mean?
WARRINGTON. A lifetime of this! Year in year out. Till you can yawn yourself decently into your grave.
ETHEL [*alarmed*]. But it won't always be like this. We shan't *live* here, Geoff and I.
WARRINGTON. Oh, yes, you will. Mrs. Cassilis was talking only at dinner of the little house she was going to furnish for you both down here, just on the edge of the Park. So that you could always be near her.
ETHEL. But Geoff has his profession.
WARRINGTON. His profession is only a name. He makes nothing at it. And never will. Geoffrey's profession is to be a country gentleman and shoot pheasants.
ETHEL. But we shall have a house in London as well.
WARRINGTON [*shaking his head*]. Not you. As long as his mother lives Geoffrey will be dependent on her, you know. He has nothing worth calling an income of his own. And he's proud. He won't accept more from her than he's obliged even if her trustees would allow her to hand over anything substantial to him on his marriage — which they wouldn't.
ETHEL [*defiantly*]. I shall refuse to live down here.
WARRINGTON. My dear, you won't be asked. You'll have to live where Mrs. Cassilis provides a house for you. Besides, Geoff will prefer it. He likes the country, and he's devoted to his mother.
ETHEL. Phew!
WARRINGTON. Happily, it won't last for ever. I dare say you'll have killed poor Mrs. Cassilis off in a dozen years or so. Though you never know how long people

will last nowadays, by the way. These modern doctors are the devil.

ETHEL. Kill her off? What do you mean? I don't want to kill Mrs. Cassilis. I like her.

WARRINGTON [*looking at her in genuine astonishment*]. My dear young lady, you don't suppose you'll be able to *stand* this sort of thing, do you? Oh, no. You'll kick over the traces, and there'll be no end of a scandal, and Geoff'll blow his brains out — if he's got any — and she'll break her heart, and that'll be the end of it.

ETHEL [*fiercely*]. It won't.

WARRINGTON. Oh, yes, it will. You don't know what Country Society is. The dulness of it! How it eats into your bones. *I* do.

ETHEL. Does it bore *you* too?

WARRINGTON. Bore? It bores me to *tears!* I'm not a bad lot really. At least, no worse than most middle-aged bachelors. But Julia thinks me an utterly abandoned character, and I take care not to undeceive her. Why? Because I find Milverton so intolerable. I used to come down every Christmas. One of those ghastly family reunions. A sort of wake without the corpse. At last I couldn't stand it, and did something perfectly outrageous. I forget what, but I know the servants all gave warning. So now I'm supposed to be thoroughly disreputable, and that ass Remenham won't have me asked to the house. Thank Heaven for that!

ETHEL. But Geoff likes the country.

WARRINGTON. I dare say. But Geoffrey and I are different. So are Geoffrey and you. You and I are town birds. He's a country bumpkin. *I* know the breed!

ETHEL [*in horror*]. And I shall have to stand this all my life! All my life! [*Savagely.*] I won't! I won't!

WARRINGTON [*calmly*]. You will!

ETHEL. I won't, I tell you! [WARRINGTON *shrugs.*] It's too sickening. [*Pause. She seems to think for a moment, then grasps him by the arm, and speaks eagerly, dropping her voice, and looking cautiously over towards the others.*] I say, let's go off to Paris, you and I, and leave all this. It'd be awful fun.

WARRINGTON [*appalled, rising*]. Hush! Hush! For God's sake. Julia'll hear.

ETHEL [*almost in a whisper*]. Never mind. What does it matter? Let's go. You'd enjoy it like anything. We'll have no end of a good time.

WARRINGTON [*shaking himself free, desperately*]. My dear young lady, haven't I just told you I'm not that sort at all? I'm a perfectly respectable person, of rather austere morality than otherwise.

ETHEL. Rot! You'll come?
[*Grasping his arm again.*]

WARRINGTON. No, I won't. I decline. I can't go off with the girl my host is going to marry. It wouldn't be decent. Besides, I don't want to go off with anybody.

ETHEL [*her spirits dropping to zero*]. You won't?

WARRINGTON [*testily*]. No, I won't. And, for goodness' sake, speak lower. Julia's listening with all her ears.

ETHEL [*with a bitter little laugh*]. Poor Major Warrington! How I scared you!

WARRINGTON. I should think you did. I'm not so young as I was. A few years ago, a little thing like that never made me turn a hair. Now I can't stand it.
[*Subsiding into chair and wiping the perspiration from his brow*].

ETHEL. You've gone through it before, then?

WARRINGTON. More than once, my dear.

ETHEL [*dismally*]. And now *you'll* look down on me, too.

WARRINGTON [*trying to cheer her up*]. On the contrary, I admire you immensely. In fact, I don't know which I admire more, your pluck or your truly marvellous self-control. To ask me to go off with you without letting Julia hear! [*Looking anxiously towards her.*] It was masterly.

ETHEL [*sighs*]. Well, I suppose I shall have to marry Geoff after all.

WARRINGTON. I suppose so. Unless you could go off with the Rector.
[*She laughs shrilly. The two ladies turn sharply and glare.*]

ETHEL. Now I've shocked your sister again.

WARRINGTON. You have. She thinks I'm flirting with you. That means I

shan't be asked down to Milverton for another five years. Thank Heaven for that! Ah, here are the billiard players.
[*He rises, with a sigh of relief. The conversation has been amusing, but not without its perils, and he is not altogether sorry to have it safely over.* ETHEL *remains seated, and does not turn round. The billiard players troop in, headed by* MABEL, GEOFFREY *holding open the door for them.*]
GEOFFREY [*to* MABEL]. You fluked outrageously, you know.
MABEL [*entering*]. I didn't.
GEOFFREY. Oh, yes, you did. Didn't she, mother?
MRS. CASSILIS [*smiling at her*]. Disgracefully.
MRS. BORRIDGE. You'll soon learn, Lady Marchmont, if you practise a bit.
LADY MARCHMONT. Do you think so?
LADY REMENHAM. Well, who won, Rector?
MRS. BORRIDGE. *I* did!
LADY REMENHAM. Indeed?
[*Turns frigidly away, losing all interest at once.*]
MRS. BORRIDGE [*obstinately cheerful and friendly*]. Why didn't *you* play, Mrs. 'Erris?
MRS. HERRIES [*frigid smile*]. I never play games.
MRS. BORRIDGE. You should learn. I'd teach you.
MRS. HERRIES [*who longs to be as rude as* LADY REMENHAM, *but has not quite the courage*]. Thank you. I fear I have no time.
[*Joins* LADY REMENHAM *again, ruffling her feathers nervously.*]
MRS. CASSILIS. Ethel, dear, we missed you sadly. I hope you haven't been dull?
ETHEL [*with hysterical laugh*]. Not at all. Major Warrington has been entertaining me.
RECTOR. I suspect Miss Borridge felt there would be no opponent worthy of her steel.
[ETHEL *shrugs her shoulders rudely. He turns away.*]
MRS. CASSILIS [*as a last resort*]. I wonder if we could have some music now. Mabel, dear, won't you sing to us?

MABEL. I've got nothing with me.
GEOFFREY. Do sing, Mabel. There'll be lots of things you know here. [*Opens the piano.*] Let me find something. Schumann?
MABEL [*shakes head*]. I think not.
[*Joins him in searching music stand.*]
MRS. CASSILIS. Sing us that Schubert song you sang when we were dining with you last, dear.
MABEL. Very well. Where's Schubert, Geoffrey?
ETHEL [*to* WARRINGTON]. Do you see that?
[*Watching* GEOFFREY'S *and* MABEL'S *heads in close proximity. Seems as if she were about to jump from her chair.* WARRINGTON *restrains her by a hand on her arm.*]
WARRINGTON. Sh. Be quiet, for Heaven's sake.
ETHEL [*hisses*]. The little *cat!*
MABEL. Here it is. Geoff, don't be silly. [*Turns to piano.*]
MRS. CASSILIS. Can you see there?
MABEL. Yes, thank you.
[*She sings two verses of Schubert's "Adieu," in German, very simply, in a small but sweet voice. While she sings the behaviour of the guests affords a striking illustration of the English attitude towards music after dinner.* GEOFFREY *stands by piano prepared to turn over when required.* LADY REMENHAM *sits on sofa in an attitude of seraphic appreciation of her daughter's efforts.* LADY MARCHMONT, *by her side, is equally enthralled — and thinks of something else.* MRS. HERRIES *gently beats time with her fan.* MRS. CASSILIS *is sweetly appreciative. The* BORRIDGES, *on the contrary, fall sadly below the standard of polite attention required of them.* ETHEL, *who has begun by glaring defiantly at* MABEL *during the first few bars of the song, rapidly comes to the conclusion that she can't sing, and decides to ignore the whole performance.* MRS. BORRIDGE *begins by settling herself*

placidly to the task of listening. She is obviously puzzled and rather annoyed when the song turns out to be German, but decides to put up with it with a shrug, hoping it will soon be over. At the end of the first verse she turns to MRS. CASSILIS *to begin to talk, but that lady, with a smile and a gesture, silences her, and the second verse begins. At this* MRS. BORRIDGE'S *jaw falls, and after a few bars, she frankly addresses herself to slumber. Her purple, good-natured countenance droops upon her shoulder as the verse proceeds, and when she wakes up at the end it is with a visible start.* WARRINGTON, *meantime, has disgraced himself in the eyes of his sister by talking to* ETHEL *during the opening bars of the second verse, and has only been reduced to silence by the stony glare which she thenceforward keeps fixed upon him till the last bar. In self-defence, he leans back in his chair and contemplates the ceiling resolutely.*]

GEOFFREY [*clapping*]. Bravo! Bravo!

RECTOR. Charming, charming.

LADY MARCHMONT [*to* LADY REMENHAM]. What a sweet voice she has.

MRS. CASSILIS. Thank you, dear.

RECTOR [*to* MABEL, *heartily*]. Now we must have another.

GEOFFREY. Do, Mabel.

MABEL. No. That's quite enough.

RECTOR [*with resolute friendliness*]. Miss Borridge, *you* sing, I'm sure.

MRS. BORRIDGE. Do, dearie. [*To* LADY REMENHAM.] My girl has a wonderful voice, Lady Remling. Quite like a professional. Old Jenkins at the Tiv. used to say she'd make a fortune in the 'alls.

LADY REMENHAM [*frigidly*]. Indeed?

ETHEL. I don't think I've any songs any one here would care for.

MRS. BORRIDGE. Nonsense, dearie. You-'ve lots of songs. Give them "The Children's 'Ome."

ETHEL [*rising*]. Well, I'll sing if you like.

GEOFFREY [*going to her*]. Shall I find you something, Ethel?

ETHEL [*snaps*]. No!

[GEOFFREY *turns away snubbed, and joins* MABEL. ETHEL *goes to the piano, where she is followed a moment later by* WARRINGTON, *who stands behind it, facing audience, and looking much amused as her song proceeds.* ETHEL *takes her seat at piano. There is a moment's pause while she darts a glance at* GEOFFREY *standing with* MABEL. *Then she seems to make up her mind, and, without prelude of any kind, plunges into the following refined ditty:*]

When Joey takes me for a walk, me an' my sister Lue,
'E puts 'is arms round both our waists, as lots o' men will do.
We don't allow no liberties, and so we tells 'im plain,
And Joey says 'e's sorry — but 'e does the same again!

(*Spoken.*) Well, we're not going to have that, you know. Not likely! We're not that sort. So we just says to 'im:

Stop that, Joey! Stow it, Joe!
Stop that ticklin' when I tell yer TOE.
You're too free to suit a girl like me,
Just you stop that ticklin' or I'll slap yer!

When Joe an' me is man an' wife — I thinks 'e loves me true,
I 'ope 'e'll go on ticklin' me — and leave off ticklin' Lue.
'E'll 'ave to leave the girls alone, and mind what 'e's about,
Or 'im an' me an' Lucy'll precious soon fall out.

(*Spoken.*) Yes, I'm not going to put up with that sort of thing once we're married. Not I. If 'e tries it on, I shall sing out straight:

Now then, all of you: [*Looks across impudently to* LADY REMENHAM.]

Stop that, Joey! Chuck it, Joe!
Stop that ticklin' when I tell yer TOE.
You're too free to suit a girl like me,
Just you stop that ticklin' or I'll slap yer!

[*Sings chorus fortissimo, joined by her delighted mother and by* WARRINGTON, *who beats time sonorously on*

the top of the piano. *For this attention she slaps him cordially on the cheek at the last line, by way of giving an artistic finish to the situation, and then rises, flushed and excited, and stands by the piano, looking defiantly at her horrified audience.*]
WARRINGTON. Splendid, by Jove! Capital!

[*That, however, is clearly not the opinion of the rest of the listeners, for the song has what is called a "mixed" reception. The ladies, for the most part, had originally settled themselves into their places prepared to listen to anything which was set before them with polite indifference. A few bars, however, suffice to convince them of the impossibility of that attitude.* LADY REMENHAM, *who is sitting on the sofa by* LADY MARCHMONT, *exchanges a horrified glance with that lady, and with* MRS. HERRIES *on the other side of the room.* MABEL *looks uncomfortable. The* RECTOR *feigns abstraction.* MRS. CASSILIS *remains calm and sweet, but avoids every one's eye, and more particularly* GEOFFREY'S, *who looks intensely miserable. But* WARRINGTON *enjoys himself thoroughly, even down to the final slap, and as for* MRS. BORRIDGE, *her satisfaction is unmeasured. She beats time to the final chorus, wagging her old head and joining in in stentorian accents, finally jumping up from her chair, clapping her hands, and crying, "That's right, Eth. Give 'em another." In fact, she feels that the song has been a complete triumph for her daughter, and a startling vindication of Old Jenkins's good opinion of her powers. Suddenly, however, she becomes conscious of the horrified silence which surrounds her. The cheers die away on her lips. She looks round the room, dazed and almost frightened, then hurriedly reseats herself in her chair, from which she has risen in her excitement, straightens her wig, and — there is an awful pause.*]

MRS. CASSILIS [*feeling she must say something*]. Won't you come to the fire, Ethel? You must be cold out there.
ETHEL. Thank you, Mrs. Cassilis. I'm not cold.
WARRINGTON. Jove, Miss Borridge, I'd no idea you could sing like that.
ETHEL [*with a sneer*]. Nor had Geoffrey.
LADY REMENHAM [*rising*]. Well, we must be getting home. Geoffrey, will you ask if the carriage is round?
GEOFFREY. Certainly, Lady Remenham. [*Rings.*]
MRS. HERRIES. We must be going, too. Come, Hildebrand. [*Rising also.*]
LADY REMENHAM. Are you coming with us, Mabel?
MRS. CASSILIS. Oh, no, I can't spare Mabel yet. She has promised to stay a few days more.
LADY REMENHAM. Very well.

[*Enter* BUTLER.]

GEOFFREY. Lady Remenham's carriage.
BUTLER. It's at the door, sir.
GEOFFREY. Very well. [*Exit* BUTLER.]
LADY REMENHAM. Good-bye, then, dear. Such a pleasant evening. Good-night, Mabel. We shall expect you when we see you. [*General leave takings.*]
MRS. HERRIES. Good-bye, Mrs. Cassilis.
MRS. BORRIDGE. Good-night, Lady Remling.

[*Holds out hand with nervous cordiality.*]

LADY REMENHAM. Good-night.

[*Sweeps past her with icy bow.* MRS. BORRIDGE *retires crushed to a chair by fire, and consoles herself with illustrated paper.*]

LADY REMENHAM [*to* WARRINGTON, *who is devoting his last moments to* MISS BORRIDGE]. Algernon.
WARRINGTON. Coming, Julia. [*To* ETHEL.] See you in London, then?
GEOFREY [*stiffly*]. You'll take another cigar, Warrington — to light you home?
WARRINGTON. Thanks. Don't mind if I do. [GEOFFREY *hands box.*]
LADY REMENHAM [*sternly*]. Algernon. We're going to get on our wraps.

[MRS. CASSILIS *and* LADY REMENham, Mrs. Herries *and the* Rector, *go out.*]

WARRINGTON. All right, Julia. I shall be ready as soon as you are.

GEOFFREY [*motioning to whisky*]. Help yourself, Warrington.

[*Goes out after the others.*]

WARRINGTON [*to* ETHEL, *after helping himself to drink*]. Well, my dear, I'm afraid you've done it *this* time!

ETHEL. Done what?

WARRINGTON. Shocked them to some purpose! It was magnificent, but it was scarcely tactics, eh?

ETHEL. I suppose not. [*Fiercely.*] But I *wanted* to shock them! Here have they been despising me all the evening for nothing, and when that detestable girl with a voice like a white mouse sang her German jargon, praising her sky-high, I said I'd show them what singing means! And I did!

WARRINGTON. You certainly did! Ha! ha! You should have seen Julia's face when you boxed my ears. If the earth had opened her mouth and swallowed you up like Korah, Dathan, and the other fellow, it couldn't have opened wider than Julia's.

ETHEL. Well, she can scowl if she likes. She can't hurt me now.

WARRINGTON. I'm not so sure of that.

ETHEL. She'll have to hurry up. We go to-morrow.

WARRINGTON. Ah, I didn't know. Well, there's nothing like exploding a bomb before you leave, eh? Only it's not always safe — for the operator.

GEOFFREY [*re-entering with* MRS. CASSILIS]. The carriage is round, Warrington. Lady Remenham's waiting.

WARRINGTON. The deuce she is! [*Swallows whisky-and-soda.*] I must fly. Good-bye again. Good-bye, Mrs. Cassilis. A thousand thanks for a most interesting evening.

[WARRINGTON *goes out with* GEOFFREY. *Pause.* ETHEL *stands sullen by fireplace.*]

MRS. BORRIDGE [*yawning cavernously*]. Well, I think I shall turn in. Good-night, Mrs. Cassilis. [*General handshakes.*] Coming, Eth?

ETHEL. In a moment, mother.

[MRS. BORRIDGE *waddles out, with a parting smile from* LADY MARCHMONT. GEOFFREY *returns from seeing* WARRINGTON *off the premises.* MRS. BORRIDGE *wrings his hand affectionately in passing.*]

LADY MARCHMONT. I must be off, too. And so must you, Mabel. You look tired out.

[*Kisses* MRS. CASSILIS. GEOFFREY *opens door for them.*]

MABEL. I am a little tired. Good-night.

[*Exeunt* LADY MARCHMONT *and* MABEL.]

GEOFFREY. Are you going, mother?

MRS. CASSILIS. Not at once. I've a couple of notes to write.

[GEOFFREY *crosses to fire.* MRS. CASSILIS *goes to writing-table, sits facing audience, and appears to begin to write notes.* GEOFFREY *goes up to* ETHEL *thoughtfully. A silence. Then he speaks in a low voice.*]

GEOFFREY. Ethel.

ETHEL [*without looking up*]. Yes.

GEOFFREY. Why did you sing that song to-night?

ETHEL [*with a sneer*]. To please Lady Remenham.

GEOFFREY. But, Ethel! That's not the sort of song Lady Remenham likes at all.

ETHEL [*impatiently*]. To shock her, then.

GEOFFREY. Ethel!

ETHEL. I think I managed it, too!

GEOFFREY. I don't understand. You're joking, aren't you?

ETHEL. Joking!

GEOFFREY. I mean you didn't really do it on purpose, to make Lady Remenham angry. I'm sure you didn't.

ETHEL [*very distinctly*]. I tell you I did it on purpose, deliberately, to shock Lady Remenham. I suppose I ought to know.

GEOFFREY [*astonished*]. But why? What made you do such a thing?

ETHEL [*savagely*]. I did it because I chose. Is that plain enough?

GEOFFREY. Still, you must have had a reason. [*No answer. Suspiciously.*] Did that fellow Warrington tell you to sing it?

ETHEL [*snaps*]. No.

GEOFFREY. I thought, perhaps. . . . Anyhow, promise me not to sing such a song again here. [*Silence.*] You will promise?

ETHEL. Pooh!

GEOFFREY. Ethel, be reasonable. You must know you can't go on doing that sort of thing here. When we are married we shall live down here. You must conform to the ideas of the people round you. They may seem to you narrow and ridiculous, but you can't alter them.

ETHEL. You don't think them narrow and ridiculous, I suppose?

GEOFFREY. No. In this case I think they are right. In many cases.

ETHEL. Sorry I can't agree with you.

GEOFFREY [*gently*]. Ethel, dear, don't let us quarrel about a silly thing like this. If you are going to marry me, you *must* take my judgment on a matter of this kind.

ETHEL [*defiantly*]. Must I!

GEOFFREY. Yes.

ETHEL. Then I won't. So there. I shall do just exactly as I please. And if you don't like it, you can do the other thing. I'm not going to be bullied by you.

GEOFFREY [*reasoning with her*]. My dear Ethel, I'm sure I am never likely to bully you, or to do or say anything that is unkind. But on a point like this I can't give way.

ETHEL. Very well, Geoff. If you think that you'd better break off our engagement, that's all.

GEOFFREY. Ethel! [*With horror.*]

ETHEL [*impatiently*]. Well, there's nothing to make faces about, is here!

GEOFFREY. You don't *mean* that. You don't mean you *want* our engagement to come to an end!

ETHEL. Never mind what I want. What do *you* want?

GEOFFREY [*astonished*]. Of course I want it to go on. You know that.

ETHEL [*gesture of despair*]. Very well, then. You'd better behave accordingly. And now, if you've finished your lecture, I'll go to bed. Good-night.

[*Is going out, with only a nod to* MRS. CASSILIS, *but she kisses her good-night gently.* GEOFFREY *holds door open for her to go out, then goes and stands by fire.* MRS. CASSILIS, *who has watched this scene while appearing to be absorbed in her notes, has risen to go to her room.*]

MRS. CASSILIS [*cheerfully*]. Well, I must be off too! Good-night, Geoffrey.
[*Kisses him.*]

GEOFFREY [*absently*]. Good-night, mother. [MRS. CASSILIS *goes slowly towards door.*] Mother.

MRS. CASSILIS [*turning*]. Yes, Geoff.

GEOFFREY. Mother, you don't think I was unreasonable in what I said to Ethel, do you?

MRS. CASSILIS [*seems to think it over*]. No, Geoff.

GEOFFREY. Or unkind?

MRS. CASSILIS. No, Geoff.

GEOFFREY. I was afraid. She took it so strangely.

MRS. CASSILIS. She's rather over-excited to-night, I think. And tired, no doubt. [*Encouragingly.*] She'll be all right in the morning.

GEOFFREY. You think I did right to speak to her about that song?

MRS. CASSILIS. Quite right, dear. Dear Ethel still has a little to learn, and, of course, it will take time. But we must be patient. Meantime, whenever she makes any little mistake, such as she made to-night, I think you should certainly speak to her about it. It will be such a help to her! I don't mean *scold* her, of course, but speak to her gently and kindly, just as you did to-night.

GEOFFREY [*despondently*]. It didn't seem to do any good.

MRS. CASSILIS. One never knows, dear. Good-night.

[*Kisses him and goes out. He stands thoughtfully looking into the fire, and the curtain falls.*]

ACT IV

SCENE. — *The morning-room at Deynham. Time, after breakfast next day. A pleasant room, with French windows at the back open on to the terrace. The sun is shining brilliantly. There is a door to hall on the left. On the opposite* side of the room is the fireplace. When the curtain rises, MABEL and GEOFFREY are on the stage. MABEL is standing by the open window. GEOFFREY looks rather out of sorts and dull.

MABEL. What a lovely day!
GEOFFREY [absently]. Not bad.
                [Pulls out cigarette case.]
MABEL. I'm sure you smoke too much, Geoffrey.
GEOFFREY [smiles]. I think not.

[Enter MRS. CASSILIS from hall.]

MRS. CASSILIS. Not gone out yet, dears? Why, Mabel, you've not got your habit on.
MABEL. We're not going to ride this morning.
MRS. CASSILIS [surprised]. Not going to ride?
MABEL. No. We've decided to stay at home to-day for a change.
MRS. CASSILIS. But why, dear?
MABEL [hesitating]. I don't know. We just thought so. That's all.
MRS. CASSILIS. But you must have some reason. You and Geoffrey haven't been quarrelling, have you?
MABEL [laughing]. Of course not.
MRS. CASSILIS. Then why aren't you going to ride?
MABEL. Well, we thought Ethel might be dull if we left her all alone.
MRS. CASSILIS. Nonsense, dears. *I'll* look after Ethel. Go up and change, both of you, at once. Ethel would be dreadfully grieved if you gave up your ride for her. Ethel's not selfish. She would never allow you or Geoffrey to give up a pleasure on her account.   [Crosses to bell.]
GEOFFREY. Well, Mabel, what do you say? [Going to window.] It is a ripping day.
MABEL. If Mrs. Cassilis thinks so.
MRS. CASSILIS. Of course I think so. Run away, dears, and get your things on. I'll tell them to send around the horses.
                       [Rings.]
GEOFFREY. All right. Just for an hour. Come on, Mabel. I'll race you to the end of the passage.
    [*They run out together, nearly upsetting* FOOTMAN *who enters at the same moment.*]
MRS. CASSILIS. Lady Mabel and Mr. Geoffrey are going out riding. Tell them to send the horses round. And tell Hallard I want to see him about those roses. I'm going into the garden now.
FOOTMAN. Very well, Madam.
    [*Exit* FOOTMAN. MRS. CASSILIS *goes out into the garden. A moment later* MRS. BORRIDGE *and* ETHEL *come in from the hall.*]
MRS. BORRIDGE [looking round, then going to easy-chair]. Mrs. Cassilis isn't here?
ETHEL [sulky]. I dare say she's with the housekeeper.
MRS. BORRIDGE. Very likely. [Picks up newspaper.] Give me a cushion, there's a good girl. [ETHEL does so.] Lady Marchmont isn't down yet, I suppose.
ETHEL. No.   [Turns away.]
MRS. BORRIDGE [putting down paper]. What's the matter, dearie? You look awfully down.
ETHEL. Nothing.
    [*Goes to the window and stares out into the sunlight.*]
MRS. BORRIDGE. I wish Lady Marchmont came down to breakfast of a morning.
ETHEL [shrugs]. Do you?
MRS. BORRIDGE. Yes. It's dull without her. She and I are getting quite chummy.
ETHEL [irritably, swinging round.] Chummy! My dear mother, Lady Marchmont's only laughing at you.
MRS. BORRIDGE. Nonsense, Ethel. Laughing at *me*, indeed! I should like to see her!
ETHEL. That's just it, mother. You never will.
MRS. BORRIDGE. Pray what do you mean by *that*, miss?
ETHEL [hopeless]. Oh, it doesn't matter.
    [*Goes to fireplace, leans arm on mantelpiece, depressed.*]
MRS. BORRIDGE. Now you're sneering at me, and I won't 'ave it — have it. [Silence.] Do you 'ear?
ETHEL. Yes, I hear.
              [Stares down at fender.]
MRS. BORRIDGE. Very well, then. Don't let me 'ave any more of it. [Grumbling to

herself.] Laughing, indeed! [*Pause. Recovering her composure.*] Where's Geoffy?
ETHEL. I don't know.
MRS. BORRIDGE. Out riding, I suppose?
ETHEL. Very likely.
MRS. BORRIDGE. 'E only finished breakfast just before us.
ETHEL. *H*e, mother.
MRS. BORRIDGE. Dear, dear, 'ow you do go on! You leave my aitches alone. *They're* all right.
ETHEL [*sighs*]. I wish they were! [*Pause.*] You've not forgotten we're going away to-day, mother?
MRS. BORRIDGE. To-day! 'Oo says so?
ETHEL. We were only invited for a week.
MRS. BORRIDGE. Were we, dearie? I don't remember.
ETHEL. *I* do. There's a train at 12.15, if you'll ask Mrs. Cassilis about the carriage.
MRS. BORRIDGE [*flustered*]. But I've not let Jane know. She won't be expecting us.
ETHEL. We can telegraph.
MRS. BORRIDGE. Can't we stay another day or two? I'm sure Mrs. Cassilis won't mind. And I'm very comfortable here.
ETHEL [*firmly*]. No, mother.
MRS. BORRIDGE. Why not?
ETHEL [*exasperated*]. In the first place, because we haven't been asked. In the second, because I don't want to.
MRS. BORRIDGE. Don't want to?
ETHEL [*snappishly*]. No. I'm sick and tired of this place.
MRS. BORRIDGE. Are you, dearie? I thought we were gettin' on first rate.
ETHEL. *Did* you? Anyhow, we're going, thank goodness, and that's enough. Don't forget to speak to Mrs. Cassilis. I'll go upstairs and pack.
[*As she is crossing the room to go out,* MRS. CASSILIS *enters from garden and meets her. She stops.* MRS. CASSILIS *kisses her affectionately.*]
MRS. CASSILIS. Going out, Ethel, dear? Good-morning. [*Greets* MRS. BORRIDGE.]
ETHEL. Good-morning.
MRS. CASSILIS [*putting her arm in* ETHEL'S *and leading her up to window*]. Isn't it a lovely day? I woke at five. I believe it was the birds singing under my window.
ETHEL. Did you, Mrs. Cassilis?

[*Enter* LADY MARCHMONT.]

LADY MARCHMONT. Good-morning, Adelaide. [*Kisses her.*] Late again, I'm afraid. [*Shakes hands with* ETHEL.]
MRS. CASSILIS [*sweetly*]. Another of your headaches, dear? I'm so sorry.
LADY MARCHMONT [*ignoring the rebuke*]. Good-morning, Mrs. Borridge. I hope *you* slept well.
MRS. BORRIDGE. Sound as a bell. But, then, I was always a onener to sleep. My old man, when 'e was alive, used to say 'e never knew any one sleep like me. And snore! Why, 'e declared it kep' 'im awake 'alf the night. But *I* never noticed it.
LADY MARCHMONT [*sweetly*]. That must have been a great consolation for Mr. Borridge.
MRS. BORRIDGE. Your 'usband snore?
LADY MARCHMONT [*laughing*]. No.
MRS. BORRIDGE. Thinks it's low, per-'aps.... They used to say snorin' comes from sleepin' with your mouth open, but *I* don't know. What do *you* think?
LADY MARCHMONT. I really don't know, dear Mrs. Borridge. I must think it over.
[LADY MARCHMONT *takes chair by* MRS. BORRIDGE. *They converse in dumb show.* ETHEL *and* MRS. CASSILIS *come down stage.*]
MRS. CASSILIS. What a pretty blouse you've got on to-day, dear.
ETHEL. Is it, Mrs. Cassilis?
MRS. CASSILIS. Sweetly pretty. It goes so well with your eyes. You've lovely eyes, you know.
ETHEL. Do you think so?
MRS. CASSILIS. Of course. So does Geoff.
ETHEL [*disengaging herself*]. Oh, Geoff — Well, I must go upstairs. [*To* MRS. BORRIDGE *in passing.*] Don't forget, mummy. [*Exit* ETHEL.]
MRS. BORRIDGE. What, dearie? Oh, yes. Ethel says we must be packin' our traps, Mrs. Cassilis.
MRS. CASSILIS [*startled*]. Packing?
MRS. BORRIDGE. Yes. She says we

mustn't outstay our welcome. She's proud, is my girlie.

MRS. CASSILIS [*with extreme cordiality*]. But you're not thinking of leaving us? Oh, you mustn't do that. Geoff would be so disappointed. And so should I.

MRS. BORRIDGE. I don't *want* to go, I'm sure. Only Ethel said —

MRS. CASSILIS. There must be some mistake. I counted on you for quite a long visit.

MRS. BORRIDGE. Ethel said we were only asked for a week.

MRS. CASSILIS. But that was before I really knew you, wasn't it. It's quite different now.

MRS. BORRIDGE [*purring delightedly*]. If you feel that, Mrs. Cassilis —

MRS. CASSILIS. Of course I feel it. I hope you'll stay quite a *long* time yet.

MRS. BORRIDGE [*complacent, appealing to* LADY MARCHMONT, *who nods sympathy*]. There! I told Ethel how it was.

MRS. CASSILIS [*anxious*]. Ethel doesn't *want* to go, does she?

MRS. BORRIDGE. Oh, no. She'd be delighted to stop on. Only she thought —

MRS. CASSILIS [*determined to leave* MRS. BORRIDGE *no opportunity to hedge*]. Very well, then. That's settled. You'll stay with us till Geoff and I go to Scotland. That won't be till the middle of August. You promise?

MRS. BORRIDGE. Thank you, Mrs. Cassilis. I call that *real* hospitable. [*Rising.*] And now I'll run upstairs and tell my girl, or she'll be packing my black satin before I've time to stop her. She's so 'asty. And I always say nothing spoils things like packing, especially satins. They do crush so.

[MRS. BORRIDGE *waddles out. As soon as the door closes,* MRS. CASSILIS *heaves a deep sigh of relief, showing how alarmed she had been lest the* BORRIDGES *should really take their departure. For a moment there is silence. Then* LADY MARCHMONT, *who has watched this scene with full appreciation of its ironic humour, speaks.*]

LADY MARCHMONT. How you fool that old woman!

MRS. CASSILIS. So do *you*, dear.

LADY MARCHMONT. Yes. You'll make me as great a hypocrite as yourself before you've done. When you first began I was shocked at you. But now I feel a dreadful spirit of emulation stealing over me.

MRS. CASSILIS [*grimly*]. There's always a satisfaction in doing a thing well, isn't there?

LADY MARCHMONT. You must feel it, then.

MRS. CASSILIS. Thanks.

LADY MARCHMONT [*puzzled*]. Do you really want these dreadful people to stay all that time?

MRS. CASSILIS. Certainly. And to come back, if necessary, in October.

LADY MARCHMONT. Good Heavens! Why?

MRS. CASSILIS [*sitting*]. My dear Margaret, as long as that woman and her daughter are here, we *may* get Geoffrey out of their clutches. I thought we should manage it last night. Last night was a terrible disillusionment for him, poor boy. But I was wrong. It was too soon.

LADY MARCHMONT. By the way, what did that amusing wretch Major Warrington advise?

MRS. CASSILIS. I didn't consult him. I'd no opportunity. Besides, I couldn't have trusted him. He might have gone over to the enemy.

LADY MARCHMONT. Yes. He was evidently attracted to the girl.

MRS. CASSILIS. I suppose so. Major Warrington isn't fastidious where women are concerned.

LADY MARCHMONT. Still, he knew, of course.

MRS. CASSILIS. Only what Lady Remenham would have told him. However, his visit wasn't altogether wasted, I think.

LADY MARCHMONT. That song, you mean?

MRS. CASSILIS. Yes. He gave poor Ethel a glimpse of the Paradise she is turning her back on for ever. London, music-hall songs, rackety bachelors. And that made her reckless. The contrast between Major Warrington and, say, our dear Rector, can hardly fail to have gone home to her.

[*Further conversation is interrupted by the entrance of* ETHEL, *in the worst of tempers.* MRS. CASSILIS *is on her guard at once.*]

ETHEL [*bursting out*]. Mrs. Cassilis —

MRS. CASSILIS [*very sweetly, rising and going to her*]. Ethel, dear, what *is* this I hear? You're not going to run away from us?

ETHEL [*doggedly*]. Indeed, we must, Mrs. Cassilis. You've had us for a week. We really mustn't stay any longer.

MRS. CASSILIS. But, my dear, it's *delightful* to have you.

MRS. BORRIDGE [*who has followed hard after her daughter and now enters, flushed and rather breathless*]. There, you see, dearie! What did I tell you?

MRS. CASSILIS. Geoff would be *terribly* distressed if you went away. He'd think I hadn't made you comfortable. He'd scold me dreadfully.

ETHEL. I don't think Geoff will care.

[MRS. BORRIDGE *appeals mutely for sympathy to* LADY MARCHMONT, *who hastens to give it in full measure.*]

MRS. CASSILIS [*great solicitude*]. My dear, you've not had any little difference with Geoff? Any quarrel?

ETHEL. No.

MRS. CASSILIS. I was so afraid —

ETHEL. Still, we oughtn't to plant ourselves on you in this way.

MRS. BORRIDGE. Plant ourselves! Really, dearie, how can you say such things? Plant ourselves!

ETHEL. Oh, do be quiet, mother.

[*Stamps her foot.*]

MRS. CASSILIS [*soothing her*]. Anyhow, you can't possibly go to-day. The carriage has gone to Branscombe, and the other horse has cast a shoe. And tomorrow there's a dinner-party at Milverton. You'll stay for *that?*

ETHEL. You're very kind, Mrs. Cassilis, but —

MRS. CASSILIS [*leaving her no time to withdraw*]. That's right, my dear. You'll stay. And next week we'll have some young people over to meet you, and you shall dance all the evening.

MRS. BORRIDGE. There, Ethel!

ETHEL [*hopeless*]. Very well. If you really wish it.

MRS. CASSILIS. Of course I wish it. I'm *so* glad. I shan't be able to part with you for a *long* time yet.

[*Kisses her tenderly. But* ETHEL *seems too depressed to answer these blandishments.*]

LADY MARCHMONT [*under her breath*]. Really Adelaide!

MRS. CASSILIS [*sweetly*]. Into the garden, did you say, Margaret? [*Taking her up towards window.*] Very well. The sun *is* tempting, isn't it?

[MRS. CASSILIS *and her sister sail out.* ETHEL *and her mother remain, the former in a condition of frantic exasperation.*]

ETHEL. Well, mother, you've done it!

MRS. BORRIDGE [*snapping. She feels she is being goaded unduly*]. Done what, dearie?

ETHEL [*impatiently*]. Oh, you know.

MRS. BORRIDGE. Do you mean about staying on here? But what could I do? Mrs. Cassilis wouldn't *let* us go. You saw that yourself.

ETHEL. You might have stood out.

MRS. BORRIDGE. I did, dearie. I stood out as long as ever I could. But she wouldn't hear of our goin'. You saw that yourself.

ETHEL. Well, mother, don't say I didn't warn you, that's all.

MRS. BORRIDGE. Warn me, dearie?

ETHEL [*breaking out*]. That I was tired of this place. Sick and tired of it! That it was time we were moving.

MRS. BORRIDGE [*placidly*]. Is that all? I'll remember. [*Pause.*] How far did you get with the packing?

ETHEL [*impatiently*]. I don't know.

MRS. BORRIDGE. You hadn't packed my black satin?

ETHEL. I don't know. Yes, I think so. I'm not sure. Don't *worry*, mother.

MRS. BORRIDGE [*lamentably*]. It'll be simply covered with creases. I know it will. Run up at once, there's a good girl, and shake it out.

ETHEL [*snaps*]. Oh, bother!

Mrs. Borridge. Then I must. How tiresome girls are! Always in the tantrums!

[*Poor old* Mrs. Borridge *ambles out grumbling.* Ethel, *left alone, sits scowling furiously at the carpet and biting her nails. There is a considerable pause, during which her rage and weariness are silently expressed. Then* Geoffrey *and* Mabel *enter, quite cheerful, in riding-things. They make a curious contrast to the almost tragic figure of sulkiness which meets their eyes.*]

Geoffrey. Hullo, Ethel! There you are, are you?

Ethel [*sulky*]. You can see me, I suppose.

Mabel. We didn't get our ride after all.

Ethel. Didn't you? [*Turns away.*]

Mabel. No. Basil has strained one of his sinews, poor darling. He'll have to lie up for a day or two.

Geoffrey. Isn't it hard luck? It would have been such a glorious day for a ride. We were going round by Long Winton and up to Tenterden's farm and —

Ethel [*snaps*]. You needn't trouble to tell me. I don't want to hear.

[*There is an awkward pause after this explosion.*]

Mabel. I think I'll go up and change my habit, Geoff.

[Geoffrey *nods, and* Mabel *goes out.* Geoffrey, *after a moment, goes up to* Ethel, *and lays a hand gently on her shoulder.*]

Geoffrey. What is it, Ethel? Is anything the matter?

Ethel [*shaking him off fiercely*]. Please don't touch me.

Geoffrey. Something has happened. What is it?

Ethel [*savagely*]. Nothing's happened. Nothing ever does happen *here*.

[Geoffrey *tries to take her hand. She pulls it pettishly away. He slightly shrugs his shoulders. A long pause. He rises slowly and turns towards door.*]

Ethel [*stopping him*]. Geoff!

Geoffrey. Yes. [*Does not turn his head.*]

Ethel. I want to break off our engagement.

Geoffrey [*swinging round, astonished, and not for a moment taking her seriously*]. My dear girl!

Ethel. I think it would be better. Better for both of us.

Geoffrey [*still rallying her*]. Might one ask why?

Ethel. For many reasons. Oh, don't let us go into all that. Just say you release me and there's an end.

Geoffrey [*more serious*]. My dear Ethel. What *is* the matter? Aren't you well?

Ethel [*impatiently*]. I'm perfectly well.

Geoffrey. I don't think you are. You look quite flushed. I wish you'd take more exercise. You'd be ever so much better.

Ethel [*goaded to frenzy by this well-meant suggestion,* Geoffrey's *panacea for all human ills*]. Geoffrey, you're simply maddening. Do please understand that I know when I'm well and when I'm ill. There's nothing whatever the matter with me. I believe you think everything in life would go right if only every one took a cold bath every morning and spent the rest of the day shooting partridges.

Geoffrey [*quite simply*]. Well, there's a lot in that, isn't there?

Ethel. Rubbish!

Geoffrey [*struck by a brilliant idea*]. It's not that silly business about the riding again, is it?

Ethel [*almost hysterical with exasperation*]. Oh, no! no! Please believe that I'm not a child, and that I know what I'm saying. *I want to break off our engagement.* I don't think we're suited to each other.

Geoffrey [*piqued*]. This is rather sudden, isn't it?

Ethel. How do you know it's sudden?

Geoffrey. Isn't it?

Ethel. No. It's not.

Geoffrey [*struck by a thought*]. Ethel, has my mother —?

Ethel. Your mother has nothing whatever to do with it.

Geoffrey. She hasn't said anything?

ETHEL. Your mother has been everything that's kind and good. In fact, if it hadn't been for her I think I should have broken it off before. But I didn't want to hurt her.

[GEOFFREY *rises and paces the room up and down for a moment in thought. Then he turns to her again.*]

GEOFFREY. Ethel, you mustn't come to a decision like this hastily. You must take time to consider.

ETHEL. Thank you. My mind is quite made up.

GEOFFREY. Still, you might think it over for a day or two — a week, perhaps. It [*hesitates*] . . . it wouldn't be fair of me to take you at your word in this way.

ETHEL. Why not?

GEOFFREY [*hesitates*]. You might — regret it afterwards.

ETHEL [*with a short laugh*]. You're very modest!

GEOFFREY [*nettled*]. Oh, I'm not vain enough to imagine you would find anything to regret in *me*. *I'm* a commonplace fellow enough. But there are other things which a girl has to consider in marriage, aren't there? Position. Money. If you broke off our engagement now, mightn't you regret these later on [*slight touch of bitterness*], however little you regret *me?*

ETHEL [*touched*]. Geoff, dear, I'm sorry I hurt you. I didn't mean to. You're a good fellow. Far too good for me. And I know you mean it kindly when you ask me to take time, and all that. But my mind's quite made up. Don't let's say any more about it.

GEOFFREY [*slowly, and a little sadly*]. You don't love me any more, then?

ETHEL. No. [*Decisively.*] I don't love you any more. Perhaps I never did love you really, Geoff. I don't know.

GEOFFREY. I loved *you*, Ethel.

ETHEL. I wonder.

GEOFFREY. You know I did.

ETHEL. You thought you did. But that's not always the same thing, is it? Many a girl takes a man's fancy for a moment. Yet people say one only loves once, don't they? [*Pause.*]

GEOFFREY [*hesitating again*]. Ethel . . . I don't know how to say it . . . You'll laugh at me again . . . But you're sure you're not doing this on *my* account?

ETHEL. On *your* account?

GEOFFREY. Yes. To spare me. Because you think I ought to marry in my own class, as Lady Remenham would say?

ETHEL. No.

GEOFFREY. Quite sure?

ETHEL [*nods*]. Quite. [*Turns away.*]

GEOFFREY [*frankly puzzled*]. Then I *can't* understand it!

ETHEL [*turning on him impatiently*]. My dear Geoff, is it impossible for you to understand that I don't *want* to marry you? That if I married you, I should be bored to death? That I *loathe* the life down here among your highly respectable friends? That if I had to *live* here with you, I should yawn myself into my grave in six months?

GEOFFREY [*astonished*]. Don't you *like* Deynham?

ETHEL. No. I detest it. Oh, it's pretty enough, I suppose, and the fields are very green, and the view from Milverton Hill is much admired. And you live all alone in a great park, and you've horses and dogs, and a butler and two footmen. But that's not enough for *me*. I want *life*, people, *lots* of people. If I lived down here, I should go blue-mouldy in three weeks. I'm town-bred, a true cockney. I want streets and shops and gas-lamps. I don't want your carriages and pair. Give me a penny omnibus.

GEOFFREY. Ethel!

ETHEL. Now you're shocked. It *is* vulgar, isn't it? But *I'm* vulgar. And I'm not ashamed of it. Now you know.

[*Another pause.* GEOFFREY, *in pained surprise, ponders deeply. At last he speaks.*]

GEOFFREY. It's all over, then?

ETHEL [*nodding flippantly*]. All over and done with. I surrender my claim to everything, the half of your worldly goods, of your mother's worldly goods, of your house, your park, your men-servants and maid-servants, your aristocratic relations. Don't let's forget your aristocratic relations. I surrender them all. There's my hand on it. [*Stretches it out.*]

GEOFFREY [*pained*]. Don't, Ethel.
ETHEL [*with genuine surprise*]. My dear Geoff, you don't mean to say you're *sorry!* You ought to be flinging your cap in the air at regaining your liberty. Why, I believe there are *tears* in your eyes! Actually tears! Let me look.
[*Turns his face to her.*]
GEOFFREY [*pulling it away sulkily*]. You don't suppose a fellow *likes* being thrown over like this, do you?
ETHEL. Vanity, my dear Geoff. Mere vanity.
GEOFFREY [*hotly*]. It's *not!*
ETHEL [*suddenly serious*]. Geoff, do you *want* our engagement to go on? Do you *want* to marry me still? [*He turns to her impulsively.*] Do you *love* me still? [*Checks him.*] No, Geoff. Think before you speak. On your honour! [GEOFFREY *is silent.*] There, you see! Come, dear, cheer up. It's best as it is. Give me a kiss. The last one.
[*She goes to* GEOFFREY *and holds up her face to be kissed. He kisses her on the forehead.*]
ETHEL. And now I'll run upstairs and tell mother. [*Laughs.*] Poor mother! Won't she make a shine!
[ETHEL *goes out recklessly.* GEOFFREY, *left alone, looks round the room in a dazed way. Takes out cigarette-case automatically, goes to writing-table for match. Just as he is lighting cigarette,* MRS. CASSILIS *enters from garden, followed a moment later by* LADY MARCHMONT. *He throws cigarette away unlighted.*]
MRS. CASSILIS. All alone, Geoffrey?
GEOFFREY. Yes, mother.
MRS. CASSILIS. Where's Ethel?
GEOFFREY. Mother — Ethel's ... [*Sees* LADY MARCHMONT. *Pause.*] Good-morning, Aunt Margaret.
LADY MARCHMONT. Good-morning.
MRS. CASSILIS. Well, dear?
GEOFFREY. Mother [*plunging into his subject*], a terrible thing has happened. Ethel was here a moment ago, and she has broken off our engagement.
LADY MARCHMONT. Broken it off!
MRS. CASSILIS [*immensely sympathetic*]. Broken it off, dear? Surely not?

GEOFFREY. Yes.
MRS. CASSILIS. Oh, *poor* GEOFFREY! [*Going to him.*] Did she say why?
GEOFFREY [*dully*]. Only that it had all been a mistake. She was tired of it all, and didn't like the country, and — that's all, I think.
MRS. CASSILIS [*anxious*]. My poor boy. And I thought her so happy with us. [*Laying hand caressingly on his shoulder as he sits with head bowed.*] You don't think we've been to blame — *I've* been to blame — in any way, do you? Perhaps we ought to have amused her more.
GEOFFREY. Not you, mother. You've always been sweet and good to her. Always. She said so.
MRS. CASSILIS. I'm glad of that, dear.
[*Enter* MRS. BORRIDGE, *furiously angry, followed by* ETHEL, *vainly trying to detain or silence her.* GEOFFREY *retreats up stage, where* MRS. BORRIDGE *for a moment does not notice him.*]
MRS. BORRIDGE [*raging*]. Where's Geoff? Leave me alone, Ethel. Where's Geoff?
ETHEL. He's not here, mother. And Mrs. Cassilis is. Do be quiet.
GEOFFREY [*coming between them*]. I'm here. What is it, Mrs. Borridge?
MRS. BORRIDGE. Oh, Geoffy, what *is* this Ethel's been telling me? You haven't reely broke off your engagement, have you?
ETHEL. Nonsense, mother. *I* broke it off, as I told you.
MRS. BORRIDGE. But you didn't mean it, dearie. It was all a mistake. Just a little tiff.
ETHEL [*firmly*]. No!
MRS. BORRIDGE [*obstinately*]. Yes, it is. It'll blow over. You wouldn't be so unkind to poor Geoffy.
ETHEL. Mother, don't be a fool. It doesn't take anybody in. Come upstairs and let's get on with our packing.
MRS. BORRIDGE [*stamps foot*]. Be quiet, Ethel, when I tell you. [ETHEL *turns away in despair.*] Lady Marchmont, won't *you* speak to her? Undutiful girl. I should like to *whip* her!
LADY MARCHMONT [*soothingly*]. Ah, well, dear Mrs. Borridge, perhaps young people know best about these things.

MRS. BORRIDGE [excited and angry]. Know best! Know best! How should they know best? They don't know *anything!* They're as ignorant as they are uppish. [*Growing tearful.*] And to think 'ow I've worked for that girl! 'Ow I've slaved for 'er, denied myself for 'er. [*Breaking down.*] I did so want 'er to be respectable. I 'aven't always been respectable myself, and I know the value of it.
[*Subsides into chair, almost hysterical, and no longer realising what she is saying.*]
ETHEL. Oh, hush, mother!
MRS. BORRIDGE [*angry again*]. I won't 'ush, so there! I'm your mother, and I won't be trod on. *I* find some one to marry you — a better match than ever you'll find for yourself, miss — and this is 'ow I'm treated! [*Begins to cry.*]
ETHEL [*taking her arm*]. Mother, mother, do come away.
MRS. BORRIDGE [*breaking down altogether*]. And now to 'ave to begin all over again. And young men ain't so green as they used to be. Not by a long way. They're cunning, most of them. They take a deal of catchin'. And I'm gettin' an old woman. Oh, she might 'ave spared me this.
MRS. CASSILIS [*almost sorry for her*]. Mrs. Borridge — Mrs. Borridge.
MRS. BORRIDGE [*refusing to be comforted*]. But she's no natural affection. That's what it is. She doesn't love 'er mother. She's 'eadstrong and wilful, and never paid the least attention to what I told 'er. [*Burst of tears.*] But I do think she might 'ave let 'im break it off. Then there'd 'ave been a breach of promise, and that's always something. That's what I always say to girls: "Leave them to break it off, dearies. And then there'll be a breach of promise, *and* damages." That's if you 've got something on paper. But [*fresh burst of tears*] she never *would* get anything on paper. She never paid the least regard to her old mother. She's an undutiful girl, and that's 'ow it is.
[*Goes off into incoherent sobs*].
BUTLER. Lady Remenham.
MRS. CASSILIS [*rising hastily*]. The drawing-room, Watson.

[*She is, however, too late to stop* WATSON *from showing in* LADY REMENHAM.]
LADY REMENHAM [*sailing in, with breezy cheerfulness*]. How do you do, Adelaide? How do you do, Margaret? I've just driven Algernon to the station, and I thought I'd leave this for you as I passed.
[*Gives book.*]
MRS. BORRIDGE. She's an undutiful daughter. That's what she is.
[*Snorting and sobbing.*]
LADY REMENHAM [*perceiving for the first time that something unusual is going on*]. Eh?
MRS. CASSILIS. Mrs. Borridge is not quite herself just now. Dear Ethel has decided that she does not wish to continue her engagement to my son, and Mrs. Borridge has only just heard the news.
LADY REMENHAM [*scarcely able to believe her ears*]. Not wish —!
MRS. CASSILIS [*hastily, checking her*]. No. This has naturally upset us all very much. It was so very sudden.
LADY REMENHAM. Well, I must say —
[*Luckily she does not do so, but takes refuge in silence.*]
MRS. BORRIDGE [*burst of grief*]. Oh, why didn't she get something on paper? Letters is best. Men are that slippy! I always told her to get something on paper.
[*Breaks down completely.*]
ETHEL. Come away, mother. [*Takes her firmly by the arm.*] Will you please order the carriage, Mrs. Cassilis?
[*Leads* MRS. BORRIDGE *off, sobbing and gulping to the last.*]
LADY REMENHAM [*sitting down, with a triumphant expression on her amiable countenance*]. Geoffrey, will you please tell the coachman to drive round to the stables? *I* shall stay to luncheon!
[*It is impossible adequately to represent the tone in which* LADY REMENHAM *announces this intention. It is that of a victorious general occupying the field, from which he has beaten the enemy with bag and baggage. Luckily,* GEOFFREY *is too depressed to notice anything. He goes out without a word — and the curtain falls.*]

JOHN GLAYDE'S HONOUR
A NEW AND ORIGINAL PLAY IN FOUR ACTS
By ALFRED SUTRO

COPYRIGHT, 1907, BY SAMUEL FRENCH

Especial notice should be taken that the possession of this book without a valid contract for production first having been obtained from Samuel French, 28-30 West 38th St., New York, confers no right or license to professionals or amateurs to produce the play publicly or in private for gain or charity. In its present form this play is intended only for students and the reading public, and no performance of it may be given except by special arrangement with Mr. French, the author's agent.

PERSONS

JOHN GLAYDE
TREVOR LERODE
HOWARD COLLINGHAM
CHRISTOPHER BRANLEY
MICHAEL SHURMUR
WALTERS
MURIEL GLAYDE
PRINCESS DE CASTAGNARY
LADY LERODE
MRS. RENNICK
DORA LONGMAN

ACT I. The dining-room of Mrs. Glayde's flat in the Avenue du Bois de Boulogne.
ACT II. John Glayde's sitting-room in the Ritz Hotel.
ACT III. Same as ACT I.
ACT IV. Trevor Lerode's studio.

JOHN GLAYDE'S HONOUR

How many a thing which we cast to the ground
When others pick it up becomes a gem?
                                    MEREDITH

ACT I

The dining-room of MRS. GLAYDE'S *flat in the Avenue du Bois de Boulogne. It is an exceedingly charming, tasteful room, dainty and delicate. At back is the fireplace; on each side of it large windows, the curtains of which have not been drawn, reveal the trees of the Avenue, with the myriad lights twinkling through. The dinner-table, oblong in shape, is in the full centre of the room. At the head of it, with their backs to the fireplace, are* MURIEL *and* TREVOR LERODE. *To the left of* TREVOR *are the* PRINCESS DE CASTAGNARY *and* HOWARD COLLINGHAM; *to the right of* MURIEL, CHRISTOPHER BRANLEY *and* MRS. RENNICK. *It is about ten o'clock at night; the illumination is chiefly from the candles on the table.*

As the curtain rises, the dinner-table has been cleared, and two men are handing round coffee and liqueurs. They go.

BRANLEY [*leaning back in his chair*]. I have dined — I have dined most amazingly well! Mrs. Glayde, I pay you my compliment. That *truite à la nage* was an achievement!

PRINCESS. Bully!

BRANLEY [*with a mock bow*]. I thank you, Princess, for that exquisite Americanism! I am a man who has known what it is to dine badly, not to dine at all, and rarely — ah, very rarely! — to dine well. To-night I have dined amazingly well. Homage to Mrs. Glayde!

MURIEL [*laughing*]. Eloquent Mr. Branley!

BRANLEY. Madam, your *chef* is an artist — I embrace him — I crown him with parsley! Thanks to him, I feel inspired.

Were Velasquez here, I would clap him on the shoulder and call him brother!

PRINCESS [*lighting a cigarette*]. That's enough, Christopher. Try some sodawater.

BRANLEY. A person came into my studio this afternoon, and haggled for a picture. I told him I'd let him know. I shall decline.

MRS. RENNICK. And why?

BRANLEY. He had a raucous voice, and squinted — he is not the man to possess my masterpieces. By that gorgeous purple trout, he shall not — no!

PRINCESS. You don't often get a chance to sell a picture, Christopher. And the people who *don't* squint aren't running after 'em.

BRANLEY. Princess, you drag me to earth — respect my wings! Mrs. Rennick [*he turns to her*], give me an appropriate sentiment — in Greek!

COLLINGHAM [*looking enquiringly at her*]. Greek?

MRS. RENNICK [*laughing*]. Yes — I'm learning. The age of the passions is past — so I study Greek!

PRINCESS. Rather a dismal alternative, isn't it?

MRS. RENNICK [*shrugging*]. One does what one can. But oughtn't we to drink to the new flat? Mr. Collingham!
[*She turns to him.*]
COLLINGHAM. Yes — a toast! [*He rises.*] Mrs. Glayde, I lift my glass — to your new home — and its most gracious mistress!

BRANLEY. Tsch, tsch — commonplace! [*He rises, followed by the others, except* MURIEL, *who leans back and laughs.*] To the wild, capricious, sparkling, storm-tossed sea, from which Venus Aphrodite Muriel

Glayde arose, on her conch-shell, in the Bois de Boulogne!
[*He empties his glass.*]
PRINCESS. To Muriel, best of pals!
MRS. RENNICK. To Muriel!
MURIEL [*turning to* TREVOR]. And you, Trevor?
TREVOR [*warmly*]. To the sweetest of hostesses, dearest of friends — the most glorious of women!
[*They all empty their glasses, then sit.* MURIEL *gives* TREVOR *the softest of glances; and, for a moment, lets her hand rest on his.*]
BRANLEY [*shaking his head in solemn disapproval*]. Sweetest, dearest, most glorious! From a painter-poet I should have expected subtler adjectives.
TREVOR [*laughing*]. You bubble, Chris, and babble —
BRANLEY. See how he plays upon words, and jingles vowels! Trifler, was there not also "bauble," which led you pleasantly to "bible," and thence to —
PRINCESS [*breaking in*]. Don't talk of bibles, please. I was religiously brought up.
BRANLEY. In Chicago — where they feed the pigs on old sermons, to give sanctimonious flavour to the pork! [*He turns, with a large gesture, to the window.*] See the good lights of old Paris twinkling in the distance! Beautiful home of Art and Lovers, Paris, I salute thee! [*To* COLLINGHAM.] Collingham, the phrase is not copyright. Let it appear to-morrow, in the column you send to the wonderful London ha'porth!
MURIEL. We've scarcely heard your voice all the evening, Mr. Collingham.
COLLINGHAM. Branley doesn't give one very much chance! And — well, the fact is, I've some rather bad news, Mrs. Glayde. Do you know that they say your husband's ill?
MURIEL [*quickly*]. No — really? Where have you heard that?
COLLINGHAM. It was cabled over from New York. Mr. Glayde had been confined to his room for a week.
BRANLEY [*filling his glass*]. Ill-mannered man, to mention husbands here!

PRINCESS [*with a grimace*]. Nasty things!
MURIEL. Mr. Glayde would have cabled me if he had been really unwell. It will only be a little game of his.
MRS. RENNICK [*wondering*]. A game?
MURIEL. The report that he is ill sends markets down; there are times when he *likes* them to go down.
PRINCESS [*admiringly*]. Oh, he's full of dodges, is the Iron King!
BRANLEY. The Iron King? Who's that?
PRINCESS. Why, John Glayde, of course — Muriel's husband. Didn't you know?
BRANLEY. How should I? Husbands don't interest me, as a rule —
MRS. RENNICK [*clapping her hands*]. John Glayde, the Iron King! Oh, it's fine! He's a great man, then, Muriel?
MURIEL [*quietly*]. He, and half a dozen others, run America.
BRANLEY. "Run America" — the pretty image! Can't you see America skipping, while John Glayde, and our Princess's father, and a few other traffickers in steel and oil and copper, hold the ropes? Jump, America! Higher, America! And America pants, breathless!
PRINCESS. Have you heard from him lately, Muriel?
MURIEL [*laughing*]. Oh, he's much too busy to write! I've been away six months — and I believe we've exchanged four letters!
BRANLEY [*to* MRS. RENNICK]. Think of it, student of Greek! Give me an irregular verb — to describe his conduct!
PRINCESS [*slyly*]. Muriel doesn't break her heart over it — does she, Trevor?
TREVOR [*coldly*]. How can I tell? She doesn't wear it on the sleeve next to me. Where's *your* husband to-night, Betsy?
PRINCESS [*indifferently*]. He's either gambling or tippling.
BRANLEY. Or protecting the choreographic arts. We've put him on an allowance.
PRINCESS [*sternly*]. We?
BRANLEY [*bowing low*]. Our friends are acquainted with the fact, most noble Princess, that you have deigned to admit

me to your counsels — to blend your inexperience of men with my most subtle knowledge. Oh, the bad deal that the respectable Mr. Huggins made, when he bartered beautiful Betsy for the Prince's coronet!
PRINCESS. And Poppa knew something about pigs, too.
BRANLEY. Also why marry an Italian Princeling, when America has kings like Mr. Glayde?
MURIEL [dryly]. Don't bother about my husband, please, Mr. Branley.
MRS. RENNICK [laughing]. I had quite forgotten that you *had* a husband, Muriel!
MURIEL. I have to pinch myself, sometimes, to remember! I've scarcely seen him, these last two or three years.
MRS. RENNICK. Really!
MURIEL. You see, he works eighteen hours a day — he does nothing but work. At home, from the first thing in the morning till the last thing at night, he's at his office, working. It has happened more than once, when we're living under the same roof, that I haven't seen him for a week at a time!
PRINCESS. *I* call that fine!
MURIEL. And then he's always running off to Chicago, or St. Louis, or somewhere — he'll go at a moment's notice. He spends his life crushing something, or fighting someone — smashing an old enterprise, or starting a new one. He's so rich that it takes a dozen clerks merely to count his money — but he's always wanting more!
PRINCESS. He gives away a lot.
MURIEL. Oh yes — millions! Schools, universities, hospitals — there he's a prince! And, more than once, when he has fought a man, and beaten him to pulp, Mr. Glayde has sent him a nice big cheque, to let him start over again!
MRS. RENNICK. Oh, isn't that generous!
BRANLEY. Wonderful! I wish he were here!
TREVOR [angrily]. Chris!
BRANLEY. I do, Trevor, I do! I'd get him to make a corner in Art — in me! There are canvases in my studio!
[*He fills his glass.*]
PRINCESS. It's not overwork *you* are suffering from, Mr. Branley!

BRANLEY [meekly]. Princess, reproach me not! This is my sentimental hour!
MRS. RENNICK [to TREVOR]. How's Muriel's portrait getting on, Mr. Lerode?
TREVOR. Nearly finished now — a few more sittings —
PRINCESS [maliciously]. You've been a long time over it, Trevor!
TREVOR [awkwardly]. A long time — I don't know — an artist isn't a bricklayer — he doesn't work by the hour! And I aim at something fine — with *such* a sitter! [*He looks ardently at* MURIEL.] I want to paint a real portrait — give the *real* Muriel — there's not only the beautiful face — I want to show the soul!
BRANLEY [sipping his glass]. It was not till 595 A.D. that the Pope allowed that women *did* have souls.
TREVOR. Shut up, Chris! [*To* MRS. RENNICK.] You've no idea how difficult it is to satisfy oneself. I've painted the whole thing out twice, and begun again —
BRANLEY. Penelope's web!
PRINCESS [laughing maliciously]. Muriel's very patient.
MURIEL [anxious to change the conversation]. Mr. Collingham, please don't look so bored. I believe you only come here to see Dora. I shall really have to send that child home, you know. She talks of nothing but you!
PRINCESS. Where *is* Dora this evening, Muriel?
MURIEL. Lady Lerode has taken her to the theatre — they're doing Antigone at the Français. But cheer up, Mr. Collingham — they'll be back soon!
MRS. RENNICK [shaking her head]. I'm not at all sure that, if Dora were *my* niece, I'd let her see so much of Mr. Collingham.
COLLINGHAM [turning to her]. And why, dear Lady Cato?
MRS. RENNICK. Now that's unkind, Mr. Collingham — I'm not eighty yet! But Dora's very impressionable; and you are — altogether too nice!
MURIEL [laughing]. You think that, Helen? Well, perhaps you're right — We'll see! And now, good people, you must make yourselves happy here — I can't take you to the drawing-room, for it's not furnished

yet. Tell me, though — *isn't* it a pretty flat?

PRINCESS [*looking around*]. I call it just lovely!

MURIEL. It's *such* a relief to be away from the hotel! All sorts of people were forever calling on me, and wanting to talk to me, because I was Mrs. Glayde!

BRANLEY. The penance of queenship! But tell me, your Majesty, does your royal husband own *all* the iron in America?

MURIEL. He's the head of the Trust that controls it. But it's not only iron — it's coal, and steel, and oil, and tobacco — he's in them all, he's in everything! Over there, one eats John Glayde, and drinks him; lights *his* cigarette with *his* matches as one leaves *his* hotel to go on board *his* train!

BRANLEY. The magnificent man! Columbus only discovered America — he swallows it! Well, here's to him — and wishing him a good digestion!

[*He raises his glass; a* FOOTMAN *enters hurriedly, and whispers to Muriel. She rises in great agitation.*]

MURIEL [*to the* FOOTMAN]. What!!! [*She turns to the others.*] My husband has come!

[*There is a general stir. The guests all rise, except* BRANLEY, *who quietly finishes his glass.* TREVOR *stands, as though thunderstruck; the* PRINCESS *deftly pulls him to her side, causing him to vacate the place next to* MURIEL.]

[JOHN GLAYDE *comes smilingly into the room. He is in immaculate evening dress, and looks pleasant and handsome.*]

MURIEL. John!

JOHN. My dear Muriel! [*He kisses her lightly on the brow.*] Ten thousand apologies for bursting in on you like this!

MURIEL. You've dined, John?

JOHN. Oh, yes — hours ago — in the train.

MURIEL. Let me introduce my friends — the Princess de Castagnary —

BRANLEY [*complacently, still seated*]. Née Betsy Huggins.

PRINCESS [*holding out her hand, which* JOHN *takes*]. We've met before, Mr. Glayde!

JOHN. Surely, surely!
[*They shake hands.*]

MURIEL. Mrs. Rennick —

BRANLEY. Ζωὴ μοῦ σὰς ἀγαπῶ —

MURIEL. Mr. Howard Collingham —

BRANLEY. Of the Press Gang.

MURIEL. Mr. Christopher Branley.

BRANLEY [*rising solemnly to his feet*]. A humble artist, sir, before dinner — a genius now. [*He bows low.*]

MURIEL. Mr. Trevor Lerode.

[JOHN *has bowed and smiled pleasantly to the others; he turns at the mention of* LERODE'S *name, and looks searchingly at him. They all sit:* JOHN *in the place before occupied by* TREVOR, *who is now at the side of the* PRINCESS. MURIEL *and* TREVOR *are nervous and excited,* JOHN *absolutely calm and unruffled.*]

JOHN. Now let me explain, first of all, how it is that I have entered in this thunderbolt fashion. [*To* MURIEL.] You may have heard that I was ill?

MURIEL. Mr. Collingham was just telling me of a report in the papers —

JOHN [*smiling*]. I allowed New York to believe that I was suffering from — measles! The fact is that a week ago I had a sudden feeling that I wanted a holiday, and would like to see my wife. But I happened to be engaged in a little financial conflict with various gentlemen over there, of whom your father, Princess, is one —

PRINCESS. Poor Poppa!

JOHN. And it wouldn't have done for me to let my intentions get abroad — when the cat's away, you know! I couldn't even cable — for my name, unfortunately, is familiar to the young ladies at the telegraph office, and it would quickly have leaked out that I was gone — to my distinct prejudice. So I had no option — but to arrive — like this.

MURIEL. You've only just come?

JOHN. We landed at Cherbourg at three. I wired you from there — but of course to the hotel.

MURIEL. Oh yes — I've only been here five days. A sudden determination — I saw this flat, and fell in love with it. I wrote you, of course. And I wouldn't leave my address at the hotel, because people pestered me so! I send every day for letters. How *did* you find out where I was?

JOHN. The invaluable Shurmur discovered that, while I was dressing at Ritz's.

MURIEL [*with vague uneasiness*]. Shurmur? Ah — he is with you?

JOHN. You know I never travel without Shurmur! [*To the others.*] A man who is half secretary and half watchdog, with something of Indian blood in him, I fancy, that makes him delight in nosing a trail! But this time the task was not very difficult, it seems.

BRANLEY. Mr. Glayde, I feel like Aladdin with the wonderful lamp — I was yearning to see you. Your wife had just been telling us of your achievements.

JOHN [*smiling*]. Which probably do not commend themselves to you! I'm by way of being an organizer, you know, and like handling brains — in bulk. [*He turns to* COLLINGHAM.] You gentlemen, I presume, are all connected with the arts?

COLLINGHAM. Mr. Lerode and Mr. Branley are both painters —

BRANLEY. And *such* painters!

COLLINGHAM. *I* am only a journalist. [*He laughs.*] Oh, don't be afraid — I'm not suggesting an interview!

MRS. RENNICK. Mr. Lerode is painting Muriel's portrait.

JOHN [*turning full on* TREVOR, *but smiling pleasantly*]. Indeed?

TREVOR [*coldly*]. Mrs. Glayde has been good enough to sit to me.

JOHN. Ah ... I shall look forward to seeing the portrait.... Where's Dora, Muriel? Gone to bed, I suppose?

MURIEL. No — she's at the theatre with Lady Lerode — Mr. Lerode's mother. But they'll be here soon. Will you have some coffee, John?

JOHN [*smiling*]. At this hour? No, thanks. But Mr. Collingham will perhaps pass me a cigarette. I see that you ladies permit. [COLLINGHAM *passes the box; he takes a cigarette and lights it.*] Thank you. Well, it's pleasant to be on terra-firma again. We had a rough crossing!

BRANLEY. Was your ironic Majesty ill?

JOHN [*coldly*]. I beg your pardon?

BRANLEY [*deprecatingly*]. Sir, I meant no offence. The truth is, the title appeals to me. I would like to be king of something, though it were but of rushlights!

PRINCESS [*rising*]. I guess you and Muriel would like to be alone. Now, Mr. Glayde, if you ruin my Poppa, I'll be very annoyed!

JOHN [*smiling*]. He shall be left with a dollar or two, Princess, for your sake!

PRINCESS. I warn you that I'll go straight to the telegraph office, and cable him that you're here!

JOHN. I mean to do a little cabling on my own account. And let's hope that Mr. Huggins will very soon be regretting that it *wasn't* measles!

PRINCESS [*with a mock grimace*]. Unpleasant man! Well, good-bye. I won't invite you to meet my Prince, because I'm not proud of him!

[*They shake hands — the* PRINCESS *goes to* MURIEL *— all have risen.*]

BRANLEY. I'll see you to your carriage, Betsy. [*He catches* JOHN'S *look of surprise.*] Er — Princess. [*He shakes hands with* MURIEL.] Mrs. GLAYDE, I shall never forget that *truite à la nage!* [*He goes to* JOHN *and shakes hands with him.*] Good-bye, Mr. Glayde. [*He holds his hand to the light.*] Not even a miserable million sticking to it! Are you coming, Trevor?

TREVOR. Yes. [*He shakes hands with* MURIEL.] I suppose you won't be able to sit to me to-morrow?

MURIEL [*quietly*]. No — not to-morrow, perhaps — but I hope the next day. I'll let you know.

TREVOR. Do. Good-bye, Mr. Glayde.

JOHN. Good-bye.

[*They bow stiffly,* JOHN *looking him squarely in the face:* TREVOR *meets his gaze unflinchingly.*]

MRS. RENNICK. [*kissing* MURIEL]. A delightful evening!

MURIEL. Don't forget you're coming to tea to-morrow!

MRS. RENNICK. Oh, no! [*She turns to* JOHN.] Good-bye, Mr. Glayde.

JOHN. Good-bye.

PRINCESS [*at the door, with* TREVOR *and* BRANLEY]. I'll drive you, if you like, Mrs. RENNICK.

MRS. RENNICK. Oh, that's awfully good of you! [*At the door.*] I never feel safe in those nasty cabs!

BRANLEY [*at the door*]. You have the resource of conjugating τύπτομαι to the cabman!

[*They go.* COLLINGHAM *has moved with outstretched hand to* MURIEL.]

MURIEL. Oh, Mr. Collingham, don't go — stay and see Dora! She'll be *so* disappointed! John — [*she turns laughingly to him*]. I must warn you that Dora's hopelessly in love with Mr. Collingham!

JOHN [*pleasantly, as he lights another cigarette*]. Really? Well, he seems a white man.

COLLINGHAM [*smiling*]. I'm glad you think so! You make up your mind quickly, Mr. Glayde?

JOHN. It's my business to know men.

COLLINGHAM. And women?

JOHN. Ah, there — my experience is too limited! . . . When do you expect Dora back, Muriel?

MURIEL [*glancing at the clock*]. It's a quarter to twelve — they'll be here in a minute or two.

[*She moves restlessly on to the balcony, and leans out.* JOHN *bends over to* COLLINGHAM, *speaking earnestly and incisively, with an entire change of manner.*]

JOHN. Will you call on me at Ritz's tomorrow, at eleven?

COLLINGHAM [*staring*]. If you wish it — certainly.

JOHN. At eleven sharp?

COLLINGHAM. Yes.

JOHN. Thank you. [*He turns, and raises his voice.*] Muriel, won't you catch cold? [MURIEL *starts, leaves the balcony, and comes into the room; he rises, and moves to her.*] Do you know, it's nearly seven months since I saw you?

MURIEL [*indifferently, as she sits beside* COLLINGHAM]. Really? But then we never see much of each other, do we?

JOHN [*standing with his back to the fireplace*]. I accept the reproach, meekly. [*To* COLLINGHAM.] Your business men over here, I suppose, Mr. Collingham, go out in the morning, somewhere about ten, after a substantial breakfast, and return home in time for dinner, and spend the evening happily with their families?

COLLINGHAM [*smiling*]. More or less.

JOHN. Well, with us, you see, there's no such thing as regular office hours. We work all the time. In England a rich man's ambition is to become a peer, mix with county families, and forget that he ever was connected with trade. In America we want power, and then more power — the thing becomes a habit: we go on, because we must. I daresay I look an old man to you — but I'm only forty. I began young.

COLLINGHAM. You've liked it?

JOHN. One enjoys the fight — brain against brain — it's chess on a rather big scale. But I'm going to retire — and turn over a new leaf! [*To* MURIEL, *who had scarcely been listening.*] Muriel, do you hear that? I intend to devote the remaining years of my life to pleasing you, and being with you.

MURIEL [*coldly*]. Indeed?

JOHN. A fact, I assure you! I intend to resign my ironic kingdom, as your facetious friend calls it, and become a private citizen again. And I've an idea we'll buy some automobiles, and do Italy together!

MURIEL [*shifting in her chair*]. This isn't the time of year for Italy.

JOHN [*lightly*]. If it's too hot in Italy we'll try Sweden or Norway — or hire a ragged regiment, perhaps, and do some camping out in the desert! What do you say? [LADY LERODE *and* DORA *come in.*] Ah, Dora!

[DORA, *a pretty girl of seventeen, rushes excitedly to him, and flings her arms round his neck.* MURIEL *goes to* LADY LERODE.]

DORA. Uncle John, Uncle John! Oh, I *am* glad to see you!

JOHN [*fondly, stroking her hair*]. Well, Doffy, my little girl — how are you?

DORA. Oh, what a lovely surprise! Lovely — that's what it is — just lovely!

MURIEL. John, let me introduce you to Lady Lerode. [*To* LADY LERODE.] My husband.

LADY LERODE [*going to him with outstretched hands*]. Delighted to welcome you over here, Mr. Glayde!

JOHN [*shaking hands with her*]. Thank you. Very good of you to take my little Dora to the theatre. Did you enjoy yourself, Dora?

DORA [*hesitating*]. Well, I mustn't say "no," because Lady Lerode took me. But, Uncle, the theatres here *are* so dull! It's all blank verse — they make love in blank verse — fancy! and kill each other in blank verse — it's *very* stupid!

COLLINGHAM [*laughing*]. Dora evidently doesn't care for the classical drama!

DORA [*coyly, over* JOHN'S *shoulder*]. Oh, Mr. Collingham, are *you* there? [*To* JOHN.] They won't take me to the really *nice* theatres, Uncle, because they say I'm too young — so I only go to the old-fogey places. But now that *you're* here, you'll show me something of life, won't you? [*She peers into his face.*] Uncle John, you're not looking well!

JOHN [*smiling*]. No?

DORA. There's a line there, right across your forehead. Take it away, Uncle John!

JOHN. Give me another kiss — that will do it!

[MURIEL *is talking at back to* COLLINGHAM *and* LADY LERODE; LADY LERODE *leaves the others, and comes to* JOHN *and* DORA.]

LADY LERODE [*gaily*]. Dora, your Mr. Collingham's going!

DORA. Oh!

[*She leaves* JOHN, *and goes quickly to the others.*]

LADY LERODE [*going close to* JOHN, *and whispering eagerly to him*]. You've not breathed a word, of course, about *my* having cabled you?

JOHN. No. But why *did* you cable?

LADY LERODE [*hastily*]. Not now — I can't tell you now. Oh, nothing serious, of course — the merest trifle! But you'll be wanting to see me. When? You'd better not call on me.

JOHN. At Ritz's to-morrow?

LADY LERODE [*surprised*]. You're staying at Ritz's?

JOHN [*shortly*]. I've engaged rooms there.

LADY LERODE. Shall we say at twelve? Will that do?

JOHN. Perfectly.

LADY LERODE. I'll be there. [*She giggles.*] Very compromising! [*Anxiously.*] And, of course — not a word —

JOHN [*quietly*]. That goes without saying.

LADY LERODE [*raising her voice to ordinary conversational tones*]. Well, good-bye, Mr. Glayde — you and Muriel must dine with us — you will, won't you? [*He bows* — *they shake hands* — *she goes to* MURIEL.] Good-bye, Muriel, my dear — I'm *so* glad to have seen your husband!

COLLINGHAM [*shaking hands with* DORA]. Good-bye, Dora.

DORA [*eagerly*]. *Isn't* he fine — don't you just love him? [*In a whisper.*] Have you spoken to him yet — about me?

COLLINGHAM [*laughing*]. Heavens! He'd send you to boarding-school! [*She makes a face at him; he laughs, pulls her hair, and goes to* JOHN, *who has been standing, quietly, looking at* MURIEL *and* LADY LERODE.] Good-bye, Mr. Glayde.

JOHN. Good-bye.

LADY LERODE [*shaking hands with* MURIEL]. Nothing, thanks, really — I *must* get home! Oh, Muriel, I *do* hope Mr. Glayde will like Trevor's portrait — don't you? It's very impressionist, of course — but the dear boy *is* so clever! Well — *au revoir!*

JOHN [*stepping forward*]. I'll see you to your carriage.

LADY LERODE. Oh, please! Mr. Collingham will do that!

JOHN. At least I'll escort you to the elevator — I beg your pardon — lift!

[JOHN, LADY LERODE, *and* COLLINGHAM *go;* MURIEL *sits, wearily.* DORA *runs to her and nestles on the arm of her chair.*]

DORA. How lovely to have Uncle John here again! Isn't it, auntie?

MURIEL [*who is staring straight before her, twisting her flowers*]. Of course.

DORA. He's not looking well, auntie: you must be *very* nice to him. Auntie, do you know, when he's there, all the other men seem to have grown quite small, except Mr. Collingham. Auntie, you'll say a word for me and Howard, won't you? Auntie, *am* I too young, do you think?

MURIEL [*wearily*]. Of course. You're only a school-girl.

DORA [*pouting*]. I'm seventeen. All the queens in the history books get married much younger than that.

MURIEL [*fretfully*]. But you're *not* a queen! Don't be silly, Dora, there's a dear child! And don't worry me now — my head aches.

[JOHN *comes back.*]

JOHN. You've a headache, Muriel? I'm sorry.

MURIEL. Oh, it's nothing.

JOHN. Now, Dora, little girl, bedtime! Why, you ought to have been in bed hours ago!

DORA. Uncle! I've *such* a lot to say to you!

JOHN [*laughing*]. It will keep! Goodnight, little girl!

DORA [*kissing him*]. That line's still there, you know! Smooth it away, Uncle, dear! [*She peers into his face:* JOHN *smiles at her.*] That's better! [*She goes to* MURIEL.] Good-night, Auntie! [*She kisses her.*] Oh, I *am* so glad Uncle John's back! Perhaps we shan't see so much of Mr. Lerode now! [*She trips off.*]

MURIEL [*biting her lip*]. The silly girl!

JOHN [*carelessly*]. She doesn't seem to like Mr. Lerode?

MURIEL. She has eyes only for Mr. Collingham. You're sure you want nothing, John?

JOHN. Oh, nothing, thanks — nothing at all. . . . [*He rises.*] Well, Muriel, let me have a look at you. . . . What a long time you've been away!

MURIEL [*dryly*]. Only six months.

JOHN. *Only* six months! It has seemed six years to me!

MURIEL. That's rather sudden, isn't it?

JOHN [*humbly*]. Don't be hard on me, Muriel. I told you I meant to turn over a new leaf. And I will!

MURIEL. You've said that before, more than once.

JOHN. I have, of course. But, this time — well, I had a twinge, a month ago, somewhere about the heart. Bad pain for a quarter of an hour — and the doctors shook their heads. Constitution of iron, they told me — but it seems I was killing myself. Rest imperative, they said — absolute rest — and I could live to a hundred. Well, I rather mean to.

MURIEL. That's wise.

JOHN. I've been quietly getting out of things since then — it's a pity old Huggins, and Marland, and Corby just selected last week for a grand attack on me — all down the line! And it may cost me a million or two. But it shows I'm in earnest, doesn't it, to have left the field like this?

MURIEL. You've lots of millions.

JOHN. Lots! And they haven't done much for us so far, have they? But they're going to.

MURIEL. How?

JOHN. Well, to begin with, we'll have a good time. And then we'll let one or two other people have a good time. There's much to be done, isn't there? And I'll forget all about business — you shall take me to concerts, show me pictures, we'll waltz off to Italy —

MURIEL [*breaking in*]. My dear John, you *are* such a hurricane! I've been in Paris six months — you suddenly arrive and want to carry me off —

JOHN. You don't seem very glad to see me, Muriel!

MURIEL. You're not going to be sentimental, John? I've had four letters from you in those six months.

JOHN. I can't write letters, unfortunately — I've lost the habit! But I've *felt* a great deal. If you knew!

MURIEL [*with a little touch of satire*]. There hasn't been much sentiment in our life these past few years!

JOHN. No, there hasn't. And it has all been my fault — I know that.

MURIEL. It wasn't to please *me*, or because *I* wished it, that you tied yourself to your desk.

JOHN. My dear Muriel, on the steamer, coming across, I've said that to myself, again and again. I realize how much I've neglected you. All I can say is that I'm sorry, and mean to mend.

MURIEL. As I've told you, it's rather sudden. You've become almost a stranger to me.

JOHN [*moving a little closer to her*]. Deal gently with me, Muriel!

MURIEL [*mechanically withdrawing from him*]. You'd like me to be frank and honest, wouldn't you? I could almost count the days that I've seen you, these past two years —

JOHN [*dropping his head*]. Yes — I suppose that's a fact. One doesn't realize it, of course. Having no children, somehow, made a great difference to me. I never spoke of it ... But I threw myself into things. One gets caught in the whirlpool.

MURIEL. And now you come to-night, like a bolt from the blue, and say, let's do this, let's do that, as though we were going off on our honeymoon —

JOHN [*eagerly*]. Why not?

MURIEL [*pettishly*]. Oh, John, don't be absurd! I'm not a railroad, for which you can sign a cheque!

JOHN. You're my wife.

MURIEL. I'm your wife, of course — merely a woman. But even a woman has to be considered a little, I think.

JOHN [*humbly*]. If you knew how full of consideration I am!

MURIEL [*with a movement*]. Well, you don't show it! I resent being hustled like this, and ordered about, and told I must pack up my trunks and rush off to Italy —

JOHN. I'm sorry, Muriel. That's not what I meant.

MURIEL. That's what you said.

JOHN. I only want ... a little ... sympathy, Muriel ...

MURIEL [*with a half laugh*]. Then, my dear John, you must — deserve it! Let me get used to you again! I'm glad to have seen you, of course —

JOHN. You'd say that to your doctor, or lawyer.

MURIEL. I'm glad to have seen you — and, as for the rest — [*With a sudden flash of anger.*] Oh, it's so like a man, to rush into a woman's life, after having absolutely neglected her for years, and then want her to take things up, exactly as they were when he left them!

JOHN [*gently*]. Muriel, I've told you —

MURIEL [*breaking in, eagerly*]. You've told me that you were caught in the whirlpool, as you call it, and to you that justifies all. But what was *I* doing, do you imagine, all that time? Did you ever stop to think how empty and dreary *my* life was?

JOHN. You had all you wanted, Muriel.

MURIEL [*scornfully*]. Diamonds, horses, motor-cars! You thought *they* were enough!

JOHN. You were proud of me, though? When I used to come and tell you —

MURIEL. I was proud of your cleverness, of course. But I wanted more than that.

JOHN. You never told me — you never complained —

MURIEL. I am not the sort of woman to go on her knees to her husband, begging for his love, when he has ceased to care for her.

JOHN [*eagerly*]. That's not true, Muriel!

MURIEL. If it isn't, it looked like it. And how was I to know? When I asked you to come away with me, spend an evening at home — there was a mine, or a tramway, or some new Trust. Love! that died years ago — you killed it — with your millions!

JOHN [*pleading*]. Muriel!

MURIEL [*looking straight before her*]. The loneliness of it, in that big empty house — oh, the loneliness! *I* had no children, either ... You went your way ...

JOHN. Yes, I've been a fool! But, Muriel — have you forgotten how happy we were, at the start, in our little flat at the Adelaide —

MURIEL [*leaning back*]. With the old Irish servant ...

JOHN [*eagerly*]. I'm glad you remember those times!

MURIEL [*shaking her head*]. I remember them as one remembers a dream. It's so long ago!

JOHN. Only twelve years.
MURIEL. Twelve years — a lifetime! I was nineteen then — nineteen! No, my dear John, let's be sensible. We two are very good friends —
JOHN [wistfully]. Only friends — nothing more? Muriel?
[He tries to take her hand, but she laughingly evades him.]
MURIEL. You'll have to begin your courting all over again! [She rises.] And now I must really go to bed — I'm dreadfully tired. I'm sorry I've no spare room to offer you — but you see I've only furnished half the flat so far —
JOHN [who has risen with her]. Don't bother about that — I'll bivouac here on the sofa — I'm an old campaigner.
MURIEL. You'd do better to go back to the hotel, I fancy — but that's as you like. And, if you want anything, one of the men is still up. So good-night.
[She holds out her hand.]
JOHN [taking it, and drawing her a little towards him]. Muriel, you say I must begin my courting all over again —
MURIEL [nodding]. Yes. And you must, too.
JOHN [with an anxiety that he cannot repress]. Is your heart . . . as free . . . as it was . . . in those days when . . .
MURIEL [taking her hand away and forcing a laugh]. Now, John, what a silly question! I'm an old woman — I'm thirty-one! Do you take me for a romantic school-girl? Whom do you think I'm in love with?
JOHN [hesitating]. Well — I don't know — from what you've been saying — there seems no reason — why you — shouldn't be —
MURIEL [merrily]. Except the very trifling one that I'm your wife! Have you forgotten that again?
JOHN [with deep earnestness]. You've been very frank and sincere with me so far, Muriel — I hope you'll continue to be so —
MURIEL [facing him squarely]. Now, what do you mean?
JOHN. I've neglected you all these years — I have, it's quite true — I've been very unwise, very wrong — the blame's all mine — I realize that. — If — [He pauses.]

MURIEL [still maintaining her cheerful tone]. If what?
JOHN [with great difficulty]. If — some other man — had taken my place — in your heart —
MURIEL [with a nervous laugh, that she strives in vain to make seem spontaneous]. My dear John!
JOHN. The fault would be mine — mine — and not — yours.
MURIEL. You seem very anxious that there should be someone! What a pity there isn't!
JOHN [looking into her eyes]. There isn't?
MURIEL [merrily]. My dear John! why do you turn that inquisitor's gaze on me? Oh, I see! [She claps her hands.] That silly little Dora spoke of Mr. Lerode coming so often! Perhaps you're jealous of Mr. Lerode! Oh, do tell!
JOHN. I don't like him.
MURIEL [dryly]. Did any husband ever like the man his wife does? Because I do like him, of course — very much. He and his mother are great friends of mine.
JOHN. And does Lady Lerode —
[He pauses.]
MURIEL. What?
JOHN. Does Lady Lerode — approve of — your friendship?
MURIEL [laughing heartily]. My dear John! Oh, you are lovely! Approve of our friendship! That's splendid, really! Why, she's almost as much a friend of mine as he is!
JOHN. It's he who is painting your portrait, though, isn't it?
MURIEL. Of course. He's a great artist. You shall begin your new career by buying one of his pictures.
JOHN [slowly]. I don't like Mr. Lerode, Muriel.
MURIEL [coldly]. Well, that's a pity, because I do. Good-night.
[She holds out her hand, which JOHN takes in his: he bends over her, and speaks eagerly.]
JOHN. Muriel, before you go — just one word. I'm relieved, of course, to find you only regard him — as a friend —
MURIEL [shrugging her shoulders]. What else?

JOHN. But *he* — is in love with you.

MURIEL [*forcing a laugh*]. What a mad idea!

JOHN. I could see it plainly enough, from the way he resented my being here, from the way he looked at you —

MURIEL [*merrily*]. Oh, John, John! My poor Iron King! Jealous, like an ordinary mortal! And, like an ordinary mortal, imagining all kinds of foolishness!

JOHN. Yes, Muriel, I'm jealous. [*With sudden passion.*] I will not let this man come between us!

MURIEL [*dryly*]. If *that* is the way you intend to begin your courting, John, I can't promise you a happy ending. [*Her voice becomes pleasant and playful again.*] Now be sensible, do! And don't worry me any more to-night — I'm so tired! If it's fine to-morrow I'll call in at the Ritz, and fetch you to lunch. Perhaps, having turned over a new leaf, you *do* mean to lunch now?

JOHN [*with deep earnestness*]. I am at your service now and always. ... Are you sitting to him to-morrow?

MURIEL. I was going to — but I've put him off, as I thought you might want me. [*She goes to the door.*] Good-night, Othello!

[*She kisses her hand lightly to him, and trips off.* JOHN *goes moodily to the table, takes a cigar, bites the end off, puts the cigar in his mouth, unlighted, and stands on the hearthrug, staring in front of him. The curtain slowly falls.*]

CURTAIN

ACT II

JOHN GLAYDE'S *sitting-room in the Ritz Hotel. It is a large apartment, furnished in usual hotel style. Against the wall, on a pedestal, is a telephone; on a small side-table, covered with a white cloth, is a tray with breakfast-things untouched.*

JOHN *is sitting in front of a writing-table, on the top of which, beneath a glass paper-weight, is a pile of cables. He has both elbows on the flap of his desk, and rests his head on his hands.*

MICHAEL SHURMUR *bustles in from the door at back. He is a short, thickset man, wearing spectacles; his hair is very black and lank, and his complexion sallow in the extreme. He wears a thick irregular moustache, of which the ends are gnawn.* JOHN *turns his head slowly as* SHURMUR *comes in.*

SHURMUR [*eagerly*]. Well?

JOHN [*languidly*]. What?

SHURMUR. How about them cables?

JOHN [*with a faint smile*]. Those, Michael — those.

SHURMUR [*lifting the paper-weight*]. You 've not looked at 'em!!

JOHN. No. Not yet.

SHURMUR [*amazed*]. Mercy on us! Then you don't know!

JOHN [*fretfully*]. Tut, tut, what is there to know? These things can wait. I'm not in the mood.

SHURMUR [*wildly*]. They kin wait, kin they? J. J. Longman has given us the skip!

JOHN [*starting to his feet*]. What!!!

SHURMUR. He's gone over to Huggins — Mr. Peter L. Huggins, of Chicago.

JOHN [*his hand nervously gripping the edge of the table*]. Jack Longman!

SHURMUR. I always told you he was a rat. They say Huggins has made him a partner.

JOHN. My sister's son, whom I took in when he was a boy!

SHURMUR [*grimly*]. Well, he's took *you* in, that's all! Read Doherty's cable. [*He ferrets among the pile.*] Huggins has got him. And I guess by this time he knows all about everything.

[*He hands the cable to* JOHN.]

JOHN [*reading it, and muttering to himself*]. Jack Longman! Jack!

SHURMUR. He'll have been reading about Judas belike — always fond of books, he was. What are you going to do?

JOHN [*who has regained his self-control, phlegmatically*]. Do? Nothing. [*He sits.*] We've made our plans.

SHURMUR. Guess you'll have to alter

them now. Longman'll be giving them tips!

JOHN. Bah — let him! They're running their heads against a brick wall, Michael.

SHURMUR. Shouldn't be surprised if they came away with a brick or two, though.

JOHN [*shrugging his shoulders*]. And then?

SHURMUR. All very well for you — but how about the others?

JOHN. What others?

SHURMUR. Them as has pinned their faith and their dollars to the name of John Glayde?

JOHN [*frowning*]. Ah!

SHURMUR. D'you know what they're saying in New York to-day — what the headlines will be in the papers? John Glayde has stolen away — bolted to Europe!

JOHN [*banging his fist on the table*]. What!

SHURMUR. D'you know what Consolidated Stock stands at? It was 102 when we left — last night it closed at 79.

JOHN [*starting to his feet again*]. 79!

SHURMUR. 79. That's the figure.

JOHN [*feverishly*]. It shall go back to-day, Michael! You're right — we must buckle to. Call up London on the telephone — by the Lord, I'll make that crew dance, over there! Call up London — get me on to Tresby — engage the line for me. Jack Longman! Huggins must have made the bribe pretty heavy — well, Huggins shall pay! Michael, all this has been only a little bit of a breeze so far — but there shall be a set-to, now, between Huggins and me, that Wall Street shall stare at!

SHURMUR [*rubbing his hands*]. Good!

JOHN. Huggins doesn't know I've been clearing out of things — Longman doesn't know — he'll be telling them all wrong. Michael, it's war now — till one of us falls — and then, by God, no mercy!

SHURMUR. We're out for blood, and we'll have it.

JOHN. We'll buy every Consolidated share that's offering — we'll buy, and buy. And we'll start an attack, right away, on every concern that Huggins controls. The London market shall have a shock to-day! It's a fight between Huggins and me — I don't care a snap for the others. By the Lord, he has tricked away Jack Longman, has he? Michael, the old man shall go on his knees for this — and eat dirt!

SHURMUR. Won't be the first time either — guess he knows the taste of it. [*He takes a cable form from the desk and sits.*] I'll cable Doherty.

JOHN. No good cabling now — it's six o'clock in New York.

SHURMUR [*writing*]. If I know Patrick Doherty, he'll not have seen the inside of his bed last night. [*He looks up.*] So J. J. Longman didn't know you had cleared out?

JOHN [*haughtily*]. Since when has it been my habit to let my clerks know what I am doing?

SHURMUR [*with a chuckle*]. Mister Longman'd have been tarnation sulky if I had called him a clerk!

JOHN. I made him, and I'll break him. What are you cabling?

SHURMUR [*reads*]. "John Glayde on top and going to roar." Guess that'll do?

[JOHN *nods.*]

SHURMUR [*rising*]. It'll give Doherty an appetite for his breakfast. [*His eyes fall on the tray.*] You don't seem to have had any?

JOHN [*shortly*]. No. Have those things taken away.

SHURMUR. Right. [*He turns to the door.*] I'll go and ring up London.

JOHN [*with a sudden change of voice and manner, his anger dying away and a certain strange nervousness coming over him*]. Have you nothing to tell me?

SHURMUR [*over his shoulder*]. You'll find it all in them cables.

JOHN [*with an effort to make his voice unconcerned*]. Is Mr. Lerode coming here?

SHURMUR [*with a shade of embarrassment*]. Yes.

JOHN. You went there?

SHURMUR. I did. He was in bed.

JOHN. What time is he coming?

SHURMUR. Didn't fix a time — said he'd look in this morning.

JOHN. What sort of place has he?

SHURMUR. What sort?
JOHN. Is he rich, or poor?
SHURMUR. Reckon he squanders his money — but he's got the money to squander. Pays his bills. Has a valet who thinks the world of him. Don't owe no money to his *concierge*.
JOHN. I want Walters. [SHURMUR *goes to the door leading to the bedroom and shouts* "Walters!" *then returns.*] Where does Mr. Lerode live?
SHURMUR. 26, Rue de Trévise. Flat.
JOHN. Studio attached?
SHURMUR. Yes.

[WALTERS *comes in: an elderly valet.*]

SHURMUR. Boss wants you. And take away them things.
[*He points to the breakfast-tray, and goes.*]
JOHN. Walters, how many rooms have I here?
WALTERS. Hotel's very full, sir — I could only get one other sitting-room.
JOHN. Where's that?
WALTERS [*pointing to the right*]. Through there, sir. It's small, but will do for people to wait.
JOHN. Tell the manager I must have another — doesn't matter where it is. I'm expecting three people this morning — Lady Lerode, Mr. Lerode, and Mr. Collingham. I don't want them to meet. You understand?
WALTERS. Yes, sir.
JOHN. I'm to be in to no one else — no one — except, of course, Mrs. Glayde, who may be coming — but not till later.
WALTERS. Very well, sir.
JOHN. And I'm on no account to be disturbed.
WALTERS. I've told them that downstairs, sir.

[*Dora bursts in from the door at back.*]

DORA [*running to* JOHN]. Uncle!
[*She flings her arms round his neck.*]
JOHN [*a little coldly*]. Dora, my dear!
[*He kisses her: then, sternly, to* WALTERS.] See to it, Walters.
WALTERS [*deprecatingly*]. I gave strict orders —

JOHN. Which have been disobeyed.
[*He makes a gesture.* WALTERS *goes, taking out the tray.*]
DORA. You're not angry with me, uncle, for coming to see you?
JOHN. I'm very busy, my child. Lots to do this morning.
DORA. Well, you see — when I found you weren't at breakfast — and I only spoke to Auntie through the keyhole — she wasn't down —
JOHN. She's all right?
DORA. Her head's still bad, she said. Why, Uncle, what*ever* made you come here, instead of —
JOHN. Don't bother, Doffy. You know the flat isn't ready yet.
DORA [*pouting*]. I thought you'd be glad to see me — I did! I dragged that stupid old Fräulein here — and oh, the trouble I had before they'd let me come up!
JOHN. You should have sent in your name, dear.
DORA. *Then* it wouldn't have been a surprise! Uncle John, Uncle John, I want to speak to you, *very seriously*, about Mr. Collingham.

[WALTERS *comes in with a card.*]

JOHN [*taking it*]. Show him in. [WALTERS *goes.*] Here *is* Mr. Collingham!
DORA [*clapping her hands*]. Oh!!! He has come — to speak about me!
JOHN [*grimly*]. I wonder.
DORA. And you mustn't think it's the money, Uncle — he doesn't care about money at all! He's an Oxford man — Oxford University — and he's been a War Correspondent — and he belongs to the Athenæum! That's a club in London, Uncle, that's full of Archbishops!
JOHN [*smiling, in spite of himself*]. Really?
DORA. And he has never made love — oh, never! In fact, it's the one thing I have against him — he *will* treat me as though I were a child! And I'm seventeen — I was seventeen last December — and that's six months ago. Don't *you* think I'm old enough, Uncle?
JOHN. But if *he* has never spoken about love?

DORA [*emphatically*]. Oh never, never!
JOHN. Then how do you know he loves you?
DORA [*coquettishly*]. It doesn't take a woman long, Uncle, to find out whether a man cares for her.
JOHN [*with sudden, deep feeling*]. Oh, you dear little fool! Why this terrible hurry to begin real life? Aren't you happy now? Haven't you all you want? O Dora, Dora, be a girl, and a little girl, as long as you can — you'll be a woman soon enough, and have to go through the mill! It will all come to you, Dora — don't be afraid — it will all come — but don't be in too great a hurry!
DORA [*clinging to him, vaguely understanding*]. Uncle, dear Uncle!
JOHN [*releasing himself gently, and speaking in normal tones again*]. That's all right — you see, a man's a bit of a philosopher! However, don't be unhappy — I like Mr. Collingham.
DORA. Oh, I'm so glad! I —
[WALTERS *comes in with* COLLINGHAM.]
WALTERS. Mr. Collingham.
JOHN. Good-morning, Mr. Collingham.
[*They shake hands.* JOHN *motions* WALTERS *to wait.*]
COLLINGHAM. Good-morning, Mr. Glayde. Ah, Dora!
[*He shakes hands with her.*]
JOHN. Walters, you will take Miss Longman to her governess.
DORA [*pouting*]. Companion, Uncle.
JOHN [*with a smile*]. Very well — companion, then. Good-bye, my child.
[*He kisses her.*]
DORA. Are you coming to lunch, Uncle?
JOHN. If I can get away — I shall be very busy this morning.
DORA. Oh, do come! [*She turns to* COLLINGHAM.] Good-bye, Mr. Collingham.
COLLINGHAM. Good-bye, Dora.
[*She goes with* WALTERS.]
COLLINGHAM [*somewhat embarrassed*]. Mr. Glayde, I feel myself in rather an awkward position — and scarcely know what you can think. Of course, I am fond of Dora — she is a very sweet child — but naturally she *is* only a child, and I'm fully aware —
JOHN [*interrupting him, with a gesture*]. Sit down, Mr. Collingham, sit down. . . . I fancy I know pretty well how matters stand between you two. And it's a thing we needn't discuss — need we? for a year or so. In the meantime we shall become better acquainted. The fact is, that when I asked you to come here, I wasn't really thinking of Dora at all. [*He pauses.*]
COLLINGHAM [*who has sat down, fidgeting*]. Ah?
JOHN. I liked your face when I saw you last night — I liked you — and I wanted to ask you a favour.
COLLINGHAM [*wondering*]. Anything I can do —
JOHN. Will you smoke?
[*He offers him the cigarette-box.*]
COLLINGHAM. No, thanks.
JOHN [*putting the box back on the table, and pacing the room*]. I met you last night for the first time — I saw you for five minutes — I want to treat you as a friend, and be treated as a friend — by you. [*He faces him suddenly.*] Will you?
COLLINGHAM. It's an honour, Mr. Glayde, that I appreciate.
JOHN. Don't let's make phrases. Are you my friend?
COLLINGHAM [*earnestly*]. Yes.
JOHN. That's good, and settled. Now tell me about Mr. Lerode.
[*He sits facing* COLLINGHAM.]
COLLINGHAM [*staring*]. Lerode?
JOHN [*quietly*]. Yes.
COLLINGHAM [*shifting uncomfortably in his chair*]. I don't quite —
JOHN. I want to know what sort of man he is. He's a friend of yours?
COLLINGHAM. Yes — we were at school together.
JOHN. You like him?
COLLINGHAM [*sturdily*]. I do. He's a good fellow — and really a fine artist. Young, of course, with the — exuberance — of youth! The artist's temperament.
JOHN [*dryly*]. What's that?
COLLINGHAM. Oh — excitable, you know — enthusiastic — and so on.
JOHN. I see.

COLLINGHAM. But he's straight — oh, straight as a die! — one can trust his word, implicitly. A bit spoiled, but that's only natural. He lost his father early.

JOHN. What was his father?

COLLINGHAM. A fashionable West End physician, who got a knighthood for something or other. As for his mother — well, you saw her last night — she's the ordinary type of frivolous society woman. In fact, she's a fool. It was a great blow to Trevor when she settled in Paris.

JOHN [*grimly*]. Not even your new Liberal Government will be able to abolish mothers. Go on.

COLLINGHAM. There's really no more to tell! He's wrapped up in his art, of course — he lives for his art — I've never known a man more single-minded, more passionately devoted —

JOHN. He sells his pictures?

COLLINGHAM. He's beginning to find a market — they think highly of him in Paris! — but he's capricious, and often refuses to sell.

JOHN. Why?

COLLINGHAM. He grows so fond of his things!

JOHN. He has money?

COLLINGHAM. A small income of his own, that his father left him. But not much.

JOHN. Mr. Branley is a friend of his?

COLLINGHAM. Oh, yes — they're inseparable.

JOHN. Branley is also a friend of the Princess's?

COLLINGHAM [*awkwardly*]. Yes...

JOHN. Merely a friend?

COLLINGHAM [*half turning away, and shrugging his shoulders*]. I never busy myself with floating gossip.

JOHN. The Prince seems a poor sort of creature?

COLLINGHAM. The usual kind of weedy aristocrat, who sells himself to an American heiress. [*Quickly.*] I beg your pardon!

JOHN. Not at all. Only please don't regard Mr. Huggins as the normal type of the American father. There *is* gossip about the Princess and Mr. Branley?

COLLINGHAM. This is an idle city, and people talk.

JOHN [*incisively*]. They talk about my wife, and Mr. Lerode?

COLLINGHAM [*alarmed, half rising*]. Mr. Glayde!

[JOHN *stops him with a gesture, and waves him back to his chair.*]

JOHN. You've seen Dora a good deal, I suppose, to have grown so fond of her?

COLLINGHAM. Your wife has been very kind to me — I've become almost an *habitué* —

JOHN. As I trust you will continue. Does Mr. Lerode live alone?

COLLINGHAM [*puzzled*]. I beg your pardon?

JOHN. Is it not the custom, in Paris, for artists to have an irregular *ménage?* We are always told so in novels.

COLLINGHAM [*with a shrug*]. Those novels are usually written by Kensington spinsters! Lerode is a man of a curiously refined temperament.

JOHN. In a word, you think a great deal of him?

COLLINGHAM. I do — yes — I like him. His mother has been trying to marry him to a Miss Hamblin —

JOHN. Ah! Who's she?

COLLINGHAM. The daughter of a wealthy English brewer, who has lately been raised to the peerage. She is studying art in Paris.

JOHN. Lady Lerode is trying, you say. Her son refuses?

COLLINGHAM. At least he is reluctant.

JOHN. Why? Is she ugly?

COLLINGHAM. A beautiful girl. And very much in love with him. But one of his reasons is — that she draws so badly!

JOHN. Not an insuperable objection. Is there no other?

COLLINGHAM [*uncomfortably*]. Lerode's not given to speaking much of his affairs.

JOHN. You've seen the portrait?

COLLINGHAM. Oh, yes. It will be fine!

JOHN. It's not finished?

COLLINGHAM. Not yet — no — not quite.

JOHN. Mr. Lerode requires many sittings?

COLLINGHAM. He really is quite a remarkable artist, you know.

JOHN. Yes. So you said. [*He rises —*

so does COLLINGHAM.] Well, Mr. Collingham, I'm exceedingly obliged to you. I appreciate your frankness, and your loyalty to your friend. I trust we shall see a good deal of each other.
COLLINGHAM. With all my heart! By the way, if you'd rather I didn't meet Dora —
JOHN. As often as you please!
COLLINGHAM. The fact is I promised to come to tea this afternoon —
JOHN. Do, by all means. I may be there, perhaps.
COLLINGHAM. Good-bye, Mr. Glayde.
JOHN. Good-bye, Mr. Collingham. And again — thank you.
[*They shake hands.* COLLINGHAM *goes.* WALTERS *comes in.*]
WALTERS. Lady Lerode is waiting, sir.
JOHN [*pointing to the right*]. In there?
WALTERS. No, sir — they've given us another sitting-room round the corner.
JOHN. Bring her in. If Mr. Lerode should come while she's here —
WALTERS. Shall I take him to the next room, sir?
JOHN. No. The other one.
WALTERS. Very well, sir.
[*He goes. The telephone bell rings.* JOHN *goes to it, and puts the receiver to his ear.*]
JOHN. Hullo. You're Shurmur? Well? You can't get on to London? How many are waiting, do you say? Two ladies and a German? Let the ladies have their turn — don't get excited, Michael — and buy the German gentleman off. Let him name his price, and pay it. Right. Good-bye.
[*He replaces the receiver on the hook, as* WALTERS *comes in with* LADY LERODE.]
WALTERS. Lady Lerode. [*He goes.*]
LADY LERODE. My dear Mr. Glayde, how are you? Really, I'm quite in a flutter! I don't know *what* you can think!
JOHN. Won't you sit down? I'm sorry I kept you waiting.
LADY LERODE [*sitting*]. Not at all — though, really, if there had only been one of last year's illustrated papers on the table, I could have imagined myself at my dentist's. The same kind of nervousness!

JOHN [*politely, as he sits, facing her*]. Indeed?
LADY LERODE [*impulsively*]. Oh, Mr. Glayde, it *was* such a relief to see you like that, last night!
JOHN. Like what?
LADY LERODE. Oh, so strong, you know, and so sensible! I've said to myself, again and again, that cable of mine might have caused no end of mischief.
JOHN. The cable — yes. I have it here.
[*He takes out his pocket-book.*]
LADY LERODE [*alarmed*]. Heavens! you keep it in there! How rash!
JOHN [*looking up at her*]. Why?
LADY LERODE. If you left your pocket-book lying about!
JOHN [*with a grim little smile*]. I don't. [*He has taken out the cable, and reads it, very slowly.*] "Lady Lerode's son painting Mrs. Glayde's portrait, strongly advise coming to Paris at once." [*He looks up at her as he folds the cable and puts it back.*] It's cryptic!
LADY LERODE. A shilling a word, you know — and they charged "at once" as two! So horribly expensive!
JOHN [*patiently*]. Very.
LADY LERODE. Well, now you're wondering *why* I cabled you.
JOHN. I am.
LADY LERODE. As I have said, you're magnificently sensible.
JOHN. Thank you.
LADY LERODE. You're a good deal older than Muriel, of course?
JOHN. Nine years.
LADY LERODE [*with a gesture of surprise*]. Only nine! — but I beg your pardon — how rude of me! Well, you see, I want Trevor to marry a Miss Hamblin — a girl who's wildly in love with him —
JOHN [*politely*]. Ah?
LADY LERODE. He *is* so handsome! And her father's a great brewer — or used to be — he turned his business into a company and it's doing very badly, but that's so lucky for him as he sold out and they made him a peer — he's enormously wealthy —
JOHN. These things happen in America, too, but we unfortunately have no peerage.
LADY LERODE. That's *such* a pity, isn't

it? But you see how important it is! He has no son — only two daughters — so the girl is a splendid match.

JOHN [without a sign of impatience]. Quite.

LADY LERODE. And I had arranged it all — brought them together — preached common-sense to Trevor — oh, it wasn't easy, I can assure you! — and then he made friends with your wife — and that spoiled everything!

JOHN. Why?

LADY LERODE. Because Miss Hamblin — silly girl! — became jealous! There's a German gentleman who lectured about Plato in London — I wish he'd come here! Plato should be a great success in Paris! But then, you see, Miss Hamblin's only twenty-two — the all-in-all period —

JOHN. What's that?

LADY LERODE. The age, don't you know, when a girl wants to feel that there isn't a corner in her lover's heart that's not papered with her photograph!

JOHN. Ah.

LADY LERODE. So naturally she resented — [She pauses.]

JOHN. What? Does she think only women should paint women's portraits?

LADY LERODE [with a languid gesture, as she fans herself with her handkerchief]. You're not helping me at all, dear Mr. Glayde!

JOHN. I am trying to, Lady Lerode. Why did you cable for me?

LADY LERODE. I've told you. Miss Hamblin was jealous.

JOHN. And have I been dragged across the Atlantic to pacify a sentimental girl's jealousy?

LADY LERODE. You must have been a little jealous yourself, Mr. Glayde, or you wouldn't have come!

JOHN. I was coming, in any event. And — let me say to you, very simply — not a thousand cables — like this — would in the slightest degree disturb — the confidence I have in my wife.

LADY LERODE [triumphantly]. Of course! Very right and proper! Quite what I should have expected of you! Want of confidence — ridiculous! It's merely that Miss Hamblin — And that's why I complimented you on being so sensible. Because I knew you wouldn't think —

JOHN. I don't. And I didn't.

LADY LERODE [with a great sigh of relief]. Of course not! Well, I shouldn't have cabled, I know. But I did — and you're here.

JOHN [looking quietly at her]. Yes, I'm here.

LADY LERODE [rising]. And there's no harm done, is there?

JOHN. I trust Miss Hamblin will be pleased.

LADY LERODE. The dear child has said to me again and again — if only Mr. Glayde would come!

JOHN. So that the dear child can now be reassured.

LADY LERODE. It will make her very happy — we shall all be very happy! [She finishes buttoning her glove.] Would you like a word of advice?

JOHN [gravely]. I never refuse advice from persons of experience.

LADY LERODE [archly]. I wonder how you mean that! But [she shakes a finger at him] oh, Mr. Glayde, Mr. Glayde, you American husbands who devote all your time to making money, and neglect your wives, and let them go abroad alone, year after year! There are lots of 'em in Paris!

JOHN. So I've heard.

LADY LERODE. I assure you! And they're not all like Muriel — she's such a dear thing — I'm ever so fond of her! But — well, you know, it's not enough for a man to give his wife diamonds, and wonderful clothes — she wants to be told how she looks in them!

JOHN. You will be glad to hear, Lady Lerode, that I intend, in the future, to become a model husband.

LADY LERODE [clapping her hands]. Splendid! And — I can tell you — I wish you were mine! Good-bye! And so many thanks! No — please stay here — it's more prudent, I think, for me to go down alone, we might meet someone! Good-bye!

[She goes, after shaking hands. JOHN stands for a moment, pensive.]

[SHURMUR *bursts breathlessly into the room.*]

SHURMUR. It's all right — we're next — we'll be on in ten minutes.

JOHN. Good. I can't telephone from here, I suppose?

SHURMUR. No. Trunk line's in the manager's office — you'll have to go down. Come now?

JOHN. No need for me to wait downstairs. You've engaged the line?

SHURMUR. Yes.

JOHN. You'll ring me up when it's free.

[WALTERS *comes in with a card, which* JOHN *takes.*]

JOHN. Show him in.

WALTERS. Yes, sir. [*He goes.*]

SHURMUR [*fidgeting*]. Lerode?

JOHN. Yes.

SHURMUR. Hadn't you better let him wait till you —

JOHN. No. I shan't keep him long.

SHURMUR. You'll come at once when I ring?

JOHN. Of course.

SHURMUR. I had to pay that German fellow fifty dollars — he had the nerve to ask five hundred!

[WALTERS *comes in with* TREVOR.]

WALTERS. Mr. Lerode. [*He goes.*]

JOHN. Good-morning, Mr. Lerode. Please sit down. Leave us, Michael.

SHURMUR. You'll come?

JOHN. I've told you. [SHURMUR *goes.* TREVOR *sits.*] Mr. Lerode, I am much obliged to you for your promptness. I trust I have not unduly disturbed you?

[TREVOR *bows, but says nothing.*]

JOHN. I will come straight to the point — I wish to speak to you about Mrs. Glayde's portrait.

[*There is a moment's silence:* TREVOR *is looking fixedly at* JOHN, *waiting for him to continue;* JOHN *goes to his desk, sits, with his back to* LERODE, *and fishes for his cheque-book.*]

JOHN. You are, I know, an artist of considerable distinction; and will, I am convinced, have produced a masterpiece. [*He has found his cheque-book, which he now spreads open before him, and dips his pen in the ink.*] Kindly name the price.

TREVOR [*blankly*]. The price?

JOHN. Your own figure. [*He smiles.*] I shall not haggle!

TREVOR [*nervously*]. The portrait is not finished, Mr. Glayde.

JOHN [*turning slowly in his chair, and facing him*]. It *is* finished, Mr. Lerode.

[*For a moment they look steadily into each other's eyes, then* JOHN *swings himself back, dips his pen in the ink again, and resumes his pleasant, conversational tone.*]

JOHN. And the price? [TREVOR *chokes, but says nothing.*] You don't care, perhaps, to name a price? You prefer to leave it to me? Very well. [*He fills in a cheque, slowly and quietly, which he hands to* TREVOR.] Here.

[TREVOR *takes the cheque, then, his eyes fixed on* JOHN; *he very quietly tears it into small pieces, which he lets drop on the floor.*]

JOHN [*without the least trace of excitement, or emotion*]. A trifle foolish, don't you think?

TREVOR [*with manifest self-control*]. The portrait was not a commission — it was I who asked Mrs. Glayde to do me the honour to sit to me. She was good enough to consent. And, I have told you, it is unfinished.

JOHN [*still in the same pleasant tones*]. I thought that I —

TREVOR [*breaking in, harshly*]. Therefore, in any event, the question of payment is not one that need at present be considered.

JOHN [*quietly*]. That, of course, will be as you wish. You prefer the portrait to remain your property — very well. Only — if, as you persist in assuring me, it is unfinished — what remains to be done must be done — from memory, Mr. Lerode.

TREVOR [*fiercely*]. Indeed?

JOHN. Yes. Mrs. Glayde will not go to your studio any more. And if, under the circumstances, you should carry your resentment so far as to refuse to visit her at the flat — I confess I shall consider you perfectly justified, Mr. Lerode.

TREVOR [*with an effort at calmness*]. Have you Mrs. Glayde's consent?

JOHN [*blandly*]. I beg your pardon?

TREVOR. It is Mrs. Glayde who is sitting to me, and not you. I ask, does Mrs. Glayde consent?

JOHN. That is a point, I fancy, into which we need scarcely enter.

TREVOR [*defiantly*]. There you will allow me to differ. What you have said has no weight with me. I take orders from Mrs. Glayde, and Mrs. Glayde alone.

[JOHN *rises, and moves slowly towards him. The telephone bell rings; as he passes he takes the receiver from the hook and lays it on the top of the instrument; then goes to* TREVOR, *who has also risen, and waits unflinchingly.*]

JOHN [*with perfect calm*]. I can quite understand, Mr. Lerode, that my request may appear somewhat unreasonable to you. But I am a good many years your senior, and I consider it to be wise. Therefore —

TREVOR [*interrupting violently*]. I have never met you till yesterday — I don't know you — I have nothing to do with you. My friendship is with Mrs. Glayde.

JOHN [*his voice for the first time becoming harsh and menacing*]. That friendship has ceased to be. You disappear from her life.

TREVOR [*with a jeer*]. Indeed?

JOHN. I assure you. Because I wish it, and command it.

[TREVOR *laughs out loud.*]

JOHN. That strikes you as amusing?

TREVOR. Intensely! You have a great many millions, Mr. Glayde; I am not aware that they have bought your wife, and I promise you they cannot buy me.

JOHN [*sternly*]. Mr. Lerode —

TREVOR [*breaking in again, bitterly*]. We need not go into the question of how you made those millions, Mr. Glayde; you come from a country where robbery on a very large scale is known as high finance. But your money has no power over me. I do not give up a friendship I value at any man's bidding. Believe it!

JOHN [*for a moment blinded by passion*]. You fool!

[*The door bursts open, and* SHURMUR *rushes in wildly.*]

JOHN [*angrily*]. Michael!

SHURMUR [*frantic with excitement*]. Why don't you come — why didn't you answer? Tresby's at the line — he's waiting —

JOHN. Let him wait!

SHURMUR. There's a panic, I tell you — come, come at once — there's not a minute to lose!

JOHN [*slowly, turning to him*]. A panic?

SHURMUR. Smashes right and left — everything toppling — come!

[*He pulls* JOHN *by the sleeve.*]

JOHN [*after a second's hesitation*]. Mr. Lerode, will you excuse me for a few minutes?

TREVOR [*haughtily*]. By all means.

JOHN. I offer you all my apologies. We will resume our conversation on my return.

[*He goes, with* SHURMUR. TREVOR *shrugs his shoulders, and, with an ironic smile, watches his departure. Scarcely has the door at back closed when the door at the right opens slowly, and* MURIEL'S *head peeps in. Seeing that* TREVOR *is alone, she rushes into the room, leaving the door open, flings her arms round his neck, and kisses him passionately. For a moment they stand locked in each other's embrace — then he breaks away nervously.*]

TREVOR. Muriel! For Heaven's sake! If he — [*He looks anxiously round him.*]

MURIEL. He's gone to his telephone. O Trevor! I heard your voice — I was waiting in there —

TREVOR. He wants me not to see you again!

MURIEL [*feverishly*]. Of course. Well, you mustn't. Tell him you won't!

TREVOR [*aghast*]. What! You consent!

MURIEL. Foolish boy! What else! Promise! Promise everything!

TREVOR [*scarcely believing his ears*]. Muriel!

MURIEL. When he comes back, be conciliatory — say that you'll do it! Have you forgotten that we're in France — that he could challenge you? And he's a dead shot — he'd kill you —

TREVOR [*in despair*]. Let him kill me! Do you think that I —

MURIEL [*stopping him eagerly*]. Hush! We must be quick. Listen. He suspects, of course, but he doesn't know. How should he? He thinks it's friendship, and he's jealous. Well, promise!

TREVOR [*completely bewildered*]. I'm not to go to the house, or you to the studio —

MURIEL [*more and more wildly*]. Promise him, promise him! I tell you he'd kill you! He might kill you now — he carries a revolver always! I fooled him last night — well, it's your turn. He means to stay with me, he says, to devote himself to me. At six o'clock this evening I'll come to you, and we'll go off together.

TREVOR [*mad with joy*]. You will?

MURIEL. Yes — to our cottage at Mantes — they know us there — no one will suspect — we'll live there quietly — he never can find us! That's the safest place. Betsy shall lend us her car, and Chris shall drive us.

TREVOR. Can we be sure of Betsy?

MURIEL. She's spiteful, but true as steel. He can't find us at Mantes — how should he? No one shall know but we four. And we'll stay down there till he's tired of looking for me — he'll soon go back to his Trusts! And, Trevor, Trevor, we'll be together now, always!

[*She throws her arms round him.*]

TREVOR [*embracing her passionately*]. Always, Muriel! For the rest of our life!

[*They kiss each other. Suddenly* TREVOR *sees an arm reaching out from the inner room, and gently, slowly, closing the door. His jaw drops, he starts wildly;* MURIEL'S *eyes follow his — their arms fall mechanically asunder; they stand, trembling with excitement. The door slowly closes.*]

TREVOR [*in a dead whisper*]. Someone closing the door! Who?

MURIEL. I don't know. Wait. Let us think. It'll be Walters — the valet.

TREVOR. He'll tell him we were together.

MURIEL. No — why should he? Besides, he's very deaf, and very stupid. And John doesn't question the servants. I'll go to him —

TREVOR [*eagerly*]. Yes — see whether he knows. . . . Or, listen — why not simply go back, and stay in there till I leave? Then —

MURIEL. You're right, you're right — I will.

TREVOR. You'd better go now. Say nothing to Walters — that's wisest. Perhaps someone else is in there?

MURIEL. I'll look. [*She goes to the door, opens it cautiously, and peeps in.*] No — no one. I'll go. Trevor! At six o'clock! And remember — promise everything!

TREVOR [*sorrowfully*]. Oh, Muriel, it's so hateful, having to tell lies!

MURIEL [*at his side again*]. Do you want him to kill you? Trevor! You will?

TREVOR [*slowly*]. Yes.

MURIEL [*taking his hand and kissing it*]. Till to-night — and then always. Always!

[*She leaves him, at the door she kisses her lips to him; then goes into the inner room, and gently closes the door.* TREVOR *paces to and fro, nervously, looking at his watch, waiting. At last* JOHN *returns.*]

JOHN. Mr. Lerode, I am sorry to have had to leave you —

TREVOR [*with an effort at courtesy*]. It was as well, perhaps. I am afraid I was rather excited . . .

JOHN. We both of us, I imagine, allowed our conversation — to drift from the point at issue. And now — what answer have you to give me?

TREVOR [*slowly*]. My visits — at Mrs. Glayde's flat — shall cease.

JOHN [*with relief*]. Ah! . . . And you will make no attempt to see her?

TREVOR. . . . I shall leave Paris to-night . . .

JOHN. That is undoubtedly wise. Mr. Lerode, before you go — it is due to you — it is due us all — that I should tell you why — I have taken this step . . .

TREVOR [*going to the door*]. It is unnecessary.

JOHN [*stopping him with a gesture*]. You are entitled to an explanation. My wife, like all women, has no idea that — while she is merely your friend — you ... love her ...

TREVOR. I don't think we need say any more, Mr. Glayde.

[*He again turns to the door.*]

JOHN. As you wish. [*With a swift, sudden movement towards him.*] I hope you are dealing straightforwardly with me — I hope it for your sake also!

TREVOR [*turning full on him, and for a moment shaking with passion*]. Mr. Glayde, Mr. Glayde!

JOHN [*coldly*]. Well?

TREVOR [*mastering himself*]. Nothing.

[*He opens the door, and goes.* JOHN *remains standing for a moment, his eyes following* TREVOR — *then he rings.*]

[WALTERS *comes in.*]

JOHN. When Mrs. Glayde comes —

WALTERS [*rather puzzled, pointing to the inner room*]. She must be waiting there now, sir. Shall I —

JOHN. Ah, she has come? All right, Walters. [WALTERS *goes;* JOHN *moves to the door and throws it open.*] Muriel! Have you been waiting long?

MURIEL [*coming into the room*]. I've just come, John. Have I disturbed you?

JOHN [*affectionately*]. Not at all. How are you to-day? Is your head better?

MURIEL. Oh, much better, thanks — much! Are you coming to lunch, John?

JOHN. I'm afraid I must send off a few cables first — my friends on the other side are playing a merry little game with me ...

MURIEL [*genuinely*]. Oh, what a shame! Are they worrying you?

JOHN. It gives me a lot of work, that's all. But I fancy I'll keep my end up! — Muriel [*he takes her hand*], I've seen Mr. Lerode — he was here just now ...

MURIEL [*affecting surprise*]. Mr. Lerode! Then it *was* his voice!

JOHN [*nodding*]. Yes. I sent for him.

MURIEL. Why?

JOHN [*very gently and deprecatingly*]. Muriel, I don't want him to see you any more ...

MURIEL [*laughing*]. My dear John! Othello again!

JOHN [*meekly*]. Yes.

MURIEL [*merrily*]. Oh, you silly man! You've not made a scene?

JOHN. No — he's quite reasonable. . . . Oh, Muriel, can you do this for me? I've no right to ask it, perhaps ...

MURIEL [*not unkindly*]. You certainly haven't! And besides, the portrait's not finished ...

JOHN [*drawing close to her*]. I don't want the portrait — I want *you!*

MURIEL [*with mild reproach*]. Mustn't I have a friend?

JOHN. I'm on my knees to you, Muriel! Of course I know well enough that this friendship is only a — passing whim — but you *do* like him, Muriel —

MURIEL [*pleasantly*]. Oh, yes, I do — very much!

JOHN. And I'm horribly, frantically jealous! [*He drops his voice.*] Because I — love you, love you!

MURIEL [*moving slightly from him*]. My dear John!

JOHN [*taking her hand*]. By the memory of those early days of ours —

MURIEL [*stopping him playfully*]. Tsch, tsch! [*She laughs, and gently withdraws her hand.*] Well, I ought to be furious with you — I ought, indeed! Poor, inoffensive Mr. Lerode! And he consented?

JOHN. Yes.

MURIEL. Really! Agreed not to see me again! Mayn't he even call?

JOHN. I'd rather he didn't.

MURIEL. And he actually agreed?

JOHN. Yes.

MURIEL. Well, *his* friendship wasn't much to boast of! He might have held out a bit longer! Never ask me to sit for my portrait again — that's all! [*She rises.*] Are you coming to lunch, John?

JOHN [*looking at his watch*]. It's only a quarter past twelve — I could be there in an hour. I *must* draft those cables. Muriel, Jack Longman has left me.

MURIEL [*genuinely distressed*]. Jack? Oh, surely not! Impossible!

JOHN. That has hit me rather hard — I loved the boy — there was nothing I wouldn't have done for him . . .

MURIEL. What can have induced him to —

JOHN. I suppose he thought advancement didn't come quickly enough — he's only twenty-four! — and Huggins, they say, has made him a partner. Don't tell Dora yet. We must break it to her . . .

MURIEL [*putting out her hand*]. Oh, John, I *am* so sorry!

JOHN [*taking her hand*]. So be gentle with me! Forgive me!

MURIEL [*pleasantly, letting her hand stay in his for a moment*]. You really don't deserve it, you know! [*She moves from him a little.*] Well — you'll be at the flat in an hour?

JOHN. Yes.

[*He makes a half-movement as though to embrace her — she evades him merrily.*]

MURIEL. I'll put lunch back, then. Au revoir.

JOHN. Au revoir . . .

[*He goes with her to the door, which opens, and* SHURMUR *enters, with a big book under his arm.*]

MURIEL. Ah, Mr. Shurmur, how are you?

SHURMUR. Quite well, thank you, Mrs. Glayde.

[*They look at each other for the briefest part of a second, then* MURIEL *goes.*]

JOHN [*following her with his eyes, then, with a half-sigh, turning to* SHURMUR]. Is that the code-book, Michael?

SHURMUR. Yes. [*He sits at the desk.*] You dictate first, and I'll translate after.

JOHN. Right. [*He sits.*] Are you ready?

SHURMUR. Yes.

[*He has spread a large sheet of paper before him, and prepares to write.*]

JOHN [*dictating*]. "Buy all Consolidated shares offering till the market has reached top figures, also shares of all subsidiary companies —"

[WALTERS *has come in at the beginning of the dictation, and has stood unobserved: he coughs discreetly, to attract attention. He is carrying a small salver, with a card upon it.*]

JOHN [*turning petulantly*]. What is it?

WALTERS [*going to him*]. Beg pardon, sir, this gentleman has called again.

[*He holds out the salver, which* JOHN *waves aside.*]

JOHN [*angrily*]. I told you I would see no one.

WALTERS [*deprecatingly*]. Yes, sir — but it's for Mrs. Glayde — he came half an hour ago —

JOHN [*turning from him*]. Well, she's not here.

WALTERS. He wants to know her address, sir.

JOHN [*dismissing him with a gesture*]. I shall have to consult her first. Say so.

WALTERS [*going*]. Yes, sir.

JOHN [*calling him back*]. Here, you had better give me the card. [WALTERS *returns and hands him the card.* JOHN *takes it.*] Mrs. Glayde hadn't come, of course, when he called before?

WALTERS. Yes, sir, but she was talking to Mr. Lerode.

JOHN [*springing to his feet*]. What!!!

WALTERS [*startled*]. Sir?

JOHN [*wildly*]. She was talking to Mr. Lerode?

WALTERS [*sheepishly*]. Yes, sir . . .

JOHN. How do you know?

WALTERS [*frightened at his violence*]. I went into the waiting-room, sir — the door was open — and I could hear them talking, sir.

JOHN [*harshly*]. Didn't you tell her this man had called?

WALTERS [*more and more embarrassed*]. No, sir . . .

JOHN. Why?

WALTERS [*his eyes on the carpet*]. Sir?

JOHN. I ask you, why didn't you tell her?

WALTERS [*groping for words*]. If you please, sir . . . I didn't think . . . Mrs. Glayde . . . would like to be . . . disturbed, sir. So I closed the door, and —

JOHN [*interrupting him violently*]. That will do. You can go.

[WALTERS *goes, sheepishly.* JOHN *stands rigid, every muscle taut, his hand gripping the chair. There is silence.* SHURMUR, *who has watched keenly through the whole scene with* WALTERS, *has his eyes fixed on* JOHN, *and sucks the top of his pen. Suddenly he turns to the desk again, and dips his pen in the ink.*]

SHURMUR [*in a matter-of-fact tone*]. "Also shares of all subsidiary companies," was where we had got to.

JOHN [*turning passionately on him*]. You know?

SHURMUR [*turning again, and eyeing him squarely*]. Yes.

JOHN. How do you know?

SHURMUR. Everyone knows — they know at his studio — common talk —

JOHN [*frantically*]. What!!!

SHURMUR. No attempt at concealment —

JOHN. And you didn't tell me!

SHURMUR [*after a moment's pause*]. There is some things one man don't tell another.

[*John drops into a chair, and covers his face with his hands.*]

SHURMUR [*turning to the desk again*]. The cable —

JOHN [*bitterly, with a groan*]. The cable!

SHURMUR [*quietly*]. "John Glayde on top, and going to roar," was the message to Doherty.

[JOHN *makes a mighty effort; he rises; the numbed muscles obey him, his hands unclasp; he tries, in a voice he cannot entirely control, a voice that does not seem his, to resume his dictation.*]

JOHN. Also ... shares of ... all ... subsidiary ...

[*He stops; he cannot go on. His head sinks on his chest, his eyes close; he stands motionless. There is silence. The curtain slowly falls.*]

CURTAIN

ACT III

Scene as in Act I. The dining-table is shut up, the windows are open: it is a magnificent June afternoon, and the sun streams into the room.

MURIEL, COLLINGHAM, *and* MRS. RENNICK *are seated:* MURIEL *on the sofa, palpably restless and distraite, and not listening to* MRS. RENNICK, *who is talking volubly.*

MRS. RENNICK. Oh, yes — all the ancient Greek statues were coloured — that's why we really don't understand them, you know. And they say those we have are only cheap copies of the *real* masterpieces — the sort of things, you know, that the Greeks allowed their servants to dust! [*Turning to* MURIEL *for a smile, she notices her inattention.*] Muriel, dear, do I bore you?

MURIEL [*recalled to herself*]. Oh, Helen, of course not! It's *most* interesting!

MRS. RENNICK. You seem so absent, and restless. Has anything —

COLLINGHAM [*who has noticed* MURIEL'S *embarrassment, throwing himself valiantly into the breach*]. Talking of servants, Mrs. Rennick, you remember that wonderful passage in which Xenophon describes the difficulty of getting good housemaids in Athens?

MRS. RENNICK [*shaking a reproachful forefinger*]. Mr. Collingham, Mr. Collingham!

COLLINGHAM [*sententiously*]. I met a man the other day — an oldish man — who told me that, in his youth, he had taken part in an expedition sent out to Peru to search for two ancient wells, known as the springs of Life and Death.

MRS. RENNICK [*throwing up her hands*]. Now what *has* that to do with the use of colour in sculpture?

COLLINGHAM [*blandly*]. Irrelevance, dear Mrs. Rennick, is the fine flower of modern conversation. Don't you remember the Academicians of Laputa, with their wonderful word-machine? One may sometimes, by chance, happen to say something apt.

Mrs. Rennick [*shifting in her chair*]. This is the mood of yours, Mr. Collingham, that I like the least!

Collingham. One should be very tolerant with moods — they reflect the individual. And the question is constant — Am I my mood, or is my mood I?

Mrs. Rennick [*turning to Muriel*]. Oh, Muriel, what *does* he mean? Muriel, you're wool-gathering again!

Collingham. I assure you, Mrs. Rennick, I have no meaning. I am simply turning the handle of the word-machine. Remember that I have to send a whole column every day to the *Courier* — and a column of sense!

Mrs. Rennick [*laughing*]. I hope so.

Collingham. You are pretending now that you don't read me?

Mrs. Rennick. I don't. I hate the papers.

Collingham. You are terribly modern, Mrs. Rennick — you care only for what is ancient. How you would devour the *Times* of Pompeii B.C.!

Mrs. Rennick [*fervently*]. Would I not!

Collingham. Have you ever met the re-incarnation crank? He is usually a very mild man, with silky hair, who neither drinks nor smokes. Tickle him, and he will confide to you what he was doing at the time that Salome danced before Herod.

Mrs. Rennick [*bending forward*]. It's a fascinating theme. I wish *I* could remember!

Collingham. You were probably Sappho,— and your photograph was on picture-postcards. Or Aspasia — who can tell? — and had pleasant evenings with Pericles when he told his wife he was dining at the Club.

Mrs. Rennick [*laughing*]. And what were you?

Collingham. Mrs. Rennick, please tell no one — but I have a profound conviction that I was William the Conqueror — the date 1066 is so strongly impressed on my memory!

Mrs. Rennick [*rising and giggling*]. You *are* a goose! Muriel — [Muriel *starts and rises*]. Muriel, I'm afraid I can't stay —

though I *should* so have liked to meet Mr. Glayde again. But you'll give me another chance, won't you?

Muriel [*shaking hands with her*]. Of course — He has been fearfully busy to-day — a lot of cables to send.

Mrs. Rennick. Remember me to him. [*She turns to* Collingham.] Ah, Mr. Collingham, you see I *do* admire Mr. Glayde, though he *is* modern! Good-bye. [*She shakes hands with him.*] And next time we meet — *please*, be sensible.

[*She goes.* Muriel *presses the bell,* Collingham *has held open the door. He returns.*]

Muriel [*sinking into a chair*]. What a relief!

Collingham [*sitting close to her*]. I thought you were rather anxious that she should go.

Muriel. She's a dear creature — but she got on my nerves to-day. How splendid you were!

Collingham. I turned on the nonsense-tap. Women hate nonsense almost as much as they do politics. [*With a sudden change of manner, his voice becoming friendly and solicitous.*] What's the matter?

Muriel [*abruptly*]. Nothing. Why?

Collingham [*bowing*]. I apologize — there's nothing the matter. Shall I go or stay?

Muriel. Stay, please, till Betsy comes. [*With a glance at the clock.*] She's late ...

Collingham [*abruptly*]. I saw Mr. Glayde this morning.

Muriel [*surprised*]. You saw him?

Collingham. Yes: he told me to call.

Muriel [*uneasily*]. Why? [*With a sigh of relief.*] Ah, of course — about Dora!

Collingham [*thoughtfully*]. He doesn't seem especially to object to my being friends with Dora. He asked me a question or two about the portrait.

Muriel [*startled*]. The portrait?

Collingham. And about Mr. Lerode. I think your husband's a splendid fellow, Mrs. Glayde. I like him tremendously.

Muriel [*indifferently*]. I'm glad.

Collingham [*fingering his gloves, and looking away from her*]. Dora will never marry me, you know — she is merely trying her wings on me; it is my privilege to be Number 1 on the list. She flashes a smile on me, and records the effect: I am the preface to the book she will some day write on love.

MURIEL [*carelessly*]. You think that?

COLLINGHAM [*nodding*]. Yes. And do you know why I mention it to you?

MURIEL. I've no idea.

COLLINGHAM. Because I've a suspicion that Nature intended me for an uncle. One of my shoulders is a little higher than the other — evidently for women to hide their heads on it while they . . . tell me things . . .

MURIEL [*wearily*]. Dear Mr. Collingham, do you want to drive me away, too? I'm like the rest of the women, you know: I don't care for nonsense.

COLLINGHAM [*with sudden earnestness*]. Well, then, I'll be very serious for a moment. I've seen the cloud that was no bigger than a man's hand — I saw it this morning . . . I am very fond of you, Mrs. Glayde — I am your friend —

MURIEL [*simply*]. Thank you.

COLLINGHAM [*looking intently at her*]. I am John Glayde's friend, too, and John Glayde's a fine man . . . [*He pauses, then reverts to his light tone.*] I wonder whether I hobnobbed with Socrates in my last incarnation but one? Anyhow, I know this — that one must be wise to be happy.

MURIEL [*impatiently*]. You give that with the air of a discovery!

COLLINGHAM. It's one of those little truths that are like America, you know — which had been there all the time — but Columbus was a fairly old man when he discovered it. . . . And now I've said all I have to say. [*He rises.*] I hear a piano. Can that be Dora?

MURIEL. They furnished two more rooms this morning.

COLLINGHAM [*listening*]. She's playing the Moonlight Sonata. How they love the moon when they're seventeen! At twenty-five, sunshine and Wagner — at forty, Chopin and candles.

[*The* PRINCESS *comes in.*]

COLLINGHAM. Ah, here's the Princess at last! I was just going to Dora to tell her that she's playing Beethoven as though it were Sousa. How is your Excellency to-day?

PRINCESS. My Excellency is well. And your Impertinence?

COLLINGHAM [*with a bow*]. Princess, when you think me impertinent, I am merely blatant modesty, masquerading!
[*He goes.*]

MURIEL [*excited*]. Betsy, Betsy, I've been in a fever, waiting for you!

PRINCESS. Sorry I couldn't come before — I was out. [*She sits.*] What's up?

MURIEL. I want you to lend me your motor.

PRINCESS. Yours out of order?

MURIEL [*at the Princess's side*]. Betsy, I'm going off with Trevor to-night —

PRINCESS [*with a jump*]. What!

MURIEL. To the cottage we have at Mantes — we'll stop there till the excitement's over.

PRINCESS [*staring*]. Are you mad?

MURIEL. We've been to it twice for a couple of days — so the people won't think it strange our staying down there — they know us, you see. And with the exception of you and Chris there's not a soul who has heard of the place — not even Trevor's valet. So we shall be safe there — and he never can find us.

PRINCESS. He? Your husband?

MURIEL [*nodding*]. And let's be quick — he may come any moment. There's an At Home at the Embassy this afternoon — the card's on the mantelpiece — I'll tell him I'm going there — I'll stop the carriage at one of those houses with two doors, take a cab, and go on to Trevor's. You'll send your car, and Chris shall drive us to Mantes.

PRINCESS [*throwing up her hands*]. Mad as a hatter!

MURIEL. Perhaps — but that can't be helped. What else can I do?

PRINCESS. What else? Why anything but that! My child, that means ruin!

MURIEL [*with a gesture of despair*]. Oh, Betsy, for Heaven's sake don't preach!

PRINCESS [*slowly*]. Preaching's not exactly in my line — and I guess the wings would have to be sewn pretty tight on an archangel for them not to come off after living a week with my Prince. But it can't be done, Muriel, my girl.

MURIEL [*fretfully*]. Betsy!

PRINCESS. Can't be, can't be. What's the use of throwing your bonnet over the windmill? You won't catch it the other side.

MURIEL [*with feverish eagerness*]. Betsy, do you understand? He came back last night — and he wants things to be as they were — and he talks of honeymoons! — He's jealous of Trevor...

PRINCESS. Don't blame him. Well?

MURIEL. He sent for him to-day — forbade him the house —

PRINCESS. Shows he's only jealous, and don't know anything.

MURIEL. He'll soon find out.

PRINCESS. Husbands never do.

MURIEL. He has that man Shurmur with him — and Shurmur knows — I could see that by the way he looked at me. And he'll tell John — if he hasn't told him already. And I'm frightened — he said he'd come to lunch —

PRINCESS. And didn't he?

MURIEL. No — he telephoned through he'd be very late.

PRINCESS. Did he give any reason?

MURIEL. It was Shurmur telephoned.

PRINCESS [*shaking her head*]. H'm... But see here — John Glayde's a very square man — he has neglected you all these years —

MURIEL [*feverishly*]. He'd forgive me, perhaps, but he'd kill Trevor.

PRINCESS. It's only in French plays that they kill lovers.

MURIEL [*wringing her hands*]. Betsy, don't! Can't you see what I am feeling? At least don't make fun of it!

PRINCESS [*stolidly*]. I'm not making fun. There'll be no killing if you give up Trevor.

MURIEL [*wildly*]. Give him up?

PRINCESS. Why not?

MURIEL. Because I love him, and can't live without him — can't live.

PRINCESS. Trevor's all right, but he don't hold a candle to John.

MURIEL. I love him.

PRINCESS. He's younger than you.

MURIEL. Three years.

PRINCESS. Three years is a lot. And he's a painter, you know — he raves about your soul, but it's your face he looks at.

MURIEL. I know, I know! You needn't tell me that it won't last for ever!

PRINCESS. For ever! Say eighteen months.

MURIEL [*putting her hands to her ears*]. Don't, Betsy, don't! It may be true — it will be, perhaps — I can't help that — I love him!

PRINCESS. You used to love John.

MURIEL. If he hadn't left me — If I'd had a child, or hadn't met Trevor — Well, it's too late for that, now. He'd kill him!

PRINCESS. I tell you he wouldn't! Give up Trevor!

MURIEL [*staring angrily at her*]. Betsy!

PRINCESS. Yes — give him up! Not morals, my dear — I'm not a moralist, worse luck — wish I were! But —

MURIEL [*with feverish determination*]. The car must be at Trevor's studio at six.

PRINCESS [*quietly*]. It shall be, of course, if you wish it. But you won't.

MURIEL [*her hands to her head*]. Oh, you'll drive me frantic!

PRINCESS. Take a week to consider.

MURIEL. A week! And what would happen, do you think, in that week?

PRINCESS. The sun would rise every morning, and set every evening. And you'd alter your mind.

MURIEL. I had to lie to him yesterday — I had to lie to-day, and shall have to again, I suppose.... Lies, lies, I've been living in lies! No! — I'll make an end. He's proud — he'll just fold his arms, and say nothing —

PRINCESS. He's not a man to talk much — but what will he do?

MURIEL. He won't be able to find us, if he should try.

PRINCESS. There's Shurmur.

MURIEL. I tell you no one can trace us down there! It's safer than trying to get on board a steamer. And, besides, Trevor can work.

PRINCESS. And you — what will you do? There are weeks, and then years —

MURIEL. I? Never mind about me. I'm done for!

PRINCESS [*throwing up her hands*]. And to think of the lots of people there are in the world, who imagine we're awfully happy, because we're rich!

MURIEL [*with a sigh*]. Yes...

PRINCESS [*with sudden energy*]. Muriel, just sit tight for two minutes, and let me talk. My father married me off to a scoundrel, a blackguard, a beast — well, *I'm* what they've made me. *You* married for love —

MURIEL. That's long ago — and he killed it!

PRINCESS. He has come back to you — give him a chance!

MURIEL [*fretfully*]. Betsy!

PRINCESS. He deserves it all — he has no right to reproach you — he has brought it on himself. And I tell you you'll find him big — he'll not beat his bosom, or squeal. Make a clean breast of it, Muriel — just go and tell him the truth. Let Trevor go back to his paint-pots, and you hunk off to Egypt with John.

MURIEL [*doggedly*]. I love Trevor.

PRINCESS. Trevor's a boy, and will change.

MURIEL. I love him.

PRINCESS. John's a good fellow — I wish *I* had married him! I'd have run straight as a die!

MURIEL [*with a wail*]. Oh, don't you see? Have you no pity? He *is* a good fellow — no one knows *how* good he is! And he's cut to the heart to-day, because his nephew has left him — Jack Longman, you know, Dora's brother. And he's sick, and he's sorry — and when he told me this morning I'd have liked to throw my arms around his neck —

PRINCESS. Why didn't you?

MURIEL. Because I love Trevor — and he must come first — before everyone! I can't reason, or argue — I love him! Oh, Betsy, don't say any more! You mean well, and I'm grateful. The time will come, I dare say, when I'll wish I had listened to you!

PRINCESS. It will.

MURIEL. But — I can't give him up!

[*A moment's silence — the* PRINCESS, *with a shrug, gives up her attempt to persuade.*]

PRINCESS. At what time do you want the car?

MURIEL. At six — at the studio.

PRINCESS [*with deep feeling*]. You're the one woman I care for — the one friend I have —

MURIEL [*with an instinctive movement towards her*]. Betsy!

PRINCESS. And I see you, with your eyes open, making a hash of things, and I can't stop you. It's hard luck!

MURIEL [*with a look at the clock*]. Is he coming at all, I wonder? It's nearly five. I must go and get ready, in case ... You'll wait?

PRINCESS. If you like.

MURIEL. If he comes while you're here, find out whether he knows.

PRINCESS. What's the use? Besides, I shan't be able to stop very long, if I'm to see about the car.

MURIEL. No, that's so. Well, good-bye, Betsy! [*She kisses her.*]

PRINCESS. I'll come down to Mantes.

MURIEL. Don't — you might be followed — Shurmur'll try everything. Good-bye.

[*She kisses her again.*]

PRINCESS. O Muriel — think!

MURIEL [*shaking her head*]. It's no good, Betsy — I must!

[*She goes.* BETSY *stands, with an unhappy look on her face.*]

[*After a moment, a footman enters with* BRANLEY.]

FOOTMAN. Mr. Branley. [*He goes.*]

BRANLEY [*very excited*]. Ah, Betsy! I thought I might find you here. I've just left Trevor. You've heard?

BETSY [*dryly*]. Yes.

BRANLEY. A nice state of things! Glayde called twice at the studio, before Trevor came in —

PRINCESS. Oh! That's bad.... And Trevor's as crazy as she, I suppose?

BRANLEY. I've argued, and prayed — it's no use.

PRINCESS. Same here. Well, you'd better not wait — John Glayde may come any moment — and I'm not at all sure that he thinks very highly of *you.*

BRANLEY [*puffing himself out*]. Preposterous!

BETSY [*eyeing him contemplatively*]. Not sure that I do, either. Well, you're to drive them to-night, and bring back the car —

BRANLEY. A mercy that Trevor was out, when Glayde called — wasn't it?

PRINCESS [*dryly*]. I wonder!

BRANLEY [*amazed*]. Betsy!

PRINCESS [*impatiently*]. Go, go. I'll look in myself at the studio, later. Don't wait.

BRANLEY [*protesting*]. Really, Betsy! —

PRINCESS [*coldly*]. I've told you to go.

[BRANLEY *shrugs his shoulders, and goes. In the corridor his voice is heard, off, as he says "How d'you do" to* JOHN GLAYDE, *whom he meets.*]

[JOHN *comes into the room, alone. His face is white and haggard, but he betrays no sign of emotion.*]

JOHN. Ah, Princess! [*They shake hands.*] Where's Muriel?

PRINCESS. She's gone to change her dress — there's an At Home at the Embassy this afternoon.

JOHN [*carelessly*]. Ah.

PRINCESS [*with an effort at flippancy*]. Not been ruining my Poppa, have you?

JOHN [*sternly*]. Don't let's talk about him.

PRINCESS. Why?

JOHN. He has got hold of a nephew of mine — a boy I was fond of.

PRINCESS. Oh, it's *he* who has done that! Muriel told me — I didn't know it was Poppa.

JOHN. Yes.

PRINCESS [*earnestly*]. Well, I'm sorry. I wish it hadn't been Poppa. Don't seem quite square, somehow. I'm real sorry, Mr. Glayde.

JOHN. I was fond of the boy.

PRINCESS. Muriel told me — she was quite cut up.

JOHN [*lifting his eyes to her*]. She was?

PRINCESS. Quite.

JOHN [*dropping his eyes again*]. Ah.

[*There is silence; the* PRINCESS *fidgets, and goes to him.*]

PRINCESS. Well, I'll leave you — I've lots to do. [*She holds out her hand.*]

JOHN [*taking it, with a keen look at her*]. You've known Muriel a long time?

PRINCESS. Ten years, off and on.

JOHN. You've been her friend?

PRINCESS. I have. Why?

JOHN [*dropping her hand*]. Oh, nothing! I've been out of her life so long — I scarcely know who her friends are.

PRINCESS [*with a touch of anger*]. Yes — you've been out of her life — you've stuck your nose to the grindstone, and merely gone for making money. Like my Poppa.

JOHN. Yes.

PRINCESS. My mother died when I was ten. I've seen quite a deal of Poppa — when he was ill. But that wasn't often.

JOHN. It's a rotten system.

PRINCESS [*with sudden impulsiveness*]. John Glayde, be very kind to Muriel!

JOHN [*looking up again, with some surprise*]. I mean to. Why do you tell me?

PRINCESS [*embarrassed*]. I don't know — it just bubbled up. You've been very cruel.

JOHN. How?

PRINCESS [*stamping her foot*]. How? You cared more for money than you did for your wife.

JOHN [*quietly*]. That's not so.

PRINCESS. We women don't analyze motives, and things — we go hard for facts. She's been in Paris six months — you wrote four times!

JOHN. I was busy.

PRINCESS. Yes — that's the cry of the American husband. Oh, it makes me tired!

JOHN. One can't undo the past.

PRINCESS. No . . . Well, be very kind to her . . . [*Impulsively.*] Are you going with her to the Embassy this evening?

JOHN. I've not been asked.

PRINCESS. As though John Glayde needed an invitation! Good-bye.

[*She holds out her hand again.*]

JOHN [*taking it, and for an instant holding*

it in his]. Good-bye, Princess. [*With a keen glance.*] Is there anything you want to tell me?

PRINCESS [*forcing a laugh*]. Gracious, what should there be! . . . I'm real sorry about your nephew. Good-bye.

JOHN. Good-bye.

[*As she goes,* DORA *and* COLLINGHAM *come in, talking and laughing.*]

PRINCESS. Ah, Dora [*she pats her cheek*], I'm just off — good-bye. Good-bye, Mr. Collingham. I'd think twice before I married him, Dora — he's very cheeky.
[*She goes.*]

DORA [*running to* JOHN, *who has sat down, and throwing her arms round his neck*]. Oh, Uncle John, how tired you look!

JOHN. Yes, I'm tired. And it has been so close to-day. How are you, Mr. Collingham? [*He nods to him.*]

COLLINGHAM [*with an anxious look at* JOHN]. One of those uncomfortable days when the air seems to have been filtered through hot flannel!

DORA. They've furnished two more rooms — you'll stay with us now, Uncle, won't you?

JOHN. We'll see. Dora, dear, run and tell your aunt I'm here.

DORA. Yes, Uncle John.

[*She kisses him and goes. There is silence.* JOHN *has his eyes fixed on the ground.* COLLINGHAM *is uncomfortable and restless.* JOHN *suddenly raises his eyes and looks at* COLLINGHAM.]

JOHN. Did you tell Mrs. Glayde of my talk with you?

COLLINGHAM [*after a second's pause, sturdily*]. Yes.

JOHN. Why?

COLLINGHAM. I'm quite a good friend of hers. And I didn't think you'd blame me.

JOHN. I don't. [*He drums his fingers on the table.*] You weren't very frank with me this morning?

COLLINGHAM [*uneasily*]. I don't understand . . .

JOHN [*bitterly*]. I have money enough to buy cities — there are things one cannot purchase!

COLLINGHAM [*eagerly*]. Don't forget what I told you about the idle gossip in Paris . . .

JOHN. You're a good fellow, Collingham. [*He stretches out his left hand, without looking at him.*]

COLLINGHAM [*taking it*]. Good-bye, Mr. Glayde.

JOHN. Good-bye. Give me your card — I may need you. [COLLINGHAM *takes a card out of his case, and gives it to him.*] You'll be in to-night?

COLLINGHAM [*hesitating*]. Yes — but —

JOHN [*with a gesture*]. Good-bye.

[COLLINGHAM *goes, with bent head.* JOHN *remains in his chair, his hands hanging limply down.* DORA *comes running back.*]

DORA. She'll be here in a minute, Uncle John — and she *does* look so lovely! — Why — where's Mr. Collingham?

JOHN. He's gone.

DORA. Gone! You've not quarrelled?

JOHN. Quarrelled! No. I like him.

DORA [*eagerly*]. I'm so glad! Uncle John, I can't tell you how good he is! He never says an unkind thing about any one, and he won't let me. He — [MURIEL *has come in —* DORA *hears the rustle of* MURIEL'S *dress, and turns.*] Oh, there's Auntie!

[*She jumps up and runs to* MURIEL, *who stands nervously at the door. She is splendidly gowned: her arms are bare to the elbow, the dress is cut rather low at the neck. In her hand she carries long, white gloves, that she unconsciously is twisting.* JOHN *does not stir, or look at her.*]

DORA [*prancing around her*]. Oh, what a splendid dress! Auntie, I'll have a dress like that next year — mayn't I?

JOHN [*with a half-turn towards* DORA]. Leave us, Dora.

DORA [*pouting*]. Uncle! Must I?

JOHN. Yes.

[DORA *goes, a little petulantly. There is constrained silence till the door closes; then* MURIEL *moves slowly towards him, and speaks, with manifest effort to keep her voice natural.*]

MURIEL. You're fearfully late, John — you couldn't come sooner, I suppose? [*He doesn't turn or look at her; his head is bent, and his eyes fixed on the ground.*] You've sent off your cables? . . . I've this tiresome affair at the Embassy . . .

JOHN [*still without looking at her, in a low, broken voice*]. I . . . know, Muriel . . .

MURIEL [*starting*]. What do you mean?

JOHN. I . . . know . . .

MURIEL [*forcing a laugh*]. You know what? John, this is absurd!

[*He slowly raises his eyes and looks at her. She mechanically retreats a step, but preserves her cheerful tone.*]

MURIEL. That silly Walters will have told you that I was talking to Mr. Lerode?

JOHN [*slowly*]. Yes . . .

MURIEL [*laughing again*]. And you imagine from that —

JOHN. No, not only from that . . .

MURIEL. You surely don't think —

JOHN [*springing to his feet, in an outburst of wild passion, and seizing her by the wrist*]. I tell you I know!

[*They look into each other's eyes for a second; he releases her: she totters back, sinks on to the sofa, and buries her face in her hands.*]

JOHN [*the whirlwind of passion dying away, his voice becoming dull and mechanical, as he stares vaguely at her*]. Don't cry — what's the use? I'm to blame, more than you . . . I left you to pick up dollars in the gutter . . . Well, I've got them — and lost you . . .

[*She lies crouched in a heap, an occasional sob breaking from her; he still stares dully at her.*]

JOHN. I stand alone, with my millions stinking around me. . . . Don't cry. . . . You couldn't tell that I loved you — that you were all I had. . . . It's not your fault. . . . I did nothing but work — it grew like a cancer. I was John Glayde, the Iron King, who endowed hospitals and universities — John Glayde, the great man whose name was in all men's mouths — John Glayde, the miserable fool, who has thrown away — you!

[*She stirs restlessly — half-raises herself as though to speak, then lets herself fall heavily back again, and sobs afresh. Her emotion is genuine, in face of his great sorrow.*]

JOHN [*with sudden passion*]. And now, if he could tear his flesh, or lop off an arm — barter the years he has left for a week with you — sell all the world, trade his money, his future, his brain, to hear you tell him you loved him . . . [*He beats his clenched fists against his forehead.*] Madman, madman!

MURIEL [*appealing, through her sobs*]. John!

JOHN. She cabled me, the woman, his mother —

MURIEL [*catching her breath*]. What!

JOHN. And I threw everything up and sailed. Would you believe it? I had never had a suspicion. We don't take out our lungs to see whether they are breathing — you were in there [*he raps his fist against his heart*] — in me, part of me. . . . Then came the cable. . . . And the week on the steamer. . . . Pacing the deck, to and fro — people there, to whom I must talk, and smile. . . . "Painting Mrs. Glayde's portrait, come at once — come at once — come at once." . . . And the boat crawling along, and the sea all around me. . . . And I saw him painting, and looking at you. . . . I saw you there with him, smiling into his eyes, telling *him* that you loved him — [*in a paroxysm of fury.*] By God, he shall pay!

MURIEL [*springing to her feet, and, in her excitement and fear, laying a hand on his arm*]. What will you do to him?

JOHN [*furiously*]. What will I do, to this painter who seduces his sitters — what will I do? [*She shrinks from him, and trembles, but never takes her eyes off him.*] Don't be afraid — I shan't harm *you*. I suppose women are like that. It was *my* fault that you no longer loved me.

MURIEL [*desperately, with sudden resolve*]. That's not true.

JOHN [*staring at her*]. What do you say?

MURIEL [*breathless*]. Not true — no. Will you listen — will you hear?

JOHN. Go on.

MURIEL. Before you came — long before — it was all over — all.

JOHN. What!!!

MURIEL [*feverishly*]. A moment of madness — I was alone, I was lonely — how could I tell that you cared for me? You never wrote, I never saw you.... Yesterday, when you came in, what do you think my one fear was, my one desire? That you never should know.... So to-day I went in and told him — told him I never would see him again — that you were here now, were going to stay with me — that you would protect me —
JOHN. Muriel!
MURIEL [*dropping her voice*]. You spoke of our honeymoon yesterday, you spoke of our early days — there was I with this load upon me, with my crime.... Between him and me all has long been over.... But I had to go on with the portrait — had to receive him, or people would talk.... [*Slowly.*] You came back, and spoke of our honeymoon — did you think *I* had forgotten?
JOHN [*dazed*]. Muriel — Muriel, Muriel! Is this true?
MURIEL [*going close to him*]. Look at me — look — look into my eyes — and see whether I'm speaking the truth!
 [JOHN *stares at her, scarcely believing his ears — she meets his gaze unflinchingly, almost with a smile; and then, with her eyes on his, she slowly draws him to her as she puts her arms round his neck. He shudders at first; at the touch of her flesh on his he yields, and sinks his head on her shoulder.*]
MURIEL [*one hand close to the head that lies on her shoulder*]. Can you forgive me? More than forgive — blot it out? I'll go away with you — Italy, anywhere — we'll be together. Leave the hotel — stay here. ... John, shall it be?
JOHN [*raising his head*]. Yes...
MURIEL. You will forgive me?
JOHN. Yes...
MURIEL. And shall we forget, and begin all over again?
JOHN [*wildly and passionately*]. Yes! Yes! Yes!
 [*He tries to take her in his arms — she evades him, with a warning forefinger.*]

MURIEL [*with a glance at the clock*]. It is half-past five — I must go to the Embassy —
JOHN [*eagerly*]. No, no!
MURIEL [*for a second contracting her eyebrows*]. I must. For an hour — that's all —
JOHN [*fondly*]. I'll go with you...
MURIEL. No, no, I'll go alone. I'll tell you why.... When I come back we shall meet as we used to meet — forget this horrible thing, never speak of it again —
JOHN [*clinging to her*]. It *is* forgotten, Muriel! Don't go — stay with me! I can't let you leave me — now!
MURIEL [*slowly, picking her words*]. I want to go out, be with people — come back, find you here — you, my husband, my [*she puts both hands to his head, swings it to her, and kisses him full on the lips*] — my lover!... Shall I not go?
JOHN [*intoxicated, in a whisper*]. Yes, Muriel, yes!... But come soon!
MURIEL [*solemn in her triumph*]. In an hour. And you'll remain here — you'll not stir from this place?
JOHN. I shall be here, counting the minutes, till you return.
 [*She takes his head again with both hands, and solemnly, possibly for the first time with a feeling of remorse, she kisses him on the brow.*]
MURIEL. Good-bye!
 [*She goes.* JOHN *follows her with his eyes; as the door closes, he sits, lets his hands fall by his side, and waits.* DORA *puts her head in at the other door and trips into the room.*]
DORA [*running to him*]. Well, Uncle, have you been nice to her? You've not scolded?
JOHN [*stroking her hair*]. No, Doffy — no.... Dora, I've some bad news for you...
DORA [*alarmed*]. Uncle!
JOHN. About your brother.
DORA [*clinging to him*]. He's not dead?
JOHN. No, no — he's well, he's quite well. But he has gone from me, Dora — left me —
DORA [*amazed*]. Left you! why?
JOHN. To make more money, I suppose

or make it more quickly. Mr. Huggins of Chicago — an enemy of mine — offered him a partnership, and Jack has gone.

DORA [*in despair*]. Oh, how wicked! After all you've done — for him, and me!

JOHN [*gently*]. The way of the world, Doffy! And I'm not sure that he has been — in a very good school... He has seen too much cutting of throats among us — we've none been over-nice, or over-scrupulous. It's a blow to me, Doffy — but I've no right to complain.

DORA [*crying*]. And will you still... keep me with you, Uncle?

JOHN [*drawing her tenderly towards him*]. My poor little girl! *You* can't help your brother leaving me! And besides — I've brought it on myself — I know that. If he wants to come back to me, he shall. I'll forgive him... too...

DORA [*burying her head on his shoulder*]. Uncle, dear Uncle!...

JOHN [*looking straight before him, as he mechanically strokes her hair*]. I've played with edged tools, and mustn't complain if one of them cuts me. I've thought myself very wise all these years — cared too much for this wretched money and the power it brought me — I didn't see that I was digging up my own happiness, building myself a great pedestal, on which I'd have to stand — alone. But at least I've found it out in time, before it was too late; and I'm going to make a change. And Jack, poor foolish Jack, who has hit me so hard — Jack shall find that I bear him no grudge, that I take it as my punishment, Doffy... for I deserve to be punished... but I mean to do better in future...

[*She vaguely realizes the sorrow in his voice, and throws her arms round him. For a second he holds her close to him; then* SHURMUR *rushes wildly into the room.*]

SHURMUR [*breathless*]. Why did you let her go?

JOHN [*starting to his feet*]. Michael!

SHURMUR [*pouring out his words*]. She stopped the carriage at a shop fifty yards away — went right through, took a cab, and gave his address —

JOHN [*staggering*]. What!!!

SHURMUR. *His* address! Yes, I tell you — yes!

JOHN [*with a roar of mad anger, seizing* SHURMUR *by the shoulders and shaking him in his agitation*]. Michael Shurmur, Michael Shurmur!

DORA [*running to him*]. Uncle!

[*Without looking at her, he seizes his hat and rushes wildly from the room.* DORA *turns, crying, to* SHURMUR *who is about to follow him.*]

DORA [*wringing her hands*]. Oh, Mr. Shurmur, what has happened?

CURTAIN

ACT IV

TREVOR LERODE'S *studio. To the left is a door opening on to a paved way, on each side of which are laurel-trees in buckets. At the end of this way is an iron gate, flanked by a low stone wall; beyond is a fairly broad road, with houses on the other side. In the studio there is a long, high window at back, looking on to the garden, which is neglected, with rank grass growing, but there are a few trees in full bloom. To the right is a door leading to another room, through which the garden can be reached. The studio has an arched roof, culminating in a top-light. The floor is stained, and covered sparsely with a few rugs. There is a sitter's platform, two or three easels, and some high-backed, antique chairs. On the wall are three or four foils, and a couple of fencers' masks. The aspect of the place is distinctly severe — it is pre-eminently a worker's studio — and there are no fal-lals or fripperies.*

As the curtain rises, CHRISTOPHER BRANLEY *is seated in a great armchair, puffing at his pipe, his legs stretched out before him.* TREVOR, *in his shirtsleeves, is kneeling on the ground, strapping canvases.*

BRANLEY. And how about clothes?

TREVOR [*looking up for an instant, but going on strapping*]. Clothes?

BRANLEY. You'll want some, won't you? That bag all you're taking?

TREVOR. Yes. Got a few down there. Besides, there are shops. [*He finishes strapping the roll of canvas, and puts it beside the other, a very long one.*] The question is, how many of these can I get into the car?

BRANLEY [*puffing at his cigarette*]. Don't see how you're going to get that long one in. The landaulette's coming.

TREVOR [*angrily*]. The landaulette! Why not the big yellow car?

BRANLEY. So that all Paris can see you driving off with her?

TREVOR [*grumbling*]. We might have had the hood up.

BRANLEY. And attract attention all round! People don't muffle themselves up on a hot day in June.

TREVOR [*laying his hand on the long canvas roll*]. I must take this canvas somehow.

BRANLEY. It's the Venus?

TREVOR. Of course. What else?

BRANLEY. Well, there's not room for her and Muriel. Have to leave one of 'em behind.

TREVOR [*angrily*]. Chris!

BRANLEY. Besides, how about the model?

TREVOR. She can come down to me there.

BRANLEY. Then you'd have John Glayde six hours after.

TREVOR. Why?

BRANLEY. If that flutter-brained little Nini goes to you at Mantes, all Montmartre will know about it in the evening.

TREVOR [*regretfully*]. That's so, of course. Come to think of it, I may as well leave the canvas here. I'll never get another model like Nini. I shan't be able to go on with it.

BRANLEY [*puffing out rings of smoke*]. Nor with anything else, as far as I can see.

TREVOR [*turning fiercely on him*]. Why the devil do you keep on saying that?

BRANLEY [*stolidly*]. Because I'm your friend.

TREVOR. To hell with your friendship, if that's the advice you give me! [BRANLEY *shrugs his shoulders.* TREVOR *hands him three small boxes of pastels, and a strap.*] Just strap up these pastels, will you?

BRANLEY [*taking them, laying down his pipe, and speaking as he straps the boxes*]. Yes — pastels are the thing. Still life, flowers — sketches of the cat purring at the window —

TREVOR. What are you driving at now?

BRANLEY [*still strapping*]. You forget that I ran away with a married woman once.

TREVOR [*with a sneer*]. Only once?

BRANLEY. Jupiter, catch me doing it again! When she wasn't making me tell her that I loved her, she was crying because of the other fellow she had left.

TREVOR [*angrily*]. D'you think Muriel's that sort?

BRANLEY. Every woman is. Wasn't I glad when Number 1 turned up!

TREVOR. You would be.

BRANLEY. We were so well hidden that he couldn't find us. I sent him an anonymous letter.

TREVOR [*putting away one roll of canvases, and trying the straps of the other*]. Brute!

BRANLEY [*laying down the boxes of pastels*]. Well, I don't know. He took Madame home, and we exchanged shots at twenty-four paces. I did the correct thing — I fired in the air.

TREVOR [*viciously, as he pulls at a strap*]. I wish he had killed you!

BRANLEY [*with a chuckle*]. Thank you. He might have, you know — he had never handled a pistol before.

TREVOR [*suddenly facing him*]. Don't you understand, you ridiculous idiot, that I love Muriel?

BRANLEY [*placidly*]. I've heard you say it often enough.

TREVOR. Say it, and mean it! She's the —

BRANLEY [*breaking in, waving his hand*]. I know, I know. Of course she is — no one's denying it. So was mine, so are they all. And if you'll only give up painting, you'll be perfectly happy.

TREVOR [*fiercely*]. Have you gone off your head? Why should I give up painting?

BRANLEY. You work from the nude

mostly, don't you? Do you think she'll ever let a nude model pose to you?

TREVOR [*scornfully*]. Do I think! You don't know her!

BRANLEY [*waving his pipe*]. You wait and see! It'll be cats at the window, flowers, and studies of old men. Oh, take it easy! There's something to be done with those.

TREVOR. I'll get a new model down there, and start the Venus over again.

BRANLEY. Yes — a dairymaid, with flat feet and a turned-up nose.

TREVOR [*turning angrily to him*]. Look here, will you understand one thing? If I had to choose, this moment, between my art and Muriel, do you think I'd hesitate?

BRANLEY. No, I don't. If you had to choose, this moment, you'd choose Muriel.

TREVOR. Very well, then — leave me alone! — Have you strapped those pastels?

BRANLEY [*picking up the boxes and handing them to him*]. The queer thing about painting is that one never gets tired of it.

TREVOR [*who has taken the pastels and laid them by the side of the canvases*]. You're not a man at all — you're a mere machine that eats and drinks —

[*He takes his coat from the chair, fetches a clothes-brush, and brushes it.*]

BRANLEY. And has sense.

TREVOR [*brushing the coat*]. Glayde will divorce her.

BRANLEY. Probably.

TREVOR. And we'll get married — and I'll work as I used to — come back to Paris —

BRANLEY. You've very little of your father's money left.

TREVOR. My pictures sell.

BRANLEY. Because you've been indifferent whether they did, or not. You've never known what it meant to pot-boil.

TREVOR [*throwing the clothes-brush violently to the ground, and striding towards him*]. I've had enough of this — do you hear — and more than enough! Stop this silly cackle of yours, with your croaking and mumbling! And I tell you this — if there *is* to be suffering, I'd rather I bore it than she. If I *have* to give up my art, and take to pot-boiling, I'll do it without a murmur, for *her* sake!

BRANLEY [*with half-closed eyes, as he puffs at his pipe*]. Now.

TREVOR. Now and always!

BRANLEY [*sitting up*]. To-morrow's a beastly word. Anything else I can do?

TREVOR [*passionately*]. Yes — be damned to you — damned, damned! Why have you been saying these horrible things? You know what my work means to me —

BRANLEY. That's just it.

TREVOR. And you imagine that she — that she — oh, Chris, I tell you, it'll take me a long time to forget this!

BRANLEY [*placidly*]. We'll hope I'm wrong.

TREVOR. Wrong! If you knew anything of women —

BRANLEY. All that I've said to you to-day you'll say to yourself by-and-by.

TREVOR. Never, I tell you — never!

Branley. Oh, not aloud, of course. Well, I've finished. [*He gets up and stretches himself.*] I've done what I could. . . . I'll see about letting the studio. Perhaps I'll take it myself.

TREVOR [*sulkily*]. I'd rather have someone else. More chance of getting some rent.

BRANLEY [*cheerfully*]. There's something in that. I'll forward your letters.

TREVOR. Don't, till you hear from me. I'll send an address.

BRANLEY. Why? If you get no letters there, they'll think it strange.

TREVOR. That's so. Don't forget, though, that I'm Mr. Matthews.

BRANLEY. Oh, I shan't forget!

[*A knock.* TREVOR *slips into his coat, runs to the door, and opens it. The* PRINCESS *is there — she comes into the room.*]

TREVOR. Princess!

PRINCESS [*quietly*]. Yes. Finished your packing?

TREVOR. I'm quite ready. [*He looks at his watch.*] She'll be here directly.

PRINCESS. Yes. [*She sits.*] Unless —
[*She pauses.*]

TREVOR. Unless what?

PRINCESS. Unless John Glayde stopped

her. I suggested his going with her to the Embassy.
TREVOR. You did!
PRINCESS. I did. Oh, without giving her away, of course! I merely nudged Providence.
TREVOR [*very white*]. I thought you were our friend?
PRINCESS. Hers more than yours, Trevor. I'd like to say one last word to you —
TREVOR [*writhing*]. Oh, for Heaven's sake! He has been going at me, the past hour!
PRINCESS [*quietly*]. When Muriel comes — if she comes — send her home.
TREVOR [*fiercely*]. Are you mad? Let her go back to him?
PRINCESS. He's worth twenty of you.
TREVOR. She loves me.
PRINCESS. You're three years younger than she — and three years is a lot. You're twenty-eight, and she's thirty-one. She'll be jealous — you'll fret — you'll both be unhappy — but it'll all fall on her. Send her back, Trevor! John Glayde has forgiven . . .
TREVOR [*stamping his foot*]. Princess!
PRINCESS [*calmly*]. Not my business, of course, but I like her. And there's something that hurts when a woman you like goes on telling lie upon lie. And it shows that it's not her real self — she wouldn't do it. Fact is, she's mad, just now. Afraid he'd kill you — that's at the root of it. And we women are fearful fools when we think we're in love. It's up to you, Trevor. Save her!
TREVOR [*tearing his hair*]. Save her! From what?
PRINCESS. From herself — the bad self that's been lying. Give her time to remember!
TREVOR. It's *you* who are mad!
PRINCESS. She thinks that she loves you now — but there's something in her that will always belong to John Glayde.
TREVOR. I love Muriel — do you understand that? — love her with all my soul!
PRINCESS. Then prove it — give her a chance.
TREVOR. I love her — and nothing shall part us!
[*The* PRINCESS *shrugs her shoulders,* *rises, and moves away.* BRANLEY, *who has been at the window, gives an exclamation and turns to* TREVOR.]
BRANLEY. Your mother's coming! She's getting out of her carriage!
TREVOR [*wildly*]. My mother!
BRANLEY. Yes.
TREVOR. Heaven! And Muriel here in a minute! Princess!
[*He turns appealingly to her.*]
PRINCESS. Yes?
TREVOR. Will you slip out through that door — you can get into the garden through the dining-room — bring Muriel in that way.
[LADY LERODE *has passed up the paved way, and gives a sharp knock.*]
PRINCESS. If she comes!
TREVOR. Of course she'll come! Will you?
PRINCESS. Yes.
[*She moves to the door.*]
TREVOR. As soon as she's here, I'll take my mother off — and come back at once. Tell her —
[*Another, and a sharper, knock.*]
PRINCESS. I will. But I hope —
[*She goes.*]
TREVOR. Chris, stand at the window, and let me know —
BRANLEY. All right.
[TREVOR *goes quickly to the door and opens it.* LADY LERODE *bounces in. She is very excited.*]
LADY LERODE. Trevor! Trevor! Can this be true?
TREVOR [*coldly*]. What?
LADY LERODE [*seeing* BRANLEY]. Ah, Mr. Branley! Mr. Branley, I'm glad you're here! *Can* you conceive it?
BRANLEY. Conceive what, Lady Lerode?
[*He has gone to the window, and stands with his back half-turned to* LADY LERODE.]
LADY LERODE [*dropping into a chair, which* TREVOR *has placed for her so that her back is to the window*]. I've just come from the Hamblins. Imagine it! He saw the girl this afternoon, and told her —
[*The outer gate clangs.* TREVOR *looks at* BRANLEY, *who nods.*]

TREVOR. She came here — I put an end to the farce — that's all.

[*The* PRINCESS, *who has in the meanwhile gone into the garden through the inner door, is seen to pass with* MURIEL, *but both keep close to the outer wall.*]

LADY LERODE [*throwing up her hands*]. Farce!

TREVOR. What else? [*He takes his hat.*] Mother, I have to go out.

LADY LERODE. Now?

TREVOR. Yes — I've an appointment.

LADY LERODE [*looking around*]. You've been packing?

TREVOR. I'm off to the country for a bit.

LADY LERODE. Mr. Branley, you're an old friend of his —

TREVOR [*impatiently*]. Come, mother — we'll talk in the carriage — you shall drive me —

LADY LERODE [*not stirring*]. The poor child is absolutely ill — hysterical. How could you!

TREVOR. I told her the truth, that's all. I hadn't seen her for weeks — she came this afternoon — it's time that she knew. Come!

[*He taps her impatiently on the shoulder.*]

LADY LERODE. It's inconceivable! And we all rejoicing at Mr. Glayde's arrival! [*With a sudden idea.*] Ah! That's why you are going away!

TREVOR. If you like. [*He throws open the door.*] Come!

LADY LERODE [*turning to* BRANLEY]. Mr. Branley! Help me!

[BRANLEY *shrugs his shoulders.*]

TREVOR. Mother, I have to catch a train. If you don't come, I'll go without you. [*He pulls her by the sleeve.*]

LADY LERODE [*to* BRANLEY]. Can you imagine anything so ridiculous? Mr. Glayde's in Paris, and he tells the girl he doesn't love her!

TREVOR [*almost dragging her out*]. Come!

LADY LERODE [*turning protestingly to him*]. My dear Trevor —

TREVOR. You can tell me all the rest in the carriage!

[*He has got her out, and closes the door. They pass down the paved way, and the outer gate clangs.*]

[*The other door slowly opens, and* MURIEL *and the* PRINCESS *come into the room.* MURIEL *is wearing a long cloak over her dress.*]

MURIEL [*to* BRANLEY]. Will he be long?

BRANLEY. Oh, no — a few minutes.

MURIEL [*taking off the cloak, which she throws on a chair*]. The car's there — Mr. Branley, will you send the chauffeur home? He didn't see me, fortunately. But I don't want him to wait.

BRANLEY [*going to the door*]. All right.

MURIEL. And don't you think it would be better — if you went off in the car yourself, perhaps, and came back in ten minutes? Then he wouldn't suspect.

BRANLEY [*nodding*]. That's a good idea. I will.

[*He goes, leaving the door open.* MURIEL *sinks into a chair.*]

PRINCESS [*standing before her*]. Well?

MURIEL [*putting both hands in front of her face*]. Don't look at me, Betsy. I'm horrible! I've done fearful things!

PRINCESS. What?

MURIEL. He wanted to come with me — I had to — [*She shakes her head, with a gesture of despair.*] Oh, terrible, terrible!

PRINCESS. What did you do?

MURIEL. Don't ask me — I've been abominable — vile. But it was my one chance — I had to seize it — I had to! But, oh, how I loathe myself!

PRINCESS. It's not too late now — there's still —

[*As she speaks, the door is pushed open, and* JOHN *appears on the threshold.* BETSY *sees him, stops short in the middle of her sentence and stares at him.* MURIEL *lifts her eyes and screams.*]

PRINCESS. Mr. Glayde!

JOHN [*coming slowly into the room, his eyes fixed on* MURIEL]. Leave us!

PRINCESS [*wringing her hands, in terror*]. Mr. Glayde, Mr. Glayde!

JOHN [*without looking at her*]. Go!

PRINCESS. I can't — I won't!

MURIEL [*rising slowly to her feet*]. Go, Betsy.

[*After a moment's hesitation, looking from one to the other, the* PRINCESS *goes, with bent head, dragging her feet, and closes the door. Her footsteps are heard on the paved way, the clang of the gate. Not till then does* JOHN *move — he walks slowly to* MURIEL, *till he almost touches her. He has never taken his eyes from her, nor she from him, from the moment he entered the room. She breathes quickly, but does not flinch.*]

JOHN. You lied to me?
MURIEL [*steadily*]. Yes.
JOHN. Why?
MURIEL. To save him.
JOHN. From what?
MURIEL. From you.
JOHN. And you put your arms round my neck, and kissed me?
MURIEL. Yes.
JOHN. That you might go alone, and come here?
MURIEL. Yes.

[*There is a moment's silence, as they stand face to face, looking into each other's eyes.*]

Muriel [*with a sudden cry*]. You have your revolver. Kill me!
JOHN [*shaking his head*]. No ... You were going off together?
MURIEL [*her voice again becoming almost mechanical, as though she were hypnotized*]. Yes.
JOHN. Where?
MURIEL. To a cottage we have at Mantes.
JOHN. This was all arranged?
MURIEL. Yes.
JOHN. When?
MURIEL. This morning, when I spoke to him.
JOHN. So it has all been lies, and lies, and lies?
MURIEL [*almost fiercely, almost triumphantly*]. All! All! All!

[*There is a moment's silence — then she bursts out passionately.*]

MURIEL. What was I to do! You would have killed him!

JOHN. Will you come back with me now?
MURIEL [*defiantly*]. No, I will not.
JOHN. You shall have your own house — live apart —
MURIEL. No. I hate you!
JOHN. Why?
MURIEL. Because you have come between us, with your strength and your cruelty! You have forced me to this — made me do these terrible things —
JOHN [*steadily*]. You will come back with me.
MURIEL. I will not — I will not!
JOHN. You were all I had in the world. Very well, that is over. I am thinking now only of you.
MURIEL. Then leave me!
JOHN. To him?
MURIEL. Yes. The man I love!
JOHN. No. That is asking too much.
MURIEL [*with a half-movement towards the door*]. I am going with him.

[*Intercepting her, in a sudden mad fit of fury, he seizes her wrist.*]

JOHN. Traitress and liar!
MURIEL [*again with an almost savage note of triumph*]. Yes.
JOHN. You could put your arms round my neck, and look into my eyes —
MURIEL. To save the man I loved.
JOHN. And you imagine that now I will let you go off with him?
MURIEL. I will never go back with you!

[*He releases her wrist, her arm falls by her side. There is silence, as they stand, breathing quickly, face to face. He passes his hand over his forehead, masters himself, then speaks slowly and quietly.*]

JOHN. I want to save you. I won't talk of disgrace, or shame — you seem dead to these things. I want to save you. I used to love you — I had faith in you — great faith. All I said to you — every word I have said — was true. *I* have not lied to you — I do not lie now. This afternoon — I believed. I looked into your eyes, and believed you. You said things to me — I believed them all. You need not have done this. It was unnecessary.
MURIEL. I did it to get away.

JOHN. You did it to get away. *How* you must hate me!

MURIEL. When you try to keep me from him.

JOHN. And all those years, when you lay in my arms, gone and forgotten! "My husband, my lover ..." You should not have done this.

MURIEL. I had no time to think.

JOHN. As you see, I am very calm. I am not using big words, or threatening. I don't talk to you of myself, of what I am feeling. I want to save you, that's all. I cannot believe that you, the woman I have known all these years, would have done what you did this afternoon, unless —

MURIEL [*breaking in, desperately*]. I would do it again — for him. I am not ashamed — I love him.

JOHN. There are limits to human endurance. Don't say that again. Where is he?

MURIEL. His mother came — he took her home. He'll be here very soon.

JOHN. You refuse to come with me?

MURIEL [*doggedly*]. Yes: I refuse.

JOHN. Then it lies between him and me.

MURIEL [*in sudden panic*]. What will you do to him?

JOHN. Since you will not come —

MURIEL. No! I will not!

JOHN. I must save you, at any cost.

MURIEL [*passionately*]. Save me! From what! From the one chance of happiness I have in the world! Go back to your Trusts, to your money! Go to your office, and scheme, and plan — break men's hearts and ruin their lives! What have we been to each other, for years! In my loneliness I have found a man who loves me — I love, and am loved!

JOHN. A love that can make you do what you did to-day is a horrible love.

MURIEL. At least it is love! I shall go with him.

JOHN. That is your last word?

MURIEL [*defiantly*]. Yes!

JOHN. Very well, then — let us wait.

MURIEL [*with a shriek*]. You mean to kill him!

JOHN [*coldly*]. Why not?

MURIEL [*frantic*]. Why not, why not? Because I adore him — you hear that, adore him! Belong to him, body and soul!

JOHN [*with a great cry, writhing, broken in two*]. Oh! Have you no pity!

[*She turns, and stares stupidly at him. He has dropped his head — she looks round as though dazed. The silence is broken by the sound of wheels, a cab that stops, the clang of the gate, then footsteps on the paved way. Neither of them speaks or stirs.* TREVOR *opens the door with his latch-key, and starts violently at seeing* JOHN.]

TREVOR. Mr. Glayde!

JOHN [*slowly raising his eyes*]. Come here.

MURIEL [*with a shriek, but not moving*]. Trevor, he will kill you!

JOHN [*quietly*]. Come.

[TREVOR *has thrown a quick glance at the foils on the wall — but moves slowly across the room to* JOHN.]

JOHN [*in dead, calm tones*]. This woman loves you. She used to be my wife. She loves you beyond everything else — honesty, truth, shame. She has made the greatest of all sacrifices for you — she has lied and betrayed ... Take her away.

MURIEL [*the nervous tension breaking, with a sudden, muffled cry, staggering against the wall*]. John!

JOHN. I shall divorce her — you can get married. I shall make provision for her, that she never may want. Take her, and help her — to lie and betray no more.

[MURIEL *covers her face with her hands.* TREVOR *stands tongue-tied, bewildered. Without looking at her, without looking at him,* JOHN GLAYDE *moves slowly to the door, and goes. His steps are heard on the stone outside, then the clang of the gate; neither of the two stirs. The curtain slowly falls.*]

THE MOLLUSC
A NEW AND ORIGINAL COMEDY IN THREE ACTS
By HUBERT HENRY DAVIES

COPYRIGHT, 1914, BY HUBERT HENRY DAVIES AS AUTHOR AND PROPRIETOR
ALL RIGHTS RESERVED

The acting rights of this play are reserved by the author. Performance is strictly forbidden unless his express consent or that of his agent has first been obtained, and attention is called to the penalties provided by law for any infringement of his rights, as follows:

"SEC. 4966: — *Any person publicly performing or representing any dramatic or musical composition for which copyright has been obtained, without the consent of the proprietor of said dramatic or musical composition, or his heirs and assigns, shall be liable for damages therefor, such damages in all cases to be assessed at such sum, not less than one hundred dollars for the first and fifty dollars for every subsequent performance, as to the court shall appear to be just. If the unlawful performance and representation be wilful and for profit, such person or persons shall be guilty of a misdemeanor, and upon conviction be imprisoned for a period not exceeding one year."* — U.S. REVISED STATUTES, *Title* 60, *Chap.* 3.

All rights reserved. Performance forbidden and right of representation reserved. Application for the right to produce this play must be made to the author's agents, the Walter H. Baker Co., 41 Winter St., Boston.

CHARACTERS

Tom Kemp
Mr. Baxter
Mrs. Baxter
Miss Roberts

The scene of the play is laid in Mrs. Baxter's sitting-room at a house some twenty or thirty miles from London.

THE MOLLUSC

ACT I

SCENE. — MRS. BAXTER'S *sitting-room. A pleasant, well-furnished room. French windows open to the garden, showing flower-beds in full bloom, it being summer-time. As the audience looks at the stage there is a door on the left-hand side at the back, and from the door a few stairs lead down to the room. Nearer and also on this side is a fireplace. Against this same wall is a flower pot on a table containing a plant in bloom. There is plenty of comfortable furniture about the room.*

It is evening after dinner. Lamps are lighted and the windows closed. MR. BAXTER, *a man about forty, is seated near a lamp reading "Scribner's Magazine." The door opens and* MISS ROBERTS *comes in. She is a pretty, honest-looking English girl about twenty-four. She comes towards* MR. BAXTER.

MISS ROBERTS. Mr. Baxter — are you very busy?
MR. BAXTER. No, Miss Roberts.
MISS ROBERTS. I want to speak to you.
MR. BAXTER. Yes. Won't you sit down?
MISS ROBERTS. Thank you. [*She does so.*] We shall soon be beginning the summer holidays, and I think after this term you had better have another governess for the girls.
MR. BAXTER. You want to leave us?
MISS ROBERTS. I don't *want* to. I shall be very sorry indeed to go. You and Mrs. Baxter have always been so kind to me. You never treated me like a governess.
MR. BAXTER. You have been with us so long. We have come to look on you as one of the family.
MISS ROBERTS. I can't tell you how often I have felt grateful. I don't want to leave you at all, and it will almost break my heart to say good-bye to the children, but I *must* go.
MR. BAXTER [*anxiously*]. You are not going to be married?
MISS ROBERTS [*smiling*]. Oh, no — nothing so interesting — I'm sorry to say.
MR. BAXTER. Have you told my wife you think of leaving?
MISS ROBERTS [*slightly troubled*]. I began to tell Mrs. Baxter several times; at the beginning of the term and three or four times since — but she was always too busy or too tired to attend to me; each time she asked me to tell her some other time — until I don't quite know what to do. That's why I've come to *you*.
MR. BAXTER [*slightly disconcerted*]. But it's not *my* place to accept your notice.
MISS ROBERTS. I know — but if I might explain to *you* —
MR. BAXTER. Certainly.
MISS ROBERTS. It's this. I can't teach the girls anything more. Gladys is nearly twelve and Margery, though she is only nine, is very bright; she often asks me the most puzzling questions — and the truth is — I have not had a good enough education myself to take them any further.
MR. BAXTER. Aren't they rather young to go to school?
MISS ROBERTS. I think you need a governess with a college education, or, at any rate, some one who doesn't get all at sea in algebra and Latin.
MR. BAXTER. I should have thought you might read and study.
MISS ROBERTS. I used to think so — but I find I haven't the time.
MR. BAXTER [*thoughtfully*]. Too much is expected of you besides your duties as

the children's governess. I've noticed that — but I don't quite see how I can interfere.

MISS ROBERTS. Please don't trouble, and don't think I'm complaining. I am always glad to be of use to Mrs. Baxter. It's not for my own sake I want a change; it's for the girls'. This is their most receptive age. What they are taught, and *how* they are taught *now*, will mean so much to them later on. I can't bear to think they may suffer all their lives through *my* ignorance.

MR. BAXTER [*politely*]. Oh — I'm sure —

MISS ROBERTS. It's very kind of you to say so — but I know what it is. I have suffered myself for want of a thorough education. Of course, I had the ordinary kind, but I was never brought up to know or do anything special. I found myself at a great disadvantage when I had to turn to, and earn my own living.

MR. BAXTER. Gladys and Margery won't have to earn their own livings.

MISS ROBERTS. No one used to think that I should have to earn mine — till one day — I found myself alone and poor — after the shipwreck — when my father and mother — and my sister —

[*She turns her head away to hide her emotion from* MR. BAXTER.]

MR. BAXTER [*kindly*]. We shall all miss you very much when you go. [*Leaning towards her.*] I shall miss you very much. [*She nods.*] We've had such good walks and talks and games of chess.

MISS ROBERTS [*brightly*]. Yes! I've enjoyed them all.

MR. BAXTER. I hope you have a nice place to go to.

MISS ROBERTS [*simply*]. I haven't any place to go to. I hoped Mrs. Baxter would help me find a new situation. I can't get one very well without her help, as this is the only place where I have ever been a governess, and after being here four years — [*smiles*] I must ask Mrs. Baxter to give me a good character.

MR. BAXTER [*meditatively*]. Four years — it doesn't seem like four years. I don't know though — in some ways it seems as if you had always been here. [*Looking at* MISS ROBERTS.] It is very honest of you to give up a good situation for a conscientious reason like this.

MISS ROBERTS. I don't know.

MR. BAXTER [*as an afterthought*]. I suppose it really is your reason for leaving?

MISS ROBERTS [*laughing*]. It's not very nice of you to compliment me on my honesty one minute and doubt it the next.

MR. BAXTER [*seriously*]. No, Miss Roberts, no. I don't doubt it. I was only wondering. I thought perhaps there might be some other reason why you find it difficult to live here — why you think it would be wiser not to stay —

MISS ROBERTS [*innocently*]. No —

MR. BAXTER. I see. Well — as I leave everything to do with the girls' education to Mrs. Baxter — perhaps you will tell *her*. Tell her what you have told *me*.

MISS ROBERTS. And — will you sit in the room?

MR. BAXTER. Why? What is going to be the difficulty?

MISS ROBERTS [*embarrassed*]. I can't explain very well to you — but if you wouldn't mind sitting in the room. [*She rises.*] I think I hear Mrs. Baxter coming.

[MRS. BAXTER *enters. She is a pretty woman about thirty-five, vague in her movements and manner of speaking. She comes down the room as she speaks.*]

MRS. BAXTER. I've been wondering where *Scribner's Magazine* is.

MR. BAXTER. I have it. Have you been looking for it?

MRS. BAXTER. No — not looking — only wondering.

MR. BAXTER. Do you want it?

MRS. BAXTER [*pleasantly*]. Not if you are reading it — though I was just halfway through a story.

MR. BAXTER. Do take it.

MRS. BAXTER [*taking magazine*]. Don't you really want it?

[*She looks about, selecting the most comfortable chair.*]

MR. BAXTER. It doesn't matter.

MRS. BAXTER [*smiling*]. Thank you. [*She sits.*] Oh, Miss Roberts, I wonder if you could get me the cushion out of that chair? [*Pointing to a chair near a window.*]

MISS ROBERTS. Certainly.
[*She brings the cushion to* MRS. BAXTER *and places it behind her back.*]
MRS. BAXTER [*settling herself*]. Thank you. Now I'm quite comfortable — unless I had a footstool.
MISS ROBERTS. A footstool?
[*She gets a footstool, brings it to* MRS. BAXTER *and places it under her feet.*]
MRS. BAXTER [*without an attempt to move while* MISS ROBERTS *is doing this*]. Don't trouble, Miss Roberts. I didn't mean *you* to do that. *I* could have done it. [*When* MISS ROBERTS *has placed the footstool.*] Oh, how kind of you, but you ought not to wait on me like this. [*Smiles sweetly.*] The paper-knife, please. Who knows where it is? [MISS ROBERTS *takes the paper-knife from* MR. BAXTER *and gives it to* MRS. BAXTER. *To* MR. BAXTER.] I didn't see you were using it, dear, or I wouldn't have asked for it. [*To* MISS ROBERTS.] As you're doing nothing, would you mind cutting some of these pages? I find there are still a few uncut. [*She gives the magazine and paper-knife to* MISS ROBERTS, *then says, smiling sweetly.*] Your fingers are so much cleverer than mine. [MISS ROBERTS *begins cutting the magazine.* MRS. BAXTER *leans back comfortably in her chair and says to* MR. BAXTER.] Why don't you get something to do?
MR. BAXTER [*rising*]. I'm going to my room to have a smoke.
[MISS ROBERTS *puts the magazine on the table and goes to* MR. BAXTER *with the paper-knife in her hand.*]
MISS ROBERTS. No, Mr. Baxter, please, I want you to help me out. I want you to stay while I tell Mrs. Baxter.
MRS. BAXTER. What's all this mystery? [*Seriously.*] Take care you don't snap that paper-knife in two, Miss Roberts.
[MR. BAXTER *sits down again.*]
MISS ROBERTS [*to* MRS. BAXTER]. I was telling Mr. Baxter before you came into the room —
MRS. BAXTER [*holding out her hand*]. Give me the paper-knife.
[MISS ROBERTS *gives her the paper-knife, which she examines carefully.*]

MISS ROBERTS. I told you at the beginning of the term, and several times since —
MRS. BAXTER. It would have been a pity if that paper-knife had been snapped in two. [*She looks up pleasantly at* MISS ROBERTS.] Yes, Miss Roberts?
MISS ROBERTS. I was saying that I thought —
[MRS. BAXTER *drops the paper-knife accidentally on the floor.*]
MRS. BAXTER. Oh, don't trouble to pick it up. [MISS ROBERTS *picks up the paper-knife and holds it in her hand.*] Oh, thank you, I didn't mean you to do that.
MISS ROBERTS. I was saying —
MRS. BAXTER. It isn't chipped, is it?
MISS ROBERTS [*nearly losing her temper*]. No.
[*She marches to the table and lays the paper-knife down.*]
MRS. BAXTER. It would have been a pity if that paper-knife had been chipped.
MISS ROBERTS [*facing* MRS. BAXTER *with determination, and speaking fast and loud*]. I said I must leave at the end of the term.
MRS. BAXTER [*blandly*]. Aren't you happy with us, Miss Roberts?
MISS ROBERTS. Oh, yes, thank you. Very.
MRS. BAXTER. Really happy, I mean.
MR. BAXTER. Miss Roberts feels that Gladys and Margery are getting too old for her to teach.
MISS ROBERTS [*glancing her gratitude to* MR. BAXTER *for helping her*]. Yes. [*To* MRS. BAXTER.] I've taught them all I know; they need some one cleverer; there ought to be a change.
MRS. BAXTER. I think you do very nicely.
MISS ROBERTS. *You* don't know how ignorant I am.
MRS. BAXTER [*sweetly*]. You do yourself an injustice, dear Miss Roberts.
[MISS ROBERTS *turns appealingly to* MR. BAXTER.]
MR. BAXTER. It was the algebra, I think you said, Miss Roberts, that you found so especially difficult?
MISS ROBERTS. Yes. I've no head for algebra.

MRS. BAXTER [*cheerfully*]. Neither have I, but I don't consider myself a less useful woman for that.
MISS ROBERTS. You're not a governess.
MRS. BAXTER. Who said I was? Don't let us wander from the point, Miss Roberts.
[MISS ROBERTS *looks appealingly at* MR. BAXTER *again.*]
MR. BAXTER. The Latin —
MISS ROBERTS. Yes, I give myself a lesson at night to pass on to them in the morning — that's no way to do, just keeping a length ahead.
MRS. BAXTER. Perhaps Mr. Baxter will help you with the Latin. Ask him.
MISS ROBERTS. I'm afraid even that —
MRS. BAXTER. Mr. Baxter's a very good Latin scholar. [*Smiling at* MR. BAXTER.] Aren't you, dear?
MR. BAXTER [*reluctantly*]. I read Virgil at school. I haven't looked at him since. After a time one's Latin gets rusty.
MRS. BAXTER [*cheerfully*]. Rub it up. We might begin now, while you're doing nothing. Ask Miss Roberts to bring you the books.
MR. BAXTER. Oh, no, dear.
MRS. BAXTER. Why shouldn't we improve our minds?
[*She leans her head back on the cushions.*]
MR. BAXTER. Not after dinner. [*To* MISS ROBERTS.] I don't see why you want to teach the girls Latin.
MISS ROBERTS. Mrs. Baxter said she wished them to have a smattering of the dead languages.
MRS. BAXTER [*complacently*]. I learnt Latin. I remember so well standing up in class and reciting "Hic — hæc — hoc" — accusative "hinc — honc — huc."
MR. BAXTER [*correcting her*]. Hoc.
MRS. BAXTER. Huc, my dear, in *my* book. And the ablative was hibus.
MR. BAXTER. Hibus!
[MR. BAXTER *and* MISS ROBERTS *both laugh.*]
MRS. BAXTER [*making wild serious guesses*]. Hobibus — no, wait a minute — that's wrong — don't tell me. [*She closes her eyes and murmurs.*] Ablative — ho — hi — hu — no; it's gone. [*She opens her eyes and says cheerfully.*] Never mind. [*To* MISS ROBERTS.] What were we talking about?
MISS ROBERTS. *My ignorance* of Latin.
MRS. BAXTER. I can't say that *my knowledge* of it has ever been of much service to me. I think Mr. Baxter is quite right. Why teach the girls Latin? Suppose we drop it from the curriculum and take up something else on Latin mornings —
MISS ROBERTS [*earnestly to* MRS. BAXTER]. I wonder if you realize how much all this means to the girls? Their future is *so* important.
MRS. BAXTER [*with the idea of putting* MISS ROBERTS *in her place*]. Of course it is important, Miss Roberts. It is not necessary to tell a mother how important her girls' future is — but I don't suppose we need settle it this evening. [*Wishing to put an end to the discussion, she rises, walks towards the table on which stands the flower pot and says amiably.*] How pretty these flowers look growing in this pot.
MISS ROBERTS. Would you rather we discussed it to-morrow, Mrs. Baxter?
MRS. BAXTER. To-morrow will be my brother's first day here, and he will have so much to tell me after his long absence. I don't think to-morrow would be a good day.
MISS ROBERTS. The day after?
MRS. BAXTER. Oh, really, Miss Roberts, I can't be pinned down like that. [*She moves towards* MR. BAXTER.] Aren't you and Miss Roberts going to play chess?
MR. BAXTER [*rising*]. Miss Roberts seems so anxious to have this thing decided. I told her that anything to do with the girls' education was left to *you*.
MRS. BAXTER. Need it be settled this minute?
MISS ROBERTS [*going towards* MRS. BAXTER]. I've tried so often to speak to you about it and something must be done.
MRS. BAXTER [*resigning herself*]. Of course — if you insist upon it — I'll do it now. I'll do anything any of you wish. [*She sits down.*] I've had a slight headache all day — it's rather worse since dinner; I really ought to be in bed, but I wanted to

be up when Tom comes. If I begin to discuss this now, I shall be in no state to receive him — but, of course — if you insist —

MISS ROBERTS. I don't want to tire you.

MRS. BAXTER. It *would* tire me very much.

MISS ROBERTS. Then I suppose we must put it off again.

MRS. BAXTER [*smiling*]. I think that would be best. We must thrash it out properly — some day.

[*She leans back in her chair.*]

MR. BAXTER [*to* MISS ROBERTS, *sighing*]. I suppose we may as well play chess?

MISS ROBERTS [*with resignation*]. I suppose so.

[MR. BAXTER *and* MISS ROBERTS *sit at a table and arrange the chess men.*]

MRS. BAXTER [*finding her place in her magazine, begins to read. After a slight pause, she says*]. What an abominable light! I can't possibly see to read. I suppose, Miss Roberts, you couldn't possibly carry that lamp over to this table, could you? [MISS ROBERTS *makes a slight movement as though she would fetch the lamp.*] It's too heavy, isn't it?

MR. BAXTER. Much too heavy!

MRS. BAXTER. I thought so. I'm afraid I must strain my eyes. I can't bear to sit idle.

MR. BAXTER [*rising*]. I'll carry the lamp over.

MRS. BAXTER [*quickly*]. No, no! You'd spill it. Call one of the servants; wouldn't that be the simplest plan?

MR. BAXTER. The simplest plan would be for you to walk over to the lamp.

MRS. BAXTER. Certainly, dear, if it's too much trouble to call one of the servants. [*She rises and carries her magazine to a chair by the lamp.*] I wouldn't have said anything about the lamp if I'd thought it was going to be such a business to move it. [*She sits and turns over a page or two while* MR. BAXTER, *who has returned to his seat, and* MISS ROBERTS *continue arranging the chess board.* MRS. BAXTER *calls gaily over her shoulder.*] Have you checkmated Mr. Baxter yet, Miss Roberts?

MISS ROBERTS. I haven't finished setting the board.

MRS. BAXTER. How slow you are. [*She turns a page or two idly, then says seriously to* MR. BAXTER.] Dear, you'll be interested to know that I don't think the housemaid opposite is engaged to young Locker. I believe it's the cook.

MR. BAXTER. Very interesting, dear. [*To* MISS ROBERTS.] It's you to play.

[*After three moves of chess,* MRS. BAXTER *says.*]

MRS. BAXTER. Oh, here's such a clever article on wasps. It seems that wasps — I'll read you what it says. [*She clears her throat.*] Wasps —

MR. BAXTER [*plaintively*]. Dulcie, dear, it's impossible for us to give our minds to the game if you read aloud.

MRS. BAXTER [*amiably*]. I'm so sorry, dear. I didn't mean to disturb you. I think you'd have found the article instructive. If you want to read it afterwards, it's page 32, if you can remember that. "Wasps and all about them." I'll dog-ear the page. Oh, I never looked out Tom's train. Miss Roberts, you'll find the time-table on the hall table. [MISS ROBERTS *rises and* MRS. BAXTER *goes on.*] Or if it isn't there, it may be —

MISS ROBERTS [*quickly*]. I know where it is. [*She goes out.*]

MRS. BAXTER. What has Miss Roberts been saying to you about leaving?

MR. BAXTER. Only what she said to you.

MRS. BAXTER. I hope she won't leave me before I get suited. I shall never find any one else to suit me. I don't know what I should do without Miss Roberts.

[MISS ROBERTS *re-enters with small time-table.*]

MISS ROBERTS. Here it is!

MRS. BAXTER [*cheerfully*]. Thank you, Miss Roberts, but I've just remembered he isn't coming by train at all; he's coming in a motor car.

MR. BAXTER. All the way from London?

MRS. BAXTER. Yes, at least I think so. It's all in his letter — who knows what I did with Tom's letter?

MISS ROBERTS [*making a slight movement as if to go*]. Shall I go and look?
MRS. BAXTER. Hush. I'm trying to think where I put it. [*Staring in front of her.*] I had it in my hand before tea. I remember dropping it — I had it again after tea; I remember thinking it was another letter, but it wasn't. That's how I know. [*Then to the others.*] I'm surprised neither of you remembers where I put it.
MISS ROBERTS. I'd better go and look.
[*She moves to go.*]
MR. BAXTER. I think I hear a motor coming.
[*He goes and looks through the window.*]
MRS. BAXTER [*in an injured tone*]. It's too late now, Miss Roberts. Mr. Baxter thinks he hears a motor coming.
MR. BAXTER. Yes, it is a car; I see the lamps. It must be Tom.
MRS. BAXTER [*smiling affectionately*]. Dear Tom, how nice it will be to see him again! [*To* MR. BAXTER.] Aren't you going to the hall to meet Tom?
MR. BAXTER. Yes, of course.
[*He goes out.*]
MRS. BAXTER. You've never seen my brother Tom.
MISS ROBERTS. No, I don't think he's been home since I came to you.
MRS. BAXTER. No, I was trying to count up this afternoon how many years it would be since Tom was home. I've forgotten again now, but I know I did it; you'd be surprised.
TOM [*outside*]. Where is she?
[*Confused greetings between* TOM *and* MR. BAXTER *are heard.* MRS. BAXTER *rises smiling, and goes towards the stairs.*]
MRS. BAXTER. That's Tom's voice.
[TOM KEMP *enters, followed by* MR. BAXTER. TOM *is a cheerful, genial, high-spirited man about forty-five; he comes downstairs, where* MRS. BAXTER *meets him. He takes her in both arms and kisses her on each cheek.*]
TOM. Well, child, how are you — bless you.

MRS. BAXTER. Oh, Tom, it *is* nice to see you again.
TOM [*holding her off and looking at her*]. You look just the same.
MRS. BAXTER. So do you, Tom. I'm so glad you haven't grown fat.
TOM [*laughing*]. No chance to grow fat out there. Life is too strenuous. [*He turns to* MR. BAXTER *and gives him a slap on the back.*] Well, Dick, you old duffer.
MRS. BAXTER. Tom.
TOM [*turning to her*]. Yes?
MRS. BAXTER. I want to introduce you to Miss Roberts.
[TOM *gives* MISS ROBERTS *a friendly hand-shake.*]
TOM. How d'you do, Miss Roberts?
MRS. BAXTER. Are you very tired, Tom?
TOM. Tired — no — never tired. [*Smiling at* MRS. BAXTER.] You look splendid.
[*He holds her by her shoulders.*]
MRS. BAXTER [*languidly*]. I'm pretty well.
TOM [*spinning* MRS. BAXTER *round*]. Never better.
MRS. BAXTER [*disliking such treatment*]. I'm pretty well.
[*She wriggles her shoulders and edges away.*]
MR. BAXTER [*to* TOM]. Have you dined?
TOM. Magnificently. Soup — fish — chops — roast beef — [*To* MISS ROBERTS.] You must live in Colorado, Miss Roberts, if you want to relish roast beef.
MR. BAXTER. But you've driven from London since dinner. [*To* MRS. BAXTER.] I suppose we can raise him a supper?
MRS. BAXTER. If the things aren't all put away.
TOM [*turning from* MISS ROBERTS]. No — see here — hold on — I dined at the Inn.
MRS. BAXTER [*smiling graciously*]. Oh, I was just going to offer to go into the kitchen and cook you something myself.
[*She sits.*]
TOM. I was late getting in and I wasn't sure what time you dined. [*To* MR. BAXTER.] Now, Dick, tell me the family history.
MR. BAXTER [*scratching his head, says slowly*]. The family history?

MRS. BAXTER [*calling out suddenly*]. His! Ablative — his.
TOM. Eh?
MRS. BAXTER [*gravely to* TOM]. Hic — hæc — hoc. His — his — his.
TOM [*looking blankly at* MISS ROBERTS *and* MR. BAXTER]. What's the matter?
MRS. BAXTER [*smiling as she explains*]. I was giving them a Latin lesson before you came.
TOM [*amused*]. You?
MRS. BAXTER [*conceitedly*]. I never think we were meant to spend all our time in frivolous conversation.
TOM [*amused, turning to* MR. BAXTER]. Dulcie, giving you a Latin lesson?
MR. BAXTER [*sadly*]. I suppose she really thinks she was by now.
TOM [*walking about*]. It's bully to be home again. I felt like a kid coming here — slipping along in the dark — with English trees and English hedges and English farms flitting by. No one awake but a few English cows, standing in the fields — up to their knees in mist. It looked like dreams — like that dream I sometimes have out there in Colorado. I dream I've just arrived in England — with no baggage and nothing on but my pyjamas.
MRS. BAXTER. What *is* he talking about?
MISS ROBERTS. I know what you mean!
TOM. I guess you've had that dream yourself. No, I mean you know how I must have felt.
MISS ROBERTS. Like a ghost revisiting its old haunts.
TOM [*sitting near* MISS ROBERTS]. Like the ghost of the boy I used to be. I thought you'd understand. You look as if you would.
MRS. BAXTER. I'm so glad you haven't married some nasty common person in America.
TOM [*chaffingly to her*]. I thought you would be. That's why I didn't do it.
[*He talks to* MISS ROBERTS.]
MRS. BAXTER [*laughing as she turns to say to* MR. BAXTER]. He's always so full of fun.
MISS ROBERTS. *I* once dreamed I was in Colorado — but it was only from one of those picture-postcards you sent. I have never travelled.

TOM. And how did Colorado look in your dreams?
MISS ROBERTS [*recalling her vision of Colorado*]. Forests —
TOM. That's right. Pine forests stretching away, away — down below there in the valley — a sea of tree-tops waving — waving — waving for miles.
MISS ROBERTS. And mountains.
TOM. Chains of mountains — great blue mountains streaked with snow — range beyond range. Oh! it's grand! it's great!
MISS ROBERTS. I should love to see it.
MRS. BAXTER. I think you are much better off where you are, Miss Roberts.
TOM. It's great, but it's not gentle like this. It doesn't make you want to cry. It only makes you want to say your prayers.
MRS. BAXTER [*laughing as she turns to* MR. BAXTER]. Isn't he droll?
MISS ROBERTS. I know what you mean.
TOM. *You* know. I thought *you'd* know. Here it comes so close to you; it's so cosy and personal. They've nothing like our orchards and lawns out there. [*Rising suddenly*.] I want to smell the garden. [*He goes to the window.*]
MR. BAXTER. No! Tom, Tom!
MRS. BAXTER. Don't open the window; we shall all catch cold.
TOM [*laughing, as he comes towards* MRS. BAXTER]. Dear old Dulcie, same as ever.
MRS. BAXTER [*smiling*]. All of us are not accustomed to living in tents and huts and such places.
TOM. What are you going to do with me in the morning?
MRS. BAXTER. We might all take a little walk, if it's a nice day.
TOM. A little walk!
MRS. BAXTER. If we're not too tired after the excitement of your arrival.
TOM. What time's breakfast?
MR. BAXTER. Quarter to nine.
MRS. BAXTER. We drift down about half-past.
TOM. What! You've got an English garden, and it's summer time and you aren't all running about outside at six o'clock in the morning?
MISS ROBERTS. I am.
TOM. *You* are? Yes, I thought *you*

would be. You and I must have a walk before breakfast to-morrow morning.

MISS ROBERTS [*smiling*]. Very well.

MRS. BAXTER. Don't overdo yourself, Miss Roberts, before you begin the duties of the day. [*To* TOM.] Miss Roberts is the children's governess.

TOM. Oh? [*To* MISS ROBERTS.] Do you rap them over the knuckles? And stick them in the corner?

MISS ROBERTS [*answering him in the same spirit of raillery*]. Oh, yes — pinch them and slap them and box their ears.

MRS. BAXTER [*leaning forward in her chair, thinking this may be true*]. I hope you don't do anything of the sort, Miss Roberts.

MISS ROBERTS. Oh, no! not really, Mrs. Baxter. [*She rises.*] I think I'll say goodnight.

TOM. Don't go to bed yet, Miss Roberts.

MRS. BAXTER [*yawning*]. It's about time we all went.

TOM [*to* MRS. BAXTER]. You, too?

MRS. BAXTER. What time is it?

TOM [*looking at his watch*]. Twenty minutes past ten.

MRS. BAXTER. How late!

TOM. Call that late?

MRS. BAXTER. Ten is our bedtime. [*She rises.*] Come along, Miss Roberts; we shan't be fit for anything in the morning if we don't bustle off to bed.

[*She suppresses a yawn.*]

MISS ROBERTS. Good-night, Mr. Baxter.

[*She shakes hands with him.*]

MR. BAXTER. Good-night.

MISS ROBERTS [*shaking hands with* TOM]. Good-night.

TOM. Good-night, Miss Roberts; sleep well.

MISS ROBERTS. I always do.

MRS. BAXTER. Will you give me the magazine off the table, Miss Roberts, to take upstairs? [TOM *goes to the table and hands the magazine to* MISS ROBERTS, *who brings it to* MRS. BAXTER. *To* MISS ROBERTS.] You and I needn't say goodnight. We shall meet on the landing.

[*Turns over the pages of the magazine.*]

MISS ROBERTS. Good-night, everybody.

TOM [*following* MISS ROBERTS *to the foot of the stairs*]. Good-night, Miss Roberts. [MISS ROBERTS *goes out.*] Nice girl, Miss Roberts.

MRS. BAXTER. She suits me very well.

MR. BAXTER. She says she is going to leave.

TOM. Leave — Miss Roberts mustn't leave!

MRS. BAXTER. I don't think she meant it. Don't sit up too late, Tom, and don't hurry down in the morning. Would you like your breakfast in bed?

TOM [*laughing*]. In bed?

MRS. BAXTER. I thought you'd be so worn out after your journey.

TOM. Heavens, no, that's nothing. Goodnight, little sister. [*He kisses her.*]

MRS. BAXTER. Good-night, Tom. It's so nice to see you again. [*Then to* MR. BAXTER.] Try not to disturb me when you come upstairs. [*Speaking through a yawn as she goes towards the door.*] Oh, dear, I'm so sleepy. [*She goes out.*]

MR. BAXTER [*smiling at* TOM]. Well, Tom!

TOM [*smiling at* MR. BAXTER]. Well, Dick, how's everything? Business pretty good?

MR. BAXTER. So so.

TOM. That's nice.

MR. BAXTER. I don't go into the city every day now — two or three times a week. I leave my partners to attend to things the rest of the time — they seem to get on just as well without me.

TOM. I dare say they would. [*Taking out his cigarette case.*] I suppose I may smoke?

MR. BAXTER [*doubtfully*]. Here?

TOM. Well, don't you smoke here?

MR. BAXTER. You may. She won't smell it in the morning. [TOM *laughs and takes out a cigarette.*] Tom, if ever you get married, don't give in to your wife's weaknesses in the first few days of the honeymoon — you'll want to then, but don't. It becomes a habit. What's the use of saying that to you? I suppose you'll never marry now. [*He sits down.*]

TOM [*quite annoyed*]. Why not? Why shouldn't I marry? I don't see why you think I shan't marry. How long has she been here? [*He lights a cigarette.*]

Mr. Baxter. Who?
Tom. Miss Roberts.
Mr. Baxter. Oh!
Tom. Weren't we talking of Miss Roberts?
Mr. Baxter. No.
Tom. Oh, well, we are now.
Mr. Baxter. She's been here about four years. I'm so sorry she wants to leave. I don't want her to go at all.
Tom. Nor do I. Rather nice for you, Dick. A pretty wife and a pretty governess. [He nudges him.]
Mr. Baxter. Tom, don't do that.
 [He defends himself by putting up his hands.]
Tom. Very well, I won't.
Mr. Baxter [embarrassed and slightly annoyed]. Why do you say that?
Tom. Only chaffing. [He sees the chessboard.] Who's been playing chess?
Mr. Baxter. Miss Roberts and I.
Tom. Does Miss Roberts play chess? I must get her to teach me — let me see if I can remember any of the moves. [He sits by the table and moves the chess men about idly as he talks.] She is far too good to be your governess.
Mr. Baxter [enthusing]. You've noticed what an unusual woman she is?
Tom. Charming!
Mr. Baxter. Isn't she?
Tom. And so pretty!
Mr. Baxter. Very pretty.
Tom. She'll make a good wife for some man.
Mr. Baxter [reluctantly]. I suppose so — sometime.
Tom. I should make love to her if I lived in the same house.
Mr. Baxter. But if you were married?
Tom. I'm not!
Mr. Baxter [slowly and thoughtfully]. No. [There is a moment's pause.]
Tom. Let's change the subject, and talk about Miss Roberts. Tell me things about her.
Mr. Baxter. She's an orphan.
Tom. Poor girl.
Mr. Baxter. She's no near relations.
Tom. Lucky fellow.

Mr. Baxter. She's wonderful with the children.
Tom. Make a good mother.
Mr. Baxter. And so nice, so interesting, so good, such a companion. I can't find a single fault in her. She's a woman in a thousand, in a million.
Tom. I say, you'd better not let Dulcie hear you talk like that.
Mr. Baxter [seriously]. I don't. [Tom laughs.] I was only saying that to show you how well she suits us.
Tom. Of course.
Mr. Baxter. How well she suits Dulcie.
Tom. Oh, Dulcie, of course.
Mr. Baxter. I can't think what Dulcie will do without her; she's got so used to her. Miss Roberts waits on Dulcie hand and foot.
Tom [indignantly]. What a shame!
Mr. Baxter. Isn't it?
Tom. Why should Dulcie be waited on hand and foot?
Mr. Baxter. I don't know. She's so — well, not exactly ill.
Tom. Ill? She's as strong as a horse, always was.
Mr. Baxter. Yes, I can't remember when she had anything really the matter with her, but she always seems so tired — keeps wanting to lie down — she's not an invalid, she's a —
Tom. She's a mollusc.
Mr. Baxter. What's that?
Tom. Mollusca, subdivision of the animal kingdom.
Mr. Baxter. I know that.
Tom. I don't know if the Germans have remarked that many mammalia display characteristics commonly assigned to mollusca. I suppose the scientific explanation is that a mollusc once married a mammal and their descendants are the human mollusc.
Mr. Baxter [much puzzled]. What are you talking about?
Tom. People who are like a mollusc of the sea, which clings to a rock and lets the tide flow over its head. People who spend all their energy and ingenuity in sticking instead of moving, in whom the instinct for what I call molluscry is as dominating as an

inborn vice. And it is so catching. Why, one mollusc will infect a whole household. We all had it at home. Mother was quite a famous mollusc in her time. She was bedridden for fifteen years, and then, don't you remember, got up to Dulcie's wedding, to the amazement of everybody, and tripped down the aisle as lively as a kitten, and then went to bed again till she heard of something else she wanted to go to — a garden party or something. Father, he was a mollusc, too; he called it being a conservative; he might just as well have stayed in bed, too. Ada, Charlie, Emmeline, all of them were more or less mollusky, but Dulcibella was the queen. You won't often see such a fine healthy specimen of a mollusc as Dulcie. I'm a born mollusc!

MR. BAXTER [surprised]. You?

TOM. Yes, I'm energetic now, but only artificially energetic. I have to be on to myself all the time; make myself do things. That's why I chose the vigorous West, and wander from camp to camp. I made a pile in Leadville. I gambled it all away. I made another in Cripple Creek. I gave it away to the poor. If I made another, I should chuck it away. Don't you see why? Give me a competence, nothing to work for, nothing to worry about from day to day — why, I should become as famous a mollusc as dear old mother was.

MR. BAXTER. Is molluscry the same as laziness?

TOM. No, not altogether. The lazy flow with the tide. The mollusc uses forces to resist pressure. It's amazing the amount of force a mollusc will use, to do nothing, when it would be so much easier to do something. It's no fool, you know, it's often the most artful creature, it wriggles and squirms, and even fights from the instinct not to advance. There are wonderful things about molluscry, things to make you shout with laughter, but it's sad enough, too — it can ruin a life so, not only the life of the mollusc, but all the lives in the house where it dwells.

MR. BAXTER. Is there no cure for molluscry?

TOM. Well, I should say once a mollusc always a mollusc. But it's like drink, or any other vice. If grappled with it can be kept under. If left to itself, it becomes incurable.

MR. BAXTER. Is Dulcie a very advanced case?

TOM. Oh, very!!!

MR. BAXTER. Oh!

TOM. But let us hope not incurable. You know better than I how far she has gone. Tell me.

MR. BAXTER [seriously]. She's certainly getting worse. For instance, I can remember the time when she would go to church twice a Sunday, walk there and back; now she drives once, and she keeps an extra cushion in the pew, sits down for the hymns and makes the girls find her places.

TOM. Do you ever tell her not to mollusc so much?

MR. BAXTER. I used to, but I've given up now.

TOM. Oh, you must never give up.

MR. BAXTER. The trouble is she thinks she's so very active.

TOM. Molluscs always think that.

MR. BAXTER. Dulcie thinks of something to be done and tells me to do it, and then, by some mental process, which I don't pretend to grasp, she thinks she's done it herself. D'you think she does that to humbug me?

TOM. I believe there's no dividing line between the conscious and subconscious thoughts of molluscs. She probably humbugs herself just as much as she humbugs you.

MR. BAXTER. Oh!

TOM. You must be firm with her. The next time she tells you to do a thing, tell her to do it herself.

MR. BAXTER. I tried that. The other day, for instance, she wanted me to set a mouse-trap in her dressing-room; well, I was very busy at the time, and I knew there were no mice there, so I refused. It meant getting the cheese and everything.

TOM [trying not to appear amused]. Of course. And what did she say when you refused to set the mouse-trap?

MR. BAXTER. She began to make me sorry for her; she has no end of ways of making me sorry for her, and I've a very tender heart; but that day I just didn't care. I had the devil in me, so I said — set it yourself.

TOM. Bravo.

MR. BAXTER. We got quite unpleasant over it.

TOM. And which of you set the mousetrap in the end?

MR. BAXTER. Miss Roberts. [TOM *rises and moves away to hide his amusement from* MR. BAXTER.] It's always like that. She makes Miss Roberts do everything. For instance, Dulcie used to play chess with me of an evening, now she tells Miss Roberts to. She used to go walks with me, now she sends Miss Roberts. Dulcie was never energetic, but we used to have some good times together; now I can't get her to go anywhere or do anything.

TOM. Not very amusing for *you*.

MR. BAXTER. It does rather take the fun out of everything.

TOM. How did you come to let her get so bad?

MR. BAXTER [*simply*]. I fell in love with her. That put me at her mercy.

[*There is a moment's silence; then* TOM *says with decision.*]

TOM. *I* must take her in hand.

MR. BAXTER. I wish you would.

TOM. I'll make her dance.

MR. BAXTER. Don't be hard on her.

TOM. No, but firm. I'll show her what firmness is. A brother is the best person in the world to undertake the education of a mollusc. His firmness will be tempered with affection, and his affection won't be undermined with sentimentality. I shall start in on Dulcie the first thing to-morrow morning.

MR. BAXTER. And now what do you say to getting our candles?

TOM [*following* MR. BAXTER *towards the stairs*]. Come along. I'm ready — must have a good night's rest if I'm to tackle Dulcie in the morning. I don't anticipate any trouble. A woman isn't difficult to deal with if you take her the right way. Leave her to me, old man. You just leave her to me!

[*They go up the stairs as the curtain falls.*]

ACT II

SCENE. — *The same scene on the following morning. The French windows are wide open, displaying a view of the garden bathed in sunshine.*

MRS. BAXTER *is lounging in an armchair reading a novel.* TOM *enters with an enormous bunch of wild flowers, foxgloves, meadow-sweet, etc.*

TOM. Look!

MRS. BAXTER. Oh, how pretty! We must put them in water. Where's Miss Roberts?

TOM. In the schoolroom. They are at their lessons.

MRS. BAXTER. Then we must wait. What a pity. I hope they won't die.

TOM. Is Miss Roberts the only person in this house who can put these flowers in water?

MRS. BAXTER. The servants are always busy in the morning.

TOM. Why can't *you* do it?

MRS. BAXTER. *I* have other things to do.

TOM. What?

MRS. BAXTER. Numerous things. Do you think a woman never has anything to do?

TOM [*coming to her and tapping her on the shoulder*]. Get up and do them yourself.

MRS. BAXTER [*amiably*]. While you sit still in this chair. All very fine!

TOM. I'll help you.

MRS. BAXTER [*rising lazily*]. Very well. Bring me the vases and some water. [*She smells the flowers.*]

TOM. Vases. [*Pointing to two vases on the mantelpiece.*] Will these do?

MRS. BAXTER. Yes. Get those.

TOM [*pointing to another vase on the table*]. And that. You must get that one. We will divide the labour. [*He gets the two vases.* MRS. BAXTER *has not stirred.*] Where's yours?

MRS. BAXTER [*smiling pleasantly*]. I thought *you* were going to get the vases.

TOM. We were going to do this work between us. Get your vase.

MRS. BAXTER [*laughing*]. Oh, Tom — what a boy you are still.

Tom. Why should I get all the vases? [*Talking seriously to her.*] You know, Dulcie, you'd feel better if you ran about a little more.

Mrs. Baxter [*pleasantly*]. You'd save time, dear, if you'd run and get that vase yourself instead of standing there telling me to.

[Tom *puts the vases on the table. Then he goes and takes up the other vase.*]

Tom. Oh, very well. It's not worth quarreling about.

Mrs. Baxter. No, don't let us quarrel the first morning you are home.

Tom [*bringing the vase and putting it before her*]. There!

Mrs. Baxter. Thank you, Tom. You'll find a tap in the wall outside the window and a little watering-can beside it.

Tom. *I* got the vases.

Mrs. Baxter. *Please* bring me the water, Tom. These poppies are beginning to droop already.

Tom. I *won't* get the water. You must get it yourself.

Mrs. Baxter [*smiling*]. Very well. Wait till I go upstairs and put on my hat.

Tom. To go just outside the window?

Mrs. Baxter. I can't go into the hot sun without a hat.

Tom. Rats!

Mrs. Baxter [*seriously*]. It's *not* rats. Dr. Ross said I must *never* go out in the sun without a hat.

Tom. That much won't hurt you.

Mrs. Baxter. *I* don't mind, of course. But *you* must take the consequences if I have a sunstroke. Dick will be furious when he hears I've been out in the sun without a hat. You wouldn't like me to make Dick furious, would you, Tom? [Tom *touches her and points to the window, then folds his arms. There is a slight pause while she waits for* Tom *to offer to go.*] If you think it's too much trouble to step outside the window, I'll go all the way upstairs for my hat. I suppose all these pretty flowers will be quite dead by the time I come back.

Tom [*exasperated*]. Oh, very well, I'll get the water. [*He goes out into the garden.*]

Mrs. Baxter [*calling*]. Try not to scratch the can, and be sure you don't leave the tap to dribble.

Tom [*outside*]. Oh, the tap's all right. [*She occupies herself by smelling the flowers.* Tom *re-enters almost immediately with a little watering-can.*]

Tom. Here's the water.

Mrs. Baxter. Thank you, Tom. Work seems like play when we do it between us. Fill the vases.

Tom. I won't.

[*He puts the can on the table.*]

Mrs. Baxter. Well, wait while I go and get an apron.

Tom. You don't want an apron for that.

Mrs. Baxter. I'm not going to risk spilling the water all down this dress; I only put it on so as to look nice for you. I won't be a minute.

Tom. Stay where you are. [*Muttering to himself as he fills the vases.*] An apron to fill three vases. You might as well put on your boots, or get an umbrella or a waterproof.

[*He is about to set the can on the floor.*]

Mrs. Baxter [*quickly*]. Don't put it on the carpet. Put it on the gravel outside.

Tom. Put it on the gravel yourself.

[Tom *holds the can for her to take. She elaborately begins to wind a handkerchief round her right hand.*]

Mrs. Baxter. It's no use both of us wetting our hands.

[Tom *grumbling goes to the window and pitches the can outside.*]

Tom. Now I hope I've scratched the can, and I'm sorry I didn't leave the tap to dribble.

Mrs. Baxter. Naughty, naughty. Do you remember, Tom, when we were all at home together, you always did the flowers?

Tom. I'm not going to do them now.

Mrs. Baxter. You did them so tastefully. No one could do flowers like you. I remember Aunt Lizzie calling one day and saying if we hired a florist to arrange our flowers, we couldn't have got prettier effects than you got.

Tom. Get on with those flowers.

Mrs. Baxter. When I did the flowers,

THE MOLLUSC

Mamma used to say the drawing-room used to look like a rubbish heap.

TOM [*loudly*]. Get on with those flowers.

MRS. BAXTER. I should so like Miss Roberts to see the way you can arrange flowers.

TOM. Get on —

MRS. BAXTER [*wheedling him*]. Do arrange one vase — only one, just to show Miss Roberts.

TOM [*weakening*]. Well, only one. You must do the other two.

[*He begins to put the flowers in water.* MRS. BAXTER *watches him a moment, then she sinks into the handiest armchair.*]

MRS. BAXTER [*after a slight pause*]. How well you do it.

TOM [*suddenly realizing the situation*]. No, no, I won't. [*He flings the flowers on the table.*] Oh, you are artful. You've done nothing; I've done everything; I got the flowers, the vases, the water — everything, and now not another stalk will I touch. I don't care if they die; their blood will be on your head, not mine.

[*He sits down and folds his arms. A pause.*]

MRS. BAXTER [*serenely*]. If you won't talk, I may as well go on reading my novel. It's on the table beside you. Would you mind passing it?

TOM. Yes, I would.

MRS. BAXTER. Throw it.

TOM. I shan't.

MRS. BAXTER. I thought you'd cheer us up when you came home, but you just sit in my chair doing nothing.

TOM [*turning on her and saying gravely*]. Dulcie, it grieves me very much to see you such a mollusc.

MRS. BAXTER. What's a mollusc?

TOM. You are.

MRS. BAXTER [*puzzled*]. A mollusc? [*Gaily.*] Oh, I know, one of those pretty little creatures that live in the sea — or am I thinking of a sea anemone?

TOM. It's dreadful to see a strong healthy woman so idle.

MRS. BAXTER [*genuinely amazed*]. I idle? Oh, you're joking.

TOM. What are you doing but idling now? [*Approaching her and saying roughly.*] Get up, and do those flowers. Get out of that chair this minute.

MRS. BAXTER [*rising and smiling*]. I was only waiting for *you*. I thought we were going to do the flowers together.

TOM. No, we won't do them together; if we do them together I shall be doing them by myself before I know where I am.

[*He sits again.*]

MRS. BAXTER. I don't call that fair, to promise to help me with the flowers, and then just to sit and watch. I don't think Colorado is improving you. You've become so lazy and underhand.

TOM [*indignantly*]. What do you mean?

MRS. BAXTER. What I mean to say is, you undertook to help me with the flowers, and now you try to back out of it. Perhaps you call that sharp in America, but in England we should call it unsportsmanlike.

TOM [*picking up the flowers and throwing them down disgustedly*]. Oh, why did I ever go and gather all this rubbish?

[MR. BAXTER *enters and comes down the stairs.*]

MR. BAXTER. Half-past eleven, dear.

MRS. BAXTER. Thank you, dear.

TOM. Half-past eleven, dear — thank you, dear — what does that mean?

MR. BAXTER. Lunch.

TOM. Already?

MR. BAXTER. Not real lunch.

MRS. BAXTER. We always have cake and milk in the dining-room at half-past eleven. We think it breaks up the morning more. Aren't you coming?

TOM. Cake and milk at half-past eleven; what an idea! No, thank you.

MRS. BAXTER. I shall be glad of the chance to sit down. I've had a most exhausting morning. [*She goes out.*]

MR. BAXTER. Have you been taking her in hand?

TOM [*pretending not to comprehend*]. I beg your pardon?

MR. BAXTER. You said you were going to take her in hand, first thing this morning.

TOM. Oh, yes, so I did. So I have done

— in a way — not seriously, of course — not the first morning.

MR. BAXTER. You said you were going to show her what firmness was.

TOM. Well, so I did, but never having had any firmness from you, she doesn't know it when she sees it. [MR. BAXTER *is about to put some of the flowers in a vase.*] What are you doing?

MR. BAXTER. They're dying for want of water.

TOM. But I said she must put them in water herself.

MR. BAXTER. Oh, I see, discipline.

TOM. Exactly.

MR. BAXTER. What happened?

TOM [*pointing to the flowers*]. Can't you see what's happened? There they are still. [*Angrily.*] We've spent hours wrangling over those damned flowers. It may seem paltry to make such a fuss over anything so trivial, but it's the principle of the thing; if I give in at the start, I shall have to give in to the finish.

MR. BAXTER. Like me.

TOM. Yes, like you. When she comes back from the dining-room, I'll make her do those flowers herself, if I have to stand over her all the morning.

MR. BAXTER [*looking at* TOM *with admiration*]. That's the spirit. If only I had begun like that the very first morning of our honeymoon.

TOM [*with great determination*]. I'll stand no nonsense. She *shall* do the flowers herself.

[MISS ROBERTS *enters.*]

MISS ROBERTS. Mrs. Baxter sent me to do the flowers.

[*She comes immediately to the table and begins putting the flowers in water.* TOM *and* MR. BAXTER *look at each other.*]

TOM [*to him*]. Shall I tell her not to?

MR. BAXTER. Then Dulcie will tell her she is to.

TOM. Then we shall have to humiliate Dulcie before Miss Roberts.

MR. BAXTER. Yes.

TOM. I don't want to do that.

MR. BAXTER. No.

TOM. I'm not giving in.

MR. BAXTER. No.

TOM. Don't gloat.

MR. BAXTER. I'm not gloating.

TOM. You are. You're gloating because I've had to give in in the way *you* always do.

MISS ROBERTS [*to* MR. BAXTER]. The girls have been asking if I thought they could have a half-holiday in honour of their uncle's arrival.

MR. BAXTER. I don't see why not.

MISS ROBERTS. If you think they'd be in the way, I might take them off to the woods for the day.

MR. BAXTER. Yes.

MISS ROBERTS. I thought as it's so fine we might take our lunch with us, and have a picnic.

TOM. Why don't we all go a picnic.

MR. BAXTER. All who?

TOM. You and I and the girls and Miss Roberts and Dulcie.

MR. BAXTER. You'll never get Dulcie on a picnic, will he, Miss Roberts?

TOM. Why not?

MR. BAXTER. Too much exertion.

MISS ROBERTS [*still busy filling the vases*]. I think Mrs. Baxter would go if Mr. Kemp asked her.

[TOM *looks at* MR. BAXTER *as soon as* MISS ROBERTS *has spoken, and* MR. BAXTER *looks dubious.*]

TOM [*in a lower voice, to* MR. BAXTER]. I don't want Miss Roberts to think that I can't master Dulcie; besides, a picnic, the very thing to make her run about, but we must approach her tactfully and keep our tempers. I lost mine over the flowers, otherwise I've not the least doubt I could have made her do them; we must humour Dulcie and cajole her. Whisk her off to the woods in a whirl of gaiety; you go dancing into the dining-room like this. [*Assuming great jollity.*] We're all going off on a picnic.

MR. BAXTER. Oh, no.

TOM. Why not?

MR. BAXTER. It wouldn't be me.

TOM. Well, er — [*glancing at* MISS ROBERTS] go and — er — [*Glancing again at* MISS ROBERTS.] Oh, go and say whatever

you like. But be jolly about it; full of the devil.
[*He takes* MR. BAXTER *by the arm and pushes him towards the stairs.*]
MR. BAXTER [*imitating* TOM *as he goes*]. We're all going off on a picnic. [*He stops at the top of the stairs and says seriously.*] It wouldn't be me. [*He exits.*]
TOM. So you're not one of the cake-and-milk brigade?
MISS ROBERTS. No.
TOM. I thought you wouldn't be.
MISS ROBERTS. Aren't you going to join them?
TOM. No, I don't want to eat cake in the middle of the morning. I'm like you. We seem to have a lot of habits in common.
MISS ROBERTS. Do you think so?
TOM. Don't you?
MISS ROBERTS. I haven't thought.
[*She takes a vase to the mantelpiece.* TOM *watches her and follows with the other vase.* MISS ROBERTS *takes the vase from* TOM *and puts it on the mantelpiece.*]
TOM. Didn't we have a nice walk together?
MISS ROBERTS. Yes; don't you love being out in the early morning?
TOM. I'm up with the sun at home out West. I live out-of-doors out there.
MISS ROBERTS. How splendid!
TOM. You're the kind of girl for Colorado.
MISS ROBERTS [*pleased*]. Am I?
TOM. Can you ride?
MISS ROBERTS. Yes, but I don't get any opportunities now.
TOM. Got a good nerve?
MISS ROBERTS. I broke a colt once; he'd thrown three men, but he never threw me!
TOM [*smiling at her*]. Well done!
MISS ROBERTS. I didn't mean to boast, but I'd love to do it again.
TOM. I should love to see you mounted on a mustang, flying through our country.
MISS ROBERTS. With the tree-tops waving down in the valley, and the great blue mountains you told us about, stretching away — away —

TOM [*watching her with admiration*]. You certainly ought to come to Colorado.
MISS ROBERTS. Nothing so thrilling could happen to me.
[*She returns to the table and picks up the remaining flowers.*]
TOM [*following her*]. Why? You've nothing to do but get on the boat and take the train from New York, and I'd meet you in Denver.
MISS ROBERTS [*laughing*]. It's so nice to have some one here to make us laugh.
TOM [*a little hurt*]. Oh, I was being serious.
MISS Roberts [*seriously*]. Do you really think Colorado would be a good place for a girl like me to go to? A governess!
TOM. Yes, yes, a girl who has to earn her own living has a better time of it out there than here, more independence, more chance, more life.
MISS ROBERTS [*thoughtfully*]. I do know an English lady in Colorado Springs, at least a great friend of mine does, and I'm sure I could get a letter to her.
TOM [*cheerfully*]. You don't want any letters of introduction; you've got me.
MISS ROBERTS [*smiling*]. Yes, but that is not quite the same thing.
TOM. No, I suppose not; no, I see: well, can't you write to your friend and tell her to send that letter on at once?
MISS ROBERTS [*amused*]. You talk as if it were all settled.
TOM. I wish it were.
MISS ROBERTS [*not noticing that he is flirting with her, she says thoughtfully*]. I wish I knew what to do about leaving here.
TOM. You told me you had already given my sister notice.
MISS ROBERTS. She won't take it.
TOM. She can't make you stay if you want to go.
MISS ROBERTS [*smiling, but serious*]. It's not as simple as that. After Mrs. Baxter has treated me so well, I should be making a poor return, if I left her before she found some one to take my place. On the other hand, my duty to the children is to leave them.
TOM. A real old-fashioned conscience.

Miss Roberts. One must think of the others.

Tom. It seems to me you're always doing that.

Miss Roberts. If you knew how I sometimes long to be free to do whatever I like just for one day! When I see other girls — girls who don't work for a living — enjoying themselves — it comes over me so dreadfully what I am missing. From the schoolroom window I can see the tennis club, and while I am giving Gladys and Margery their geography lesson, I hear them calling "Play! Fifteen love!" and see the ball flying and the girls in their white dresses, talking to such nice-looking young men.

Tom. Um, yes. Don't *you* ever talk to any of those nice-looking young men?

Miss Roberts. Of course not.

Tom. How's that?

Miss Roberts. Governesses never do. We only pass them by as we walk out with the children, or see the backs of their heads in church. Or, if we are introduced, as I was to one at the Rectory one day — the occasion is so unusual we feel quite strained and nervous — and can't appear at our best. So that they don't want to pursue the acquaintance even if they could.

Tom. You don't seem strained and nervous as you talk to me.

Miss Roberts [*innocently*]. You don't seem like the others. [*She meets his eyes — smiles at him and says.*] I must go back to the schoolroom. [*She rises.*]

Tom [*rising and coming to* Miss Roberts]. Not yet. Don't go yet. I want you to stay here — talking to me. You are sure to hear my little nieces shrieking about in the garden when they have done their cake.

[Mrs. Baxter *enters followed by* Mr. Baxter.]

Mrs. Baxter. Oh, I hurried back to finish the flowers, but I see you have done them. Thank you.

Miss Roberts. You asked me to do them, Mrs. Baxter.

Mrs. Baxter [*smiling*]. Oh, no, Miss Roberts — I think you are mistaken. I only said they were there waiting to be done.

[*She sits in an armchair and begins to read a novel.*]

Tom [*in an undertone to* Mr. Baxter]. Have you told her about the picnic?

Mr. Baxter. There was no suitable opportunity — so —

Tom. You're a coward! [*He pushes past him.* Tom *then motions to* Mr. Baxter *to speak to* Mrs. Baxter. *He refuses.* Tom, *assuming great cheerfulness, addresses* Mrs. Baxter.] We are all going off on a picnic.

Mrs. Baxter [*pleasantly*]. Oh.

Tom. Yes. We four and the girls. [*Whispering to* Mr. Baxter.] Back me up.

Mr. Baxter [*rubbing his hands together, and trying to assume jollity*]. Won't that be fun?

Mrs. Baxter [*brightly*]. I think it would be great fun —

Tom. Ah.

Mrs. Baxter. — Some day.

Tom. Why not to-day?

Mrs. Baxter. Why to-day?

Tom [*at a loss for an answer, appeals to* Mr. Baxter *and* Miss Roberts]. Why to-day?

Miss Roberts. In honour of Mr. Kemp's arrival, and it's such a fine day — and —

Mrs. Baxter. You will find the girls in the schoolroom — dear.

Tom [*very jolly*]. Shall she go and get them ready?

Mrs. Baxter [*innocently*]. What for?

Tom. The picnic.

Mrs. Baxter. I thought it had been decided not to go to-day.

Mr. Baxter [*losing his temper*]. Oh, Dulcie — you know quite well —

Tom [*signing to* Mr. Baxter *to keep quiet*]. Sh! [*Turning to* Mrs. Baxter *and pretending to make a meek, heartfelt appeal.*] Please let us go to-day. It's in honour of my arrival. I shall be *so* hurt if I don't have a picnic in honour of my arrival.

Mrs. Baxter. Suppose it rains.

Tom [*at a loss for an answer, appealing to the others*]. Suppose it rains?

Miss Roberts [*at the window*]. I can't see a single cloud.

MR. BAXTER. The glass has gone up.
TOM. It won't rain if we take plenty of umbrellas and mackintoshes and our goloshes.
MRS. BAXTER. I think we are all too tired.
TOM [*scouting the idea*]. Too tired!
[MR. BAXTER *and* TOM *get together*.]
MRS. BAXTER. I suppose it is the excitement of Tom's arrival which is making us feel so next-dayish.
TOM. Next-dayish!
MRS. BAXTER. *You* especially. *You* were very irritable over the flowers. You ought to go and lie down.
[*She takes up her novel and opens it as if she considered the argument over.* MISS ROBERTS *watches them anxiously.* MR. BAXTER *makes an emphatic gesture, expressing his strong feelings on the subject.*]
TOM [*clutching his arm*]. We *must* keep our tempers. We *must* keep our tempers.
MR. BAXTER. Shall we poke fun at her?
TOM. No, no, we'll try a little coaxing first. [*He takes a chair, places it close beside* MRS. BAXTER *and sits. Smiling affectionately at* MRS. BAXTER.] Dear Dulcie.
MRS. BAXTER [*smiling affectionately at* TOM *and patting his knees*]. Dear Tom.
TOM. We shall have such a merry picnic.
MRS. BAXTER. It *would* have been nice, wouldn't it?
TOM. Under a canopy of green boughs with the sunbeams dropping patterns on the carpet of moss at our feet.
MRS. BAXTER. Spiders dropping on our hats.
TOM. Dear, interesting little creatures, and so industrious.
MRS. BAXTER. Ants up our arms.
TOM [*laughing*]. Lizards up our legs. Frogs in our food. Oh, we shall get back to Nature. [TOM *and* MRS. BAXTER *both laugh heartily, both in the greatest good-humour.* MR. BAXTER *and* MISS ROBERTS *also laugh.*] Then it's settled.
MRS. BAXTER. Yes, dear — it's settled.
TOM [*thinking he has won*]. Ah!

MRS. BAXTER. We'll all stay quietly at home.
[*She resumes the reading of her book.* TOM *is in dismay.*]
MR. BAXTER. The girls will be greatly disappointed.
TOM [*with emotion*]. Poor girls! A day in the woods. [*With mock pathos.*] Think what that means to those poor girls.
MRS. BAXTER [*rising and saying seriously to* MISS ROBERTS]. Miss Roberts, you might go to the schoolroom and tell Gladys and Margery that Mamma says they may have a half-holiday and go for a picnic in the woods.
[TOM *winks at* MR. BAXTER. *The three look at each other agreeably surprised.*]
MISS ROBERTS [*moving towards the stairs*]. Thank you. Thank you very much, Mrs. Baxter. I'll go and get them ready at once. [*She goes out.*]
TOM. I knew we only had to appeal to her heart.
MR. BAXTER. We shall want twelve hard-boiled eggs.
TOM. And some ginger-beer.
MR. BAXTER. A ham.
TOM. A few prawns.
MRS. BAXTER [*looking out of the window to which she has strolled*]. I am glad Miss Roberts and the girls have got such a fine day for their picnic.
[TOM *and* MR. BAXTER *look at each other in dismay.*]
MR. BAXTER [*after a pause*]. After leading us on to believe —
TOM [*in great good-humour*]. Can't you see she's teasing us? [*Going to* MRS. BAXTER, *he playfully pinches her ear.*] Mischievous little puss!
MRS. BAXTER [*gravely to* MR. BAXTER]. Dear, I should like to speak to you.
MR. BAXTER. Shall we go to my room?
MRS. BAXTER. I don't see why we need trouble to walk across the hall. [*Glances at* TOM.] We may get this room to ourselves by and by. [*She sits down.*]
TOM [*cheerfully taking the hint*]. All right — all right. I'll go and make preparations for the picnic. Don't keep us

waiting, Dulcie. Prawns — hams — ginger-beer — [*He runs off.*]

MR. BAXTER [*slightly peevish*]. I wish you would enter more into the spirit of the picnic. It would do you good to go to a picnic.

MRS. BAXTER. I don't like the way Tom is carrying on with Miss Roberts. Last evening they monopolized the conversation. This morning — a walk before breakfast. Just now — as soon as my back is turned — at it again. I don't like it — and it wouldn't do me any good at all to go to a picnic.

MR. BAXTER. Tom seems so set on our going.

MRS. BAXTER. Tom is set on making *me* go. Tom has taken upon himself to reform my character. He thinks I need stirring up.

MR. BAXTER [*embarrassed*]. What put such an idea as that into your head?

MRS. BAXTER [*looking him straight in the eye*]. The clumsy way you both go about it. [MR. BAXTER *looks exceedingly uncomfortable.*] ... It wouldn't deceive any woman. It wouldn't suit me at all if Tom became interested in Miss Roberts. I could never find another Miss Roberts. She understands my ways so well, I couldn't possibly do without her; not that I'm thinking of myself; I'm thinking only of her good. It's not right for Tom to come here turning her head, and I don't suppose the climate of Colorado would suit her.

MR. BAXTER. I don't think we need worry yet. They only met yesterday.

MRS. BAXTER. That is so like you, dear — to sit still and let everything slip past you like the — what was that funny animal Tom mentioned — the mollusc. I prefer to take action. We must speak to Tom.

MR. BAXTER. You'll only offend him if you say anything to him.

MRS. BAXTER. I've no intention of saying anything. I think it would come much better from you.

MR. BAXTER [*with determination*]. I shan't interfere.

MRS. BAXTER [*trying to work on his feelings*]. It's not often I ask you to do anything for me, and I'm not strong.

MR. BAXTER [*feeling uncomfortable*]. I shouldn't know what to say to Tom, or how to say it.

MRS. BAXTER [*approaching* MR. BAXTER]. You know the way men talk to each other. Go up to him and say, "I say, old fellow, that little governess of ours. Hands off, damn it all." [MRS. BAXTER *nudges* MR. BAXTER *in a masculine way.* MR. BAXTER *laughs and retreats a little.* MRS. BAXTER *is mightily offended.*] I don't consider that trifling with a young girl's affections is food for laughter.

MR. BAXTER [*trying to conceal his amusement*]. I think I'll go and join Tom.

MRS. BAXTER. Will you tell him we wish him to pay less [MISS ROBERTS *enters*] attention to — [*She sees* MISS ROBERTS.]

MR. BAXTER. We'll see. [*He goes out.*]

MRS. BAXTER. I know what *that* means.

MISS ROBERTS [*coming to* MRS. BAXTER]. If you please, Mrs. Baxter, I'm having such trouble with Gladys and Margery. They want to go to the picnic in their Sunday hats, and I say they must go in their everyday ones.

MRS. BAXTER. If there's going to be any trouble about the matter, let them have their own way.

MISS ROBERTS. Thank you.
[*She is going out.*]

MRS. BAXTER. Oh, Miss Roberts. [MISS ROBERTS *stops.*] I want a word with you before you start off on your picnic. Sit down dear. [MISS ROBERTS *sits down.*] You know how devoted I am to my brother Tom.

MISS ROBERTS [*with smiling enthusiasm*]. I don't wonder. He's delightful. So amusing, so easy to get on with.

MRS. BAXTER. Yes, but of course we all have our faults, and a man who gets on easily with one will get on easily with another. Always mistrust people who are easy to get on with.

MISS ROBERTS [*solemnly*]. Oh — do you mean he isn't quite honest?

MRS. BAXTER [*indignantly*]. Nothing of the sort. You mustn't twist my meanings in that manner. You might get me into great trouble.

MISS ROBERTS. I'm so sorry, but I

thought you were warning me against him.

MRS. BAXTER [*confused*]. Yes — no — yes — and no. [*Recovering herself.*] I am sure you will take what I'm going to say as I mean it, because — [*smiles at her*] I am so fond of you. Ever since you came to us I have wished to make you one of the family. When I say one of the family, I mean in the sense of taking your meals with us. Mr. Baxter and the girls and I are so much attached to you. We should like to keep you with us always.

MISS ROBERTS. I *must* leave at the end of the term.

MRS. BAXTER. We won't go into all that now.

MISS ROBERTS. But —

MRS. BAXTER [*smiling and raising her hand in protestation, says politely*]. Try not to interrupt. [*Seriously.*] I should say that a man of Tom's age who has never married would be a confirmed bachelor. He might amuse himself here and there with a pretty girl, but he would never think of any woman seriously.

MISS ROBERTS [*embarrassed*]. I can't think why you are saying this to me.

MRS. BAXTER [*plunging at last into her subject*]. To speak quite frankly — as a sister — I find your attitude towards my brother Tom a trifle too encouraging. Last evening, for instance, you monopolized a good deal of the conversation — and this morning you took a walk with him before breakfast — and altogether — [*very sweetly*] it looks just a little bit as if you were trying to flirt — doesn't it?

MISS ROBERTS [*with suppressed rage*]. I'm not a flirt!

MRS. BAXTER. I didn't say you were — I said —

MISS ROBERTS. I'm *not* a flirt — I'm *not!*

MRS. BAXTER. We'll say no more about it. It was very hard for me to have to speak to you. You have no idea how difficult I found it.

MISS ROBERTS. Mrs. Baxter, you have often been very kind to me, and I don't want to forget it — but I'd rather not be treated as one of the family any more. I want my meals in the schoolroom, and I mustn't be expected to sit in the drawing-room.

MRS. BAXTER. Upsetting the whole machinery of the house.

MISS ROBERTS. I can't go on meeting him at table and everywhere.

MRS. BAXTER. I don't see why not.

MISS ROBERTS. I shouldn't know where to look or what to say.

MRS. BAXTER. Look out of the window and converse on inanimate objects.

MISS ROBERTS [*mumbles angrily*]. I will not look out of the window and converse on inanimate objects.

MRS. BAXTER [*putting up a warning hand*]. Hush, hush, hush!

MISS ROBERTS. Please understand I won't be one of the family, and I won't go to the picnic.

[*She goes hurriedly into the garden.*]

MRS. BAXTER. Oh, oh, naughty girl!

[TOM *and* MR. BAXTER *enter.*]

TOM. Cook thinks the large basket and the small hamper will suffice. She *said* suffice.

MRS. BAXTER. I'm very sorry, Tom, but it is out of the question for us to go to a picnic to-day.

MR. BAXTER. Oh, Dulcie.

TOM. Too late to back out.

MRS. BAXTER. *I* haven't backed out. It's Miss Roberts.

TOM. We can't have a picnic without Miss Roberts.

MR. BAXTER. What's the matter with her?

MRS. Baxter [*solemnly*]. Miss Roberts and I have had *words*.

[TOM *whistles quietly.*]

MR. BAXTER. What about?

MRS. BAXTER. Never you mind.

TOM. Oh, it can't be such a very dreadful quarrel between two such nice sensible women. I guess you were both in the right. [*To* MR. BAXTER.] I guess they were both in the wrong. [*Taking* MRS. BAXTER *by the arm and cajoling her.*] Come along. Tell us all about it.

MRS. BAXTER [*withdrawing her arm*]. No, Tom, I can't.

Tom. Then suppose I go to Miss Roberts and get her version.

Mrs. Baxter [*in dismay*]. Oh, no, that wouldn't do at all.

Tom. I only want to make peace. [*To Mr. Baxter.*] Wouldn't it be better if they told me and let me make it up for them?

Mr. Baxter. Why you?

Tom. A disinterested person.

Mrs. Baxter. But you are not.

[*Putting her hand over her mouth.*]

Tom [*turns quickly to* Mrs. Baxter]. What?

Mrs. Baxter. I'm not going to say any more. [*She sits down.*]

Tom [*seriously*]. You *must*. If your quarrel concerns *me*, I have a right to know all about it.

Mr. Baxter [*motioning to* Mrs. Baxter]. You are only putting ideas into their heads.

Tom [*turning sharply on* Mr. Baxter]. Putting what ideas into their heads? [*It dawns upon him what the subject of the quarrel has been.*] Oh! [*To* Mrs. Baxter.] You don't mean to say you spoke to her about — [*He stops, embarrassed.*] What have you said to her?

Mrs. Baxter. I decline to tell you.

Tom. Then I shall ask *her*. [*Going.*]

Mrs. Baxter [*quickly*]. No, no, Tom. I — prefer to tell you myself. I spoke very nicely to her. I forget how the conversation arose, but I think I did say something to the effect that young girls ought to be careful not to have their heads turned by men years older than themselves. [*She looks significantly at* Tom, *who turns away angrily.*] Instead of thanking me, she stamped and stormed and was very rude to me — very rude. I simply said [*in a very gentle tone*], Oh, Miss Roberts! [*Rousing herself as she describes* Miss Roberts' *share in the scene.*] But she went on shouting, "I won't go to the picnic, I won't go to the picnic!" and bounced out of the room. It just shows you how you can be deceived in people, and I have been so good to that girl.

Tom [*coming towards* Mrs. Baxter]. I'm very angry — with you — very angry.

Mrs. Baxter. I simply gave her a word of counsel which she chose to take in the wrong spirit.

Tom. You interfered. You meddled. It's too bad of you, Dulcie. It's unbearable.

Mr. Baxter [*watching* Tom]. The way you take it any one would think you had fallen in love with our Miss Roberts since yesterday.

Mrs. Baxter. Yes — wouldn't any one?

Tom [*addressing them both*]. Would there be anything so strange in that? Perhaps I have, I don't know — perhaps as you imply I'm old enough to know better. I don't know. All I know is, I think her the most charming girl I ever met. I've not had time to realize what this is; one must wait and see; give the seed a chance to produce a flower — not stamp on it. [*To* Mrs. Baxter.] You might have left things alone, when all was going so pleasantly. I was just beginning to think — beginning to feel — wondering if perhaps — later on — Now you've spoilt everything.

Mrs. Baxter [*tearful and angry*]. I won't stay here to be abused. [*Going to the window.*] You've done nothing else all the morning. I'm tired of being taken in hand and improved. No one likes to be improved.

[Mrs. Baxter *goes out through the window.*]

Tom. I don't want to be unkind to her — but you know how a man feels. He doesn't like any one meddling when he's just beginning to —

Mr. Baxter [*showing embarrassment all through the early part of this scene*]. I agree with Dulcie. It would not be suitable for you to marry Miss Roberts.

Tom. She's as good as any of us.

Mr. Baxter [*hesitatingly*]. It's not that. Miss Roberts from her position here — alone in the world but for us — and having lived here so long — is — in a sense — under my protection.

Tom. I don't see that, but go on.

Mr. Baxter. I feel — in a certain degree — responsible for her. I think it is my duty — and Dulcie's duty — to try and stop her making what we both feel would be an unsuitable marriage.

Tom. It's a little early to speak of our marriage, but why should it be unsuitable?
Mr. Baxter. We don't wish her to marry you.
Tom. Why? Give me a reason.
Mr. Baxter. Why do you press me for a reason?
Tom. Because this is very important to me. You have constituted yourself her guardian. I have no objection to *that*, but I want to get at your objection to me as a husband to her. I'm in a position to marry. I'd treat her well if she'd have me. We'd be as happy as the day is long in our little home in the mountains —
Mr. Baxter [*unable to restrain himself*]. You married to her? Oh, no — oh, no, I couldn't bear that.
[*He sinks into a chair and leans his head on his hands.*]
Tom [*completely taken aback*]. Dick, think what you're saying.
Mr. Baxter. I couldn't help it. You made me say it — talking of taking her away — right away where I shall never see her again. I couldn't stand my life here without her.
Tom. Dick, Dick!
Mr. Baxter. She knows nothing of how I feel; it's only this moment I realized myself what she is to me.
Tom. Then from this moment you ought never to see her again.
Mr. Baxter. That's impossible!
Tom. Think of Dulcie, and the girl herself; she can't live in the house with you both now.
Mr. Baxter. She's lived with us for four years, and no one has ever seen any harm in it; nothing is changed.
Tom. From the moment you realized what she is to you, everything is changed.
Mr. Baxter. There has never been anything to criticize in my conduct to Miss Roberts, and there won't be anything.
Tom. She is the object of an affection, which you, as a married man, have no right to feel for her. I don't blame you entirely. I blame Dulcie, for throwing you so much together. I remember all you said last evening. Dulcie used to play chess with you, now she tells Miss Roberts to; Dulcie used to go for long walks with you, now she sends Miss Roberts. Out of your forced companionship has sprung this, which she ought to have foreseen.
Mr. Baxter. Nothing is confessed or understood; I don't see that Miss Roberts is in any danger.
Tom. She is alone. She has no confidant, no friend, no outlet for the natural desires of youth, for love, for some one to love. She finds you sympathetic — you know the rest.
Mr. Baxter. It is jealousy that is at the bottom of your morality.
Tom. It won't do, Dick. It's a most awful state of things.
Mr. Baxter. If you think that, I wonder you stay here.
Tom. Very well, if you mean I ought to clear out. [*He goes towards the door.*]
Mr. Baxter [*following after* Tom]. No, Tom. Look here, I didn't mean that; but, you see, you and I can't discuss this without losing our tempers, so if your visit to us is to continue mutually pleasant, as I hope it will, we'd better avoid the topic in future.
Tom. Then you mean to keep Miss Roberts here indefinitely — compromised?
Mr. Baxter. It's no use going over the ground; we don't see things from the same point of view, so don't let us go on discussing. [*He goes up the stairs and then turns to* Tom.] Tom, you might trust me.
[Mr. Baxter *goes out.* Tom *remains in deep thought, then suddenly makes a determined movement, then stops and sighs.*]

[Miss Roberts *enters from the garden. She hesitates timidly when she sees him.*]

Miss Roberts. Mrs. Baxter sent me to get her magazine.
Tom. Where is my sister?
Miss Roberts. Sitting in the garden.
[*She takes up the magazine and is going out again.*]
Tom. I — [Miss Roberts *stops.*] I want to tell you something.
Miss Roberts. I can't stay.
Tom. I ask you as a great favour to me to hear me.
Miss Roberts. I ought not to stay.

Tom. I didn't think you'd refuse me when I asked you like that.

Miss Roberts [*hesitating*]. I can't stay long.

Tom. Won't you sit down while I tell you? [*He indicates a chair.* Miss Roberts *comes to the chair and sits.*] I want to tell you about myself, and my life in Colorado.

Miss Roberts [*nervously*]. I don't think I can stay if it's just to talk and hear stories of Colorado.

Tom [*smiling*]. Did you have enough of my stories this morning?

Miss Roberts. Oh, no, I was quite interested in what you said, but I —

Tom. You *were* interested. I knew it by your eyes. Why, you even thought you'd like to go there yourself sometime.

Miss Roberts. I've changed my mind. I've quite given up that idea now.

Tom. You'd like it out there. I'm sure you would; it's a friendly country; no one cares who you are, but only what you are, so you soon make friends. That's right. That gives every one a chance, and it's good in this way, it makes a man depend on himself, it teaches him to think clearly and decide quickly; in fact he has to keep wide awake if he wants to succeed. That's the kind of training I've had. I've been from mining camp to mining camp — I've tried my luck in half the camps in California and Colorado. Sometimes it was good, sometimes bad, but take it altogether, I've done well. [*Making the next point clearly and delicately.*] I've got something saved up, and I can always make good money, anywhere west of Chicago. [*Laughing.*] Now I'm talking like a true American; they always begin by telling you how much they've got. You'll forgive me, won't you? It's force of habit. Now what was I saying? [*Seriously.*] We learn to decide quickly in everything; you find me somewhat abrupt; it's only that. I make up my mind all at once, and once it's made up, that's finished — I don't change. [*Hesitating slightly.*] The first time I saw you I made up my mind — I said that's the girl for me, that's the girl I want for my wife. [*Leans towards her.*] Will you be my wife?

Miss Roberts [*rising and very much moved and distressed*]. Oh, no, I can't. I didn't know that was coming, or I wouldn't have listened, I wouldn't indeed.

Tom [*following her*]. I've been too abrupt. I warned you I was like that; I make up my mind I want something, and the next thing is, I go straight away and ask for it. That's too quick for you. You want time to think — well, take time to think it over. [Miss Roberts *turns to him quickly.*] Don't tell me yet; there's no hurry. I'm not going back for a month or two.

Miss Roberts. I'm very much obliged to you for asking me to marry you, but I can't.

Tom. Never?

Miss Roberts. No, never! I don't think so.

Tom. Eh? That sounds like hope.

Miss Roberts [*quickly*]. I didn't mean it to sound like hope.

Tom. It didn't seem that way last evening when we were talking about the forests and the mountains, and I was telling you how it felt to be back — or this morning when we were getting flowers, or afterwards when we sat here, while they were eating their cake and milk; it seemed to me we were getting on famously.

Miss Roberts [*appealingly*]. Oh, please don't go on. I can't bear it. You only distress me. [*She sobs.*]

Tom. Oh! [*Pausing and looking at her, he sees that she means it and is really distressed.*] I'm sorry.

[*He goes out abruptly.* Miss Roberts *is weeping bitterly.*]

[Mr. Baxter *enters. He comes downstairs towards her and looks down at her with affectionate concern.* Miss Roberts *does not notice his presence till he speaks.*]

Mr. Baxter. What is it?

Miss Roberts [*trying to control her sobs*]. Nothing.

Mr. Baxter. You are in trouble. You are in great trouble — can't you tell me — can't I do anything?

Miss Roberts. No.

Mr. Baxter. Wouldn't it do you good

to tell somebody? Don't you want some one to tell it all to?

MISS ROBERTS.. I want — [*She falters.*]

MR. BAXTER. What is it you want?

MISS ROBERTS. I think I want a mother. [*The effort of saying this brings on her tears afresh; she stands weeping bitterly.* MR. BAXTER *puts his arm about her and draws her gently to him. She yields herself naturally and sobs on his shoulder.* MR. BAXTER *murmurs and soothes her.*]

MR. BAXTER. Poor child! Poor child! [*While they are in this sentimental position* TOM *and* MRS. BAXTER *appear at the window. They see* MR. BAXTER *and* MISS ROBERTS, *but are unseen by them.* MISS ROBERTS *disengages herself from* MR. BAXTER *and goes out sobbing without perceiving* TOM *and* MRS. BAXTER. MR. BAXTER *watches* MISS ROBERTS *off, then turns and sees* MRS. BAXTER *for the first time; he becomes very embarrassed under her steady, disapproving eyes. To* MRS. BAXTER.] Do you want me to explain?

MRS. BAXTER [*coldly*]. Not at present, thank you, Richard.

MR. BAXTER. I was only —

MRS. BAXTER. Not now. I prefer to consider my position carefully before expressing my astonishment and indignation.

MR. BAXTER. Well, if you won't let me explain —

[*He turns to the window and sees* TOM. *He looks appealingly at him.* TOM *ignores him and walks past him.* MR. BAXTER *shrugs his shoulders and goes out through the window.*]

MRS. BAXTER. I don't know which of them I feel angriest with.

TOM. Dick, of course.

MRS. BAXTER [*tearfully*]. For thirteen years no man has ever kissed me — except you — and Dick — and Uncle Joe — and Dick's brothers — and old Mr. Redmayne — and the Dean when he came back from the Holy Land. [*Working herself into a rage.*] I'll never speak to Dick again. I'll bundle Miss Roberts out of the house at once.

TOM. Do it discreetly. Send her away certainly, but don't do anything hastily.

MRS. BAXTER. I'm not the woman to put up with that sort of thing.

TOM [*persuasively*]. Don't be hard on her; don't be turning her into the street; make it look as if she were going on a holiday. Pack her off somewhere with the children for a change of air, this afternoon.

MRS. BAXTER. It's most inconvenient; everything will be upside down. [*Calming herself, she sits in an armchair.*] You're right. I mustn't be too hasty; better wait a few days, till the end of the term, or even till after we come home from the seaside, then pack her off. [*Pause.*] Unless it blows over.

TOM [*astonished and going to her quickly*]. Blows over! It won't blow over while *she's* in the house. [*Very seriously.*] You're up against a serious crisis. Take warning from what you saw and save your home from ruin. [MRS. BAXTER, *awed and impressed by this, listens attentively.*] You've grown so dependent on Miss Roberts, you've almost let her slip into your place; if you want to keep Dick, you must begin an altogether different life, not to-morrow — [MRS. BAXTER *shakes her head.*] Not next week — [MRS. BAXTER *shakes her head again.*] Now! [MRS. BAXTER'S *face betrays her discontent at the unattractive prospect he offers her.*] *You* be his companion, *you* play chess with him, *you* go walks with him, sit up with him in the evenings, get up early in the morning. Be gay and cheerful at the breakfast table. When he goes away, see him off; when he comes home, run to meet him. Learn to do without Miss Roberts, and make him forget her.

MRS. BAXTER. Very well. [*Rising.*] She shall leave this house directly — directly I recover.

TOM. Recover from what?

MRS. BAXTER. From the shock. Think of the shock I've had; there's sure to be a reaction. I shouldn't wonder if I had a complete collapse. It's beginning already. [*She totters and goes towards staircase.*] Oh, dear, I feel so ill. Please call Miss Roberts.

TOM. You were going to learn to do without Miss Roberts.

Mrs. Baxter. That was before I was ill. I can't be ill without Miss Roberts.

[*Puts her hand to her side, turns up her eyes and groans as she totters out.*]

Tom. Oh! Oh! You mollusc!

THE CURTAIN FALLS

ACT III

Scene. — *The same scene one week later. The only difference to the appearance of the room is that there is the addition of an invalid couch with a little table beside it.*

Tom is in an armchair reading a newspaper. Miss Roberts comes in carrying two pillows, a scent bottle, and two fans. The pillows she lays on the couch.

Miss Roberts. She is coming down to-day.

Tom [*betraying no interest at all*]. Oh!

Miss Roberts. Aren't you pleased?

Tom. I think it's about time.

Miss Roberts. How unsympathetic you are — when she has been so ill. For a whole week she has never left her room.

Tom. And refuses to see a doctor.

Miss Roberts. She says she doesn't think a doctor could do anything for her.

Tom. Except make her get up. Oh, no! I forgot — it's their business to keep people in bed.

Miss Roberts. You wouldn't talk like that if you'd seen her as I have, lying there day after day, so weak she can only read the lightest literature, and eat the most delicate food.

Tom. She won't let me in her room.

Miss Roberts. She won't have any one but Mr. Baxter and me.

Tom. It's too monstrous. What actually happened that day?

Miss Roberts. Which day?

Tom. The day you turned me down. [*Miss Roberts looks at him, troubled. He looks away sadly.*] What happened after that?

Miss Roberts. I was still upset when Mr. Baxter came in and tried to comfort me.

Tom [*grimly*]. I remember.

Miss Roberts. You know he's a kind, fatherly little man.

Tom. Oh — fatherly!

Miss Roberts. Yes, I wept on his shoulder just as if he'd been an old woman.

Tom. Ah! An old woman! I don't mind that.

Miss Roberts. Then I went to the schoolroom. Presently in walked Mrs. Baxter. She seemed upset, too, for all of a sudden she flopped right over in the rocking-chair.

Tom. The only comfortable chair in that room.

Miss Roberts. Oh, don't say that. Then I called Mr. Baxter; when he came, she gripped his hand and besought him never to leave her. I was going to leave them alone together, when she gripped my hand and besought me never to leave her either.

Tom. Did you promise?

Miss Roberts. Of course. I thought she was dying.

Tom [*scouting the idea*]. Dying? What made you think she was dying?

Miss Roberts. She said she was dying.

Tom. Well, what happened after she gripped you both in her death struggles?

Miss Roberts. We got her to bed, where she has remained ever since.

Tom. And here we are a week later, all four of us just where we were, only worse. What's to be done?

Miss Roberts. We must go on as we are for the present.

Tom. Impossible!

Miss Roberts. Till you go. Then Mr. Baxter and I —

Tom. More impossible!

Miss Roberts [*innocently*]. Poor Mr. Baxter; he will miss you when you go; I shall do my best to comfort him.

Tom. That's most impossible.

Miss Roberts. He must have some one to take care of him, while his wife is ill.

Tom. You don't really think she has anything the matter with her?

Miss Roberts. I can't imagine any one

who is not ill stopping in bed a week; it must be so boring.

TOM. To a mollusc there is no pleasure like lying in bed feeling strong enough to get up.

MISS ROBERTS. But it paralyzes everything so. Mr. Baxter can't go to business; I never have an hour to give to the girls; they're running wild and forgetting the little I ever taught them. I can't believe she would cause so much trouble deliberately.

TOM. Not deliberately, no. It suited Dulcie to be ill, so she kept on telling herself that she was ill till she thought she was, and if we don't look out, she will be. It's all your fault.

MISS ROBERTS. Oh — how?

TOM. You make her so comfortable, she'll never recover till you leave her.

MISS ROBERTS. I've promised never to leave her till she recovers.

TOM. A death-bed promise isn't binding if the corpse doesn't die.

MISS ROBERTS. I don't think you quite understand how strongly I feel my obligation to Mrs. Baxter. Four years ago I had almost nothing, and no home; she gave me a home; I can't desert her while she is helpless, and tells me twenty times a day how much she needs me.

TOM. She takes advantage of your old-fashioned conscience.

MISS ROBERTS. I wish she would have a doctor.

TOM [with determination]. She shall have me.

MISS ROBERTS. But suppose you treat her for molluscry, and you find out she has a real illness — think how dreadful you would feel.

TOM. That's what I've been thinking. That's why I've been sitting still doing nothing for a week. I do believe I'm turning into a mollusc again. It's in the air. The house is permeated with molluscular microbes. I'll find out what is the matter with Dulcie to-day; if it's molluscry I'll treat her for it myself, and if she's ill she shall go to a hospital.

MISS ROBERTS [going to the bottom of the stairs]. I think I hear her coming downstairs. Yes, here she is. Don't be unkind to her.

TOM. How is one to treat such a woman? I've tried kindness — I've tried roughness — I've tried keeping my temper — I've tried losing it — I've tried the serious tack — and the frivolous tack — there isn't anything else. [As MR. and MRS. BAXTER appear.] Oh! for Heaven's sake look at this!

[He takes his paper and sits down, ignoring them both. MR. BAXTER is carrying MRS. BAXTER in his arms. MRS. BAXTER is charmingly dressed as an invalid, in a peignoir and cap with a bow. She appears to be in the best of health, but behaves languidly.]

MRS. BAXTER [as MR. BAXTER carries her down the stairs]. Take care of the stairs, Dick. Thank you, darling! How kind you are to me. [Nods and smiles to MISS ROBERTS.] Dear Miss Roberts! [To MR. BAXTER.] I think you'd better put me down, dear — I feel you're giving way. [He lays her on the sofa. MISS ROBERTS arranges the cushions behind her head.] Thank you — just a little higher with the pillows; and mind you tuck up my toes. [MISS ROBERTS puts some wraps over her — she nods and smiles at TOM.] And what have you been doing all this week, Tom?

TOM [gruffly, without looking up]. Mollusking.

MRS. BAXTER [laughs and shakes her hand playfully at TOM]. How amusing Tom is. I don't understand half his jokes. [She sinks back on her cushions with a little gasp.] Oh, dear, how it tires me to come downstairs. I wonder if I ought to have made the effort. [TOM laughs harshly.]

MR. BAXTER [reprovingly]. Tom!

[MISS ROBERTS also looks reprovingly at TOM.]

MRS. BAXTER. Have you no reverence for the sick?

TOM. You make me sick.

MRS. BAXTER. Miss Roberts, will you give me my salts, please?

MISS ROBERTS. They're on the table beside you, Mrs. Baxter.

MRS. BAXTER. Hand them to me, please. [MISS ROBERTS picks up the salts where *they stand within easy reach of* Mrs. Baxter *if she would only stretch out her hand.* Mr. Baxter *makes an attempt to get the salts.*] Not you, Dick; you stay this side, and hold them to my nose. The bottle is so heavy. [Miss Roberts *gives the salts to* Mrs. Baxter, *who gives them to* Mr. Baxter, *who holds them to* Mrs. Baxter's *nose.*] Delicious!

Tom [*rising quickly and going towards* Mrs. Baxter]. Let me hold it to your nose. I'll make it delicious.

Mrs. Baxter [*briskly*]. No, thank you; take it away, Miss Roberts. I've had all I want.

[*She gives the bottle to* Miss Roberts.]

Tom. I thought as much.

Mrs. Baxter [*feebly*]. My fan.

Mr. Baxter [*anxiously*]. A fan, Miss Roberts — a fan!

[Miss Roberts *takes a fan and gives it to* Mr. Baxter.]

Mrs. Baxter. Is there another fan?

Mr. Baxter [*anxiously*]. Another fan, Miss Roberts — another fan!

[Miss Roberts *gets another fan.*]

Mrs. Baxter. If you could make the slightest little ruffle of wind on my right temple.

[Miss Roberts *stands gently fanning* Mrs. Baxter's *right temple.* Mr. Baxter *also fans her.* Tom *twists his newspaper into a fan.*]

Tom. Would you like a ruffle of wind on your left temple?

Mrs. Baxter [*briskly*]. No, no — no more fans — take them all away — I'm catching cold. [Miss Roberts *takes the fan from* Mr. Baxter *and lays both fans on the table.* Mrs. Baxter *smiles feebly at* Mr. Baxter *and* Miss Roberts. Tom *goes back to his chair and sits.*] My dear kind nurses!

Miss Roberts. Is there anything else I can do for you?

Mrs. Baxter. No, thank you. [*They turn away.*] Yes, hold my hand. [Miss Roberts *holds her hand. Then to* Mr. Baxter.] And you hold this one.

[Mr. Baxter *holds* Mrs. Baxter's *other hand. She closes her eyes.*]

Tom. Would you like your feet held?

Mr. Baxter [*holding up his hands to silence* Tom]. Hush, she's trying to sleep.

Tom [*going to her says in a hoarse whisper*]. Shall I sing you to sleep?

[Mr. Baxter *pushes* Tom *away.* Tom *resists.*]

Mr. Baxter. Come away — she'll be better soon. [*They leave her.*] Oh, Tom, if you knew how I blame myself for this; it's all through me she's been brought so low; ever since the day she caught me comforting Miss Roberts. How she must have suffered, and she's been so sweet about it.

Mrs. Baxter [*opens her eyes*]. I don't feel any better since I came downstairs.

[Miss Roberts *comes back to the sofa.*]

Mr. Baxter. I wish you'd see a doctor.

Mrs. Baxter. As if a country doctor could diagnose me.

Tom. Have a baronet from London.

Mrs. Baxter. Later on, perhaps, unless I get well without.

Tom. Then you do intend to recover?

Mrs. Baxter. We hope, with care, that I may be able to get up and go about as usual in a few weeks' time.

Tom. When I've gone back to Colorado? [*He pushes* Mr. Baxter *out of the way and approaches* Mrs. Baxter.] I guess you'd be very much obliged to me if I cured you.

Mrs. Baxter [*speaking rapidly and with surprising energy*]. Yes, Tom, of course I should. But I've no confidence in you, and Dr. Ross once said a doctor could do nothing for a patient who had no confidence in him. [*Smiling at* Tom.] I'm so sorry, Tom; I wish I had confidence in you.

Tom. I have confidence in myself enough for two.

Mrs. Baxter. Dr. Ross said that wasn't at all the same thing. I wish you'd stand farther off; you make it so airless when you come so close.

[*She waves him off with her hand.*]

Tom. I'm not going to touch you.

Mrs. Baxter [*relieved*]. Oh, well, that's another matter. I thought you were going to force me up. Try to rather. Do what you like, as long as you don't touch me or make me drink anything I don't like. I mean that I ought not to have.

MR. BAXTER. I wish we could think of some way to make our darling better.

TOM. I've heard of people who couldn't get up having their beds set on fire.

[*He picks up a box of matches and goes towards* MRS. BAXTER. MR. BAXTER *and a hand of* MISS ROBERTS *— serenely*]. My dear ones, he doesn't understand — he wouldn't really do it.

TOM. Wouldn't he? [*He puts the matches back.*]

MRS. BAXTER. To show him I'm not afraid, leave me alone with him.

TOM. Going to try and get round me, too? That's no good.

MRS. BAXTER [*affectionately to* MR. BAXTER *and* MISS ROBERTS]. You need a rest, I'm sure — both of you. Miss Roberts, will you go to the library for me, and change my book?

MISS ROBERTS. With pleasure.

MRS. BAXTER. Bring me something that won't tax my brain.

MISS ROBERTS [*soothingly*]. Yes, yes, something trashy — very well.

[*She goes out.*]

MR. BAXTER [*impulsively*]. I need a walk too. I'll go with Miss Roberts.

[*About to follow her.*]

MRS. BAXTER [*quickly pulling him back*]. No, you won't, Dick. I want you to go upstairs and move my furniture. The washstand gets all the sun, so I want the bed where the washstand is, and the washstand where the bed is. I wouldn't trouble you, dear, but I don't like to ask the servants to push such heavy weights.

MR. BAXTER. I'll do anything, dear, to make you more comfortable.

MRS. BAXTER. Do it quietly, so that I shan't be disturbed by the noise as I lie here. [*Closes her eyes.*]

MR. BAXTER. Darling.

[*He kisses her tenderly on the brow, then tiptoes to the stairs motioning* TOM *to keep quiet.* TOM *stamps heavily on the ground with both feet.* MR. BAXTER, *startled, signs to* TOM *to keep quiet; then goes out.*]

MRS. BAXTER [*smiling and murmuring*]. Dear Dick!

TOM. Poor Dick!

MRS. BAXTER [*plaintively*]. Poor Dulcie!

TOM. Look here, Dulciebella, it's no use trying to get round me. I know you. I've seen you grow up. Why, even in your cradle you'd lie by the hour, gaping at the flies, as if the world contained nothing more important. I used to tickle you, to try and give you a new interest in life, but you never disturbed yourself till bottle time. And afterwards; don't I know every ruse by which you'd make other people run about, when you thought you were playing tennis, standing on the front line, tipping at any ball that came near enough for you to spoil — [*he thumps the cushions*] and then taking all the credit if your partner won the set. [*Again he thumps the cushions. Each time* MRS. BAXTER *looks startled and attempts to draw them from him.*] And if a ball was lost, would you help to look for it? [TOM *gesticulates —* MRS. BAXTER *watches him in alarm.*] Not you. You'd pretend you didn't see where it went. Those were the germs of mulluscry in infancy — and this is the logical conclusion — you lying there with a bow in your cap — [*he flicks her cap with his hand*] having your hands held.

MRS. BAXTER [*in an injured tone*]. You have no natural affection.

TOM. I've a solid, healthy, brotherly affection for you, without a spark of romance.

MRS. BAXTER. Other people are much kinder to me than you are.

TOM. Other people only notice that you look pretty and interesting lying there — they wouldn't feel so sorry for you if you were ugly — [MRS. BAXTER *smiles.*] You know that; that's why you stuck that bow in your bonnet. [*He flicks her cap again.*] You can't fool me. [*Moves away.*]

MRS. BAXTER [*sweetly, yet maliciously*]. No, dear, I saw that the morning you made me do the flowers.

Tom [*exasperated at the remembrance of his failure*]. Get up! [*Thumps the table.*]

Mrs. Baxter. I can't get up.

Tom. Lots of people think every morning that they can't get up, but they do.

Mrs. Baxter. Lots of people do lots of things I don't.

Tom. How you can go on like this after what you saw — Dick and Miss Roberts a week ago — after the warning I gave you then. I thought the fundamental instinct in any woman was self-preservation, and that she would make every effort to keep her husband by her. You don't seem to care — to indulge your molluscry you throw those two more and more together.

Mrs. Baxter. I don't see how you make that out.

Tom. There they are, both spending the whole of their time waiting on you.

Mrs. Baxter. In turns — never together — and I always have one or the other with me.

Tom [*taking it all in, he laughs and says with admiration and astonishment*]. Oh! Oh! I see. Lie still, hold them both to you and hold them apart. That's clever.

Mrs. Baxter. *Your* way was to pack Miss Roberts off; the result would have been that Dick would be sorry for her and blame me. *My* way, Dick is sorry for me, and blames himself, as long as Miss Roberts is here to remind him.

Tom. You can't keep this game up forever.

Mrs. Baxter [*complacently*]. When I feel comfortable in my mind that the danger has quite blown over — [*She suddenly remembers she is giving herself away too much.*] Oh, but, Tom, I hope you don't think I planned all this like a plot, and got ill on purpose?

Tom. Who knows? It may have been a plot, or suggestions may have arisen like bubbles in the subconscious caverns of your mollusc nature.

Mrs. Baxter [*offended*]. It was bubbles.

Tom. You don't know which it was any more than anybody else. Think what this means for the others — there's your husband growing ill with anxiety, neglecting his business — your children running wild when they ought to be at school — Miss Roberts wasting her life in drudgery. All of them sacrificed so that you may lie back and keep things as they are. But you can't keep things as they are; they'll get worse, unless you get on to yourself and buck up. It's that, or the break up of your home. Now Miss Roberts' presence in the house has ceased to be a danger — [Mrs. Baxter *smiles*] for the moment. But you wait! Wait till this invalid game is no longer a novelty, and Dick grows tired of being on his best behaviour — or wait till he finds himself in some trouble of his own, then see what happens. He won't turn to you, he'll spare you — he'll turn to his friend, his companion, the woman he has come to rely on — because you shirked your duties on to her, and pushed her into your place. And there you'll be left, lying, out of it, a cypher in your own home.

Mrs. Baxter [*pleasantly*]. Do you know, Tom, I sometimes think you would have made a magnificent public speaker.

[Tom *is angry. He conveys to the audience by his manner in the next part of the scene that he is trying a change of tactics. He sits.*]

Tom. I wonder where those two are now?

Mrs. Baxter. Miss Roberts has gone to the library, and Dick is upstairs moving my furniture.

Tom [*gazing up at the ceiling*]. I haven't heard any noise of furniture being moved about.

Mrs. Baxter [*smiling*]. I asked him to do it quietly.

Tom. Miss Roberts has had more than time to go to the library and back.

Mrs. Baxter [*growing uneasy and sitting up*]. You don't think he's gone too?

Tom [*in an offhand way*]. That's what I should do. Pretend to you I was going upstairs to move furniture, and I should move out after her.

Mrs. Baxter. It's the first time I've let them out of my sight together since — [*She sits bolt upright.*] Go and see if they're coming. [*She points to the window.*]

Tom. They'd be careful not to be seen from this window.

Mrs. Baxter [*excitedly*]. They may be in the arbour.

Tom. It's a very good place.

Mrs. Baxter. Go and look.

Tom. I won't.

Mrs. Baxter. Then I will!
[*She springs off the couch and runs towards the window.*]

Tom. I thought I should make you get up.

Mrs. Baxter [*brought suddenly to realize what she has done*]. Oh!

Tom. Now that you are up, better go and look in the arbour.

Mrs. Baxter. If I do catch them again, of course there will be only one thing for me to do.

Tom. What's that?

Mrs. Baxter. The girls and I must come out and rough it with you in Colorado.
[*She goes out through the window.*]

Tom [*protesting vehemently*]. No, you don't! I won't have that! Not at any price. There's no room for you in Colorado. Oh, dear! What a dreadful thought! [Miss Roberts *comes in wearing her hat and carrying the library book in her hand.*] Thank goodness, they were not in the arbour.

Miss Roberts. What?

Tom. Oh, never mind, never mind.

Miss Roberts [*surprised at not seeing* Mrs. Baxter *on the couch*]. Why, where is she?

Tom. Gone for a chase round the garden.

Miss Roberts. A chase?

Tom. A wild-goose chase. Leave her alone — she needs exercise. You see I was right; she was mollusking.

Miss Roberts. And she wasn't really ill?

Tom [*quickly*]. Now seize this opportunity to give her notice. Have a plan. Know where you're going to or we shall have — "Dear Miss Roberts — stay with us till you find a place" — and the whole thing over again.

Miss Roberts [*taking off her hat, says thoughtfully*]. I don't know where I can go at a moment's notice. I suppose you don't actually know of any one in Colorado who wants a governess?

Tom. No, I can't say I do.

Miss Roberts. Then I suppose it must be the Governesses' Home.

Tom [*kindly*]. We shall hear from you from time to time, I hope?

Miss Roberts [*pleased*]. Oh, yes, if you wish to.

Tom. You'll write sometimes — [Miss Roberts *looks up hopefully. But when he says* "*to my sister,*" *she is disappointed*] to my sister?

Miss Roberts [*disappointed*]. Oh, yes.

Tom. And in that way I shall hear of you.

Miss Roberts [*sadly*]. If you remember to ask. But people so soon forget, don't they?

Tom. I shan't forget. I don't want you to forget me.

Miss Roberts. It won't make much difference to you in Colorado whether you're remembered or forgotten by me.

Tom. I like to know there are people here and there in the world who care what happens to me.

Miss Roberts [*faltering*]. That's something, isn't it?

Tom. It's a real thing to a man who lives out of his own country; we spend a lot of time just thinking of the folks at home.

Miss Roberts. Do you?

Tom [*looks at her face*]. How young you are — there isn't a line in your face. [*She smiles at him.*] You will let me hear how you get on? [*Moves away.*]

Miss Roberts [*disappointed*]. If there's anything to tell. Some people have no history.

Tom. Yours hasn't begun yet — your life is all before you.

Miss Roberts. A governess's life isn't much.

Tom. You won't always be a governess. You'll marry a young man, I suppose. I hope he'll be worthy of you.

Miss Roberts [*wistfully*]. Would he have to be young for that?

Tom. It's natural; I suppose it's right — anyway, it can't be helped. A man doesn't realize that he's growing old with the rest of the world; he notices that his friends are. He can't see himself — so he doesn't notice that he, too — he gets a shock now and then — but... well, then he gets busy about something else and forgets.

MISS ROBERTS. Forgets?

TOM. Or tries to. I almost wish I'd never come to England. It was easier out there to get busy and forget.

MISS ROBERTS. You'll find that easy enough when you go back.

TOM [shaking his head]. Too much has happened; more than I can forget. But I must buck up because I have to be jolly as a duty to my neighbours, and then your letters — they'll cheer me. And when that inevitable letter arrives to tell me you've found happiness, I shall send you my kindest thoughts and best wishes, and try not to curse the young devil whoever he is. So you see we can always be friends, can't we? In spite of the blunder I made a week ago. Don't quite forget me — [taking her hands and shaking them] when he comes along.

[He goes and sits on the couch disconsolately.]

MISS ROBERTS. Shall I tell you something?

TOM. What?

MISS ROBERTS. Oh, no — I can't!

TOM. You must now you've begun.

MISS ROBERTS. I daren't.

TOM. I want you to.

MISS ROBERTS. Well, don't look at me.

TOM. I'm ready.

[He looks at her, and then turns his back to her.]

MISS ROBERTS. Suppose there was a girl, quite young, and not bad-looking, and she knew that her chief value as a person was her looks and her youth, and a man — oh, I don't know how to say this —

TOM. I'm not looking.

MISS ROBERTS. He had great value as a person. He was kind and sensible, and brave, and he had done things. He wasn't young, but he couldn't have lived and still had a smooth face, so she liked him all the better for not having a smooth face — his face meant things to a girl, and if he wanted to give her so much — such great things — don't you think she'd be proud to give him her one little possession, her looks and her youth?

TOM. You don't mean us?

[He turns to her.]

MISS ROBERTS [overcome with confusion]. Don't look at me. I'm ashamed. [Covers her face with her hands. TOM goes to her, gently draws her hands from her face and holds them both in his.] I wouldn't have dared to tell you only I couldn't let you go on thinking what you were thinking. When you asked me to marry you a week ago and I said "No" — it was only because I was so hurt — my pride was hurt and I thought — oh, never mind now — I wanted to say "Yes" all the time.

TOM [looking at her and saying to himself, as if he scarcely believed it]. I am really going to take her with me to Colorado.

[Kisses her.]

[After a slight pause, MR. BAXTER enters limping painfully.]

MR. BAXTER. I've sprained my ankle — moving that washstand.

TOM. Oh, my poor old chap — what can we do for you?

MISS ROBERTS. You ought to have some lint and a bandage. [To TOM.] You'll find it in a cupboard in the spare room — your room.

TOM. All right — hold on while I go and get it.

[He puts MR. BAXTER's hand on the post of the stairs; then he goes out.]

MISS ROBERTS. Hold on to me, Mr. Baxter. [She supports him.]

[MRS. BAXTER enters from the garden without seeing MR. BAXTER and MISS ROBERTS.]

MRS. BAXTER. They're not in the arbour. [Catching sight of them.] What, again?

MISS ROBERTS. He's sprained his ankle.

MRS. BAXTER [rushing to him]. Sprained his ankle — oh, my poor Dick!

MR. BAXTER [looking surprised at MRS. BAXTER]. What, you up — running about?

MRS. BAXTER. I've taken a sudden turn for the better.

MR. BAXTER [mournfully]. I wish you'd taken it a bit sooner; making me move that damned old washstand. [Then, suddenly.] Oh, my foot!

Mrs. Baxter. Let me help you to my couch. [Tom *comes in with bandages.*]
Mr. Baxter. You wouldn't know how. [*Pushes her away.* Mrs. Baxter *gives an exclamation of horror. Turning to* Miss Roberts.] Miss Roberts!
Mrs. Baxter. Let me!
Mr. Baxter. No, no — not now. [*As* Miss Roberts *assists him to the sofa.*] You see, she's used to helping people, and you're not.
[Miss Roberts *kneels and begins to untie his shoe-lace.*]
Mrs. Baxter [*to* Tom]. He refuses my help.
Tom. He turns to the woman he has come to rely on. Now is your chance. Seize it; you may never get another.
Mr. Baxter. I want a pillow for my foot.
Miss Roberts [*rising*]. A pillow for your foot?
Tom [*to* Mrs. Baxter]. Go on — go on — get it.
Mrs. Baxter [*running for the pillow*]. A pillow for his foot. [*She anticipates* Miss Roberts, *snatches the pillow and brings it to* Mr. Baxter, *then, looking indignantly at* Miss Roberts, *she raises* Mr. Baxter's *sprained foot with one hand as she places the pillow under it with the other.* Mr. Baxter *utters a yell of pain.*] Oh, my poor Dick, I'm so sorry. Did I hurt you?
Mr. Baxter [*looking at her in wonder*]. Why, Dulcie, but it seems all wrong for me to be lying here, while you wait on me.
Mrs. Baxter. I want you to rely on me, dear, so that when you're in trouble, you'll turn to me. What can I do for your poor foot? We must get some — some —
Tom. Bandages.
[*Throwing bandages to* Mrs. Baxter.]

Mrs. Baxter. Yes, and some — some arnica. Miss Roberts never thought of arnica.
Miss Roberts. I'll go and look for it.
[*She makes a slight movement.*]
Mrs. Baxter [*pleasantly*]. Don't trouble, Miss Roberts, I will go myself directly. [*Then to* Mr. Baxter.] You know, dear, we must learn to do without Miss Roberts.
Tom. You'll have to. She's coming back to Colorado with me.
Mrs. Baxter [*going to* Miss Roberts]. Tom, this is news. Dear Miss Roberts, I'm so glad.
Mr. Baxter [*holding out his hand to* Tom]. So am I.
[Tom *shakes hands with* Mr. Baxter.]
Mrs. Baxter. But oh, how we shall miss you.
Miss Roberts. I hope I'm not being selfish!
Mrs. Baxter. Oh, no, no, dear. I'm glad you're going to make Tom happy. We shall do very well here; it's high time the children went to school. I've been thinking about it for a long time. [*She kneels by* Mr. Baxter.] And now that I'm so much better, I shall be able to do more for my husband, play chess with him — go walks with him — Tom shall never have another chance to call me a mollusc.
Tom. Bravo! Bravo!
Mr. Baxter. Dulcie!
Mrs. Baxter. Dearest!
Miss Roberts [*to* Tom]. You've worked a miracle!
Tom [*quietly to* Miss Roberts]. Were those miracles permanent cures? [*Shakes his head.*] We're never told! We're never told!

CHAINS
A PLAY, IN FOUR ACTS
By ELIZABETH BAKER

Elizabeth Baker does not supply a List of Persons for this play. For convenience such a list for *Chains* may be found in the notes on the play in the Appendix.

ENTERED AT THE LIBRARY OF CONGRESS, WASHINGTON, U.S.A.
ALL RIGHTS RESERVED

Reprinted by arrangement with Sidgwick and Jackson, Ltd., London.

Caution. Professionals and amateurs are hereby warned that this play is fully copyrighted under the existing laws of the United States, and no one is allowed to produce this play without first having obtained permission of Samuel French, 25 West 45th St., New York City, U.S.A.

CHAINS

ACT I

SCENE. — *Sitting-room at 55 Acacia Avenue. The principal articles of furniture are the centre table, set for dinner for three, and a sideboard on the right. There are folding doors at the back, leading to the front room, partly hidden by curtains; on the left a low French window leading into the garden. On the right is a fire burning; and above it a door into the kitchen.*

The furniture of the room is a little mixed in style. A wicker armchair is on one side of the fireplace, a folding carpet-chair on the other. The other chairs, three at the table and two against the walls, are of bent wood. The sideboard is mahogany. The carpet-square over oilcloth is of an indeterminate pattern in subdued colours, dull crimson predominating. Lace curtains at window. Family photographs, a wedding group and a cricket group, and a big lithograph copy of a Marcus Stone picture, are on the walls. There is a brass alarm clock on the mantelpiece and one or two ornaments. A sewing-machine stands on a small table near the window; and on the edge of this table and on the small table on the other side of the window are pots of cuttings. A couple of bookshelves hang over the machine. A small vase of flowers stands in the centre of the dinner table.

LILY WILSON, *much worried, is laying the centre table. She is a pretty, slight woman, obviously young, wearing a light cotton blouse, dark skirt and big pinafore. The front door is heard to close.* CHARLEY WILSON *enters. He is an ordinary specimen of the city clerk, dressed in correct frock-coat, dark trousers, carefully creased, much cuff and a high collar.*

LILY. Here you are, then. [*She puts up her face and they kiss hurriedly.*] Did I hear Mr. Tennant with you?

CHARLEY. Met on the step.
LILY. How funny! Well, that's nice. We can have dinner almost directly.
CHARLEY [*putting down his hat carefully on sideboard, and stretching himself slowly, with evident enjoyment*]. Saturday, thank the Lord!
LILY [*laughing prettily*]. Poor thing!
CHARLEY [*looking at his silk hat*]. I should like to pitch the beastly thing into the river. [*He shakes his fist at it. Then he stretches his neck as if to lift it out of the collar and shaking down his cuffs till he can get a fine view of them, regards them meditatively.*] Pah!
LILY [*anxiously*]. What's the matter with them? Are they scorched?
CHARLEY. Scorched! No, they're white enough. Beastly uniform!
LILY. But you must wear cuffs, dear.
CHARLEY. A chap came to the office to-day in a red tie. Old Raffles had him up, and pitched into him. Asked him if he was a Socialist. Chap said he wasn't, but liked red. "So do I," says the Boss, "but I don't wear a golf coat in the city!" Thought he was awfully smart, and it did make Poppy swear.
LILY. Who's Poppy, dear.
CHARLEY. Popperwell. He almost left there and then. Said he should wear whatever tie he liked.
LILY. It would have been rather silly of him, wouldn't it? He's so sure there.
CHARLEY. That's what *he* said. He thought better ‚of it and swallowed it. Well — dinner ready?
LILY. Waiting.
CHARLEY [*going out*]. I'll be down in a jiffy.

[LILY *goes to the fire.* TENNANT *heard outside whistling a bar of the song "Off to Philadelphia." He comes in. He is a broad-shouldered young fellow, a little shy in his manner with women.*]

TENNANT. Nice day, Mrs. Wilson.

LILY. Beautiful.
TENNANT. I've brought you home the paper, if you'd like it. It's the Daily Mirror.
LILY. Oh, thank you. I do like the pictures. Charley is getting so dreadfully serious now in his reading, and won't buy it. He takes the Daily Telegraph. He thinks the gardening notes are so good.
TENNANT. He's luxurious. It's a penny.
LILY. Oh, he shares it with somebody. [Pause.]
TENNANT. How goes the garden?
LILY. It's rather trying — I should like to give up those peas and things, and have chickens. They would be so useful.

[LILY goes out. TENNANT takes a map out of his pocket and stands studying it. CHARLEY and LILY enter together. CHARLEY has made a wonderful change into a loose, rather creased suit of bright brown, flannel shirt with soft collar, flowing tie and old slippers. A pipe is sticking out of one pocket, and a newspaper out of the other. They sit down, and LILY tries not to look worried as CHARLEY laboriously cuts the small joint which she has brought in with her and put before him. He splashes the gravy a little and has to use the sharpener. LILY serves vegetables.]

CHARLEY. I think I shall get one of Robertson's pups.
LILY. It would be lovely.
CHARLEY. He's got one he'll let me have cheap.
TENNANT. I saw them last night. They're a good breed. Make fine house-dogs.
CHARLEY. That's what you want round here. A quiet neighbourhood like this is A 1 for burglars.
LILY. You don't think we shall have any, do you?
CHARLEY. No. 24 had 'em the other night.
TENNANT. What were they after?
LILY. 24? That's the new people. What a shame!
CHARLEY. Wanted the wedding presents.
LILY. And Mrs. Thompson told me they had real silver at 24.
CHARLEY. Trust the burglars for knowing that. They won't risk their skins for electro. So we shan't have 'em.
LILY. Charley! You forget the biscuit barrel and the tray.
TENNANT. Where's the Bobby?
LILY. There's only one about here.
CHARLEY. They don't have Bobbies for burgles in these sort of places, only for rows. And we don't have rows. We're too respectable.
LILY. I think it's so mean of burglars to come to people like us.
CHARLEY [with a burst of laughter]. Let 'em go to Portman Square, you say?
LILY. Well, of course, it's wrong to steal at all; but it doesn't seem quite so bad. [She stops, a little confused.]
TENNANT. Of course it isn't.
CHARLEY [lying back comfortably in his chair]. Going away Sunday?
TENNANT. No — the fact is —
LILY. Maggie is coming round this afternoon. Shall we ask the Leslies for whist to-night?
CHARLEY. All right. Don't make it too early, though. [Looking out of the French windows into the garden.] I've got to get in my peas.
TENNANT. Green peas?
CHARLEY. Green peas in that patch? My dear chap, don't I wish I could!
LILY [to TENNANT]. Have some more?
TENNANT. No, thanks.
CHARLEY. For one thing, there's the soil! It's rotten. Then there're the sparrows . . .
LILY. Some of them are so tame, dear, and they don't seem to care a bit for the cat next door.
CHARLEY [bitterly]. They don't care for anything. I wish they'd take a fancy to a few snails.
LILY. They don't eat snails.
CHARLEY. You spoil 'em. — She gives 'em soaked bread all through the winter, and then expects me to grow things. Lord!
[LILY collects plates. TENNANT goes out. CHARLEY lights pipe. CHARLEY goes to window, where he

stands *leaning against the post and smoking.*]
LILY. The baby across the road is such a darling, Charley.
CHARLEY. Is it?
LILY. The girl was out with it this morning, and I called her over.
CHARLEY. What is it?
LILY. It's a boy. [CHARLEY's *replies are without interest and he continues to gaze out into the garden.*] They're going to call him Theodore Clement Freeman. It's rather a lot, isn't it?
CHARLEY. What's he got it all for?
LILY. After her father and his father and Freeman is a family name.
CHARLEY. What did they want to give 'em all to *him* for? They should keep some for the next.
LILY. Charley!
CHARLEY. It's silly. Still, it's their business.
LILY. It might be a girl.
CHARLEY. Well — there's the others.
LILY. Charley!
CHARLEY. My dear girl, why not?
LILY. I don't like you to speak like that.
CHARLEY. I — [*Stops suddenly, looks at her, and comes over. He takes her face between his hands.*] You silly! [*Kisses her.*]
  [LILY *goes out with a tray of things singing.* CHARLEY *rolls up his sleeves and goes into the garden.*]
[TENNANT *comes in and looks round.* CHARLEY *comes to the window with a spade.*]
TENNANT. You — er — busy?
CHARLEY [*lighting his pipe*]. Um! Want a job? There's a nice little lot of squirming devils under that flower-pot that want killing. Take your time over it.
TENNANT. Thanks. My fancy doesn't lie in gardening.
CHARLEY. Filthy soil, this.
TENNANT. Mrs. Wilson would like to keep chickens.
CHARLEY. Not if I know it! I'd rather go into a flat. [*Leaning against the door and smoking thoughtfully.*] I could chuck the lot sometimes. These two-penny-halfpenny back yards make me sick. [*Pause.*] I'd give something for a piece of good land. Something to pay you for your labour. [*Rousing.*] Well — going out?
TENNANT [*uneasily*]. Yes — presently.
CHARLEY [*turning to look at him*]. What's up?
TENNANT. I've — er — got some news for you.
CHARLEY. Anything wrong?
TENNANT. No — no! The fact is — I'm going to hook it.
CHARLEY [*astonished*]. Hook it? Where to?
TENNANT. I'm sick of the whole show. I can't stand it any longer.
CHARLEY [*trying to realise the situation*]. Do you mean you've left Molesey's?
TENNANT. Yes. I'm going to leave England — and so, you see, I've got to leave here — your place.
CHARLEY. Leave England? Got a crib?
TENNANT. No, nothing.
CHARLEY. What are you going for then?
TENNANT. Because I'm sick of it.
CHARLEY. So am I, and so are others. Do you mean you are just going out because you want a change?
TENNANT. That's about it. I've had enough of grind.
CHARLEY. Well, perhaps you'll get grind somewhere else.
TENNANT. It'll be a change of grind then. That's something.
CHARLEY. Canada?
TENNANT. No, Australia.
CHARLEY. Phew! That's a long shot. Got any friends there?
TENNANT. No.
CHARLEY. It's a bit risky, isn't it?
TENNANT. Of course it's risky. But who wouldn't have a little risk instead of that beastly hole every day for years? Scratch, scratch, scratch, and nothing in the end, mind you?
CHARLEY [*ironically*]. You might become a junior partner.
TENNANT [*ignoring the remark*]. Suppose I stay there. They'll raise the screw every year till I get what they think is enough for me. Then you just stick. I

suppose I should marry and have a little house somewhere, and grind on.

CHARLEY [*looking round*]. Like me.

[LILY *heard singing off* R.]

TENNANT. No offence, old chap. It's all right for some. It suits you. You're used to it. I want to see things a bit before I settle. [CHARLEY *is silent. His pipe has gone out and he is staring at the floor.*] So I thought I'd go the whole plunge. I've got a little cash, of course, so I shan't starve at first, anyhow. [CHARLEY *makes no remark.* TENNANT *becomes apologetic.*] I'm — I feel a bit of a beast — but the fact is — I — it was decided in a hurry — I — er — CHARLEY *looks up.*] I'm going on Monday.

CHARLEY. On Monday! Why, that's the day after to-morrow.

TENNANT. Yes, I know. It was like this. I heard of a man who's going Monday — a man I know — and it came over me all at once, why shouldn't I go too? I went to see him Friday — kept it dark here till I'd seen the guv'nor, and now it's all fixed. I'm awfully sorry to have played you like this —

CHARLEY. Oh, rot! That's nothing. But I say, it's the rummest go I ever heard of. What did Molesey say?

TENNANT. Slapped me on the back! What d'ye think of that? I thought he'd call me a fool. He pointed out that I could stay there for ever, if I liked — which was jolly decent of him — but when I said I'd rather not, thanks muchly, he banged me on the back, and said he wished he could do the same and cut the office. He didn't even stop the money for notice.

CHARLEY. Did he give you a £5 note?

TENNANT [*laughing*]. You don't want much. The old chap was quite excited, asked me to write — how's that? [*Pause.*] [*Rising.*] The thing is — I can't see why I didn't go before. Why did I ever go into the beastly office? There was nobody to stop me going to Timbuctoo, if I liked. I say, will you tell Mrs. Wilson?

CHARLEY. She's only in the kitchen. Lil! — Lil! [*Shouting.*]

LILY [*from outside*]. Yes, dear.

CHARLEY. Come here! Here's news.

[LILY *enters, wiping her hands on her pinafore and smiling.*]

LILY. Yes?

CHARLEY [*waving his pipe towards* TENNANT]. What d'ye think *he's* going to do?

LILY [*studying* TENNANT *seriously*]. Do? How —

TENNANT [*nervously*]. I — I'm going to leave you, Mrs. Wilson.

LILY. To leave us? [*With enlightenment.*] You're going to be married!

TENNANT. Good Heavens, no! Not that!

CHARLEY. Whatever made you think of that?

LILY. What else could he do?

TENNANT. I'm going abroad.

[*Going over to garden door.*]

CHARLEY. He's going to seek his fortune. Lucky dog!

LILY. Have you got a good appointment, Mr. Tennant?

TENNANT. No, nothing. I'm going on the chance.

LILY. Whatever for? Didn't you like Molesey's?

TENNANT. Oh, they were good enough and all that, but I got sick of the desk. I'm going farming.

LILY. And throwing up a good situation?

TENNANT. I suppose you'd call it good.

LILY. It was so sure. You'd have been head clerk in time. I'm sure you would. It does seem such a pity.

TENNANT. Sounds a bit foolish, I expect.

LILY. Of course you must get tired of it sometimes. But to throw it up altogether! I do hope you won't be sorry for it. Charley gets tired of it sometimes — don't you, dear?

CHARLEY [*from the garden door*]. Just a bit — now and then.

LILY. Everybody does, I expect. It would be very nice, of course, to see other places and all that — but you can always travel in your holidays.

CHARLEY. How far on the Continong can you go in a fortnight, Lil?

TENNANT. I don't think you quite understand. It isn't so much that I want to see things — though that'd be jolly — but I want a change of work.

LILY [*sympathetically*]. It *is* trying to do the same thing over and over again. But then the hours are not so very long, are they?

CHARLEY. Nine to six, with an hour for lunch and tea thrown in. Count your blessings, Freddy.

LILY [*reproachfully, and crossing to him*]. You know, Charley, we've often talked it over, and you've said how regular the hours were.

CHARLEY. So they are.

[CHARLEY *disappears for a moment into garden, but is now and again to be seen outside the door with a flower-pot or some other thing for the garden.*]

LILY. And you have the evenings, and they give you Saturday morning at Molesey's as you get on, don't they?

TENNANT. Yes, it's all true, Mrs. Wilson — but I can't stand it. Anybody can have the job.

CHARLEY. It's the spring, Freddy. That's the matter with you.

LILY. I do hope you won't be sorry for it. It would be so dreadful if you failed, after giving up such a good situation. Of course we are very sorry to lose you, Mr. Tennant — you have been so kind.

TENNANT [*hastily and with much embarrassment*]. Oh, please don't.

LILY. And we have always got on so very well together. I'm sure it will be very difficult to get anyone to suit us so well again. But you won't forget us and if we have your address, we can write sometimes —

CHARLEY. And if anything striking occurs, I'll send a cable. The novelty will be worth it. [*Coming just inside the door with the spade in his hand.*] For the rest, I'll describe one day and you can tick it off for the whole lot of the others. Rise at 7, breakfast; catch the 8.30, City — [*The doorbell is heard.*] Who on earth —!

[*He goes into the garden.*]

LILY. Maggie, I expect. [*She goes out.*]

[TENNANT, *after making a step towards the garden, turns to the door, only to meet* MAGGIE MASSEY *and* LILY. MAGGIE *is of medium height, well-proportioned, good-looking without being pretty.*]

MAGGIE [*shaking hands with* TENNANT]. How do you do?

LILY. What *do* you think, Maggie? Mr. Tennant is going to leave us. Guess what for!

MAGGIE. He's going to be married?

CHARLEY. Good Lord! There's another.

MAGGIE. Hullo, Charles, you there!

LILY. He's going to leave England.

MAGGIE. How nice for him!

LILY [*emphatically*]. Nice! But he's got nothing to do there!

MAGGIE [*to* TENNANT]. Are you going to emigrate?

TENNANT. Yes; I'm going to Australia to try my luck.

CHARLEY. Isn't he an idiot?

MAGGIE. Do you think so?

CHARLEY. Throwing up a nice snug little place at Molesey's and rushing himself on to the already overstocked labour market of the Colonies.

MAGGIE. You are really going on your luck?

TENNANT. Yes.

MAGGIE. How fine!

LILY. Maggie! Think of the risk!

MAGGIE. He's a man. It doesn't matter.

LILY. If he'd been out of work, it would have been so very different.

MAGGIE. That would have spoilt the whole thing. I admire his pluck.

LILY. Well, he's got no one depending on him, so he will suffer alone.

MAGGIE. You're not very encouraging, Lil. I have heard of a married man doing the same.

CHARLEY [*quickly*]. Who was that?

LILY. How very foolish!

MAGGIE. Oh, he was already out of work.

LILY. That is different — although even then —

MAGGIE. His wife went to live with her people again and he went out to the Colonies and made a home for her.

LILY [*sceptically*]. How did he do that?

MAGGIE. I don't know. *You* are quite free to do as you like, aren't you, Mr. Tennant? How does that feel?

TENNANT. I have only just started to think about it. Directly the idea came into my head, off I had to go.

[CHARLEY, *who has stood listening, turns slowly and walks away.*]

MAGGIE. You are lucky to have found it out in time.

TENNANT. In time?

MAGGIE. Before you got too old to do anything. [*Pause.*]

CHARLEY [*near the garden window, but outside*]. Climb on to the dustbin, only mind the lid's on tight.

TENNANT. That's Leslie coming over. I'll go. [*Goes.*]

[*Enter from the garden* MORTON LESLIE, *a big fair man, clean-shaven, lazy and good-natured.* CHARLEY *follows.*]

LESLIE. I nearly smashed your husband, Mrs. Wilson... Good-day, Miss Maggie — and I'm sure I've absolutely killed Mr. Wilson's beans.

CHARLEY. If you don't the birds will — and if they don't the worms will — and — how can you expect anything to grow in that garden?

LESLIE. I thought it was such an excellent Small Holding! What about the carrots?

CHARLEY. Pah! Carrots! Why not peaches? Come on, Leslie! I've got the papers in the other room.

[CHARLEY *lifts the curtain and they go into front room.*]

LILY. I'm afraid Charley must be tired. He seems quite irritable.

MAGGIE. So am I when I get home from business. [*Throwing out her arms and smiling at* LILY.] No more shop for me in a month or two, Lil.

LILY [*excitedly*]. You're going to marry Mr. Foster? [MAGGIE *nods.*] Oh, how lovely! How nice for you, dear! I am so glad. What did mother say?

MAGGIE [*with a little laugh*]. Mother is charmed.

LILY. Everybody is, of course. He is such a nice man. He will spoil you, Maggie. You lucky girl!

MAGGIE. Yes, I suppose I am.

LILY. You don't like to show it, of course, dear.

MAGGIE. Don't I? You should have seen me last night! I took off my shop collar and apron and put them on the floor and danced on them — till mother came to see what was the matter.

LILY. You *must* be fond of him, dear.

MAGGIE. No, I'm *not*, particularly.

LILY. Maggie!

MAGGIE [*walking up and down*]. That's funny now. I didn't mean to say that. It just came. [*A pause.*] How queer! [*A pause.*] Well, it's the truth, anyway. At least, it's not quite true. When I came here to-day I was awfully happy about it — I am fond of him at least — I — well — he's very nice — you know. [*Irritably.*] What did you want to start this for, Lil?

LILY [*aggrieved*]. *I* start it? I did nothing.

MAGGIE. I was so satisfied when I came.

LILY [*soothingly and taking her sister's hat and coat from her*]. You're a little tired, dear. We'll have an early cup of tea. Have you got your ring, dear? [MAGGIE *holds out her left hand.*] How sweet! Sapphires! He must be rich, Maggie. [*Pause.*]

MAGGIE. I wish I was a good housekeeper, Lil.

LILY [*reassuring*]. Oh, you'll soon learn, dear; and his other housekeeper wasn't very good.

MAGGIE. I wasn't thinking of that.

LILY. But you talked of housekeeping, dear.

MAGGIE. Yes, but that's quite different from being married. If I could cook decently, I would have left the shop before.

LILY. But you *are* going to leave the shop!

MAGGIE [*unheeding*]. Or if I understood anything about the house properly, but I couldn't be even a mother's help unless I could wash.

LILY. I don't know what you mean, Maggie. You haven't got to wash. You know Mr. Foster can afford to send it all out. [*Sighing enviously.*] That must be nice.

MAGGIE. I heard of a girl the other day, Fanny White — you know her — she's gone to Canada.

LILY. Canada! Who's talking about Canada? What's that to do —?

MAGGIE. I was envious. She used to be with us at the shop.

LILY [*impatiently*]. Yes, I know. Well, you've done better than she, anyway, Maggie, if she *is* going to Canada. She'll only be a servant, after all. What else can she do? And then in the end she'll marry some farmer man and have to work fearfully hard — I've heard about the women over there — and wish she had *never* left England. While here are you, going to marry a rich man who's *devoted* to you, with plenty of money and long holidays, and your own servant to begin with! Really, Maggie —!

MAGGIE [*stretching a little and smiling*]. Isn't it gorgeous? [*Shaking herself.*] Well — it must be Mr. Tennant's fault. He shouldn't get mad ideas into his head —

LILY. And he really is mad. Throwing up a most *excellent* situation. My dear, I call him just stupid!

CHARLEY [*lifting the curtain and coming forward with* LESLIE]. There's no hurry.

LESLIE. Oh, I'll start on it to-night. My wife's gone away and left me for the day, and I'm a forsaken grass widower.

LILY [*laughing*]. Poor Mr. Leslie! Won't you come in here to-night? Don't you think it would be very nice, Charley, as Mr. Tennant is going so soon —

LESLIE. Tennant? Where's he going?

MAGGIE. *You'll* never guess.

LESLIE. He's leaving you? He's going to get married?

CHARLEY [*impatiently*]. You're as bad as a woman!

MAGGIE. I thought you more brilliant, Mr. Leslie.

LESLIE. I thought of the happiest thing that could happen to a man, Miss Maggie.

LILY. No, it's not marrying. He's going abroad.

LESLIE. Got a fortune?

MAGGIE. He's just going to try his luck. He's emigrating.

LESLIE. What a fool! He's got the sack, I suppose?

MAGGIE. No. He's thrown it up.

LESLIE. Thrown up a safe job? Oh, he's an ass, a stupid ass! You surely don't ask me to come and wish good luck to an ass?

MAGGIE. You can help with a dirge then.

LESLIE. Much more like it. But, I say, is it really true? He must have got something to go to?

CHARLEY. He hasn't. He's got a little cash, of course. He's always been a careful beast.

LESLIE. And he's going to throw it away! And then I suppose he'll be out of work over there, and we shall be hearing of the unemployment in the Colonies! It's just this sort of thing that makes a man a Conservative. It's what I call getting off the ladder and deliberately kicking it down.

CHARLEY. Well, I don't then. I think he's a lucky chap to be able to do something he likes. He's got some pluck.

LILY. Why, dear, you know you think it's very silly of him!

LESLIE [*laughing*]. You must look after your husband, Mrs. Wilson, I can see. He'll be running away. Well, so long, old chap! I'll come back later. Just give me a hitch over the wall. You'll be sorry about those beans next week

[*Pause. They go out. A crash is heard.*]

CHARLEY. Hullo! What's up?

LESLIE [*in the distance*]. Smashed a box of tomato plants. Phew!

[LILY, *laughing, goes out with* MAGGIE. *A long whistle —* CHARLEY *comes back into the room and stands looking into the fire. Pause.*]

[*Enter* TENNANT.]

TENNANT. I'm just going round to Carter's. Anything you want? [*Pause.*] I suppose Leslie had something to say about me?

CHARLEY. He doesn't want to come *with* you. [TENNANT *laughs.*] You don't seem to know much about it, but I suppose you've fixed on a town. Sydney?

TENNANT. No, Brisbane. [*Pulling out a map.*] The chap I know is cattle-raising. Look! [*He opens the map on the table: they both lean over it,* CHARLEY's *burnt-out pipe still in his hand.*] We're going to Brisbane, then this way [*moving his finger*] across Queensland. He knows something at Merivale — here — see — in the Darling district. Then we shall push on to Maronoa — that's the county — we're going to a tiny place — Terramoa — but of course I mayn't get anything —

CHARLEY [*who is practically lying over the map*]. Not fruit-farming then? That's more my line.

TENNANT. No. If ever you thought of that — see — this is a good district — I heard of a man there once — see — this way — Ship to Sydney — Vineyards and all sorts — suit you.

CHARLEY. U-m! Or one could go this way. [*Pointing with his pipe.*]
[LILY's *voice heard calling "Charley"* — TENNANT *stands upright.*]

LILY [*enters — laughing*]. Charley! What are you doing? [CHARLEY *jumps up and* TENNANT *folds up the map.*] Looking at the plans?

TENNANT. I'm off. [*Goes out.*]

LILY. Finished gardening already, dear?

CHARLEY [*putting on his coat*]. Don't feel like it.

LILY [*holding out a newspaper*]. Look here, dear, this will do for us, I think.

CHARLEY [*glancing round*]. What is it?

LILY. An advertisement. [*Reading.*] "Wanted, by Young Man, board — residence in quiet family within easy reach of city. Western suburb preferred." I must answer it.

CHARLEY. I say — give Tennant a chance to get out first.

LILY. But he is going, dear, so there's no risk. And it's such a good chance. Besides, we can ask Mr. Tennant for a reference.

CHARLEY [*sharply*]. No, don't. Surely we can exist a week without anybody.

LILY. Oh, yes! Only I thought — it's a pity to miss — You don't want Mr. Tennant to go, do you, dear? He is nice company for you.

CHARLEY. He's a nice chap. But you needn't get lodgers to keep me company.

LILY [*laughs*]. What an idea! Of course not.

CHARLEY [*going to her and turning her face towards him*]. I say, Lil, aren't you ever dull here?

LILY. No — well — hardly ever. There's always something to do. What a question!

CHARLEY. Don't you ever get sick of it? It's jolly hard work sometimes. [*He takes her hands and looks at them, stroking them as if unconsciously.*] Why, they're getting quite rough. [*She pulls them away.*]

LILY. It's the washing, dear. It does roughen your hands.

CHARLEY [*taking them again and kissing them*]. They weren't rough when we married.

LILY [*she turns away*]. You silly boy, of course they weren't. I never did washing at home. What do you think, dear? Maggie is going to be married.

CHARLEY [*with little interest*]. To Foster?

LILY. Yes. Isn't she lucky? He's quite well off.

CHARLEY. So *she* won't do the washing. I shall never be rich.

LILY. You'll be head clerk one of these days.

CHARLEY. One of these days!

LILY. And then we'll have a servant.

CHARLEY. Perhaps I shall never be head clerk.

LILY. Oh, yes, you will!

CHARLEY. I don't know that I'm excited at the idea — a sort of policeman over the other chaps. I'd rather be as I am.

LILY. But think of the position — and the money! [CHARLEY *nods gloomily — he walks to garden door.*] Where's your ambition, dear?

CHARLEY. Perfectly safe. No fear of that getting lost. The man who built that road [*pointing out of the window*] ought to be hanged.

LILY. They're not very pretty, those houses. Mrs. Freeman told me this morning that they're going to raise our rents a little.

CHARLEY [*turning round sharply*]. What? That's because they've brought the fares down. Just like 'em.

LILY. I was thinking this morning, dear, that perhaps we could take two boarders. It would help a little. That little room at the back, over the scullery, would do nicely with a single bed.

CHARLEY. That's where I keep my cuttings and things.

LILY. Yes, dear, but you could have half the coal shed. We never fill it.

CHARLEY. I don't want the coal shed. I say — must we have two?

LILY. It would make things better, dear.

CHARLEY. But it's beastly, choking up your house with a lot of fellers. *You* don't like it, do you?

LILY. No, dear, of course not.

CHARLEY. You don't seem much put out.

LILY. It's no good being cross about it, dear, is it? If it's got to be done, we may as well make the best of it.

CHARLEY. Oh, make the best of it. [*Fretfully.*] You might at least seem vexed.

LILY [*patiently*]. Of course I don't like it, dear, and of course I'd much rather be alone with you and have all my house to myself — though really the boarders don't worry much, you know. They are always home late and only have meals with us.

CHARLEY. Who wants 'em at meals? I don't, if you do!

LILY [*pathetically*]. You are very unkind. I never said I wanted them. I'm only doing my best to make things smooth. You might help me, Charley.

[*She turns away.*]

CHARLEY [*crossing to* LILY *and patting her on her hand*]. I'll be all right later. But I say it is a bit thick. An Englishman's home is his castle. I like that! Why, the only place where you can be alone is the bedroom. We'll be letting that next. [*He laughs sarcastically.*]

LILY [*shocked*]. Charley! What are you saying?

CHARLEY. Ha, ha, what a joke! The —

well, never mind. The day we let the bathroom, Lil — I'm off to the Colonies. [*He stops, suddenly struck with a thought.*]

LILY. You silly boy.

CHARLEY. Supposing I did, eh?

LILY. We're not going to let the bathroom, so you needn't suppose anything.

CHARLEY [*abstractedly — sitting on a corner of the table*]. Why not?

LILY. Did you speak, dear?

CHARLEY [*starting*]. Eh? — No, no! — nothing.

[LILY *goes, closing door.*]

CURTAIN

ACT II

SCENE. — *Sitting-room at 55 Acacia Avenue. The folding doors between front and back parlour are opened, with red curtains looped up. The front parlour, a glimpse of which is visible between curtains, is in full light and a corner of the piano can be seen. The furniture in this room is of the imitation Sheraton variety. There is an ornamental overmantel with photographs and vases, and a marble clock in the middle of the mantelpiece.*

Someone is playing the piano, and LILY, *standing beside it, is singing in a sweet but rather weak voice,* "*Sing me to sleep.*" *No one is in the back parlour, but through the curtains can be seen* MORTON LESLIE, *lolling on mantelpiece,* SYBIL FROST, *a pretty fair-haired girl, much given to laughing at everything;* PERCY MASSEY, *a good-looking, somewhat weak youth of perhaps twenty-one or twenty-two, sitting very close to* SYBIL, *and* TENNANT, *standing in the bay window.*

CHARLEY *comes in quietly through the side door into the back parlour during the singing. When* LILY *comes to the refrain of the song, everyone except* CHARLEY *joins in. He stays in the back parlour and sitting down in the shadow, lights a cigarette.* LILY *sits down amid a good deal of clapping and words of admiration.*]

SYBIL. I do love that song.

PERCY. Now you sing something.

SYBIL [*with a giggle*]. I couldn't really — you know I couldn't.

PERCY. Oh, yes, you can — that nice little coon thing you sang at the Richards.

SYBIL. I've got a cold.

MAGGIE [*crossing from piano*]. Of course you have.

SYBIL [*laughing*]. But it's quite true. Really. And I couldn't really sing after Mrs. Wilson.

LILY. Sybil! Do sing, *please*.

LESLIE. We're all waiting, Miss Frost.

SYBIL. Oh, please — I can't. Let some one else sing first.

[MAGGIE *comes to the doorway and catches sight of* CHARLEY. *She comes in. In the front parlour* SYBIL *can be seen still resisting, while* LILY, LESLIE, *and* PERCY MASSEY *beseech her.*]

MAGGIE. You here — all alone?

CHARLEY. 'Um.

MAGGIE. What's the matter?

CHARLEY. Nothing.

MAGGIE. Why didn't you come into the front room?

CHARLEY. I can hear quite as well here.

MAGGIE. Got the hump?

CHARLEY. What for? Head's a bit nasty, so I'm smoking it off.

MAGGIE. It isn't that — it's all this about Tennant.

CHARLEY [*irritably*]. I'm not grieving over him, if that's what you mean.

MAGGIE. As if I did! and as if you'd confess if you were. Are you sick of everything?

CHARLEY. Sick! I'd cut the whole beastly show to-morrow if —

[*He stops suddenly.*]

[LILY's *voice can be heard distinctly from the front room.*]

LILY. Well, we'll ask Mr. Tennant to sing first.

SYBIL. Oh, I can't sing, really —

CHARLEY. Why doesn't the girl sing when she's asked?

MAGGIE. She says she has a cold.

[*She laughs a little.*]

CHARLEY. Rot! Affectation, I call it.

MAGGIE. Percy's awfully smitten, isn't he?

CHARLEY [*surprised*]. With her?

MAGGIE. Of course. But you haven't noticed that. Lily's been arranging it.

CHARLEY. But he's such a kid.

MAGGIE. He's twenty-two.

CHARLEY. What's that?

MAGGIE. Lots of men marry at twenty-two.

CHARLEY. More fools they! Getting tied up before they've seen anything.

MAGGIE [*thoughtfully*]. I can never understand why a man gets married. He's got so many chances to see the world and do things — and then he goes and marries and settles down and is a family man before he's twenty-four.

CHARLEY. It's a habit.

MAGGIE. If I were a man I wouldn't stay in England another week. I wouldn't be a quill-driver all my life. [CHARLEY *gets up and walks restlessly up and down the room.*] If I were a man —

CHARLEY. Men can't do everything.

MAGGIE. I say, don't you think it's fine of Mr. Tennant to throw up everything and take the risk?

CHARLEY. I'd do the same if . . .

LILY [*coming forward a little*]. Where's Charley? Oh, never mind, I daresay he's got a lantern and is looking for worms or something. Are you ready, Mr. Tennant?

MAGGIE. I wonder what Lil would say if you did!

[CHARLEY *stops dead and looks at* MAGGIE.]

CHARLEY. If I *did?* What are you talking about?

MAGGIE. Why shouldn't you?

CHARLEY. Why shouldn't I? Aren't there a thousand reasons?

MAGGIE. There's Lily, certainly — but . . .

CHARLEY. She wouldn't understand. She'd think I was deserting her. [*A pause.*] But that's not all. I might manage her — I don't know — but — you see, I've got a berth I can stay in all my life . . . [TENNANT *starts singing the first verse of "Off to Philadelphia."*] It's like throwing up a dead cert. And then . . .

MAGGIE. It *would* be a splash.

CHARLEY. Yes — and think of all your people? What'd they say? They'd say I was running away from Lil — of course, it would seem like it . . . [*Another pause.*] It's impossible. I might never get anything to do — and then — [*His voice is suddenly drowned as the front room party sing the chorus "With my Knapsack," etc. Knock at front door.*] I —

MAGGIE. I believe I heard a knock.

[*She goes out in corridor as* TENNANT *commences the second verse.*]

[CHARLEY *sits on the edge of the table watching and listening. The door opens and* MAGGIE *enters, followed by* FENWICK. FENWICK *is a man of middle age, short and slight, with a quiet, rather crushed manner.*]

MAGGIE. Mr. Fenwick didn't want to come in when he heard all the singing. He thought we had a party.

[*She goes through curtains.*]

CHARLEY. Oh, it's nothing — a sort of family sing-song.

FENWICK. Miss Massey would have me come in — but really I'd rather come some other —

CHARLEY. Stuff! Sit down. I'll pull the curtains if it's anything special you've come about. I thought it was perhaps over those geranium cuttings. Afterwards, if you feel like it, we'll go and join them. [*Draws curtains and turns up light.*] Freddy Tennant — you know him, don't you he's going to seek his fortune in the Colonies.

FENWICK. Is he?

CHARLEY. Yes, and we'll drink his health. What's up?

FENWICK. I didn't see you at the train to-day.

CHARLEY. No, you were late. I came on with Malcolm.

FENWICK. The chief sent for me.

CHARLEY. Wasn't a rise, I suppose?

FENWICK. Do I look like it? It's the other thing.

CHARLEY. Docking?

FENWICK [*nodding first and then speaking slowly*]. He said he'd sent for me as senior of my department. The company has had a bad year and they can't give the usual rises.

CHARLEY. None?

FENWICK. None. Haven't you had a letter?

CHARLEY. No. I say, have I got the sack?

FENWICK. No, you haven't. But they're offering you the same alternative they offered me — stay on at less — or go.

CHARLEY [*walking up and down*]. What are you going to do?

FENWICK. What can I do? Stay, of course — what else is there?

CHARLEY. Sit down under it?

FENWICK. What else?

[*Postman's knock.*]

CHARLEY. There's the postman. Wait a bit.

[*He goes out, and the voices in the other room can be distinctly heard laughing, while someone is playing a waltz tune very brilliantly.*]

[CHARLEY *comes back with a letter in his hand, closes door and music dies down.*]

CHARLEY. Here it is.

[*He opens and reads it, then throws it on the table.*]

FENWICK. A bit of a blow, isn't it?

CHARLEY. I didn't expect it. Did you?

FENWICK. Not until last week when Morgan started making enquiries as to salaries, et cetera. Then I guessed.

CHARLEY. We can't do anything.

FENWICK. Of course not.

CHARLEY. But I say, you know, it's all rot about a bad year. Don't expect we've been exactly piling it up, but it's nothing to grumble about.

FENWICK. That doesn't affect us, anyway. We've got to do as we're told. I fancy old Morgan is hit, too. He was sugary, but of course he had to obey the instructions of the directors and so on.

CHARLEY. It's no good swearing at him.

FENWICK. It's no good swearing at anybody. What's a Board? Where is it?

[*The curtains part and* LILY *appears in the opening.*]

LILY. Charley — are you there? Are you never coming back? Oh, Mr. Fenwick! [FENWICK *rises; shake hands.*]

FENWICK. Good-evening. I'm afraid I'm an awful nuisance, but I just called to see your husband about a little business.

LILY. You'll stay to supper, won't you? You and Charley can sit and talk business the whole time. I'm afraid Charley doesn't like music very much — do you, dear?

CHARLEY. Oh, sometimes.

LILY [*big laugh from behind curtains*]. You should hear Mr. Leslie. He's so funny, he's been giving Mr. Tennant advice what to do when he's a lonely bachelor in Australia. He made us *roar* with laughter. [*Goes back laughing.*]

CHARLEY. Silly ass!

FENWICK [*startled*]. What?

CHARLEY. That chap Leslie! It'd do him good to go to Australia for a bit. He'd stick to his berth if they docked his screw to ten bob. He's got no pride in him.

FENWICK. Well, we — at least, I — can't say much — I'm going to stay on. You, too, I suppose.

CHARLEY [*with a sort of defiance*]. Why should I? What's to hinder me leaving? Why shouldn't I go to Morgan and say, "Look here — just tell those directors that I won't stand it! I'm not going to be put up or down — take this or that — at their will and pleasure."

[*There is a burst of laughter from the inner room.*]

FENWICK. That's all very well — and if you've got something else —

CHARLEY [*fiercely*]. I haven't — not an idea of one — but why should that hinder? Look at Tennant, he's chucked his job and no one wanted to take off anything.

FENWICK [*quite undisturbed*]. Tennant? Oh, he's going to the Colonies? Very risky. I nearly went there myself once.

CHARLEY. Why didn't you quite?

FENWICK. Various things. All my people were against it. Oh, well, what was the good of going? It was only a passing fancy, I dare say. Once you leave a place the chances are you won't get another. There are so many of us....

CHARLEY. Of course, it's safe and it's wise and it's sensible and all that — but it's *damnable*.

FENWICK. It's come suddenly to you — I've almost got used to the idea. [*With a little laugh.*] You do, you know, after a little. You're young.... [*With sigh.*] Well, there it is. [*A pause.*] But I'd looked for that rise. It'll make a difference. [*Pulling himself together.*] However, it can't be helped. We've got something left and I'm safe, and that's more than a good many people can say. I'm sorry I came to-night, Wilson.

[LESLIE's *voice can be heard, shouting out a comic song.*]

[*Smiling.*] Life doesn't seem to worry him.

CHARLEY. Won't you stay and have supper?

FENWICK. Thanks, no. I don't feel exactly sociable.

CHARLEY [*with a short laugh*]. Neither do I, old chap. Fact is, I was feeling a bit off when you came.

FENWICK. You're a little restless, but it'll work off. Look at me. I felt like that once.

[*They go out. The curtains are pulled wide and* LESLIE *and* PERCY MASSEY *enter.* TENNANT *can be seen in the front parlour.*]

LESLIE. May we interrupt? [*Looking around.*] Empty was the cradle.

[*Re-enter* CHARLEY.]

LESLIE. Where's the business?

CHARLEY. Fenwick's been, but he's just gone.

LESLIE. Fenwick? Wasn't cheerful company, was he?

CHARLEY [*crossly*]. What's the matter with him?

LESLIE. He never is, that's all.

CHARLEY. He isn't exactly boisterous. He nearly emigrated once, he tells me.

TENNANT [*coming forward*]. Why didn't he quite?

LESLIE. Not enough devil in him. Hundreds of 'em almost go.

CHARLEY. Did you?

LESLIE [*with energy*]. I'm comfortable enough where I am. I've been telling this chap here he's a fool, but he won't believe me. He says he'd rather be a fool in the Colonies than a wise man here. Don't know what he means quite, but it sounds rather smart. [*Waving his pipe oracularly as he faces the three men.*] I've known lots of chaps who've wanted to go. The guv'nor is unpleasant or there's too much overtime or they get jealous of their girl or something of that sort and off they must go. I've known a few who went — and sorry they were, too. You can't do anything out there. Read the emigration books, read your papers. Failure all along the line. Market overcrowded. Only capitalists need apply — the Colonies don't want you —

CHARLEY. Neither does England —

LESLIE. Of course not, but — [*waving his arm impressively*] — but you're here and got something. That's the whole point. My advice is — stick where you are. Tennant's a stupid ass to give up a decent berth; he deserves to fail. Of course, we should all like to see the world. *I* should—

TENNANT. It's more than that.

CHARLEY. Yes, yes, you don't understand. It isn't the idea of travelling — it's because you want to feel — oh! [*He stretches out his arms.*] I don't suppose you ever feel so —

LESLIE. Can't say I do.

TENNANT. Aren't you ever sick of the thing, Leslie?

CHARLEY. And don't you ever want to pitch all the ledgers into the dustbin and burn the stools?

LESLIE. Never — though I've met many that have. I tell you, it's a good thing to have a safe berth nowadays. Many fellows would only be too glad to pick up Tennant's berth — or yours, Wilson. Think of the crowds that will answer the advertisement at Molesey's — Last week our firm wanted a man to do overtime work, and they don't pay too high a rate — I can tell you. They had five hundred and fifteen applications — five hundred and fifteen! Think of that! And that's what would happen to you if you went, Wilson, and that'll be the end of Tennant. Sorry to be unpleasant — but truth —

TENNANT. But there's room on the land —

LESLIE. Land! What on earth can a bally clerk do with a spade? He'd be trying to stick it behind his ear — [*Shout of laughter from* PERCY MASSEY.] He's got no muscle — he's got a back that would break if he stooped — he'd always have a cold in his nose —

CHARLEY. Shut it, Leslie. You can't call Tennant exactly anæmic. And look at this. [*He strips off his coat and turns back his shirt sleeves to display his arms.*] How's that?

[TENNANT *looks on with interest.* LESLIE *comes near and pinches* CHARLEY's *arm, while* PERCY MASSEY *looks on smilingly.*]

LESLIE. All right for a back garden. I suppose you think you're an authority on the land question 'cause you grow sweet peas?

CHARLEY [*digging his hands into the pockets without turning down his sleeves again*]. I don't think anything of the kind. What I do know is that if I had a chance I could farm land with anybody. Do you think I chose this beastly business of quill-driving because it's the best work I know. Do you?

LESLIE. I don't suppose you chose it at all. Your father chose it for you.

PERCY [*to* CHARLEY]. Well, I say, what's the matter with it?

CHARLEY. You wait till you're a few years older.

LESLIE. Wilson's caught the land fever. Take up an allotment — that'll cure you. Your garden isn't big enough. Have you got that map, Tennant?

TENNANT. It's in my room. Shall we go up?

LESLIE. Is there a fire?

TENNANT. No.

LESLIE. Bring it down, there's a good chap. I like to take things comfortable. I'll wait down here.

[TENNANT *goes out.* LESLIE *rises; goes back to the front room.*]

PERCY. I say, Charley —

CHARLEY. Well?

PERCY. I've got a rise.

CHARLEY. Congratulations — wish I had.
PERCY. Foster's given me Beckett's job.
CHARLEY. And Beckett?
PERCY. Well, he's got the sack, you know. It's a bit rough on him, but I couldn't help it, could I?
CHARLEY. I suppose you're doing it cheaper?
PERCY. That's about the line. I'm awfully sorry for Beckett. He's not young, and it's awfully hard to get anything when you're middle-aged.
CHARLEY. So I believe. Well, anyhow, you're in luck — aren't you?
PERCY. Yes, it's sooner than I thought. [*They sit in silence.* TENNANT *re-enters, and goes into inner room.*] I say, Charley, what did you start on?
CHARLEY. Eh? What d'ye mean?
PERCY. You — and — and Lily — you know. [CHARLEY *looks at him steadily.*]
CHARLEY. Oh, that's it, is it?
PERCY. You didn't begin with a house, of course.
CHARLEY. You know as well as I do that we had three rooms — and jolly small ones.
PERCY. Still you were comfortable.
CHARLEY. It was warm — winter and summer.
PERCY. It wasn't very expensive?
CHARLEY. You have to choose your housekeeper carefully.
PERCY. If you're going to chaff —
CHARLEY. Don't be an idiot. You've now got ninety, I suppose. You can manage on that.
PERCY. You really think so?
CHARLEY. I know from experience.
PERCY. You don't ask who the lady is?
CHARLEY. Sybil is a pretty little girl.
PERCY. Well, I suppose you did guess a bit.
CHARLEY. Not me! Maggie and Lil did it between them.
PERCY. Did it?
CHARLEY. Made the match — Maggie told me.
PERCY [*indignantly*]. They did nothing of the kind. I met Sybil here and ...
CHARLEY. 'Um — um!

PERCY. We just came together — it was bound to be.
[*There is a sound of laughter outside and* LILY *and* SYBIL *are seen carrying in cakes and lemonade.*]
CHARLEY. She *is* pretty —
PERCY. Yes, in rather an unusual —
CHARLEY. But so are others.
PERCY. I say, old man.
CHARLEY. Well, aren't they? I suppose you won't listen to advice.
PERCY. What about?
CHARLEY. You're too young to marry.
PERCY. I'm twenty-three. So were you when you were married.
CHARLEY. I was too young.
PERCY. Do you mean ...
CHARLEY [*impatiently*]. Oh, don't look so scandalised. No, I'm not tired of Lily. It's not that at all — but, are you satisfied to be a clerk all your life?
PERCY. I say, Tennant's upset you. Of course I'm satisfied to be a clerk.
CHARLEY. But *are* you?
PERCY [*impatiently*]. Don't I say so?
CHARLEY. Have you ever felt a desire to kick your hat into the fire? Have you?
PERCY. No! Not yet!
CHARLEY. Not yet. There you are — but you will. Don't you ever want to see anything more of the world — did you ever have that feeling?
PERCY [*a little thoughtfully*]. Well, I did once. I wanted to go out with Robinson. But the dad wouldn't consent. It was a bit risky, you know, and this job came along — and so I wouldn't go.
CHARLEY. Did Robinson come back?
PERCY. No, he's got a decent little place out there.
CHARLEY. They don't all fail, then?
PERCY. Of course not — but lots do. I might be one of those.
CHARLEY. Well, the thing is if you ever thought of doing anything now's your time. You can't do it afterwards. Take my tip and don't get engaged yet. You're too young to decide such an important question.
PERCY. No younger than you were — and I must say ...

CHARLEY. Don't be so touchy — can't you see I'm talking to you for your good?

PERCY. I think you're crazed.

CHARLEY [*sharply*]. Why am I crazed, as you call it? Isn't it because I know a little what your life is going to be? Haven't I gone backwards and forwards to the City every day of my life since I was sixteen and am I crazed because I suggest it's a bit monotonous? [*Going close to* PERCY *and putting his hand on his shoulder solemnly.*] I'm not saying she isn't the right girl for you — I'm only suggesting that perhaps she isn't! She's pretty and she's handy ...

PERCY. I say! I won't have that.

CHARLEY. Don't. Pass it over. It's just this — think — and don't marry the first pretty girl and live in three rooms because your brother-in-law did it.

PERCY. She wasn't — the first pretty girl ...

SYBIL [*appearing at opening and smiling demurely*]. Mrs. Wilson says — Oh, Mr. Wilson, have you been fighting?

CHARLEY [*suddenly remembering that he has his coat off*]. I beg your pardon. [*He pulls it on hastily.*] [*To* PERCY.] Remember!

PERCY [*with his eyes on* SYBIL]. Rot! [*Goes back with* SYBIL.]

LILY [*coming towards him*]. Who said anything about fighting? Now I suppose you've been arguing with everybody and shouted at them. You do get so cross when you argue — don't you, dear? Supper is quite ready. I sent Sybil to tell you. ...

CHARLEY. Sybil's feeding Percy. She's got all her work cut out.

LILY. How rude you are! Do you know, I'm quite angry with you. You've hardly been in the whole evening.

CHARLEY. Fenwick ...

LILY. Yes, I saw him. He looks so lifeless, don't you think?

CHARLEY. He says I shall grow like him.

LILY. What an idea! Why, how could you?

[*The company move about the two rooms, the men handing refreshments to the women — they all come more forward.*]

LESLIE. What do you think —? I lost the 8.15 this morning!

CHARLEY. Should have thought it would have waited for you.

LESLIE. I left the house at the usual time, and there was a confounded woman at the station with about five trunks and a paper parcel, who took up the whole doorway. [*Much laughing from* SYBIL *and an encouraging smile from* LILY.] By the time I got over, the train was gone. Never did such a thing in my life before.

LILY. *You* haven't sung to us, Charley, dear.

MAGGIE. He's tired.

LILY. Not too tired for that, are you?

SYBIL. Oh, do, Mr. Wilson, I know you sing splendidly. Per — Mr. Massey told me so.

PERCY. S'sh! don't give me away — he's my brother-in-law.

CHARLEY. Not to-night, Lil — I — I'm a little hoarse.

LILY. That's being out in the garden at all hours.

LESLIE. Don't say that, Mrs. Wilson. Your husband wants to go as a farmer in the Colonies — and you'll discourage him.

LILY. You silly man, Mr. Leslie. [*To* CHARLEY.] You must have something hot when you go to bed, dear.

LESLIE. I love being a little ill. My wife's an awfully good nurse.

SYBIL. I believe you put it on sometimes, Mr. Leslie.

LESLIE. Well, do you know — I believe I do. Ladies won't put their pretty fingers round your neck for nothing. But if you have a little hoarseness — not too much to be really unpleasant — or a headache is a very good thing — it is delightful — I always say to myself:

"O woman — in our hours of ease —
Uncertain, coy and hard to please,
When pain and anguish wring the brow,
A ministering angel thou."

LILY. We ought to have "Auld Lang Syne" —

TENNANT. Please don't.

LILY. It would be so nice for you to remember. [*Going up* L.] Yes, we must.

Come. [*She puts out her hands and makes them all form a ring, with hands crossed and all round table.* TENNANT *and* CHARLEY *join most reluctantly and are not seen to sing a note.*] There! That's better.

SYBIL. Now I must go, Mrs. Wilson.

LILY. Must you really? Come and get your things. [*They go out.*]

[*A tapping is heard at the window in the near room —* MAGGIE *runs and opens it.*]

VOICE. Is my husband there, Mrs. Wilson?

LESLIE. Y — es. I'm here. Coming, darling.

[SYBIL *and* LILY *re-enter.*]

LESLIE. My wife has sent for me home, Mrs. Wilson.

MAGGIE. Are you going over the wall?

SYBIL. Oh, do, Mr. Leslie — I should love to see you.

LESLIE. If it will give you any pleasure it shall be done, though I am not at my best on the fence.

[*They all crowd round — he shakes hands, smiling profusely, and disappears through the window.*]

VOICE. Mind the flower-pot. No — not there — that's the dustbin. Not the steps.

[*There is a great shout to announce his safe arrival.*]

LESLIE. Safe!

SYBIL. I do think he is so funny!

LILY. Yes, isn't he? Are you going by 'bus?

PERCY. I'm going Miss Frost's way.

SYBIL [*much surprised*]. Are you really?

MAGGIE. How extraordinary!

[*Much kissing between* SYBIL, LILY, *and* MAGGIE. SYBIL *and* PERCY *go out.*]

LILY. She's so sweet, isn't she? And Percy's so awfully gone.

MAGGIE [*as they start clearing away the dishes*]. Very. So he was over Daisy Mallock and Ruby Denis — and who's the other girl with the hair?

LILY. The hair? What do you mean?

MAGGIE. The one with the hair all over her eyes — nice hair, too.

LILY. Gladys Vancouver? Poor Percy — I'm afraid he is a little bit of a flirt.

MAGGIE. He's got nothing else to do with his evenings.

LILY. And then people like Mr. Tennant think it's a dull life.

MAGGIE. Well, good-night all. No, don't come out, Mr. Tennant — I'm quite a capable person.

TENNANT. Oh, but I shall — if you'll allow me.

MAGGIE. I'd rather you didn't — still, if you will.

[*They go out with* LILY. CHARLEY *looks round and sighs with relief — he walks round, looks out of the window, then at the garden — he takes up the paper, but after trying in vain to settle to it, throws it on the floor — he re-fills his pipe and lights it.*]

[*Re-enter* TENNANT.]

TENNANT. Well. [*He pauses, but* CHARLEY *does not stir.*] I say, Wilson, I never thought you'd take it like this. [CHARLEY *does not answer, but only shifts restlessly.*] I thought you'd think I was a fool, too. In fact I was half ashamed to say anything about it. It wouldn't do for most people, you know. I'm in an exceptional position, and even in spite of that they call me an ass. I've got a little cash, too.

CHARLEY [*quickly*]. So have I.

TENNANT. Yes, but the cases are different. I can rough it.

CHARLEY. Let me have the chance to rough it.

TENNANT. You're married. [CHARLEY *does not reply.*] You're settled. Your friends are here. I've got nothing and nobody to worry about. [*They both smoke in silence.*] I say, don't sit up and think. Go to bed.

CHARLEY. I'm going soon. Don't stay up, old chap.

TENNANT. You'll get over it.

[*He goes out.*]

[*Enter* LILY — *she pulls down blind and fastens catch of window.*]

LILY. I'm going up now. Don't be long. You look so tired.

CHARLEY [*irritably*]. Oh, don't fret about me. I'm a little worried, that's all.

LILY [*timidly*]. Did Mr. Fenwick bring bad news? He looked miserable enough.

CHARLEY [*looking at her steadily*]. Yes, I'm not going to have that rise.

LILY. Oh, dear — what a shame! Why?

CHARLEY. Lots of reasons — but that's all.

LILY. Of course, you're worried. Still — it might have been worse. You might have been sent away.

CHARLEY. Yes.

LILY. It's very disheartening — after all we'd planned to do with it. You won't be able to have the greenhouse, now, will you, dear?

CHARLEY [*with a short laugh*]. What's the good of a greenhouse in that yard? It isn't that.

LILY [*a little timidly*]. But we can manage very well, dear. We — you remember what I said this morning — about the other lodger.

CHARLEY. Oh, don't, for Heaven's sake. It isn't losing the cash I mind; it's having to give in like this. I want to go to them and tell them to do their worst and get somebody else.

LILY. But, dear, you might lose your place.

CHARLEY. I should.

LILY. But that — we couldn't afford that, could we? Why, we can manage quite well as we are. I can be very careful still —

CHARLEY. I'm tired of going on as we've been going.

LILY. What do you want to do?

CHARLEY. I — I want to go away.

[*Pause.*]

LILY. And leave me?

CHARLEY [*suddenly remembering*]. Oh — er —

LILY. It's just that horrid Mr. Tennant —

CHARLEY. It's nothing to do with him — at least . . .

LILY. I said it was. He wants you to go with him — and you want to go — you're tired of me —

CHARLEY [*going up to her and trying to speak gently, but being very irritated — his voice is sharp*]. Oh, don't cry . . . you don't understand. Look, Lil, supposing I went and you came out afterwards.

LILY. You want to go without me.

CHARLEY. I couldn't take you, dear, but I would soon send for you; it wouldn't be long.

LILY. You want to go without me. You're tired of me.

CHARLEY. Oh, don't cry, Lil. I didn't say I was going. Of course I don't want to leave you, dear. You mustn't take any notice.

[*Attempting to take her in his arms.*]

LILY [*turning away from him, sobs*]. But you do . . .

CHARLEY. I don't want to go because I want to leave you . . .

LILY. But you said . . .

CHARLEY. Never mind what I said. [*He kisses her and pets her like a child.*] Come, go to bed. It's the news — and the excitement about Tennant — and all that. Come, go back to bed and I'll be up in a few minutes.

[CHARLEY *leads her to the door and coaxes her outside and stands at the door a few seconds, then he comes back into the room, stands still, looking round. He goes to the front parlour and hunts over the chairs and the piano as if in search of something. Finally he picks up a paper off the floor and brings to table — it is the map of Australia. He opens it on the table and leans over it, his pipe unnoticed burning out in his left hand.*]

CURTAIN

ACT III

SCENE. — *The sitting-room at "Sunnybank," Hammersmith. There is no centre table, but there are various small ones against the wall and in the window. There is a piano, a tall palm in the window, and one or two wicker chairs that creak. The rest of the furniture is upholstered in saddlebags with anti-*

macassars over the sofa head and armchairs. Gramophone in the corner. Big mirror over mantelpiece. Gilt clock in glass case and lustres.
MRS. MASSEY *is sleeping in one armchair.* MR. MASSEY *is asleep on sofa, pulled across centre.* MAGGIE *sits reading at small table.* MAGGIE *softly rises and goes to fire. She pokes it and a piece of coal falls out.* MRS. MASSEY *turns her head.*

MAGGIE. I'm so sorry, mother, I tried to poke it gently.

MRS. MASSEY. I was hardly asleep, my dear.

MAGGIE. Mother! — you've been sleeping for half an hour!

MRS. M. It didn't seem like it, dear. Why, your father's asleep.

MAGGIE. Isn't that extraordinary!

MRS. M. [*admiringly*]. How soundly he sleeps! What's the time?

MAGGIE. Four o'clock.

MRS. M. I should have thought they'd have been here now.

MAGGIE. Not Percy and Sybil, I hope. You don't expect *them*, until the last minute, do you?

MRS. M. No, dear — of course not.

MAGGIE. I wouldn't walk the streets this afternoon for any man.

MRS. M. I don't suppose they find it cold.

MAGGIE. Oh, I dare say they're sitting in the Park.

MRS. M. I hope they won't be late for tea. I shall want mine soon.

MAGGIE. I'll put on the kettle now and when Lil and Charley come, we will have tea and not wait for the others. We'll have it cosily in here.

[*She goes out, returning with kettle, which she puts on fire. Sits close to* MRS. MASSEY.]

MAGGIE. Mother!

MRS. M. Yes.

MAGGIE. Mother, did you love father when you married him — very much, I mean, very, very much!

MRS. M. [*much astonished*]. What a question! Of course.

MAGGIE. More than any other man you'd ever seen?

MRS. M. Of course!

MAGGIE. More than everything and everybody?

MRS. M. *Of course!*

MAGGIE. Well, there's something wrong with me, then — or else with Walter. I don't feel a bit like that. There's no "of course" with me. I wouldn't go and sit in the Park with him this afternoon for anything.

MRS. M. I suppose you've quarrelled?

MAGGIE. No, we haven't. I wish we had.

MRS. M. Maggie! Don't talk like that.

MAGGIE. But I do. He wants me to marry him next month.

MRS. M. And a very good thing, too.

MAGGIE. He says he's found a house, and wants me to go and look at it. *I* don't want to see it.

MRS. M. What's come over you lately? You used to be satisfied. Walter is very nice and attentive — in fact, quite devoted.

MAGGIE. Yes, I know. Just like he was to his first wife, I expect.

MRS. M. You've such an absurd prejudice against widowers, Maggie. You're jealous.

MAGGIE. I'm not. Not a bit. But I do wish he would do something, and not worry about getting married.

MRS. M. The poor man is doing something, I should think, running after you every spare minute, and house hunting.

MAGGIE. I would much rather he went to Australia — or somewhere.

MRS. M. That's that absurd Tennant man again. You're not in love with *him*, I hope?

MAGGIE [*promptly*]. Not a scrap! I find him rather dull.

MRS. M. Then what is it?

MAGGIE. I should like Walter to go out and seek his fortune instead of getting it in a coal merchant's office.

MRS. M. He mightn't come back.

MAGGIE [*thoughtfully*]. Perhaps he wouldn't. [*Click of gate.*]

MRS. M. There's the gate, Maggie.

[MAGGIE *goes out. She comes back*

in a moment, followed by LILY. LILY *goes to her mother and kisses her. She looks at her father.*]
LILY. Father asleep?
MAGGIE. What a question! Shall I take your hat and coat? [LILY *takes them off and hands them to* MAGGIE.] You're shivering! Sit close to the fire. Aren't you well?
LILY [*in a pathetic voice*]. Yes, I'm well, thank you.
MRS. M. Are you alone?
LILY. Charley is coming on. He's gone to the station with Mr. Tennant.
MRS. M. To see him off?
LILY. No — Mr. Tennant goes to-morrow.
[MAGGIE *goes out with hat and coat. She brings back with her a tray, with cloth, etc., and prepares for tea on a small table.*]
MRS. M. Have you got another lodger?
LILY. No. We — we've got to have two.
MRS. M. Two? What for?
[MAGGIE *stops to listen.*]
LILY. They've reduced Charley's salary.
MRS. M. [*sitting up energetically*]. Reduced it? What for?
LILY. I don't know — I . . . oh, I'm so miserable.
[*She suddenly covers her face with her hands and sobs.*]
MAGGIE [*stooping over her*]. Lil, dear, you're not crying over *that*, are you?
LILY [*sobbing*]. Oh, no, no! It doesn't matter. We can make room for two lodgers quite well. I don't mind the work.
MAGGIE. Then what is it?
MRS. M. I suppose you and Charley have quarrelled?
MAGGIE. Tell us, dear.
LILY. Charley — wants — to go away — and leave me.
MRS. M. What? What's this?
LILY [*looking apprehensively round at the sleeping figure*]. Hush! don't wake father!
MAGGIE. He won't wake till the teacups rattle. Charley wants to leave YOU!
MRS. M. I *knew* they'd quarrelled.
LILY. We haven't — not exactly — but he's been so *funny* ever since Mr. Tennant

said he was going to Australia. He wants to go, too.
MRS. M. What next? Charley ought to be ashamed of himself. Go to Australia, indeed! He forgets he is married.
LILY. I don't want him to stay just because he's married, if he wants to leave me.
MAGGIE. You are quite *wrong*, I'm sure, Lil. He doesn't want to leave you at all. He wants to leave his work.
MRS. M. Perhaps he does. So do other people very often. Suppose we all stopped work when we didn't like it? A pretty muddle the world would be in. Charley is forgetting there is such a thing as duty.
LILY. He's very unhappy — and I — can't make him happy.
MRS. M. So he ought to be miserable with such ideas in his head. I never heard of such a thing! The sooner Mr. Tennant goes the better. He's been putting Charley up to this, I suppose?
MAGGIE. You don't know Mr. Tennant, mother. He's not that sort.
MRS. M. Then what made Charley think of it at all?
MAGGIE. It's just a feeling you get sometimes, mother. You can't help it. Office work is awf'lly monotonous.
MRS. M. Of course it is. So is all work. Do you expect work to be pleasant? Does anybody ever like work? The idea is absurd. Anyone would think work was to be pleasant. You don't come into the world to have pleasure. We've got to do our duty, and the more cheerfully we can do it, the better for ourselves and everybody else.
LILY. I — I didn't mean to tell you.
MRS. M. He ought to be talked to.
LILY. Don't say anything, please — not yet. Perhaps after tea we can all talk about it, and it may do him good.
[MAGGIE *goes out.* LILY *starts to arrange the tea-cups.* MR. MASSEY *rouses.*]
[*Re-enter* MAGGIE *with teapot.*]
MASSEY. Tea?
MAGGIE. Yes, daddy.
MASSEY. In here? There's no room.

MAGGIE. It's cosey. I'll bring yours to the sofa.

MASSEY. Where am I to put it? — on the floor?

MAGGIE. I'll bring up a table for you if you must have one. You wouldn't do for a Society gentleman. Can't you balance a cup on your knee?

MASSEY. I don't mean to try. Hope you haven't got out those finnicky little cups. I want my own.

MAGGIE. I've got your own — here.

[*She holds up a very big breakfast cup, plain white with gilt band.*]

MASSEY. I didn't hear you come in, Lil. Where's Charley?

LILY. Coming on.

MASSEY. What've you done with Foster, Mag?

MAGGIE. He's not coming.

[MAGGIE *takes tea round.*]

MASSEY. Gone away for the week end?

MAGGIE [*taking a cup for herself and sitting down beside* LILY]. Oh, no! He's not coming. That's all. Lily and I are grass widows. It's a very nice feeling.

MASSEY. It's all right about you, but Lil looks a bit off. You've got a cold. Your eyes are red.

LILY. Yes, father.

MRS. M. You've dropped some bread and butter on the carpet, Alfred.

MASSEY [*irritably*]. Of course I have! I knew I should.

MAGGIE [*running to pick it up*]. Percy hasn't come back with Sybil yet, dad. We expect they're sitting in the Park.

MASSEY [*his attention taken from his grievance*]. What, in this weather?

MAGGIE. The seats will be dry and they sit close together, you know. I've often seen them do it.

MASSEY [*chuckling*]. You have, have you? And what about yourself? What about yourself? You! Lord! what a nest of turtle doves it is — nothing but billing and cooing!

MAGGIE. Especially Percy.

MASSEY. P'raps so. He's young at it. Well, he'll be the next, I suppose. And you, too, Mag?

MAGGIE. I'm in no hurry.

MRS. M. [*a little impatiently to* MAGGIE]. Don't talk like that, my dear.

MASSEY. Of course she says she isn't. She's a modest young woman — I never heard *you* say you were in a hurry, my dear.

MRS. M. Of course I shouldn't — to you.

MASSEY. Ha, ha! You put on the shy business then. Lord! these women. [MAGGIE *moves towards table.*] Come, now, Mag, confess! You think of it sometimes.

MAGGIE. I think of it a lot.

MASSEY. There you are! There you are! What did I say?

MAGGIE. And what do you think I think about it?

MASSEY. How should I know. Wedding, I suppose. I bet you never think of anything else after the wedding day.

MAGGIE [*slowly*]. I think of the wedding dress, and the bridesmaids, and the pages. Shall I have pages, Mum?

MRS. M. Maggie!

MAGGIE. I suppose I shan't. I think of the house I'm going to have, daddy — and the furniture, and I'm going to have a cat and a dog —

MASSEY [*slyly*]. Nothing else, of course. Just a cat and a dog. Ha, ha!

MRS. M. Alfred, don't suggest. It isn't nice.

MASSEY. A cat and dog — ha, ha, ha!

MAGGIE. Don't laugh, daddy. I'm telling you the solemn truth — I think most of all that I shall never, never, never have to go into a shop again.

MASSEY. I wish old Foster could hear you.

MAGGIE. Why?

MASSEY. He'd say — "And where do I come in?"

MAGGIE. Well, of course he'll be there. I wish —

MRS. M. Maggie, my dear — I should like a little more tea! Have you got some more hot water?

MAGGIE. I'll get some. [*Goes out.*]

MASSEY. It's all very well for her to chaff, but she ain't quite natural about this affair of hers. She ought to be more pleased — excited like.

MRS. M. I think they've had a little quarrel. People often do. She's a little bit down about it. We've had a talk about it.
MASSEY. Well, she can't have any quarrel about him himself. He's all right, and got a jolly soft job, too. He'll make her a good husband. He's insured for £500.
MRS. M. Is he? That's very nice. If anything happened to him, she'd be all right.
MASSEY. He's a thoughtful sort of chap. Of course he's not exactly young, but he's steady.
MRS. M. The poor child is jealous of his first wife.
MASSEY. You don't say so? Jealous, is she? That's all right — that's a healthy feeling. I'm glad she's jealous, but she'll get over it once she's married. Jealous! Lord! Fancy, Mag, too — I wouldn't have thought it. He'll be head clerk, one of these days — he can stay at Whitakers all his life. He told me.
LILY. Do you think he'll ever get tired of it?
MRS. M. What an idea!
MASSEY [roaring]. Tired! Tired of what? A good job? Why ever should he be? He couldn't have anything better — Ten to half-past five every day of his life, except Saturdays, and then it's *one* — and three weeks' holiday. Think of that?
LILY. But, I —

[*Enter* MAGGIE *with hot water. The doorbell is heard.*]

MRS. M. Let them in, Lily, my dear — it's Percy and Syb. [LILY *goes out.*]

[*Re-enter* LILY *a moment after, followed by* PERCY *and* SYBIL. SYBIL *kisses* MRS. MASSEY *and* MAGGIE.]

SYBIL. Aren't we dreadfully late, Mrs. Massey? I'm *so* sorry!
PERCY. Awfully sorry, but my watch is —
MAGGIE. Don't blame the poor thing — it's all right.
MASSEY. The watch, was it? Come here, my girl! [SYBIL *goes to him with giggling shyness. He takes her face between his hands.*] *Was* it the watch? Not a bit of it! It was this — [*He pats her cheek*] these roses. Lucky young dog! Percy! [*He kisses her.*]
MAGGIE. Rather cold in the Park, isn't it?
PERCY. Not very.
MAGGIE. There's a northeast wind. Still, you can find a sheltered seat.
PERCY. Just beyond the glass house thing.
MAGGIE. What did I tell you?
 [*Looking triumphantly round.*]
SYBIL [*covering her cheeks*]. What a tease you are, Maggie!
MASSEY. Don't listen to her!
PERCY. You're only giving yourself away, Mag. What do you know about sheltered seats and glass houses?
MAGGIE. It wasn't exactly guess work.
 [*Click of gate.*]
MRS. M. There's Walter.
MAGGIE. What?
MASSEY. Isn't she surprised? Now isn't she surprised? Fancy! Walter!
MAGGIE. He said he wasn't coming. [*She looks out of the window.*] Charley is with him.
LILY. Will you open the door, Maggie?
MAGGIE [*almost at the same moment*]. Go to the door, Percy.
PERCY. Well, you're two dutifully loving young women, I must say.
MAGGIE. You forget — we're used to it. [PERCY *goes out.*] Come, Sybil, and take off your things.
 [*Exeunt* SYBIL *and* MAGGIE.]

Enter WALTER FOSTER, *a man of about thirty-five, prosperous-looking, rather stout of build, and fair.* CHARLEY *also enters, and* PERCY.]

FOSTER [*looking round for* MAGGIE]. Good-afternoon.
 [*Shakes hands with* MRS. M. *and* MASSEY.]
MRS. M. She's gone up with Sybil, Walter.
FOSTER. Oh! I was afraid she was out, perhaps.
MASSEY. Well, Charles, you're not looking spry.

CHARLEY. I'm a bit seedy — nothing much.

MASSEY. And when's that madman lodger of yours going, eh?

CHARLEY. To-morrow.

MASSEY. Of all the fools he's the biggest I know.

[*The door opens, and* SYBIL *and* MAGGIE *come back.*]

MAGGIE. I was just telling Sybil, Percy, that tea is laid in the sitting-room. We didn't know when you'd be in.

[*She crosses up to* FOSTER *and lifts her face to be kissed.*]

SYBIL. Isn't she dreadful?

MASSEY. Well, you won't be alone, don't you worry. Charley here wants some tea, and Lil will have to see he gets it, won't you, Lil?

LILY. Yes, Dad.

MAGGIE [*to* FOSTER]. Have you had tea?

FOSTER. Yes, thanks.

[*Exeunt all, except* MASSEY, MAGGIE, *and* FOSTER.]

MASSEY [*finally he looks at the* TWO, *then at the clock; poking the fire, then humming a little*]. Have you seen the *Argus*, Mag?

MAGGIE. In the kitchen. I'll get it.

[*Makes a move to the door.*]

MASSEY. No, no, I'm going out. [*Goes.*]

MAGGIE. Father calls that tact.

FOSTER [*coming over to her*]. What?

MAGGIE. Didn't you notice? He does n't want the *Argus*, really.

FOSTER [*just understanding*]. You mean he's left us together?

MAGGIE. Yes.

FOSTER. Awfully kind of him! I say, Maggie, you don't mind my coming, do you? I really had to. We — hadn't made arrangements about Tuesday.

[MAGGIE *laughing a little sadly.*]

MAGGIE. And you couldn't write them? You are very good to me, Walter.

FOSTER. Don't talk like that. [*A pause.*] Maggie, I — you haven't kissed me yet.

MAGGIE. I did — when you came in.

FOSTER. No — I kissed *you*.

MAGGIE. I'm sorry — I — I don't care for kissing in front of people.

FOSTER [*getting bolder*]. There's no one here now. [MAGGIE *rises, turns, and looking at him very straight, then lifts her face — pause — and going to him, kisses him on the lips. He keeps her close to him till she gently moves herself away.*] I've got something here — you said the other day you wanted — you would like one of those Dutch brooches. [*He puts his hand in his coat pocket and brings out a little parcel.*] Here it is!

MAGGIE [*unfastens it*]. It *is* good of you! You are so thoughtful! [*She looks at him.*] I suppose —

[*She kisses him again. Delighted, he keeps hold of her hand. She looks at him and then at her hand imprisoned in his, and then away at the fire.*]

FOSTER. What's the matter, dear?

MAGGIE [*impatiently drawing her hand away*]. It's still the mood. I can't help it. I don't feel like love-making.

FOSTER. All right, dear — I won't bother you.

MAGGIE. Perhaps if you did bother — no, never mind. You know I asked you not to come to-day.

FOSTER. Yes.

MAGGIE. Well, I had no reason, except that I didn't feel like it. But I ought to feel like you always, oughtn't I?

FOSTER. You're different from me. I always feel like you.

MAGGIE. Walter, I don't want to settle down. I want to go and — and do things.

FOSTER. What things, dear?

MAGGIE. Oh, I don't know. [*A pause.*] Did you ever go abroad?

FOSTER. Yes, to Paris, once at Easter.

MAGGIE. Oh! just for a holiday. Would n't you just love to go out and try your luck? Have a change? — Do something with your hands? Aren't you ever tired of what you are doing?

FOSTER. I can't say I am, really. Why should I? The work is not too hard. But you like change. I have a good salary, you know, dear. When we are married you can go about a lot, you'll be quite free.

MAGGIE. No, I shan't.

FOSTER. But you can have a servant and all that, you know.

MAGGIE. Oh, yes — yes — I understand.

FOSTER. If I went abroad — suppose it, for instance — I shouldn't have you, should I?

MAGGIE. No, and a good thing for you. You deserve something better. You know — you *know*, Walter, that I don't love you half or a quarter as you love me.

FOSTER. Yes, I know that. But you don't love anybody else.

MAGGIE. No. Have you ever thought that I'm really marrying you to get out of the shop?

FOSTER. Of course not. Of course you are glad to leave the shop because you don't like it. You are so tied.

MAGGIE. I should love to be absolutely independent, quite — altogether free for a whole year. Oh!

FOSTER [*a little hurt*]. You will be free when you are married to me, Maggie. You can do anything you like.

MAGGIE [*looking at him despairingly for a moment, then suddenly going up to him*]. You are a dear! — you are, really! Marry me quick, Walter! [*He takes her in his arms delightedly.*] Quick — or — or —

FOSTER. Or what? [*Very tenderly.*]

MAGGIE. Or I shall run away.

FOSTER. And where would you run to?

MAGGIE. Perhaps if I'd known where to run to — I should have gone before.

FOSTER. Dearest, don't talk like that!

MAGGIE [*turning away a little*]. But I don't! I'm safe! [MASSEY *is heard outside the door, coughing and making a noise. Enters.*] I'm afraid you've caught a cold in the kitchen, daddy. I thought you went for the *Argus*.

MASSEY. So I did. [*He looks down at it.*]

MAGGIE. And you've brought the *Family Herald*. [*She takes it from him.*]

[*Enter* MRS. MASSEY, CHARLEY, LILY, PERCY, *and* SYBIL.]

MRS. M. Play something, Lily.

[LILY *goes to piano and picks out some music.* SYBIL *and* PERCY *occupy one big chair between them.* CHARLEY *stands idly at window, turning over an album.*]

PERCY. Going to church, mother?

MRS. M. No, dear, it's a very nasty night. Such a cold wind.

PERCY. Last Sunday it was the rain — and the week before it was foggy, and the week before —

SYBIL. Don't be such a very rude boy! [*She puts her hand over his mouth and he takes it and holds it.*]

MRS. M. [*complacently*]. You're a bad boy to make fun of your old mother. I went to church this morning.

PERCY. You're getting a oncer, mother.

MRS. M. Well, I should only go to sleep if I went.

PERCY. Think of the example you set if you put in an appearance.

MRS. M. Yes, dear; I have thought of that, but it wouldn't do for them to see me asleep.

FOSTER [*who always has the effect of trying to smooth things over*]. I'm sure it is better for you to rest, Mrs. Massey, than walk such a distance twice a day!

MRS. M. Yes, it is rather a long way. It's quite a quarter of an hour's walk, and I don't care to ride on Sundays.

[LILY *plays, choosing the mournful hymn,* "Abide with me," CHARLEY *fidgets, goes to the piano and then back again to the window.*]

MASSEY. Can't you find a seat, Charles? You look uncomfortable.

CHARLEY. Plenty, thanks. Sybil only has half a one.

SYBIL. Oh, Mr. Wilson.

[*She fidgets away from* PERCY, *who pulls her back again.* LILY *has played the tune through. She stops.*]

MRS. M. That's such a nice tune, don't you think, Walter?

FOSTER. Very! — rather plaintive, but soothing.

[LILY *starts another — this time* "Sun of my Soul."]

CHARLEY. For Heaven's sake, Lil, play something cheerful.

[LILY *stops, turns undecidedly on the stool, looks round imploringly at* CHARLEY, *turns a few pages and then rises and goes out of the room hurriedly.*]

SYBIL. She's crying!

MASSEY. What?

MRS. M. You've hurt her, Charley, speaking like that. There was nothing to get cross about. She came this afternoon crying.

CHARLEY. I've done nothing! I —

[*Exit* MRS. MASSEY *in much indignation.*]

MASSEY. Had a tiff?

CHARLEY. A tiff — we don't tiff.

MASSEY. Well, then, don't shout at her like that. [*To* SYBIL.] Here — are you sure she was crying?

SYBIL. Yes, quite.

MASSEY. That's queer. She didn't use to.

CHARLEY. She's been worrying, I expect. Women worry so quick.

MASSEY. What's she got to worry about? A bit hysterical, perhaps.

[*Re-enter* MRS. MASSEY.]

MASSEY. Is she better?

MRS. M. She's got a headache, she says. But it isn't that; I know what's the matter. When she came to-day she could hardly speak —

CHARLEY [*interrupting*]. Is she worrying over me?

MASSEY. What's she got to worry over you about?

CHARLEY. I happened to say — I got the hump, I think . . . I feel a bit restless . . .

MRS. M. [*hotly*]. You know what it is well enough. You want to go away with that Tennant man and leave your wife —

MASSEY [*shouting*]. What!

[SYBIL *looks shocked,* PERCY *astonished, while* FOSTER *tries to pretend he didn't hear.*]

MRS. M. The poor child's breaking her heart because she says he wants to leave her.

CHARLEY. I never said anything of the kind — I never thought of such a thing, I —

MRS. M. *Do* you want to go away with that man?

MASSEY. I should think you're mad, both of you, to talk about it. Go with who? What for? What're you talking about?

MRS. M. Lily told me distinctly this afternoon that Charley wanted to go to Australia. She nearly cried her eyes out. Of course that means he wants to leave her. What else could it mean? She said he'd been funny and she was miserable. I said Charley ought to be ashamed of himself to want to go away like that, and so I think.

MASSEY [*sitting up very straight and looking angry*]. What's all this, Charley? What . . .

[FOSTER *on tiptoe slowly goes to door.*]

CHARLEY. Don't go, Foster. Let's have all the family in. You're going to be part of it some day.

FOSTER [*sitting down again*]. I'm quite ready to go.

CHARLEY. No, don't. Let's have it out. You may as well know, all of you.

MRS. M. [*with a resignation of despair*]. Then you do want — to go and leave her? It's disgraceful!

CHARLEY [*angrily*]. What stuff you all talk! I —

MRS. M. Do you or do you not want to go?

CHARLEY. Yes, I do!

[*General consternation.*]

MRS. M. There! I said so.

[*Enter* MAGGIE.]

MRS. M. How's the poor dear?

MAGGIE. She says her head is better and she will come down in a minute. What's the matter?

MRS. M. Charley wants to go to Australia and leave his wife. He's *told* us so.

CHARLEY. Well, suppose it was true, wouldn't it be better than going without telling you? But it isn't true.

MASSEY. Do you want to take Lil with you?

CHARLEY. How could I?

[*Enter* LILY — *all mutter words of encouragement. General movement towards her. Everybody offers chairs in sympathy. She sits by her father.*]

CHARLEY. Look here now, just listen!

It's quite true I want to go. I want to do as Tennant's done, chuck everything and try my luck in the Colonies. As soon as I had a fair start, Lil would come out.

MASSEY [*interrupting*]. Yes, and suppose you failed? You should have thought of that before you married. You can't run off when you like when you've a wife.

CHARLEY [*excitedly*]. But why not?

MRS. M. [*interrupting*]. Why not? — just hear him.

CHARLEY. It's that I'm just sick of the office and the grind every week and no change! — nothing new, nothing happening. Why, I haven't seen anything of the world. I just settled down to it — why? — just because other chaps do, because it's the right thing. I only live for Saturday —

PERCY. So do I! — so does everybody!

CHARLEY. But they shouldn't —

PERCY. You don't mean to suggest, I hope, that we ought to *like* our work, do you?

MASSEY. Do you suppose I like plumbing? Do you think I ever did? No, but I stuck to it, and now look at me, got a nice little bit in the bank and bought my own house. [*Looks proudly round.*] Of course, I hated it, just as you do.

MAGGIE. Then why didn't you try something else, daddy?

MASSEY. I like that! What could I do? I was taught plumbing. We don't have choice. Your grandfather put me to it, and of course I stuck to it.

MAGGIE. But why didn't you ask for a choice?

MASSEY. Me! Why should I do such a thing? Father was a plumber, and if it was good enough for him, it was good enough for me. Suppose I had thrown it up and gone to Canada for a lark? A *nice* thing for my family. [*To* MAGGIE.] You wouldn't have had the education you've had, my girl. We've got to live somehow, and if you get a good job stick to it, say I — none of your highty flighty notions. Live 'em down!

FOSTER [*gently*]. We all have moments of discontent, I fancy, but we get over them.

MAGGIE [*turns to* FOSTER]. Did you ever have any?

FOSTER. A long time ago, but I'm quite safe now, dear.

[MAGGIE *shrugs her shoulders and turns half away impatiently.*]

CHARLEY. I never said you couldn't live them down. I never said, did I, that I was going away? I only said I should like to. Did I ever say more, Lil?

LILY [*meekly*]. No, dear.

MRS. M. But you shouldn't want to. It's ridiculous.

CHARLEY. It wasn't till Tennant started about his going —

MRS. M. I knew it was that man Tennant —

CHARLEY. . . . that I thought of it. But if he threw up his job, I thought, why shouldn't I?

MASSEY. Because he's a fool, you needn't be another.

MAGGIE. He's not a fool, and I wish Charley could go, too.

LILY. Maggie, how can you?

MAGGIE [*crossing to fireplace*]. Why should a young man be bound down to one trade all his life? I wish I were a man — I'd —

MRS. M. Well, you're not, so it doesn't matter.

CHARLEY. Of course it must make a difference my being married.

MASSEY. Remember your wife's here and don't talk as if you were sorry about it.

CHARLEY [*turning on them fiercely*]. For Heaven's sake, can't you listen fair? My wife needn't go to her father for protection from me? I'm not a scoundrel just because I've got an idea, am I? [*A pause — nobody answers.*] But I'll tell you what, marriage shouldn't tie a man up as if he was a slave. I don't want to desert Lily — she's my wife and I'm proud of it — but because I married, am I never to strike out in anything? People like us are just cowards. We seize on the first soft job — and there we stick, like whipped dogs. We're afraid to ask for anything, afraid to ask for a rise even — we wait till it comes. And when the boss says he won't give you one

— do we up and say, "Then I'll go somewhere where I can get more." Not a bit of it! What's the good of sticking on here all our lives? Why shouldn't somebody risk something sometimes? We're all so jolly frightened — we've got no spunk — that's where the others get the hold over us — we slog on day after day and when they cut our wages down we take it as meek as Moses. We're not men, we're machines. Next week I've got my choice — either to take less money to keep my job or to chuck it and try something else. You say — everybody says — keep the job. I expect I shall — I'm a coward like all of you — but what I want to know is, why can't a man have a fit of restlessness and all that, without being thought a villain?

FOSTER. But after all, we undertake responsibilities when we marry, Mr. Wilson. We can't overlook them.

CHARLEY. I don't want to. But I don't think we ought to talk as if when a man gets married he must always bring in just the same money.

FOSTER. If you have the misfortune to have your salary reduced, nobody would blame you.

CHARLEY. I don't know. I felt a bit of a beast when I had to tell Lil about that.

MAGGIE [*suddenly*]. If you went away, Lily could come and live with us.

MRS. M. [*scandalised*]. How could she? Everybody would think she was divorced or something.

FOSTER. Live with *us*, dear?

MAGGIE [*impatiently*]. No, here, I meant.

CHARLEY. I've got a little cash put by that she could live on. *Don't cry, Lil, for Heaven's sake!* Can't any of you see my point — or won't you?

MASSEY. I suppose you're a Socialist.

CHARLEY. Doesn't anybody but a Socialist ever have an idea?

MASSEY. They're mostly mad, if that's what you mean. And they're always talking about the wickedness of the boss and the sweetness of the working man.

CHARLEY. I never said anything about either, and I'm not a Socialist.

PERCY. You'll be better when Tennant's gone.

CHARLEY [*viciously*]. Just you wait till you're two years older, my boy.

FOSTER. You see it isn't as if you had any prospects in the Colonies. Has Mr. Tennant?

CHARLEY. He's got an introduction to a firm.

MASSEY. What's the good of that?

LILY [*tearfully*]. Perhaps I could go with Charley. I'm quite willing to — rough it a little.

MAGGIE. You'd help him more by staying here.

MRS. M. He doesn't want her. He said so.

LILY [*still tearfully*]. If Charley really means it — I think — I —

MRS. M. My dear, don't think anything about it. It's worrying you and making you ill — you want nursing, not frightening.

[*This with a glare of indignation at* CHARLEY.]

LILY. I'm all right.

CHARLEY [*suddenly dropping his defiance*]. Oh, let's go home, Lil. You're tired.

MRS. M. Have you just noticed that?

MAGGIE. Mother!

MRS. M. She's my child, and if her husband won't think of her, I must.

LILY. Mother, dear, Charley means all right. I'm sure he does. Yes, dear — I'm quite ready to go.

FOSTER [*with the air of pouring oil on troubled waters*]. Well, at any rate, it needn't be settled to-night. Perhaps after a night's rest —

MAGGIE [*vehemently*]. I like impulse.

MASSEY. I expect you do. You don't know what's good for you.

MAGGIE. Well, at any rate, daddy, you can't say I have much. There's not much chance at Jones & Freeman's.

PERCY. So you've caught it, too, Mag.

SYBIL. Don't tease.

[*Enter* LILY, *dressed for going out, also* MRS. MASSEY. LILY *goes round, kissing and shaking hands, with a watery smile and a forced tearful cheerfulness.*]

CHARLEY [*without going all round and calling from the door*]. Good-night, all!
  [*Exeunt* LILY *and* CHARLEY.]
MRS. M. Well, I must say —
PERCY. Oh, let's drop it, mother. Play something, Maggie.
MAGGIE. I don't want to.
MRS. M. Walter would like to hear something, wouldn't you, Walter?
FOSTER. If Maggie feels like it.
MAGGIE. She doesn't feel like it.
MASSEY. Be as pleasant as you can, my girl — Charley's enough for one evening.
  [MAGGIE *goes to the piano and sitting down plays noisily with both pedals on, the chorus, "Off to Philadelphia."*]
MRS. M. Maggie, it's Sunday!
MAGGIE. I forgot!
MRS. M. You shouldn't forget such things — Sybil, my dear —
SYBIL. I don't play.
MASSEY. Rubbish! Come on!
  [SYBIL *goes to the piano and* PERCY *follows her.*]
PERCY [*very near to* SYBIL *and helping to find the music*]. Charley is a rotter! What d'ye think he was telling me the other day?
SYBIL. I don't know.
PERCY. Told me to be sure I'd got the right girl.
SYBIL. Brute!
PERCY. What do you think I said? Darling!   [*Kisses her behind music.*]
MASSEY [*looking round*]. Take a bigger sheet.
  [SYBIL *sits at piano quickly and plays the chorus to "Count your many Blessings." To which they all sing —*]

Count your blessings, count them one by one,
Count your blessings, see what God has done.
Count your blessings, count them one by one,
And it will surprise you what the Lord has done.

CURTAIN

ACT IV

SCENE. — *Sitting-room at 55 Acacia Avenue. Early morning.*
  LILY *discovered, cutting sandwiches. Ring at door.* LILY *admits* MAGGIE, *who is dressed for the shop.*

LILY [*rather nervously*]. You, Maggie! How early. What is it?
MAGGIE. I've come to help Mr. Tennant off, Lil. Where's Charley? Is he up?
LILY. Oh, yes. [MAGGIE *goes to the garden door and stands looking out.*] He's been up a long while.
MAGGIE. So the great day has come. [*Turning.*] Is Charley going, or isn't he, Lil?
LILY [*nervously and avoiding* MAGGIE'S *eyes*]. No, of course not.
MAGGIE. Why not?
LILY. Because — why, how can he? [*Tearfully.*] Don't speak in that tone, Maggie.
MAGGIE. He would have decided to go, if you had encouraged him.
LILY. I *did* encourage him. You heard me last night. I told him — and I told him again after we got home — "If you want to go, I'll never stand in your way."
MAGGIE. Yes, I heard. Is that how you told him last night?
LILY. It doesn't matter how I said it. He'll get over it. Everybody says he will — except you. And how could he go? It's just an idea he's got over Mr. Tennant.
MAGGIE [*angrily*]. Of course it's Mr. Tennant. Everybody speaks as if Mr. Tennant was a wicked person going round tempting poor husbands to desert their wives. "It's all that Mr. Tennant." "What a blessing when that man goes," etc., etc., as if he had a bad character. The truth is, that he's done a jolly good thing. He's stirred us all up. He's made us dissatisfied.
LILY. What's the good of that? Nobody can make things different if they wanted to.
MAGGIE. Don't talk nonsense. Hasn't

he made things different himself? [*Getting a little heroic.*] Heaps of fellows in London go on doing the same old thing, in the same old way, only too glad if it's safe. Look how everybody runs for the Civil Service. Why? Because it's safe, of course, and because they'll get a pension. Look at the post office clerks and Somerset House and lawyer's clerks and bank clerks —

LILY. Bank clerks don't get pensions —

MAGGIE. I know they don't, but once in a bank, always in a bank. Is there anything to look forward to — and aren't they all just — exactly *alike?* I once went past a lot of offices in the city — I don't know what sort of offices they were. But the windows had dingy drab blinds, and inside there were rows and *rows* of clerks, sitting on high stools, bending over great books on desks. And over each there was an electric light under a green shade. There they were scribbling away — and outside there was a most beautiful sunset. I shall never, never, forget those men.

LILY. They don't have long hours.

MAGGIE [*promptly*]. Nine to six.

LILY. I always thought it was ten to four.

MAGGIE. Don't you believe it. That's what I thought once. You're thinking of the bank clerks, of course. My dear, the doors close at half-past three or four — but the clerks — why, they never see the daylight.

LILY. In the summer they do.

MAGGIE [*impressively*]. I don't care what you say, or what anybody says, it's not right. And if the men have got used to it, it's all the worse. They want stirring up — and it's the women who've got to do the stirring.

LILY. Whatever can *they* do?

MAGGIE. Lots. It's the women who make the men afraid. In the old days the women used to help the men on with their armour and give them favours to wear, and send them forth to fight. That's the spirit we want now. Instead of that we say to the men: — "I shouldn't trouble, my dear, if I were you. You're safe here. Do be careful."

LILY. You're very unjust. Look at the Boer War, and how brave the women were then.

MAGGIE. That isn't the only kind of war. Is a soldier to be the only kind of man, that a woman's going to encourage? Can't she help the man who wants to make a better thing of life? Oh, what a lovely chance you had and didn't take it, Lill.

LILY. How can you talk like that! What a fuss you're making over a little thing.

MAGGIE. It wasn't a little thing. Here is Charley, with all sorts of "go" in him and fire and energy. Why couldn't you go to him and say, "I'm proud of you. Throw up the horrid business and go and seek your fortune." It was all he wanted, I do believe. Instead of which, he's got every blessed person against him — wife, mother-in-law, father-in-law, and all his friends and relations, and everything he can have. Everybody thinks him mad.

LILY. *You* ought to have married him, I should think!

MAGGIE. Don't get spiteful, Lil!

LILY. Wait till you're married yourself to Walter —

MAGGIE. I'm not going to marry Walter.

LILY [*struck with astonishment*]. You're not going to marry Walter? Maggie!

MAGGIE. I've broken it off. I did it last night.

LILY. Whatever for? Did you quarrel? You were a little touchy last night, I thought — but Walter is so good tempered.

MAGGIE. I'm sure it's very good of him, but I don't wish to be forgiven and taken back. It was all through Mr. Tennant.

LILY [*anxiously*]. You don't love *him?*

MAGGIE [*exasperated*]. No, I'm not in love with *anybody;* but all last week I was thinking and thinking, and it wasn't till last night that I found I was just marrying — to get away from the shop!

LILY. But he was *devoted* to you and so kind.

MAGGIE. I don't want kindness. My shopwalker is very kind where I am, and I don't see any need to change.

LILY. How extraordinary you talk!

MAGGIE. Well, when I heard Charley talking last night, I thought what a fool I

was to throw up one sort of — cage — for another.
LILY. But you *are* free when you're married —
MAGGIE. Nobody is — more especially the woman. But the thing is, I shouldn't want to be, if I loved the man. But I don't love Walter, only his house. Now, I can leave the shop any day, when I've saved enough — and run away. But I couldn't run away from Walter.
LILY [*horrified*]. Run away —
MAGGIE [*suddenly beginning to laugh*]. Can you see me? Running away from Walter? *Walter!* Oh!
[*She laughs, but* LILY *looks very grave.*]
LILY. You don't take the matter seriously.
MAGGIE. It shows how seriously I do take it. Have you ever heard of any girl, throwing up a good match, who wasn't dead serious?

[TENNANT *enters.*]

TENNANT. Good-morning. Oh, good-morning, Miss Massey.
LILY. You're ready for breakfast, aren't you? [*Goes out.*]
MAGGIE. Aren't you surprised to see me here? I wanted to give you a send-off.
TENNANT. Awfully good of you.
MAGGIE. You're quite a hero in my eyes, you know, and I feel I must cheer or do something extra.

[LILY *comes in with porridge.*]

LILY. You'll have some, won't you, Maggie?
MAGGIE. Thanks. Here, I'll pour out the tea. [LILY *goes out.*]
MAGGIE [*to* TENNANT]. Aren't you just frightfully excited?
TENNANT. Can't say I am.
MAGGIE [*sighing and looking admiringly at him*]. I should be *wild*, absolutely wild, if I were going.
TENNANT. I'm going to chance it, you know. There's no fortune waiting for me.
MAGGIE. That's the point of it. You know it's awfully unsettling, all this talk about Australia. You've made me so dissatisfied. I don't feel I can go back to the shop.
TENNANT [*easily*]. You'll get over that.
MAGGIE. Oh, I suppose so.

[LILY *enters with toast and puts it down beside him.*]

TENNANT [*turning*]. Please don't bring anything else, Mrs. Wilson. I can't eat it.
LILY. But it's such a journey to the boat.
TENNANT. Oh, that's nothing — besides, I've got these sandwiches.
[*Laying his hand on the package near him.*]
LILY. Are you sure there are enough? I can soon cut some more.
TENNANT. Heaps, thanks. [*Earnestly.*] Really, I shan't know what to do with them.
LILY. I'll put you an apple or two in.
TENNANT. No, don't —
LILY. Oh, but they won't take up much room.
TENNANT [*resignedly*]. Thanks very much.

[CHARLEY *enters.*]

LILY. Oh, there you are. You'll have breakfast now, dear, won't you?
CHARLEY. I'll have it later. You here, Mag?
MAGGIE. Of course. Do you think this great event could go off without me?
[LILY *and* MAGGIE *go out.*]
TENNANT [*smilingly*]. Miss Massey seems to think it's a sort of picnic.
CHARLEY [*absently*]. Does she?
TENNANT. She'd marry well out there, I dare say.
CHARLEY. Would she?
TENNANT. She looks strong and healthy. Her sort get snapped up in no time.
CHARLEY. You're catching the 10.15, aren't you?
TENNANT [*surprised*]. Yes. Why? Coming to the station?
CHARLEY. There's another just after twelve —
[TENNANT, *who has been swinging his chair backwards, comes to a pause as* CHARLEY *comes up to him.*]

TENNANT. Is there? I don't know. But what —

CHARLEY [*lowering his voice*]. Look here, old chap, suppose I come, too?

TENNANT. What!

CHARLEY [*who keeps his voice rather low the whole time, though visibly excited*]. Don't shout! I haven't told anybody — but I mean it. I want you to look out for me at Plymouth.

TENNANT. But, Wilson — I say — you —

CHARLEY. Don't! It's all settled. There's no use arguing. I've made up my mind. I'm going to leave here as usual and coming on by the second train and pick you up at Plymouth. Don't stare like that — I've thought it all out —

TENNANT. But your wife — your people here — you can't do it. When I've gone, you'll get over it.

CHARLEY. Get over it? I'm not going to get over anything. I've been a coward, see? — and now I'm going to cut and run. It's no good telling *Lil* — she wouldn't understand — but when I'm out there and get something and making a tidy little place for her, she'll be all right. She's nervous — the women are like that, you know — they can't help it — and her people, too — well, they're old, and when you're old, you're afraid.

TENNANT [*interrupting*]. You mean to go! to-day?

CHARLEY. Why not? Why not? If I put it off, I'll never go. It wants a bit of doing, and if you don't do these things at the time, well, you give in. I've packed a bag with some things — I did it this morning.

TENNANT. That's why you were up so early —

CHARLEY. I have written a note to Lil. [*Argumentatively.*] It's the only thing to do — there's no other way — I say, Freddy, you'll stand by me? It's easy for chaps like you —

[MORTON LESLIE *crosses behind sitting-room window.*]

TENNANT [*uneasily*]. Well — you know best —

CHARLEY. Of course — it's the only thing — [*The door opens and voices can be heard outside, laughing.*] Who's this coming? It's that ass . . .

[*He rises as* MAGGIE, LILY, *and* MORTON LESLIE *enter.*]

LESLIE [*a little short of breath*]. Where's that fool? Thought I'd come and give you a good-bye kiss, old fellow. I would cry, but I've only brought one handkerchief.

MAGGIE. Lily will lend you one of Charley's. But won't you miss the 8.15? Do be careful.

LESLIE. Miss Maggie, I'll tell you a great, an awful secret. [*He goes to her and says in a loud whisper.*] I mean to miss it.

MAGGIE. I don't believe it — you couldn't do such a thing.

LESLIE [*to* CHARLEY]. Well, Wilson, how is it? You look —

CHARLEY [*curtly*]. I'm all right. You don't expect me to laugh all the time, do you?

LESLIE. Certainly not. I'm afraid you're still pining for the flesh-pots — or is it cocoanuts —

CHARLEY. No, it's gourds —

TENNANT. Tin mugs, you mean.

LESLIE. Take my word for it, before a week's out, you'll be thankful you're sitting opposite your own best tea service, on a Sunday afternoon.

CHARLEY. I say, it's about time you were off, Freddy.

TENNANT [*looking at his watch*]. So it is.

LILY [*to* TENNANT]. You're sure you've got everything.

LESLIE. *Don't* forget to write, please — and *do* let us know what boat you're coming back by.

TENNANT [*laughing*]. Shut up! Where did I put my cap?

[*They all make a rush for the cap, and* MAGGIE *brings it from the hall.*]

CHARLEY [*picking up a paper off the table*]. Here, is this yours?

TENNANT. Another map — it doesn't matter. Burn it.

CHARLEY. Australia!

TENNANT [*looking at* CHARLEY]. Put it in the fire.

CHARLEY [*defiantly*]. It might be useful. [*He opens it and fixes it with a pin against the wall.*]

LILY. Now we shall be able to follow your travels, shan't we?
LESLIE. The time has come! Well, good-bye — old man. Allow me to prophesy you'll soon be back — remember what I said —
MAGGIE [*from the door*]. It's a most glorious morning! The sun is shining for you, Mr. Tennant — and there's not a cloud in the sky.
LESLIE. I hope you won't lose *all* your money —
MAGGIE. The sea will be all beautiful with the dearest little ripples.
LESLIE. And if by any wonderful stroke of luck you do make anything, let us know. Good-bye.
MAGGIE. All the men are running off to the city — but *you're* going to Australia.
[TENNANT *is rushed out.* LILY *and* CHARLEY *follow him.* MAGGIE *runs in quickly and opens the sitting-room window, through which* TENNANT *can be seen shaking hands again and again with* CHARLEY *and* LILY.]
MAGGIE. Good luck!
LESLIE [*shouting through window*]. Give my love to What's-his-name, the Prime Minister!
MAGGIE [*singing*]. "For I've lately got a notion for to cross the briny ocean."
LESLIE [*joining*]. "And I'm off to Philadelphia in the morning."
[LESLIE *drawls out the last word, bursts out laughing and turns away.*]
MAGGIE. Anybody would think you were excited.
LESLIE. If a man *will* be a fool, Miss Maggie, he may as well go away a happy fool. A cheer costs nothing. So much for him. Now it's me.
MAGGIE. How many trains *have* you missed?
LESLIE [*seriously*]. Quite two, I should think. But I promise you it shan't happen again. [*Goes out.*]
[CHARLEY *and* LILY *enter.*]
LILY [*wiping her eyes*]. So he's gone. Poor man, I do hope he'll get on all right.
CHARLEY [*easily and in a brighter tone*]. He'll be all right. He can stand a little roughing.
LILY. It was such a pity you couldn't get the time to go and see him off, dear.
CHARLEY. Oh, that's nothing.
LILY. I'll have breakfast ready for you soon. [*Goes out.*]
CHARLEY. There's no hurry.
[MAGGIE *is looking at the map.*]
MAGGIE. It's a big place.
CHARLEY. Um. A chance to get some fresh air there.
MAGGIE [*turning*]. So you're not going, after all?
CHARLEY. Oh — er — how can I, Mag?
MAGGIE. It means such a lot, of course.
CHARLEY. Courage or cheek — I don't know which. Of course, it's quite a mad idea — any fool can see that.
MAGGIE. You're not a fool. It's the others who're fools. If only you could hold out a little longer. Lil would be all right. She might fret a little at first — but she's the clinging sort —
CHARLEY. But think what everybody would say!
MAGGIE. You're getting over it already!
CHARLEY. What else can I do? I — I — shall settle down.
MAGGIE. Settle down! Charley — why should you? *I've* refused to settle down. Why can't you?
CHARLEY. What do you mean? What's it got to do with you?
MAGGIE [*triumphantly*]. I've refused to marry Walter.
CHARLEY [*surprised, but not particularly interested*]. What on earth for?
MAGGIE. It was all through Mr. Tennant —
CHARLEY. Tennant? You're —
MAGGIE [*impatiently*]. Oh, dear, NO. I'm not pining for him. But I found out, when there was all this talk about Mr. Tennant, that I was marrying Walter because I wanted to be safe and was afraid of risk. Then I made up my mind I wouldn't do that. I tell you because — if a girl can risk things — surely a man —
CHARLEY. There wasn't any risk for you with Walter. I can't see it.
MAGGIE. A woman isn't tested in the

same way as a man. It's the only way I have —

CHARLEY. Well, you know best, and if you don't like him — but everybody thought you did. I must say you've been rather hard on Foster. You led him on. I should have thought it was rather a good thing for you. Still . . .

MAGGIE [*sighing*]. So it's no good, then, saying anything?

CHARLEY [*uneasily*]. No — er — [*Turning to her.*] Mag! What would you really think of me if I did?

MAGGIE. What? [*Looks at him for a second.*] Charley — will you — after all?

CHARLEY. Supposing I don't give in — supposing I did go —

MAGGIE. Do you mean it?

CHARLEY. Are you sure about Lil — I'm ready to throw up everything —

MAGGIE. I would look after her — she would be all right in a week — I would do anything —

CHARLEY. But if I go it must be at once — at once, you understand.

MAGGIE. Yes, yes . . .

CHARLEY. And if Lil thinks me a brute beast for leaving her like this — in this way — you'll explain — you'll stick up for me —

MAGGIE. This way? I don't —

CHARLEY. I'm going to-day, Mag. I've arranged everything. I couldn't stand it. I had to go. I've written to Lil. She'll be all right for money — I've thought of that and I shall soon send for her. I know I shall, and then she'll be glad I did it. I look a brute, but, Mag, it's got to be. [*Postman's knock on front door.*] Hush! Here comes Lil — don't breathe a word —

MAGGIE. To-day!

[LILY *enters with letters.*]

LILY. Here's the post. Two for you, dear.

[*Gives letters to* CHARLEY, *who, however, doesn't look at them, but goes up to map.*]

MAGGIE [*quickly*]. I'll call back for you, to go to the station.

CHARLEY. All right.

[MAGGIE *goes out hurriedly.*]

LILY. I'm sure you're ready for breakfast now, dear — and you won't have very much time.

CHARLEY. I'm not very hungry.

LILY. It was so nice of Mr. Leslie to come in like that, wasn't it?

CHARLEY. Yes. He means all right.

LILY [*as he eats*]. They're very nice neighbours. I think we're very lucky to have them.

CHARLEY. Um. You were up very early. You'll be tired to-night.

LILY. These things don't often happen, do they, and I can keep better hours in future. We generally go along so regularly, don't we?

CHARLEY [*suddenly turning from his breakfast*]. Yes.

LILY. I've been thinking, dear, that we shall feel a little dull to-night without Mr. Tennant. Shall we go to the theatre? — something light —

CHARLEY. Oh — no — I don't think so —

LILY. Shall we ask the Leslies for whist?

CHARLEY [*rising*]. No — not them — it doesn't matter, Lil — unless you'd rather.

LILY. Oh, I shall be quite happy at home, by ourselves. I am so glad you would prefer that, dear.

[*She goes up to him.*]

CHARLEY. I haven't been up to much in the company line lately, have I?

LILY. You'll be better now, dear. What time shall you be home?

CHARLEY. Oh — er — you know my usual —

LILY. Yes, dear. Don't be late. I've got something to tell you — which will please you, I think.

CHARLEY. Have you?

LILY. Would you like to hear it now?

CHARLEY. Is it important?

LILY. *Is* it important? You'll have to be such a good man soon, dear — you'll have to set a good example.

CHARLEY [*uneasily*]. What do you mean?

LILY. Can't you guess? How dull you are! Bend down and let me tell you.

[*She pulls down his face and whispers.*]

CHARLEY [*pulling himself away*]. What! God! [*Taking her by the arms.*] CHARLEY [*turning away a second, and then turning back*]. Is that true?
LILY. Yes, dear.
CHARLEY. Lil — I . . .
LILY. You *are* pleased! But of course you are.
CHARLEY. Of course, dear.
LILY. Isn't it lovely to think of! And can't you imagine mother as grandmamma! Won't she be a fuss! Why, you're quite overcome. There! Go away and get ready. You didn't open your letters. There's the door. I suppose it's Maggie back.
    [LILY *goes out, and re-enters a moment after with* MAGGIE. *They meet* CHARLEY *going out, and* MAGGIE, *looking at him, almost stops him.*]
MAGGIE. What have you been saying to Charley, Lil?
LILY. Why?
MAGGIE. I thought he looked a little — upset . . .
LILY. He is rather. He's quite overcome, in fact. But then he would be, of course.
    [MAGGIE *closes door, still looking at* LILY.]
MAGGIE. What about?
LILY. What could I tell him, that would make him more pleased than anything else?
MAGGIE. I'm sure I don't know.
LILY. What generally happens when people are married?
MAGGIE. That! [*Pause.*] Lily!
LILY. Charley is delighted.
MAGGIE [*unconsciously speaking her thought*]. So you've *got* him, after all.
LILY [*indignant*]. Maggie!!
MAGGIE. Why did you tell him *now?*
    [LILY *goes out, a little indignant.*]
[CHARLEY *enters from kitchen, dressed for the office.*]
MAGGIE. Charley!
CHARLEY. What's up? Don't rot, Mag!
MAGGIE. And now —
CHARLEY. Oh, let's drop it. I was a fool all along — a bit of a beast, too — it's done with . . .
MAGGIE. But —
CHARLEY. What's the good of talking? Don't make me out more of a brute than I am! No, the thing was meant to be! I was mad. After all, a man can't do just what he likes! It's better as it is. If this hadn't happened I should have done it — and a pretty mess, I daresay, I'd have been in — and dragged her in, too —
MAGGIE. If —

    [LILY *enters.*]

MAGGIE. . . . I don't think I can wait for you, after all, Charley.
CHARLEY. Don't trouble.
MAGGIE. Good-bye.   [*She goes.*]
LILY. You didn't open your letters, dear.
CHARLEY. What are they?
LILY [*tearing one open*]. About the new lodger — very quick replies . . .
CHARLEY [*hastily*]. Oh, leave them over.
LILY. Ready?
CHARLEY [*moving his neck uneasily in the high collar*]. Yes — this beastly collar.
LILY. It's a pity they make you wear such things.
CHARLEY. I've got a short neck. I suppose you shouldn't be a clerk, if you've got a short neck. It doesn't fit the collars.
LILY. What an idea!
    [CHARLEY *stands looking at the map a moment. Suddenly he tears it down and throws it into the fire.*]
CHARLEY. Good-bye, Lil.
    [*He kisses her.*]
LILY. Good-bye, dear. [*He picks up his silk hat and gloves and puts the hat on as he reaches the door.* LILY *runs to the door.*] Good-bye.
CHARLEY [*from outside*]. Good-bye.
    [*There is a sound of the front door slamming.* LILY *starts chorus of hymn:*]
Count your blessings, count them one by one.
Count your blessings, see what God has done, etc.

CURTAIN

KINDLING

A COMEDY DRAMA IN THREE ACTS

By CHARLES KENYON

COPYRIGHT, 1914, BY E. J. BOWES

ALL RIGHTS RESERVED

Caution: Professionals and amateurs are hereby warned that KINDLING *being fully protected under the copyright laws of the United States, is subject to royalty, and anyone presenting the play without the consent of the owner or his authorized agents will be liable to the penalties by law provided. Application for the amateur right to produce* KINDLING *must be made to Samuel French, 28–30 West Thirty-Eighth Street, New York City. Application for the professional acting rights must be made to the American Play Company, 33 West Forty-Second Street, New York.*

Especial notice should be taken that the possession of this book without a valid contract for production first having been obtained from the publisher, confers no right or license to professionals or amateurs to produce the play publicly or in private for gain or charity.

In its present form this play is dedicated to the reading public only, and no performance, representation, production, recitation, or public reading may be given except by special arrangement with Samuel French, the publishers of the separate edition.

This play may be presented by amateurs upon payment of a royalty of Twenty-Five Dollars for each performance, payable to Samuel French, one week before the date when the play is given.

Whenever the play is produced the following notice must appear on all programs, printing and advertising for the play: "Produced by special arrangement with Samuel French of New York."

Attention is called to the penalty provided by law for any infringement of the author's rights, as follows:

*"*SECTION 4966: — *Any person publicly performing or representing any dramatic or musical composition for which copyright has been obtained, without the consent of the proprietor of said dramatic or musical composition, or his heirs and assigns, shall be liable for damages thereof, such damages, in all cases to be assessed at such sum, not less than one hundred dollars for the first and fifty dollars for every subsequent performance, as to the court shall appear to be just. If the unlawful performance and representation be wilful and for profit, such person or persons shall be guilty of a misdemeanor, and upon conviction shall be imprisoned for a period not exceeding one year." — U.S. Revised Statutes: Title 60, Chap. 3.*

CHARACTERS

MAGGIE SCHULTZ
HEINRICH SCHULTZ, *her husband, a stevedore*
MRS. BATES
STEVE, *Mrs. Bates's son*
MRS. BURKE SMITH
MR. HOWLAND, *her business manager*
ALICE, *her niece*
DR. TAYLOR, *an interne from a public hospital*
RAFFERTY
DONOVAN

SCENE: Home of Schultz, in a New York tenement.
TIME: Present.

ACT I: Morning in autumn.
ACT II: Late afternoon. Two weeks later.
ACT III: Forty minutes later.

KINDLING

ACT I

DISCOVERED: BATES *is at the wash tub, scrubbing and rinsing clothes in a pail.* STEVE *comes downstairs and is about to cross the landing when* MRS. BATES *sees him.*

BATES [*washing at tub — turns and sees* STEVE *coming downstairs*]. Steve! Will ye take this basket o' wash upstairs to our place before ye g' out?

STEVE [*lounging in the doorway, rolling cigarette*]. I'd like to, Mud, but I couldn't lift a dollar bill before breakfast.

BATES [*crossly*]. Go on, then. Faith, do ye ever do anything ye poor mother asks ye?

STEVE [*good-humoredly*]. God help me, if I did *everythin'* ye asked me. [*Crosses down* R. *to stove.*] Say, you got some kind of heat in here, ain't ye?

BATES. Ye'd better keep out o' here now. Ye know what Heinie said — he didn't want ye to ever come in his place. Be careful now — he means it.

STEVE [*with a laugh*]. Say! You must have a life size piture o' what that Dutch boob can do to *me!*

BATES. I know what he'll *do* all right.

STEVE. If Dutch don't like me, what are you hangin' around here fer? Ye got a home o' yer own upstairs, ain't ye? Why don't ye stay in it?

[*Crosses up* C. *to mirror above window — up* R. *and starts brushing hair.*]

BATES. If ye was any account on earth, ye'd pack the wather upstairs fer me so I could, instead of havin' me comin' down here botherin' the Schultzes.

STEVE [*cheerfully*]. The water ought to be piped up there — there ought to be a fasset on every floor. The law says that.

BATES. Well, you're doin' nothin' else. Chase down and see that the landlord obeys the law.

STEVE [*turns down* C.]. What do I want to mix up in it fer? *You* pay the rent, don't ye?

BATES [*in angry disgust*]. Ah, get out o' me sight!

STEVE [*yawning*]. Well! Me to the street fer a stiff drink an' a fat breakfast. [*He steps out into the landing and is about to go down the stairs, but he sees somebody coming up the stairs and steps back into the room again. To* MRS. BATES.] Say — here's somethin' pretty nice comin' up here.

BATES. What d'ye mean?

STEVE. That nice little fancy squab from Fift' Avenue.

[BATES *goes out on the landing and looks down.*]

BATES [*speaking downstairs*]. Oh, good-mornin', miss. Come right up. [*To* STEVE, *who is* R. *of doorway*]. You get out. Go on, get out!

[STEVE *loiters in the room until* ALICE *appears in the doorway. She is a young woman of about twenty, fashionably dressed. She hesitates on seeing* STEVE. BATES *throws* STEVE *a look.* STEVE *ogles* ALICE, *who enters, avoiding him. He goes out and downstairs.*]

STEVE [*as he exits*]. Oh, you kid!

ALICE [*crossed down* C. R. *of* BATES *at tub*]. Good-morning. You're Mrs. Bates who lives upstairs, aren't you?

BATES [*washing at tub*]. Yes. I'm the lady from right over here. I drop down into Maggie's place sometimes to do me washin'!

ALICE. I see. I was expecting to find Mrs. Schultz at home.

BATES. She ain't been here since I came down.

ALICE. I don't believe we know each other?

BATES. Sure I've seen ye around the buildin' the last two weeks. Ye're doin' tinement work.

[*Brings down chair* C. *to* ALICE, *crosses to wash-boiler on stove* R.]

ALICE [*sitting*]. Oh, not exactly that. I've been helping poor Mrs. Simons look after her sick child. She expected me this morning to come and stay with it while she went out, but I find I won't be able to for an hour or so, and I thought Mrs. Schultz might take my place.

BATES [*poking clothes in boiler with stick*]. Sure, I'm thin' ye won't be bothered many mornin's watchin' that kid.

ALICE. No. Doctor Taylor says it isn't going to live.

BATES. Faith, the young doctor didn't have to feel the child's pulse to find that out.

ALICE. What do you mean?

BATES. He only had to glance at the place the child was tryin' to live in.

[*Takes clothes from wash-boiler on broomstick, dropping same into bucket.*]

ALICE. I know, it's terrible! It's an outrage! [*She pauses, troubled.* BATES *grunts her approval.*] Mrs. Bates, I've induced my aunt to come down this morning.

BATES. Yer aunt?

ALICE. Yes — Mrs. Burke Smith; that's why I can't go to Mrs. Simons' now. She'll be here with Mr. Howland, who manages her business affairs. [ALICE *rises, crosses* R.] I mean to take them over this building from top to bottom and show them everything.

BATES. That sounds as if your aunt had money.

ALICE. More than she knows what to do with!

BATES. And ye're hopin' she'll spill some around here, eh?

ALICE. Yes.

BATES [*still busy fishing out clothes from wash-boiler on stove*]. Faith, that ain't the cure for the troubles of this place! It's the owners of the buildin' should give us what we pay for.

ALICE [*thoughtfully*]. That's very true,

MRS. BATES. The owners of this building *must* do their duty. [*Quickly — fearing lest she has said too much.*] Of course we shouldn't judge them too harshly. Property like this is usually in the hands of agents. And sometimes the owner doesn't know what the real conditions are. I can't think they'd shirk their moral responsibility if they did.

BATES. I guess the wise agent ain't puttin' them kind o' words in the contract.

ALICE [*after a moment of troubled thought*]. I had no idea myself until a few weeks ago. It was Doctor Taylor who told me.

BATES. Faith, he kicks enough, but that's all he can do.

ALICE. I suppose you've wondered why I come down here so often?

BATES. The doctor said you were interested in humanity. [*Snickering.*] I'm thinkin' the young feller looks on himself as quite a crowd.

ALICE [*crosses to vase on shelf and puts flowers she is wearing in vase and sets it on bureau with flowers in it. Embarrassed*]. Well! One evening at dinner he happened by the merest chance to tell me of his work down here, and of the terrible condition that prevailed. The next morning I came down to see for myself!

BATES. And that got ye interested in humanity? [*Crosses back to tub. Dryly.*] Ah! He's a nice young feller.

ALICE [*crosses to* C. R. *of tub*]. Well, the more I've come here, the more I've realized something must be done! Finally, I spoke to my aunt. She wasn't deeply impressed.

BATES [*half disgust*]. I guess not!

ALICE. She thinks it's one of my fads, but I've induced her to come down and see for herself, and I hope — [*She breaks off with troubled apprehension. Crosses up* R.] Well, we'll see. [*As if desiring to change the subject.*] You can't say when Mrs. Schultz will be back, then?

BATES. Faith, I can't keep track of Maggie these days. She's actin' kind o' queer lately.

ALICE [*crosses down to* BATES]. Why — is anything troubling her? She hasn't quarreled with Mr. Schultz?

BATES. I ain't heard of it, but ye can't tell — his father was Dutch. Lately he's stormin' round because he thinks he ain't gettin' his rights here in the buildin'. He's heard the doctor talk.
ALICE. The doctor shouldn't say things to make people discontented.
BATES. The child's got to spout his learnin' somewhere. He'd blow up if he didn't!
ALICE [*smiles*]. I know. He's very earnest.
BATES. Uh huh. [*She glances up at* ALICE *and they both laugh.*] He's a fine bye.
ALICE [*going toward the door. Embarrassed*]. Well, I'll come back again when my aunt comes; I mean to show her everything.
  [*She passes out.* STEVE *is on the landing holding door. She passes him without looking at him. Goes upstairs.*]
STEVE [*indicating* ALICE; *coming down, toothpick in mouth, speaking to* BATES]. Pretty fine, huh?
BATES [*at tub*]. Ye hadn't better get fresh with her.
STEVE [R. *of* BATES *and tub*]. Awh, Hell! Skoits love it!
BATES [*at tub*]. Maybe *your* kind do.
STEVE [*turning to* BATES]. My kind?
BATES. It's a dangerous road ye're traveling, Steve. Ye ought to be plyin' an honest trade like Heinie. Sure, it's breakin' me heart to see ye doin' what ye are!
STEVE [*good-naturedly. Flicks soapsuds from tub at* MRS. BATES, C.]. Fergit it!
BATES. I try to take pride in ye, but yer a good-fer-nothin' lad! and it'll be the end of me some day . . .
STEVE [*good-naturedly*]. Aw, dry up! I ain't a dub — some day I'll set ye up in a sunny flat, and buy ye phoney curls till yer head aches. How's that?
BATES [*alarmed*]. Where d'ye mean to get the money, Steve?
STEVE [*turns up* C.]. Don't *you* fret.
BATES [*alarmed*]. Steve!

[MAGGIE *enters from downstairs, carrying some kindling in her apron. She crosses to stove wearily and starts putting the sticks of wood in the top of stove.* STEVE *sits on table up* C.]

BATES. Oh, there ye are! That young lady was here asking fer ye. Did ye see her? [*No answer.*] Maggie, don't ye hear nothin' I say to ye lately?
MAGGIE. What'd ye say?
BATES. I said that young lady, Miss Alice, was askin' fer ye.
STEVE [*up* C. *sitting on table by window*]. Say, she's some looker all right. I seen that kid doctor downstairs. He's comin' up here.
  [MAGGIE *sits in chair before stove down* R.]
STEVE [*getting off table*]. I'd like t' pipe her loose on Fourteenth Street — I'd have her doin' the turkey trot in the Brighton before midnight.
BATES. That ain't no way to talk about a good woman.
STEVE [*down to* C.] That's the only kind I have on me staff. [*Crosses down to* MAGGIE *at stove — above chair in which* MAGGIE *sits.*] Say, angel face, you're the only good girl I know. Any time ye get tired lookin' at the face of that crazy Dutch husband of yours . . .
BATES [*puts some of her washing on chair* C.]. Steve, shut up — get upstairs now. Heinie don't want ye in his place nor talkin' to Maggie anyhow.
STEVE [*good-naturedly to* MAGGIE]. Hear that? Yer Dutch husband says I can't talk to ye. [*Crosses back to* C. *As he crosses up.*] Ain't it hell to be hated?
BATES. What ye want here anyhow?
STEVE [*up* C.]. It's freezing up there . . . gimme somethin' for the fire.
BATES. Maggie, can ye give the bye some wood so he'll get out . . . Maggie!
MAGGIE. I just put the last piece in the fire.
STEVE [*dumping clothes off chair* C., *sitting*]. Then I sits here till me mother gits the strength t' chop some more.
BATES [*picking up clothes*]. Let him stay in a few minutes till I finish me washin'.
MAGGIE. I don't care what he does.

STEVE. O, you little dare-devil.

BATES [*busy washing*]. There ought to be some wood around here somewhere. Maggie, what ye doin' with that baby cradle?

MAGGIE. What cradle?

BATES [*at tub*]. The one ye was packin' home from the furniture factory fire last week ... don't ye remember ... with one leg busted off? Let Steve break it up for you.

MAGGIE. I ain't choppin' that up.

BATES [*at tub*]. Sure you can't sell it. Tain't worth nothin' ... there's plenty of cradles layin' empty around here. [*Pause.*] What's the matter?

MAGGIE. Oh, nothin'. How's that sick kid downstairs?

BATES. Sure if it's still alive, it's nearly dead.

MAGGIE. And only three years old.

BATES. Sure it might 'a' spent the time better niver bein' born at all. What's the use? They say they're comin' for it with the ambulance and the poor little divil too near dead to enjoy the ride.

TAYLOR [*downstairs off stage* L. *Calling loudly*]. Hey there ... anybody home?

BATES. There's the young doctor now.

[TAYLOR *enters up* R. C., *carrying a doctor's medicine satchel and a baby.*]

BATES. Hello, Doctor.

[*The* DOCTOR *is a young man of about twenty-five. He carries a small baby wrapped in a cheap gray blanket.*]

TAYLOR [*to* BATES *up* C.]. Good-morning! Will you keep this kid here awhile? Its mother has to go to the drug-store for the other one.

BATES. Sure it's a great way ye have o' holdin' a baby. [*Snatching it from him.*] Gimme it. [*Holding it admiringly.*] Ain't it a fat rosy one? Don't ye be triflin' with this child. It's the only healthy one in the buildin'. [*Handing it to* MAGGIE, *who places baby in clothes-basket,* L. *of table up* C. DOCTOR *puts satchel and hat on table up* C. DOCTOR *crosses down* R. *to stove.*] Put it away, Maggie, where he can't get at it.... Carryin' a baby around with its head below its feet.... [*Going to tub.*] Was ye tryin' to teach it to skin the cat? Sure ye better try raisin' a family before ye try curin' one.

MAGGIE. Say, Doctor, you goin' to take the other one to the hospital?

TAYLOR. I guess it isn't worth while.

MAGGIE. What ails it? Do you know?

TAYLOR. Improper sanitation.

BATES [*at tub, scornfully*]. Improper sanitation ... a hell of a lot you know!

TAYLOR [*laughing*]. What!

BATES. Some of them dude babies uptown might catch improper sanitation from ridin' too fast in automobeels or overfeedin'. But the divil of a disease wid a name like that will yez find in this district! [*Wringing clothes.*] That baby's sufferin' from a severe attack of bein' born down here where he shouldn't be born!

MAGGIE [*up* C. *by table. To* TAYLOR]. 'Tain't so. Somethin's wrong inside, ain't it?

TAYLOR. I guess about everything's wrong inside.

BATES [*at tub*]. No doubt ye'll soon be takin' out some of the child's plumbin'?

TAYLOR. It's the plumbing here in the house that's doing the business, if any one should ask you.

STEVE [*jumping up impatiently and making for the door*]. Awh!

BATES. Where yer goin', Steve?

STEVE [*in disgust, turning to door*]. Upstairs where it's cold. Gee, ye're a healthy bunch of grave-diggers.

[*He exits into the hall and upstairs.*]

TAYLOR [*starting for the door, laughing*]. Well, see you later.

BATES. Good-day, Doctor.

TAYLOR [*stopping, as if struck by a sudden thought*]. Oh, by the way — you haven't seen two ladies and a gentleman here to-day?

BATES. How's that?

[MAGGIE *crosses to window* R.]

TAYLOR. There's a gentleman and two ladies.

BATES [*shyly*]. And one's a young lady?

TAYLOR [*down* C. *anxiously*]. Yes, that's it!

BATES. They're expected shortly.
TAYLOR [*brightening up*]. Sure? How do you know?
BATES. From the way you're loafin' around.
TAYLOR [*with a half-embarrassed laugh*]. Nothing gets by you, Bates, does it? Well, so long — I'm busy.
[*He leaves his medicine case on the table up C. by window C. as if unconscious of it and again starts for the door.*]
BATES. Oh, Doctor.
TAYLOR [*pausing*]. Eh?
BATES [*winking at MAGGIE*]. Ain't he the cute one? [*Pointing to the medicine case.*] I suppose it's a shame to tell ye, ye're forgettin' yer little pill box!
TAYLOR [*trying to look surprised*]. Gee whiz!
BATES [*laughing at him and imitating his start*]. Gee whiz!... D'ye notice the sudden start of surprise? He was savin' that for the young lady. Sure, here's a better excuse than that. [*She picks up the wash basket up C. into which MAGGIE had placed the baby.*] Here's me basket of wash with the child on top. [*Putting the basket in his arms.*] Carry it upstairs to *my* place. I'm thinkin' it's got a high fever. When yer friends come in, ye kin just be bringin' him back to life.
TAYLOR [*laughing*]. But see here...
BATES. Drop in here for some hot water.
[*Nudging him in the ribs, handing clothes-basket to TAYLOR.*]
TAYLOR. But suppose they ask to see the kid. He doesn't look very feverish.
BATES. Wait till *you've* had him a while.
TAYLOR [*starting for the door, carrying the basket and medicine case and laughing*]. You're a wonder!
MAGGIE [*at window R.*]. Say, Doctor —
TAYLOR [*pausing*]. Yes.
MAGGIE. What made that other one sick? Ye ain't told me yet?
TAYLOR [*offhand*]. Just living down here. It's enough to kill a horse!
[*Exits and upstairs.* MAGGIE *turns away to hide the effect his words have had upon her.*]
MAGGIE [*crosses down to BATES at tub*].

Other kids are born down here. This place is good enough for them to live in, ain't it?
BATES. Aw, Maggie, will ye fergit it?
MAGGIE. They're grown up all right, and they're happy and good as any other kids. Ain't they? Well, ain't they?
BATES [*at tub*]. Yes... look at them with their little bits of wizened bodies and chalky faces. D'ye suppose any one of them could be a policeman? Then look at my bye Steve — can lick any one in the ward. He was born and raised in Wyoming. Sure, a kid from here wouldn't stand no chance wid him.
[MAGGIE *crosses thoughtfully to stove.*]
STEVE [*coming hurriedly downstairs and enters*]. Say, Mud, how about some wood for the fire? Get busy, will ye?
[*Sits on corner of table up C. swinging foot.*]
BATES [*crossly*]. If ye were a good lad, ye'd be out in the street gettin' me some.
STEVE [*good-humoredly*]. If I was a good lad, I'd be takin' yer wash home Saturday nights instead of me dame to the theatre. Now rustle me up some wood, will ye?
[*Sitting on table up C. and accidentally kicking cradle, which is concealed under table by tablecloth which hangs down in front of it.*] What's this? [*Pulling cradle from under table.*] Here's where Stevie gets some steam heat. Here's that cradle youse two was gassin' about.
MAGGIE [*at him, savagely*]. You leave that cradle alone!
STEVE [*catches a glimpse of baby clothes in it, and goes off into peals of laughter as he steps back.* MAGGIE *throws herself protectingly over the cradle. Laughing. Crosses R. to window*]. This is no place for a young feller.
[HEINIE *is heard coming upstairs.*
BATES *gives a start, then suddenly hurries toward window up C.*]
BATES. Hark! Somebody's comin'. [*She looks out the window.*] It's Heinie. [MAGGIE *looks up, startled —* STEVE *stops laughing —* MAGGIE *hurriedly hiding the cradle under the table again —* BATES *frightened.*] Steve — get out! Get out, will ye, or there'll be a fight.
[STEVE *has started for the door, but*

finds that he has no time to get out. Turning back into the room with bravado, he crosses down to stove.]
STEVE. Well, I'm lookin' for it!

[HEINIE *enters.* HEINIE *then looks at* MAGGIE *up* C. *by table, who is trying to control her agitation.*]

HEINIE. Hello, Maggie! [*No one answers.*] What's the matter with ye?
MAGGIE. Nothing!
HEINIE. Yes, they is.
MAGGIE. Why, no. I...
BATES. Why, it was nothin', Heinie. She...

[*Steps, accidentally knocks down poker which is leaning against the stove. As she fails for an answer,* HEINIE *looks at* BATES *keenly.*]

HEINIE [*turns, sees* STEVE. *Pause — to* MAGGIE]. You go in there a minute. [*Takes* MAGGIE L. *to exit. As* HEINIE *crosses* L. *with* MAGGIE, STEVE *picks up poker from floor.*]
MAGGIE. Heinie...I...
HEINIE [*urging her — kindly*]. Go on ahead.

[MAGGIE *exits* L. HEINIE *crosses below tub to* C., *where he meets* STEVE. *While* HEINIE's *back is turned,* BATES *motions frantically to* STEVE *to get out.* HEINIE *turns and advances toward* STEVE, *who holds the poker behind his back.*]

BATES [*frantically*]. Why, Heinie, it's nothing —

[HEINIE *plants himself squarely before* STEVE, *who crosses to* C. *to meet him.*]

HEINIE [HEINIE *and* STEVE, *eye to eye*]. A while ago you came to my wife with a line of talk about goin' to work in a dance-hall as a waitress — I heard about it, and ye was careful to keep out of my sight. Now I told yer mother ye wasn't to come into this place or speak to Maggie.
STEVE (C.). Aw, I was only joshin'.

[BATES *crosses below* STEVE, R.]

HEINIE [*cutting him short*]. Well, you don't pull that josh in my home, see! What's more, you keep out of it!
STEVE. Aw, I just come in fer some wood.

HEINIE. Get out into the street and chop yer own. Women don't work for your kind in this place. Just get that — your game won't go.
STEVE [*defiantly*]. What game?
HEINIE. Bringin' young girls down to your dance-hall. Makin' 'em drink, plyin' a trade so dirty low even the dogs in the street wouldn't mix with ye.
STEVE [*threatening him with the poker*]. Why, damn ye!
HEINIE [*seeing poker is in* STEVE's *hand. Undisturbed*]. Put that down.
STEVE. Maybe I'd like to hold it.
HEINIE. Put it down!
STEVE [*dropping it and speaking with meaning*]. All right, I don't need it.
BATES [*behind* STEVE, *touching his arm pleadingly*]. Boys, boys!
STEVE [*angrily*]. You shut up! [*To* HEINIE.] Now what ye gotta say?

[MRS. BATES *picks up poker from floor.*]

HEINIE. Just this: If you know what's good for ye, don't ye ever show yer mug in this place again, and if ye ever try yer con talk with Maggie, like ye passed her a while ago...
STEVE. Well?
HEINIE [*in a cold, steely voice*]. You're a pretty handsome feller; I guess ye need yer looks in yer business, don't ye?
STEVE. It's me stock and trade.
HEINIE. Well, if I ever see ye in here again, or in speakin' distance of Maggie, I won't stop to ask ye what yer talkin' about...
STEVE. What'll ye do?
HEINIE. I'll spoil yer stock and trade! Ye got that? Now, get out!
STEVE. As this is your shanty, ye gotta perfect right t' order me out. [*Sneeringly as he moves toward door.* HEINIE *crosses* L. *below tub.*] Ye show ye good senses to let it go at that.

[*As* STEVE *goes up,* MRS. BATES *places poker by stove.*]

HEINIE. And don't ye ever come back!
STEVE [*at door*]. We'll see about that when the time comes. [*He goes out.*]
BATES [*crosses* C.]. Steve won't come in again, I'll see to that!

HEINIE [*to* BATES. *Crosses below tub*]. Do it! Ye're a good friend of our'n, Bates. Don't let him come in and spoil it. Any dog what's in the business he is . . .
BATES. Wait, Heinie . . . he's *my boy*.
HEINIE. All right, we'll drop it!
BATES. What ye comin' home at this time for?
HEINIE [*crosses down* R.]. The Walkin' Delegate's jawin' with the Bosses.
BATES [*crosses to tub*]. The stevedores goin' to be called out?
HEINIE. Looks that way.
BATES. Aw, what a shame!
HEINIE. Rotten news for Maggie.
BATES [*glancing apprehensively toward other room*]. Ump. Yes . . . Say, Heinie, I hear McKenzie wants a man to tend his stable. . . . It'll come in handy if you're laid off. I told Steve about it, but he wouldn't go. Why don't ye chase down before any one else does?
HEINIE [*crosses up* R.]. I will! Thanks for the tip!
BATES. That's all right. Hope ye get it. Ye'd better hurry.
HEINIE. No use telling Maggie I'm out of work till I know fer sure.

[*He goes out and downstairs.* BATES *crosses up to table up* C. *under which the cradle is concealed — looks thoughtfully at baby cap which she picks out of it.* MAGGIE *enters.*]

BATES [*drops cap back on cradle. Goes to her tenderly.* Down, L. C.]. Maggie, darlint, is it thrue? Aw, Maggie, Maggie. An' to think what I was sayin' to ye a while ago. [*Crosses down* L.] What does Heinie say?
MAGGIE. He don't know.
BATES [R. *of tub*]. It's time ye tould him.
MAGGIE [*crosses* L., *still to* L. *of tub*]. I don't dare. Heinie thinks like you do. A kid ain't got a chance down here. Up till a while ago, he used t' feel like I did.
BATES. He'd uv welcomed it, eh?
MAGGIE. We used to talk about it nights — how happy our home ud be with kids — somethin' to hold him and me together forever — somethin' to work fer. It ud be a real home, then, no matter where it was, or how poor it was. Then one day the health officer said somethin', and that started him thinkin'. Then he started readin' things up to find out fer himself. An' now he's fierce against it. He says bringin' kids into the world in places like this is worse than murder. Think of it, Bates, worse than murder. [*Crosses above tub.*]
BATES [*impatiently*]. Ah!
MAGGIE. I fought against believin' it. But now you say it's so. The doc says it's so, an' I can see it in that sick kid downstairs. [*Breaking down.*] Oh, it's awful!
[*Crosses up* L.]
BATES. Sure, it's a foine state of mind ye're gettin' in.
MAGGIE. Heinie'll be wild at me.
BATES. Sure, he'll be kissin' ye till ye're smilin' an' tickled to death. Tell him right out. If he's got any objections, he can be takin' ye away, he can.
MAGGIE [*coming down* C. R. *of tub. Surprised*]. Take me away?
BATES. Do ye think this is the only place of residence in the world?
MAGGIE. What d'ye mean?
BATES. What's the matter with Wyoming? Shure it's the paradise o' babies. Look at Steve. When Steve was a baby he used to sleep in the sagebrush like a regular little Moses.
MAGGIE [*vaguely — sitting in chair* C., *which she brings down*]. Wyoming — it's a terrible way off, ain't it? Say, I bet it's a beautiful place —
BATES. It ain't keepin' any tourists away from the Garden of Eden — but to my mind, it's got it on this place.
MAGGIE [*rapturously*]. It's all covered over with grass out there, ain't it? An' there's trees an' brooks an' lakes — an' ye can jest take ye lunch and go off on a picnic whenever ye want and lay around an' pick roses . . .
BATES. All the pickin' ye'll do at picnics'll be the shells off'n hard boiled eggs. There ain't no roses in Wyoming.
MAGGIE [*with a shade of disappointment*]. Oh —
BATES. No, dearie, it's a hard, rugged country, an' ye got to scrap for a livin' jes' like ye do here — but ye got the color in yer

cheek and the sparkle in yer eye to scrap with. An' that's where me bye Steve was born —

MAGGIE [*breathlessly*]. And he grew strong and husky!

BATES. And the night he come into the world the thunder was crashin' among the peaks and the wind was shriekin' and rippin' board after board off the house, and the cattle outside was a bellowin' — but above it all — loud and strong — came the howl o' me baby, and I thanked the good Lord fer it. For I knew he'd come into the world to last —

MAGGIE. Yes, yes!

BATES. — Like the rocks and the prairies and the mountains . . .

MAGGIE [*passionately*]. Come into the world to last — that's what *I* want — that's what *I* want.

BATES. And it's what's expected of ye. If ye bring a life into the world, ye got to start it right — it's yer everlastin' duty.

MAGGIE [*rises. Crosses to above stove* R. *thoughtfully*]. My everlastin' duty. [*Eagerly turning.*] Say, d'ye think Heinie'd quit his job and go?

BATES. I can put yez next to a scheme to land yez both in Wyoming and set yez up fer a hundred dollars at the most.

MAGGIE [*crosses to Bates. Eagerly*]. Ye can?

BATES. Ever hear tell o' homesteadin'? Well, there's certain land the Government ain't got no use fer, so it gives little pieces to the poor people, and tells them to go and live happy ever afther.

MAGGIE. They give it to ye, to *own?*

BATES. Wait till ye see the *land*.

MAGGIE. Then if we get a hundred, we can set up in Wyoming?

BATES. That's the game.

MAGGIE. Heinie's got to do it. I'll help him — I'll work, too. Gee, think of it — livin' out there in the sunshine an' flowers.

BATES. Fergit the flowers.

MAGGIE. Heinie's got to do it. Tell him about it when he comes home to-night, will ye?

BATES. An' *you'll* be tellin' him about the other?

[STEVE *opens door and enters. In the hallway behind* STEVE *are* MR. HOWLAND *and* MRS. BURKE SMITH, *in the order named.*]

STEVE [*speaking as he enters, winking at* MAGGIE *and* BATES]. I sold these guys tickets to come in an' see the Morgue, d'ye mind?

[HOWLAND *enters, crosses down* R. *He is a man about forty, quietly but fashionably dressed, patronizing to all but* MRS. BURKE SMITH, *to whom he dances obsequious attention.*]

HOWLAND [*at doorway*]. May we come in?

BATES [*at tub*]. Ask Maggie. It's her place.

[MRS. BURKE SMITH *enters — a woman of fifty, pompous and haughty, pushes forward and assumes the initiative. Crosses down* R.]

MRS. BURKE SMITH. Good-morning, my good people.

MAGGIE [*embarrassed. Up* C.]. Good-mornin'.

BATES [*very busy, washing*]. Marnin'.

STEVE [*at door up* R. C. *imitating sideshow spieler*]. Folks, it's the juiciest show on the Boardwalk. When ye've seen enough, step out by the door on the right, tell yer friends about it and come again.

[*All but* BATES *look horrified. She giggles.* STEVE *exits laughing.* MRS. BURKE SMITH *and* HOWLAND *turn to look at* STEVE.]

MRS. BURKE SMITH. I believe the fellow is drunk.

BATES. Aw, go on, he's humorous.

MRS. BURKE SMITH [*turning to* HOWLAND — *sitting* R. *in rocking-chair which* HOWLAND *has turned toward* C.]. Well?

HOWLAND [*reading from memorandum book*]. Let me see — No. 18. Oh! This is Schultz and his wife.

MRS. BURKE SMITH. Oh, yes. I remember Alice mentioning them particularly. Which one of you is Maggie.

MAGGIE. Me, ma'am.

MRS. BURKE SMITH. I'm glad to see

you, Maggie. Mr. Howland is taking me through the building. My niece has interested me in the work down here. She speaks most highly of you and your husband.

MAGGIE. Thanks, ma'am.

[*Alice enters.*]

ALICE. Oh, here you are, Aunt.... Good-morning, Maggie. [*To* MRS. BURKE SMITH.] I didn't mean to miss you downstairs.

MRS. BURKE SMITH. We're getting on quite well.

HOWLAND. A most remarkable chap showed us up. .

MRS. BURKE SMITH [*to* MAGGIE]. I'm desirous of assisting those among you who show a disposition to better yourselves.

MAGGIE [*undecided how to take it*]. Yes'm.

MRS. BURKE SMITH. Of course, we realize that to a few of you assistance in the form of donations is humiliating.

ALICE [*touching her arm*]. Auntie, dear.

MRS. BURKE SMITH [*to* MAGGIE]. Your husband is working now?

MAGGIE. Yes'm, he's a stevedore, down on the docks.

MRS. BURKE SMITH. Splendid! Does he drink?

MAGGIE. Not to hurt. Jes' a little sometimes when he's tired.

MRS. BURKE SMITH. Really, you know, that's very intelligent. It's a positive pleasure to find these occasional examples of the poor emerging from the thralldom of narrow thinking. [*To* MAGGIE.] I judge your husband reads a bit.

MAGGIE. Up to Cooper Union most every night.

HOWLAND [*unenthusiastically*]. Oh!

MRS. BURKE SMITH. Make a note of reading matter.

[HOWLAND *makes note.*]

ALICE [*speaking to* MRS. BURKE SMITH *aside*]. Auntie, these people might be sensitive ...

MRS. BURKE SMITH. You insisted on my coming down here, didn't you?

ALICE. Yes, but ...

MRS. BURKE SMITH. Then if I am to assist them, I must investigate in my own way.

[ALICE *gives a little gesture of hopelessness and crosses up* R. *again.*]

MRS. BURKE SMITH [*turns to* MAGGIE]. My dear, your husband's desire for knowledge should be encouraged, but along beneficial lines. Much of our magazine reading is most sinister in effect.

MAGGIE [*in a fog*]. What'm?

ALICE. Some of the stories he reads make him sad.

MAGGIE. He does get grouchy sometimes.

MRS. BURKE SMITH [*to* MAGGIE]. Have you any children?

MAGGIE. No'm.

MRS. BURKE SMITH. That's very sensible.

ALICE. Oh, Auntie.

MAGGIE [*in a trembling voice*]. That's what Heinie says.

MRS. BURKE SMITH. Your husband is quite right. Having children in your sphere is an economic error.

[MAGGIE *turns and weeps on* MRS. BATES' *shoulder.*]

HOWLAND. Evidently we have touched upon a sensitive point.

[BATES *puts her arms about* MAGGIE.]

MRS. BURKE SMITH [*to* MAGGIE, *a little irritably*]. My dear, we all have our burdens to bear. Come, now, you mustn't cry.

BATES. She ain't crying. She's laughin'. [*Whispering to* MAGGIE *as* HEINIE *enters from the hall.*] Dry up. Here's Dutch.

HEINIE [*eyes the visitors half-angrily, half-curiously, then nods*]. Good-morning.

HOWLAND. You are Schultz, I presume?

HEINIE. Well?

MAGGIE [*going to him*]. Heinie, what ye home now fer — what's wrong?

HEINIE [*looking at her keenly*]. What's wrong with you? Ye been cryin'.

MAGGIE. No, I ain't.

HEINIE. Yes, ye have.

HOWLAND. We were discussing a rather painful topic.

HEINIE [*sharply*]. Well, ye needn't... she's happy jus' as she is...

MAGGIE [*intervening hurriedly*]. Sure, I'm all right. What ye home from work fer?

HEINIE. Strike.

MAGGIE. Strike — are ye gonna lay off work?

HEINIE. For a while.

MAGGIE. Oh, Heinie —

HOWLAND [*to* MRS. BURKE SMITH]. That means a stand-off for the rent. [*Crosses up to* HEINIE.] I suppose nothing could induce you to return to work?

[ALICE *crosses down* R. *back of* MRS. BURKE SMITH *as* HOWLAND *crosses* C.]

HEINIE. Say, I'm crazy about layin' off —

HOWLAND. You working-men are merely the tools of demagogues — you are refusing to work at their command, and your wife here is the victim.

MAGGIE [*interrupting*]. Oh, that's all right. Strikes ain't nothin' fer us to tide over — we've done it before — only —

HEINIE. Maggie, what's ailin' ye?

MAGGIE. Nothin' — only we was savin' up so fast. We had twenty-seven dollars in the bank — pretty soon we'd 'a' had a hundred dollars. I was kind o' — kind o' stuck on savin' a hundred, but now —

[*Bravely attempts to smile.*]

HEINIE [*tenderly*]. Don't you fret, Maggie.

MAGGIE [*smiling up at him*]. I ain't got no kick comin' — you know that.

HOWLAND [*turns to* HEINIE, C.]. But what I would impress is — the futility — the folly of the whole business —

HEINIE [*angrily*]. Say, what d'ye think — [*He checks himself and turns away with a laugh of contempt.*] Gee —

[*Turns up with* MAGGIE.]

BATES. Let him tell ye, Dutch — he's the original sure-cure kid.

MRS. BURKE SMITH [*surveying* MRS. BATES *haughtily*]. Does this woman belong here?

[HEINIE *and* MAGGIE *cross* L. *at back, toward door* L.]

BATES [L. *Scrubbing, in her best society manner*]. Introduce us, Dutch — we've been spakin' but we ain't met —

HOWLAND [C.]. Er — this is Mrs. Burke Smith.

BATES [*brightening up*]. Oh, ye're a Burke, are ye? [*Getting very gracious.*] Sure, now an' I like ye better fer that — I was a Burke, too, before I married Batsy. Tell us, d'ye iver hear from the ould counthry?

[*She offers to shake hands with* MRS. BURKE SMITH. MRS. BURKE SMITH *and* HOWLAND *stand aghast.* HEINIE *exits hurriedly into the other room, holding his hand over his mouth.* MAGGIE *catches* MRS. BATES *by dress and urges her back to tub.*]

MAGGIE. Ye mustn't mind 'em, ma'am. Heinie feels bad about the strike, that's why he hadda leave the room. [*A burst of laughter from the next room causes* MAGGIE *to hurriedly shut the door.* ALICE *and* HOWLAND *exchange glances, ill at ease.*] And Mrs. Bates ain't just herself neither.

[BATES *bristles up indignantly.*]

MRS. BURKE SMITH. It is quite apparent that you are blessed with finer perception than those others. [*To* HOWLAND.] I feel it my duty to do something.

HOWLAND. Really!

[*Crosses up to window* R.]

MRS. BURKE SMITH [*motioning to* MAGGIE]. One moment, my dear...

[BATES *takes wash tub up* C. *and sets it between table and cupboard.*]

MRS. BURKE SMITH [*turning to* MAGGIE]. You do plain sewing?

MAGGIE. Yes'm.

MRS. BURKE SMITH. Come a little closer. [MAGGIE *approaches below bench.*] I'm going to let you come to my house to sew.

MAGGIE [*hesitatingly*]. Why —

MRS. BURKE SMITH. You wish to work, don't you?

MAGGIE. Heinie never used to want me to work, but now he's layin' off, I guess maybe I better. I'll ask him.

[*She starts toward door* L.]

MRS. BURKE SMITH. Yes, do. [*Rises.*] We have other visits to make in the building. [*Starts for door up* R.]

KINDLING

[DOCTOR TAYLOR *bursts into room. Starts as in surprise at them.*]

TAYLOR. Why...
[*Alice becomes confused.* MRS. BURKE SMITH *eyes him coldly.*]

BATES [*throwing up her hands in mock surprise*]. Gee whiz!

TAYLOR. Why, how do you do, everybody? [*Up* C. L. *of* MRS. BURKE SMITH.] Quite a surprise to find you here.

MRS. BURKE SMITH [*dryly*]. Quite! I can imagine!

TAYLOR. I've got a sick child upstairs.

MRS. BURKE SMITH [*frigidly*]. Really?

TAYLOR. So I dropped in here for some hot water.

MRS. BURKE SMITH [*crosses down* B. C.]. I hope you obtained the hot water.

TAYLOR [*to* MRS. BATES]. I'd like it boiling, please. It wasn't half hot enough before.

BATES [*with a wink*]. Lave it to me, Docthor.
[*Gets tin pail from table above stove. She crosses to stove and pours some water into a small tin pail from teakettle on floor above stove.*]

TAYLOR [*to* MRS. BURKE SMITH; *down* C. *to* L. *of* BURKE SMITH]. Your niece is becoming quite familiar with the work down here.

MRS. BURKE SMITH [*coldly*]. So it seems.

TAYLOR. It is quite a science, you know. It's great to think she's been able to interest you. I know she felt discouraged at first —

MRS. BURKE SMITH. Really!

TAYLOR. — thought you looked on it all as a fad.

MRS. BURKE SMITH [*dryly*]. I shouldn't call it that exactly.

TAYLOR. What induced you to consider it seriously enough to come down?

MRS. BURKE SMITH. I thought she needed a chaperon.
[*Crosses up* R. *to* HOWLAND *at window.*]

TAYLOR. Oh!

BATES [*crosses to* DOCTOR, C.]. Here ye are, Docthor; bilin'.
[*She hands him the pail.* MRS. BATES *crosses to wash bench* L. *back of* DOCTOR.]

TAYLOR [*smiling at* ALICE]. Good-morning. [*Crosses up to* MRS. BURKE SMITH.] Good-morning. We hope you'll come down again.

MRS. BURKE SMITH [*turns with surprising graciousness*]. Good-morning, Doctor Taylor. [*She extends to him her hand, from which the glove is turned back.* TAYLOR *is about to take it, when she suddenly dips her finger into the pail of water which he is holding.*] Just as I thought. Stone cold.

TAYLOR [*to* BATES, *reproachfully*]. Mrs. Bates, how could you!

BATES [*looking at* MRS. BURKE SMITH]. I'd hate to say what chilled it.
[MRS. BURKE SMITH *and* HOWLAND *exchange a look of disgust.* TAYLOR *exits hurriedly, bursting with laughter.*]

MRS. BURKE SMITH [*quite angry, to* ALICE]. You have seen the last of that young man, my dear.

ALICE. Yes, Auntie.

MRS. BURKE SMITH [*curtly, to* MAGGIE. MAGGIE *is down* L. *with* BATES]. I pay five dollars a week. You take your meals at the house. You can come up whenever you're ready — [*To* ALICE, *as she goes toward the door.*] Come along!
[*She goes out, followed by* ALICE, *downstairs;* HOWLAND *crosses up to door.*]

HOWLAND [*pausing for a final word with* MAGGIE]. I hope you will seize the opportunity to profit by this uplift.
[HOWLAND *exits and downstairs.*]

BATES. It's a holdup — [MAGGIE *crosses* R. *to stove.*] Can ye beat the loikes of that?

MAGGIE. What you mixin' in this fer? D'ye want me to lose the job?

BATES. It's a foine illigint job she's offerin' ye — five dollars a week. The high-toned robber.

MAGGIE. Just the same, I got t' have it, ain't I?

BATES. And a lot more with it if ye're goin' to Wyoming.

MAGGIE. I'm gonna get a hundred dollars, I don't care how.

BATES. It's yer duty to start the little

thing proper — because it can't start itself. It's the way of beasts what's always good parents — if ye need anythin' fer yer young — take it.

MAGGIE. Ye tell me to steal?

BATES. Bless ye, no. Shave it off unnoticeable like.

MAGGIE. Do ye think I don't know nothin' about the Ten Commandments?

BATES. Lookin' out fer yer own's followin' the rules of nature an' I bet the Lord made the rules of nature long before He made them Ten Commandments.

MAGGIE. Ye can talk and talk all ye like, but yer conscience tells ye yer wrong. Ye know it does.

BATES. It's plain the loikes o' you ain't got the price of a conscience and a healthy baby too, so make up yer mind which you'll have.

MAGGIE. Why, I'd think about it till I died. I wouldn't dare look Heinie in the face — [*A sudden thought strikes her.*] The Bible says, the sins o' the fathers is visited on the children — an' if I'm a thief —

BATES. Maybe ye can beat the thievin' instincts out o' the young one, but ye can't beat the health into him if he grow up around here.

MAGGIE. Suppose I got caught?

BATES. Ye won't. I'll be prayin' for ye night and day.

HEINIE [*enters from room* R.]. Well, have they beat it? I s'pose they was here offerin' charity.

BATES. To thimselves.

[*She begins gathering up her wash.*]

MAGGIE [*anxiously*]. Say, Heinie, is the strike apt to last long?

HEINIE. Now, tell me what's wrong with ye?

MAGGIE [*her agitation increases under his gaze*]. Me — why — nothin'.

HEINIE. I know better; what was they sayin' to her, Bates?

BATES. The lady is goin' to give Maggie an uplift — ain't that nice?

MAGGIE. She's offerin' me a job sewin' — I can earn somethin' while ye layin' off.

HEINIE. For how much?

MAGGIE. Five a week —

HEINIE [*sarcastically*]. Fine — what's the hours?

MAGGIE. I just go to the house and stay all day —

HEINIE. Nothin' doin'.

MAGGIE. But, Heinie, we need it.

HEINIE. Not that bad. She can try her charity slave-drivin' on some one else.

MAGGIE. But — Heinie —

HEINIE. If ye want to work awhile, and maybe ye'd better just a little, while I'm layin' off — I can get ye something easy around the factory for ten a week.

MAGGIE. Yes — I know — but —

[*She looks at* MRS. BATES.]

BATES [*up* C.]. Maybe she'd rather be takin' the other, Dutch —

MAGGIE. Yes, I — I —

HEINIE [L.]. What? For half the money?

BATES. Ye be forgittin' the uplift. Ye better think it over, it has foine possibilities. [*She looks at* MAGGIE *and nods toward* HEINIE *significantly.*] So long.

[MRS. BATES *exits upstairs.*]

HEINIE. Nix, nothin' doin' —

MAGGIE. You oughtn't to make 'em mad —

HEINIE. I can look after this ranch without the help o' charity — who asked 'em in here?

MAGGIE. Why, they're just people what likes comin' around doin' good.

HEINIE [*sneers*]. Same's their children likes feedin' monkeys in the park — The poverty and trouble o' me and my family ain't made for the pleasure of no man. They can go and do their [*gets paper from mantel*] playin' somewheres else.

[*Sits on stool below bench* L. C.]

MAGGIE [*pleadingly*]. They could do so much for us if ye'd only let them, and we need their help; honest we need their help. [*Crosses* L. *to* HEINIE, *hesitatingly.*] Say, Heinie, how'd ye like to pull out o' here?

HEINIE [*in surprise*]. Huh?

MAGGIE. An' go to Wyoming?

HEINIE. Wyoming?

MAGGIE [*sits on wash bench,* L., *eagerly*]. A hundred dollars is all we need. The Government gives ye the land for nuthin', and it's nice and healthy out there. O' course, ye mustn't expect too much, there ain't no roses. But it's fine and healthy and there ain't no sickness, an' that's what yer always growlin' about.

HEINIE. Me private car's in the repair shop — say — what got yer started on Wyoming?

MAGGIE. Mrs. Bates was tellin' of it. Look at Steve, he was born out there.

HEINIE [*in contempt*]. That skunk?

MAGGIE. Well, anyhow, he's husky and —

HEINIE. Did ye think o' earnin' the price workin' for them ducks at five a week?

MAGGIE. No! [*Positively.*] No, I don't want to work for them. [*Rises.*] You can take me down and get me that job at the factory.

HEINIE. Soon as the noon whistle blows we'll go right over. [*Rises. Crosses to her*, R.] Don't you bother, little girl, I know how ye feel —

MAGGIE. Dear old Heinie.

HEINIE. Some day — the minute I can get the price, I'll take ye away, anywheres ye like, so we can have a real home an' live like human bein's — then ye'll be happy, won't you?

MAGGIE. Sure — but — but — that won't be for a long time — will it?

HEINIE. Maybe in a couple of years.

MAGGIE. Oh! [*After a pause.*] But, Heinie, things ain't so bad here — ye just imagine it.

HEINIE. Do I? Well, the health officer says if folks live in dumps like this they get consumption.

MAGGIE. We can't help it.

HEINIE [*sits on stool below tub*]. You're right — it don't help — grumblin' only it makes me sore.

MAGGIE. Well, maybe things could be better — but yer feelin's ain't changed, Heinie, have they? Heinie, lemme show ye somethin'. [*She gets a book of Mother Goose rhymes from the bureau drawer up* L. *Crosses down to bench.*] Remember, it — the night you brought this home — I learned one of the rhymes an' you learned one. [*Turning the page.*] Here's the one I learned. [*Turning another page.*] And here's the one you learned. I bet ye forgot yours already.

HEINIE [*laughing, he tugs almost sheepishly at the top of his shoe*]. Not on yer life. [*He recites 'Bye, Baby Bunting,' hesitatingly, looking foolish.*]

Bye, baby bunting, papa's gone a-hunting
To get a little rabbit skin
To wrap his baby buntin' in.

[*Sheepish laugh.*]

MAGGIE. Oh, Heinie, you don't know how happy it all made me. I knew what it meant. It meant ye loved me. Heinie, are things different now?

HEINIE. Why, honey, the only difference is — I care more an' more for ye every day.

MAGGIE. Heinie!

HEINIE. An' I feel just as I did the day I brought that kid book home. An' I always will. Don't ye ever forget that. But I come to see, fixed as we are, down here, it's wrong.

MAGGIE. Oh, but Heinie, look at the kids that are born down here. They're happy, ain't they?

HEINIE [*rises*]. Yes, look at 'em!

MAGGIE [*pleadingly*]. Other people down here's satisfied with 'em.

HEINIE. Because they don't know what a terrible thing they're doin'.

MAGGIE. Is it a terrible thing? Ain't it your crazy way of seein' things?

HEINIE. Do ye think when them kids grow up to see their sickly half-baked bodies don't give 'em no chance with other people they'll thank the fools what brought 'em into the world? Why, how'd yer like ter have a kid of yer own cursin' yer fer the very life you give it?

MAGGIE [*rising from arm of wash bench*]. No, no, don't say that.

HEINIE. I'd rather kill it when it was born than send it up against a game like that.

MAGGIE [*shrilly*]. Shut up, will ye? Shut up —

HEINIE [*suspiciously, approaching her, both down* L.]. Say, what's ther matter with ye?

MAGGIE [*trembling, evading his eye*]. It's them awful things you say — ye oughtn't to say 'em, Heinie, ye oughtn't to say 'em, even if they are true.

[*Buries her head on his breast, sobbing.*]

HEINIE. That's all right, honey, don't ye cry. We'll pull out o' here yet. There, now, put on yer hat and coat and I'll take ye over to the factory.

[MRS. BATES *enters, up* R. C.]

BATES. Your sassiety friends is returnin'.

HEINIE [*sulkily*]. What do they want?

BATES. Comin' back to see if Maggie wants the job.

HEINIE [*angrily*]. Tell 'em no.

[*He goes into next room* L. *and slams door after him.*]

BATES. Well?

MAGGIE. I couldn't.

BATES. God save us, child —

MAGGIE. Oh, I was too scared. He said if one come he'll kill it —

BATES [*starts* L.]. I'll talk to the pig-headed Dutchman.

MAGGIE [*stopping her*]. No, no, don't say a word — not now.

BATES. What else can ye do?

MAGGIE. I'll tell him — I'll — Oh, tell him to-morrow. Say, maybe if I'd go up to the house and tell that woman about myself, maybe she'd help me.

BATES [*skeptically*]. Huh! [*She hears* STEVE *coming downstairs.*] Here they come back.

[MAGGIE *goes slowly to chair down* U. R. *of tub and sits.*]

[STEVE *enters.*]

BATES [*whispering*]. Steve — go away; Heinie's here.

STEVE [*leaning against the door jamb, to* BATES]. Beat it upstairs, some one wants to see ye about their wash. [BATES *exits and upstairs.*] Hurry up! [*Still standing by the closed door — speaking to* MAGGIE *in a low voice.*] Where's yer husband?

MAGGIE [*nods toward the other room*]. In there.

STEVE. Come here —

[MAGGIE *does not move.*]

MAGGIE. Well?

STEVE. Say, did I get the dope right? Ye goin' to work for them guys?

MAGGIE. I don't know — why?

STEVE. Me mother was sayin' ye was hard up fer money —

MAGGIE. I am —

STEVE. Bad?

MAGGIE. Awful —

STEVE. Yer know where ter git it, don't ye?

MAGGIE. You can't tell me.

STEVE. I don't mean what you mean — listen here — that place yer goin' to work in is a cinch.

MAGGIE. Aw, cut that!

STEVE. I ain't askin' ye to steal. Come here — I can't holler at ye. Just get the dope on the place an' give it to me.

MAGGIE. What for?

STEVE. I'd like to know what it looks like, that's all. Say, if it happens to look good, you won't have no kick comin' —

MAGGIE. Say, who do you think you're talkin' to!

STEVE. Come here, ye little idiot — talk won't hurt ye — listen here; if ye tell me how pretty the house looks inside — after I take a look at it, I might be able to slip ye a couple o' hundred. Ye might be able to use it.

MAGGIE [*almost to herself*]. A hundred's all I need.

STEVE [*laughing*]. Sure, I wouldn't have ye feel bad about it. I tell ye — [*Crosses down.*] You slip a note under my pillow givin' me a plan of the house an' I'll treat ye right. [BATES *is heard returning, coming downstairs.*] Cheese it, here's Mud.

[*He leans against the door jamb, grinning.*]

[MRS. BATES *enters.*]

BATES [*speaking angrily to* STEVE]. What d'ye mean by sendin' me chasin' upstairs when there's no one there?

STEVE. Ye needed the exercise, Mud. The kid doctor said he could love ye for ye money, if ye wasn't so fat — [*Meaningly*] I'll be upstairs, Maggie.

[STEVE *laughs at her with brutal good nature and exits.*]

BATES [*angrily*]. What's he up to, Maggie?

MAGGIE [*still sitting, as if about to tell*

her]. He comes down here — [*Then suddenly becomes evasive.*] Oh, I don't know — he's drunk, I guess. He better keep out o' here, or Heinie'll beat him up.

BATES. The young imp — bad cess to him.

[HEINIE *enters from* L.]

HEINIE. Ain't ye ready yet?

MAGGIE. Why, no, I — Oh, Heinie, I want to wait and tell the people I don't want the job. I got to tell 'em nice that I don't want it —

[BATES R. HEINIE L. MAGGIE C.]

BATES [R. C.]. Sure an' ye can write to 'em, Maggie. I got the address — she left me a card where to go fer medicine for the sick kid. [*She reads the card which she takes from her shirtwaist.*] Mrs. Burke Smith, her house is 1914 Fifth Avenue, and the business address is 62 Wall Street.

HEINIE [*looking up suddenly*]. What's the last address? [*He snatches the card from* MRS. BATES *and reads it.*] 62 Wall Street is her office, is it? Well, of all the brassy nerve —

MAGGIE. Now, what's ailin' ye —

[HEINIE *crosses to* MAGGIE *below wash bench.* BATES *crosses up* C. *to table* C. *Anxious for fear she has urged* MAGGIE *too strongly.*]

HEINIE. It's a fine bunch of man-killin' saints ye'd like ter be bowin' and scrapin' to around here. Say, if that guy shows his mug in here, I'll tear him to a pulp. And I'll bounce the old woman out on her neck — I mean it. [*Derisively.*] Say, they're good to ye, ain't they?

MAGGIE [*defiantly*]. Yes.

HEINIE. They're crazy to pull ye out o' this rat hole and see ye live like a human bein', ain't they?

MAGGIE. Yes.

HEINIE. They're eatin' their hearts out 'cause we ain't livin' in gold palaces on Fifth Avenue, and when ye get through kissin' the ground they walk on, they're goin' to fix ye up fine and dandy, ain't they?

MAGGIE [*blindly*]. Yes! Yes! Yes!

HEINIE. That's what you think, but I'll put ye wise. Do ye know who owns this rat hole ye live in? Do ye know who pulls down rent for block after block o' dumps like this? Do ye know who sidesteps fire laws and tenement laws — makes ye breathe dirt, who'd send yer kids coughin' and spittin' to hell if ye dared to have any?

MAGGIE [*aghast*]. What d'ye mean?

HEINIE. I mean that angel of charity on the stairs — that Mrs. Burke Smith, of 62 Wall Street!

MAGGIE [*a strange hardening on her face — speaking quietly*]. Say, that's on the level? That woman owns this house?

HEINIE. The whole block pays her blood money so she can come down here in her glad rags and diamonds an' chuck it at us in charity.

MAGGIE [*half to herself — lost in thought*]. Gee!

HEINIE. Now are ye wise to the deal you're gettin'? [*After waiting for her to say more —* MAGGIE *in deep thought, her face gradually hardening — after watching her curiously for a moment.*] Come on, let's fergit it and go to the factory. [*He opens the door and stands waiting.*] Ain't ye comin'? Git on yer things.

[*Comes toward* MAGGIE. MAGGIE, *absorbed in her own thoughts, makes no move.*]

MAGGIE. Gimme that card.

[*She takes card from him.*]

HEINIE [*to* MAGGIE]. What's got into ye? [*Down* C.]

MAGGIE [*a stubborn expression on her face*]. Goin' to take the job, that's all.

HEINIE. After all I jus' told ye?

MAGGIE. Yep.

HEINIE. Don't believe me, eh?

MAGGIE. Yep.

HEINIE. Then what's ailin' ye?

MAGGIE. I'm jus' goin', that's all. Can if I want, can't I?

HEINIE [*losing temper completely*]. Sure, ye can.

MAGGIE. All right.

HEINIE [*crosses* L.]. Go anywhere ye like. Go on up to that bunch, and git played for a sucker. Maybe ye'll come back with some kind of sense banged into ye. I'm tired of talkin' to ye.

[*He rushes into room* L., *in a*

temper, slamming the door after him. BATES *follows* MAGGIE *up to door up* R., *after watching her nervously.*]

MAGGIE. Lend me a nickel for car-fare. [*Pause in which* MAGGIE *slips on her jacket up* R. BATES *fumbles in her pocket, takes out her purse, and gives* MAGGIE *a coin. Puts coin in her pocket.*] Thanks, so long! [*She goes out into the landing and calls upstairs*]. So long, Steve!

STEVE [*after a pause,* STEVE *is heard coming down a step or two*]. What's that?

MAGGIE. I said "So long" — I'm gonna work for them people.

[*She goes down the stairs.*]

CURTAIN

ACT II

SCENE: Same scene as Act I.
TIME: Two weeks later.

The curtain rises on an empty stage. Wash boiler has been emptied and placed behind stove — wash tub is off — wash bench is up by window R. *A kitchen table stands where wash bench stood down* L. C. *with chair either side of it. Tea-kettle is on the stove, also pot of boiling potatoes, also pot of boiling coffee, loaf of bread in bread box on table up* C., *bottle of milk on fire escape, package of uncooked liver off stage* L.

There is a knock at the hall door, then another knock — RAFFERTY *opens door cautiously and steps into the room. He crosses* L *stealthily, gives it a hasty inspection, then goes into the next room* L., *returns almost immediately. He hears some one coming up the stairs, he looks through stairway window and discovers it is* STEVE, *so he ceases his examination and stands in* U. R. *corner of room. In a moment* STEVE *comes up the stairs and enters. He is slightly intoxicated and has an unlighted cigar in his mouth. He crosses room and looks in door* L., *starts back to hall and faces* RAFFERTY, *who has come down* C.

Note: The following scene should be played slowly and deliberately.

STEVE [*startled into a look of suspicion at seeing* RAFFERTY]. Oh! [*Quickly recovering himself — crossing close to* RAFFERTY *with an air of bravado.*] Well, see who's here.

RAFFERTY [*smiling sardonically*]. Surprised?

STEVE [*mumbling*]. Thought me mother was here. [*A little defiantly under* RAFFERTY'S *gaze.*] What you doin' here?

RAFFERTY. Oh, just blew in to see my friend Schultz.

STEVE [*half believing*]. Friend o' yours — huh?

RAFFERTY [*after* STEVE *eyes him awhile with covert glances*]. Sure — what else do ye suppose I'd come up here for? [*With a sharp glance.*] Any idea?

STEVE [*stares at him a moment, then begins to smile insolently*]. Sure I know.

RAFFERTY. What for?

STEVE. Ye come all the way upstairs jest to gimme a light. [RAFFERTY *gives him light.*] Ye're a nice little fella.

RAFFERTY [*as he gets whiff of the smoke*]. What's this — Africanos?

STEVE [*with bravado*]. Twenty-five straight. [*Taking cigar from his pocket and handing it to* RAFFERTY.] Have one?

RAFFERTY [*studying the cigar*]. Ain't we living high nowadays?

STEVE. I ain't afraid to spend money.
[*Crosses down* L. C.]

RAFFERTY [*dryly*]. Sure, and ye ain't afraid to get money; come easy, go easy, eh, Steve?

STEVE [*stopped by* RAFFERTY'S *reply*]. You got the idea — almost.

RAFFERTY [*carelessly — crosses below table to chair* L. *of it*]. See ye ain't been workin' down to the dance-hall lately. [*Sits.*]

STEVE. Who said I ain't?
[*Crosses to* R. *of table* L. C.]

RAFFERTY. I didn't see ye there last night.

STEVE [*suspiciously*]. What kind of a con is that? You wasn't there last night.

RAFFERTY. I know I wasn't. I was on the corner of Central Park West and 87th Street — [*glances at* STEVE *out of the corner of his eye to see the effect.* STEVE *is just about to sit, but stands again*] — about eleven-thirty. [*Lights cigar.*]

STEVE [*betrays a slight start by halting his cigar halfway to his lips, then — speaking easily. Sits* R. *of table*]. That so? Well, don't feel bad. It was dark and nobody could see ye.

RAFFERTY [*whittles a match*]. Guess that's why nobody saw me cross the Park on Fifth Avenue about eight.

[*He watches* STEVE *keenly to see how he takes this.*]

STEVE [*imperturbably*]. Maybe ... and maybe that's why ye didn't see me sittin' in the Brighton from five-thirty up to that time — that seems to be what's worrying you.

RAFFERTY. Oh, I saw you all right. [*After a few puffs of his cigar.*] Say, what the hell does a fella that can't hit a spot ball stand around a pool table for two hours for? That was the rankest play to git noticed I ever looked at.

STEVE. Well, I was noticed at five-thirty, wasn't I? Well, I never git up before three in the afternoon. Takes me a couple of hours to git dressed, git breakfast, and git to Harlem. So now nursey knows just where little baby was all the time.

RAFFERTY. But yesterday baby couldn't sleep and got up at noon. It *worried nursey.*

STEVE. Oh — ye was takin' that much notice, was ye? Well, now I'm gonna tell ye somethin' to make ye feel bad. Some o' you wise guys thought Haggerty was playin' the New Orleans ponies in the back of his saloon, and ye had a nice little raid all framed up for one o'clock — didn't ye?

RAFFERTY [*smilingly*]. I heard about it.

STEVE. Well, them smart Alecs come rushing back through the bar an' there was two doors [*laughing gleefully*]. Sure enough the boobs goes in the wrong door.

RAFFERTY [*with amusement*]. An' somebody turned the key on 'em.

STEVE [*with a wink of confidence*]. Neat, huh? Well, that guy with the key was — [*pause and satisfied smirk*] — baby.

RAFFERTY [*seeming to enjoy it*]. Bully for you. [*Laughs lightly.*] I hear there was a ripe guy in there with whiskers [*puff*] — from Indiana.

STEVE. Hear about him? Well, after the place got pinched, I couldn't lose him. He wanted to hand me his roll, 'fraid they'd take it for evidence. Well, I lights out, and this guy clings to me all the way up Seventh Avenue, so I begins to think I kin git him up to Harlem sittin' in a nice little poker game.

RAFFERTY [*sharply*]. But instead ye lost him in the subway crowd at two-thirty.

STEVE [*mystified, but guarded*]. How the hell do you know?

RAFFERTY. Well, that guy with the whiskers was nursey. So you see she's worryin' about where you were for three hours till you showed up in Harlem.

STEVE. There's a picture puzzle for ye. Find six saloons with — Stevie inside between Harlem and Houston Street.

RAFFERTY. [*Rising, crosses* R. *below table.*] So that's the best you can give me, is it? Well, I'll try.

[MRS. BATES *coming downstairs — appears in the doorway. She has a shawl over her head and carries a small basket for bundles.*]

BATES. [RAFFERTY *turns to see who it is.*] Oh, Steve! [BATES *stops in doorway, surprised at seeing* RAFFERTY.] Ah, there you are.

STEVE [*still seated at the table, his back toward her*]. Huh!

BATES. I'm goin' to the grocery.

STEVE [*without looking up*]. Well, go ahead.

BATES. I'm needin' some change.

STEVE [*irritably, rises, crosses* L. *below table*]. Can't ye see I'm busy?

RAFFERTY. I won't wait.

[RAFFERTY *goes toward door.*]

BATES [*entering* L. *of* RAFFERTY]. Ye're wantin' to see somebody?

RAFFERTY [*laughing*]. Oh, that's all right.

[*He goes out and downstairs, laughing as he goes.*]

BATES. Who is that, Steve?

STEVE [*crosses* R. *above table*]. Oh, that's a loose-mouthed guy named Bill Rafferty.

BATES [*startled*]. Rafferty! He's a plain-clothes cop, ain't he?

STEVE [*angrily, looks through window stairs*]. He's a bum imitation of one.
BATES [*alarmed*]. What's he doin' here?
STEVE [*crosses down* C. *irritable and restless*]. Come in to see Dutch.
BATES. What's a plain-clothes man botherin' Dutch about?
STEVE [*crosses* L. *door down* L.]. Well, how do I know? — that's his business.
BATES. Ye're sure it isn't you he's after?
STEVE [*sarcastically, down* L.]. Sure — by appointment. Here in Dutch's place.
BATES. Ye seemed talking awful serious about somethin'. [STEVE *does not answer, but runs up and opens door, up* R. — *looking downstairs.*] What's the matter, Steve? I can see by yer manner ye're scared.
STEVE [*slams door angrily, crosses down* R.]. Quit yer gassin', can't ye? Ye're enough to make any one crazy with yer questionin'.
BATES. You bin doin' somethin'?
STEVE. I tell ye nobody's got nothin' on me. Now shut up. [*As* TAYLOR *is seen coming up the stairs and looks in window.*] Cheese it — somebody's comin'.

[DOCTOR TAYLOR *enters.*]

TAYLOR [*crosses down to stove*]. Good-afternoon, Mrs. Bates. Saw you had a fire in here. Don't mind if I warm my fingers, do you?
[*He warms his hands over the stove.*]
BATES. Are ye on the way to see the sick child, Doctor?
TAYLOR. How is he to-day?
BATES [C.]. He's always better when yer friend Miss Alice is lookin' after him.
TAYLOR [*with studied innocence crosses* C. *to* BATES]. That's so — this is her day down here, isn't it? — Thursday.
[STEVE *moves down* R. *to stove restlessly — strikes match on stove, lights cigarette.*]
BATES [*with a dry smile*]. Maybe that's why ye come two hours earlier than usual.
TAYLOR [*who has been laughing at* BATES'S *last remark, turns and nods to* STEVE. STEVE *moves up* R.]. How are you?
[STEVE *answers with a grunt, goes out of the room and up the stairs.* DOCTOR *crosses to stove* R.]

BATES [L. C., *sighs. Sits* R. *of table* L. C.]. Oh, dear.
TAYLOR [R. *nodding his head after* STEVE]. Anything wrong?
BATES. Was there iver a toime when there wasn't somethin' wrong?
TAYLOR. How's Maggie getting on at Burke Smith's?
BATES. Why, not so good, I guess. She wasn't able to go to work to-day.
TAYLOR. What's the trouble?
BATES. Faith, she's worked to death. [DOCTOR *crosses to stove.*] I never saw a swell job yet there wasn't a bug in it. [*Notices* TAYLOR *poking the fire.*] Oh, Doctor, dear, be gentle with that coal.
[*Starts* R. *toward him.*]
TAYLOR. Eh?
BATES. Ye know ye can't jab at that in the free-and-easy way ye jab yer patients. [*Crosses to* L. C.] We'd like to have it last longer.

[ALICE *enters.*]

ALICE [*shaking* TAYLOR'S *hand*]. Oh! you are here already, are you?
[*Down* C.]
BATES [*mockingly taking her tone*]. Oh! Such a world of surprises.
TAYLOR [*to* ALICE]. Thought I had better get down here before you had my patient entirely cured. How is the kid?
ALICE. It's asleep now. You mustn't go up there yet awhile — you're not in a hurry, are you?
[*Crosses to stove below* RALPH. *After* MRS. BATES *speaks.*]
BATES [*answering for* TAYLOR]. Oh, not a little bit. [*Picking up her basket from table.*] But I'll be goin' about me errands. [*Nudging* TAYLOR.] Shure, if the baby will help ye out by goin' to sleep, it's up to me to help ye out, too — I'll see ye later.
[*She goes out and downstairs.* ALICE *is fixing fire.*]
TAYLOR [*indicating* BATES]. Nice, cheery party. This would be a sad place with her off the premises — [*smiling at* ALICE *as she turns to him*] — except on Thursdays.
ALICE. You'd better add that.
TAYLOR. How are things at the house

now? Have they quieted down since yesterday?

ALICE. Not a bit. Auntie was having a long talk to a man from the Police Station when I left — I do wish she would let the matter drop.

TAYLOR. Having a yeggman prowling about the house picking up jewelry is a pretty serious business — get much?

ALICE [depreciatingly]. The man was frightened away before it really became serious. Why, Auntie would never have missed the things if she did not know the house had been robbed.

TAYLOR. Aren't you making rather light of it?

ALICE [very seriously]. I'm trying to, Ralph. [Crosses L. below TAYLOR to table.] I want it dropped.

TAYLOR [surprised]. Dropped! Oh, come now. [Crosses C. after her.] That's overdoing our humanitarian purpose just a little.

ALICE. I don't mean to do that, Ralph, but I know that if this matter is pushed any further the punishment will fall on innocent shoulders.

TAYLOR. Whose?

ALICE. Maggie's. [Sits R. of table L.]

TAYLOR [becoming thoughtful]. Oh — I see —

ALICE. She took occasion to leave us yesterday, just about the time this thing happened — well, every one instantly concluded that she had a hand in it.

TAYLOR. French leave?

ALICE. You know Maggie. She's a strange girl — she wasn't happy at Auntie's — her husband opposed her working there. It wasn't surprising to have her leave without saying a word, especially as she had received her wages that morning — it's just an unfortunate coincidence.

TAYLOR [skeptically]. Just the same, it looks black for Maggie.

ALICE [reproachfully]. Ralph, how can you say that? [Turns away from him.]

TAYLOR [crosses back of ALICE and sits on R. end of table]. Well, see the way the thing was worked out — a wash basin is broken in your aunt's house — somebody telephones for the plumber — pretty soon a chap comes in — says he is the plumber, robs the house, and makes his escape just as the real plumber arrives. That couldn't possibly be done without an inside confederate. Who broke the wash basin?

ALICE [reluctantly]. Maggie.

TAYLOR. There you are.

ALICE [firmly]. Ralph, that girl is innocent.

TAYLOR. I'd like to believe it.

ALICE. You must, Ralph — facts or no facts — you must.

TAYLOR [with deep admiration, on table]. What a staunch friend you are — by Jove — it's worth being in trouble just to have you stand by one.

ALICE [smiling at him]. Is it? Then you stand by me and we will stand by Maggie together.

TAYLOR [grasping her hand]. Done!

ALICE [sits — very earnestly]. And don't think it's a blind, girlish sentiment on my part — I know it's the right thing to do, because whatever the real facts are — at heart Maggie is good — she may have had some battle to fight, some problem to face that was too big for her, but she's done her level best to do right — I know that.

TAYLOR [gives an appreciative grunt]. Does Maggie know she is under suspicion?

ALICE. I don't think so. I haven't seen her since.

TAYLOR [looking at her musingly, taking her hand]. Bill, you are a big woman.

ALICE [smiling]. You haven't called me "Bill" since we were kiddies.

TAYLOR [absently]. Funny how it slipped out. You know I sometimes wonder . . .

ALICE. Wonder what?

TAYLOR. Well, I have floated around here as some kind of a model-chap with a high-sounding humanitarian object.

ALICE. I hope you have.

TAYLOR. But somehow all my feelings for humanity seem to concentrate into one little emotional, overcharged capsule on Thursdays.

ALICE [laughing at him, crosses R.]. And you don't know what on earth to do with the capsule — what a pity!

TAYLOR [*realizing he is thwarted*]. Now if you don't mind my starting again, perhaps I could frame this up more intelligently.

ALICE [*patting him friendly on the arm*]. I'll let you frame it up some other time, Ralph.

TAYLOR. You mean that?

[*Following her quickly to* C.]

ALICE [*turns to stop him*]. But down here we must give all our time to these poor people. We have our own world in which to think of ourselves.

TAYLOR. But down here is where I found you — I mean the woman you really are — why, I knew you up town — just as I know other women — no better, but when I saw you here — [*taking her hand*] Come on, Bill. Let's brighten up this old shack with radiance of our own.

ALICE. Can we, Ralph?

TAYLOR. You stand by folks in trouble, don't you? Well, I'm in trouble now, the worst kind — stand pat.

ALICE [*her hands on his shoulders — she whispers to him*]. I love you.

[*Letting him kiss her.*]

TAYLOR. Bill! [*Embrace.*]

ALICE. But I had no idea of letting you be so irresistible in work hours.

[DOCTOR *starts to embrace her again.*]

[STEVE *comes running down the stairs, carrying an old satchel containing silverware, in a black cloth bag.*]

ALICE [*drawing away from* TAYLOR]. Be careful — some one is coming.

[*Crosses to* C.]

[STEVE *hurries downstairs. He crosses the landing and starts to descend the lower flight.*]

TAYLOR. It's only Steve — he's going downstairs.   [*Starts to embrace her again.*]

VOICE [*outside*]. Miss Alice!

[*She stops him again. He crosses to* L. C.]

ALICE [*opening door — in hall — calling upstairs*]. Yes!

VOICE [*upstairs*]. The baby's woke, miss — he's crying for ye.

ALICE. Come, Ralph, and see if you don't think the little chap looks better.

RALPH. All right.

[*They exit and upstairs.* STEVE, *after* ALICE *and* TAYLOR *are out of sight, darts back across the landing, and comes hurriedly into the room. He carries a small, cheap satchel, places it on the table and opens it, takes out a cloth bag containing silverware, and goes into the next room. Returns immediately without the bag. He is barely in the room when* MAGGIE *enters from downstairs.* STEVE *is a bit disconcerted at meeting her, but gains his composure immediately.* MAGGIE *eyes* STEVE *sullenly.*]

STEVE. Jest come upstairs?

MAGGIE. Yes.

[*Puts package of liver on table up* C.]

STEVE. See a tall guy in a blue suit and a red moustache waitin' around anywheres?

MAGGIE [*disinterestedly*]. I don't know — [*Then, as if half remembering.*] Yes, I guess so — if Heinie catches ye in here, ye know what'll happen to ye — what ye doin' aroun' here anyhow?

STEVE. Sort of wonderin' how ye panned out. Lichtenstein give ye what I said he oughta on the brooch?

MAGGIE. He gimme a hundred and thirteen dollars.

STEVE. An' you shoutin' yer head off coz I made ye take it fer ye share. Ye see? — I knowed what it was worth.

[*Crosses* L.]

MAGGIE. I wasn't kickin' about that.

STEVE [*above table* L. C.]. I know — ye didn't trust me — [*Injured, turns face front.*] Nobody ever trusts me.

MAGGIE. I told ye Miss Alice was the one friend I got in the world — I didn't want nothin' stole she had.

STEVE [*sarcastically*]. Nothin' to it at all. I can break into a house an' rob it in six minutes, an' play favorites while I'm doin' it. Gee, youse women are a scream.

MAGGIE. Anyhow ye might a gimme somethin' that wasn't hers for my share.

[*Takes off hat and coat and hangs them on hooks up* R. *Puts on apron.*]

STEVE [*crosses* R.]. Ye couldn't 'a' soaked nothin' else and got away with it, ye little idiot — but I notice, when it comes down to brass tacks, yer after the money all right.

MAGGIE. I hadda ... I hadda. There wasn't nothin' else for it. It meant everything in the world to me. I hadda — that's all.

STEVE. Aw, quit yer snivellin'. Take it from me if ye wanta keep out o' jail ye wanta sack that long face o' yours. People is gettin' to think things around here.

MAGGIE [crosses c. to STEVE in a panic]. Steve ...

STEVE. Soft pedal. You're all right. I told ye I was takin' all the risk, didn't I?

MAGGIE. Yes.

STEVE. Well, I am. So I'm blowin' out o' town. Nobody'll notice you if ye keep ye head shut.

MAGGIE [frightened]. Oh, Steve, if they git ye ...

STEVE [sneeringly and menacingly]. Oh! so that's why ye're scared for me, was it? Well, don't ye fret — but if they git anythin' out o' ye — if ye squeal — I'll fix ye good and plenty — don't forget I got a little note ye left under me pillow. [Takes note from his pocket.] If I go up the river, you go, too — see?

[BATES enters from downstairs. STEVE crosses L. and taking cigar stump he left on table in first scene, lights it at door, down L.]

BATES [putting down her bundle basket and gasping for breath]. Thank the Lord, that errand's done. Steve, every toime I come by I see ye here.

STEVE [leaning carelessly against door jamb down L.]. Me and Maggie was jest gassin' friendly. Wasn't we, Maggie?

BATES [crosses to above table L.; seeing the bag on the table, looks at STEVE]. What's me beg doin' here?

[MAGGIE gets platter from cupboard up L.]

STEVE. Ye know, Mud, I was all fixed to go t' Europe, but there ain't a bunk left on the Lusitania, so take t' bag away.

[MAGGIE crosses to table down R. above stove with liver and platter.]

BATES [looking in the bag]. There's nothin' in it. What divilment are ye up to, anyhow?

STEVE. Ye bin saying fer so long that me next suit of panjamas would be furnished by the State, I didn't see no use in takin' any.

BATES. Steve — talk serious — are ye goin' away?

[MAGGIE at stove preparing to fry liver.]

STEVE [in mock confidence]. Now this is dead on the level ... no joshin'? I am goin' to Newport and rent meself out as a little brother of the rich.

BATES [anxiously]. Steve, if ye're in some kind of trouble and have to git out, won't ye tell me about it? Don't keep me worryin'; tell me where ye're goin'.

STEVE [crosses below table to c.]. I don't know where I'm goin'. But don't worry. If a telegram comes, collect, don't accept it, it's just a signal I'm in good health — see — so long. [Goes out on the landing and down a couple of steps. Suddenly darts back into the room.] Say! There's a hopeful guy down there waitin' for some money I owe 'm. [Crosses to window up R. Opens window and steps out on fire-escape.] If he's waitin' there to-morrow mornin', chase down and feed him some breakfast.

[He waves his hand to them, pulls down the window, and goes down the fire-escape.]

MAGGIE [startled]. Why did he do that?

BATES [irritably, with anxiety crosses to table for bag]. Faith, I don't know. He's up to somethin', I can tell by his manner. Whenever he jokes that way, it's to hide his bein' scared — it's some kind of trouble he's in. [Knock at the door.] Who's there?

[ALICE enters.]

ALICE [in doorway]. May I come in? [To MAGGIE]. How do you do, Maggie?

MAGGIE [nervously at stove]. How d' do, miss?

ALICE [down L. c.]. I thought you might be in now. You little runaway, what made you leave us like that?

MAGGIE. Why — why, I was tired; I didn't think you'd mind.

ALICE [sweetly]. Of course, no one

minded, but we couldn't imagine where you had gone. You'll come back to us when you feel rested, won't you? I should be dreadfully disappointed if you didn't. When I came home late in the afternoon, I waited in my room expecting you would be in for our usual chat, and when you didn't come, I was positively lonesome, I have become so used to them.

MAGGIE. Thank ye for missin' me.

ALICE. So I have come down to have a good chat with you here.

MAGGIE [*frightened*]. What about?

ALICE. Oh, everything. [*Crosses* R. *nearer* MAGGIE.] I felt you were not exactly happy at our house. Why didn't you confide in me?

MAGGIE. Why, there wasn't nothin' to confide.

ALICE. Haven't we agreed to be friends and help each other? Won't you tell me what the trouble is?

MAGGIE. Oh, I want to tell ye — [*Then, looking away.*] But —

ALICE. But what?

MAGGIE. I can't — that's all.

ALICE. I understand, dear, you have some problem that you must solve alone; we all have those and I know you'll do the best you can.

MAGGIE. Oh, I wanta be good — I mean the way you call good — but sometimes there's somethin' you gotta do that's greater.

ALICE. Greater than doing right?

MAGGIE. That's the word — right — that's what I'm drivin' at — bein' right's greater 'n bein' good — and it's different. It's easy enough bein' good — 'cause everybody agrees about it, but in doin' right, there's nothin' to back you up but yer own sense — [*With a sob*]. Oh, it's awful hard.

ALICE. Whatever your problem is, I'm glad you decided to solve it by doing right.

MAGGIE [*gratefully*]. Somehow, I knew if it was up to you, you'd decide my way too. It's thinkin' that keeps me goin' now.

ALICE. And you'll always turn to me in case — well, if anything should happen. If you should ever need a friend, promise that I shall be the first one that you will come to; will you do that?

MAGGIE. Oh, Miss Alice.

ALICE. No matter what the trouble is, come to me — [*Rising.*] Well, I must go now. Good-bye, dear. Don't forget. [*She goes toward the door.* MAGGIE *rises, crosses up to door, up* R. C. *after her.*]

[HEINIE *enters. On seeing* ALICE, *he stands, cap in hand, waiting for her to speak.*]

ALICE [R. *of him, graciously*]. How do you do, Mr. Schultz?

HEINIE [*with cool civility*]. How are ye, ma'm?

ALICE. Maggie and I have just been having a talk.

HEINIE [*crosses down* L. *of table*]. Another one o' them talks where she comes out cryin' huh?

ALICE. Oh, I hope not [MAGGIE *crosses up to table* C. *To* MAGGIE.] You'll be more cheerful now, won't you?

MAGGIE. Oh, yes'm.

HEINIE [*down* L.]. Well, she ain't workin' for your crowd now, so I guess ye hadn't better bother about it.

MAGGIE [*up* R. C. L. *of* ALICE]. Oh, Heinie. [*To* ALICE.] He don't mean that. miss — sure he don't.

ALICE. I know, dear. It's all right. Good-bye. [*Exit.*]

MAGGIE. Heinie, you oughtn't to said that. [*Crosses to stove.*]

HEINIE. Come now, don't bother about them; we're through with that bunch for good. Say, I've got some bully good news for ye.

MAGGIE. Yes —

HEINIE. The strike's called off.

MAGGIE [*only half interested*]. That so?

HEINIE. And somethin' better than that. Work on the docks is going to be rushed; that means I can earn enough to take you out to Wyoming in less than a month.

MAGGIE. In less than a month?
[*With a half-suppressed cry as she realizes the futility of all she has done, she stands staring straight ahead.*]

HEINIE. Well — ye don't seem awful tickled to hear it.

MAGGIE [*repeating as if dazed*]. You can raise the money in less than a month?

HEINIE [*taking off his coat*]. Yes. Easy. Workin' night shifts, and Sundays — that's double pay.

MAGGIE [*in agony*]. Why didn't you tell me before —

HEINIE. Tell ye — why, didn't I jest find out fer myself?

MAGGIE [*looking away to hide her tears*]. Yes, o' course.

[HEINIE *goes out in the landing to the sink, rolling up his sleeves, humming cheerfully.*]

HEINIE [*coming back into room*]. Where's the soap, Maggie?

MAGGIE. I brought it in here — Steve's always swipin' it.

HEINIE [*getting it*]. Oh, Steve likes soap, does he? I guess it'll take more than soap to get his hands clean. [*Going out to the sink again.*] Poor old Steve, ye know I feel so good our own troubles are over, I could almost feel sorry for him. [MAGGIE *busies herself about the stove. In a moment* HEINIE *comes in and dries his hands on the roller towel, up* R. *Coming down.*] No more frettin' now fer us, eh, Maggie? We're goin' to have money in the bank, ain't we? Oh, say, here's somethin' good. [MAGGIE *at stove, starts to look in oven.*] Do ye know Lichtenstein, the pawnbroker?

MAGGIE [*terrified, shuts oven door*]. Why d'ye ask me that?

HEINIE. Well, he said ye came into his shop last night and hocked a diamond brooch.

MAGGIE [*with a dry throat*]. Me, hock a diamond?

HEINIE. Yes, for a hundred and thirteen dollars. Say — what do ye know about that?

[*Crosses* L. *He laughs uproariously.*]

MAGGIE [*mumbling*]. I think he's crazy.

HEINIE. Yes, he seed you on the street with me once. [*Up* R. *combing hair.*] I guess the party must have looked somethin' like ye. Well, I told him we wasn't soakin' the family jools just yet.

[*Putting on coat.*]

MAGGIE [*with a long breath of relief*]. I'm goin' to give ye yer supper now — you must be awfully hungry.

[*Crosses* L. C.]

HEINIE [*crosses to her*]. Well, what ye got that's good? Ye know there ain't no harm in loosenin' up a bit now that things are gonna come easy.

[*There is a knock on the door.* HEINIE *opens it.* RAFFERTY *is standing in the hall.* MAGGIE *gets red tablecloth from cupboard and puts it on the table.*]

HEINIE. Hello, Rafferty! how's everything?

[*Crosses down* R. *above chair before stove.*]

RAFFERTY [*in doorway, looking past* HEINIE *at* MAGGIE, *who is* L. *setting table*]. Pretty fine; how are you?

HEINIE [*notices that* RAFFERTY *is staring at* MAGGIE]. Oh, this is my wife.

RAFFERTY [*nods bluntly*]. How are ye, ma'm? [MAGGIE *nods.*] Ye ain't seen that fella Steve around here, have ye?

HEINIE [*grimly*]. No, sir. He don't come in here — he knows what he'll get.

RAFFERTY [*with another keen look at* MAGGIE]. Oh! I see — an' ye ain't seen him anywhere round to-day?

HEINIE. Nope.

RAFFERTY [*to* MAGGIE]. Have you, Mrs. Schultz?

MAGGIE. Why, yes. [*Rattled.*] Er — no, I don't know.

HEINIE [*laughing*]. Well, which is it?

MAGGIE. No, I ain't seen 'm.

RAFFERTY [*dryly*]. Oh!

HEINIE. Nothin' doin', I guess, Bill.

RAFFERTY. Thanks. I'll take a look upstairs. [*With another keen glance at* MAGGIE.] Good-afternoon, ma'm.

[RAFFERTY *goes upstairs and* HEINIE *shuts the door.*]

MAGGIE [*nervous, bringing two cups and saucers from cupboard to table*]. Heinie, who is that man?

HEINIE [*sits in chair before fire, reads paper*]. That's Bill Rafferty, a plain-clothes cop. [MAGGIE *is unable to control a start of terror.*] Wonder what that fella Steve has been up to now.

MAGGIE [*at table with feverish agitation*]. Heinie, ye know ye got me all worked up again about goin' to Wyoming — now ye seein' yer way clear.

HEINIE [*burying himself in a newspaper*]. That so?

MAGGIE [*hesitatingly*]. I'd like to go sooner if we could.

HEINIE. Can't ye wait three or four weeks? [*Looking up and noticing her agitation.*] What's ailin' ye?

MAGGIE [*hysterically, crosses* C.]. Oh, I hate this place — I hate it — I can't stand it.

HEINIE [*puzzled, rising, and crossing to her* C.]. I know ye don't like it, but ye been here long enough to git used to it — an' I'm doin' the best I can.

MAGGIE. I know ye are, Heinie, but —

HEINIE. There — ye mustn't let yerself go that way. [*Consoling her.*] Aw, ye're all fidgetty and tired out. If ye hadn't quit that Burke Smith woman you'd 'a' been down and out soon. Now jest keep a lookin' ahead — the time'll go before ye know it. You sit down there an' rest and I'll set the table.

[*He pushes her into the chair he has just occupied before stove* R. *and starts setting the table, getting things from cupboard up* L. C.]

MAGGIE [*after waiting to get up courage to speak*]. But, Heinie — s'pose we can go — s'pose we can — will ye?

HEINIE. I'll do anythin' in the world I can fer ye, but I couldn't get the money any sooner to save my life.

MAGGIE. I know ye can't, Heinie — but — jest supposen I could fix it, would ye be willin' to start to-night?

HEINIE [*setting table, looking at her in amazement*]. You!

MAGGIE. Would ye? There's a train at eleven.

HEINIE. You fix it?

MAGGIE [*rising*]. Yes — I can git the money.

HEINIE [*continues to set table*]. You can get the money — you?

MAGGIE. Yes, I — I got it.

HEINIE [*stops suddenly*]. What!

MAGGIE. A hundred.

HEINIE. You got —

MAGGIE [*indicating dress pocket*]. Right here — Now, will ye start to-night? There's a train goes at eleven.

HEINIE [*crosses to her*]. Wait a minute — where'd ye get that?

MAGGIE. I borrowed it.

HEINIE. Who from?

MAGGIE. Miss Alice.

HEINIE. The lady what jest left?

MAGGIE. Yes.

HEINIE. Why — she didn't say nothin' —

MAGGIE [*hastily*]. She didn't want nothin' said about it. She's a good friend o' mine — she lent me the money.

HEINIE. She lent ye a hundred dollars? What could ye give her for security?

[*Coming down* R. *of table.*]

MAGGIE. I didn't give her nothin'. She jest took my word we'd pay it back soon as we could.

HEINIE. Well, how about the interest?

MAGGIE. Oh, there wasn't nothin' said about interest. She just took my word for it — we'd pay her back whenever we could.

HEINIE. Hold on there. Well, I'll have to see her an' find out. We can't take charity.

MAGGIE [*stopping him, frightened*]. No, no. Ye mustn't see her, Heinie.

HEINIE. Why not?

MAGGIE. She don't want no one else to know. It's a secret between me an' her.

HEINIE. Well — but — I —

MAGGIE. I'll write her to-morrow about the interest.

HEINIE. Say, she's dead white, though.

MAGGIE [*very earnestly*]. She is, Heinie — she's the best woman in the world. I'd die fer her. Now, Heinie, can't we get out to-night? I've went and borrowed the money.

HEINIE [*indulgently*]. Well, if we can't get out to-night, we'll go jus' as soon as we can.

MAGGIE. No, I want to go to-night. I'm goin' in now and start packin'.

[*Starts for door down* L.]

HEINIE. Wait — I got to straighten this out with her before I start —

MAGGIE [*halted at door, toward* HEINIE *again*]. But, Heinie — you can't, it's a secret —

HEINIE. But she might 'a' knowed I'd ask about that hundred —

MAGGIE [*above table* L.]. But don't ye understand —
HEINIE. Yes — I understand — she don't want the story passed around.
MAGGIE. No. She don't want it spoke of even to her, and if ye go an' do it, I'm never goin' to speak to ye again.
HEINIE. Well, there's no use gettin' mad about it — tell me what was the real reason —
MAGGIE. But ain't I tellin' ye . . .
HEINIE. Are ye sure she lent ye this money — it ain't no charity?
MAGGIE. Oh, Heinie!
HEINIE. Well, I'm goin' to find out.
[*He goes out on hall landing.*]
HEINIE [*calling upstairs*]. Oh, Miss Alice —
ALICE'S VOICE [*from upper stairway*]. Yes.
HEINIE. Could I see ye a minute, please? When ye come downstairs?
[MAGGIE *stands transfixed with fear, back of table* L.]
ALICE. Certainly; we're on our way down now.
[ALICE *appears in doorway.*]
HEINIE. Could I speak to ye alone, please?
ALICE [*a little surprised*]. Why — yes. [*Speaking off.*] Ralph, wait for me downstairs?
[*She comes into the room down* R.]
HEINIE [*somewhat embarrassed, comes down* C.]. First — I want to say — I'm sorry for bein' gruff awhile ago.
ALICE. Oh, I knew you were disturbed about something.
HEINIE. No, it wasn't that, mam, I was sizin' ye up with the rest o' that bunch that comes down here. I didn't know ye was different — but Maggie's just been tellin' me.
ALICE. That I am always to be her friend — I hope you'll let me be a friend of yours, too, Mr. Schultz.
HEINIE. Why, yes, of course. But Maggie's just been tellin' me the kind of friend ye are — and the big white thing ye done fer us, and I wanted to see ye and thank ye.

ALICE. But I haven't been able to do much yet except to offer my friendship —
[*She glances at* MAGGIE *and notices her strange appearance,* MAGGIE *looking a piteous appeal.*]
HEINIE. I know; Maggie said you didn't want it spoke of — that's why I asked to see ye alone — but I wanted to thank ye, and ask ye about the interest —
ALICE [*puzzled*]. Interest?
HEINIE. Yes, it wasn't just clear how much it is.
ALICE. What interest?
HEINIE. Why, the interest on the loan — on the hundred — [*As* ALICE *looks still more puzzled.*] Ye meant it to be a regular business loan — [*glancing toward* MAGGIE] Maggie said.
[*He catches a look between* MAGGIE *and* ALICE, *a dawning light on* ALICE'S *part, appeal and terror on* MAGGIE'S.]
ALICE [*looking away*]. Why, yes — certainly — of course, Mr. Schultz.
HEINIE [*looking at them both*]. Why — what's wrong?
ALICE [*who has fully recovered herself*]. You see, I don't know much about such things, so I decided to leave that entirely to you.
HEINIE. Would ten per cent be about right?
ALICE. Yes, I should think so.
HEINIE [*who is still puzzled, after a moment's thought*]. You're sure that's all right, ma'm?
ALICE. Absolutely.
HEINIE. Say, it's an awful big thing ye're doin' fer us, miss. Yer givin' us a chance fer go out to Wyoming and start life all over again and live like a man and woman should — that means a lot — especially to Maggie, and ye let us have the money in a way we ain't ashamed to take it. Of course I can't thank ye right, like I should. God bless ye is all I can say — an' I give ye my word of honor to send it back to ye, interest and all, out o' the first money we make.
ALICE [*crosses to him and offers her hand*]. I am confident that you will, Mr. Schultz. [*Gives him her hand.*] I hope you will have

great success in your new life in Wyoming. [*Turning to* MAGGIE, *crosses below table;* HEINIE *crosses above,* ALICE *to above chair* R.] Remember, dear, you are going far away to a new country, to start life anew; above all things remember that — to start life anew. And if anything happens — if you should ever need me, you'll let me know, you've promised me that — haven't you?
[MAGGIE *nods, scarcely able to keep from sobbing.*]
MAGGIE. Thank ye.
ALICE. Good-bye, Maggie. [*Crosses up.*] Good-bye, Mr. Schultz. [*Goes out.*]
HEINIE. That's funny . . .
[*Leaning on back of chair down* R.]
MAGGIE. What ye mean?
HEINIE. Oh — nothing. . . .
MAGGIE [*crosses to stove.* HEINIE *moves* C.]. Will ye sit down now and eat yer supper?
HEINIE. What ye got that's good? [MAGGIE *lifts piece of liver from frying-pan with fork.*] Liver, eh? Say, we'll have real beef in Wyoming, won't we? That is, if I can ever hit a cow — maybe I won't be a greenhorn.
MAGGIE. Oh, ye'll learn quick enough.
HEINIE [*crosses and sits* R. *of table*]. Yes — just the same I bet them cowboys has a gay time with me.
MAGGIE. Mrs. Bates can put ye on to all the ropes.
HEINIE. That's right, she can; let's have her down. [*Crosses up to hall.* MAGGIE *crosses up after him and stands with him in doorway.*] Oh, Batesey, are ye eatin'?
BATES'S VOICE [*upstairs*]. Sometimes —
HEINIE. Well, come on down and eat with us.
[*Crosses to bring down chair up* L. *to above table.* MAGGIE *back to stove.*]
BATES [*coming downstairs. In doorway*]. Well, what's all this? Some one send ye a basket?
HEINIE. Somethin' better 'an that; we're goin' out to Wyoming and we want ye to tell us all the angles. I don't want them cowboys out there to think I'm a rube. [BATES *comes into room.*]

BATES [*sits above table*]. So ye're really goin', are ye? I hears the strike was off. How soon can ye raise the money?
HEINIE [*sits* R. *of table*]. We got it already.
BATES. No?
HEINIE. Yes, Maggie got a loan of a hundred dollars from that young woman.
[BATES *throws a sharp look at* MAGGIE, *who looks away.*]
BATES. Ain't she a darlint? I knew she'd do it.
HEINIE. You knew it.
BATES. Yes, she was talkin' to me upstairs.
HEINIE. Why, Maggie said it was a secret.
BATES [*realizing her slip*]. Shure it was. She told me the secret.
[MAGGIE *puts boiled potatoes in bowl. At stove.*]
HEINIE. Well, anyhow we're gettin' out o' here, and we got Maggie to thank fer it. I couldn't 'a' done it in a thousand years.
BATES. No, I guess you couldn't.
MAGGIE [*to table with potatoes. To* BATES]. Have a potato?
HEINIE. Put another cup on fer Batesey, Maggie.
[MAGGIE *gets milk from fire-escape* R. *and coffee from stove.*]
MAGGIE. She can have mine, we only got two.
HEINIE. Well, use that silver mug the woman gave ye. [*He goes to shelf in cupboard up* L. C. *and takes down a little silver baby's mug containing baby ribbon and four little gold baby pins.* MAGGIE *crosses and sits* L. *of table.*] Ye know I'm sorry she give ye that. That's plain charity.
MAGGIE. I wish you'd let up on that.
HEINIE. Well, maybe I am hip on it, but —
BATES. Ye'll use the mug all the same.
HEINIE. Just the same; it's the first time I've touched it. [*Seeing something inside of it.*] What's all this junk in here? [*Pulls out pink baby ribbon, places on table. Empties gold pins in palm of hand.*] Hello — little gold pins — four of 'em. Did the lady give ye them, too?

MAGGIE. Yes.
HEINIE. I'd think ye'd be ashamed to take things like that.
MAGGIE. They ain't worth nothin'.
HEINIE. Just the same I think ye'd better send all that junk back.
BATES. Shure, an' offend the lady after she's made the loan? Lord, Dutch is Dutch and ye can't kill it.
HEINIE. Well, anyhow I don't like it.
BATES. Oh, for Heaven's sake, if ye're goin' away, talk about that and quit yer squabblin'.
HEINIE. All right, Batesey, tell us about Wyoming. Don't ye wish ye was goin' back there to see the hills and the trees and the grass —
BATES. Now don't start on that again. There ain't no roses in Wyoming.
HEINIE. Well, anyhow, we're goin' now for sure.
BATES. Oh, begorra, touch wood, touch wood, quick. An' stop yer braggin' — if ye was fallin' from a balloon and started talkin' that way, somethin' would stop ye.
HEINIE. Well, we got the money and that's what does the business — ain't it?
MAGGIE. Heinie, what are we loafin' around here for? It's five o'clock now an' I want to git packed. Suppose ye go an' buy the tickets now, and while you're gone Bates an' me will do the packin'.
HEINIE. Well, of all the crazy stunts — why don't ye wait till to-morrow, anyhow.
BATES [*breaking out*]. Oh, Heinie, humor the child: can't ye see she's nervous?
HEINIE. All right, I'll go git the tickets and if you can git ready — we'll beat it.
MAGGIE. Yes, and hurry back, will ye, Heinie? So's we can go an' wait down at the station.
HEINIE. Wait at the station? — what's the matter with ye? Ye said the train didn't start before eleven o'clock to-night.
BATES. Trains have been missed before, ain't they? I suppose ye'll go flyin' down the last minute in a taxicab.
HEINIE. Gee, you women! What do ye want to set around the station all night fer? What d'ye think we are, a couple of dago emi-*grants*?
MAGGIE. Now, Heinie, you go on.

HEINIE [*rising*]. All right, hon, I'll get right back with the tickets. And if we got time on our hands, we can amuse ourselves walkin' around seein' the sights. Say, maybe I'll take ye to see a movin'-picture show; how's that?
MAGGIE [*dancing with delight*]. Oh, Heinie, will ye? We'll be ready an' waitin' when ye git back. Bates, you pull them bags out of the other room. Oh, Heinie, you're so good, you're so good.
 [*Throws arms about* HEINIE's *neck.*
 BATES *exits door* L.]
HEINIE [*laughing*]. Now hold on here, don't get too excited or ye won't finish up nothin'.
MAGGIE. Don't ye worry about me.
 [*Sits at table, starts to eat.*]
HEINIE. Oh, say, have ye got the stuff that takes us?
MAGGIE. The money?
HEINIE. Yes.
MAGGIE [*takes money from her dress and hands it to him*]. Here ye are — now will ye hurry? [*Butters bread.*]
HEINIE. Hurry! Ye bet I will. [*Goes to* L., *takes hat off hook. After counting bills at door up* R. *Coming down.*] Now, Maggie, tell us about this money.
MAGGIE. What?
HEINIE. How'd you come by it?
MAGGIE. How'd I come by it?
HEINIE. Yes!
MAGGIE. I just told ye —
HEINIE. That lady give you a hundred and *thirteen dollars?*
MAGGIE. Oh, I give ye thirteen dollars too much, didn't I?
HEINIE. Yes, how's that?
MAGGIE [*stammering*]. Why — why — ye see I had thirteen dollars extra.
HEINIE. Ye had? Where did ye git it?
MAGGIE. I bin workin', ain't I?
HEINIE. Ye didn't have it yesterday.
MAGGIE. Yes, I had, but I didn't tell ye.
HEINIE. Why not?
MAGGIE. Why — I — I was savin' for Wyoming — I was afraid ye'd laugh at me so —
 [*Starts to drink again. She falters under his cold look of disbelief.*]
HEINIE. That's pretty thin.

MAGGIE [*becoming panic-stricken*]. What ye mean?
HEINIE. Now don't make me ask questions.
MAGGIE. What's the matter with ye? What ye drivin' at?
HEINIE. I can't help puttin' two and two together. Now don't stall; explain.
MAGGIE. Explain what?
HEINIE. How this come to a hundred and thirteen dollars.
MAGGIE [*still sitting*]. Why, I did — I —
HEINIE. A hundred and thirteen dollars — the exact amount o' money Lichtenstein handed a woman that looked like you, that hocked a dimon brooch.
MAGGIE [*rising angrily*]. Why, ye crazy thing! Ye ain't sayin' that woman was me, are ye?
HEINIE. No, I'm jest puttin' it up to you.
MAGGIE. Yes, just because some woman gets a hundred and thirteen dollars on a dimon pin and Lichtenstein says she looks like me, I can't help that, can I?
[*Pushes chair* R. *of table out of the way and moves to* R. *of table.*]

[BATES *enters with telescope basket, etc.*]

BATES. For the land's sake, what's wrong now! [*Places bags on floor up* L.]
MAGGIE. Some woman gets a hundred and thirteen dollars from Lichtenstein —
HEINIE. An' looked like you —
MAGGIE. He don't even know me.
BATES [*to* HEINIE]. Can't ye see it's just a coincidence?
HEINIE. All right. Now you get out a minute, Bates, I want to talk to Maggie alone. [BATES *exits.* HEINIE *crosses* L. *and closes door after* BATES. MAGGIE *goes to* R. *in fear.* HEINIE *crosses* R. *to* MAGGIE.] Now we'll drop Lichtenstein; we'll say ye saved the thirteen. Now tell us about the hundred.
MAGGIE. I did — I told you that Miss Alice —
HEINIE. Aw, wait a minute! When I thanked her for that hundred, she didn't know what I was talkin' about. She done the best she could to shield ye, but she didn't give ye that money.

MAGGIE. That's right, don't use no sense about it — just make up yer mind, bull-headed, I'm lyin' to ye.
HEINIE. Well, just because things don't strike me as bein' right, I oughtn't to talk to you like that. Now, Maggie, git on yer hat.
MAGGIE. What fer?
HEINIE. Ye're comin' with me.
MAGGIE. What ye mean? Where?
HEINIE. To Lichtenstein's.
MAGGIE [*quickly*]. No, I won't.
HEINIE. Do ye hear, put on yer hat!
MAGGIE. I won't be made a fool of like that.
HEINIE [*his mind satisfied*]. That's enough for me. [*Throwing down his cap. Starts toward* MAGGIE. *Savagely.*] Now you tell me about that —
MAGGIE [*in fear*]. Now ye needn't start in again — I — I didn't tell ye the thing just as it was.
HEINIE. No, I guess not. [*Putting her off.*] Now tell us about the brooch.
MAGGIE. Well, it was me that hocked it. Miss Alice gimme it. It belonged to her.
HEINIE. Go on.
MAGGIE. Well, she wanted to lend me the money to go to Wyoming — she didn't happen to have it on hand, so she let me have the brooch to raise it on. [*As he stares at her coldly and unbelievingly.*] Well, that's clear, ain't it?
HEINIE [*breaking out angrily*]. Yes, it's perfectly clear. It's lies, lies, lies from start to finish. [*Gripping her by the arms savagely.*] But I'll get the truth out o' ye before I'm through.
MAGGIE. Heinie, don't hurt me.
HEINIE [*menacingly*]. Will ye tell me?
MAGGIE [*sniveling*]. Ye's a nice one, ain't ye? Ye're tryin' to make me say I took somethin' when I didn't! She give me the brooch, I tell ye.
HEINIE [*releasing her*]. Aw, women of her kind don't do things like that. If she hadn't 'a' had the money, she'd 'a' got it some other way than through a hock shop ... if ye wasn't so tangled up in lies ye'd see how funny the whole thing sounds. She didn't give ye that brooch. You stole it, didn't ye? [*Shaking her.*] Didn't ye?

MAGGIE. Not exactly.
HEINIE. Not exactly.
MAGGIE. I'd like to tell ye the truth, but — ye make it so hard fer me.
HEINIE [*releasing his grip and speaking calmly*]. Go on, then.
MAGGIE. I — I wouldn't steal from Miss Alice — she's the best friend I got — if ye knew, ye'd understand.
HEINIE. Aw, don't beat about the bush.
MAGGIE. Well, yesterday afternoon Mrs. Burke Smith's house got robbed.
HEINIE. Robbed, was it?
MAGGIE. Yes, by a fake plumber. A wash basin got busted — they telephoned for a man to come and fix it — by and by this fella come. He started workin' in the room next to the one I was sewin' in, and then he sneaks downstairs and was robbin' the house when the doorbell rings and the real plumber shows up. Well, he comes rushin' through the room, an' tells me what he is an' says if I'll help him get out he'll divide with me. I dunno why I did it, but I hid him till the coast was clear and he made his getaway. I dunno why I did it, it all happened so sudden — but that's just how it was, Heinie.
HEINIE. An' ye didn't know this fake plumber before?
MAGGIE. No, Heinie, no.
HEINIE. Never saw him before in yer life?
MAGGIE. No, never, o' course not.
HEINIE. An' how about that sink, didn't you bust it?
MAGGIE. Why, it was cracked already — a bottle fell off the shelf and busted through. [*With a sickly smile of fear and desperation.*] An old yellow bottle. I dunno what was in it.
HEINIE. So! You bust a sink by accident, an' this guy happens along just at the right time, robs the house, divides with ye, and nothin' was fixed up beforehand. So that's why ye couldn't be coaxed away from that place. Why ye'd stayed there and worked yerself sick. Ye was fixin' a deal with a thief, meetin' him time and again. How do I know there wasn't somethin' more back of it? Somethin' more than just robbin' the house.

MAGGIE [*shrilly*]. Don't you dare!
HEINIE. Well, I take that back. Now, tell me, who was the fella? Who was the man?
MAGGIE [*bowed head*]. Steve . . .
HEINIE. Steve! [*He pauses until he masters himself, then speaks to her quietly*]. Ye got the ticket fer the pin? [*She takes it from her pocket and hands it to him.*] It belongs to the young lady?
MAGGIE [*head still bowed and averted*]. Yes.
HEINIE. An' she didn't even let on when she found it out. Oh! [*Bitterly.*] She pitied ye, I guess — she pitied both of us. [*After struggling for composure.*] The brooch all Steve gave ye?
MAGGIE. Yes.
HEINIE. How about that silver mug, them gold pins and things?
MAGGIE. Oh, they was just knockin' about. Nobody wanted it. It didn't matter.
HEINIE. Didn't matter? My God, what's got into ye, anyway?
MAGGIE [*turns toward* HEINIE]. You put the idea into my head.
HEINIE [*stunned*]. *Me!*
MAGGIE. Yes! — you showed me the game we was up against! I was satisfied with things as they was till then. You think I'm just a weak fool that Steve got to help him. Well, now. I'll tell ye somethin'. Ye're wrong!
HEINIE [*puzzled by her defiance*]. Just what ye drivin' at?
MAGGIE. I mean that I finally woke up to what I had comin' to me. Them people owned our home, they owned us, and if I dared to bring a life into the world they owned that, too. Well, they went too far, so I went up there and took what I needed — what was mine — I had a right to, I tell ye.
HEINIE. Right?
MAGGIE. Yes, a right — to my share o' life, just as they have, just as any animal has. I didn't ask for comfort, I didn't ask for happiness; that's fer their kind uptown — that's the law, but there's some things they've got to let me have; me — and the lowest animal livin'; you're a man, ain't ye? and you're goin' to have food and

drink. Ye got a right to live and ye'll steal an' murder to do it. Well, I'm a woman and God give me a greater right even than that. He give me the power to give life — an' there's no want o' my body or soul cries out so loud. It will be satisfied, my greatest right o' all — then them people come down here an' warn me, warn me that if I dared to bring a life into the world it'd be smothered out — burned up like so much kindlin', and for what, their comfort, their pleasure; think of it — I'm a thief, I'm rotten, and in their eyes I lowered myself; well, just let 'em think so — in my own eyes I raised myself way above 'em, way far above 'em.

HEINIE. [*Pick up speech quickly here to kill applause.*] Well, how about this — [*taking baby ribbon from table*]. Junk? Ye didn't swipe that to get yer needs of life, did ye? Ye wasn't buyin' yer passage to Wyoming with six yards o' that, was ye? No, ye took it because ye was a natural born thief.

MAGGIE. Ye don't understand —

[*No break in* HEINIE'S *speech —* MAGGIE *going* R. *and ejaculates.*]

HEINIE. A thief, I tell you, and couldn't help yourself. Ye'll take stuff like that — junk ye got no use for — just because ye can't keep yer hands off it — [*Waving ribbon in her face.*] Will ye tell me why ye steal baby ribbon, baby pins — and baby mu— [MAGGIE *bowed head under denunciation, raises eyes to* HEINIE *at last "baby." In sudden enlightenment he stops and falls back a step, his hands across his brows as she stands before him, trembling.*] My God — my God — [HEINIE *keeps gaze on* MAGGIE, *who bows head in shame. His voice husky with awe and reverence.*] Why didn't ye tell me, Maggie — why didn't ye tell me?

MAGGIE [*piteous whimper, turning away from him*]. I — I was too scared. Ye said if one come ye'd kill it.

HEINIE [*bitterly, voice breaking*]. God bless ye, little girl. I love ye for it.

[MAGGIE *totters into his arms,* C. *He takes her sobbing in his arms — comforts her.*]

CURTAIN

ACT III

SCENE: *The same. Evening. The lamp is lighted on dresser up* L. *The gas in hallway is lighted. Dishes are removed from table and placed in dishpan on table* R., *above stove — baby ribbon is in cradle under table up* C.

TIME: *Forty minutes later.*

DISCOVERED: HEINIE *is standing up* L. *with book in hand;* MAGGIE *is up* R. *by window.*

MAGGIE [*crosses to table up* C.]. Look, Heinie, I ain't showed you the cradle yet.

[*Pulls out cradle from under the table. There is a knock at the door.* HEINIE *and* MAGGIE *are both startled.*]

HEINIE. Who's there?

[MAGGIE *goes toward rocker* R. HEINIE *to above rocker, sort of shielding* MAGGIE *from view of* RAFFERTY. *The door opens and* RAFFERTY *lounges in doorway. The manner of both* HEINIE *and* MAGGIE *becomes strange and on the defensive.*]

RAFFERTY [*good-humoredly*]. Stayin' in to-night, huh?

HEINIE. Yes. Come in?

RAFFERTY. No; jes' stopped to say hello.

HEINIE. Glad to have ye!

[*There is a strange, awkward pause in which* RAFFERTY *eyes him furtively and keenly, his glance finally traveling to the window of the fire-escape — his manner becoming easy again as he addresses them.*]

RAFFERTY [*coming down* C.]. Hear the strike's off.

HEINIE. Start work to-morrow.

RAFFERTY. That so? [*Pause.*] Too bad it wasn't sooner. [*Pause. Throwing a quick glance at him.*] Must got down pretty low, huh?

HEINIE. Oh, me and Maggie had enough to see us through.

RAFFERTY [*thoughtfully*]. Ye did, eh? That's more than lots of 'em had.

HEINIE. We'd set some money aside.

RAFFERTY. Oh, I see. That's a good idea. [*There is another awkward pause.*]

HEINIE. Find your man?
RAFFERTY. Who — Steve?
HEINIE. Yes. You was huntin' fer him, wasn't you?
RAFFERTY. He ain't the best friend you got, is he?
HEINIE. Not a bit of it —
RAFFERTY. He's a pretty fresh guy, but, believe me, when I put him in the tank he stays to get his hair cut.
MAGGIE [*from chair*]. Then ye ain't seen him yet?
RAFFERTY [*crosses down to see her*]. No. Have you?
MAGGIE. No.
RAFFERTY. He's left the building. [*Watching her closely for the effect of his words.*] And he didn't do it by the front door, neither.
MAGGIE [*faintly*]. How d'ye suppose ye came to miss him?
RAFFERTY [*sourly*]. Maybe them fire-escapes is no good fer fire, but they're good to fool a guy like me — jes' once, that's all!
HEINIE. Think he beat it that way?
RAFFERTY. I got a hunch.
HEINIE. Well, if he's out o' the building it won't be so easy to find him.
RAFFERTY. That's right. Well — [*ominously*] I'll have to be satisfied with what I can get for the present. But I won't go to sleep on the fire-escape again. That's a cinch! [*Shifts his position as if about to go.*] Well —
HEINIE. Why don't you set down?
RAFFERTY. No, I guess I'll be wanderin'. Good-night.
    [*He saunters down the stairs.* HEINIE *goes over and shuts the door, then begins to walk the room with troubled thought.*]
MAGGIE [*after watching for a while nervously*]. What ye thinkin' about?
HEINIE. Huh? Why, jes' figurin'.
MAGGIE. Figurin' what?
HEINIE [*trying to brighten up*]. It'll take just twenty-eight days workin' double-time to earn the money.
MAGGIE [*not satisfied*]. What else was you thinkin' about?
HEINIE. Why — nothin' else. Why?
MAGGIE. Yes you was.

HEINIE [*trying to speak easily*]. Well, I was thinkin' I was glad Steve was out o' the way, bad as I want to see him sent up. Now there's no danger of his talkin'.
MAGGIE [*her anxiety increasing*]. D'ye think everythin'll be all right now that Steve's gone?
HEINIE. Sure everythin'll be all right — that is, as soon as we give the brooch back to the young lady. [*Trying to change the subject. Above stove.*] That's a good stove, ain't it? [*Looking about.*] What d'ye think we oughta get on the stuff in this place, Maggie?
MAGGIE. What d'ye think Rafferty came in that way for?
HEINIE [*trying to speak easily*]. Why — he jes' dropped in.
MAGGIE. What for?
HEINIE. He was up at Bates's place. I heard him nosin' around up there.
MAGGIE. He's come in here twice like that to-day.
HEINIE [*crosses* C.]. He was lookin' for Steve the first time.
MAGGIE. Oh, he knows Steve ain't in the buildin'.
HEINIE. Well, he ain't known it long, because he —
    [ALICE *comes upstairs past hall window.*] Oh, there's the young lady now. [*Coming to* MAGGIE *and putting his arm around her with affectionate encouragement.*] Now we're goin' to clear our hands and our minds of the whole business, ain't we? In five minutes we'll be square with the world.
    [*There is a knock at the door, and* HEINIE *crosses and opens it.*]

[ALICE *enters — her manner is sweet and cheerful.*]

ALICE [*crosses down* C.]. Good-evening, Mr. Schultz. Good-evening, Maggie. [*Looks about.*] Why, you haven't done much packing yet, have you? I wanted to hear more of your new plans for Wyoming. The Doctor was coming this way in his car, so I made him bring me. [*To* HEINIE.] Tell me — when did you decide to be a cowboy?
HEINIE [L.]. . . . It's for Maggie's sake, we're goin', miss.

ALICE. Oh, I think it's a splendid idea — to go out and start life anew — a good, healthy, wholesome life! [*To* MAGGIE, *very sincerely.*] I want you to go out with every good wish that I can give you. That's why I came down here to see you. But why haven't you started to get ready? I thought you were going at once?

HEINIE. Oh, not yet awhile. In about a month.

ALICE [*to* HEINIE]. Surely, it won't take a month to get ready? I rushed down. I thought you were going, say . . . to-morrow. [*To* MAGGIE.] I thought perhaps Mr. Schultz would be out buying the tickets and seeing friends, and you and I might pack up together and have a nice cozy little chat . . . talking over your new plans.

HEINIE. Oh, I see what yer drivin' at, miss . . . you want to see Maggie alone.

ALICE. Now that you've guessed it, may I?

HEINIE. And talk over that money business of this afternoon that you couldn't understand?

ALICE [*embarrassed*]. Why —

HEINIE. Well, we can both talk to you about it now. You see Maggie and me have straightened it out between ourselves.

ALICE [*serious, looking at them both*]. Have you?

HEINIE. She's told me everythin'.

MAGGIE. Oh, Miss Alice, what did ye think of me?

ALICE [*to* MAGGIE]. I knew that you were in some deep trouble, but whatever it was you were doing your best — and eventually you would do the right thing.

HEINIE. She *was* doin' her best, miss. I'll answer for that!

ALICE. That's why I've come down to see if I couldn't help you.

MAGGIE. But stealin' wasn't the worst of it, miss. I turned against you — that hurt me worse than the stealin'.

ALICE. Tell me everything, dear.

MAGGIE. You see I was in with that fella that robbed your house. He give me a dimon brooch that belonged to you for my share. Oh, I begged him to gimme somethin' else, but he wouldn't. Forgive me.

HEINIE [*raising tablecloth and revealing cradle up* C.]. That was the reason, miss.

ALICE. Maggie!

MAGGIE. Oh, Miss Alice, if ye only seen what I seen — them things layin' empty — the little bodies carried away and the mothers cryin' over them, and I was scared — scared that if I didn't get away from this place, mine'd be empty like that too — [*She breaks down sobbing violently.*]

ALICE. I forgive you. I do forgive you — there — there! [*Turning to* HEINIE.] Now we must think of what's to be done. [MAGGIE *crosses to window* R., *opens it and sits on bench before it. Man off stage with fan to stimulate the blowing curtains.*]

ALICE [*her manner becoming purposeful*]. It was a pin with four diamonds, wasn't it?

HEINIE. I ain't seen it, miss.

ALICE [*to* MAGGIE]. Are you sure it was mine? [MAGGIE *nods her head "yes."* ALICE *turns to* HEINIE.] Mr. Schultz, I want you to reconsider and take Maggie away at once.

HEINIE. I can't do that, miss.

ALICE. I want you to take the money that you have — [*As he protests.*] Merely as a *loan* from me. As we agreed upon this afternoon, and take Maggie — away from here as soon as you possibly can.

HEINIE. That's kind of ye — but — Maggie, put down the window, you'll catch cold — [MAGGIE *pulls down window, also shade*], but we couldn't do that, miss —

ALICE. But, Mr. Schultz?

HEINIE. You must understand, we'd neither of us feel right starting out that way. There's only one thing to do — redeem the brooch and give it back to ye. I'll do it to-night.

ALICE. But if I ask you as a favor to me —

HEINIE. I'll have to refuse — honest, miss, we don't need the money that bad. Ye see, the strike's off — I can earn enough inside of a month . . . that'll be time enough.

ALICE. But there *isn't* time, Mr. Schultz.

HEINIE [*surprised at her insistency*]. Why not?

ALICE. You see my aunt doesn't take

my view of this. I've tried to make her see, but —
HEINIE. You mean she suspects Maggie?
ALICE. Maggie left just about the time this thing happened. So far, they've been able to trace nothing, but can't you see the danger? Won't you take the money and go?
HEINIE. Takin' the money wouldn't help us, ma'm, an', if we have to keep out of the way, why, I guess New York's big enough for that.
ALICE [troubled over it, starts up R.]. I'm sorry that you won't. [After thinking rapidly for a moment.] I think you'd better let me have the ticket.
                    [Down toward HEINIE.]
HEINIE. Better let me redeem it for you, miss.
ALICE. I'll take it, please.
       [HEINIE hands her the ticket.]
HEINIE [handing her the money]. An' here's the money we got on it. A hundred and thirteen. [ALICE takes it.]
ALICE [studying the ticket]. Lichtenstein's? Where is that?
HEINIE. Just two blocks down the street. I'd like to save ye the trouble, miss.
ALICE. It's no trouble. I'll have the Doctor take me down in his car. You've spoken of this to no one? No one suspects?
HEINIE. No one.
ALICE. Very well; you've returned this to me. We're square. So no matter what any one asks you, you know nothing about it? Will you promise me that?
HEINIE. Sure — thanks.
              [ALICE goes to door C.]
ALICE [at door]. Good-bye, Maggie. I'll be back very soon. [Exit.]
HEINIE [with a sigh of great relief]. There! Now, don't ye feel better?
MAGGIE. I'm scared —
HEINIE. Well, I ain't goin' to let that bother ye long. Just you put on yer hat an' coat. I'll have ye out of this fix in about two minutes.
MAGGIE [hurriedly putting on her hat and coat]. Where're ye takin' me?
HEINIE [gets cap from hook L.]. You can thank your friend Mrs. Burke Smith for a nice little outin' in Jersey.

MAGGIE [delightedly]. In the country?
HEINIE. Yes — my foreman lives over there with his mother. I'll take ye over and board you out with them for a couple of weeks.
MAGGIE [happily]. Ain't it great? What'll I take with me?
HEINIE. Don't you take nothin'. We'll leave everythin' right here just as if we were goin' for a walk. Then nobody'll suspect nothin'. [Pinching her cheek.] You want to spend your time over there learning how to tell ducks from turkeys.
MAGGIE. It ain't a-goin' to take me long.
HEINIE. Come on, then. [In the doorway, stopping to look at her.] This suits you right down to the ground, don't it?
MAGGIE. Gee! I'm crazy about it.
HEINIE. Give us a kiss, then!
[She lets him kiss her. They start out of the doorway, when HEINIE stops her.] Wait! [Whispers to her.] Go back in the room. [MAGGIE comes back into the room and stands trembling with fear. HEINIE locks door.] Sh-h!
[He pulls down curtain of hall window.]
MAGGIE. What is it?
HEINIE. Be quiet!
[He stands a moment as if trying to collect his thoughts. Then turns down the lamp L. Stage dark except for light from stove. HEINIE dashes over to the other window and raises shade. A man is standing outside on the fire-escape. With a suppressed oath, HEINIE jerks down the curtain. He steps back into the center of the room. There is a sharp knock on the door. Silence. The knock is repeated.]
RAFFERTY'S VOICE [in sharp command]. Schultz! Open up!
HEINIE [in a low voice to MAGGIE]. Now keep yer head shut! Whatever happens, keep yer head shut!
[MAGGIE takes off hat and coat, tosses them into corner down R., and sits on seat below stove. As if realizing the futility of not opening the

door, he steps over and turns the key, then steps back.]

[*The door is flung open and* RAFFERTY *comes in followed by* HOWLAND. HOWLAND *down* L. *of table,* RAFFERTY, C., HEINIE, R. C.]

RAFFERTY [*sharply*]. Light up!
 [HEINIE *crosses* L. *and turns up lamp. Then to* R. C. RAFFERTY *raises curtain of the hall window, then crosses to the* R. *window and raises shade. He nods to the man on the fire-escape to come in. The other man raises the window and climbs into the room, and pulls down the window after him.*]

RAFFERTY [*to the other officer*]. Did they try it? [*Nodding toward the window.*]

DONOVAN [*plain-clothes man*]. Sure!

RAFFERTY [*looking at* HEINIE]. They ought to run an elevator down there. [*To the plain-clothes man.*] That's the woman.

MAGGIE [*shrinking back*]. No! No!

HEINIE [*steps forward*]. What you want with my wife?

RAFFERTY. I don't want her. Headquarters does.

HEINIE. What you got agin' Maggie? Well, spit it out!

RAFFERTY. You was working for Mrs. Burke Smith, wasn't you, Maggie?

MAGGIE. Yes!

RAFFERTY. What made you pull out?

MAGGIE. I was tired.

HEINIE. I told her to quit.

RAFFERTY. What for?

HEINIE [*to* HOWLAND]. Seein' the value you put on life down here, I didn't want to have her take a chance on one o' your own homes.

RAFFERTY [*impatiently*]. Aw — cut that talk! [*To* MAGGIE.] Did you know the house was robbed about the time you left?

MAGGIE. No!

RAFFERTY. By a guy that passed himself off as a plumber — come to fix a broken sink. You broke that sink, didn't ye?

MAGGIE. I — I didn't mean to. Heinie can pay for it!

RAFFERTY. That's all right. This guy is a good friend of yours ain't he?

HEINIE. No, he ain't.

RAFFERTY. So you know who I mean, do ye?

HEINIE [*realizing his slip*]. No, I don't. But you can't tell me she knows anybody like that.

RAFFERTY [*to* MAGGIE]. Steve's a good friend of yours, ain't he?

HEINIE. He wouldn't dare to open his face to her.

RAFFERTY. Yes, he dared — this afternoon.

HEINIE. That's a lie!

RAFFERTY. Right here . . . now, shut up! [*Turning suddenly on* MAGGIE.] Where's that diamond brooch, Maggie? [MAGGIE *quivers, but says nothing.*] Well —

HEINIE [*pause*]. So, the house gets robbed, and jes' because Maggie quits the job it's up to her, is it? Well, you got to pull somethin' better than that before you go any farther, see!

RAFFERTY. If you don't like it here, we'll do it at headquarters. [*A little less sternly.*] Now, for your own sake, this bluff don't go. Cut it! She was on the inside for Steve. We got all his stuff — he soaked it in a Harlem pawn-shop. But there's a diamond brooch and some cheap stuff missing. [*To* MAGGIE.] Now, that was your share. Where'd you put it?

RAFFERTY [*as she does not answer*]. Well, you know how it is — the quicker you come through — the quicker you get out! [*There is another pause.* RAFFERTY *looks about the room, finally he notices the travelling-bag and pasteboard boxes up* L.] Hello, what's all this? Goin' away, huh?

HEINIE. We was, but changed our mind.

RAFFERTY. You're frank about it. Where was you goin' to?

HEINIE. Wyoming.

HOWLAND. That's a long walk when you haven't got the money.

RAFFERTY. Yes — what did you expect to go on, Dutch?

HEINIE. Maggie borrowed the money, but when we changed our minds about goin' she give it back.

RAFFERTY [*cynically*]. Oh, she borrowed

some money and gave it back? That's good! [*Turning to* MAGGIE.] Who'd you borrow it from, Maggie?

MAGGIE. Why — why, the lady told me not to tell.

HOWLAND [*impatiently*]. What damned tommy-rot! [*To* RAFFERTY.] Can't you see they're stalling? Well! What do you want to do — keep me here all night?

RAFFERTY [*to* HOWLAND]. Now just a minute — I'm doin' this! [*To* HEINIE.] Maggie tell you she borrowed it?

HEINIE. I know it's so.

RAFFERTY. I guess you're straight, Dutch — but I guess your wife's got you buffaloed.

HEINIE. You think so, eh? Well, the party what made the loan blew out of here not five minutes ago.

RAFFERTY. They did, eh? [*Turning to* MAGGIE.] You'd better tell us the party's name, Maggie. For your own good.

HEINIE. Sure, I'll tell ye! [*Turning to* HOWLAND.] It's that young lady from your house.

HOWLAND [*amazed*]. What! Miss Alice?

HEINIE. Yes, what d'ye know about that?

RAFFERTY [*observing* HOWLAND'S *amazement*]. Yes, what d'ye know about that?

HOWLAND. Why, it's preposterous! The brooch belongs to the very person he speaks of.

RAFFERTY [*surprised*]. Oh, it does, eh?

HOWLAND. Can't you see they're involving things simply to gain time?

RAFFERTY. Didn't you know the lady was in the habit of loaning these people money?

HOWLAND. I most certainly did not!

RAFFERTY. Now we're getting down to facts.

HOWLAND [*amazed*]. Do you mean to tell me you believe this fellow's yarn?

RAFFERTY. Why shouldn't I?

HOWLAND. But what proof has he?

RAFFERTY. Just at present what proof have you?

HOWLAND. Well, great Scott!

RAFFERTY. Now suppose you ring up your house and get this thing straight from the young woman.

HEINIE. Sure. Ask her; she'll tell ye.

[ALICE *enters up* R. C., *crosses down* R. *of* RAFFERTY. RAFFERTY *crosses up and beckons for plain-clothes man to cross* L. *to him.*]

HOWLAND. Why, what on earth are you doing down here?

ALICE [*sweetly*]. Why, several things. I've come to see the sick child, and I've come to see Maggie.

HOWLAND. Your aunt will be furious!

ALICE. Then you will have the satisfaction of seeing her so. She'll be here shortly.

HOWLAND. I hope you haven't dragged her down here to-night?

ALICE. That's exactly what Doctor Taylor is trying to do. If he's able.

RAFFERTY [*coming down* L. *to* ALICE]. This the lady?

HOWLAND. Yes.

RAFFERTY [*to* ALICE]. Did you lend Maggie any money?

ALICE. Why, yes. That is ... I did, but they returned it to me.

HOWLAND. For just what did you lend the money?

ALICE. Why, to go to Wyoming.

RAFFERTY. That fits.

ALICE. What's it all about?

RAFFERTY. Then she didn't raise the money on your jewelry?

ALICE. On my jewelry? [*Turning to* HOWLAND *indignantly.*] Oh, I see! Merely because Maggie left our house at the time of the robbery, you've come here to persecute her. Really, Mr. Howland, I can't believe that my aunt will tolerate any such brutality. It's cruel and it's inhuman!

HOWLAND. There is no desire to persecute. We merely wish to get back some of the articles that were stolen.

ALICE. Nearly everything that man took has been recovered. Is there anything still missing of such great value that you must still hound this woman against whom you have no evidence?

RAFFERTY. Wasn't your brooch valuable?

ALICE [*in a surprised manner*]. My brooch?

HOWLAND. Yes — we discovered after you left the house this morning that your jewel box had been rifled.

ALICE. My jewel box?

HOWLAND. No doubt you were too tender-hearted to tell us about it last night.

ALICE. My jewel box?

RAFFERTY [*puzzled*]. Say, didn't you know about it?

ALICE. My jewel box?

HOWLAND [*impatiently*]. Yes, yes. A diamond brooch.

[ALICE *unbuttons her coat, exposing brooch, which* MAGGIE *sees.*]

ALICE. Do you mean this?

MAGGIE. That's it! That's it!

RAFFERTY [*to* HOWLAND]. Do you mean that?

HOWLAND [*thunderstruck*]. Why, yes!

RAFFERTY [*flying off the handle*]. Well, good God, what are we coming to? Juggin' people for goods she's got on her back?

HOWLAND [*to* RAFFERTY]. Now, just a minute. [*To* ALICE.] You didn't wear that brooch from the house this morning. Your aunt said so.

ALICE. Really, Mr. Howland, I don't believe I require such violent enlightenment concerning my own actions.

HOWLAND. Well, I beg your pardon, but —

ALICE [*turning to* RAFFERTY]. I took my brooch to the jeweler's to be fixed yesterday afternoon.

RAFFERTY [*suspiciously*]. Say, if Maggie never saw that brooch before, how did she know it just now?

ALICE. She's often helped me dress at the house.

RAFFERTY. Um — um, very good friends, ain't ye?

ALICE. Very.

RAFFERTY. When were you down here last?

ALICE. Yesterday.

RAFFERTY. Huh?

ALICE [*quickly*]. This morning early.

RAFFERTY [*grinning. To plain-clothes man*]. What d'ye know about this, anyhow? [*The other officer shrugs his shoulders. Eyeing* HOWLAND *in disgust.*] Say, you don't want a detective — you want a lady's maid. [*To assistant.*] Rubber around the other room.

[RAFFERTY *turns up stage. Assistant exits* L.]

[TAYLOR *enters up* R.]

ALICE [*crosses to* TAYLOR]. Ralph, did you bring her?

TAYLOR. She's on the stairs — so cross she wouldn't even let me help her up.

ALICE [*to* MAGGIE]. I've brought her down to help you, dear.

TAYLOR [*going out to landing, speaking downstairs*]. This is the last flight.

ALICE [*to* RAFFERTY]. Aunt will take things in hand now.

RAFFERTY. Oh, ain't that nice?

[MRS. BURKE SMITH *comes into the room.* TAYLOR *comes in after her.*]

MRS. BURKE SMITH [*flustered and out of breath*]. Oh, dear! Somebody give me something to sit on, please!

ALICE [*crosses down* R. *of* MRS. BURKE SMITH. HOWLAND *places a chair for* MRS. BURKE SMITH *and she sinks into it* R. *of table*]. Oh, Aunt, I knew you'd consent to come.

MRS. BURKE SMITH. Consent? I was dragged. Literally dragged here by the doctor.

HOWLAND [L. *of table*]. My dear Mrs. Burke Smith, I'm afraid you've been put to a great deal of unnecessary trouble.

MRS. BURKE SMITH. I know that, but what could I do? These young ones have no consideration for one's feeling, and I was so comfortably settled for the evening.

ALICE. Oh, Aunt, if you knew what it means!

MRS. BURKE SMITH. I know what it means — all this excitement; a perfectly wretched, restless night! [*Giving* ALICE *a look of reproach.*] And of course, I know you're back of it! You never think of others! [*With a sigh of martyrdom.*] Well, now that I'm here, what's wanted of me? What's the situation?

[ALICE *crosses up to* TAYLOR *by table up* C.]

RAFFERTY [*crosses down* R. *of* MRS. SMITH]. I'll tell you the situation. As far as the Schultzes go, you ain't got a look-in.

HOWLAND. What do you mean by that? Haven't we a warrant from the judge?

RAFFERTY. Yes, and when the judge hears the cock-and-bull story you handed him to get it, you'll find yourself mighty liable for contempt.

MRS. BURKE SMITH. What are you saying? That we haven't told the truth?

RAFFERTY. This man told the judge that he had absolute knowledge that Maggie had your brooch. And now one of your own family stalks in here wearing it.

MRS. BURKE SMITH. Impossible!

ALICE [crosses down C. R. of RAFFERTY]. Yes, Auntie, I had it!

MRS. BURKE SMITH. Oh, you did? Then why didn't you tell me? [To RAFFERTY.] But that makes no difference. Things have been disappearing continually for the past week.

[ALICE crosses up to TAYLOR again up C.]

RAFFERTY. Then you'd better go home and take the trouble to hunt them up.

MRS. BURKE SMITH. My good man —

RAFFERTY. My good woman — what do you think the police force is — something to play with? Something to break into honest men's houses whenever the sweet fancy strikes you?

HOWLAND. You're decidedly impertinent, young man.

RAFFERTY. That'll be about all from you. Now clear out, the whole lot o' ye!

HOWLAND [to MRS. BURKE SMITH]. Suppose I take you home now? I'll see what can be done with this matter later.

MRS. BURKE SMITH. Perhaps as no articles of any value have been found, we'd better not prosecute these people. [Pointing to RAFFERTY. Rising.] But I want that man reported for impertinence! That's much more important just now. Mr. Howland, please call a cab. I just couldn't survive going back in the Doctor's machine!

[She moves toward the door accompanied by HOWLAND.]

[DONOVAN enters from the other room, carrying a cloth bag of silver which STEVE had left.]

PLAIN-CLOTHES MAN. Here ye are!

RAFFERTY [looking at it]. Silverware. [Calling to HOWLAND and MRS. BURKE SMITH.] Here! [They turn in hallway, come back in doorway.] This from your place? [RAFFERTY up to table up C.]

MRS. BURKE SMITH [crossing and looking at them]. Every bit of it! [Looking at MAGGIE, who stands astounded.] She shows her guilt — look at her face!

RAFFERTY. That settles it. [To plainclothes man.] Call the wagon.

[RALPH and ALICE follow MRS. BURKE SMITH and HOWLAND in from hallway and stand about table up C., looking at silverware.]

ALICE [starting over toward her aunt]. Oh, Aunt, you won't let them. [To plainclothes man.] Wait! Wait, please!

[MAGGIE down R., HEINIE L. of her; DONOVAN up L.; RAFFERTY R. of him; ALICE R. of RAFFERTY; MRS. BURKE SMITH R. of ALICE; TAYLOR R. of MRS. BURKE SMITH; HOWLAND above TAYLOR, grouped around table up C. At their discovery of the package, MAGGIE and HEINIE are both dumfounded. MAGGIE crosses in terror to HEINIE. HEINIE's amazement has given way to bitter anger at this fresh proof of MAGGIE's untruthfulness. He turns on her accusingly.]

MAGGIE [to HEINIE, in low, terrified voice]. What'll I do?

HEINIE [bitterly]. Why didn't ye tell me?

MAGGIE [frantically]. I never saw them things before.

HEINIE [unbelievingly]. How did they get here, then?

MAGGIE [dazed]. I... I don't know.

HEINIE. What do ye wanta lie to me again for? Don't ye see this breaks down everythin' between us?

MAGGIE. No — no — I ain't lying to ye — I — [Struck by sudden thought.] Steve!!!

HEINIE. What!!!

MAGGIE. I caught him in here, this afternoon.

[Turns toward others, about to speak.]

HEINIE [quickly checking her]. Wait! Don't ye know it'll just make matters worse if you ring him in now?

MAGGIE. Maybe the judge won't send me up for long. Promise ye'll be waitin' for me when I get out.

HEINIE. You ain't a-gonna git sent up. [To MAGGIE in a low voice.] Now just sit down here an' keep yer head shut.

[MAGGIE sits in wonder. HOWLAND crosses down L. of table, MRS. BURKE SMITH R. of it. ALICE and TAYLOR up C. L. of table.]

RAFFERTY [crosses down C.]. Well, Maggie, ye'd better tell us all ye know.

HEINIE. Ye needn't always talk to Maggie; talk to me.

RAFFERTY. Well, how about it, Dutch?

HEINIE. Well, how about it? I took it.

RAFFERTY. You!

MAGGIE [starting up]. What!

HEINIE. Did yer think fer a minute that Maggie —

[The others have all turned to HEINIE at the new turn of affairs.]

RAFFERTY. Just where do you come in?

HEINIE. I give Steve the lay of the house.

MRS. BURKE SMITH [quickly]. It might easily have been this fellow. He used to come to the house to fetch his wife!

MAGGIE. Will you listen to me?

RAFFERTY. All right, Dutch. I'll have to take ye.

[Hand on HEINIE's shoulder and starts for door.]

MAGGIE. Here — wait — [Dragging cradle from under the table up C. and snatching up baby ribbon out of it.] Here, look at this stuff, baby ribbon. D'ye think Heinie'd steal stuff like that?

[MRS. BURKE SMITH crosses down below table to HOWLAND.]

HEINIE [interrupting her]. Wait a minute. [To RAFFERTY, aside.] Let me talk to her a minute. [RAFFERTY nods assent, and HEINIE goes down to MAGGIE.] Maggie, you got to let me go! You got to!

MAGGIE [clinging to him]. No, no!

HEINIE. It was all my fault. I scared ye into it.

MAGGIE. No, no, you're all I got in the world.

HEINIE. Listen, honey ... there's somethin' else. Our little baby, he can't be born in jail. We can't start him off wrong like that.

MAGGIE [standing off and looking at him strangely]. So, that's your reason?

HEINIE. We can do that much for it!

MAGGIE [half to herself]. Jail! It's as good as the gutter, ain't it?

HEINIE. We'll make the best of it, honey.

MAGGIE [her scorn rising. Crosses R.]. The best of it? So, I got my choice, have I? Whether my child will be born in jail or in the gutter.

HEINIE. Now, don't lose yer head, Maggie ...

MAGGIE [shrilly, hysterically]. I ain't losin' my head.... I'm just gettin' on to myself the kind of a fool I been.

HOWLAND. Oh, come, now, this noise won't save you!

MAGGIE. That man was goin' to jail in my place, because o' that. [Pointing to the cradle.] He didn't want his baby born there. Think of it, to save his baby from the shame of jail ... why don't ye tell him it ain't no use? You know it ain't.

MRS. BURKE SMITH. What do you mean?

MAGGIE. What chance has it got, can ye tell me? It's comin' inter the world weaklin', to be shoved into the gutter ... You can't save it.

HEINIE. Maggie ...

MAGGIE. Oh, what's the use! I fought ... I lied ... I stole ... I wanted to give my baby a chance — that was right, wasn't it? I wanted it healthy an' strong an' decent. But it ain't no use — it ain't no use. There's somethin' wrong somewhere, I tell ye ... an' mine ... mine's ... to be the scum o' the earth cursin' me for the very life I give it.

HEINIE. Maggie ...

MAGGIE. Them's yer own words. Ye all told me, an' it's the truth.... Ye rubbed it in till I've gone crazy with it. Now I'm scared. I'm scared o' what's comin' — I can't face it — [Down on knees

at cradle.] It's too much to ask of me ... it's too much to ask of any woman. [*Takes baby clothes in hands, presses to face.*] It ain't no use, it ain't no use.
   [*Throws herself upon the cradle sobbing. She lies over the cradle exhausted by her passion, moaning.* MRS. BURKE SMITH, *hysterically, sits* L. *of table.*]
HEINIE [*quietly as he kneels beside her*]. Rafferty, ask these people to git out, will ye — I want to talk to my wife alone —
   [RAFFERTY *beckons for them to leave.* MRS. BURKE SMITH *crosses below table to* R. *of table.* TAYLOR *crosses up and into hallway,* HOWLAND *up to table up* C. HEINIE *takes* MAGGIE *to rocker, where she sinks limply.*]
ALICE [*stepping forward, down* C. R. *of* MRS. BURKE SMITH]. Wait, please. [*To* MRS. BURKE SMITH.] Aunt, I had you dragged down here, and you said the excitement would cause you a wretched night. Will you blame me for this or for other wretched nights if you've been brought to see — to understand —
   [MRS. BURKE SMITH *brokenly turns and speaks to* HOWLAND.]
RAFFERTY. Well, what do you want done?
HOWLAND. Mrs. Burke Smith has decided to withdraw the charge.
   [RAFFERTY *motions for* DONOVAN *to go downstairs.*]
ALICE. Oh, Aunt!
   [*Her head on* MRS. BURKE SMITH'S *shoulder.*]
MRS. BURKE SMITH [*controlling her emotion with an effort*]. I looked on things down here too casually ... I didn't know ... I didn't realize ...
   [MRS. BURKE SMITH *exits downstairs, followed by* TAYLOR *and* HOWLAND. RAFFERTY *at door shakes his head in disgust.*]
RAFFERTY. It's a shame things has to be like this.

ALICE [*crosses to* HEINIE]. Mr. Schultz! Will you grant me a great favor?
HEINIE [*back of rocker*]. Anything, miss!
ALICE [*handing* HEINIE *two railroad tickets*]. I got these for you.
HEINIE. The passage?
ALICE. Will you go? [*As he hesitates.*] My first request and you refuse it?
HEINIE [*choking*]. You got to let us pay ye back.
ALICE. Yes, and with interest. I shall be a regular old miser about the interest.
   [ALICE *crosses to table* L. *and gets gloves, then starts up* C. HEINIE *gets stool from above stove, brings to* L. *of rocker, sits and takes* MAGGIE'S *head on shoulder.*]
RAFFERTY [*to* ALICE, *crosses up* C. *to her*]. Say, you're a pretty smart young woman, ain't ye?
ALICE [*defiantly*]. Am I?
RAFFERTY. So your brooch was in the jeweler's? I'll hand Dutch the price of a brooch if he can tell me what jeweler's you had it in.
ALICE. The charge has been dropped, I believe.
RAFFERTY. That's why I'm tippin' ye off now. I don't want you to think me any more of a rube sheriff than necessary.
ALICE. You mean you don't believe my brooch was at the jeweler's?
RAFFERTY. Well, I give the best imitation I could of a credulous man! But when the other junk showed up — why —
   [*He looks at her meaningly.*]
ALICE [*understanding*]. Oh, I see. Thank you, Mr. Rafferty.
   [*Shakes hands with him.*]
RAFFERTY. Well, good-night and good luck to ye. [*Exits, and downstairs.*]
ALICE [*crosses down* R. *to* HEINIE *and* MAGGIE]. Good-night, Maggie, and good-bye. [*Exits up* R. *and downstairs.*]
MAGGIE. Heinie! Maybe there's roses in Wyoming.

CURTAIN

HINDLE WAKES
A PLAY IN THREE ACTS
BY STANLEY HOUGHTON

ALL RIGHTS RESERVED
Reprinted by arrangement with Sidgwick and Jackson, Ltd.

CHARACTERS

CHRISTOPHER HAWTHORN, *a slasher at Daisy Bank Mill*
MRS. HAWTHORN, *his wife*
FANNY HAWTHORN, *their daughter, a weaver at Daisy Bank Mill*
NATHANIEL JEFFCOTE, *owner of Daisy Bank Mill*
MRS. JEFFCOTE, *his wife*
ALAN JEFFCOTE, *their son*
SIR TIMOTHY FARRAR, *Chairman of the Education Committee at Hindle*
BEATRICE FARRAR, *his daughter*
ADA, *maid at Bank Top*

ACT I. Scene 1. Kitchen of the Hawthorns' house, 137, Burnley Road, Hindle. Bank Holiday, Monday, August 6th. 9 P.M.

Scene 2. Breakfast-room of the Jeffcotes' house, Bank Top, Hindle Vale. The same night. 10.30 P.M.

Scene 3. Breakfast-room at the Jeffcotes'. The same night. 1 A.M.

ACT II. Breakfast-room at the Jeffcotes'. Tuesday, August 7th. 8 P.M.

ACT III. Breakfast-room at the Jeffcotes'. Tuesday, August 7th. 9 P.M.

NOTE. The scene for Act I, Scene 1, should be very small, as a contrast to the room at the Jeffcotes'. It might well be set inside the other scene so as to facilitate the quick change between Scenes 1 and 2, Act I.

NOTE ON THE LANCASHIRE DIALECT

This play is about Lancashire people. In the smaller Lancashire towns it is quite usual for well-to-do persons, and for persons who have received good educations at grammar schools and technical schools, to drop more or less into dialect when familiar, or when excited, or to point a joke. It is even usual for them to mix their speech with perfect naturalness. "You" and "thou" may jostle one another in the same sentence, as, for instance: "You can't catch it, I tell thee." As a general rule they will miss out a good many "h's," and will pronounce vowels with an open or flat sound. The final consonants will usually be clipped. At the same time it is unnecessary laboriously to adopt any elaborate or fearsome method of pronunciation. The Lancashire dialect of to-day — except amongst the roughest class in the most out-of-the-way districts — has had many of its corners rubbed off. It varies in its accents, too, in each separate town, that it may be attempted with impunity by all save the most incompetent. The poorest attempt will probably be good enough to pass muster as "Manchester," which has hardly a special accent of its own, but boasts a tongue composed of all the other Lancashire dialects mixed up, polished and made politer, and deprived of their raciness.

HINDLE WAKES

ACT I

Scene 1

The scene is triangular, representing a corner of the living-room kitchen of No. 137, Burnley Road, Hindle, a house rented at about 7s. 6d. a week. In the left-hand wall, low down, there is a door leading to the scullery. In the same wall, but further away from the spectator, is a window looking on to the backyard. A dresser stands in front of the window. About half-way up the right-hand wall is the door leading to the hall or passage. Nearer, against the same wall, a high cupboard for china and crockery. The fireplace is not visible, being in one of the walls not represented. However, down in the L. corner of the stage is an arm-chair, which stands by the hearth. In the middle of the room is a square table, with chairs on each side. The room is cheerful and comfortable. It is nine o'clock on a warm August evening. Through the window can be seen the darkening sky, as the blind is not drawn. Against the sky an outline of roof-tops and mill chimneys. The only light is the dim twilight from the open window. Thunder is in the air. When the curtain rises CHRISTOPHER HAWTHORN, *a decent, white-bearded man of nearly sixty, is sitting in the arm-chair smoking a pipe.* MRS. HAWTHORN, *a keen, sharp-faced woman of fifty-five, is standing gazing out of the window. There is a flash of lightning and a rumble of thunder far away.*

MRS. HAWTHORN. It's passing over. There'll be no rain.

CHRISTOPHER. Ay! We could do with some rain. [*There is a flash of lightning.*]

CHRISTOPHER. Pull down the blind and light the gas.

MRS. HAWTHORN. What for?

CHRISTOPHER. It's more cosy-like with the gas.

MRS. HAWTHORN. You're not afraid of the lightning?

CHRISTOPHER. I want to look at that railway guide.

MRS. HAWTHORN. What's the good? We've looked at it twice already. There's no train from Blackpool till five-past ten, and it's only just on nine now.

CHRISTOPHER. Happen we've made a mistake.

MRS. HAWTHORN. Happen we've not. Besides, what's the good of a railway guide? You know trains run as they like on Bank Holiday.

CHRISTOPHER. Ay! Perhaps you're right. You don't think she'll come round by Manchester?

MRS. HAWTHORN. What would she be doing coming round by Manchester?

CHRISTOPHER. You can get that road from Blackpool.

MRS. HAWTHORN. Yes. If she's coming from Blackpool.

CHRISTOPHER. Have you thought she may not come at all?

MRS. HAWTHORN [*grimly*]. What do you take me for?

CHRISTOPHER. You never hinted.

MRS. HAWTHORN. No use putting them sort of ideas into your head.

[*Another flash and a peal of thunder.*]

CHRISTOPHER. Well, well, those are lucky who haven't to travel at all on Bank Holiday.

MRS. HAWTHORN. Unless they've got a motor-car, like Nat Jeffcote's lad.

CHRISTOPHER. Nay. *He's* not got one.

MRS. HAWTHORN. What? Why, I saw him with my own eyes setting out in it last Saturday week after the mill shut.

CHRISTOPHER. Ay! He's gone off these Wakes with his pal George Ramsbottom. A couple of thick beggars, those two!

MRS. HAWTHORN. Then what do you mean telling me he's not got a motor-car?

CHRISTOPHER. I said he hadn't got one of his own. It's his father's. You don't catch Nat Jeffcote parting with owt before his time. That's how he holds his lad in check, as you might say.

MRS. HAWTHORN. Alan Jeffcote's seldom short of cash. He spends plenty.

CHRISTOPHER. Ay! Nat gives him what he asks for, and doesn't want to know how he spends it either. But he's *got* to ask for it first. Nat can stop supplies any time if he's a mind.

MRS. HAWTHORN. That's likely, isn't it?

CHRISTOPHER. Queerer things have happened. You don't know Nat like I do. He's a bad one to get across with.

[*Another flash and gentle peal.*
MRS. HAWTHORN *gets up.*]

MRS. HAWTHORN. I'll light the gas.

[*She pulls down the blind and lights the gas.*]

CHRISTOPHER. When I met Nat this morning he told me that Alan had telegraphed from Llandudno on Saturday asking for twenty pounds.

MRS. HAWTHORN. From Llandudno?

CHRISTOPHER. Ay! Reckon he's been stopping there. Run short of brass.

MRS. HAWTHORN. And did he send it?

CHRISTOPHER. Of course he sent it. Nat doesn't stint the lad. [*He laughs quietly.*] Eh, but he *can* get through it, though!

MRS. HAWTHORN. Look here. What are you going to say to Fanny when she comes?

CHRISTOPHER. Ask her where she's been.

MRS. HAWTHORN. Ask her where she's been! Of course we'll do that. But suppose she won't tell us?

CHRISTOPHER. She's always been a good girl.

MRS. HAWTHORN. She's always gone her own road. Suppose she tells us to mind our own business?

CHRISTOPHER. I reckon it *is* my business to know what she's been up to.

MRS. HAWTHORN. Don't you forget it. And don't let her forget it either. If you do I promise you I won't.

CHRISTOPHER. All right. Where's that postcard?

MRS. HAWTHORN. Little good taking heed of that.

[CHRISTOPHER *rises and gets a picture postcard from the dresser.*]

CHRISTOPHER [*reading*]. "Shall be home before late on Monday. Lovely weather." [*Looking at the picture.*] North Pier, Blackpool. Very like, too.

MRS. HAWTHORN [*suddenly*]. Let's have a look. When was it posted?

CHRISTOPHER. It's dated Sunday.

MRS. HAWTHORN. That's nowt to go by. Anyone can put the wrong date. What's the post-mark? [*She scrutinises it.*] "August 5th, summat P.M." I can't make out the time.

CHRISTOPHER. August 5th. That was yesterday, all right. There'd only be one post on Sunday.

MRS. HAWTHORN. Then she was in Blackpool up to yesterday, that's certain.

CHRISTOPHER. Ay!

MRS. HAWTHORN. Well, it's a mystery.

CHRISTOPHER [*shaking his head*]. Or summat worse.

MRS. HAWTHORN. Eh? You don't think *that*, eh?

CHRISTOPHER. I don't know what to think.

MRS. HAWTHORN. Nor me neither.

[*They sit silent for a time. There is a rumble of thunder, far away. After it has died away a knock is heard at the front door. They turn and look at each other.* MRS. HAWTHORN *rises and goes out in silence. In a few moments* FANNY HAWTHORN *comes in, followed by* MRS. HAWTHORN. FANNY *is a sturdy, determined, dark little girl, with thick lips, a broad, short nose, and big black eyes. She is dressed rather smartly, but not very tastefully. She stands by the table unpinning her hat and talking cheerfully.* MRS. HAWTHORN *stands by the door and* CHRISTOPHER

remains in his chair. Both look at FANNY *queerly.*]
FANNY. Well, you didn't expect me as soon as this, I'll bet. I came round by Manchester. They said the trains would run better that way to-night. Bank Holiday, you know. I always think they let the Manchester trains through before any of the others, don't you?
MRS. HAWTHORN. We didn't see how you were to get here till past ten if you came direct. We've been looking up in the Guide.
FANNY. No. I wasn't for coming direct at any price. Mary wanted to.
CHRISTOPHER. Mary!
[CHRISTOPHER *is about to rise in astonishment, but* MRS. HAWTHORN *makes signs to him behind* FANNY'S *back.*]
MRS. HAWTHORN. Oh! So Mary Hollins wanted to come back the other way, did she?
FANNY. Yes. But I wasn't having any. They said the Manchester trains would be — oh! I've told you all that already.
MRS. HAWTHORN. So you've had a good time, Fanny.
FANNY. Rather! A fair treat. What do *you* think?
MRS. HAWTHORN. Was Mary Hollins with you all the time?
FANNY. Of course she was.
[*She steals a puzzled glance at* MRS. HAWTHORN.]
MRS. HAWTHORN. And she came back with you to-night?
FANNY. Yes.
MRS. HAWTHORN. And where's she gone now?
FANNY. She's gone home of course. Where else should she go?
[*There is a short pause.*]
CHRISTOPHER [*quietly*]. You're telling lies, my girl.
FANNY. What, father?
CHRISTOPHER. That's not the truth you've just been saying.
FANNY. What's not the truth?
CHRISTOPHER. You didn't spend the week-end in Blackpool with Mary Hollins.
FANNY. Who says I didn't?

CHRISTOPHER. I say so.
FANNY. Why do you think I didn't, father?
CHRISTOPHER. Well, did you?
FANNY. Yes, I did.
[CHRISTOPHER *turns helplessly to his wife.*]
MRS. HAWTHORN. All right, Chris, wait a minute. Look here, Fanny, it's no use trying to make us believe you've been away with Mary.
FANNY. What? I can bring you any number of folk out of Hindle who saw us in Blackpool last week.
MRS. HAWTHORN. Last week, happen. Not this week-end?
FANNY. Yes.
MRS. HAWTHORN. Bring them, then.
FANNY. How can I bring them to-night? They've most of them not come back yet.
MRS. HAWTHORN. Tell us who to ask, then.
FANNY [*thinking*]. Ask Polly Birtwistle. Or Ethel Slater.
MRS. HAWTHORN. Yes. After you've got at them and given them a hint what to say.
FANNY. Of course if you'll believe that it's no use asking Mary. You'd only say *she* was telling lies as well.
[*There is a pause.*]
FANNY. Will you go round and see Mary?
CHRISTOPHER. No.
MRS. HAWTHORN. Fanny, it's no use seeing Mary. You may as well own up and tell us where you've been.
FANNY. I've been to Blackpool with Mary Hollins.
MRS. HAWTHORN. You've not. You weren't there this week-end.
FANNY. Why, I sent you a picture post-card on Sunday.
MRS. HAWTHORN. Yes, we got that. Who posted it?
FANNY. I posted it myself at the pillar-box on the Central Pier.
[*There is a pause. They do not believe her.*]
FANNY [*flaring up*]. I tell you I've been all week-end at Blackpool with Mary Hollins.

CHRISTOPHER [*quietly*]. No, you've not.
FANNY [*pertly*]. Well, that's settled then. There's no need to talk about it any more.
  [*A pause.* FANNY *nervously twists her handkerchief.*]
FANNY. Look here. Who's been saying I didn't?
CHRISTOPHER. We know you didn't.
FANNY. But you can't know.
MRS. HAWTHORN. As certain as there's a God in Heaven we know it.
FANNY. Well, that's not so certain after all.
CHRISTOPHER. Fanny! Take heed what you're saying.
FANNY. Why can't you speak out? What do you know? Tell me that.
MRS. HAWTHORN. It's not for us to tell you anything. It's for you to tell us where you've been.
FANNY [*mutinously*]. I've told you.
  [*They do not speak.* FANNY *rises quickly.*]
MRS. HAWTHORN. Where are you going?
FANNY. Are you trying to hinder me from going out when I please, now? I'm going to see Mary Hollins.
MRS. HAWTHORN. What for?
FANNY. To fetch her here. You shall see her whether you like it or not.
CHRISTOPHER. Fanny, I've already seen Mary Hollins.
  [FANNY *turns and stares at him in surprise.*]
FANNY. When?
CHRISTOPHER. This morning.
FANNY. She was at Blackpool this morning.
CHRISTOPHER. So was I.
FANNY [*amazed*]. What were you doing there?
CHRISTOPHER. I went there with Jim Hollins. We went on purpose to see Mary.
FANNY. So it's Mary as has given me away, is it?
CHRISTOPHER [*nodding, slowly*]. Yes. You might say so.
FANNY [*angrily*]. I'll talk to her.
CHRISTOPHER. It wasn't her fault. She couldn't help it.

MRS. HAWTHORN. Now will you tell us where you've been?
FANNY. No, I won't. I'll see Mary first. What did she say to you?
CHRISTOPHER. When I told thee I went with Jim Hollins to Blackpool, I didn't tell thee quite everything, lass. [*Gently.*] Mary Hollins was drowned yesterday afternoon.
FANNY. What!
  [*She stares at* CHRISTOPHER *in horror.*]
CHRISTOPHER. It was one of them sailing boats. Run down by an excursion steamer. There was over twenty people on board. Seven of them was drowned.
FANNY. Oh! My poor Mary!
  [FANNY *sinks down into her chair and stares dully at* CHRISTOPHER.]
MRS. HAWTHORN. You didn't know that?
FANNY [*shaking her head*]. No, no.
  [*She buries her head in her arms on the table and begins to sob.*]
MRS. HAWTHORN. Now then, Fanny.
  [*She is about to resume her inquisition.*]
CHRISTOPHER. Hold on, mother. Wait a bit. Give her a chance.
MRS. HAWTHORN [*waving him aside*]. Now then, Fanny. You see you've been telling lies all the time. [FANNY *sobs.*]
MRS. HAWTHORN. Listen to me. You weren't at Blackpool this week-end.
FANNY [*to herself*]. Poor, poor Mary!
MRS. HAWTHORN [*patiently*]. You weren't at Blackpool this week-end.
  [FANNY *sobs.*]
MRS. HAWTHORN. Were you?
FANNY [*sobbing*]. N — no.
  [*She shakes her head without raising it.*]
MRS. HAWTHORN. Where were you?
FANNY. Shan't tell you.
MRS. HAWTHORN. You went away for the week-end? [*No answer.*] Did you go alone? [*No answer.*] You didn't go alone, of course. [*No answer.*] Who did you go with?
FANNY. Leave me alone, mother.
MRS. HAWTHORN. Who did you go with? Did you go with a fellow?
  [FANNY *stops sobbing. She raises*

her head the tiniest bit so that she can see her mother without seeming to do so. *Her eyes are just visible above her arm.* MRS. HAWTHORN *marks the movement, nevertheless.*]
MRS. HAWTHORN [*nodding*]. Yes. You went with a chap?
FANNY [*quickly dropping her head again*]. No, I didn't.
MRS. HAWTHORN [*roughly*]. You little liar, you did! You know you did! Who was he?
 [MRS. HAWTHORN *seizes* FANNY *by the shoulder and shakes her in exasperation.* FANNY *sobs.*]
MRS. HAWTHORN. Will you tell us who he was?
FANNY [*sharply*]. No, I won't.
 [*There is a slight pause.*]
CHRISTOPHER. This is what happens to many a lass, but I never thought to have it happen to a lass of mine!
MRS. HAWTHORN. Why didn't you get wed if you were so curious? There's plenty would have had you.
FANNY. Chance is a fine thing. Happen I wouldn't have had them!
MRS. HAWTHORN. Happen you'll be sorry for it before long. There's not so many will have you now, if this gets about.
CHRISTOPHER. *He* ought to wed her.
MRS. HAWTHORN. Of course he ought to wed her, and shall too, or I'll know the reason why! Come now, who's the chap?
FANNY. Shan't tell you.
MRS. HAWTHORN. Look here.
 [*She places her hand on* FANNY'S *arm.* FANNY *turns round fiercely and flings it off.*]
FANNY. Leave me alone, can't you? You ought to be thankful he did take me away. It saved my life, anyhow.
MRS. HAWTHORN. How do you make that out?
FANNY. I'd have been drowned with Mary if I hadn't gone to Llandudno.
MRS. HAWTHORN. Llandudno? Did you say —? [*She stops short.*]
CHRISTOPHER. Why mother, that's —
MRS. HAWTHORN [*cutting him short*]. Be quiet, can't you?
 [*She reflects for a moment, and then sits down at the other side of the table, opposite* FANNY.]
MRS. HAWTHORN [*with meaning*]. When you were in Llandudno did you happen to run across Alan Jeffcote?
 [FANNY *looks up and they stare hard at each other.*]
FANNY [*at length*]. How did you know?
MRS. HAWTHORN [*smiling grimly*]. I didn't. You've just told me.
FANNY [*gives a low moan*]. Oh!
 [*She buries her head and sobs.*]
MRS. HAWTHORN [*to* CHRISTOPHER]. Well. What do you think of her now?
CHRISTOPHER [*dazed*]. Nat Jeffcote's lad!
MRS. HAWTHORN. Ay! Nat Jeffcote's lad. But what does that matter? If it hadn't been him it would have been some other lad.
CHRISTOPHER. Nat and me were lads together. We were pals.
MRS. HAWTHORN. Well, now thy girl and Nat's lad are pals. Pull thyself together, man. What art going to do about it?
CHRISTOPHER. I don't know, rightly.
MRS. HAWTHORN. Aren't you going to give her a talking-to?
CHRISTOPHER. What's the good?
MRS. HAWTHORN. What's the good? Well, I like that! My father would have got a stick to me. [*She turns to* FANNY.] Did he promise to wed you?
FANNY [*in a low voice*]. No.
MRS. HAWTHORN. Why not?
FANNY. Never asked him.
MRS. HAWTHORN. You little fool! Have you no common sense at all? What did you do it for if you didn't make him promise to wed you? [FANNY *does not reply.*]
MRS. HAWTHORN. Do you hear me? What made you do it? [FANNY *sobs.*]
CHRISTOPHER. Let her be, mother.
MRS. HAWTHORN. She's turned stupid. [*To* FANNY.] When did you go? [*No answer.*] Did you go in his motor-car? [*No answer.*] Where did you stay?
 [*There is no answer, so she shakes* FANNY.]
Will you take heed of what I'm saying? Haven't you got a tongue in your head? Tell us exactly what took place.

FANNY. I won't tell you anything more.
MRS. HAWTHORN. We'll see about that.
CHRISTOPHER [*rising*]. That's enough, mother. We'll leave her alone to-night. [*He touches* FANNY *on the shoulder.*] Now then, lass, no one's going to harm thee. Stop thy crying. Thou'd better get upstairs to bed. Happen thou's fagged out.
MRS. HAWTHORN. You *are* soft. You're never going to let her off so easy?
CHRISTOPHER. There's plenty of time to tackle her in the morning. Come, lass.

[FANNY *rises and stands by the table, wiping her eyes.*]

Get to bed and have some sleep, if thou can.

[*Without a word* FANNY *slowly goes to the door and out of the room. She does not look at either of them.*]

MRS. HAWTHORN. Now then. What's to be done?
CHRISTOPHER. Ay! That's it.
MRS. HAWTHORN. You'll have to waken up a bit if we're to make the most of this. I can tell you what's the first job. You'll have to go and see Nathaniel Jeffcote.
CHRISTOPHER. I'll see him at the mill to-morrow.
MRS. HAWTHORN. To-morrow! You'll go and see him to-night. Go up to the house at Bank Top. If Alan's come home with Fanny he'll be there as well, and you can kill two birds with one stone.
CHRISTOPHER. It's a nasty job.
MRS. HAWTHORN. It's got to be done, and the sooner the better. How would it be if I come with you?
CHRISTOPHER [*hastily*]. Nay. I'll go alone.
MRS. HAWTHORN. I'm afraid you'll be too soft. It's a fine chance, and don't you forget it.
CHRISTOPHER. A fine chance?
MRS. HAWTHORN. To get her wed, thou great stupid. We're not going to be content with less. We'll show them up if they turn nasty.
CHRISTOPHER. He *ought* to wed her. I don't know what Nat'll say.
MRS. HAWTHORN. Look here, if you're not going to stand out for your rights I'll come myself. I'm not afraid of Nat Jeffcote, not if he owned twenty mills like Daisy Bank.
CHRISTOPHER. I'm not afraid of him, neither, though he's a bad man to tackle. [*He rises.*] Where's my hat?

[MRS. HAWTHORN *gives him his hat and stick, and he goes to the door.*]

MRS. HAWTHORN. I say. I wonder if she's done this on purpose, after all. Plenty of girls have made good matches that way.
CHRISTOPHER. She said they never mentioned marriage. You heard her.
MRS. HAWTHORN. Well, he mightn't have gone with her if she had. Happen she's cleverer than we think!
CHRISTOPHER. She always was a deep one.
MRS. HAWTHORN. That's how Bamber's lass got hold of young Greenwood.
CHRISTOPHER. But there was a — He couldn't help it, so well.
MRS. HAWTHORN. Yes. [*She reflects.*] Ah, well. You never know what may happen.

[CHRISTOPHER *goes out followed by* MRS. HAWTHORN *as the curtain falls.*]

SCENE 2

The breakfast-room at Nathaniel Jeffcote's house, Bank Top, Hindle Vale, is almost vast, for the house is one of those great old-fashioned places standing in ample grounds that are to be found on the outskirts of the smaller Lancashire manufacturing towns. They are inhabited by wealthy manufacturers who have resisted the temptation to live at St. Anne's-on-the-Sea, or Blackpool. In the wall facing the spectator is the door from the hall, which when the door is open can be seen distinctly, a big square place. The fireplace is in the right-hand wall, and a bow window in the left-hand one. The furniture is solid and costly, but the room is comfortable and looks as if it is intended to be lived in. A table stands in the middle, a sideboard near the door, arm-chairs near the hearth, whilst other chairs and furniture (including a bookcase filled with stand-

ard works) complete the rather ponderous interior. The Jeffcotes use the breakfast-room for all meals except ceremonious ones, when the dining-room is requisitioned and an elaborate dinner is substituted for the high tea which Nathaniel persists in regarding as an essential of comfort and homeliness. It is about 10.30 on the same Bank Holiday evening. The room is well lighted by gas, not electricity, but of course there is no fire.

NATHANIEL JEFFCOTE and his wife are sitting alone in the room. He is a tall, thin, gaunt, withered, domineering man of sixty. When excited or angry he drops into dialect, but otherwise his speech, though flat, is fairly accurate. MRS. JEFFCOTE has even more fully adapted herself to the responsibilities and duties imposed by the possession of wealth. She is a plump, mild, and good-natured woman. She sits under the chandelier embroidering, whilst her husband sits in an arm-chair by the empty hearth working calculations in a small shiny black notebook, which he carries about with him everywhere, in a side pocket.

MRS. JEFFCOTE. I asked Mrs. Plews to let me have a look through Hindle Lodge to-day.

JEFFCOTE [*looking up*]. Eh? What's that?

MRS. JEFFCOTE. Mrs. Plews is leaving Hindle Lodge at Christmas.

JEFFCOTE. What of it?

MRS. JEFFCOTE. I was thinking it would do very well for Alan when he gets married.

JEFFCOTE. Is Alan talking about getting married?

MRS. JEFFCOTE. Beatrice was mentioning it last week.

JEFFCOTE. How long have they been engaged? A year?

MRS. JEFFCOTE. Eleven months. I remember it was on September the 5th that it happened.

JEFFCOTE. How on earth can you remember that?

MRS. JEFFCOTE. Because September the 5th is your birthday.

JEFFCOTE. Is it? [*He grunts.*] Well, eleven months isn't so long after all. Let 'em wait a bit longer.

MRS. JEFFCOTE. I thought we might be speaking for the Lodge.

JEFFCOTE. What do they want with a house like the Lodge? Isn't there plenty of room here? We've got four living-rooms and fourteen bedrooms in this house, and there's never more than three of them going at the same time.

MRS. JEFFCOTE. Really, Nat! They'll want a house of their own, no matter how many bedrooms we've got empty, and it's only natural.

JEFFCOTE. There's no hurry as far as I can see. Alan won't be twenty-five till next March, will he?

MRS. JEFFCOTE. You were only twenty-two when you married me.

JEFFCOTE. I didn't marry a girl who'd been brought up like Beatrice Farrar. I married a girl who could help me to make money. Beatrice won't do that. She'll help to spend it, likely.

MRS. JEFFCOTE. Well, he'll have it to spend. What's money for?

JEFFCOTE. Money's power. That's why I like money. Not for what it can buy.

MRS. JEFFCOTE. All the same, you've always done yourself pretty well, Nat.

JEFFCOTE. Because it pays in the long run. And it's an outward sign. Why did I buy a motor-car? Not because I wanted to go motoring. I hate it. I bought it so that people could see Alan driving about in it, and say, "There's Jeffcote's lad in his new car. It cost five hundred quid." Tim Farrar was so keen on getting his knighthood for the same reason. Every one knows that him and me started life in a weaving shed. That's why we like to have something to show 'em how well we've done. That's why we put some of our brass into houses and motors and knighthoods and fancy articles of the kind. I've put a deal of brass into our Alan, and Tim Farrar's put a deal into his Beatrice, with just the same object in view.

[*There is a short pause.* JEFFCOTE

goes on with his reckoning and MRS. JEFFCOTE *with her sewing. Then she speaks quietly.*]

MRS. JEFFCOTE. I was wondering what you intend to do for Alan when he gets married.

JEFFCOTE. Do for him? What do you mean?

MRS. JEFFCOTE. He doesn't get a regular salary, does he?

JEFFCOTE [*suspiciously*]. Has Alan been putting you up to talk to me about this?

MRS. JEFFCOTE. Well, Nat, if he has —?

JEFFCOTE. Why can't he talk to me himself?

MRS. JEFFCOTE [*placidly continuing*]. You're not such a good one to tackle. I daresay he thought I should do it better than he would.

JEFFCOTE. I don't keep him short, do I?

MRS. JEFFCOTE. No. But Sir Timothy will expect him to show something more definite before the wedding.

JEFFCOTE. Tim Farrar don't need to be afraid. I hope he'll leave his lass as much as I shall leave Alan. That lad'll be the richest man in Hindle some day.

MRS. JEFFCOTE. I daresay. Some day! That's not much good to set up house on. Why don't you take him into partnership?

JEFFCOTE. Partnership?

MRS. JEFFCOTE. You always say he works hard enough.

JEFFCOTE [*grudgingly*]. Well enough.

MRS. JEFFCOTE. I suppose it comes to this. You don't want to take him into partnership because it would mean parting with some of that power you're so fond of.

JEFFCOTE. He mightn't work so well if he was his own master.

MRS. JEFFCOTE. But if you gave him a junior partnership he wouldn't be his own master. You'd see to that.

JEFFCOTE [*jocularly dropping into dialect*]. Eh, lass! thou'd better come and manage mill thyself.

MRS. JEFFCOTE. I shouldn't make such a bad job of it, neither! Remember that if you take him in you'll have less work to do yourself. He'll share the responsibility.

JEFFCOTE. Hold on a bit. The owd cock's not done with yet.

MRS. JEFFCOTE. If Beatrice starts talking about the date —

JEFFCOTE. Oh, if you'll stop your worritting I daresay I'll take the lad into partnership on his wedding-day.

MRS. JEFFCOTE. Can I tell Sir Timothy that?

JEFFCOTE. If you like. I told him myself six months ago.

MRS. JEFFCOTE. You *are* a caution, Nat, indeed you are! Why couldn't you tell me so at once, instead of making a fool of me like this?

JEFFCOTE. I like to hear thee talking, lass.

[*Having brought off this characteristic stroke of humour,* JEFFCOTE *resumes his work. The door opens and* ADA *comes in.*]

ADA. If you please, sir, there's someone to see you.

JEFFCOTE [*absorbed*]. Eh?

MRS. JEFFCOTE. Who is it, Ada?

ADA. His name's Hawthorn, ma'am.

MRS. JEFFCOTE. It'll be Christopher Hawthorn, Nat.

JEFFCOTE. What does he want coming so late as this? Fetch him in here.

[ADA *goes out.*]

Can't be owt wrong at the mill, seeing it's Bank Holiday.

[ADA *shows in* CHRISTOPHER, *who stands near the door.*]

MRS. JEFFCOTE. Good-evening, Mr. Hawthorn.

CHRISTOPHER. Good-evening, Mrs. Jeffcote.

JEFFCOTE [*rising*]. Well, Chris!

CHRISTOPHER. Well, Nat!

[*These two old comrades address each other by their first names although master and man.*]

JEFFCOTE. Sit down. The rain's held off.

CHRISTOPHER. Ay! [*He is obviously ill at ease.*]

MRS. JEFFCOTE. Where have you been these Wakes.

CHRISTOPHER. Nowhere.

MRS. JEFFCOTE. What? Stopped at home?

CHRISTOPHER. Ay! Somehow we don't

seem quite as keen on Blackpool as we used to be. And the missus was badly last week with her leg, and what with one thing and another we let it drift this time round. You've not been away, either?

MRS. JEFFCOTE. No, we went to Norway in June, you know.

CHRISTOPHER. Ay! so you did. That must be a fine place — from the pictures.

MRS. JEFFCOTE. Alan is away, though. He is motoring in North Wales. We expect him back to-night.

JEFFCOTE. Business is too bad to go away, Chris. I was down in Manchester Tuesday and Friday. It isn't Wakes in Manchester, thou knows!

CHRISTOPHER. Anything doing?

JEFFCOTE. I landed ten sets of those brown jacconets on Friday. Five for October and five for November.

CHRISTOPHER. For the forty-four inch looms?

JEFFCOTE. Ay! And hark you, Chris! they're complaining about the tint. Not bright enough, they say in India. They've sent a pattern over this mail. You'd better have a look at it to-morrow. We've got to give them what they want, I reckon.

CHRISTOPHER. I don't think they do know what they want in India, Nat.

JEFFCOTE. You're about right there, Chris.

[*A pause.* CHRISTOPHER *looks uncomfortably at* MRS. JEFFCOTE.]

JEFFCOTE [*at length*]. When are you going to bed, mother?

MRS. JEFFCOTE [*taking the hint*]. Any time now.

JEFFCOTE. That's right. Just reach me the whisky before you go.

[MRS. JEFFCOTE *gets a bottle of whisky, a syphon and glasses from the sideboard cupboard.*]

MRS. JEFFCOTE. Are you going to sit up for Alan?

JEFFCOTE. Why? Hasn't he got his latchkey?

MRS. JEFFCOTE. I expect so.

JEFFCOTE. Then I reckon he'll be able to find the keyhole, and if he can't he won't thank me for sitting up to welcome him.

MRS. JEFFCOTE [*smiling*]. You do talk some nonsense, Nat. Good-night, Mr. Hawthorn.

CHRISTOPHER [*rising*]. Good-night, Mrs. Jeffcote.

[MRS. JEFFCOTE *goes out of the room.*]

JEFFCOTE. Have a drink, Chris?

CHRISTOPHER. No, thanks, Nat.

JEFFCOTE [*incredulously*]. Get away!

CHRISTOPHER. Well — just a small one, then.

[JEFFCOTE *pours out two drinks.*]

JEFFCOTE. Light your pipe, Chris.

CHRISTOPHER. Ay! Thanks.

[*He does so.*]

JEFFCOTE. It's a long while since we had a quiet chat together. We don't see so much of each other as we did thirty years ago?

CHRISTOPHER. No. You've other fish to fry, I reckon.

JEFFCOTE. I'm always right glad to see you. How long have you been taping for me, Chris?

CHRISTOPHER. I came to you in '95. I remember because Joe Walmesley's shed was burnt down the same year.

JEFFCOTE. Ay! That was during the General Election, when Tories knocked out Mark Smethurst in Hindle. Joe was speaking at one of Mark's meetings when they come and told him his mill was afire. That was the only time I ever saw Joe Walmesley cry.

CHRISTOPHER. He was fond of them looms, was Joe!

JEFFCOTE. You missed your way, Chris, you did indeed, when you wouldn't come in with me and put your savings into Trafalgar Mill.

CHRISTOPHER. That's what the missus is never tired of telling me.

JEFFCOTE. You might have been my partner these fifteen years instead of only my slasher.

CHRISTOPHER. You'd never have got on with a partner, Nat. You're too fond of your own way.

JEFFCOTE. You're right there. I've been used to it for a good while now.

CHRISTOPHER. You don't remember Daisy Bank being built, Nat?

JEFFCOTE. No. I was living over Blackburn way then.

CHRISTOPHER. I was only a lad at the time. I used to come along the river bank on Sundays with the other lads. There were no weaving sheds in Hindle Vale in those days, nothing but fields all the way to Harwood Bridge. Daisy Bank was the first shed put up outside Hindle proper. They called it Daisy Bank because of the daisies in the meadows. All the side of the brow falling away towards the river was thick with them. Thick dotted it was, like the stars in the sky of a clear night.

JEFFCOTE. Look here, old lad, thou didn't come up here at this time of night just to talk about daisies.

CHRISTOPHER. Eh?

JEFFCOTE. You've come up here with a purpose, haven't you?

CHRISTOPHER. That's so, Nat.

JEFFCOTE. I could see that. That's why I sent the missus to bed. I know you of old. What is it that's troubling you? Get it off your chest!

CHRISTOPHER. It's about my lass.

JEFFCOTE. Hullo!

CHRISTOPHER. I'm worried about her.

JEFFCOTE. What's she been doing?

CHRISTOPHER. Getting into trouble.

JEFFCOTE. What sort of trouble?

CHRISTOPHER [*troubled*]. Well, thou knows — there's only one sort of trouble —

JEFFCOTE. Ay — ay! With a lad?

CHRISTOPHER. Ay!

[*There is a slight pause.*]

CHRISTOPHER. It's only by chance we found it out. The missus is in a fine way about it, I can tell you!

JEFFCOTE. Then it's proper serious, like?

CHRISTOPHER. They've been away together, these Wakes.

JEFFCOTE [*whistling*]. Humph! She's a cool customer. What art going to do in the matter?

CHRISTOPHER. That's what I've come up to see thee about. I wasn't for coming to-night, but missus, she was set on it.

JEFFCOTE. Quite right, too. I'll help thee any road I can. But you mustn't take it too much to heart. It's not the first time a job like this has happened in Hindle, and it won't be the last!

CHRISTOPHER. That's true. But it's poor comfort when it's your own lass that's got into trouble.

JEFFCOTE. There's many a couple living happy to-day as first come together in that fashion.

CHRISTOPHER. Wedded, you mean?

JEFFCOTE. Ay! Wedded, of course. What else do you think I meant? Does the lad live in Hindle?

CHRISTOPHER. Ay!

[*He does not know how to break it to* JEFFCOTE.]

JEFFCOTE. Whose shed does he work at?

CHRISTOPHER. Well, since you put it that way, he works at yours.

JEFFCOTE. At Daisy Bank? Do I know him?

CHRISTOPHER. Ay! You know him well.

JEFFCOTE. Then by Gad! I'll have it out with him to-morrow. If he doesn't promise to wed thy Fanny I'll give him the sack!

CHRISTOPHER [*dazed*]. Give him the sack!

JEFFCOTE. And I'll go further. If he'll be a decent lad and make it right with her at once, I'll see that he's well looked after at the mill. We're old pals, Chris, and I can't do no fairer than that, can I?

CHRISTOPHER. No.

JEFFCOTE. Now, then, who's the chap?

CHRISTOPHER. Thou'll be a bit surprised-like, I reckon.

JEFFCOTE. Spit it out!

CHRISTOPHER. It's thy lad, Alan.

JEFFCOTE [*sharply*]. What? [*A slight pause.*] Say that again.

CHRISTOPHER. Thy lad, Alan.

JEFFCOTE. *My* lad?

CHRISTOPHER. Ay!

[*After a short pause,* JEFFCOTE *springs up in a blazing rage.*]

JEFFCOTE. Damn you, Chris Hawthorn! why the devil couldn't you tell me so before?

CHRISTOPHER. I were trying to tell thee, Nat —

JEFFCOTE. Trying to tell me! Hasn't thou got a tongue in thy head that thou mun sit there like a bundle of grey-cloth while I'm making a fool of myself this road? [*He paces up and down in his agitation.*] Here! How do you know it's Alan? Who says it's Alan?

CHRISTOPHER. Fanny.

JEFFCOTE. Fanny, eh? How do you know she's not lying?

CHRISTOPHER [*stoutly*]. You can settle it soon enough by asking Alan. I thought to have found him here to-night.

JEFFCOTE. He's not come home yet?

CHRISTOPHER. No.

JEFFCOTE. And a good job for him, too!

CHRISTOPHER. Wouldn't he fetch Fanny back, think you?

JEFFCOTE. Would he, the dickens! He's not altogether without sense. Do you think he'd run her in the car through Hindle market-place and up Burnley Road and set her down at your house for all the folk to see?

CHRISTOPHER. No.

JEFFCOTE [*suddenly flaring up again*]. The bally young fool! I'd like to break his silly neck for him! And that lass of thine is just as much to blame as he is! I've marked her — the hot-blooded little wench!

CHRISTOPHER. I can't defend her. She's always been a bit of a mystery to her mother and me. There's that in her veins as keeps her restless and uneasy. If she sees you want her to do one thing she'll go right away and do t'other out of pure cussedness. She won't be driven, not any road. I had a dog just like her once.

JEFFCOTE. Eh, old lad, it's a good job you never had any boys if you don't know how to manage a girl!

CHRISTOPHER. Happen I could have managed lads better. I never could clout a girl properly.

JEFFCOTE. I can manage my lad without clouting. Always could.

CHRISTOPHER. Folk are different, you see. Happen you couldn't have managed our Fanny.

JEFFCOTE. I'd have had a damn good try! Where is she now?

CHRISTOPHER. At the house. She was overdone, and I sent her to bed to get her out of range of the missus's tongue. She was talking rather bitter, like.

JEFFCOTE. She had a sharp way with her when she was Sarah Riley, had your missus, and I reckon it won't have improved with the passing of years! I shouldn't wonder if it was your missus who got the truth out of Fanny.

CHRISTOPHER. So it was.

JEFFCOTE. And what *did* she get out of her? Let's be knowing just what took place.

CHRISTOPHER. I can tell you nowt save that they stayed in Llandudno. You'll have to go to your lad for the rest of the story.

JEFFCOTE. All right. I'll see you to-morrow at the mill. There's nowt more to be done to-night.

CHRISTOPHER. Maybe it's a queer fancy, but I'd like to have seen him to-night. There's no chance of him coming in shortly, think you?

JEFFCOTE. He may come in the next five minutes, or he may not come home at all. There's no telling what may happen on Bank Holiday.

CHRISTOPHER. Then it's no use me waiting a while?

JEFFCOTE. Nay, you can't wait here. I'm going to bed. I'm not going to let this business spoil a night's rest. I'd advise you to look on it in the same light.

CHRISTOPHER. Ah, Nat, but it's not so hard on you as it is on me!

JEFFCOTE. Is it not? How do you know what plans of mine will come to naught through this job? [*More kindly.*] Come, old lad, thou mun clear out. Thou can do nowt here.

CHRISTOPHER. Well, I've not said all that my missus told me to say, and I doubt she'll be on my track, but I reckon it's a bit too previous afore we've seen the lad.

JEFFCOTE. If your wife wants to say anything to me, she's welcome. You'd better fetch her up here to-morrow night, and bring Fanny along as well. I'll be ready for you by then.

CHRISTOPHER. To-morrow night?

JEFFCOTE. About nine o'clock. Do you understand?

CHRISTOPHER. Ay! [*He goes to the door, and* JEFFCOTE *rises.*] My wife said —

JEFFCOTE [*curtly*]. I can guess all that thy wife said. You can tell her this from me. I'll see you're treated right. Do you hear? [JEFFCOTE *opens the door.*]

CHRISTOPHER. I can't ask for more than that.

JEFFCOTE. I'll see you're treated right. [*They go into the hall out of sight.* ADA *comes into the room with a tray which she places on the table. The tray holds bread, cheese, butter, a bottle of beer and a tumbler.*]

JEFFCOTE [*out of sight in the hall*]. I'm not afraid of thy wife, if *you* are.

[*The front door bangs.* JEFFCOTE *returns into the room and sees the tray, which he examines irritably.*]

JEFFCOTE. What's this for?

ADA. Mr. Alan's tray, sir. We always leave it when he's out late.

JEFFCOTE [*flaring up*]. Take it away!

ADA. Take it away, sir?

JEFFCOTE. Yes. Do you hear? Take the damned thing away!

ADA. What about Mr. Alan's supper, sir?

JEFFCOTE. Let him do without.

ADA. Yes, sir.

[ADA *takes the tray out.* JEFFCOTE *watches her, and then goes to the window to see if it is fastened.* MRS. JEFFCOTE, *mostly undressed and attired in a dressing-wrap, appears in the hall.*]

MRS. JEFFCOTE. Nat?

JEFFCOTE. What do *you* want?

MRS. JEFFCOTE. Is anything the matter?

JEFFCOTE. Why?

MRS. JEFFCOTE. I thought I heard you swearing, that's all.

JEFFCOTE. Happen I was.

MRS. JEFFCOTE. You've not quarrelled with Christopher Hawthorn?

JEFFCOTE. No, we're the best of friends. He only wanted my opinion about summat.

MRS. JEFFCOTE. What had you got to swear about, then?

JEFFCOTE. I was giving him my opinion.

MRS. JEFFCOTE. Well, but —

JEFFCOTE. That's enough. Get along to bed with you. Maybe I'll tell you all about it to-morrow. Maybe I won't!

MRS. JEFFCOTE. Well, I'm glad it's no worse. I thought you were coming to blows.

[MRS. JEFFCOTE *goes out and upstairs.* JEFFCOTE *sees the two glasses of whisky and soda which neither of the men has remembered to touch. He takes his own and drinks it.* ADA *appears.*]

ADA. Please, sir, do you want anything else?

JEFFCOTE. No. Get to bed. [*She is going.*] Have the other girls gone upstairs yet?

ADA. Yes, sir.

JEFFCOTE. And you've fastened the back door?

ADA. Yes, sir.

JEFFCOTE. Good-night.

ADA. Good-night, sir.

[ADA *goes upstairs.* JEFFCOTE *slowly drinks the second glass of whisky and soda. He puts both the empty glasses on the sideboard and looks round the room. He turns out all the gases except one, which he leaves very low. He goes out into the hall, leaving the breakfast-room door open, and is seen to go out of sight to the front door, as if to assure himself that it is on the latch. Then he turns the hall gas very low indeed, and goes upstairs.*]

CURTAIN

SCENE 3

The curtain rises again immediately. The scene is the same room about two hours later, that is to say at about one o'clock in the morning. Everything looks just the same. At first there is silence. Then is heard the scratching noise of a latch-key being inserted into the front door. The process takes some time. At last the door is heard to open, and someone stumbles in, making rather too much noise. The door is closed very quietly. A match is struck in the hall, out of sight. It goes out at once. Then a figure is dimly seen to appear in the doorway of the breakfast-room, lean against the jamb and look around. It is ALAN JEFFCOTE, who if he could be seen distinctly would be found a well-made, plump, easy-going young fellow, with a weak but healthy and attractive face and fair hair. He is of the type that runs to stoutness after thirty, unless diet and exercise are carefully attended to. At present he is too fond of luxury and good living to leave any doubt that this pleasant fellow of twenty-five will be a gross, fleshly man at forty. He is dressed by a good Manchester tailor, and everything he has is of the best. He does not stint his father's money. He has been to the Manchester Grammar School and Manchester University, but he has not lost the characteristic Hindle burr in his accent, though he speaks correctly as a rule. He does not ever speak affectedly, so that his speech harmonises with that of the other characters. This is important, for though he has had a far better education than any of the other characters except BEATRICE, he is essentially one of them, a Hindle man. He has no feeling that he is provincial, or that the provinces are not the principal asset of England. London he looks upon as a place where rich Lancashire men go for a spree, if they have not time to go to Monte Carlo or Paris. Manchester he looks upon as the centre or headquarters for Lancashire manufacturers, and therefore more important than London. But after all he thinks that Manchester is merely the office for Hindle and the other Lancashire towns, which are the actual source of wealth. Therefore Hindle, Blackburn, Bolton, Oldham, and the rest are far more important in his eyes than London or Manchester, and perhaps he is right. Anyhow, the feeling gives him sufficient assurance to stroll into the most fashionable hotels and restaurants, conscious that he can afford to pay for whatever he fancies, that he can behave himself, that he can treat the waiters with the confidence of an aristocrat born — and yet be patently a Lancashire man. He would never dream of trying to conceal the fact, nor indeed could he understand why anybody should wish to try and conceal such a thing. He is now slightly intoxicated, not seriously drunk, only what he would himself describe as "a bit tight." He strikes another match and lurches towards the gas, only to find that it is already lighted. He blows out the match and tries to turn up the gas. As he reaches up he knocks a small bronze vase off the end of the mantel-piece. It falls into the fire-irons with an appalling crash.

ALAN. Curse it!

[He turns up the gas and clumsily picks up and replaces the vase. He sees on the mantel-piece a couple of letters addressed to him. He tears them open, stares at them, and crams them unread into his pocket. Then he gazes at the table as if in search of something.]

ALAN. Where's that tray? Where the devil's that tray?

[He shakes his head and proceeds to look in the sideboard cupboard for food. He can find none, so he turns to the whisky and soda, and fills one of the empty glasses. This he puts on the mantel-piece, and then he sits in the arm-chair by the hearth, sinks back and holds his head in his hands. He seems to be going to sleep.

In the hall is observed a flickering light, coming nearer by degrees. Old NATHANIEL JEFFCOTE appears, a lean picturesque figure in pyjamas and dressing-gown, carrying in one hand a lighted bedroom candle and in the other a poker. He comes to the door of the room, stands at the threshold and contemplates his son. At length ALAN seems to feel that he is not alone, for he slowly steals a glance round to the door, and encounters his father's stern gaze.]

ALAN. Hello! [He smiles amiably.] Thought you were in bed.

JEFFCOTE. So it's you, is it? What are you making all this din about?

ALAN. 'S not my fault. You don't s'pose I did it on purpose, do you?

JEFFCOTE. I'll not have you coming in and raising Cain at this time of night. It's enough to waken the dead!

ALAN. I can't help it. They go and stick that beastly thing up there! [*He points to the vase.*] Can't blame me for knocking it over. 'S not my fault. [*He hiccoughs.*] I can't help it.

JEFFCOTE. Are you drunk?

ALAN [*rising and standing with his back to the hearth in a dignified way*]. You've never seen me drunk yet! [*He hiccoughs.*]

[JEFFCOTE *approaches him and scrutinises him by the light of the candle.*]

JEFFCOTE. I've never seen thee nearer drunk, anyhow. Thou didn't drive the car home in this state, surely?

ALAN. No fear!

JEFFCOTE. Where have you left it?

ALAN. At "George and Dragon," in Hindle.

JEFFCOTE. I see. You've been at "George and Dragon"? Didn't they chuck you out at eleven?

ALAN. Ay! Then we went round to the Liberal Club.

JEFFCOTE. Who's "we"?

ALAN. Me and George Ramsbottom.

JEFFCOTE. Has George Ramsbottom been with you this week-end?

ALAN. No. I met him at the "Midland" at Manchester. We had a bit of dinner together.

JEFFCOTE. Ah! Where's George Ramsbottom been during the week-end?

ALAN. After his own devices.

JEFFCOTE. Humph! Like thyself, no doubt?

ALAN. Happen!

JEFFCOTE. What's thou been up to these Wakes?

ALAN. Nothing. Why?

JEFFCOTE [*holding the candle up to* ALAN'S *face*]. Hast been with a girl?

ALAN [*flinching slightly*]. No.

JEFFCOTE. Thou hardened young liar!

ALAN [*staggered*]. Why?

JEFFCOTE [*looking hard at him*]. Chris Hawthorn's been here to-night.

ALAN [*vaguely*]. Chris Hawthorn?

JEFFCOTE. Ay!

[ALAN *cannot bear his father's gaze. He is not able to keep up the pretence of coolness any longer. He turns towards the arm-chair and stumbles into it, his attitude of collapse denoting surrender.*]

JEFFCOTE. Thou cursed young fool! I could find it in my heart to take a strap to thee, so I could. Why hadn't thou the sense to pay for thy pleasures, instead of getting mixed up with a straight girl? I've never kept thee short of brass. And if thou must have a straight girl, thou might have kept off one from the mill. Let alone her father's one of my oldest friends.

ALAN. What does he say?

JEFFCOTE. Say? What dost thou think he said? Does thou think as he come up here to return thanks?

ALAN. But — but, how did he know?

JEFFCOTE. The lass has told them, so it appears.

ALAN. She promised not to.

JEFFCOTE. Happen she did. And what then?

ALAN. What's going to be done?

JEFFCOTE. I said I'd see him treated right.

ALAN [*brightening*]. What'll they take?

JEFFCOTE [*dangerously*]. I said I'd see them treated right. If thou expects I'm going to square it with a cheque, and that thou's going to slip away scot free, thou's sadly mistaken.

ALAN. What do you want me to do?

JEFFCOTE. I know what thou's going to do. Thou's going to wed the lass.

ALAN. What do you say?

JEFFCOTE. Thou's heard me all right.

ALAN. Wed her? Fanny Hawthorn!

JEFFCOTE. Ay! Fanny Hawthorn.

ALAN. But I cannot.

JEFFCOTE. Why not?

ALAN. You know — Beatrice — I can't!

JEFFCOTE. Thou mun tell Beatrice it's off.

ALAN. How can I do that?

JEFFCOTE. That's thy look-out.

ALAN [*rising and holding on to the mantelpiece*]. Look here. I can't do it. It isn't fair to Beatrice.

JEFFCOTE. It's a pity thou didn't think of that before thou went to Llandudno!
ALAN. But what can I tell her?
JEFFCOTE. Thou mun tell her the truth if thou can't find owt better to say.
ALAN. The truth!
[ALAN *again collapses in the chair. A pause.*]
JEFFCOTE. What's done is done. We've got to stand by it.
ALAN. Father! I don't want to wed Fanny. I want to wed Beatrice.
JEFFCOTE. Dost thou love Beatrice?
ALAN. Yes.
JEFFCOTE. I'm glad of it. It's right that thou should suffer as well as her.
[ALAN *is overcome, and drops into dialect as he pleads.*]
ALAN. Father, thou'll not make me do it! Thou'll not make me do it! I cannot. I'd have all the folk in Hindle laughing at me.
[ALAN *breaks down, excitement and drink combined being too much for him.*]
JEFFCOTE [*brusquely*]. Come now, pull thyself together.
ALAN. Ay! It's easy talking that road.
JEFFCOTE. Thou art a man, now. Not a kid!
ALAN. It's me that's got to go through it. It doesn't hurt thee if I wed Fanny Hawthorn.
JEFFCOTE. Does it not?
ALAN. No.
JEFFCOTE. So thou thinks it easy for me to see thee wed Fanny Hawthorn? Hearken! Dost know how I began life? Dost know that I started as tenter in Walmesley's shed when I were eight years of age, and that when the time comes I shall leave the biggest fortune ever made in the cotton trade in Hindle? Dost know what my thought has been when labouring these thirty years to get all that brass together? Not what pleasure I could get out of spending, but what power and influence I were piling up the while. I was set on founding a great firm that would be famous not only all over Lancashire but all over the world, like Horrockses or Calverts or Hornbys of Blackburn. Dost think as I weren't right glad when thou goes and gets engaged to Tim Farrar's lass? Tim Farrar as were Mayor of Hindle and got knighted when the King come to open the new Town Hall. Tim Farrar that owns Lane End Shed, next biggest place to Daisy Bank in Hindle. Why, it were the dearest wish of my heart to see thee wed Tim Farrar's lass; and, happen, to see thee running both mills afore I died. And now what falls out? Lad as I'd looked to to keep on the tradition and build the business bigger still, goes and weds one of my own weavers! Dost think that's no disappointment to me? Hearken! I'd put down ten thousand quid if thou could honestly wed Beatrice Farrar. But thou can't honestly wed her, not if I put down a million. There's only one lass thou can honestly wed now, and that's Fanny Hawthorn, and by God I'm going to see that thou does it!

[JEFFCOTE *stalks out of the room with his candle and his poker, which he has never put down, and* ALAN *remains huddled up and motionless in a corner of the arm-chair.*]

CURTAIN

ACT II

The scene is again the breakfast-room at the JEFFCOTES' *house. It is shortly after 8 P.M. on the day following that on which the First Act took place. The evening meal, tea, is just over. Only* MR. *and* MRS. JEFFCOTE *have partaken of it.* ADA *has almost finished clearing away, there is a loaded tray on the sideboard and the coloured cloth is not yet spread, although the white cloth has been removed.* MRS. JEFFCOTE *is sitting by the hearth, and* JEFFCOTE *is standing with his back to the empty fireplace filling his pipe. It is not yet dark, but the light is fading.*

JEFFCOTE [*to* ADA]. Come now, lass, be sharp with your siding away.
[ADA *is about to spread the coloured cloth.* MRS. JEFFCOTE *rises and assists her.*]

Mrs. Jeffcote. Give me that end, Ada. [*They spread the cloth whilst* Jeffcote *lights his pipe, and then* Ada *hurries out with the tray.*]

Jeffcote. That girl wants wakening up.

Mrs. Jeffcote. What are you in such a hurry about, Nat?

Jeffcote. I've got summat to say to you.

Mrs. Jeffcote. Something to say to me. Why couldn't you say it whilst we were having tea?

Jeffcote. It's not quite the sort of thing to say before the servant.

Mrs. Jeffcote [*surprised*]. Why, Nat, what is it?

Jeffcote. Last night you were talking of taking Hindle Lodge for Alan?

Mrs. Jeffcote. Yes. I was going to call on Mrs. Plews this afternoon, only it came on wet.

Jeffcote [*briefly*]. Don't go.

Mrs. Jeffcote. Why not?

Jeffcote. There's no need.

Mrs. Jeffcote. Surely, Nat, you've not changed your mind again?

Jeffcote. Alan won't want to live in a place like Hindle Lodge.

Mrs. Jeffcote. His wife will.

Jeffcote. How do you know that?

Mrs. Jeffcote. I've asked her.

Jeffcote. Nay, you've not.

Mrs. Jeffcote. Why, Nat, I mentioned it to Beatrice only a week ago.

Jeffcote. Happen you did. Alan's not going to marry Beatrice.

Mrs. Jeffcote [*dumbfoundered*]. Not going to marry — [*She stops.*]

Jeffcote. That's what I said.

Mrs. Jeffcote. Why? Have they quarrelled?

Jeffcote. No.

Mrs. Jeffcote. Then, what's the matter? What has happened? When did you get to know about it?

Jeffcote. I first got to know about it last night.

Mrs. Jeffcote. That was what you were talking to Alan about when you went downstairs last night?

Jeffcote. Aye!

Mrs. Jeffcote. And you said you were lecturing him on coming home so late. Why didn't you tell me the truth?

Jeffcote. I knew you'd learn it soon enough, and I didn't want to spoil your night's rest.

Mrs. Jeffcote. Why didn't you tell me to-day, then?

Jeffcote. I've been at the Mill all day.

Mrs. Jeffcote. You could have told me as soon as you came home.

Jeffcote. I didn't want to spoil your tea for you.

Mrs. Jeffcote [*wiping her eyes*]. As if that mattered!

Jeffcote. Well, then, I didn't want to spoil *my* tea.

Mrs. Jeffcote. Oh! Nat, what is it that's happened?

Jeffcote. To put it in a nutshell, Alan's not going to marry Beatrice because another girl has a better right to him.

Mrs. Jeffcote. But how can that be? He's been engaged to Beatrice for nearly a year.

Jeffcote [*grimly*]. Ay! He's only been engaged to Beatrice. With the other girl he's gone a step further.

Mrs. Jeffcote. He's not gone and got wed already?

Jeffcote. No. He's not got wed. He dispensed with the ceremony.

Mrs. Jeffcote. Dispensed with it?

Jeffcote. Did without.

Mrs. Jeffcote [*shocked*]. Oh, Nat!

Jeffcote. Ay. He spent last week-end with a girl at Llandudno.

Mrs. Jeffcote. The creature!

Jeffcote. Eh?

Mrs. Jeffcote [*indignantly*]. Why are such women allowed to exist?

Jeffcote [*scratching his head*]. Thou mun ask me another. I never looked on it in that light before.

Mrs. Jeffcote. And at Llandudno, too, of all places. Why, I've been there many a time.

Jeffcote. What's that got to do with it?

Mrs. Jeffcote. I shall never be able to fancy it again! And I'm so fond of the place.

Jeffcote. That's a pity. Happen

you'll get over the feeling when they're married.

Mrs. Jeffcote. But Nat, it's impossible! Alan can't marry a woman of that sort!

Jeffcote. She's not a woman of that sort. She's a straight girl.

Mrs. Jeffcote. How can you call her that?

Jeffcote. Well, you know what I mean. It's not been a matter of business with her.

Mrs. Jeffcote. I don't see that that makes things any better. There might have been some excuse for her if it had been a matter of business. Really, Nat, you must see that the woman is not fit to marry Alan!

Jeffcote. Not quite so fast. You don't even know who she is yet.

Mrs. Jeffcote. Whoever she is, if she's not above going away for the week-end with a man she can't be fit to marry our son.

Jeffcote. Not even when our son's the man she's been away with?

Mrs. Jeffcote. That has nothing to do with the case. It is evident that she is a girl with absolutely no principles.

Jeffcote. Dash it all! at that rate some folk might say that Alan's not fit to marry her because of what he's done.

Mrs. Jeffcote. Well, if you can't see the difference —

[*He does not choose to. She shrugs her shoulders and continues.*]

I'm surprised at you, Nat, I really am. You seem to take a delight in being perverse and making difficulties.

Jeffcote. Upon my soul, mother, I'd no idea thou were such an unscrupulous one before. Don't you want to do what's right?

Mrs. Jeffcote. Can't you offer the girl some money?

Jeffcote. Would you think that right treatment?

Mrs. Jeffcote. She wouldn't object. She'd jump at it.

Jeffcote. Shall I tell you who she is?

Mrs. Jeffcote. Of course you'll tell me who she is. Though that won't make me much wiser, for I don't suppose I've ever heard her name before.

Jeffcote. What makes you think that?

Mrs. Jeffcote. I'm sure nobody I know would do a thing like that.

Jeffcote. She's not exactly a friend of yours, but her father is a very old friend of mine. His name's Christopher Hawthorn.

Mrs. Jeffcote [*open-mouthed*]. What!

Jeffcote. And the lass is his daughter Fanny.

Mrs. Jeffcote. Fanny Hawthorn! Do you mean to tell me that the lad's going to marry one of our own weavers? Why, Nat, you must be out of your senses!

Jeffcote [*stubbornly*]. 'Think so?

Mrs. Jeffcote. Why, all the folk in Hindle will be laughing at us.

Jeffcote. Anything else?

Mrs. Jeffcote. I should just think I have got something else. What about Timothy Farrar, for instance? Have you thought what he'll say?

Jeffcote. What does it matter what Tim Farrar says?

Mrs. Jeffcote. There's Beatrice.

Jeffcote. Ay! there's Beatrice. I'm right sorry for that girl. But there's the other girl to be considered, mind you.

Mrs. Jeffcote. Does Beatrice know yet?

Jeffcote. No. I told Alan we'd go up to Farrar's to-night and have it out with them.

Mrs. Jeffcote. Perhaps he's there now.

Jeffcote. Nay. He'll not be back from Manchester yet. He was stopping later because Raleigh's had got a cable in from India, and it wasn't translated when I left. Business before pleasure, mother!

Mrs. Jeffcote. Then, thank goodness, it's not too late.

Jeffcote. What do you mean by that?

Mrs. Jeffcote. This affair has got to be stopped.

Jeffcote. Now, old lass, don't thou start meddling with what doesn't concern thee.

Mrs. Jeffcote. That's a nice thing! It concerns me as much as you. I've a right to have my say when it comes to a wife for Alan, and I'll not give way without a struggle to a girl like Fanny Hawthorn.

Jeffcote. Come, now, what's wrong with her, after all?

Mrs. Jeffcote. She's a girl without any character.

Jeffcote. Now, I should say she's a girl with a good deal of character.

Mrs. Jeffcote. The wrong sort.

Jeffcote. How do you know that? We don't know what made her go away with Alan.

Mrs. Jeffcote. I do. It was one of two things. Either she's thoroughly wicked, or else she was simply trying to make him marry her, and whichever it was it's evident she's no fit wife for Alan.

Jeffcote. Alan should have thought of that earlier.

Mrs. Jeffcote. You are taking much too serious a view of this affair, Nat; you are, indeed. Mind you, I'm not defending what Alan's done. I'm as shocked as anyone. I know it's a sin, and a grievous one too. What puzzles me is how he could do it. I wonder what made him. I don't know where he got it from. I'm sure he didn't get it from my side of the family!

Jeffcote. Happen he got it from Adam.

Mrs. Jeffcote. Very well, then, all the more reason why you should overlook it.

Jeffcote. We can't overlook them sort of things in Lancashire same as we could in the Garden of Eden.

Mrs. Jeffcote. If you can't overlook it altogether there's no reason why you should want to punish the lad like this. It's just cruelty, that's what it is, to make him marry a girl out of the Mill.

Jeffcote. You mean she's beneath him?

Mrs. Jeffcote. Of course she's beneath him.

Jeffcote. It's queer what short memories some folks have! What was my father, I should like to know? And thine, too, if it comes to that? Why, I wore clogs myself until I was past twenty.

Mrs. Jeffcote. Yes, and if you don't look out your grandson will wear them again. Don't forget the old saying: "There's three generations from clogs to clogs."

Jeffcote. A man may wear worse things than clogs. They're grand tackle for keeping the feet out of the wet.

Mrs. Jeffcote. Don't talk so foolishly, Nat! I know as well as you do that before you die you're hoping to see Alan a big man. Member for Hindle, perhaps. You know whether a wife like Fanny Hawthorn would be a hindrance to him or not.

Jeffcote. If a man's wife gets in the road of his career, then his career will have to suffer.

Mrs. Jeffcote. And everyone knows what that means. He'll be blaming her all the time for standing in his light, and' so his home life will be ruined as well.

Jeffcote. Marriage is a ticklish business anyhow. There's always the chance of a bust-up.

Mrs. Jeffcote. Chance, indeed! It's as sure as Fate if Alan marries Fanny, and you know that. They'll be separated in five years. We've seen cases like that before.

Jeffcote. And shall again, I've little doubt.

Mrs. Jeffcote. Well, Alan's shan't be one of them if I can help it.

Jeffcote. But you can't, old lass. I wear the breeches in this house.

Mrs. Jeffcote. I'll be no party to it, anyhow! It shan't be said that I didn't lift my voice against the wedding.

[Mrs. Jeffcote *is nearly sobbing by this time. The room is in semi-darkness.* Jeffcote *listens.*]

Jeffcote. There's the front door. It'll be Alan. Come now, mother, don't make a scene.

[Mrs. Jeffcote *wipes her eyes.* Ada *comes in.*]

Ada. If you please, ma'am, Sir Timothy Farrar and Miss Beatrice.

Mrs. Jeffcote. Oh! [*A pause.*] Mr. Alan hasn't come in yet?

Ada. No, ma'am.

Mrs. Jeffcote. Are they in the drawing-room?

Ada. Yes, ma'am.

Mrs. Jeffcote. Very well.

[Ada *withdraws.*]

Mrs. Jeffcote. Dear me, Nat, this is very awkward. Why doesn't Alan come home? It's too bad of him, it is indeed.

Jeffcote. He's ashamed to face his mother, happen?

Mrs. Jeffcote. He should know his mother better than that.

Jeffcote. Then he's trying to drive it too late to go up to Farrar's to-night.

Mrs. Jeffcote. That's more likely.

Jeffcote. Very well. He's reckoned without his dad. If he's too much of a coward to face the music himself, I'll do it for him.

Mrs. Jeffcote. What are you going to do?

Jeffcote. Just go and send Tim Farrar in here, while you keep Beatrice company in the other room.

Mrs. Jeffcote. Are you going to tell him?

Jeffcote. Ay!

Mrs. Jeffcote. But what shall I say to Beatrice?

Jeffcote. Say nowt.

Mrs. Jeffcote. But I can't talk to her just as if nothing has happened. It would be like deceiving her. I'm not cut out for a hypocrite.

Jeffcote. All right. Tell her everything. She'll have to know some time.

Mrs. Jeffcote [pleading]. Need she ever know?

Jeffcote. Whatever falls out, it's not going to be hushed up.

Mrs. Jeffcote. Strike a light, Nat. [He lights the gas.] Do I look as if I'd been crying?

Jeffcote. Why? Have you been crying?

Mrs. Jeffcote. No.

Jeffcote. It doesn't show. Nothing to speak of.

[Mrs. Jeffcote goes out, and Jeffcote lights the other gas-jets, until the room is brightly illuminated. He gets out the whisky and soda. Sir Timothy Farrar, a portly red-faced, rough Lancashire man of fifty-nine or so, with a scrubby growth of hair under his chin, appears in the doorway. He is much the coarsest and commonest person in the play.]

Jeffcote [curtly]. How do, Tim.

Sir Timothy. How do, Nat.

Jeffcote [nodding to a chair]. Sit you down.

Sir Timothy [choosing the best chair]. Ay — ay!

Jeffcote [holding out a cigar-box]. The old brand.

Sir Timothy [choosing the best cigar with deliberation]. I'll have a drop of whisky, too, Nat.

Jeffcote. Help yourself. [Jeffcote places the whisky handy, and then closes the door.] So they've made you Chairman of Hindle Education Committee, Tim?

Sir Timothy. Ay! Why not? Thou knows I were reet mon for the job.

Jeffcote. Thou's not done much studying since thou were eight year of age.

Sir Timothy. Happen I haven't. But I'm going to take damn good care that Hindle new Technical School is the finest in Lancashire. Or Yorkshire either, if it comes to that!

Jeffcote. Why not finest in England whilst you are about it?

Sir Timothy. If it's finest in Lancashire and Yorkshire it goes without saying it's finest in England. They don't know how to spend money on them in the South. Besides, what should they want with Technical Schools in them parts? They don't *make* anything to speak of.

Jeffcote. They're a poor lot, it's true.

Sir Timothy. I were in London all last week.

Jeffcote. Corporation business?

Sir Timothy. Ay!

Jeffcote. Expenses paid?

Sir Timothy. Ay!

Jeffcote. That's the style.

Sir Timothy. Where's the lad?

Jeffcote. Not got home yet.

Sir Timothy. Beatrice were expecting him to telephone all day, but he didn't. So as soon as we'd done eating she were on pins and needles to look him up.

Jeffcote. He was coming round to your place to-night.

Sir Timothy. I told the lass he'd be sure to. She hasn't seen him for ten days, thou knows, and that seems a long time when it's before the wedding. It doesn't seem so long afterwards. That reminds me! Have you seen *The Winning Post* this week?

JEFFCOTE. Nay. I rarely look at it.
SIR TIMOTHY. There's a tale in this week — it'll suit thee down to the ground.
JEFFCOTE. Hold on a bit. There's something I've a mind to tell you.
SIR TIMOTHY. Let me get mine off my chest first. It's about a fellow who took a girl away for the week-end —
JEFFCOTE. So's mine.
SIR TIMOTHY. Oh! It's the same one. [*He is disappointed.*]
JEFFCOTE. Nay, it isn't.
SIR TIMOTHY. How do you know?
JEFFCOTE. Mine's true.
SIR TIMOTHY. True, is it? [*He considers.*] Well, let's hear it. Who's the fellow?
JEFFCOTE. Chap out of Hindle.
SIR TIMOTHY [*looking him in the face*]. Here! Who's been giving me away?
JEFFCOTE. Eh?
SIR TIMOTHY. I say who's been giving me away?
JEFFCOTE. Thee? [*He stares at* SIR TIMOTHY *and then breaks into a roar of laughter.*] Thou's given thyself away, Tim Farrar. I wasn't talking about thee at all.
SIR TIMOTHY [*wiping his brow*]. Eh! I thought as someone had seen us at Brighton. I don't mind thee knowing, but if the wrong person gets hold of that sort of thing all Hindle is apt to hear about it. Well, who's the chap?
JEFFCOTE. Our Alan.
SIR TIMOTHY. What! The young devil! I'd like to give him a reet good hiding.
JEFFCOTE. Come. Thou'rt a nice man to talk, after what I've just learned.
SIR TIMOTHY. Hang it all, it's different with me! I'm not engaged to be wed. Why, I haven't even got a wife living. [*Fuming.*] The young beggar!
JEFFCOTE. I thought I'd better tell thee first.
SIR TIMOTHY. Ay — ay! I'll talk pretty straight to him.
JEFFCOTE. Perhaps you'll choose to tell Beatrice yourself.
SIR TIMOTHY. Tell who?
JEFFCOTE. Beatrice.
SIR TIMOTHY. Why? What's it got to do with her?

JEFFCOTE. Someone will have to tell her. She'll have to know sooner or later.
SIR TIMOTHY. God bless my soul, Nat Jeffcote! hast thou told thy missus everything thou did before thou got wed?
JEFFCOTE. I'd nowt to tell her.
SIR TIMOTHY. I always thought there was summat queer about thee, Nat. [*He shakes his head.*] Well, I'm not going to have Bee told of this affair, and that's flat. It's all over and done with.
JEFFCOTE. It's not all over. You don't understand. This girl is a decent girl, thou knows. Daughter of Chris Hawthorn.
SIR TIMOTHY. What! Him as slashes for thee?
JEFFCOTE. Ay!
SIR TIMOTHY. I've seen her. A sulky-looking wench. Well, I cannot see what difference it makes who the girl was. I reckon Alan's not going to marry her.
JEFFCOTE. That's just what he is going to do.
SIR TIMOTHY. What!
JEFFCOTE. You heard what I said.
SIR TIMOTHY. But he's going to marry my Beatrice.
JEFFCOTE. If he does he'll be had up for bigamy.
SIR TIMOTHY. Do you mean to say he's going to throw her over?
JEFFCOTE. There's no need to put it that way.
SIR TIMOTHY. There's no other way to put it if he weds Fanny Hawthorn.
JEFFCOTE. What else can he do?
SIR TIMOTHY. There's ways and means.
JEFFCOTE. For instance —
SIR TIMOTHY. It's only a question of money.
JEFFCOTE. Have you forgotten who she is?
SIR TIMOTHY. She's one of thy weavers. That'll cost thee a trifle more.
JEFFCOTE. She's daughter of one of my oldest friends.
SIR TIMOTHY. I'm one of thy oldest friends, likewise. What about my lass? Have you thought what a fool she'll look?
JEFFCOTE. I'm sorry. But t'other girl must come first. I think well enough of

Beatrice to know she'll see it in that light when it's put to her.

SIR TIMOTHY. And who's going to put it to her, I should like to know?

JEFFCOTE. You can put it to her yourself, if you've a mind.

SIR TIMOTHY. Dang it! It's a nice awkward thing to talk to a lass about. Here! before I go any further with this job I want to see Alan, and know for certain what he's going to do.

JEFFCOTE. He'll do what I tell him.

SIR TIMOTHY. I doubt it! I know he's a fool, but I don't think he's such a fool as all that.

[*The door opens and* ALAN *looks in.*]

SIR TIMOTHY. Why — talk of the devil —

ALAN. Hello, Sir Timothy! Has Bee come with you?

JEFFCOTE. She's with your mother in the drawing-room.

ALAN. Right.

[ALAN *is withdrawing when* JEFFCOTE *calls him back.*]

JEFFCOTE. Here! I say! Just wait awhile. We've summat to say to you.

[ALAN *comes in reluctantly.*]

JEFFCOTE. Anything fresh in Manchester?

ALAN. No.

JEFFCOTE. Nowt for us in that cable?

ALAN. No.

JEFFCOTE. You're very late.

ALAN. I got something to eat in Manchester. [*He is for withdrawing again.*]

JEFFCOTE. Hold on a bit. You'd better shut the door and sit down.

SIR TIMOTHY. Now then, what's all this I hear tell about thee?

ALAN [*to* JEFFCOTE]. Have you been telling him?

JEFFCOTE. Ay!

ALAN. You'd no right to!

JEFFCOTE. Hello!

ALAN. It was my business.

JEFFCOTE. It was your business right enough, but if I'd left it to you it wouldn't have been done. I can see that you weren't for going up to Farrar's to-night.

ALAN. No, I wasn't.

JEFFCOTE [*grimly*]. I knew it.

ALAN. And that's just why you hadn't any right to tell Sir Timothy.

JEFFCOTE. You young fool! What was the good of hanging back? Sir Timothy had got to be told some time, I reckon.

ALAN. Why?

JEFFCOTE. Why? You don't suppose he's going to see you throw his Beatrice over without knowing why?

ALAN. Who says I'm going to throw his Beatrice over?

JEFFCOTE [*looking hard at him*]. I say so.

ALAN. Happen it would be better if you'd stick to what concerns you in future.

JEFFCOTE [*rising*]. What the deuce dost thou mean by talking to me that road?

SIR TIMOTHY [*rising*]. Here! hold on a bit. Don't go shouting the lad down, Nat Jeffcote. I want to hear what he's got to say.

ALAN. If father hadn't opened his mouth there'd have been no call to say anything. It wasn't me who started to make difficulties.

SIR TIMOTHY. I'll bet it wasn't. You'd have let the thing slide?

ALAN. I'd have tried to settle it.

SIR TIMOTHY. Then I take it thou's no desire to wed Fanny Hawthorn?

ALAN. I don't think it's necessary.

SIR TIMOTHY. No more do I.

JEFFCOTE [*to* ALAN]. I thought we had this out last night. Were you so drunk that you couldn't take in what I said?

ALAN. No.

JEFFCOTE. Why did you not speak out then?

ALAN. You never gave me a chance. You did all the talking yourself.

SIR TIMOTHY. I'd be ashamed to say that. I'd like to see the man as could shut *my* mouth when I'd had too much to drink. *Thou* couldn't do it, Nat, fond of shouting as thou art!

ALAN. He's not your father.

SIR TIMOTHY. Art afraid of him?

ALAN. No.

SIR TIMOTHY. Then stand up to him. I'll back thee up.

ALAN. I've told him I'm not going to wed Fanny. What more does he want?

JEFFCOTE. You've made up your mind?
ALAN. Yes.
JEFFCOTE. Very well. I've rarely been beat up to now, and I'm not going to be beat by my own lad!
SIR TIMOTHY. Hang it all, Nat, thou cannot take him by the scruff of the neck and force him to wed where he doesn't want to!
JEFFCOTE. No, that's true. And no one can force me to leave my brass where I don't want to.
SIR TIMOTHY. Thou's not serious?
JEFFCOTE. I am that.
SIR TIMOTHY. Thou wouldn't care to leave Daisy Bank outside the family.
JEFFCOTE. It wouldn't go outside the family if I left it to his cousin Travis.
SIR TIMOTHY [grimacing]. Thou art a queer chap, Nat!
ALAN. So it comes to this. If I don't marry Fanny you'll leave your brass to Travis?
JEFFCOTE. That's it.
ALAN. I see. [He thinks a moment.] And would Travis be expected to take Fanny over along with the mill?
 [JEFFCOTE winces, and makes as if to reply angrily, but he thinks better of it and remains grimly silent. A pause.]
ALAN. Very well. Leave it to Travis. I'm going to stick to Beatrice.
JEFFCOTE. Right. You haven't thought what you and Beatrice are going to live on, have you?
ALAN. I'm not such a fool that I can't earn my own living.
JEFFCOTE. What you'll earn won't go very far if you have to keep a girl like Beatrice.
ALAN. Beatrice and I can manage like you and mother did.
JEFFCOTE. No, you can't. You haven't been brought up to it.
ALAN. Then Sir Timothy will help us.
JEFFCOTE. Sir Timothy? Oh, ay! [He laughs sardonically.] I'd like to hear what Tim Farrar thinks of the situation now.
SIR TIMOTHY [scratching his head]. It's not straight of thee, Nat. Thou's not acting right.
JEFFCOTE. I've put thee in a bit of a hole, like?
SIR TIMOTHY. Thou's made it very awkward for me.
ALAN. I like that! It was you who told me to stand up to father. You said you'd back me up.
SIR TIMOTHY. Oh, ay! I'll back thee up all right. But there's no good in losing our tempers over this job, thou knows. I don't want to see a split 'twixt thee and thy father.
ALAN. If I don't mind, I don't see why you should.
SIR TIMOTHY. Lord bless thee! if thou art bent on a row, have it thy own way. But thy father's one of my oldest friends, think on, and I'm not going to part from him for thy sake. *Thou* can quarrel with him if thou's a mind to, but don't expect me to do the same.
ALAN. You're trying to draw out, now.
SIR TIMOTHY. I'll stand in at anything in reason, but I'll be no party to a bust-up. Besides, now I come to think of it, I'm not sure thou's treated my Beatrice right.
ALAN. Hello!
SIR TIMOTHY. No, I'm not. When a chap's engaged he ought to behave himself. From the way thou's been carrying on thou might be married already.
ALAN. Look here! You knew all this five minutes ago, when you told me to stand up to my father. What's happened to change you?
SIR TIMOTHY. Thou's very much mistaken if thou thinks I've changed my mind because thy father's leaving the Mill to thy cousin Travis. I'm not the man to do that sort of thing. Besides, what do I care about thy father's brass? I'm worth as much as he is.
JEFFCOTE [pleasantly]. That's a lie, Tim Farrar.
SIR TIMOTHY. Lie or not, I'm worth enough to be able to snap my fingers at thy brass. I'll not see my lass insulted by thy lad, not if thou were ten times as rich as thou makes out!
ALAN [exasperated]. But don't you see —
SIR TIMOTHY. No, I don't.

JEFFCOTE. Yes, you do. You're only trying to draw a red-herring across the track.
SIR TIMOTHY. Be damned to that for a tale!
JEFFCOTE. It's right.
SIR TIMOTHY. Dost take me for a mean beggar?
JEFFCOTE. No. I take thee for a business man. I never think of thee as owt else.
SIR TIMOTHY [*with heat*]. Dost tell me thou can believe I don't wish Alan to marry Bee just because of what thou's said about leaving thy brass?
JEFFCOTE. I do.
[*A pause.* SIR TIMOTHY *looks hard at* JEFFCOTE.]
SIR TIMOTHY. Well! And why not?
JEFFCOTE. Don't ask me. I don't object.
ALAN. Aren't you ashamed to say that?
SIR TIMOTHY. No. And if thou'd been in weaving as long as I have, thou wouldn't either. Thou's got to keep an eye on the main chance.
ALAN. But you've got plenty of money yourself. Quite enough for the two of us.
SIR TIMOTHY [*whimsically*]. Well, blow me if thou aren't the best business man of the lot! Thou comes along and asks me for my daughter and my money. And what does thou offer in exchange? Nowt but thyself! It isn't good enough, my lad.
ALAN. Good enough or not, it's the best I can do.
SIR TIMOTHY. It won't do for me.
ALAN. I shan't bother about you.
SIR TIMOTHY. Eh? What's that?
ALAN I don't want to marry you. I shall leave it to Beatrice.
SIR TIMOTHY. Bee'll do what I tell her. Thou can take that from me.
ALAN. No, thanks. I'll ask her myself. I don't care a hang for the pair of you. I'm going to stick to Beatrice if she'll have me. You can cut us off with a shilling if you've a mind to, both of you.
SIR TIMOTHY [*worried*]. Hang it! Thou knows I cannot do that with my Bee. I call it taking a mean advantage of me, that I do!

JEFFCOTE. Why cannot you cut off your lass?
SIR TIMOTHY. Thou knows well enough that I cannot.
JEFFCOTE. I could.
SIR TIMOTHY. I don't doubt it. But, thank God, I'm not like thee, Nat Jeffcote. I sometimes think thou'st got a stone where thy heart should be by rights.
JEFFCOTE. Happen, I've got a pair of scales.
SIR TIMOTHY. That's nowt to boast of. I'd as soon have the stone.
[*The door opens and* MRS. JEFFCOTE *looks in.*]
MRS. JEFFCOTE [*seeing* ALAN]. Beatrice wants to speak to you, Alan.
[MRS. JEFFCOTE *enters, followed by* BEATRICE FARRAR, *a determined, straightforward girl of about twenty-three.*]
SIR TIMOTHY [*to* BEATRICE]. Now, my lass —
BEATRICE. Father, I want to speak to Alan.
SIR TIMOTHY. I'd like to have a word with thee first, Bee.
BEATRICE. Afterwards, father.
SIR TIMOTHY. Ay! but it'll be too late afterwards, happen!
JEFFCOTE. Come, Tim, thou can't meddle with this job.
SIR TIMOTHY [*worried*]. I call it a bit thick!
BEATRICE. Please, father.
MRS. JEFFCOTE. Come into the drawing-room, Sir Timothy. You can smoke there, you know.
SIR TIMOTHY [*grumbling*]. A bit thick!
[*He is led out by* MRS. JEFFCOTE.
JEFFCOTE *is following, when he turns in the doorway.*]
JEFFCOTE. I'll overlook all you've said to-night if you'll be guided by me. But it's your last chance, mind.
ALAN. All right.
JEFFCOTE [*half to himself*]. I never fancied thy cousin Travis.
[SIR TIMOTHY *returns to the doorway.*]
SIR TIMOTHY [*indignantly*]. Here! What's all this? Thou wouldn't let me

stop behind! What's thou been saying to Alan?

JEFFCOTE. Telling him not to make a fool of himself.

SIR TIMOTHY. I don't call it fair —

JEFFCOTE. Come along. Don't *thee* make a fool of thyself, either.

[JEFFCOTE *draws* SIR TIMOTHY *out of the room. After they have gone* ALAN *closes the door, and then turns slowly to* BEATRICE. *They do not speak at first. At last* BEATRICE *almost whispers.*]

BEATRICE. Alan!

ALAN. So they've told you?

BEATRICE. Yes.

ALAN. Perhaps it's as well. I should have hated telling you.

BEATRICE. Alan, why did you —?

ALAN. I don't know. It was her lips.

BEATRICE. Her lips?

ALAN. I suppose so.

BEATRICE. I — I see.

ALAN. I'm not a proper cad, Bee. I haven't been telling her one tale and you another. It was all an accident, like.

BEATRICE. You mean it wasn't arranged?

ALAN. No, indeed, it wasn't. I shouldn't like you to think that, Bee. I ran across her at Blackpool.

BEATRICE. You didn't go to Blackpool to meet her?

ALAN. On my oath I didn't! I went there in the car with George Ramsbottom.

BEATRICE. What became of him?

ALAN. Him? Oh! George is a pal. He made himself scarce.

BEATRICE. Just as you would have done, I suppose, if he had been in your place?

ALAN. Of course! What else can a fellow do? Two's company, you know. But old George would be all right. I daresay he picked up something himself.

BEATRICE. You knew her before you met her at Blackpool?

ALAN. Of course. There's not so many pretty girls in Hindle that you can miss one like Fanny Hawthorn. I knew her well enough, but on the straight, mind you. I thought she looked gay, that was all. I'd hardly spoken to her before I ran into her at the Tower at Blackpool.

BEATRICE. So you met her at the Tower?

ALAN. Yes. We'd just had dinner at the Metropole Grill-room, George and I, and I daresay we had drunk about as much champagne as was good for us. We looked in at the Tower for a lark, and we ran into Fanny in the Ball-room. She had a girl with her — Mary — Mary — something or other. I forget. Anyhow, George took Mary on, and I went with Fanny.

BEATRICE. Yes?

ALAN. Next day I got her to come with me in the car. We went to Llandudno.

BEATRICE. Yes?

ALAN. There's not much more to say.

BEATRICE. And I've got to be satisfied with that?

ALAN. What else do you want me to tell you?

BEATRICE. Didn't you ever think of me?

ALAN. Yes, Bee, I suppose I did. But you weren't there, you see, and she was. That was what did it. Being near her and looking at her lips. Then I forgot everything else. Oh! I know. I'm a beast. I couldn't help it. I suppose you can never understand. It's too much to expect you to see the difference.

BEATRICE. Between me and Fanny?

ALAN. Yes. Fanny was just an amusement — a lark. I thought of her as a girl to have a bit of fun with. Going off with her was like going off and getting tight for once in a way. You wouldn't care for me to do that, but if I did you wouldn't think very seriously about it. You wouldn't want to break off our engagement for that. I wonder if you can look on this affair of Fanny's as something like getting tight — only worse. I'm ashamed of myself, just as I should be if you caught me drunk. I can't defend myself. I feel just an utter swine. What I felt for Fanny was simply — base — horrible —

BEATRICE. And how had you always thought of me?

ALAN. Oh, Bee, what I felt for you was something — higher — finer —

BEATRICE. Was it? Or are you only trying to make yourself believe that?

ALAN. No. I respected you.

BEATRICE [*thinking*]. I wonder which

feeling a woman would rather arouse. And I wonder which is most like love?

ALAN. All the time, Bee, I have never loved anyone else but you.

BEATRICE. You say so now. But, forgive me, dear, how am I to know? You have given Fanny the greater proof.

ALAN. I'm trying to show you that Fanny was one thing, you were another. Can't you understand that a fellow may love one girl and amuse himself with another? [*Despondently.*] No, I don't suppose you ever can?

BEATRICE. I think I can. We were different kinds of women. On separate planes. It didn't matter to the one how you treated the other.

ALAN. That's it. Going away with Fanny was just a fancy — a sort of freak.

BEATRICE. But you have never given me any proof half so great as that.

ALAN. Haven't I? I'll give it you now. You know that father says I am to marry Fanny?

BEATRICE. Your mother told me he wished it.

ALAN. Wished it! He's set his mind on it. He won't leave me a farthing unless I marry her.

BEATRICE. What did you tell him?

ALAN. If you can't guess that you haven't much confidence in me.

BEATRICE. That's hardly my fault, is it?

ALAN. No. Well, I told him I'd see him damned first — or words to that effect.

BEATRICE [*with a movement of pleasure*]. You did?

ALAN. Yes. Is that good enough for you, Bee? You wanted proof that it is you I love. I've chucked away everything I had to expect in the world rather than give you up. Isn't that good enough for you?

BEATRICE. Alan!

ALAN [*quickly clasping her*]. Bee, in a way I've been faithful to you all the time. I tried hard enough to forget all about you, but I couldn't. Often and often I thought about you. Sometimes I thought about you when I was kissing Fanny. I tried to pretend she was you. She never guessed, of course. She thought it was her I was kissing. But it wasn't. It was you. Oh, the awfulness of having another girl in my arms and wanting you! [BEATRICE *does not answer. She closes her eyes, overcome.*] Bee, you'll stick to me, although I shan't have a penny? I'll get to work, though. I'll work for you. You won't have any cause to reproach me. If only you'll stick to me. If only you'll tell me you forgive me!

BEATRICE [*at length*]. Could you have forgiven me if I had done the same as you?

ALAN [*surprised*]. But — you — you couldn't do it!

BEATRICE. Fanny Hawthorn did.

ALAN. She's not your class.

BEATRICE. She's a woman.

ALAN. That's just it. It's different with a woman.

BEATRICE. Yet you expect me to forgive you. It doesn't seem fair!

ALAN. It isn't fair. But it's usual.

BEATRICE. It's what everybody agrees to.

ALAN. You always say that you aren't one of these advanced women. You ought to agree to it as well.

BEATRICE. I do. I can see that there *is* a difference between men and women in cases of this sort.

ALAN. You can?

BEATRICE. Men haven't so much self-control.

ALAN. Don't be cruel, Bee. There's no need to rub it in!

BEATRICE. I'm not being personal, Alan. I'm old-fashioned enough to really believe there is that difference. You see, men have never had to exercise self-control like women have. And so I'm old-fashioned enough to be able to forgive you.

ALAN. To forgive me, and marry me, in spite of what has happened, and in spite of your father and mine?

BEATRICE. I care nothing for my father or yours. I care a good deal for what has happened, but it shows, I think, that you need me even more than I need you. For I do need you, Alan. So much that nothing on earth could make me break off our engagement, if I felt that it was at all possible to let it go on. But it isn't. It's impossible.

ALAN. Impossible? Why do you say that? Of course it's not impossible.

BEATRICE. Yes, it is. Because to all intents and purposes you are already married.

ALAN. No, Bee!

BEATRICE. You say I'm old-fashioned. Old-fashioned people used to think that when a man treated a girl as you have treated Fanny it was his duty to marry her.

ALAN. You aren't going to talk to me like father, Bee?

BEATRICE. Yes. But with your father it is only a fad. You know it isn't that with me. I love you, and I believe that you love me. And yet I am asking you to give me up for Fanny. You may be sure that only the very strongest reasons could make me do that.

ALAN. Reasons! Reasons! Don't talk about reasons, when you are doing a thing like this!

BEATRICE. You may not be able to understand my reasons. You have always laughed at me because I go to church and believe things that you don't believe.

ALAN. I may have laughed, but I've never tried to interfere with you.

BEATRICE. Nor I with you. We mustn't begin it now, either of us.

ALAN. Is this what your religion leads you to? Do you call it a Christian thing to leave me in the lurch with Fanny Hawthorn? When I need you so much more than I've ever done before?

BEATRICE. I don't know. It's not what I can argue about. I was born to look at things just in the way I do, and I can't help believing what I do.

ALAN. And what you believe comes before me?

BEATRICE. It comes before everything. [*A pause.*] Alan, promise that you'll do what I wish.

ALAN. You love me?

BEATRICE. If I love anything on earth I love you.

ALAN. And you want me to marry Fanny?

BEATRICE. Yes. Oh, Alan! can't you see what a splendid sacrifice you have it in your power to make? Not only to do the right thing, but to give up so much in order to do it. [*A pause.*] Alan, promise me.

ALAN [*nodding sullenly*]. Very well.

BEATRICE [*gladly*]. You have sufficient courage and strength?

ALAN. I'll do what you ask, but only because I can see that your talk is all humbug. You don't love me. You are shocked by what I did, and you're glad to find a good excuse for getting rid of me. All right. I understand.

BEATRICE [*in agony*]. You don't — you don't understand.

ALAN. Faugh! You might have spared me all that goody-goody business.

BEATRICE [*faintly*]. Please —

ALAN. You don't care for me a bit.

BEATRICE [*passionately*]. Alan! You don't know what it's costing me.

[ALAN *looks at her keenly, and then seizes her violently and kisses her several times. She yields to him and returns his embrace.*]

ALAN [*speaking quickly and excitedly*]. Bee, you're talking nonsense. You can't give me up — you can't give me up, however much you try.

[BEATRICE *tears herself away from him.*]

BEATRICE. You don't know me. I can. I will. I shall never be your wife.

ALAN. I won't take that for an answer — Bee —

BEATRICE. No, no, no! Never, never! whilst Fanny Hawthorn has a better right to you than I have.

[*There is a long pause. At length comes a knock at the door.*]

ALAN. Hello!

[JEFFCOTE *puts his head inside.*]

JEFFCOTE. Nine o'clock.

ALAN. What of it?

JEFFCOTE. Hawthorns are due up here at nine.

ALAN [*shortly*]. Oh!

BEATRICE. Is my father there?

JEFFCOTE. Ay! [*Calling.*] Tim!

[SIR TIMOTHY *appears in the doorway.*]

SIR TIMOTHY. Well? Fixed it up, eh?

BEATRICE. Alan and I are not going to be married, father. [*There is a pause.*]

JEFFCOTE. Ah!
SIR TIMOTHY. I'm sure it's all for the best, lass.
BEATRICE. Are you quite ready, father? I want you to take me home.
SIR TIMOTHY. Ay — ay! Shall I get thee a cab, Bee?
BEATRICE. I'd rather walk, please. [BEATRICE *goes to the door.*] I'll write to you, Alan.
[*She goes out, followed by* SIR TIMOTHY.]
JEFFCOTE. So you've thought better of it?
ALAN. Seems so.
JEFFCOTE. And you'll wed Fanny Hawthorn, I take it?
ALAN [*laconically*]. Ay!
JEFFCOTE. Thou'rt a good lad, Alan. I'm right pleased with thee.
[ALAN *bursts into a loud peal of mirthless laughter.* JEFFCOTE *stares at* ALAN *in surprise.*]
JEFFCOTE. What's the matter?
ALAN. Nothing, father.
[*He flings himself listlessly into an arm-chair.* JEFFCOTE, *after another look at him, scratches his head and goes out.*]

CURTAIN

ACT III

The Scene is the same as in the previous Act, the time a few minutes later. The room is empty. ADA *opens the door and shows in* MRS. HAWTHORN, CHRISTOPHER, *and* FANNY, *who file in silently and awkwardly. Instead of a hat,* FANNY *is wearing the shawl that Lancashire weavers commonly wear when going to the Mill.*

ADA [*glancing back at them from the door*]. Will you take a seat, please.
[ADA *goes out.* CHRISTOPHER *and* MRS. HAWTHORN *sit on chairs placed against the back wall.* FANNY *remains standing.*]
MRS. HAWTHORN. Fanny, sit you down.
[FANNY *silently seats herself. They are all three in a row along the back wall, very stiff and awkward.*]
[*Presently* JEFFCOTE *enters. The* HAWTHORNS *all rise. He greets the three drily.*]
JEFFCOTE [*nodding*]. 'Evening, Chris. [*To* MRS. HAWTHORN.] Good-evening. [*He stops in front of* FANNY.] Good-evening, lass.
[*He eyes her from tip to toe with a searching stare. She returns it quite simply and boldly.*]
JEFFCOTE [*satisfied*]. Ay!
[*He turns away to the hearth, where he takes his stand just as* MRS. JEFFCOTE *comes in. She is stiff and ill at ease.*]
MRS. JEFFCOTE [*to them all without looking at them*]. Good-evening.
[MRS. HAWTHORN *and* CHRISTOPHER *murmur a greeting, and* MRS. JEFFCOTE *passes on to the fire, having cut them as nearly as she dared.* ALAN *lounges in sheepishly. He does not say anything, but nods to the three in a subdued way, and sits down sullenly on the* L., *far away from his father and mother.*]
JEFFCOTE [*to the* HAWTHORNS]. Sit down.
[*They are about to sit against the wall as before, but he stops them.*]
JEFFCOTE. Not there. Draw up to the table.
[*They seat themselves round the table. The disposition of the characters is as follows. On the extreme* L. *is* ALAN, *in a big arm-chair. Sitting on the left of the table is* FANNY. *Behind the table,* MRS. HAWTHORN. *On the right of the table,* CHRISTOPHER. *Further to the right, in an arm-chair near the hearth, is* MRS. JEFFCOTE. *As for* JEFFCOTE, *he stands up with his back to the empty fireplace. Thus he can dominate the scene and walk about if he feels inclined.*]
JEFFCOTE. Well, here we are, all of us. We know what's brought us together. It's not a nice job, but it's got to be gone

through, so we may as well get to business right away.

CHRISTOPHER. Ay!

JEFFCOTE. We don't need to say owt about what's happened, do we?

MRS. HAWTHORN. No, I don't see as we need.

MRS. JEFFCOTE. Excuse me. I think we do. I know hardly anything of what has happened.

MRS. HAWTHORN. It's admitted by them both.

MRS. JEFFCOTE. But what is admitted by them both? It's rather important to know that.

MRS. HAWTHORN. You're hoping that we won't be able to prove owt against Alan. You think that happen he'll be able to wriggle out of it.

JEFFCOTE. There'll be no wriggling out. Alan has got to pay what he owes, and I don't think there's any doubt what that is. It's true I've only heard his version. What's Fanny told you?

CHRISTOPHER. Nowt.

JEFFCOTE. Nowt?

CHRISTOPHER. Nowt.

JEFFCOTE. How's that?

MRS. HAWTHORN. She's turned stupid, that's why.

JEFFCOTE. I'll have to have a go at her, then. [*To* FANNY.] It seems my lad met you one night in Blackpool and asked you to go to Llandudno with him?

FANNY. Yes. What then?

JEFFCOTE. He was drunk?

FANNY. No. He wasn't what you'd call drunk.

JEFFCOTE. As near as makes no matter, I'll bet.

FANNY. Anyhow, he was sober enough next morning when we went away.

JEFFCOTE. And where did you stay at Llandudno? Did he take you to an hotel?

[FANNY *does not reply.*]

MRS. HAWTHORN [*sharply*]. Now, then, Fanny.

JEFFCOTE. Come, lass, open thy mouth.

ALAN. All right, father. I'll answer for Fanny. We stopped at St. Elvies Hotel, Saturday till Monday.

JEFFCOTE. What did you stop as?

ALAN. Man and wife.

MRS. HAWTHORN [*gratified*]. Ah!

ALAN. You'll find it in the register if you go there and look it up.

JEFFCOTE [*to* MRS. JEFFCOTE]. There. Are you satisfied?

MRS. JEFFCOTE. Quite, thank you, Nat. That was all I wanted to know. I didn't want there to be any mistake.

CHRISTOPHER. There's one thing bothering me. That postcard. It was posted in Blackpool on Sunday. I don't see how you managed it if you left on Saturday.

FANNY. I wrote it beforehand and left it for Mary to post on Sunday morning.

MRS. HAWTHORN. So Mary was in at all this!

FANNY. If Mary hadn't been drowned you'd never have found out about it. I'd never have opened my mouth, and Alan knows that.

MRS. HAWTHORN. Well, Mary's got her reward, poor lass!

CHRISTOPHER. There's more in this than chance, it seems to me.

MRS. HAWTHORN. The ways of the Lord are mysterious and wonderful. We can't pretend to understand them. He used Mary as an instrument for His purpose.

JEFFCOTE. Happen. But if He did it seems cruel hard on Mary, like. However, it's all over and done with, and can't be mended now, worse luck! These two young ones have made fools of themselves. That don't matter so much. The worst feature of it is they've made a fool of me. We've got to decide what's to be done. [*To* MRS. HAWTHORN] I gave Chris a message for you last night.

MRS. HAWTHORN. Yes, you said as how you'd see us treated right.

JEFFCOTE. That's it. That's what I'm going to do. Now what do you reckon is the right way to settle this job?

MRS. HAWTHORN. He ought to marry her. I'll never be satisfied with owt less.

JEFFCOTE. That's your idea, too, Chris?

CHRISTOPHER. Ay!

JEFFCOTE. It's mine as well. [MRS. HAWTHORN *nods eagerly.*] Before I knew who the chap was I said he should wed her, and I'm not going back on that now I find he's my own son. The missus there doesn't see it in the same light, but she'll have to make the best of it. She's in a minority of one, as they say.

MRS. HAWTHORN. Then we may take it that Alan's agreeable?

JEFFCOTE. Whether he's agreeable or not I cannot say. He's willing, and that'll have to be enough for you.

MRS. HAWTHORN. You'll excuse me mentioning it, but what about the other girl?

JEFFCOTE. What other girl? Has he been carrying on with another one as well?

MRS. JEFFCOTE. She means Beatrice. Alan was engaged to Miss Farrar.

MRS. HAWTHORN. Yes, that's it. What about her?

JEFFCOTE. That's off now. No need to talk of that.

CHRISTOPHER. The lad's no longer engaged to her?

MRS. JEFFCOTE. No.

MRS. HAWTHORN. And he's quite free to wed our Fanny?

JEFFCOTE. He is so far as we know.

MRS. HAWTHORN. Then the sooner it's done the better.

JEFFCOTE. We've only to get the licence.

CHRISTOPHER [*brokenly*]. I'm sure — I'm sure — we're very grateful.

MRS. HAWTHORN [*wiping her eyes*]. Yes, we are indeed. Though, of course, it's only what we'd a right to expect.

CHRISTOPHER. I'm sure, Mrs. Jeffcote, that you'll try and look on Fanny more kindly in time.

MRS. JEFFCOTE. I hope I shall, Mr. Hawthorn. Perhaps it's all for the best. More unlikely matches have turned out all right in the end.

MRS. HAWTHORN. I'm sure there's nothing can be said against Fanny save that she's got a will of her own. And after all, there's a many of us have that.

CHRISTOPHER. She's always been a good girl up to now. You can put trust in her, Alan.

JEFFCOTE. It's evidently high time Alan got wed, that's all I can say, and it may as well be to Fanny as to anyone else. She's had to work at the loom for her living, and that does no woman any harm. My missus has worked at the loom in her time, though you'd never think it to look at her now, and if Fanny turns out half as good as her, Alan won't have done so badly. Now we've got to settle when the wedding's to be.

MRS. JEFFCOTE. What *sort* of wedding is it to be?

JEFFCOTE. You women had better fix that up.

MRS. JEFFCOTE. It ought to be quiet.

JEFFCOTE. It'll be quiet, you may lay your shirt on that! We shan't hold a reception at the Town Hall this journey.

MRS. JEFFCOTE. I should prefer it to take place at the Registrar's.

MRS. HAWTHORN. No. I'll never agree to that. Not on any account.

MRS. JEFFCOTE. Why not?

MRS. HAWTHORN. No. In church, if you please, with the banns and everything. There's been enough irregular work about this job already. We'll have it done properly this time.

ALAN. I should like to hear what Fanny says.

MRS. HAWTHORN. Fanny'll do what's thought best for her.

ALAN. Anyhow, we'll hear what she thinks about it, if you please.

FANNY. I was just wondering where I come in.

MRS. HAWTHORN. Where you come in? You're a nice one to talk! You'd have been in a fine mess, happen, if you hadn't had us to look after you. You ought to be very thankful to us all, instead of sitting there hard like.

JEFFCOTE. You'd better leave it to us, lass. We'll settle this job for you.

FANNY. It's very good of you. You'll hire the parson and get the licence and make all the arrangements on your own without consulting me, and I shall have nothing to do save turn up meek as a lamb at the church or registry office or whatever it is.

JEFFCOTE. That's about all you'll be required to do.

FANNY. You'll look rather foolish if that's just what I won't do.

Mrs. Hawthorn. Don't talk silly, Fanny.

Jeffcote. What does she mean by that?

Mrs. Hawthorn. Nothing. She's only showing off, like. Don't heed her.

Mrs. Jeffcote. I beg your pardon. We will heed her, if you please. We'll see what it is she means by that.

Jeffcote. Hark you, lass. I'm having no hanky-panky work now. You'll have to do what you're bid, or maybe you'll find yourself in the cart.

Christopher. Fanny, you'll not turn stupid now?

Fanny. It doesn't suit me to let you settle my affairs without so much as consulting me.

Mrs. Hawthorn. Consulting you! What is there to consult you about, I'd like to know? You want to marry Alan, I suppose, and all we're talking about is the best way to bring it about.

Fanny. That's just where you make the mistake. I don't want to marry Alan.

Jeffcote. Eh?

Fanny. And what's more, I haven't the least intention of marrying him.

Mrs. Hawthorn. She's taken leave of her senses!

[*They are all surprised.* Alan *is puzzled.* Mrs. Jeffcote *visibly brightens.*]

Jeffcote. Now, then, what the devil do you mean by that?

Fanny. I mean what I say, and I'll trouble you to talk to me without swearing at me. I'm not one of the family yet.

Jeffcote. Well, I'm hanged!

[*He is much more polite to* Fanny *after this, for she has impressed him. But now he rubs his head and looks round queerly at the others.*]

Christopher. Why won't you wed him? Have you got summat against him?

Fanny. That's my affair.

Mrs. Hawthorn. But you must give us a reason.

[Fanny *remains obstinately silent.*]

Christopher. It's no good talking to her when she's in this mood. I know her better than you do. She won't open her mouth, no, not if she was going to be hung.

Jeffcote. Dost thou mean to tell me that all us folk are to stand here and let this girl beat us?

Christopher. Fanny'll get her own way.

Jeffcote. We'll see.

Mrs. Jeffcote. Why shouldn't she have her own way? I don't think we have any right to press her; I don't really.

Mrs. Hawthorn. All you're after is to get Alan out of the hole he's in. You don't care about Fanny.

Mrs. Jeffcote. I'm sorry for Fanny, but of course I care more about my own child.

Mrs. Hawthorn. Well, and so do we.

Mrs. Jeffcote. After all, she knows better than we do whether she wants to marry Alan.

Jeffcote. Now then, Alan, what's the meaning of this?

Alan. I don't know, father.

Jeffcote. You've not been getting at her to-day and wheedling her into this?

Alan. Good Lord, no! What would have been the good of that? Besides, I never thought of it.

Jeffcote. Well, *I* can't account for it!

Alan. Look here, father, just let me have a talk to her alone. It's not likely she'll care to speak with all you folk sitting round.

Jeffcote. Do you reckon she'll open her mouth to you?

Alan. I can but try, though it's true she never takes much notice of what I say.

Jeffcote. We'll give you fifteen minutes. [*He looks at his watch.*] If thou cannot talk a lass round in that time thou ought to be jolly well ashamed of thyself. I know I could have done it when I was thy age. Mother, you'd better show Chris and his missus into t'other room for a bit.

[Mrs. Jeffcote *goes to the door.*]

Mrs. Jeffcote. Will you come this way, please?

[Mrs. Jeffcote *goes out, followed by* Christopher.]

Mrs. Hawthorn. Now, Fanny, think on what you're doing. For God's sake, have a bit of common sense!

[Fanny *is silent.* Mrs. Hawthorn *goes out.*]

JEFFCOTE. Fifteen minutes. And if you're not done then we shall come in whether or not. [JEFFCOTE *goes out.*]
ALAN. Look here, Fanny, what's all this nonsense about?
FANNY. What nonsense?
ALAN. Why won't you marry me? My father's serious enough. He means it when he says he wants you to. He's as stupid as a mule when he once gets an idea into his head.
FANNY. As if I didn't know that. He's like you, for that matter!
ALAN. Well, then, what are you afraid of?
FANNY. Afraid? Who says I am afraid?
ALAN. I don't see what else it can be.
FANNY. You can't understand a girl not jumping at you when she gets the chance, can you?
ALAN. I can't understand you not taking me when you get the chance.
FANNY. How is it you aren't going to marry Beatrice Farrar?
ALAN. I can't marry both of you.
FANNY. Weren't you fond of her?
ALAN. Very.
FANNY. But you were fonder of me — Eh?
ALAN. Well —
FANNY. Come, now, you must have been or you wouldn't have given her up for me.
ALAN. I gave her up because my father made me.
FANNY. Made you? Good Lord, a chap of your age!
ALAN. My father's a man who will have his own way.
FANNY. You can tell him to go and hang himself. He hasn't got any hold over you.
ALAN. That's just what he has. He can keep me short of brass.
FANNY. Earn some brass.
ALAN. Ay! I can earn some brass, but it'll mean hard work and it'll take time. And, after all, I shan't earn anything like what I get now.
FANNY. Then all you want to wed me for is what you'll get with me? I'm to be given away with a pound of tea, as it were?

ALAN. No. You know I like you, Fanny — I'm fond of you.
FANNY. You didn't give up Beatrice Farrar because of me, but because of the money.
ALAN. If it comes to that, I didn't really give her up at all. I may as well be straight with you. It was she that gave me up.
FANNY. What did she do that for? Her father's plenty of money, and she can get round *him*, I'll bet, if you can't get round *yours*.
ALAN. She gave me up because she thought it was her duty to.
FANNY. You mean because she didn't fancy my leavings.
ALAN. No. Because she thought you had the right to marry me.
FANNY. Glory! She must be queer!
ALAN. It was jolly fine of her. You ought to be the first to see that.
FANNY. Fine to give you up? [*She shrugs her shoulders, and then admits grudgingly.*] Well, I reckon it was a sacrifice of a sort. That is, if she loves you. If I loved a chap I wouldn't do that.
ALAN. You would. You're doing it now.
FANNY. Eh?
ALAN. Women are more unselfish than men and no mistake!
FANNY. What are you getting at?
ALAN. I know why you won't marry me.
FANNY. Do you? [*She smiles.*] Well, spit it out, lad!
ALAN. You're doing it for my sake.
FANNY. How do you make that out?
ALAN. You don't want to spoil my life.
FANNY. Thanks! Much obliged for the compliment.
ALAN. I'm not intending to say anything unkind, but of course it's as clear as daylight that you'd damage my prospects, and all that sort of thing. You can see that, can't you?
FANNY. Ay! I can see it now you point it out. I hadn't thought of it before.
ALAN. Then, that isn't why you refused me?
FANNY. Sorry to disappoint you, but it's not.
ALAN. I didn't see what else it could be.

FANNY. Don't you kid yourself, my lad! It isn't because I'm afraid of spoiling *your* life that I'm refusing you, but because I'm afraid of spoiling *mine!* That didn't occur to you?

ALAN. It didn't.

FANNY. You never thought that anybody else could be as selfish as yourself.

ALAN. I may be very conceited, but I don't see how you can hurt yourself by wedding me. You'd come in for plenty of brass, anyhow.

FANNY. I don't know as money's much to go by when it comes to a job of this sort. It's more important to get the right chap.

ALAN. You like me well enough?

FANNY. Suppose it didn't last? Weddings brought about this road have a knack of turning out badly. Would you ever forget it was your father bade you marry me? No fear! You'd bear me a grudge all my life for that.

ALAN. Hang it! I'm not such a cad as you make out.

FANNY. You wouldn't be able to help it. It mostly happens that road. Look at old Mrs. Eastwood — hers was a case like ours. Old Joe Eastwood's father made them wed. And she's been separated from him these thirty years, living all alone in that big house at Valley Edge. Got any amount of brass, she has, but she's so lonesome-like she does her own housework for the sake of something to occupy her time. The tradesfolk catch her washing the front steps. You don't find me making a mess of my life like that.

ALAN. Look here, Fanny, I promise you I'll treat you fair all the time. You don't need to fear that folk'll look down on you. We shall have too much money for that.

FANNY. I can manage all right on twenty-five bob a week.

ALAN. Happen you can. It's not the brass altogether. You do like me, as well, don't you?

FANNY. Have you only just thought of that part of the bargain?

ALAN. Don't be silly. I thought of it long ago. You *do* like me? You wouldn't have gone to Llandudno with me if you hadn't liked me?

FANNY. Oh! yes, I liked you.

ALAN. And don't you like me now?

FANNY. You're a nice, clean, well-made lad. Oh, ay! I like you right enough.

ALAN. Then, Fanny, for God's sake, marry me, and let's get this job settled.

FANNY. Not me!

ALAN. But you must. Don't you see it's your duty to.

FANNY. Oh! come now, *you* aren't going to start preaching to me?

ALAN. No. I don't mean duty in the way Beatrice did. I mean your duty to me. You've got me into a hole, and it's only fair you should get me out.

FANNY. I like your cheek!

ALAN. But just look here. I'm going to fall between two stools. It's all up with Beatrice, of course. And if you won't have me I shall have parted from her to no purpose; besides getting kicked out of the house by my father, more than likely!

FANNY. Nay, nay! He'll not punish you for this. He doesn't know it's your fault I'm not willing to wed you.

ALAN. He may. It's not fair, but it would be father all over to do that.

FANNY. He'll be only too pleased to get shut of me without eating his own words. He'll forgive you on the spot, and you can make it up with Beatrice to-morrow.

ALAN. I can never make it up with Bee!

FANNY. Get away!

ALAN. You won't understand a girl like Bee. I couldn't think of even trying for months, and then it may be too late. I'm not the only pebble on the beach. And I'm a damaged one, at that!

FANNY. She's fond of you, you said?

ALAN. Yes. I think she's very fond of me.

FANNY. Then she'll make it up in a fortnight.

ALAN [*moodily*]. You said *you* were fond of me once, but it hasn't taken you long to alter.

FANNY. All women aren't built alike. Beatrice is religious. She'll be sorry for you. I was fond of you in a way.

ALAN. But you didn't ever really love me?

FANNY. Love you? Good Heavens, of

course not! Why on earth should I love you? You were just someone to have a bit of fun with. You were an amusement — a lark.

ALAN [*shocked*]. Fanny! Is that all you cared for me?

FANNY. How much more did you care for me?

ALAN. But it's not the same. I'm a man.

FANNY. You're a man, and I was your little fancy. Well, I'm a woman, and *you* were *my* little fancy. You wouldn't prevent a woman enjoying herself as well as a man, if she takes it into her head?

ALAN. But do you mean to say that you didn't care any more for me than a fellow cares for any girl he happens to pick up?

FANNY. Yes. Are you shocked?

ALAN. It's a bit thick; it is really!

FANNY. You're a beauty to talk!

ALAN. It sounds so jolly immoral. I never thought of a girl looking on a chap just like that! I made sure you wanted to marry me if you got the chance.

FANNY. No fear! You're not good enough for me. The chap Fanny Hawthorn weds has got to be made of different stuff from you, my lad. My husband, if ever I have one, will be a man, not a fellow who'll throw over his girl at his father's bidding! Strikes me the sons of these rich manufacturers are all much alike. They seem a bit weak in the upper storey. It's their fathers' brass that's too much for them, happen! They don't know how to spend it properly. They're like chaps who can't carry their drink because they aren't used to it. The brass gets into their heads, like!

ALAN. Hang it, Fanny, I'm not quite a fool.

FANNY. No. You're not a fool altogether. But there's summat lacking. You're not man enough for me. You're a nice lad, and I'm fond of you. But I couldn't ever marry you. We've had a right good time together, I'll never forget that. It *has* been a right good time, and no mistake! We've enjoyed ourselves proper! But all good times have to come to an end, and ours is over now. Come along, now, and bid me farewell.

ALAN. I can't make you out rightly, Fanny, but you're a damn good sort, and I wish there were more like you!

FANNY [*holding out her hand*]. Good-bye, old lad.

ALAN [*grasping her hand*]. Good-bye, Fanny! And good luck! [*A slight pause.*]

FANNY. And now call them in again.

ALAN [*looking at his watch*]. Time's not up yet.

FANNY. Never heed! Let's get it over.

[ALAN *goes out, and* FANNY *returns to her chair and sits down. Presently* ALAN *comes in and stands by the door, whilst* MRS. JEFFCOTE, MRS. HAWTHORN, *and* CHRISTOPHER *file in and resume their original positions. Last of all comes* JEFFCOTE, *and* ALAN *leaves the door and goes back to his chair.* JEFFCOTE *comes straight behind the table.*]

JEFFCOTE. Well? What's it to be? [ALAN *and* FANNY *look at each other.*] Come. What's it to be? You, Fanny, have you come to your senses?

FANNY. I've never left them, so far as I know.

JEFFCOTE. Are you going to wed our Alan or are you not?

FANNY. I'm not.

JEFFCOTE. Ah!

MRS. HAWTHORN. Well!

ALAN. It's no good, father. I can't help it. I've done all I can. She won't have me.

JEFFCOTE. I'm beat this time! I wash my hands of it! There's no fathoming a woman. And these are the creatures that want us to give them votes!

[*After this* JEFFCOTE *does not attempt to influence the discussion.*]

MRS. HAWTHORN [*in a shrill voice*]. Do you tell us you're throwing away a chance like this?

FANNY. You've heard.

MRS. HAWTHORN. I call it wicked, I do, indeed! I can see you are downright bad, through and through! There's one thing I tell you straight. Our house is no place for thee after this.

FANNY. You're not really angry with me because of what I've done. It's because I'm not going to have any of Mr. Jeffcote's money that you want to turn me out of the house.

Mrs. Hawthorn. It's not! It's because you choose to be a girl who's lost her reputation, instead of letting Alan make you into an honest woman.

Fanny. How can he do that?

Mrs. Hawthorn. By wedding you, of course.

Fanny. You called him a blackguard this morning.

Mrs. Hawthorn. So he is a blackguard.

Fanny. I don't see how marrying a blackguard is going to turn me into an honest woman!

Mrs. Hawthorn. If he marries you he won't be a blackguard any longer.

Fanny. Then it looks as if I'm asked to wed him to turn him into an honest man?

Alan. It's no use bandying words about what's over and done with. I want to know what's all this talk of turning Fanny out of doors?

Christopher. Take no heed of it! My missus don't rightly know what she's saying just now.

Mrs. Hawthorn. Don't she? You're making a big mistake if you think that. Fanny can go home and fetch her things, and after that she may pack off!

Christopher. That she'll not!

Mrs. Hawthorn. Then I'll make it so hot for her in the house, and for thee, too, that thou'll be glad to see the back of her!

Fanny. This hasn't got anything to do with Mr. and Mrs. Jeffcote, has it?

[Fanny *rises*.]

Alan. It's got something to do with me, though! I'm not going to see you without a home.

Fanny [*smiling*]. It's right good of you, Alan, but I shan't starve. I'm not without a trade at my finger-tips, thou knows. I'm a Lancashire lass, and so long as there's weaving sheds in Lancashire I shall earn enough brass to keep me going. I wouldn't live at home again after this, not anyhow! I'm going to be on my own in future. [*To* Christopher.] You've no call to be afraid. I'm not going to disgrace you. But so long as I've to live my own life I

don't see why I shouldn't choose what it's to be.

Christopher [*rising*]. We're in the road here! Come, Sarah!

Jeffcote. I'm sorry, Chris. I've done my best for thee.

Christopher. Ay! I know. I'm grateful to thee, Nat. [*To* Mrs. Jeffcote.] Good-night, ma'am.

Mrs. Jeffcote. Good-night.

[Mrs. Hawthorn *and* Christopher *go out, the former seething with suppressed resentment. Neither says anything to* Alan. Jeffcote *opens the door for them and follows them into the hall. As* Fanny *is going out,* Mrs. Jeffcote *speaks.*]

Mrs. Jeffcote. Good-bye, Fanny Hawthorn. If ever you want help, come to me.

Fanny. Ah! You didn't want us to wed?

Mrs. Jeffcote. No.

Fanny. You were straight enough.

Mrs. Jeffcote. I'm sure this is the best way out. I couldn't see any hope the other way.

Fanny. Good-bye.

[Mrs. Jeffcote *holds out her hand, and they shake hands. Then* Fanny *goes out with* Alan. *There is a slight pause.* Mrs. Jeffcote *goes to the door and looks into the hall, and then returns to her chair. Soon* Jeffcote *comes in.*]

Mrs. Jeffcote. Have they gone?

Jeffcote. Ay!

[Jeffcote *sits down in an armchair and fills his pipe.*]

Mrs. Jeffcote. Where's Alan?

Jeffcote. Don't know.

Mrs. Jeffcote. What are you going to do about him?

Jeffcote. Don't know.

[Alan *opens the door and looks in. He is wearing a light burberry mackintosh and a soft felt hat.*]

Mrs. Jeffcote. Where are you going to, Alan?

Alan. I'm just running round to Farrar's.

Jeffcote [*surprised*]. To Farrar's?

Alan. To see Beatrice.

MRS. JEFFCOTE [*not surprised*]. You're going to ask her to marry you?

ALAN [*laconically*]. Happen I am!

JEFFCOTE. Well, I'm damned! Dost thou reckon she'll have thee?

ALAN. That remains to be seen.

JEFFCOTE. Aren't you reckoning without me!

ALAN. Can't help that.

[JEFFCOTE *grunts*.]

ALAN. Hang it! be fair. I've done my best. It's not my fault that Fanny won't have me.

JEFFCOTE. Well, if Beatrice Farrar can fancy thee, it's not for me to be too particular.

ALAN. Thank you, father.

JEFFCOTE. Get along! I'm disgusted with thee!

[ALAN *slips out of the door.*]

MRS. JEFFCOTE. Beatrice will have him.

JEFFCOTE. How do you know that?

MRS. JEFFCOTE. She loves him; she told me.

JEFFCOTE. There's no accounting for tastes! [*He ruminates.*] So Beatrice loves him, does she? Eh! but women are queer folk! Who'd have thought that Fanny would refuse to wed him?

MRS. JEFFCOTE. It *is* strange. It makes you feel there *is* something in Providence after all.

CURTAIN

RUTHERFORD AND SON
A PLAY IN THREE ACTS
By GITHA SOWERBY

ENTERED AT THE LIBRARY OF CONGRESS, WASHINGTON, U.S.A.
ALL RIGHTS RESERVED

CHARACTERS

JOHN RUTHERFORD.
JOHN, } *his sons.*
RICHARD,
JANET, *his daughter.*
ANN, *his sister.*
MARY, *young John's wife.*
MARTIN.
MRS. HENDERSON.

SCENE — Living-room in John Rutherford's house.

Two days elapse between Acts I and II.
One night between Acts II and III.

RUTHERFORD AND SON

ACT I

John Rutherford's *house stands on the edge of the moor, far enough from the village to serve its dignity and near enough to admit of the master going to and from the Works in a few minutes — a process known to the household as "going across." The living-room, in which the family life has centred for generations, is a big square room furnished in solid mahogany and papered in red, as if to mitigate the bleakness of a climate that includes five months of winter in every year. There is a big table in the middle of the room covered with a brown cloth at which the family take their meals. An air of orderliness pervades the room, which perhaps accounts for its being extremely uncomfortable. From above the heavy polished sideboard the late* John Rutherford *looks down from his frame and sees the settle and arm-chair on either side of the fire, the marble clock on the mantelpiece, the desk with its brass inkstand and neatly arranged bundles of papers precisely as he saw them in life.*

On this particular evening in December, Ann Rutherford *is sitting by the fire alternately knitting and dozing. She is a faded, querulous woman of about sixty, and wears a black dress with a big flat brooch and a cap with lilac ribbons.* Mary Rutherford, *a gentle, delicate-looking woman of twenty-six, is seated on the settle opposite to her making a baby's cap; she is bending forward to catch the light of the fire on her work, for the lamp has not yet been brought in.*

Presently Janet *comes in carrying a silver basket and a pair of carpet slippers. She is a heavy dark woman, some ten years older than* Mary, *with an expressionless tired face and monotonous voice. All her movements are slipshod and aimless, and she seldom raises her eyes. She is dressed in a dark dress of some warm material with white collar and cuffs.*

Janet [*glancing at the clock*]. He's not back yet.

Ann. No.... If you mean your father.

Janet [*folding up the brown cloth preparatory to laying the table*]. Who else should I mean?

Ann. You might mean any one.... You always talk about he and him, as if there was no one else in the house.

Janet. There isn't.

Ann. Answer me back, that's the way. [Janet *makes no reply. She puts the silver basket on the table and comes to the fire with the slippers.*] There — put his slippers down to warm. The Committee room's cold as ice, and he'll come in like the dead.

Mary [*looking up from her work for a moment*]. I believe it's going to freeze to-night — the chimneys are flaring so.

[Janet *drops the shoes one by one on to the hearthrug without stooping.*]

Ann. They'll never warm there! I never seed sic a feckless lass. [*Stoops laboriously and sets them up against the fender.*] Is the dinner all right?

Janet. Susan's let the pie get burnt, but I've scraped the top off — he won't notice. The girdle cake's as tough as leather. She'll have to do a fresh one — if there's time.

Ann. You might ha' seen to things a bit.

Janet. I have. There wouldn't ha' been a pie at all if I hadn't. The oven damper's gone wrong.

Ann. Answer me — answer yer aunt!

You and your dampers — and there you are a-laying the table and ye know weel enough yer father's forbid you to do things like a servant.

JANET. What else is there to do? I can't sit and sew all day.

ANN. I'm sure I'm never done finding fault from morning to night with one thing and another.

JANET. Don't then.

ANN. And a nice thing if I didn't! Nothing ever done in the house unless I see to it — that's what it comes to.

JANET [*spreading the cloth*]. You'll drop your stitches.

ANN. You never stir yourself, nor Mary neither, for that matter.

MARY. I can't do much else with Tony to look after, Miss Rutherford.

JANET. There's no need for her to do anything. It's not her business.

ANN. Nor anybody's business, it seems to me. [*Subsiding.*] I don't know what's come to Susan nowadays, she's that daft — a head like a sieve, and that clumsy-handed.

JANET. Susan's got a man.

ANN. Well, I never!

JANET. That's what she says. It's one of the men at the Works. He hangs about on his way home from the night shift — when she ought to be doing the rooms. . . . Susan's happy . . . that's why she forgot to take the milk out of the can. There's no cream for the pudding.

ANN. And he's so particular about his cream.

JANET. He'll have to do without for once. And what with the pie burnt — and the girdle cake like leather, if he comes in before the other's ready — I should think we'll have a fair evening.

[*She leaves the room.*]

ANN. Eh, dearie — dearie. Sic doings!

MARY [*absorbed in her cap*]. Never mind, Miss Rutherford.

ANN. Never mind! It's well for you to talk.

MARY. Janet'll see that it's all right. She always does, though she talks like that.

ANN. Her and her sulky ways. There's no doing anything with her of late. She used to be bad enough as a lass, that passionate and hard to drive. She's ten times worse now she's turned quiet.

MARY. Perhaps she's tired with the long walks she takes. She's been out nearly two hours this afternoon in the rain.

ANN [*turning to her knitting*]. What should she have to put her out — except her own tempers.

MARY [*trying to divert her attention*]. Miss Rutherford, look at Tony's cap; I've nearly finished it.

ANN [*still cross*]. It's weel enough. Though what he wants wi' a lot o' bows standing up all over his head passes me.

MARY. They're butterfly bows.

ANN. Butterfly bows! And what'll butterfly bows do for'n? They'll no keep his head warm.

MARY. But he looks such a darling in them. I'll put it on to-morrow when I take him out, and you'll see.

ANN. London ways — that's what it is.

MARY. Do north-country babies never have bows on their caps?

ANN. Not in these parts. And not the Rutherfords anyway. Plain and lasting — that's the rule in this family, and we bide by it, babies and all. But you can't be expected to know, and you like a stranger in the hoose.

[JANET *comes in carrying a lamp and a loaf on a trencher, which she puts on the table.*]

MARY. I've been here nearly three months.

ANN. And this very night you sit wasting your time making a bit trash fit for a monkey at a fair. A body would think you would ha' learned better by now.

JANET [*quietly*]. What's the matter with Mary now?

ANN. We can talk, I suppose, without asking your leave?

JANET. It was you that was talking. Let her be.

ANN. And there you've been and put the loaf on as if it was the kitchen — and you know weel enough that gentlefolk have it set round in bits.

JANET. Gentle folk can do their own ways. [*She goes out to fetch the knives.*]

ANN [*she gets up laboriously and goes to the table*]. I'll have to do it myself as usual. [*She cuts the bread and sets it round beside the plates.*]

MARY [*who has gone to the window and is looking out at the winter twilight*]. If I'm a stranger, it's you that makes me so.

ANN. Ye've no cause to speak so, lass. ... I'm not blamin' you. It's no' your fault that you weren't born and bred in the north country.

MARY. No. I can't change that. ... I wonder what it's like here when the sun shines!

ANN [*who is busy with the bread*]. Sun?

MARY. It doesn't look as if the summer ever came here.

ANN. If ye're looking for the summer in the middle o' December ye'll no' get it. Ye'll soon get used to it. Ye've happened on a bad autumn for your first, that's all.

MARY. My first.

ANN. Ye're a bit saft wi' livin' in the sooth, nae doubt. They tell me there's a deal of sunshine and wickedness in them parts.

MARY. The people are happier, I think.

ANN. Mebbees. Bein' happy'll make no porridge. [*She goes back to her chair.*]

MARY. I lived in Devonshire when I was a child, and everywhere there were lanes. But here — it's all so old and stern — this great stretch of moor, and the fells — and the trees — all bent one way, crooked and huddled.

ANN [*absorbed in her knitting*]. It's the sea-wind that does it.

MARY. The one that's blowing now?

ANN. Aye.

MARY [*with a shiver*]. Shall I draw the curtains?

ANN. Aye.

[*MARY draws the curtains. After a silence she speaks again gently.*]

MARY. I wonder if you'll ever get used to me enough to — like me?

ANN [*with the north-country dislike of anything demonstrative*]. Like you! Sic a question — and you a kind of a relation.

MARY. Myself, I mean.

ANN. You're weel enough. You're a bit slip of a thing, but you're John's wife, and the mother of his bairn, and there's an end.

MARY. Yes, that's all I am! [*She takes up her work again.*]

ANN. Now you're talking.

MARY [*sewing*]. Don't think I don't understand. John and I have been married five years. All that time Mr. Rutherford never once asked to see me; if I had died, he would have been glad.

ANN. I don't say that. He's a proud man, and he looked higher for his son after the eddication he'd given him. You mustn't be thinking such things.

MARY [*without bitterness*]. Oh, I know all about it. If I hadn't been Tony's mother, he would never have had me inside his house. And if I hadn't been Tony's mother, I wouldn't have come. Not for anything in the world.... It's wonderful how he's picked up since he got out of those stuffy lodgings.

ANN [*winding up her wool*]. Well, Mr. Rutherford's in the right after all.

MARY. Oh, yes. He's in the right.

ANN. It's a bitter thing for him that's worked all his life to make a place i' the world to have his son go off and marry secret-like. Folk like him look for a return from their bairns. It's weel known that no good comes of a marriage such as yours, and it's no wonder that it takes him a bit of time to make up his mind to bide it. [*Getting up to go.*] But what's done's done.

[*Young JOHN RUTHERFORD comes in while she is speaking. He is delicate-looking and boyish in speech and manner — attractive, in spite of the fact that he is the type that has been made a gentleman of and stopped half-way in the process.*]

JOHN [*mimicking her tone*]. So it is, Aunt Ann. Dinner's late, isn't it?

ANN. He's not back yet. He's past his time. I'm sure I hope nothing's happened.

JOHN. What should have happened?

ANN. Who's to tell that he hasn't had an accident. Things do happen.

JOHN. They do indeed. He may have jumped into a furnace.

ANN. Ah, you may joke. But you never know. You never know.
[*She wanders out, with the vague intention of seeing to the dinner.*]
JOHN. Cheery old soul, Aunt Ann. No one's ever five minutes late but she kills and buries them. [*Pause.*] What's she been saying to you?
MARY [*sewing*]. She's been talking about — us.
JOHN. I should have thought that subject was about threadbare by now. [*Pause.*] What's she say?
MARY. The usual things. How angry your father still is, and how a marriage like ours never comes to good —
JOHN. Oh, rot. Anyway, we needn't talk about it.
[*She looks quickly up at him and her face changes.*]
MARY. Some one's always talking about it.
JOHN. Who is?
MARY. Miss Rutherford — any of them. Your father would, if he ever spoke to me at all. He looks it instead.
JOHN. Oh, nonsense; you imagine things. The Guv'nor's like that with us all — it's always been so; besides, he doesn't like women — never notices them. [*Trying to make it all right.*] Look here, I know it's rather beastly for you just now, but it'll be all right in time. Things are going to change, so don't you worry, little woman.
MARY. What are we going to do?
JOHN. Do? What should we do?
MARY. Anything. To get some money of our own. To make some sort of life for ourselves, away from here.
JOHN. You wait till I get this invention of mine set going. As for getting away, please remember it was you who insisted on coming. I never wanted you to.
MARY. I had to come. Tony was always ailing in London.
JOHN. You never left me alone till I'd crawled to the Guv'nor and asked to come back.
MARY. What else was there left to do? You couldn't find work —
JOHN. If you'd had patience and waited, things would have been all right.

MARY. I've waited five years. I couldn't go on earning enough when Tony came.
JOHN [*sulkily*]. Well, you couldn't expect me to ask the Guv'nor to keep us all three. And if I had stayed in London with you instead of coming back when he gave me the chance, what good would it have done? I'd have missed the biggest thing of my life — I know that.... Anyway, I do hate this going back over it all. Beastly, sordid —
MARY [*looking before her*]. I couldn't go on. I'd done it so long — long before you knew me. Day after day in an office. The crowded train morning and night — bad light — bad food — and because I did that my boy is small and delicate. It's been nothing else all along — the bare struggle for life. I sometimes think that it's the only reality in the world.
JOHN [*ill-humoured*]. Whether it's the only reality or not, I call it a pretty deadly way of looking at things.
MARY. It is deadly. I didn't know how deadly till I began to care for you and thought it was going to be different.
JOHN. The old story.
MARY. No, no, we won't look back. But oh, John, I do so dreadfully want things for Tony. [JOHN *begins to move about the room.*] I didn't mind when there was only ourselves. But when he was coming I began to think, to look at the other children — children of people in our position in London — taught to work before they'd had time to learn what work means — with the manhood ground out of them before ever it came. And I thought how that was what we had to give our child, you and I.... When your father forgave you for marrying me, and said you might come here, it seemed like a chance. And there's nothing, nothing — except this place you call home.
JOHN. Hang it all —
MARY. Oh, I know it's big — there's food and warmth, but it's like a prison! There's not a scrape of love in the whole house. Your father! — no one's any right to be what he is — never questioned, never answered back — like God! and the rest of you just living round him — neither chil-

dren, nor men and women — hating each other.

JOHN [*turning to look at her with a sort of wonder*]. Don't exaggerate. Whatever has set you off talking like this?

MARY. Because I'm always thinking about it.

JOHN. You've never had a home of your own, and you don't make excuses for family life — everybody knows it's like that more or less.

MARY. And you've lived with it always — you can't see it as I do.

JOHN. I do see it. And it's jolly unpleasant — I'm not arguing about that —

MARY. Don't you see that life in this house is intolerable?

JOHN. Well, frankly, no, I don't. That is, I don't see why you should find it so. It's all very well to abuse my people, and I sympathise with you in a way — no one dislikes them more than I do. I know Janet's got a filthy temper, and Aunt Ann — well, she hasn't moved on with the rest of us, poor old soul, that's the long and the short of it. As for the Guv'nor — it's no use beginning to apologise for *him*.

MARY. Apologise!

JOHN. Well, that's about what you seem to expect. I've told you I quite see that it isn't over pleasant for you, and you might leave it at that, I think. You do drive at one so... and you seem to forget how ill I've been.

MARY. I don't forget. But don't you see we may go on like this for twenty years doing nothing?

JOHN. Do you suppose I wouldn't have done something? Do you suppose I didn't mean to do something, if I hadn't been knocked over just at the critical moment? [*Injured.*] Do you suppose I wouldn't rather have been working than lying on my back all these weeks?

MARY [*quietly*]. How about all the other weeks?

JOHN. Good Heavens, what more could I do than I have done? Here have I hit on a thing worth thousands — a thing that any glass-maker would give his ears to have the working of. And you talk to me about making money — and a life of our own. Good Lord! we're going to be rich — rich, once it's set going.

MARY [*unimpressed*]. Have you told Mr. Rutherford about it?

JOHN. Yes. At least, I've told him what it is.... I haven't told him how it's done — naturally.... He won't listen to me — it's like talking to a lump of granite. He'll find he'll have to listen before long.... I've set Martin on to him.

MARY. Why Martin?

JOHN. Because he helped me to work it out. And because he happens to be the one person in the world the Guv'nor ever listens to.

MARY [*looking up*]. He trusts Martin, doesn't he? Absolutely.

JOHN. Oh, Lord! yes. Martin can do no wrong. The Guvnor'll listen to him all right.

MARY [*resuming her work*]. When is he going to tell him?

JOHN. Oh, directly he gets a chance. He may have done it already.

MARY [*putting down her sewing*]. To-day? Then Martin really believes there's something in it?

JOHN [*indignantly*]. Something in it! My dear Mary, I know you don't mean to be, but you are most fearfully irritating. Here have I told you over and over again that I'm going to make my fortune, and because some one else agrees with me you're kind enough to believe what I say. One would think you had no faith in me.

MARY [*giving it up as hopeless*]. I'm sorry. We won't talk of it any more. I've said it all so often — said it till you're sick of hearing it, and it's no good.

JOHN. Molly, don't be cross.... I don't mean to be a brute, but it is a bit disappointing, isn't it? when I really have found the right thing at last, to find you so lukewarm about it. Because it really *is* this time. It'll change everything; and you shall do what you like and enjoy yourself as much as you want to — and forget all about those filthy years in Walton Street. [*He comes to her and puts his arm round her.*] There, don't be a little fool. What are you making?

MARY. A cap for Tony.

JOHN. Dear little beggar, isn't he?
MARY. Yes.... Don't say things to please me, John.
JOHN. I'm not. I do think he's a dear little beggar. [*Pleased with himself.*] We'll be as happy as kings by and by.
MARY. As happy as we were at first?
JOHN. Happier — we'll have money.
MARY. We couldn't be happier. [*She sits with her hands in her lap, her mouth wistful.*] What a pair of babies we were, weren't we?
JOHN. Oh, I don't know.
MARY. What — blunderers! I thought it was so different — and I dare say you did, too, though you never said so. I suppose it's really true what they think here — that we'd no business to marry and have a child when we'd nothing to give him when he came.
JOHN. What a little worrit you are.
MARY. I do worry, John — you don't know how much.
JOHN. But what about?
MARY. Tony.
JOHN. You funny little thing. Surely there's time enough to think about Tony; he's just four months old.
MARY. Yes, but to me — I suppose every woman thinks about her baby like that — till he's a boy and a man and a child all in one — only he never grows old. [*In a practical tone.*] How long will it take?
JOHN. How long will what take?
MARY. Your invention. [*Looks up quickly.*] I mean — don't be cross — will it be months — or years before it *pays?*
JOHN [*moving away*]. I really can't say — it depends. If the Guv'nor has the sense to see things my way — it depends.
[*He takes a cigarette.*]
MARY. I see. You will work at it, won't you? *Make it go?*
JOHN [*striking a light*]. There's no work to be done. All I've got to do is to sit down and let some one pay for it.
MARY. Sit down? It seems so much to us, doesn't it? *Everything* —
JOHN [*who has burnt his finger*]. It means my getting the whip-hand of the Guv'nor for once in my life. [*Irritably.*] And it means my getting away from your incessant nagging at me about the kid — and money.
MARY. John!
JOHN [*sharply*]. After all, it isn't very pleasant for me having you dependent on the Guv'nor and being reminded of it every other day. I don't choose this kind of life, I can tell you. If you're sick of it, God knows I am.

[*While he is speaking* ANN *drifts into the room again.*]

ANN. There you are — smoking again; and you know what the doctor said. Mary, tell him he's not to.
MARY. John must do as he likes.
JOHN. I must have something; my nerves are all on edge.
ANN. Weel, ye can't expect to be right all of a sudden. When I think o' the Sunday night ye was so bad, I never thought to see ye standin' there now.
JOHN [*injured*]. I shouldn't worry about that. I don't suppose any one would have been much the worse if I had pegged out.
ANN. Whatever makes you say a thing like that?
JOHN. Mary. Yes, you do, Mary. To hear you talk one would think I was no good. How do you suppose I've made an invention if I were the rotter you think me?
MARY. I didn't say that — I didn't say that.
ANN. An invention's weel enough if you're not mistaken.
JOHN. Mistaken!
ANN. Ah, but older people nor you make mistakes. There was old Green — I mind him fiddlin' on wi' a lot of old cogs and screws half his time, trying to find oot the way to prevent a railway train going off the line. And when he did find it and took it to show it to some one as knawed aboot such things, it was so sartin sure not to go off the line that the wheels wouldn't turn roond at all. A poor, half-baked body he was, and his wife without a decent black to show herself in o' Sundays.
JOHN. I'll undertake that my wheels will go round.

ANN. If it's such a wonderful thing, why hasn't some one thought of it afore? Answer me that.

JOHN. You might say that of any new idea that ever came into the world.

ANN. Of course, if you set up to know more about glass-making than your father that's been at it ever since he was a bairn...

JOHN. It isn't a case of knowing. I've a much better chance because I don't know. It's the duffers who get hold of the best things — stumble over them in the dark, as I did. It makes my blood run cold to think how easily I could have missed it, of all the people who must have looked straight at it time after time, and never seen it. [Contemptuously.] Hullo, Dick!

[RICHARD RUTHERFORD has come in from the hall. He wears the regulation clergyman's clothes and looks older than JOHN, though he is in reality the younger by a couple of years. He is habitually overworked, and his face has the rather pathetic look of an overweighted youth that finds life too much for its strength. His manner is extremely simple and sincere, which enables him to use priggish phrases without offence. He comes to the table while JOHN is speaking, looks from him to ANN, then at the butter, sugar, and bread in turn.]

DICK [very tired]. Dinner?
JOHN [mimicking him]. Not imminent.
DICK. Will it be long?
ANN [crossly]. Ye'll just have to bide quiet till it comes.
DICK [gently]. Ah!... In that case I think I'll just —
[He takes a piece of bread and moves towards the door.]
ANN. You look fair done.
DICK. I've had a tiring day. [To MARY.] Where is Janet?
MARY. In the kitchen. [She looks at him intently.] Why did you ask? Do you want her?
DICK [uncertainly]. No, no. I thought she might have gone out. It's best for her not to go out after dark.

ANN. You can't sit in your room i' this cold.
DICK. I'll put on a coat. It's quiet there.
JOHN. You'll have time to write your sermon before he comes in, I dare say.
DICK [simply]. Oh, I've done that, such as it is.
[He leaves the room, eating his bread as he goes.]
JOHN [irritably]. This is a damned uncomfortable house. I'm starving.
ANN. It's Committee day.
JOHN. He'll be having the whole Board on his toes as usual, I suppose.
ANN. That Board 'll be the death of him. When I think of the old days when he'd no one to please but himself!
JOHN. He's stood it for five years. I wouldn't — being badgered by a lot of directors who know as much about glass-making as you do.
ANN. That's all very well. But when you borrow money you've got to be respectful one way and another. If he hadn't gone to the Bank how would Rutherford's ha' gone on?
JOHN [who has taken up the newspaper and is half reading it as he talks]. Why should it go on?
ANN [sharply]. What's that?
JOHN. Why didn't he sell the place when he could have made a decent profit.
ANN [scandalised]. Sell Rutherford's? Just you let your father hear you.
JOHN. I don't care if he does. I never can imagine why he hangs on — working his soul out year after year.
ANN [conclusively]. It's his duty!
[She resumes her knitting.]
JOHN. Duty — rot! He likes it. He's gone on too long. He couldn't stop and rest if he tried. When I make a few thousands out of this little idea of mine I'm going to have everything I want, and forget all about the dirt and the ugliness, the clatter and bang of the machinery, the sickening hot smell of the furnaces — all the things I've hated from my soul.
ANN [who has become absorbed in a dropped stitch]. Aye weel... there's another strike at Rayner's, they tell me.

JOHN. Yes. Eight hundred men. That's the second this year.

ANN. You don't think it'll happen here, do you?

JOHN. I can't say. They're smashing things at Rayner's.

ANN. It'll no' come here. The men think too much of your father for that.

JOHN. I'm not so sure.

ANN. There was the beginnings of a strike once, years ago, and he stopped it then. The men at the furnaces struck work — said it was too hard for 'n. And your father he went doon into the caves and took his coat off afore them all, and pitched joost half as much coal again as the best of 'em — now!

JOHN. Yes, that's the sort of argument they can see — it catches hold of the brute in them. If the Guv'nor had sat quietly in his office and sent his ultimatum through the usual channels, he would have been the owner of Rutherford's, and the strike would have run its course. Shovelling coal in his shirt with his muscles straining, and the sweat pouring off him, he was "wor John" — and there's three cheers for his fourteen stone of beef and muscle. That was all very well — thirty years ago.

ANN. And what's to hinder it now?

JOHN. Oh, the Guv'nor was a bit of a hero then — an athlete, a runner. The men who worked for him all the week crowded to see him run on Saturday afternoons, Martin's told me. But when all's said and done, Rutherford's is a money-making machine. And the Guv'nor's the only man who doesn't know it. He's getting old.

ANN [crossly]. To hear you talk a body would think we were all going to die to-morrow. Your father's a year younger nor me — now! And a fine up-standing man forbye.

JOHN [who is looking at himself in the glass above the mantelpiece]. Oh, he know how to manage a pack of savages.

ANN. There's not one of 'em to-day or thirty years ago but'll listen to him.

JOHN. He'd knock any one down who didn't.

[JANET comes in with a tray and begins to set cups and saucers on the table.]

ANN. They all stood by him when the trouble came, every one of 'em. And he's climbed up steady ever since, and never looked ahint him. And now you've got your invention it'll no be long now — if it's all you think it. Ah, it 'ud be grand to see Rutherford's like old times again.

JOHN. Rutherford's.... [He speaks half seriously, half to tease ANN.] Aunt Ann, have you ever in your life — just for a moment at the back of your mind — wished Rutherford's at the bottom of the Tyne?

[ANN gazes at him in silence. When she speaks again it is as to a foolish child.]

ANN. Are you taking your medicine reg'lar?

JOHN. Yes. But have you ever heard of Moloch? No. — Well, Moloch was a sort of a god — some time ago, you know, before Dick and his kind came along. They built his image with an ugly head ten times the size of a real head, with great wheels instead of legs, and set him up in the middle of a great dirty town. [JANET, busy at the table, stops to listen, raising her eyes almost for the first time.] And they thought him a very important person indeed, and made sacrifices to him — human sacrifices — to keep him going, you know. Out of every family they set aside one child to be an offering to him when it was big enough, and at last it became a sort of honour to be dedicated in this way, so much so, that the victims gave themselves gladly to be crushed out of life under the great wheels. That was Moloch.

[There is a silence. JANET speaks eagerly.]

JANET. Where did you get that?

JOHN. Get what?

JANET. What you've been saying.

JOHN. Everybody knows it.

JANET. Dedicated — we're dedicated — all of us — to Rutherford's. And being respected in Grantley.

ANN. Talk, talk — chatter, chatter.

Words never mended nothing that I knows on.

JOHN [*who is tired of the subject*]. Talk — if I hadn't you to talk to, Aunt Ann, or Mary, I think I'd talk to the door-post.

JANET [*who has slipped back into her dull listlessness*]. And just as much good would come of it, I dare say.

ANN. And who are you to say it? You got no book-learning like him — and no invention neither.

JANET [*who is laying forks round the table*]. How do you know he's got an invention?

ANN. Because he says so, o' course — how else? It's a secret.

JANET. John always had a secret. He used to sell them to me when we were little. And when I'd given him whatever it was he'd taken a fancy to, there was no secret. Nothing worth paying for, anyway.

JOHN. Oh, shut up.

ANN [*as if they were children*]. Now, now. Don't quarrel.

JANET. We're not quarrelling.

JOHN. Yes, we are. And you began it.

JANET. I didn't. I only said what any one can see. [*Scornfully*]. *You* make an invention. Likely.

JOHN. A lot you know about it.

JANET. If you did, you'd muck it somehow, just as you do everything.

ANN [*querulously*]. Bairns! Bairns! One would think you'd never growed up.

JOHN [*angrily to* JANET]. I wish you'd keep quiet if you can't say anything decent. You never open your mouth except to say something disagreeable. First there's Mary throwing cold water, then you come in.

JANET. I'm not any more disagreeable than any one else. We're all disagreeable if it comes to that. All except Susan.

ANN. Susan's not one of the family! A common servant lass.

JANET. Like me.

ANN [*using the family threat*]. Just you let your father hear you.

JANET. We do the same things.

ANN. Susan's *paid* for it. Whoever gave you a farthing?

JANET [*bitterly*]. Aye!

ANN. Has she made another girdle cake?

JANET. I didn't notice. She's probably talking to her young man at the gate.

JOHN. Susan with a young man!

ANN. Yes, indeed — a nice thing, and her turned forty.

JOHN. Ugliest woman I ever saw bar none. Who is it? Not Martin surely! [JANET *stops suddenly and looks at him.*] I've noticed he's been making excuses to come about lately, and he's taken the cottage at the Tarn.

JANET [*with a sudden stillness*]. It isn't Martin.

JOHN. Well, if it is, the Guv'nor would soon put a stop to it.

JANET. Put a stop to what?

JOHN. Martin getting married — if it's that he's after.

JANET. What right's he to interfere?

JOHN. Right — nonsense. Martin practically lives at the Works as it is. If he had a wife he'd get to be just like the other men — hankering after going home at the proper time, and all that.

ANN [*preparing to leave the room*]. You and your gossip — and the dinner spoiling every minute. [*With a parting shot at* JANET.] It's a good thing nobody's married you — a nice hoose you'd make without me to look to everything. [*She fusses out.*]

JOHN. Married! Cheer up, Janet! Thirty-five last birthday, isn't it?

MARY. John!

JANET [*her voice hard*]. No, it isn't. It's thirty-six.

JOHN. You'll make a happy home for some one yet. No one's asked you so far, I suppose?

JANET. Who's there been to ask me?

JOHN. Oh, I don't know. I suppose you have been kept pretty close. Other girls manage it, don't they?

JANET. I don't know other girls.

JOHN. Mary caught me.

JANET. I don't know anybody — you know that. No one in Grantley's good enough for us, and we're not good enough for the other kind.

JOHN. Speak for yourself.

JANET. Oh, we're all alike; don't you fret. Why hasn't young Squire Earnshaw invited you to shoot with him again? He did once — when none of his grand friends were there. [JOHN *pretends not to hear.*] I know why.

JOHN. Oh, you know a lot, don't you?

JANET. It was because you pretended — pretended you knew the folk he talked about, because you'd shown them over the Works once when father was away. Pretended you said "parss" for pass every day. I heard you. And I saw the difference. Gentlemen are natural. Being in company doesn't put them about. They don't say "thank you" to servants neither, not like you do to Susan.

JOHN. Oh, shut up, will you?

JANET. I wouldn't pretend, whatever I did — mincing round like a monkey.

ANN [*coming in from the kitchen*]. Now, now. That's the door, isn't it?

[*They all listen. A voice is heard outside, then the outer door opens.*]

JOHN. Father.

JANET. Martin.

[*There is the sound of a stick being put into the umbrella stand; then* JOHN RUTHERFORD *comes in, followed by* MARTIN. *He is a heavily built man of sixty, with a heavy lined face and tremendous shoulders — a typical north country man. There is a distinct change in the manner of the whole family as he comes in and walks straight to his desk as if the door had scarcely interrupted his walk.* MARTIN *is a good-looking man of the best type of working-man. Very simple in manner and bearing — about forty years of age. He touches his forelock to the family and stands beside the door with nothing servile in either action.*]

RUTHERFORD [*talking as he comes in*]. . . . and it's got to be managed somehow. Lads are wanted and lads'll have to be found. Only six out of the seventeen shops started the first shift o' Monday.

MARTIN. Grey couldn't start at all last week for want o' lads.

RUTHERFORD. What's got them? Ten years ago you could have had fifty for the asking, and taken your pick. And now here's the work waiting to be done, and half the hands we want to do it lounging about Grantley with their hands in their breeches' pockets, the beggars. What do they think they're bred for?

MARTIN. There's too many of 'em making for the towns, that's it. It's lighter work.

RUTHERFORD. Just remind me to give the men a word o' wages time o' Saturday. They got to keep their lads at home as long as they're wanted at Rutherford's. [*Turning papers and a bunch of keys out of his pocket on to the desk.*] The new lear man's shaping all right then.

MARTIN. Dale? Knows as much aboot a pot-arch as I knows aboot a flying-machine.

RUTHERFORD. Why didn't you tell me before?

MARTIN. I thought I'd wait to give him a trial. I took a look at the flues myself to make sure it wasn't them at fault. He can't get the heat up properly, and the pots are put into the furnaces afore they're furnace heat. They'll all be broke one o' these days.

RUTHERFORD. We'd better take on Ford.

MARTIN. He finishes at Cardiff Saturday.

RUTHERFORD. He'll do, I suppose?

MARTIN [*feeling in his pocket and pulling out a leather purse or bag*]. You couldn't get a better man for the job in all Tyneside. There's the ten pound young Henderson had out o' the cash-box.

[*He counts it out on the desk.*]

RUTHERFORD. What! He's given it up?

MARTIN. Aye. Leastways, I took it off him.

RUTHERFORD. Has he owned to it?

MARTIN. Sure enough. Said he hadn't gone for to do it. Cried like a bairn, he did.

JOHN [*from his arm-chair by the fire*]. Henderson? Has he been stealing?

MARTIN. Aye, Mr. John. I caught him at it i' the office — at dinner-time when there's nobody much aboot — wi' his hands i' the box.

JOHN. Dirty little sweep! Have you kicked him out?

RUTHERFORD [*pausing with his hand on his cash-box*]. I suppose there's no doubt he's a bad 'un?

MARTIN. Bred and born.

RUTHERFORD. No use giving him another chance.

MARTIN. Throwed away on the likes o' him.

RUTHERFORD [*locking the box and putting it in a drawer*]. Ah.... Well, if he comes back, turn him away. Everything ready for the pot-setting in the morning?

MARTIN. Aye, sir. The night shift'll set four when they stop, and the other shift'll set the others a bit later.

RUTHERFORD. You'll be there to see them do it?

MARTIN. Surely.

RUTHERFORD [*with a curious softening in his voice*]. When'll you get your rest?

MARTIN. Plenty o' time for that, sir.

RUTHERFORD [*crossing to the fire*]. We'll have you on strike one o' these days, Martin.

MARTIN [*turning to go*]. Not me, sir. When you begin to spare yourself you can begin to think about sparing me. And next week things'll go easier.... Is that all for the night, sir?

RUTHERFORD [*wearily*]. Aye. Goodnight to ye. [*He has taken his pipe from the rack above the mantelpiece and is filling it.*] You've further to go now ye're in the Tarn Cottage.

[*There is a slight pause before* MARTIN *replies.*]

MARTIN. Aye. A bit, mebbee.

RUTHERFORD [*lighting his pipe*]. I — should ha' — thought you'd had done better to stick to your old one — near at hand; but you know your own business best.

MARTIN. It's weel enough.

ANN. Now Martin's here, can he no take a look at the range? Susan canna get the oven to go.

JANET [*to* ANN]. The oven's all right.

RUTHERFORD [*with a complete change of voice and manner*]. Now what's that got to do with Martin?

ANN [*subsiding*]. He could tell Baines to send up a man i' the mornin'.

RUTHERFORD. That's not Martin's business — you must send word to Baines himself.

MARTIN. I could easy take a look at it while I'm here, sir. It 'ud save you sending.

RUTHERFORD [*wearily*]. Oh, all right. If you want a job.

ANN. Janet, go and show Martin.

[MARTIN *turns at the door and looks for her to pass out before him.*]

JANET [*standing motionless*]. Susan can show him. [MARTIN *goes, closing the door.*]

RUTHERFORD. Any letters?

ANN [*flurried*]. Yes. They're somewheres. Janet —

RUTHERFORD [*with the sudden irritation of a tired man*]. Bless me, can't I have a simple thing like that done for me? How often have I said to put them in one place and stick to it? [JANET *discovers the letters on the small table by the door and brings them to him. He sits on the settle and stretches out his legs.*] Here, take them off for me. I'm dead beat. [*After a moment's silent revolt she kneels and begins to unlace his boots. He looks at her bent sullen face.*] Ah! sulky, are ye? [*She makes no answer.*] 'Ud like to tell me to take them off myself, I dare say. And I been working the day long for you. [*Getting irritated at her touch.*] Spoilt — that's what you are, my lass. [*Opening a letter.*] What's this? A polite letter from the vicar, eh? Damn polite — a new organ — that's his trouble — thinks I'd like to help pay for it. [*He throws it across the hearthrug to* JOHN.] There's a job for you — you're idle enough. Write and tell His Reverence to go to the devil and ask him for an organ. Or mebbee Richard'll like to do it, as he's his curate. [*To* JANET.] Let be, let be.

[*He takes his boots off painfully one with the other.*]

ANN [*plaintively*]. I'm sure the vicar came in pleasant enough not a week gone, and asked for 'ee —

RUTHERFORD. Asked for my money, you mean. They're civil enough when they want anything, the lot of them. [*To* JANET — *sarcastically, as she carries the boots away.*] Thank 'ee kindly.

[*He gets up and puts his slippers on.* ANN *speaks in a flurried whisper to* JOHN.]

ANN. John, you've got your father's chair.

JOHN [*gets up*]. Sorry.

RUTHERFORD [*drags the chair up to the table, and sits down as if he were tired out. He looks at* JOHN *with a curiously interested expression as he lounges across*]. Feeling better?

JOHN [*uneasy and consequently rather swaggering*]. Oh, I'm still a bit shaky about the knees.

RUTHERFORD. You'll be coming back to work, I suppose. There's plenty to be done. How's the little lad?

JOHN. I don't know — all right, I suppose. Isn't he, Mary?

MARY. Mr. Rutherford asked you.

JOHN. But I don't know.

[RUTHERFORD *looks at* MARY, *she at him; there is a pause.*]

RUTHERFORD [*busy with his letters*]. I thought Gibson had forbidden you to smoke?

[JOHN *rebels for a moment, then throws his cigarette into the fire, with an action like a petted child.*]

JOHN. I must do something.

RUTHERFORD. What have you been busy with to-day? ... This — metal o' yours? Eh?

JOHN [*evasively*]. Aunt Ann's been talking about it.

ANN [*meaning well*]. We've joost been saying how it'll all come right now — all the bother. John'll do it — Rutherford's 'll be itself again.

RUTHERFORD. Martin tells me you've hit on a good thing — a big thing. ... I've got to hear more about it, eh?

JOHN. If you like.

RUTHERFORD. What's that?

[*He looks up slowly under his eyebrows — a long curious look, as if he saw the first possibility of opposition.*]

JOHN [*going over to the fireplace*]. Can't we have dinner?

ANN. You're getting back your appetite. That's a good sign.

RUTHERFORD. Dinner can wait. [*He sweeps a space clear on the table and puts his letters down.* JANET *presently sits down resigned to a family row.* MARY *listens throughout intently, her eyes constantly fixed on* JOHN.] I'm a business man, and I like to know how I stand. [*Launching at* JOHN.] Now — what d'ye mean?

JOHN. I don't understand you, sir.

RUTHERFORD. What's there to understand?

JOHN [*his manner gradually slipping into that of a child afraid of its father*]. Well, I've been away from the Works for two months. Before we begin to talk about the other thing, I'd like to know what's doing.

RUTHERFORD. What's that got to do with it? You never have known what's doing.

JOHN. I think I ought to be told — now.

RUTHERFORD. Now! That's it, is it? You want a bone flung to your dignity! Well, here it is. Things are bad.

JOHN. Really bad?

RUTHERFORD. For the present. These colliery strikes one on top of another, for one thing. Rayner's drew the ponies out of the pit this afternoon.

JOHN. It'll about smash them, won't it?

RUTHERFORD. Mebbee. The question is how it affects us.

JOHN. Oh! We get coal from them?

RUTHERFORD. I should have thought you'd ha' picked up that much — in five years.

JOHN. Stoking isn't my business.

RUTHERFORD. You might have noticed the name on the trucks — you see it every day of your life. Well, yes — we get our coal from them. ... What then?

JOHN. Well — what's going to happen? *How* bad is it?

RUTHERFORD. I said — bad for the present. The balance-sheet for the year's just been drawn up and shows a loss of four thousand on last year's working. It's not a big loss, considering what's been against us — those Americans dumping all that stuff in the spring — we had to stop that little game, and it cost us something to do it. Then the price of materials has gone up, there's a difference there. [*Irritably, answering his own thoughts.*] It's not *ruin*, bless us — it's simply a question of work and sticking together; but the Bank's rather more difficult to manage than usual. There's not one of 'em would sacrifice a shilling of their own to keep the old place going — they want their fees reg'lar. That's their idea of the commercial enterprise they're always talking about. It's the pulse they keep their finger on — when it misses a beat, they come crowding round with their hands up like a lot of damned old women.... Well, well! Something's wanted to pull things together.... Now — this idea of yours. Martin tells me it's worth something.

JOHN [nettled]. Worth something? It's worth thousands a year to any one who works it properly.

RUTHERFORD [with his half smile]. Thousands! That's a fair margin. [Drily.] What's your calculation in figures?

JOHN. That depends on the scale it's worked on.

RUTHERFORD [as to a child]. Yes — so I supposed. What's your preliminary cost?

JOHN [getting nervous]. Nothing — as far as I know. I can't say for certain — something like that.

RUTHERFORD. Something like nothing; and on something like nothing you're going to show a profit of thousands a year on a single metal. [Drily.] Sounds like a beautiful dream, doesn't it? About your cost of working now — that should run you into something?

JOHN [who is getting annoyed]. Thirty per cent less than what you're working at now.

RUTHERFORD. Indeed.... May I ask where and how you've carried out your experiments?

JOHN [uneasily]. I didn't mention it to you. A year ago I got a muffle furnace. I've worked with it from time to time, in the old pot-loft.

RUTHERFORD. Paid for it by any chance?

JOHN. Not yet.

RUTHERFORD. How did you manage for coals now?

JOHN. I — took what I wanted from the heap.

RUTHERFORD. Ah, and your materials — I suppose you took what you wanted of those too? Well, I've no objection, if you can make it good. [Suddenly.] What's your receipt?

JOHN. I haven't — I'm not prepared to say.

[There is a silence. ANN lowers her knitting with an alarmed look.]

RUTHERFORD [heavily]. A week or two ago in this room you told me it was perfected — ready for working to-morrow.

JOHN. Yes — I told you so.

RUTHERFORD [suppressed]. What d'ye mean?... Come, come, sir — I'm your father, I want an answer to my question — a plain answer, if you can give one.

JOHN [in a high-pitched, nervous voice]. I — I'm a business man, and I want to know where I stand. [RUTHERFORD breaks into a laugh.] Oh, you turn me into an impudent school-boy, but I'm not. I'm a man, with a thing in my mind worth a fortune.

ANN. John! [Asserting her authority.] You must tell your father.

JOHN [very excited]. I shan't tell him till I've taken out my patent, so there!

[There is a pause — RUTHERFORD stares at his son.]

RUTHERFORD [heavily]. What d'ye mean?

JOHN. I mean what I say. I want my price.

RUTHERFORD. Your price — your price? [Bringing his fist down on the table.] Damn your impudence, sir. A whippersnapper like you to talk about your price.

JOHN [losing his temper]. I'm not a whippersnapper. I've got something to sell and you want to buy it, and there's an end.

RUTHERFORD. To buy? To sell? And this to your father?

JOHN. To any man who wants what I've made.

[There is a dead silence on this, broken only by an involuntary nervous movement from the rest of the family. Then RUTHERFORD speaks without moving.]

RUTHERFORD. Ah! So that's your line, is it?... This is what I get for all I've done for you.... This is the result of the schooling I give you.

JOHN [with an attempt at a swagger]. I suppose you mean Harrow

RUTHERFORD. It was two hundred pound — that's what I mean.

JOHN. And you gave me a year of it!

RUTHERFORD. And a lot of good you've got of it. . . . What ha' you done with it? Idled your time away wi' your books o' poetry when you should ha' been working. Married a wife who bears you a bairn you can't keep. [*At a movement from* MARY.] Aye — hard words, mebbee. What will you do for your son when the time comes? I've toiled and sweated to give you a name you'd be proud to own — worked early and late, toiled like a dog when other men were taking their ease — plotted and planned to get my chance, taken it and held it when it come till I could ha' burst with the struggle. Sell! You talk o' selling to me, when everything you'll ever make couldn't pay back the life I've given to you!

JOHN. Oh, I know, I know.

ANN. You mustn't answer your father, John.

JOHN. Well, after all, I didn't ask to be born.

RUTHERFORD. Nor did the little lad, God help him.

JOHN [*rapidly*]. Look here, father — why did you send me to Harrow?

RUTHERFORD. Why? To make a gentleman of you, and because I thought they'd teach you better than the Grammar School. I was mistaken.

JOHN. They don't turn out good clerks and office boys.

RUTHERFORD. What's that?

JOHN. I've been both for five years. Only I've had no salary.

RUTHERFORD. You've been put to learn your business like any other young fellow. I began at the bottom — you've got to do the same. There'll not be two masters at Rutherford's while I'm on my legs.

JOHN. That's it, that's it. You make a servant of me.

RUTHERFORD. What do you suppose your work's worth to Rutherford's? Tell me that.

JOHN. What's that matter now? I've done with it. I've found a way out.

RUTHERFORD. A way out — of what?

JOHN [*rather taken aback*]. Well — you don't suppose I'd choose to live here all my life?

ANN [*taking it personally*]. And why not, pray?

RUTHERFORD. Your father has lived here, and your grandfather before you. It's your inheritance — can't you realise that? — what you've got to come to when I'm under ground. We've made it for you, stone by stone, penny by penny, fighting through thick and thin for close on a hundred years.

JOHN. Well, after all, I can't help what you and grandfather chose to do.

RUTHERFORD. *Chose* to do! There's no chose to do. The thing's there. You're my son — my son that's got to come after me.

JOHN. Oh, it's useless. Our ideas of life are utterly different.

RUTHERFORD. Ideas of life! What do you know about life?

JOHN. Oh, nothing, of course.

RUTHERFORD. If you did, you'd soon stop having ideas about it. Life! I've had nigh on sixty years of it, and I'll tell you. Life's *work* — keeping your head up and your heels down. Sleep, and begetting children, rearing them up to work when you're gone — that's life. And when you know better than the God who made you, you can begin to ask what you're going to get by it. And you'll get more work and six foot of earth at the end of it.

JOHN. And that's what you mean me to do, is it?

RUTHERFORD. It's what you've got to do — or starve. You're my son — you've got to come after me.

JOHN. Look here, father. You tell me all this. Just try and see things my way for once. Take the Works. I know you've done it all, built it up, and all that — and you're quite right to be proud of it. But I — I don't like the place, that's the long and the short of it. It's not worth my while. After all, I've got myself to think of — my own life. If I'd done that sooner, by Jove! I'd have been a jolly sight better off. I'd not have married, for one thing. [*With a glance at* MARY.] Not that I regret that. You talk about what you did when you were young. You've told me the sort of time you've had — nothing but grind, grind, since the time you could do anything. And what have you got by it? What have you got? I have myself to think of. I want a run for my money — your money, I suppose it is — other fellows do. And I've made this thing myself, off my own bat — and — and — [*ending lamely*] — I don't see why I shouldn't have a look in.... On my own account....

[*There is an uncomfortable silence.*]

RUTHERFORD [*in a new tone*]. You're going to take out a patent, you say?

JOHN [*taking this as friendly*]. Yes.

RUTHERFORD. Know anything about Patent Law?

JOHN. Well, no — not yet.

RUTHERFORD. It's very simple, and wonderfully cheap — three pound for three years. At the end of three years, you can always extend the time if you want to — no difficulty about that.

JOHN. Oh, no.

RUTHERFORD. But you can't patent a metal.

JOHN. I don't see why not.

RUTHERFORD. What's the use if you do?

JOHN. It's the same as anything else. I take out a patent for a certain receipt, and I can come down on any one who uses it.

RUTHERFORD. And prove that they've used it?

JOHN. They have to find out what it is first. It's not likely I'm going to give the show away. [*Pause.*]

RUTHERFORD. But you want to sell, you say.

JOHN. Yes.

RUTHERFORD. How are you going to do that without giving it away? ... Suppose you go to one of the big chaps — Miles of Cardiff, for example. "Here you are," you say. "I've got an idea worth a fortune. Give me a fortune and I'll tell you what it is." He's not going to buy a pig in a poke any more than I am. People have a way of thinking they're going to make their fortunes, d'ye see? But those people aren't generally the sort you let loose in your glass-house.

JOHN. Of course, I shall make inquiries about all that. I can't say till I know.

RUTHERFORD. Do you remember a little thing of mine — an invention you would call it. Did ye ever happen to see it?

JOHN. Yes. Martin showed it to me once.

RUTHERFORD. What's your opinion of that now — as a business man?

JOHN. Of course, it had the makings of a good thing — any one could see that.

RUTHERFORD. Nobody did. I was nineteen at the time — a lad. Like you, I hadn't the money to run it myself. Clinton, the American people, got hold of it, and sold seven hundred thousand the first six months in New York alone. [*He gets up and addresses the room, generally.*] Dinner in ten minutes.

JOHN. Surely you could have got some one to take it up — an obvious thing like that?

RUTHERFORD [*drily*]. That's how it worked out in my case.

[*He moves slowly to the door.*]

JOHN. You don't believe I can do what I say.

RUTHERFORD. I can't tell — nor can you.

JOHN [*high-handed*]. Oh, very well, then. What are we talking about?

RUTHERFORD. You undertake to produce ordinary white metal at a third of the usual cost — that's it, isn't it? You've worked this out in a muffle furnace. My experience of muffle furnaces is that they're excellent for experimenting in a very small way. A child can hit on an idea for a metal — provided he's materials at his command, and knows a bit about chemistry. But no man living can estimate the cost of that idea until it's worked out on a big scale. Your receipt, as it stands, isn't worth the paper it's written on.

[*As* RUTHERFORD *moves again towards the door* JOHN *makes a movement to stop him.*]

JOHN. Father, look here. Here's an offer.

RUTHERFORD. Thank you kindly.

JOHN. If you'll let me have a pot in one of the big furnaces for a trial — I swear to you, on my honour, I'll let you see the result without touching it, after I've put in the materials. You can clay the pots up — seal them, if you like. Let me do it tomorrow; I can't stand hanging on like this.

RUTHERFORD. To-morrow! Impossible.

JOHN. Why not?

RUTHERFORD. You can't come down to the Works in this weather. You'd catch cold, and be laid up again.

JOHN. The day after then — next week — or, why not? — let Martin do it.

RUTHERFORD. Martin?

[*He turns to look at* JOHN, *struck by a new thought.*]

JOHN. Why not? He can do it as well as I can.

RUTHERFORD. Martin? . . . He knows, then?

JOHN [*surprised*]. Why, he talked to you about it, didn't he?

RUTHERFORD. Yes, yes. But — he's got the receipt?

JOHN. Yes — there's no difficulty at all. Let him mix the metal and clay her up, and you can open her yourself. Then you'll see. You'll take Martin's word for it, I suppose? Only, for Heaven's sake, give me a fair chance.

RUTHERFORD [*moving suddenly*]. Fair chance be damned, sir. You've said your say, and I've said mine. Think it over!

[*He goes out, leaving* JOHN *standing staring after him.*]

JOHN [*under his breath as the door closes*]. Oh, go to the devil!

ANN. For shame to speak so. Just let him hear you. And there, dinner'll be as dry as a bone, and I've waited so long I don't feel as if I could touch a morsel. You might keep your business till we'd had something to eat, I think. [*She hurries out.*]

JANET [*with a sort of admiration*]. Now you've done it.

JOHN. Done it! I've jolly well let him know what I think — and high time, too. [*Brokenly.*] It isn't fair — it isn't fair. Old bully. What am I going to do?

JANET [*dropping into her usual tone*]. What you've always done, I suppose.

JOHN. What's that?

JANET. Say you're sorry. It's the soonest way back.

JOHN. I'm not going back. Sooner than give in, I'll starve. I don't care. I'll go to London, Canada, anywhere. He shan't have me, to grind the life out of me by inches — and he shan't have my metal. If he thinks he's going to pick my brains and give me nothing for it, he'll find himself jolly well mistaken. I don't care. Once and for all, I'm going to make a stand. And he can jolly well go to the devil.

[MARY *speaks for the first time, in a low voice.*]

MARY. What are you making a stand for?

JOHN [*stopping to look at her*]. Good Lord, Mary, haven't you been listening?

MARY. Yes, I've been listening. You said you wanted your price. What is your price?

JANET. All the profits and none of the work — that's John's style.

[*She sits on settle, her chin on her hands.*]

JOHN. A lot you know about it.

[MARY *speaks again.*]

MARY. If you get your price, what will you do with it?

JANET. He won't get it.

JOHN [*to* JANET]. Do you suppose I'm going to sit down under his bullying?

JANET. You've done it all your life.

JOHN. Well, here's an end of it then.

JANET. No one ever stands out against father for long — you know that — or else they get so knocked about they don't matter any more. [*She looks at* MARY, *who has made an involuntary movement.*] Oh, I don't mean he hits them — that's not his way.

JOHN. Oh, don't exaggerate.

JANET. Exaggerate — look at mother! You were too young — I remember — [*To* MARY.] You've been here nigh on three months. If you think you're going to change this house with your soft ways, you're mistaken. Nothing'll change us now — nothing. We're made that way — set — and we've got to live that way.

[*Slowly.*] You think you can make John do something. If ever he does it'll be for fear of father, not for love of you.

JOHN. What do you mean? [*In a high voice.*] If you think I'm going to give in —

JANET. You've said that three times. I know you're going to give in.

JOHN. Well, I'm not — so there.

JANET. What will you do then?

JOHN. That's my business. Curse Rutherford's! Curse it!

JANET [*to* MARY]. That's what he'll do. That's what he's been doing these five years. And what's come of it? He's dragged you into the life here — and Tony — that's all.... I knew all the time you'd have to come in the end, to go under, like the rest of us.

MARY [*quickly*]. No, no —

JANET. Who's going to get you out of it?... John?... You're all getting excited about this metal. I don't know whether it's good or bad, but anyway it doesn't count. In a few days John'll make another row for us to sit round and listen to. In a few days more he'll threaten father to run away. He can't, because he's nothing separate from father. When he gives up his receipt, or whatever it is, it'll go to help Rutherford's — not you or me or any one, just Rutherford's. And after a bit he'll forget about it — let it slide like the rest of us. We've all wanted things, one way and another, and we've let them slide. It's no good standing up against father.

JOHN. Oh, who listens to you? Come along, Mary [*moving to the door*]. Disagreeable old maid!

[*He goes out.* MARY *stands in the same place looking at* JANET.]

MARY. Oh, Janet, no one's any right to be what he is — no one's any right.

JOHN [*calling from the hall*]. Mollie! I want you. [*Irritably.*] Mollie!

MARY. Coming!

[*She follows him.* JANET *remains in the same attitude — her chin on her hands, staring sullenly before her. Suddenly she bows her face in her arms and begins to cry.*]

[MARTIN *comes in from the kitchen on his way out. As he reaches the door leading to the hall, he sees her and stops.*]

MARTIN [*in a whisper*]. My lass!

[*She starts and gets up quickly.*]

JANET. Martin! Martin!

[*He blunders over to her and takes her in his arms with a rough movement, holding her to him — kisses her with passion and without tenderness, and releases her suddenly. She goes to the fireplace, and leans her arms on the mantelpiece, her head on them — he turns away with his head bent. They stand so.*]

MARTIN [*as if the words were dragged from him*]. Saturd'y night — he's away to Wickham — at the Tarn.... Will ye come?

JANET. Yes.

[MARTIN *goes to the door at back. As he reaches it* JOHN RUTHERFORD *comes into the room with some papers in his hand. In crossing between the two, he stops suddenly as if some thought had struck him.*]

MARTIN. Good-night, sir.

RUTHERFORD. Good-night. [*He stands looking at* JANET *till the outer door shuts.*] Why don't you say good-night to Martin? It 'ud be more civil — wouldn't it?

JANET. I have said it. [*Their eyes meet for a moment — she moves quickly to the door.*] I'll tell Susan you're ready.

[RUTHERFORD *is left alone. He stands in the middle of the room with his papers in his hand — motionless, save that he turns his head slowly to look at the door by which* MARTIN *has gone out.*]

ACT II

It is about nine o'clock in the evening. The lamp is burning on the large table. Bedroom candlesticks are on the small table between the window and door.

JOHN RUTHERFORD *is sitting at his desk. He has been writing, and now sits staring in front of him with a heavy brooding face. He does not hear* DICK *as he comes in quietly and goes to the table to light his candle — then changes his mind, looks at his father, and comes to the fire to warm his hands. He looks, as usual, pale and tired.* RUTHERFORD *becomes suddenly aware of his presence, upon which* DICK *speaks in a gentle, nervous tone.*

DICK. I should rather like to speak to you, if you could spare me a minute.

RUTHERFORD. What's the matter with *you?*

DICK. The matter?

RUTHERFORD. You're all wanting to speak to me nowadays — what's wrong with things?... [*Taking up his pen.*] What's the bee in your bonnet?

DICK [*announcing his news*]. I have been offered the senior curacy at St. Jude's, Southport.

RUTHERFORD. Well — have you taken it?

DICK [*disappointed*]. I could not do so without your consent. That's what I want to speak to you about — if you could spare me a minute.

RUTHERFORD [*realising*]. Ah! that means you're giving up your job here?

DICK. Exactly.

RUTHERFORD. Ah.... Just as well, I dare say.

DICK. You will naturally want to know my reasons for such a step. [*He waits for a reply and gets none.*] In the first place, I have to consider my future. From that point of view there seems to be a chance — of more success. And lately — I have had it in my mind for some time past — somehow my work among the people here hasn't met with the response I once hoped for.... I have done my best — and it would be ungrateful to say that I had failed utterly when there are always the few who are pleased when I drop in.... But the men are not encouraging.

RUTHERFORD. I dare say not.

DICK. I have done my best. Looking back on my three years here, I honestly cannot blame myself; and yet — failure is not the less bitter on that account.

RUTHERFORD [*almost kindly*]. Well — perhaps a year or two at a Theological College wasn't the best of trainings for a raw hell like Grantley. It always beats me — whenever a man thinks it's his particular line to deal with humanity in the rough, he always goes to school like a bit of a lad to find out how to do it.

DICK. Ah! you don't understand.

RUTHERFORD. You mean I don't see things your way — well, that's not worth discussing. [*He goes back to his writing.*]

DICK. I have sometimes wondered if your not seeing things my way has had anything to do with my lack of success among your people. For they are your people.

RUTHERFORD. What d'ye mean?

DICK [*sincerely*]. Not only the lack of religious example on your part — even some kind of Sunday observance would have helped — to be more in touch — but all through my ministry I have been conscious of your silent antagonism. Even in my active work — in talking to the men, in visiting their wives, in everything — I have always felt that dead weight against me, dragging me down, taking the heart out of all I do and say, even when I am most certain that I am right to do and say it.   [*He ends rather breathlessly.*]

RUTHERFORD [*testily*]. What the devil have you got hold of now?

DICK. Perhaps I haven't made it clear what I mean.

RUTHERFORD [*deliberately*]. I've never said a word against you or for you. And I've never heard a word against you or for you. Now!... As for what you call your work, I don't know any more about it than a bairn, and I haven't time to learn. I should say that if you could keep the men out of the public-houses and hammer a little decency into the women it might be a good thing. But I'm not an expert in your line.

DICK [*bold in his conviction*]. Father — excuse me, but sometimes I think your point of view is perfectly deplorable.

RUTHERFORD. Indeed! Frankly, I don't realise the importance of my point of view or of yours either. I got my work to do in the world — for the sake o' the argument, so have you — we do it or we don't do it. But what we think about it either way, doesn't matter.

DICK [*very earnestly*]. It matters to God.

RUTHERFORD. Does it. — Now run along — I'm busy.

DICK. This is all part of your resentment — your natural resentment — at my having taken up a different line to the one you intended for me.

RUTHERFORD. Resentment — not a bit. Wear your collar-stud at the back if you like, it's all one to me. You can't make a silk purse out of a sow's ear — you were no good for my purpose, and there's an end. For the matter o' that, you might just as well never ha' been born — except that you give no trouble either way.... Where's John?

DICK. I don't know. His candle is here.... I am still absolutely convinced that I chose the better part.

RUTHERFORD. Probably. There are more ways than one of shirking life, and religion's one of them. If you want my blessing, here it is. As long as you respect my name and remember that I made a gentleman of ye, ye can go to the devil in your own way.

DICK. Then I have your consent to accept St. Jude's?

RUTHERFORD [*writing*]. Aye. Just ring the bell before you go. I want my lamp.

[DICK *does so, depressed and disappointed. On his way to his candle he hesitates.*]

DICK. By the way — I'm forgetting — Mrs. Henderson wants to see you.

RUTHERFORD. And who's Mrs. Henderson?

DICK. William's mother.

RUTHERFORD. William?... The chap who's been pilfering my money? Oh, that matter's settled.

DICK. Oh!... Yes.

RUTHERFORD. Good-night. Did you ring?

DICK. Yes. I rang. Good-night. [*There is a silence, broken by the scratching of* RUTHERFORD'S *pen.* DICK *summons up his courage and speaks again.*] I'm afraid I told Mrs. Henderson she might call to-night.

RUTHERFORD. Did ye now?

DICK. Yes.

RUTHERFORD. And what the devil did ye do that for, if one may inquire?

DICK. She is one of my parishioners — in my district. She came to me — asked my help.

RUTHERFORD. Told you the usual yarn, I suppose. More fool you, to be taken in by it. I can't see her.

DICK. We don't know that it isn't true. The boy has been led astray by bad companions to bet and gamble. It's a regular gang — George Hammond's one, Fade's another.

RUTHERFORD. I know them. Two of the worst characters and the best workers we've got.

DICK. However that may be, the mother's in great grief, and I promised to intercede with you to give her son another chance.

RUTHERFORD. Then you'd no business to promise anything of the kind. The lad's a young blackguard. Bless my soul — look at the head he's got on him! As bad an egg as you'll find in all your parish, and that's saying a good deal.

DICK. I'm afraid it is — God help them. But — [*A series of slow heavy knocks on the outer door are heard, ending with a belated single one.*] I'm afraid that *is* Mrs. Henderson.

RUTHERFORD [*going on with his writing*]. Aye, it sounds like her hand. Been drowning her trouble, mebbee.

DICK [*after another knock*]. Well. She's here.

RUTHERFORD. You'd better go and tell her to go away again.

DICK. Yes. [*He makes an undecided move towards the door; stops.*] The woman ought to have a fair hearing.

RUTHERFORD [*losing patience*]. Fair hearing! She's badgered Martin till he's had to turn her out, and on the top of it all you come blundering in with your talk of a fair hearing — [*he gets up and swings to the door, pushing* DICK *aside*]. Here — let be.

DICK [*speaking with such earnestness that*

Rutherford *stops to look at him*]. Father — one moment.... Don't you think — don't you think it might be better to be friendly with her? To avoid unpleasantness? And gossip afterwards —

Rutherford. What? God help you for a fool, Richard. One would think I'd nothing to do but fash myself about this young blackguard and speak soft to his mother — [*he goes out into the hall and is heard opening the door*]. Now, Mrs. Henderson — you've come about your lad. You've had my answer.

[Mrs. Henderson *is heard speaking apparently on the mat.*]

Mrs. Henderson. Oh, if you please, sir — if you could just see your way to sparin' me a minute I'd take it kindly, that I would. And I come all the way from home on me two feet — and me a poor widder woman.

[*She drifts imperceptibly just inside the room. She is a large and powerful woman with a draggled skirt and a shawl over her head, and she is slightly drunk.* Rutherford *follows her in and stands by the open door, holding the handle.*]

Rutherford. Well, then, out with it. What ha' ye got to say?

Mrs. Henderson. It's my lad Bill as has been accused o' takin' your money —

Rutherford. Ten pounds.

Mrs. Henderson. By Mr. Martin, sir.

Rutherford. What then?

Mrs. Henderson. And not another living soul near to say the truth of it.

Rutherford. Martin's my man, Mrs. Henderson. What he does, he does under my orders. Besides, Martin and your son both say he took it. They've agreed about it.

Mrs. Henderson. Aye, when he was scared out of his life he owned to it. I'm not denying he owned to it —

Rutherford. Oh, that's it, is it? He wants to go back on it? Why did he give up the money?

Mrs. Henderson. He was that scared, sir, o' being sent to the gaol and losing his place and all, what wi' Mr. Martin speaking that harsh to him, and all, and him a bit of a lad —

Rutherford. I see. In that case I owe him ten pounds?

Mrs. Henderson. Eh?

Rutherford. I've took ten pounds off him, poor lad, all his honest savings mebbee. Good-night, Mrs. Henderson.

Mrs. Henderson. Ah, Mr. Rutherford, sir, don't 'ee be hard on us — don't 'ee now. We all got summat to be overlooked — every one on us when ye get down to it — and there's not a family harder working nor more respected in Grantley. Mr. Richard here'll speak for us.

Rutherford. Speak for them, Richard.

Dick. I ... I do believe they are sincerely trying to do better.

Rutherford. Just so — better not rake up bygones. My time's short, Mrs. Henderson, and you've no business to come up to the house at this time o' night, as you know well enough.

Mrs. Henderson. Aye, sir, begging your pardon. I'm sure I'd be the last to intrude on you and the family if it warn't for —

Rutherford. I dare say. What did Martin say to you when you intruded into the glass-house?

Mrs. Henderson. What did he say to me?

Rutherford [*impatiently*]. Aye.

Mrs. Henderson [*fervently*]. Far be it from me to repeat what he did say. God forbid that I should dirty my mouth wi' the words that man turned on me! before the men too, and half of 'em wi' their shirts off and me a decent woman. [*Violently.*] "Hawd yer whist," I says to 'n. "Hawd yer whist for a shameless — "

Rutherford. That'll do, that'll do — that's enough. You can take what Martin said from me. The matter's ended. [Dick *makes an appealing movement.*] Five years ago your son was caught stealing coppers out o' the men's coats — men poorer than himself. Don't forget that. I knew about it well enough. I gave him another chance because he was a young 'un, and because you ought to ha' taught him better.

Mrs. Henderson. Me? Taught him better! That I should ever hear the like!

Rutherford. I gave him another

chance. He made the most of it by robbing me the first time he thought he was safe not to be caught. Every man's got a right to go to the devil in his own way, as I've just been telling Mr. Richard here, and your son Bill's old enough to choose his. I don't quarrel with him for that. But lads that get their fingers in my till are no use to me. And there's an end!

DICK. Father! If you talk to her like this —

RUTHERFORD. It's you that's brought her to hear me — you must take the consequences.

DICK. No one is wholly bad — we have no right to say the lad is past hope, to condemn him utterly.

MRS. HENDERSON. Thank 'ee kindly, Mr. Richard, sir — it's gospel truth every word of it. My son's as good a son as ever a lone woman had, but he's the spittin' image of his father, that easily led. And now to have him go wrong and all through keeping bad company and betting on the racing — just as he might ha' laid a bit on you, sir, in your young days and won his money too, sir, along o' your being sartain sure to win.

RUTHERFORD. Well, I would have done my best to get him his money. But if I'd lost he'd ha' had to take his beating and pay up like a man and no whining about it. You take an interest in running?

MRS. HENDERSON [fervently]. Aye, sir, and always has done ever since I was a bit lass. And many's the Saturday me and my old man's gone down to the ground to see you run.

RUTHERFORD. You don't happen to have heard who's won the quarter-of-a-mile at Broughton, do you?

DICK. Father!

MRS. HENDERSON. I did hear as it was Dawson, sir, as I was passing.

RUTHERFORD. Ah. Shepherd was overtrained. What time did he do — Dawson?

MRS. HENDERSON. I don't know, sir.

RUTHERFORD. I made him a shade worse than six under at his trial. Shepherd should have been that.

DICK. Father, please! Do let us talk this matter out seriously.

RUTHERFORD. Seriously? What more?

DICK. You see, it is as I said. I am sure Mrs. Henderson will answer for her son's good conduct if you will consent to take him back — won't you, Mrs. Henderson? Just this once. Your kindness may make all the difference, reform him altogether, who knows? He's had his lesson and I hate to preach, but — there is such a thing as repentance.

RUTHERFORD [drily]. That's all right. You say what you think! And don't misunderstand me. I've no objection to Bill Henderson repenting, but I won't have him doing it in my Works, d'ye see? There's nothing spreads so quick as a nice soft feeling like that, and — who knows — we might have half-a-dozen other young blacklegs at the same game? Now, Mrs. Henderson, go home like a sensible woman and send your lad away from Grantley. He'll soon find his feet if he's a mind to go straight. Keep him clear o' the pit towns — put him on a farm somewhere, where there aren't so many drinks going. And if I were you [looking at her], why not go with him yourself?

MRS. HENDERSON [after a pause, suddenly truculent]. Me? Me leave Grantley? Me go to a place where I'm not respected and not a friend to speak for me? In Grantley I was born and in Grantley I'll live, like yourself. And beggin' your pardon, though you are the master, I'll joost take the liberty o' choosin' my own way.

RUTHERFORD. Quite right — quite right. When you've lived and had your bairns and got drunk in a place you're apt to get attached to it. I'm that way myself. But it's just as well to change your drinks once in a while. It's only a friendly word of advice I'm giving you. Take it or leave it.

MRS. HENDERSON [bridling]. And so I will take it or leave it. Much obliged to 'ee.

RUTHERFORD. And now go home, like a good woman.

MRS. HENDERSON [tossing her head with an unsteady curtsey]. And so I will, and a lot I got for my trouble — thank 'ee for nothing.

RUTHERFORD. Thank me for not prosecuting your son, as I might ha' done.

MRS. HENDERSON [*working herself up*]. Prosecute! Prosecute my son! And why didn't ye do it? Ye darena'— that's why. You're feared o' folks talkin' — o' things said i' the court. And ye took and hided him and him a bit of a lad, and not a decent woman in Grantley but's crying shame on ye!

RUTHERFORD [*good-humouredly*]. Now, Richard, this is where you come in. You brought her here.

MRS. HENDERSON [*very shrill*]. You let him off easy, did you? You give him another chance, did you? My lad could ha' had you up for assault — that's what he'd ha' done if he'd had a mind, and quite right too. It's him that's let you off, mind that. And you may thank your devil's luck you're not up afore the magistrate this next Assizes that ever is, and printed in the paper for all the countryside to mock at.

RUTHERFORD. Go on, Richard. She's your parishioner. Turn her out.

MRS. HENDERSON. Him turn me out? A bit of a preaching bairn no stronger nor a linty — him with his good noos and his sojers-o'-Christ-arise! Whee was it up and ran away from old Lizzie Winter like a dawg wi' a kettle tied to his tail?

RUTHERFORD [*quietly without turning*]. We'll have all your secrets in a minute. Are you going, Mrs. Henderson?

MRS. HENDERSON. I'll go when it pleases me, and not afore!

RUTHERFORD. Are you going —

[*He gets up and moves towards her in a threatening manner.*]

MRS. HENDERSON [*retreating*]. Lay hands on me! Lay hands on a helpless woman! I'll larn ye! I'll larn ye to come on me wi' yer high ways. Folks shall hear tell on it, that they shall, and a bit more besides. I'll larn ye, sure as I'm a living creature.... I'll set the police on ye, as sure as I'm a living woman....

RUTHERFORD [*to* DICK, *contemptuously*]. Hark to that — hark to it.

MRS. HENDERSON. You think yourself so grand wi' your big hoose, and your high ways. And your grandfather a potman like my own. You wi' your son that's the laughing-stock o' the parish, and your daughter that goes wi' a working man ahint your back! And so good-night to 'ee.

[*The outer door bangs violently. There is a pause.* DICK *speaks in a voice scarcely audible.*]

DICK. What was that? ... She said something — about Janet.

RUTHERFORD [*impatiently*]. Good God, man — don't stand staring there as if the house had fallen.

DICK [*shaking*]. I told you to be careful — I warned you — I knew how it would be.

RUTHERFORD. Warned me! You're fool enough to listen to what a drunken drab like that says!

DICK. She's not the only one —

RUTHERFORD [*looking at him*]. What d'ye mean? What's that?

DICK. People are talking. I've — heard things.... It isn't true — it can't be — it's too dreadful.

RUTHERFORD. Heard things — what ha' ye heard?

DICK. It isn't true.

RUTHERFORD. Out with it.

DICK. Lizzie Winter that time — called out something. I took no notice, of course. ... Three nights ago as I was coming home — past a public-house — the men were talking. I heard something then.

RUTHERFORD. What was it you heard?

DICK. There was his name, and Janet's. Then one of them — George Hammond, I think it was — said something about having seen him on the road to the Tarn late one evening with a woman with a shawl over her head — Martin!

RUTHERFORD. Martin!

DICK [*trying to reassure himself*]. It's extremely unlikely that there is any truth in it at all. Why, he's been about ever since we were children. A servant, really. No one's ever thought of the possibility of such a thing. They *will* gossip, and one thing leads to another. It's easy to put two and two together and make five of them. That's all it is, we'll find. Why, even I can recall things I barely noticed at the time — things that might point to its being true — if it weren't so utterly impossible.

RUTHERFORD [hoarsely]. Three nights gone. In this very room —

DICK. What? [running on again]. They've seen some one like Janet, and started the talk. It would be enough.

RUTHERFORD [speaking to himself]. Under my roof —

DICK. After dark on the road with a shawl — all women would look exactly alike.... It's a pity he's taken the Tarn Cottage.

RUTHERFORD [listening again]. Eh?

DICK. I mean it's a pity it's happened just now.

RUTHERFORD. A good mile from the Works.

DICK. You can't see it from the village.

RUTHERFORD. A good mile to walk, morn and night.

DICK. No one goes there.

RUTHERFORD. A lone place — a secret, he says to himself. Martin...

[He stands by the table, his shoulders stooped, his face suddenly old. DICK makes an involuntary movement towards him.]

DICK. Father! Don't take it like that, for Heaven's sake — don't look so broken.

RUTHERFORD. Who's broken... [he makes a sign to DICK not to come near]. Him to go against me. You're only a lad — you don't know. You don't know.

[JOHN comes into the room, evidently on his way to bed.]

JOHN [idly]. Hullo! [Stops short, looking from one to the other.] What's the matter?

RUTHERFORD [turning on him]. And what the devil do you want?

JOHN. Want? — nothing... I thought you were talking about me, that's all.

RUTHERFORD. About you, damn you — go to bed, the pair o' ye.

DICK. Father —

RUTHERFORD. Go to bed. There's men's work to be done here — you're best out o' the way — [he goes to his desk and speaks down the tube]. Hulloh there — Hulloh!

DICK. Wouldn't it be better to wait to talk things over? Here's John — you may be able to settle something — come to some arrangement.

RUTHERFORD. Who's that? Gray — has Martin gone home? Martin! Tell him to come across at once — I want him. Aye — to the house — where else? Have you got it? Tell him at once.

JOHN [suspicious]. I rather want a word with Martin myself. I think I'll stay.

RUTHERFORD. You'll do as you're bid.

JOHN. What do you want Martin for at this time of night?

RUTHERFORD. That's my business.

JOHN. About my metal —

RUTHERFORD. Your metal! What the devil's your metal got to do with it?

[Breaks off.]

JOHN [excited]. Martin's got it. You know that. You're sending for him. Martin's honest — he won't tell you.

DICK. Here's Janet.

[JANET has come in in answer to the bell and stands by the door sullen and indifferent, waiting for orders.]

JANET. Susan's gone to bed. [As the silence continues she looks round.] The bell rang.

DICK [looking at RUTHERFORD]. Some time ago. The lamp — father wanted his lamp. [She goes out.]

JOHN [rapidly]. It's no use going on like this, settling nothing either way. Sooner or later we've got to come to an understanding.... [DICK makes a movement to stop him.] Oh, shut up, Dick!

[He breaks off at a look from RUTHERFORD.]

RUTHERFORD. I want to have it clear. You heard what I said, three days past?

JOHN. Yes, of course.

RUTHERFORD. You still ask your price?

JOHN. I told you — the thing's mine — I made it.

RUTHERFORD [to JOHN]. You've looked at it — fair and honest.

DICK. Oh, what is the use of talking like this now? Father! you surely must see — under the circumstances — it isn't right — it isn't decent.

JOHN. It's perfectly fair and just, what

I ask. It benefits us both, the way I want it. You've made your bit. Rutherford's has served its purpose — and it's coming to an end — only you don't see it, Guv'nor. Oh, I know you're fond of the old place and all that — it's only natural — but you can't live for ever — and I'm all right — if I get my price . . .

RUTHERFORD. So much down for yourself — and the devil take Rutherford's.

JOHN. You put it that way —

RUTHERFORD. Yes or no?

JOHN. Well — yes.

[*A knock is heard at the outer door.*]

DICK. That's Martin, father —

JOHN. I'll stay and see him — I may as well.

RUTHERFORD. To-morrow — to-morrow I'll settle wi' ye.

[JOHN *looks at him in amazement;* DICK *makes a sign to him to come away; after a moment he does so.*]

JOHN [*turning as he reaches the door*]. Thanks, Guv'nor — I thought you'd come to see things my way. [*They go out.*]

RUTHERFORD. Come in.

[MARTIN *comes in, cleaning his boots carefully on the mat — shuts the door after him and stands cap in hand.* RUTHERFORD *sits sunk in his chair, his hands gripping the arms.*]

MARTIN. I came up as soon as I could get away. [*Pause.*]

RUTHERFORD [*as if his lips were stiff*]. You've stayed late.

MARTIN. One o' the pots in Number Three Furnace ran down, and I had to stay and see her under way.

RUTHERFORD. Sit down. . . . Help yourself.

MARTIN. Thank 'ee, sir. [*He comes to the table and pours out some whisky, then sits with his glass resting on his knee.*] Winter's setting in early.

RUTHERFORD. Aye —

MARTIN. There's a heavy frost. The ground was hardening as I came along . . . . They do say as Rayner's'll be working again afore the week's out.

RUTHERFORD. Given in — the men?

MARTIN. Aye — the bad weather'll have helped it. Given a fine spell the men 'ud ha' hung on a while longer — but the cold makes 'em think o' the winter — turns the women and bairns agin them.

RUTHERFORD. Ah!

MARTIN. I thought you'd like to hear the coal 'ud be coming in all right, so I just went over to have a word wi' White the Agent this forenoon. [*He drinks, then as the silence continues, looks intently at* RUTHERFORD.] You sent for me?

[JANET *comes in carrying a reading-lamp. She halts for a moment on seeing* MARTIN. *He gets up awkwardly.*]

MARTIN [*touching his forelock*]. 'Evenin'.

JANET. Good-evening.

[*She sets the lamp on the desk.* RUTHERFORD *remains in the same position till she goes out, closing the door. There is a moment's silence, then* MARTIN *straightens himself, and they look at each other.*]

MARTIN [*hoarsely*]. You're wanting summat wi' me?

RUTHERFORD. I want the receipt of Mr. John's metal.

MARTIN [*between amazement and relief*]. Eh?

RUTHERFORD. You've got it.

MARTIN. Aye —

RUTHERFORD. Then give it me.

MARTIN. I cannot do that, sir.

RUTHERFORD. What d'ye mean?

MARTIN. It's Mr. John's own — what belongs to him — I canna do it.

RUTHERFORD. On your high horse, eh, Martin? You can't do a dirty trick — you can't, eh?

MARTIN. A dirty trick. Ye'll never be asking it of me — you never will —

RUTHERFORD. I am asking it of ye. We've worked together five and twenty years, master and man. You know me. You know what there is'll stop me when I once make up my mind. I'm going to have this metal, d'ye understand. Whether Mr. John gives it me or I take it, I'm going to have it.

MARTIN. It's Mr. John's own; if it's ever yourn, he must give it to ye himself. It's not for me to do it. He's found it, and it's his to do what he likes wi'. For me to go behind his back — I canna do it.

[*They look at each other; then* RUTHERFORD *gets out of his chair and begins to pace up and down with his hands behind him. He speaks deliberately, with clumsy gestures and an air of driving straight to a goal.*]

RUTHERFORD. Sit down.... Look how we stand. We've seven years' losing behind us, slow and sure. We've got the Bank that's poking its nose into this and that, putting a stop to everything that might put us on our legs again — because o' the risk.... Rutherford's is going down — down — I got to pull her up somehow. There's one way out. If I can show the directors in plain working that I can cover the losses on the first year and make a profit on the second, I've got 'em for good and all.

MARTIN. That's so — and Mr. John'll see it, and ye'll come to terms —

RUTHERFORD. Mr. John's a fool. My son's a fool — I don't say it in anger. He's a fool because his mother made him one, bringing him up secret wi' books o' poetry and such-like trash — and when he'd grown a man and the time was come for me to take notice of him, he's turned agin me —

MARTIN. He'll come roond — he's but a bit lad yet —

RUTHERFORD. Turned agin me — agin me and all I done for him — all I worked to build up. He thinks it mighty clever to go working behind my back — the minute he gets the chance he's upon the hearthrug dictating his terms to me. He knows well enough I've counted on his coming after me. He's all I got since Richard went his ways — he's got me there.... He wants his price, he says — his price for mucking around with a bit of a muffle furnace in his play-hours — that's what it comes to.

MARTIN. Aye — but he's happened on a thing worth a bit.

RUTHERFORD. Luck! Luck! What's he done for it? How long has he worked for it — tell me that — an hour here and a bit there — and he's got it! I've slaved my life long, and what have I got for it? Toil and weariness. That's what I got — bad luck on bad luck battering on me — seven years of it. And the worst bit I've had yet is that when it turns it's put into my son's hands to give me or not, if you please, as if he was a lord.

MARTIN. He'll come roond — lads has their notions — we all want to have things for ourselves when we're young, all on us —

RUTHERFORD. Want — want — lad's talk! What business has he to want when there's Rutherford's going to the dogs?

MARTIN. That canna be, it canna — he'll have to see different.

RUTHERFORD. He won't see different.

MARTIN. He'll learn.

RUTHERFORD. When it's too late. Look here, Martin, we can't go on — you know that as well as I do — leastways you've suspected it. Ten years more as things are'll see us out. Done with! Mr. John's made this metal — a thing, I take your word for it, that's worth a fortune. And we're going to sit by and watch him fooling it away — selling it for a song to Miles or Jarvis, that we could break to-morrow if we had half a chance. And they'll make on it, make on it — while Rutherford's'll grub on as we've been grubbing for the last seven years. I'm speaking plain now — I'm saying what I wouldn't say to another living man. We can't go on. You've been with me through it all. You've seen me do it. You've seen the drag and the struggle of it — the days when I've nigh thrown up the sponge for very weariness — the bit o' brightness that made me go on — the times when I've stood up to the Board, sick in the heart of me, with nothing but my will to turn 'em this way or that. And at the end of it — I come up against this — a bit o' foolishness — just foolishness — and all that I done'll break on that — just that.

MARTIN. Nay — nay —

RUTHERFORD. I'm getting old, they say — old — there's new ways in the trade, they say. And in their hearts they see me out of it — out o' the place I built afore they learnt their letters, many of 'em —

MARTIN. That'll never be.

RUTHERFORD. Why not — when you've got but to put your hand in your pocket to save the place and you don't do it. You're with them — you're with the money-grubbing little souls that can't see beyond the next shilling they put in their pockets, that's content to wring the old place dry, then leave it to the rats — you're with a half-broke puppy like Mr. John that wants to grab his bit for himself and clear out. Twenty-five years ... and you go sniveling about what Mr. John thinks of ye — what's right for you to do. Everybody for himself — his pocket or his soul, it's all one. And Rutherford's loses her chance through the lot o' ye. Blind fools!

MARTIN. You blame me — you put me i' the wrong. It's like as if I'd have to watch the old place going down year by year, and have it on my mind that I might ha' saved her. But Mr. John's got his rights.

RUTHERFORD. You think I'm getting this metal for myself against Mr. John?

MARTIN. I'm loath to say it.

RUTHERFORD. Answer me —

MARTIN. Mr. John'll see it that way.

RUTHERFORD. Stealing like, out o' his pocket into mine. When men steal, Martin, they do it to gain something. If I steal this, what'll I gain by it? If I make money, what'll I buy with it? Pleasure, mebbee? Children to come after me — glad o' what I done? Tell me anything in the wide world that'd bring me joy, and I'll swear to you never to touch it.

MARTIN. If you think what you're saying, it's a weary life you got to face.

RUTHERFORD. If you give it to me, what'll you gain by it? Not a farthing shall you ever have from me — no more than I get myself.

MARTIN. And what'll Mr. John get for it?

RUTHERFORD. Rutherford's — when I'm gone. [*After a silence.*] He'll thank you in ten years — he'll come to laugh at himself — him and his price. He'll see the Big Thing one day, mebbee, like what I've done. He'll see that it was no more his to keep than 'twas yours to give nor mine to take.... It's Rutherford's.... Will you give it me?

MARTIN [*facing him*]. If I thought that we'd make a farthing out of it, either on us —

RUTHERFORD. Will ye give it me —

[MARTIN *stands looking at him, then slowly begins to feel in his pockets.*]

RUTHERFORD. Got it — on you?

MARTIN [*taking out a pocket-book*]. He'll never forgi' me, Mr. John won't — never i' this world.... It should be somewheres. He'll turn agin me — it'll be as if I stole it.

RUTHERFORD. Got it?

MARTIN. Nay, I mun' ha' left it up hame. Aye, I call to mind now — I locked it away to keep it safe.

RUTHERFORD. Can ye no' remember it? Think, man — *think!*

MARTIN. Nay, I canna be sure. I canna call the quantities to mind.

RUTHERFORD [*violently*]. Think — think — you must know!

MARTIN [*wonderingly*]. I can give it 'ee first thing i' the morning.

RUTHERFORD. I want it to-night.... No, no — leave it — you might get it wrong — better make sure — bring it up in the morning. Good-night to 'ee — good-night. And remember — I take your word to bring it — no going back, mind ye —

MARTIN. Nay, nay. [*Turning to go.*] I doubt if Mr. John'll ever see it in the way you do. If you could mebbee explain a bit when he hears tell of it — put in a word for me, belike —

RUTHERFORD. I'm to bed.

MARTIN. I take shame to be doing it now.

RUTHERFORD. Off wi' ye — off wi' ye — wi' your conscience so delicate and tender. Keep your hands clean, or don't let any one see them dirty — it'll do as well.

MARTIN. He worked it out along o' me. Every time it changed he come running to show me like a bairn wi' a new toy.

RUTHERFORD. It's for Rutherford's....

MARTIN. Aye, for Rutherford's — Good-night, sir. [*He goes out.*]

[*After a pause,* JANET *comes in to put things straight for the night. She goes into the* hall and is heard putting the chain on the outer door — comes back, locking the inner door — then takes the whisky decanter from the tray and locks it in the sideboard, laying the key on the desk. RUTHERFORD stands on the hearthrug. As she takes up the tray he speaks.]

RUTHERFORD. How long has this been going on atween you and Martin?
[She puts the tray down and stands staring at him with a white face.]
JANET. How long?
RUTHERFORD. Answer me.
JANET. September — about when Mary and Tony came. [There is a long silence. When it becomes unbearable she speaks again.] What are you going to do? [He makes no answer.] You must tell me what you're going to do?
RUTHERFORD. Keep my hands off ye.
JANET. You've had him here.
RUTHERFORD. That's my business.
JANET [speaking in a low voice as if she were repeating a lesson]. It wasn't his fault. It was me. He didn't come after me. I went after him.
RUTHERFORD. Feel — proud o' yourself?
JANET. You can't punish him for what isn't his fault. If you've got to punish any one, it's me. . . .
RUTHERFORD. How far's it gone?
JANET [after a pause]. Right at first. I made up my mind that if you ever found out, I'd go right away, to put things straight. [She goes on presently in the same toneless voice.] He wanted to tell you at the first. But I knew it would be no use. And once we'd spoken — every time was just a little more. So we let it slide. . . . It was I said not to tell you.
RUTHERFORD. Martin . . . that I trusted as I trust myself.
JANET. I'll give him up.
RUTHERFORD. You can't give him back to me. He was a straight man. What's the good of him now? You've dragged the man's heart out of him with your damned woman's ways. [She looks at him.]
JANET. You haven't turned him away — you couldn't do that!

RUTHERFORD. That's my business.
JANET. You couldn't do that — not Martin . . .
RUTHERFORD. Leave it — leave it. . . . Martin's my servant, that I pay wages to. I made a name for my children — a name respected in all the countryside — and you go with a working-man. To-morrow you leave my house. D'ye understand. I'll have no light ways under my roof. No one shall say I winked at it. You can bide the night. To-morrow when I come in I'm to find ye gone. . . . Your name shan't be spoke in my house . . . never again.
JANET. Yes. [She stands looking down at the table, then slowly moves to go, her feet dragging — stops for a moment and says in a final tone, almost with a sigh of relief.] Then there'll be no need for anybody to know it was Martin —
RUTHERFORD. No need to know! Lord, you drive me crazy! With all Grantley telling the story — my name in every public-house.
JANET. When I'm gone. [Looking up.] What did you say?
RUTHERFORD. It's all over the place by now. Richard's heard it — your own brother. . . . You've been running out o' night, I suppose. Somebody's seen.
JANET. What's Dick heard?
RUTHERFORD. What men say about women like you. They got a word.
JANET. The men. . . . Oh God!
RUTHERFORD. Aye — you say that now the thing's done — you'll whine and cry out now you done your worst agin me.
JANET. Let me be.
RUTHERFORD. You're going to put things straight, are ye — you're going to walk out comfortable wi' your head up and your fine talk!
JANET. I'm ready to stand by it.
RUTHERFORD. It's not you that's got to stand by it — it's me! What ha' you got to lose? Yourself, if you've a mind to. That's all. It's me that's to be the laughing-stock — the Master whose daughter goes wi' a working-man like any Jenny i' the place —
JANET. Oh! You stand there. *To* drive me mad —

RUTHERFORD. That'll do — that'll do. I've heard enough. You've confessed, and there's an end.

JANET. Confessed? As if I'd stolen something. [*Brokenly.*] You put it all on to me, every bit o' the wrong.

RUTHERFORD. Ah, you'll set to and throw the blame on Martin now. I thought we'd come to it.

JANET. No, no. I've taken that. But ... you make no excuse.... You think of this that I've done separate from all the rest — from all the years I done as you bid me, lived as you bid me.

RUTHERFORD. What's that to do wi' it? I'm your father! I work for 'ee.... I give 'ee food and clothes for your back! I got a right to be obeyed — I got a right to have my children live respectable in the station where I put them. You gone wrong. That's what you done. And you try to bring it up against me because I set you up i' the world. Go to bed!

JANET. Oh, you've no pity.... [*She makes a movement to go, then turns again as if for a moment.*] I was thirty-six. Gone sour. Nobody'd ever come after me. Not even when I was young. You took care o' that. Half of my life was gone, well-nigh all of it that mattered.... What have I had of it, afore I go back to the dark? What have I had of it? Tell me that. Tell me!

RUTHERFORD. Where's the man as 'ud want you wi' your sulky ways?

JANET. I've sat and sewed — gone for a walk — seen to the meals — every day — every day.... That's what you've given me to be my life — just that!

RUTHERFORD. Talk, talk, talk! Fine words to cover up the shame and disgrace you brought on me —

JANET. On you?

RUTHERFORD. Where'd you ha' been if I hadn't set you up?

JANET. Down in the village — in amongst it, with the other women — in a cottage — happy, mebbee.

RUTHERFORD [*angrily*]. I brought you up for a lady as idle as you please — you might ha' sat wi' your hands afore you from morn till night if ye'd had a mind to.

JANET. Me a lady? What do ladies think about, sitting the day long with their hands before them? What have they in their idle hearts?

RUTHERFORD. What more did you want, in God's name?

JANET. Oh, what more! The women down there know what I wanted ... with their bairns wrapped in their shawls and their men to come home at night-time. I've envied them — envied them their pain, their poorness — the very times they hadn't bread. Theirs isn't the dead empty house, the blank o' the moors, they got something to fight, something to be feared of. They got life, those women we send cans o' soup to out o' pity when their bairns are born. Me a lady! with work for a man in my hands, passion for a man in my heart! I'm common — common.

RUTHERFORD. It's a lie! I've risen up. You can't go back on it — my children can't go back.

JANET. Who's risen — which of us?

RUTHERFORD. You say that because you've shamed yourself, and you're jealous o' them that keep decent like gentlefolk —

JANET. Dick — that every one laughs at? John — with his manners?

RUTHERFORD. Whisht wi' your wicked tongue!

JANET. Who's Mary? A little common work-girl — no real gentleman would ha' looked at.... You think you've made us different by keeping from the people here. We're just the same as they are! Ask the men that work for you — ask their wives that curtsey to us in the road. Do you think they don't know the difference? We're just the same as they are — common, every one of us. It's in our blood, in our hands and faces; and when we marry, we marry common —

RUTHERFORD. Marry! Common or not, nobody's married you that I can see —

JANET. Leave that — don't you say it!

RUTHERFORD. It's the truth, more shame to 'ee.

JANET [*passionately*]. Martin loves me honest. Don't you come near! Don't you touch that!... You think I'm sorry you've found out — you think you've done for me when you use shameful words on me and turn me out o' your house. You've let me out o' gaol! Whatever happens to me now, I shan't go on living as I lived here. Whatever Martin's done, he's taken me from you. You've ruined my life, you with your getting on. I've loved in wretchedness, all the joy I ever had made wicked by the fear o' you.... [*Wildly.*] Who are you? Who are you? A man — a man that's taken power to himself, power to gather people to him and use them as he wills — a man that'd take the blood of life itself and put it into the Works — into Rutherford's. And what ha' you got by it — what? You've got Dick, that you've bullied till he's a fool — John, that's waiting for the time when he can sell what you've done — and you got me — me to take your boots off at night — to wellnigh wish you dead when I had to touch you.... Now!... Now you know!

ACT III

It is about eleven o'clock on the following morning. JANET *is sitting at the table with a shawl about her shoulders talking in low tones to* MARY, *who is opposite.*

JANET [*after a pause*]. You mean that you guessed?
MARY. Yes.
JANET. You knew all the time, and you didn't tell? Not even John?
MARY. Why should I tell him?
JANET. I would ha' told Martin if it had been you.
MARY. Not John.
JANET. It was good of you. You've always been better to me than I've been to you.
MARY. What are you going to do?
JANET. He says I'm to go. He's to come in and find me gone, and no one's to speak of me any more. Not John, nor Dick, nor Aunt Ann — I'm never to set foot in this room again. Never to lock up and give him the keys last thing. Never to sit the long afternoon through in the window, till the chimneys are bright in the dark. I've done what women are shamed for doing — and all the night I've barely slept for the hope in my heart.
MARY. Hope?
JANET. Of things coming. I had a dream — a dream that I was in a place wi' flowers, in the summer-time, white and thick like they never grow on the moor — but it was the moor — a place near Martin's cottage. And I dreamt that he came to me with the look he had when I was a little lass, with his head up and the lie gone out of his eyes. All the time I knew I was on my bed in my room here — but it was like as if sweetness poured into me, spreading and covering me like the water in the tarn when the rains are heavy in the fells.
MARY. Is Mr. Rutherford very angry?
JANET. He won't never hear my name again. Oh, last night I said things to him, when he blamed me so — things he can't never forget. I was wild — mad with the bitterness of it. He made it all ugly with the things he said. I told him what I never looked to tell him, though I'd had it in my heart all these years. All the time I was speaking I was dead with shame that he should know, and I had to go on. But afterwards — it was as if I'd slipped a burden, and I was glad he knew, glad that Dick heard it in the street, glad that he sneaked of me behind my back — glad! For, when I'd got over the terror of it, it came to me that this was what we'd been making for ever since you came without knowing it, that we were to win through to happiness after all, Martin and I, and everything come right. Because I've doubted. Men's lives are different to ours. And sometimes, when we've stolen together, and afterwards I've seen his face and the sadness of it, I've wondered what I had to give him that could count against what he'd lost.
MARY. But that's done with now.
JANET. Yes! That's why I dreamt of him so last night. It was as if all that was best in me was in that dream — what I was as a bairn, and what I'm going to be. He couldn't help but love me. It was a message — I couldn't have thought of it by myself. It's something that's come to

me, here. [*Putting her hands on her breast.*] Part of me.

[MARY *looks at her with a new understanding. After a pause she speaks again, very gently.*]

MARY. Where are you going when Martin comes for you?

JANET. I don't know yet. He'll say what to do.

MARY. Have you got your things ready?

JANET [*as if she scarcely heard*]. Yes.

MARY. I could see to them for you.

JANET. They're all ready. I put them together early in the box mother had.

[*She breaks off, listening.*]

MARY. Janet, if ever the time should be when you want help — and it does happen sometimes even to people who are very happy — remember that I'll come when you ask me — always.

JANET. He's coming now!

[*She sits listening, her eyes bright.* MARY *goes out quietly, closing the door.*]

[MARTIN *comes in from the hall.*]

JANET [*very tenderly*]. Martin!

[*He stands in the doorway, his cap in his hands, his head bent. He looks spent, broken, and at the sight of him the hope dies slowly out of her face.*]

MARTIN. Is Mr. John about?

JANET. I don't know.

MARTIN. I mun see 'n. I got summat to say to 'n.

JANET. He's down at the Works, mebbee —

MARTIN. I canna seek him there — I got summat to say to 'n.

JANET. You could give a message.

MARTIN. Nay. It's summat that's got to be said to his face — like a man.

JANET. Have you nothing to say to me, Martin — to my face like a man?

MARTIN. What should there be to say betwixt you and me? It's all said long since.

JANET. He's turned you away?

[*He raises his eyes and looks at her for the first time.*]

MARTIN. Aye. You've said it. What I've been trying to tell myself these three months past. Turned away I am, sure enough. Twenty-five year. And in a minute it's broke. Wi' two words.

JANET. He'll call you back. He can't do without you, Martin. He's done it in anger like he was last night. He'll call you back.

MARTIN. He never calls no one back. He's a just man, and he's in the right of it. Anger — there's no anger in a face that's twisting like a bairn's — white as if it was drained o' the blood. There's no anger in a man that stands still where he is, when he might ha' struck and killed and still been i' the right.

[JANET *gets up slowly and goes to the fire.*]

JANET. Come and get warm by the fire. It's a bitter cold morning. Come and get warm.

[*He moves slowly across and sits on the settle. She kneels beside him, takes his hands and begins to rub them.*]

JANET [*as if he were a child*]. Your hands are as cold, as cold — like frozen. It's all fresh and new to you now, my dear, the surprise of it. It'll pass — and by-and-by you'll forget it — be glad, mebbee. Did you get your breakfast?

MARTIN. Aye.

JANET. What have you been doing — since?

MARTIN. Walking — walking. Up on the fell I been — trying to get it clear —

JANET. On the fell, in such weather! That's why you're so white and weary. You should have come to me, my honey — you should ha' come straight to me. I would ha' helped you, my dear — out of my love for 'ee.

MARTIN. There's no help.

JANET. You say that now because your heart's cold with the trouble. But it'll warm again — it'll warm again. I'll warm it out of my own heart, Martin — my heart that can't be made cold, not if he killed me. Why, last night he was just the same with me as he's been with you. I know it all — there's nothing you feel that I don't know. We'll face it together, you and me, equal — and by-and-by it'll be different. What we done was for love — people give up everything for love, Martin; every day they say there's some one in the world that does it. Don't 'ee take on so — don't 'ee.

MARTIN. Twenty-five year —

JANET. Don't 'ee, my dear.

MARTIN [*brokenly*]. I'd rather ha' died than he turn me away. I'd ha' lost everything in the world to know that I was true to'n, like I was till you looked at me wi' the love in your face.

JANET. Everything in the world. . . . I gave you joy — joy for the toil he gave you, softness for his hardness.

MARTIN [*without bitterness*]. Aye, you were ready. And you gave the bitter with the sweet. Every time there was him to face, wi' a heart like lead.

JANET. It was a power — a power that came, stronger than us both.

MARTIN. You give me the word.

JANET. You took away my strength. [*There is a silence. He sits looking dully at the fire.*] Any one might think me light. It isn't true. I never had any one but you, never. All my life I've been alone. When I was a little lass I wasn't allowed to play with the other bairns, and I used to make signs to tell them I wanted to. You'd never have known I loved you if I hadn't given you the word — and all our happiness, all that's been between us, we'd never have had it — gone through our lives seeing each other, speaking words that didn't matter, and grown old and never known what was sleeping in our hearts under the dullness. I wasn't light. It was only that I couldn't be shamed for you.

MARTIN. Nay, nay, it was a great love ye gave me — you in your grand hoose wi' your delicate ways. But it's broke me.

JANET. But — it's just the same with us. Just the same as ever it was.

MARTIN. Aye. But there's no mending, wi' the likes o' him.

JANET. What's there to mend? What's there to mend except what's bound you like a slave all the years? You're *free* — free for the first time since you were a lad mebbee — to make a fresh start.

MARTIN. A fresh start? Wi' treachery and a lyin' tongue behind me?

JANET. With our love that nothing can break. Oh, my dear, I'll help 'ee. Morning, noon, and night I'll work for 'ee, comfort 'ee. We'll go away from it all, you and me together. We'll go to the south, where no one's heard tell of Rutherford's or any of us. I'll love 'ee so. I'll blind your eyes wi' love so that you can't look back.

MARTIN [*looking up.*] Aye. There's that.

JANET. We'll begin again. We'll be happy — happy. You and me, free in the world! All the time that's been'll be just like a dream that's past, a waiting time afore we found each other — the long winter afore the flowers come out white and thick on the moors —

MARTIN. He'll be lookin' to me to right ye. He'll be lookin' for that.

JANET. To right me?

MARTIN. Whatever's been, they munna say his daughter wasn't made an honest woman of. He'll be lookin' for that.

[*There is a silence. She draws back slowly, dropping her hands.*]

JANET. What's he to do with it? [*He looks at her, not understanding.*] Father — what's he to do with it?

MARTIN. It's for him to say — the Master.

JANET. Master!

MARTIN. What's come to ye, lass?

JANET. It's time you left off doing things because of him. You're a free man. He's not your master any more.

MARTIN. What's wrong wi' ye?

JANET. You'll right me because of him. You'll make an honest woman of me because he's looking for it. He can't make you do as he bids you now. He's turned you away. He's not your master any more. He's turned you away.

MARTIN. Whisht — whisht. [*He sinks his head in his hands.*] Nay, but it's true. I'll never do his work again. But I done it too long to change — too long.

JANET. He's done with you — that's how much he cares. I wouldn't ha' let you go, not if you'd wronged me.

MARTIN. Twenty-five years ago he took

me from nothing. Set me where I could work my way up — woke the lad's love in me till I would ha' died for him — willing. It's too long to change.

JANET [*passionately*]. No — no.

MARTIN. I'll never do his work no more; but it's like as if he'd be my master just the same — till I die —

JANET. No, no, not that! You mustn't think like that! You think he's great because you've seen him at the Works with the men — everybody doing as he bids them. He isn't great — he's hard and cruel — cruel as death.

MARTIN. What's took you to talk so wild?

JANET [*holding him*]. Listen, Martin. Listen to me. You've worked all your life for him, ever since you were a little lad. Early and late you've been at the Works — working — working for him.

MARTIN. Gladly!

JANET. Now and then he gie you a kind word — when you were wearied out mebbee — and your thoughts might ha' turned to what other men's lives were, wi' time for rest and pleasure. You didn't see through him, you wi' your big heart, Martin. You were too near to see, like I was till Mary came. You worked gladly, mebbee — but all the time your life was going into Rutherford's — your manhood into the place he's built. He's had you, Martin — like he's had me, and all of us. We used to say he was hard and ill-tempered. Bad to do with in the house — we fell silent when he came in — we couldn't see for the little things — we couldn't see the years passing because of the days. And all the time it was our lives he was taking bit by bit — our lives that we'll never get back.

MARTIN. What's got ye to talk so wild?

[*He moves from her as she talks and clings to him.*]

JANET. Now's our chance at last! He's turned us both away, me as well as you. We two he's sent out into the world together. Free. He's done it himself, of his own will. It's ours to take, Martin — our happiness. We'll get it in spite of him. He'd kill it if he could.

MARTIN. Whisht, whisht! You talk wild!

JANET. Kill it, kill it! He's gone nigh to it as it is. [*As he makes a movement to rise.*] Martin, Martin, I love 'ee. I'm old — with the lines on my face — but it's him that's made me so. I'm bitter-tongued and sharp — it's him that's killed the sweetness in me, starved it till it died. He's taken what should have been yours to have your joy of. Stolen it — remember that — and say he's in the right! Say it when you wish me young and bonny. Say it as I shall when I look in your face for the love that can't wake for me.

MARTIN. Bide still, bide still!

JANET. I wouldn't ha' turned against you, not if you'd nigh killed me — and you set his love up against mine! Martin!

[*He gets up, not roughly, but very wearily, and moves away from her.*]

MARTIN. It bain't the time, it bain't the time. I been a bad servant. Faithless. We can twist words like we done all along to make it seem different, but there it stands. Leave him, when you talk to me. Leave him.... Mebbee he's had his mind full of a big work when you've took a spite at him.

JANET. Ah!

MARTIN. Womenfolk has their fancies, and mebbee they don't know the harshness that's in the heart of every man that fights his way i' the world when he comes into the four walls of his bit hoose of a night and sees the littleness of it. [*Standing by the table.*] I'm a plain man with no book larning, and mebbee I don't see far. But I've watched the Master year in year out, and I never seed him do a thing, nor say a thing, that he warn't in the right of. And there's not a man among them that can say different. [*Taking up his cap.*] I'll be seekin' Mr. John.

JANET [*speaks in a dull, toneless voice, kneeling where he left her*]. He says I have to be gone by the time he come in. Where am I to go to?

[*He turns to look at her with a puzzled face.*]

MARTIN. Aye. There's that.

JANET. Where am I to go to?

MARTIN. It would be best to go a bit away — where ye wouldna' be seen for a while.

JANET. Where's a place — far enough?

MARTIN. There's Horkesley — up the line. Or Hillgarth yonder. He's not likely to be knawed thereaboots.

JANET. I haven't any money.

[MARTIN *slowly counts out some coins on the table.*]

MARTIN. It'll be a hard life for you, and you not used to it. Work early and late — wi' a bairn mebbee. Bitter cold i' the winter mornings wi' the fire to light and the breakfast to get, and you not used to it; we mun just bide it, the pair on us. Make the best of it. I've saved two hundred pounds. There'll be summat to get along on whilst I look for a job. Afterwards we mun just bide it. [*There is a silence.*]

JANET [*without bitterness*]. Take up your money.

MARTIN [*puzzled*]. It's for you, lass.

JANET. Take up your money. I'll have no need of it.

[*After a moment he picks it up and returns it to his pocket.*]

JANET [*still kneeling*]. After all, you'd give the world to ha' been true to him — you'd give me, that you said was the world. He'd have you back if it wasn't for me. He needs you for the Works. If I was out of it there'd be no more reason — you'd go back, and people would think it all a mistake about you and me. Gossip. After a bit he'd forget and be the same. Because he needs you for the Works. Men forgive men easy where it's a woman, they say, and you could blame me, the pair of you. Me that gave you the word.

[MARY *comes in hurriedly.*]

MARY. John's coming. He's coming across from the Works.

[MARTIN *turns to face the door.* JANET *does not move.*]

[JOHN *comes in excited and nervous.*]

JOHN [*awkwardly*]. Hullo! [*He looks at* JANET *and speaks to* MARTIN.] What are you here for?

MARTIN. Mr. John — I summat to say to you — summat I must say afore I go.

JOHN. You'd better keep quiet, I should think. Oh, I know! I've been with the Guv'nor, and he's told me plain enough. You'd better keep quiet.

MARY. John, you must listen.

JOHN. I tell you I know! The less we talk about it the better; I should think you would see that — the whole beastly, disreputable business. I can't stay — I can't talk calmly, if you can — I'm better out of it.

[*He makes for the door.* MARTIN *stops him.*]

MARTIN. Mr. John.... You been wi' the Master. What was it he told you — plain enough?

JOHN [*significantly*]. What was it!

MARTIN. Did he tell you he'd got your metal? [JOHN *looks at him.*]

JOHN. Are you mad?

MARTIN. I've give it him — I took it him this morning, and when he got it safe he turned me away. That's what I got to say.

JOHN [*sharply*]. I don't believe it! You can't have! You haven't got the quantities!

MARTIN. The paper I took the last trial we made —

JOHN [*his voice high-pitched with excitement*]. Don't — don't play the fool.

MARTIN. I'm speaking God's truth, and you'd best take it. Yesterday night he sent for me — and I give it him, because he asked me for it. He was i' the right, yesterday night — I don't call to mind how. And just now I give it him. That's what I got to say.

[JOHN *stands staring at him speechless.* MARTIN, *having said what he came to say, turns to go.* MARY, *suddenly realising what it all means, makes an involuntary movement to stop him.*]

MARY. Martin! You've given the receipt to Mr. Rutherford! He's got it — he'll take the money from it!... You're sure of what you say, Martin? You haven't made a mistake?

MARTIN. Mistake?

MARY. You may have got it wrong —

the quantities, or whatever it is. It all depends on that, doesn't it? The least slip would put it all wrong, wouldn't it?

MARTIN [*tired out and dull*]. There's no mistake.

MARY [*with a despairing movement*]. Oh! you don't know what you've done!

JOHN [*almost in tears*]. He knows well enough — you knew well enough. You're a thief — you're as bad as he is — you two behind my back. It was mine — the only chance I had. Damn him! Damn him! You've done for yourself, that's one thing — you're done for! You'll not get anything out of it now, not a farthing. He's twisted you round his finger, making you think you'd have the pickings, has he? And then thrown you out into the street for a fool and worse. You're done for! . . . You've worked with me, seen it grow. I never thought but to trust you as I trusted myself — and you *give it away* thinking to make a bit behind my back! You'll not get a farthing now — not a farthing — you're done for.

MARTIN. Hard words, Mr. John, from you to me. But I done it, and I mun bide by it.

JOHN. Oh, clear out — don't talk to me. By Heaven! I'll be even with him yet.

MARTIN. I done it — but it bain't true what you think, that I looked to make a bit. I give it to him, but I had no thought o' gain by what I done. . . . It's past me — it's all past me — I canna call it to mind, nor see it plain. But I know one thing, that I never thought to make a penny. [*Suddenly remembering.*] It was for Rutherford's — that's what he said — I mind it now. He said, for Rutherford's — and I seed it yesterday night. It was as clear as day — yesterday night.

[*No one answers. After a moment he goes out. As the outer door closes* JOHN *suddenly goes to* RUTHERFORD'S *desk and begins pulling out drawers as if searching for something.*]

MARY [*watching him*]. What are you doing?

JOHN. Where's the key, curse it!

MARY [*sharply*]. You can't do that!

JOHN. Do what? I'm going to get even.

MARY. Not money! You can't take his money!

JOHN [*unlocking the cash-box*]. Just be quiet, will you? He's taken all I have. [*He empties the money out on to the desk, his hands shaking.*] Fifteen — twenty — twenty-three. And it's twenty-three thousand he owes me more like, that he's stolen. Is there any more — a sixpence I've missed, that'll help to put us even? Twenty-three quid — curse him! And he stood and talked to me not an hour ago, and all the time he *knew!* He's mean, that's what he is — mean and petty-minded. No one else could have done it — to go and get at Martin behind my back because he knew I was going to be one too many for him.

MARY [*imploringly*]. Put it back! Oh, put it back!

JOHN. Oh, shut up, Mollie.

MARY. Don't take it, John.

JOHN. I tell you it's mine, by right — you don't understand. . . . How am I to get along if I don't?

MARY. You've not got to do this, John — for Tony's sake. I don't care what he's done to you — you've not got to do it.

JOHN. Don't make a tragedy out of nothing. It's plain common sense! [*Angrily.*] And don't look at me as if I were stealing. It's mine, I tell you. I only wish there were a few thousands — I'd take them!

MARY. John, listen to me. I've never seriously asked you to do anything for me in my life. Just this once — I ask you to put that money back.

JOHN. My dear girl, don't be so foolish —

MARY [*compelling him to listen to her*]. Listen! You're Tony's father! I can't help it if you think I'm making a tragedy out of what seems to you a simple thing. One day he'll know — some one'll tell him that you stole money — well, then, that you took money that wasn't yours, because you thought you had the right to it. What will it be like for him? Try and realise — we've no right to live as we like — we've had our day together, you and I — but it's past, and we know it. He's what matters

now — and we've got to live decently for him — keep straight for him —
JOHN [*answering her like an angry child*]. Then *do* it! I've had enough — I'm sick of it.

[JANET, *who all this time has been kneeling where* MARTIN *left her, gets up suddenly, stumbling forward as if she were blind. The other two stop involuntarily and watch her as she makes for the door, dragging her shawl over her head. As the outer door shuts on her,* MARY *with a half-cry makes a movement to follow her.*]

MARY. Janet!
JOHN. Oh, let her be!
MARY [*facing the door*]. Where's she going to?
JOHN. I'm not going to argue — I've done that too long — listening to first one and then another of you. What's come of it? You wouldn't let me go out and sell the thing while it was still mine to sell. I might have been a rich man if I'd been let to go my own way! You were always dragging me back, everything I did — with your talk. Tony — you're perpetually cramming him down my throat, till I'm sick of the very name of the poor little beggar. How much better off is he for your interfering? Give up this and give up that — I've lost everything I ever had by doing as you said. Anybody would have bought it, anybody! and made a fortune out of it — and there it is, lost! gone into Rutherford's, like everything else. Damn the place! Damn it! Oh, let him wait! I'll be even with him. I came back once because I was a soft fool — this time I'll starve sooner.
MARY. You're going away?
JOHN. Yes, I'm going for good and all.
[*She stands looking at him.*]
MARY. Where are you going to?
JOHN. London — anywhere. Canada probably — that's the place to strike out on your own —
MARY. You mean to work, then?
JOHN [*impatiently*]. Of course. We can't live for ever on twenty-three quid.
MARY. What are you going to work at?
JOHN. Anything — as long as I show him —

MARY. But what — what?
JOHN. Oh, there'll be something. Damn it, Mary, what right have you to catechise?
MARY. Don't, please. I'm not catechising; I want to know. It's a question of living. What are you going to do when you've spent what you've got?
JOHN [*trying not to look shamefaced as he makes the suggestion*]. You could go back to Mason's for a bit — they'd be glad enough to have you.
MARY. Go back?
JOHN [*resentfully*]. Well, I suppose you won't mind helping for a bit till I see my way. What was the screw you got?
MARY. Twenty-five.
JOHN. That would help if the worst came to the worst.
MARY. We lived on it before.
JOHN. We could put up at the same lodgings for a bit. They're cheap.
MARY. Walton Street.
JOHN [*loudly*]. Anyway, I'm going to be even with him — I'll see him damned before I submit. I've put up with it long enough for your sake — I'm going to get a bit of my own back for once. After all, I'm his son — you can't count Dick; when I'm gone he'll begin to see what he's lost. Why, he may as well *sell* Rutherford's outright — with no one to come after him. He's worked for that — all his life! Lord! I'd give something to see his face when he comes in and asks for me!

[MARY *makes no answer, as indeed there is none to make. She speaks again, not bitterly, but as one stating a fact.*]

MARY. So that's your plan. [*There is a silence, in which he cannot meet her eyes. She repeats, without hope.*] John, once more — from my soul I ask you to do what I wish.
JOHN [*impatiently*]. What about?
MARY. The money. To put it back. [*He makes a movement of desperate irritation.*] No, don't answer just for a moment. You don't know how much depends on this — for us both. Our future life — perhaps our last chance of happiness together — you don't know what it may decide.
JOHN. I tell you you don't understand.

[*There is a blank silence. He moves uncomfortably.*] You can't see. What's twenty-three quid!
[*She makes a despairing movement.*]
MARY [*in a changed voice*]. I'm afraid you'll find it rather a burden having me and Tony — while you're seeing your way, I mean.
JOHN. A burden? You? Why, you've just said you could help at Mason's —
MARY. I can't go out all day and leave Tony.
JOHN. Old Mrs. What's-'er-name would keep an eye on him.
MARY. It would free you a good deal if we weren't with you.
JOHN. Of course if you won't do anything to help —
MARY [*after a pause*]. How would it be if you went alone? Then — when you've seen your way — when you've made enough just to live decently — you could write and we could come to you. Somewhere that would do for Tony — wherever it may be.
JOHN. In a month or two.
MARY. In a month or two.
JOHN [*awkwardly*]. Well, perhaps it would be better — as you suggest it. I really don't exactly see how I'm going to manage the two of you. . . . You mean — stay on here in the meantime.
MARY. Yes — stay on here.
JOHN. But the Guv'nor — I'm afraid it'll be pretty rotten for you without me.
MARY. That's all right.
JOHN [*irritably*]. All these stupid little details — we lose sight of the real issue. That's settled, then.
MARY. Yes — settled. [*She moves, passing her hand over her eyes.*] How are you going?
JOHN [*relieved*]. What's the time now? Close on twelve!
MARY. You're not thinking of going now — at once!
JOHN. There's the one o'clock train. I'll get old Smith to drive me to the Junction — it doesn't stop.
MARY. There won't be time to pack your things.

JOHN. Send them after me.
MARY. You've no food to take with you.
JOHN. That doesn't matter; I'll get some on the way.
MARY [*suddenly*]. You can't go like this! We must talk — we can't end it all like this.
JOHN. I must — I didn't know it was so late — he'll be in to dinner. Cheer up, dear, it's only for a little while. I hate it too, but it wouldn't do for him to find me here. It would look — weak.
MARY. No, no — you're right — you mustn't meet — it would do no good. [*She stands undecided for a moment, then goes quickly into the hall and brings his overcoat.*] It's bitter cold. And it's an open trap, isn't it?
JOHN. I shall be all right. [*She helps him on with the coat.*] It won't be long — the time'll pass before you know where you are; it always does — I haven't time to see the kid — it's the only thing to be done — other fellows make their fortunes every day, why shouldn't I?
MARY [*as if he were a child*]. Yes, yes, why shouldn't you?
JOHN. Something'll turn up — and I've got the devil's own luck at times — you'll see. I've never had a chance up to now. Some day you'll believe in me. [*He sees her face and stops short.*] Mollie — !
[*Takes her in his arms. She breaks down, clinging to him.*]
MARY. Oh, my dear — if I could!
JOHN [*moved*]. I will do it, Mollie — I swear I will. Something'll turn up, and it'll all come right — we'll be as happy as kings, you see if we aren't. Don't, dear, it's only for a little while. . . . Well, then — will you come with me now?
MARY. No, no, that can't be. Go, go — he'll be in directly. Go now.
[*She goes with him to the outer door.*]

[ANN RUTHERFORD *comes in on her way through the room.*]

ANN. Who is it's got the door open on such a day? And the wind fit to freeze a body's bones! [*The outer door is heard closing.* MARY *comes in slowly, very pale.*] Come in, come in, for the Lord's sake.

[*Looking at her.*] What be ye doing out there?
MARY. He's gone.
ANN [*cross with the cold*]. Gone, gone, this one and that — John? And what'll he be gone for? I never seed such doings, never!
MARY. Shall I make up the fire?
ANN. And you all been and let it down. Nay, nay, I'll do it myself. It'll not be up for ten minutes or more. Such doings. What'll he be gone for?
MARY. He's had a quarrel with his father.
ANN [*putting logs on, half-whimpering*]. A fine reason for making folks talk — bringing disgrace on the house, and all Grantley talking, and to-morrow Sunday — I never seed the like, never!
MARY. It's no use crying.
ANN. It's weel enough for you to talk — you bain't one of the family, a stranger like you. You don't know. When you've come up i' the world and are respected there's nothing pleases folk better than to find something agin you. What am I to say when I'm asked after my nevvy? Tell me that. And him gone off without so much as a change to his back — it aren't respectable. And there's Janet not ten minutes since gone along the road wi' her shawl over her head like a common working lass. Where it's to end, I'm sure I can't tell.
MARY. Perhaps it is ended.
ANN. Perhaps half the work's left and the house upset. Susan'll be giving notice just now — her and her goings on. As if lasses weren't hard enough to get — and there's dinner and all —
MARY. Do you want the table laid?
ANN. It'd help — though you've no call to do it — you got your own troubles — the little lad'll be wanting you mebbee.
MARY. He's still asleep. I'll leave the door open and then I shall hear him.
[*She opens the door, listening for a moment before she comes back into the room.*]
ANN. Janet'll be back, mebbee, afore you've finished. Such doings — everything put wrong. I'll go and fetch the bread.

[*She wanders out, talking as she goes.* MARY *takes the red cloth off the table, folds it, takes the white one from the drawer in the sideboard, and spreads it. As she is doing so,* JOHN RUTHERFORD *comes in. He stands looking at her for a moment, then comes to the fire.*]
RUTHERFORD [*as he passes her*]. Dinner's late.
MARY [*going on with her work*]. It'll be ready in a few minutes.
RUTHERFORD. It's gone twelve.
[*She makes no answer. He takes his pipe off the chimney-piece and begins to fill it. As he is putting his tobacco-pouch back into his pocket his eyes fall on the table; he stops short.*]
RUTHERFORD. You've laid a place short. [*Raising his voice.*] D'ye hear me, you've laid a — [*She looks at him.*]
MARY. No.
[*She goes to the sideboard and spreads a cloth there. He stands motionless staring at the table.*]
RUTHERFORD. Gone. Trying to frighten me, is he? Trying a bit o' bluff — he'll show me, eh? And all I got to do is to sit quiet and wait for him to come back — that's all I got to do.
MARY [*quietly*]. He won't come back.
RUTHERFORD. Won't he! He'll come back right enough when he feels the pinch — he'll come slinking back like a whipped puppy at nightfall, like he did afore. I know him — light — light-minded like his mother afore him. [*He comes to his desk and finds the open cash-box.*] Who's been here? Who's been here? [*He stands staring at the box till the lid falls from his hand.*] Nay — he'll not come back, by God!
MARY [*hopelessly*]. He thought he had the right — he believed he had the right after you'd taken what was his.
RUTHERFORD. I'd sooner have seen him in his grave.
MARY. He couldn't see.
RUTHERFORD. Bill Henderson did that because he knowed no better. And my son knowed no better, though I made a gentleman of him. Set him up. I'm done with

him — done with him. [*He drops heavily into the arm-chair beside the table and sits staring before him. After a long silence he speaks again.*] Why haven't you gone, too, and made an empty house of it?

MARY. I'm not going.

RUTHERFORD. Not going, aren't you? Not till it pleases you, I take it — till he sends for you?

MARY. He won't send for me.

RUTHERFORD [*quickly*]. Where's the little lad?

MARY. Asleep upstairs. [*After a pause she speaks again in level tones.*] I've lived in your house for nearly three months. [*He turns to look at her.*] Until you came in just now you haven't spoken to me half-a-dozen times. Every slight that can be done without words you've put upon me. There's never a day passed but you've made me feel that I'd no right here, no place.

RUTHERFORD. You'll not die for a soft word from the likes o' me.

MARY. Now that I've got to speak to you, I want to say that first — in case you should think I'm going to appeal to you, and in case I should be tempted to do it.

RUTHERFORD. What ha' ye got to ask of me?

MARY. To ask — nothing. I've a bargain to make with you.

RUTHERFORD [*half truculent*]. Wi' me?

MARY. You can listen — then you can take it or leave it.

RUTHERFORD. Thank ye kindly. And what's your idea of a bargain?

MARY. A bargain is where one person has something to sell that another wants to buy. There's no love in it — only money — money that pays for life. I've got something to sell that you want to buy.

RUTHERFORD. What's that?

MARY. My son. [*Their eyes meet in a long steady look. She goes on deliberately.*] You've lost everything you have in the world. John's gone — and Richard — — and Janet. They won't come back. You're alone now and getting old, with no one to come after you. When you die, Rutherford's will be sold — somebody'll buy it and give it a new name, perhaps, and no one will even remember that you made it. That'll be the end of all your work. Just — nothing. You've thought of that. I've seen you thinking of it as I've sat by and watched you. And now it's come. . . . Will you listen?

RUTHERFORD. Aye.

[*She sits down at the other end of the table, facing him.*]

MARY. It's for my boy. I want — a chance of life for him — his place in the world. John can't give him that, because he's made so. If I went to London and worked my hardest, I'd get twenty-five shillings a week. We've failed. From you I can get what I want for my boy. I want — all the good common things: a good house, good food, warmth. He's a delicate little thing now, but he'll grow strong like other children. I want to undo the wrong we've done him, John and I. If I can. Later on there'll be his schooling — I could never save enough for that. You can give me all this — you've got the power. Right or wrong, you've got the power. . . . That's the bargain. Give me what I ask, and in return I'll give you — him. On one condition. I'm to stay on here. I won't trouble you — you needn't speak to me or see me unless you want to. For ten years he's to be absolutely mine, to do what I like with. You mustn't interfere — you mustn't tell him to do things or frighten him. He's mine. For ten years more.

RUTHERFORD. And after that?

MARY. He'll be yours.

RUTHERFORD. To train up. For Rutherford's? You'd trust your son to me?

MARY. Yes.

RUTHERFORD. After all? After Dick, that I've bullied till he's a fool? John, that's wished me dead?

MARY. In ten years you'll be an old man; you won't be able to make people afraid of you any more.

RUTHERFORD. Ah! Because o' that? And because I have the power?

MARY. Yes. And there'll be money for his clothes — and you'll leave the Works to him when you die.

[*There is a silence. He sits motionless, looking at her.*]

RUTHERFORD. You've got a fair notion of business — for a woman.

MARY. I've earned my living. I know all that that teaches a woman.

RUTHERFORD. It's taught you one thing — to have an eye to the main chance.

MARY. You think I'm bargaining for myself?

RUTHERFORD. You get a bit out of it, don't you?

MARY. What?

RUTHERFORD. A roof over your head — the shelter of a good name — your keep — things not so easy to come by, my son's wife, wi' a husband that goes off and leaves you to live on his father's charity.

[*There is a pause.*]

MARY [*slowly*]. There'll be a woman living in the house — year after year, with the fells closed round her. She'll sit and sew at the window and see the chimney flare in the dark; lock up, and give you the keys at night —

RUTHERFORD. You've got your bairn.

MARY. Yes, I've got him! For ten years. [*They sit silent.*] Is it a bargain?

RUTHERFORD. Aye. [*She gets up with a movement of relief. As he speaks again, she turns, facing him.*] You think me a hard man. So I am. But I'm wondering if I could ha' stood up as you're standing and done what you've done.

MARY. I love my child. That makes me hard.

RUTHERFORD. I used to hope for my son once, like you do for yours now. When he was a bit of a lad, I used to think o' the day when I'd take him round and show him what I had to hand on. I thought he'd come after me — glad o' what I'd done. I set my heart on that. And the end of it's just this — an empty house — we two strangers, driving our bargain here across the table.

MARY. There's nothing else.

RUTHERFORD. You think I've used him badly? You think I've done a dirty thing about this metal?

MARY. It was his.

RUTHERFORD. I've stolen it behind his back — and I'm going to make money out of it?

MARY. I don't know — I don't know.

RUTHERFORD. It'll come to your son.

MARY. Yes.

RUTHERFORD. Because I done that, he'll have his chance, his place i' the world. What would ha' gone to the winds, scattered and useless, 'll be his. He'll come on, young and strong, when my work's done, and Rutherford's'll stand up firm and safe out o' the fight and the bitterness — Rutherford's that his grandfather gave his life to build up.

MARY [*stopping him with a gesture*]. Hush!

RUTHERFORD. What is it? [*They both listen.*] The little lad. He's waking!

[MARY *runs out. The room is very silent as* RUTHERFORD *sits sunk in his chair, thinking.*]

THE UNCHASTENED WOMAN
A MODERN COMEDY IN THREE ACTS
By LOUIS KAUFMAN ANSPACHER

COPYRIGHT, 1916, BY LOUIS KAUFMAN ANSPACHER

COPYRIGHT, 1912, AS A DRAMATIC COMPOSITION

All rights reserved, including that of translation into foreign languages, including the Scandinavian.

All acting rights, both professional and amateur, are reserved, in the United States, Great Britain, and all countries of the Copyright Union, by Louis Kaufman Anspacher. Performances forbidden and right of representation reserved. Piracy or infringement will be prosecuted in accordance with the penalties provided by the United States Statutes: Sec. 4966, U.S. Revised Statutes, Title 60, Chap. 3.

Application for the right of performing this play should be made to the author.

Persons desiring to read this play professionally in public should first apply to the author.

PERSONS OF THE PLAY

Arranged in the order of their first entrances

HUBERT KNOLLYS
MRS. MURTHA, *a charwoman*
MISS SUSAN AMBIE
CAROLINE KNOLLYS, *wife of Hubert Knollys*
LAWRENCE SANBURY
HILDEGARDE SANBURY, *his wife*
MISS EMILY MADDEN
MICHAEL KRELLIN

TIME: *The Present*
PLACE: *New York City*

THE UNCHASTENED WOMAN

ACT I

The play opens in a morning in October. It is about ten o'clock. The first act presents the drawing-room of the KNOLLYS' *house, situated on a corner in the fashionable fifties, New York City. The room is spacious, but a little old-fashioned. Up stage, at the right, is a large arch opening on a hall, which leads out to the front door off stage at the right. In the center of the arch there are three steps leading to a platform, from which a flight of stairs rises, going left, and leading to the rooms above. The balustrade continues on a level with the stage, and indicates that the stairs lead also downward from the front hall to the basement.*

In the middle of the right wall is a large marble mantelpiece, with an open fireplace. Above the mantel hangs an old family portrait. On the wall below the mantel hangs an ornamental Venetian mirror. In the rear wall of the room, toward the left, is a mahogany door, leading to the basement. Between this door and the arch stands a large bookcase, filled with books in expensive bindings. The left wall of the room is pierced by two large windows, with practical shades and blinds.

A library table and three chairs occupy the center of the room, under a heavy chandelier. There is a large divan chair with cushions and a footstool placed down left of the room. Set on an angle in front of the fireplace is a Davenport. Below this, also on an angle is a settle. Several of the chairs and the Davenport are covered with linen slips or sheets, which indicate that the house has not been occupied for some time. The size and visible appointments of the room must suggest the atmosphere of large, though rather formal, luxury.

The curtain rises on an empty stage. Dim light sifts through the closed blinds. There is a pause, and then the front door of the house is heard to open and close. A moment later HUBERT KNOLLYS *enters from the hall, through the arch, putting his keys into his pocket. He is followed by* MRS. MURTHA. HUBERT KNOLLYS *is a tall and distinguished-looking man of fifty-three. He is dressed in a morning suit and a Panama hat. He carries a whisky and a couple of soda bottles under his arm. He also has a newspaper.* MRS. MURTHA *is an elderly Irish woman.*

HUBERT. Phew! It's close in here! [*Goes to a window which he opens and lets in the sunlight, then he turns and looks at* MRS. MURTHA.] Is your name Agnes Murtha?

MURTHA. No. That's me daughter. D'ye see, Agnes was comin', the Lord love her, but she had a fall yesterday —

HUBERT. Oh, too bad.

[*He begins removing the slips from the furniture.*]

MURTHA [*undoing her bonnet and showing her white head*]. Yis — She's a foine eddication, so she has; but she bez a little weak in th' knee. So Oi came over mesilf, as soon as Oi heard from Mrs. Sanbury.

HUBERT [*seeing her white hair*]. Perhaps you're not strong enough —

MURTHA. Oi'm as shtrong as ivir Oi wuz. [*She energetically takes a slip from a piece of furniture.*]

HUBERT. The whole house must be got in shape.

MURTHA. Yis, m'am. [*Awed.*] An' do yez own th' whole house entoire? [*He nods quizzically.*] Ah, glory be to God fer that!

HUBERT [*going to open the second window*]. I'll tend to the windows on this floor. [*Looking out, then turning.*] Oh, catch that ice-man and get him to leave a piece of ice.

MURTHA. Now do you be shtandin' there, son, so he don't get away. Oi'll let him in.

[*She starts to go off through the arch.*]

HUBERT [*pointing to the door*]. No, this way through the basement.

[MURTHA *scrambles off quickly.* HUBERT *pauses, looking out, sees the ice-man, whistles and gesticulates to him to wait and go down into the house. During this,* SUSAN AMBIE *enters from the hall through the arch.* SUSAN *is a woman of forty-five. She has the soul of a chaperon. She enters in nervous haste.*]

HUBERT. Why, Miss Ambie! [*Shaking hands.*] Where's Caroline?

SUSAN. Get your hat and come right down to the dock with me.

HUBERT. I'm never missed unless there's been some trouble. What is it?

SUSAN. Your wife has been grossly insulted, as I was! It's unheard of!

HUBERT [*dawning*]. Ah! trouble with the customs. Is that it?

SUSAN [*indignantly*]. They have dared to suspect us, your wife and me!

HUBERT. You mean they've found you out. You too!

SUSAN. I'm not speaking for myself. When I saw they were going to be disagreeable, I declared everything. But suddenly I realized that a vulgar inspector woman had been watching Caroline. I saw her take Carrie off! All your wife's trunks are held!

HUBERT [*grimly relieved*]. Good!

SUSAN [*recoiling with a stare*]. Carrie's told me many things; but I never believed that you could be so heartless!

HUBERT. I've been prepared for this for many years. If she will do things in her own high-handed way, she'll have to stand the consequences. That's why I never meet her.

SUSAN. Then you refuse to go?

HUBERT. I refuse to be made a cat's-paw. That is, when I can help it.

SUSAN. Oh!

HUBERT. What is there for me to do? You must have made false declarations.

SUSAN. We didn't know they'd be so strict with us. We're not tradespeople or importers, or —

HUBERT. No, you're worse. Two women without even the wretched excuse of poverty, attempting to defraud the Government!

SUSAN. Mr. Knollys!

HUBERT. Ha! The cold sweat isn't worth the money.

[*Wipes his brow.*]

SUSAN. I don't know what she'll do!

HUBERT. She'll come home chastened in spirit, I hope, after having profited by this experience.

SUSAN. I really believe you're glad she's in trouble!

HUBERT. Not that. But I shall be glad if this population of a hundred million citizens in their corporate capacity are able, for once in her life, to demonstrate to my good wife that she can't do everything she likes with everybody. I've tried, her friends have tried, society has tried, perhaps the *Government* will succeed.

SUSAN. Well, if I can't make you see your duty —

HUBERT [*interrupting*]. The question of my duty to my wife is one that I do not care to discuss even with you.

SUSAN. It's none of my business, I suppose . . .

HUBERT [*bluntly*]. Quite so.

SUSAN [*fixes her hat*]. Then I'll go back alone. Carrie's my dearest friend — [*Then, in a bravado of accusing tearfulness.*] And I can't help it if I'm not strong enough to stand by quietly and see her die of mortification!

HUBERT [*sarcastically*]. You might advise her to appeal to them for clemency.

SUSAN. She can't find less of it there than here!

[*He turns and goes up.* SUSAN *is about to exit when* CAROLINE KNOLLYS *enters from the hall.* CAROLINE is a woman of forty, very young looking, handsome, commanding, and self-possessed. She is faultlessly gowned.]

SUSAN [with a cry]. Oh, Carrie!

CAROLINE [entering]. Oh, there you are, Susan. How are you, Hubert? [Shakes hands with him. Then to SUSAN.] I didn't know what became of you.

SUSAN. I came right here.

CAROLINE. You should have told me. Ninette and I looked every place.

SUSAN. I didn't want those men to see us together.

CAROLINE. Nonsense!

SUSAN. And I thought —

CAROLINE [interrupting]. You didn't think. You went right off your head.

HUBERT [expectantly]. Well?

CAROLINE [to HUBERT]. You seem to thrive in my absence. [To SUSAN.] Doesn't he?

HUBERT. I return the doubtful compliment. The same to you, and many of them.

CAROLINE. Thank you. [To SUSAN.] You got through quickly, didn't you?

SUSAN. When I saw they were going to be disagreeable, I declared everything.

CAROLINE. What!

SUSAN. What could I do?

CAROLINE [shrugging her shoulders]. I told you exactly what to do.

SUSAN. But when that woman searched me, I —

CAROLINE. You lost your nerve.

SUSAN. Oh, Carrie, I'm not thinking of myself. What did they do to you?

HUBERT [expectantly]. Yes, what did they do to you?

CAROLINE. To me? Why, what's the matter?

SUSAN [relieved]. Nothing, dear, if you're all right. How brave you are!

CAROLINE. Don't be absurd!

HUBERT [breaking in]. I should hardly call it bravery. This was bound to come some time. I've always said so. I've always feared it.

CAROLINE [calmly]. Feared what?

HUBERT. Miss Ambie's told me everything!

CAROLINE [with a sharp look at SUSAN]. Oh, indeed! Then there's nothing for me to say. [Rises to cross.]

HUBERT [nettled]. Caroline, I want to know exactly what has happened; so if there's anything that can be done now, I —

CAROLINE [sarcastically]. My dear Hubert, I'm really sorry to disappoint you; but there's nothing to be done.

HUBERT. And how about your difficulty with the trunks?

CAROLINE [smiling]. Sorry again. There's been no difficulty.

HUBERT. Then why did you send for me?

CAROLINE. I didn't send for you.

HUBERT. You didn't!

[He looks at SUSAN inquiringly.]

SUSAN. I know, but —

CAROLINE. Whenever we are away from you, Hubert, we grow so accustomed to depend on the chivalry and courtesy of men, that on our return, Susan forgets, and has to learn her lesson of self-dependence over again. You must forgive her. Really, Susan, you gave yourself too much concern.

SUSAN. My dear, I was so frightened. Didn't that woman search you?

CAROLINE. Me? Oh, no! I very soon put her in her place. And then, besides, I was careful to have nothing dutiable on my person.

HUBERT. Where *are* your trunks?

CAROLINE. I couldn't carry them with me, all nine of them. They'll be here shortly, I suppose.

[She stands before the Venetian mirror, takes off her hat and fixes her hair.]

HUBERT. Caroline, there's been quite enough of this bantering. *Did* you make a declaration?

CAROLINE. Sufficient for all practical purposes.

HUBERT. And what does that mean?

CAROLINE. I've done exactly as I've always done. I refused to argue the matter. I settled. Of course, as the law puts a premium on *dishonesty*, I found it expedient to —

HUBERT [interrupting]. To what?

CAROLINE [smiling]. To pay the premium.

HUBERT. It isn't only a question of expediency. It's downright lying!
CAROLINE [sarcastically]. Behold the moralist!
HUBERT [continuing]. And it's a question of decent, honest citizenship!
CAROLINE. But I'm not a citizen; and I don't care to be. If *you* were honest, you'd confess you're only irritated, Hubert, because you can't say: "I told you so." So don't moralize; it doesn't suit you; and don't talk like a husband the first day I arrive. That doesn't suit me.
[HUBERT *is about to say something, but is interrupted by the entrance of* MRS. MURTHA *from the basement.* CAROLINE *looks at her with an amused smile.*]
MURTHA. Mr. Knowllez, the motor-man from the taxicab is ashkin' if you'll be wantin' him to wait any longer.
SUSAN. Oh, that's my cab! He's been there all this time! [*She flounces to the hall.*]
HUBERT. Wait, I'll —
SUSAN [*with acerbity*]. No, thank you.
[*Exits.*]
MURTHA. An' th' oice man will be wantin' twenty cints fer th' oice. [*To* CAROLINE.] Shure, it's the grand box ye have.
HUBERT [*giving her money*]. Here.
[MURTHA *goes to door.*] Oh, you can fetch up some glasses now, with ice in them; if you will.
MURTHA. Yis, sor.
[*Exits hastily.*]
CAROLINE [*amazed*]. Where did you get her?
HUBERT. At a place that calls itself the "Co-operative Servant Agency."
CAROLINE. That must be the new name for the "Zoo." Have you a match?
HUBERT. Yes.
CAROLINE [*opening her cigarette case*]. Will you smoke?
HUBERT. Thank you, I prefer my own.
CAROLINE. These are contraband.
HUBERT. The kind you like.
CAROLINE. Yes.
[*He strikes a match for* CAROLINE. *She lights her cigarette.*]
HUBERT. Well, didn't you have a good time abroad?

CAROLINE. Certainly.
[*He sits at left of table, and lights his cigarette. She sits at right.*]
HUBERT. But you changed your plans rather unexpectedly?
CAROLINE. I hope that hasn't inconvenienced you.
HUBERT. Not at all.
[SUSAN *enters from the hall.*]
SUSAN. I hate America!
HUBERT. Eh?
SUSAN. When you sail up the harbor and see the Statue of Liberty, you feel a tremendous emotion of patriotism; but when you see your first cab charge, you want to turn around and go right back to Europe. I told the man there was something the matter with his meter! It jumped ten cents while I was arguing with him!
CAROLINE. Did you pay?
SUSAN. I *had* to!
CAROLINE. Then don't complain. Pay or complain; but don't do both. It isn't economical.
[MURTHA *enters, carrying three glasses awkwardly.*]
MURTHA. Here ye are, Mr. Knowllez!
[CAROLINE *opens the newspaper on the table and begins to read.*]
HUBERT. Thank you, that will do.
MURTHA [*putting down the glasses*]. Shure, they'll do. [*She suddenly stares as she sees* CAROLINE *smoking.*] Ah, fer th' love o' God! [CAROLINE *looks up.* MURTHA *continues:*] Shure, Oi do be fergittin' mesilf when Oi be passin' rhemarks wid your hushband. [*Catching* CAROLINE's *eye.*] Oh, Lord, yis, m'am.
[*She wilts away and exits to basement.* HUBERT *opens the whisky bottle.*]
HUBERT. Miss Ambie, will you have a Scotch and soda?
SUSAN. No, thank you, it always makes me silly. I'll go directly to my room.
CAROLINE [*not looking up from the newspaper*]. Take the front room on the third floor.
SUSAN. Don't worry about me. I'll have Ninette arrange your things.

CAROLINE [*turning over the paper*]. Thank you, dear. [SUSAN *exits up stairs.*]

HUBERT. She's going to stay here?

CAROLINE. Yes.

HUBERT. Oh, then, in that case — [*He ostentatiously doubles his drink.*] How do you stand her?

CAROLINE. She pays her own way and is very useful.

HUBERT [*sarcastically*]. I dare say; but to me she's simply an interfering nuisance. [*Pours soda into his whisky.*]

CAROLINE [*still reading*]. No. She's a constitutional altruist. That is, she has the soul of a servant.

HUBERT. A Scotch and soda?

CAROLINE. I never take it in the morning.

HUBERT [*drinking*]. I always forget.

CAROLINE [*looking up*]. The Homestead stock at sixty-four?

HUBERT. It closed at seventy yesterday.

CAROLINE. What made the slump?

HUBERT. A series of muck-raking articles about Factory Reform, and a lot of talk about Child Labor.

CAROLINE. I hope you're not embarrassed.

HUBERT. I've got to keep buying *in* to steady them.

CAROLINE [*putting down the paper*]. I'll lend you, Hubert; but I won't invest.

HUBERT [*ironically*]. Really, Caroline, your generosity overwhelms me.

CAROLINE. Not at all. I know you have collateral.

HUBERT. I still hope to worry along without placing myself under *financial* obligations to you.

CAROLINE [*placing both her elbows on table and looking at him narrowly*]. Hubert, I've often thought you resented my having independent means.

HUBERT. It's foolish of me; but I believe it might have made some difference in our lives, if you'd been —

CAROLINE [*interrupting*]. If I'd been dependent upon you for everything. If I had had no individuality of my own, or the means of keeping it intact. In other words, if I'd been poor. Is that what you mean?

HUBERT. No. But the superfluous wealth you've had has deprived us both of at least *one* of the real things. If we'd been poor together, there might have been something in our lives ... something we've missed — something at any rate *I've* missed. Some mutuality — some interest together. [*Rising.*] Here we are, two people who have lived for twenty odd years together, and who have never really had even a trouble in common!

CAROLINE [*with a remote smile*]. What trouble would you like to have me share with you? [*Pause.*]

HUBERT [*with a changed tone*]. Oh, none.

CAROLINE [*laughing*]. Hubert, don't be romantic toward your wife. That's waste. You're neither old enough nor young enough to play that sketch convincingly. You're neither dawn nor twilight; and Romance needs something undiscovered, something in possibility, something not yet precipitated into noonday commonplace reality. And you and I — we know too much about each other to really carry that off without laughing in our sleeves. You say it isn't money. Oh, then I fear something has gone wrong with some object of your affection.

HUBERT. Please!

CAROLINE. Then what is it?

HUBERT. I — I was about to speak of Elsie and Stephen.

CAROLINE [*carelessly*]. Oh, yes. How are the happy couple?

HUBERT. I'm afraid our daughter's not very happy. Stephen is a fool.

CAROLINE. I can't help that.

HUBERT. Have Elsie down here with us a little while —

CAROLINE [*interrupting*]. Impossible!

HUBERT. She might occupy her old rooms.

CAROLINE. I have other plans.

HUBERT. But a little motherly counsel from you might —

CAROLINE [*waving the discussion aside*]. Oh, Elsie and Stephen bore me to extinction, — both of them. I did my best for her — gave her a coming out, a season in Newport and —

HUBERT [*interrupting*]. Then married her off, made her a settlement and got rid of her. Gad! A girl of nineteen married!

CAROLINE. How old was I?

HUBERT. Well, our married life is nothing to boast of.

CAROLINE. Pardon, my dear Hubert, we've made a brilliant success of marriage. We ought to be grateful to the institution. It has given both of us the fullest liberty — a liberty that I've enjoyed; and you've —

HUBERT [*interrupting*]. Yes, you've always done exactly what you wanted.

CAROLINE [*meaningly*]. And you?

HUBERT. It makes no difference where we begin, we always wind up at the same place; don't we?

CAROLINE. Because you have abused your liberty.

HUBERT. Yes, I admit, it's my fault — if you like, *all* my fault. It's useless to go back over the old ruptures and recriminations. The prime mistake in both our lives was that we ever married. Well, we did. After about two years of doves, we had several years of cat and dog — and —

CAROLINE. I beg your pardon, in which class of animals do you place me?

HUBERT. We won't quarrel about the phrase. You refused divorce or separation at a time in life when we might have got one without making ourselves ridiculous.

CAROLINE. Divorce is always ridiculous. I made up my mind you'd never get free for anything *I* should do.

HUBERT. Yes, you've always been very careful about that. It isn't morality; but you never cared to relinquish an advantage. You refused divorce for your own reasons; and I agreed with you for Elsie's sake. Then Elsie married — a great relief to you; and we both agreed that the altitude of ideal husband and wife was too high for *me* to breathe in. You never cared about me; yet you were always very anxious that nobody else should. In the real significance of marriage, you have broken all your vows but one. I have kept all my vows —

CAROLINE [*sharply*]. Eh?

HUBERT. But one.

CAROLINE. Ah!

HUBERT [*continuing*]. That one violation of mine has given you the whip hand over me for these long years.

CAROLINE. Have you broken with that woman?

HUBERT. What woman?

CAROLINE. That Madden woman — Emily Madden.

HUBERT. You know nothing whatever about her.

CAROLINE. Pardon, I have taken the trouble to gather all the intimate details.

HUBERT. Indeed?

CAROLINE. And my friends have seen you every place with her. That's all I really care about.

HUBERT. And they will continue to see us; whenever Miss Madden does me the honor to accompany me.

CAROLINE [*resuming her newspaper*]. Oh, very well. I shall continue to condone everything; because I do not wish the elaborate structure I have built for many years to be destroyed. Our marriage stands as a temple to the Gods of Convention. The priests are hypocrites; but be careful not to make the *congregation* laugh. That's all I ask of you. Quite simple, isn't it?

HUBERT. Yes, simple as all heartless things are.

[*Pause. She reads.* HUBERT *walks up as* SUSAN AMBIE *enters from upstairs.*]

SUSAN. Carrie, I tried to 'phone the Intelligence Offices; but your 'phone isn't connected.

[*She looks accusingly at* HUBERT.]

HUBERT [*irritated*]. Excuse me. [*Goes to door, then turns.*] Oh, Miss Ambie, there's a prize of fifty dollars for the first *good* news that you announce. [*Exits.*]

SUSAN [*sentimentally*]. I can see by your face, dear, you've had a scene.

CAROLINE. No. Just our annual understanding.

SUSAN [*curiously*]. You don't have to tell me, Carrie. [*Pause.*] Has he broken with that Madden woman?

CAROLINE [*smiling*]. I hope not.

SUSAN. It's wonderful that all this hasn't made you bitter.

CAROLINE. Bitter? [*Laughing.*] I am very grateful to Miss Madden.

SUSAN [*quickly*]. Oh, Carrie, you didn't tell *him* that, did you?

CAROLINE [*laughs*]. Oh, dear, no! I never let him forget that at any moment I could name Miss Madden as a co-respondent. She is a weapon in my hands.

SUSAN [*admiringly*]. What a wonderful person you are! Only —

CAROLINE. Only what?

SUSAN. Only be careful, dear. Don't give *him* a weapon against *you*.

CAROLINE. In what way?

SUSAN. Of course you'd never think about it; and it's quite as well you shouldn't as long as I can do that for you. But be careful, dear, about Lawrence Sanbury.

CAROLINE. Don't be absurd. You were practically always with me.

SUSAN [*with a nervous whimper*]. Oh, no, I failed you, Carrie; I should have dragged along no matter how ill I was.

CAROLINE [*bluntly*]. Get that idea out of your head.

SUSAN. But if he should ever learn about your last days alone with Lawrence in the mountains...

CAROLINE. He'll never learn it.

SUSAN. And there is a *Mrs.* Sanbury, too!

CAROLINE [*impatiently*]. Of course! Susan, I've know artists all my life, and I've never had to bother with their wives; at least...

[MURTHA *enters excitedly from the hall.*]

CAROLINE. Would you mind knocking on the door before you enter a room?

MURTHA [*pointing innocently to the arch*]. But there isn't any door, me dear.

CAROLINE. What is it?

MURTHA. Me great friend and sishter, Mrs. Sanbury, is here wid her hushband! They be a-wantin' to see you!

SUSAN [*frightened*]. She's here!

CAROLINE. Tell them I'm at home.

MURTHA [*going to the arch*]. Why wouldn't you be? Shure, Oi told thim that already.

SUSAN [*anxiously*]. Oh, Carrie! She's here!

CAROLINE [*severely*]. Don't be an ass!

MURTHA [*calling out into the hall*]. Come, Lord bless yer lovin' hearts! It's roight in here, yer to come! [*Reëntering.*] Shure Oi'd trust her wid a million dollars. It was Mrs. Sanbury, it was, that sint me to you.

CAROLINE. Oh, I've *her* to thank for *you*, have I?

MURTHA. Yis, m'am. Shure ye have.

[LAWRENCE *and* HILDEGARDE SANBURY *enter from the hall. He is a handsome, vital-looking man of twenty-five. He has a quick and ingenuous, volatile manner.* HILDEGARDE, *his wife, is a woman of thirty, of sympathetic and responsive nature, full of exuberant gratitude to* CAROLINE, *whom she has never met. In dress* HILDEGARDE *is the exact opposite of* CAROLINE. *She is scrupulously neat, but* CAROLINE *is a perfect conscience of every allure of fashion. They enter followed by* MURTHA, *who goes up rear.* LAWRENCE *nods to* SUSAN.]

CAROLINE [*to* HILDEGARDE]. I'm very glad you've come.

LAWRENCE. Hildegarde, this is Mrs. Knollys.

[HUBERT *enters quietly from the door leading to the basement. He is unnoticed amid the greetings. He goes nonchalantly towards window at left.*]

HILDEGARDE. When I heard Larrie was coming to you, I just couldn't stay at home.

LAWRENCE. She wouldn't. So we —

HILDEGARDE [*interrupting*]. Oh, Larrie, you must let *me* speak! You've had Mrs. Knollys all to yourself for six long weeks — [HUBERT *turns as* LAWRENCE *goes to* SUSAN.] You see I've heard so much about you. Larrie wrote me reams and reams of letters right from the beginning.

CAROLINE [*purringly*]. Yes.

HILDEGARDE. Oh, yes! I've followed you every step you've taken.

[SUSAN *looks anxious and laughs a little hysterically.*]

CAROLINE [*noticing* HUBERT'S *presence*]. Indeed!

HILDEGARDE [*seeing* CAROLINE'S *face change*]. I hope we haven't intruded!

CAROLINE. Not at all. Oh, Hubert, let me present you to Mr. and Mrs. Sanbury.

HUBERT. Ah! How do you do?

[*They exchange greetings.*]

CAROLINE. I've persuaded Mr. Sanbury to accept the commission to remodel the house.

HUBERT [*surprised*]. Oh, have you!

[*Pause.*]

HILDEGARDE [*continuing to* CAROLINE]. Oh, it was wonderful for Larrie to be with you. You were eyes to him in Italy.

CAROLINE. Let me present you to Miss Ambie. [*Pointedly.*] She was with us too.

[HUBERT *notes this closely, though seeming not to listen.*]

HILDEGARDE [*surprised*]. Oh, *were* you? [*Goes immediately to* SUSAN.] Larrie wrote me you were taken ill in Switzerland, and that he and Mrs. Knollys went on alone.

SUSAN [*nervously*]. Oh, dear, no, I mean . . . I . . . It was really nothing serious.

HILDEGARDE. I hope you've recovered.

SUSAN. Oh, perfectly, thank you. I didn't miss much of the trip . . . You see it was really only . . .

CAROLINE [*seeing* HUBERT'S *eye on them*]. Oh, Susan, it's nearly twelve. [*To the others.*] Excuse me. [*Again to* SUSAN.] You might hail a taxi and settle the matter of servants for me.

SUSAN [*anxiously*]. Yes, yes, but hadn't I better — ?

CAROLINE [*decisively, going to the hall with* SUSAN]. The club for luncheon. One o'clock. [SUSAN *exits.*]

MURTHA [*coming up from rear*]. Ah, it do be good to see thim together again, eh?

CAROLINE. Did you want to ask me anything?

MURTHA. If it's a chambermaid ye want, me daughter Agnes —

CAROLINE. Would you mind closing the door?

MURTHA. Ah, not at all.

[*She crosses and closes the door, then returns.*]

CAROLINE [*cuttingly*]. I mean *behind* you.

MURTHA [*catching* CAROLINE'S *eye and meaning*]. Oh, yis, m'am.

[*She exits.*]

CAROLINE [*motioning* HILDEGARDE *to a chair*]. Do I understand you run an Intelligence Office?

HILDEGARDE. I've organized a general employment bureau in connection with the tenements.

LAWRENCE. But, my dear, it's hardly fair to Mrs. Knollys to send this old —

HILDEGARDE [*interrupting*]. We sent her daughter Agnes. You understand, only the derelicts come to us; but you'll see, Mrs. Murtha will do her work well.

CAROLINE. Tell me, do you really *live* among these people?

HILDEGARDE. Yes, at the model tenement. Have you ever seen one?

CAROLINE. No!

HILDEGARDE. I'd be delighted to show you around.

CAROLINE. Yes. Miss Ambie and I will come sometime together.

HILDEGARDE. Do, and take luncheon with us at our co-operative dining-room.

LAWRENCE [*to* CAROLINE]. I wouldn't expect too much. You see, it's a fad of hers — Democracy and the Underdog.

HILDEGARDE. Oh, no, that's my real work.

HUBERT [*coming into the conversation*]. What?

HILDEGARDE. We believe in giving the poor people better living conditions first; so that then they will be better able to fight for other things.

HUBERT. Yes, and make them discontented all along the line.

HILDEGARDE [*fervently*]. If only we could make them sufficiently discontented!

HUBERT [*taking up the newspaper*]. I should say you were succeeding very well. Have you seen this series of furious articles on Factory Reform?

HILDEGARDE [*looking at paper*]. Yes.

HUBERT. What do you think of them?

HILDEGARDE. I ought to approve of them.

HUBERT. Why?

HILDEGARDE. Because I wrote them.

HUBERT [*amazed*]. What! You?

HILDEGARDE. Yes. They're mine.
HUBERT. You label these articles reform, but they read pretty much like anarchy to me.
HILDEGARDE. Do you know about our present factory conditions?
HUBERT [grimly]. Somewhat, to my cost. You've made me one of your horrible examples.
HILDEGARDE. What!!
HUBERT. I own the majority stock in the Homestead Mills.
LAWRENCE [nervously]. Good Lord, Hildegarde! Your crowd haven't been attacking Mr. Knollys, have they?
HILDEGARDE [to LAWRENCE]. No one was mentioned by name. [To HUBERT.] Your manager refused to show his stock sheet to our committee; so we simply wrote up the mill.
HUBERT. Our manager has to compete with others. We give these people work. We don't force our hands to come to us.
HILDEGARDE. That's it. The whole system is wrong. The State must remedy it. Individuals can't. You've got to resort to the means of your lowest and most unscrupulous competitor; or leave the field.
HUBERT. Do you mind answering a few questions?
HILDEGARDE. Not at all.
HUBERT [to CAROLINE and LAWRENCE]. Excuse us. [He and HILDEGARDE go toward the hall. He takes some clippings from his pocket.] In the first place, you stated . . .

[They exit and pass out of sight, going toward the right, in earnest conversation. CAROLINE is sitting in the large divan chair at the left. LAWRENCE comes toward her.]

LAWRENCE [enthusiastically]. Isn't she splendid!
CAROLINE [softly ironical]. You treat us all alike; don't you?
LAWRENCE. How?
CAROLINE [quietly]. She, too, is older than you. Isn't she?
LAWRENCE. Oh, a year or two. That doesn't matter.
CAROLINE. How chivalrous you are. But for your sake, she ought to be wiser.

LAWRENCE. What do you mean?
CAROLINE. Her radical theories about Democracy and — the great Unwashed. . . . Do you agree with them?
LAWRENCE. I'm an artist. I take no side whatever.
CAROLINE. But don't you see, you'll *have* to take a side?
LAWRENCE. Why?
CAROLINE. People of our class won't support you, if your wife attacks the very sources from which they pay you.
LAWRENCE [with sudden anxiety]. Oh, perhaps Mr. Knollys will resent what Hildegarde has done, and won't care to give me the work. Is that what you mean?
CAROLINE. I mean your wife mustn't add to my difficulties.
LAWRENCE [sincerely distressed]. Oh, Lord! In wrong the first crack out of the box; and I wanted you so much to like each other!
CAROLINE. Tell me — is she really as frank as she seems?
LAWRENCE. Why, yes. What makes you ask that?
CAROLINE. I was a little startled when I learned you'd written her so definitely about our tour in Italy.
LAWRENCE [relieved]. Oh, that's all right. Hildegarde thinks nothing about that.
CAROLINE. But she mustn't give everybody credit for so much sympathetic understanding.
[With a glance toward the hall.]
LAWRENCE. You mean your husband!
CAROLINE [quickly]. Don't speak so loudly! [With a change to a seductive, problematical manner.] I haven't told you everything about my life. I thought you guessed.
LAWRENCE. Why, surely, he wouldn't dare to misjudge you, would he?
CAROLINE. We move in a society that does not trust itself, so it is always suspicious.
LAWRENCE. I hope you'll forgive me. I'm just a fool about these things.
CAROLINE [seeing HUBERT and HILDEGARDE approaching]. Pst! Say nothing more.

HUBERT [*re-entering from the hall. To* HILDEGARDE]. If I'm on top, I know I'll treat the laborer as well as I can afford. If he's on top, I can't expect so much in return. They get a living wage.

HILDEGARDE. You'd better take a trip down South and see how well they live.

HUBERT. Perhaps I shall. And then I'll want to see you again.

HILDEGARDE. Do! [*To the others.*] Until then we part, good, class-conscious, cordial enemies.

HUBERT [*pointing to the newspaper*]. Very well. And how about these articles?

HILDEGARDE. To-morrow we begin on your competitors.

HUBERT. Good! That's fair play.

CAROLINE. Hubert, would you mind showing Mr. Sanbury about the house?

HUBERT. Now?

CAROLINE. Yes. Mrs. Sanbury will remain with me. [HILDEGARDE *nods.*]

HUBERT. We'll go this way.

LAWRENCE. Excuse me.

[LAWRENCE *and* HUBERT *exit through hall and are seen mounting the stairs.*]

CAROLINE [*points to a chair in the full light*]. You don't mind the light?

HILDEGARDE. Oh, not at all.

CAROLINE [*speaking as she pulls up the shade full upon* HILDEGARDE]. I'm sure we shall understand each other thoroughly; because we both want your husband to succeed.

HILDEGARDE. It's fine of you to be so interested. He's never had a chance to prove what he can do.

CAROLINE [*sitting with her back to the light*]. My interest will excuse many personal questions. [*Charmingly.*] He being so young, we can discuss him and his future from the same point of view.

HILDEGARDE. Yes, Larrie for all his twenty-five years is just a great big boy.

CAROLINE. How did you come to live there in the tenements?

HILDEGARDE. Surely Larrie has told you!

CAROLINE. But I never trust a husband to tell me all about his home. [*Insinuatingly.*] If the wife loves him very much, he never really knows his circumstances.

HILDEGARDE. We've had no secrets from each other. We struggled on together right from the beginning. I sometimes got disheartened, but Larrie never did.

CAROLINE. Ah! Did *he* decide to live there?

HILDEGARDE. No. I lived there first, and when we married, we decided to settle there together, so I might continue my work.

CAROLINE. But do you think the tenement is quite the — ah — the atmosphere for him to work in?

HILDEGARDE. He hasn't complained; and offices cost lots of money.

CAROLINE. Yes.

HILDEGARDE. Your commission will enable him to start in business for himself; and then we hope to afford a better place.

CAROLINE. Yes. But have you ever considered how your very work in the world might hinder him?

HILDEGARDE [*puzzled*]. In what way?

CAROLINE. Art has always been the luxury of a leisure class. It has always been supported by the patronage of wealth; and you can't expect that the people whom you attack, and *publicly* attack, are going to reply by using their influence to promote your husband.

HILDEGARDE. Then Lawrence must work his way without their influence.

CAROLINE [*with narrowing eyes*]. In the school of adversity, eh?

HILDEGARDE [*proudly*]. That school has brought out the best in many artists!

CAROLINE. And has killed thousands of others that we never hear of. My dear, the school of adversity is a very good school; provided you don't matriculate too early and continue too long.

HILDEGARDE. I'd rather continue just as we are now to the end of our days, than have him sell his soul and abandon all he's stood for.

CAROLINE. *You* would; but how about *him?*

HILDEGARDE. He would too!

CAROLINE. Perhaps I know him better than you do.

HILDEGARDE. I don't think so.

CAROLINE. Then some day, you may have to reproach yourself for his failure.
HILDEGARDE. I?
CAROLINE. Yes.
HILDEGARDE. Why should he fail?
CAROLINE. Just because of his unusual qualities. The world at best is a cruel place. It gives its prizes to the ordinary. It martyrizes the exceptional person, because it doesn't understand him, and what it doesn't understand, it fears; and what it fears, it destroys, or worse than that, it allows to die unnoticed. The world will make your husband suffer, *just because he is exceptional.*
HILDEGARDE. I can't believe that!
CAROLINE [*sarcastically*]. One must, indeed, be an optimist to be a fanatic. With your help I hoped to place him where I know he belongs. But I cannot, if you oppose it. [*Pause.*]
HILDEGARDE. I don't see how *I* stand in his way!
CAROLINE. You have already made a difficulty with my husband.
HILDEGARDE. How?
CAROLINE. My dear, you can hardly expect my husband to give your husband an expensive commission, when you spend your time writing articles that lower the value of the most important investment he holds.
HILDEGARDE. Then Lawrence will have to choose.
CAROLINE. Oh, no. You mustn't put that on him. You mustn't bind him by his love for you. For if he fails to choose properly, you will be forced to bear the burden of his bitterness. And there's nothing so bitter in the world as an artist's bitterness. [*Looking at her closely.*] It won't come now. I grant you a few years more of his hopeful illusions and youthful courage; but then your awakening will come ... when you are gray — at heart, and he still in his prime; but with the sources of his faith run dry — eaten with disappointments, sick with postponements, his inspiration festered by discouragement; while he still knocks listlessly at the doors, which would be open to him now; but will be closed hereafter, when his opportunities have passed him by.
HILDEGARDE. That can't be true!
CAROLINE [*continuing ruthlessly*]. And in the cruel retrospect, then *his* awakening will come; and he will see that it has been [*cynically*] what you call your "life-work" that has hindered him. And then, what will his love for you be worth to *you* or *him?*
HILDEGARDE [*obstinately*]. He has his work, I have mine. It's for him to choose.
CAROLINE. And is your muck-raking worth his career? Knowing that he loves you now, and will be influenced by you, have you a right to make him choose?
HILDEGARDE. No more than you!
CAROLINE. There is this difference: — *I* do it for his sake purely.
HILDEGARDE. So do I!
CAROLINE. I doubt it.
HILDEGARDE [*passionately*]. Don't you think it would be easier for me to see him settled? I've walked the floor at night! I've agonized over his career, while he's been sleeping like a child!
CAROLINE [*quickly*]. Ah, then there *have* been secrets!
HILDEGARDE [*continuing*]. Yes! I've made it a point of honor not to allow him to spend one cent on me! [*Suddenly.*] You're looking at this dress! I know it's shabby — You've noticed it — He hasn't ...
CAROLINE. My dear, you mustn't feel sensitive about your clothes!
HILDEGARDE [*choking back her tears*]. It's the first time that I ever was!
CAROLINE. You must let me give you a gown or two.
HILDEGARDE [*recoiling*]. Oh, no! I couldn't accept them — I couldn't!
CAROLINE. But, my dear —
HILDEGARDE [*proudly*]. Excuse me, don't presume!
CAROLINE. I hoped you'd understand. Your husband's profession has a social side. There are people he must meet — people that will be of use to him. I want to arrange it. You won't object?
HILDEGARDE. Oh, no!
CAROLINE. It's always easy for a man — a dress suit and there you are. But we

women are at a disadvantage without the proper equipment, and . . .

HILDEGARDE. Please leave me out of all your calculations. I shan't complicate matters.

CAROLINE. My dear, I merely intended to save you from embarrassment.

HILDEGARDE. I am very grateful. But I repeat, it's impossible I should accept anything from you. We belong to two totally different orders.

CAROLINE. Then as you're unwilling to meet the social requirements, you will understand perfectly, if you're not included in . . .

HILDEGARDE. Certainly. I shall not expect to be invited.

CAROLINE. I must compliment you, Mrs. Sanbury. You're stronger than I thought you were.

[Pause. The two women look at each other. HILDEGARDE is dazed. CAROLINE is smilingly confident.]

LAWRENCE [coming downstairs]. We'll have a jolly job introducing Queen Victoria to the Renaissance. You've plenty of room; that is, if you'll let me smash the conventional partitions.

CAROLINE [meaningly]. I always like to smash conventional partitions, provided the outside walls remain intact. Have you explained to Hubert?

LAWRENCE. He couldn't follow the sketch.

CAROLINE [with a veiled sneer]. You'll have to build models before he can see.

LAWRENCE [after a slight hesitation]. Will you really need models?

CAROLINE. I am afraid so. How long would it take you?

LAWRENCE. Well, you know, I've left my old firm; and I'll first have to look about for larger quarters.

HILDEGARDE [involuntarily]. Oh!

LAWRENCE [confidently]. I've been thinking of changing. It's only been a question of the proper place.

CAROLINE [knowingly smiling at HILDEGARDE]. Oh, of course. But I've an idea. In insisting upon models, I appreciate I am asking the unusual; but I want to expedite matters.

LAWRENCE. Yes . . . Yes . . .

CAROLINE. You've seen the fourth storey?

LAWRENCE. Yes.

CAROLINE. Couldn't you build your models there?

LAWRENCE [eagerly]. Splendidly! [Relieved.] That would solve everything; wouldn't it, Hildegarde? [To CAROLINE.] And I could consult with you at every step.

CAROLINE. Yes. . [To HILDEGARDE.] And in that way, we needn't interfere with your plans at the tenement.

HILDEGARDE. Oh!

CAROLINE. Perhaps you'd better advise with your wife before you decide. I'll speak with Hubert. Excuse me.

[She exits through the hall.]

LAWRENCE. [Watches her out of the tail of his eye. As soon as she is off, his manner changes, and he comes to HILDEGARDE in hushed excitement. He takes her hands and speaks quickly.] I'm glad, old girl, you didn't butt into any of my bluffs! I got a cold sweat when she spoke about models! [Wiping his brow.] Phew! That was a poser! But did you see me do it? [Imitating his former manner.] "Just looking for a proper place." [With a flourish of his hand.] Money no object. Did you see me? With not enough to the good to keep the sheriff off any place for a single month! [Sitting.] That fourth storey is too good to be true! [Devoutly.] God bless the ugliness of Queen Victoria! God bless the rich with big houses and small families! Don't wake me!

HILDEGARDE. Then you're going to accept her top floor?

LAWRENCE [flabbergasted to an echo]. Am I going to accept her . . . ? Watch me! I've never told you; but I haven't been able to work there in the tenements. This address alone will get me credit for materials. And right now, I'm in no position to deny her anything.

HILDEGARDE. Evidently.

LAWRENCE [rubbing his chin]. Gosh! The old man was pretty mum about the plan. [Suddenly.] He may be sore about those articles of yours! I hope they haven't queered it.

HILDEGARDE. Oh, I fancy she'll arrange it.

LAWRENCE. I hope she will. [*Suddenly.*] Golly, you don't seem to realize what this job means to me!

HILDEGARDE. Perhaps I do, even more than you.

LAWRENCE [*intensely*]. Money! That's what it means... Money! A thing we've never had, and a thing we've got to get!

HILDEGARDE. Is money everything?

LAWRENCE. Yes, now — everything.... Money! I want money — money to be free to do things — money to get things for you. Do you think I like to see you wearing rags like this?
[*Pointing to her dress.*]

HILDEGARDE [*with a quick pain*]. Oh, as for me —

LAWRENCE. I've had enough of the tenements! I've never told you —

HILDEGARDE. Larrie!!

LAWRENCE [*excitedly*]. That's all right, my dear. You're a fanatic about some things. I don't interfere with you, and you mustn't interfere with me! [*Change.*] Perhaps you'd better go.... I mean if you're not in sympathy with the scheme, for God's sake, don't hang on.

HILDEGARDE [*slowly*]. There's lots that I could say, Larrie....

LAWRENCE. Yes, I know, but not here. Listen — Open your head! I've got to nail this job. I want to do it on my own hook. Then if I take it to a firm, I collar some of the swag and get some credit for my work.... I may never wing a chance to start like this again. [*She is about to say something but he continues.*] We're broke — and no instalment until the plans and models are accepted. Here I get a place rent free, materials on tick, with Lawrence Sanbury I-N-C upon the signs.... I'll incorporate my debts. Otherwise, back again into an old thirty a week job to sweat for the other fellow all my life. [*Quickly giving* HILDEGARDE *her coat.*] Hildegarde, here — take your rags and run.

HILDEGARDE [*quietly*]. Shall I wait luncheon?

LAWRENCE. Hang luncheon! I'm going to eat this job.

HILDEGARDE. But on your first day home, after...

LAWRENCE. There'll be lots of days like this coming. [*Holding her coat.*] Here — here she comes. Just say good-by.

[*Enter* CAROLINE *from the hall.*]

CAROLINE. Well, I've spoken with my husband.

LAWRENCE [*restrained*]. Yes...?

CAROLINE. He thinks it an admirable plan for you to work here.

LAWRENCE [*relieved*]. Ah, then that's settled!

CAROLINE. So we can begin immediately ... that is ... if —
[*Looks at* HILDEGARDE.]

HILDEGARDE. I was just going. [CAROLINE *is silent.*] Good-by, Mrs. Knollys.

CAROLINE [*with feigned surprise*]. Oh! [*Then in a commonplace tone.*] Good-by. I shan't forget your invitation to the tenements.

LAWRENCE. Excuse me, Hildegarde, I'll be home — ah — shortly.

[HILDEGARDE *goes quickly to the arch, and exits through the hall.* LAWRENCE *makes a move to follow her, then pauses perplexed.* CAROLINE *watches him narrowly.*]

LAWRENCE [*scratching his head*]. By Jove! What makes a fellow a brute sometimes to the woman he cares for?

CAROLINE [*slowly*]. It's the artist in *you*, Lawrence, that is instinctively unscrupulous toward anything that hinders its development.

LAWRENCE. But Hildegarde wouldn't hinder me!

CAROLINE. Not intentionally, certainly not. She's an exceptional person. [*Sitting.*] I'm sorry she doesn't like me.

LAWRENCE [*fighting against his own conviction*]. What makes you think she doesn't like you?

CAROLINE. She has her — ah — principles. Unfortunately they oppose everything I stand for.

LAWRENCE. You don't know her, she...

CAROLINE. Perhaps not, and I'm so sorry; for I hoped we should agree about you.

LAWRENCE. But she must see how much you mean to me, and —
CAROLINE. Perhaps you've been too frank with her.
LAWRENCE. I never conceal anything from Hildegarde.
CAROLINE [ironically]. No....
LAWRENCE [continuing]. And I'd hate any person that made me lie! [Sitting disconsolately.] What can I do?
CAROLINE. That you must decide yourself. You stand at a crossing, Lawrence. The one road means the old limitations and the commonplace: the other leads to freedom and opportunity. It's difficult to choose, because she loves you ... dearly.
LAWRENCE. Of course she does!
CAROLINE. Therefore it's quite natural she should resent any one having the power to do for you what she would like to do; but can't. I'd feel that way myself, if ...
LAWRENCE. If what?
CAROLINE. If I loved you the way she does. If I weren't ambitious for your *great* work!
LAWRENCE. But she wants me to do big work.
CAROLINE [shaking her head]. You feel things in you that she never dreamed of. That's why ... [With a change.] But I oughtn't make you conscious.
LAWRENCE. What is it?
CAROLINE [with a show of reluctance]. That's why you aren't at your best, when you're with her. Now there, I've said it.
LAWRENCE. But I haven't had the chance of really explaining to her all I want to do, and ...
CAROLINE [unscrupulously]. An *artist* justifies himself by *doing:* not explaining! Consider everything that helps you to your end as good. That is the conscience of an artist. His work is always greater than his life.
LAWRENCE. By Jove, I always see clearer when I talk to you!
CAROLINE [passionately]. I am unscrupulous for the best in you!
LAWRENCE [taking her hands]. You're wonderful!

CAROLINE. I mustn't be mistaken in you!
LAWRENCE [kissing her hands]. You won't be.
CAROLINE. I have a problem too, because of you.
LAWRENCE [dropping her hands]. Yes, I know.
CAROLINE. And you must justify *me* as well. We made a compact. Have you forgotten it?
LAWRENCE. The afternoon we left Florence.
CAROLINE. And climbed the hills toward Fiesole ... alone.
LAWRENCE [rapt]. In the flaming orange scarfs of mist, with the whole world behind us in the valley.
CAROLINE. Where you said the world should always be for the artist with the vision and the will to create a new form of art. You were splendid then!
LAWRENCE. And afterward, the long ride on to Brescia and Como and —
CAROLINE. Psch! That lies behind us. [Pause. With a change.] I thought that memory belonged to us alone.
LAWRENCE. It does!
CAROLINE [raising her finger]. You shared it.
LAWRENCE. Forget that, please.
CAROLINE. I hope the others will.
MURTHA'S VOICE [upstairs]. Will I hang the things up here, sir?
HUBERT'S VOICE [upstairs]. Yes, just put them in the closet, please.
CAROLINE [quickly to LAWRENCE]. Sit down. [He starts to sit in a chair near her. She points to one at right of stage.] No; over there. [He goes quickly to the other side. She continues.] We'll lunch together. The Colony Club at one o'clock.
LAWRENCE. I thought that Hildegarde might —
CAROLINE [interrupting peremptorily]. I *must* see you.
LAWRENCE. But on my first day home —
CAROLINE [impatiently]. Between Susan's nervousness and your thoughtlessness, I ...
LAWRENCE. Very well.

[*Enter* HUBERT *from the hall.*]

HUBERT. H'm! Still talking over plans?

LAWRENCE [*rising, embarrassed*]. Yes ... yes ... and I want to thank you, Mr. Knollys.

HUBERT. Me? For what?

LAWRENCE. The fourth storey. It'll be a great help to me.

[HUBERT *looks perplexed.*]

CAROLINE. You know, I have asked Mr. Sanbury to build his models there.

HUBERT [*grimly*]. Ah ... have you! I didn't know.

LAWRENCE [*filling in the awkward pause*]. Then you can see exactly how the rooms will look.

HUBERT. Oh, as for me ... [*Smiles.*] Quite so. Very kind of you — very. Where's your wife?

LAWRENCE. She's already gone.

HUBERT [*sarcastically*]. If you should see her again, you might tell her that I've decided to go South immediately.

LAWRENCE [*jerking at his watch.*] Yes — ah ... She'll be delighted to hear that ... and ... ah ... I was delighted to meet you, Mr. Knollys; and if you'll excuse me — I'll — I'll ... be going now.

[*He stands awkwardly.* HUBERT *goes to the hall, then turns to* LAWRENCE.]

HUBERT. Good-morning.

LAWRENCE. Oh, good-by, Mrs. Knollys. [*To* HUBERT.] Good-by, Mr. Knollys.

CAROLINE. Good-by.

[HUBERT *nods.* LAWRENCE *exits. Pause.*]

HUBERT [*laughing softly*]. Caroline, I think your latest is a light-weight!

CAROLINE [*changing the subject*]. You're going South?

HUBERT. I hope you'll endure my absence. [*Pause.*] What was your object in giving your young man the impression that you had to consult me in anything?

CAROLINE. I generally consult you.

HUBERT. Yes. After you've completed your arrangements. It's your house. I've nothing to say. But I see now why you needed Elsie's room.

[*A furious knock is heard in the hall. They both start as* MURTHA *enters.*]

MURTHA [*proudly*]. Ah, did ye hear me knock?

CAROLINE. What is it?

MURTHA. A young lady's in th' front hall. [*To* HUBERT.] She wants to see you, Mr. Knowllez.

HUBERT. To see me?

MURTHA [*hesitating*]. She says she's from th' Cushtoms office, so she says.

HUBERT [*grimly to* CAROLINE]. I fancy it's about your trunks.

CAROLINE [*to* MURTHA]. Send her in here.

MURTHA. Shure Oi will — whoy wouldn't Oi? [*Exits to hall.*]

HUBERT. Why should the young lady want to see me?

CAROLINE. Have you money with you?

HUBERT [*taking out his bill case*]. Yes.

CAROLINE [*with a smile*]. I gave her my card.

HUBERT. But —

CAROLINE [*taking his bill case and going to window*]. Let me see. All she's come for is more money.

[HUBERT *during the above goes toward the hall.* CAROLINE'*s back is to him.*]

[EMILY MADDEN *enters nervously from the right. She is a young woman of about twenty-eight.* HUBERT *makes a quick recoil of amazement and a half-smothered exclamation:* "*Emily!*" *She, seeing* CAROLINE, *gives him a quick gesture of silence.*]

EMILY [*in a breathless staccato and a forbidding manner*]. This is Mr. Knollys, I believe.

HUBERT. Yes.

CAROLINE [*turning and coming down*]. I hope you've had no difficulty.

EMILY. You evidently did not understand.

CAROLINE. Oh, I see. In that case, why, of course, I wish to pay you for any further —

EMILY [*violently*]. Please!

HUBERT. Caroline!

CAROLINE. Oh!

EMILY. Mrs. Knollys, all your trunks are held.

CAROLINE [*savagely*]. The insolence!

EMILY. It was the only way to save you from a charge of smuggling and . . .

CAROLINE. Indeed!

EMILY. I couldn't make you realize it. That's why I've come to see your husband.

CAROLINE [*with a smile*]. Thank you very much.

HUBERT. Caroline, you'd better let me settle this.

CAROLINE [*crossing to the hall*]. By all means. You always settle things so adequately. [*To* EMILY.] Good-morning. [*She starts to go upstairs, then turns and says significantly to* HUBERT:] Oh, your purse!

[*She throws it gracefully over the balustrade. He, standing below, catches it. She continues upstairs. He watches her out of sight, then turns and comes down to* EMILY.]

HUBERT [*giving way to his astonishment*]. Emily! I'm all in the dark! How are you mixed up in this?

EMILY [*quickly*]. I left the newspaper and got a position in the Customs. This morning I saw her name on the list of passengers. She fell into the hands of one of the sourest old inspectors. He found some jewels in a sachet bag. Then he caught her in a lie. As usual, he asked her to reconsider her declaration. She refused . . .

HUBERT [*unconsciously*]. The damned fool!

EMILY. Then he insisted she be searched.

HUBERT. Naturally.

EMILY. As I was standing there, the officers deputed me to look her over.

HUBERT [*appalled*]. But she didn't know who you were, did she?

EMILY. Oh, no, but I took the chance to tell her of the penalty: ten thousand dollars' fine, or two years' imprisonment, or both.

HUBERT. I hope that sobered her!

EMILY. Judge for yourself. She said she had a list, and gave me this envelope. [*Giving him an envelope out of her bag.*] Open it.

HUBERT [*opening it*]. Two one-hundred-dollar bills.

EMILY. One for my partner. There were two of us.

HUBERT [*putting envelope on table*]. The same old game.

EMILY. I felt like throwing it into her face; but then I thought of you, and held my temper. The inspectors were waiting.

HUBERT. What did you do?

EMILY. I told your wife I'd tend to everything, and got her off. Then I reported for her that she had reconsidered, had nothing on her person, she was ill and didn't know what things were dutiable; and therefore wanted all her stuff to be appraised.

HUBERT. Good! And then?

EMILY. Then I tried to 'phone you everywhere, and finally I had to take the chance of even meeting — her again, and come right here to tell you.

HUBERT. You little thoroughbred.

EMILY. Hubert, do nothing until you hear from them. Dispute nothing, but make her stick to the story that I framed up for her, and pay on their appraisal. I hope I've done right.

HUBERT. Right! I don't know how to thank you.

EMILY. Return this to your wife with my compliments. [*Points to envelope.*]

HUBERT. I guess you're all in, Emily.

EMILY. Oh, don't mind about me.

HUBERT. Filthy business, this. [*Suddenly anxious.*] There'll be no consequences for you?

EMILY. I guess not.

HUBERT [*walking about*]. I don't know how it is. She never learns. She does exactly what she pleases. Experience means nothing to her; because in some way she always manages to get protected, no matter what she does. She's skated over thin ice all her life — she *courts* the danger signals; and just when anybody else would fall through, an unknown somebody reaches her a hand out of the universe and lands her safe! Gad! and to think that it was you that helped her!

EMILY. I don't think that would appeal to her sense of humor.

HUBERT. Did she bring over much stuff?

EMILY. They said about six thousand, offhand.

HUBERT. Six thou... Phew! Well, that's *her* affair. But sit down a moment. [*He puts her on settle, then sits at right of the table.*] Tell me, how did *you* get into the Customs office?

EMILY. I got tired of the paper. My friend Hildegarde Sanbury suggested the Customs, and helped me get it.

HUBERT. Oh, Mrs. Sanbury's a friend of yours.

EMILY. Yes, why?

HUBERT. They were here this morning.

EMILY. Were they? Isn't Hildegarde fine?

HUBERT. Tell me about *him!*

EMILY. You mean Lawrence?

HUBERT. Yes.

EMILY. They say he's a genius, full of all wonderful things, and just waiting for his opportunity to express them.

HUBERT. Yes, just the type!

EMILY. What type?

HUBERT. Do you know where he and Caroline met?

EMILY. I've no idea; except that they spent some time together in Italy.

HUBERT. What was he doing there?

EMILY. Studying and making sketches. Hildegarde slaved and saved every cent she could to send him over.

HUBERT. So this is her latest!

EMILY. What do you mean?

HUBERT. I wonder if I can explain it. Caroline has a mania for depredating the next generation. She poses to herself as the heroine of a belated romance.

EMILY. But she knows Lawrence is married, doesn't she?

HUBERT. She prefers them married. Takes all the perfume and the blossoms, and lets the wife grub at the roots. She likes to be the destiny and let the wife assume the utility. Does he love his wife?

EMILY. Why, of course, devotedly. That's the finest thing about him.

HUBERT. Better yet. She enjoys making a test of her power.

EMILY [*impulsively*]. Hildegarde's the best in the world, Hubert, and...

HUBERT. Then I pity her.

EMILY. You don't mean your wife will hurt Hildegarde, do you?

HUBERT [*bitterly*]. She won't bleed; that is, outwardly. She'll just wake up and find her happiness evaporated.

EMILY. You mustn't allow it. She's just a child before a sophisticated person.

HUBERT [*desperately*]. What can I do? Caroline has done this all her life; and as she operates under the protection of my name, I've had apparently to stand by and sanction it.

EMILY. Can't you stop her?

HUBERT [*again walking about*]. How? You'd respect her if she showed one real emotion. She's physically chaste; but is absolutely unchastened in soul; and yet she feeds on the souls of others. That's how she keeps young. She's a mental *Bluebeard*, and I'm the hotel clerk for her castle... I know where all her miserable relics hang... What rooms and what days of their lives they've offered her!

EMILY. Why, this is horrible, Hubert!

HUBERT [*continuing*]. I'd give my eyes to stop her! If not for the sake of others, for my own sake! She's broken me! I tried to get free for years at the beginning. But she plays so absolutely safe... She protects herself so completely that she is unassailable.

EMILY. Can't *he* be warned?

HUBERT. Not if she gets him first. Her kind of poison strikes them blind. There's nothing to be done for him. Just *you* keep out of her way.

EMILY. Don't worry. I will. Well, I must get back to work.

[*She starts to go again.*]

HUBERT. My dear, why will you work? Why won't you let me take care of you?

EMILY. I wish to earn my own living, Hubert. You know that.

HUBERT. Yes. But I want to ask you... Why have you avoided me for this long time?

EMILY. Hubert, I didn't want to write it; but it's over between us.

HUBERT [*after a pause*]. Yes, I've realized that.

EMILY [*very tenderly*]. Hubert, I've no reproach to make you; and I don't want you to reproach me, or to feel any bitterness. What we gave was a free gift from both — a free gift and no regrets. A break had to come some time, I suppose; and as soon as I met *him*, I — I realized that it had to come right away. [*Looking away from* HUBERT.] He asked no questions; but that's why you haven't seen or heard from me. Hubert, I'm going to marry Michael Krellin.

HUBERT [*after a pause*]. Good luck to you. [*He takes her hand in both of his.*] But I thought you didn't believe in marriage.

EMILY. Neither did he. But I'm afraid we both believe in marriage now. I can't tell you how it happened; but it's *different*, Hubert... That's all... I know you'll understand.

[HUBERT *nods and releases her hand. She goes toward the hall.*]

HUBERT. Emily... [*She stops and turns.*] We've been good chums for a long time; and, do you know, you've never allowed me to give you anything?

EMILY. That was our agreement, Hubert.

HUBERT. Yes; but I want you to promise me this. If you should ever get into a blind alley, and need anything, a friend or money, and need it without strings, I want you to think of me. I'd like to feel you'd do that much for the sake of Auld Lang Syne.

EMILY [*coming to him*]. All right. I promise. [*Extends her hand.*] Good-by.

HUBERT [*quietly, as he takes her hand*]. Krellin's a very lucky fellow.

EMILY. That's like you, Hubert.

HUBERT. I'll call you a cab.

EMILY. Never mind. Don't come with me, please. I'll run right along. [*She turns and says very tenderly:*] Good-by.

HUBERT. Good-by.

[*She exits through the hall. After she is off,* HUBERT *stands looking after her until the front door is heard to close. He drops his hands disconsolately and walks mechanically to the table at center. His eyes fall upon the envelope still lying there. He takes it up. His mood changes.*

He gets a sudden idea. He looks up, throws the envelope down on the table again with an angry gesture, and goes with vehement determination toward the stairs. He pauses at the bottom of the stairs, shakes his head perplexed, and then decides upon a different attack. He calls very pleasantly:]

HUBERT. Ah, Caroline!

CAROLINE [*upstairs*]. Yes.

HUBERT. I'd like to see you for a moment.

CAROLINE. Are you alone?

HUBERT [*still pleasantly*]. Yes. Oh, yes.

CAROLINE. I'll be right down.

[HUBERT *walks round the room gathering his confident anger with every step. He hears her coming, controls his humor, and stands with his hands behind him, full of exultant exasperation, as she enters.*]

CAROLINE. Did you settle it?

HUBERT [*deliberately giving her a chair*]. One moment.

CAROLINE. Susan is waiting me for luncheon.

HUBERT [*decidedly*]. Very sorry.

CAROLINE [*inquiringly*]. Well?

HUBERT. Very sorry, but I'm afraid *I'll* need some of your time this afternoon.

CAROLINE [*after sitting, looks up demurely*]. What for?

HUBERT [*with great distinctness*]. The Customs office.

CAROLINE. Oh, no. You ventured to criticize me. You asked me to leave it to you. I do.

HUBERT [*losing control*]. About six thousand dollars' duty for you to pay!

CAROLINE. I? Perfectly ridiculous! I settled it. Of course, if you...

HUBERT [*angrily*]. You did, eh?

CAROLINE [*laughing*]. If you were fool enough to let that woman —

HUBERT. If "that woman" treated you as you deserve —

CAROLINE. I think I treated her very well.

HUBERT. It was only out of consideration for me that she —

CAROLINE. Oh, for *you!*
HUBERT. Yes, for me. If "that woman" didn't happen to be a friend of mine, you might be publicly disgraced by now as well as I!
CAROLINE [*laughing*]. A friend of yours! Why, really, Hubert, I must say you have strange friends — A woman that would use her friendship to extort money...
HUBERT [*enraged*]. Listen to me! Your trunks are in the hands of the appraisers. You've been caught in a ridiculous lie; and she —
CAROLINE [*triumphantly*]. She can't say that, because *I bribed her!* Your friend!
HUBERT [*flinging the envelope on the table*]. There's your two hundred dollars, and you'll have to pay six *thousand* dollars on your trunks, and be grateful to *Miss Madden* for having saved you!
CAROLINE. To whom?
HUBERT [*with great confidence*]. Miss Emily Madden, the woman you maligned.
CAROLINE [*in a moment of rage*]. She looked me over! She dared!
HUBERT [*gloating*]. It was Miss Madden. [*He walks away from her, turns with supreme elation.*] Yes.
CAROLINE [*in a peal of laughter*]. Then I understand perfectly why she came to you! But I'm not so easy. The matter of the trunks was settled. [*Walking to the hall*]. Of course, if you feel that you are subject to her extortions, or that perhaps you want to give her a token of your gratitude, that's *your* affair. [*Turning to him.*] It would really be indelicate of you to insist that *I* should pay your *mistress!*
HUBERT [*foiled and following her furiously*]. You... [*Chokes.*]
CAROLINE [*very pleasantly*]. Good-morning. Susan is waiting.
[*She exits as the Curtain descends.*]

ACT II

The stage presents the combined kitchen and living-room of the SANBURY *flat in the model tenements, New York City. The whole atmosphere betrays great neatness, but equal constriction and narrowness of quarters. At the first glance, the room is apparently all doors. The walls are done in waterproof white. There is a window in the rear wall, a little to the left. This opens on a fire-escape, and gives a view of other tenements in the rear. There is a shade over the window, which is further hung with chintz curtains, that are visibly cheap, but in good taste as far as the design is concerned. In front of the window is an upholstered window-seat. To the left of the window is a small serving table, with cruets of vinegar and oil, and a salad-bowl upon it. Below this table hang sundry cooking utensils. Next to the table stands the gas-stove with a coffee-pot upon it. High on the wall above the gas-stove is a gas-meter of the kind commonly in use in the tenements. It is automatic, and releases a supply of gas only when a quarter is dropped into it. At the left of the stove and in the corner of the room is a combination sink and wash-tub of white porcelain ware. The dwellers in the tenements use the wash-tub as an ice-box. At the opening of the act, a four-fold screen hides both the sink and the stove from view. However, above the screen, a towel rack with clean dish towels is visible. In the upper left wall of the room is a door leading to* LAWRENCE'S *bedroom. Below this, there is a combination wall book-case and mirror. The book shelf is jammed with well-used books. Directly underneath the book-case stands a flat table upon which are a typewriter and a telephone.*

In the rear wall of the room, to the right of the window, is the door leading from the hall. To the right of this is the dumb-waiter shaft, with a sliding panel door. In the right wall of the room is the entrance to HILDEGARDE'S *bedroom. A little below this, is the door leading to the bathroom.*

There is an electric bell above the hall door, another electric bell above the dumb-waiter. Next to the dumb-waiter is a speaking tube, which rejoices in a very shrill whistle.

Running around the whole room is a

plate shelf with colored plates upon it. There are framed pictures of Tolstoy, Ruskin, and Prince Kropotkin conspicuously hung upon the walls.

At the center of the room is a large mission table, set with a plate, knife, cup and saucer, napkin, and a bowl of fruit. The morning newspaper lies opened. Between the dumb-waiter and the door to HILDEGARDE'S *room is a large mission cupboard. There are five chairs in the room. Three are around the table, and one is placed before the typewriting stand. There is a hatrack upon the wall next to the hall door.*

It is about eleven-thirty in the morning, some weeks after the preceding act. The blind is up, and the room is very light.

[*Off rear a hand-organ is heard playing.* HILDEGARDE *is discovered at the typewriter. She works on, disregarding the hum of incoherent tenement life about her. The organ stops. A street vendor is heard hoarsely crying his wares:*]

VENDOR'S VOICE [*off*]. Apples! Apples! Ten cents a qu-a-art!

WOMAN'S VOICE [*off*]. Hey-hey! Epples! Yas — you! Noomber seven! A helfft quart!

VENDOR'S VOICE [*off*]. All right, number seven!

WOMAN'S VOICE [*off*]. I schick de nikkel down.

[*The* VENDOR'S *voice ceases. Suddenly the sound of a window crashing is heard quite close.* HILDEGARDE *pauses attentively.* LAWRENCE *bursts into the room from the left. He appears in a dressing gown, with a ball in his hand. He is shaved, but still has lather on his face.*]

LAWRENCE. Look here!

HILDEGARDE. Was it your window?

LAWRENCE. Almost my *head.* Say, does anybody own those brats?

HILDEGARDE. [*Goes quickly to the window, throws it up and calls out:*] Vincent! Joey! Don't run away. I told you, you mustn't play ball in the court. I'll have to tell your mothers.

LAWRENCE [*giving her the ball, which she puts on a shelf*]. A lot of good that'll do.

HILDEGARDE. It's hard to be severe with them. [LAWRENCE *goes toward the bathroom.*] They oughtn't play in the street. Little Jamie Kirk was killed by a car last week.

LAWRENCE. There's plenty of them left. [*The dumb-waiter whistle gives a piercing scream.*] What's loose again? [*He opens the tube, listens and yells down.*] No! We don't want any apples!

HILDEGARDE [*opening dumb-waiter*]. Wait, Lawrence. [*She calls down quietly.*] Mrs. Pannakin is number seven on the other side. [*Shuts dumb-waiter door.*] Will you have breakfast now?

LAWRENCE. What time is it?

HILDEGARDE [*taking screen away from stove*]. About half-past eleven.

[*She tries to light gas-stove.*]

LAWRENCE. We've got to hurry. [*Turning.*] What's the matter now?

HILDEGARDE. The meter. Have you a quarter?

LAWRENCE [*giving her a coin*]. No credit there, eh!

[*He goes into bathroom. She gets up on chair and puts coin in the meter, winds it and proceeds to heat the coffee.*]

HILDEGARDE [*calling to him*]. It'll be ready in a moment. You finish dressing.

[LAWRENCE *enters from the bathroom with a towel, drying his face.*]

LAWRENCE. What have you ordered for lunch?

HILDEGARDE. I told Mrs. Pannakin to take especial pains to-day.

LAWRENCE [*grimly disgusted*]. Mrs. Knollys will enjoy one of Mrs. Pannakin's co-operative dinners; where all the last week's vegetables co-operate to make this week's soups! I wonder why they want to come here anyway.

HILDEGARDE [*slowly*]. I can't imagine.

LAWRENCE [*reproachfully*]. *You* invited them. I tried to head it off.

HILDEGARDE. They are your friends;

and you know I never miss a chance of interesting rich people in this philanthropy. Go, dear, and finish dressing.

[*He exits to his room. She takes a script from the typewriter, folds and signs it, then addresses it in an envelope, and stamps it. She hums while she works.*]

[LAWRENCE *re-enters carrying his collar, tie, coat, and vest. He wrestles with his collar and then throws the other things down.*]

LAWRENCE. This life is killing me! I'm as nervous as a cat!

HILDEGARDE. Didn't you sleep well?

LAWRENCE [*pointing to the typewriter*]. Sleep! What time was it when you began banging that instrument of torture?

HILDEGARDE. I had to get my copy ready for this evening's edition.

LAWRENCE [*continuing to dress*]. What is it?

HILDEGARDE. A report of last evening's Labor Meeting for Krellin's column.

LAWRENCE. You know, you'll have to stop this kind of thing. That's if you care anything for me.

[*She gets butter out of improvised ice-box in the wash-tubs.*]

HILDEGARDE [*cheerfully*]. My little writing and my job here are at present our only means of support.

[*She puts butter on table.*]

LAWRENCE. Oh, don't rub it in. [*With a change.*] I'm sorry enough to see you slave the way you do; but Krellin and your friends are attacking the very people from whom I'm going to get my living.

HILDEGARDE [*cheerfully*]. Yes, Mrs. Knollys took the trouble to inform me of that some weeks ago.

LAWRENCE. Well, they don't *like* to hear how their money is made.

HILDEGARDE. There's very little danger of their listening to me.

LAWRENCE. And how about Mr. Knollys?

HILDEGARDE. He and I understand each other completely.

LAWRENCE. Yes, no doubt. But this is how it's worked out for me. I've finished the preliminary plans, and should have got the first instalment to begin my work three days ago.

HILDEGARDE. Well?

LAWRENCE [*continuing*]. Your articles have driven him down South, to look over that factory of his.

HILDEGARDE. Oh, I'm glad of that.

LAWRENCE. I'm glad you're glad. But I get not a cent till he O.K.'s the plans.

HILDEGARDE [*cutting bread for him*]. When does he get back?

LAWRENCE. He was expected yesterday. [*Turning away.*] Oh, I don't want a lot of breakfast. I'm rickety! I'm all in! Just give me some coffee!

HILDEGARDE [*getting coffee from gas-stove*]. It's ready now. [*Pouring it.*] Where do you go to-night?

LAWRENCE. Mrs. Millette.

HILDEGARDE. Mrs. Who?

LAWRENCE. Millette — what's the difference what her name is? Mrs. Knollys says she wants to build a house.

HILDEGARDE. Good.

LAWRENCE. I'm invited to dine with her and go to the play to-night to talk things over.

HILDEGARDE. Any prospects?

LAWRENCE [*with a tone of justification*]. There's a social side to my job. You must see that. I've got to make that solid first.

HILDEGARDE. Yes. [*Pause.*]

LAWRENCE. Why? You're not offended that you're not asked, are you?

HILDEGARDE. Oh, dear, no; I'm thinking only of what they'll think of you.

LAWRENCE. In what way?

HILDEGARDE. I don't want you to be known as the kind of man these women can invite without his wife.

LAWRENCE. And I don't want to be known as the kind of man that always drags his wife about, either.

[*He opens the newspaper.*]

HILDEGARDE. It's an affront to you, not to me. [*The bell rings over the hall door. Opening the door.*] Oh, thank you. [*Takes letters from some one outside.*] Wait; will you drop this in the mail for me? [*She fetches her typewritten article and an orange. As she passes* LAWRENCE *she says:*] These are for you. [*She gives him some letters. Then she returns to the door and gives the letter and the orange to the little girl evidently standing outside.*] Here, Annie. Thank you. [*She closes the door.*]

LAWRENCE [*reading a letter which he has opened during the above business*]. From my old firm. [*Proudly.*] They offer me a raise of ten a week if I'll come back.

HILDEGARDE [*looking through her mail*]. Bills, bills, bills.
[*She sits at her typewriting table.*]

LAWRENCE. They'll have to wait. I've got to. [*Showing his letter.*] How would you answer them?

HILDEGARDE. That you must decide yourself.

LAWRENCE [*pointing to the bills humorously*]. Say, ain't it the devil how the money goes?

HILDEGARDE [*with a smile*]. I can manage the necessities; if you'll keep down the luxuries.

LAWRENCE [*looking at a bill*]. Seven dollars and fifty cents for flowers.
[*Looks up at her.*]

HILDEGARDE. To whom did you send them?

LAWRENCE. Mrs. Knollys, of course. She needs flowers. Always has them. [*With attempted justification.*] I eat two meals a day on her; I've got to keep my end up some way.

HILDEGARDE. Certainly, by all means.

LAWRENCE [*with another letter*]. Tailor's bill. One hundred and twenty-five cold plunks. [*Boyishly.*] That's the swell dress suit, all right. [*Looks at her.*] Do you know, I'm sometimes tempted to drop in and see my old firm; not that I'm aching to go back to them, but —

HILDEGARDE. You might call on them, and tell them what you're doing.

LAWRENCE. What do you think?

HILDEGARDE. I'd play the game out for all it's worth. It's no use weakening now.

LAWRENCE [*pointing to bills*]. What will we do with these?

HILDEGARDE [*encouragingly*]. We'll meet them with your first instalment.
[*The bell over the dumb-waiter rings loudly.*]

LAWRENCE [*going to dumb-waiter*]. I'll open.
[*He opens door. The bell continues its ringing.*]

VOICE [*below, yelling up*]. Sanbury?

LAWRENCE [*shouting down*]. Yes. [*Roaring.*] Take your finger off that bell!
[*Bell stops.*]

VOICE [*cheerily*]. Thought you might be a-hangin' out the wash!

LAWRENCE. No, I'm not hangin' out the wash! What do you want?

VOICE. Look out! It's coming up!!
[LAWRENCE *just ducks back as the dumb-waiter shoots up.*]

HILDEGARDE. It's the grape-fruit and salad from the grocer's. [LAWRENCE *takes it off.*] Put them in there.
[*He puts them as she indicates inside the wash-tubs.*]

LAWRENCE. What time is it now?

HILDEGARDE. After twelve. You'll have to hurry.

LAWRENCE [*suddenly*]. Say, can't we have the screens up? [*Putting them hastily back before the stove.*] And you know, there's nothing very handsome about this view.
[*Jerks down the blind over window rear.*]

HILDEGARDE. Larrie, please don't fuss.
[*He has gone quickly for his coat hanging on a peg behind his door. He re-enters struggling into his coat.*]

LAWRENCE. Say, my room looks like hell!

HILDEGARDE. Agnes will clear it up while I'm setting the table.

LAWRENCE [*nervously*]. Where is she? You know she never comes when you want her!

HILDEGARDE [*clearing table quietly*]. She'll be here.

LAWRENCE [*attempting to fix a picture straight on the wall*]. Have all your orders come?

HILDEGARDE. Yes. Please don't get nervous.

LAWRENCE [*turning nervously*]. Well, I'm only trying to help *you* out. I pass the grocer's.

HILDEGARDE [*pausing*]. You silly boy. I guess you can't help fussing.

LAWRENCE. I like things to be right. [*Suddenly.*] Are you going to wear that dress?

HILDEGARDE. What's the matter with my dress?

LAWRENCE [*dubiously*]. Oh, I suppose it's all right; only I thought your green — and honestly now, your feet aren't as big as that. It's those Consumer's League boots, just like your gloves! You'd wear anything with a Trade Union label on it, wouldn't you? No matter what it looked like!

HILDEGARDE. They won't see my feet.

LAWRENCE. Won't they? [*Exploding.*] That skirt hikes!!

HILDEGARDE [*with an obvious effort to be patient*]. I'll be all right; if you'll only get out before you make *me* nervous. [*A bell rings. He goes toward dumb-waiter again. Lifting the blind he has pulled down.*] No. That's the door. I guess it's Agnes.

LAWRENCE. I hope so. [*He opens the hall door and* MURTHA *bounds into the room.*] Oh, Lord!

MURTHA [*effusively*]. Th' top o' th' marnin' to you, Mishter Sanbury! [*Seeing* HILDEGARDE.] Ah, Sishter! Shure, yer hushband do be lookin' loike a capitalisht to-day. [*Shakes both her hands.*]

LAWRENCE. Where's Agnes?

MURTHA [*with feigned surprise*]. Ah, Agnes, is it? [*Cunningly.*] Shure, she's all roight. She do be havin' th' gran' good loock to-day!

LAWRENCE. Where is she?

MURTHA. She's got a job to-day, yis, wid Mishter Curtis, her auld boss.

HILDEGARDE. Why didn't you tell me she couldn't come?

MURTHA. Oi wouldn't dishappoint ye. Oi know yer goin' to have a shindy; and is it any wonder that Oi'm here before th' wind.

HILDEGARDE [*practically*]. Then go right to Mr. Sanbury's room and clear it up.

MURTHA. Shure Oi will; whoy wouldn't Oi? [*She exits left with aged agility.*]

LAWRENCE. Can't you get rid of her?

HILDEGARDE. I've got to have somebody.

LAWRENCE. Mrs. Knollys hates the sight of her. [*To the ceiling.*] Oh, we're going to have a lovely party!

HILDEGARDE [*nervously*]. Then call it off entirely.

LAWRENCE. I tried to. But she was determined to come here to-day.

HILDEGARDE [*abruptly*]. Then stop complaining! I wish you'd go! [*Seeing the futility of chiding him, she changes to a very reassuring manner.*] Now go, dear. You look very handsome.

[*She adjusts his necktie and goes with him toward hall door. He has his hands in his pockets.*]

LAWRENCE. Do I look like ready money?

HILDEGARDE [*laughing*]. Yes.

LAWRENCE [*shamefaced*]. Well, I haven't got any. Mine's in the gas meter.

HILDEGARDE. How much will you need?

LAWRENCE. I've got to get those dames here, haven't I? And I might be stuck for a taxicab. You know, such things *have* happened!

HILDEGARDE [*going to cupboard*]. Wait. [*She brings out a china bank and shakes it.*]

LAWRENCE. What's that?

HILDEGARDE. My linen bank. [*Shaking it.*] There must be several dollars in it.

[*She breaks it with a knife; and a mass of small coins is exposed.*]

LAWRENCE [*sweeping up the coins*]. I feel like a man that's robbed a nursery.

[*As he puts them uncounted into his pocket, some of them roll on the floor.*]

HILDEGARDE. The grocer will be glad to give you bills.

LAWRENCE. It 'ud take me an hour to count up this chicken feed. [*Suddenly.*] There's some on the floor. [*As he starts to lean over, his soft hat falls from his head. He steps on it.*] Gad!! Sure thing! This is my lucky day!

[*He punches his hat savagely.*]

HILDEGARDE. I'll pick it up. [*She does so.*] Larrie, dear, will you let me say something? And you won't get angry?

LAWRENCE [*defensively*]. Well . . . ?

HILDEGARDE [*going to him*]. Dearest, first try to be calm — for your own sake, don't be irritated. It's unbecoming.

LAWRENCE. Oh, I'm all right; but all these little things . . .

HILDEGARDE. I know, dear, it *is* hard; but for the sake of my pride in you, be careful about showing any impatience to me, particularly in front of Mrs. Knollys. I don't care how angry you get when we're alone. I understand. *She* doesn't. And judging from the last time she saw us together, she might think . . .

LAWRENCE. Please don't refer to that again. I thought you had forgotten it. [*Contritely.*] I lost my head.

HILDEGARDE. If you remember it, I shall forget it. [*She kisses him.*] Now, good-by, dear.

LAWRENCE. Good-by.

[*He exits through the hall door, as* MURTHA *re-enters from his room at the left.*]

MURTHA. That's done.

HILDEGARDE. Then you can lay the table.

MURTHA. Shure Oi will, me dear.

[*She goes quickly to the cupboard for the necessary things. While* MURTHA *is busied at the table, center,* HILDEGARDE *gets the salad and grapefruit from wash-tubs. She cleans and prepares them during the following scene.*]

HILDEGARDE. You know, Mrs. Murtha, it isn't quite honest for you to say that Agnes will go to places, and then you go to them yourself.

MURTHA [*busying herself at table*]. No, ma'm.

[*She crosses herself with a mechanically devout expression.*]

HILDEGARDE. Then why do you do it?

MURTHA. Whoy wouldn't Oi? There's Aggie, th' Lord love her, can hardly keep herself, and Tim's no good at all, and Mary in th' hoshpital, and Joey wid th' haughty lady that he's married and th' twins!

HILDEGARDE. But aren't you getting a little too old for . . . ?

MURTHA [*interrupting savagely*]. There yer sayin' it! And d'ye see, if Oi wuz to tell thim: "It's me, ma'm, that's lookin' fer th' job," Oi'd nivir git it! And a little loi loike that doan't hurrt. [*Wheedling.*] Fer Oi'm as shtrong as ivir Oi wuz.

HILDEGARDE [*with a sigh of futility*]. The knives on the *right* side.

MURTHA [*very gently*]. Yis, ma'm.

[*Pause.*]

HILDEGARDE. Have you ever waited on a table?

MURTHA. Me! Naw, ma'm.

HILDEGARDE [*pausing*]. Then perhaps —

MURTHA [*confidently, while* HILDEGARDE *works at straightening out the table*]. Ah, ye jusht tell me what to do, and Oi kin do it. Shure, Oi'm not wan av thim thick Micks.

HILDEGARDE. Then first of all you must roll down your sleeves.

MURTHA [*obeying like a child*]. Yis, ma'm. Yer a laidy. Oi can't say naw liss than that.

HILDEGARDE [*smiling*]. What is a lady?

MURTHA. Ha! A laidy is wan av thim that has all th' beer an' skittles, an' doan't have to do no worrk. [*Laughing.*] Shure, Oi allus says moy auld man's th' loocky laidy av our house. Me an' his chilthren does th' worrk fer him; an' he schmokes in th' corner all day long.

HILDEGARDE. Well, *I* don't smoke in the corner all day long.

MURTHA. Ah, doan't ye be lishtenin' to me gush!

HILDEGARDE. You just bring the things from Mrs. Pannakin to me.

MURTHA. Yis, ma'm.

HILDEGARDE. And if there's anything you don't know how to do, you just ask me quietly, and I'll tell you.

MURTHA. Yis, ma'm. [*She pricks up her ears.*] What wuz that!!! [*She makes a dive for the window rear and looks out.*] That's Mickey Doolan! Shure it's Doolan!! [*She flings open the window. As she does so, a violent quarrel in Irish between a man and woman is heard.* MURTHA *yells out:*] Mickey! Mickey!! You lave her be! [*Solemnly.*] Moy Gawd! He's hit her, th' poor woman, and she wid th' young un comin'! [*She jumps up on the sill.*] Mickey! Mickey!! You lave her be!! Fer th' love o' God and th' shame o' man, you let her be!! You dhrunken pesht!

[*During the above speech,* HILDEGARDE *has tried vainly to hold* MURTHA *back and stop her yelling; but* MURTHA *has got speechless with rage. She tears loose from* HILDEGARDE, *goes through the window and is heard clattering down the fire-escape execrating* DOOLAN.]

HILDEGARDE [*calling*]. Mrs. Murtha!! Wait — Mrs. Murtha!!!

[MURTHA *has disappeared into the mêlée. The row is heard suddenly to increase with* MURTHA'S *advent. A woma.1's shrill scream is heard, and then a man's growl. The row increases.* HILDEGARDE, *seeing the futility of trying to control things at a distance, decides to follow. She also exits over the fire-escape, and descends.* MURTHA'S *high voice is heard above the noise, calling for "Tim." Then some other women's voices are heard in high excitement calling. A hushed subsidence due to* HILDEGARDE'S *appearance follows. Finally an absolute pause of silence. Then a key is heard turning in the lock of door from the hall. The door opens. Whistling is heard on the steps. The whistling evidently is paced to keep time with some one climbing slowly up stairs.*]

[LAWRENCE *enters.*]

BOYS' VOICES [*outside, heard as the door opens*]. Give us the ball! You got it!

LAWRENCE. Go on, boys, chase yourselves. [*To* CAROLINE.] Come in.

[CAROLINE *enters.*]

BOYS' VOICES [*derisively*]. Git a haircut! Git a hair-cut! G'wan, you dude!

LAWRENCE [*closing the door*]. This is the living-room. Plain living and high thinking.

CAROLINE [*laughing*]. I should admit it's rather high.

LAWRENCE [*calling*]. Hildegarde! We're here! [*To* CAROLINE.] Sit down, please.

CAROLINE [*not sitting*]. Are you sure that she expected me?

LAWRENCE. Certainly. She may be in my room.

[*Crosses left and opens his door.*]

CAROLINE [*crossing*]. I want to see where you sleep.

LAWRENCE. Behold my couch of dreams.

CAROLINE [*murmuring*]. You poor boy!

LAWRENCE [*closing window rear*]. I don't care where I sleep, as long as I've a place to *work* in.

[*He starts to pull down the blind.*]

CAROLINE. What's there?

LAWRENCE [*cheerfully*]. Excellent view of a fire-escape and Mrs. Pannakin's kitchen, where our nectar and ambrosia are prepared; which later you are to be privileged to taste.

CAROLINE [*after looking*]. Ah!

LAWRENCE. [*He pulls down the blind. Then he goes toward* HILDEGARDE'S *room at right, calling.*] Hildegarde!

CAROLINE [*insinuatingly*]. Do you object to this little chat with me alone?

LAWRENCE. Of course not! But I wanted to leave you here with Hildegarde, while I looked for Miss Ambie. She may have trouble finding us.

CAROLINE. I hope so. [*He looks at her.*] I have trouble enough in losing her.

LAWRENCE [*laughing*]. Do you know, you sometimes perplex me terribly?

CAROLINE [*sitting*]. Do I? [*Smiles.*] Sit down and let me look at you. [*He sits and looks at her inquiringly.*] I want to see if I can fit you into this environment. How do you manage it?

LAWRENCE. Oh, Caroline, you're so used to luxury, you can't understand how a little plain living rather helps a fellow to dream true. That's why I didn't want you to come down. I was afraid it would discourage you.

CAROLINE [*slowly and with a caressing glance*]. It has made many things about you very clear to me.

LAWRENCE. There's nothing complex about me.

CAROLINE. Yes, if you can do what you have done down here, what will you do, when —? Oh, it's only because you are *you* that all this squalor hasn't killed your genius!

LAWRENCE [*humorously*]. Oh, come now, Caroline, it's hard for me not to agree with you when you speak of me as a genius and all that. I tell you frankly I adore it; but I'm really quite an ordinary sort of a chap. I've got enough ambition and enthusiasm to draw cheques on my future. I hope I've learned my job; so if the big things come along, I'll be able to measure up to my opportunities. And — when I'm with you, I feel my luck is with me.

CAROLINE. Then my faith in you does really help you, does it?

LAWRENCE. How can you ask that?

CAROLINE. Keep your confidence, Lawrence, but remember that patience is a virtue of the underlings. *I* don't possess that virtue; and you cannot afford to.

LAWRENCE. What's that to do with it?

CAROLINE [*vehemently*]. Oh, I can't bear to see you in circumstances like these! I can't lie to you! It's useless to disguise it. I hate to see you pulling down the blinds! I hate anything that ties you here! The world is full of people that can plod and wait for opportunities. *We've* got to *make* them and before it is too late! I knew that you had wings the first time that I saw you. I hate the idea of a half a loaf, when by the right of the power in you, you are entitled to the whole! I hate even the patchwork you're doing on my house! [*She rises.*]

LAWRENCE. Don't say that! The work you've given me has enabled me to leave my firm with a free conscience.

CAROLINE [*smiling*]. What have *you* to do with conscience? People have conscience only when they *fail*.

LAWRENCE [*rising*]. By Jove, you have a liberating way of saying things!

CAROLINE. Have I helped to liberate you?

LAWRENCE. I've chucked a lot of litter since I've met you.

CAROLINE. That's right. I love to hear you say that. Oh, I want to see you free — free from all the petty scruples that would hinder you! That's my work now. For while you're building houses, *I* shall be building your career.

[LAWRENCE *takes her enthusiastically and impulsively into his arms, and kisses her full on the mouth. He looks at her as if hypnotized. She is full of the disguised triumph in her seduction. They pause.* LAWRENCE *becomes thoughtful with a disturbing realization of what he has done.*]

LAWRENCE. I beg your pardon.

CAROLINE. For what?

LAWRENCE. Forgive me. I had no right to —

CAROLINE [*interrupting*]. You have a right to everything if you only want it *enough!* [*Passionately.*] I want *you* — [*Quickly correcting herself.*] I *want* you to succeed; and we shall find a means. [*Suddenly.*] You must get that studio immediately.

LAWRENCE [*dazed*]. What — ?

CAROLINE [*in a low voice*]. You can't work any longer at my house. [*He looks up.*] Hubert arrives to-day.

LAWRENCE [*absently*]. Good!

CAROLINE. A little less enthusiasm, please.

LAWRENCE. I mean, then I can get his O.K. on the plans.

CAROLINE. You'll get your first instalment to-morrow. You've got to draw up plans of an Italian country house for Edwalyn Millette.

LAWRENCE. She has decided?

CAROLINE. She will. She has money; and I can tell her exactly what she thinks she wants. [*Humorously.*] There I can help *you* too. You'll need your studio. [*Dreamily.*] I know exactly how we'll furnish it. I know just where I shall sit and pour your tea. [*The bell rings over the door. They start.*] And we won't have bells like that!

LAWRENCE. That's Hildegarde. [*Turning.*] I'll tell her of the studio.

CAROLINE [*quickly*]. Not a word. Leave that to me. [*He hesitates.*] Oh, we drive to Edwalyn's Long Island place this afternoon. I want you to see the grounds before you dine with her to-night.

LAWRENCE. Oh, all right. [*He opens the door to the hall, and discovers* SUSAN AMBIE.] Come in, Miss Ambie.

SUSAN [*entering, her hat awry*]. Oh,

there you are! [*Grieved.*] Well, Carrie, I *must say* —
CAROLINE. We decided you weren't coming.
SUSAN [*looking at her watch*]. I thought I was on time.
CAROLINE. Think again, my dear.
LAWRENCE. Did you have trouble finding us?
SUSAN [*straightening her hat and speaking to* LAWRENCE]. You oughtn't let those children play ball in the street. Their ball just missed me!
CAROLINE. Too bad! Too bad!
SUSAN. Carrie, I've something I must say to you . . .
  [*Looks significantly at* LAWRENCE.]
LAWRENCE. Excuse me. I'll hunt up Hildegarde. She may be in her office.
  [*As soon as* LAWRENCE *exits,* SUSAN *betrays a most uncontrolled and nervous anxiety. She is nervous almost to the point of incoherency.*]
CAROLINE. Well, what is it?
SUSAN. Carrie, I'm sorry . . . but I haven't slept! I can't take any more responsibility. That's all.
CAROLINE. Then don't.
SUSAN [*on the raw*]. They ask me if I'm blind!!
CAROLINE. Well, if you're not, what do you care?
SUSAN [*gushily*]. People are talking about you and Lawrence. Of course, *I* understand — but . . .
CAROLINE [*interrupting*]. If you give your time thinking about what other people say, you'll never have time for anything else.
SUSAN [*impatiently*]. But people know that Hubert's been away . . . and they see you and Lawrence together everywhere, and . . .
CAROLINE. There's comfort in that. Just think what they imagine when they don't see us.
SUSAN. My dear, you can't stop wicked tongues from wagging. . . . Of course, I tried to defend you all I could. . . . People are saying that you've lost your head over this young architect that you have *living* with you in your house. *Everybody's* talking —

CAROLINE. Everybody has nothing else to do.
SUSAN. Where is his wife? Perhaps *she's* heard things and *means* to be rude!
CAROLINE. Rude to *me?* She couldn't be.
SUSAN. You know, Lawrence tried to discourage our coming. What *can* you and she have in common?
CAROLINE [*meaningly*]. Nothing! Lawrence sees that already. When *she* realizes that we can have *nothing in common* — not even her — well, the rest is easy.
SUSAN [*alarmed*]. Carrie! You're up to something mad! [CAROLINE *laughs.*] I haven't seen you look or act like this, not since . . . Italy! [*Suddenly with a cry.*] Yes, they're right! It's true!!
CAROLINE [*calmly*]. What?
SUSAN. You've lost your head about him.
CAROLINE [*recklessly*]. Oh, there's no law against a woman losing her *head*.
SUSAN. But his wife! What do you mean to do?
CAROLINE. I? Nothing.
SUSAN. Carrie, come back with me. We'll leave our cards; and we'll have done our duty.
CAROLINE. Go if you like.
SUSAN [*with a nervous whimper*]. I won't desert you, Carrie!
CAROLINE [*rising*]. Oh, then shut up!
SUSAN. Don't be rash, dear; she may know more than you think.
CAROLINE. In big things I do nothing underhand.
  [*There is heard a fearful shaking of the window.*]
SUSAN. What's that!!
CAROLINE. I'll see.
  [*She goes toward window, rear, pulls up the blind. The person outside on the fire-escape flings up the window and scrambles into the room.*]
SUSAN [*tearfully, during* CAROLINE'S *movement*]. I don't know what we're doing here anyway!
CAROLINE [*seeing* MURTHA]. The gorilla!
SUSAN [*frightened*]. Carrie, this is the way out!

[MURTHA *has scrambled into the room talking incoherently to herself. She looks rather damaged, and is carrying her apron and purse in her hand. Her hair is tousled and her eye is red.*]

MURTHA [*recognizing* CAROLINE]. Ah, fer th' love o' God, Mrs. Knowllez, is it you! D'ye see me oye! [*Pointing to it.*] That's phwat ye git whin ye come interferin' between a hushband and a woife! Shure, it wuz *her* that guv me that. [*Laughing.*] Hah, there wuz wigs on th' green! I licked him wance before, and Mrs. Doolan she knows it, moind ye; and whin I wuz trou' wid him, a dog wouldn't ha' lapped his blood!

[CAROLINE *and* SUSAN *have tried in vain to retreat before* MURTHA'S *stream of hysterical verbiage.*]

SUSAN [*completely appalled*]. Yes, that's all very interesting . . . !
[*Retreats around table.*]

MURTHA. Now doan't ye moind me. Shure Oi'm only talkin' to mesilf, and Oi couldn't foind a bigger fool to talk to. [*She opens a purse she still carries in her hand, sees her money.*] Ah, that's all roight.
[*She puts purse down on the table.* CAROLINE *and* SUSAN *are chasséing toward the door, which is suddenly opened and* HILDEGARDE *is heard talking to some one at the entrance.*]

HILDEGARDE [*calling in*]. Mrs. Murtha, go bathe that eye in cold water.

MURTHA [*subdued immediately*]. Yis, ma'm. [*She goes to the sink and does so.*]

HILDEGARDE [*continuing to some one outside*]. No, Doolan; if you're sobered up at four o'clock, come to my office. The ejection officer will be there. [*She closes the door sharply as she enters, then suddenly sees* CAROLINE *and* SUSAN. *She continues with complete composure.*] Oh! [*Shakes hands with* CAROLINE.] I'm sorry I wasn't here to receive you. [*Shakes hands with* SUSAN.] I hope you'll forgive me. There's been an unfortunate difficulty with a couple of our tenants. Excuse me!

CAROLINE. Certainly.

[HILDEGARDE *exits into her room.* CAROLINE *and* SUSAN *look at each other while the noise of running water is heard at the sink, where* MURTHA *is bathing her eye.* SUSAN *is frightened.* CAROLINE *is enjoying her usual parasitic amusement.*]

SUSAN. What do you think, Carrie?

CAROLINE. The worse it is, the better I like it.

[HILDEGARDE *immediately re-enters with a small bottle and some lint, which she puts down on the table.*]

HILDEGARDE [*to* CAROLINE *and* SUSAN]. Won't you lay off your wraps in Larrie's room? [*Pointing left.* SUSAN *passes and enters the room at left.*] I'm sure there's more excitement than real injury.

[CAROLINE *goes toward room.* HILDEGARDE *takes a bowl from plate rack and moves to* MURTHA.]

CAROLINE [*to* SUSAN *whose train is still visible, showing the smallness of the room*]. Susan, go in.

SUSAN [*excitedly*]. I can't walk through the wall, my dear.
[*The train is, however, snatched in, and* CAROLINE *enters, closing the door behind her.*]

MURTHA. Oh, me oye — me oye!

HILDEGARDE [*to* MURTHA]. Now, quick, let me look at that eye.

MURTHA. Shure Oi will, me dear!

HILDEGARDE. Bathe it with this stuff. Here, use this too. [*Going to table to get the lint pad, she sees* MURTHA'S *purse.*] Oh, you've found your purse. Where was it?

MURTHA [*guiltily*]. I must ha' dhropped it runnin' down.

HILDEGARDE. You see you were wrong to accuse Mrs. Doolan. That only made more trouble.

MURTHA [*cannily*]. It wuz th' loocky thing thim Polacks didn't know 'twas loyin' jusht outside their window.

[LAWRENCE *enters from the hall door.*]

LAWRENCE [*to* HILDEGARDE]. Where have you been?

MURTHA [*groaning*]. Oh, Mother! Me oye . . . me oye . . . .
[*She sits wretchedly at the left.*]

LAWRENCE. What's the matter!

MURTHA [*in a loud regretful tone*]. If I had only hit him whin he thripped!!
HILDEGARDE. There's been trouble with the Doolans.
LAWRENCE. In here?
HILDEGARDE. No. And everything is all right now.
LAWRENCE. Yes, but where are the ladies?
HILDEGARDE [*trying to quiet him by her tone*]. In your room, laying off their wraps.
[*During the above, MURTHA has been fighting over the battle in pantomime, while bathing her eye, and mumbling to herself.*]
LAWRENCE. Did you get anybody else to help you?
HILDEGARDE [*barely holding her nerves*]. I've been quelling a riot!
LAWRENCE [*pointing to MURTHA*]. What are you going to do with her?
HILDEGARDE. Go to Mrs. Pannakin's, and see if *she* won't serve the dinner herself.
LAWRENCE. I was just there looking for *you!* I asked her then . . .
HILDEGARDE. Well . . . ?
LAWRENCE [*throwing up his hands and speaking to the ceiling*]. She can't come! She isn't dressed! And dinner's ready!!
HILDEGARDE [*to MURTHA*]. Go to Mrs. Pannakin's, smooth your hair, borrow an apron, and bring in the dinner.
MURTHA [*rising*]. Oh, yis, ma'm. [*With a savage gesture.*] The durrty A.P.A.! [*She crosses to the hall door muttering.*] Oh, Lord, I'm as blind as Doolan's goat! I'll nivir see out o' that oye again. . . . To hit me whin Oi wasn't lookin' . . . [*She exits.*]
LAWRENCE. Good Lord!
[*He swings around the room in an ecstasy of exasperation.*]
HILDEGARDE [*going to him*]. Larrie, no matter what happens, don't be betrayed into any rudeness to me before Mrs. Knollys.

[*The door, left, opens and SUSAN enters.*]

HILDEGARDE. The excitement has subsided. Won't you sit here? [*She fixes a chair at her right.* SUSAN *sits with her back to the door.* CAROLINE *enters.*] And, Mrs. Knollys, won't you sit there? [*She motions* CAROLINE *to the chair at LAWRENCE's right. He helps her. She faces the door.* HILDEGARDE *faces the audience.* LAWRENCE *has his back to the audience. Note: the LADIES have just removed their wraps.* CAROLINE *has not taken off her gloves.*] Don't mind my jumping up. [*She gets bread and butter from the wash-tubs.*] How is Mr. Knollys?
CAROLINE. Well, thank you, the last I heard.
HILDEGARDE. [*Puts the bread on table and helps them to butter. To* CAROLINE.] Let me help you. We hear the Homestead Mills are going to begin work again. I'm glad. Sugar?
CAROLINE [*waving a "no"*]. And the percentage on investments lowered again.
[*They all, except* CAROLINE, *eat grape-fruit.*]
SUSAN [*changing the conversation*]. Mrs. Sanbury, have you any nerves left?
HILDEGARDE. This is by no means a typical day.
CAROLINE. No?
HILDEGARDE. Many of the workmen living here are idle. Unfortunately, they drink.
CAROLINE. If that is how they spend their leisure, why agitate for shorter hours and bigger pay?
SUSAN [*vigorously*]. What good bread!
HILDEGARDE. Many laboring people drink because they have to work, and —
CAROLINE [*interrupting sarcastically*]. Precisely, and they don't like it. I agree with you so far.
HILDEGARDE. Perhaps. But oftener they get the habit of drink because they haven't decent food.
LAWRENCE [*rising*]. That being the case, ladies, I propose we fortify ourselves against the possible vagaries of our coöperative cook.
[*He goes to tubs and takes out bottles.*]
SUSAN [*looking*]. Your what?
HILDEGARDE [*to SUSAN*]. Perhaps Larrie has told you, this is a coöperative dining-room. Several of the people living here chip in to pay the rent.

LAWRENCE [to CAROLINE]. A little Scotch?

[*She refuses it. He helps* SUSAN.]

CAROLINE [to HILDEGARDE]. A sort of socialistic mess.

SUSAN [*incredulously*]. But you're not Socialists, are you?

[*She drops her bread and knife.*]

HILDEGARDE. Not all of us.

SUSAN [*reassured and beginning to eat again*]. Oh, that's better.

HILDEGARDE. But then we've got an Anarchist or two among us.

SUSAN [*anxiously, pausing in a mouthful*]. Oh!

HILDEGARDE [*continuing*]. All interested in improving conditions.

SUSAN [*approving charitably*]. Ah.

[*She resumes eating.*]

LAWRENCE [*rising*]. Psch! [*Mysteriously.*] It's coming! [SUSAN *is apprehensive, as he goes to the hall door and opens it.*] I've got a long-distance nose! The soup!!

[*He returns to his chair as* MURTHA *enters carrying four soup-bowls on a very presentable tray. She never takes her eyes from* HILDEGARDE. MURTHA *is very neat and important.* HILDEGARDE *motions her to serve her first.* MURTHA *does so.*]

SUSAN [*seeing* MURTHA]. Oh, she's all right again. I'm glad.

HILDEGARDE [to MURTHA]. Then serve Mrs. Knollys.

CAROLINE [*waving a gloved hand*]. I never eat soup.

[MURTHA *goes to* SUSAN *and helps her, then* LAWRENCE. *She stands awkwardly for a moment, but very quietly.*]

HILDEGARDE [to MURTHA]. You can come back in a moment and clear off the bowls.

MURTHA. Yis, ma'm.

HILDEGARDE. Leave the door ajar.

[MURTHA *is about to exit, carrying the tray with* CAROLINE'S *bowl of soup on it, when she is passed in the door by* MICHAEL KRELLIN. KRELLIN *is a Russian by birth, but speaks English with a scrupulous, scholarly exactness, though with a slightly foreign accent. Physically, he is of medium height, lithe and slender in figure, rapid and exact in his movements. His dress is clean but careless. Everything about him betokens a fearless definiteness of mind. He has a shock of curly hair. His face is pale, his eyes are very keen; and when he looks at a person, he is likely to peer a little closer into their faces than the usual man. His speech is fluent and incisive. He is mentally a combination of the political dreamer and the practical meliorist, who has saved his optimism by fighting for the next reform at his hand. His manner is above all things humorous and easy, with a sort of detached impersonal impertinence. He has the assurance of the platform orator.*]

MURTHA [*meeting him at the door*]. Good marnin', Mishter Krellin.

KRELLIN. Good morning. Eh? Wait! [*Stops* MURTHA *and peers into the tray.*]

LAWRENCE [to CAROLINE]. There's our Anarchist. [HILDEGARDE *rises.*]

KRELLIN [*continuing to* MURTHA]. Here ... Hello — Hello! I'll take that soup.

[*He has already deftly lifted it from the tray.*]

MURTHA. Doan't let yer modesty wrong you. [*She exits.*]

KRELLIN [*joyously*]. Hildegarde, Hildegarde! I've news for you! Good news!

[*He goes immediately to the cupboard, puts down his soup-bowl deftly, pulls out a drawer, finds his napkin with a cheap ring on it, picks out a knife, fork, and spoon, puts the napkin in his mouth, takes the bowl, with knife, fork, and spoon in one hand, then picks up a chair with his remaining hand and advances toward the table.*]

HILDEGARDE [*hesitatingly*]. Yes, Michael ...

KRELLIN [*during the above business*]. Just wait. I'm as hungry as a wolf. All night at the office.

HILDEGARDE. You must be tired, Michael.
KRELLIN [*his voice is merry, but his body is relaxed*]. Not very.
[*He puts down his chair between* SUSAN'S *and* HILDEGARDE'S, *and places his eating paraphernalia on the table.* SUSAN *draws away, as he sits down.* CAROLINE *is imperturbed.* LAWRENCE *is annoyed.*]
KRELLIN [*peering near-sightedly at* SUSAN]. Oh, you're having a party. I didn't see. [*Rising.*] Pardon, I am very near-sighted; and I have broken my glasses. [*About to withdraw.*] I'll step in later.
HILDEGARDE. Wait, Michael. [*To* CAROLINE *and* SUSAN.] Mr. Krellin is one of our friends.
KRELLIN. Yes, yes. I only wanted to ask; did you finish your article?
HILDEGARDE. Yes. It's gone. What's the news?
KRELLIN. You'll have to write a special. Despatches from the South tell of the final settlement by arbitration with the Homestead Mills. Another victory!
[*He shakes* HILDEGARDE'S *hands enthusiastically.*]
HILDEGARDE. Splendid, but —
[*Turns toward* CAROLINE.]
KRELLIN [*continuing*]. A ten-hour day, and a dollar ninety cents!
LAWRENCE. The Homestead Mills! those are . . . [*Turns to* CAROLINE.]
CAROLINE. Yes, I'm interested.
HILDEGARDE. My friend is one of the reporters on the *Echo*. He's just had news. May I present him?
CAROLINE. And which way has the strike been settled?
KRELLIN [*coming toward her*]. You will be glad to hear in favor of the shorter hour and the living wage. Another milestone passed!
HILDEGARDE. Mrs. Knollys, this is Mr. Krellin. A member of our coöperative club. We don't usually have the pleasure of seeing him till dinner time.
KRELLIN [*has leaned toward* CAROLINE]. Mrs. Knollys . . . Knollys? [*Peers at her, then at* HILDEGARDE, *then again at* CAROLINE.] I am delighted to find *you* here. [*Laughs softly.*] God is a great dramatist!
CAROLINE. Why?
KRELLIN. I've seen you before, Madame; and I've heard of your husband.
HILDEGARDE [*quickly*]. And this is Miss Ambie.
KRELLIN [*bowing*]. Ah, yes . . . Miss Ah . . . [*He goes toward her.*]
SUSAN [*frightened*]. How do you do! . . .
[KRELLIN *sits between* HILDEGARDE *and* SUSAN. *Pause.*]
KRELLIN [*partially rising with his knife in hand and peering*]. Is that the butter? [*He takes some and puts it on bread.* To CAROLINE, *as he settles back in his chair.*] Mrs. Knollys, I put you on your guard. Before you know it, Hildegarde will persuade you to invest in tenements and make you a five per cent philanthropist.
LAWRENCE [*decidedly*]. No, she won't! She —
KRELLIN [*interrupting*]. Wait! She will induce you to put up better dwellings for the poor; so they can live a little more decently on their miserable wages. You will feel charitable toward them, because they will give you a steady five per cent; and the workingmen will be made more contented with conditions, that otherwise they might be encouraged to radically change.
SUSAN [*horrified*]. But don't you believe in charity?
KRELLIN [*throwing up his hands*]. Ah, I see! Another sentimentalist. I surrender!
SUSAN. I'm no such thing!
KRELLIN [*gracefully looking at* SUSAN *and* CAROLINE]. But neither of you is old enough to be the real conservative.
CAROLINE [*smiling*]. You're a radical?
KRELLIN. I am a social physician, whose prescriptions nobody respects, because I do not believe in wasting time disguising or trying to cure *symptoms*. *Poverty is the real disease.*
CAROLINE. Other people have a name for your kind of man.
KRELLIN. They call us lots of names. Which one?
CAROLINE. They call you "muck rakers."

KRELLIN [*good-humoredly*]. Oh, that never offends me. To make all beautiful things grow, there must be some one to stir up ... ah ... unappetizing things about the roots. We do that. [*Pointing to* CAROLINE.] Unfortunately, however, it is the "other" people that wear the flowers. So! [*He eats his soup.*]

LAWRENCE. You mustn't take him seriously, Mrs. Knollys.

KRELLIN. Never listen to the artists. *They* must take nothing seriously; else they could find very little beauty in anything. They are spiritual toy-makers and seducers. They gather the flowers and forget the roots. At least don't take them seriously when they *speak*. Admire them when they *do;* because they are permitted to do, and don't know *how* to speak. Listen to *us* when *we* speak; because the Government will allow us no other liberty. [*Eats.*]

LAWRENCE. Nonsense, Michael.

KRELLIN [*appealing to* CAROLINE]. You see, that is my great misfortune. My friends never know when I am in earnest. What else is there to eat?

[*At this moment* MURTHA *appears with a tray on which are chops and vegetables.*]

HILDEGARDE [*to* MURTHA]. Take these things off before you serve the chops.

[MURTHA, *without a word, puts the tray on the cupboard, and deftly removes the empty soup-bowls.*]

KRELLIN [*to* HILDEGARDE]. Emmy will be late.

[MURTHA *during the next speeches serves chops.*]

CAROLINE [*resuming*]. Do you take yourself seriously, Mr. Krellin?

KRELLIN [*with a quick glance*]. That means *you* don't. But I did once. That's why I left Russia.

HILDEGARDE. Mr. Krellin wrote a book for the Radical movement, and the Government didn't like it.

CAROLINE. Wise Government.

[*Henceforward* LAWRENCE *and* CAROLINE *form a party against* HILDEGARDE *and* KRELLIN.]

KRELLIN. Yes, my friends, the enemy, were making Russia too hot for me; and Siberia has always been too cold; and —

CAROLINE [*interrupting*]. So you decided to make trouble over here.

[SUSAN *has got an eating devil and is despatching food.*]

KRELLIN. Precisely.

CAROLINE. And in that work, do you take *other* people seriously?

KRELLIN. Sometimes. You see, I am neither an artist [*bowing to* LAWRENCE] nor [*bowing to* SUSAN] a sentimentalist.

SUSAN [*putting down her knife and fork*]. Now he means me again, Carrie!

CAROLINE [*to* KRELLIN]. Then you and I might understand each other.

KRELLIN. Ah — you mustn't ask me to take *you* seriously, Mrs. Knollys; that would be too much to ask.

CAROLINE. Why?

KRELLIN. You see, I know you. You're a spoiled American woman; which means you take neither our Government nor yourself seriously. I don't blame you; neither do I. In other words, *we* have a sense of humor. And then you are a *Saxon* woman; which means, to a Russian, that you have elevated hypocrisy until it takes rank with a virtue. Otherwise you could never do as you do. [*He eats.*]

LAWRENCE [*growing nervous*]. For Heaven's sake, stop him!

HILDEGARDE. Please, Michael, eat.

LAWRENCE [*to* CAROLINE]. He's our interminable talker.

HILDEGARDE [*laughing a little nervously and speaking to* CAROLINE]. People say anything they think here.

KRELLIN [*in the midst of a mouthful*]. Yes, *when* they think! [*Then to* SUSAN.] *When* they think!

HILDEGARDE. But we try to argue about *principles*, not persons.

CAROLINE. But I'm not interested in principles.

KRELLIN [*to* CAROLINE]. Right you are! Only involve people in *principles*, and you keep them harmless.

CAROLINE [*to* KRELLIN]. But do go on. You said you saw me once before.

KRELLIN. Yes. I was detailed at the dock when you arrived.

CAROLINE [*not so pleasantly*]. Oh.
[SUSAN *puts down her knife and fork again.*]
KRELLIN [*continuing*]. And a dear, a very dear friend persuaded me to lose fifteen dollars on your account.
CAROLINE. That was a very *dear* friend, indeed.
KRELLIN. Ah, yes, I had a beautiful article written, which, for *her* sake, I was weak enough to drop ... an article about the humor and hypocrisy of the American woman — with special reference to yourself, Mrs. Knollys ...
[LAWRENCE *is fearful, pushes back his chair.* CAROLINE *has waved aside the chop and peas that* MURTHA *has offered her.*]
KRELLIN [*to* MURTHA]. Bring that to me. I've had no breakfast. [*During the next speeches he has the business of taking* CAROLINE'S *chop, etc.*] Shall I continue?
LAWRENCE [*decidedly*]. No!
CAROLINE. By all means.
KRELLIN [*to the others*]. You see, she already treats me as an artist. I amuse her.
CAROLINE. Immensely.
KRELLIN. That's why I permit myself to speak. Well, to resume: strange to say, I wrote that the people whose fortunes have been made in industries protected by the Government are always the very ones most eager to evade the customs imposed by that Government to *protect* their industries.
SUSAN [*fearfully*]. Carrie!
KRELLIN [*impatiently*]. Miss Nambie — Miss Pambie — Miss ...
SUSAN. *Ambie* is my name.
KRELLIN. Pardon, quite so. I do not include you; because on that day you personally *lost* your sense of humor. [*To* CAROLINE.] Your money is made in protected tin plate. Your husband's in protected woollen mills. [*Laughs.*] You see, you have a sense of humor and a genius for hypocrisy. [*Seriously.*] You don't *respect* a Government that will let your factories work the *poor* the way they do. Neither do I. And so you refuse to pay the customs to support that Government. No more do I!

LAWRENCE. Michael!
KRELLIN [*continuing unperturbed*]. I admire you! Your personal discernment and your sense of humor were almost worth six thousand dollars to you. I admire you personally — fifteen dollars' worth; and that's a great deal for a man who is saving up in order to get married.
CAROLINE [*quietly leading him on*]. Oh, you still believe in marriage. That's interesting.
KRELLIN. You mean, as soon as we are *inconsistent* we are interesting. [*Wisely.*] *You* believe in conventions that you do not observe; *I* for a time observe conventions in which I do not believe.
SUSAN [*horrified*]. Don't you believe in marriage?
KRELLIN [*bowing to her*]. Oh, yes, as all the *un*married people do.
SUSAN. I'm sure I don't know what you mean, but it makes me very uncomfortable.
LAWRENCE [*laughing*]. Gag him!
HILDEGARDE. I'll mix the salad.
[*She gets the salad bowl.* MURTHA *helps her.*]
CAROLINE. Then you believe in *women* too?
KRELLIN. Boundlessly. And in every capacity of citizenship. [SUSAN *pushes back her chair with an exclamation of disgust.* KRELLIN *continues to* CAROLINE.] I believe especially in *one*, the one I'm going to marry. I believe in eugenics and endowed maternity — in everything that makes for a superior humanity. [*To* SUSAN.] I believe that by our foolish laws we can sometimes save people from doing what they'd like to *do*. [*To* CAROLINE.] I should like to save people from being what they *are*. I believe — Oh — I believe that I'm a stupid fool for telling you sincerely all that I do believe in — and —
[*To* HILDEGARDE.] Don't put too much vinegar in the dressing.
SUSAN [*outraged*]. I've listened long enough!
CAROLINE. Why, Susan! What's broke loose in you?
SUSAN. I'm bound to protest!
KRELLIN. Ah, then there's hope for you.
SUSAN [*scathingly*]. Oh, I'm not clever!

but I think your ideas are perfectly ridiculous and detestable — all of them!

KRELLIN. Thank you. I would have doubt of them if you thought otherwise.

SUSAN [continuing]. And as for women as citizens — women voting and doing the work of men... Well, it's bad enough now as it is, when they happen to hold office under the Government...

KRELLIN [amused]. I remember. You had difficulty.

SUSAN [unheeding his interruption]. Yes, we had an experience at the customs!

CAROLINE [warningly]. Susan!

SUSAN [impetuously]. There was a hussy there when we arrived... Of all the insolence in office... Hah! If I had my way...

[Stops breathlessly.]

KRELLIN. You didn't have your way. That was the trouble, wasn't it?

SUSAN. Well, I'd like to meet her some time face to face — That's all; when she didn't have her little badge upon her; and without the authority of the Government behind her — I'd...

KRELLIN. Yes — yes. Excuse me.

[The door to the hall has opened and EMILY MADDEN appears. KRELLIN has risen alertly.]

SUSAN [bewildered]. What's the matter?

[She continues to talk to CAROLINE.]

KRELLIN [at the door with EMILY]. Ah, Emmy, you're late.

[He starts to bring her down. She resists a little, seeing strangers present.]

CAROLINE [seeing EMILY]. Susan, you're a fool!

SUSAN [seated with her back to the door, doesn't see EMILY. She continues to talk to CAROLINE, mournfully]. I had no right to drink that whisky. It always makes me silly. [She suddenly turns, following CAROLINE'S glance, and exclaims, terrified:] There she is!! Don't you see her? [Crumpled.] Oh, Carrie, it's gone to my head!!

[She makes a mad clutch at her head.]

CAROLINE. Keep quiet!

LAWRENCE [to CAROLINE]. I'm so sorry. [Then savagely to HILDEGARDE.] Now, you see!...

[He becomes incoherent and swings up rear, sees MURTHA, stops short and goes to window.]

KRELLIN [bringing EMILY down]. Emily, there is a lady here who has just expressed a great desire to meet you.

EMILY [advancing a step]. Oh, then, I'd be deligh —

[She stops and recoils as she recognizes CAROLINE.]

SUSAN [waving her hands]. I've had quite enough! I've had quite enough!!

[She rises as if to go.]

KRELLIN [gallantly]. Mrs. Knollys, Miss Madden is the reason for my belief in marriage.

CAROLINE [amused and pausing]. Oh! That is remarkable.

[She suddenly realizes that a weapon has been placed in her hands; she immediately becomes calm. EMILY is in silent desperation.]

KRELLIN [proudly]. It was due to her persuasion that the article I wrote about you was never published in the papers.

CAROLINE [to EMILY]. I am glad of this opportunity to thank Miss Madden for that, and [significantly] for many other favors.

EMILY [uncertainly]. Oh, I am sure... I...

KRELLIN [to EMILY]. I needed you, my dear, to save me from Miss Ambie and defend the Government. Miss Ambie agrees with you about the Government. [To SUSAN.] No?

SUSAN [vehemently]. I don't!

KRELLIN [to EMILY]. She does not! Another convert! [Gesture of amusement.] While Mrs. Knollys and I maintain the Government is ridiculous. [To CAROLINE.] No? [Suddenly remembering.] I'll get a chair.

[He looks for one, but there are no more.]

CAROLINE [to KRELLIN]. Don't bother, please. Miss Madden can occupy my place.

EMILY. Oh, no!

HILDEGARDE [to CAROLINE]. Please

don't disturb yourself. [To LAWRENCE.] Larrie, get a chair from your room.
[LAWRENCE *immediately exits left.*]
CAROLINE. It won't be a new experience for Miss Madden. She has already *occupied my place* before this, many times; and for a long time, I have been accustomed to yield to her.
KRELLIN [*perplexed*]. Is that so! How?
EMILY [*in terror*]. Oh, Michael, why did I come here!!
KRELLIN. What's the matter, Emmy?
CAROLINE [*to* EMILY]. Have no fear, Miss Madden. Your intended husband believes in women "boundlessly," and "in every capacity." He has a sense of humor and admires hypocrites. He will be consistent to his views; but I am sure he will allow me to be equally consistent with mine.
KRELLIN. Carte blanche! [*Seeing* LAWRENCE *re-enter with the chair.*] Here we are. Now we can listen.
CAROLINE. I have no principles, but I have some prejudices. And either Miss Madden or I must leave the room.
SUSAN. Oh, Carrie!
KRELLIN. What do you mean! That isn't argument. That is evasion!
LAWRENCE [*quickly*]. Emily and Michael, you've said about enough! Now please go! [*He bangs down the chair.*]
HILDEGARDE [*to* LAWRENCE]. By no means. Mrs. Knollys will be good enough to explain herself.
KRELLIN. What is your reason, Mrs. Knollys?
CAROLINE [*charmingly*]. Since you insist, it is simply because I refuse to sit at the same table with my husband's *mistress*.
KRELLIN [*dawning*]. Ha!!
HILDEGARDE [*simultaneously*]. Oh!
KRELLIN [*fiercely*]. That's a lie! A black, malicious lie!!
CAROLINE. Oh, no!
KRELLIN [*continuing*]. She doesn't even *know* your husband!
CAROLINE [*confidently taunting*]. Ask her!
KRELLIN. Madame, I am not here to insult her myself; but to defend her against *your attempt* to do so.

CAROLINE. Ask her, and you will learn it was for my *husband's* sake that your article was suppressed. But he, no doubt, has *paid* Miss Madden for any loss *you* may have suffered. Come, Susan. [*To* HILDEGARDE.] I've had a most delightful luncheon. My wrap, Lawrence.
[*He exits left.*]
KRELLIN [*quietly aggressive*]. Mrs. Knollys, of course you cannot go until I have relieved your mind from any misapprehensions you may have concerning your husband.
CAROLINE. But unfortunately I seem to affect Miss Madden disagreeably.

[LAWRENCE *re-enters with wraps.*]

MURTHA [*suddenly coming up from rear*]. Fer th' love o' Gawd, th' poor gurrl's goin' t' faint!! [*She takes* EMILY *in her arms.*]
EMILY [*weakly*]. Take me home, Michael . . . Oh . . . !
MURTHA. Now, there, there, there, dearie, doan't ye moind . . .
KRELLIN [*to* MURTHA]. Yes, take Miss Madden home!!
EMILY. No! Not without you, Michael!!
SUSAN [*terrified*]. Carrie, Carrie! Come with me! Come home!! I'm sorry we ever came! These awful people!!
[*Gets into her wrap.*]
LAWRENCE. Come, Mrs. Knollys. [*Then to* KRELLIN *and* EMILY.] If *they* haven't sense enough to go!
KRELLIN [*fiercely to* CAROLINE]. You cannot go!
LAWRENCE [*to* KRELLIN]. What do you mean?
KRELLIN. I have something to say to Mrs. Knollys!
SUSAN [*as he comes forward*]. Carrie, if you don't come, I . . . [*Weeps in fright.*] God knows what they will do!
HILDEGARDE [*beseechingly*]. Michael, go with Emily!
KRELLIN [*shaking his mane*]. Mrs. Knollys has permitted herself to utter a filthy, vicious lie! And I —
HILDEGARDE [*going to him*]. But this is not the time to —
KRELLIN [*in fury*]. A filthy LIE!!

LAWRENCE [*to* KRELLIN]. See here, you can't use that kind of language to my friend!

KRELLIN [*savagely to* LAWRENCE]. Your friend! You little lap-dog! I want nothing from you! Just look to yourself!!

[*He flings* LAWRENCE *aside*.]

HILDEGARDE [*imploringly*]. Michael, go with Emily. She *needs* you.

[*She turns him around, and he sees* EMILY *being helped to the door by* MURTHA.]

EMILY [*as she leaves with* MURTHA]. Michael... Michael...

KRELLIN [*with suppressed vehemence*]. Mrs. Knollys, I shall give myself the pleasure of continuing this conversation in the presence of your husband.

[*He bows and exits, after* MURTHA *and* EMILY.]

SUSAN [*incoherently*]. Carrie, here are your things! Here! Of all the frightful experiences! [*Spinning around*.] Where's my glove? You must get out of this!!

HILDEGARDE. Mrs. Knollys, *I* must have a word with you.

SUSAN [*dizzily*]. Now *she's* going to begin! Why did we ever...?

LAWRENCE [*angrily*]. Hildegarde, don't you think you'd better drop it?

HILDEGARDE [*meaningly*]. It isn't only in reference to *Miss Madden* that I wish to speak.

SUSAN [*hysterically*]. I knew it, Carrie! [*To* HILDEGARDE.] But you're wrong! No matter what you think.... People have such vile minds! [*Specifically*.] I was with Mrs. Knollys all the time, except once when I took sick.... Your husband knows it — and so does Mr. Knollys...

LAWRENCE. What are you talking about?

SUSAN [*continuing*]. And if her kindness is to be misinterpreted — then —

LAWRENCE [*angrily*]. Say, Miss Ambie, what's on your mind?

CAROLINE [*to* LAWRENCE]. Psch!

SUSAN [*collapsing*]. Oh, everybody's crazy!

LAWRENCE [*disgusted*]. You're right there. [*He turns helplessly*.] Hildegarde, I hope that... Oh, what's the use!

CAROLINE [*abruptly*]. Quite so, Lawrence; get Susan home.

[SUSAN *has got rapidly to the hall door*.]

LAWRENCE. But, Hildegarde, I —

CAROLINE. Please go. I wish to talk with your wife. [LAWRENCE *takes his hat*.] Send the motor back for me immediately. [*He crosses to the door. There is a look full of crowded meaning between* HILDEGARDE *and* CAROLINE; *then* CAROLINE *continues to* LAWRENCE.] Oh, and remember you have engagements for this afternoon.

[LAWRENCE *exits with* SUSAN. HILDEGARDE *closes the door after him. There is a pause of sizing up between the two women*.]

CAROLINE [*amused*]. You're not going to lock me in; I hope.

HILDEGARDE [*gravely*]. No. But after you leave this room, I want you to pass out of our lives forever.

CAROLINE. *Your* life? That's very simple. You have something else to say to me?

HILDEGARDE. So many things — I hardly know where to begin.

CAROLINE. Let me help you. We'll eliminate Miss Madden.

HILDEGARDE. We will *not* eliminate Miss Madden. We have a different sense of values, you and I; but we both are *married* women. Emily is different. She has nothing but her friends, Michael and me. And we together will force you to retract.

CAROLINE. Retract the truth! What else?

HILDEGARDE. And make a full apology to her.

CAROLINE. I have never apologized in my life.

HILDEGARDE. Then you have a new experience in store for you. [*Pause*.] What was your purpose in coming here to-day?

CAROLINE [*with charming frankness*]. You know. My interest in your husband.

HILDEGARDE. And now, you think you can eliminate *me*.

CAROLINE. Why? Your husband has his own career; and you are sensible.

HILDEGARDE. It's a dangerous thing to interfere with other people's lives.

CAROLINE. Yes. We discussed that some time ago.

HILDEGARDE. You told me then that I might hinder him — that my very work in the world might be an obstacle. Since then I've left him free. I haven't influenced him —

CAROLINE. Oh, don't make virtues of your inabilities.

HILDEGARDE. You mean?

CAROLINE. Don't boast of what you *couldn't* do. You know you couldn't keep him here. Don't say you didn't *want* to. That would be weak.

HILDEGARDE. I don't wish to speak of Lawrence. I wish to speak of you. I am told the world of art needs women of your kind. You have everything — wealth, influence, position. You hold patronage and opportunity in your hands.

CAROLINE [*interrupting*]. Why don't you add: "You hold my husband too"? In other words, that you regret your bargain; and you want me to send him back to you.

HILDEGARDE [*scornfully*]. Oh, no! But don't make the price for your patronage so high, that a man must sacrifice his self-respect to gain the prize you offer.

CAROLINE [*quietly, after a look*]. I never dreamed that you'd be jealous; are you?

HILDEGARDE [*fervently*]. Yes, I am jealous — jealous *for* him, but not *of* him!

CAROLINE. I've given him the opportunity. *He* has chosen.

HILDEGARDE. He hasn't!

CAROLINE. Then why are you so anxious?

HILDEGARDE [*continuing*]. To choose, one must be independent. He isn't. He thinks he dare not choose against you. He fears to jeopardize commissions. There's where you make unscrupulous use of your advantages!

CAROLINE [*with a smile*]. My dear Mrs. Sanbury, I may be mistaken; but you seem bent on telling me your husband doesn't care for me. Is that what you mean?

HILDEGARDE. No. [*Suddenly.*] What are you trying to make me think?

CAROLINE. Think what you like. *I* make no disguises. But I marvel at you.

HILDEGARDE. At me!

CAROLINE. I thought you weren't a feminine woman. You're interested in so many things besides your husband. I've interested myself in him. If, in that interest, you think that *he* has gone beyond what you expected; why not speak to *him?*

HILDEGARDE. He's lost his senses! You've blinded him!

CAROLINE. I thought I had *opened* his eyes. You see, Love isn't blind. The trouble is, it sees too much! [*Obliterating her with a glance.*] It sometimes sees things that aren't there at all. It isn't *my* fault if *now* he sees things as they are. I open everybody's eyes. That's my profession. [*Significantly.*] I've opened *yours*, I hope. I've opened Mr. Krellin's. [*She laughs.*]

HILDEGARDE. Yes, and tried wantonly to destroy his faith in Emily, as now you're trying to destroy my faith in Lawrence.

CAROLINE. Ah, then you *are* afraid!

HILDEGARDE [*uncertainly*]. Afraid of what!

CAROLINE. You fear to lose your husband's love. Of course, you'll struggle.

HILDEGARDE. I never struggle for what is mine.

CAROLINE. Hum.

HILDEGARDE [*nervously*]. I'm not afraid of Lawrence. Your insinuations don't affect me — you . . .

CAROLINE. Indeed. Then why this argument?

HILDEGARDE [*amazed*]. You'd like to make me think my husband is your lover! [*She draws a sharp breath.*]

CAROLINE. And if that were the case — What then? [*Pause.*]

HILDEGARDE. Oh, no! You wouldn't boast of it!

CAROLINE [*quietly*]. I never boast. Only the insecure do that.

HILDEGARDE. It's a lie! It's a lie!! It's a lie!!!

CAROLINE. Ask him.

HILDEGARDE. You mean you would have me ask my husband such a question?

CAROLINE. Why not?

HILDEGARDE [*suddenly calm, and seeing through* CAROLINE]. Because it isn't important enough, Mrs. Knollys.

CAROLINE. You mean, your husband's fidelity isn't important to you?

HILDEGARDE. Oh, yes, but there's far more at stake. For his sake, I've stepped aside. I've given you every chance with him; because you may have helped him. ... I don't know. You've taken his time, his mind, his work, his energy. He has amused you, fed your vanity and gratified your sense of power over people. I've been patient. I've left him free to choose. For if a woman like you can take the rest of him from me, he isn't worth my energy to keep. I don't want even a part of him, if anything is withheld —

CAROLINE [with an amused sneer]. And what have *I* to do with your ideal of marriage?

HILDEGARDE. I don't approve of the way that you make use of the protection of your husband's name!

CAROLINE. Then you'd better see my husband. [She goes toward the hall door.]

HILDEGARDE. Perhaps I shall.

CAROLINE. He'll be delighted to discuss Miss Madden. Mr. Krellin also wants to speak with him. He'll welcome you both, I'm sure. [Turning casually.] He's just back from the South. He'll be in splendid humor after all you've done for him in shutting up the mills. Good-by.

[She exits in smiling good humor.]

[HILDEGARDE stands by the table and slowly sinks into a chair. The hum of tenement life becomes audible. A baby is heard crying; and every detail that can be developed, pointing to the barren squalor of her life is emphasized as in contrast with the elegance of MRS. KNOLLYS'. HILDEGARDE sits lost in thought, while the hubbub swings around her. Suddenly the telephone begins to ring. HILDEGARDE doesn't notice it at first. The bell continues. HILDEGARDE seems to come to her senses with a start. She goes to the 'phone, takes receiver and listens mechanically.]

HILDEGARDE. Yes.... This is Mrs. Sanbury.... Who is this?... Oh, Miss Ambie.... Yes.... Mrs. Knollys has just left.... [Coldly.] I quite understand. Yes.... Good-by.... [Suddenly.] Wait! Hello! [Quietly.] Is Mr. Sanbury still there? [MURTHA has entered softly from the hall, and goes to clear up the table.] ... Yes. ... I should like to speak with him. [Pause. She speaks very tenderly.] Is this you, Larrie?... I'm sorry; but it couldn't be helped.... She s just left.... Yes. ... Nothing has happened.... I'd just like to speak with you; as soon as you can get here.... Larrie!... What?... You can't?... [Long breath.] Then I'll wait for you.... This evening too...? ... Well, listen, Larrie, you *must* come. ... No.... I can't speak of it over the 'phone.... I must see you; and as quickly as possible.... But this is important too! [Pause.] No! I can't wait! ... Do you understand, Larrie, I *won't* wait!!!

[She claps up the receiver and crosses to her room exclaiming hysterically: "I won't wait!! I won't wait!!"

MURTHA goes on quietly clearing up the dishes at the table. HILDEGARDE is heard pulling out drawers violently and pushing them back again. MURTHA shakes her head sorrowfully. She has cannily sensed the situation. HILDEGARDE reënters, carrying a small satchel, which she places on a chair next to the table. During the following scene she packs it with a dressing-gown, toothbrush, hairbrush and comb, slippers, nightgown, etc. Several times during the scene she exits rapidly to her room for these toilet articles, and returns, without interrupting the dialogue.]

MURTHA [as HILDEGARDE enters carrying her satchel]. Ye ain't goin' away; are ye?

HILDEGARDE [jamming things into the grip]. Yes ... yes ...

MURTHA [suddenly]. Ah, where's me head! I saw th' Doolans. They've got a date wid you, they say.

HILDEGARDE [going to her room]. I don't want to see them.

MURTHA [calling after HILDEGARDE]. Th' agent says he's goin' to throw him out.

HILDEGARDE. He deserves it.

MURTHA. Ah, but jisht a word from you.... Moy, th' poor woman an' th' fambly....
HILDEGARDE [*entering and continuing her packing*]. I can't help them.
MURTHA. Doolan wanted to come here to apologoize; but Oi told him he'd bedther not. He'd be met on th' door-sthep wid a lump av his death!
HILDEGARDE. You can tell them the ejection officer will tend to them.
[*She exits again and immediately re-appears.*]
MURTHA. Shure, it's not *you* that's talkin', dearie; and Oi can't go down there! Th' avvicer would see me oye, and know th' Doolans done it.... Oh, where's that shtuff? They say it's goin' blue on me.... An' you wouldn't have thim turned out in th' shtreet....
HILDEGARDE [*pointing to the shelf above the sink*]. It's over there. You'd better take it with you.
MURTHA. Thank ye. [*Tenderly coaxing.*] Go on now, you. Go on now, shishter.... Take him back and let him shtay.
HILDEGARDE. After what they've done to you, it seems queer that you ...
MURTHA. Shure ye can't be angry wid th' min-folks.... They're chilthren all av thim. [*Piling up dishes.*] Some gits crazy over the *booze*, and some gits crazy over *polyteecks* ... and some gits crazy over *wimmin* ... [*Picking up all the dishes*] and th' resht gits crazy over nothin' at all. [*Coaxingly.*] Go on now.... Give iviry body anither chanct. That's what I allus says. [*Singing out.*] Ha! Now there's moy Tim — Ha! Oi could ha' left him any toime this forty years fer what he done to me — and what he *didn't* do.... G'wan now, dearie, give th' man anither chanct. [HILDEGARDE *leaves the grip.*] Th' Lord love ye, that's roight ... and it's th' gran' good heart ye have. [HILDEGARDE *goes toward door of her room.* MURTHA *continues with a wise and tender canniness.*] And ... ah ... ye'll not be needin' these things roight away.... [*She throws the grip into her room.*] You'd bedther shleep here fer to-night.... [HILDEGARDE *has exited sobbing brokenly.* MURTHA *returns to the work of clearing up the table. She shakes her head and exclaims:*] Shure, they're chilthren! Ivery blessed wan of thim — just chilthren.

CURTAIN

ACT III

The scene is the same as Act II. It is about eight-thirty of the evening of the same day. The table has been cleared and everything is restored to order. The door of HILDEGARDE'S *room is open. There are no lights on the stage, but the scene is dimly lit by the glow of lights from the flats in the rear.*

[*After the rise of the curtain,* KRELLIN *enters from the hall door, and goes immediately to the telephone on the typewriting desk.*]

KRELLIN [*with the 'phone*]. Hello — give me seven-one-one Plaza — yes, if you please. No, seven-*one*-one.

[*Enter* LAWRENCE *from the hall, flinging the door back.*]

KRELLIN. Say, be quiet, will you?
LAWRENCE [*nervously*]. Oh, that you, Krellin? Where's Hildegarde?
[*He turns on a light over the table.*]
KRELLIN. Psch! [*To 'phone.*] Hello, seven-one-one Plaza? Yes. Mr. Krellin of the *New York Echo* would like to speak with Mr. Knollys.
LAWRENCE [*startled*]. See here, Krellin, you'd better drop it.
KRELLIN [*to 'phone*]. Then I'll ring up again — yes, later.
[*As soon as* LAWRENCE *has gathered that* HUBERT *is out, he makes a gesture of relief and flings into* HILDEGARDE'S *room. He finds her bag and immediately reënters carrying it.* KRELLIN, *in the interim, has hung up the receiver.*]
LAWRENCE. What does this mean? Where is she?
[*He drops the bag and goes uncertainly toward his room at the left, and opens the door.*]

KRELLIN. Have you been drinking?
LAWRENCE [*fiercely*]. That's my business!
KRELLIN. H'm! Have you any other?
LAWRENCE [*coming towards him*]. I want to know where my wife is; and I want to know why you're telephoning my friends!
KRELLIN. Because I won't let your friends treat my Emmy the way you let them treat your wife.
LAWRENCE. Don't you interfere between Hildegarde and me! Because, if you do, by God, I'll —
KRELLIN. I don't mix in with you. I have my own score to settle with Mr. Knollys and his wife.
LAWRENCE [*seriously*]. Krellin, I advise you to leave Mr. Knollys out of it.
KRELLIN. Ah, you are afraid, eh?
LAWRENCE. It isn't me — it's —
[*He hesitates.*]
KRELLIN [*violently*]. So! You too!! That woman has made you believe that Emmy — [*He goes toward* LAWRENCE *angrily, but stops and laughs.*] I don't wonder Mrs. Knollys thinks all women are like she is!
LAWRENCE [*violently*]. You —!
KRELLIN [*quietly*]. All the more am I determined now.
LAWRENCE [*at his wits' end*]. There'll be an awful mix-up! I don't know what to do! [*Sits down blankly.*]
KRELLIN. Don't think that I don't know why you're afraid of Mr. Knollys. It isn't business — it isn't Emmy — it's you. [*Scathingly.*] I am ashamed of you! You'd let this lie rest on my Emmy's shoulders, rather than have the truth revealed about yourself. Of course you don't want the truth to come out. But you see, *I'm* different. I don't fear the truth. And if your conduct with Mrs. Knollys cannot stand her husband's or your wife's investigation, I am sorry. That is all.
LAWRENCE. Get that idea out of your head! I don't fear the truth. It's Hildegarde I'm thinking of, and only Hildegarde.
KRELLIN [*scornfully*]. You've thought so much of her these last four months, since —

LAWRENCE. I have. We're down to rock-bottom, Krellin. We're full of debts — even my life-insurance is gone. I've given up my job. We've pawned everything that we could raise a cent on; and Hildegarde's stood by me. That's why you can't go on and spoil things now, by dragging Mr. Knollys in. [KRELLIN *laughs scornfully.*] I know it looks as if I had neglected Hildegarde; but *she* understands. I've had to hold on to this one chance, tooth and toe-nail. [*Desperately.*] I won't let anything interfere with it! Not you, nor Hildegarde — nor Emily — nor —
KRELLIN [*interrupting*]. Is that so! Well, no matter what it costs to you or anybody else, we make Mrs. Knollys eat those lying words she said about my Emmy. So.
[KRELLIN *exits through the hall door.* LAWRENCE *stands perplexed for a moment, then goes decidedly to the 'phone and rings up.*]
LAWRENCE. Hello — give me one-four-three-three Plaza — yes — in a hurry, please. [*Pause.*] Central, they *must* answer. It's a private wire and they are expecting me to ring them up. [*Pause. Then with an exaggerated change to a very polite manner.*] Oh, hello — Is that you, Caroline? I've been very busy — yes — all afternoon. Yes, I'm so sorry, but I shan't be able to get back — Nothing's happened to my *voice;* but — ah — the fact is I've had an accident ... only my ankle — Oh, nothing serious — I'm sure, so don't be alarmed. ... Yes, getting out of the cab. ... I'm telephoning from a drug store. ... Yes, it *is* painful; but I'm sure it's only wrenched. ... Yes, I'll ring up my doctor as soon as I get home. ... I shall be quite alone. ... Please don't worry. ... Oh, I can tend to everything. [*Pause.*] I've already telephoned to Mrs. Millette. ... Mercy, no, I wouldn't have a nurse touch me. ... Yes, I'll telephone in the morning ... yes, then as soon as he has left, I'll ring you up and tell you what his diagnosis is. ... Hildegarde? ... No, I haven't seen her. ... Oh, not because of anything that happened here. ... She's — she left this afternoon to spend the

week-end with some friends — yes — somewhere in the country — Westchester. . . . No, I shan't send for her. . . . Yes, if there's anything — but — Oh, thank you so much. . . . Good-by.

[*He rings off. During the last part of the above speech,* HILDEGARDE *has quietly entered from the hall door.*]

LAWRENCE [*relieved and confused*]. Oh — Westchester! — I mean, I've just been telephoning.

HILDEGARDE. I didn't expect to see you this evening.

[*She goes to her typewriting desk for some letters, etc.*]

LAWRENCE. Well, there was something in the sound of your voice over the 'phone that made me nervous; and I lied out of my engagements. As usual, said the first foolish thing that came into my mind. Now I'll have to stick to it, I suppose.

HILDEGARDE. Why do you always lie these days?

LAWRENCE. I never lie to *you.*

HILDEGARDE. Is *that* really the truth?

LAWRENCE. Why, yes!

HILDEGARDE. Why did you say I was in Westchester?

LAWRENCE. I didn't know where you'd gone to, and —

HILDEGARDE. Didn't you say I'd gone to Westchester because you were afraid that Mrs. Knollys would be jealous of your spending an evening alone with me?

LAWRENCE. What have you got in your head? [*She looks at him. He continues.*] I had to say something to get out of things. Then I come home and find your bag packed. Where *are* you going?

HILDEGARDE. I think it best I go away a little while.

LAWRENCE. Away? Where to?

HILDEGARDE. I haven't decided. I was going to leave a note for you; but Michael told me you were here; so I —

LAWRENCE [*bursting*]. Michael! Do you know what he's doing? And just now, of all times! When everything depends on Mr. Knollys!

HILDEGARDE. Yes, I advised him.

LAWRENCE. What! [*Pause.*] Hildegarde, suppose what Mrs. Knollys said about Emily is true?

HILDEGARDE [*turning sharply*]. Larrie!

LAWRENCE. Well, I said, *suppose* it's true.

HILDEGARDE. It's not. And even if it were, *she's* not the one to make the accusation.

LAWRENCE. Why not? [*Pause.*] What's in your mind? *Krellin's* been saying things!

HILDEGARDE. Oh, no.

LAWRENCE. I know it. Why, just a moment ago he said that I was afraid to meet Mr. Knollys.

HILDEGARDE. Afraid? Why?

LAWRENCE. He thinks that I —

[*He hesitates.*]

HILDEGARDE [*in a level tone*]. What —?

LAWRENCE. That I've forgotten you. [*Recklessly.*] Oh, I don't care what he thinks, except that I don't want *you* to get wrong-headed. I thought at least, *you'd* understand. There's not a thing I've done that anybody can't question.

HILDEGARDE. That's ambiguous, Larrie; but I shan't question you.

LAWRENCE. I mean that anybody can't investigate. I've never *really* lied to you; have I?

HILDEGARDE. No — not lied exactly — just disguised things to make it easier for me. . . . Oh, yes, Larrie, my clothes, my work, our home, our life together, *your* work and all the circumstances and people that have come between us.

LAWRENCE. Oh, those things! I don't mean them.

HILDEGARDE. What do you mean?

LAWRENCE [*blurting it out*]. I mean Car — Mrs. Knollys. That's what *you* mean; and that's what Krellin means.

HILDEGARDE [*tremulously*]. Yes.

[*She turns away.*]

LAWRENCE. I want to explain everything, right from the beginning — everything. [*She moves away. He follows.*] I want you to know the whole truth, and nothing *but* the truth; and then you can judge for yourself. Oh, I'm not proud of what I've had to do; but there isn't a single thing that you can't know about — or that

I'm really ashamed of — I swear! [*There is a knock at the hall door.* LAWRENCE, *after a gesture of impatience, continues:*] If that's Krellin, tell him I want to be alone with you. He can't telephone. He's got to leave Mr. Knollys out of this. I don't want Knollys to get wrong-headed too!
[*He has followed* HILDEGARDE *who has moved up to the door.*]
HILDEGARDE [*at door, to* LAWRENCE]. Please!
[*She opens the door and discovers* HUBERT KNOLLYS *standing there.*]
HUBERT [*to* HILDEGARDE]. I couldn't find the bell.
LAWRENCE [*retreating*]. Oh, Lord!
HUBERT. Mrs. Sanbury, I'm very glad to see you.
[*Extends his hand. She takes it.*]
HILDEGARDE. I've been hoping you'd come. [LAWRENCE *is surprised.*]
HUBERT. Thank you.
LAWRENCE. Yes — we —
HUBERT [*laconically to* LAWRENCE]. Oh — how are you?
LAWRENCE [*embarrassed*]. Oh, finely . . . been pretty busy since you left; but —
HUBERT [*abruptly*]. Yes, so I hear. [*He turns to* HILDEGARDE *and points to a chair.*] May I?
HILDEGARDE [*nodding*]. Let me take your things.
[LAWRENCE *takes his hat and coat.*]
HUBERT [*sitting and speaking to* HILDEGARDE]. I've just got back from the South.
LAWRENCE [*effusively*]. Yes, we heard you were away.
HUBERT [*turning quietly*]. I was rather of the opinion that you *knew* I was away.
LAWRENCE. Yes, to be sure — of course. Did you have a successful trip of it?
HUBERT [*ironically*]. Have you had time to read the papers?
LAWRENCE. I was interested and all that; though I haven't followed the strike very closely. A little out of my line, you know. So if you're going to talk economics, hadn't I better —?
[*He starts toward his room.*]
HUBERT [*interrupting*]. There are some things I wish to discuss with your wife. I'd rather you'd be here. That is, if you don't mind.
LAWRENCE [*vaguely*]. By all means — not at all.
[HILDEGARDE *turns anxiously to* HUBERT.]
HUBERT [*to* HILDEGARDE]. You know, it was due a little to your suggestion, I went South.
HILDEGARDE. And?
HUBERT. We've increased the operatives' salaries and killed the child labor.
HILDEGARDE. We know about the splendid settlement you forced.
HUBERT [*grimly*]. I couldn't have done it by myself. You opened fire on my competitors. That made it easy. It looked like a general lock-out; so I called a committee of the managers, and we all agreed to meet the strikers' terms. Alone, I would have made a Quixotic failure. Well, we've yielded. You've kept *your* word; I've kept mine. Now we'll see what the workers will do with more money and shorter hours. Personally, I think they'll invest in more phonographs and liquor; and their children will continue to go barefoot.
HILDEGARDE. Perhaps. But the use of time and money must be learned.
HUBERT. They'll have their chance. Now, for the matter that brings me here immediately. [*He takes out a letter.*] I received this by messenger this afternoon — from Miss Madden.
HILDEGARDE. Yes.
HUBERT. Miss Madden urges me to see *you*.
HILDEGARDE. She told me.
HUBERT. So I am here to do anything I can in the way of reparation.
HILDEGARDE. There's only one possible reparation. Your wife must withdraw her statement absolutely. The circumstances are such that —
HUBERT. I know.
HILDEGARDE. What can have been her motive?
HUBERT. There is no question of Miss Madden's innocence. She suffers from two misfortunes. Firstly, she is a very dear friend of mine; and, secondly, she was of

service to my wife. Gratitude makes some natures resentful. I, however, feel a great obligation to Miss Madden for averting a scandal, that my wife's ignorance of the law nearly precipitated.

HILDEGARDE. Mr. Krellin helped her hush the matter up. But now, unless your wife withdraws her statements, he is determined to publish everything.

HUBERT. So his telegram informed me. But Mr. Krellin's threat could have very little weight either with Mrs. Knollys or with me.

HILDEGARDE. Why?

HUBERT. You must surely see that, after doing all he could to keep the matter from the press, it would be ridiculous for Krellin now to make an exposure. His own conduct couldn't stand investigation. [*Pause.*] Will not my personal apology for Mrs. Knollys to Mr. Krellin and Miss Madden suffice?

HILDEGARDE. Considering the accusation and the way you are involved, I should say not.

HUBERT. Perhaps you're right. [*Rises.*] I suggested it merely to show you how really powerless we are. A money damage for defamation is out of the question —

HILDEGARDE. Quite.

HUBERT. Then what do you propose?

HILDEGARDE [*firmly*]. That right here, and before the very people in whose presence Mrs. Knollys *made* the accusation, she must *retract* and with full apologies. Nothing less.

HUBERT [*involuntarily*]. I'd love to see it!

LAWRENCE. Hildegarde!

HUBERT [*to* HILDEGARDE]. Your husband's exclamation proves that he and I know my wife much better than you do, Mrs. Sanbury. *He* appreciates her force of will. [*To* LAWRENCE.] Don't you, sir?

[LAWRENCE *looks on guard and says nothing.*]

HILDEGARDE. Is your wife absolutely indifferent to the social consequences of her own conduct?

HUBERT [*sitting*]. Ah! Why do you ask?

HILDEGARDE. Because immediately after having accused Emily, she did her best to make *me* believe my husband had become her lover.

HUBERT [*attempting to be surprised*]. What!!

LAWRENCE [*bounding out of his skin*]. Hildegarde!! [*To* HUBERT.] This is outrageous!

HILDEGARDE. Yes.

[LAWRENCE *is open-mouthed.*]

HUBERT [*to* HILDEGARDE]. Are you sure you're not mistaken?

HILDEGARDE. Oh, no. On the contrary, she took the greatest pains to impress it on me with all the malicious insolence of triumph she could command.

HUBERT. But — why do you tell *me* this?

HILDEGARDE. To ask you to use it as you think best, to help me to force your wife to make just reparation to my friend.

LAWRENCE [*finding his voice*]. It's all a damnable lie! A wholesale rotten —!

HUBERT [*interrupting*]. Pardon, I should reserve such language until you have a better right to use it.

LAWRENCE. Wh-what do you mean?

HUBERT. Remember, sir, the lady you are speaking of is still *my* wife.

LAWRENCE [*wildly*]. I can't help *that!* I have *my* wife to consider, Mr. Knollys, and —

HUBERT [*scornfully*]. Indeed!

LAWRENCE [*continuing*]. And with all deference to *your* wife, I must repeat that if *your* wife said those things to *my* wife, your wife uttered a lie!!

HILDEGARDE. So I told her myself.

HUBERT [*promptly*]. You did that to shield your husband.

LAWRENCE [*vehemently*]. And I protest that if *your* wife —

HUBERT [*sternly to* LAWRENCE]. Keep quiet!

LAWRENCE [*spinning about*]. For God's sake, some one do me the favor to tell me that one of us is blind or deaf or —

HUBERT [*severely*]. Sit down!!

LAWRENCE [*landing into a chair and wailing*]. She's old enough to be my mother!

HUBERT [*to* HILDEGARDE]. Did she say anything further? Come!

HILDEGARDE. She wantonly taunted me with my failure to hold my husband. When I told her I did not believe her, she even urged me to question him. I refused. Please to observe I have not questioned him.

LAWRENCE [*imploringly*]. Oh, why didn't you?

HUBERT [*to* HILDEGARDE]. Why did you *not* question him?

HILDEGARDE. Because — simply because I did not believe your wife.

LAWRENCE [*fervently*]. Thank God!

HUBERT. But if you do not believe her statements, why repeat them to me?

HILDEGARDE. To serve my friend, I shall deliberately *choose to believe* your wife; and if you will help me —

HUBERT [*interjecting*]. Rely on that.

HILDEGARDE. Then I shall act as if everything she said were absolutely true.

LAWRENCE. Oh, Hildegarde! How *can* you!

HILDEGARDE [*to* HUBERT]. In that way we can turn her arrow against Emily into a boomerang to recoil upon herself.

HUBERT. Hum. Then you will name her as a co-respondent?

HILDEGARDE [*genuinely frightened*]. What! You mean divorce my — divorce Larrie?

HUBERT. Yes.

LAWRENCE [*to* HILDEGARDE]. See here! *I'm* the one that your damned boomerang is hitting!

HUBERT [*to* HILDEGARDE]. That is unavoidable.

LAWRENCE. See here! —

HILDEGARDE [*expostulatingly to* HUBERT]. BUT don't you see that I do *not* believe her? She did it to provoke a jealous quarrel; and if I judge her rightly, she will withdraw her insults rather than endure disgrace. It won't have to go that far! D-don't you see that?

HUBERT. Thank you for your assurance, but I must differ with you.

LAWRENCE [*to* HUBERT]. Why? — do you think that I —?

HUBERT [*calmly*]. I think there is an important person that you both have so far overlooked — myself. [*To* LAWRENCE.] You have chosen to protect my wife by calling her a liar. [*To* HILDEGARDE.] You protect your husband by calling her a liar, too. It seems *my* attitude has been neglected. [HILDEGARDE *is appalled.*]

LAWRENCE [*bravely*]. Well —?

HUBERT. Yes. Here's where *you* come in.

LAWRENCE [*crumpling*]. What do you intend to do?

HUBERT. I choose to believe these statements for my *own* sake.

HILDEGARDE. You can't! You can't!!

LAWRENCE [*to* HUBERT]. You don't mean to say! — [*To* HILDEGARDE, *wildly.*] He believes it! He believes it!

HUBERT [*quietly*]. I always believe my wife when she affirms, *never* when she denies.

HILDEGARDE [*stupefied*]. But, Mr. Knollys, you don't *really* think that . . .

HUBERT [*interrupting*]. My dear lady, you are too gullible. [*To* LAWRENCE.] Now, I want the truth, and I expect it manfully.

[*He approaches* LAWRENCE, *who retreats.*]

LAWRENCE. This is perfectly ridiculous!

HUBERT [*taking out a note-book*]. Please have the courtesy to remember that it is *you* who has made us both ridiculous; and don't thrust it down our throats. [*Consulting his book.*] You spent at least a week with Caroline alone in Italy.

LAWRENCE. That isn't true! Susan Ambie . . .

HUBERT [*promptly*]. I have seen Miss Ambie. She did more than confess. She attempted to defend it.

LAWRENCE. Miss Ambie is a fool!

HUBERT. Quite so. [*Continuing.*] Do you admit being alone with Mrs. Knollys?

LAWRENCE [*pausing*]. Why — I —

HILDEGARDE [*gone white*]. Don't deny it, Larrie.

HUBERT [*to* HILDEGARDE]. I heard you say some weeks ago you had letters to that effect.

LAWRENCE [*imploringly*]. Hildegarde!

HILDEGARDE. Yes. I have them.

HUBERT. Very good. I trust you to produce them at the proper time. [*To* LAWRENCE.] You crossed on the same steamer.

LAWRENCE [*grasping at a straw*]. Miss Ambie was with us!

HUBERT. Yes; and since your arrival on October 5th you have devoted all your time, practically day and night, to each other.

LAWRENCE [*angrily*]. I won't stand here and have you say such things about your wife!

HUBERT. Am I to be the only one who does *not* say them?

LAWRENCE. She simply —

HUBERT [*with feigned anger*]. Pray do not explain my wife to me. [*Continuing from his note-book.*] On October 7th you actually installed yourself under my roof — a most tasteless procedure, which I refused to countenance. I went South. You thought, no doubt, that openness would disarm suspicion. It doesn't work. As part of that same plan, my wife openly confesses her infatuation to your wife, boasts of her power, and then further openly denounces an innocent woman, in order to produce the impression that her own actions are not subject to criticism. Truly, this is the very blindness of infatuation. [*Laughs.*] I admire your brass — but really it won't do. The rest of us are not so blind. I compliment you on your conquest [*ironically*]. But how long did you imagine I would allow this to continue?

LAWRENCE. Mr. Knollys, all that I can say is —

HUBERT [*scathingly*]. At least, sir, have the courage of your actions. [*Snapping his book closed, and looking at* HILDEGARDE, *who sees she has awakened a Frankenstein.*] I have a further list of rendezvous, which I shall not ask you to verify in the presence of your wife!

LAWRENCE. My wife knows everything that can be said about me!

HUBERT. I doubt it. In any case, your protection until now has been your wife's credulity. We shall see. When my lawyer —

LAWRENCE [*interrupting*]. All right. *Get* your lawyer. Now I'll thank you, Mr. Knollys, to leave me alone with my wife, who's never doubted me, and has no reason to doubt me now. I *have* the courage of my actions! I'll bring the whole thing right into the open — and if *you* can stand it, *I* can.

[*The two men look each other squarely in the eye. Suddenly the bell rings over the hall door.*]

HUBERT [*turning to* HILDEGARDE]. Is that your bell?

[HILDEGARDE *goes directly to the hall door, opens it and discloses* MRS. KNOLLYS. *She is magnificently dressed in a long opera cloak over her evening gown. She has also a heavy veil about her head.* CAROLINE *enters swiftly, then stands appalled.*]

HUBERT [*recognizing her*]. Ah, Caroline! [*Surprise of all.* CAROLINE *undoes her veil and faces him.*] You come most apropos. [*Sarcastically.*] Did you call to see Mrs. Sanbury?

CAROLINE [*after a pause*]. I ... I have called for *you*. [*She comes into the room.*]

HUBERT. Indeed! How is that?

CAROLINE. I am on my way to the opera. I assumed that Miss Madden had summoned you. I thought I'd pick you up.

HUBERT. How kind of you. But may I ask why you assumed that I'd be here in Mrs. Sanbury's apartment?

CAROLINE. Quite naturally. Mrs. Sanbury is the only other person interested, with you, in deceiving Mr. Krellin and whitewashing Miss Madden.

HILDEGARDE. Mrs. Knollys, my husband telephoned you that I had gone to Westchester; so you couldn't have expected to see *me*.

[LAWRENCE *is desperate.*]

HUBERT [*to* CAROLINE]. Oh, you expected to find *Mr.* Sanbury alone. [*After a glance at* LAWRENCE, *he turns to* HILDEGARDE.] Well, then, Mrs. Sanbury, let us no longer intrude. Will you direct me to Miss Madden?

HILDEGARDE [*moves to the hall door, then turns*]. Mrs. Knollys, I think it only fair to tell you, that I have repeated to Mr.

Knollys the whole substance of your conversation with me this afternoon.

[HUBERT *opens the door.* HILDEGARDE *exits; and he follows, closing the door behind him.* LAWRENCE *is standing stupefied down left.* CAROLINE *is at center. Pause.*]

CAROLINE [*in an unsteady voice*]. I think I'm going to faint.

LAWRENCE [*putting her into chair at the table, anxiously*]. Oh, don't! For Heaven's sake, don't do that. [*She sits.*] I'll get you a glass of water. [*He goes quickly to the tubs and pours one out of a bottle. Coming to her.*] Here, drink this. Is there anything else I can get you? [*She sips the water.*] Shan't I send for some one?

CAROLINE [*ironically*]. For whom?

[*She drinks the water.*]

LAWRENCE. You feel better now, don't you? Shall I get you some salts?

[*He moves quickly toward* HILDEGARDE'S *room.*]

CAROLINE. No. I'll be all right. [*Suddenly.*] You walk very well.

LAWRENCE [*stopping*]. Why, yes, I — Shall I get you home?

CAROLINE [*caustically*]. No. I have no trouble with *my* ankle.

LAWRENCE [*suddenly remembering*]. Oh, forgive me, Caroline.

CAROLINE [*in a rage*]. Don't call me Caroline! I imagined you here alone, in pain, too ill to telephone — I thought you might be glad to see me. I lost my prudence. [LAWRENCE *turns away.*] How much of what you've said to me for all these months is true? What did you mean by taking me into your arms to-day and . . . Agh —!! [*She turns from him.*]

LAWRENCE [*simply*]. I've done a great wrong.

CAROLINE [*sarcastically*]. And when did you discover that?

LAWRENCE. After I kissed you to-day — the way I did.

CAROLINE. That's why you left so suddenly.

LAWRENCE. Yes.

CAROLINE. And came right back to *her?*

LAWRENCE. I tried to find her, but I couldn't. I was frantic. I looked every place. I really thought that she had left me. [*In a low voice.*] And I thought that I deserved it. Then I telephoned to you; and she came in.

CAROLINE. The kiss that woke *your* prudence put *mine* to sleep. How strange! And you were thinking all the time of *her!*

[*She laughs hysterically.*]

LAWRENCE. Why, yes. Always! My work, my ambition — even my gratitude to you has been for her sake.

CAROLINE. Then I was merely the ladder on which you proposed to climb and pluck the golden fruit for *her!*

LAWRENCE. I've been a miserable cad! I know what you must think of me!

CAROLINE. And what do *they* think of you?

LAWRENCE. Oh, how can I tell you? Your husband insists upon putting the worst interpretation upon everything!

CAROLINE. You mean?

LAWRENCE. I did all I could to make him see that he was wrong in doubting *you.* [*A withering look from* CAROLINE.] Oh, but what made you tell those outrageous falsehoods about us to Hildegarde?

CAROLINE [*rising in a cold rage*]. The word falsehood can only be applied to *your* attitude to me. I took you for an artist, eager to rise above and to be free from the commonness and squalor of your surroundings, and I was willing to help you. But I find you only a little entrepreneur, afraid of your conscience, and satisfied with your mutton! Well, return to it! [*She moves away, then turns.*] I have one more direction to give you. Kindly refrain from any further defense of me. I wish to speak to my husband. Will you tell him I am waiting?

[LAWRENCE *exits through the hall door.*]

[CAROLINE *pauses in intense thought, then gathers herself together, takes her vanity-box from her opera bag, opens the mirror and scrutinizes herself closely. She adjusts her hair, smooths her eyebrows, and puts a little rouge on her lips. She regains her absolute composure by a supreme effort.* HUBERT *enters. He is very self-possessed.*]

THE UNCHASTENED WOMAN

HUBERT. You wished to see me?
CAROLINE [*charmingly*]. I have been waiting.
HUBERT. For what?
CAROLINE. If you've quite finished your visit, I thought perhaps you would enjoy an hour at the opera.
[*She gives him her cloak.*]
HUBERT [*taking the cloak*]. No, thank you.
CAROLINE. You wish to go right home?
HUBERT. For the present I have decided to — ah — live at the club.
CAROLINE. Very well. Can I drop you there?
HUBERT. No. [*Putting her cloak on a chair.*] I shall need you here.
CAROLINE. Oh, then our meeting was most fortunate.
HUBERT. Yes. I was wondering how to get you here.
CAROLINE. As it is probably the last time I shall ever come, if there's anything that you would like me to do for you while I am —
HUBERT [*interrupting her, admiringly*]. Caroline, you're magnificent! We'd better get right to the point. [*Looking at his watch.*] I needn't detain you very long. I've told Miss Madden and the others to — ah — come downstairs in five minutes.
CAROLINE [*acting as if perplexed*]. I wonder what she can have to say to me; or [*incredulously*] do *you* want me to meet her again?
HUBERT. I am afraid I shall be obliged to insist upon it. I have already satisfied Mr. Krellin.
CAROLINE. Dear, dear! That must have been fatiguing; but how very nice! I believe he wants to marry her.
HUBERT. Yes.
CAROLINE. A very amusing man. Too bad! But how am I concerned?
HUBERT. In the presence of all the people before whom you made your accusation against Miss Madden, I should like you to retract it and apologize.
CAROLINE [*very graciously*]. My dear Hubert, I consider that you've never had any fault to find with me in any of your former affectionate waywardnesses. Of course, I have regretted them, but my pride has never been involved till now. *This* adventure is different. You might at least have chosen a woman of your class. I closed my eyes even to *this*, until the unfortunate woman was forced upon me in a manner I felt obliged to resent. I'm very sorry. I know so little of how these people act. You might have put me on my guard. Now you wish me to apologize to her for having said the truth. [*She laughs.*] Really, Hubert, don't you think you ask too much?
HUBERT. I have assured them you would do so. That was the purpose of my visit.
CAROLINE [*still smiling*]. I'm very sorry to disappoint the audience and perplex the impresario. [*Distinctly.*] You may cut my salary if you like, but I give no performance this evening. [*Rises.*]
HUBERT [*gracefully*]. Having heard you once, the audience refuses a substitute.
CAROLINE. Then I suggest you reimburse them.
HUBERT. No, that won't do.
CAROLINE. Have you tried?
HUBERT. I explained that you came here with the best intentions, and that you would fulfil their expectations.
CAROLINE [*merrily*]. I couldn't keep my face straight in the tragic parts.
HUBERT. I must really insist that you be serious.
CAROLINE. It's no use my trying.
HUBERT [*looking at his watch*]. We're wasting time.
CAROLINE. Hubert, you're so good-humored, you almost make me feel that you're in earnest.
HUBERT. I am.
CAROLINE. And if I still refuse?
HUBERT. Then you force me to resort to measures that we both decided were ridiculous. I have waited for this moment for twenty-five long years. For all that time *you've* held the whip; *I've* had to canter to your wish. But now, my dear, if you do not retract your statement and protect Miss Madden absolutely, *I* shall sue for a divorce and name your — latest as a co-respondent.

CAROLINE [*calmly*]. You can't.

HUBERT. I have persuaded Mrs. Sanbury to allow me to assume the suit.

CAROLINE [*slowly*]. So, you stand with her.

HUBERT. Precisely.

CAROLINE. I compliment you on your associate.

HUBERT. You left me no choice.

CAROLINE. Well?

HUBERT. It's been your policy to overlook *my* trespasses; but note *I* have not condoned either in private or in public. That is why I do not wish to appear with you in our box to-night — that is why I left your house, as soon as ever I discovered the — intrigue; and I shall not return. Whatever was lacking in my evidence, Mrs. Sanbury and others have supplied.

CAROLINE. Go on.

HUBERT. I should like to settle matters amicably, but really, my dear, it's no longer in my power. If *I* do not sue for the divorce, Mrs. Sanbury *will;* and she will name *you* as a co-respondent. That might be more annoying.

CAROLINE. I have done nothing!

HUBERT. You have always told me that our Society deals in appearances; and you have done sufficient here and abroad to create a prima facie case. The burden will rest upon you to prove that we are wrong.

CAROLINE [*snapping her fingers*]. That for your appearances!

HUBERT. They are far more damning than any you may know about me and Miss Madden. Come, you're too much a thoroughbred and too wise a woman not to know when you are beaten.

CAROLINE [*leaning forward*]. Let me understand you. If I give Miss Madden a certificate of virtue, you will withhold the suit. That is your price, is it?

HUBERT. As far as I'm concerned, yes. I can make no bargain for Mrs. Sanbury.

CAROLINE. Then what's the use of my withdrawing anything, if she —?

HUBERT. You will have me *with* you instead of *against* you.

CAROLINE. And what of that?

HUBERT. If I stand by and make no objection to Sanbury's attentions, who else can? They become immediately innocent, and her proceeding is discouraged; but if I join with her — which I mean to do unless you meet my terms, you become immediately defenseless and every suspicion is justified. [*A movement from* CAROLINE.] Without me, to whom can you appeal for help? To Society? It would rend you and rejoice in it, as you have rended others. You can ill afford to have your name publicly coupled with this young Sanbury's in any dirty proceeding.

CAROLINE [*sharply driving a bargain*]. In other words, if *I* protect Miss Madden from the truth, *you* will protect *me* from a lie.

HUBERT. Precisely; and we all enter into our usual, polite conspiracy of silence. I advise you to reflect.

CAROLINE [*rising*]. I shall. I'll think it over. [*She sits in the chair down left.*]

HUBERT [*with his watch*]. You've just two minutes to decide.

CAROLINE [*ominously*]. Hubert, I advise you not to humiliate me before these people.

HUBERT. It's either these few people here, or the grinning congregation you will be forced to face alone, in your Temple of Convention. [*Pause.*] I know what this must mean to you. [CAROLINE *shudders.*] You've been hard hit to-day. [*He goes toward her.*] With all your bravado, I know you're covering a wound. I believe that you seriously cared about this young man. For the first time in your life you've cared about anything outside of yourself. That's why you forgot yourself and went so wrong. [*She looks up at him.*] Oh! There's hope in that. I didn't think that it was *in* you. You made yourself vulnerable for him, and the disillusionment has come, and hurt you far more than you will ever confess. [*He turns away.*] And then I'd like to spare you for another reason. After all, you are the mother of my child, and we've negotiated something of a life since we were young together. [*Pause.*]

CAROLINE [*rising*]. Send them in!

[*He goes to the hall door, opens it and makes a gesture to them outside.*]

HUBERT [to CAROLINE]. They're coming now.

CAROLINE. [A malicious expression crosses her face. It passes. She turns and asks:] Do you want to stay and see me take my medicine?

HUBERT [bowing]. I know that you will do it gracefully.

[LAWRENCE enters from the hall. CAROLINE turns immediately toward the audience. LAWRENCE is very uncomfortable as he passes HUBERT. LAWRENCE is followed by KRELLIN and EMILY. KRELLIN is uneasily defiant. EMILY looks down. HILDEGARDE is the last to enter. She looks uncertainly at HUBERT. CAROLINE is the only one who is completely self-possessed. HILDEGARDE closes the door. The others have gathered awkwardly around the table, center. CAROLINE stands in her position down left. There is an awkward pause. HUBERT turns to CAROLINE, who shrugs her shoulders gaily and turns away.]

HUBERT [to all]. Hum — As I explained to you, my wife so much regretted her unfortunate mistake that she was unwilling to allow the night to pass before she came down personally to rectify it. [To KRELLIN and EMILY.] You have assured me that her personal retraction will be satisfactory. My wife desires to make it.

KRELLIN [taking out a paper]. Mr. Knollys, I have drawn up a paper for your wife to sign.

HUBERT. But —

CAROLINE. Hubert!

[She passes him and goes to the table, center.]

KRELLIN. I think that she will find it accurate.

[KRELLIN puts the paper on the table, center, and takes out his fountain pen, which he lays carefully next to it. CAROLINE sits at the table, takes the paper and reads aloud.]

CAROLINE. "November twenty-ninth, nineteen-fifteen. I, Mrs. Hubert Knollys, having permitted myself to make a certain disparaging, slanderous, and criminal statement [HUBERT would interfere. She continues] on this date, concerning the chastity of Miss Emily Madden — in the presence of Mr. Krellin, Mrs. Sanbury, and Mr. Sanbury, do herewith wish to recant it absolutely, and to state over my signature that my statement was groundless. To wit: I said that Miss Madden was improperly intimate with my husband, Mr. Hubert Knollys. I now declare this statement to be absolutely false, mistaken, and unwarranted. Signed" — [She looks up questioningly. KRELLIN points to the bottom of the page.] Here?

KRELLIN. Please.

CAROLINE [while writing]. In addition, I wish to make my humble apology for any misinterpretation I may have made in regard to Miss Madden's... generous services to my husband and to me. At least I've learned that lies are futile, and that truth crushed to earth will rise again. [She rises. EMILY sinks down into a chair at the right. The rest of them shift in an embarrassed way. CAROLINE folds the signed retraction, leans toward KRELLIN and asks gently:] Is there anything else? [Pause.]

LAWRENCE [coming forward]. Mrs. Knollys... [CAROLINE passes him, disdaining to reply. He then turns to MR. KNOLLYS.] Considering the circumstances, I think it better that I resign the contract for remodeling your house.

HUBERT. Very well. Then — ah... Caroline, if you've quite finished... that is...

CAROLINE [taking her cloak, which he holds for her]. Yes. I told Morgan to wait. [With a little shiver.] I'm afraid it's raining. Hubert, will you please see if the motor is at the door?

[HUBERT gives her a swift, suspicious look. She meets his returning glance with an assuring smile. Pause.]

HUBERT. Yes, certainly. [He quickly takes his hat and coat from the hatrack at the door, then turns.] Good-night. Good-night.

KRELLIN [picking up the signed paper]. Good-night.

[HUBERT exits. CAROLINE sweeps

around as if to follow HUBERT, *but pauses a second to look mockingly at* EMILY, *who is still seated at the right, with bowed head.* CAROLINE'S *soft laugh is interrupted by* KRELLIN, *who speaks just as she has got to the door.*]

KRELLIN. Mrs. Knollys... [*She turns in the door, with her hand on the knob.*] You have signed this paper. [*Triumphantly.*] But I wish you to know that, for me, this was not in the least necessary. I had no belief whatever in your assertions. It was only because they distressed Miss Madden that I exacted this satisfaction.

CAROLINE [*graciously*]. Quite so... Quite so. It's a pity that I cannot go further and silence all rumors about a little trip on the Chesapeake Miss Madden made with Mr. Knollys on his yacht... [*Looking at* EMILY.] Or any malicious innuendoes about my husband's too frequent visits at odd hours to her apartment in East Thirtieth Street. [*A movement from* KRELLIN.] Don't be alarmed! When rumors of this kind come to you, I want you to feel sure that I am always at your service to help you to discredit them.

[EMILY *has cowered under* CAROLINE'S *speech.* KRELLIN *starts for the door with an inarticulate cry of rage and surprise.*]

CAROLINE [*very graciously*]. Good-night.
[*She closes the door behind her.*]

KRELLIN. Stop! Wait!!

[EMILY *has quickly risen, and intercepts him.*]

EMILY. Michael! Please!

KRELLIN. But, Emmy, this is worse!!

EMILY. You can do nothing more!

KRELLIN. This time I'll...!

EMILY. No, no! I'm done for! I've got to give you up! What she said is true!!

KRELLIN. What!

HILDEGARDE. Oh!

EMILY. I couldn't have stood it any longer! I'm glad the truth is out!!... I'm glad...

[KRELLIN *makes over to her, takes her by the shoulders and peers into her face. She sinks under his gaze.*

He recoils with an almost savage exclamation.]

HILDEGARDE. Stop, Michael!

KRELLIN [*tearing up the retraction*]. Women! Women! [*Then, with a bitter cry.*] Faith is a virtue only when it is blind; and then it makes a fool of you... a fool!

EMILY. No, Michael, *I'm* the fool! I should have trusted you... I should have told you everything. *You* would have understood. But how can you forgive me for the *lie* I've *acted!* [*She goes toward him.*] But don't... don't lose your faith in other women, because *I've* been a fool... [*She turns sobbing toward the door.*] Yes, I'm the fool... I'm the fool... [*She exits.*]

HILDEGARDE. Michael, go with Emily.

KRELLIN [*with infinite pity*]. So, my poor little Emmy. Oh, we primitive males! We create idols, and when the truth comes, what do we find? Only pitiful humanity! [*He goes to the door and turns with a wry smile.*] But you see, all of us together, fighting blindly, were not strong enough to fight against the *truth!* [*He suddenly breaks out into an hysterical laugh.*] God is a great humorist!... A great humorist!!

[*He exits through hall door. As soon as the door closes on* KRELLIN, HILDEGARDE *also breaks out into a bitter laugh of disillusionment.*]

LAWRENCE [*frightened at her laughter*]. How can you laugh?

HILDEGARDE. Because I, too, have been a fool! And when one's faith is dead, one needs a sense of humor. [*Grimly.*] So, she spoke the truth, your friend Mrs. Knollys — the truth about *you* as well.

LAWRENCE. Hildegarde, if she told you that I had ever been unfaithful to you, she lied.

HILDEGARDE. Did she lie when she said your nature couldn't stand poverty — that you couldn't work in this environment — that you had to court the rich to get your chance to rise — that I, with my principles and my work, stood in your way? Did she lie about your *character?* Oh, no, she showed me the truth.

LAWRENCE. Hildegarde, you frighten

me! How can we live together if you believe such things?

HILDEGARDE. Do you think that I could speak like this, if I didn't realize that we *can't* live together?

LAWRENCE [*terrified*]. Hildegarde!

HILDEGARDE. I see it now. It's been a huge mistake, our marrying. I've got to leave you.

LAWRENCE. Why — why?

HILDEGARDE. You can't live *my* way any more. You've got another call. I won't live *your* way. I try not to judge; but I can't approve of what you do.

LAWRENCE. Then you really believe all that she said about me?

HILDEGARDE. How little you understand!

LAWRENCE. But she lied — she lied!!

HILDEGARDE. I know she's neither big enough nor small enough to really give herself; but there's much more at stake than physical fidelity. She's seduced you away from your *self* — from every ideal I built my faith in — from everything that consecrated us.

LAWRENCE. But you're my *wife;* aren't you?

HILDEGARDE. You're not the man I married; and this isn't the kind of life together that we contemplated.

LAWRENCE [*agonized*]. But you love me; don't you?

HILDEGARDE. How far off that sounds!

LAWRENCE [*imploringly*]. What are you saying!

HILDEGARDE. Larrie, you've become a stranger. Something in me has withered. I believe it's dead.

LAWRENCE. No — no — will you listen?

HILDEGARDE. Oh, don't explain. I've had my fill of that. I'm not blaming you.

LAWRENCE [*choking*]. Listen!

HILDEGARDE. You'll only end by asking for something that I cannot give. I can't help it, Larrie; but the truth is, we don't need or want each other any longer.

LAWRENCE. But I want *you!* I can't live without you. I'd give up everything 1 ever hoped to get, to have you happy as you were!

HILDEGARDE. We never used to think about happiness. It just came.

LAWRENCE [*with a cry*]. I wish I'd never met her! It's all been futile!

HILDEGARDE. No. It hasn't been. She's taught us both a great deal.

LAWRENCE. What's the good of that, if I've lost *you?*

HILDEGARDE [*continuing*]. And then I like to think the factory people are a little happier for our knowing Mr. Knollys.

LAWRENCE [*reproachfully and helplessly*]. How cruel you are! What do I care about all those things? It's only *you,* Hildegarde! [*Going to her.*] You! You! [*Tearfully.*] You're all I want! [*Weeping.*] If I lose you, what will become of me? [*Clutching her childishly and accusingly.*] I'll just lose myself! [*Shaking her.*] Don't you see that I *belong* to you? Don't you see *that!* Don't punish me any more. [*Hoarsely shaken with sobs, he falls and clutches her knees.*] You can't treat me like this! I can't stand it! I've been wrong; but don't punish me for what I couldn't help!

[LAWRENCE *has delivered this last speech in a torrent of choking tears and with a sobbing incoherent vehemence.*]

HILDEGARDE. Larrie — Larrie. . . . Don't be absurd. [*Comforting him.*] Don't cry, Larrie — you foolish, foolish boy!

LAWRENCE [*still holding her tightly*]. And you won't leave me?

HILDEGARDE [*helplessly*]. How can I? You're such a child.

[*She takes him in her arms.*]

CURTAIN

THE CIRCLE
A COMEDY IN THREE ACTS
By W. SOMERSET MAUGHAM

COPYRIGHT, 1921, BY GEORGE H. DORAN COMPANY

All applications regarding the Performance Rights of this play should be addressed to The American Play Company, 33 West 42d Street, New York.

PERSONS OF THE PLAY

CLIVE CHAMPION-CHENEY
ARNOLD CHAMPION-CHENEY, M.P.
LORD PORTEOUS
EDWARD LUTON
LADY CATHERINE CHAMPION-CHENEY
ELIZABETH
MRS. SHENSTONE

The action takes place at Aston-Adey, Arnold Champion-Cheney's house in Dorset.

THE CIRCLE

ACT I

The Scene is a stately drawing-room at Aston-Adey, with fine pictures on the walls and Georgian furniture. Aston-Adey has been described, with many illustrations, in "Country Life." It is not a house, but a place. Its owner takes a great pride in it, and there is nothing in the room which is not of the period. Through the French windows at the back can be seen the beautiful gardens which are one of the features.

It is a fine summer morning.

[ARNOLD *comes in. He is a man of about thirty-five, tall and good-looking, fair, with a clean-cut, sensitive face. He has a look that is intellectual, but somewhat bloodless. He is very well dressed.*]

ARNOLD [*calling*]. Elizabeth! [*He goes to the window and calls again.*] Elizabeth! [*He rings the bell. While he is waiting he gives a look round the room. He slightly alters the position of one of the chairs. He takes an ornament from the chimney-piece and blows the dust from it.*]

[*A* FOOTMAN *comes in.*]

ARNOLD. Oh, George! see if you can find Mrs. Cheney, and ask her if she'd be good enough to come here.

FOOTMAN. Very good, sir.
    [*The* FOOTMAN *turns to go.*]

ARNOLD. Who is supposed to look after this room?

FOOTMAN. I don't know, sir.

ARNOLD. I wish when they dust they'd take care to replace the things exactly as they were before.

FOOTMAN. Yes, sir.

ARNOLD [*dismissing him*]. All right.
    [*The* FOOTMAN *goes out.* ARNOLD *goes again to the window and calls.*]

ARNOLD. Elizabeth! [*He sees* MRS. SHENSTONE.] Oh, Anna, do you know where Elizabeth is?

[MRS. SHENSTONE *comes in from the garden. She is a woman of forty, pleasant and of elegant appearance.*]

ANNA. Isn't she playing tennis?

ARNOLD. No, I've been down to the tennis court. Something very tiresome has happened.

ANNA. Oh?

ARNOLD. I wonder where the deuce she is.

ANNA. When do you expect Lord Porteous and Lady Kitty?

ARNOLD. They're motoring down in time for luncheon.

ANNA. Are you sure you want me to be here? It's not too late yet, you know. I can have my things packed and catch a train for somewhere or other.

ARNOLD. No, of course we want you. It'll make it so much easier if there are people here. It was exceedingly kind of you to come.

ANNA. Oh, nonsense!

ARNOLD. And I think it was a good thing to have Teddie Luton down.

ANNA. He is so breezy, isn't he?

ARNOLD. Yes, that's his great asset. I don't know that he's very intelligent, but, you know, there are occasions when you want a bull in a china shop. I sent one of the servants to find Elizabeth.

ANNA. I daresay she's putting on her shoes. She and Teddie were going to have a single.

ARNOLD. It can't take all this time to change one's shoes.

ANNA [*with a smile*]. One can't change one's shoes without powdering one's nose, you know.

[Elizabeth *comes in. She is a very pretty creature in the early twenties. She wears a light summer frock.*]

Arnold. My dear, I've been hunting for you everywhere. What *have* you been doing?

Elizabeth. Nothing! I've been standing on my head.

Arnold. My father's here.

Elizabeth [*startled*]. Where?

Arnold. At the cottage. He arrived last night.

Elizabeth. Damn!

Arnold [*good-humouredly*]. I wish you wouldn't say that, Elizabeth.

Elizabeth. If you're not going to say "Damn" when a thing's damnable, when are you going to say "Damn"!

Arnold. I should have thought you could say, "Oh, bother!" or something like that.

Elizabeth. But that wouldn't express my sentiments. Besides, at that speech day when you were giving away the prizes you said there were no synonyms in the English language.

Anna [*smiling*]. Oh, Elizabeth! it's very unfair to expect a politician to live in private up to the statements he makes in public.

Arnold. I'm always willing to stand by anything I've said. There *are* no synonyms in the English language.

Elizabeth. In that case I shall be regretfully forced to continue to say "Damn" whenever I feel like it.

[Edward Luton *shows himself at the window. He is an attractive youth in flannels.*]

Teddie. I say, what about this tennis?

Elizabeth. Come in. We're having a scene.

Teddie [*entering*]. How splendid! What about?

Elizabeth. The English language.

Teddie. Don't tell me you've been splitting your infinitives.

Arnold [*with the shadow of a frown*]. I wish you'd be serious, Elizabeth. The situation is none too pleasant.

Anna. I think Teddie and I had better make ourselves scarce.

Elizabeth. Nonsense! You're both in it. If there's going to be any unpleasantness we want your moral support. That's why we asked you to come.

Teddie. And I thought I'd been asked for my blue eyes.

Elizabeth. Vain beast! And they happen to be brown.

Teddie. Is anything up?

Elizabeth. Arnold's father arrived last night.

Teddie. Did he, by Jove! I thought he was in Paris.

Arnold. So did we all. He told me he'd be there for the next month.

Anna. Have you seen him?

Arnold. No! he rang me up. It's a mercy he had a telephone put in the cottage. It would have been a pretty kettle of fish if he'd just walked in.

Elizabeth. Did you tell him Lady Catherine was coming?

Arnold. Of course not. I was flabbergasted to know he was here. And then I thought we'd better talk it over first.

Elizabeth. Is he coming along here?

Arnold. Yes. He suggested it, and I couldn't think of any excuse to prevent him.

Teddie. Couldn't you put the other people off?

Arnold. They're coming by car. They may be here any minute. It's too late to do that.

Elizabeth. Besides, it would be beastly.

Arnold. I knew it was silly to have them here. Elizabeth insisted.

Elizabeth. After all, she *is* your mother, Arnold.

Arnold. That meant precious little to her when she — went away. You can't imagine it means very much to me now.

Elizabeth. It's thirty years ago. It seems so absurd to bear malice after all that time.

Arnold. I don't bear malice, but the fact remains that she did me the most irreparable harm. I can find no excuse for her.

Elizabeth. Have you ever tried to?

ARNOLD. My dear Elizabeth, it's no good going over all that again. The facts are lamentably simple. She had a husband who adored her, a wonderful position, all the money she could want, and a child of five. And she ran away with a married man.

ELIZABETH. Lady Porteous is not a very attractive woman, Arnold. [*To* ANNA.] Do you know her?

ANNA [*smiling*]. "Forbidding" is the word, I think.

ARNOLD. If you're going to make little jokes about it, I have nothing more to say.

ANNA. I'm sorry, Arnold.

ELIZABETH. Perhaps your mother couldn't help herself — if she was in love?

ARNOLD. And had no sense of honour, duty, or decency? Oh, yes, under those circumstances you can explain a great deal.

ELIZABETH. That's not a very pretty way to speak of your mother.

ARNOLD. I can't look on her as my mother.

ELIZABETH. What you can't get over is that she didn't think of you. Some of us are more mother and some of us more woman. It gives me a little thrill when I think that she loved that man so much. She sacrificed her name, her position, and her child to him.

ARNOLD. You really can't expect the said child to have any great affection for the mother who treated him like that.

ELIZABETH. No, I don't think I do. But I think it's a pity after all these years that you shouldn't be friends.

ARNOLD. I wonder if you realise what it was to grow up under the shadow of that horrible scandal. Everywhere, at school, and at Oxford, and afterwards in London, I was always the son of Lady Kitty Cheney. Oh, it was cruel, cruel!

ELIZABETH. Yes, I know, Arnold. It was beastly for you.

ARNOLD. It would have been bad enough if it had been an ordinary case, but the position of the people made it ten times worse. My father was in the House then, and Porteous — he hadn't succeeded to the title — was in the House too; he was Under-Secretary for Foreign Affairs, and he was very much in the public eye.

ANNA. My father always used to say he was the ablest man in the party. Every one was expecting him to be Prime Minister.

ARNOLD. You can imagine what a boon it was to the British public. They hadn't had such a treat for a generation. The most popular song of the day was about my mother. Did you ever hear it! "Naughty Lady Kitty. Thought it such a pity . . ."

ELIZABETH [*interrupting*]. Oh, Arnold, don't!

ARNOLD. And then they never let people forget them. If they'd lived quietly in Florence and not made a fuss the scandal would have died down. But those constant actions between Lord and Lady Porteous kept on reminding everyone.

TEDDIE. What were they having actions about?

ARNOLD. Of course my father divorced his wife, but Lady Porteous refused to divorce Porteous. He tried to force her by refusing to support her and turning her out of her house, and heaven knows what. They were constantly wrangling in the law courts.

ANNA. I think it was monstrous of Lady Porteous.

ARNOLD. She knew he wanted to marry my mother, and she hated my mother. You can't blame her.

ANNA. It must have been very difficult for them.

ARNOLD. That's why they've lived in Florence. Porteous has money. They found people there who were willing to accept the situation.

ELIZABETH. This is the first time they've ever come to England.

ARNOLD. My father will have to be told, Elizabeth.

ELIZABETH. Yes.

ANNA [*to* ELIZABETH]. Has he ever spoken to you about Lady Kitty?

ELIZABETH. Never.

ARNOLD. I don't think her name has passed his lips since she ran away from this house thirty years ago.

TEDDIE. Oh, they lived here?

ARNOLD. Naturally. There was a house-party, and one evening neither Porteous nor my mother came down to dinner. The rest of them waited. They couldn't make it out. My father sent up to my mother's room, and a note was found on the pin-cushion.

ELIZABETH [*with a faint smile*]. That's what they did in the Dark Ages.

ARNOLD. I think he took a dislike to this house from that horrible night. He never lived here again, and when I married he handed the place over to me. He just has a cottage now on the estate that he comes to when he feels inclined.

ELIZABETH. It's been very nice for us.

ARNOLD. I owe everything to my father. I don't think he'll ever forgive me for asking these people to come here.

ELIZABETH. I'm going to take all the blame on myself, Arnold.

ARNOLD [*irritably*]. The situation was embarrassing enough anyhow. I don't know how I ought to treat them.

ELIZABETH. Don't you think that'll settle itself when you see them?

ARNOLD. After all, they're my guests. I shall try and behave like a gentleman.

ELIZABETH. I wouldn't. We haven't got central heating.

ARNOLD [*taking no notice*]. Will she expect me to kiss her?

ELIZABETH [*with a smile*]. Surely.

ARNOLD. It always makes me uncomfortable when people are effusive.

ANNA. But I can't understand why you never saw her before.

ARNOLD. I believe she tried to see me when I was little, but my father thought it better she shouldn't.

ANNA. Yes, but when you were grown up?

ARNOLD. She was always in Italy. I never went to Italy.

ELIZABETH. It seems to me so pathetic that if you saw one another in the street you wouldn't recognise each other.

ARNOLD. Is it my fault?

ELIZABETH. You've promised to be very gentle with her and very kind.

ARNOLD. The mistake was asking Porteous to come too. It looks as though we condoned the whole thing. And how am I to treat him? Am I to shake him by the hand and slap him on the back? He absolutely ruined my father's life.

ELIZABETH [*smiling*]. How much would you give for a nice motor accident that prevented them from coming?

ARNOLD. I let you persuade me against my better judgment, and I've regretted it ever since.

ELIZABETH [*good-humouredly*]. I think it's very lucky that Anna and Teddie are here. I don't foresee a very successful party.

ARNOLD. I'm going to do my best. I gave you my promise and I shall keep it. But I can't answer for my father.

ANNA. Here is your father.

[MR. CHAMPION-CHENEY *shows himself at one of the French windows.*]

C.-C. May I come in through the window, or shall I have myself announced by a supercilious flunkey?

ELIZABETH. Come in. We've been expecting you.

C.-C. Impatiently, I hope, my dear child.

[MR. CHAMPION-CHENEY *is a tall man in the early sixties, spare, with a fine head of gray hair and an intelligent, somewhat ascetic face. He is very carefully dressed. He is a man who makes the most of himself. He bears his years jauntily. He kisses* ELIZABETH *and then holds out his hand to* ARNOLD.]

ELIZABETH. We thought you'd be in Paris for another month.

C.-C. How are you, Arnold? I always reserve to myself the privilege of changing my mind. It's the only one elderly gentlemen share with pretty women.

ELIZABETH. You know Anna.

C.-C. [*shaking hands with her*]. Of course I do. How very nice to see you here! Are you staying long?

ANNA. As long as I'm welcome.

ELIZABETH. And this is Mr. Luton.

C.-C. How do you do? Do you play bridge?

LUTON. I do.

C.-C. Capital. Do you declare without top honours?
LUTON. Never.
C.-C. Of such is the kingdom of heaven. I see that you are a good young man.
LUTON. But, like the good in general, I am poor.
C.-C. Never mind; if your principles are right, you can play ten shillings a hundred without danger. I never play less, and I never play more.
ARNOLD. And you — are you going to stay long, father?
C.-C. To luncheon, if you'll have me.
[ARNOLD *gives* ELIZABETH *a harassed look.*]
ELIZABETH. That'll be jolly.
ARNOLD. I didn't mean that. Of course you're going to stay for luncheon. I meant, how long are you going to stay down here?
C.-C. A week.
[*There is a moment's pause. Everyone but* CHAMPION-CHENEY *is slightly embarrassed.*]
TEDDIE. I think we'd better chuck our tennis.
ELIZABETH. Yes. I want my father-in-law to tell me what they're wearing in Paris this week.
TEDDIE. I'll go and put the rackets away. [TEDDIE *goes out.*]
ARNOLD. It's nearly one o'clock, Elizabeth.
ELIZABETH. I didn't know it was so late.
ANNA [*to* ARNOLD.] I wonder if I can persuade you to take a turn in the garden before luncheon.
ARNOLD [*jumping at the idea*]. I'd love it.
[ANNA *goes out of the window, and as he follows her he stops irresolutely.*]
I want you to look at this chair I've just got. I think it's rather good.
C.-C. Charming.
ARNOLD. About 1750, I should say. Good design, isn't it? It hasn't been restored or anything.
C.-C. Very pretty.
ARNOLD. I think it was a good buy, don't you?

C.-C. Oh, my dear boy! you know I'm entirely ignorant about these things.
ARNOLD. It's exactly my period ... I shall see you at luncheon, then.
[*He follows* ANNA *through the window.*]
C.-C. Who is that young man?
ELIZABETH. Mr. Luton. He's only just been demobilised. He's the manager of a rubber estate in the F.M.S.
C.-C. And what are the F.M.S. when they're at home?
ELIZABETH. The Federated Malay States. He joined up at the beginning of the war. He's just going back there.
C.-C. And why have we been left alone in this very marked manner?
ELIZABETH. Have we? I didn't notice it.
C.-C. I suppose it's difficult for the young to realise that one may be old without being a fool.
ELIZABETH. I never thought you that. Everyone knows you're very intelligent.
C.-C. They certainly ought to by now. I've told them often enough. Are you a little nervous?
ELIZABETH. Let me feel my pulse. [*She puts her finger on her wrist.*] It's perfectly regular.
C.-C. When I suggested staying to luncheon Arnold looked exactly like a dose of castor oil.
ELIZABETH. I wish you'd sit down.
C.-C. Will it make it easier for you? [*He takes a chair.*] You have evidently something very disagreeable to say to me.
ELIZABETH. You won't be cross with me?
C.-C. How old are you?
ELIZABETH. Twenty-five.
C.-C. I'm never cross with a woman under thirty.
ELIZABETH. Oh, then I've got ten years.
C.-C. Mathematics?
ELIZABETH. No. Paint.
C.-C. Well?
ELIZABETH [*reflectively*]. I think it would be easier if I sat on your knees.
C.-C. That is a pleasing taste of yours, but you must take care not to put on weight. [*She sits down on his knees.*]
ELIZABETH. Am I boney?

C.-C. On the contrary.... I'm listening.
ELIZABETH. Lady Catherine's coming here.
C.-C. Who's Lady Catherine?
ELIZABETH. Your — Arnold's mother.
C.-C. Is she?
[*He withdraws himself a little and* ELIZABETH *gets up.*]
ELIZABETH. You mustn't blame Arnold. It's my fault. I insisted. He was against it. I nagged him till he gave way. And then I wrote and asked her to come.
C.-C. I didn't know you knew her.
ELIZABETH. I don't. But I heard she was in London. She's staying at Claridge's. It seemed so heartless not to take the smallest notice of her.
C.-C. When is she coming?
ELIZABETH. We're expecting her in time for luncheon.
C.-C. As soon as that? I understand the embarrassment.
ELIZABETH. You see, we never expected you to be here. You said you'd be in Paris for another month.
C.-C. My dear child, this is your house. There's no reason why you shouldn't ask whom you please to stay with you.
ELIZABETH. After all, whatever her faults, she's Arnold's mother. It seemed so unnatural that they should never see one another. My heart ached for that poor lonely woman.
C.-C. I never heard that she was lonely, and she certainly isn't poor.
ELIZABETH. And there's something else. I couldn't ask her by herself. It would have been so — so insulting. I asked Lord Porteous, too.
C.-C. I see.
ELIZABETH. I daresay you'd rather not meet them.
C.-C. I daresay they'd rather not meet me. I shall get a capital luncheon at the cottage. I've noticed you always get the best food if you come in unexpectedly and have the same as they're having in the servants' hall.
ELIZABETH. No one's ever talked to me about Lady Kitty. It's always been a subject that everyone has avoided. I've never even seen a photograph of her.

C.-C. The house was full of them when she left. I think I told the butler to throw them in the dust-bin. She was very much photographed.
ELIZABETH. Won't you tell me what she was like?
C.-C. She was very like you, Elizabeth, only she had dark hair instead of red.
ELIZABETH. Poor dear! it must be quite white now.
C.-C. I daresay. She was a pretty little thing.
ELIZABETH. But she was one of the great beauties of her day. They say she was lovely.
C.-C. She had the most adorable little nose, like yours....
ELIZABETH. D'you like my nose?
C.-C. And she was very dainty, with a beautiful little figure; very light on her feet. She was like a *marquise* in an old French comedy. Yes, she was lovely.
ELIZABETH. And I'm sure she's lovely still.
C.-C. She's no chicken, you know.
ELIZABETH. You can't expect me to look at it as you and Arnold do. When you've loved as she's loved you may grow old, but you grow old beautifully.
C.-C. You're very romantic.
ELIZABETH. If everyone hadn't made such a mystery of it I daresay I shouldn't feel as I do. I know she did a great wrong to you and a great wrong to Arnold. I'm willing to acknowledge that.
C.-C. I'm sure it's very kind of you.
ELIZABETH. But she loved and she dared. Romance is such an illusive thing. You read of it in books, but it's seldom you see it face to face. I can't help it if it thrills me.
C.-C. I am painfully aware that the husband in these cases is not a romantic object.
ELIZABETH. She had the world at her feet. You were rich. She was a figure in society. And she gave up everything for love.
C.-C. [*dryly*]. I'm beginning to suspect it wasn't only for her sake and for Arnold's that you asked her to come here.
ELIZABETH. I seem to know her already.

I think her face is a little sad, for a love like that doesn't leave you gay, it leaves you grave, but I think her pale face is unlined. It's like a child's.

C.-C. My dear, how you let your imagination run away with you!

ELIZABETH. I imagine her slight and frail.

C.-C. Frail, certainly.

ELIZABETH. With beautiful thin hands and white hair. I've pictured her so often in that Renaissance Palace that they live in, with old Masters on the walls and lovely carved things all round, sitting in a black silk dress with old lace round her neck and old-fashioned diamonds. You see, I never knew my mother; she died when I was a baby. You can't confide in aunts with huge families of their own. I want Arnold's mother to be a mother to me. I've got so much to say to her.

C.-C. Are you happy with Arnold?

ELIZABETH. Why shouldn't I be?

C.-C. Why haven't you got any babies?

ELIZABETH. Give us a little time. We've only been married three years.

C.-C. I wonder what Hughie is like now!

ELIZABETH. Lord Porteous?

C.-C. He wore his clothes better than any man in London. You know he'd have been Prime Minister if he'd remained in politics.

ELIZABETH. What was he like then?

C.-C. He was a nice-looking fellow. Fine horseman. I suppose there was something very fascinating about him. Yellow hair and blue eyes, you know. He had a very good figure. I liked him. I was his parliamentary secretary. He was Arnold's godfather.

ELIZABETH. I know.

C.-C. I wonder if he ever regrets!

ELIZABETH. I wouldn't.

C.-C. Well, I must be strolling back to my cottage.

ELIZABETH. You're not angry with me?

C.-C. Not a bit.

[*She puts up her face for him to kiss. He kisses her on both cheeks and then goes out. In a moment* TEDDIE *is seen at the window.*]

TEDDIE. I saw the old blighter go.

ELIZABETH. Come in.

TEDDIE. Everything all right?

ELIZABETH. Oh, quite, as far as he's concerned. He's going to keep out of the way.

TEDDIE. Was it beastly?

ELIZABETH. No, he made it very easy for me. He's a nice old thing.

TEDDIE. You were rather scared.

ELIZABETH. A little. I am still. I don't know why.

TEDDIE. I guessed you were. I thought I'd come and give you a little moral support. It's ripping here, isn't it?

ELIZABETH. It is rather nice.

TEDDIE. It'll be jolly to think of it when I'm back in the F.M.S.

ELIZABETH. Aren't you homesick sometimes?

TEDDIE. Oh, everyone is now and then, you know.

ELIZABETH. You could have got a job in England if you'd wanted to, couldn't you?

TEDDIE. Oh, but I love it out there. England's ripping to come back to, but I couldn't live here now. It's like a woman you're desperately in love with as long as you don't see her, but when you're with her she maddens you so that you can't bear her.

ELIZABETH [*smiling*]. What's wrong with England?

TEDDIE. I don't think anything's wrong with England. I expect something's wrong with me. I've been away too long. England seems to me full of people doing things they don't want to because other people expect it of them.

ELIZABETH. Isn't that what you call a high degree of civilisation?

TEDDIE. People seem to me so insincere. When you go to parties in London they're all babbling about art, and you feel that in their hearts they don't care twopence about it. They read the books that everybody is talking about because they don't want to be out of it. In the F.M.S. we don't get very many books, and we read those we have over and over again. They mean so much to us. I don't think the people over there are half so clever as the people at home, but one gets to know them better. You see, there are so few of us that we have to make the best of one another.

ELIZABETH. I imagine that frills are not much worn in the F.M.S. It must be a comfort.

TEDDIE. It's not much good being pretentious where everyone knows exactly who you are and what your income is.

ELIZABETH. I don't think you want too much sincerity in society. It would be like an iron girder in a house of cards.

TEDDIE. And then, you know, the place is ripping. You get used to a blue sky and you miss it in England.

ELIZABETH. What do you do with yourself all the time?

TEDDIE. Oh, one works like blazes. You have to be a pretty hefty fellow to be a planter. And then there's ripping bathing. You know, it's lovely, with palm trees all along the beach. And there's shooting. And now and then we have a little dance to a gramophone.

ELIZABETH [pretending to tease him]. I think you've got a young woman out there, Teddie.

TEDDIE [vehemently]. Oh, no!

[She is a little taken aback by the earnestness of his disclaimer. There is a moment's silence, then she recovers herself.]

ELIZABETH. But you'll have to marry and settle down one of these days, you know.

TEDDIE. I want to, but it's not a thing you can do lightly.

ELIZABETH. I don't know why there more than elsewhere.

TEDDIE. In England if people don't get on they go their own ways and jog along after a fashion. In a place like that you're thrown a great deal on your own resources.

ELIZABETH. Of course.

TEDDIE. Lots of girls come out because they think they're going to have a good time. But if they're empty-headed, then they're just faced with their own emptiness and they're done. If their husbands can afford it they go home and settle down as grass-widows.

ELIZABETH. I've met them. They seem to find it a very pleasant occupation.

TEDDIE. It's rotten for their husbands, though.

ELIZABETH. And if the husbands can't afford it?

TEDDIE. Oh, then they tipple.

ELIZABETH. It's not a very alluring prospect.

TEDDIE. But if the woman's the right sort she wouldn't exchange it for any life in the world. When all's said and done it's we who've made the Empire.

ELIZABETH. What sort is the right sort?

TEDDIE. A woman of courage and endurance and sincerity. Of course, it's hopeless unless she's in love with her husband.

[He is looking at her earnestly and she, raising her eyes, gives him a long look. There is silence between them.]

TEDDIE. My house stands on the side of a hill, and the cocoanut trees wind down to the shore. Azaleas grow in my garden, and camellias, and all sorts of ripping flowers. And in front of me is the winding coast line, and then the blue sea. [A pause.] Do you know that I'm awfully in love with you?

ELIZABETH [gravely]. I wasn't quite sure. I wondered.

TEDDIE. And you? [She nods slowly.] I've never kissed you.

ELIZABETH. I don't want you to.

[They look at one another steadily. They are both grave.]

[ARNOLD comes in hurriedly.]

ARNOLD. They're coming, Elizabeth.

ELIZABETH [as though returning from a distant world]. Who?

ARNOLD [impatiently]. My dear! My mother, of course. The car is just coming up the drive.

TEDDIE. Would you like me to clear out?

ARNOLD. No, no! For goodness' sake stay.

ELIZABETH. We'd better go and meet them, Arnold.

ARNOLD. No, no; I think they'd much better be shown in. I feel simply sick with nervousness.

[ANNA *comes in from the garden.*]
ANNA. Your guests have arrived.
ELIZABETH. Yes, I know.
ARNOLD. I've given orders that luncheon should be served at once.
ELIZABETH. Why? It's not half-past one already, is it?
ARNOLD. I thought it would help. When you don't know exactly what to say you can always eat.
[*The* BUTLER *comes in and announces.*]
BUTLER. Lady Catherine Champion-Cheney! Lord Porteous!
[LADY KITTY *comes in followed by* PORTEOUS, *and the* BUTLER *goes out.* LADY KITTY *is a gay little lady, with dyed red hair and painted cheeks. She is somewhat outrageously dressed. She never forgets that she has been a pretty woman and she still behaves as if she were twenty-five.* LORD PORTEOUS *is a very bald, elderly gentleman in loose, rather eccentric clothes. He is snappy and gruff. This is not at all the couple that Elizabeth expected, and for a moment she stares at them with round, startled eyes.* LADY KITTY *goes up to her with outstretched hands.*]

LADY KITTY. Elizabeth! Elizabeth!. [*She kisses her effusively.*] What an adorable creature! [*Turning to* PORTEOUS.] Hughie, isn't she adorable?
PORTEOUS [*with a grunt*]. Ugh!
[ELIZABETH, *smiling now, turns to him and gives him her hand.*]
ELIZABETH. How d'you do?
PORTEOUS. Damnable road you've got down here. How d'you do, my dear? Why d'you have such damnable roads in England?
[LADY KITTY'S *eyes fall on* TEDDIE *and she goes up to him with her arms thrown back, prepared to throw them around him.*]
LADY KITTY. My boy, my boy! I should have known you anywhere!
ELIZABETH [*hastily*]. That's Arnold.
LADY KITTY [*without a moment's hesitation*]. The image of his father! I should have known him anywhere! [*She throws her arms round his neck.*] My boy, my boy!
PORTEOUS [*with a grunt*]. Ugh!
LADY KITTY. Tell me, would you have known me again? Have I changed?
ARNOLD. I was only five, you know, when — when you . . .
LADY KITTY [*emotionally*]. I remember as if it was yesterday. I went up into your room. [*With a sudden change of manner.*] By the way, I always thought that nurse drank. Did you ever find out if she really did?
PORTEOUS. How the devil can you expect him to know that, Kitty?
LADY KITTY. You've never had a child, Hughie; how can you tell what they know and what they don't?
ELIZABETH [*coming to the rescue*]. This is Arnold, Lord Porteous.
PORTEOUS [*shaking hands with him*]. How d'you do? I knew your father.
ARNOLD. Yes.
PORTEOUS. Alive still?
ARNOLD. Yes.
PORTEOUS. He must be getting on. Is he well?
ARNOLD. Very.
PORTEOUS. Ugh! Takes care of himself, I suppose. I'm not at all well. This damned climate doesn't agree with me.
ELIZABETH [*to* LADY KITTY]. This is Mrs. Shenstone. And this is Mr. Luton. I hope you don't mind a very small party.
LADY KITTY [*shaking hands with* ANNA *and* TEDDIE]. Oh, no, I shall enjoy it. I used to give enormous parties here. Political, you know. How nice you've made this room!
ELIZABETH. Oh, that's Arnold.
ARNOLD [*nervously*]. D'you like this chair? I've just bought it. It's exactly my period.
PORTEOUS [*bluntly*]. It's a fake.
ARNOLD [*indignantly*]. I don't think it is for a minute.
PORTEOUS. The legs are not right.
ARNOLD. I don't know how you can say that. If there is anything right about it, it's the legs.
LADY KITTY. I'm sure they're right.

PORTEOUS. You know nothing whatever about it, Kitty.

LADY KITTY. That's what you think. *I* think it's a beautiful chair. Hepplewhite?

ARNOLD. No, Sheraton.

LADY KITTY. Oh, I know. *The School for Scandal.*

PORTEOUS. Sheraton, my dear. Sheraton.

LADY KITTY. Yes, that's what I say. I acted the screen scene at some amateur theatricals in Florence, and Ermeto Novelli, the great Italian tragedian, told me he'd never seen a Lady Teazle like me.

PORTEOUS. Ugh!

LADY KITTY [*to* ELIZABETH]. Do you act?

ELIZABETH. Oh, I couldn't. I should be too nervous.

LADY KITTY. I'm never nervous. I'm a born actress. Of course, if I had my time over again I'd go on the stage. You know, it's extraordinary how they keep young. Actresses, I mean. I think it's because they're always playing different parts. Hughie, do you think Arnold takes after me or after his father? Of course I think he's the very image of me. Arnold, I think I ought to tell you that I was received into the Catholic Church last winter. I'd been thinking about it for years, and last time we were at Monte Carlo I met such a nice monsignore. I told him what my difficulties were and he was too wonderful. I knew Hughie wouldn't approve, so I kept it a secret. [*To* ELIZABETH.] Are you interested in religion? I think it's too wonderful. We must have a long talk about it one of these days. [*Pointing to her frock.*] Callot?

ELIZABETH. No, Worth.

LADY KITTY. I knew it was either Worth or Callot. Of course, it's line that's the important thing. I go to Worth myself, and I always say to him, "Line, my dear Worth, line." What *is* the matter, Hughie?

PORTEOUS. These new teeth of mine are so damned uncomfortable.

LADY KITTY. Men are extraordinary. They can't stand the smallest discomfort. Why, a woman's life is uncomfortable from the moment she gets up in the morning till the moment she goes to bed at night. And d'you think it's comfortable to sleep with a mask on your face?

PORTEOUS. They don't seem to hold up properly.

LADY KITTY. Well, that's not the fault of your teeth. That's the fault of your gums.

PORTEOUS. Damned rotten dentist. That's what's the matter.

LADY KITTY. I thought he was a very nice dentist. He told me *my* teeth would last till I was fifty. He has a Chinese room. It's so interesting; while he scrapes your teeth he tells you all about the dear Empress Dowager. Are you interested in China? I think it's too wonderful. You know they've cut off their pigtails. I think it's such a pity. They were so picturesque.

[*The* BUTLER *comes in.*]

BUTLER. Luncheon is served, sir.

ELIZABETH. Would you like to see your rooms?

PORTEOUS. We can see our rooms after luncheon.

LADY KITTY. I must powder my nose, Hughie.

PORTEOUS. Powder it down here.

LADY KITTY. I never saw anyone so inconsiderate.

PORTEOUS. You'll keep us all waiting half an hour. I know you.

LADY KITTY [*fumbling in her bag*]. Oh, well, peace at any price, as Lord Beaconsfield said.

PORTEOUS. He said a lot of damned silly things, Kitty, but he never said that.

[LADY KITTY's *face changes. Perplexity is followed by dismay, and dismay by consternation.*]

LADY KITTY. Oh!

ELIZABETH. What is the matter?

LADY KITTY [*with anguish*]. My lipstick!

ELIZABETH. Can't you find it?

LADY KITTY. I had it in the car. Hughie, you remember that I had it in the car.

PORTEOUS. I don't remember anything about it.

THE CIRCLE 443

LADY KITTY. Don't be so stupid, Hughie. Why, when we came through the gates I said: "My home, my home!" and I took it out and put some on my lips.

ELIZABETH. Perhaps you dropped it in the car.

LADY KITTY. For heaven's sake send some one to look for it.

ARNOLD. I'll ring.

LADY KITTY. I'm absolutely lost without my lip-stick. Lend me yours, darling, will you?

ELIZABETH. I'm awfully sorry. I'm afraid I haven't got one.

LADY KITTY. Do you mean to say you don't use a lip-stick?

ELIZABETH. Never.

PORTEOUS. Look at her lips. What the devil d'you think she wants muck like that for?

LADY KITTY. Oh, my dear, what a mistake you make! You *must* use a lip-stick. It's so good for the lips. Men like it, you know. I couldn't *live* without a lipstick.

[CHAMPION-CHENEY *appears at the window holding in his upstretched hand a little gold case.*]

C.-C. [*as he comes in*]. Has anyone here lost a diminutive utensil containing, unless I am mistaken, a favourite preparation for the toilet?

[ARNOLD *and* ELIZABETH *are thunderstruck at his appearance and even* TEDDIE *and* ANNA *are taken aback. But* LADY KITTY *is overjoyed.*]

LADY KITTY. My lip-stick!

C.-C. I found it in the drive and I ventured to bring it in.

LADY KITTY. It's Saint Antony. I said a little prayer to him when I was hunting in my bag.

PORTEOUS. Saint Antony be blowed! It's Clive, by God!

LADY KITTY [*startled, her attention suddenly turning from the lip-stick*]. Clive!

C.-C. You didn't recognize me. It's many years since we met.

LADY KITTY. My poor Clive, your hair has gone quite white!

C.-C. [*holding out his hand*]. I hope you had a pleasant journey down from London.

LADY KITTY [*offering him her cheek*]. You may kiss me, Clive.

C.-C. [*kissing her*]. You don't mind, Hughie?

PORTEOUS [*with a grunt*]. Ugh!

C.-C. [*going up to him cordially*]. And how are you, my dear Hughie?

PORTEOUS. Damned rheumatic if you want to know. Filthy climate you have in this country.

C.-C. Aren't you going to shake hands with me, Hughie?

PORTEOUS. I have no objection to shaking hands with you.

C.-C. You've aged, my poor Hughie.

PORTEOUS. Some one was asking me how old you were the other day.

C.-C. Were they surprised when you told them?

PORTEOUS. Surprised! They wondered you weren't dead.

[*The* BUTLER *comes in.*]

BUTLER. Did you ring, sir?

ARNOLD. No. Oh, yes, I did. It doesn't matter now.

C.-C. [*as the* BUTLER *is going*]. One moment. My dear Elizabeth, I've come to throw myself on your mercy. My servants are busy with their own affairs. There's not a thing for me to eat in my cottage.

ELIZABETH. Oh, but we shall be delighted if you'll lunch with us.

C.-C. It either means that or my immediate death from starvation. You don't mind, Arnold?

ARNOLD. My dear father!

ELIZABETH [*to the* BUTLER]. Mr. Cheney will lunch here.

BUTLER. Very good, ma'am.

C.-C. [*to* LADY KITTY]. And what do you think of Arnold?

LADY KITTY. I adore him.

C.-C. He's grown, hasn't he? But then you'd expect him to do that in thirty years.

ARNOLD. For God's sake let's go in to lunch, Elizabeth!

ACT II

The Scene is the same as in the preceding Act. It is afternoon. When the curtain rises PORTEOUS *and* LADY KITTY, ANNA *and* TEDDIE *are playing bridge.* ELIZABETH *and* CHAMPION-CHENEY *are watching.* PORTEOUS *and* LADY KITTY *are partners.*

C.-C. When will Arnold be back, Elizabeth?

ELIZABETH. Soon, I think.

C.-C. Is he addressing a meeting?

ELIZABETH. No, it's only a conference with his agent and one or two constituents.

PORTEOUS [*irritably*]. How anyone can be expected to play bridge when people are shouting at the top of their voices all round them, I for one cannot understand.

ELIZABETH [*smiling*]. I'm so sorry.

ANNA. I can see your hand, Lord Porteous.

PORTEOUS. It may help you.

LADY KITTY. I've told you over and over again to hold your cards up. It ruins one's game when one can't help seeing one's opponent's hand.

PORTEOUS. One isn't obliged to look.

LADY KITTY. What was Arnold's majority at the last election?

ELIZABETH. Seven hundred and something.

C.-C. He'll have to fight for it if he wants to keep his seat next time.

PORTEOUS. Are we playing bridge, or talking politics?

LADY KITTY. I never find that conversation interferes with my game.

PORTEOUS. You certainly play no worse when you talk than when you hold your tongue.

LADY KITTY. I think that's a very offensive thing to say, Hughie. Just because I don't play the same game as you do you think I can't play.

PORTEOUS. I'm glad you acknowledge it's not the same game as I play. But why in God's name do you call it bridge?

C.-C. I agree with Kitty. I hate people who play bridge as though they were at a funeral and knew their feet were getting wet.

PORTEOUS. Of course you take Kitty's part.

LADY KITTY. That's the least he can do.

C.-C. I have a naturally cheerful disposition.

PORTEOUS. You've never had anything to sour it.

LADY KITTY. I don't know what you mean by that, Hughie.

PORTEOUS [*trying to contain himself*]. Must you trump my ace?

LADY KITTY [*innocently*]. Oh, was that your ace, darling?

PORTEOUS [*furiously*]. Yes, it was my ace.

LADY KITTY. Oh, well, it was the only trump I had. I shouldn't have made it anyway.

PORTEOUS. You needn't have told them that. Now she knows exactly what I've got.

LADY KITTY. She knew before.

PORTEOUS. How could she know?

LADY KITTY. She said she'd seen your hand.

ANNA. Oh, I didn't. I said I could see it.

LADY KITTY. Well, I naturally supposed that if she could see it she did.

PORTEOUS. Really, Kitty, you have the most extraordinary ideas.

C.-C. Not at all. If anyone is such a fool as to show me his hand, of course I look at it.

PORTEOUS [*fuming*]. If you study the etiquette of bridge, you'll discover that onlookers are expected not to interfere with the game.

C.-C. My dear Hughie, this is a matter of ethics, not of bridge.

ANNA. Anyhow, I get the game. And rubber.

TEDDIE. I claim a revoke.

PORTEOUS. Who revoked?

TEDDIE. You did.

PORTEOUS. Nonsense. I've never revoked in my life.

TEDDIE. I'll show you. [*He turns over the tricks to show the faces of the cards.*] You threw away a club on the third heart trick and you had another heart.

PORTEOUS. I never had more than two hearts.

TEDDIE. Oh, yes, you had. Look here. That's the card you played on the last trick but one.

LADY KITTY [*delighted to catch him out*]. There's no doubt about it, Hughie. You revoked.

PORTEOUS. I tell you I did not revoke. I never revoke.

C.-C. You did, Hughie. I wondered what on earth you were doing.

PORTEOUS. I don't know how anyone can be expected not to revoke when there's this confounded chatter going on all the time.

TEDDIE. Well, that's another hundred to us.

PORTEOUS [*to* CHAMPION-CHENEY]. I wish you wouldn't breathe down my neck. I never can play bridge when there's somebody breathing down my neck.

[*The party have risen from the bridge-table, and they scatter about the room.*]

ANNA. Well, I'm going to take a book and lie down in the hammock till it's time to dress.

TEDDIE [*who has been adding up*]. I'll put it down in the book, shall I?

PORTEOUS [*who has not moved, setting out the cards for a patience*]. Yes, yes, put it down. I never revoke. [ANNA *goes out.*]

LADY KITTY. Would you like to come for a little stroll, Hughie?

PORTEOUS. What for?

LADY KITTY. Exercise.

PORTEOUS. I hate exercise.

C.-C. [*looking at the patience*]. The seven goes on the eight.

[PORTEOUS *takes no notice.*]

LADY KITTY. The seven goes on the eight, Hughie.

PORTEOUS. I don't choose to put the seven on the eight.

C.-C. That knave goes on the queen.

PORTEOUS. I'm not blind, thank you.

LADY KITTY. The three goes on the four.

C.-C. All these go over.

PORTEOUS [*furiously*]. Am I playing this patience, or are you playing it?

LADY KITTY. But you're missing everything.

PORTEOUS. That's my business.

C.-C. It's no good losing your temper over it, Hughie.

PORTEOUS. Go away, both of you. You irritate me.

LADY KITTY. We were only trying to help you, Hughie.

PORTEOUS. I don't want to be helped. I want to do it by myself.

LADY KITTY. I think your manners are perfectly deplorable, Hughie.

PORTEOUS. It's simply maddening when you're playing patience and people won't leave you alone.

C.-C. We won't say another word.

PORTEOUS. That three goes. I believe it's coming out. If I'd been such a fool as to put that seven up I shouldn't have been able to bring these down.

[*He puts down several cards while they watch him silently.*]

LADY KITTY and C.-C. [*together*]. The four goes on the five.

PORTEOUS [*throwing down the cards violently*]. Damn you! why don't you leave me alone? It's intolerable.

C.-C. It was coming out, my dear fellow.

PORTEOUS. I know it was coming out. Confound you!

LADY KITTY. How petty you are, Hughie!

PORTEOUS. Petty, be damned! I've told you over and over again that I will not be interfered with when I'm playing patience.

LADY KITTY. Don't talk to me like that, Hughie.

PORTEOUS. I shall talk to you as I please.

LADY KITTY [*beginning to cry*]. Oh, you brute! You brute!

[*She flings out of the room.*]

PORTEOUS. Oh, damn! now she's going to cry.

[*He shambles out into the garden.* CHAMPION-CHENEY, ELIZABETH, *and* TEDDIE *are left alone. There is a moment's pause.* CHAMPION-CHENEY *looks from* TEDDIE *to* ELIZABETH, *with an ironical smile.*]

C.-C. Upon my soul, they might be married. They frip so much.

ELIZABETH [*frigidly*]. It's been nice of you to come here so often since they arrived. It's helped to make things easy.

C.-C. Irony? It's a rhetorical form not much favoured in this blessed plot, this earth, this realm, this England.

ELIZABETH. What exactly are you getting at?

C.-C. How slangy the young women of the present day are! I suppose the fact that Arnold is a purist leads you to the contrary extravagance.

ELIZABETH. Anyhow, you know what I mean.

C.-C. [*with a smile*]. I have a dim, groping suspicion.

ELIZABETH. You promised to keep away. Why did you come back the moment they arrived?

C.-C. Curiosity, my dear child. A surely pardonable curiosity.

ELIZABETH. And since then you've been here all the time. You don't generally favour us with so much of your company when you're down at your cottage.

C.-C. I've been excessively amused.

ELIZABETH. It has struck me that whenever they started fripping you took a malicious pleasure in goading them on.

C.-C. I don't think there's much love lost between them now, do you?

[TEDDIE *is making as though to leave the room.*]

ELIZABETH. Don't go, Teddie.

C.-C. No, please don't. I'm only staying a minute. We were talking about Lady Kitty just before she arrived. [*To* ELIZABETH.] Do you remember? The pale, frail lady in black satin and old lace.

ELIZABETH [*with a chuckle*]. You are a devil, you know.

C.-C. Ah, well, he's always had the reputation of being a humorist and a gentleman.

ELIZABETH. Did *you* expect her to be like that, poor dear?

C.-C. My dear child, I hadn't the vaguest idea. You were asking me the other day what she was like when she ran away. I didn't tell you half. She was so gay and so natural. Who would have thought that animation would turn into such frivolity, and that charming impulsiveness lead to such a ridiculous affectation?

ELIZABETH. It rather sets my nerves on edge to hear the way you talk of her.

C.-C. It's the truth that sets your nerves on edge, not I.

ELIZABETH. You loved her once. Have you no feeling for her at all?

C.-C. None. Why should I?

ELIZABETH. She's the mother of your son.

C.-C. My dear child, you have a charming nature, as simple, frank, and artless as hers was. Don't let pure humbug obscure your common sense.

ELIZABETH. We have no right to judge. She's only been here two days. We know nothing about her.

C.-C. My dear, her soul is as thickly rouged as her face. She hasn't an emotion that's sincere. She's tinsel. You think I'm a cruel, cynical old man. Why, when I think of what she was, if I didn't laugh at what she has become I should cry.

ELIZABETH. How do you know she wouldn't be just the same now if she'd remained your wife? Do you think your influence would have had such a salutary effect on her?

C.-C. [*good-humouredly*]. I like you when you're bitter and rather insolent.

ELIZABETH. D'you like me enough to answer my question?

C.-C. She was only twenty-seven when she went away. She might have become anything. She might have become the woman you expected her to be. There are very few of us who are strong enough to make circumstances serve us. We are the creatures of our environment. She's a silly, worthless woman because she's led a silly, worthless life.

ELIZABETH [*disturbed*]. You're horrible to-day.

C.-C. I don't say it's I who could have prevented her from becoming this ridiculous caricature of a pretty woman grown old. But life could. Here she would have had the friends fit to her station, and a decent activity, and worthy interests. Ask her what her life has been all these years among divorced women and kept women and the men who consort with them. There is no more lamentable pursuit than a life of pleasure.

ELIZABETH. At all events she loved and she loved greatly. I have only pity and affection for her.

C.-C. And if she loved what d'you think she felt when she saw that she had ruined Hughie? Look at him. He was tight last night after dinner and tight the night before.

ELIZABETH. I know.

C.-C. And she took it as a matter of course. How long do you suppose he's been getting tight every night? Do you think he was like that thirty years ago? Can you imagine that that was a brilliant young man, whom everyone expected to be Prime Minister? Look at him now. A grumpy sodden old fellow with false teeth.

ELIZABETH. You have false teeth, too.

C.-C. Yes, but damn it all, they fit. She's ruined him and she knows she's ruined him.

ELIZABETH [*looking at him suspiciously*]. Why are you saying all this to me?

C.-C. Am I hurting your feelings?

ELIZABETH. I think I've had enough for the present.

C.-C. I'll go and have a look at the gold-fish. I want to see Arnold when he comes in. [*Politely.*] I'm afraid we've been boring Mr. Luton.

TEDDIE. Not at all.

C.-C. When are you going back to the F.M.S.?

TEDDIE. In about a month.

C.-C. I see. [*He goes out.*]

ELIZABETH. I wonder what he has at the back of his head.

TEDDIE. D'you think he was talking at you?

ELIZABETH. He's as clever as a bagful of monkeys.

[*There is a moment's pause. TEDDIE hesitates a little and when he speaks it is in a different tone. He is grave and somewhat nervous.*]

TEDDIE. It seems very difficult to get a few minutes alone with you. I wonder if you've been making it difficult?

ELIZABETH. I wanted to think.

TEDDIE. I've made up my mind to go away to-morrow.

ELIZABETH. Why?

TEDDIE. I want you altogether or not at all.

ELIZABETH. You're so arbitrary.

TEDDIE. You said you — you said you cared for me.

ELIZABETH. I do.

TEDDIE. Do you mind if we talk it over now?

ELIZABETH. No.

TEDDIE [*frowning*]. It makes me feel rather shy and awkward. I've repeated to myself over and over again exactly what I want to say to you, and now all I'd prepared seems rather footling.

ELIZABETH. I'm so afraid I'm going to cry.

TEDDIE. I feel it's all so tremendously serious and I think we ought to keep emotion out of it. You're rather emotional, aren't you?

ELIZABETH [*half smiling and half in tears*]. So are you for the matter of that.

TEDDIE. That's why I wanted to have everything I meant to say to you cut and dried. I think it would be awfully unfair if I made love to you and all that sort of thing, and you were carried away. I wrote it all down and thought I'd send it you as a letter.

ELIZABETH. Why didn't you?

TEDDIE. I got the wind up. A letter seems so — so cold. You see, I love you so awfully.

ELIZABETH. For goodness' sake don't say that.

TEDDIE. You mustn't cry. Please don't, or I shall go all to pieces.

ELIZABETH [*trying to smile*]. I'm sorry. It doesn't mean anything really. It's only tears running out of my eyes.

TEDDIE. Our only chance is to be awfully matter-of-fact.

[*He stops for a moment. He finds it quite difficult to control himself. He clears his throat. He frowns with annoyance at himself.*]

ELIZABETH. What's the matter?

TEDDIE. I've got a sort of lump in my throat. It is idiotic. I think I'll have a cigarette. [*She watches him in silence while he lights a cigarette.*] You see, I've never been in love with anyone before, not really. It's knocked me endways. I don't know how I can live without you now.... Does that old fool know I'm in love with you?

ELIZABETH. I think so.

TEDDIE. When he was talking about Lady Kitty smashing up Lord Porteous' career I thought there was something at the back of it.

ELIZABETH. I think he was trying to persuade me not to smash up yours.

TEDDIE. I'm sure that's very considerate of him, but I don't happen to have one to smash. I wish I had. It's the only time in my life I've wished I were a hell of a swell so that I could chuck it all and show you how much more you are to me than anything else in the world.

ELIZABETH [*affectionately*]. You're a dear old thing, Teddie.

TEDDIE. You know, I don't really know how to make love, but if I did I couldn't do it now because I just want to be absolutely practical.

ELIZABETH [*chaffing him*]. I'm glad you don't know how to make love. It would be almost more than I could bear.

TEDDIE. You see, I'm not at all romantic and that sort of thing. I'm just a common or garden business man. All this is so dreadfully serious and I think we ought to be sensible.

ELIZABETH [*with a break in her voice*]. You owl!

TEDDIE. No, Elizabeth, don't say things like that to me. I want you to consider all the *pros* and *cons*, and my heart's thumping against my chest, and you know I love you, I love you, I love you.

ELIZABETH [*in a sigh of passion*]. Oh, my precious!

TEDDIE [*impatiently, but with himself, rather than with* ELIZABETH]. Don't be idiotic, Elizabeth. I'm not going to tell you that I can't live without you and a lot of muck like that. You know that you mean everything in the world to me. [*Almost giving it up as a bad job.*] Oh, my God!

ELIZABETH [*her voice faltering*]. D'you think there's anything you can say to me that I don't know already?

TEDDIE [*desperately*]. But I haven't said a single thing I wanted to. I'm a business man and I want to put it all in a business way, if you understand what I mean.

ELIZABETH [*smiling*]. I don't believe you're a very good business man.

TEDDIE [*sharply*]. You don't know what you're talking about. I'm a first-rate business man, but somehow this is different. [*Hopelessly.*] I don't know why it won't go right.

ELIZABETH. What are we going to do about it?

TEDDIE. You see, it's not just because you're awfully pretty that I love you. I'd love you just as much if you were old and ugly. It's you I love, not what you look like. And it's not only love; love be blowed! It's that I *like* you so tremendously. I think you're such a ripping good sort. I just want to be with you. I feel so jolly and happy just to think you're there. I'm so awfully *fond* of you.

ELIZABETH [*laughing through her tears*]. I don't know if this is your idea of introducing a business proposition.

TEDDIE. Damn you, you won't let me.

ELIZABETH. You said "Damn you."

TEDDIE. I meant it.

ELIZABETH. Your voice sounded as if you meant it, you perfect duck!

TEDDIE. Really, Elizabeth, you're intolerable.

ELIZABETH. I'm doing nothing.

TEDDIE. Yes, you are, you're putting me off my blow. What I want to say is perfectly simple. I'm a very ordinary business man.

ELIZABETH. You've said that before.

TEDDIE [*angrily*]. Shut up. I haven't got a bob besides what I earn. I've got no position. I'm nothing. You're rich and you're a big pot and you've got everything that anyone can want. It's awful cheek my saying anything to you at all. But after all there's only one thing that really matters in the world, and that's love. I love you. Chuck all this, Elizabeth, and come to me.

ELIZABETH. Are you cross with me?

TEDDIE. Furious.

ELIZABETH. Darling!

TEDDIE. If you don't want me tell me so at once and let me get out quickly.

ELIZABETH. Teddie, nothing in the world matters anything to me but you. I'll go wherever you take me. I love you.

TEDDIE [all to pieces]. Oh, my God!

ELIZABETH. Does it mean as much to you as that? Oh, Teddie!

TEDDIE [trying to control himself]. Don't be a fool, Elizabeth.

ELIZABETH. It's you're the fool. You're making me cry.

TEDDIE. You're so damned emotional.

ELIZABETH. Damned emotional yourself. I'm sure you're a rotten business man.

TEDDIE. I don't care what you think. You've made me so awfully happy. I say, what a lark life's going to be!

ELIZABETH. Teddie, you are an angel.

TEDDIE. Let's get out quick. It's no good wasting time. Elizabeth.

ELIZABETH. What?

TEDDIE. Nothing. I just like to say Elizabeth.

ELIZABETH. You fool!

TEDDIE. I say, can you shoot?

ELIZABETH. No.

TEDDIE. I'll teach you. You don't know how ripping it is to start out from your camp at dawn and travel through the jungle. And you're so tired at night and the sky's all starry. It's a fair treat. Of course I didn't want to say anything about all that till you'd decided. I'd made up my mind to be absolutely practical.

ELIZABETH [chaffing him]. The only practical thing you said was that love is the only thing that really matters.

TEDDIE [happily]. Pull the other leg next time, will you? I should have to have one longer than the other.

ELIZABETH. Isn't it fun being in love with some one who's in love with you?

TEDDIE. I say, I think I'd better clear out at once, don't you? It seems rather rotten to stay on in — in this house.

ELIZABETH. You can't go to-night. There's no train.

TEDDIE. I'll go to-morrow. I'll wait in London till you're ready to join me.

ELIZABETH. I'm not going to leave a note on the pin-cushion like Lady Kitty, you know. I'm going to tell Arnold.

TEDDIE. Are you? Don't you think there'll be an awful bother?

ELIZABETH. I must face it. I should hate to be sly and deceitful.

TEDDIE. Well, then, let's face it together.

ELIZABETH. No, I'll talk to Arnold by myself.

TEDDIE. You won't let anyone influence you?

ELIZABETH. No.

[He holds out his hand and she takes it. They look into one another's eyes with grave, almost solemn affection. There is the sound outside of a car driving up.]

ELIZABETH. There's the car. Arnold's come back. I must go and bathe my eyes. I don't want them to see I've been crying.

TEDDIE. All right. [As she is going.] Elizabeth.

ELIZABETH [stopping]. What?

TEDDIE. Bless you.

ELIZABETH [affectionately]. Idiot!

[She goes out of the door and TEDDIE through the French window into the garden. For an instant the room is empty.]

[ARNOLD comes in. He sits down and takes some papers out of his despatch-case. LADY KITTY enters. He gets up.]

LADY KITTY. I saw you come in. Oh, my dear, don't get up. There's no reason why you should be so dreadfully polite to me.

ARNOLD. I've just rung for a cup of tea.

LADY KITTY. Perhaps we shall have the chance of a little talk. We don't seem to have had five minutes by ourselves. I want to make your acquaintance, you know.

ARNOLD. I should like you to know that it's not by my wish that my father is here.

LADY KITTY. But I'm so interested to see him.

ARNOLD. I was afraid that you and Lord Porteous must find it embarrassing.

LADY KITTY. Oh, no. Hughie was his greatest friend. They were at Eton and Oxford together. I think your father has improved so much since I saw him last. He wasn't good-looking as a young man, but now he's quite handsome.

[*The* FOOTMAN *brings in a tray on which are tea-things.*]

LADY KITTY. Shall I pour it out for you?

ARNOLD. Thank you very much.

LADY KITTY. Do you take sugar?

ARNOLD. No. I gave it up during the war.

LADY KITTY. So wise of you. It's so bad for the figure. Besides being patriotic, of course. Isn't it absurd that I should ask my son if he takes sugar or not? Life is really very quaint. Sad, of course, but oh, so quaint! Often I lie in bed at night and have a good laugh to myself as I think how quaint life is.

ARNOLD. I'm afraid I'm a very serious person.

LADY KITTY. How old are you now, Arnold?

ARNOLD. Thirty-five.

LADY KITTY. Are you really? Of course, I was a child when I married your father.

ARNOLD. Really. He always told me you were twenty-two.

LADY KITTY. Oh, what nonsense! Why, I was married out of the nursery. I put my hair up for the first time on my wedding-day.

ARNOLD. Where is Lord Porteous?

LADY KITTY. My dear, it sounds too absurd to hear you call him Lord Porteous. Why don't you call him — Uncle Hughie?

ARNOLD. He doesn't happen to be my uncle.

LADY KITTY. No, but he's your godfather. You know, I'm sure you'll like him when you know him better. I'm so hoping that you and Elizabeth will come and stay with us in Florence. I simply adore Elizabeth. She's too beautiful.

ARNOLD. Her hair is very pretty.

LADY KITTY. It's not touched up, is it?

ARNOLD. Oh, no.

LADY KITTY. I just wondered. It's rather a coincidence that her hair should be the same colour as mine. I suppose it shows that your father and you are attracted by just the same thing. So interesting, heredity, isn't it?

ARNOLD. Very.

LADY KITTY. Of course, since I joined the Catholic Church I don't believe in it any more. Darwin and all that sort of thing. Too dreadful. Wicked, you know. Besides, it's not very good form, is it?

[CHAMPION-CHENEY *comes in from the garden.*]

C.-C. Do I intrude?

LADY KITTY. Come in, Clive. Arnold and I have been having such a wonderful heart-to-heart talk.

C.-C. Very nice.

ARNOLD. Father, I stepped in for a moment at the Harveys' on my way back. It's simply criminal what they're doing with that house.

C.-C. What are they doing?

ARNOLD. It's an almost perfect Georgian house and they've got a lot of dreadful Victorian furniture. I gave them my ideas on the subject, but it's quite hopeless. They said they were attached to their furniture.

C.-C. Arnold should have been an interior decorator.

LADY KITTY. He has wonderful taste. He gets that from me.

ARNOLD. I suppose I have a certain *flair*. I have a passion for decorating houses.

LADY KITTY. You've made this one charming.

C.-C. D'you remember, we just had chintzes and comfortable chairs when we lived here, Kitty.

LADY KITTY. Perfectly hideous, wasn't it?

C.-C. In those days gentlemen and ladies were not expected to have taste.

ARNOLD. You know, I've been looking

at this chair again. Since Lord Porteous said the legs weren't right I've been very uneasy.

LADY KITTY. He only said that because he was in a bad temper.

C.-C. His temper seems to me very short these days, Kitty.

LADY KITTY. Oh, it is.

ARNOLD. You feel he knows what he's talking about. I gave seventy-five pounds for that chair. I'm very seldom taken in. I always think if a thing's right you feel it.

C.-C. Well, don't let it disturb your night's rest.

ARNOLD. But, my dear father, that's just what it does. I had a most horrible dream about it last night.

LADY KITTY. Here is Hughie.

ARNOLD. I'm going to fetch a book I have on Old English furniture. There's an illustration of a chair which is almost identical with this one.

[PORTEOUS *comes in.*]

PORTEOUS. Quite a family gathering, by George!

C.-C. I was thinking just now we'd make a very pleasing picture of a typical English home.

ARNOLD. I'll be back in five minutes. There's something I want to show you, Lord Porteous. [*He goes out.*]

C.-C. Would you like to play piquet with me, Hughie?

PORTEOUS. Not particularly.

C.-C. You were never much of a piquet player, were you?

PORTEOUS. My dear Clive, you people don't know what piquet is in England.

C.-C. Let's have a game then. You may make money.

PORTEOUS. I don't want to play with you.

LADY KITTY. I don't know why not, Hughie.

PORTEOUS. Let me tell you that I don't like your manner.

C.-C. I'm sorry for that. I'm afraid I can't offer to change it at my age.

PORTEOUS. I don't know what you want to be hanging around here for.

C.-C. A natural attachment to my home.

PORTEOUS. If you'd had any tact you'd have kept out of the way while we were here.

C.-C. My dear Hughie, I don't understand your attitude at all. If I'm willing to let bygones be bygones why should you object?

PORTEOUS. Damn it all, they're not bygones.

C.-C. After all, I am the injured party.

PORTEOUS. How the devil are you the injured party?

C.-C. Well, you did run away with my wife, didn't you?

LADY KITTY. Now, don't let's go into ancient history. I can't see why we shouldn't all be friends.

PORTEOUS. I beg you not to interfere, Kitty.

LADY KITTY. I'm very fond of Clive.

PORTEOUS. You never cared two straws for Clive. You only say that to irritate me.

LADY KITTY. Not at all. I don't see why he shouldn't come and stay with us.

C.-C. I'd love to. I think Florence in spring-time is delightful. Have you central heating?

PORTEOUS. I never liked you, I don't like you now, and I never shall like you.

C.-C. How very unfortunate! because I liked you, I like you now, and I shall continue to like you.

LADY KITTY. There's something very nice about you, Clive.

PORTEOUS. If you think that, why the devil did you leave him?

LADY KITTY. Are you going to reproach me because I loved you? How utterly, utterly, utterly detestable you are!

C.-C. Now, now, don't quarrel with one another.

LADY KITTY. It's all his fault. I'm the easiest person in the world to live with. But really he'd try the patience of a saint.

C.-C. Come, come, don't get upset, Kitty. When two people live together there must be a certain amount of give and take.

PORTEOUS. I don't know what the devil you're talking about.

C.-C. It hasn't escaped my observation

that you are a little inclined to frip. Many couples are. I think it's a pity.

PORTEOUS. Would you have the very great kindness to mind your own business?

LADY KITTY. It is his business. He naturally wants me to be happy.

C.-C. I have the very greatest affection for Kitty.

PORTEOUS. Then why the devil didn't you look after her properly?

C.-C. My dear Hughie, you were my greatest friend. I trusted you. It may have been rash.

PORTEOUS. It was inexcusable.

LADY KITTY. I don't know what you mean by that, Hughie.

PORTEOUS. Don't, don't, don't try and bully me, Kitty.

LADY KITTY. Oh, I know what you mean.

PORTEOUS. Then why the devil did you say you didn't?

LADY KITTY. When I think that I sacrificed everything for that man! And for thirty years I've had to live in a filthy marble palace with no sanitary conveniences.

C.-C. D'you mean to say you haven't got a bathroom?

LADY KITTY. I've had to wash in a tub.

C.-C. My poor Kitty, how you've suffered!

PORTEOUS. Really, Kitty, I'm sick of hearing of the sacrifices you made. I suppose you think I sacrificed nothing. I should have been Prime Minister by now if it hadn't been for you.

LADY KITTY. Nonsense!

PORTEOUS. What do you mean by that? Everyone said I should be Prime Minister. Shouldn't I have been Prime Minister, Clive?

C.-C. It was certainly the general expectation.

PORTEOUS. I was the most promising young man of my day. I was bound to get a seat in the Cabinet at the next election.

LADY KITTY. They'd have found you out just as I've found you out. I'm sick of hearing that I ruined your career. You never had a career to ruin. Prime Minister! You haven't the brain. You haven't the character.

C.-C. Cheek, push, and a gift of the gab will serve very well instead, you know.

LADY KITTY. Besides, in politics it's not the men that matter. It's the women at the back of them. I could have made Clive a Cabinet Minister if I'd wanted to.

PORTEOUS. Clive?

LADY KITTY. With my beauty, my charm, my force of character, my wit, I could have done anything.

PORTEOUS. Clive was nothing but my political secretary. When I was Prime Minister I might have made him Governor of some Colony or other. Western Australia, say. Out of pure kindliness.

LADY KITTY [*with flashing eyes*]. D'you think I would have buried myself in Western Australia? With my beauty? My charm?

PORTEOUS. Or Barbadoes, perhaps.

LADY KITTY [*furiously*]. Barbadoes! Barbadoes can go to — Barbadoes.

PORTEOUS. That's all you'd have got.

LADY KITTY. Nonsense! I'd have India.

PORTEOUS. I would never have given you India.

LADY KITTY. You would have given me India.

PORTEOUS. I tell you I wouldn't.

LADY KITTY. The King would have given me India. The nation would have insisted on my having India. I would have been a vice-reine or nothing.

PORTEOUS. I tell you that as long as the interests of the British Empire — Damn it all, my teeth are coming out!

[*He hurries from the room.*]

LADY KITTY. It's too much. I can't bear it any more. I've put up with him for thirty years and now I'm at the end of my tether.

C.-C. Calm yourself, my dear Kitty.

LADY KITTY. I won't listen to a word. I've quite made up my mind. It's finished, finished, finished. [*With a change of tone.*] I was so touched when I heard that you never lived in this house again after I left it.

C.-C. The cuckoos have always been

very plentiful. Their note has a personal application which, I must say, I have found extremely offensive.

LADY KITTY. When I saw that you didn't marry again I couldn't help thinking that you still loved me.

C.-C. I am one of the few men I know who is able to profit by experience.

LADY KITTY. In the eyes of the Church I am still your wife. The Church is so wise. It knows that in the end a woman always comes back to her first love. Clive, I am willing to return to you.

C.-C. My dear Kitty, I couldn't take advantage of your momentary vexation with Hughie to let you take a step which I know you would bitterly regret.

LADY KITTY. You've waited for me a long time. For Arnold's sake.

C.-C. Do you think we really need bother about Arnold? In the last thirty years he's had time to grow used to the situation.

LADY KITTY [with a smile]. I think I've sown my wild oats, Clive.

C.-C. I haven't. I was a good young man, Kitty.

LADY KITTY. I know.

C.-C. And I'm very glad, because it has enabled me to be a wicked old one.

LADY KITTY. I beg your pardon.

[ARNOLD comes in with a large book in his hand.]

ARNOLD. I say, I've found the book I was hunting for. Oh! isn't Lord Porteous here?

LADY KITTY. One moment, Arnold. Your father and I are busy.

ARNOLD. I'm so sorry.

[He goes out into the garden.]

LADY KITTY. Explain yourself, Clive.

C.-C. When you ran away from me, Kitty, I was sore and angry and miserable. But above all I felt a fool.

LADY KITTY. Men are so vain.

C.-C. But I was a student of history, and presently I reflected that I shared my misfortune with very nearly all the greatest men.

LADY KITTY. I'm a great reader myself. It has always struck me as peculiar.

C.-C. The explanation is very simple. Women dislike intelligence, and when they find it in their husbands they revenge themselves on them in the only way they can, by making them — well, what you made me.

LADY KITTY. It's ingenious. It may be true.

C.-C. I felt I had done my duty by society and I determined to devote the rest of my life to my own entertainment. The House of Commons had always bored me excessively and the scandal of our divorce gave me an opportunity to resign my seat. I have been relieved to find that the country got on perfectly well without me.

LADY KITTY. But has love never entered your life?

C.-C. Tell me frankly, Kitty, don't you think people make a lot of unnecessary fuss about love?

LADY KITTY. It's the most wonderful thing in the world.

C.-C. You're incorrigible. Do you really think it was worth sacrificing so much for?

LADY KITTY. My dear Clive, I don't mind telling you that if I had my time over again I should be unfaithful to you, but I should not leave you.

C.-C. For some years I was notoriously the prey of a secret sorrow. But I found so many charming creatures who were anxious to console that in the end it grew rather fatiguing. Out of regard to my health I ceased to frequent the drawing-rooms of Mayfair.

LADY KITTY. And since then?

C.-C. Since then I have allowed myself the luxury of assisting financially a succession of dear little things, in a somewhat humble sphere, between the ages of twenty and twenty-five.

LADY KITTY. I cannot understand the infatuation of men for young girls. I think they're so dull.

C.-C. It's a matter of taste. I love old wine, old friends, and old books, but I like young women. On their twenty-fifth birthday I give them a diamond ring and tell them they must no longer waste their youth and beauty on an old fogey like me.

We have a most affecting scene, my technique on these occasions is perfect, and then I start all over again.

LADY KITTY. You're a wicked old man, Clive.

C.-C. That's what I told you. But, by George! I'm a happy one.

LADY KITTY. There's only one course open to me now.

C.-C. What is that?

LADY KITTY [with a flashing smile]. To go and dress for dinner.

C.-C. Capital. I will follow your example.

[As LADY KITTY goes out ELIZABETH comes in.]

ELIZABETH. Where is Arnold?

C.-C. He's on the terrace. I'll call him.

ELIZABETH. Don't bother.

C.-C. I was just strolling along to my cottage to put on a dinner jacket. [As he goes out.] Arnold. [Exit C.-C.]

ARNOLD. Hulloa! [He comes in.] Oh, Elizabeth, I've found an illustration here of a chair which is almost identical with mine. It's dated 1750. Look!

ELIZABETH. That's very interesting.

ARNOLD. I want to show it to Porteous. [Moving a chair which has been misplaced.] You know, it does exasperate me the way people will not leave things alone. I no sooner put a thing in its place than somebody moves it.

ELIZABETH. It must be maddening for you.

ARNOLD. It is. You are the worst offender. I can't think why you don't take the pride that I do in the house. After all, it's one of the show places in the county.

ELIZABETH. I'm afraid you find me very unsatisfactory.

ARNOLD [good-humouredly]. I don't know about that. But my two subjects are politics and decoration. I should be a perfect fool if I didn't see that you don't care two straws about either.

ELIZABETH. We haven't very much in common, Arnold, have we?

ARNOLD. I don't think you can blame me for that.

ELIZABETH. I don't. I blame you for nothing. I have no fault to find with you.

ARNOLD [surprised at her significant tone]. Good gracious me! what's the meaning of all this?

ELIZABETH. Well, I don't think there's any object in beating about the bush. I want you to let me go.

ARNOLD. Go where?

ELIZABETH. Away. For always.

ARNOLD. My dear child, what *are* you talking about?

ELIZABETH. I want to be free.

ARNOLD [amused rather than disconcerted]. Don't be ridiculous, darling. I daresay you're run down and want a change. I'll take you over to Paris for a fortnight if you like.

ELIZABETH. I shouldn't have spoken to you if I hadn't quite made up my mind. We've been married for three years and I don't think it's been a great success. I'm frankly bored by the life you want me to lead.

ARNOLD. Well, if you'll allow me to say so, the fault is yours. We lead a very distinguished, useful life. We know a lot of extremely nice people.

ELIZABETH. I'm quite willing to allow that the fault is mine. But how does that make it any better? I'm only twenty-five. If I've made a mistake, I have time to correct it.

ARNOLD. I can't bring myself to take you very seriously.

ELIZABETH. You see, I don't love you.

ARNOLD. Well, I'm awfully sorry. But you weren't obliged to marry me. You've made your bed and I'm afraid you must lie on it.

ELIZABETH. That's one of the falsest proverbs in the English language. Why should you lie on the bed you've made if you don't want to? There's always the floor.

ARNOLD. For goodness' sake don't be funny, Elizabeth.

ELIZABETH. I've quite made up my mind to leave you, Arnold.

ARNOLD. Come, come, Elizabeth, you must be sensible. You haven't any reason to leave me.

ELIZABETH. Why should you wish to keep a woman tied to you who wants to be free?

ARNOLD. I happen to be in love with you.

ELIZABETH. You might have said that before.

ARNOLD. I thought you'd take it for granted. You can't expect a man to go on making love to his wife after three years. I'm very busy. I'm awfully keen on politics and I've worked like a dog to make this house a thing of beauty. After all, a man marries to have a home, but also because he doesn't want to be bothered with sex and all that sort of thing. I fell in love with you the first time I saw you and I've been in love ever since.

ELIZABETH. I'm sorry, but if you're not in love with a man his love doesn't mean very much to you.

ARNOLD. It's so ungrateful. I've done everything in the world for you.

ELIZABETH. You've been very kind to me. But you've asked me to lead a life I don't like and that I'm not suited for. I'm awfully sorry to cause you pain, but now you must let me go.

ARNOLD. Nonsense! I'm a good deal older than you are and I think I have a little more sense. In your interests as well as in mine I'm not going to do anything of the sort.

ELIZABETH [with a smile]. How can you prevent me? You can't keep me under lock and key.

ARNOLD. Please don't talk to me as if I were a foolish child. You're my wife and you're going to remain my wife.

ELIZABETH. What sort of a life do you think we should lead? Do you think there'd be any more happiness for you than for me?

ARNOLD. But what is it precisely that you suggest?

ELIZABETH. Well, I want you to let me divorce you.

ARNOLD [astounded]. Me? Thank you very much. Are you under the impression I'm going to sacrifice my career for a whim of yours?

ELIZABETH. How will it do that?

ARNOLD. My seat's wobbly enough as it is. Do you think I'd be able to hold it if I were in a divorce case? Even if it were a put-up job, as most divorces are nowadays, it would damn me.

ELIZABETH. It's rather hard on a woman to be divorced.

ARNOLD [with sudden suspicion]. What do you mean by that? Are you in love with some one?

ELIZABETH. Yes.

ARNOLD. Who?

ELIZABETH. Teddie Luton.

[He is astonished for a moment, then bursts into a laugh.]

ARNOLD. My poor child, how can you be so ridiculous? Why, he hasn't a bob. He's a perfectly commonplace young man. It's so absurd I can't even be angry with you.

ELIZABETH. I've fallen desperately in love with him, Arnold.

ARNOLD. Well, you'd better fall desperately out.

ELIZABETH. He wants to marry me.

ARNOLD. I daresay he does. He can go to hell.

ELIZABETH. It's no good talking like that.

ARNOLD. Is he your lover?

ELIZABETH. No, certainly not.

ARNOLD. It shows that he's a mean skunk to take advantage of my hospitality to make love to you.

ELIZABETH. He's never even kissed me.

ARNOLD. I'd try telling that to the horse marines if I were you.

ELIZABETH. It's because I wanted to do nothing shabby that I told you straight out how things were.

ARNOLD. How long have you been thinking of this?

ELIZABETH. I've been in love with Teddie ever since I knew him.

ARNOLD. And you never thought of me at all, I suppose.

ELIZABETH. Oh, yes, I did. I was miserable. But I can't help myself. I wish I loved you, but I don't.

ARNOLD. I recommend you to think very carefully before you do anything foolish.

ELIZABETH. I have thought very carefully.

ARNOLD. By God! I don't know why I don't give you a sound hiding. I'm not sure if that wouldn't be the best thing to bring you to your senses.

ELIZABETH. Oh, Arnold, don't take it like that.

ARNOLD. How do you expect me to take it? You come to me quite calmly and say: "I've had enough of you. We've been married three years and I think I'd like to marry somebody else now. Shall I break up your home? What a bore for you! Do you mind my divorcing you! It'll smash up your career, will it? What a pity!" Oh, no, my girl, I may be a fool, but I'm not a damned fool.

ELIZABETH. Teddie is leaving here by the first train to-morrow. I warn you that I mean to join him as soon as he can make the necessary arrangements.

ARNOLD. Where is he?

ELIZABETH. I don't know. I suppose he's in his room.

[ARNOLD *goes to the door and calls.*]

ARNOLD. George!

[*For a moment he walks up and down the room impatiently.* ELIZABETH *watches him.*]

[*The* FOOTMAN *comes in.*]

FOOTMAN. Yes, sir.

ARNOLD. Tell Mr. Luton to come here at once.

ELIZABETH. Ask Mr. Luton if he wouldn't mind coming here for a moment.

FOOTMAN. Very good, madam.

[*Exit* FOOTMAN.]

ELIZABETH. What are you going to say to him?

ARNOLD. That's my business.

ELIZABETH. I wouldn't make a scene if I were you.

ARNOLD. I'm not going to make a scene. [*They wait in silence.*] Why did you insist on my mother coming here?

ELIZABETH. It seemed to me rather absurd to take up the attitude that I should be contaminated by her when . . .

ARNOLD [*interrupting*]. When you were proposing to do exactly the same thing. Well, now you've seen her what do you think of her? Do you think it's been a success? Is that the sort of woman a man would like his mother to be?

ELIZABETH. I've been ashamed. I've been so sorry. It all seemed dreadful and horrible. This morning I happened to notice a rose in the garden. It was all over-blown and bedraggled. It looked like a painted old woman. And I remembered that I'd looked at it a day or two ago. It was lovely then, fresh and blooming and fragrant. It may be hideous now, but that doesn't take away from the beauty it had once. That was real.

ARNOLD. Poetry, by God! As if this were the moment for poetry!

[TEDDIE *comes in. He has changed into a dinner jacket.*]

TEDDIE [*to* ELIZABETH]. Did you want me?

ARNOLD. *I* sent for you. [TEDDIE *looks from* ARNOLD *to* ELIZABETH. *He sees that something has happened.*] When would it be convenient for you to leave this house?

TEDDIE. I was proposing to go to-morrow morning. But I can very well go at once if you like.

ARNOLD. I do like.

TEDDIE. Very well. Is there anything else you wish to say to me?

ARNOLD. Do you think it was a very honourable thing to come down here and make love to my wife?

TEDDIE. No, I don't. I haven't been very happy about it. That's why I wanted to go away.

ARNOLD. Upon my word, you're cool.

TEDDIE. I'm afraid it's no good saying I'm sorry and that sort of thing. You know what the situation is.

ARNOLD. Is it true that you want to marry Elizabeth?

TEDDIE. Yes. I should like to marry her as soon as ever I can.

ARNOLD. Have you thought of me at all? Has it struck you that you're destroying my home and breaking up my happiness?

TEDDIE. I don't see how there could be much happiness for you if Elizabeth doesn't care for you.

ARNOLD. Let me tell you that I refuse to have my home broken up by a two penny-halfpenny adventurer who takes advantage of a foolish woman. I refuse to allow myself to be divorced. I can't prevent my wife from going off with you if she's determined to make a damned fool of herself, but this I tell you: nothing will induce me to divorce her.

ELIZABETH. Arnold, that would be monstrous.

TEDDIE. We could force you.

ARNOLD. How?

TEDDIE. If we went away together openly, you'd have to bring an action.

ARNOLD. Twenty-four hours after you leave this house I shall go down to Brighton with a chorus-girl. And neither you nor I will be able to get a divorce. We've had enough divorces in our family. And now get out, get out, get out!

[TEDDIE *looks uncertainly at* ELIZABETH.]

ELIZABETH [*with a little smile*]. Don't bother about me. I shall be all right.

ARNOLD. Get out! Get out!

ACT III

The Scene is the same as in the preceding Acts. It is the night of the same day as that on which takes place the action of the second Act.

[CHAMPION-CHENEY *and* ARNOLD, *both in dinner jackets, are discovered.* CHAMPION-CHENEY *is seated.* ARNOLD *walks restlessly up and down the room.*]

C.-C. I think, if you'll follow my advice to the letter, you'll probably work the trick.

ARNOLD. I don't like it, you know. It's against all my principles.

C.-C. My dear Arnold, we all hope that you have before you a distinguished political career. You can't learn too soon that the most useful thing about a principle is that it can always be sacrificed to expediency.

ARNOLD. But supposing it doesn't come off? Women are incalculable.

C.-C. Nonsense! Men are romantic. A woman will always sacrifice herself if you give her the opportunity. It is her favourite form of self-indulgence.

ARNOLD. I never know whether you're a humorist or a cynic, father.

C.-C. I'm neither, my dear boy; I'm merely a very truthful man. But people are so unused to the truth that they're apt to mistake it for a joke or a sneer.

ARNOLD [*irritably*]. It seems so unfair that this should happen to me.

C.-C. Keep your head, my boy, and do what I tell you.

[LADY KITTY *and* ELIZABETH *come in.* LADY KITTY *is in a gorgeous evening gown.*]

ELIZABETH. Where is Lord Porteous?

C.-C. He's on the terrace. He's smoking a cigar. [*Going to window.*] Hughie!

[PORTEOUS *comes in.*]

PORTEOUS [*with a grunt*]. Yes? Where's Mrs. Shenstone?

ELIZABETH. Oh, she had a headache. She's gone to bed.

[*When* PORTEOUS *comes in* LADY KITTY *with a very haughty air purses her lips and takes up an illustrated paper.* PORTEOUS *gives her an irritated look, takes another illustrated paper and sits himself down at the other end of the room. They are not on speaking terms.*]

C.-C. Arnold and I have just been down to my cottage.

ELIZABETH. I wondered where you'd gone.

C.-C. I came across an old photograph album this afternoon. I meant to bring it along before dinner, but I forgot, so we went and fetched it.

ELIZABETH. Oh, do let me see it! I love old photographs.

[*He gives her the album, and she, sitting down, puts it on her knees and begins to turn over the pages. He stands over her.* LADY KITTY *and* PORTEOUS *take surreptitious glances at one another.*]

C.-C. I thought it might amuse you to see what pretty women looked like five-and thirty years ago. That was the day of beautiful women.

ELIZABETH. Do you think they were more beautiful then than they are now?

C.-C. Oh, much. Now you see lots of pretty little things, but very few beautiful women.

ELIZABETH. Aren't their clothes funny?

C.-C. [*pointing to a photograph*]. That's Mrs. Langtry.

ELIZABETH. She has a lovely nose.

C.-C. She was the most wonderful thing you ever saw. Dowagers used to jump on chairs in order to get a good look at her when she came into a drawing-room. I was riding with her once, and we had to have the gates of the livery stable closed when she was getting on her horse because the crowd was so great.

ELIZABETH. And who's that?

C.-C. Lady Lonsdale. That's Lady Dudley.

ELIZABETH. This is an actress, isn't it?

C.-C. It is, indeed. Ellen Terry. By George! how I loved that woman!

ELIZABETH [*with a smile*]. Dear Ellen Terry!

C.-C. That's Bwabs. I never saw a smarter man in my life. And Oliver Montagu. Henry Manners with his eye-glass.

ELIZABETH. Nice-looking, isn't he? And this?

C.-C. That's Mary Anderson. I wish you could have seen her in *A Winter's Tale*. Her beauty just took your breath away. And look! There's Lady Randolph. Bernal Osborne — the wittiest man I ever knew.

ELIZABETH. I think it's too sweet. I love their absurd bustles and those tight sleeves.

C.-C. What figures they had! In those days a woman wasn't supposed to be as thin as a rail and as flat as a pancake.

ELIZABETH. Oh, but aren't they laced in? How could they bear it?

C.-C. They didn't play golf then, and nonsense like that, you know. They hunted, in a tall hat and a long black habit, and they were very gracious and charitable to the poor in the village.

ELIZABETH. Did the poor like it?

C.-C. They had a very thin time if they didn't. When they were in London they drove in the Park every afternoon, and they went to ten-course dinners, where they never met anybody they didn't know. And they had their box at the opera when Patti was singing or Madame Albani.

ELIZABETH. Oh, what a lovely little thing! Who on earth is that?

C.-C. That?

ELIZABETH. She looks so fragile, like a piece of exquisite china, with all those furs on and her face up against her muff, and the snow falling.

C.-C. Yes, there was quite a rage at that time for being taken in an artificial snowstorm.

ELIZABETH. What a sweet smile, so roguish and frank, and debonair! Oh, I wish I looked like that! Do tell me who it is!

C.-C. Don't you know?

ELIZABETH. No.

C.-C. Why — it's Kitty.

ELIZABETH. Lady Kitty! [*To* LADY KITTY.] Oh, my dear, do look! It's too ravishing. [*She takes the album over to her impulsively.*] Why didn't you tell me you looked like that? Everybody must have been in love with you.

[LADY KITTY *takes the album and looks at it. Then she lets it slip from her hands and covers her face with her hands. She is crying.*]

ELIZABETH [*in consternation*]. My dear, what's the matter? Oh, what have I done? I'm so sorry.

LADY KITTY. Don't, don't talk to me. Leave me alone. It's stupid of me.

[ELIZABETH *looks at her for a moment perplexed, then, turning round, slips her arm in* CHAMPION-CHENEY'S *and leads him out on to the terrace.*]

ELIZABETH [*as they are going, in a whisper*]. Did you do that on purpose?

[PORTEOUS *gets up and goes over to* LADY KITTY. *He puts his hand on her shoulder. They remain thus for a little while.*]

PORTEOUS. I'm afraid I was very rude to you before dinner, Kitty.

LADY KITTY [*taking his hand which is on her shoulder*]. It doesn't matter. I'm sure I was very exasperating.

PORTEOUS. I didn't mean what I said, you know.
LADY KITTY. Neither did I.
PORTEOUS. Of course I know that I'd never have been Prime Minister.
LADY KITTY. How can you talk such nonsense, Hughie? No one would have had a chance if you'd remained in politics.
PORTEOUS. I haven't the character.
LADY KITTY. You have more character than anyone I've ever met.
PORTEOUS. Besides, I don't know that I much wanted to be Prime Minister.
LADY KITTY. Oh, but I should have been so proud of you. Of course you'd have been Prime Minister.
PORTEOUS. I'd have given you India, you know. I think it would have been a very popular appointment.
LADY KITTY. I don't care twopence about India. I'd have been quite content with Western Australia.
PORTEOUS. My dear, you don't think I'd have let you bury yourself in Western Australia?
LADY KITTY. Or Barbadoes.
PORTEOUS. Never. It sounds like a cure for flat feet. I'd have kept you in London.
[*He picks up the album and is about to look at the photograph of Lady Kitty. She puts her hand over it.*]
LADY KITTY. No, don't look.
[*He takes her hand away.*]
PORTEOUS. Don't be so silly.
LADY KITTY. Isn't it hateful to grow old?
PORTEOUS. You know, you haven't changed much.
LADY KITTY [*enchanted*]. Oh, Hughie, how can you talk such nonsense?
PORTEOUS. Of course you're a little more mature, but that's all. A woman's all the better for being rather mature.
LADY KITTY. Do you really think that?
PORTEOUS. Upon my soul I do.
LADY KITTY. You're not saying it just to please me?
PORTEOUS. No, no.
LADY KITTY. Let me look at the photograph again. [*She takes the album and looks at the photograph complacently.*] The fact is, if your bones are good, age doesn't really matter. You'll always be beautiful.

PORTEOUS [*with a little smile, almost as if he were talking to a child*]. It was silly of you to cry.
LADY KITTY. It hasn't made my eyelashes run, has it?
PORTEOUS. Not a bit.
LADY KITTY. It's very good stuff I use now. They don't stick together either.
PORTEOUS. Look here, Kitty, how much longer do you want to stay here?
LADY KITTY. Oh, I'm quite ready to go whenever you like.
PORTEOUS. Clive gets on my nerves. I don't like the way he keeps hanging about you.
LADY KITTY [*surprised, rather amused, and delighted*]. Hughie, you don't mean to say you're jealous of poor Clive?
PORTEOUS. Of course I'm not jealous of him, but he does look at you in a way that I can't help thinking rather objectionable.
LADY KITTY. Hughie, you may throw me down stairs like Amy Robsart; you may drag me about the floor by the hair of my head; I don't care, you're jealous. I shall never grow old.
PORTEOUS. Damn it all, the man was your husband.
LADY KITTY. My dear Hughie, he never had your style. Why, the moment you come into a room everyone looks and says: "Who the devil is that?"
PORTEOUS. What? You think that, do you? Well, I daresay there's something in what you say. These damned Radicals can say what they like, but, by God, Kitty! when a man's a gentleman — well, damn it all, you know what I mean.
LADY KITTY. I think Clive has degenerated dreadfully since we left him.
PORTEOUS. What do you say to making a bee-line for Italy and going to San Michele?
LADY KITTY. Oh, Hughie! It's years since we were there.
PORTEOUS. Wouldn't you like to see it again — just once more?
LADY KITTY. Do you remember the first time we went? It was the most heavenly place I'd ever seen. We'd only left England a month, and I said I'd like to spend all my life there.

PORTEOUS. Of course I remember. And in a fortnight it was yours, lock, stock and barrel.

LADY KITTY. We were very happy there, Hughie.

PORTEOUS. Let's go back once more.

LADY KITTY. I daren't. It must be all peopled with the ghosts of our past. One should never go again to a place where one has been happy. It would break my heart.

PORTEOUS. Do you remember how we used to sit on the terrace of the old castle and look at the Adriatic? We might have been the only people in the world, you and I, Kitty.

LADY KITTY [*tragically*]. And we thought our love would last for ever.

[*Enter* CHAMPION-CHENEY.]

PORTEOUS. Is there any chance of bridge this evening?

C.-C. I don't think we can make up a four.

PORTEOUS. What a nuisance that boy went away like that! He wasn't a bad player.

C.-C. Teddie Luton?

LADY KITTY. I think it was very funny his going without saying good-bye to any-one.

C.-C. The young men of the present day are very casual.

PORTEOUS. I thought there was no train in the evening.

C.-C. There isn't. The last train leaves at 5.45.

PORTEOUS. How did he go then?

C.-C. He went.

PORTEOUS. Damned selfish I call it.

LADY KITTY [*intrigued*]. Why did he go, Clive?

[CHAMPION-CHENEY *looks at her for a moment reflectively.*]

C.-C. I have something very grave to say to you. Elizabeth wants to leave Arnold.

LADY KITTY. Clive! What on earth for?

C.-C. She's in love with Teddie Luton. That's why he went. The men of my family are really very unfortunate.

PORTEOUS. Does she want to run away with him?

LADY KITTY [*with consternation*]. My dear, what's to be done?

C.-C. I think you can do a great deal.

LADY KITTY. I? What?

C.-C. Tell her, tell her what it means.

[*He looks at her fixedly. She stares at him.*]

LADY KITTY. Oh, no, no!

C.-C. She's a child. Not for Arnold's sake. For her sake. You must.

LADY KITTY. You don't know what you're asking.

C.-C. Yes, I do.

LADY KITTY. Hughie, what shall I do?

PORTEOUS. Do what you like. I shall never blame you for anything.

[*The* FOOTMAN *comes in with a letter on a salver. He hesitates on seeing that* ELIZABETH *is not in the room.*]

C.-C. What is it?

FOOTMAN. I was looking for Mrs. Champion-Cheney, sir.

C.-C. She's not here. Is that a letter?

FOOTMAN. Yes, sir. It's just been sent up from the "Champion Arms."

C.-C. Leave it. I'll give it to Mrs. Cheney.

FOOTMAN. Very good, sir.

[*He brings the tray to* CLIVE, *who takes the letter. The* FOOTMAN *goes out.*]

PORTEOUS. Is the "Champion Arms" the local pub?

C.-C. [*looking at the letter*]. It's by way of being a hotel, but I never heard of any-one staying there.

LADY KITTY. If there was no train I suppose he had to go there.

C.-C. Great minds. I wonder what he has to write about! [*He goes to the door leading on to the garden.*] Elizabeth!

ELIZABETH [*outside*]. Yes.

C.-C. Here's a note for you.

[*There is silence. They wait for* ELIZABETH *to come. She enters.*]

ELIZABETH. It's lovely in the garden to-night.

C.-C. They've just sent this up from the "Champion Arms."

ELIZABETH. Thank you.

(*Without embarrassment she opens*

the letter. *They watch her while she reads it. It covers three pages. She puts it away in her bag.*]

LADY KITTY. Hughie, I wish you'd fetch me a cloak. I'd like to take a little stroll in the garden, but after thirty years in Italy I find these English summers rather chilly. [*Without a word* PORTEOUS *goes out.* ELIZABETH *is lost in thought.*] I want to talk to Elizabeth, Clive.

C.-C. I'll leave you. [*He goes out.*]

LADY KITTY. What does he say?

ELIZABETH. Who?

LADY KITTY. Mr. Luton.

ELIZABETH [*gives a little start. Then she looks at* LADY KITTY.] They've told you?

LADY KITTY. Yes. And now they have I think I knew it all along.

ELIZABETH. I don't expect you to have much sympathy for me. Arnold is your son.

LADY KITTY. So pitifully little.

ELIZABETH. I'm not suited for this sort of existence. Arnold wants me to take what he calls my place in Society. Oh, I get so bored with those parties in London. All those middle-aged painted women, in beautiful clothes, lolloping round ball-rooms with rather old young men. And the endless luncheons where they gossip about so-and-so's love affairs.

LADY KITTY. Are you very much in love with Mr. Luton?

ELIZABETH. I love him with all my heart.

LADY KITTY. And he?

ELIZABETH. He's never cared for any-one but me. He never will.

LADY KITTY. Will Arnold let you divorce him?

ELIZABETH. No, he won't hear of it. He refuses even to divorce me.

LADY KITTY. Why?

ELIZABETH. He thinks a scandal will re-vive all the old gossip.

LADY KITTY. Oh, my poor child!

ELIZABETH. It can't be helped. I'm quite willing to accept the consequences.

LADY KITTY. You don't know what it is to have a man tied to you only by his hon-our. When married people don't get on they can separate, but if they're not mar-ried it's impossible. It's a tie that only death can sever.

ELIZABETH. If Teddie stopped caring for me I shouldn't want him to stay with me for five minutes.

LADY KITTY. One says that when one's sure of a man's love, but when one isn't any more — oh, it's so different. In those cir-cumstances one's got to keep a man's love. It's the only thing one has.

ELIZABETH. I'm a human being. I can stand on my own feet.

LADY KITTY. Have you any money of your own?

ELIZABETH. None.

LADY KITTY. Then how can you stand on your own feet? You think I'm a silly, frivolous woman, but I've learned some-thing in a bitter school. They can make what laws they like, they can give us the suffrage, but when you come down to bed-rock it's the man who pays the piper who calls the tune. Woman will only be the equal of man when she earns her living in the same way that he does.

ELIZABETH [*smiling*]. It sounds rather funny to hear you talk like that.

LADY KITTY. A cook who marries a but-ler can snap her fingers in his face be-cause she can earn just as much as he can. But a woman in your position and a woman in mine will always be dependent on the men who keep them.

ELIZABETH. I don't want luxury. You don't know how sick I am of all this beauti-ful furniture. These over-decorated houses are like a prison in which I can't breathe. When I drive about in a Callot frock and a Rolls-Royce I envy the shop-girl in a coat and skirt whom I see jumping on the tail-board of a bus.

LADY KITTY. You mean that if need be you could earn your own living?

ELIZABETH. Yes.

LADY KITTY. What could you be? A nurse or a typist. It's nonsense. Luxury saps a woman's nerve. And when she's known it once it becomes a necessity.

ELIZABETH. That depends on the wo-man.

LADY KITTY. When we're young we think we're different from everyone else, but when we grow a little older we discover we're all very much of a muchness.

ELIZABETH. You're very kind to take so much trouble about me.

LADY KITTY. It breaks my heart to think that you're going to make the same pitiful mistake that I made.

ELIZABETH. Oh, don't say it was that, don't, don't.

LADY KITTY. Look at me, Elizabeth, and look at Hughie. Do you think it's been a success? If I had my time over again do you think I'd do it again? Do you think he would?

ELIZABETH. You see, you don't know how much I love Teddie.

LADY KITTY. And do you think I didn't love Hughie? Do you think he didn't love me?

ELIZABETH. I'm sure he did.

LADY KITTY. Oh, of course in the beginning it was heavenly. We felt so brave and adventurous and we were so much in love. The first two years were wonderful. People cut me, you know, but I didn't mind. I thought love was everything. It *is* a little uncomfortable when you come upon an old friend and go towards her eagerly, so glad to see her, and are met with an icy stare.

ELIZABETH. Do you think friends like that are worth having?

LADY KITTY. Perhaps they're not very sure of themselves. Perhaps they're honestly shocked. It's a test one had better not put one's friends to if one can help it. It's rather bitter to find how few one has.

ELIZABETH. But one has some.

LADY KITTY. Yes, they ask you to come and see them when they're quite certain no one will be there who might object to meeting you. Or else they say to you: "My dear, you know I'm devoted to you, and I wouldn't mind at all, but my girl's growing up — I'm sure you understand; you won't think it unkind of me if I don't ask you to the house?"

ELIZABETH [*smiling*]. That doesn't seem to me very serious.

LADY KITTY. At first I thought it rather a relief, because it threw Hughie and me together more. But you know, men are very funny. Even when they are in love they're not in love all day long. They want change and recreation.

ELIZABETH. I'm not inclined to blame them for that, poor dears.

LADY KITTY. Then we settled in Florence. And because we couldn't get the society we'd been used to we became used to the society we could get. Loose women and vicious men. Snobs who liked to patronize people with a handle to their names. Vague Italian Princes who were glad to borrow a few francs from Hughie and seedy countesses who liked to drive with me in the Cascine. And then Hughie began to hanker after his old life. He wanted to go big game shooting, but I dared not let him go. I was afraid he'd never come back.

ELIZABETH. But you knew he loved you.

LADY KITTY. Oh, my dear, what a blessed institution marriage is — for women, and what fools they are to meddle with it! The Church is so wise to take its stand on the indi — indi —

ELIZABETH. Solu —

LADY KITTY. Bility of marriage. Believe me, it's no joke when you have to rely only on yourself to keep a man. I could never afford to grow old. My dear, I'll tell you a secret that I've never told a living soul.

ELIZABETH. What is that?

LADY KITTY. My hair is not naturally this colour.

ELIZABETH. Really.

LADY KITTY. I touch it up. You would never have guessed, would you?

ELIZABETH. Never.

LADY KITTY. Nobody does. My dear, it's white, prematurely of course, but white. I always think it's a symbol of my life. Are you interested in symbolism? I think it's too wonderful.

ELIZABETH. I don't think I know very much about it.

LADY KITTY. However tired I've been I've had to be brilliant and gay. I've never let Hughie see the aching heart behind my smiling eyes.

ELIZABETH [*amused and touched*]. You poor dear.

LADY KITTY. And when I saw he was attracted by some one else the fear and the jealousy that seized me! You see, I didn't dare make a scene as I should have done if I'd been married — I had to pretend not to notice.

ELIZABETH [taken aback]. But do you mean to say he fell in love with anyone else?

LADY KITTY. Of course he did eventually.

ELIZABETH [hardly knowing what to say]. You must have been very unhappy.

LADY KITTY. Oh, I was, dreadfully. Night after night I sobbed my heart out when Hughie told me he was going to play cards at the club and I knew he was with that odious woman. Of course, it wasn't as if there weren't plenty of men who were only too anxious to console me. Men have always been attracted by me, you know.

ELIZABETH. Oh, of course, I can quite understand it.

LADY KITTY. But I had my self-respect to think of. I felt that whatever Hughie did I would do nothing that I should regret.

ELIZABETH. You must be very glad now.

LADY KITTY. Oh, yes. Notwithstanding all my temptations I've been absolutely faithful to Hughie in spirit.

ELIZABETH. I don't think I quite understand what you mean.

LADY KITTY. Well, there was a poor Italian boy, young Count Castel Giovanni, who was so desperately in love with me that his mother begged me not to be too cruel. She was afraid he'd go into a consumption. What could I do? And then, oh, years later, there was Antonio Melita. He said he'd shoot himself unless I — well, you understand I couldn't let the poor boy shoot himself.

ELIZABETH. D'you think he really would have shot himself?

LADY KITTY. Oh, one never knows, you know. Those Italians are so passionate. He was really rather a lamb. He had such beautiful eyes.

[ELIZABETH *looks at her for a long time and a certain horror seizes her of this dissolute, painted old woman.*]

ELIZABETH [hoarsely]. Oh, but I think that's — dreadful.

LADY KITTY. Are you shocked? One sacrifices one's life for love and then one finds that love doesn't last. The tragedy of love isn't death or separation. One gets over them. The tragedy of love is indifference.

[ARNOLD *comes in.*]

ARNOLD. Can I have a little talk with you, Elizabeth?

ELIZABETH. Of course.

ARNOLD. Shall we go for a stroll in the garden?

ELIZABETH. If you like.

LADY KITTY. No, stay here. I'm going out anyway. [*Exit* LADY KITTY.]

ARNOLD. I want you to listen to me for a few minutes, Elizabeth. I was so taken aback by what you told me just now that I lost my head. I was rather absurd and I beg your pardon. I said things I regret.

ELIZABETH. Oh, don't blame yourself. I'm sorry that I should have given you occasion to say them.

ARNOLD. I want to ask you if you've quite made up your mind to go.

ELIZABETH. Quite.

ARNOLD. Just now I seem to have said all that I didn't want to say and nothing that I did. I'm stupid and tongue-tied. I never told you how deeply I loved you.

ELIZABETH. Oh, Arnold!

ARNOLD. Please let me speak now. It's so very difficult. If I seemed absorbed in politics and the house, and so on, to the exclusion of my interest in you, I'm dreadfully sorry. I suppose it was absurd of me to think you would take my great love for granted.

ELIZABETH. But, Arnold, I'm not reproaching you.

ARNOLD. I'm reproaching myself. I've been tactless and neglectful. But I do ask you to believe that it hasn't been because I didn't love you. Can you forgive me?

ELIZABETH. I don't think that there's anything to forgive.

ARNOLD. It wasn't till to-day when you talked of leaving me that I realized how desperately in love with you I was.

ELIZABETH. After three years?

ARNOLD. I'm so proud of you. I admire you so much. When I see you at a party, so fresh and lovely, and everybody wondering at you, I have a sort of little thrill because you're mine, and afterwards I shall take you home.

ELIZABETH. Oh, Arnold, you're exaggerating.

ARNOLD. I can't imagine this house without you. Life seems on a sudden all empty and meaningless. Oh, Elizabeth, don't you love me at all?

ELIZABETH. It's much better to be honest. No.

ARNOLD. Doesn't my love mean anything to you?

ELIZABETH. I'm very grateful to you. I'm sorry to cause you pain. What would be the good of my staying with you when I should be wretched all the time?

ARNOLD. Do you love that man as much as all that? Does my unhappiness mean nothing to you?

ELIZABETH. Of course it does. It breaks my heart. You see, I never knew I meant so much to you. I'm so touched. And I'm so sorry, Arnold, really sorry. But I can't help myself.

ARNOLD. Poor child, it's cruel of me to torture you.

ELIZABETH. Oh, Arnold, believe me, I have tried to make the best of it. I've tried to love you, but I can't. After all, one either loves or one doesn't. Trying is no help. And now I'm at the end of my tether. I can't help the consequences — I must do what my whole self yearns for.

ARNOLD. My poor child, I'm so afraid you'll be unhappy. I'm so afraid you'll regret.

ELIZABETH. You must leave me to my fate. I hope you'll forget me and all the unhappiness I've caused you.

ARNOLD. [*There is a pause.* ARNOLD *walks up and down the room reflectively. He stops and faces her.*] If you love this man and want to go to him I'll do nothing to prevent you. My only wish is to do what is best for you.

ELIZABETH. Arnold, that's awfully kind of you. If I'm treating you badly, at least I want you to know that I'm grateful for all your kindness to me.

ARNOLD. But there's one favour I should like you to do me. Will you?

ELIZABETH. Oh, Arnold, of course I'll do anything I can.

ARNOLD. Teddie hasn't very much money. You've been used to a certain amount of luxury, and I can't bear to think that you should do without anything you've had. It would kill me to think that you were suffering any hardship or privation.

ELIZABETH. Oh, but Teddie can earn enough for our needs. After all, we don't want much money.

ARNOLD. I'm afraid my mother's life hasn't been very easy, but it's obvious that the only thing that's made it possible is that Porteous was rich. I want you to let me make you an allowance of two thousand a year.

ELIZABETH. Oh, no, I couldn't think of it. It's absurd.

ARNOLD. I beg you to accept it. You don't know what a difference it will make.

ELIZABETH. It's awfully kind of you, Arnold. It humiliates me to speak about it. Nothing would induce me to take a penny from you.

ARNOLD. Well, you can't prevent me from opening an account at my bank in your name. The money shall be paid in every quarter whether you touch it or not, and if you happen to want it, it will be there waiting for you.

ELIZABETH. You overwhelm me, Arnold. There's only one thing I want you to do for me. I should be very grateful if you would divorce me as soon as you possibly can.

ARNOLD. No, I won't do that. But I'll give you cause to divorce me.

ELIZABETH. You!

ARNOLD. Yes. But of course you'll have to be very careful for a bit. I'll put it through as quickly as possible, but I'm afraid you can't hope to be free for over six months.

ELIZABETH. But, Arnold, your seat and your political career!

ARNOLD. Oh, well, my father gave up

his seat under similar circumstances. He's got along very comfortably without politics.

ELIZABETH. But they're your whole life.

ARNOLD. After all one can't have it both ways. You can't serve God and Mammon. If you want to do the decent thing you have to be prepared to suffer for it.

ELIZABETH. But I don't want you to suffer for it.

ARNOLD. At first I rather hesitated at the scandal. But I daresay that was only weakness on my part. Under the circumstances I should have liked to keep out of the Divorce Court if I could.

ELIZABETH. Arnold, you're making me absolutely miserable.

ARNOLD. What you said before dinner was quite right. It's nothing for a man, but it makes so much difference to a woman. Naturally I must think of you first.

ELIZABETH. That's absurd. It's out of the question. Whatever there's to pay I must pay it.

ARNOLD. It's not very much I'm asking you, Elizabeth.

ELIZABETH. I'm taking everything from you.

ARNOLD. It's the only condition I make. My mind is absolutely made up. I will never divorce you, but I will enable you to divorce me.

ELIZABETH. Oh, Arnold, it's cruel to be so generous.

ARNOLD. It's not generous at all. It's the only way I have of showing you how deep and passionate and sincere my love is for you. [*There is a silence. He holds out his hand.*] Good-night. I have a great deal of work to do before I go to bed.

ELIZABETH. Good-night.

ARNOLD. Do you mind if I kiss you?

ELIZABETH [*with agony*]. Oh, Arnold!

[*He gravely kisses her on the forehead and then goes out.* ELIZABETH *stands lost in thought. She is shattered.*]

[LADY KITTY *and* PORTEOUS *come in.* LADY KITTY *wears a cloak.*]

LADY KITTY. You're alone, Elizabeth?

ELIZABETH. That note you asked me about, Lady Kitty, from Teddie ...

LADY KITTY. Yes?

ELIZABETH. He wanted to have a talk with me before he went away. He's waiting for me in the summer house by the tennis court. Would Lord Porteous mind going down and asking him to come here?

PORTEOUS. Certainly. Certainly.

ELIZABETH. Forgive me for troubling you. But it's very important.

PORTEOUS. No trouble at all.

[*He goes out.*]

LADY KITTY. Hughie and I will leave you alone.

ELIZABETH. But I don't want to be left alone. I want you to stay.

LADY KITTY. What are you going to say to him?

ELIZABETH [*desperately*]. Please don't ask me questions. I'm so frightfully unhappy.

LADY KITTY. My poor child!

ELIZABETH. Oh, isn't life rotten? Why can't one be happy without making other people unhappy?

LADY KITTY. I wish I knew how to help you. I'm simply devoted to you. [*She hunts about in her mind for something to do or say.*] Would you like my lip-stick?

ELIZABETH [*smiling through her tears*]. Thanks. I never use one.

LADY KITTY. Oh, but just try. It's such a comfort when you're in trouble.

[*Enter* PORTEOUS *and* TEDDIE.]

PORTEOUS. I brought him. He said he'd be damned if he'd come.

LADY KITTY. When a lady sent for him? Are these the manners of the young men of to-day?

TEDDIE. When you've been solemnly kicked out of a house once I think it seems rather pushing to come back again as though nothing had happened.

ELIZABETH. Teddie, I want you to be serious.

TEDDIE. Darling, I had such a rotten dinner at that pub. If you ask me to be serious on the top of that I shall cry.

ELIZABETH. Don't be idiotic, Teddie. [*Her voice faltering.*] I'm so utterly wretched.

[*He looks at her for a moment gravely.*]

TEDDIE. What is it?

ELIZABETH. I can't come away with you, Teddie.

TEDDIE. Why not?

ELIZABETH [*looking away in embarrassment*]. I don't love you enough.

TEDDIE. Fiddle!

ELIZABETH [*with a flash of anger*]. Don't say "Fiddle" to me.

TEDDIE. I shall say exactly what I like to you.

ELIZABETH. I won't be bullied.

TEDDIE. Now look here, Elizabeth, you know perfectly well that I'm in love with you, and I know perfectly well that you're in love with me. So what are you talking nonsense for?

ELIZABETH [*her voice breaking*]. I can't say it if you're cross with me.

TEDDIE [*smiling very tenderly*]. I'm not cross with you, silly.

ELIZABETH. It's harder still when you're being rather an owl.

TEDDIE [*with a chuckle*]. Am I mistaken in thinking you're not very easy to please?

ELIZABETH. Oh, it's monstrous. I was all wrought up and ready to do anything, and now you've thoroughly put me out. I feel like a great big fat balloon that some one has put a long pin into. [*With a sudden look at him.*] Have you done it on purpose?

TEDDIE. Upon my soul I don't know what you're talking about.

ELIZABETH. I wonder if you're really much cleverer than I think you are.

TEDDIE [*taking her hands and making her sit down*]. Now tell me exactly what you want to say. By the way, do you want Lady Kitty and Lord Porteous to be here?

ELIZABETH. Yes.

LADY KITTY. Elizabeth asked us to stay.

TEDDIE. Oh, I don't mind, bless you. I only thought you might feel rather in the way.

LADY KITTY [*frigidly*]. A gentlewoman never feels in the way, Mr. Luton.

TEDDIE. Won't you call me Teddie? Everybody does, you know.

[LADY KITTY *tries to give him a withering look, but she finds it very difficult to prevent herself from smiling.* TEDDIE *strokes* ELIZABETH'S *hands. She draws them away.*]

ELIZABETH. No, don't do that. Teddie, it wasn't true when I said I didn't love you. Of course I love you. But Arnold loves me, too. I didn't know how much.

TEDDIE. What has he been saying to you?

ELIZABETH. He's been very good to me, and so kind. I didn't know he could be so kind. He offered to let me divorce him.

TEDDIE. That's very decent of him.

ELIZABETH. But don't you see, it ties my hands. How can I accept such a sacrifice? I should never forgive myself if I profited by his generosity.

TEDDIE. If another man and I were devilish hungry and there was only one mutton chop between us, and he said, "You eat it," I wouldn't waste a lot of time arguing. I'd wolf it before he changed his mind.

ELIZABETH. Don't talk like that. It maddens me. I'm trying to do the right thing.

TEDDIE. You're not in love with Arnold; you're in love with me. It's idiotic to sacrifice your life for a slushy sentiment.

ELIZABETH. After all, I did marry him.

TEDDIE. Well, you made a mistake. A marriage without love is no marriage at all.

ELIZABETH. *I* made the mistake. Why should he suffer for it? If anyone has to suffer it's only right that I should.

TEDDIE. What sort of a life do you think it would be with him? When two people are married it's very difficult for one of them to be unhappy without making the other unhappy too.

ELIZABETH. I can't take advantage of his generosity.

TEDDIE. I daresay he'll get a lot of satisfaction out of it.

ELIZABETH. You're being beastly, Teddie. He was simply wonderful. I never knew he had it in him. He was really noble.

TEDDIE. You are talking rot, Elizabeth.

ELIZABETH. I wonder if you'd be capable of acting like that.

TEDDIE. Acting like what?

ELIZABETH. What would you do if I

were married to you and came and told you I loved somebody else and wanted to leave you?

TEDDIE. You have very pretty blue eyes, Elizabeth. I'd black first one and then the other. And after that we'd see.

ELIZABETH. You damned brute!

TEDDIE. I've often thought I wasn't quite a gentleman. Had it ever struck you?

[*They look at one another for a while.*]

ELIZABETH. You know, you are taking an unfair advantage of me. I feel as if I came to you quite unsuspectingly and when I wasn't looking you kicked me on the shins.

TEDDIE. Don't you think we'd get on rather well together?

PORTEOUS. Elizabeth's a fool if she don't stick to her husband. It's bad enough for the man, but for the woman — it's damnable. I hold no brief for Arnold. He plays bridge like a fool. Saving your presence, Kitty, I think he's a prig.

LADY KITTY. Poor dear, his father was at his age. I daresay he'll grow out of it.

PORTEOUS. But you stick to him, Elizabeth, stick to him. Man is a gregarious animal. We're members of a herd. If we break the herd's laws we suffer for it. And we suffer damnably.

LADY KITTY. Oh, Elizabeth, my dear child, don't go. It's not worth it. It's not worth it. I tell you that, and I've sacrificed everything to love. [*A pause.*]

ELIZABETH. I'm afraid.

TEDDIE [*in a whisper*]. Elizabeth.

ELIZABETH. I can't face it. It's asking too much of me. Let's say good-bye to one another, Teddie. It's the only thing to do. And have pity on me. I'm giving up all my hope of happiness.

[*He goes up to her and looks into her eyes.*]

TEDDIE. But I wasn't offering you happiness. I don't think my sort of love tends to happiness. I'm jealous. I'm not a very easy man to get on with. I'm often out of temper and irritable. I should be fed to the teeth with you sometimes, and so would you be with me. I daresay we'd fight like cat and dog, and sometimes we'd hate each other. Often you'd be wretched and bored stiff and lonely, and often you'd be frightfully homesick, and then you'd regret all you'd lost. Stupid women would be rude to you because we'd run away together. And some of them would cut you. I don't offer you peace and quietness. I offer you unrest and anxiety. I don't offer you happiness. I offer you love.

ELIZABETH [*stretching out her arms*]. You hateful creature, I absolutely adore you!

[*He throws his arms round her and kisses her passionately on the lips.*]

LADY KITTY. Of course the moment he said he'd give her a black eye I knew it was finished.

PORTEOUS [*good-humouredly*]. You are a fool, Kitty.

LADY KITTY. I know I am, but I can't help it.

TEDDIE. Let's make a bolt for it now.

ELIZABETH. Shall we?

TEDDIE. This minute.

PORTEOUS. You're damned fools, both of you, damned fools! If you like you can have my car.

TEDDIE. That's awfully kind of you. As a matter of fact I got it out of the garage. It's just along the drive.

PORTEOUS [*indignantly*]. How do you mean, you got it out of the garage?

TEDDIE. Well, I thought there'd be a lot of bother, and it seemed to me the best thing would be for Elizabeth and me not to stand upon the order of our going, you know. Do it now. An excellent motto for a business man.

PORTEOUS. Do you mean to say you were going to steal my car?

TEDDIE. Not exactly. I was only going to bolshevise it, so to speak.

PORTEOUS. I'm speechless. I'm absolutely speechless.

TEDDIE. Hang it all, I couldn't carry Elizabeth all the way to London. She's so damned plump.

ELIZABETH. You dirty dog!

PORTEOUS [*spluttering*]. Well, well, well! ... [*Helplessly.*] I like him, Kitty, it's no good pretending I don't. I like him.

TEDDIE. The moon's shining, Elizabeth. We'll drive all through the night.

PORTEOUS. They'd better go to San Michele. I'll wire to have it got ready for them.

LADY KITTY. That's where we went when Hughie and I ... [*Faltering.*] Oh, you dear things, how I envy you!

PORTEOUS [*mopping his eyes*]. Now don't cry, Kitty. Confound you, don't cry.

TEDDIE. Come, darling.

ELIZABETH. But I can't go like this.

TEDDIE. Nonsense! Lady Kitty will lend you her cloak. Won't you?

LADY KITTY [*taking it off*]. You're capable of tearing it off my back if I don't.

TEDDIE [*putting the cloak on* ELIZABETH]. And we'll buy you a tooth-brush in London in the morning.

LADY KITTY. She must write a note for Arnold. I'll put it on her pincushion.

TEDDIE. Pincushion be blowed! Come, darling. We'll drive through the dawn and through the sunrise.

ELIZABETH [*kissing* LADY KITTY *and* PORTEOUS]. Good-bye. Good-bye.

[TEDDIE *stretches out his hand and she takes it. Hand in hand they go out into the night.*]

LADY KITTY. Oh, Hughie, how it all comes back to me! Will they suffer all we suffered? And have we suffered all in vain?

PORTEOUS. My dear, I don't know that in life it matters so much what you do as what you are. No one can learn by the experience of another because no circumstances are quite the same. If we made rather a hash of things perhaps it was because we were rather trivial people. You can do anything in this world if you're prepared to take the consequences, and consequences depend on character.

[*Enter* CHAMPION-CHENEY, *rubbing his hands. He is as pleased as Punch.*]

C.-C. Well, I think I've settled the hash of that young man.

LADY KITTY. Oh!

C.-C. You have to get up very early in the morning to get the better of your humble servant.

[*There is the sound of a car starting.*]

LADY KITTY. What is that?

C.-C. It sounds like a car. I expect it's your chauffeur taking one of the maids for a joy-ride.

PORTEOUS. Whose hash are you talking about?

C.-C. Mr. Edward Luton's, my dear Hughie. I told Arnold exactly what to do and he's done it. What makes a prison? Why, bars and bolts. Remove them and a prisoner won't want to escape. Clever, I flatter myself.

PORTEOUS. You were always that, Clive, but at the moment you're obscure.

C.-C. I told Arnold to go to Elizabeth and tell her she could have her freedom. I told him to sacrifice himself all along the line. I know what women are. The moment every obstacle was removed to her marriage with Teddie Luton, half the allurement was gone.

LADY KITTY. Arnold did that?

C.-C. He followed my instructions to the letter. I've just seen him. She's shaken. I'm willing to bet five hundred pounds to a penny that she won't bolt. A downy old bird, eh? Downy's the word. Downy.

[*He begins to laugh. They laugh, too. Presently they are all three in fits of laughter.*]

[THE CURTAIN FALLS]

THE HAIRY APE
A COMEDY OF ANCIENT AND MODERN LIFE
IN EIGHT SCENES
BY EUGENE O'NEILL

COPYRIGHT, 1922, BY BONI & LIVERIGHT, INC.

ALL RIGHTS RESERVED

Reprinted by special arrangement

Caution — All persons are hereby warned that the play published in this volume is fully protected under the copyright laws of the United States and all foreign countries, and is subject to royalty, and any one presenting said play in any form whatsoever without consent of the Author or his recognized agents will be liable to the penalties by law provided. Applications for the acting rights must be made to the American Play Company, Inc., 44 West 42d Street, New York City.

CHARACTERS

ROBERT SMITH, "YANK"
PADDY
LONG
MILDRED DOUGLAS
HER AUNT
SECOND ENGINEER
A GUARD
A SECRETARY OF AN ORGANIZATION
STOKERS, LADIES, GENTLEMEN, ETC.

SCENES

SCENE   I: The firemen's forecastle of an ocean liner — an hour after sailing from New York.
SCENE   II: Section of promenade deck, two days out — morning.
SCENE   III: The stokehole. A few minutes later.
SCENE   IV: Same as Scene I. Half an hour later.
SCENE   V: Fifth Avenue, New York. Three weeks later.
SCENE   VI: An island near the city. The next night.
SCENE   VII: In the city. About a month later.
SCENE VIII: In the city. Twilight of the next day.

TIME — The Modern.

THE HAIRY APE

SCENE ONE

SCENE — *The firemen's forecastle of a transatlantic liner an hour after sailing from New York for the voyage across. Tiers of narrow, steel bunks, three deep, on all sides. An entrance in rear. Benches on the floor before the bunks. The room is crowded with men, shouting, cursing, laughing, singing — a confused, inchoate uproar swelling into a sort of unity, a meaning — the bewildered, furious, baffled defiance of a beast in a cage. Nearly all the men are drunk. Many bottles are passed from hand to hand. All are dressed in dungaree pants, heavy ugly shoes. Some wear singlets, but the majority are stripped to the waist.*

The treatment of this scene, or of any other scene in the play, should by no means be naturalistic. The effect sought after is a cramped space in the bowels of a ship, imprisoned by white steel. The lines of bunks, the uprights supporting them, cross each other like the steel framework of a cage. The ceiling crushes down upon the men's heads. They cannot stand upright. This accentuates the natural stooping posture which shovelling coal and the resultant over-development of back and shoulder muscles have given them. The men themselves should resemble those pictures in which the appearance of Neanderthal Man is guessed at. All are hairy-chested, with long arms of tremendous power, and low, receding brows above their small, fierce, resentful eyes. All the civilized white races are represented, but except for the slight differentiation in color of hair, skin, eyes, all these men are alike.

The curtain rises on a tumult of sound. YANK *is seated in the foreground. He seems broader, fiercer, more truculent, more powerful, more sure of himself than the rest. They respect his superior strength — the grudging respect of fear. Then, too, he represents to them a self-expression, the very last word in what they are, their most highly developed individual.*

VOICES. Gif me trink dere, you!
'Ave a wet!
Salute!
Gesundheit!
Skoal!
Drunk as a lord, God stiffen you!
Here's how!
Luck!
Pass back that bottle, damn you!
Pourin' it down his neck!
Ho, Froggy! Where the devil have you been?
La Touraine.
I hit him smash in yaw, py Gott!
Jenkins — the First — he's a rotten swine —
And the coppers nabbed him — and I run —
I like peer better. It don't pig head gif you.
A slut, I'm sayin'! She robbed me aslape —
To hell with 'em all!
You're a bloody liar!
Say dot again!
[*Commotion. Two men about to fight are pulled apart.*]
No scrappin' now!
To-night —
See who's the best man!
Bloody Dutchman!
To-night on the for'ard square.

I'll bet on Dutchy.
He packa da wallop, I tella you!
Shut up, Wop!
No fightin', maties. We're all chums, ain't we?
[*A voice starts bawling a song.*]

"Beer, beer, glorious beer!
Fill yourselves right up to here."

YANK [*for the first time seeming to take notice of the uproar about him, turns around threateningly — in a tone of contemptuous authority*]. Choke off dat noise! Where d'yuh get dat beer stuff? Beer, hell! Beer's for goils — and Dutchmen. Me for somep'n wit a kick to it! Gimme a drink, one of youse guys. [*Several bottles are eagerly offered. He takes a tremendous gulp at one of them; then, keeping the bottle in his hand, glares belligerently at the owner, who hastens to acquiesce in this robbery by saying:*] All righto, Yank. Keep it and have another.

[YANK *contemptuously turns his back on the crowd again. For a second there is an embarrassed silence. Then* —]

VOICES. We must be passing the Hook.
She's beginning to roll to it.
Six days in hell — and then Southampton.
Py Yesus, I vish somepody take my first vatch for me!
Gittin' seasick, Square-head?
Drink up and forget it!
What's in your bottle?
Gin.
Dot's nigger trink.
Absinthe? It's doped. You'll go off your chump, Froggy!
Cochon!
Whiskey, that's the ticket!
Where's Paddy?
Going asleep.
Sing us that whiskey song, Paddy.

[*They all turn to an old, wizened Irishman who is dozing, very drunk, on the benches forward. His face is extremely monkey-like with all the sad, patient pathos of that animal in his small eyes.*]

Singa da song, Caruso Pat!
He's gettin' old. The drink is too much for him.
He's too drunk.

PADDY [*blinking about him, starts to his feet resentfully, swaying, holding on to the edge of a bunk*]. I'm never too drunk to sing. 'Tis only when I'm dead to the world I'd be wishful to sing at all. [*With a sort of sad contempt.*] "Whiskey Johnny," ye want? A chanty, ye want? Now that's a queer wish from the ugly like of you, God help you. But no matther. [*He starts to sing in a thin, nasal, doleful tone:*]

Oh, whiskey is the life of man!
Whiskey! O Johnny!
      [*They all join in on this.*]
Oh, whiskey is the life of man!
Whiskey for my Johnny!
      [*Again chorus*]
Oh, whiskey drove my old man mad!
Whiskey! O Johnny!
Oh, whiskey drove my old man mad!
Whiskey for my Johnny!

YANK [*again turning around scornfully*]. Aw hell! Nix on dat old sailing ship stuff! All dat bull's dead, see? And you're dead, too, yuh damned old Harp, on'y yuh don't know it. Take it easy, see. Give us a rest. Nix on de loud noise. [*With a cynical grin.*] Can't youse see I'm tryin' to tink?

ALL [*repeating the word after him as one with the same cynical amused mockery*]. Think!

[*The chorused word has a brazen metallic quality as if their throats were phonograph horns. It is followed by a general uproar of hard, barking laughter.*]

VOICES. Don't be cracking your head wid ut, Yank.
You gat headache, py yingo!
One thing about it — it rhymes with drink!
Ha, ha, ha!
Drink, don't think!
Drink, don't think!
Drink, don't think!

[*A whole chorus of voices has taken up this refrain, stamping on the floor, pounding on the benches with fists.*]

THE HAIRY APE

YANK. [*taking a gulp from his bottle — good-naturedly*]. Awright. Can de noise. I got yuh de foist time.
[*The uproar subsides. A very drunken sentimental tenor begins to sing:*]

"Far away in Canada,
Far across the sea,
There's a lass who fondly waits
Making a home for me —"

YANK [*fiercely contemptuous*]. Shut up, yuh lousey boob! Where d'yuh get dat tripe? Home? Home, hell! I'll make a home for yuh! I'll knock yuh dead. Home. T'hell wit home! Where d'yuh get dat tripe? Dis is home, see? What d'yuh want wit home? [*Proudly.*] I runned away from mine when I was a kid. On'y too glad to beat it, dat was me. Home was lickings for me, dat's all. But yuh can bet your shoit noone ain't never licked me since! Wanter try it, any of youse? Huh! I guess not. [*In a more placated but still contemptuous tone.*] Goils waitin' for yuh, huh? Aw, hell! Dat's all tripe. Dey don't wait for noone. Dey'd double-cross yuh for a nickel. Dey're all tarts, get me? Treat 'em rough, dat's me. To hell wit 'em. Tarts, dat's what, de whole bunch of 'em.

LONG [*very drunk, jumps on a bench excitedly, gesticulating with a bottle in his hand*]. Listen 'ere, Comrades! Yank 'ere is right. 'E says this 'ere stinkin' ship is our 'ome. And 'e says as 'ome is 'ell. And 'e's right! This is 'ell. We lives in 'ell, Comrades — and right enough we'll die in it. [*Raging.*] And who's ter blame, I arsks yer? We ain't. We wasn't born this rotten way. All men is born free and ekal. That's in the bleedin' Bible, maties. But what d'they care for the Bible — them lazy, bloated swine what travels first cabin? Them's the ones. They dragged us down 'til we're on'y wage slaves in the bowels of a bloody ship, sweatin', burnin' up, eatin' coal dust! Hit's them's ter blame — the damned capitalist clarss!
[*There had been a gradual murmur of contemptuous resentment rising among the men until now he is interrupted by a storm of catcalls, hisses, boos, hard laughter.*]

VOICES. Turn it off!
Shut up!
Sit down!
Closa da face!
Tamn fool! (*Etc.*)

YANK [*standing up and glaring at* LONG]. Sit down before I knock yuh down! [LONG *makes haste to efface himself.* YANK *goes on contemptuously.*] De Bible, huh? De Cap'tlist class, huh? Aw nix on dat Salvation Army-Socialist bull. Git a soap-box! Hire a hall! Come and be saved, huh? Jerk us to Jesus, huh? Aw g'wan! I've listened to lots of guys like you, see. Yuh're all wrong. Wanter know what I t'ink? Yuh ain't no good for noone. Yuh're de bunk. Yuh ain't got no noive, get me? Yuh're yellow, dat's what. Yellow, dat's you. Say! What's dem slobs in de foist cabin got to do wit us? We're better men dan dey are, ain't we? Sure! One of us guys could clean up de whole mob wit one mit. Put one of 'em down here for one watch in de stokehole, what'd happen? Dey'd carry him off on a stretcher. Dem boids don't amount to nothin'. Dey're just baggage. Who makes dis old tub run? Ain't it us guys? Well den, we belong, don't we? We belong and dey don't. Dat's all. [*A loud chorus of approval.* YANK *goes on.*] As for dis bein' hell — aw, nuts! Yuh lost your noive, dat's what. Dis is a man's job, get me? It belongs. It runs dis tub. No stiffs need apply. But yuh're a stiff, see? Yuh're yellow, dat's you.

VOICES [*with a great hard pride in them*].
Righto!
A man's job!
Talk is cheap, Long.
He never could hold up his end.
Divil take him!
Yank's right. We make it go.
Py Gott, Yank say right ting!
We don't need noone cryin' over us.
Makin' speeches.
Throw him out!
Yellow!
Chuck him overboard!
I'll break his jaw for him!

[*They crowd around* LONG *threateningly.*]

YANK [*half good-natured again — contemptuously*]. Aw, take it easy. Leave him alone. He ain't woith a punch. Drink up. Here's how, whoever owns dis. [*He takes a long swallow from his bottle. All drink with him. In a flash all is hilarious amiability again, back-slapping, loud talk, etc.*]

PADDY [*who has been sitting in a blinking, melancholy daze, suddenly cries out in a voice full of old sorrow*]. We belong to this, you're saying? We make the ship to go, you're saying? Yerra then, that Almighty God have pity on us! [*His voice runs into the wail of a keen, he rocks back and forth on his bench. The men stare at him, startled and impressed in spite of themselves.*] Oh, to be back in the fine days of my youth, ochone! Oh, there was fine beautiful ships them days — clippers wid tall masts touching the sky — fine strong men in them — men that was sons of the sea as if 'twas the mother that bore them. Oh, the clean skins of them, and the clear eyes, the straight backs and full chests of them! Brave men they was, and bold men surely! We'd be sailing out, bound down round the Horn maybe. We'd be making sail in the dawn, with a fair breeze, singing a chanty song wid no care to it. And astern the land would be sinking low and dying out, but we'd give it no heed but a laugh, and never a look behind. For the day that was, was enough, for we was free men — and I'm thinking 'tis only slaves do be giving heed to the day that's gone or the day to come — until they're old like me. [*With a sort of religious exaltation.*] Oh, to be scudding south again wid the power of the Trade Wind driving her on steady through the nights and the days! Full sail on her! Nights and days! Nights when the foam of the wake would be flaming wid fire, when the sky'd be blazing and winking wid stars. Or the full of the moon maybe. Then you'd see her driving through the gray night, her sails stretching aloft all silver and white, not a sound on the deck, the lot of us dreaming dreams, till you'd believe 'twas no real ship at all you was on but a ghost ship like the Flying Dutchman they say does be roaming the seas forevermore widout touching a port. And there was the days, too. A warm sun on the clean decks. Sun warming the blood of you, and wind over the miles of shiny green ocean like strong drink to your lungs. Work — aye, hard work — but who'd mind that at all? Sure, you worked under the sky and 'twas work wid skill and daring to it. And wid the day done, in the dog watch, smoking me pipe at ease, the lookout would be raising land maybe, and we'd see the mountains of South Americy wid the red fire of the setting sun painting their white tops and the clouds floating by them! [*His tone of exaltation ceases. He goes on mournfully.*] Yerra, what's the use of talking? 'Tis a dead man's whisper. [*To* YANK *resentfully.*] 'Twas them days men belonged to ships, not now. 'Twas them days a ship was part of the sea, and a man was part of a ship, and the sea joined all together and made it one. [*Scornfully.*] Is it one wid this you'd be, Yank — black smoke from the funnels smudging the sea, smudging the decks — the bloody engines pounding and throbbing and shaking — wid divil a sight of sun or a breath of clean air — choking our lungs wid coal dust — breaking our backs and hearts in the hell of the stokehole — feeding the bloody furnace — feeding our lives along wid the coal, I'm thinking — caged in by steel from a sight of the sky like bloody apes in the Zoo! [*With a harsh laugh.*] Ho-ho, divil mend you! Is it to belong to that you're wishing? Is it a flesh and blood wheel of the engines you'd be?

YANK [*who has been listening with a contemptuous sneer, barks out the answer*]. Sure ting! Dat's me! What about it?

PADDY [*as if to himself — with great sorrow*]. Me time is past due. That a great wave wid sun in the heart of it may sweep me over the side sometime I'd be dreaming of the days that's gone!

YANK. Aw, yuh crazy Mick! [*He springs to his feet and advances on* PADDY *threateningly — then stops, fighting some queer struggle within himself — lets his hands fall to his sides — contemptuously.*] Aw, take it

THE HAIRY APE

easy. Yuh're aw right, at dat. Yuh're bugs, dat's all — nutty as a cuckoo. All dat tripe yuh been pullin' — Aw, dat's all right. On'y it's dead, get me? Yuh don't belong no more, see. Yuh don't get de stuff. Yuh're too old. [*Disgustedly.*] But aw say, come up for air onct in a while, can't yuh? See what's happened since yuh croaked. [*He suddenly bursts forth vehemently, growing more and more excited.*] Say! Sure! Sure I meant it! What de hell — Say, lemme talk! Hey! Hey, you old Harp! Hey, youse guys! Say, listen to me — wait a moment — I gotter talk, see. I belong and he don't. He's dead but I'm livin'. Listen to me! Sure I'm part of de engines! Why de hell not! Dey move, don't dey? Dey're speed, ain't dey? Dey smash trou, don't dey? Twenty-five knots a hour! Dat's goin' some! Dat's new stuff! Dat belongs! But him, he's too old. He gets dizzy. Say, listen. All dat crazy tripe about nights and days; all dat crazy tripe about stars and moons; all dat crazy tripe about suns and winds, fresh air and de rest of it — Aw hell, dat's all a dope dream! Hittin' de pipe of de past, dat's what he's doin'. He's old and don't belong no more. But me, I'm young! I'm in de pink! I move wit it! It, get me! I mean de ting dat's de guts of all dis. It ploughs trou all de tripe he's been sayin'. It blows dat up! It knocks dat dead! It slams dat offen de face of de oith! It, get me! De engines and de coal and de smoke and all de rest of it! He can't breathe and swallow coal dust, but I kin, see? Dat's fresh air for me! Dat's food for me! I'm new, get me? Hell in de stokehole? Sure! It takes a man to work in hell. Hell, sure, dat's my fav'rite climate. I eat it up! I git fat on it! It's me makes it hot! It's me makes it roar! It's me makes it move! Sure, on'y for me everyting stops. It all goes dead, get me? De noise and smoke and all de engines movin' de woild, dey stop. Dere ain't nothin' no more! Dat's what I'm sayin'. Everyting else dat makes de woild move, somep'n makes it move. It can't move witout somep'n else, see? Den yuh get down to me. I'm at de bottom, get me! Dere ain't nothin' foither. I'm de end. I'm de start! I start somep'n and de woild moves! It — dat's me! — de new dat's moiderin' de old! I'm de ting in coal dat makes it boin; I'm steam and oil for de engines; I'm de ting in noise dat makes yuh hear it; I'm smoke and express trains and steamers and factory whistles; I'm de ting in gold dat makes it money! And I'm what makes iron into steel! Steel, dat stands for de whole ting! And I'm steel — steel — steel! I'm de muscles in steel, de punch behind it! [*As he says this he pounds with his fist against the steel bunks. All the men, roused to a pitch of frenzied self-glorification by his speech, do likewise. There is a deafening metallic roar, through which* YANK'S *voice can be heard bellowing.*] Slaves, hell! We run de whole woiks. All de rich guys dat tink dey're somep'n, dey ain't nothin'! Dey don't belong. But us guys, we're in de move, we're at de bottom, de whole ting is us! [PADDY *from the start of* YANK'S *speech has been taking one gulp after another from his bottle, at first frightenedly, as if he were afraid to listen, then desperately, as if to drown his senses, but finally has achieved complete indifferent, even amused, drunkenness.* YANK *sees his lips moving. He quells the uproar with a shout.*] Hey, youse guys, take it easy! Wait a moment! De nutty Harp is sayin' somep'n.

PADDY [*is heard now — throws his head back with a mocking burst of laughter*]. Ho-ho-ho-ho-ho —

YANK [*drawing back his fist, with a snarl*]. Aw! Look out who yuh're givin' the bark!

PADDY [*begins to sing the "Miller of Dee" with enormous good-nature*].

"I care for nobody, no, not I,
And nobody cares for me."

YANK [*good-natured himself in a flash, interrupts* PADDY *with a slap on the bare back like a report*]. Dat's de stuff! Now yuh're gettin' wise to somep'n. Care for nobody, dat's de dope! To hell wit 'em all! And nix on nobody else carin'. I kin care for myself, get me! [*Eight bells sound, muffled, vibrating through the steel walls as if some enormous brazen gong were imbedded in the heart of the ship. All the men jump up mechanically, file through the door silently close upon each other's heels in what is very like a prisoners' lockstep.* YANK *slaps* PADDY *on the back.*] Our watch, yuh old Harp! [*Mockingly.*] Come on down in hell. Eat up de coal dust. Drink in de heat. It's it, see! Act like yuh liked it, yuh better — or croak yuhself.

PADDY [*with jovial defiance*]. To the divil wid it! I'll not report this watch. Let thim log me and be damned. I'm no slave the like of you. I'll be sittin' here at me ease, and drinking, and thinking, and dreaming dreams.

YANK [*contemptuously*]. Tinkin' and dreamin', what'll that get yuh? What's tinkin' got to do wit it? We move, don't we? Speed, ain't it? Fog, dat's all you stand for. But we drive trou dat, don't we? We split dat up and smash trou — twenty-five knots a hour! [*Turns his back on* PADDY *scornfully.*] Aw, yuh make me sick! Yuh don't belong!

[*He strides out the door in rear.* PADDY *hums to himself, blinking drowsily.*]

CURTAIN

SCENE TWO

SCENE — *Two days out. A section of the promenade deck.* MILDRED DOUGLAS *and her aunt are discovered reclining in deck chairs. The former is a girl of twenty, slender, delicate, with a pale, pretty face marred by a self-conscious expression of disdainful superiority. She looks fretful, nervous, and discontented, bored by her own anemia. Her aunt is a pompous and proud — and fat — old lady. She is a type even to the point of a double chin and lorgnettes. She is dressed pretentiously, as if afraid her face alone would never indicate her position in life.* MILDRED *is dressed all in white.*

The impression to be conveyed by this scene is one of the beautiful, vivid life of the sea all about — sunshine on the deck in a great flood, the fresh sea wind blowing across it. In the midst of this, these two incongruous, artificial figures, inert and disharmonious, the elder like a gray lump of dough touched up with rouge, the younger looking as if the vitality of her stock had been sapped before she was conceived, so that she is the expression not of its life energy but merely of the artificialities that energy had won for itself in the spending.

MILDRED [*looking up with affected dreaminess*]. How the black smoke swirls back against the sky! Is it not beautiful?

AUNT [*without looking up*]. I dislike smoke of any kind.

MILDRED. My great-grandmother smoked a pipe — a clay pipe.

AUNT [*ruffling*]. Vulgar!

MILDRED. She was too distant a relative to be vulgar. Time mellows pipes.

AUNT [*pretending boredom, but irritated*]. Did the sociology you took up at college teach you that — to play the ghoul on every possible occasion, excavating old bones? Why not let your great-grandmother rest in her grave?

MILDRED [*dreamily*]. With her pipe beside her — puffing in Paradise.

AUNT [*with spite*]. Yes, you are a natural born ghoul. You are even getting to look like one, my dear.

MILDRED [*in a passionless tone*]. I detest you, Aunt. [*Looking at her critically.*] Do you know what you remind me of? Of a cold pork pudding against a background of linoleum tablecloth in the kitchen of a — but the possibilities are wearisome.

[*She closes her eyes.*]

AUNT [*with a bitter laugh*]. Merci for your candor. But since I am and must be your chaperone — in appearance, at least — let us patch up some sort of armed truce. For my part you are quite free to indulge any pose of eccentricity that beguiles you — as long as you observe the amenities —

MILDRED [*drawling*]. The inanities?

AUNT [*going on as if she hadn't heard*]. After exhausting the morbid thrills of social service work on New York's East Side — how they must have hated you, by the way, the poor that you made so much poorer in their own eyes! — you are now bent on making your slumming international.

THE HAIRY APE

Well, I hope Whitechapel will provide the needed nerve tonic. Do not ask me to chaperone you there, however. I told your father I would not. I loathe deformity. We will hire an army of detectives and you may investigate everything — they allow you to see.

MILDRED [*protesting with a trace of genuine earnestness*]. Please do not mock at my attempts to discover how the other half lives. Give me credit for some sort of groping sincerity in that at least. I would like to help them. I would like to be some use in the world. Is it my fault I don't know how? I would like to be sincere, to touch life somewhere. [*With weary bitterness.*] But I'm afraid I have neither the vitality nor integrity. All that was burnt out in our stock before I was born. Grandfather's blast furnaces, flaming to the sky, melting steel, making millions — then father keeping those home fires burning, making more millions — and little me at the tail-end of it all. I'm a waste product in the Bessemer process — like the millions. Or rather, I inherit the acquired trait of the by-product, wealth, but none of the energy, none of the strength of the steel that made it. I am sired by gold and damned by it, as they say at the race track — damned in more ways than one.

[*She laughs mirthlessly.*]

AUNT [*unimpressed — superciliously*]. You seem to be going in for sincerity to-day. It isn't becoming to you, really — except as an obvious pose. Be as artificial as you are, I advise. There's a sort of sincerity in that, you know. And, after all, you must confess you like that better.

MILDRED [*again affected and bored*]. Yes, I suppose I do. Pardon me for my outburst. When a leopard complains of its spots, it must sound rather grotesque. [*In a mocking tone.*] Purr, little leopard. Purr, scratch, tear, kill, gorge yourself and be happy — only stay in the jungle where your spots are camouflage. In a cage they make you conspicuous.

AUNT. I don't know what you are talking about.

MILDRED. It would be rude to talk about anything to you. Let's just talk. [*She looks at her wrist watch.*] Well, thank goodness, it's about time for them to come for me. That ought to give me a new thrill, Aunt.

AUNT [*affectedly troubled*]. You don't mean to say you're really going? The dirt — the heat must be frightful —

MILDRED. Grandfather started as a puddler. I should have inherited an immunity to heat that would make a salamander shiver. It will be fun to put it to the test.

AUNT. But don't you have to have the captain's — or someone's — permission to visit the stokehole?

MILDRED [*with a triumphant smile*]. I have it — both his and the chief engineer's. Oh, they didn't want to at first, in spite of my social service credentials. They didn't seem a bit anxious that I should investigate how the other half lives and works on a ship. So I had to tell them that my father, the president of Nazareth Steel, chairman of the board of directors of this line, had told me it would be all right.

AUNT. He didn't.

MILDRED. How naïve age makes one! But I said he did, Aunt. I even said he had given me a letter to them — which I had lost. And they were afraid to take the chance that I might be lying. [*Excitedly.*] So it's ho! for the stokehole. The second engineer is to escort me. [*Looking at her watch again.*] It's time. And here he comes, I think.

[*The SECOND ENGINEER enters. He is a husky, fine-looking man of thirty-five or so. He stops before the two and tips his cap, visibly embarrassed and ill-at-ease.*]

SECOND ENGINEER. Miss Douglas?

MILDRED. Yes. [*Throwing off her rugs and getting to her feet.*] Are we all ready to start?

SECOND ENGINEER. In just a second, ma'am. I'm waiting for the Fourth. He's coming along.

MILDRED [*with a scornful smile*]. You don't care to shoulder this responsibility alone, is that it?

SECOND ENGINEER [*forcing a smile*]. Two

are better than one. [*Disturbed by her eyes, glances out to sea — blurts out.*] A fine day we're having.

MILDRED. Is it?

SECOND ENGINEER. A nice warm breeze —

MILDRED. It feels cold to me.

SECOND ENGINEER. But it's hot enough in the sun —

MILDRED. Not hot enough for me. I don't like Nature. I was never athletic.

SECOND ENGINEER [*forcing a smile*]. Well, you'll find it hot enough where you're going.

MILDRED. Do you mean hell?

SECOND ENGINEER [*flabbergasted, decides to laugh*]. Ho-ho! No, I mean the stokehole.

MILDRED. My grandfather was a puddler. He played with boiling steel.

SECOND ENGINEER [*all at sea — uneasily*]. Is that so? Hum, you'll excuse me, ma'am, but are you intending to wear that dress?

MILDRED. Why not?

SECOND ENGINEER. You'll likely rub against oil and dirt. It can't be helped.

MILDRED. It doesn't matter. I have lots of white dresses.

SECOND ENGINEER. I have an old coat you might throw over —

MILDRED. I have fifty dresses like this. I will throw this one into the sea when I come back. That ought to wash it clean, don't you think?

SECOND ENGINEER [*doggedly*]. There's ladders to climb down that are none too clean — and dark alleyways —

MILDRED. I will wear this very dress and none other.

SECOND ENGINEER. No offence meant. It's none of my business. I was only warning you —

MILDRED. Warning? That sounds thrilling.

SECOND ENGINEER [*looking down the deck — with a sigh of relief*]. There's the Fourth now. He's waiting for us. If you'll come —

MILDRED. Go on. I'll follow you. [*He goes.* MILDRED *turns a mocking smile on her aunt.*] An oaf — but a handsome, virile oaf.

AUNT [*scornfully*]. Poser!

MILDRED. Take care. He said there were dark alleyways —

AUNT [*in the same tone*]. Poser!

MILDRED [*biting her lips angrily*]. You are right. But would that my millions were not so anemically chaste!

AUNT. Yes, for a fresh pose I have no doubt you would drag the name of Douglas in the gutter!

MILDRED. From which it sprang. Good-by, Aunt. Don't pray too hard that I may fall into the fiery furnace.

AUNT. Poser!

MILDRED [*viciously*]. Old hag!

[*She slaps her aunt insultingly across the face and walks off, laughing gaily.*]

AUNT [*screams after her*]. I said poser!

CURTAIN

SCENE THREE

SCENE — *The stokehole. In the rear, the dimly-outlined bulks of the furnaces and boilers. High overhead one hanging electric bulb sheds just enough light through the murky air laden with coal dust to pile up masses of shadows everywhere. A line of men, stripped to the waist, is before the furnace doors. They bend over, looking neither to right nor left, handling their shovels as if they were part of their bodies, with a strange, awkward, swinging rhythm. They use the shovels to throw open the furnace doors. Then from these fiery round holes in the black a flood of terrific light and heat pours full upon the men who are outlined in silhouette in the crouching, inhuman attitudes of chained gorillas. The men shovel with a rhythmic motion, swinging as on a pivot from the coal which lies in heaps on the floor behind to hurl it into the flaming mouths before them. There is a tumult of noise — the brazen clang of the furnace doors as they are flung open or slammed shut, the grating, teeth-gritting grind of steel against steel, of crunching coal. This clash of sounds stuns one's ears with its rending dissonance. But there is order in it, rhythm, a mechanical regulated recurrence, a tempo. And rising above all, making the air hum with the quiver of liberated energy, the roar of leaping flames in the furnaces, the monotonous throbbing beat of the engines.*

As the curtain rises, the furnace doors are shut. The men are taking a breathing spell. One or two are arranging the coal behind them, pulling it into more accessible heaps. The others can be dimly made out leaning on their shovels in relaxed attitudes of exhaustion.

PADDY [*from somewhere in the line — plaintively*]. Yerra, will this divil's own watch nivir end? Me back is broke. I'm destroyed entirely.

YANK [*from the center of the line — with exuberant scorn*]. Aw, yuh make me sick! Lie down and croak, why don't yuh? Always beefin', dat's you! Say, dis is a cinch! Dis was made for me! It's my meat, get me! [*A whistle is blown — a thin, shrill note from somewhere overhead in the darkness.* YANK *curses without resentment.*] Dere's de damn engineer crackin' de whip. He tinks we're loafin'.

PADDY [*vindictively*]. God stiffen him!

YANK [*in an exultant tone of command*]. Come on, youse guys! Git into de game! She's gittin' hungry! Pile some grub in her! Trow it into her belly! Come on now, all of youse! Open her up!

[*At this last all the men, who have followed his movements of getting into position, throw open their furnace doors with a deafening clang. The fiery light floods over their shoulders as they bend round for the coal. Rivulets of sooty sweat have traced maps on their backs. The enlarged muscles form bunches of high light and shadow.*]

YANK [*chanting a count as he shovels without seeming effort*]. One — two — tree — [*His voice rising exultantly in the joy of battle.*] Dat's de stuff! Let her have it! All togedder now! Sling it into her! Let her ride! Shoot de piece now! Call de toin on her! Drive her into it! Feel her move! Watch her smoke! Speed, dat's her middle name! Give her coal, youse guys! Coal, dat's her booze! Drink it up, baby! Let's see yuh sprint! Dig in and gain a lap! Dere she go-o-es —

[*This last in the chanting formula of the gallery gods at the six-day bike race. He slams his furnace door shut. The others do likewise with as much unison as their wearied bodies will permit. The effect is of one fiery eye after another being blotted out with a series of accompanying bangs.*]

PADDY [*groaning*]. Me back is broke. I'm bate out — bate —

[*There is a pause. Then the inexorable whistle sounds again from the dim regions above the electric light. There is a growl of cursing rage from all sides.*]

YANK [*shaking his fist upward — contemptuously*]. Take it easy dere, you! Who d'yuh tinks runnin' dis game, me or you? When I git ready, we move. Not before! When I git ready, get me!

VOICES [*approvingly*]. That's the stuff!
Yank tal him, py golly!
Yank ain't affeerd.
Goot poy, Yank!
Give him hell!
Tell 'im 'e's a bloody swine!
Bloody slave-driver!

YANK [*contemptuously*]. He ain't got no noive. He's yellow, get me? All de engineers is yellow. Dey got streaks a mile wide. Aw, to hell wit him! Let's move, youse guys. We had a rest. Come on, she needs it! Give her pep! It ain't for him. Him and his whistle, dey don't belong. But we belong, see! We gotter feed de baby! Come on!

[*He turns and flings his furnace door open. They all follow his lead. At this instant the* SECOND *and* FOURTH ENGINEERS *enter from the darkness on the left with* MILDRED *between them. She starts, turns paler, her pose is crumbling, she shivers with fright in spite of the blazing heat, but forces herself to leave the* ENGINEERS *and take a few steps nearer the men. She is right behind* YANK. *All this happens quickly while the men have their backs turned.*]

YANK. Come on, youse guys! [*He is turning to get coal when the whistle sounds again in a peremptory, irritating note. This drives* YANK *into a sudden fury. While the other men have turned full around and stopped dumfounded by the spectacle of* MILDRED *standing there in her white dress,* YANK *does not turn far enough to see her. Besides, his head is thrown back, he blinks upward through the murk trying to find the owner of the whistle, he brandishes his shovel murderously over his head in one hand, pounding on his chest, gorilla-like, with the other, shouting:*] Toin off dat whistle! Come down outa dere, yuh yellow, brass-buttoned, Belfast bum, yuh! Come down and I'll knock yer brains out! Yuh lousey, stinkin', yellow mut of a Catholic-moiderin' bastard! Come down and I'll moider yuh! Pullin' dat whistle on me, huh? I'll show yuh! I'll crash yer skull in! I'll drive yer teet' down yer troat! I'll slam yer nose trou de back of yer head! I'll cut yer guts out for a nickel, yuh lousey boob, yuh dirty, crummy, muck-eatin' son of a —

[*Suddenly he becomes conscious of all the other men staring at something directly behind his back. He whirls defensively with a snarling, murderous growl, crouching to spring, his lips drawn back over his teeth, his small eyes gleaming ferociously. He sees* MILDRED, *like a white apparition in the full light from the open furnace doors. He glares into her eyes, turned to stone. As for her, during his speech she has listened, paralyzed with horror, terror, her whole personality crushed, beaten in, collapsed, by the terrific impact of this unknown, abysmal brutality, naked and shameless. As she looks at his gorilla face, as his eyes bore into hers, she utters a low, choking cry and shrinks away from him, putting both hands up before her eyes to shut out the sight of his face, to protect her own. This startles* YANK *to a reaction. His mouth falls open, his eyes grow bewildered.*]

MILDRED [*about to faint — to the* EN-GINEERS, *who now have her one by each arm — whimperingly*]. Take me away! Oh, the filthy beast!

[*She faints. They carry her quickly back, disappearing in the darkness at the left, rear. An iron door clangs shut. Rage and bewildered fury rush back on* YANK. *He feels himself insulted in some unknown fashion in the very heart of his pride. He roars:* God damn yuh! *And hurls his shovel after them at the door which has just closed. It hits the steel bulkhead with a clang and falls clattering on the steel floor. From overhead the whistle sounds again in a long, angry, insistent command.*]

CURTAIN

SCENE FOUR

SCENE — *The firemen's forecastle.* YANK'S *watch has just come off duty and had dinner. Their faces and bodies shine from a soap and water scrubbing but around their eyes, where a hasty dousing does not touch, the coal dust sticks like black make-up, giving them a queer, sinister expression.* YANK *has not washed either face or body. He stands out in contrast to them, a blackened, brooding figure. He is seated forward on a bench in the exact attitude of Rodin's "The Thinker." The others, most of them smoking pipes are staring at* YANK *half-apprehensively, as if fearing an outburst; half-amusedly, as if they saw a joke somewhere that tickled them.*

VOICES. He ain't ate nothin'.
 Py golly, a fallar gat gat grub in him.
 Divil a lie.
 Yank feeda da fire, no feeda da face.
 Ha-ha.
 He ain't even washed hisself.
 He's forgot.
 Hey, Yank, you forgot to wash.

YANK [*sullenly*]. Forgot nothin'! To hell wit washin'.

VOICES. It'll stick to you.

It'll get under your skin.
Give yer the bleedin' itch, that's wot.
It makes spots on you — like a leopard.
Like a piebald nigger, you mean.
Better wash up, Yank.
You sleep better.
Wash up, Yank.
Wash up! Wash up!

YANK [*resentfully*]. Aw say, youse guys. Lemme alone. Can't youse see I'm tryin' to tink?

ALL [*repeating the word after him as one with cynical mockery*]. Think!

[*The word has a brazen, metallic quality as if their throats were phonograph horns. It is followed by a chorus of hard, barking laughter.*]

YANK [*springing to his feet and glaring at them belligerently*]. Yes, tink! Tink, dat's what I said! What about it?

[*They are silent, puzzled by his sudden resentment at what used to be one of his jokes. YANK sits down again in the same attitude of "The Thinker."*]

VOICES. Leave him alone.
He's got a grouch on.
Why wouldn't he?

PADDY [*with a wink at the others*]. Sure I know what's the matther. 'Tis aisy to see. He's fallen in love, I'm telling you.

ALL [*repeating the word after him as one with cynical mockery*]. Love!

[*The word has a brazen, metallic quality as if their throats were phonograph horns. It is followed by a chorus of hard, barking laughter.*]

YANK [*with a contemptuous snort*]. Love, hell! Hate, dat's what. I've fallen in hate, get me?

PADDY [*philosophically*]. 'Twould take a wise man to tell one from the other. [*With a bitter, ironical scorn, increasing as he goes on.*] But I'm telling you it's love that's in it. Sure what else but love for us poor bastes in the stokehole would be bringing a fine lady, dressed like a white quane, down a mile of ladders and steps to be havin' a look at us?

[*A growl of anger goes up from all sides.*]

LONG [*jumping on a bench — hecticly*]. Hinsultin' us! Hinsultin' us, the bloody cow! And them bloody engineers! What right 'as they got to be exhibitin' us 's if we was bleedin' monkeys in a menagerie? Did we sign for hinsults to our dignity as 'onest workers? Is that in the ship's articles? You kin bloody well bet it ain't! But I knows why they done it. I arsked a deck steward 'o she was and 'e told me. 'Er old man's a bleedin' millionaire, a bloody Capitalist! 'E's got enuf bloody gold to sink this bleedin' ship! 'E makes arf the bloody steel in the world! 'E owns this bloody boat! And you and me, comrades, we're 'is slaves! And the skipper and mates and engineers, they're 'is slaves! And she's 'is bloody daughter and we're all 'er slaves, too! And she gives 'er orders as 'ow she wants to see the bloody animals below decks and down they takes 'er!

[*There is a roar of rage from all sides.*]

YANK [*blinking at him bewilderedly*]. Say! Wait a moment! Is all dat straight goods?

LONG. Straight as string! The bleedin' steward as waits on 'em, 'e told me about 'er. And what're we goin' ter do, I arsks yer? 'Ave we got ter swaller 'er hinsults like dogs? It ain't in the ship's articles. I tell yer we got a case. We kin go ter law —

YANK [*with abysmal contempt*]. Hell! Law!

ALL [*repeating the word after him as one with cynical mockery*]. Law!

[*The word has a brazen metallic quality as if their throats were phonograph horns. It is followed by a chorus of hard, barking laughter.*]

LONG [*feeling the ground slipping from under his feet — desperately*]. As voters and citizens we kin force the bloody governments —

YANK [*with abysmal contempt*]. Hell! Governments!

ALL [*repeating the word after him as one with cynical mockery*]. Governments!

[*The word has a brazen metallic*

quality as if their throats were phonograph horns. It is followed by a chorus of hard, barking laughter.]
LONG [*hysterically*]. We're free and equal in the sight of God —
YANK [*with abysmal contempt.*] Hell! God!
ALL [*repeating the word after him as one with cynical mockery*]. God!
[*The word has a brazen metallic quality as if their throats were phonograph horns. It is followed by a chorus of hard, barking laughter.*]
YANK [*witheringly*]. Aw, join de Salvation Army!
ALL. Sit down! Shut up! Damn fool! Sea-lawyer!
[LONG *slinks back out of sight.*]
PADDY [*continuing the trend of his thoughts as if he had never been interrupted — bitterly*]. And there she was standing behind us, and the Second pointing at us like a man you'd hear in a circus would be saying: In this cage is a queerer kind of baboon than ever you'd find in darkest Africy. We roast them in their own sweat — and be damned if you won't hear some of thim saying they like it!
[*He glances scornfully at* YANK.]
YANK [*with a bewildered uncertain growl*]. Aw!
PADDY. And there was Yank roarin' curses and turning round wid his shovel to brain her — and she looked at him, and him at her —
YANK [*slowly*]. She was all white. I tought she was a ghost. Sure.
PADDY [*with heavy, biting sarcasm*]. 'Twas love at first sight, divil a doubt of it! If you'd seen the endearin' look on her pale mug when she shrivelled away with her hands over her eyes to shut out the sight of him! Sure, 'twas as if she'd seen a great hairy ape escaped from the Zoo!
YANK [*stung — with a growl of rage*]. Aw!
PADDY. And the loving way Yank heaved his shovel at the skull of her, only she was out the door! [*A grin breaking over his face.*] 'Twas touching, I'm telling you! It put the touch of home, swate home in the stokehole.

[*There is a roar of laughter from all.*]
YANK [*glaring at* PADDY *menacingly*]. Aw, choke dat off, see!
PADDY [*not heeding him — to the others.*] And her grabbin' at the Second's arm for protection. [*With a grotesque imitation of a woman's voice.*] Kiss me, Engineer dear, for it's dark down here and me old man's in Wall Street making money! Hug me tight, darlin', for I'm afeerd in the dark and me mother's on deck makin' eyes at the skipper! [*Another roar of laughter.*]
YANK [*threateningly*]. Say! What yuh tryin' to do, kid me, yuh old Harp?
PADDY. Divil a bit! Ain't I wishin' myself you'd brained her?
YANK [*fiercely*]. I'll brain her! I'll brain her yet, wait 'n' see! [*Coming over to* PADDY *— slowly.*] Say, is dat what she called me — a hairy ape?
PADDY. She looked it at you if she didn't say the word itself.
YANK [*grinning horribly*]. Hairy ape, huh? Sure! Dat's de way she looked at me, aw right. Hairy ape! So dat's me, huh? [*Bursting into rage — as if she were still in front of him.*] Yuh skinny tart! Yuh white-faced bum, yuh! I'll show yuh who's a ape! [*Turning to the others, bewilderment seizing him again.*] Say, youse guys. I was bawlin' him out for pullin' de whistle on us. You heard me. And den I seen youse lookin' at somep'n and I tought he'd sneaked down to come up in back of me, and I hopped round to knock him dead wit de shovel. And dere she was wit de light on her! Christ, yuh coulda pushed me over with a finger! I was scared, get me? Sure! I tought she was a ghost, see? She was all in white like dey wrap around stiffs. You seen her. Kin yuh blame me? She didn't belong, dat's what. And den when I come to and seen it was a real skoit and seen de way she was lookin' at me — like Paddy said — Christ, I was sore, get me? I don't stand for dat stuff from nobody. And I flung de shovel — on'y she'd beat it. [*Furiously.*] I wished it'd banged her! I wished it'd knocked her block off!
LONG. And be 'anged for murder or

'lectrocuted? She ain't bleedin' well worth it.
YANK. I don't give a damn what! I'd be square wit her, wouldn't I? Tink I wanter let her put somep'n over on me? Tink I'm goin' to let her git away wit dat stuff? Yuh don't know me! Noone ain't never put nothin' over on me and got away wit it, see! — not dat kind of stuff — no guy and no skoit neither! I'll fix her! Maybe she'll come down again —
VOICE. No chance, Yank. You scared her out of a year's growth.
YANK. I scared her? Why de hell should I scare her? Who de hell is she? Ain't she de same as me? Hairy ape, huh? [With his old confident bravado.] I'll show her I'm better'n her, if she on'y knew it. I belong and she don't, see! I move and she's dead! Twenty-five knots a hour, dat's me! Dat carries her but I make dat. She's on'y baggage. Sure! [Again bewilderedly.] But, Christ, she was funny lookin'! Did yuh pipe her hands? White and skinny. Yuh could see de bones trough 'em. And her mush, dat was dead white, too. And her eyes, dey was like dey'd seen a ghost. Me, dat was! Sure! Hairy ape! Ghost, huh? Look at dat arm! [He extends his right arm, swelling out the great muscles.] I coulda took her wit dat, wit' just my little finger even, and broke her in two. [Again bewilderedly.] Say, who is dat skoit, huh? What is she? What's she come from? Who made her? Who give her de noive to look at me like dat? Dis ting's got my goat right. I don't get her. She's new to me. What does a skoit like her mean, huh? She don't belong, get me! I can't see her. [With growing anger.] But one ting I'm wise to, aw right, aw right! Youse all kin bet your shoits I'll git even wit her. I'll show her if she tinks she — She grinds de organ and I'm on de string, huh? I'll fix her! Let her come down again and I'll fling her in de furnace! She'll move den! She won't shiver at nothin', den! Speed, dat'll be her! She'll belong den! [He grins horribly.]
PADDY. She'll never come. She's had her belly-full, I'm telling you. She'll be in bed now, I'm thinking, wid ten doctors and nurses feedin' her salts to clean the fear out of her.
YANK [enraged]. Yuh tink I made her sick, too, do yuh? Just lookin' at me, huh? Hairy ape, huh? [In a frenzy of rage.] I'll fix her! I'll tell her where to git off! She'll git down on her knees and take it back or I'll bust de face offen her! [Shaking one fist upward and beating on his chest with the other.] I'll find yuh! I'm comin', d'yuh hear? I'll fix yuh, God damn yuh!
[He makes a rush for the door.]
VOICES. Stop him!
He'll get shot!
He'll murder her!
Trip him up!
Hold him!
He's gone crazy!
Gott, he's strong!
Hold him down!
Look out for a kick!
Pin his arms!
[They have all piled on him and, after a fierce struggle, by sheer weight of numbers have borne him to the floor just inside the door.]
PADDY [who has remained detached]. Kape him down till he's cooled off. [Scornfully.] Yerra, Yank, you're a great fool. Is it payin' attention at all you are to the like of that skinny sow widout one drop of rale blood in her?
YANK [frenziedly, from the bottom of the heap]. She done me doit! She done me doit, didn't she? I'll git square wit her! I'll get her some way! Git offen me, youse guys! Lemme up! I'll show her who's a ape!

CURTAIN

SCENE FIVE

SCENE — *Three weeks later. A corner of Fifth Avenue in the Fifties on a fine, Sunday morning. A general atmosphere of clean, well-tidied, wide street; a flood of mellow, tempered sunshine; gentle, genteel breezes. In the rear, the show windows of two shops, a jewelry establishment on the corner, a furrier's next to it. Here the adornments of extreme wealth are tantalizingly displayed.*

The jeweler's window is gaudy with glittering diamonds, emeralds, rubies, pearls, etc., fashioned in ornate tiaras, crowns, necklaces, collars, etc. From each piece hangs an enormous tag from which a dollar sign and numerals in intermittent electric lights wink out the incredible prices. The same in the furrier's. Rich furs of all varieties hang there bathed in a downpour of artificial light. The general effect is of a background of magnificence cheapened and made grotesque by commercialism, a background in tawdry disharmony with the clear light and sunshine on the street itself.

Up the side street YANK *and* LONG *come swaggering.* LONG *is dressed in shore clothes, wears a black Windsor tie, cloth cap.* YANK *is in his dirty dungarees. A fireman's cap with black peak is cocked defiantly on the side of his head. He has not shaved for days and around his fierce, resentful eyes — as around those of* LONG *to a lesser degree — the black smudge of coal dust still sticks like make-up. They hesitate and stand together at the corner, swaggering, looking about them with a forced, defiant contempt.*

LONG [*indicating it all with an oratorical gesture*]. Well, 'ere we are. Fif' Avenoo. This 'ere's their bleedin' private lane, as yer might say. [*Bitterly.*] We're trespassers 'ere. Proletarians keep orf the grass!

YANK [*dully*]. I don't see no grass, yuh boob. [*Staring at the sidewalk.*] Clean, ain't it? Yuh could eat a fried egg offen it. The white wings got some job sweepin' dis up. [*Looking up and down the avenue — surlily.*] Where's all de white-collar stiffs yuh said was here — and de skoits — *her* kind?

LONG. In church, blarst 'em! Arskin' Jesus to give 'em more money.

YANK. Choich, huh? I useter go to choich onct — sure — when I was a kid. Me old man and woman, dey made me. Dey never went demselves, dough. Always got too big a head on Sunday mornin', dat was dem. [*With a grin.*] Dey was scrappers for fair, bot' of dem. On Satiday nights when dey bot' got a skinful dey could put up a bout oughter been staged at de Garden. When dey got trough dere wasn't a chair or table wit a leg under it. Or else dey bot' jumped on me for somep'n. Dat was where I loined to take punishment. [*With a grin and a swagger.*] I'm a chip offen de old block, get me?

LONG. Did yer old man follow the sea?

YANK. Naw. Worked along shore. I runned away when me old lady croaked wit de tremens. I helped at truckin' and in de market. Den I shipped in de stokehole. Sure. Dat belongs. De rest was nothin'. [*Looking around him.*] I ain't never seen dis before. De Brooklyn waterfront, dat was where I was dragged up. [*Taking a deep breath.*] Dis ain't so bad at dat, huh?

LONG. Not bad? Well, we pays for it wiv our bloody sweat, if yer wants to know!

YANK [*with sudden angry disgust*]. Aw, hell! I don't see noone, see — like her. All dis gives me a pain. It don't belong. Say, ain't dere a backroom around dis dump? Let's go shoot a ball. All dis is too clean and quiet and dolled-up, get me! It gives me a pain.

LONG. Wait and yer'll bloody well see —

YANK. I don't wait for noone. I keep on de move. Say, what yuh drag me up here for, anyway? Tryin' to kid me, yuh simp, yuh?

LONG. Yer wants to get back at her, don't yer? That's what yer been sayin' every bloomin' 'our since she hinsulted yer.

YANK [*vehemently*]. Sure ting I do! Didn't I try to git even wit her in Southampton? Didn't I sneak on de dock and wait for her by de gangplank? I was goin' to spit in her pale mug, see! Sure, right in her pop-eyes! Dat woulda made me even, see? But no chanct. Dere was a whole army of plain clothes bulls around. Dey spotted me and gimme de bum's rush. I never seen her. But I'll git square wit her yet, you watch! [*Furiously.*] De lousey tart! She tinks she kin get away wit moider — but not wit me! I'll fix her! I'll tink of a way!

LONG [*as disgusted as he dares to be*]. Ain't that why I brought yer up 'ere — to show yer? Yer been lookin' at this 'ere 'ole affair wrong. Yer been actin' an' talkin' 's if it was all a bleedin' personal matter between yer and that bloody cow. I wants to convince yer she was on'y a representative of 'er clarss. I wants to awaken yer bloody clarss consciousness. Then yer'll see it's 'er clarss yer've got to fight, not 'er alone. There's a 'ole mob of 'em like 'er, Gawd blind 'em!

YANK [*spitting on his hands — belligerently*]. De more de merrier when I gits started. Bring on de gang!

LONG. Yer'll see 'em in arf a mo', when that church lets out. [*He turns and sees the window display in the two stores for the first time.*] Blimey! Look at that, will yer? [*They both walk back and stand looking in the jeweler's.* LONG *flies into a fury.*] Just look at this 'ere bloomin' mess! Just look at it! Look at the bleedin' prices on 'em — more'n our 'old bloody stokehole makes in ten voyages sweatin' in 'ell! And they — her and her bloody clarss — buys 'em for toys to dangle on 'em! One of these 'ere would buy scoff for a starvin' family for a year!

YANK. Aw, cut de sob stuff! T' hell wit de starvin' family! Yuh'll be passin' de hat to me next. [*With naïve admiration.*] Say, dem tings is pretty, huh? Bet yuh dey'd hock for a piece of change aw right. [*Then turning away, bored.*] But, aw hell, what good are dey? Let her have 'em. Dey don't belong no more'n she does. [*With a gesture of sweeping the jeweler's into oblivion.*] All dat don't count, get me?

LONG [*who has moved to the furrier's — indignantly*]. And I s'pose this 'ere don't count neither — skins of poor, 'armless animals slaughtered so as 'er and 'ers can keep their bleedin' noses warm!

YANK [*who has been staring at something inside — with queer excitement*]. Take a slant at dat! Give it de once-over! Monkey fur — two t'ousand bucks! [*Bewilderedly.*] Is dat straight goods — monkey fur? What de hell —?

LONG [*bitterly*]. It's straight enuf. [*With grim humor.*] They wouldn't bloody well pay that for a 'airy ape's skin — no, nor for the 'ole livin' ape with all 'is 'ead, and body, and soul thrown in!

YANK [*clenching his fists, his face growing pale with rage as if the skin in the window were a personal insult*]. Trowin' it up in my face! Christ! I'll fix her!

LONG [*excitedly*]. Church is out. 'Ere they come, the bleedin' swine. [*After a glance at* YANK's *lowering face — uneasily.*] Easy goes, comrade. Keep yer bloomin' temper. Remember force defeats itself. It ain't our weapon. We must impress our demands through peaceful means — the votes of the on-marching proletarians of the bloody world!

YANK [*with abysmal contempt*]. Votes, hell! Votes is a joke, see. Votes for women! Let dem do it!

LONG [*still more uneasily*]. Calm, now. Treat 'em wiv the proper contempt. Observe the bleedin' parasites, but 'old yer 'orses.

YANK [*angrily*]. Git away from me! Yuh're yellow, dat's what. Force, dat's me! De punch, dat's me every time, see! [*The crowd from church enter from the right, sauntering slowly and affectedly, their heads held stiffly up, looking neither to right nor left, talking in toneless, simpering voices. The women are rouged, calcimined, dyed, overdressed to the nth degree. The men are in Prince Alberts, high hats, spats, canes, etc. A procession of gaudy marionettes, yet with something of the relentless horror of Frankensteins in their detached, mechanical unawareness.*]

VOICES. Dear Doctor Caiaphas! He is so sincere!
What was the sermon? I dozed off.
About the radicals, my dear — and the false doctrines that are being preached.
We must organize a hundred per cent American bazaar.

And let everyone contribute one one-hundredth per cent of their income tax. What an original idea! We can devote the proceeds to rehabilitating the veil of the temple. But that has been done so many times.

YANK [*glaring from one to the other of them — with an insulting snort of scorn*]. Huh! Huh!

[*Without seeming to see him, they make wide detours to avoid the spot where he stands in the middle of the sidewalk.*]

LONG [*frightenedly*]. Keep yer bloomin' mouth shut, I tells yer.

YANK [*viciously*]. G'wan! Tell it to Sweeney! [*He swaggers away and deliberately lurches into a top-hatted gentleman, then glares at him pugnaciously.*] Say, who d'yuh tink yuh're bumpin'? Tink yuh own de oith?

GENTLEMAN [*coldly and affectedly*]. I beg your pardon.

[*He has not looked at* YANK *and passes on without a glance, leaving him bewildered.*]

LONG [*rushing up and grabbing* YANK'S *arm*]. 'Ere! Come away! This wasn't what I meant. Yer'll 'ave the bloody coppers down on us.

YANK [*savagely — giving him a push that sends him sprawling*]. G'wan!

LONG [*picks himself up — hysterically*]. I'll pop orf, then. This ain't what I meant. And whatever 'appens, yer can't blame me. [*He slinks off left.*]

YANK. T' hell wit youse! [*He approaches a lady — with a vicious grin and a smirking wink.*] Hello, Kiddo. How's every little ting? Got anyting on for tonight? I know an old boiler down to de docks we kin crawl into. [*The lady stalks by without a look, without a change of pace.* YANK *turns to others — insultingly.*] Holy smokes, what a mug! Go hide yuhself before de horses shy at yuh. Gee, pipe de heinie on dat one! Say, youse, yuh look like de stoin of a ferryboat. Paint and powder! All dolled up to kill! Yuh look like stiffs laid out for de boneyard! Aw, g'wan, de lot of youse! Yuh give me de eye-ache. Yuh don't belong, get me! Look at me, why don't youse dare? I belong, dat's me! [*Pointing to a skyscraper across the street which is in process of construction — with bravado.*] See dat building goin' up dere? See de steel work? Steel, dat's me! Youse guys live on it and tink yuh're somep'n. But I'm *in* it, see! I'm hoistin' engine dat makes it go up! I'm it — de inside and bottom of it! Sure! I'm steel and steam and smoke and de rest of it! It moves — speed — twenty-five stories up — and me at de top and bottom — movin'! Youse simps don't move. Yuh're on'y dolls I winds up to see 'm spin. Yuh're de garbage, get me — de leavins — de ashes we dump over de side! Now, whata yuh gotto say? [*But as they seem neither to see nor hear him, he flies into a fury.*] Bums! Pigs! Tarts! Bitches! [*He turns in a rage on the men, bumping viciously into them but not jarring them the least bit. Rather it is he who recoils after each collision. He keeps growling.*] Git off de oith! G'wan, yuh bum! Look where yuh're goin', can't yuh? Git outa here! Fight, why don't yuh? Put up yer mits! Don't be a dog! Fight or I'll knock yuh dead!

[*But, without seeming to see him, they all answer with mechanical affected politeness:* I beg your pardon. *Then a cry from one of the women, they all scurry to the furrier's window.*]

THE WOMAN [*ecstatically, with a gasp of delight*]. Monkey fur! [*The whole crowd of men and women chorus after her in the same tone of affected delight.*] Monkey fur!

YANK [*with a jerk of his head back on his shoulders, as if he had received a punch full in the face — raging*]. I see yuh, all in white! I see yuh, yuh white-faced tart, yuh! Hairy ape, huh? I'll hairy ape yuh!

[*He bends down and grips at the street curbing as if to pluck it out and hurl it. Foiled in this, snarling with passion, he leaps to the lamp-post on the corner and tries to pull it up for a club. Just at that moment a bus is* heard rumbling up. A fat, high-hatted, spatted gentleman runs out from the side street. He calls out plaintively:* "Bus! Bus! Stop there!" *and runs full tilt into the bending, straining* YANK, *who is bowled off his balance.]

YANK [*seeing a fight — with a roar of joy as he springs to his feet*]. At last! Bus, huh? I'll bust yuh!

[*He lets drive a terrific swing, his fist landing full on the fat gentleman's face. But the gentleman stands unmoved as if nothing had happened.*]

GENTLEMAN. I beg your pardon. [*Then irritably.*] You have made me lose my bus.

[*He claps his hands and begins to scream:* Officer! Officer! *Many police whistles shrill out on the instant and a whole platoon of policemen rush in on* YANK *from all sides. He tries to fight, but is clubbed to the pavement and fallen upon. The crowd at the window have not moved or noticed this disturbance. The clanging gong of the patrol wagon approaches with a clamoring din.*]

CURTAIN

SCENE SIX

SCENE — *Night of the following day. A row of cells in the prison on Blackwell's Island. The cells extend back diagonally from right front to left rear. They do not stop, but disappear in the dark background as if they ran on, numberless, into infinity. One electric bulb from the low ceiling of the narrow corridor sheds its light through the heavy steel bars of the cell at the extreme front and reveals part of the interior.* YANK *can be seen within, crouched on the edge of his cot in the attitude of Rodin's "The Thinker." His face is spotted with black and blue bruises. A blood-stained bandage is wrapped around his head.*

YANK [*suddenly starting as if awakening from a dream, reaches out and shakes the bars — aloud to himself, wonderingly*]. Steel. Dis is de Zoo, huh?

[*A burst of hard, barking laughter comes from the unseen occupants of the cells, runs back down the tier, and abruptly ceases.*]

VOICES [*mockingly*]. The Zoo? That's a new name for this coop — a damn good name!

Steel, eh? You said a mouthful. This is the old iron house.

Who is that boob talkin'?

He's the bloke they brung in out of his head. The bulls had beat him up fierce.

YANK [*dully*]. I musta been dreamin'. I tought I was in a cage at de Zoo — but de apes don't talk, do dey?

VOICES [*with mocking laughter*]. You're in a cage aw right.

A coop!

A pen!

A sty!

A kennel!

[*Hard laughter — a pause.*]

Say, guy! Who are you? No, never mind lying. What are you?

Yes, tell us your sad story. What's your game?

What did they jug yuh for?

YANK [*dully*]. I was a fireman — stokin' on de liners. [*Then with sudden rage, rattling his cell bars.*] I'm a hairy ape, get me? And I'll bust youse all in de jaw if yuh don't lay off kiddin' me.

VOICES. Huh! You're a hard-boiled duck, ain't you!

When you spit, it bounces!

[*Laughter.*]

Aw, can it. He's a regular guy. Ain't you?

What did he say he was — a ape?

YANK [*defiantly*]. Sure ting! Ain't dat what youse all are — apes?

[*A silence. Then a furious rattling of bars from down the corridor.*]

A VOICE [*thick with rage*]. I'll show yuh who's a ape, yuh bum!

VOICES. Ssshh! Nix!

Can de noise! Piano! You'll have the guard down on us!

YANK [*scornfully*]. De guard? Yuh mean de keeper, don't yuh?

[*Angry exclamations from all the cells.*]

VOICE [*placatingly*]. Aw, don't pay no attention to him. He's off his nut from the beatin'-up he got. Say, you guy! We're waitin' to hear what they landed you for — or ain't yuh tellin'?

YANK. Sure, I'll tell youse. Sure! Why de hell not? On'y — youse won't get me. Nobody gets me but me, see? I started to tell de Judge and all he says was: "Toity days to tink it over." Tink it over! Christ, dat's all I been doin' for weeks! [*After a pause.*] I was tryin' to git even wit someone, see? — someone dat done me doit.

VOICES [*cynically*]. De old stuff, I bet. Your goil, huh? Give yuh the double-cross, huh? That's them every time! Did yuh beat up de odder guy?

YANK [*disgustedly*]. Aw, yuh're all wrong! Sure dere was a skoit in it — but not what youse mean, not dat old tripe. Dis was a new kind of skoit. She was dolled up all in white — in de stokehole. I tought she was a ghost. Sure. [*A pause.*]

VOICES [*whispering*]. Gee, he's still nutty. Let him rave. It's fun listenin'.

YANK [*unheeding — groping in his thoughts*]. Her hands — dey was skinny and white like dey wasn't real but painted on somep'n. Dere was a million miles from me to her — twenty-five knots a hour. She was like some dead ting de cat brung in. Sure, dat's what. She didn't belong. She belonged in de window of a toy store, or on de top of a garbage can, see! Sure! [*He breaks out angrily.*] But would yuh believe it, she had de noive to do me doit. She lamped me like she was seein' somep'n broke loose from de menagerie. Christ, yuh'd oughter seen her eyes! [*He rattles the bars of his cell furiously.*] But I'll get back at her yet, you watch! And if I can't find her I'll take it out on de gang she runs wit. I'm wise to where dey hangs out now. I'll show her who belongs! I'll show her who's in de move and who ain't. You watch my smoke!

VOICES [*serious and joking*]. Dat's de talkin'! Take her for all she's got! What was this dame, anyway? Who was she, eh?

YANK. I dunno. First cabin stiff. Her old man's a millionaire, dey says — name of Douglas.

VOICES. Douglas? That's the president of the Steel Trust, I bet. Sure. I seen his mug in de papers. He's filthy with dough.

VOICE. Hey, feller, take a tip from me. If you want to get back at dat dame, you better join the Wobblies. You'll get some action then.

YANK. Wobblies? What de hell's dat?

VOICE. Ain't you ever heard of the I.W.W.?

YANK. Naw. What is it?

VOICE. A gang of blokes — a tough gang. I been readin' about 'em to-day in the paper. The guard give me the *Sunday Times*. There's a long spiel about 'em. It's from a speech made in the Senate by a guy named Senator Queen. [*He is in the cell next to* YANK'S. *There is a rustling of paper.*] Wait'll I see if I got light enough and I'll read you. Listen. [*He reads:*] "There is a menace existing in this country to-day which threatens the vitals ot our fair Republic — as foul a menace against the very life-blood of the American Eagle as was the foul conspiracy of Catiline against the eagles of ancient Rome!"

VOICE [*disgustedly*]. Aw hell! Tell him to salt de tail of dat eagle!

VOICE [*reading*]. "I refer to that devil's brew of rascals, jailbirds, murderers, and cutthroats who libel all honest working men by calling themselves the Industrial Workers of the World; but in the light of their nefarious plots, I call them the Industrious *Wreckers* of the World!"

YANK [*with vengeful satisfaction*]. Wreckers, dat's de right dope! Dat belongs! Me for dem!

VOICE. Ssshh! [*Reading:*] "This fiendish organization is a foul ulcer on the fair body of our Democracy —"

VOICE. Democracy, hell! Give him the boid, fellers — the raspberry! [*They do.*]

VOICE. Ssshh! [*Reading:*] "Like Cato I say to this Senate, the I.W.W. must be destroyed! For they represent an ever-present dagger pointed at the heart of the greatest nation the world has ever known, where all men are born free and equal, with equal opportunities to all, where the Founding Fathers have guaranteed to each one happiness, where Truth, Honor, Liberty, Justice, and the Brotherhood of Man are a religion absorbed with one's mother's milk, taught at our father's knee, sealed, signed, and stamped upon in the glorious Constitution of these United States!"

[*A perfect storm of hisses, catcalls, boos, and hard laughter.*]

VOICES [*scornfully*]. Hurrah for de Fort' of July!
Pass de hat!
Liberty!
Justice!
Honor!
Opportunity!
Brotherhood!

ALL [*with abysmal scorn*]. Aw, hell!

VOICE. Give that Queen Senator guy the bark! All togedder now — one — two — tree —

[*A terrific chorus of barking and yapping.*]

GUARD [*from a distance*]. Quiet there, youse — or I'll git the hose.

[*The noise subsides.*]

YANK [*with a growling rage*]. I'd like to catch dat Senator guy alone for a second. I'd loin him some trute!

VOICE. Ssshh! Here's where he gits down to cases on the Wobblies. [*Reads:*] "They plot with fire in one hand and dynamite in the other. They stop not before murder to gain their ends, nor at the outraging of defenceless womanhood. They would tear down society, put the lowest scum in the seats of the mighty, turn Almighty God's revealed plan for the world topsy-turvy, and make of our sweet and lovely civilization a shambles, a desolation where man, God's masterpiece, would soon degenerate back to the ape!"

VOICE [*to* YANK]. Hey, you guy. There's your ape stuff again.

YANK [*with a growl of fury*]. I got him. So dey blow up tings, do dey? Dey turn tings round, do dey? Hey, lend me dat paper, will yuh?

VOICE. Sure. Give it to him. On'y keep it to yourself, see. We don't wanter listen to no more of that slop.

VOICE. Here you are. Hide it under your mattress.

YANK [*reaching out*]. Tanks. I can't read much, but I kin manage. [*He sits, the paper in the hand at his side, in the attitude of Rodin's "The Thinker." A pause. Several snores from down the corridor. Suddenly* YANK *jumps to his feet with a furious groan as if some appalling thought had crashed on him — bewilderedly.*] Sure — her old man — president of de Steel Trust — makes half de steel in de world — steel — where I tought I belonged — drivin' trou — movin' — in dat — to make *her* — and cage me in for her to spit on! Christ! [*He shakes the bars of his cell door till the whole tier trembles. Irritated, protesting exclamations from those awakened or trying to get to sleep.*] He made dis — dis cage! Steel! *It* don't belong, dat's what! Cages, cells, locks, bolts, bars — dat's what it means! — holdin' me down wit him at de top! But I'll drive trou! Fire, dat melts it! I'll be fire — under de heap — fire dat never goes out — hot as hell — breakin' out in de night —

[*While he has been saying this last he has shaken his cell door to a clanging accompaniment. As he comes to the "breakin' out" he seizes one bar with both hands and, putting his two feet up against the others so that his position is parallel to the floor like a monkey's, he gives a great wrench backwards. The bar bends like a licorice stick under his tremendous strength. Just at this moment the* PRISON GUARD *rushes in, dragging a hose behind him.*]

GUARD [*angrily*]. I'll loin youse bums to wake me up! [*Sees* YANK.] Hello, it's you, huh? Got the D.Ts., hey? Well, I'll cure 'em. I'll drown your snakes for yuh! [*Noticing the bar.*] Hell, look at dat bar bended! On'y a bug is strong enough for dat!

YANK [*glaring at him*]. Or a hairy ape, yuh big yellow bum! Look out! Here I come! [*He grabs another bar.*]

GUARD [*scared now — yelling off left*]. Toin de hose on, Ben! — full pressure! And call de others — and a strait-jacket! [*The curtain is falling. As it hides* YANK *from view, there is a splattering smash as the stream of water hits the steel of* YANK'S *cell.*]

CURTAIN

SCENE SEVEN

SCENE — *Nearly a month later. An I.W.W. local near the waterfront, showing the interior of a front room on the ground floor, and the street outside. Moonlight on the narrow street, buildings massed in black shadow. The interior of the room, which is general assembly room, office, and reading-room, resembles some dingy settlement boys' club. A desk and high stool are in one corner. A table with papers, stacks of pamphlets, chairs about it, is at center. The whole is decidedly cheap, banal, commonplace, and unmysterious as a room could well be. The* SECRETARY *is perched on the stool making entries in a large ledger. An eye shade casts his face into shadows. Eight or ten men, longshoremen, iron workers, and the like, are grouped about the table. Two are playing checkers. One is writing a letter. Most of them are smoking pipes. A big signboard is on the wall at the rear, "Industrial Workers of the World — Local No. 57."*

[YANK *comes down the street outside. He is dressed as in Scene Five. He moves cautiously, mysteriously. He comes to a point opposite the door; tiptoes softly up to it, listens, is impressed by the silence within, knocks carefully, as if he were guessing at the password to some secret rite. Listens. No answer. Knocks again a bit louder. No answer. Knocks impatiently, much louder.*]

SECRETARY [*turning around on his stool*]. What the devil is that — someone knocking? [*Shouts:*] Come in, why don't you? [*All the men in the room look up.* YANK *opens the door slowly, gingerly, as if afraid of an ambush. He looks around for secret doors, mystery, is taken aback by the commonplaceness of the room and the men in it, thinks he may have gotten in the wrong place, then sees the signboard on the wall and is reassured.*]

YANK [*blurts out*]. Hello.

MEN [*reservedly*]. Hello.

YANK [*more easily*]. I tought I'd bumped into de wrong dump.

SECRETARY [*scrutinizing him carefully*]. Maybe you have. Are you a member?

YANK. Naw, not yet. Dat's what I come for — to join.

SECRETARY. That's easy. What's your job — longshore?

YANK. Naw. Fireman — stoker on de liners.

SECRETARY [*with satisfaction*]. Welcome to our city. Glad to know you people are waking up at last. We haven't got many members in your line.

YANK. Naw. Dey're all dead to de woild.

SECRETARY. Well, you can help to wake 'em. What's your name? I'll make out your card.

YANK [*confused*]. Name? Lemme tink.

SECRETARY [*sharply*]. Don't you know your own name?

YANK. Sure; but I been just Yank for so long — Bob, dat's it — Bob Smith.

SECRETARY [*writing*]. Robert Smith. [*Fills out the rest of card.*] Here you are. Cost you half a dollar.

YANK. Is dat all — four bits? Dat's easy. [*Gives the* SECRETARY *the money.*]

SECRETARY [*throwing it in drawer*].

THE HAIRY APE

Thanks. Well, make yourself at home. No introductions needed. There's literature on the table. Take some of those pamphlets with you to distribute aboard ship. They may bring results. Sow the seed, only go about it right. Don't get caught and fired. We got plenty out of work. What we need is men who can hold their jobs — and work for us at the same time.

YANK. Sure.

[*But he still stands, embarrassed and uneasy.*]

SECRETARY [*looking at him — curiously*]. What did you knock for? Think we had a coon in uniform to open doors?

YANK. Naw. I tought it was locked — and dat yuh'd wanter give me the once-over trou a peep-hole or somep'n to see if I was right.

SECRETARY [*alert and suspicious, but with an easy laugh*]. Think we were running a crap game? That door is never locked. What put that in your nut?

YANK [*with a knowing grin, convinced that this is all camouflage, a part of the secrecy*]. Dis burg is full of bulls, ain't it?

SECRETARY [*sharply*]. What have the cops got to do with us? We're breaking no laws.

YANK [*with a knowing wink*]. Sure. Youse wouldn't for woilds. Sure. I'm wise to dat.

SECRETARY. You seem to be wise to a lot of stuff none of us knows about.

YANK [*with another wink*]. Aw, dat's aw right, see. [*Then, made a bit resentful by the suspicious glances from all sides.*] Aw, can it! Youse needn't put me trou de toid degree. Can't youse see I belong? Sure! I'm reg'lar. I'll stick, get me? I'll shoot de woiks for youse. Dat's why I wanted to join in.

SECRETARY [*breezily, feeling him out*]. That's the right spirit. Only are you sure you understand what you've joined? It's all plain and above board; still, some guys get a wrong slant on us. [*Sharply.*] What's your notion of the purpose of the I.W.W.?

YANK. Aw, I know all about it.

SECRETARY [*sarcastically*]. Well, give us some of your valuable information.

YANK [*cunningly.*] I know enough not to speak outa my toin. [*Then, resentfully again.*] Aw, say! I'm reg'lar. I'm wise to de game. I know yuh got to watch your step wit a stranger. For all youse know, I might be a plain-clothes dick, or somep'n, dat's what yuh're tinkin', huh? Aw, forget it! I belong, see? Ask any guy down to de docks if I don't.

SECRETARY. Who said you didn't?

YANK. After I'm 'nitiated, I'll show yuh.

SECRETARY [*astounded*]. Initiated? There's no initiation.

YANK [*disappointed*]. Ain't there no password — no grip nor nothin'?

SECRETARY. What'd you think this is — the Elks — or the Black Hand?

YANK. De Elks, hell! De Black Hand, dey're a lot of yellow backstickin' Ginees. Naw. Dis is a man's gang, ain't it?

SECRETARY. You said it! That's why we stand on our two feet in the open. We got no secrets.

YANK [*surprised, but admiringly*]. Yuh mean to say yuh always run wide open — like dis?

SECRETARY. Exactly.

YANK. Den yuh sure got your noive wit youse!

SECRETARY [*sharply*]. Just what was it made you want to join us? Come out with that straight.

YANK. Yuh call me? Well, I got noive, too! Here's my hand. Yuh wanter blow tings up, don't yuh? Well, dat's me! I belong!

SECRETARY [*with pretended carelessness*]. You mean change the unequal conditions of society by legitimate direct action — or with dynamite?

YANK. Dynamite! Blow it offen de oith — steel — all de cages — all de factories, steamers, buildings, jails — de Steel Trust and all dat makes it go.

SECRETARY. So — that's your idea, eh? And did you have any special job in that line you wanted to propose to us.

[*He makes a sign to the men, who get up cautiously one by one and group behind* YANK.]

YANK [*boldly*]. Sure, I'll come out wit it.

I'll show youse I'm one of de gang. Dere's dat millionaire guy, Douglas —

SECRETARY. President of the Steel Trust, you mean? Do you want to assassinate him?

YANK. Naw, dat don't get yuh nothin'. I mean blow up de factory, de woiks, where he makes de steel. Dat's what I'm after — to blow up de steel, knock all de steel in de woild up to de moon. Dat'll fix tings! [Eagerly, with a touch of bravado.] I'll do it by me lonesome! I'll show yuh! Tell me where his woiks is, how to git there, all de dope. Gimme de stuff, de old butter — and watch me do de rest! Watch de smoke and see it move! I don't give a damn if dey nab me — long as it's done! I'll soive life for it — and give 'em de laugh! [Half to himself.] And I'll write her a letter and tell her de hairy ape done it. Dat'll square tings.

SECRETARY [stepping away from YANK]. Very interesting.

[He gives a signal. The men, huskies all, throw themselves on YANK, and before he knows it they have his legs and arms pinioned. But he is too flabbergasted to make a struggle, anyway. They feel him over for weapons.]

MAN. No gat, no knife. Shall we give him what's what and put the boots to him?

SECRETARY. No. He isn't worth the trouble we'd get into. He's too stupid. [He comes closer and laughs mockingly in YANK's face.] Ho-ho! By God, this is the biggest joke they've put up on us yet. Hey, you Joke! Who sent you — Burns or Pinkerton? No, by God, you're such a bonehead I'll bet you're in the Secret Service! Well, you dirty spy, you rotten agent provocator, you can go back and tell whatever skunk is paying you blood-money for betraying your brothers that he's wasting his coin. You couldn't catch a cold. And tell him that all he'll ever get on us, or ever has got, is just his own sneaking plots that he's framed up to put us in jail. We are what our manifesto says we are, neither more nor less — and we'll give him a copy of that any time he calls. And as for you — [He glares scornfully at YANK, who is sunk in an oblivious stupor.] Oh, hell, what's the use of talking? You're a brainless ape.

YANK [aroused by the word to fierce but futile struggles]. What's dat, yuh Sheeny bum, yuh!

SECRETARY. Throw him out, boys.

[In spite of his struggles, this is done with gusto and éclat. Propelled by several parting kicks, YANK lands sprawling in the middle of the narrow cobbled street. With a growl he starts to get up and storm the closed door, but stops bewildered by the confusion in his brain, pathetically impotent. He sits there, brooding, in as near to the attitude of Rodin's "Thinker" as he can get in his position.]

YANK [bitterly]. So dem boids don't tink I belong, neider. Aw, to hell wit 'em! Dey're in de wrong pew — de same old bull — soapboxes and Salvation Army — no guts! Cut out an hour offen de job a day and make me happy! Gimme a dollar more a day and make me happy! Tree square a day, and cauliflowers in de front yard — — ekal rights — a woman and kids — a lousey vote — and I'm all fixed for Jesus, huh? Aw, hell! What does dat get yuh? Dis ting's in your inside, but it ain't your belly. Feedin' your face — sinkers and coffee — dat don't touch it. It's way down — at de bottom. Yuh can't grab it, and yuh can't stop it. It moves, and everyting moves. It stops and de whole woild stops. Dat's me now — I don't tick, see? — I'm a busted Ingersoll, dat's what. Steel was me, and I owned de woild. Now I ain't steel, and de woild owns me. Aw, hell! I can't see — it's all dark, get me? It's all wrong! [He turns a bitter mocking face up like an ape gibbering at the moon.] Say, youse up dere, Man in de Moon, yuh look so wise, gimme de answer, huh? Slip me de inside dope, de information right from de stable — where do I get off at, huh?

A POLICEMAN [who has come up the street in time to hear this last — with grim humor]. You'll get off at the station, you boob, if you don't get up out of that and keep movin'.

YANK [looking up at him — with a hard,

THE HAIRY APE

bitter laugh]. Sure! Lock me up! Put me in a cage! Dat's de on'y answer yuh know. G'wan, lock me up!
POLICEMAN. What you been doin'?
YANK. Enuf to gimme life for! I was born, see? Sure, dat's de charge. Write it in de blotter. I was born, get me!
POLICEMAN [*jocosely*]. God pity your old woman! [*Then matter-of-fact.*] But I've no time for kidding. You're soused. I'd run you in but it's too long a walk to the station. Come on now, get up, or I'll fan your ears with this club. Beat it now! [*He hauls* YANK *to his feet.*]
YANK [*in a vague mocking tone*]. Say, where do I go from here?
POLICEMAN [*Giving him a push — with a grin, indifferently*]. Go to hell.

CURTAIN

SCENE EIGHT

SCENE — *Twilight of the next day. The monkey house at the Zoo. One spot of clear gray light falls on the front of one cage so that the interior can be seen. The other cages are vague, shrouded in shadow from which chatterings pitched in a conversational tone can be heard. On the one cage a sign from which the word "gorilla" stands out. The gigantic animal himself is seen squatting on his haunches on a bench in much the same attitude as Rodin's "Thinker."*

[YANK *enters from the left. Immediately a chorus of angry chattering and screeching breaks out. The gorilla turns his eyes, but makes no sound or move.*]

YANK [*with a hard, bitter laugh*]. Welcome to your city, huh? Hail, hail, de gang's all here! [*At the sound of his voice the chattering dies away into an attentive silence.* YANK *walks up to the gorilla's cage and, leaning over the railing, stares in at its occupant, who stares back at him, silent and motionless. There is a pause of dead stillness. Then* YANK *begins to talk in a friendly confidential tone, half-mockingly, but with a deep undercurrent of sympathy.*] Say, yuh're some hard-lookin' guy, ain't yuh? I seen lots of tough nuts dat de gang called gorillas, but yuh're de foist real one I ever seen. Some chest yuh got, and shoulders, and dem arms and mits! I bet yuh got a punch in eider fist dat'd knock 'em all silly! [*This with genuine admiration. The gorilla, as if he understood, stands upright, swelling out his chest and pounding on it with his fist.* YANK *grins sympathetically.*] Sure, I get yuh. Yuh challenge de whole woild, huh? Yuh got what I was sayin' even if yuh muffed de woids. [*Then bitterness creeping in.*] And why wouldn't yuh get me? Ain't we both members of de same club — de Hairy Apes! [*They stare at each other — a pause — then* YANK *goes on slowly and bitterly.*] So yuh're what she seen when she looked at me, de white-faced tart! I was you to her, get me? On'y outa de cage — broke out — free to moider her, see? Sure! Dat's what she tought. She wasn't wise dat I was in a cage, too — worser'n yours — sure — a damn sight — 'cause you got some chanct to bust loose — but me — [*He grows confused.*] Aw, hell! It's all wrong, ain't it? [*A pause.*] I s'pose yuh wanter know what I'm doin' here, huh? I been warmin' a bench down to de Battery — ever since last night. Sure. I seen de sun come up. Dat was pretty, too — all red and pink and green. I was lookin' at de skyscrapers — steel — and all de ships comin' in, sailin' out, all over de oith — and dey was steel, too. De sun was warm, dey wasn't no clouds, and dere was a breeze blowin'. Sure, it was great stuff. I got it aw right — what Paddy said about dat bein' de right dope — on'y I couldn't get in it, see? I couldn't belong in dat. It was over my head. And I kept tinkin' — and den I beat it up here to see what youse was like. And I waited till dey was all gone to git yuh alone. Say, how d'yuh feel sittin' in dat pen all de time, havin' to stand for 'em comin' and starin' at yuh — de white-faced, skinny tarts and de boobs what marry 'em — makin' fun of yuh, laughin' at yuh, gittin' scared of yuh — damn 'em! [*He pounds on the rail with his fist. The gorilla rattles the bars of his cage and snarls. All the other monkeys set up an angry chattering in the darkness.* YANK *goes on excitedly.*]

Sure! Dat's de way it hits me, too. On'y yuh're lucky, see? Yuh don't belong wit 'em and yuh know it. But me, I belong wit 'em — but I don't, see? Dey don't belong wit me, dat's what. Get me? Tinkin' is hard — [*He passes one hand across his forehead with a painful gesture. The gorilla growls impatiently.* YANK *goes on gropingly.*] It's dis way, what I'm drivin' at. Youse can sit and dope dream in de past, green woods, de jungle and de rest of it. Den yuh belong and dey don't. Den yuh kin laugh at 'em, see? Yuh're de champ of de woild. But me — I ain't got no past to tink in, nor nothin' dat's comin', on'y what's now — and dat don't belong. Sure, you're de best off! Yuh can't tink, can yuh? Yuh can't talk neider. But I kin make a bluff at talkin' and tinkin' — a'most git away wit it — a'most! — and dat's where de joker comes in. [*He laughs.*] I ain't on oith and I ain't in heaven, get me? I'm in de middle tryin' to separate 'em, takin' all de woist punches from bot' of 'em. Maybe dat's what dey call hell, huh? But you, yuh're at de bottom. You belong! Sure! Yuh're de on'y one in de woild dat does, yuh lucky stiff! [*The gorilla growls proudly.*] And dat's why dey gotter put yuh in a cage, see? [*The gorilla roars angrily.*] Sure! Yuh get me. It beats it when you try to tink it or talk it — it's way down — deep — behind — you 'n' me we feel it. Sure! Bot' members of dis club! [*He laughs — then in a savage tone.*] What de hell! T' hell wit it! A little action, dat's our meat! Dat belongs! Knock 'em down and keep bustin' 'em till dey croaks yuh wit a gat — wit steel! Sure! Are yuh game? Dey've looked at youse, ain't dey — in a cage? Wanter git even? Wanter wind up like a sport 'stead of croakin' slow in dere? [*The gorilla roars an emphatic affirmative.* YANK *goes on with a sort of furious exaltation.*] Sure! Yuh're reg'lar! Yuh'll stick to de finish! Me' n' you, huh? — bot' members of this club! We'll put up one last star bout dat'll knock 'em offen deir seats! Dey'll have to make de cages stronger after we're trou! [*The gorilla is straining at his bars, growling, hopping from one foot to the other.* YANK *takes a jimmy from under his coat and forces the lock on the cage door. He throws this open.*] Pardon from de governor! Step out and shake hands! I'll take yuh for a walk down Fif' Avenoo. We'll knock 'em offen de oith and croak wit de band playin'. Come on, Brother. [*The gorilla scrambles gingerly out of his cage. Goes to* YANK *and stands looking at him.* YANK *keeps his mocking tone — holds out his hand.*] Shake — de secret grip of our order. [*Something, the tone of mockery, perhaps, suddenly enrages the animal. With a spring he wraps his huge arms around* YANK *in a murderous hug. There is a crackling snap of crushed ribs — a gasping cry, still mocking, from* YANK.] Hey, I didn't say, kiss me. [*The gorilla lets the crushed body slip to the floor; stands over it uncertainly, considering; then picks it up, throws it in the cage, shuts the door, and shuffles off menacingly into the darkness at left. A great uproar of frightened chattering and whimpering comes from the other cages. Then* YANK *moves, groaning, opening his eyes, and there is silence. He mutters painfully.*] Say — dey oughter match him — wit Zybszko. He got me, aw right. I'm trou. Even him didn't tink I belonged. [*Then, with sudden passionate despair.*] Christ, where do I get off at? Where do I fit in? [*Checking himself as suddenly.*] Aw, what de hell! No squakin', see! No quittin', get me! Croak wit your boots on! [*He grabs hold of the bars of the cage and hauls himself painfully to his feet—looks around him bewilderedly — forces a mocking laugh.*] In de cage, huh? [*In the strident tones of a circus barker.*] Ladies and gents, step forward and take a slant at de one and only — [*His voice weakening —* one and original — Hairy Ape from de wilds of —

[*He slips in a heap on the floor and dies. The monkeys set up a chattering, whimpering wail. And, perhaps, the Hairy Ape at last belongs.*]

CURTAIN

MARY THE THIRD
A COMEDY IN PROLOGUE AND THREE ACTS
By RACHEL CROTHERS

COPYRIGHT, 1923, BY RACHEL CROTHERS
ALL RIGHTS RESERVED

CHARACTERS

MARY THE FIRST. 1870
WILLIAM

MARY THE SECOND. 1897
ROBERT
RICHARD

MARY THE THIRD. 1923
MOTHER
GRANNY
FATHER
BOBBY
LYNN
HAL
LETTIE
MAX
NORA

MARY THE THIRD

PROLOGUE

MARY THE FIRST

TIME: 1870.
The stage is hung in dark curtains, the center is lighted and the figures which walk into the light are framed by darkness.
An old mahogany sofa, upholstered in black hair cloth, is the only furniture in the scene.
A girl of twenty sits on it — dressed in an evening gown of the period. The skirt voluminous with ruffles and lace. Her arms, bosom, and shoulders are bare — but the fashion of her hair is demure and maidenly with the proverbial curl and rose.
She fans nervously with her diminutive fan, waiting and watching. She is soft and pretty and flower-like. Her voice is sweet. Shyness and modesty are her manner. Her movements are graceful and coy and mincing — full of a conscious charm.
An orchestra from a seductive distance is playing an enticing polka.

A tall, good-looking fellow of twenty-five — in the evening dress of the period — comes quickly into the scene.

MARY. Good gracious! How did you know I was here?
WILLIAM. You told me you would be.
MARY. I didn't! The idea of you thinking such a thing!
WILLIAM [*heavy, honest, and simpleminded*]. I thought you said as soon as you finished that dance with Hiram, you'd come in here.
MARY. I may have said I *might* but I didn't say I *would*.
WILLIAM. Well, I hoped you would.
MARY. Where's Lucy? I didn't suppose you'd be looking for *me* when you were dancing with *her*.
WILLIAM. I finished.

MARY. Aren't you going to dance this one with her? It's your favorite polka and now no one in the world dances the polka so well as Lucy, of course.
WILLIAM. No one but you.
MARY. Oh, that's what you *used* to say. But you can't say that any more. Go on. Don't keep her waiting.
WILLIAM. Who's waiting for *you?*
MARY. I won't tell you.
WILLIAM. It's Hiram. How many times have you danced with him?
MARY. How do I know?
WILLIAM. Every other dance. Is this his, too?
MARY. I'm not dancing with anybody this time. I'm just sitting here resting. It's so sweet and quiet. Listen! Isn't the music sweet? I shall always think of you, William, when I hear that music. We've danced to it so many, many times. Oh, I oughtn't to have said that.
WILLIAM. Why not?
MARY. I mustn't say those things now. And you must go. There mustn't be any more of these sweet little stolen moments under the stairs. This is really good-bye, William, isn't it?
WILLIAM. No, it's not. Unless *you* want it to be.
MARY. Oh, *me!* Don't say me. What have I to do with it?
WILLIAM. Everything. It all depends on you whether it's good-bye or not.
MARY. Then of course it's good-bye. Dear, dear little Lucy! I hope you'll be happy with her, William. Good-bye.
[*Giving him her hand daintily, and drawing it away at once.*]
WILLIAM. What are you goin' on like this for? Nothing's going to be any different for you and me.

MARY. Oh, do you suppose for a minute she'll ever let you dance with me again?

WILLIAM. She can't help herself.

MARY. Oh, you don't know her — as I do. I love Lucy very, *very* dearly. She doesn't mean to be —

WILLIAM. What?

MARY. Nothing. I ought not to have said that.

WILLIAM. Said what? What are you hiding?

MARY. Oh, I'm not *hiding* anything about Lucy. Good gracious! I wouldn't have you think *that* for *any*thing. Oh, dear. Oh, dear! Rather than have you think that, I'll tell you right out what was on my mind. I only meant that under her sweet little purring ways, she's very, *very* strong and stubborn and always gets what she wants. She won't let you be my dear old friend any more. She's been very cold to me lately and there can't be any reason for it unless it's because she doesn't like you to like me — even a little bit.

WILLIAM. She can't stop that.

MARY. You mustn't say that. It's all over now.

WILLIAM. It never would have been over if you hadn't preferred Hiram and his money.

MARY. Oh, don't blame me. But it *is* over. So let's not talk about it. Let's just be happy for a moment here . . . in this sweet little corner where we've sat so many, many times.

WILLIAM. We'll sit here again sometimes, too.

[*Trying to take her hand which she finally allows him to do after a modest struggle.*]

MARY. Oh, never, *never!* I'm not that kind of a girl. You ought to know that, William. You ought to know that I will be loyal to Lucy always — above everything. Nothing shall ever dim my devotion to her. Dear, dear little Lucy! I must be true to her.

WILLIAM. What about being true to me? You can't throw me away like an old shoe — just because I'm getting married. I'm not going to throw you away, let me tell you.

MARY. Oh, but you're a great, big, strong man. You can do as you please and still control your feelings. I'm only a weak little thing. I wouldn't dare try to go on seeing you after you are married. I might not be able to hide my feelings.

WILLIAM. Hide what feelings? What kind of feelings have you got for me, Mary?

MARY [*turning away and brushing a tear from her cheek*]. No kind. Good-bye, William! You must go.

WILLIAM. I won't go until you tell me just what you mean and just how you're feeling.

MARY. No — No — it's too late.

WILLIAM. It's not too late. I'm not tied up yet. We can change things.

MARY. Oh, no — no — Lucy!

WILLIAM. I've got more money than Hiram has now. More than he ever will have. Granddad left me rich, Mary. I'm a rich man now. If I thought you still cared for me the way you once did — nothing could hold me back from getting you.

MARY. Oh, William — William, you mustn't say that. [*Taking the rose from her hair, smelling it and holding it to her lips.*] Take this and keep it and look at it sometimes when it's faded and think of me. Perhaps I'll be faded, too. Isn't it pretty?

WILLIAM. Not half so pretty as you are.

MARY. Oh!

WILLIAM. Your cheek is much softer and pinker.

MARY. How can you say such a thing! It couldn't be. See. Look! [*Holding the rose to her cheek and bending near him. He kisses her cheek.*] Oh — how could you! How could you, William! Oh — you're hurting my arm! You're going to make it black and blue. There, look at that red spot. Kiss it and make it well. Oh, no — I mustn't say that. [WILLIAM *kisses her forearm, her elbow, her shoulder, and her throat.*] Oh, William — you mustn't!

WILLIAM. I won't let anybody else have you. Are you engaged to Hiram?

MARY. Oh, what does it matter?

WILLIAM. I never have loved any other girl. I never will.

MARY. And do you think I've ever loved any other man? Oh, I ought not to have said that. But I will say it, just this once before we part forever. I loved you as no girl ever loved a man.

WILLIAM. God!

[*Bending over her hands and holding them to his lips.*]

MARY. We must be brave, William, and say good-bye.

WILLIAM [*kneeling before her, his head bowed in her hands*]. I can't — I can't — don't ask it.

MARY. It's too late. You're pledged to another. You must be true to her and live a beautiful life, William.

WILLIAM. I ain't going to do it. You're my fate. I'll blow my brains out if you don't marry me. I'll kill anybody else that gets you.

MARY [*sobbing*]. But fate is parting us.

WILLIAM. Look here. I'll have the horses ready in an hour. You go home and put on your riding habit and meet me at the cross-roads in an hour.

MARY. No, no, William. I couldn't — I couldn't.

WILLIAM [*still on his knees*]. You've got to. We can't let life treat us like this. We've got to take hold of things. Nothing can stop us. This is meant to be.

MARY. Then it would be wrong to let anything separate us. It's stronger than we are, William. Eternal and beautiful like the stars. But, oh, I can't do it, William. Never — never in this world can I do it. I'm not sure that it would be right. I'll be behind the oak tree. It's bigger than the maple.

WILLIAM [*getting up*]. You angel!

MARY. Don't you bring Fleetfoot. I'm afraid of her. Bring Silver Star. Will you love me forever?

WILLIAM. Forever and ever.

MARY. In this world and the next?

WILLIAM. Longer than eternity.

MARY. There never has been a love as great as this. I feel it. I know it. Oh, William, I love you so! I love you!

[*They are locked in each other's arms; their lips pressed together as the light fades.*]

MARY THE SECOND

TIME: 1897.

The light comes on again and shows the same sofa with a tall, fair, rather æsthetic-looking boy standing by it.

He wears evening clothes of the period and is examining closely a dance program, checking off numbers with a small pencil.

An orchestra is playing Sousa's "Washington Post" twostep with great swing and pomp.

A dark boy, more sturdy in appearance, also wearing evening clothes, comes into the scene quickly.

ROBERT [*as he comes on with smiling self-assurance*]. Hello, Richard. Who's the dude dancing with Mary?

RICHARD [*with injured dignity*]. I thought she was dancing with you.

ROBERT. No, I have this next one with her.

RICHARD. Oh, no. *I* have it.

ROBERT. You're off your trolley. It's mine.

RICHARD. You're mistaken. She has it with me.

ROBERT. You better go find her, then. I think I'll wait here.

[*Throwing himself on the sofa.*]

RICHARD. You seem to be very sure of yourself.

ROBERT. You bet I'm sure.

RICHARD. You're not going to stay here and make a scene, are you — over a little thing like this?

ROBERT. I haven't anything to make a scene about. I'm just waiting to dance with Mary. If that's painful to you, why not *withdraw* so you won't suffer so much?

[*The orchestra changes to "Daisy Belle" and* ROBERT *sings a verse with a gaiety intended to madden* RICHARD.]

Daisy, Daisy, give me your answer true,
I'm half crazy all for the love of you.
It won't be a stylish marriage —
I can't afford a carriage,
But you'll look neat — upon the seat —
Of a bicycle built for two.

RICHARD. Oh, don't! It's bad enough to have to dance to anything so vulgar — without hearing the words.

ROBERT. I'm stuck on the words.

RICHARD. You probably are. They're just about suited to your vocabulary.

ROBERT. What's the matter with my vocabulary?

RICHARD. Nothing. I dare say it expresses everything you think — very adequately.

ROBERT. Meaning my intellect is not so colossal as yours.

RICHARD. I couldn't be so rude as that.

ROBERT. Suppose you clear out then before I say something so rude you won't care to hear it.

RICHARD. You're making a fool of yourself.

ROBERT [*rising quickly*]. I'll show you who's the fool!

MARY [*coming into the scene out of breath*]. Oh, I'm nearly dead! Mamma *made* me dance with that old man.

[MARY *is the perfect Gibson type — in dress and hair and figure.*]

ROBERT. He's got cheek asking you. He must think he's a young masher. Come on, this one is ours.

RICHARD. It's *mine*, Mary.

MARY. Oh — which one *is* it?

ROBERT AND RICHARD. The tenth — a twostep.

MARY. No, this is an extra. Isn't it?

ROBERT. No, it isn't. Let me see your card.

RICHARD. Let *me* see it.

MARY [*hiding her program*]. *No!*

ROBERT [*showing her his*]. Look at this. There it is — the tenth — perfectly plain.

RICHARD [*showing his card*]. Nothing could be plainer than this.

MARY. That's funny. Well — the *next* one is an extra. One of you can have *that*.

ROBERT. It's mine, anyway.

MARY. I'll tell you what let's do. Let's divide *this* one. I'll dance the first half with you, Robert, and the other half with you, Richard.

ROBERT. I don't see why I should give up half my dance.

RICHARD. Oh, give it all to him. You're wasting time talking about it.

MARY. Now, boys, don't be silly. I'll stay here and sit it out. The first half is Richard's. Go on, Robert. I want to talk to Richard.

ROBERT. Rats! I make myself pretty tired doing this.

MARY. It's a sweet thing for you to do. Ta-ta.

[*She turns her back to* RICHARD *and blows a small kiss to* ROBERT.]

ROBERT. I'll be back in a jiffy.

[*He goes out.*]

MARY [*sitting on the sofa*]. Now we can talk.

RICHARD. How *could* you?

MARY. How could I what?

RICHARD. I don't care anything about the old program. [*Going to her and tearing the program in two.*] I want to know what you said you'd tell me to-night.

MARY. I'm not going to tell you anything when you're in that kind of a humour.

RICHARD. What kind of a humour did you expect me to be in?

MARY. The kind you were last night — when you're different and not like anybody else.

RICHARD. You were different — too — you made me believe you *would* marry me and to-night you've hardly looked at me.

MARY. But I'm thinking every minute.

RICHARD. What are you thinking?

MARY. Life is wonderful. I want to live it wonderfully.

RICHARD. We'll live it wonderfully — together. Our souls are like one soul.

MARY. Yes, but our dispositions aren't. Sometimes we feel alike. When you read poetry to me we're awfully high and exalted, but when we're just going along in an every-day way we aren't a bit alike.

RICHARD. Well, it's better to be alike and feel alike on the heights than in commonplace things that don't matter.

MARY. But I believe they do matter. I wonder which matters the most.

RICHARD. Which are the more important in the world — the great things or the little things?

MARY. Oh, of course, of course — but

the trouble is when you do ordinary little things that I don't like, I forget the great ones and I could just —
RICHARD. Just what?
MARY. Just kill you.
RICHARD. But that's your fault, dearest — not mine.
MARY. I wonder. I wonder if it *is* my fault when I hate you and yours when I love you. I do love you sometimes — Richard.
RICHARD. Oh, Mary, we belong to each other. We were *meant* for each other — in our *real* selves.
MARY. But I'm not sure which *is* my real self. You see, Richard, it's this way. Now listen and see if I can make you understand. Sometimes you're the most wonderful thing in the world. You say things that no one else says — and you think and feel and understand — and then sometimes —
RICHARD. It's you who don't understand. Listen, dearest —
ROBERT [*dashing in*]. Time's up. Slide, Kelly, slide! You must have said everything you ever thought of by this time.
RICHARD. Oh, time doesn't matter. [*Rising slowly.*] A minute — or eternity are all alike.
ROBERT. You don't say! I'll take mine done up in sixty-minute parcels, thank you — and you've had more than your share. Skip.
RICHARD [*looking at* MARY *as he goes*]. Eternity.
ROBERT [*after* RICHARD *has gone*]. Dick's got 'em again. What in the name of Heaven do you scrape up to talk to him about?
MARY. Oh, lots of things.
ROBERT. Does he spout poetry to you *all* the time?
MARY. It wouldn't hurt you to have a little poetry, too.
ROBERT [*laughing and sitting beside* MARY]. All right. I'll get some. Anything you say. What more do you want me to have?
MARY. You don't think much about —
ROBERT. About what?
MARY. Oh, about things that aren't just *things*.
ROBERT. What?
MARY. You see, you don't even know what I'm talking about.
ROBERT. How can I tell what you're thinking when you don't *say* anything.
MARY. That's just it. You ought to be able to.
ROBERT. Well, all right. I'll find out how it's done if that's what you want.
MARY. Oh!
ROBERT. What's the matter, little girl? I'll give you anything on earth and the moon and stars thrown in. Honest, Mary, no man ever loved a girl the way I love you. And I'll never change. *That's* the point.
MARY. What if you did? It would be horrible.
ROBERT. But I wouldn't. I couldn't. How could I? You're meant for me. You're mine. We suit each other. Don't you trust me, Mary?
MARY. Oh, yes, I trust you — but getting married is forever and ever and ever.
ROBERT. Of course.
MARY. And Oh — unless two people *do* love each other — Oh, in the most wonderful way — that *nothing* can change —
ROBERT. Like us.
MARY. Now, listen, Robert. I want to make you understand.
ROBERT [*taking her in his arms*]. You don't need to. I do understand. I know all about it. [*He covers her face with kisses.*] I'll make you the happiest girl in the world. I love you. And we'll never change. Never.
MARY [*clinging to him*]. Oh, if it could be that way, Robert!
ROBERT. Of course it will be that way. Nobody ever loved anybody the way I love you. You're going to marry me, aren't you? You know you are! *Say* it!
MARY. Yes.
ROBERT. Do you love me?
MARY. Oh, I do, Robert — and we must make it the most wonderful love that was ever in the world.
[*He folds her in his arms as the light fades.*]

ACT I

TIME: 1923. *Summer.*
PLACE: *The living room in the Robert Hollister house.*

It is the conventional room of conventional success — filled with a certain amount of beauty and comfort produced by money rather than individual taste.

The walls are made by the same draperies used in the first two scenes — with the frames of the doors and windows set in.

The furniture is a mixture of old and new — brought into harmony in dull tones. The sofa that is seen in the first scenes is now upholstered in chintz.

Late afternoon in summer.

AT CURTAIN, MARY THE FIRST, *at seventy-five, and* MARY THE SECOND, *now forty-five, are in the room.*

GRANNY — MARY THE FIRST — *sits on the sofa, still somewhat the pretty and spoiled darling — still a trace of coquetry in her soft blue frock. She is knitting a blue woolen scarf on large needles.* MOTHER, MARY THE SECOND *— grown into a handsome full-blown rose — wears a gown and hat in good style and unobtrusive prettiness. She comes in by the long window — a little warm, a little bored and tired.*

MOTHER. Hello, Mother.
GRANNY. Back?
MOTHER. Oh — It's hot!
   [*Sitting listlessly in a comfortable chair.*]
GRANNY [*after an elaborate search for her ball of wool*]. Who was there?
MOTHER. Oh, everybody.
GRANNY. Did you have a good time?
MOTHER. Not very.
GRANNY. You're a funny woman, Mary. I don't see why you ever go to a party. You're so indifferent about it.
MOTHER. What else is there to do?
GRANNY. When I was your age I never missed a party. Euchre was a much better game than bridge too. Much more sociable. You could talk all you wanted to, and I usually took the prize.
MOTHER. I'll bet you did, Mother.
GRANNY. Did you play for money?
MOTHER. Yes.
GRANNY. How much did you win?
MOTHER. I lost.
GRANNY. Serves you right. Ladies and gentlemen didn't act like professional gamblers when I was your age. Mary, let me tell you something. From something I heard Mary drop the other day I wouldn't be at all surprised if *she* plays for money too — sometimes.
MOTHER. I shouldn't be surprised if she does?
GRANNY. Do you know she does?
MOTHER. How can she help it, Mother? Everybody else does.
GRANNY. You could put your foot down hard and forbid it.
   [MOTHER *smiles again and reaches for the afternoon paper on the low table near her — and opens it indifferently.*]
GRANNY. I know Robert doesn't know. Aren't you going to tell him?
MOTHER. I don't think so.
GRANNY. You ought to. At least he'd try to put a stop to it. Robert certainly does *try* to make his children what they ought to be. He certainly tries harder than you do, Mary. Don't you think he'd try if you told him? [MARY, *reading, doesn't hear.*] Mary!
MOTHER. Uh? What? I beg your pardon, Mother.
GRANNY. I say, don't you think Robert would try?
MOTHER. Try what?
GRANNY. Try to put a stop to Mary's playing cards for money, if he knew.
MOTHER. I expect he would. He's tried to put a stop to almost everything else she does.
GRANNY. You don't help him much. You're certainly not bringing your children up the way I brought *you* up.
MOTHER. And do you think you did a good job on me?
GRANNY. At least I did a better one than you're doing on *her.* Look here! [*Drawing a box of cigarettes out from under one pillow and a box of matches from an-*

other.] Look here! It isn't enough to have them laid out on every table in the house. They're stuck under everything you touch. I expect to find them in my own bed some night. Why she hasn't set the house afire long ago I don't see for the life of me.

MOTHER. I don't either.

GRANNY. And look at *this!*

MOTHER. What?

GRANNY. A hole burned right through this sofa by one of those abominable things.

MOTHER. Oh, that's a shame.

GRANNY. I should think it is. It's *my sofa,* too, you know. It came out of Aunt Fannie's house. I sat on it in her house the night I told your father I'd marry him.

MOTHER. Well — that was a great moment for us all, wasn't it?

GRANNY. Yes, it was. You needn't be sarcastic. And here's Mary abusing it. Sitting on it morning, noon, and night with boys — boys — *boys.* Do you know how many boys she *has* sat on it with?

MOTHER. No, I don't. I served my time at sitting on it, myself.

GRANNY. That's what I say. All sorts of things have happened on this sofa and here she is treating it like — with no respect at all.

MOTHER. Were you taking care of the sofa when you were sitting on it?

GRANNY. Of course I was. And so were you. I didn't *allow* you to abuse it. You were *taught* to take care of things.

MOTHER. I don't seem to remember that.

GRANNY. Seems to me you're forgetting a great many things you ought to remember. Seems to me you're getting very hard and worldly as you grow older.

MOTHER. Nonsense, Mother! There's nothing hard about *me.* I wish there were.

GRANNY. You wish there were! There you are! That's a hard thing to say. You're getting more like everybody else — callous — just *callous.* You let things slip and you're not holding up strict enough standards to your children.

MOTHER. Yes, I know. Let's not start that, please.

GRANNY. There you go! You don't care a fig about what I say. There was a time when people thought what I said was of some importance, and listened to it — too.

MOTHER. Oh, Mother dear, I *do* listen.

GRANNY. You have no more respect for my opinion than that.

[*Flicking her fingers.*]

BOBBY [*dashing in from the outside*]. Mother, are you through with the car?

MOTHER. Y-e-s — but what do you —

BOBBY. I left my racket out at the club. I want to dash out and get it. [*He starts out and turns back.*] Oh, Granny, another button's busted off this coat. Will you sew it on, please? [*Putting it on the table.*]

GRANNY. Yes, dearie. Don't put it there. Give it to me. You can't put anything down in this house if you ever expect to get it back.

BOBBY [*going to give her the button*]. See — it came off here and it sort of took a chunk of the coat with it.

GRANNY. You bad thing! I s'pose I can darn it. Here, you keep it. I mended sixteen pairs of socks for you this morning.

BOBBY. Thanks.

MOTHER. Mind you're back in time for dinner, Bobby. Your father will probably want the car to-night.

BOBBY. I'll hurry.

MOTHER. And don't drive too fast, Bobby.

GRANNY. I'll never go with you again if you drive the way you did yesterday.

BOBBY. Oh, you think anything over five miles an hour is too fast.

[*He hurries out.*]

GRANNY. Bobby's a sweet child, but he's getting to be a ripsnorter too — just about as bad as Mary. Both of them are as wild as colts.

MOTHER. Well — after all, they're my children, and if I don't mind the things they do, I don't know why you should.

GRANNY. Your children! Anybody would think I hadn't brought up a family of children of my own.

MOTHER. I expect you were a much better mother than I am, dear.

GRANNY. I *know* I was. You're shutting your eyes to things that are right under your nose. Robert does try. I will say that for him. Robert's peculiar in some ways, but I must say he does try to bring up his children right.

MOTHER [*seeing a letter on the desk and opening it to read*]. Robert is always right.

GRANNY. I don't say that. But he certainly is as right as most men are. As men go, he's a very fine man. You're a very fortunate woman.

MARY. As women go, I suppose I am.

GRANNY. I sometimes think you don't appreciate him, Mary. I sometimes do.

MOTHER. I've spent my life appreciating Robert.

GRANNY. I don't know why you wouldn't... a man who has succeeded as he has and put you in this beautiful house.

MOTHER [*sitting at the desk to write a note*]. He certainly did *put* me in it.

GRANNY. Uh? What do you mean by that? You're getting so sort of nifty and highty-tighty lately I don't know what you mean half the time.

MOTHER. Well, I don't mean much of anything. I wouldn't worry about that.

GRANNY. You're not living up to the principles I brought you up with.

MOTHER. Mother — if you'd only acknowledge that what you brought me up with hasn't any more to do with the case now than I have with the North Pole — and stop stewing about it — you'd be a much happier person.

GRANNY. Why, Mary McDougal Hollister! That I should live to hear you say that! What's happened to you? You're different lately. What is it? Is anything wrong?

MOTHER. Everything's just exactly as it always was.

GRANNY. I should hope so. You're a happy woman. If you're not, you ought to be ashamed of yourself. When I was your age, it was the fashion to be happy. Women loved their husbands and appreciated their blessings. Or if they didn't they didn't air it from the house-tops.

MOTHER. No — they just lied along and covered things up.

GRANNY. Well, land knows *you* haven't anything to cover up. That's one sure thing. [*A pause.*] Have you?

MOTHER [*sealing her letter and getting up*]. Of course not.

GRANNY. Then what's the use acting as if you had? The thing for you to think about is your children and how to keep them from being contaminated by the terrible things that are going on. You aren't half strict enough with Mary. I tell you she's in danger — actual downright danger, and you don't seem to see it at all.

MOTHER. We're *all* in danger. You're in danger of becoming a fussy old woman. I'm in danger of being swamped by the hateful ugliness of — respectable — everyday life. If Mary's got anything more dangerous than that to face, she'll wriggle through somehow, I s'pose.

[*Taking her hat and going to the hall door.*]

GRANNY. And make a muddle of it. *She* doesn't know what's good for her. It's your business to make her see who's the right one for her to marry, and make her marry him.

MOTHER. Did your mother make you marry Father?

GRANNY. She didn't have to. I *knew* he was the best and I took him. Didn't I help you to take Robert?

MOTHER. No, you didn't, and I didn't take him — I was taken. Mary won't be taken — and she won't take. She wants something different.

GRANNY. Wants? Wants? What does she want?

MOTHER. Something that *comes*. Something you nor I ever had.

GRANNY. I think you're out of your head lately! I'm going to take Mary in hand myself.

MOTHER. No, you won't, Mother. I must ask you, please — to let Mary alone.

MARY [*coming in quickly through one of the long windows*]. Mother — I've got a great scheme.

[MARY *is twenty — slender and straight as a boy. She wears a slip of a frock — which leaves her free — and she vibrates with vitality and eagerness — rather dynamically interested in her own affairs. She pitches her hat into a chair as she comes in.*]

MOTHER. Have you, dear? What?

MARY. Some of us are going camping — Lettie and Max and Lynn and Hall and I — and do all our own cooking and cleaning up and everything — and see how really awfully well and decently we *can* do it. We think — we know, in fact — it's the best way in the world — the only way to really know each other — you know — to see each other all the time — in a sort of messy way — doing things we don't like to do — and sort of getting right down at realities, you know — vital stuff.

MOTHER. I see. But why do you want to know each other so well? Why take such risks?

GRANNY. I think as much! It's hard enough to like anybody when they're all dressed up and on their good behavior, let alone when they're all dirty and eating bad food.

MARY. That's just it, Granny. That's the point exactly. It's a magnificent test.

MOTHER. But why not let well enough alone?

MARY. Because you see — some of us — all of us, in fact — are in love with some of the others — and we're going to take this way of finding out — just what kind of love it is, and what we're going to do with it. See?

GRANNY. You take my advice and pick out the best one and stay at home with him, and wear your good clothes every day.

MARY [*going to* GRANNY *to chuck her under the chin*]. I bet you were the worst kind of a vamp, Granny.

GRANNY. I was a very modest, maidenly girl, through and through and *through.*

MOTHER. Who's going with you? Who are the chaperons, I mean.

MARY. That's the point. We're not going to have any.

MOTHER. Oh —

GRANNY. What?

MARY. It would be the same old thing if we did, and put the whole scheme on the blink.

MOTHER. But you don't mean —

MARY. Nobody would be natural. It would be the cut-and-dried conventional stuff, and that's just what we don't want. We want to see each other as we really are.

GRANNY. You mean go way off alone — boys and girls *together* — without any older people?

MARY. Yes.

GRANNY. Are you stark, staring crazy?

MARY. Not at all. I think it's a great idea. People don't *know* each other before they're married. That's why most marriages are merely disappointing experiments instead of lifetime mating. That's why the experimenting ought to be done *before* marriage.

MOTHER. We'll talk about it after while, dear.

MARY. Oh, Mother — why wait to *talk?*

GRANNY. Yes, *why?* Tell her now that it's an unheard-of, immoral, *disgraceful* idea to have even come into a nice girl's head. Tell her that — this minute.

MOTHER. Wait, Mother.

MARY. Immoral? Disgraceful? Why, pray? Why?

GRANNY. Because it outrages all the decencies. What would you do at night, I'd like to know?

MARY. We'd go to bed and sleep — as decently as we do at home in our own beds.

MOTHER. Now, now, dear.

MARY. If you can't think of anything but *that*, Granny, you *have* got an evil mind.

MOTHER. Mary!

MARY. We aren't going away just so we can sleep together. We could stay right at home and do that, let me tell you.

MOTHER. Mary!

GRANNY [*rising in shocked excitement*]. Are you going to *do* something? Don't you know *now* you must do something, or are you just going to go on sitting still?

MOTHER. Mother, will you *please* let me —

MARY. If I could just talk to Mother alone once, Granny, without you interfering, I might be able to make her understand something.

MOTHER. Mary — be quiet! Aren't

you ashamed to speak to your grandmother like that?

GRANNY. No, she's not. There's no shame in her. She's brazen and disrespectful, and you *let* her be.

MARY. She isn't *letting* me be *any*thing. I'm myself, Granny. Can't you understand that? And I'm talking about something very important to me which you don't understand at all.

MOTHER. Mary — that will *do*, I say. Tell your grandmother you're sorry, and don't let this happen again.

MARY [*going to* GRANNY *reluctantly*]. I'm sorry, Granny. I really am. I didn't mean to be disrespectful. Will you forgive me?

GRANNY [*bursting into tears*]. No, I won't. You're an impertinent little minx, and I don't want you to speak to me.

MOTHER. Oh, Mother dear, don't take it that way.

MARY. I said I was sorry.

GRANNY. Don't touch me! Nobody loves me. Nobody appreciates me.

MARY. Please forgive me.

GRANNY. Let me alone. You've broken my heart.

[*She goes out into the hall sobbing.*]

MOTHER. Now see what you've done.

MARY [*closing the door*]. Grandmother's the limit. She really is.

MOTHER. She's dear and sweet, and you have no business to say wild things you know will shock her.

MARY. What's wild about what I said?

MOTHER. You know as well as I do. Decent people don't *do* those things.

MARY [*throwing herself on the sofa*]. Because they don't is no reason it wouldn't be a darned good idea if they did.

MOTHER. Oh — *dearest!*

MARY. If nobody ever did anything that had never been done before, we'd be a sweet set of dubs. People are dull enough as it is, goodness knows — without setting that up as the law to live by.

MOTHER. You're talking from very lofty heights. Unfortunately we have to live in the valleys of common sense.

MARY. That's the way you always get out of everything, Mother. I want to *try* things. What else is life for?

MOTHER. You can't try things the whole world knows have nothing but danger and disaster in them.

MARY. Do you mean to say I couldn't go any place with anybody and not stay *myself* — just as I am now — unless I *wanted* to be something else? And then if I wanted to, why, of course I *would*, and that would be my own affair, anyway.

MOTHER. Mary! Stop it. If I thought for a minute you *meant* that stuff, I'd be terribly frightened. But you don't.

MARY. Certainly I mean it. And I've just about decided that free love is the only solution to the whole business, anyway.

MOTHER. What on earth are you talking about?

MARY. I don't know that I *could* live all my life with one man — however much I loved him. Of course you and Father are satisfied with each other because you've never had anything else. But you don't know *what* you might have been, Mother, if you'd lived with a lot of men. Experience — constructive experience — is the only developing progressive thing in the world.

MOTHER. There's nothing new about the relations between men and women and there's nothing true or right but the same old things that have always been true. I'm afraid you've been reading too much new stuff — trying to be clever and advanced. Don't, dear — don't.

MARY. Gosh, Mother — you don't suppose anything I've read in a book cuts any ice? I'm talking about *me* myself, and how I feel and what I want. Hal and Lynn both have qualities that attract me enormously — and I want to find out if I want to marry either one of them. I wouldn't be satisfied to be happy just in the way you and Father are happy. I want something that is beautiful, and beautiful all the time.

MOTHER. Nothing is beautiful *all* the time. If you're going on a quest for that, you might as well stay at home.

MARY. Mother, are you and Father really happy?

MOTHER [startled]. Of course! Why on earth do you say that?
MARY. Lots and lots of times I — Nothing.
MOTHER. What do you mean?
MARY. There isn't anything really wrong, is there? You do love each other, don't you?
MOTHER [evading MARY's eyes]. Don't be silly. Of course we do. Now see here, Mary — you can't expect me to take your scheme seriously . . .
MARY. But I do. What if I must do it, Mother? What if I must to *express* myself — to find myself? After all, it's my life, you know.
MOTHER. Mary, if you'll promise me to stop thinking about this nonsense, I won't tell your Father, but if you don't — I will — and he'll — I don't know *what* he will do.
MARY. I do. I know every snort and gesture, but that won't make any difference if I think my happiness —

[LYNN *comes through the lower window followed by* HAL. LYNN *is the prototype of* ROBERT HOLLISTER — HAL *of* RICHARD, *seen in the Prologue.*]

LYNN. Hello, Mary! Hello, Mrs. Hollister!
MARY. Hello, Lynn!
MOTHER. Hello.
HAL. Hello.
MARY. Come in — come in. Pray do.
HAL. What's the matter?
MARY. I've just told Mother the scheme.
LYNN. It doesn't seem to have made a hit.
MOTHER. It's too silly to talk about. You two boys ought to be men of the world enough to make Mary realize how impossible it is — instead of putting such ideas into her head.
MARY. They didn't, Mother. I put them into theirs.
MOTHER. Then get them out. I trust you boys, you know, and when I come back into this room I expect you both to give me your word of honor that the whole thing is off.

[*She goes out — closing the door.*]

MARY. Mother's difficult because she's so nice. Give me a light — somebody.

[*Going to sit on the sofa and taking a cigarette. Both boys strike matches and sit — one on either side of her, lighting their own cigarettes.*]

MARY [*going on after a long puff and throwing back her head to blow the smoke — crossing her legs and folding her arms*]. It's almost impossible to talk to her or get anywhere with her, because she's a perfectly happy inexperienced woman, the most dangerous kind.
LYNN. Dangerous? I wouldn't exactly call your mother dangerous.
MARY. She's dangerous because she's contented, and therefore not progressive — stupid.
LYNN. Oh.
HAL [*slowly and importantly*]. Of course — I get that.
MARY. And she represents such an awful lot of women. They haven't moved an inch for ages.
LYNN. Your mother's a peach, though.
MARY. Of course she is — a perfect darling. I'm crazy about her. That's why this thing is so hard.
LYNN. Then give it up. Hang it, I'm not so mad about it, you know.
MARY. I knew you'd be the first one to back out.
HAL. So did I.
LYNN. I'm not backing out.
HAL. Yes, you are. Give it up, old man. It's not your gait, anyway. Just drop it.
LYNN. And let you stick? Not much. Don't worry about my gait. I'll keep up all right.
MARY. Is the first thing that Mother says going to knock it all out of you?
LYNN. No — but people are going to talk like blazes, and I can't stand to have you talked about, Mary.
MARY. Oh, Lord, Lynn! Do we have to begin all over to convince you?
HAL. You see, old man, you're not really with us. You're only going because you don't want to be left out. You don't see it as something important to the improvement of the whole question of love and marriage.

LYNN. Take it from me, Max and Lettie aren't up in the clouds the way you two are — you're fooling yourselves there — *hard*.

HAL. I don't agree with you. I think Mary and I have succeeded in making them see that — that —

LYNN. That what?

HAL. That if they haven't the courage to lead their own lives regardless of other people's moth-eaten convictions — they will never get anywhere or be any further along than their fathers and mothers.

MARY. Of course, to me it's thrilling — positively thrilling. I've never done anything in my life that I like so much. It's so simple — so absolutely simple — merely to go off and live naturally and freely for two weeks — doing a thing we know in the bottom of our souls is *right*, and knowing perfectly well the whole town is going to explode with horror. Then we'll march back again with our heads well up and prove that we're finer and more intelligent people than we were before we went away. I think it's big — you know.

LYNN. Y-e-s — but what if it never was understood and accepted. It would be terribly hard on you two girls.

HAL. Even so — it would be worth it. They'd both be doing something great. Wreckage of the individual doesn't count in the world's work.

LYNN. Not so long as the *other* fellow happens to be the wreck.

MARY. Now, listen. We've all reached the point where we think it's worth doing. I've even decided I *must* do it — in spite of Mother. But if we're going to get away with it, we've got to do it quickly before the others back out and spill the whole business. I think we'd better go to-night — after the party. We'll all be out late — anyway — and nobody watching the time and expecting us. I'll get word to Letitia, and we can pack now and put the stuff in — in your garage, Lynn, and all start off together.

HAL. Great!

LYNN. No — we've got to be foxy getting out of the garage — not get together till we're out of town — then when we're out on the road, let 'er go.

MARY. I can hardly wait! And now — you boys have to promise me — utterly and absolutely — that you won't make love to me the whole time we're gone. It's going to be a square deal for everybody, and don't forget this — I may not want to marry either one of you — and you may not want to marry me, after all. You *do* understand — don't you?

HAL. *I* do. Certainly. You're magnificent, Mary. If we haven't enough of your spirit in us to rise to this, we're rotters. If you *do* find that Lynn's the one to make you happy, I shall understand, and if I can't take you by the hand, old man, and wish you luck — I shall be horribly disappointed in myself.

LYNN. And if the same thing happens to *me*, I hope I'll have the guts to clear out and not stop to wish anything on anybody.

MARY [*getting up and standing between them*]. You're splendid — both of you. Shake. [*The boys clasp hands and she puts hers over theirs.*] Skip now before Mother comes back — and avoid the issue. Bye-bye — see you to-night.

[*The boys go.* MARY *goes to the hall door — about to open it.* HAL *comes back.*]

HAL [*in a whisper*]. Mary!

MARY. Oh! — I thought you'd gone.

HAL. Just a minute.

MARY. What do you want?

[*They go to the sofa and sit.* MARY *turns on the light in the lamp which is behind the sofa — the rest of the room is in shadow — with the same effect as in the scenes in the Prologue.*]

HAL. I just want to say this, dear — that whatever happens — I'll be with you and you can count on me and my love — and above all on my *friendship*.

MARY. I know I can, old dear. I know that, and it gives me such a wonderful feeling of security — your understanding, I mean.

HAL. That's what I wanted to be sure of. That you *do* feel that.

MARY. Oh, I do — I do.

HAL. Of course I know your soul belongs to *me*, Mary — whatever happens. We may get lost from each other, and confused and entangled — but *that* will remain through eternity — that our souls have found each other and understood.

MARY. Yes, I know, dear. I know.

HAL. And I'm sure of *you* — *now* in reality. No love as great as mine could fail to find its completion. *You* will be sure, too. I'm not afraid. I love you, Mary. I love you as no man ever loved before.

MARY. If I were sure of that!

HAL. You *will* be. Will you kiss me, Mary, as a consecration to our ideal?

MARY. Of course.
   [*She kisses him with a very honest and unfeeling smack on the lips.*]

HAL [*rising with a sigh*]. That will live through eternity.
   [*He goes.* MARY *goes to the door again.* LYNN *comes to the other window.*]

LYNN. Mary!

MARY. Oh — I thought you'd gone.

LYNN [*coming in*]. I waited. I knew Hal would come back to say something. Just a minute, Mary. Come here. [*They sit on the sofa.*] I came back to say this — that if I wasn't *dead sure* I'm going to get you, I wouldn't go a *step* on this tom-fool expedition.

MARY. Now —

LYNN. Listen! I'm going to take care of you and pull this thing off *right*, and you're going to come back engaged to *me*.

MARY. Now if you're going with any fixed ideas, you can't go at all. It's going to be growth and freedom.

LYNN. I don't need to grow. I *know* what *I* want. I love you.

MARY. But that isn't enough. You don't know that it will last forever.

LYNN. Of *course* it will. When people love the way *I* do, it's *got* to last. You *do* love me, don't you?

MARY. Yes — I do — in a way — very, very much. But not in *all* ways. It isn't the great love that embraces everything — that envelops and sweeps one away — so there's no doubt about anything.

LYNN. Tell me how much you do love me and I'll take a chance on the rest.

MARY. I think — I *think* I'd rather you were the father of my children than any man I ever saw.

LYNN. Well, then, what difference does anything else make?

MARY. But that isn't everything.

LYNN. What else *is* there?

MARY. Beautiful — mystic — far-away things. Please go. I'm afraid Mother will come and spoil everything.

LYNN [*catching her hand*]. Kiss me.

MARY. No!

LYNN. Why not?

MARY. I don't want to.

LYNN. Well, if I've got to act like a dead man for two weeks — you might kiss me once — now.

MARY. No.

LYNN [*taking her by the arms*]. You've got to!

MARY. If you do, I'll hate you.

LYNN. Did you kiss Hal?

MARY. None of your business.

LYNN. But *did* you!

MARY [*pulling away from him*]. Do you want Mother to catch you here? Don't! I'll run around the house and get upstairs.
   [*She darts out the upper window and* LYNN *the lower. After a moment* MOTHER *opens the hall door and comes in — turning on the lights. She hesitates, is about to go back into the hall when* BOBBY *comes in quickly through the lower window.*]

BOBBY. Mother — have you got seventeen dollars? I need it quick.

MOTHER. No. Why?

BOBBY. I ran into a fellow and smashed his fender. He'll settle for that and keep quiet and I can get 'em at the garage to fix our car to-night — if you'll keep Dad from wanting it.

MOTHER. Oh, Bobby — *again!* This is awful.

BOBBY. It's hell. Have you got the seventeen?

MOTHER. I don't know. I don't think so.

BOBBY. Go see — please, Ma, and it'll be all right. The fellow's waitin' 'round the corner.

MOTHER. But I don't believe —

FATHER [*coming in through the window*]. Bobby, a fellow out at the gate asked me if you'd just come in here. What does he want?
[ROBERT HOLLISTER *is fifty — a solid, successful man with a very agreeable manner when he is agreeable, and a man who, not so successful and sure, might have been a very delightful person.*]
BOBBY. Oh — he — just — He's got a car out there he wants to show me.
FATHER. Indeed! That will be profitable to him.
BOBBY. Well — I guess I can *look* at it — can't I?
FATHER [*going to the desk, where he sits turning on the light and opening his paper*]. I guess you can. Why don't you go out and look? You can't see it in here, can you?
BOBBY. I'm going.
[*He looks expressively at* MOTHER *and she starts to the door as* GRANNY *comes in.*]
GRANNY [*her pride and her feathers still somewhat ruffled*]. Is that child in here? Because if she is, I won't come in a step.
FATHER. What's the matter with *you*, Granny?
GRANNY [*sitting on the sofa*]. A good deal. I want to talk to you, Robert.
MOTHER. A — don't talk to him now, Mother.
GRANNY. Why not? Can't I even *talk* when I want to?
BOBBY. Mother! Ahem!
[MOTHER *looks at* BOBBY, *who nods frantically for her to go.*]
MOTHER. Robert's tired now. Wait till after dinner.
FATHER. Let's get it over with now — whatever it is. I'd like to rest after dinner. I want a long ride. Bobby, you get the car out and have it here so I won't lose any time. We'll all go for a long ride in the country.
BOBBY. Yes, Father.
MOTHER. Oh — that's too bad, Robert.
FATHER. What's too bad?
MOTHER. I promised the car to someone else this evening.

FATHER. You did? And what in the name of common sense did you do that for when you know it's the only recreation I have? The only way I can cool off and get a good night's sleep.
MOTHER. But it's for a poor sick woman who has *no* way of getting out.
FATHER. She hasn't? Well, I haven't either. I'd be a poor sick man if I didn't have *some* little outing. You don't seem to have thought of that. Is the poor sick woman going to drive my car herself?
MOTHER. No — Bobby's going to take her.
FATHER. Then take her for half an hour, Bobby, and be back here sharp — understand?
BOBBY. Yes, Father.
[MOTHER *starts to the door again.* GRANNY *snivels.*]
FATHER. Now, Granny, what is it? Out with it.
GRANNY. She —
MOTHER. Bobby, bring me a handkerchief out of my top bureau drawer — in the box in the right-hand corner. You know, you can get it.
[BOBBY, *suddenly understanding, starts to the hall door.*]
FATHER. How about that fellow waiting out there?
BOBBY. I'll see him as soon as I get Mother's handkerchief.
FATHER [*to* GRANNY]. Has Mary been doing something to upset you again?
GRANNY. She —
MOTHER. Oh, she didn't mean to, Mother. She didn't mean to hurt your feelings.
GRANNY. Oh, never mind my feelings. I'm used to that. I think Robert ought to know things and I think it's my duty to tell him. You're so slack yourself. Mary's very slack, Robert.
FATHER. What have you been slack about now, Mary?
MOTHER. Mother doesn't realize that girls can't be *just* the way they were when she was a girl.
GRANNY. Fiddlesticks! Right and wrong haven't changed a bit and no amount of angling and twisting and dodging can get away from facts.

FATHER. Well — well — what are the facts in this case? Come to the point.
GRANNY. Mary's got —
MOTHER. Please, don't talk about it now. I'll tell Father at the right time.
GRANNY. The right time! The right time is *now*, this minute, before any harm's done. Putting things off is your worst —
FATHER. For Heaven's sake, what *is* it? [*They both start to talk.*] Now don't both talk at once. Christopher! It's enough to be in court all day without hearing cases all night, too. What is it? Now you first, Mary. Wait, Mother.
GRANNY. Oh, yes, I can wait. I'm used to that.
MOTHER. It's only a very foolish idea Mary has in her head, and I know I can get it out if I go at it in the right way — without making a row about it.
GRANNY. That's what you always say, Mary — and it don't very often succeed, so far as I can see. This time it's too serious to fool with. It's got to be nipped in the bud.
FATHER. There's a good deal in what your mother says, you know, Mary. You are pretty soft and undecided. That's your besetting sin.
MOTHER. If anybody's *hard* with her now, it *will* be serious. It's got to be handled very carefully. She believes she's right with all her —
GRANNY. Shucks! She doesn't anything of the kind. It's a dangerous —
MOTHER. That's why we must avoid the danger, and —
FATHER. Now, see here, Mary. Tell me what it is and I'll settle it without any squeamish nonsense. What danger is she in?
GRANNY. That's the way to talk, Robert. I knew you'd settle it. You tell him the truth, Mary, or I will.
FATHER [*looking at* MOTHER]. Well —
MOTHER. It's already settled.
FATHER. Uh?
MOTHER. It's all right. She won't do it.
FATHER. Won't do what?
GRANNY. How do you know she won't?
MOTHER. Because I know. I trust her.

MARY [*coming in quickly from the hall*]. Mother, will you hook me, please?
[*She wears a charming evening gown — very simple. Her lovely young body is free and somewhat exposed. An evening cape is thrown over her arm.*]
MARY. Hello, Father.
FATHER. Hello, daughter.
MARY. I got all my bills straight, Dad — and I haven't overdrawn my allowance a penny for three months. Pretty good — uh?
FATHER. Yes, I must say you do pretty well in that line. You've got a good mind if you'd just use it — instead of throwing it away.
MARY. What makes you think I'm throwing it away?
FATHER. I wouldn't have to *think* much to see that.
MARY. I think you have a perfectly corking mind, Father — but you don't always use it the way I think you ought to.
FATHER. And what's this I hear about some new idea you have in your head?
MOTHER. Robert — *please!*
[FATHER *shrugs his shoulders and goes back to his paper.*]
MARY. Mother, your hands are shaking. Can't you find the hooks?
GRANNY. I don't know why she couldn't. There's nothing to the whole dress *but* the hooks.
MARY. Are you still cross at me, Granny? I'm awfully sorry. I'll be good.
GRANNY. I don't know how you can expect to be good in that dress.
MARY. What's the matter with this dress? It's a love. Isn't it, Mother?
MOTHER. It's very pretty, dear.
GRANNY. Yes, you uphold her in her nakedness, instead of making her put on clothes enough.
MARY. Oh, Granny!
GRANNY. I'll wager you haven't got a sign of a petticoat on.
MARY. Of course I haven't.
FATHER [*looking over his paper*]. What's the reason you haven't?
MARY. Heavens — nobody wears a petticoat, Father.

GRANNY. I do. Look at her. She might just as well be stark naked for all the good her clothes are doing her.

MARY. You needn't talk, Granny. I think it's much better to show my back than the way you used to show your front. Thanks, dearest. [*As her mother holds the cape, a whistle is heard from outside.*] That's Lynn. Good-night, everybody. Good-night, Granny. [*Kissing* GRANNY's *cheek.*] Good-night, Dad. [*Kissing the top of his head.*] Good-night, Mother dear.
[*Putting her arms around her mother.*]

FATHER. Where are you going?

MARY. To Lettie's for dinner and a dance at the club afterwards.

FATHER. What time will you be in?

MARY. Why — I don't know.

FATHER. I don't want it to be so late as it was last night, mind you. Understand?

MARY. Yes, Father.

FATHER. And listen to me — if you've got any *new* kind of dare-devil recklessness in your head, you get it out or you'll reckon with me. Understand?

MARY. Yes, Father.

GRANNY. Aren't you going to put anything over your head?

MARY. Goodness, no, Granny. It's roasting.

GRANNY. Mary, are you going to let her go out in the night air without putting anything on her head?

MARY. Oh —

FATHER. Put something over your head. Do you hear?

MARY. I haven't anything to *put*.

MOTHER [*snatching up the scarf* GRANNY *was knitting*]. Here, dear.

GRANNY. My fascinator! You'll ravel it all out.

MOTHER. I'll fasten it, Mother. It won't hurt it a bit. Good-night, dear.

GRANNY. How do you know she won't take it off the minute she's out of sight?

MOTHER [*holding* MARY]. Because I trust her — always — anywhere.

MARY. Good-night, Mother dear. You *are* a darling.

[MARY *starts out. She comes back impulsively throwing her arms about her mother.*]

MOTHER. What is it, dearest?

MARY. Nothing. Good-night.
[*She kisses her mother and goes out quickly.* BOBBY *has come back through the upper window during this scene and sits sprawling in a chair.*]

GRANNY. Where's your mother's handkerchief, Bobby?

BOBBY. Oh — I forgot. I went out to see the fella.

GRANNY. I'll wager it wasn't a handkerchief she sent you for at all. I expect it was something else — something you ought not to have.

FATHER. What's that?
[MOTHER *moves a chair up to the desk and sits with her back to* FATHER *as she reads.*]

GRANNY. I say I expect —

FATHER. I heard what you said. What have you been doing, Bobby?

BOBBY. Nothing.

FATHER. What about the fellow's car? What did you think of it?

BOBBY. Oh — I didn't think much of it.

FATHER [*still looking over the paper*]. I got the repair bills to-day on *my* car, and, by Jove, if they aren't cut in two this next month, I'll sell the damn thing. I never saw anything like it.

BOBBY. Well, I don't make the bills, Father.

FATHER. Oh, no. The car just walks out and gets itself out of commission. I'll sell it, I tell you. I'm not made of money, you know. All the bills were terrific this month, Mary. Something's got to be done.

GRANNY. Well, I don't run up the bills. I'm a *very* little eater if you mean *me*, Robert.

FATHER. I don't mean anybody. But you might control things, Mary, and keep them within bounds.

MARY. Oh, I do try to, Robert — I do.

GRANNY. You're not as careful a housekeeper as I was, Mary.

MOTHER. No — and eggs aren't ten cents a dozen now, either.

FATHER. We've got to cut down. That's all there is about it.

BOBBY. That's what you always say the first day of the month, Dad.

FATHER. The whole country's going to collapse if we don't look out — with this reckless extravagance. Everybody's living beyond their income — everybody. Same wild looseness there is in every other direction. There's a general lowering of standards and ideals that is undermining society and civilization.

GRANNY. That's just what I was saying to Mary this afternoon. She don't see it. She don't see it creeping into her own children.

FATHER. Creeping in — striding in, you mean.

GRANNY. Yes, that's it.

MOTHER. You can't expect your own children to be different from other people's, you know.

FATHER. I do expect it, by Jove. If I had my way they would be. If I had my way they'd all be at home this evening.

GRANNY. That's what I say. It certainly is a lovely, *lovely, happy* home, and they ought all to be *in* it.

NORA [*a neat maid — opening the hall door*]. Dinner is served.

MOTHER. There's dinner and you two aren't ready. Run along, Bobby, and get ready for dinner — and *hurry*. Why *will* you two *always* wait till dinner is on the table before you move? Hurry, Bobby, *hurry*. [BOBBY *rises and shambles out.*] Come, Robert.

FATHER. It might wait a little for me.

MOTHER. You simply *cannot* have decent food and keep it waiting. You've done it all your life, and it's terribly irritating.

FATHER [*rising reluctantly*]. I have to rush all day. I would like peace and relaxation at home.

MOTHER. Here's your hat, Robert.

FATHER [*as he goes into the hall*]. I don't want it.

GRANNY [*trotting after him*]. We're going to have chicken to-night, and I declare it is a shame we aren't all here to eat it. I de believe in a family all being 'round the table together when night comes.

[MOTHER *ends the procession — going out with* FATHER'S *hat as*

THE CURTAIN FALLS

ACT II

SCENE I

SCENE: *The scene is dark, showing a motor, a roadster, facing the audience. The whir of the motor is heard.* LYNN, MARY, *and* HAL *are in the car.* LYNN *is driving.* MARY *sits next him and* HAL *beside her.*

MARY. She's only going forty. Step on her, Lynn.

LYNN. Are Max and Lettie right behind us?

HAL. Yes, they're sticking.

MARY. Oh, isn't it wonderful! I never was so happy in my life!

LYNN. We're ten miles out now. Ought to do it in three hours.

MARY. Easy! Isn't it wonderful driving at night when nobody gets in the way!

HAL. Everything's wonderful when nobody gets in the way.

MARY. Now she's sixty! Gosh, isn't it great!

HAL. You can't keep this up, Lynn.

LYNN. What's the reason I can't? She's just beginning.

HAL. For God's sake, don't stop or turn. They're right behind us.

MARY. I hope you're not afraid, Hal.

HAL. Of course I'm not. But there is a limit, you know.

LYNN [*bending over the wheel*]. No, there isn't! Gee, it feels good to let her out!

MARY. It's marvelous! I never was so alive before. Isn't it glorious to know nothing can stop us! We're free! I feel as if we were part of the wind and sky. I think we're going right on up, through the sky, into the stars.

HAL. Yes, we may do that sooner than you think. For Heaven's sake, let up a little, Lynn. You've lost your head.

LYNN. Not a bit! She's a good little wagon. This is easy for 'er.

MARY. Don't spoil it, Hal. This is the way everything always ought to be — going with all we've got and nobody saying "*don't*." Oh, aren't you glad we did it? Don't you know now we're right, Lynn?

LYNN. *This* part of it's all right.

HAL. Of course we're right. But let's go slow enough to enjoy it.

MARY. But, Hal, I thought this was what you wanted, moving swiftly, alone, leaving the world behind. The world's asleep, and we're running away from it out into the unknown.

HAL. This isn't spiritual exaltation. This is just reckless foolhardiness. Not what *I* came for.

LYNN. Do you want us to let you out?

HAL. Don't be funny.

MARY. Buck up, Hal. You're *free!* For the first time in your life.

HAL. There goes my hat!

MARY. Never mind. What's a hat?

HAL. You're doing everything you can to queer the whole idea.

LYNN. I'm taking you *to* the idea as fast as I can. Do you want to go back and get your hat?

MARY. Shut up, boys! This is glorious! Doesn't everything we've left seem a thousand times worse and more ordinary and piffling than it ever did before? Oh, there's a rabbit! Don't hit him, Lynn. Oooo!

[*Screaming and hiding her face against* HAL.]

LYNN. Look out, boy! Whew! Never touched him.

HAL. Stop it, Lynn! I can't *stand* it!

LYNN. Nothing to be afraid of.

MARY. He can't help it. Shut your eyes, Hal, and put your head on my shoulder.

LYNN. Here, here, none of that. Where's your nerve, Hal?

MARY. He's got a great deal more nerve about some things than you have. Gee, if you were both mixed up together into one man, you'd be pretty good. See the stars. We *are* going up — up — right into them. This is life! Go on, Lynn! *Step on her!*

[LYNN *bends lower over the wheel with a set face.* HAL *is holding on, sick with fear.* MARY *sits between them, her head thrown back, ecstatically happy.*]

CURTAIN

SCENE II

TIME: *Four o'clock the next morning.*
PLACE: *The living room again.*
AT CURTAIN: *The light of early morning comes through the windows. After a moment five figures are seen crossing the upper window outside. They come to the lower window.* HAL *opens it cautiously and comes in quickly, carrying* MARY'S *suitcase which he puts on the floor above the chair at left C.* LYNN *carries* MARY *in.* LETITIA *and* MAX *follow.* LETITIA *is a pretty girl of the flapper type. She wears* MAX'S *topcoat over her evening gown and his cap on her bobbed hair.* MAX *is a rather flamboyant and good-looking youth. The three boys are in evening clothes.*

HAL. Put her over here, Lynn.

[LYNN *puts the limp* MARY *in the armchair at the left. The others come close, bending over her.*]

LETITIA [*kneeling beside* MARY]. How are you now, honey?

HAL. Don't try to talk, Mary. How do you feel?

LETITIA. Thank goodness, we got her home! I never was so frightened in my life. I thought you were going to die, Peaches.

HAL. How is the pain now, dear? Just as bad?

LYNN. Mary, I'm going to call a doctor.

MARY. No!

LYNN. Then I'm going to call your mother.

MARY. No!

LETITIA. Yes, we will. We must, honey. It's perfectly awful to see you like this.

MARY. No!

LYNN. Then how *is* the pain?

MARY [*suddenly sitting up*]. There never was a pain.
THE OTHERS. What?
MARY. I didn't have a bit.
THE OTHERS. What?
LETITIA. She's out of her head. Don't you know me, lamb? It's Tish.
MARY. I wanted to get you home. I knew I must do something desperate, so I had appendicitis.
LETITIA. You wanted to get me *home?*
MARY. Yes.
LETITIA. After raising heaven and earth to get me to go? Oh, she *is* out of her head.
HAL. No, she isn't. She's arrived at something important. Speak to us freely, Mary. We must be honest or it's all futile.
MAX. She needs a drink.
LYNN. Shut up, Max. What do you mean, Mary?
MARY. Sit down just a minute and I'll tell you. Ssh!
LETITIA. Oh don't push me.
[*There is a general commotion.*]
MARY. Do be quiet. Don't wake anybody up — for Heaven's sake. I suddenly knew I'd been all wrong — that the only thing to do was to get you back.
LETITIA. Do you mean it was all a joke?
LYNN. Ssh!
LETITIA. Did you never intend to —
MARY. No, no — no! Listen! Sit down, all of you — please.
LETITIA. Nobody wants to sit down.
HAL [*sitting on the floor near* MARY]. Yes, we do. Yes, we do. Don't be so emotional, Letitia. You have no mental poise at all.
LETITIA. No, and I don't want any. I'm sick of trying to act like a highbrow. I'm not one. I'm a human being.
HAL. Well, you might control your human feelings long enough to see what Mary's mental attitude is now. This reaction is very important.
MAX [*lying on the floor in front of the others*]. What the devil's it all about, anyway?
LYNN. Well, listen — listen, and you may find out.

LETITIA. We listened enough while you were working us up to *do* it, Mary. I don't want to listen while you *un*work us again.
MAX. Come on, sweetie. Sit down. Don't be peevish!
LETITIA. I think it's just too awful to come home in this perfectly flat way.
[*Sitting with a flop.*]
HAL. Wait, Lettie, till you find out how it is. This may be the beginning of something greater. I'm sure it is, Mary.
MAX. Stop chewing the rag, Lettie.
LYNN. Oh, for Heaven's sake, be quiet. Go on, Mary.
LETITIA. Yes, do. We're all sitting at your feet as usual — waiting for you to tell us why you changed your mind.
MARY. I *didn't* change my mind. It was something much bigger than that.
MAX. Must have been *colossal* to make you turn turtle like this.
[*They are all sitting on the floor in a circle about* MARY. *Each has lighted a cigarette.*]
MARY. The whole world and life and what it means suddenly flashed before me, and —
LETITIA. I thought that flashed before you long ago. I thought that was why we —
LYNN. Sh!
HAL. Wait, Lettie, wait.
MARY. I knew that we were wrong. That we were destroying something — hurting something.
LYNN. You bet we were! I'm darned thankful we're back. We're well out of a nasty mess, let me tell you.
MARY. Oh, *you* don't understand, Lynn. It isn't that at all. I mean that we were absolutely right in what we believed, but we've got to be big enough not to hurt other people with it.
HAL. Oh, Mary, that is so weak.
MARY. I never *wanted* to do anything so much in my life, but I just suddenly saw it the way Mother and Father would — and knew how it would seem to them.
MAX. You knew that in the first place, didn't you?
MARY. No — not actually — in the real

way. None of us thought of it from their side.

HAL. Oh, Mary, their side doesn't count. We know we're thinking way beyond the general level of thought, and if we don't act on it we're not advancing.
[*He hits* LETITIA'S *nose with a gesture.*]

LETITIA. Oh, Hal, my nose!
[*There is general noise and confusion.* MARY *hushes them.*]

LYNN. I don't see any use advancing so far that everybody thinks you're a *lunatic.*

MARY. But because we *do* see further than other people — we must be a — magnanimous. They can't help it — you know — these deep prejudices, and after all — they *are* our parents.

HAL. Personally, I think parents are much overrated — and given entirely too much importance in the general scheme. Though I believe if my father had lived he would have been a great man.

LYNN. I suppose *you're* very much like him.

HAL. They say so. [*The others laugh.*] We're the next generation, and the *next generation must go on.* We know that marriage *as is* — is a failure — a gigantic human failure — and we also know that it's getting worse.

MAX. You don't have to do much profound thinking to know that. Look at our own crowd. Every damned one of 'em divorced or ought to be. What's the use of being married at all?

LETITIA. Yes — love — yes — but we've said all that long ago and often. The discussion in hand at the moment is — was it a mistake for Mary to bring us back or not?

MARY. The point is — we have no right to make our parents suffer.

LETITIA. Suffer! Mother does anything *she* pleases — regardless of me. She's been married twice now, and it isn't at all impossible that she will be again. She won't hesitate to rip things up — in spite of the fact that I've just got used to calling this one Father, and just got so — I sort of can stand him. I don't see what I owe to them — and, anyway, I don't think they'd suffer a darned bit no matter what became of me.

HAL. My mother is entirely sympathetic with our idea — of course. She knows Father would have left her sometime without a moment's notice, if he had lived. He wouldn't have vulgarized it with a quarrel or a divorce. *He* was *way* in advance of his time.

MAX. My father and mother are so old school — it would do them good to get a shock. If I want to try out Lettie in a *new* way — it's none of their business.

LETITIA. Try *me* out? I'm trying *you* out. Don't forget that, my lamb.

MAX [*kissing her hand*]. Excuse me, darling.

HAL. If we never did anything except what our parents want us to do, the world wouldn't move much.

MARY. Yes, but we've got to begin all over again and *make* them understand, and *tell* them what we're going to do. It was the sneaking away I couldn't stand.

LETITIA [*getting up*]. You certainly have put me in a sweet hole. I wrote a note and stuck it on Mother's pin-cushion. I'm going to feel clever when they find me in bed in the morning in the same old way.

MARY. Oh, Lettie, I *am* so sorry.

LETITIA. Oh, don't mind me. Come on, Max. I might as well marry you *first.* Why not? You've got more money than anybody I know.
[*Going up toward the window dragging her coat after her.*]

MARY. Oh, Tish, don't give up like that. We aren't through yet — we're just beginning.

LETITIA. I'm afraid you'll have a hard time inflating me again, Mary. I feel as though I had started off on wings and come back in a wheelbarrow. Are you coming or staying, Max?

MAX. You bet I'm coming. [*He hurries to the window.*] So long! This is all right, you know. Good luck, fellers — I've got *my* girl. [*He goes after* LETITIA.]

LYNN. Of course it's all right. It's turned out the best thing in the world. And you were a brick — a brick, Mary, to do it.

MARY. It isn't all right. I've made it worse than ever — and nobody really understands what I meant at all.

LYNN. *I* do.

HAL. Have I ever misunderstood you, Mary? But I do think you were weak, dear girl. I do think you let sentiment — pure sentiment — run away with you, after you've been so strong and done such good — *individual* thinking.

LYNN. Oh, cool off and let's get down to solid rock.

HAL. Oh, yes, solid rock! That's what we're all chained to. I don't expect you to feel this as I do, Lynn. You couldn't.

LYNN. I *hope* not.

HAL. I'm not going to pretend that I'm not disappointed in you, Mary. But this isn't the end. You *will* do it yet — and in a still wider, fuller way. Anybody who's got the idealism you have, can't go back to the sordid conventional old rut.

LYNN. Start the car, old man, I'll be right out.

HAL. Thanks. I'll walk home.

MARY. Hal — you're not angry with me?

HAL. No — not angry, but hurt and horribly — *horribly* disappointed. You were thinking with distinction — and now you've gone back to the ordinary level of the average girl. Of course I'm disappointed. [*He goes out.*]

LYNN. It's turned out the best thing in the world. I love you more than ever, Mary. And you love me — don't you, dear?

MARY. Don't ask me now — please. I'm just beginning to find out something.

LYNN. You needn't expect me to believe for a minute that you hauled us off on this wild-goose chase and then hauled us back again, because you got afraid of public opinion, and hurting people — and that stuff.

MARY. You don't —

LYNN. You say you had a sudden flash — well, it must have flashed on you which *one of us* you wanted to marry, and God knows it couldn't have been Hal — I give you credit for that — so, in all modesty, it must have been me.

MARY. I can't talk about it now. I want to think. The thing that brought me back is more important than *that* just now.

LYNN. Just what *did* bring you back? Tell me.

MARY. I will try to make you understand — sometime.

LYNN. I'll stop on my way downtown in the morning.

MARY. Then hurry. I want to lock the window.

LYNN. Well, tell me this. Even if you haven't found out yet, you want *me* — aren't you *dead sure* you don't want Hal?

MARY. Please go.

LYNN. But I want *you* and I want you harder than ever. Talk about going up into the stars! I went up and I'm still there and I'm going to stay. When you sat there close to me — making me go faster — when your hair blew in my face — I didn't care whether we smashed into eternity or not. We were together — alone.

MARY. We weren't. Hal was there.

LYNN. Same thing. You weren't the only one who got a flash of what it all means. It was only you and me and space — that was *life*, all right — and I'm going to keep on living it — *up there* — in the stars.

MARY. But we can't. It's too high.

LYNN. Not with *you*.

MARY. We had to come down.

LYNN. Well, what of it! When I think what you went out to find — and that you even let me go with you to try to find it — I — my head swims. I can't say it, Mary — but I *know* what you want — because I've found it. I couldn't wish anything more wonderful for you than for you to love someone the way I love you.

MARY. Oh, Lynn! I wanted to go on with you forever. I wanted to push Hal out of the way and go on and on — and never stop — with *you*.

LYNN. Mary!

MARY. I wanted to get inside your coat — close to you — away from everything else in the world.

LYNN. And that's right where you're going to stay.

MARY. And then I got afraid — of myself — of you — of everything.

LYNN. Dear!

MARY. And then I wanted to come home — and now I don't know what I want. We've lost that wild sweet something. It's gone and I'm afraid it will never come back.

LYNN. You wanted to come home because you knew that you loved me. All that wild stuff's over. We don't need it. I love you, and I'm coming over the first thing in the morning, to tell your father and mother.

MARY. Oh — I s'pose you might as well. There's nothing else to do.

LYNN. What's the matter, dear? Aren't you happy?

MARK. I was — out there.

LYNN. And you will be here. We've got the star dust and we're going to hold on to it — tight.

MARY. Do you think we can?

LYNN. Certainly we can — nothing as great as this can get away from us.

MARY. We mustn't let it, Lynn — we mustn't let it. Go now — please. [*He holds her a moment — kisses her — and goes out quickly.* MARY *fastens the window — starts to the hall door and sees* BOBBY *asleep on the couch.*] Bobby, what are you doing there? [*She goes to the couch and shakes him.*] Bobby! Wake up. I bet you're just pretending to be asleep. I'll bet you heard everything. Bobby — *get up!*

BOBBY. Uh?

MARY. What are you doing down here this time of night?

BOBBY [*half waking*]. I came down to unlock the window for you — and I want to give you a tip.

MARY. What about?

BOBBY. They're on the war-path. You've done it once too often. What the devil do you mean staying out so late? A girl can't get away with stuff like that — chasing 'round all night.

MARY. Oh, a girl — a girl! What's the reason I can't come in when I please?

[*Sitting on the couch beside* BOBBY.]

BOBBY. Because you *can't*. Dad's foaming at the mouth. Gramma told him about your dope for goin' campin'.

MARY. She didn't!

BOBBY. She did.

MARY. If Grandma could only hold her tongue *once* in a while!

BOBBY. I wish she'd let me hold it for her once in a while. I'd pull it out.

MARY. What did Father say?

BOBBY. He's going to send you away.

MARY. What? Where?

BOBBY. Oh — just away. [*Waving his arm.*] Anywhere out of this pernicious town with its pernicious influences.

MARY. Lordie, doesn't it make you tired?

BOBBY. You were a chump if you thought you could get away with that. You never would have had the nerve to do it, anyway.

MARY. We *did* it. We were there — at the place where we were going to stay.

BOBBY. When?

MARY. To-night. We went sixty miles an hour some of the time. It was marvelous.

BOBBY. You're a queer nut, Mary. What in "h" did you get yourself into that kind of a —

MARY. Because I'm *tired* of doing just what everybody else does because they think anything different is wrong. I came back for Mother and Father's sake — but if they're going to act up about it, I wish I'd *stayed*.

BOBBY. Well, gosh — you can't blame them much. Your rep won't be worth two cents if it gets out. Dad hit the ceiling so hard he hasn't come down yet. Honest, Mary, he *is* going to do something. Don't let 'em know you *did* go. He'll sizzle you. You'll have to dope up some reason why you stayed out all night.

MARY. I *won't*. Why should I? The way Mother and Father *make* you lie is sickening. Why can't they let me alone? I don't say anything to them about the things *they* do.

BOBBY. Wouldn't you *like* to, though?

MARY. *Wouldn't* I? Just to let go and tell 'em a few things.

BOBBY. I'd like to shoot a few at Dad — square in the eye — what I like about him and what I don't.

MARY. Exactly.

BOBBY. If I could just once let him know that I'm *on* to him, I could listen to his favorite remarks about my character with more equanimity.
MARY. I know. *We're* always wrong. They *never* are.
BOBBY. And the worst of it is you can't tell 'em.
MARY. Tell? You might as well try to tell God He's wrong.
BOBBY. If Dad didn't take it as a matter of religion that I ought to give him the paper! If *once* in a while, he'd say, "Here, Bob, you take it" — I'd be crazy about giving it to him.
MARY. Of course. And if I could only *talk* to Mother. I did try. I did try to make her see. She doesn't know at all what I want and what I think and feel. I know a great deal more about life and what's going on this minute than she does. They've never done anything thrilling or had any fun themselves and they don't expect anybody else to.
BOBBY [*with a chuckle*]. Oh, I don't know. They must have been pretty devilish — buggy-ridin' Sunday afternoons.
MARY. Yes — looking for wild flowers. Mother never had any beau but Father, I s'pose, and she just married him and settled down and there you are. Anything *I* do is wrong because *they* haven't done it. [*Giving* BOBBY *a poke to make him move over and sitting closer to him.*] Listen, Bobby. I came back for *them*. I wanted to do this thing more than I ever wanted anything in my life — but just as I was the happiest and the surest I heard Mother say — "I trust you — always — anywhere" — and she stayed right there with me — nearer than she's ever been before and I — well — I came back.
BOBBY. Darn good job you did, too. I could have told you before you started your idea was bunk.
MARY. Oh, of course it all seems silly to you. You aren't old enough to know what it means.
BOBBY. Slush! I'm eighteen — you're only twenty.
MARY. Yes, but those two years make all the difference in the world.

BOBBY. Ho—o— Don't you fool yourself — I know a thing or two. Those fellows are big chumps if they were goin' off to let you size them up like that and take your choice.
MARY. Well — anyway — here I am — back — as Lettie says — in the same old flat way. You see — I began to think about Mother and Father somehow. They're narrow and old-fashioned, but they're *good*.
BOBBY. Yea — they're all right — even if they do scrap sometimes.
MARY. Sometimes I'm sort of worried about them.
BOBBY. I know. Sometimes it's rotten.
MARY. But home and the family and you and me are the most important things in the world to them. After all, we're awfully lucky to have such parents. Lots of them are running around on the loose, you know.
BOBBY. You bet your sweet life they are!
MARY. And a really, truly home like ours *is* wonderful — and I just couldn't do anything to hurt it. They're good and they love us, and they *do* love each other. I guess I *will* just sneak upstairs and tell one more lie to keep them happy. Don't you ever really peep that I really *did* go. Don't — for their sakes, old man.
BOBBY. I'm with you. Go to it, Sis. [*She takes up her suitcase.*] St! They're coming! — Beat it! [MARY *starts to the hall door.*] Look out! You can't do that. — You're caught. [MARY *drops the suitcase.* BOBBY *turns out the light and rolls under the sofa.*]

MOTHER *comes in quickly from the hall — runs to the lower window and peers out. She wears a negligee — her hair disordered.*]

FATHER [*from the hall*]. Are they there?
MOTHER. No.
FATHER [*coming in — in bathrobe and slippers*]. I told you so. He's gone after her, then. They're in cahoots. He knew all the time where she was.
MOTHER. I hope so.
FATHER. You do? You hope he lied to me steadily for hours?

MOTHER. Yes — if he knew where she is.

FATHER [*he paces about restlessly irritable with apprehension*]. There you are. No wonder they lie.

MOTHER. They don't lie.

FATHER. They don't lie — don't they?

MOTHER. No, they don't.

FATHER. No, they don't. They just go on deceiving you and getting away with it because you shut your eyes to it.

MOTHER. You wouldn't telephone any place again, would you?

FATHER. What good would that do? We've tried every place. Lettie's gone. Those good-for-nothing boys are gone. Of course that's what it means. She's bolted — right under your nose.

MOTHER. I won't believe it. She *couldn't*. She wouldn't do it without telling me.

FATHER. Telling you? She *did* tell you.

MOTHER. She only said she was *thinking* about it. She was honest enough to tell me that — and I could have persuaded —

FATHER. Honest your foot! She's fooled you — deceived you. She does all the time.

MOTHER [*coming away from the window*]. Do you think Bobby *has* gone after her?

FATHER. He must have. He must have gone . . . to warn her that I know and that I'm going to punish her. I think he's gone to tell her that and bring her back.

MOTHER. Listen! I thought the 'phone was going to ring.

FATHER. I tell you I'm going to change things. I'm through. I won't be made a fool of by my own children. What's the matter with 'em? Where dō they get it, anyway? I sometimes think it's something in *you* they get their looseness from, Mary.

MOTHER. I expect it is.

FATHER [*his voice rising*]. I don't believe you *try*. You're not firm enough. If you'd kept *at* it — day in and day out, since they were born — impressing the principles of —

MOTHER. Don't yell so! I'm not deaf. You'll raise the neighbors.

FATHER. I'll raise the roof. I'll raise heaven and earth. I won't *have* such children. What *do* you teach them — anyway?

MOTHER [*going back to the window*]. I don't teach them anything. What difference does it make? I want to *know where she is*.

FATHER. She's *gone*. That's what she is. She's disgraced us.

MOTHER. I don't believe it.

FATHER. No — you never face facts. That's what's put us where we are. She's *gone off just the way she told you she was going to.*

MOTHER. Try to get Lettie's house once more.

FATHER. No use getting that maid out of bed again. She's told us *fifteen times* now there's *nobody at home*. Of course that blatherskite of a Lettie — has chosen a time to go off when her mother and father *are* away — but yours did it right before your eyes.

MOTHER [*going back to her chair again*]. Don't keep on saying that. *Do* something.

FATHER. Why didn't *you* do something at the right time? Why in the name of Heaven haven't you controlled her?

MOTHER. Because *I don't know how*.

FATHER. Why don't you know how? It's your job. Why can't you run your house and your children as well as I run my office? Good Lord, she's only a young girl. You're more than twice her age. Why can't you manage her?

MOTHER. You're more than *three times* Bobby's age. Why don't you manage him?

FATHER. I do.

MOTHER. No, you don't.

FATHER. Besides, he's a boy. He's got to have experience. It wouldn't hurt him to go off on a spurt like this.

MOTHER. It would. It would. I couldn't bear it.

FATHER. You undermine everything I say to him anyway — with your softness. *I* don't know what's the matter. It's not *my* fault. What in the name of Heaven *is* the matter? Why have we *got* such rotten children?

[*He sinks into a chair — putting his head in his hands.*]

MARY THE THIRD

MOTHER [*after a pause*]. We don't know what kind of children we have.
FATHER. What?
MOTHER. We don't know them. We don't know how to take care of them. We don't come any place near it.
FATHER. Speak for yourself. Don't blame *me* because *you've failed*.
MOTHER. Of course *you* haven't — in *any* way.
FATHER. No — I don't think I have.
MOTHER. You're always *right* about *everything*.
FATHER. Well, what am I wrong about *now?* Haven't I told you from the beginning all the things you've let her do would —
MOTHER. Yes — yes — yes — you have!
FATHER. It's because you haven't done what I wanted that —
MOTHER. You're only thinking about wha*t you* want — and not about what's righ*t* for them at all.
FATHER. Well, is this right? This and everything that's led up to it?
MOTHER. No — but you wouldn't have made it any better by being hard and pigheaded.
FATHER [*getting up*]. Have you made it any better by being so weak and sloppy you let this happen?
MOTHER. She didn't mean any *harm*.
  [*Beginning to cry with quiet heart-broken tears.*]
FATHER. Oh, no — no harm — just disgraced us. That's all.
MOTHER. Poor child! She was trying to find the unfindable thing — a perfect love. I went through it myself floundering around in the dark — trying to choose.
FATHER. I think you did pretty well for yourself — choosing.
MOTHER. Oh, yes — it was wise choosing —
FATHER. You regret it — do you?
MOTHER. Don't you?
FATHER. If I do, I've got the decency not to say so.
MOTHER. If you could have seen what we'd be like in twenty-five years — would you have chosen *me?*

FATHER. If you feel that way about it — whose fault is it?
MOTHER. Or even *ten*. Did we have ten years that were worth *anything?*
FATHER. Are you blaming *me?*
MOTHER. At the end of *five* we were a failure — jogging along — letting out the worst side of ourselves for the other to live with.
FATHER. You're saying a lot of wild things. You haven't had one of these spells for years.
MOTHER. No — because I've just about given up *trying* to tell the truth to you about *anything*.
FATHER. That's so, all right. You certainly are not any too keen about telling the *truth*.
MOTHER. Because you can't stand it. Your nature can't stand the truth.
FATHER. Oh, don't excuse your lies and deceit and weakness by *my nature*.
MOTHER. Don't think I wouldn't be glad to be honest — to honestly be *myself*. You think I'm weak. Well, you couldn't *stand* my strength.
FATHER. What?
MOTHER. We *can't* speak the truth to each other. We haven't anything to speak it with.
FATHER. I'm flabbergasted at you. You seem to have lost what sense you did have. You disappoint me terribly.
MOTHER [*with a sudden outburst as her suffering gets beyond her control*]. Of course I do. Don't you think you disappoint *me?*
FATHER. You haven't come along the way I thought you were going to. I can't *count* on you. You aren't *there*. Sometimes I think you aren't the woman I married at all.
MOTHER. And sometimes I think you're a man I *couldn't* have married. Sometimes I loathe everything you think and say and do. When you grind out that old stuff, I could *shriek*. I can't breathe in the same room with you. The very sound of your voice drives me insane. When you tell me how right you are — I could strike you.
FATHER. Mary!
MOTHER. Oh!

[*She screams as she suddenly sees the suitcase.*]

FATHER. My God — what's the matter?

MOTHER. Her suitcase! That wasn't here when I was in this room before. She *is* here. Mary — my darling — where are you?

[*She rushes out of the room.* FATHER *goes after her. After a pause* MARY *comes slowly from behind the curtain — stricken white and dumbfounded.*]

MARY. Bobby! They hate each other.

BOBBY. Uh.

MARY. How can they ever speak to each other again!

BOBBY. D'know.

MARY. I didn't know it was like this. And you can tell it's been going on — sort of smothered.

BOBBY. It sure has busted out now.

MARY. It makes me — all gone — inside.

BOBBY. Nothing to hang on to.

MARY. Father and Mother! I wish I hadn't come back.

BOBBY. I'd like to light out myself.

MARY. *Our* father and mother! I can't believe it!

BOBBY [*going close to* MARY]. We can't let 'em know we know.

MARY. How can we help it?

BOBBY. I guess plenty of parents fight.

MARY. But *ours*! I always thought they were so *good!* Oh, Bobby!

[*She drops her head on his shoulder and is shaken with sobs.*]

MOTHER [*calling from the hall*]. Mary — Mary — where are you? [*Rushing back into the room.*] Oh, my dearest — where were you? Where have you been? What have you been doing?

FATHER [*having come in after* MOTHER]. Now, young lady! This is the last time! Where have you been? What have you been doing?

MARY. Nothing wrong.

MOTHER. How *could* you? Do you know what time it is?

FATHER. It's morning. That's what time it is — and you've been out all night. This is the last time you're going to do a thing like this. And I know your *new* idea — what you were planning to do.

MOTHER. Robert — wait.

FATHER. I almost thought you'd done it to-night. If you're reckless enough to have wanted to do it at all — I almost thought maybe you'd started off to-night.

MARY. I did.

FATHER. What?

MOTHER. Oh, no — Mary — you didn't. You didn't do that.

FATHER. You what?

MARY. I — went — to-night — all of us, to the place we were going to stay.

MOTHER. Mary —

MARY. And then we came back.

MOTHER. You don't mean you went to *stay?* You didn't expect to do that?

MARY. Yes, I did.

FATHER. I'm not surprised. This is the *end.* You've gone too far. I'm going to send you away.

MOTHER. Oh, Robert — no, you're not. Wait!

FATHER. Why should I wait? I've waited too long. I'm going to send you where you'll live a decent normal life till you come to your senses. The thing you planned to do is a brazen outrage.

MOTHER. She didn't do it. She came home.

FATHER. Much *home* means to her! You've abused it all — everything your mother and I have taught you to respect and hold sacred — thrown it away. Why you came back at all I don't see.

MARY. I came back for a very silly reason.

FATHER. I'll bet you did — nothing with any good in it.

MARY. No — not a bit.

MOTHER. My dearest — don't say that. You came back because you love us.

MARY [*breaking a little, but controlling herself quickly*]. Yes — I did, Mother.

MOTHER. Because you were sorry and didn't want to hurt us.

FATHER. Hurt us! You've wounded us so we'll never get over it. You've destroyed everything your mother and I have held up to you as right — all our standards — the sanctity of the home.

MARY. Oh, *rot*, Father.
MOTHER. Mary! Stop it! You're out of your senses.
MARY. I came home for that and found it was a joke.
FATHER. What do you mean?
MARY. We heard you — Bobby and I. We were here in this room.
FATHER. Heard us what?
MARY. Heard you say things to each other that makes everything you're talking about now *disgusting*.
MOTHER. Oh, my child!
FATHER. You heard us discussing *you* and what you've done. You heard us say how pained we are.
MARY. We heard you *fight*.
MOTHER. Mary — don't — don't! You don't understand, dear child. Your father and I were only excited. I honor and respect your father above everything on earth.
FATHER. Your mother and I have had a lifetime of devotion — with the highest ideals of married life. We didn't think we'd live to see our own children desecrate all that we've lived for.
MARY. Oh, don't! We heard. We know. You told each other the *truth*. What's the good of trying to plaster it over for us?
FATHER. There's nothing left. This is the result of the wild life you've been leading.
BOBBY. Why do you keep going on about *her?* It's you two that have smashed everything up.
FATHER. Stop! She's disgraced us.
BOBBY. She's not the one that's done the disgracin'.
MARY. I don't see how Bobby and I can ever hold up our heads again.
MOTHER. Don't, child — don't.
MARY. What's the use of anything when everything we ever thought and believed about *you* isn't true?
BOBBY. We *know we're rotten* — plenty of times — but we always thought you were —
MARY. We always thought you were good.
FATHER. How *dare* you? Is nothing sacred to you?
MARY. A lot of things used to be. We always thought there was something between you and Mother, sort of holy — and different — that most people didn't have at all. How do you s'pose we feel when we know that it isn't so? I don't see that it makes much difference what *we* do — anyway — when everything's all wrong with *you*.

[*She goes swiftly out of the room as her sobs begin to come.* FATHER *turns away to the window.* MOTHER *sits helpless and dazed.* BOBBY *lowers his head — ashamed to look at either one of them as*

THE CURTAIN FALLS

ACT III

TIME: *Three hours later.*
The dining-room.
The same curtains are used for the walls — with the same doors and windows placed in a different arrangement. The table is set for breakfast.

FATHER *sits at the right, holding the newspaper so that it completely hides him from* MOTHER *who sits opposite, trying to drink her coffee, and making a pretense of reading a few letters.*

Mother [*forcing herself to speak*]. We must make them know it was never — quite so bad before.
FATHER. Oh, I guess they've come to their senses by this time.
MOTHER. No matter *how* you feel towards me, make them think —
FATHER. I don't know that it makes much difference what they think.
MOTHER. It's the only thing that *does* make much difference.
FATHER. The point is, what are we going to do with her? And I've made up my mind.
MOTHER. To what? What are you going to do? [*A pause.*] You wouldn't do anything without telling me? You —

[NORA *enters from the pantry with a small platter of scrambled eggs. She puts the platter on the serving table.*]

FATHER. Thank you, Nora.
[NORA *looks from one to the other*

— *scenting something wrong — removes the fruit plates and serves the eggs.* Mr. Hollister *takes some,* Mrs. Hollister *refuses,* Nora *goes out.*]

Mother. You wouldn't do anything without telling me?

Father. What good will it do to tell you?

Mother. But you can't —

Father. *You* didn't tell *me.* And it's because you didn't that this whole thing has come about. You've shown you haven't the strength and decision to compete with your children. There's nothing left but for me to take hold and —

Mother. Be careful.

[Granny *enters from the hall cheerful and chipper. She wears an agreeable little lavender frock and a pink fluffy shoulder shawl.*]

Granny. Good-morning.

Mother. Good-morning, Mother.

Granny. I said good-morning, Robert.

Father [*from behind the paper*]. Oh — good-morning.

Granny [*opening her napkin with cheerful fussiness*]. The paper must be even more entertaining than usual. Didn't I get any letters, Mary?

Mother. No — nothing.

Granny. Who are yours from?

Mother. Oh, nobody in particular.

Granny. They must be from *somebody.* Pass me the sugar, Robert, please. Isn't there anything you want me to read, Mary?

Mother. Oh — here's one from Cousin Maria.

Granny. Funny she didn't write it to me. She owes me one. Sugar — sugar, Robert. [*Poking* Robert's *arm, then opening the letter.*] I don't see why Maria *will* use this paper. I've told her twice I don't like it. [Robert *passes the sugar to* Granny.] Thank you, Robert. [*Patting his hand and smiling at him in her most irresistible way.*] Feel a little grumpy this morning? Didn't sleep well, I expect. Mary, are you going to give me any coffee or not? Is your coffee all right, Robert?

Nobody's paying any attention to you. I believe in petting a man a little in the morning till he gets the creaks out, and sort of warmed up. I'm always sorry for a man when he has to leave his comfortable home and start off for the day. Goodness! Maria's writing gets worse and worse. I can't read a word she says. Read it to me, Mary.

Mother. I will after breakfast, Mother.

Granny. You aren't eating a thing. At least, you do come down to the table. I'm glad you're not like the lazy women who lie in bed and have their *own* breakfasts and let their husbands come down to the table. I think breakfast is the nicest meal of the day and the time people ought to be the cheeriest. Where are the children? You certainly do let them lag behind, Mary.

Mother. They were up late. I'm letting them sleep.

Granny. It wouldn't hurt them to come and see their father. I know a man likes to see his family 'round him before he starts off for the day. Does Maria say anything about coming?

Mother. Um — sort of a hint.

Granny. Well, just don't you take it. I love Maria dearly, but I can't stand her in the same house. There's nothing she hasn't got her nose in — [Nora *enters*] just boss, boss, boss. Maria's got money. Let her stay at home and spend it. Don't you say so, Robert? Do put down that old paper, Robbie, and eat your breakfast. What's the news?

Father. Oh — nothing.

Granny. I never saw a man in my life who found any news in the paper after having his head stuck in it for a week. [Nora *serves the eggs to* Granny.] Oh! Scrambled eggs again! I wonder if she stirred cream in these? Did you tell Lizzie what I said, Nora?

Nora. Yes, m'am.

Granny. What did she say?

Nora. Well —

Granny. Lizzie's a mule. It's the only way they're fit to eat. [Nora *goes out.*] See how tough these are? [*She takes a bite of egg complacently and looks from* Mother

to FATHER.] What *is* the matter? What's the matter, Mary?
MOTHER. Why, nothing, Mother.
GRANNY. You two had a tiff? What if you have? This is another day. You have to begin all over again.
FATHER. It looks like rain.
GRANNY. Does it? [*A pause*.]
FATHER. We need rain. The country needs it badly.
GRANNY. Yes, I s'pose it does.
FATHER [*after another pause*]. It's been the driest spell we've had for some time.
GRANNY [*with a chuckle*]. Robert's doing pretty well, Mary. You might say *something*.
MOTHER. I have a headache, Mother. I can't talk.

[NORA *enters, with more eggs and toast*.]

GRANNY. If I'd stopped talking to your father every time I had a headache, many a thing would have happened that didn't. I hope you two haven't quarreled over Mary. You have to stand *together* to control her. That's the only way you'll ever —

[MARY *comes in from the hall — solemnly followed by* BOBBY.]

MOTHER. Good-morning, dear. Good-morning, Bobby.
BOBBY AND MARY. Good-morning.
GRANNY. Good-morning. Good-morning. Good-morning. [*They seat themselves*.] Aren't you going to kiss me good-morning?
MARY. Do you want me to?
GRANNY. No — I don't especially want you to — but I think you ought to.
MARY. I don't see why.
GRANNY. I'm not so anxious to be kissed, young lady — but I believe in keeping up appearances.
MARY. I don't.
GRANNY. Um — you'll get over that — the longer you live.
MOTHER. Eat your breakfast, dear.

[*As* NORA *serves the eggs again*.]

MARY. No, thank you, Nora.
MOTHER. Oh —
MARY. No — just some coffee, Mother.
FATHER. No, thank you, Nora.

[BOBBY *falls upon his breakfast eagerly*. MOTHER *pours two cups of coffee*. NORA *serves the coffee to* MARY *and* BOBBY, *and goes out*.]

GRANNY. You're all awfully silly. I don't know why you can't go on eating, just because there was a little — *discussion* last night. You needn't be nifty at me, Missy, because I told your father. I did it for your own good.
MARY. Oh, that's a very small thing, Granny. Forget it.
GRANNY. Then what *is* the matter? Why can't you start off the day like a happy family ought to?
MARY. Because we're not a happy family.
MOTHER. Mary —
GRANNY. Then why don't somebody tell me what's the matter?
MARY. I should think you'd know.
FATHER. That will do. We won't discuss it now. But I've come to a decision.
MARY. About you and Mother?
FATHER. About you. I'm going to send you where you will learn the important things of life and learn to conform to the opinions of those who know.
MARY. Where am I to learn that?
FATHER. At a school I know of — a very fine one.
MARY. And are you and Mother going on in the same way?
FATHER. What do you mean?
MARY. I'm perfectly willing to go away to school or any old place if it will help. Bobby and I talked it all over. If you and Mother want a divorce, we'll see you through.
GRANNY. She's out of her senses.
FATHER. Don't put me and your Mother in the same class with the rotten set you've been running with. We don't tear up the ties of a lifetime just because we've had — a — hard places — sometimes.
MARY. Do you mean you've patched it up? We won't *let* you.
FATHER. *Stop*, I say.
MARY. Mother, do you prefer to stick together and hate each other?
MOTHER. You have a wrong impression. We were only wrought up over —

[BOBBY *starts to leave the table*.]

MARY. Bobby, for Heaven's sake, speak up. Tell them what *you* think.

FATHER [*shouting at* BOBBY]. Are you a part of this rubbish?

BOBBY. I know how you feel, Dad. I used to feel that way about it myself. But I changed my mind last night — after I saw how things are. We'll buck up and do anything — so long as it's got to be. Don't mind us.

FATHER. This is *insufferable*.

MARY. Go on, Bobby.

GRANNY. I can't stand it!

BOBBY. There's nothin' the matter with a divorce — it's the havin' to have it that's rotten — and when you do — why you just *got*-a. So let's get at it and get done with it.

FATHER. You leave the room. Go upstairs. [*To* MARY.] To-night I'll try to make you see straight. I can't say anything more now.

MOTHER [*shaking her head at* NORA, *who starts in from the pantry*]. No — Nora. Don't come in at all. [NORA *goes out.*]

MARY. I won't go away a step — to school or any place else — till you and Mother are settled.

FATHER. You'll do as I say.

MARY. And leave Mother wretched like this?

FATHER. Your mother is *not* wretched.

MARY. Yes, she is, and so are you, Father.

FATHER. I'm not.

MARY. Mother, do you want to go on living with Father or *not?*

[MOTHER *bursts into tears.*]

FATHER. You've made her hysterical. She can't speak.

GRANNY. Well, *I* can! Hold up your head, Mary, and tell us you're a happy woman. [*To* MARY *the* THIRD.] You ought to thank your lucky stars your father and mother get along as well as they do. Life's not all skittles and beer, let me tell you — and you ought to be put to bed on bread and water till you get over this romantic notion of wanting to be *happy* every minute.

MOTHER. You don't understand, you children. Your father and I are sorry we quarreled last night, but you're making too much of it entirely. Stop it. It's over and ended.

MARY. You're crawling out of it, Mother. Now's your chance. We all *know*. You can't go back to the same old thing, because we *do* know.

FATHER. If reason won't control you, something else will. You've made it impossible for us to let you stay at home. You've outraged everything that goes to make a home.

MARY. That's what *we* think *you've* done.

BOBBY. There isn't any home when you and Mother are like this.

FATHER. Do you set yourselves up against us?

MARY. Say something, Bobby.

BOBBY. What more is there to say? We've told you we don't want you to go on tryin' to keep up the bluff for *our sakes*. And you surely don't want to for yourselves. So what is there to it but to get together and quit? We're only tellin' you that we want you and Mother to be happy, and go to it. [*He goes out of the room.*]

FATHER. If it comes to defiance — you'll both go away.

MARY. Very well. We'll meet you halfway. We'll go if you and Mother get a divorce.

FATHER. I'll settle you to-night.

[*He goes out.*]

MARY. Oh, Mother, don't cry.

GRANNY. What do you expect her to do? It's the awfullest thing I ever heard of any child doing to any parent — ever — anywhere.

MARY. Oh, Lord, I don't see anything to cry about. Let's get some action.

MOTHER. I think the best thing to do *is* for you to go away for a while, dear. Till we get over this.

MARY. Mother — do you actually mean you *want* to go on living with Father?

GRANNY. Listen to her! Who *else* would she live with?

MARY. Granny, will you keep out of this — *please?* I'm trying to help Mother.

MOTHER. Oh, don't you two quarrel. I can't stand any more.

MARY THE THIRD

GRANNY. We're not quarreling. Come here, honey — come here. [*Drawing a chair out from the table and sitting.*] Now, listen, dearie. I know more in a minute about men than you and your mother put together. It won't be necessary for you or anybody else to go away — or upset our peace and comfort, if you'll just use your wits. A little tact and wheedling goes further with a man than all the storming in the world. You can get anything on earth out of your father if you'll just manage him. Let him *think* you're giving up to him, and you'll get your own way every time.

MARY. I think that's perfectly disgusting, Granny.

GRANNY. Now — now — don't be saucy. I'm trying to help you.

MARY. I don't need to be helped. It's Mother.

GRANNY. Well, the only way you can help her is to calm your father down. Rub him the right way till all this blows over.

MARY. Blows over? If you don't know how it is, you ought to. They don't *love* each other. Bobby and I found it out last night, and we can't stand this twaddle and mush about home and the family when we know Mother and Father ought not to even be in the same house. Is that the truth, Mother — or isn't it.

GRANNY. It's new-fangled nonsense. Modern selfishness. That's what it is. A man and woman have no right to expect to be happy *all* the time — every minute — day and night. You *have* to have a good fight now and then to clear the air. Your grandfather and I had plenty. You women now-a-days don't know how to manage men. That's what's the matter with you. Of course they get the best of you because you're trying to make 'em think you know as much as they do, and they won't *stand* it. You're such simpletons. You oughtn't to let 'em *ever* see how smart you are. Why, I had my way about everything on earth. The madder your grandfather got, the more I cried and the softer I was. I just twisted him round my finger — like that. And he thought I was right under his thumb.

MARY. Oh, Granny — how can you! Mother isn't Father's mistress, you know.

GRANNY [*putting her hands over her face*]. Oh! I never used that word in my life!

MARY. It's a perfectly good word. Mother and Father undertook the greatest relationship in the world and it hasn't been a success — so the only thing for them to do is to start another kind of life entirely. Isn't that so, Mother?

GRANNY. No, it's not! What would become of the rest of us?

MARY. Us? What have we got to do with it? It's their own inner, closest life. It's not *right* for them to live together. It's not decent. It's absolutely *immoral*.

GRANNY. I won't listen to such talk! It's godless and heathenish! [*Going to* MOTHER.] Mary, you come upstairs and I'll help you. I can help you to bear anything you've got to bear with Christian fortitude as a good and noble wife should. I never dreamed you were silly enough to *let* yourself be unhappy. Heaven knows, you've got enough to be happy with — and if you're as clever as you ought to be you'll take the bit in your own teeth and he'll come trotting right along. There ain't a man on earth as smart as a woman if she just uses what God gave her — and there's no young chit can teach *me* any tricks!

[*She goes out with her head well up, closing the door.*]

MARY. Now, Mother — let's decide what to do.

MOTHER. Mary, you *must* stop this. You're making a tragedy out of just a little hard place that your father and I have to get over in our own way.

MARY. *Was* there someone else you ought to have married — or just the ideal man of your dreams?

MOTHER. Oh, we always like to think it might have been different with someone else — when we fail. I *have* failed — utterly.

MARY [*kneeling quickly by her mother and throwing her arms about her*]. I adore you, Mother. I didn't know till last night how much I loved you. I'm lots older than you are. Really I am. You're just a little girl and I'm going to take care of you.

MOTHER. I wish I were.

MARY. But still I *am* awfully sorry for Father. You do get on his nerves. He's bored. Father's bored to death with you, Mother. You're disappointed and disillusioned in him — but I do think it's more your fault than his.

MOTHER. Oh — Mary — Why?

MARY. Women will have to change marriage — men never will. At least, you've come a long way ahead of Granny. Her marriage was on a very *low plane*, of course. You haven't stood up to Father and looked into his eyes — levelly — without conditions and silly compromise because he's a man and you're a woman.

MOTHER. Go on.

MARY. The interesting side of you — as a *person* — you haven't given to Father at all. He said last night, "You don't come through. You aren't there." He *is* there — in his way. There's *his* side too.

MOTHER. Oh-h — don't think I don't know that.

MARY. But you *are* going to stand up now and keep a stiff lip and come through with *this*.

MOTHER. I don't see anything but blankness before me. And there's Mother. She has to have a home.

MARY [*looking deeply at her mother*]. You mean you haven't any *money* without Father? That you and Granny are dependent on him? [MOTHER *nods*.] All that is so horrible ... so disreputable!

MOTHER. *Mary!*

MARY. It *is!* It's *buying* things with *you*. Don't let it go on, Mother. We'll fix it some way. I'll help you.

MOTHER. I'm not young. I can't go out and make my own living.

MARY. But you *ought* to be able to. That's the point to the whole business. I shall *have* my own money. I'll *make it*. I shall live with a man because I love him and only as long as I love him. I shall be able to take care of myself *and* my children if necessary. Anything else gives the man a horrible advantage, of course. It makes the woman a kept woman.

MOTHER. Oh, you —

MARY. Why it *does*, Mother. The biggest, fairest, most chivalrous man on earth can't feel the same towards a woman who lives with him only because she has to be taken care of — as he does to one who lives with him because she loves him. Unless it's love and only love —

FATHER [*coming back into the room*]. I want to speak to your mother.

[*After a slight pause* MARY *goes out*.]

FATHER. The boy's hard hit. He's taken this thing terribly seriously. We've got to do something about it.

MOTHER. And the girl?

FATHER. Oh — She's excited — but *he* is actually suffering. As you say, we've got to make them see they're mistaken ...

MOTHER. But *are* they?

FATHER. Then you meant everything you said to me last night?

MOTHER. And you meant everything you said to me?

FATHER. We were all stirred up.

MOTHER. Yes — enough to speak the truth.

FATHER. Well — what are you going to do? Let them go on — thinking what they think?

MOTHER. They've made their own solution.

FATHER. You mean ... [*She nods.*] You don't think for a second we ... [*A pause.*] We haven't done anything people get — divorces for, Mary.

[*His voice growing a little hoarse.*]

MOTHER. We've done the worst of all things.

FATHER. What?

MOTHER. We haven't made it a success — and it *might* have been.

FATHER. Oh — we've been careless. We need more self-control, I s'pose.

MOTHER. Self-control is a poor substitute for love.

FATHER. It's impossible to think of you and me — not together. It used to be all right. We've got to go back and begin all over again.

MOTHER. Go back to what?

FATHER. See here, Mary — some of the

nonsense that child spouted has got hold of you. Don't let any of her silly...

MOTHER. She isn't silly. She's brutal because she's so young — but she's honest and —

FATHER. She's the product of this damnable modern loose-thinking.

MOTHER. And she's thinking nearer the truth than *we* ever did. She's got something dangerous and ridiculous in *one* hand and something big and real in the other.

FATHER. Oh, you can't take her seriously?

MOTHER. You say we must go back. Go back to what? Our accidental love affair — when we didn't know each other at all? We *do* know each other now. How can we go on after this? *I* can't.

FATHER. What about me? I've got something to say about this — too — you know. I won't have my home broken up. Good God, Mary! Nothing means anything to me but you and the children! I won't have —

LYNN [*coming in from the veranda quickly*]. Good-morning. Good-morning, Mrs. Hollister. I'm glad you haven't gone yet, Mr. Hollister. I want to say to you both that I've come back to my senses good and hard. Mary's up in the clouds about the whole business, but I've come down with a thud and know where my feet are. I know the good old way is the *only* way — like you two did it. *You* didn't need any experiments to make you know you loved each other for good and all, did you? You *knew* you'd stick to the end, and be crazy about each other forever — didn't you? And you've proved it. And that's what got Mary, you know. She sort of seemed to realize for the first time what marriage means, and she came back for your sakes. [MOTHER *and* FATHER *turn away.*] Honest, I'm not stringin' you. I know you want to kick me, Mr. Hollister, but I've come to you in the good old way to say I'd like to marry your daughter and ask your *consent*. I *know* I can make her happy — and I *know* we were meant for each other, and I know we'll make a go of it the same way you have, and I hope you'll back me up and help me to get her.

[*He forces* MR. HOLLISTER *to give him his hand, and shakes it vigorously and confidently.*]

FATHER [*to* MOTHER — *trying to get his hand away while* LYNN *shakes it*]. Bring Mary down here and let's get at this thing. [MOTHER *goes out, closing the door.*] Has she promised to marry you?

LYNN. Yes. Don't you think I'd make her a good husband, Mr. Hollister?

FATHER. How do I know what kind of a husband you'd make?

LYNN. But with your experience, don't you think if a girl marries a solid, practical man who can take care of her —

FATHER. I don't think that has anything to do with the case.

LYNN. But if we're —

HAL [*coming in from the veranda*]. Good-morning, Mr. Hollister. Hello, Lynn.

LYNN. Hello.

HAL. I was going in to your office this morning, Mr. Hollister, to see you.

FATHER. *Indeed!*

HAL. I want you to know that I'm sorry we didn't go through with it last night.

FATHER. Ah!

HAL. Because it *looks* like a failure doesn't change *me* in the least.

FATHER. That's important.

HAL. I *know* we were right.

LYNN. Oh, cool off, Hal. It's all over now, and Mr. Hollister doesn't care anything about what *we* think.

HAL. Excuse me — it *isn't* all over. And what I think is more important than ever. I want you to know, Mr. Hollister, that I love your daughter too much to marry her in the old blind accidental lottery that *your* marriage was.

FATHER. What?

HAL. It *was* a lottery, wasn't it? Just good luck that it turned out as it has? It might have gone the other way for anything you really know about each other, mightn't it? You've just had the luck of one in a thousand that you've loved each other devotedly and continuously all these years — haven't you? I'm sure you're a big enough man to acknowledge *that*.

LYNN. I think Mr. Hollister's bored stiff with us, if you ask me.

HAL. I suppose he is. But you've said

your say, I'll bet, and I want him to know —

FATHER. I don't want to know *anything*.

HAL. But it's only fair to let me say that I'll stand up for my convictions before the whole town, if necessary. I know that unless we change the entire attitude of men and women towards each other — there won't be any marriage in the future. Unless we open our eyes to what happiness and decency really are — unless we lift ourselves to another plane of thought entirely —

FATHER. Oh, shut up about your plane of thought! You don't know any more what you're talking about than an unborn baby. Until you've *lived* — until you've gone through the mill — you don't know *yourself*, let alone anybody else. You don't know what kind of a fool you may be, or how you may ball things up.

HAL. That's just why we ought not to marry till we know —

FATHER. It's not the damned ideas that will get you anywhere — it's yourself. If you're ever lucky enough to have a woman love you, you take care of that *one love* — and don't be so cocksure of yourselves. If you — [MARY *comes in from the hall.*] Now, see here, Mary, which one of these boys do you intend to marry?

MARY. Neither.

FATHER. You didn't start off on that outlandish idea last night without intending to marry *one* of them?

MARY. I hoped it would be one of them, of course. That's what I was going to find out.

FATHER. You couldn't have found that out by staying at home, I suppose, in a normal, natural way?

MARY. I admit I found out a great deal more about it after I got home than I could have any other way.

HAL. How, Mary?

FATHER. Never mind that. You can't go as far as this with the most important thing in your life and drop it as if it was nothing at all. You can't go as far as this without having some indication as to which one of these boys you *prefer*. Now, which one *is* it? What are you hesitating about?

MARY. I'm not hesitating at all. I know now if I'd gone off with each one of you *alone* for a year — we wouldn't have *known* each other. Now I know it takes most of one's life to do that.

HAL. Then we were right. I can't talk to you here, Mary, before other people — but you know I'd rather lose you than have you make a mistake.

MARY [*taking his hand quickly in both of hers*]. Thank you, Hal. [*He goes out.*]

LYNN. Mary, what's changed you since last night? What are you going to do?

MARY. Father, listen! This is what I've just told Mother. When I got home I told Lynn I loved him — and I do. I love him so much I can't live without him. I was going to marry him — quick. But now I wouldn't marry him for anything on earth.

FATHER. Why not?

LYNN. What do you mean?

MARY. Marriage is a disgusting, sordid business affair that I wouldn't go into for anything.

LYNN. Mary!

MARY. But if you want me to, Lynn, I'll live with you till we're *sure* what we really mean to each other, and when we *know*, we'll either be married or quit.

LYNN. Good Heavens, Mary! You don't know what you're talking about.

FATHER. Is this the kind of muck and filth you've been thinking about?

LYNN. Why, you never even dreamed of such a thing.

MARY. I didn't think I'd actually do it, 'til I found out how horrible a perfectly good and respectable marriage can be.

FATHER. Haven't you any decency about anything?

MARY. I'm sorry, Dad, but Lynn's got to know. He's got to know why I won't marry him. It's because of Father and Mother, Lynn. I don't believe in marriage.

BOBBY [*coming in quickly*]. I've got Mother to say she'll do it.

[*He stops, seeing* LYNN.]

FATHER. Do what?

LYNN. Do you want me to go?

MARY. Don't go 'way. Wait on the porch. [LYNN *goes out onto the terrace.*]

FATHER [to BOBBY]. Do what?
BOBBY. Leave you.
FATHER. You —
       [He tries to speak, but stops helplessly.]
BOBBY. I've bucked her up to that and I'm going with her and take care of her, Father. You needn't worry about that part of it. But don't spoil it now — will you? Don't say anything to make her lose her nerve.
. MARY. You won't, will you, Father? That's splendid, Bobby.
FATHER [broken and unbelievingly]. Your mother didn't tell you — she'd leave me, did she?
BOBBY. Yes, she did.
       [FATHER goes slowly to the other end of the table and sits.]
MARY. You won't do anything to stop her — will you?
BOBBY. I'm thinking about you, Dad, just as much as I am about Mother. I know you want her to go. You just hate to come straight out and say so. Now's your chance — do it.
FATHER. Are you children blaming me for the whole thing?
BOBBY AND MARY. No!!!
MARY. Of course not, Father!
BOBBY. You bet we're not! I can see that it's hard livin' with a woman. Imagine one man living all his life with Gra'ma.
FATHER [getting hold of himself again and rising]. You're acting like lunatics — both of you. If you've made your mother think I want her to leave me —
BOBBY. If *I* have? I like *that!* You mean if *you* have.
FATHER. You don't know anything — you young whippersnapper. Your mother's the finest woman in the world. I'd lay down my life for her. Your poor dear mother!
       [BOBBY and MARY look at each other — surprised and slightly disgusted at FATHER'S sudden sentiment.]
MARY. For goodness' sake, don't get sentimental *now*, Father — just as Mother's getting some spine.
BOBBY. I think as much. I worked like the devil to get her to come to the point.
FATHER [quite himself again]. Now, see here. If you think for one minute anything you say is going to — [MOTHER opens the door and comes slowly into the room.] Mary — you haven't let anything these children have said influence you?
BOBBY. If you don't do what you said you were going to, Mother — I'm going to clear out. I won't live here.
MARY. And you know what I'm going to do, Mother. I've told Father, too.
FATHER. Be quiet — both of you. Now, Mary dear — tell them there's nothing in this nonsense. Tell them they've kicked up a fuss over nothing and we're going right on with our customary happy life. Assert yourself — and tell them they're entirely mistaken. [A pause.] Come — come — go on — dearest.
       [FATHER tries to be sure of himself, and assumes a slightly affectionate gaiety. MARY and BOBBY look at each other, half disgusted, half ready to laugh.]
MOTHER. I'm going away.
FATHER. You're not. I won't have it.
BOBBY. Go on, Mother.
FATHER. Be quiet, I say. What in the name of common sense do you think life is, anyway? Your mother and I haven't done anything to get a divorce for.
BOBBY. Of course you haven't beaten her or broken the eighth commandment — or any —
MARY. The *seventh*, Bobby.
BOBBY. Uh? Well — but what you have done is a thousand times rottener, and if you're going to keep right on, I'm leavin'. How about it, Mother?
MOTHER. They're rebelling against the ugliness — and meanness — the cruelty and pettiness. They think it doesn't have to be. They're saying very foolish things — but they're true — they're true. I'm going.
BOBBY. And I'm goin' with you.
MOTHER. No. I'm going alone. It's the only way we can find the truth about ourselves, Robert, or anything else. Where's Lynn?
MARY. Out there.

MOTHER. Call him in.
MARY [*going to the window*]. Lynn!

[LYNN *comes in.*]

MOTHER. Mary, I don't ask you *not* to do what you say you're going to — for I know I haven't given you anything better — but I ask you to wait. It isn't our marriage that was wrong — it's what we've done with it.

LYNN. I'm not afraid, Mary — I'll make you happy.

MARY. How do you know you will?

BOBBY. That's what. I thought the thing you were up to was all hot air and bunk — but I begin to believe there's a good deal in it. I know one thing, by golly — *I'll* never take a chance. I'll never take a chance of being where you and Father are. If you two couldn't make a go of it, I'd like to know who *can*. I don't see why men and women don't stop *tryin'* to live together — anyway.

[*He starts to go.*]

MOTHER [*stopping* BOBBY *with her hand and going to the door*]. Oh, no — that isn't it. It's we — ourselves and what *we've* done — that are wrong.

[*She goes out.* BOBBY *follows.*
FATHER *goes to the door.*]

MARY [*putting her hand on* FATHER's *arm*]. Let her go, Dad. Let her go.

FATHER. But I'll bring her back.

MARY. Do you mean you love her?

FATHER. You've got an awful lot to learn, little girl.

MARY [*suddenly throwing her arms about his neck*]. Make her love you, Dad. Make it all over. If you could! If you could!

[FATHER, *too moved to speak, holds her close for a moment and goes out — closing the door.*]

LYNN [*going down to* MARY — *after a pause*]. Gosh, I'm sorry. It's the last thing in the world I would have expected to happen.

MARY. Why didn't they know in the first place? Can anybody ever know?

[*Sitting in her father's place at the table.*]

LYNN. We know. [*Sitting in* MOTHER's *place at the table.*] We were *meant* for each other. No man ever loved a girl the way I love you.

MARY. I bet that's what Father said to Mother. I bet that's what *everybody* says. It makes me sort of sick.

LYNN. But we're different. We *know* what we've got.

MARY. How do we know we do? What if *the* very things you like in me now — you'd hate sometime. What if the things I think are strong and stunning in you now, I'd think were pig-headed and kickable after a while?

LYNN. How could we? People couldn't be better suited to each other than we are.

MARY. I suppose they thought that, too. Twenty-five years Mother and Father have been looking at each other across the table. And most of that time they've wished they were looking at somebody else.

LYNN. Oh, Mary, you don't —

MARY. If they hadn't been married, if they hadn't been *tied* to each other, or if Mother could have walked out and taken care of herself at any minute, they would have had to *please* each other in order to *hold* each other.

LYNN. I know. You're dead right. But what if they hadn't been married? You and Bobby wouldn't have thanked them much for bringing you into the world without any name or anything to put your feet on.

MARY. I don't see that they've given us so darned much to put our feet on now. They've smashed everything I ever believed about love and marriage.

LYNN. Oh — your mother said it — there's nothing the matter with marriage — it's what people do with it. What's the use trying to bust up the best thing we've got? Why don't we begin to make marriage better instead of chucking it? Why don't we make it honest and decent and fair — and if we have made a mistake we'll quit.

MARY. Lynn — you're *marvelous!*

LYNN. You angel!

MARY. Oh, *don't!* I bet Grandfather called Granny an angel — and knelt at her feet while he was saying it.

LYNN. Well, old pal — we're going to be

side by side — both on the same level — both on the square.

MARY. And just as free as though we weren't married at all.

LYNN. Absolutely.

MARY. No hold on each other but love.

LYNN. None.

MARY. And the minute that's gone — we're through.

LYNN. That's the stuff.

MARY. Give me your hand on that, old man. [*They clasp hands.*] But, Lynn, I wouldn't marry you if I didn't *know* that ours *is* the love that will last forever. There *can't* be any doubt about a love as great as ours, can there, dear?

LYNN [*drawing her onto his knees*]. You *bet* there can't.

MARY. I *do* think we're safe, because we've been intelligent about it. I adore the way your hair grows at the side, dearest.

LYNN. Your eyes are the most beautiful things in the world. They have in them *everything* I want.

MARY [*putting her arms about his neck*]. I love you.

LYNN. I love you.

MARY. And we must make it the most wonderful love that was ever in the world.

[*She kisses his lips.*]

THE CURTAIN FALLS

ICEBOUND
A PLAY
By OWEN DAVIS

COPYRIGHT, 1922, 1923, BY OWEN DAVIS

ALL RIGHTS RESERVED

Reprinted by permission of the publishers, Little, Brown and Company

No performance of this play, professional or amateur — or public reading of it — may be given without the written permission of the author and the payment of royalty. Application for the rights of performing "Icebound" must be made to Sam H. Harris, Sam H. Harris Theatre, New York City.

CHARACTERS

HENRY JORDAN
EMMA, *his wife*
NETTIE, *her daughter by a former marriage*
SADIE FELLOWS, *once Sadie Jordan, a widow*
ORIN, *her son*
ELLA JORDAN, *the unmarried sister*
DOCTOR CURTIS
JANE CROSBY, *a second cousin of the Jordans*
JUDGE BRADFORD
BEN JORDAN
HANNAH
JIM JAY

ACT ONE. The parlor of the Jordan homestead, 4 P.M., October, 1922.

ACT TWO. The sitting-room of the Jordan homestead, two months later.

ACT THREE. Same as Act One, late in the following March.

ICEBOUND

ACT ONE

SCENE: *The parlor of the Jordan Homestead at Veazie, Maine.*

It is late October, and through the two windows at the back one may see a bleak countryside, the grass brown and lifeless, and the bare limbs of the trees silhouetted against a gray sky. Here, in the room that for a hundred years has been the rallying-point of the Jordan family, a group of relatives are gathered to await the death of the old woman who is the head of their clan. The room in which they wait is as dull and as drab as the lives of those who have lived within its walls. Here we have the cleanliness that is next to godliness, but no sign of either comfort or beauty, both of which are looked upon with suspicion as being sign-posts on the road to perdition.

In this group are the following characters: HENRY JORDAN, *a heavy-set man of fifty, worn by his business cares into a dull sort of hopeless resignation;* EMMA, *his wife, a stout and rather formidable woman of forty, with a look of chronic displeasure;* NETTIE, *her daughter by a former marriage, a vain and shallow little rustic beauty;* SADIE, *a thin, tight-lipped woman of forty, a widow and a gossip;* ORIN, *her son, a pasty-faced boy of ten with large spectacles;* ELLA, *a "maiden lady" of thirty-six, restless and dissatisfied.*

ELLA *and* SADIE, *true Jordans by birth, are a degree above* EMMA *in social standing, at least they were until* HENRY'S *marriage to* EMMA *made her a somewhat resentful member of the family. In* EMMA'S *dialogue and in her reactions, I have attempted a rather nice distinction between the two grades of rural middle-class folk; the younger characters here, as in most other communities, have advanced one step.*

Rise: At rise there is a long silence; the occupants of the room are ill at ease. EMMA *is grim and frowning.* NETTIE *sits with a simper of youthful vanity, looking stealthily at herself from time to time in a small mirror set in the top of her cheap vanity case.* ELLA *and* SADIE *have been crying and dab at their eyes a bit ostentatiously.* HENRY *makes a thoughtful note with a pencil, then returns his notebook to his pocket and warms his hands at the stove.*

There is a low whistle of a cold autumn wind as some dead leaves are blown past the window. ORIN, *who has a cold in his head, sniffs viciously; the others, with the exception of his mother, look at him in remonstrance. An eight-day clock in sight, through the door to the hall, strikes four.*

EMMA [*sternly*]. Four o'clock.

HENRY [*looks at watch*]. Five minutes of. That clock's been fast for more'n thirty years.

NETTIE [*looks at wrist watch*]. My watch says two minutes after.

HENRY. Well, it's wrong!

EMMA [*acidly*]. You gave it to her yourself, didn't you?

SADIE [*sighs*]. Good Land! What does it matter?

NETTIE [*offended*]. Oh! Doesn't it? Oh!

ELLA. Maybe it does to you. She ain't your blood relation.

EMMA. Nettie loves her grandma, don't you, dear?

NETTIE. Some folks not so far off may get fooled before long about how much grandma and I was to each other.

EMMA [*sternly*]. You hush!

[*Again there is a pause, and again it is broken by a loud sniff from* ORIN,

as the women look at him in disgust.
SADIE *speaks up in his defense.*]
SADIE. He's got kind of a cold in his head.
HENRY. The question is, ain't he got a handkerchief?
SADIE. Here, Orin!
[*She hands him her handkerchief.*]
ELLA. The idea! No handkerchief when you've come expectin' some one to die!
ORIN. I had one, but I used it up.
[*He blows his nose.*]
HENRY. After four. Well, I expect they'll have to close the store without me.
ELLA. I left everything just as soon as Jane sent me word!
SADIE. Why should Jane be with her instead of you or me, her own daughters?
HENRY. You girls always made her nervous, and I guess she's pretty low. [*He looks at his watch again.*] I said I'd be back before closin' time. I don't know as I dare to trust those boys.
EMMA. You can't tell about things, when Sadie's husband died, we sat there most all night.
SADIE [*angrily*]. Yes, and you grudged it to him, I knew it then, and it isn't likely I'm going to forget it.
ELLA. Will was a good man, but even you can't say he was ever very dependable.
EMMA. My first husband died sudden [*she turns to* NETTIE] — you can't remember it, dear.
ELLA. *You* didn't remember it very long, it wa'n't much more'n a year before you married Henry.
HENRY [*sighs*]. Well, he was as dead then as he's ever got to be. [*He turns and glances nervously out window.*] I don't know but what I could just run down to the store for a minute, then hurry right back.
SADIE. You're the oldest of her children, a body would think you'd be ashamed.
HENRY. Oh, I'll stay.
[*There is a silence.* ORIN *sniffs.* ELLA *glares at him.*]
ELLA. Of course he *could* sit somewheres else.
[SADIE *puts her arm about* ORIN *and looks spitefully at* ELLA. DOCTOR CURTIS, *an elderly country physician, comes down the stairs and enters the room; all turn to look at him.*]
DOCTOR. No change at all. I'm sendin' Jane to the drugstore.
ELLA [*rises eagerly*]. I'll just run up and sit with mother.
[SADIE *jumps up and starts for door.*]
SADIE. It might be better if I went.
ELLA. Why might it?
[*They stand glaring at each other before either attempts to pass the* DOCTOR, *whose ample form almost blocks the doorway.*]
SADIE. *I've* been a wife and a mother.
DOCTOR. Hannah's with her, you know. I told you I didn't want anybody up there but Jane and Hannah.
ELLA. But we're her own daughters.
DOCTOR. You don't have to tell me, I brought both of you into the world. The right nursing might pull her through, even now; nothing else can, and I've got the two women I want. [*He crosses to* HENRY *at stove.*] Why don't you put a little wood on the fire?
HENRY. Why — I thought 'twas warm enough.
ELLA. Because you was standin' in front of it gettin' all the heat.
[HENRY *fills the stove from wood basket.*]

[JANE CROSBY *enters on stairs and crosses into the room.* JANE *is twenty-four, a plainly dressed girl of quiet manner. She has been "driven into herself," as one of our characters would describe it, by her lack of sympathy and affection, and as a natural result she is not especially articulate; she speaks, as a rule, in short sentences, and has cultivated an outward coldness that in the course of time has become almost aggressive.*]

JANE. I'll go now, Doctor; you'd better go back to her. Hannah's frightened.
DOCTOR. Get it as quick as you can, Jane; I don't know as it's any use, but we've got to keep on tryin'.

JANE. Yes.

[*She exits;* DOCTOR *warms his hands.*]

DOCTOR. Jane's been up with her three nights. I don't know when I've seen a more dependable girl.

ELLA. She ought to be.

HENRY. If there's any gratitude in the world.

DOCTOR. Oh, I guess there is; maybe there'd be more if there was more reason for it. It's awful cold up there, but I guess I'll be gettin' back.

[*He crosses toward door.*]

HENRY. Doctor! [*He looks at his watch.*]

DOCTOR [*stops in doorway*]. Well?

HENRY. It's quite a bit past four, I don't suppose — I don't suppose you can tell —

DOCTOR. No, I can't tell.

[*He turns and exits up the stairs.*]

ELLA. There's no fool like an old fool.

SADIE. Did you hear him? "Didn't know when he'd seen a more dependable girl than her!"

EMMA. Makes a lot of difference who's goin' to depend on her. I ain't, for one.

NETTIE. If I set out to tell how she's treated me lots of times, when I've come over here to see grandma, nobody would believe a word of it.

SADIE. Mother took her in out of charity.

ELLA. And kept her out of spite.

HENRY. I don't know as you ought to say that, Ella.

ELLA. It's my place she took, in my own mother's house. I'd been here now, but for her. I ain't goin' to forget that. No! Me, all these years payin' board and slavin' my life out, makin' hats, like a nigger.

NETTIE [*smartly*]. Oh! So *that's* what they're like. I've often wondered!

ELLA [*rises*]. You'll keep that common little thing of your wife's from insultin' me, Henry Jordan, or I won't stay here another minute.

EMMA [*angry*]. Common!

NETTIE. Mother!

HENRY [*sternly*]. Hush up! All of yer!

SADIE. It's Jane we ought to be talkin' about.

EMMA. Just as soon as you're the head of the family, Henry, you've got to tell her she ain't wanted here!

HENRY. Well — I don't know as I'd want to do anything that wasn't right. She's been here quite a spell.

SADIE. Eight years!

ELLA. And just a step-cousin, once removed.

HENRY. I guess mother's made her earn her keep. I don't know as ever there was much love lost between 'em.

EMMA. As soon as your mother's dead, you'll send her packing.

HENRY. We'll see. I don't like countin' on mother's going; that way.

SADIE [*hopefully*]. Grandmother lived to eighty-four.

HENRY. All our folks was long lived; nothin' lasts like it used to — Poor mother!

ELLA. Of course she'll divide equal, between us three?

HENRY [*doubtfully*]. Well, I don't know!

SADIE. Orin is her only grandchild; she won't forget that.

HENRY. Nettie, there, is just the same as my own. I adopted her legal, when I married Emma.

EMMA. Of course you did. Your mother's too — just a woman to make distinctions!

NETTIE. Yes, and the funny part of it is grandma may leave me a whole lot, for all any of *you* know.

ELLA. Nonsense! She'll divide equally between us three; won't she, Henry?

HENRY [*sadly*]. She'll do as she pleases, I guess we all know that.

ELLA. She's a religious woman, she's *got* to be fair!

HENRY. Well, I guess it would be fair enough if she was to remember the trouble I've had with my business. I don't know what she's worth, she's as tight-mouthed as a bear trap, but I could use more'n a third of quite a little sum.

ELLA. Well, you won't get it. Not if I go to law.

EMMA. It's disgusting. Talking about money at a time like this.

HENRY. I like to see folks reasonable. I don't know what you'd want of a third of all mother's got, Ella.

SADIE [*to* ELLA]. You, all alone in the world!

ELLA. Maybe I won't be, when I get that money.

SADIE. You don't mean you'd get married?

EMMA. At your age!

ELLA. I mean I never had anything in all my life; now I'm going to. I'm the youngest of all of you, except Ben, and he never was a real Jordan. I've never had a chance; I've been stuck here till I'm most forty, worse than if I was dead, fifty times worse! Now I'm going to buy things — everything I want — I don't care what — I'll buy it, even if it's a man! Anything I want!

NETTIE. A *man!*

[NETTIE *looks at* ELLA *in cruel amazement, and all but* ORIN *burst into a laugh —* ELLA *turns up and hides her face against the window as* ORIN *pulls at his mother's skirt.*]

ORIN. Mum! Mum! I thought you told me not to laugh, not once, while we was here!

HENRY. You're right, nephew, and we're wrong, all of us. I'm sorry, Ella, we're all sorry.

ELLA [*wipes her eyes*]. Laugh if you want to — maybe it won't be so long before I do some of it myself.

HENRY [*thoughtfully*]. Equally between us three? Well, poor mother knows best of course. [*He sighs.*]

SADIE. She wouldn't leave *him* any, would she — Ben?

ELLA [*shocked*]. Ben!

HENRY [*in cold anger*]. She's a woman of her word; no!

SADIE. If he was here he'd get around her; he always did!

HENRY. Not again!

SADIE. If she ever spoiled anybody it was him, and she's had to pay for it. Sometimes it looks like it was a sort of a judgment.

HENRY. There hasn't been a Jordan before Ben, who's disgraced the name in more'n a hundred years; he stands indicted before the Grand Jury for some of his drunken devilment. If he hadn't run away, like the criminal he is, he'd be in the State's Prison now, down to Thomaston. Don't talk *Ben* to me, after the way he broke mother's heart, and hurt my credit!

NETTIE. I don't remember him very well. Mother thought it better I shouldn't come around last time he was here; but he looked real nice in his uniform.

SADIE. It was his bein' born so long after us that made him seem like an outsider; father and mother hadn't had any children for years and years! Of course I never want to sit in judgment on my own parents, but I never approved of it; it never seemed quite — what I call proper.

NETTIE [*to* EMMA]. Mother, don't you think I'd better leave the room?

SADIE [*angrily*]. Not if half the stories I've heard about you are true, I don't.

HENRY. Come, come, no rows! Is this a time or place for spite? We've always been a united family, we've always got to be, — leavin' Ben out, of course. You can't make a silk purse out of a sow's ear.

ORIN. Mum! Say, Mum! [*He pulls at* SADIE'S *dress.*] Why should anybody want to make a silk purse out of a sow's ear?

ELLA. Can't you stop that boy askin' such fool questions?

SADIE. Well, as far as that goes, why should they? It never sounded reasonable to me.

HENRY [*sternly*]. Decent folks don't reason about religion; they just accept it.

ORIN. You could make a skin purse out of a sow's ear, but I'll be darned if you could make a silk purse out of one. I'll bet God couldn't.

HENRY. Are you going to let him talk about God like that, like he was a real person?

ELLA. I don't know as a body could expect any better; his father was a Baptist!

SADIE [*angrily*]. His father was a good man, and if he talked about God different from what you do, it was because he knew more about him. And as for my being here at all [*she rises with her arms about* ORIN] — I wouldn't do it, not for anything less than my own mother's deathbed.

HENRY. This family don't ever agree on nothin' but just to differ.

EMMA. As far as I see, the only time you ever get together is when one of you is dead.

ELLA. Maybe that's the reason I got such a feelin' against funerals.

[*The outside door opens and* JANE *enters, a druggist's bottle in her hand; she is followed by* JOHN BRADFORD, *a man of about thirty-five. He is better dressed than any of the others and is a man of a more cosmopolitan type — a New-Englander, but a university man, the local judge, and the leading lawyer of the town.*]

JANE. I met Judge Bradford on the way.

JUDGE [JOHN BRADFORD]. Court set late. I couldn't get here before. Jane tells me that she's very low.

HENRY. Yes.

JUDGE. I can't realize it; she has always been so strong, so dominant.

ELLA. In the midst of life we are in death.

ORIN. Say, Mum, that's in the Bible too!

SADIE. Hush!

ORIN. Well, ain't it?

SADIE. Will you hush?

HENRY. It's our duty to hope so long as we can.

JUDGE. Yes, of course.

JANE. I'll take this right up.

[*She exits up the stairs.*]

JUDGE [*removes his coat*]. I'll wait.

SADIE. She can't see you; she ain't really what a body could call in her right mind.

JUDGE. So Jane said.

[*He crosses to stove and warms his hands.*]

ELLA [*sighs*]. It's a sad time for us, Judge!

JUDGE. She was always such a wonderful woman.

HENRY. An awful time for us. Did you come up Main Street, Judge?

JUDGE. Yes.

HENRY. Did you happen to notice if my store was open?

JUDGE. No.

HENRY. Not that it matters.

SADIE. Nothing matters now.

HENRY. No — Mother wasn't ever the kind to neglect things; if the worst does come she'll find herself prepared. Won't she? Won't she, Judge?

JUDGE. Her affairs are, as usual, in perfect order.

HENRY. In every way?

JUDGE [*looks at him coldly*]. Her will is drawn and is on deposit in my office, if that is what you mean.

HENRY. Well — that *is* what I mean — I'm no hypocrite.

EMMA. He's the oldest of the family. He's got a right to ask, hasn't he?

JUDGE. Yes.

HENRY [*honestly*]. If I could make her well by givin' up everything I've got in the world, or ever expect to git, I'd do it!

SADIE. All of us would.

HENRY. If it's in my mind at all, as I stand here, that she's a rich woman, it's because my mind's so worried, the way business has been, that I'm drove most frantic; it's because, well — because I'm human; because I can't help it.

ELLA [*bitterly*]. You're a man! What do you think it's been for me!

SADIE [*with arm about* ORIN]. His father didn't leave much, you all know that, and it's been scrimp and save till I'm all worn to skin and bone.

ELLA. Just to the three of us, that would be fair.

HENRY. Judge! My brother's name ain't in her will, is it? Tell me that? Ben's name ain't there!

JUDGE. I'd rather not talk about it, Henry.

ELLA. She'd cut him off, she said, the last time he disgraced us, and she's a woman of her word.

SADIE [*eagerly, to* JUDGE]. And the very next day she sent for you because I was here when she telephoned; and you came to her that very afternoon because I saw you from my front window cross right up to this door.

JUDGE. Possibly. I frequently drop in to discuss business matters with your mother for a moment on my way home.

SADIE. It was five minutes to four when

you went in that day, and six minutes to five when you came out, by the clock on my mantel.

JUDGE. Your brother has been gone for almost two years. Your memory is very clear.

ELLA. So's her window.

NETTIE. I know folks in this town that are scared to go past it.

SADIE [to her]. I know others that ought to be.

HENRY [discouraged]. Every time you folks meet there's trouble.

[JANE *enters down the stairs and into the room.*]

JUDGE [looks at her]. Well, Jane?

JANE. No change. It's — it's pitiful, to see her like that.

[SADIE *sobs and covers her face.*]

HENRY. It's best we should try to bear this without any fuss, she'd 'a' wanted it that way.

SADIE. She didn't even want me to cry when poor Will died, but I did; and somehow I don't know but it made things easier.

HENRY. When father died she didn't shed a tear; she's been a strong woman, always.

[*The early fall twilight has come on and the stage is rather dim, the hall at right is in deep shadow; at the end of* HENRY's *speech the outside door supposedly out at right is opened, then shut rather violently.*]

ELLA [startled]. Some one's come in.

SADIE. Nobody's got any right —

[*She rises as some one is heard coming along the hall.*]

HENRY [sternly]. Who's that out there? Who is it?

ORIN. Mum! Who is it!

[*He clings to his mother, afraid, as all turn to the door, and* BEN *Jordan steps into the room and faces them with a smile of reckless contempt.* BEN *is the black sheep of the Jordan family, years younger than any of the others, a wild, selfish, arrogant fellow, handsome, but sulky and defiant. His clothes are cheap and dirty and he is rather pale and looks dissipated. He doesn't speak, but stands openly sneering at their look of astonishment.*]

JANE [quietly]. I'm glad you've come, Ben.

BEN [contemptuously]. You are?

JANE. Yes, your mother's awful sick.

BEN. She's alive?

JANE. Yes.

BEN. Well [*he looks contemptuously about*] — Nobody missin'. The Jordans are gathered again, handkerchiefs and all.

HENRY. You'll be arrested soon as folks know you've come.

BEN [scornfully]. And I suppose you wouldn't bail me out, would you, Henry?

HENRY [simply]. No, I wouldn't.

BEN. God! You're still the same, all of you. You stink of the Ark, the whole tribe. It takes more than a few Edisons to change the Jordans!

ELLA. How'd you get here? How'd you know about mother?

BEN [nods at JANE]. She sent me word, to Bangor.

SADIE [to JANE]. How'd you get to know where he was?

JANE [quietly]. I knew.

HENRY. How'd you come; you don't look like you had much money?

BEN. She sent it. [*He nods toward* JANE.] God knows, it wasn't much.

ELLA [to JANE]. Did mother tell you to — ?

BEN. Of course she did!

JANE [quietly]. No, she didn't.

HENRY. You sent your own money?

JANE. Yes, as he said it wasn't much, but I didn't have much.

BEN [astonished]. Why did you do it?

JANE. I knew she was going to die; twice I asked her if she wanted to see you, and she said no —

HENRY. And yet you sent for him?

JANE. Yes.

HENRY. Why?

JANE. He was the one she really wanted. I thought she'd die happier seeing him.

ELLA. You took a lot on yourself, didn't you?

JANE. Yes, she's been a lonely old

woman. I hated to think of her there, in the churchyard, hungry for him.

BEN. I'll go to her.

JANE. It's too late; she wouldn't know you.

BEN. I'll go.

JANE. The Doctor will call us when he thinks we ought to come.

BEN [*fiercely*]. I'm going now.

HENRY [*steps forward*]. No, you ain't.

BEN. Do you think I came here, standin' a chance of bein' sent to jail, to let *you* tell me what to do?

HENRY. If she's dyin' up there, it's more'n half from what you've made her suffer; you'll wait here till we go to her together.

EMMA. Henry's right.

SADIE. Of course he is.

ELLA. Nobody but Ben would have the impudence to show his face here, after what he's done.

BEN. I'm going just the same!

HENRY. No, you ain't.

[*Their voices become loud.*]

EMMA. Henry! Don't let him go!

SADIE. Stop him.

ELLA [*grows shrill*]. He's a disgrace to us. He always was.

HENRY. You'll stay right where you are. [*He puts his hand heavily on* BEN'S *shoulder* — BEN *throws him off fiercely.*]

BEN. Damn you! Keep your hands off me!

[HENRY *staggers back and strikes against a table that falls to the floor with a crash.* NETTIE *screams.*]

JANE. Stop it — stop! You must!

JUDGE. Are you crazy? Have you no sense of decency?

[DOCTOR CURTIS *comes quickly downstairs.*]

DOCTOR. What's this noise? I forbid it. Your mother has heard you.

HENRY [*ashamed*]. I'm sorry.

BEN [*sulkily*]. I didn't mean to make a row.

HENRY. It's him. [*He looks bitterly at* BEN.] He brings out all the worst in us. He brought trouble into the world with him when he came, and ever since.

[HANNAH, *a middle-aged servant, comes hastily halfway downstairs and calls out sharply.*]

HANNAH. Doctor! Come, Doctor!

[*She exits up the stairs, as the* DOCTOR *crosses through the hall and follows her.*]

ORIN [*afraid*]. Is she dead, Mum? Does Hannah mean she's dead!

[SADIE *hides her head on his shoulder and weeps.*]

JANE. I'll go to her. [*She exits.*]

ELLA [*violently*]. She'll go. There ain't scarcely a drop of Jordan blood in her veins, and *she's* the one that goes to mother.

EMMA [*coldly*]. Light the lamp, Nettie; it's gettin' dark.

NETTIE. Yes, mother.

[*She starts to light lamp.*]

HENRY. I'm ashamed of my part of it, makin' a row, with her on her deathbed.

BEN. You had it right, I guess. I've made trouble ever since I came into the world.

NETTIE. There!

[*She lights lamp; footlights go up.*]

JUDGE [*sternly*]. You shouldn't have come here; you know that, Ben.

BEN. I've always known that, any place I've been, exceptin' only those two years in the Army. That's the only time I ever was in right.

JUDGE [*sternly*]. I would find it easier to pity you if you had any one to blame besides yourself.

BEN. Pity? Do you think I want your pity? [*There is a pause.*]

[JANE *is seen on stairs, they all turn to her nervously as she comes down and crosses into room. She stops at the door looking at them.*]

HENRY [*slowly*]. Mother — mother's gone!

JANE. Yes.

[*There is a moment's silence broken by the low sobs of the women who for a moment forget their selfishness in the presence of death.*]

HENRY. The Jordans won't ever be the same; she was the last of the old stock, mother was — No, the Jordans won't ever be the same.

[DOCTOR CURTIS *comes downstairs and into the room.*]

DOCTOR. It's no use tryin' to tell you what I feel. I've known her since I was a boy. I did the best I could.

HENRY. The best anybody could, Doctor, we know that.

DOCTOR. I've got a call I'd better make [*he looks at watch*] — should have been there hours ago, but I hadn't the heart to leave her. Who's in charge here?

HENRY. I am, of course.

DOCTOR. I've made arrangements with Hannah; she'll tell you. I'll say good-night now.

HENRY. Good-night, Doctor.

JANE. And thank you.

DOCTOR. We did our best, Jane.
[*He exits.*]

SADIE. He's gettin' old. When Orin had the stomach trouble a month ago, I sent for Doctor Morris. I felt sort of guilty doin' it, but I thought it was my duty.

JUDGE. You will let me help you, Jane?

JANE. Hannah and I can attend to everything. Henry! [*She turns to him.*] You might come over for a minute this evening and we can talk things over. I'll make the bed up in your old room, Ben, if you want to stay.

EMMA [*rises and looks at* JANE *coldly*]. Now, Henry Jordan, if she's all through givin' orders, maybe you'll begin.

ELLA. Well, I should say so. Let's have an understandin'.

SADIE. You tell her the truth, Henry, or else one of us will do it for you.

HENRY [*hesitates*]. Maybe it might be best if I should wait until after the funeral.

ELLA. You tell her now, or I will.

JANE. Tell me what?

HENRY. We was thinkin', now that mother's dead, that there wasn't much use in your stayin' on here.

JANE. Yes? [*She looks at him intently.*]

HENRY. We don't aim to be hard, and we don't want it said we was mean about it; you can stay on here, if you want to, until after the funeral, maybe a little longer, and I don't know but what between us, we'd be willing to help you till you found a place somewheres.

JANE. You can't help me, any of you. Of course, now she's dead, I'll go. I'll be glad to go.

ELLA. Glad!

JANE [*turns on them*]. I hate you, the whole raft of you. I'll be glad to get away from you. She was the only one of you worth loving, and she didn't want it.

EMMA. If that's how you feel, I say the sooner you went the better.

HENRY. Not till after the funeral. I don't want it said we was hard to her.

JUDGE [*quietly*]. Jane isn't going at all, Henry.

HENRY. What's that?

ELLA. Of course she's going.

JUDGE. No, she belongs here in this house.

HENRY. Not after I say she don't.

JUDGE. Even then, because it's hers.

SADIE. Hers?

JUDGE. From the moment of your mother's death, everything here belonged to Jane.

HENRY. Not everything.

JUDGE. Yes, everything — your mother's whole estate.

BEN. Ha! Ha! Ha!
[*He sits at right laughing bitterly.*]

JANE. That can't be, Judge, you must be wrong. It's a mistake.

JUDGE. No.

HENRY. My mother did this?

JUDGE. Yes.

HENRY. Why? You've got to tell me why!

JUDGE. That isn't a part of my duties.

HENRY. She couldn't have done a thing like that without sayin' why. She said something, didn't she?

JUDGE. I don't know that I care to repeat it.

HENRY [*fiercely*]. You must repeat it!

JUDGE. Very well. The day that will was drawn she said to me, "The Jordans are all waiting for me to die, like carrion crows around a sick cow in a pasture, watchin' till the last twitch of life is out of me before they pounce. I'm going to fool them," she said, "I'm going to surprise them; they are all fools but Jane — Jane's no fool."

BEN [*bitterly*]. No — Ha! Ha! Ha! Jane's no fool!

JUDGE. And she went on — [*He turns to* JANE] You'll forgive me, Jane; she said, "Jane is stubborn, and set, and wilful, but she's no fool. She'll do better by the Jordan money than any of them."

ELLA. We'll go to law, that's what we'll do!

SADIE. That's it, we'll go to law.

HENRY [*to* JUDGE]. We can break that will; you know we can!

JUDGE. It's possible.

HENRY. Possible! You *know*, don't yer! You're supposed to be a good lawyer.

JUDGE. Of course if I *am* a good lawyer, you can't break that will, because you see I drew it.

ELLA. And we get nothing, not a dollar, after waitin' all these years?

JUDGE. There are small bequests left to each of you.

SADIE. How much?

JUDGE. One hundred dollars each.

ELLA [*shrilly*]. One hundred dollars.

JUDGE. I said that they were small.

BEN. You said a mouthful!

ELLA. Ha! Ha! Ha! Ha! Ha!
[*She laughs wildly.*]

HENRY [*sternly*]. Stop your noise, Ella.

ELLA. I — Ha! Ha! Ha! — I told you I was going to have my laugh, didn't I? Ha! Ha! Ha!

ORIN [*pulls* SADIE'S *dress*]. Mum! What's she laughin' for?

SADIE. You hush!

EMMA [*faces them all in evil triumph*]. If anybody asked me, I'd say it was a judgment on all of yer. You Jordans was always stuck up, always thought you was better'n anybody else. I guess I ought to know, I married into yer! — You a rich family? — You the salt of the Earth? — You Jordans! You paupers! — Ha! Ha! Ha!

ORIN [*pulls* SADIE'S *skirt*]. Aint she still dead, Mum! Ain't grandma still dead?

SADIE [*angrily*]. Of course she is.

ORIN. But I thought we was all goin' to cry!

SADIE. Cry, then, you awful little brat.
[*She slaps his face and he roars loudly; she takes him by the arm and yanks him out of the room, followed by* HENRY, EMMA, NETTIE, *and* ELLA — *through his roars, they all speak together as they go.*]

EMMA [*to* HENRY]. One hundred dollars! After all your blowin'.

HENRY. It's you, and that child of yourn; you turned her against me.

NETTIE. Well, I just won't spend my hundred dollars for mournin'. I'll wear my old black dress!

ELLA. And me makin' hats all the rest of my life — just makin' hats!

[*The front door is heard to shut behind them.* JANE, BEN, *and* JUDGE *are alone.* JUDGE *stands by stove.* JANE *is up by window, looking out at the deepening twilight.* BEN *sits at right.*]

BEN. Ha! Ha! Ha! "Crow buzzards" mother called us — the last of the Jordans — crow buzzards — and that's what we are.

JUDGE. You can't stay here, Ben; you know that as well as I do. I signed the warrant for your arrest myself. It's been over a year since the Grand Jury indicted you for arson.

BEN. You mean you'll give me up?

JANE. You won't do that, Judge; you're here as her friend.

JUDGE. No, but if it's known he's here, I couldn't save him, and it's bound to be known.

JANE [*to* BEN]. Were you careful coming?

BEN. Yes.

JUDGE. It's bound to be known.

BEN. He means they'll tell on me. [*He nods his head toward door.*] My brother, or my sisters.

JUDGE. No, I don't think they'd do that.

BEN. Let 'em! What do I care? I'm sick of hiding out, half starved! Let 'em do what they please. All I know is one thing — when they put her into her grave her sons and daughters are goin' to be standin' there, like the Jordans always do.

JANE [*quietly*]. Hannah will have your

room ready by now. There are some clean shirts and things that was your father's; I'll bring them to you.

BEN [*uneasily*]. Can I go up there, just a minute?

JANE. To your mother?

BEN. Yes.

JANE. If you want to.

BEN. I do.

JANE. Yes, you can go.

[BEN *turns and exits up the stairs.* JANE *crosses and sits by stove, sinking wearily into the chair.*]

JUDGE. And she left him nothing, just that hundred dollars, and only that because I told her it was the safest way to do it. I thought he was her one weakness, but it seems she didn't have any.

JANE. No.

JUDGE. She was a grim old woman, Jane.

JANE. I think I could have loved her, but she didn't want it.

JUDGE. And yet she left you everything.

JANE. I don't understand.

JUDGE. She left a sealed letter for you. It's in my strong box; you may learn from it that she cared more about you than you think.

JANE. No.

JUDGE. There was more kindness in her heart than most people gave her credit for.

JANE. For her own, for Uncle Ned, who never did for her, for Ned, for the Jordan name. I don't understand, and I don't think I care so very much; it's been a hard week, Judge.

[*She rests her head against the back of the chair.*]

JUDGE. I know, and you're all worn out.

JANE. Yes.

JUDGE. It's a lot of money, Jane.

JANE. I suppose so.

JUDGE. And so you're a rich woman. I am curious to know how you feel?

JANE. Just tired.

[*She shuts her eyes. For a moment he looks at her with a smile, then turns and quietly fills the stove with wood as* BEN *comes slowly downstairs and into the room.*]

BEN. If there was only something I could do for her.

JUDGE. Jane's asleep, Ben.

BEN. Did she look like that, unhappy, all the time?

JUDGE. Yes.

BEN. Crow buzzards! God damn the Jordans!

[*Front door bell rings sharply;* BEN *is startled.*]

JUDGE. Steady there! It's just one of the neighbors, I guess. [*Bell rings again as* HANNAH *crosses downstairs and to hall.*] Hannah knows enough not to let any one in.

BEN [*slowly*]. When I got back, time before this, from France, I tried to go straight, but it wasn't any good, I just don't belong —

[HANNAH *enters, frightened.*]

HANNAH. It's Jim Jay!

BEN [*to* JUDGE]. And you didn't think my own blood would sell me?

[JIM JAY, *a large, kindly man of middle age, enters.*]

JIM. I'm sorry, Ben, I've come for you!

[JANE *wakes, startled, and springs up.*]

JANE. What is it?

JIM. I got to take him, Jane.

BEN [*turns fiercely*]. Have you!

JIM [*quietly*]. I'm armed, Ben — better not be foolish!

JANE. He'll go with you, Mr. Jay. He won't resist.

JIM [*quietly*]. He mustn't. You got a bad name, Ben, and I ain't a-goin' to take any chances.

BEN. I thought I'd get to go to her funeral, anyway, before they got me.

JIM. Well, you could, maybe, if you was to fix a bail bond. You'd take bail for him, wouldn't you, Judge?

JUDGE. It's a felony; I'd have to have good security.

JANE. I'm a rich woman, you said just now. Could I give bail for him?

JUDGE. Yes.

BEN [*to her*]. So the money ain't enough. You want all us Jordans fawnin' on you for favors. Well, all of 'em but me will; by mornin' the buzzards will be flocking round you thick! You're going to hear a lot about how much folks love you, but you ain't goin' to hear it from me.

JANE [*turns to him quietly*]. Why did you come here, Ben, when I wrote you she was dying?

BEN. Why did I come?

JANE. Was it because you loved her, because you wanted to ask her to forgive you, before she died — or was it because you wanted to get something for yourself?

BEN [*hesitates*]. How does a feller know why he does what he does?

JANE. I'm just curious. You've got so much contempt for the rest, I was just wondering? You were wild, Ben, and hard, but you were honest — what brought you here?

BEN [*sulkily*]. The money.

JANE. I thought so. Then when you saw her you were sorry, but even then the money was in your mind — well — it's mine now. And you've got to take your choice — you can do what I tell you, or you'll go with Mr. Jay.

BEN. Is that so? Well, I guess there ain't much doubt about what I'll do. Come on, Jim!

JIM. All right. [*He takes a pair of handcuffs from his pocket.*] You'll have to slip these on, Ben.

BEN [*steps back*]. No — wait [*He turns desperately to* JANE] — What is it you want?

JANE. I want you to do as I say.

BEN [*after a look at* JIM *and the handcuffs*]. I'll do it.

JANE. I thought so. [*She turns to* JUDGE.] Can you fix the bond up here?

JUDGE. Yes. [*He sits at table and takes pen, ink, and paper from a drawer.*] I can hold court right here long enough for that.

JIM. This is my prisoner, Judge, and here's the warrant.

[*He puts warrant on table.*]

JANE. First he's got to swear, before you, to my conditions.

BEN. What conditions?

JANE. When will his trial be, Judge?

JUDGE. Not before the spring term, I should think — say early April.

JANE. You'll stay here till then, Ben; you won't leave town! You'll work the farm — there's plenty to be done.

BEN [*sulkily*]. I don't know how to work a farm.

JANE. I do. You'll just do what I tell you.

BEN. Be your slave? That's what you mean, ain't it?

JANE. I've been about that here for eight years.

BEN. And now it's your turn to get square on a Jordan!

JANE. You'll work for once, and work every day. The first day you don't I'll surrender you to the Judge, and he'll jail you. The rest of the Jordans will live as I tell them to live, or for the first time in any of their lives, they'll live on what they earn. Don't forget, Ben, that right now I'm the head of the family.

JUDGE [*to* BEN]. You heard the conditions? Shall I make out the bond?

BEN [*reluctantly*]. Yes.

[*He sits moodily at right, looking down at the floor.* JANE *looks at him for a moment, then turns up to window.*]

JANE. It's snowing!

JIM. Thought I smelled it. [*He buttons his coat.*] Well, nothin' to keep me, is there, Judge?

JUDGE. No. [*He starts to write out the bond with a rusty pen.*] This pen is rusty!

JIM. I was sorry to hear about the old lady. It's too bad, but that's the way of things.

JUDGE [*writes*]. Yes.

JIM. Well — It's early for snow, not but what it's a good thing for the winter wheat.

[*He exits.*]

CURTAIN

ACT TWO

SCENE: *Sitting-room of the Jordan homestead some two months later.*

This room also shows some traces of a family's daily life, and to that extent is less desolate than the "parlor" of the

First Act, although the stern faith of the Puritan makes no concession to the thing we have learned to call "good taste." The old-fashioned simplicity seen in such a room as this has resulted from poverty, both of mind and of purse, and has nothing akin to the simplicity of the artist; as a matter of fact, your true descendants of the settlers of 1605 would be the first to resent such an implication; to them the arts are directly connected with heathen practices, and any incense burned before the altars of the Graces still smells to them of brimstone.

At back center folding doors, now partly open, lead to dining-room. In this room may be seen the dining-table, back of the table a window looking out on to the farmyard, now deep in midwinter snow. At right is an open fireplace with a log fire. Below fireplace a door to hall. Up left door to small vestibule in which is the outside door. Down left a window overlooking a snowbound countryside. The clock above the fireplace is set for quarter-past four. Several straight-backed chairs and a woodbox by fireplace. A sewing-table and lamp at center. A sewing-machine near window at left. A wall cupboard on the wall right of the doors to the dining-room. An old sofa down left, two chairs at right. When the door at left, in vestibule, is opened, one may see a path up to the door, between two walls of snow.

Discovered: ELLA *sits right at sewing-machine, hemming some rough towels.* ORIN *and* NETTIE *are by fireplace* SADIE *sits right of center.* SADIE *and* ORIN *are dressed for outdoors.* NETTIE'S *coat, hat, and overshoes are on a hat-rack by door at left.* ORIN, *as the curtain goes up, is putting a log on the fire.*]

SADIE [*acidly to* ELLA]. Why shouldn't he put wood on the fire if he wants to?

ELLA [*at sewing-machine*]. Because it ain't your wood.

SADIE. No, it's *hers!* Everything is hers!

ELLA. And maybe she just don't know it.

NETTIE [*at fireplace*]. Ah! [*She bends closer to the fire as the log blazes up.*] I do love a good fire! Oh, it's nice to be warm!

SADIE. There's somethin' sensual about it.

NETTIE. Mother told me that the next time you started talkin' indecent, I was to leave the room.

SADIE. Tell your mother I don't wonder she's sort of worried about you. I'd be if you was *my* daughter.

ELLA. I don't see why you can't let Nettie alone!

NETTIE. She's always picking on me, Aunt Ella! To hear her talk, anybody would think I was terrible.

SADIE. I know more about what's going on than some folks think I do.

NETTIE. Then you know a lot. I heard Horace Bevins say a week ago that he did n't know as it was any use tryin' to have a Masonic Lodge in the same town as you.

SADIE. They never was a Bevins yet didn't have his tongue hung from the middle; the day his mother was married she answered both the responses.

ORIN. Mum! Mum! Shall I take my coat off; are we going to stay, Mum?

SADIE. No, we ain't going to stay. I just want to see Cousin Jane for a minute.

ELLA. She's in the kitchen with Hannah.

SADIE. Watchin' her, I bet! I wonder Hannah puts up with it.

ELLA. If you was to live with Jane for a spell, I guess you'd find you had a plenty to put up with.

SADIE. It's enough to make the Jordans turn in their graves, all of 'em at once.

ELLA. I guess all she'd say would be, "Let 'em if it seemed to make 'em any more comfortable."

[JANE *enters. She has apron on and some towels over her arm.*]

JANE. Are those towels finished?

ELLA. Some is! Maybe I'd done all of 'em if I'd been a centipede.

JANE. Oh! I didn't see you, Sadie.

SADIE. Oh! Ha, ha! Well, I ain't surprised.

JANE [*with* ELLA, *selecting finished towels*]. Well, Orin, does the tooth still hurt you?

ORIN. Naw, it don't hurt me none now. I got it in a bottle.

[*He takes small bottle from pocket.*]

NETTIE. Oh, you nasty thing. You get away!

SADIE [*angrily*]. What did I tell you about showin' that tooth to folks!

JANE. Never mind, Orin, just run out to the barn and tell your Uncle Ben we've got to have a path cleared under the clotheslines.

ORIN. All right.

[*He crosses toward door.*]

JANE. Hannah's going to wash tomorrow, tell him. I'll expect a good wide path.

ORIN. I'll tell him. [*He exits.*]

SADIE. I must say you keep Ben right at it, don't you?

JANE. Yes. [*She takes the last finished towel and speaks to* ELLA.] I'll come back for more.

SADIE [*as* JANE *crosses*]. First I thought he'd go to jail before he'd work, but he didn't, did he?

JANE. No. [*She exits right.*]

SADIE. Yes. No! Yes. No! Folks that ain't got no more gift of gab ain't got much gift of intellect. I s'pose Hannah's out there.

ELLA. Yes, she keeps all of us just everlastingly at it.

SADIE. When Jane comes back, I wish you and Nettie would leave me alone with her, just for a minute.

ELLA [*as she works over sewing-machine*]. It won't do you much good; she won't lend any more money.

SADIE. Mother always helped me. I've got a right to expect it.

ELLA [*as she bites off a thread*]. Expectin' ain't gettin'.

SADIE. I don't know what I'll do.

ELLA. You had money out of her; so has Henry.

SADIE [*shocked*]. You don't mean to say your father's been borrowin' from her.

[*This to* NETTIE.]

NETTIE. He's always borrowin'. Did n't he borrow the hundred dollars grandma left me? I'm not going to stand it much longer.

ELLA. Henry's havin' trouble with his business.

SADIE. We're fools to put up with it. Everybody says so. We ought to contest the will.

ELLA. Everybody says so but the lawyers; they won't none of 'em touch the case without they get money in advance.

SADIE. How much money? Didn't your father find out, Nettie?

NETTIE. The least was five hundred dollars.

ELLA. Can you see us raisin' that?

SADIE. If we was short, we might borrow it from Jane.

ELLA. We'd have to be smarter'n I see any signs of; she's through lendin'.

SADIE. How do you know?

ELLA. I tried it myself.

SADIE. What do you want money for? Ain't she takin' you in to live with her?

ELLA. I don't call myself beholden for that. She had to have some one, with Ben here, and her unmarried, and next to no relation to him.

NETTIE. Everybody's callin' you the chaperon! [*She laughs.*] Not but what they ought to be one with *him* around; he's awful good-lookin'.

SADIE. You keep away from him. He's no blood kin of yours, and he's a bad man, if he is a Jordan. Always makes up to everything he sees in petticoats, and always did.

NETTIE. Thanks for the compliment, but I'm not looking for any jailbirds.

ELLA. It will be awful, Ben in State's Prison — and I guess he'll have to go, soon as he stands his trial.

SADIE. He got drunk and had a fight with the two Kimbal boys, and they licked him, and that night he burned down their barn; everybody knows it.

ELLA. He's bad, all through, Ben is.

NETTIE. He'll get about five years, father says. I guess that will take some of the spunk out of him.

[*A sound in the hall at right.*]

ELLA. Hush! I think he's coming.

[BEN *enters at right with a big armful of firewood and crosses and drops it heavily into woodbox, then turns and looks at them in silence.*]

SADIE. Seems kind of funny, your luggin' in the wood.

BEN [*bitterly*]. Does it?

SADIE. Did you see Orin out there?

BEN. Yes, he went along home.

SADIE. How do you like workin'?

BEN. How do you think I like it? Workin' a big farm in winter, tendin' the stock and milking ten cows. How do I like it?

[*As he stands by fire,* NETTIE *looks up at him.*]

NETTIE. I think it's just a shame!

SADIE [*turns to* ELLA]. Are you going to make towels all the afternoon?

ELLA. I am 'til they're done, then I expect she'll find somethin' else for me to do.

NETTIE [*to* BEN]. Do you know I'm sorry for you, awful sorry?

[*She speaks low.* ELLA *and* SADIE *are at the other side of the room.*]

BEN. Then you're the only one.

NETTIE. Maybe I am, but I'm like that.

BEN. Another month of it, then State's Prison, I guess. I don't know as I'll be sorry when the time comes.

NETTIE. Oh, Uncle Ben! No, I'm not goin' to call you *that*. After all, you're not really any relation, are you? I mean to me?

BEN. No.

NETTIE [*softly*]. I'm just going to call you Ben!

BEN. You're a good kid, Nettie.

NETTIE. Oh, it isn't that, Ben, but it does just seem too awful.

[*As she looks up at him, the outside door opens and* HENRY *and* EMMA *enter. They see* NETTIE *and* BEN *together by the fire.*]

EMMA [*sternly*]. Nettie!

NETTIE [*sweetly*]. Yes, mother?

EMMA. You come away from him.

BEN [*angrily*]. What do you mean by that?

EMMA. You tell him, Henry.

HENRY. I don't know as it's any use to —

EMMA [*sternly*]. Tell him what I mean.

HENRY [*to* BEN]. Emma thinks, considerin' everything, that it's best Nettie shouldn't talk to you.

BEN. Why don't you keep her at home, then? You don't suppose I want to talk to her.

EMMA. Oh, we ain't wanted here, I guess. We know that, not by you, or by *her*; — and Henry's the oldest of the Jordans. All this would be his, if there was any justice in the world.

NETTIE. Father wouldn't have taken that hundred dollars grandma left me if there had been any justice in the world. That's what I came here for, not to talk to him. To tell Cousin Jane what father did, and to tell her about Nellie Namlin's Christmas party, and that I've got to have a new dress. I've just got to!

SADIE. A new dress, and my rent ain't paid. She's got to pay it. My Orin's got to have a roof over his head.

HENRY. I don't know as you've got any call to be pestering Jane all the time.

ELLA. She's always wantin' something.

SADIE. What about you? Didn't you tell me yourself you tried to borrow from her?

ELLA. I got a chance to set up in business, so as I can be independent. I can go in with Mary Stanton, dressmakin'. I can do it for two hundred dollars, and she's got to give it to me.

HENRY. You ought to be ashamed, all three of you, worryin' Jane all day long. It's more'n flesh and blood can stand!

NETTIE [*to him*]. Didn't you say at breakfast you was coming here to-day to make Cousin Jane endorse a note for you? Didn't you?

EMMA [*fiercely*]. You hush!

BEN [*at back by window*]. Ha! Ha! Ha! Crow buzzards.

HENRY. Endorsing a note ain't lending money, is it? It's a matter of business. I guess my note's good.

BEN. Take it to the bank without her name on it and see how good it is.

EMMA. You don't think we want to ask her favors, but Henry's in bad trouble and she'll just have to help us this time.

BEN. There's one way out of your troubles. One thing you could all do, for a change, instead of making Jane pay all your bills. I wonder you haven't any of you thought of it.
HENRY. What could we do?
BEN. Go to work and earn something for yourselves.
SADIE. Like you do, I suppose.
EMMA. The laughing-stock of all Veazie!
ELLA. Everybody's talkin' about it, anywhere you go.
NETTIE. Jane Crosby's White Slave, that's what they call you. Jane Crosby's White Slave.
BEN [fiercely]. They call me that, do they?
ELLA [to NETTIE]. Why can't you ever hold your tongue?
BEN [in cold anger]. I've been a damned fool. I'm through.

[HANNAH enters.]

HANNAH. She wants you.
BEN. Jane?
HANNAH. Yes.
BEN. I won't come.
HANNAH. There'll be another row.
BEN. Tell her I said I wouldn't come.
[He sits.]
HANNAH. She's awful set, you know, when she wants anything.
BEN. You tell her I won't come.
HANNAH. Well, I don't say I hanker none to tell her, but I'd rather be in my shoes than yourn. [She exits.]
SADIE. Well, I must say I don't blame you a mite.
EMMA. If the Jordans is a lot of slaves, I guess it's pretty near time we knew it.
HENRY [worried]. She'll turn you over to Judge Bradford, Ben: he'll lock you up. It ain't goin' to help me none with the bank, a brother of mine bein' in jail.
BEN. So they're laughing at me, are they, damn them!
NETTIE [at door right]. She's coming!

[There is a moment's pause and JANE enters door right. HANNAH follows to door and looks on eagerly.]

JANE. I sent for you, Ben.

BEN. I won't budge.
JANE [wearily]. Must we go through all this again?
BEN. I ain't going to move out of this chair to-day. You do what you damned please.
JANE. I am sorry, but you must.
BEN. Send for Jim Jay, have me locked up, do as you please. Oh, I've said it before, but this time I mean it.
JANE. And you won't come?
BEN. No.
JANE. Then I'll do the best I can alone.
[She crosses up to wall closet and opens it and selects a large bottle, and turns. BEN rises quickly.]
BEN. What do you want of that?
JANE. It's one of the horses. I don't know what's the matter with her. She's down in her stall, just breathing. She won't pay any attention to me.
BEN. Old Nellie?
JANE. Yes.
BEN. What you got? [He steps to her and takes the bottle from her and looks at it.] That stuff's no good. Here! [He steps to cabinet and selects another bottle.] If you hadn't spent five minutes stalling around, I might have had a better chance.
[He exits quickly at left.]
HANNAH. I allers said 'twas easier to catch flies with honey than 'twas with vinegar.
HENRY. What's Ben know about horses?
JANE. A lot.
HENRY. I didn't know that.
JANE. Neither did Ben, six weeks ago.
[She exits.]
HENRY. Mother was like that, about animals. I guess Ben sort of takes after her.
EMMA [shocked]. Ben! Like your mother!
HANNAH. Of course he is. He's the "spit and image of her." [She exits.]
NETTIE. She made him go! It wouldn't surprise me a mite if she'd pushed that old horse over herself.

[JANE enters.]

JANE. He wouldn't let me in the barn. [For the first time in the play, she laughs *lightly.*] Well [*she looks about at them*] — we have quite a family gathering here this afternoon. I am wondering if there is any — special reason for it?

HENRY. I wanted to talk with yer for just a minute, Jane.

SADIE. So do I.

JANE. Anybody else? [*She looks about.*]

ELLA. I do.

NETTIE. So do I.

JANE. I've a lot to do; suppose I answer you all at once. I'm sorry, but I won't lend you any money.

HENRY. Of course, I didn't think they'd call that note of mine; it's only five hundred, and you could just endorse it.

JANE. No!

SADIE. I was going to ask you —

JANE. No!

ELLA. I got a chance to be independent, Jane, and —

JANE. No. I haven't any money. I won't have before the first of the month.

EMMA. No money!

HENRY. I bet you're worth as much to-day as you was the day mother died.

JANE. To a penny. I've lived, and run this house, and half supported all of you on what I've made the place earn. Yesterday I spent the first dollar that I didn't have to spend. I mean, on myself. But that's no business of yours. I *am* worth just as much as the day I took the property, and I'm not going to run behind, so you see, after all, I'm a real Jordan.

EMMA. Seems so, I never knew one of 'em yet who didn't seem to think he could take it with him.

HENRY. Well, Jane, I don't know as it's any use tryin' to get you to change your mind?

JANE. I'm sorry.

EMMA. You can leave that for us to be. I guess it's about the only thing we've got a right to. Get your things on, Nettie!

NETTIE. I'm going to stay a while with Aunt Ella; I won't be late.

HENRY. I don't know what I'm goin' to do about that note. I s'pose I'll find some way out of it.

JANE. I hope so.

EMMA. Thank yer. Of course we know there's always the poorhouse. Come, Henry.

[*She exits at left, leaving the outside door open.*]

HENRY. Emma is a little upset. I hope you won't mind her talk. I guess her part of it ain't any too easy.

[*He exits, shutting the door.*]

ELLA [*to* JANE]. Poor Henry! Of course I s'pose you're right not to lend it to him. But I don't know as *I* could do it, but I'm sensitive.

JANE. Perhaps it's harder to say no than you think.

[*Hannah enters.*]

HANNAH. I got everything ready for to-morrow's wash, but the sheets off your bed, Miss Ella.

ELLA. Good Land! I forgot 'em. Nettie will bring 'em right down.

NETTIE [*to* JANE]. After that, I'm going to stay and help Aunt Ella. I was wondering if you'd be here all the afternoon.

JANE. Yes.

NETTIE [*charmingly*]. Nothing special, you know. I'd just like to have a little visit with you.

[*She exits at left with* ELLA.]

HANNAH [*looks after her*]. Every time I listen to that girl I get fur on my tongue.

JANE. Fur?

HANNAH. Like when my dyspepsia's coming. There's two things I can't abide, her and cucumbers.

[*She crosses to door left.*]

JANE. Hannah!

HANNAH [*stops*]. Well?

JANE [*rather shyly*]. We are going to have rather a special supper to-night.

HANNAH [*doubtfully*]. We are?

JANE. Yes. That's why I had you roast that turkey yesterday.

HANNAH [*firmly*]. That's for Sunday!

JANE. No, it's for to-night.

HANNAH [*angrily*]. Why is it?

JANE. It's my birthday.

HANNAH. I didn't know that.

JANE. No, it isn't exactly a national holiday, but we'll have the turkey, and I'll get some preserves up, and I want you to bake a cake, a round one. We'll have

candles on it. I got some at the store this morning.
HANNAH [*shocked*]. Candles?
JANE. Yes.
HANNAH. Who's going to be to this party?
JANE [*a little self-conscious*]. Why — just — just ourselves.
HANNAH. Just you and Mr. Ben and Miss Ella?
JANE. Yes.
HANNAH. You don't want candles on that cake, you want crape on it.
[*She exits door left.*]

[JANE *crosses up and starts to clear the dining-room table of its red table-cover, as* BEN *enters door left.*]

BEN [*cheerfully*]. Well, I fixed Old Nellie up. [*He puts his bottle back in its place in the wall cabinet.*] Just got her in time. Thought she was gone for a minute, but she's going to be all right.
JANE. That's good.
[*She folds the tablecloth up and puts it away.*]
BEN [*in front of fire*]. She knew what I was doin' for her too; you could tell by the way she looked at me! She'll be all right, poor old critter. I remember her when she was a colt, year before I went to high school.
[*Jane crosses into room, shutting the dining-room door after her.*]
JANE. You like animals, don't you, Ben?
BEN [*surprised*]. I don't know. I don't like to see 'em suffer.
JANE. Why?
BEN. I guess it's mostly because they ain't to blame for it. I mean what comes to 'em ain't their fault. If a woman thinks she's sick, 'til she gets sick, that's her business. If a man gets drunk, or eats like a hog, he's got to pay for it, and he ought to. Animals live cleaner than we do anyhow — and when you do anything for 'em they've got gratitude. Folks haven't.
JANE. Hand me that sewing basket, Ben.
[*She has seated herself at left center by table.* BEN *at left of table, hands her the basket as she picks up some sewing.*]

BEN. It's funny, but except for a dog or two, I don't remember carin' nothin' for any of the live things, when I lived here, I mean.
JANE. I guess that's because you didn't do much for them.
BEN. I guess so — Sometimes I kind of think I'd like to be here when spring comes — and see all the young critters coming into the world — I should think there'd be a lot a feller could do, to make it easier for 'em.
JANE. Yes.
BEN. Everybody's always makin' a fuss over women and their babies. I guess animals have got some feelings, too.
JANE [*sewing*]. Yes.
BEN. I *know* it — Yes, sometimes I sort of wish I could be here, in the spring.
JANE. You'll be a big help.
BEN. I'll be in prison. [*He looks at her. She drops her head and goes on sewing.*] You forgot that, didn't yer?
JANE. Yes.
BEN. What's the difference? A prison ain't just a place; it's bein' somewheres you don't want to be, and that's where I've always been.
JANE. You liked the army?
BEN. I s'pose so.
JANE. Why?
BEN. I don't know, there was things to do, and you did 'em.
JANE. And some one to tell you what to do?
BEN. Maybe that's it, somebody that knew better'n I did. It galled me at first, but pretty soon we got over in France, an' I saw we was really doin' something, then I didn't mind. I just got to doin' what I was told, and it worked out all right.
JANE. You liked France, too?
BEN. Yes.
JANE. I'd like to hear you tell about it.
BEN. Maybe I'll go back there some time. I don't know as I'd mind farming a place over there. Most of their farms are awful little, but I don't know but what I'd like it.
JANE. Farming is farming. Why not try it here?

BEN. Look out there! [*He points out of the window at the drifted snow.*] It's like that half the year, froze up, everything, most of all the people. Just a family by itself, maybe. Just a few folks, good an' bad, month after month, with nothin' to think about but just the mean little things, that really don't amount to nothin', but get to be bigger than all the world outside.

JANE [*sewing*]. Somebody must do the farming, Ben.

BEN. Somebody like the Jordans, that's been doin' it generation after generation. Well, look at us. I heard a feller, in a Y.M.C.A. hut, tellin' how Nature brought animals into the world, able to face what they had to face —

JANE. Yes, Ben?

BEN. That's what Nature's done for us Jordans, — brought us into the world half-froze before we was born. Brought us into the world mean, and hard, so's we could live the hard, mean life we have to live.

JANE. I don't know, Ben, but what you could live it different.

BEN. They *laugh* over there, and sing, and God knows when I was there they didn't have much to sing about. I was at a rest camp, near Nancy, after I got wounded. I told you about the French lady with all those children that I got billeted with.

JANE. Yes.

BEN. They used to *sing*, right at the table, and laugh! God! It brought a lump into my throat more'n once, lookin' at them, and rememberin' the Jordans!

JANE. I guess there wasn't much laughing at your family table.

BEN. Summers nobody had much time for it, and winters — well, I guess you know.

JANE. Yes.

BEN. Just a few folks together, day after day, and every little thing you don't like about the other raspin' on your nerves 'til it almost drives you crazy! Most folks quiet, because they've said all the things they've got to say a hundred times; other folks talkin', talkin', talkin' about nothing. Sometimes somebody sort of laughs, and it scares you; seems like laughter needs the sun, same as flowers do. Icebound, that's what we are all of us, inside and out.

[*He stands looking grimly out window.*]

JANE. Not all. I laughed a lot before I came here to live.

BEN [*turns and looks at her*]. I remember, you were just a little girl.

JANE. I was fourteen. See if there's a spool of black sewing cotton in that drawer.

BEN [*looking in drawer*]. You mean thread?

JANE. Yes.

BEN. This it?

[*He holds up a spool of white thread.*]

JANE. Would you call that black?

BEN [*looks it over*]. No — it ain't black. [*He searches and finds black thread.*] Maybe this is it!

JANE. Maybe it is! [*She takes it.*] You were with that French family quite a while, weren't you?

BEN. Most a month; they was well off, you know; I mean, they was, before the war. It was a nice house.

JANE [*sewing*]. How nice?

BEN [*hesitates*]. I don't know, things — well — useful, you know, but nice, not like this. [*He looks about.*]

JANE [*looks around with a sigh*]. It's not very pretty, but it could be. I could make it.

BEN. If you did, folks would be sayin' you wasn't respectable.

JANE. Tell me about the dinner they gave you the night before you went back to your company.

BEN. I told you.

JANE. Tell me again.

BEN [*smiles to himself at the remembrance*]. They was all dressed up, the whole family, and there I was with just my dirty old uniform.

JANE. Yes.

BEN [*lost in his recollections*]. It was a fine dinner, but it wasn't that. It was their doin' so much for me, folks like that — I've sort of pictured 'em lots of times since then.

JANE. Go on.

BEN. All of the young ones laughing and

happy, and the mother too, laughing and tryin' to talk to me, and neither one of us knowing much about what the other one was sayin'. [*He and* JANE *both laugh.*]

JANE. And the oldest daughter? The one that was most grown up?

BEN. She was scared of me somehow, but I don't know as ever I've seen a girl like her, before or since.

JANE. Maybe 'twas that dress you told me about; seems to me you don't remember much else about her; not so much as what color her hair was, only just that that dress was blue.

BEN [*thoughtfully*]. Yes.

JANE [*sewing*]. Sometimes you say dark blue!

[*She is watching him closely through half-shut eyes.*]

BEN [*absently*]. I guess so.

JANE. And then I say, dark as something I point out to you, that isn't dark at all, and you say, "No, lighter than that!"

BEN [*absently*]. Just — sort of blue.

JANE. Yes, sort of blue. It had lace on it, too, didn't it?

BEN. Lace? Maybe — yes, lace.

JANE. There's more than one blue dress in the world.

BEN. Like enough. Maybe there's more'n one family like that lady's, but I'll be damned if they live in Veazie. [*He crosses and opens cupboard and selects a bottle.*] I might as well run out and see how the old mare is getting on.

[*He selects bottle from shelf.*]

JANE. And you've got to shovel those paths for the clothes lines yet.

BEN. I know.

JANE. Well, don't forget.

BEN. It ain't likely you'll let me.

[*He exits at door right.* JANE *laughs softly to herself, and runs to closet and takes out a large cardboard box, and, putting it on the table, she cuts the string and removes the wrapping paper, then lifts the cover of the box and draws out a dainty light-blue gown with soft lace on the neck and sleeves. She holds it up joyfully, then, covering her own dress with it, she looks at herself in a mirror on wall. As she stands smiling at her reflection, there is a sharp knock on the outside door.* JANE *hastily returns dress to box and, as the knock is repeated, she puts the box under the sofa at left and crosses and opens the outside door.*]

[JUDGE BRADFORD *enters.*]

JANE. Oh, it's you, Judge! Come in.

JUDGE. I thought I'd stop on my way home and see how you were getting on, Jane.

JANE. I'll take your coat.

JUDGE. I'll just put it here. [*He puts coat on chair.*] Have you time to sit down a minute?

JANE. Of course. [*They sit.*]

JUDGE [*looks at her*]. That isn't a smile on your lips, is it, Jane?

JANE. Maybe —

JUDGE [*laughingly*]. I'm glad I came!

JANE. It's my birthday.

JUDGE. Why, Jane! [*He crosses to her and holds out his hand. She takes it.*] Many happy returns!

JANE [*thoughtfully*]. Many — happy returns — that's a lot to ask for.

JUDGE. You're about twenty-two, or twenty-three, aren't you?

JANE. Twenty-three.

JUDGE. Time enough ahead of you. [*His eye falls on the box, imperfectly hidden under the sofa; out of it a bit of the blue dress is sticking.*] Hello! What's all that?

JANE. My birthday present.

JUDGE. Who gave it to you?

JANE. I did.

JUDGE. Good! It's about time you started to blossom out.

JANE. I ordered a lot of things from Boston; they'll be here to-morrow.

JUDGE. I suppose that one's a dress?

JANE. Yes.

JUDGE [*bends over to look*]. Light blue, isn't it?

JANE [*smiles*]. Just sort of blue — with lace on it.

JUDGE. Oh, you're going to wear it, I suppose, in honor of your birthday?

JANE [*startled*]. To-night — oh, no — soon maybe, but not to-night.

JUDGE [*smiles*]. How soon?
JANE. Soon as I dare to; not just yet.
JUDGE. You have plenty of money; you ought to have every comfort in the world, and some of the luxuries.
JANE [*gravely*]. Judge! I want you to do something for me.
JUDGE. And of course I'll do it.
JANE. I want you to get Ben off. I want you to fix it so he won't go to State's Prison.
JUDGE. But if he's guilty, Jane?
JANE. I want you to go to old Mr. Kimbal for me and offer to pay him for that barn of his that Ben burned down. Then I want you to fix it so he won't push the case, so's Ben gets off.
JUDGE. Do you know what you are asking of me?
JANE. To get Ben off.
JUDGE. To compound a felony.
JANE. Those are just words, Judge, and words don't matter much to me. I might say I wasn't asking you to compound a felony, I was askin' you to save a sinner, but those would be just words too. There's nobody else; you've *got* to help me.
JUDGE [*thoughtfully*]. I've always thought a lot could be done for Ben, by a good lawyer.
JANE. It doesn't matter how, so long as it's done.
JUDGE. He was drinking, with a crowd of young men; the two Kimbal boys jumped on him and beat him up rather badly. That's about all we know, aside from the fact that Ben was drunk, and that that night the Kimbals' barn was set on fire.
JANE. Just so long as you can get him off, Judge.
JUDGE. I think a case of assault could be made against the Kimbal boys, and I think it would stand.
JANE. What of it?
JUDGE. It is quite possible that the old man, if he knew that action was to be taken against his sons, and if he could be tactfully assured of payment for his barn, say by Ben, in a year's time, might be persuaded to petition to have the indictment against Ben withdrawn. In that event, I think the chances would be very much in Ben's favor.
JANE. I don't care what names you call it, so long as it's done. Will you fix it?
JUDGE. Well, it's not exactly a proper proceeding for a Judge of the Circuit Court.
JANE. I knew you'd do it.
JUDGE. Yes, and I think you knew why, didn't you?
JANE. Ever since she's died, you've helped me about everything. Before she died you were just as good to me, and nobody else was.
JUDGE. I am glad you said that, because to clear me from the charge of being what poor Ben calls "one of the crow buzzards," and I don't want you to think me that.
JANE. No, you're not that.
JUDGE. I love you, Jane.
JANE. No!
JUDGE. Yes — I've done that for a long while. Don't you think you could get used to the thought of being my wife?
JANE [*gently*]. No.
JUDGE. I think I could make you happy.
JANE. No.
JUDGE. I am afraid being happy is something you don't know very much about.
JANE. No.
JUDGE. It isn't a thing that I am going to hurry you over, my dear, but neither is it a thing that I am going to give up hoping for.
JANE. When you told me, that day, that Mrs. Jordan had left me all her money, I couldn't understand; then, afterwards, you gave me the letter she left for me. I want you to read it.
JUDGE. What has her letter to do with us?
JANE. Maybe, reading it, you'll get to know something you've got a right to know, better than I could tell it to you.
JUDGE. Very well.
JANE. It's here. [*She opens drawer, and selects a letter in a woman's old-fashioned handwriting, from a large envelope of papers.*] She was a cold woman, Judge. She never let me get close to her, although I tried. She didn't love me. I was as sure of it then as I am now. [*She holds out the letter.*] Read it.

JUDGE. If it's about the thing I've been speaking of, I'd rather hear it in your voice.

JANE [reads]. "My dear Jane, the doctor tells me I haven't long to live, and so I'm doing this, the meanest thing I think I've ever done to you. I'm leaving you the Jordan money. Since my husband died, there has been just one person I could get to care about; that's Ben, who was my baby so long after all the others had forgotten how to love me. And Ben's a bad son, and a bad man. I can't leave him the money; he'd squander it, and the Jordans' money came hard."

JUDGE. Poor woman! It was a bitter thing for her to have to write like that.

JANE [reads on]. "If squandering the money would bring him happiness, I'd face all the Jordans in the other world and laugh at them, but I know there's only just one chance to save my boy — through a woman who will hold out her heart to him and let him trample on it, as he has on mine."

JUDGE [in sudden fear]. Jane!

JANE [reads on]. "Who'd work, and pray, and live for him, until as age comes on, and maybe he gets a little tired, he'll turn to her. And you're that woman, Jane; you've loved him ever since you came to us. Although he doesn't even know it. The Jordan name is his, the money's yours, and maybe there'll be another life for you to guard. God knows it isn't much I'm leaving you, but you can't refuse it, because you love him, and when he knows the money is yours, he will want to marry you. I'm a wicked old woman. Maybe you'll learn to forgive me as time goes on — It takes a long time to make a Jordan."

[JANE *drops her hand to her side.*] Then she just signed her name.

JUDGE. Is the damnable thing she says there true?

JANE. Yes, Judge.

JUDGE. And you're going to do this thing for her?

JANE. No, for him.

JUDGE [bitterly]. He isn't worth it.

JANE. I guess you don't understand.

JUDGE. No.

[*He crosses and picks up his coat.*]

JANE. You can't go like that, angry. You have to pay a price for being a good man, Judge — I need your help.

JUDGE. You mean *he* needs my help?

JANE. Yes, and you'll have to give it to him, if what you said a little while ago was true.

JUDGE [after a pause]. It *was* true, Jane. I'll help him. [*He picks up his hat.*]

JANE. I've an errand at the store. I'll go with you.

[*She takes hat and coat from rack and puts them on.*]

JUDGE. Is it anything I could have sent up for you?

JANE [putting on coat]. I guess not. You see, I've got to match a color.

JUDGE. Another new dress?

JANE [they start toward door]. Just a ribbon, for my hair.

JUDGE. I didn't know women still wore ribbons in their hair.

JANE. It seems they do — in France.

[*They exit together at left to the outside door and off.*]

[NETTIE *and* ELLA *enter quickly, after a slight pause,* NETTIE *running in from right, followed more sedately by* ELLA.]

NETTIE. You see! I was right! She went with him.

[*She has run to window left and is looking out.*]

ELLA. That's what money does. If mother hadn't left her everything, he wouldn't have touched her with a ten-foot pole.

NETTIE. Well, if she's fool enough to stay in this place, I guess he's about the best there is.

ELLA. Then trust her for gettin' him; by the time she gets through in Veazie, this town will be barer than Mother Hubbard's cupboard by the time the dog got there. [*Her eye falls on* JANE's *box, partly under sofa.*] What's that?

[*She bends over, looking at it.*]

NETTIE. What?

ELLA. I never saw it before. [*She draws it out.*] Looks like a dress. See! Blue silk!

NETTIE. Open it.

ELLA [*hesitates*]. Must be hers! Maybe she wouldn't like it.

NETTIE. Maybe she wouldn't know it.

ELLA. A cat can look at a king!
[*She opens the box and holds up the blue dress.*]

NETTIE. Oh! Oh!

ELLA [*really moved*]. Some folks would say a dress like that wasn't decent, but I wouldn't care, not if it was mine, and it might have been mine — but for her.

NETTIE. Yours! Grandma wouldn't have left her money to you. She hated old people. Everybody does. She'd have left it to me; but for Jane Crosby!

ELLA [*looks at dress*]. I always wanted a dress like this; when I was young, I used to dream about one, but mother only laughed. For years I counted on gettin' me what I wanted, when she died; now I never will.

NETTIE [*fiercely*]. I will — somehow!

ELLA. Maybe, but not me. Oh, if I could have the feelin' of a dress like that on me, if I could wear it once, where folks could see me — Just once! Oh, I know how they'd laugh — I wouldn't care —

NETTIE [*almost in tears*]. I can't stand it if she's going to wear things like that.

ELLA. I'll put it back.
[*She starts to do so.*]

NETTIE [*catches her hand*]. Not yet.

ELLA. I guess the less we look at it, the better off we'll be.
[*There is a ring at the front door.*]

NETTIE. Who's that?

ELLA. Here! [*She hands the box to* NETTIE.] Shove it back under the sofa. I'll go and see. [*She turns and crosses to door left and out to the vestibule.* NETTIE, *with the box in her arms, hesitates for a moment, then turns and exits at right, taking the box with her.* ELLA *opens the outside door at left, showing* ORIN *on the doorstep.* ELLA *looks at him angrily.*] For time's sake, what are you ringing the bell for?

ORIN. Mum says for me not to act like I belonged here.

ELLA. Well, I'm goin' to shut the door. Git in or git out!

ORIN. I got a note. [*He enters room as* ELLA *shuts door.*] It's for her.

ELLA [*holds out hand*]. Let me see it.

ORIN. Mum said not to let on I had nothin' if you came nosin' around.

[JANE *enters from left.*]

JANE. I just ran across to the store. I haven't been five minutes.
[*She takes coat off.*]

ELLA. He's got a note for you, from Sadie.

JANE. Oh, let me see it, Orin.

ORIN [*gives her note*]. She said, if you said is they an answer, I was to say yes, they is.

JANE. Just a minute.
[*She opens note and reads it.*]

ELLA. I must say she didn't lose much time.

JANE [*after reading note*]. Poor Sadie! Wait, Orin! [*She sits at table and takes checkbook from the drawer and writes.*] Just take this to your mother.

ELLA. You don't mean you're goin' to —

JANE. Be quiet, Ella. Here, Orin. [*She hands him check.*] Don't lose it, and run along.

ORIN. All right. Mum said we was goin' to have dinner early, and go to a movie! Good-night.

JANE [*again writing in checkbook*]. Good-night. [ORIN *exits.*]

ELLA. So you sent her her rent money, after all?

JANE. Here!
[*She rises and hands a check to* ELLA.]

ELLA. What's that?

JANE. Two hundred dollars. You can try that dressmaking business if you want to, Ella.

ELLA [**Looks at check**]. Two hundred dollars!

JANE. You needn't thank me.

ELLA. That ain't it. I was just wonderin' what's come over you all of a sudden.

[*Ben enters.*]

JANE. It's my birthday, that's all. Did you know it was my birthday, Ben?

BEN [*carelessly*]. Is it? I shoveled them damned paths!
[*He crosses and sits by fire.*]

JANE. Ella's going into the dressmaking business, Ben.

BEN [*moodily*]. What of it?
ELLA. That's what I say. It ain't much of a business.
[*She exits at right; outside it grows to dusk.*]
JANE. Are you tired?
BEN. Maybe.
[*He stretches his feet out toward fire.*]
JANE. You've done a lot of work to-day.
BEN. And every day.
JANE. I don't suppose you know how much good it's done you, how well you look!
BEN. Beauty's only skin deep.
JANE. Folks change, even in a few weeks, outside and in. Hard work don't hurt anybody.
BEN. I got chilblains on my feet. The damned shoes are stiffer than they ever was.
JANE. Icebound, you said. Maybe it don't have to be like that. Sometimes, just lately, it's seemed to me that if folks would try, things needn't be so bad. All of 'em try, I mean, for themselves, and for everybody else.
BEN. If I was you, I'd go out somewheres and hire a hall.
JANE. If you'd put some pork fat on those shoes to-night, your feet wouldn't hurt so bad.
BEN. Maybe.
[*He sits looking moodily into the fire. After a moment's hesitation, JANE crosses and sits in the chair beside his. The evening shadows deepen around them but the glow from the fire lights their faces.*]
JANE. I'm lonesome to-night. We always made a lot of birthdays when I was a girl. .
BEN. Some do.
JANE. Your mother didn't. She found me once trying, the day I was fifteen. I remember how she laughed at me.
BEN. All the Jordans have got a sense of humor.
JANE. She wasn't a Jordan, not until she married your father.
BEN. When a woman marries into a family, she mostly shuts her eyes and jumps in all over.

JANE. Your mother was the best of the whole lot of you. Anyway, I think so.
BEN. I *know* it. I always thought a lot of her, in spite of our being relations.
JANE. She loved you, Ben.
BEN. She left me without a dollar, knowin' I was going to State's Prison, and what I'd be by the time I get out.
JANE. Maybe some day you'll understand why she did it.
BEN. Because she thought you'd take better care of the money than any of the rest of us.
JANE. And you hate me because of that, the way all the rest of the Jordans do?
BEN. Sometimes.
JANE [*sadly*]. I suppose it's natural.
BEN. But I ain't such a fool as Henry, and the women folks. They think you took advantage and fooled her into what she did. I thought so at first, now I don't.
JANE. What do you think now, Ben?
BEN. She'd watched you; she knew you were worth more'n all of us in a lump. I know it, too, but some way it riles me worse than if you wasn't.
JANE. That's silly!
BEN [*with growing resentment*]. Don't you suppose I know what you've been doin' to me? Tryin' to make a man of me. Tryin' to help me. Standing up to me and fightin' me every day, tryin' to teach me to be decent. Workin' over me like I was a baby, or somethin', and you was tryin' to teach me how to walk. Gettin' me so upset that every time I don't do what I ought to do, I get all het up inside; I never was so damned uncomfortable in all my life.
JANE. And I never was so happy.
BEN. I s'pose God knew what he was about when he made women.
JANE. Of course he did.
BEN. Anyhow, he gave 'em the best of it, all right.
JANE. You don't mean that! You *can't!*
BEN. I do. Let a man get miserable, and he *is* miserable. A woman ain't really happy no other way.
JANE. Maybe you think I'm having an easier time right now than you are.
BEN. I know it.
JANE. They all hate me, and they all

want something, all the time. I can't say yes, and it's hard to always say no. Then there's the farm, big, and poor, and all worked out. The Jordans have been taking their living out of this soil for more than a hundred years, and never putting anything back.

BEN. Just themselves, that's all.

JANE. Worked right, like they do out West, this place could be what it ought to be. How can I do that? It needs a man.

BEN. I been thinkin' lately things could be done a whole lot different.

JANE. By a man, if he loved the old place — You Jordans robbed this soil always. Suppose one of you tried to pay it back — it would mean work and money, for a couple of years maybe, then I guess you'd see what gratitude meant.

BEN. It could be done; it ought to be.

JANE. By you, Ben!

BEN. No — I guess I ain't got the judgment.

JANE. You've got it, if you'd learn to use it.

BEN. Anyhow, I've got just a month, that's all.

JANE. Maybe you'll have more.

BEN. I'm as good as convicted as I sit here. I've only got a month.

JANE. Then help me for that month. We could plan how to start out in the spring. I've got books that will help us, and I can get more. We could do a lot!

BEN. I don't know but what we could!

JANE [bends toward him]. Will you shake hands on it? [She offers her hand.]

BEN [surprised]. What for?

JANE. Oh, just because we never have.

BEN. We ain't goin' to change *every-thing*, are we?

JANE. One thing. We're going to be friends.

BEN [takes her hand awkwardly]. You're a good sport, game as a man, gamer, maybe.

JANE. And now for the surprise.

BEN. The what?

JANE [draws her hand away and rises]. You'll see. I want you to sit right here, until I open those doors.
   [She points to doors to dining-room.]

BEN. I wasn't thinkin' of movin'.

JANE. Just sit right there.

BEN. And do what?

JANE. Think.

BEN. What of?

JANE. Oh, anything — so long as it's pleasant — of the spring that's coming —

BEN. In the prison down at Thomaston.

JANE. Of France, then, of the family that was so good to you — of the beautiful lady — of the daughter, if you want to, the one that was most grown up — and of the wonderful blue dress. Just shut your eyes and think, 'til I come back!
   [She exits through doors to dining-room and closes the doors after her. BEN sits in glow from the fire, his eyes closed. In a moment the door at right is thrown open and NETTIE stands in the doorway, the light from the hall falling on her. She has on JANE's blue dress and is radiant with youth and excitement.]

NETTIE. Ben! Look at me! Look, Ben!

BEN. What?

NETTIE. Look, Ben!
   [He looks at her and for a moment sits in stupid wonder, then rises slowly to his feet.]

BEN. It's — It's Nettie!

NETTIE. Did you ever see anything so lovely, did you?

BEN. You're — you're a woman, Nettie!

NETTIE. Of course I am, you stupid!

BEN [crosses down to her]. God! How I've starved for somethin' pretty to look at! God! How I've starved for it!

NETTIE. That's why I came down, I wanted you to see! I waited there in the hall till she went out.

BEN. And you've been here all the time, and I haven't so much as looked at you!

NETTIE [softly]. You've been in trouble, Ben!

BEN. I'll get out of that somehow! I'm going to make a fight. I ain't goin' to let 'em take me now.

NETTIE. Honest, Ben?

BEN. Not now. Oh, you pretty kid! You pretty little thing!
   [He catches her fiercely in his arms.

NETTIE. You mustn't, Ben!
BEN [*triumphant*]. Mustn't! You don't know me!
NETTIE. Just one then! [*She holds up her lips, and as he kisses her ardently, the dining-room doors back of them open and* JANE *stands in the doorway, looking at them. She has removed her apron and has made some poor attempt at dressing up. Back of her we see the table bravely spread for the festive birthday party. There is a large turkey and other special dishes, and a round cake on which blaze twenty-three tiny candles. They turn their heads, startled, as* JANE *looks at them, and* BEN *tightens his arms defiantly about* NETTIE.] Let me go!
BEN [*holding her and looking past her to* JANE]. No! [*Then to* JANE.] Why are you looking at me like that?
NETTIE. Let me go.
BEN [*to* JANE]. To hell with your dream of grubbing in the dirt. Now I know what I want, and I'm going to get it.
NETTIE. Let go, dear. [*She draws away.*] I'm ashamed about wearin' your dress, Cousin Jane. I'll take it right off.
JANE. You needn't. I guess I don't want it any more. [*For the first time her eyes leave* BEN'S *face. She turns and steps past them to the door at right and calls.*] Supper's ready, Ella!
[HANNAH *enters at back in dining-room with a plate of hot biscuits.*]

CURTAIN

ACT THREE

SCENE: *Same as Act One. Parlor at the Jordans', two months later.*
At rise the characters are grouped exactly as they were at the opening of the play. The white slip covers, however, have been removed from the chairs, and the backing through the window shows partly melted snowdrifts. HENRY *sighs; the clock strikes two.* HENRY *looks at his watch.*
There is a pause. The outside door slams and BEN *enters and looks about.*

BEN. Well — here we all are again.
SADIE [*sadly*]. Yes.

HENRY. I ain't been in this room before since the funeral.
SADIE. And I ain't, and the last time before that was when father died.
EMMA. I sat right here, in the same chair I'm settin' in now, but to your grandfather's funeral, right after I married Henry, I was treated like one of the poor relations! I had to stand up.
HENRY. I remember; it made considerable trouble.
ELLA. I don't know as it was ever what I called a cheerful room.
HENRY [*severely*]. A parlor's where a person's supposed to sit and think of God, and you couldn't expect it to be cheerful!
ELLA [*looks about*]. Seems like we'd had trouble and disgrace enough in this family without her takin' all the slip covers off of the chairs and sofa!
EMMA. It ain't *right!*
SADIE. That Boston woman that's building the house over on Elm Street ain't so much as goin' to have a parlor. I stopped her right on the street and asked her what she was plannin' to do soon as the first of 'em died.
EMMA. What did she say?
SADIE. Said she tried not to think about such things.
HENRY [*sternly*]. We got Atheists enough in this town right now.
BEN. Well, if Jane's coming, I wish she'd come; this ain't exactly my idea of pleasant company.
ELLA. She says we're all to wait in here for Judge Bradford.
SADIE. What did she send for us for?
ELLA. I don't know.
EMMA. Why didn't you ask her?
ELLA. I did, and she most bit my head off.
BEN. She most bites mine off every time I see her. I must say she's changed, Jane has; she ain't the same girl at all she was a few weeks ago.
NETTIE. She's actin' just awful, especially to me!
SADIE. Of course, I'd be the last one to say anything against her, but —
BEN. But nothin'! There ain't one of you here fit to tie her shoes!

SADIE. *We* ain't?

BEN. And I ain't! The only difference between us is I ain't worth much and I know it, and you ain't worth nothin' and you don't.

EMMA. I guess you'd better be careful how you talk!

NETTIE. If anybody says anything about Jane lately, that's the way he always talks! The worse she treats him, the better he seems to like it.

SADIE. Well, I don't know as I'm surprised more about his insultin' the rest of us, but it's sort of comical his talkin' that way about you, Nettie.

EMMA. Nettie! What's Nettie got to do with him?

SADIE. Oh! Excuse me! I didn't know 'twas supposed to be a secret.

EMMA. What is?

SADIE. About the way those two have been carryin' on together!

HENRY. What!

EMMA. Ben and Nettie!

NETTIE [afraid]. Stop her, Ben, can't you?

BEN. If I knew a way to stop women like her, I'd patent it and get rich!

EMMA [sternly]. Him and Nettie?

SADIE. They passed my house together *once* a week ago Wednesday, *once* the Tuesday before that, and *twice* the Sunday after New Year's.

HENRY. Together!

SADIE. And Eben Tilden's boy told Abbie Palsey that Tilly Hickson heard Aaron Hamlin say he'd seen 'em together at the picture show!

HENRY [to BEN]. Is it true?

EMMA. You've been with him after all I told you!

BEN. It ain't going to hurt her none just to talk to me, is it?

EMMA. Them that touches pitch gets defiled!

HENRY [to NETTIE]. I want you to tell me everything that's took place between you two.

SADIE. Wait!

HENRY. What?

SADIE. Orin! Leave the room!

NETTIE. He don't have to leave the room. I don't care who knows what happened!

HENRY. Go on, then.

NETTIE. Well — Ben and I — We — Just for a few days — anyway, it was all his fault.

BEN. She threw me down because I was going to prison.

NETTIE. He said he'd get out of it somehow, but he can't, and I just won't have folks laughing at me!

BEN. It's all right, it never meant nothin' to her, and I guess it didn't mean much to me. It's just as well it's over.

NETTIE. It's a whole lot better.

HENRY. Well — what's passed is passed. Folks that plant the wind reap the whirlwind! There's no use cryin' over spilled milk.

ORIN. Say, Mum! What do you s'pose Uncle Henry thinks he means when he says things?

HENRY. Somehow I can't help wishin' you was my son for just about five minutes.

[HANNAH and JUDGE BRADFORD enter.]

HANNAH. They're all in here, Judge.

JUDGE. Good-afternoon.

HENRY. How are you, Judge?

SADIE. It's a mild day; winter's most over. — Stop scratching yourself.

[This last to ORIN, who seems to be uneasy and frequently scratches himself.]

HANNAH [at door]. I'll tell her you're here, Judge. She'll be right down.

[Hannah exits.]

ELLA. Won't you sit?

JUDGE. Thanks. [He sits by table.]

HENRY. What's it about? Why did she say we was to all be here at two o'clock?

JUDGE. She will probably be able to answer that question herself, Ben.

SADIE [to ORIN]. Don't.

ORIN. What?

SADIE. Scratch!

ORIN. Oh.

[JANE enters. The JUDGE rises.]

JUDGE. Well, Jane?

JANE. Don't get up, Judge.

JUDGE. Will you sit here?
[JUDGE *turns to get a chair for* JANE. ORIN *scratches himself.* ELLA *rises.*]
ELLA. What is the matter with this brat?
ORIN. I itch!
SADIE. It's warm, and he's got on his heavy flannels! He's as clean as you are!
[JANE *and* JUDGE *sit.*]
BEN. You said to heat this room up and wait here for you and the Judge. Why? I got my stock to tend.
HENRY. It's a bad time for me to get away from the store; what was it you wanted of us?
JANE. I'm afraid it isn't going to be easy to tell you.
JUDGE. Won't you let me do it, Jane?
JANE. No. I've come to know that your mother didn't really want that I should have the Jordan money.
SADIE. What's that?
JANE. I put it as simply as I could.
BEN. You mean a later will's been found?
JUDGE. No.
JANE. In a way, Judge, it's like there had. Your mother left me a letter dated later than the will.
ELLA. Leavin' the money different?
JANE. Tellin' what she really wanted.
BEN. Well, what did she want?
JANE. It was like she left me all her money in trust, so I could keep it safe until the time she was hopin' for come, and in a way it did come, not quite like she wanted it, but near enough so I can give up a burden I haven't strength enough to carry any more. [*She stops.*]
JUDGE. Let me finish, Jane. Jane has asked me to draw a deed of gift, making the Jordan property over to Ben.
BEN. Why?
JANE. She wanted you to have it.
BEN. Why didn't she will it to me, then?
JANE. She was afraid to trust you.
BEN. Well?
JANE. You've learned to work; you'll keep on working.
HENRY. You mean to say my mother wanted him to have it all?
JANE. Yes.

HENRY. I am a religious man, but there was a time when even Job gave up! So — all our money goes to Ben — and he can't even buy himself out of prison!
JANE [*after a pause*]. Ben isn't going to prison.
BEN. Why? Who's to stop it?
JUDGE [*after a look from* JANE]. Kimbal agreed not to press the charge against you. It seems that there were certain extenuating circumstances. A motion has been made for the dismissal of the indictment, and it won't be opposed.
BEN. Why did he? Who fixed this thing.
JANE. Judge Bradford did.
[*She looks at* JUDGE.]
BEN [*slowly*]. It means a lot to me. There's things I'd like to do. I haven't dared to think about 'em lately — now I'll do 'em. [*There is a pause.*]
HENRY. Well, Ben, so you've got the money! I guess maybe it's better than her havin' it; after all, blood's thicker than water! We'll help you any way we can and — er — of course you'll help us.
BEN. Why will I?
HENRY. We're brothers, Ben! We're old Jordans!
BEN. What was we when I got back from France? There was a band met us boys at the station. I was your brother all right that day, only somehow, in just a little while, you forgot about it. I was a Jordan when I was hidin' out from the police, and all that kept me from starvin' was the money Jane sent me! I was your brother the night mother died, and you said you wouldn't go my bail.
ELLA. You ain't going to be hard, Ben!
BEN. I'm the head of the family now, ain't I, and you can bet all you've got I'm going to be a real Jordan.
HENRY. I think, Ben —
BEN. From now on, there ain't nobody got any right to think in this house but just me! So run along home, the whole pack of you, and after this, when you feel like you must come here — come separate.
ELLA. Turn us out, Ben?
BEN. Sure, why not?
NETTIE [*crosses to him. Sweetly*]. There

ain't any reason why *we* can't be friends, is there?

BEN. Well, I don't know. There's only one way I could ever get to trust you.

NETTIE. What way, Ben?

BEN. I'd have to go to jail for five years and see if you'd wait for me!

EMMA. It's an awful thing for a mother to have a fool for a child.

ELLA [*goes upstage with* NETTIE]. Well, I must say you made a nice mess of things!

NETTIE [*exits with* ELLA]. Well, I don't care! I don't see how anybody would expect me to be a mind-reader!

SADIE. Come, Orin — say good-by to your Uncle Ben.

ORIN. What will I do that for?

SADIE. Because I tell you to!

ORIN. Yesterday you told me he wasn't worth speakin' to!

SADIE. Are you going to move, you stupid little idiot? [*She drags him out.*]

ORIN [*as they go*]. What did I say? You let me alone!

HENRY. I was wonderin', Ben, how you'd feel about endorsing that note of mine.

BEN. You was?

HENRY. Yes, I don't know what I'm going to do about it.

BEN. As far as I care, you can go nail it on a door. [HENRY *and* EMMA *start to exit.*] No, hold on, I'll pay it.

HENRY. You will!

BEN. Yes; I don't know as it would do me much good at the bank, havin' a brother of mine in the poorhouse.

[BEN *laughs as* HENRY *and* EMMA *exit.*]

JUDGE. Well, Ben? "Uneasy lies the head that wears a crown."

BEN [*down to stove*]. Depends on the head. Mine's thick, I guess. Anyhow, none of them is going to bother it. I'm boss here now.

JUDGE. You'll find a copy here of the inventory of the estate, and other legal papers. Everything is in order.

JANE. And my accounts, Ben; you'll find the exact amount your mother left. I spent some money about six weeks ago, on myself, but I've been careful ever since, and I've made up for it.

BEN. You said, Judge, she didn't have to go by that letter of my mother's, if she didn't want to? She didn't have to give anything back at all?

JUDGE. No, she didn't.

BEN. Then if I was you — [*to* JANE] I wouldn't talk so much about the little you spent on yourself. I guess to look at you it wasn't much.

JANE. Yes, it was.

BEN. Well, we'll fix things so you can keep on spendin'. Only let's see somethin' come of it. I never was so damned sick of anything in my life as I am of that old black dress of yours!

[*Crosses stage up and over right.*]

JANE. I've got plenty of clothes upstairs. I'm sorry now I ever bought them, but I'll take them with me when I go.

BEN. Go? Go where?

JANE. To Old Town. I've got a place there, clerking in the Pulp Mill.

BEN. You!

JANE. Yes.

BEN. But what about me?

JUDGE. Don't you think Jane has done about enough for you?

BEN. She's done a lot, she's given up the money. I don't know as I like that; 'course I like gettin' it, but not if she's going away.

JANE. I couldn't stay now, and I wouldn't want to.

BEN. I don't suppose you remember about plannin' what you and me was to do with this old farm?

JANE. I remember.

BEN. Well — then what are you going away for?

JANE. Because I couldn't be happy here, Ben — It's been harder than anything I ever thought could come to anybody, the last few weeks here — and so I'm going. [*She turns to* JUDGE.] I'll go upstairs and get my things. I'll stop at your office, Judge, on the way to the station.

JUDGE. Thank you, Jane.

BEN. You're goin' to-day? Before I order my new farm machinery or anything?

You're goin' to leave me with all this work on my hands?
JANE. Yes, Ben. [*She exits.*]
BEN. Well — that's a lesson to me! Oh, she's a good woman! I ain't denyin' that — but she's fickle!
JUDGE. You're a fool, Ben!
BEN. I been doin' kitchen police around this town for quite a spell now, Judge, but from this day on I ain't goin' to take that sort of talk from anybody.
JUDGE. I assure you that you won't have to take any sort of talk at all from me.
[*He starts for the door.*]
BEN. I didn't mean that. I don't want you to think I ain't grateful for all you've done for me.
JUDGE [*coldly*]. I have done nothing for you.
BEN. If it wasn't for you, I'd want to die; that's what I did want. I was afraid of that prison, just a coward about it. Now I'm a free man, with a big life openin' out ahead of me — I got everything in the world right here in my two hands, everything — and I owe it to you!
JUDGE. I am very glad to say that you don't owe me anything. I don't like you, I haven't forgiven you for what you did to your mother's life. Nor for a worse thing, one you haven't brains enough to even know you've done. Don't be grateful to me, Ben, please. I think nothing could distress me more than that.
BEN. You've been a good friend to me.
JUDGE. I haven't meant to be; as I said, I don't like you. I haven't any faith in you. I don't believe in this new life of yours. You made a mess of the old one, and I think you will of the new.
BEN. No matter what you say, you can't get away from me. I'll be grateful till I die. But for you I'd have gone to that damned prison!
JUDGE. But for Jane.
BEN. How Jane?
JUDGE. How Jane? Jane went your bond the day your mother died. Jane took you in and taught you how to work, made you work, taught you through the one decent spot in you something of a thing you'd never know, self-respect. Worked over you, petted you, coaxed you — held you up — Then you hurt her — but she kept on — She went herself to Kimbal, after he had refused me, and got his help to keep you out of prison — then, against my will, against the best that I could do to stop her, she turns over all this to you — and goes out with nothing — and you ask, "How Jane?"
BEN. Why? Why has she done this, all this, for me?
[*The* JUDGE *looks at* BEN *with contempt and turns and exits.* BEN *is left in deep thought.*]
[JANE *comes downstairs dressed for a journey with a handbag, etc. She enters.*]
JANE. Good-by, Ben. [*She crosses to him, her hand out.*] Good-by. Won't you say good-by?
BEN. First, there's some things I got to know about.
JANE [*smiles*]. I guess there's not much left for us to say, Ben.
BEN [JANE *crosses to door, but he gets ahead of her*]. There's things I got to know. [*She looks at him, but does not speak.*] The Judge tells me 'twas you got Kimbal to let me go free. [*He looks at her — she half turns away.*] Answer me. [*Pause.*] The Judge tells me you gave up what was yours — to me — without no other reason than because you wanted me to have it. That's true, ain't it? [*Pause.*] You sent me every cent you had, when you knew mother was dying, then you went bail for me, like he said — and did all them other things. I don't know as any woman ever did any more — I want to know why!
JANE. Why do you think?
BEN. I don't know — I sort of thought — sort of hoped —
JANE [*bravely*]. It was because I loved her, Ben —
BEN. Oh.
[*He turns away disappointed.*]
JANE. You're forgetting, I guess, how long we was alone here — when you was in France — then the months we didn't know where you was, when the police was looking for you — She used to make me promise if ever I could I'd help you.

BEN. Well — all I've got to say is you're no liar.

JANE. Good-by. [*She turns to go.*]

BEN. Wait. [*Closes door.*] Let's see that letter you said she left for you.

JANE. No. I won't do that. I've done enough; you're free, you've got the money and the farm.

BEN [*crosses in front of table and sits left of table*]. They ain't worth a damn with you gone — I didn't know that till just now, but they ain't.

JANE. It's sort of sudden, the way you found that out.

BEN. Oh, it don't take long for a man to get hungry — it only takes just a minute for a man to die; you can burn down a barn quick enough, or do a murder; it's just living and getting old that takes a lot of time — Can't you stay here, Jane?

JANE. There's Nettie.

BEN. Nettie — that couldn't stand the gaff — that run out on me when I was in trouble.

JANE. It doesn't matter what folks do, if you love 'em enough.

BEN. What do you know about it? I suppose you've been in love a lot of times?

JANE. No.

BEN. Then you be quiet and let an expert talk. I was lonesome and I wanted a woman; she was pretty and I wanted to kiss her — that ain't what I call love.

JANE. You. You don't even know the meaning of the word.

BEN. That don't worry me none — I guess the feller that wrote the dictionary was a whole lot older'n I am before he got down to the L's.

JANE. You've got good in you, Ben, deep down, if you'd only try. [BEN *turns.*] I know, it's always been that way! You've never tried for long; you've never had a real ambition.

BEN. When I was a kid I wanted to spit farther than anybody.

JANE. Good-by. [*She starts up to door.*]

BEN. And so you're going to break your word? [JANE *turns, hurt.*]

BEN. I don't know what 'twas you promised mother, but you've broke your word. No man ever needed a woman more'n I need you, and you're leaving me.

JANE. That isn't fair.

BEN. It's true, ain't it; truth ain't always fair — You ain't helped me none, you've hurt me — worse than bein' broke, worse than bein' in jail.

JANE. It don't seem like I could stand to have you talk like that.

BEN. What you done you done for her. I didn't count, I never have, not with you.

JANE. When you've been trying to do a thing as long as I have, it gets to be a part of you.

BEN. You done it all for her — well — she's dead — you'd better go.

JANE. Maybe I had, but if I do it will be with the truth between us. Here's the letter she left for me, Ben — I got a feeling somehow like she was here with us now, like she wanted you to read it. [*She holds it out.*] It's like she was guiding us from the grave — Read it.

[*Crosses up to window.*]

BEN [*reads*]. "My dear Jane: The doctor tells me I haven't long to live and so I am doing this, the meanest thing I think I've ever done to you. I'm leaving you the Jordan money. Since my husband died there has been just one person I could get to care about, that's Ben, who was my baby so long after all the others had forgotten how to love me. [*He mumbles the letter to himself, then brings out the words.*] Hold out her heart and let him trample on it, as he has on mine."

[*Slowly he breaks down, sobbing bitterly.*]

JANE. Don't, Ben —

BEN. Look what I done to her! Look what I done!

JANE [*hand on his shoulder*]. Oh, my dear — my dear!

BEN. I did love her, more'n she thought, more'n I ever knew how to tell her!

JANE [*kneels beside him*]. It wasn't all your fault — you were a lonely boy — she never said much — she was like you, Ben, ashamed to show the best that's in you.

BEN [*bitterly*]. The best in me. I ain't fit that you should touch me, Jane — you'd better go.

JANE. Not if you need me, Ben, and I think you do.

BEN. I love you — more'n I ever thought I could — tenderer — truer — but I'm no good — you couldn't trust me — I couldn't trust myself.

JANE. Spring's coming, Ben, everywhere, to you and me, if you would only try.

BEN. Can a feller change — just 'cause he wants to?

JANE. I don't want you changed. I want you what you are, the best of you — just a man that loves me — if you do love me, Ben.

BEN. Can't you help me to be fit?

JANE. I'm going to do the thing I always meant to do — good times and bad, Ben, I'm going to share with you.

BEN. God knows I —

JANE. Hush, Ben — I don't want another promise.

BEN. What do you want?

JANE. You said I was a good sport once — you shook hands on what we'd do to bring this old place back — there's plenty to be done. I'll stay and help you if you want me.

BEN. A good sport? [*He takes her hand.*] I'll say you're all of that.

[HANNAH *enters.*]

HANNAH. If you ain't careful you'll miss that train.

JANE. That's just what I want to do.

HANNAH. You ain't going?

JANE. I'm never going, Hannah.

HANNAH. You going to marry him?

BEN. You bet your life she is!

HANNAH. I guess you'll be mighty happy — marriage changes folks — and any change in him will be a big improvement.

[*She picks up* JANE's *bag and exits* — JANE *and* BEN *laugh.*]

CURTAIN

THE ADDING MACHINE
A PLAY IN SEVEN SCENES
By ELMER L. RICE

COPYRIGHT, 1923, BY DOUBLEDAY, PAGE & COMPANY

Reprinted by special arrangement with the author and The Theatre Guild

All rights reserved, including that of translation into foreign languages, including the Scandinavian

CAST OF CHARACTERS

Mr. Zero
Mrs. Zero
Messrs. One, Two, Three, Four, Five, Six,
  and their respective wives
Daisy Diana Dorothea Devore
The Boss
Policeman
Two Attendants
Judy O'Grady
A Young Man
Shrdlu
A Head
Lieutenant Charles
Joe

THE ADDING MACHINE

SCENE ONE

SCENE: *A bedroom.*
A small room containing an "installment plan" bed, dresser, and chairs. An ugly electric light fixture over the bed with a single glaring naked lamp. One small window with the shade drawn. The walls are papered with sheets of foolscap covered with columns of figures.
MR. ZERO is lying in the bed, facing the audience, his head and shoulders visible. He is thin, sallow, undersized, and partially bald. MRS. ZERO *is standing before the dresser arranging her hair for the night. She is forty-five, sharp-featured, gray streaks in her hair. She is shapeless in her long-sleeved cotton nightgown. She is wearing her shoes, over which sag her ungartered stockings.*

MRS. ZERO [*as she takes down her hair*]. I'm gettin' sick o' them Westerns. All them cowboys ridin' around an' foolin' with them ropes. I don't care nothin' about that. I'm sick of 'em. I don't see why they don't have more of them stories like *For Love's Sweet Sake.* I like them sweet little love stories. They're nice an' wholesome. Mrs. Twelve was sayin' to me only yesterday, "Mrs. Zero," says she, "what I like is one of them wholesome stories, with just a sweet, simple little love story." "You're right, Mrs. Twelve," I says. "That's what I like, too." They're showin' too many Westerns at the Rosebud. I'm gettin' sick of them. I think we'll start goin' to the Peter Stuyvesant. They got a good bill there Wednesday night. There's a Chubby Delano comedy called *Sea-Sick.* Mrs. Twelve was tellin' me about it. She says it's a scream. They're havin' a picnic in the country and they sit Chubby next to an old maid with a great big mouth. So he gets sore an' when she ain't lookin' he goes and catches a frog and drops it in her clam chowder. An' when she goes to eat the chowder the frog jumps out of it an' right into her mouth. Talk about laugh! Mrs. Twelve was tellin' me she laughed so she nearly passed out. He sure can pull some funny ones. An' they got that big Grace Darling feature, *A Mother's Tears.* She's sweet. But I don't like her clothes. There's no style to them. Mrs. Nine was tellin' me she read in *Pictureland* that she ain't livin' with her husband. He's her second, too. I don't know whether they're divorced or just separated. You wouldn't think it to see her on the screen. She looks so sweet and innocent. Maybe it ain't true. You can't believe all you read. They say some Pittsburgh millionaire is crazy about her and that's why she ain't livin' with her husband. Mrs. Seven was tellin' me her brother-in-law has a friend that used to go to school with Grace Darling. He says her name ain't Grace Darling at all. Her right name is Elizabeth Dugan, he says, an' all them stories about her gettin' five thousand a week is the bunk, he says. She's sweet, though. Mrs. Eight was tellin' me that *A Mother's Tears* is the best picture she ever made. "Don't miss it, Mrs. Zero," she says. "It's sweet," she says. "Just sweet and wholesome. Cry!" she says, "I nearly cried my eyes out." There's one part in it where this big bum of an Englishman — he's a married man, too — an' she's this little simple country girl. An' she nearly falls for him, too. But she's sittin' out in the garden, one day, and she looks up and there's her mother lookin' at her, right out of the clouds. So that night she locks the door of her room. An' sure enough, when everybody's in bed, along comes this big bum of an Englishman an' when she won't let him in what does he do but go an' kick open the door. "Don't miss it, Mrs. Zero," Mrs. Eight was tellin' me. It's at the Peter Stuyvesant Wednesday night, so don't be tellin' me you want to go to the Rosebud. The Eights seen it downtown at the Strand. They go downtown all the time. Just like us — nit! I guess by the time it gets to the Peter Stuyvesant all that part about kickin' in the door will be cut out. Just like they cut out that big cabaret scene in *The Price of Virtue*. They sure are pullin' some rough stuff in the pictures nowadays. "It's no place for a young girl," I was tellin' Mrs. Eleven, only the other day. An' by the time they get uptown half of it is cut out. But you wouldn't go downtown — not if wild horses was to drag you. You can wait till they come uptown! Well, I don't want to wait, see? I want to see 'em when everybody else is seein' them an' not a month later. Now don't go tellin' me you ain't got the price. You could dig up the price all right, all right, if you wanted to. I notice you always got the price to go to the ball game. But when it comes to me havin' a good time then it's always: "I ain't got the price, I gotta start savin'." A fat lot you'll ever save! I got all I can do now makin' both ends meet an' you talkin' about savin'. [*She seats herself on a chair and begins removing her shoes and stockings.*] An' don't go pullin' that stuff about bein' tired. "I been workin' hard all day. Twice a day in the subway's enough for me." Tired! Where do you get that tired stuff, anyhow? What about me? Where do I come in? Scrubbin' floors an' cookin' your meals an' washin' your dirty clothes. An' you sittin' on a chair all day, just addin' figgers an' waitin' for five-thirty. There's no five-thirty for me. I don't wait for no whistle. I don't get no vacations neither. And what's more I don't get no pay envelope every Saturday night neither. I'd like to know where you'd be without me. An' what have I got to show for it? — slavin' my life away to give you a home. What's in it for me, I'd like to know? But it's my own fault, I guess. I was a fool for marryin' you. If I'd 'a' had any sense, I'd 'a' known what you were from the start. I wish I had it to do over again, I hope to tell you. You was goin' to do wonders, you was! You wasn't goin' to be a book-keeper long — oh, no, not you. Wait till you got started — you was goin' to show 'em. There wasn't no job in the store that was too big for you. Well, I've been waitin' — waitin' for you to get started — see? It's been a good long wait, too. Twenty-five years! An' I ain't seen nothin' happen. Twenty-five years in the same job. Twenty-five years to-morrow! You're proud of it, ain't you? Twenty-five years in the same job an' never missed a day! That's somethin' to be proud of, ain't it? Sittin' for twenty-five years on the same chair, addin' up figures. What about bein' store-manager? I guess you forgot about that, didn't you? An' me at home here lookin' at the same four walls an' workin' my fingers to the bone to make both ends meet. Seven years since you got a raise! An' if you don't get one to-morrow, I'll bet a nickel you won't have the guts to go an' ask for one. I didn't pick much when I picked you, I'll tell the world. You ain't much to be proud of. [*She rises, goes to the window, and raises the shade. A few lighted windows are visible on the other side of the closed court. Looking out for a moment.*] She ain't walkin' around to-night, you can bet your sweet life on that. An' she won't be walkin' around any more nights, neither. Not in this house, anyhow. [*She turns away from the window.*] The dirty bum! The idea of her comin' to live in a house with respectable people. They should 'a' gave her six years, not six months. If I was the judge I'd of gave her life. A bum like that. [*She approaches the bed and stands there a moment.*] I guess you're sorry she's gone. I guess you'd like to sit home every night an' watch her goin's-on. You're somethin' to be proud of, you are! [*She stands on the bed and turns out the light.* . . . *A thin stream of moonlight filters in from the court. The two figures are dimly visible.* MRS. ZERO *gets into bed.*] You'd better not start nothin'

THE ADDING MACHINE

with women, if you know what's good for you. I've put up with a lot, but I won't put up with that. I've been slavin' away for twenty-five years, makin' a home for you an' nothin' to show for it. If you was any kind of a man you'd have a decent job by now an' I'd be gettin' some comfort out of life — instead of bein' just a slave, washin' pots an' standin' over the hot stove. I've stood it for twenty-five years an' I guess I'll have to stand it twenty-five more. But don't you go startin' nothin' with women — [*She goes on talking as the curtain falls.*]

SCENE TWO

SCENE: *An office in a department store. Wood and glass partitions. In the middle of the room, two tall desks back to back. At one desk on a high stool is* ZERO. *Opposite him at the other desk, also on a high stool, is* DAISY DIANA DOROTHEA DEVORE, *a plain, middle-aged woman. Both wear green eyeshades and paper sleeve protectors. A pendent electric lamp throws light upon both desks.* DAISY *reads aloud figures from a pile of slips which lie before her. As she reads the figures,* ZERO *enters them upon a large square sheet of ruled paper which lies before him.*

DAISY [*reading aloud*]. Three ninety-eight. Forty-two cents. A dollar fifty. A dollar fifty. A dollar twenty-five. Two dollars. Thirty-nine cents. Twenty-seven fifty.

ZERO [*petulantly*]. Speed it up a little, cancha?

DAISY. What's the rush? To-morrer's another day.

ZERO. Aw, you make me sick.

DAISY. An' you make me sicker.

ZERO. Go on. Go on. We're losin' time.

DAISY. Then quit bein' so bossy. [*She reads.*] Three dollars. Two sixty-nine. Eighty-one fifty. Forty dollars. Eight seventy-five. Who do you think you are, anyhow?

ZERO. Never mind who I think I am. You tend to your work.

DAISY. Aw, don't be givin' me so many orders. Sixty cents. Twenty-four cents. Seventy-five cents. A dollar fifty. Two fifty. One fifty. One fifty. Two fifty. I don't have to take it from you and what's more I won't.

ZERO. Aw, quit talkin'.

DAISY. I'll talk all I want. Three dollars. Fifty cents. Fifty cents. Seven dollars. Fifty cents. Two fifty. Three fifty. Fifty cents. One fifty. Fifty cents.

[*She goes bending over the slips and transferring them from one pile to another.* ZERO *bends over his desk, busily entering the figures.*]

ZERO [*without looking up*]. You make me sick. Always shootin' off your face about somethin'. Talk, talk, talk. Just like all the other women. Women make me sick.

DAISY [*busily fingering the slips*]. Who do you think you are, anyhow? Bossin' me around. I don't have to take it from you, and what's more I won't.

[*They both attend closely to their work, neither looking up.*]

ZERO. Women make me sick. They're all alike. The judge gave her six months. I wonder what they do in the work-house. Peel potatoes. I'll bet she's sore at me. Maybe she'll try to kill me when she gets out. I better be careful. Hello, Girl Slays Betrayer. Jealous Wife Slays Rival. You can't tell what a woman's liable to do. I better be careful.

DAISY. I'm gettin' sick of it. Always pickin' on me about somethin'. Never a decent word out of you. Not even the time o'day.

ZERO. I guess she wouldn't have the nerve at that. Maybe she don't even know it's me. They didn't even put my name in the paper, the big bums. Maybe she's been in the work-house before. A bum like that. She didn't have nothin' on that one time — nothin' but a shirt. [*He glances up quickly, then bends over again.*] You make me sick. I'm sick of lookin' at your face.

DAISY. Gee, ain't that whistle ever goin' to blow? You didn't used to be like that. Not even good mornin' or good evenin'. I ain't done nothin' to you. It's the young girls. Goin' around without corsets.

ZERO. Your face is gettin' all yeller. Why don't you put some paint on it? She was puttin' on paint that time. On her cheeks and on her lips. And that blue stuff on her eyes. Just sittin' there in a shimmy puttin' on the paint. An' walkin' around the room with her legs all bare.

DAISY. I wish I was dead.

ZERO. I was a goddam fool to let the wife get on to me. She oughta get six months at that. The dirty bum. Livin' in a house with respectable people. She'd be livin' there yet, if the wife hadn't o' got on to me. Damn her!

DAISY. I wish I was dead.

ZERO. Maybe another one'll move in. Gee, that would be great. But the wife's got her eye on me now.

DAISY. I'm scared to do it, though.

ZERO. You oughta move into that room. It's cheaper than where you're livin' now. I better tell you about it. I don't mean to be always pickin' on you.

DAISY. Gas. The smell of it makes me sick.

[ZERO *looks up and clears his throat.*]

DAISY [*looking up, startled*]. Whadja say?

ZERO. I didn't say nothin'.

DAISY. I thought you did.

ZERO. You thought wrong.

[*They bend over their work again.*]

DAISY. A dollar sixty. A dollar fifty. Two ninety. One sixty-two.

ZERO. Why the hell should I tell you? Fat chance of you forgettin' to pull down the shade!

DAISY. If I asked for carbolic they might get on to me.

ZERO. Your hair's gettin' gray. You don't wear them shirt-waists any more with the low collars. When you'd bend down to pick somethin' up —

DAISY. I wish I knew what to ask for. Girl Takes Mercury After All-Night Party. Woman In Ten-Story Death Leap.

ZERO. I wonder where'll she go when she gets out. Gee, I'd like to make a date with her. Why didn't I go over there the night my wife went to Brooklyn? She never woulda found out.

DAISY. I seen Pauline Frederick do it once. Where could I get a pistol, though?

ZERO. I guess I didn't have the nerve.

DAISY. I'll bet you'd be sorry then that you been so mean to me. How do I know, though? Maybe you wouldn't.

ZERO. Nerve! I got as much nerve as anybody. I'm on the level, that's all. I'm a married man and I'm on the level.

DAISY. Anyhow, why ain't I got a right to live? I'm as good as anybody else. I'm too refined, I guess. That's the whole trouble.

ZERO. The time the wife had pneumonia I thought she was goin' to pass out. But she didn't. The doctor's bill was eighty-seven dollars. [*Looking up.*] Hey, wait a minute! Didn't you say eighty-seven dollars?

DAISY [*looking up*]. What?

ZERO. Was the last you said eighty-seven dollars?

DAISY [*consulting the slip*]. Forty-two fifty.

ZERO. Well, I made a mistake. Wait a minute. [*He busies himself with an eraser.*] All right. Shoot.

DAISY. Six dollars. Three fifteen. Two twenty-five. Sixty-five cents. A dollar twenty. You talk to me as if I was dirt.

ZERO. I wonder if I could kill the wife without anybody findin' out. In bed some night. With a pillow.

DAISY. I used to think you was stuck on me.

ZERO. I'd get found out, though. They always have ways.

DAISY. We used to be so nice and friendly together when I first came here. You used to talk to me then.

ZERO. Maybe she'll die soon. I noticed she was coughin' this mornin'.

DAISY. You used to tell me all kinds o' things. You were goin' to show them all. Just the same, you're still sittin' here.

ZERO. Then I could do what I damn please. Oh, boy!

DAISY. Maybe it ain't all your fault

neither. Maybe if you'd had the right kind o' wife — somebody with a lot of common-sense, somebody refined — me!

ZERO. At that, I guess I'd get tired of bummin' around. A feller wants some place to hang his hat.

DAISY. I wish she would die.

ZERO. And when you start goin' with women you're liable to get into trouble. And lose your job maybe.

DAISY. Maybe you'd marry me.

ZERO. Gee, I wish I'd gone over there that night.

DAISY. Then I could quit workin'.

ZERO. Lots o' women would be glad to get me.

DAISY. You could look a long time before you'd find a sensible, refined girl like me.

ZERO. Yes, sir, they could look a long time before they'd find a steady meal-ticket like me.

DAISY. I guess I'd be too old to have any kids. They say it ain't safe after thirty-five.

ZERO. Maybe I'd marry you. You might be all right, at that.

DAISY. I wonder — if you don't want kids — whether — if there's any way —

ZERO [*looking up*]. Hey! Hey! Can't you slow up? What do you think I am — a machine?

DAISY [*looking up*]. Say, what do you want, anyhow? First it's too slow an' then it's too fast. I guess you don't know what you want.

ZERO. Well, never mind about that. Just you slow up.

DAISY. I'm gettin' sick o' this. I'm goin' to ask to be transferred.

ZERO. Go ahead. You can't make me mad.

DAISY. Aw, keep quiet. [*She reads.*] Two forty-five. A dollar twenty. A dollar fifty. Ninety cents. Sixty-three cents.

ZERO. Marry you! I guess not! You'd be as bad as the one I got.

DAISY. You wouldn't care if I did ask. I got a good mind to ask.

ZERO. I was a fool to get married.

DAISY. Then I'd never see you at all.

ZERO. What chance has a guy got with a woman tied around his neck?

DAISY. That time at the store picnic — the year your wife couldn't come — you were nice to me then.

ZERO. Twenty-five years holdin' down the same job!

DAISY. We were together all day — just sittin' around under the trees.

ZERO. I wonder if the boss remembers about it bein' twenty-five years.

DAISY. And comin' home that night — you sat next to me in the big delivery wagon.

ZERO. I got a hunch there's a big raise comin' to me.

DAISY. I wonder what it feels like to be really kissed. Men — dirty pigs! They want the bold ones.

ZERO. If he don't come across I'm goin' right up to the front office and tell him where he gets off.

DAISY. I wish I was dead.

ZERO. "Boss," I'll say, "I want to have a talk with you." "Sure," he'll say, "sit down. Have a Corona Corona." "No," I'll say, "I don't smoke." "How's that?" he'll say. "Well, boss," I'll say, "it's this way. Every time I feel like smokin' I just take a nickel and put it in the old sock. A penny saved is a penny earned, that's the way I look at it." "Damn sensible," he'll say. "You got a wise head on you, Zero."

DAISY. I can't stand the smell of gas. It makes me sick. You coulda kissed me if you wanted to.

ZERO. "Boss," I'll say, "I ain't quite satisfied. I been on the job twenty-five years now and if I'm gonna stay I gotta see a future ahead of me." "Zero," he'll say, "I'm glad you came in. I've had my eye on you, Zero. Nothin' gets by me." "Oh, I know that, boss," I'll say. That'll hand him a good laugh, that will. "You're a valuable man, Zero," he'll say, "and I want you right up here with me in the front office. You're done addin' figgers. Monday mornin' you move up here."

DAISY. Them kisses in the movies — them long ones — right on the mouth —

ZERO. I'll keep a-goin' right on up after

that. I'll show some of them birds where they get off.

DAISY. That one the other night — *The Devil's Alibi* — he put his arms around her — and her head fell back and her eyes closed — like she was in a daze.

ZERO. Just give me about two years and I'll show them birds where they get off.

DAISY. I guess that's what it's like — a kinda daze — when I see them like that, I just seem to forget everything.

ZERO. Then me for a place in Jersey. And maybe a little Buick. No tin Lizzie for mine. Wait till I get started — I'll show 'em.

DAISY. I can see it now when 1 kinda half-close my eyes. The way her head fell back. And his mouth pressed right up against hers. Oh, Gawd! it must be grand!

[*There is a sudden shrill blast from a steam whistle.*]

DAISY AND ZERO [*together*]. The whistle!

[*With great agility they get off their stools, remove their eye-shades and sleeve protectors and put them on the desks. Then each produces from behind the desk a hat —* ZERO, *a dusty derby,* DAISY, *a frowsy straw....* DAISY *puts on her hat and turns toward* ZERO *as though she were about to speak to him. But he is busy cleaning his pen and pays no attention to her. She sighs and goes toward the door at the left.*]

ZERO [*looking up*]. G'night, Miss Devore.

[*But she does not hear him and exits.* ZERO *takes up his hat and goes left. The door at the right opens and the* Boss *enters — middle-aged, stoutish, bald, well-dressed.*]

THE BOSS [*calling*]: Oh — er — Mister — er —

[ZERO *turns in surprise, sees who it is and trembles nervously.*]

ZERO [*obsequiously*]. Yes, sir. Do you want me, sir?

BOSS. Yes. Just come here a moment, will you?

ZERO. Yes, sir. Right away, sir.

[*He fumbles his hat, picks it up, stumbles, recovers himself, and approaches the* Boss, *every fibre quivering.*]

BOSS. Mister — er — er —

ZERO. Zero.

BOSS. Yes, Mr. Zero. I wanted to have a little talk with you.

ZERO [*with a nervous grin*]. Yes, sir, I been kinda expectin' it.

BOSS [*staring at him*]. Oh, have you?

ZERO. Yes, sir.

BOSS. How long have you been with us, Mister — er — Mister —

ZERO. Zero.

BOSS. Yes, Mister Zero.

ZERO. Twenty-five years to-day.

BOSS. Twenty-five years! That's a long time.

ZERO. Never missed a day.

BOSS. And you've been doing the same work all the time?

ZERO. Yes, sir. Right here at this desk.

BOSS. Then, in that case, a change probably won't be unwelcome to you.

ZERO. No, sir, it won't. And that's the truth.

BOSS. We've been planning a change in this department for some time.

ZERO. I kinda thought you had your eye on me.

BOSS. You were right. The fact is that my efficiency experts have recommended the installation of adding machines.

ZERO [*staring at him*]. Addin' machines?

BOSS. Yes, you've probably seen them. A mechanical device that adds automatically.

ZERO. Sure. I've seen them. Keys — and a handle that you pull.

[*He goes through the motions in the air.*]

BOSS. That's it. They do the work in half the time and a high-school girl can operate them. Now, of course, I'm sorry to lose an old and faithful employee —

ZERO. Excuse me, but would you mind sayin' that again?

BOSS. I say I'm sorry to lose an employee who's been with me for so many years —

[*Soft music is heard — the sound of the mechanical player of a distant merry-go-round. The part of the* floor upon which the desk and stools are standing begins to revolve very slowly.]

Boss. But, of course, in an organization like this, efficiency must be the first consideration —

[The music becomes gradually louder and the revolutions more rapid.]

Boss. You will draw your salary for the full month. And I'll direct my secretary to give you a letter of recommendation —

Zero. Wait a minute, Boss. Let me get this right. You mean I'm canned?

Boss [barely making himself heard above the increasing volume of sound]. I'm sorry — no other alternative — greatly regret — old employee — efficiency — economy — business — business — BUSINESS —

[His voice is drowned by the music. The platform is revolving rapidly now. Zero and the Boss face each other. They are entirely motionless save for the Boss's jaws, which open and close incessantly. But the words are inaudible. The music swells and swells. To it is added every off-stage effect of the theatre: the wind, the waves, the galloping horses, the locomotive whistle, the sleighbells, the automobile siren, the glass-crash. New Year's Eve, Election Night, Armistice Day, and the Mardi-Gras. The noise is deafening, maddening, unendurable. Suddenly it culminates in a terrific peal of thunder. For an instant there is a flash of red and then everything is plunged into blackness.]

CURTAIN

SCENE THREE

Scene: The Zero dining-room. Entrance door at right. Doors to kitchen and bedroom at left. The walls, as in the first scene, are papered with foolscap sheets covered with columns of figures. In the middle of the room, up-stage, a table set for two. Along each side wall, seven chairs are ranged in symmetrical rows.

[At the rise of the curtain Mrs. Zero is seen seated at the table looking alternately at the entrance door and a clock on the wall. She wears a bungalow apron over her best dress.

After a few moments, the entrance door opens and Zero enters. He hangs his hat on a rack behind the door and coming over to the table seats himself at the vacant place. His movements throughout are quiet and abstracted.]

Mrs. Zero [breaking the silence]. Well, it was nice of you to come home. You're only an hour late and that ain't very much. The supper don't get very cold in an hour. An' of course the part about our havin' a lot of company to-night don't matter. [They begin to eat.] Ain't you even got sense enough to come home on time? Didn't I tell you we're goin' to have a lot o' company to-night? Didn't you know the Ones are comin'? An' the Twos? An' the Threes? An' the Fours? An' the Fives? And the Sixes? Didn't I tell you to be home on time? I might as well talk to a stone wall. [They eat for a few moments in silence.] I guess you musta had some important business to attend to. Like watchin' the score-board. Or was two kids havin' a fight an' you was the referee? You sure do have a lot of business to attend to. It's a wonder you have time to come home at all. You gotta tough life, you have. Walk in, hang up your hat, an' put on the nose-bag. An' me in the hot kitchen all day, cookin' your supper an' waitin' for you to get good an' ready to come home! [Again they eat in silence.] Maybe the boss kept you late to-night. Tellin' you what a big noise you are and how the store couldn't 'a' got along if you hadn't been pushin' a pen for twenty-five years. Where's the gold medal he pinned on you? Did some blind old lady take it away from you or did you leave it on the seat of the boss's limousine when he brought you home? [Again a few moments of silence.] I'll bet he gave you a big raise, didn't he? Promoted you from the third floor to the fourth, maybe. Raise? A fat chance you got o' gettin' a raise. All they gotta do is put an ad in the paper. There's ten thousand like you layin' around the streets. You'll be holdin' down the same job at the end of another twenty-five years — if you ain't forgot how to add by that time.

[*A noise is heard off-stage, a sharp clicking such as is made by the operation of the keys and levers of an adding machine.* ZERO *raises his head for a moment, but lowers it almost instantly.*]

MRS. ZERO. There's the door-bell. The company's here already. And we ain't hardly finished supper. [*She rises.*] But I'm goin' to clear off the table whether you're finished or not. If you want your supper, you got a right to be home on time. Not standin' around lookin' at scoreboards. [*As she piles up the dishes,* ZERO *rises and goes toward the entrance door.*] Wait a minute! Don't open the door yet. Do you want the company to see all the mess? An' go an' put on a clean collar. You got red ink all over it. [ZERO *goes toward bedroom door.*] I should think after pushin' a pen for twenty-five years, you'd learn how to do it without gettin' ink on your collar. [ZERO *exits to bedroom.* MRS. ZERO *takes dishes to kitchen talking as she goes.*] I guess I can stay up all night now washin' dishes. You should worry! That's what a man's got a wife for, ain't it? Don't he buy her her clothes an' let her eat with him at the same table? An' all she's gotta do is cook the meals an' do the washin' an' scrub the floor, an' wash the dishes, when the company goes. But, believe me, you're goin' to sling a mean dish-towel when the company goes to-night!

[*While she is talking* ZERO *enters from bedroom. He wears a clean collar and is cramming the soiled one furtively into his pocket.* MRS. ZERO *enters from kitchen. She has removed her apron and carries a table cover which she spreads hastily over the table. The clicking noise is heard again.*]

MRS. ZERO. There's the bell again. Open the door, cancha?

[ZERO *goes to the entrance door and opens it.*

Six men and six women file into the room in a double column. The men are all shapes and sizes, but their dress is identical with that of ZERO *in every detail. Each, however, wears a wig of a different color. The women are all dressed alike, too, except that the dress of each is of a different color.*]

MRS. ZERO [*taking the first woman's hand*]. How de do, Mrs. One.
MRS. ONE. How de do, Mrs. Zero.

[MRS. ZERO *repeats this formula with each woman in turn.* ZERO *does the same with the men except that he is silent throughout. The files now separate, each man taking a chair from the right wall and each woman one from the left wall. Each sex forms a circle with the chairs very close together. The men — all except* ZERO — *smoke cigars. The women munch chocolates.*]

SIX. Some rain we're havin'.
FIVE. Never saw the like of it.
FOUR. Worst in fourteen years, paper says.
THREE. Y' can't always go by the papers.
TWO. No, that's right, too.
ONE. We're liable to forget from year to year.
SIX. Yeh, come t' think, last year was pretty bad, too.
FIVE. An' how about two years ago?
FOUR. Still this year's pretty bad.
THREE. Yeh, no gettin' away from that.
TWO. Might be a whole lot worse.
ONE. Yeh, it's all the way you look at it. Some rain, though.
MRS. SIX. I like them little organdie dresses.
MRS. FIVE. Yeh, with a little lace trimmin' on the sleeves.
MRS. FOUR. Well, I like 'em plain myself.
MRS. THREE. Yeh, what I always say is the plainer the more refined.
MRS. TWO. Well, I don't think a little lace does any harm.
MRS. ONE. No, it kinda dresses it up.
MRS. ZERO. Well, I always say it's all a matter of taste.

Mrs. Six. I saw you at the Rosebud Movie Thursday night, Mr. One.
One. Pretty punk show, I'll say.
Two. They're gettin' worse all the time.
Mrs. Six. But who was the charming lady, Mr. One?
One. Now don't you go makin' trouble for me. That was my sister.
Mrs. Five. Oho! That's what they all say.
Mrs. Four. Never mind! I'll bet Mrs. One knows what's what, all right.
Mrs. One. Oh, well, he can do what he likes — 'slong as he behaves himself.
Three. You're in luck at that, One. Fat chance I got of gettin' away from the frau even with my sister.
Mrs. Three. You oughta be glad you got a good wife to look after you.
The Other Women [in unison]. That's right, Mrs. Three.
Five. I guess I know who wears the pants in your house, Three.
Mrs. Zero. Never mind. I saw them holdin' hands at the movie the other night.
Three. She musta been tryin' to get some money away from me.
Mrs. Three. Swell chance anybody'd have of gettin' any money away from you.
[General laughter.]
Four. They sure are a loving couple.
Mrs. Two. Well, I think we oughta change the subject.
Mrs. One. Yes, let's change the subject.
Six [sotto voce]. Did you hear the one about the travellin' salesman?
Five. It seems this guy was in a sleeper.
Four. Goin' from Albany to San Diego.
Three. And in the next berth was an old maid.
Two. With a wooden leg.
One. Well, along about midnight —
[They all put their heads together and whisper.]
Mrs. Six [sotto voce]. Did you hear about the Sevens?
Mrs. Five. They're gettin' a divorce.
Mrs. Four. It's the second time for him.
Mrs. Three. They're two of a kind, if you ask me.
Mrs. Two. One's as bad as the other.
Mrs. One. Worse.
Mrs. Zero. They say that she —
[They all put their heads together and whisper.]
Six. I think this woman suffrage is the bunk.
Five. It sure is! Politics is a man's business.
Four. Woman's place is in the home.
Three. That's it! Lookin' after the kids, 'stead of hangin' around the streets.
Two. You hit the nail on the head that time.
One. The trouble is they don't know what they want.
Mrs. Six. Men sure get me tired.
Mrs. Five. They sure are a lazy lot.
Mrs. Four. And dirty.
Mrs. Three. Always grumblin' about somethin'.
Mrs. Two. When they're not lyin'!
Mrs. One. Or messin' up the house.
Mrs. Zero. Well, believe me, I tell mine where he gets off.
Six. Business conditions are sure bad.
Five. Never been worse.
Four. I don't know what we're comin' to.
Three. I look for a big smash-up in about three months.
Two. Wouldn't surprise me a bit.
One. We're sure headin' for trouble.
Mrs. Six. My aunt has gall-stones.
Mrs. Five. My husband has bunions.
Mrs. Four. My sister expects next month.
Mrs. Three. My cousin's husband has erysipelas.
Mrs. Two. My niece has St. Vitus's dance.
Mrs. One. My boy has fits.
Mrs. Zero. I never felt better in my life. Knock wood!
Six. Too damn much agitation, that's at the bottom of it.
Five. That's it! — too damn many strikes.
Four. Foreign agitators, that's what it is.
Three. They ought be run outa the country.

Two. What the hell do they want, anyhow?
One. They don't know what they want, if you ask me.
Six. America for the Americans is what I say!
All [*in unison*]. That's it! Damn foreigners! Damn dagoes! Damn Catholics! Damn sheenies! Damn niggers! Jail 'em! shoot 'em! hang 'em! lynch 'em! burn 'em!   [*They all rise.*]
All [*sing in unison*].

"My country 'tis of thee,
Sweet land of liberty!"

Mrs. Four. Why so pensive, Mr. Zero?
Zero [*speaking for the first time*]. I'm thinkin'.
Mrs. Four. Well, be careful not to sprain your mind.
[*Laughter.*]
Mrs. Zero. Look at the poor men all by themselves. We ain't very sociable.
One. Looks like we're neglectin' the ladies.
[*The women cross the room and join the men, all chattering loudly. The door-bell rings.*]
Mrs. Zero. Sh! The door-bell!
[*The volume of sound slowly diminishes. Again the door-bell.*]
Zero [*quietly*]. I'll go. It's for me.
[*They watch curiously as Zero goes to the door and opens it, admitting a policeman. There is a murmur of surprise and excitement.*]
Policeman. I'm lookin' for Mr. Zero.
[*They all point to Zero.*]
Zero. I've been expectin' you.
Policeman. Come along!
Zero. Just a minute.
[*He puts his hand in his pocket.*]
Policeman. What's he tryin' to pull? [*He draws a revolver.*] I got you covered.
Zero. Sure, that's all right. I just want to give you somethin'.
[*He takes the collar from his pocket and gives it to the Policeman.*]
Policeman [*suspiciously*]. What's that?
Zero. The collar I wore.
Policeman. What do I want it for?
Zero. It's got blood-stains on it.

Policeman [*pocketing it*]. All right, come along!
Zero [*turning to* Mrs. Zero]. I gotta go with him. You'll have to dry the dishes yourself.
Mrs. Zero [*rushing forward*]. What are they takin' you for?
Zero [*calmly*]. I killed the boss this afternoon.
[*Quick curtain as the* Policeman *takes him off.*]

SCENE FOUR

Scene: *A court of justice. Three bare white walls without door or windows except for a single door in the right wall. At the right is a jury-box in which are seated* Messrs. One, Two, Three, Four, Five, *and* Six *and their respective wives. On either side of the jury box stands a uniformed officer. Opposite the jury box is a long, bare oak table piled high with law books. Behind the books* Zero *is seated, his face buried in his hands. There is no other furniture in the room.*

[*A moment after the rise of the curtain, one of the officers rises and, going around the table, taps* Zero *on the shoulder.* Zero *rises and accompanies the* Officer. *The* Officer *escorts him to the great empty space in the middle of the court-room, facing the jury. He motions to* Zero *to stop, then points to the jury and resumes his place beside the jury-box.* Zero *stands there looking at the jury, bewildered and half afraid. The Jurors give no sign of having seen him. Throughout they sit with folded arms, staring stolidly before them.*]

Zero [*beginning to speak; haltingly*]. Sure I killed him. I ain't sayin' I didn't, am I? Sure I killed him. Them lawyers! They give me a good stiff pain, that's what they give me. Half the time I don't know what the hell they're talkin' about. Objection sustained. Objection overruled. What's the big idea, anyhow? You ain't heard me do any objectin', have you? Sure not! What's the idea of objectin'?

THE ADDING MACHINE

You got a right to know. What I say is if one bird kills another bird, why, you got a right to call him for it. That's what I say. I know all about that. I been on the jury, too. Them lawyers! Don't let 'em fill you full of bunk. All that bull about it bein' red ink on the bill-file. Red ink nothin'! It was blood, see? I want you to get that right. I killed him, see? Right through the heart with the bill-file, see? I want you to get that right — all of you. One, two, three, four, five, six, seven, eight, nine, ten, eleven, twelve. Twelve of you. Six and six. That makes twelve. I figgered it up often enough. Six and six makes twelve. And five is seventeen. And eight is twenty-five. And three is twenty-eight. Eight and carry two. Aw, cut it out! Them damn figgers! I can't forget 'em. Twenty-five years, see? Eight hours a day, exceptin' Sundays. And July and August half-day Saturday. One week's vacation with pay. And another week without pay if you want it. Who the hell wants it? Layin' around the house listenin' to the wife tellin' you where you get off. Nix! An' legal holidays. I nearly forgot them. New Year's, Washington's Birthday, Decoration Day, Fourth o' July, Labor Day, Election Day, Thanksgivin', Christmas. Good Friday if you want it. An' if you're a Jew, Young Kipper an' the other one — I forget what they call it. The dirty sheenies — always gettin' two to the other bird's one. An' when a holiday comes on Sunday, you get Monday off. So that's fair enough. But when the Fourth o' July comes on Saturday, why, you're out o' luck on account of Saturday bein' a half-day anyhow. Get me? Twenty-five years — I'll tell you somethin' funny. Decoration Day an' the Fourth o' July are always on the same day o' the week. Twenty-five years. Never missed a day, and never more'n five minutes late. Look at my time card if you don't believe me. Eight twenty-seven, eight thirty, eight twenty-nine, eight twenty-seven, eight thirty-two. Eight an' thirty-two's forty an' — Goddam them figgers! I can't forget 'em. They're funny things, them figgers. They look like people sometimes.

The eights, see? Two dots for the eyes and a dot for the nose. An' a line. That's the mouth, see? An' there's others remind you of other things — but I can't talk about them, on account of there bein' ladies here. Sure I killed him. Why didn't he shut up? If he'd only shut up! Instead o' talkin' an' talkin' about how sorry he was an' what a good guy I was an' this an' that. I felt like sayin' to him: "For Christ's sake, shut up!" But I didn't have the nerve, see? I didn't have the nerve to say that to the boss. An' he went on talkin', sayin' how sorry he was, see? He was standin' right close to me. An' his coat only had two buttons on it. Two an' two makes four an' — aw, can it! An' there was the bill-file on the desk. Right where I could touch it. It ain't right to kill a guy. I know that. When I read all about him in the paper an' about his three kids I felt like a cheap skate, I tell you. They had the kids' pictures in the paper, right next to mine. An' his wife, too. Gee, it must be swell to have a wife like that. Some guys sure is lucky. An' he left fifty thousand dollars just for a rest-room for the girls in the store. He was a good guy, at that. Fifty thousand. That's more'n twice as much as I'd have if I saved every nickel I ever made. Let's see. Twenty-five an' twenty-five an' twenty-five an' — aw, cut it out! An' the ads had a big, black border around 'em; an' all it said was that the store would be closed for three days on account of the boss bein' dead. That nearly handed me a laugh, that did. All them floor-walkers an' buyers an' high-muck-a-mucks havin' me to thank for gettin' three days off. I hadn't oughta killed him. I ain't sayin' nothin' about that. But I thought he was goin' to give me a raise, see? On account of bein' there twenty-five years. He never talked to me before, see? Except one mornin' we happened to come in the store together and I held the door open for him and he said "Thanks." Just like that, see? "Thanks!" That was the only time he ever talked to me. An' when I seen him comin' up to my desk, I didn't know where I got off. A big guy like that comin' up to my desk. I felt like I was chokin' like, and all of a sudden I got a kind o' bad taste in my mouth like when you get up in the mornin'. I didn't have no right to kill him. The district attorney is right about that. He read the law to you, right out o' the book. Killin' a bird — that's wrong. But there was that girl, see? Six months they gave her. It was a dirty trick tellin' the cops on her like that. I shouldn't 'a' done that. But what was I gonna do? The wife wouldn't let up on me. I hadda do it. She used to walk around the room, just in her undershirt, see? Nothin' else on. Just her undershirt. An' they gave her six months. That's the last I'll ever see of her. Them birds — how do they get away with it? Just grabbin' women, the way you see 'em do in the pictures. I've seen lots I'd like to grab like that, but I ain't got the nerve — in the subway an' on the street an' in the store buyin' things. Pretty soft for them shoe-salesmen, I'll say, lookin' at women's legs all day. Them lawyers! They give me a pain, I tell you — a pain! Sayin' the same thing over an' over again. I never said I didn't kill him. But that ain't the same as bein' a regular murderer. What good did it do me to kill him? I didn't make nothin' out of it. Answer yes or no! Yes or no, me elbow! There's some things you can't answer yes or no. Give me the once-over, you guys. Do I look like a murderer? Do I? I never did no harm to nobody. Ask the wife. She'll tell you. Ask anybody. I never got into trouble. You wouldn't count that one time at the Polo Grounds. That was just fun like. Everybody was yellin', "Kill the empire! Kill the empire!" An' before I knew what I was doin' I fired the pop bottle. It was on account of everybody yellin' like that. Just in fun like, see? The yeller dog! Callin' that one a strike — a mile away from the plate. Anyhow, the bottle didn't hit him. An' when I seen the cop comin' up the aisle, I beat it. That didn't hurt nobody. It was just in fun like, see? An' that time in the subway. I was readin' about a lynchin', see? Down in Georgia. The took the nigger an' they tied him to a tree. An' they poured kerosene on him and lit a big fire under him. The dirty nigger! Boy, I'd of liked to been there, with a gat in each hand, pumpin' him full of lead. I was readin' about it in the subway, see? Right at Times Square where the big crowd gets on. An' all of a sudden this big nigger steps right on my foot. It was lucky for him I didn't have a gun on me. I'd of killed him sure, I guess. I guess he couldn't help it all right on account of the crowd, but a nigger's got no right to step on a white man's foot. I told him where he got off all right. The dirty nigger. But that didn't hurt nobody, either. I'm a pretty steady guy, you gotta admit that. Twenty-five years in one job an' I never missed a day. Fifty-two weeks in a year. Fifty-two an' fifty-two an' fifty-two an' — They didn't have t' look for me, did they? I didn't try to run away, did I? Where was I goin' to run to! I wasn't thinkin' about it at all, see? I'll tell you what I was thinkin' about — how I was goin' to break it to the wife about bein' canned. He canned me after twenty-five years, see? Did the lawyers tell you about that? I forget. All that talk gives me a headache. Objection sustained. Objection overruled. Answer yes or no. It gives me a headache. And I can't get the figgers outta my head, neither. But that's what I was thinkin' about — how I was goin' t' break it to the wife about bein' canned. An' what Miss Devore would think when she heard about me killin' him. I bet she never thought I had the nerve to do it. I'd of married her if the wife had passed out. I'd be holdin' down my job yet, if he hadn't o' canned me. But he kept talkin' an' talkin'. An' there was the bill-file right where I could reach it. Do you get me? I'm just a regular guy like anybody else. Like you birds now. [*For the first time the* JURORS *relax, looking indignantly at each other and whispering.*] Suppose you was me, now. Maybe you'd 'a' done the same thing. That's the way you oughta look at it, see? Suppose you was me —

THE JURORS [*rising as one and shouting in unison*]. *GUILTY!*

[ZERO *falls back, stunned for a moment by their vociferousness. The* JURORS *right-face in their places and* file quickly out of the jury-box and toward the door in a double column.]

ZERO [*recovering speech as the* JURORS *pass out at the door*]. Wait a minute. Jest a minute. You don't get me right. Jest give me a chance an' I'll tell you how it was. I'm all mixed up, see? On account of them lawyers. And the figgers in my head. But I'm goin' to tell you how it was. I was there twenty-five years, see? An' they gave her six months, see?

[*He goes on haranguing the empty jury-box as the curtain falls.*]

SCENE FIVE

SCENE: *A graveyard in full moonlight. It is a second-rate graveyard — no elaborate tombstones or monuments — just simple headstones and here and there a cross. At the back is an iron fence with a gate in the middle. At first no one is visible, but there are occasional sounds throughout: the hooting of an owl, the whistle of a distant whippoorwill, the croaking of a bull-frog, and the yowling of a serenading cat.*

[*After a few moments two figures appear outside the gate — a man and a woman. She pushes the gate and it opens with a rusty creak. The couple enter. They are now fully visible in the moonlight —* JUDY O'GRADY *and a* YOUNG MAN.]

JUDY [*advancing*]. Come on, this is the place.

YOUNG MAN [*hanging back*]. This! Why, this here is a cemetery.

JUDY. Aw, quit yer kiddin'!

YOUNG MAN. You don't mean to say —

JUDY. What's the matter with this place?

YOUNG MAN. A cemetery!

JUDY. Sure. What of it?

YOUNG MAN. You must be crazy.

JUDY. This place is all right, I tell you. I been here lots o' times.

YOUNG MAN. Nix on this place for me!

JUDY. Ain't this place as good as another? Whaddya afraid of? They're all dead ones here! They don't bother you.

[*With sudden interest.*] Oh, look, here's a new one.

YOUNG MAN. Come on out of here.

JUDY. Wait a minute. Let's see what it says. [*She kneels on a grave in the foreground and putting her face close to headstone spells out the inscription.*] Z-E-R-O. Z-e-r-o. Zero! Say, that's the guy —

YOUNG MAN. Zero? He's the guy killed his boss, ain't he?

JUDY. Yeh, that's him, all right. But what I'm thinkin' of is that I went to the hoose-gow on account of him.

YOUNG MAN. What for?

JUDY. You know, same old stuff. Tenement House Law. [*Mincingly.*] Section blaa-blaa of the Penal Code. Third offense. Six months.

YOUNG MAN. And this bird —

JUDY [*contemptuously*]. Him? He was mamma's white-haired boy. We lived in the same house. Across the airshaft, see? I used to see him lookin' in my window. I guess his wife musta seen him, too. Anyhow, they went and turned the bulls on me. And now I'm out and he's in. [*Suddenly.*] Say — say —

[*She bursts into a peal of laughter.*]

YOUNG MAN [*nervously*]. What's so funny?

JUDY [*rocking with laughter*]. Say, wouldn't it be funny — if — if — [*She explodes again.*] That would be a good joke on him, all right. He can't do nothin' about it now, can he?

YOUNG MAN. Come on out of here. I don't like this place.

JUDY. Aw, you're a bum sport. What do you want to spoil my joke for?

[*A cat yammers mellifluously.*]

YOUNG MAN [*half hysterically*]. What's that?

JUDY. It's only the cats. They seem to like it here all right. But come on if you're afraid. [*They go toward the gate. As they go out.*] You nervous men sure are the limit.

[*They go out through the gate. As they disappear,* ZERO's *grave opens suddenly and his head appears.*]

ZERO [*looking about*]. That's funny! I thought I heard her talkin' and laughin'.

But I don't see nobody. Anyhow, what would she be doin' here? I guess I must 'a' been dreamin'. But how could I be dreamin' when I ain't been asleep? [*He looks about again.*] Well, no use goin' back. I can't sleep, anyhow. I might as well walk around a little.

[*He rises out of the ground, very rigidly. He wears a full-dress suit of very antiquated cut and his hands are folded stiffly across his breast.*]

ZERO [*walking woodenly*]. Gee! I'm stiff! [*He slowly walks a few steps, then stops.*] Gee, it's lonesome here! [*He shivers and walks on aimlessly.*] I should 'a' stayed where I was. But I thought I heard her laughin'.

[*A loud sneeze is heard.* ZERO *stands motionless, quaking with terror. The sneeze is repeated.*]

ZERO [*hoarsely*]. What's that?

A MILD VOICE. It's all right. Nothing to be afraid of.

[*From behind a headstone* SHRDLU *appears. He is dressed in a shabby and ill-fitting cutaway. He wears silver-rimmed spectacles and is smoking a cigarette.*]

SHRDLU. I hope I didn't frighten you.

ZERO [*still badly shaken*]. No-o. It's all right. You see, I wasn't expectin' to see anybody.

SHRDLU. You're a newcomer, aren't you?

ZERO. Yeh, this is my first night. I couldn't seem to get to sleep.

SHRDLU. I can't sleep, either. Suppose we keep each other company, shall we?

ZERO [*eagerly*]. Yeh, that would be great. I been feelin' awful lonesome.

SHRDLU [*nodding*]. I know. Let's make ourselves comfortable.

[*He seats himself easily on a grave.* ZERO *tries to follow his example, but he is stiff in every joint and groans with pain.*]

ZERO. I'm kinda stiff.

SHRDLU. You mustn't mind the stiffness. It wears off in a few days. [*He seats himself on the grave beside* ZERO *and produces a package of cigarettes.*] Will you have a Camel?

ZERO. No, I don't smoke.

SHRDLU. I find it helps keep the mosquitoes away.

[*He lights a cigarette.*]

SHRDLU [*suddenly taking the cigarette out of his mouth*]. Do you mind if I smoke, Mr. — Mr. — ?

ZERO. No, go right ahead.

SHRDLU [*replacing the cigarette*]. Thank you. I didn't catch your name.

[ZERO *does not reply.*]

SHRDLU [*mildly*]. I say I didn't catch your name.

ZERO. I heard you the first time. [*Hesitantly.*] I'm scared if I tell you who I am and what I done, you'll be off me.

SHRDLU [*sadly*]. No matter what your sins may be, they are as snow compared to mine.

ZERO. You got another guess comin'. [*He pauses dramatically.*] My name's Zero. I'm a murderer.

SHRDLU [*nodding calmly*]. Oh, yes, I remember reading about you, Mr. Zero.

ZERO [*a little piqued*]. And you still think you're worse than me?

SHRDLU [*throwing away his cigarette*]. Oh, a thousand times worse, Mr. Zero — a million times worse.

ZERO. What did you do?

SHRDLU. I, too, am a murderer.

ZERO [*looking at him in amazement*]. Go on! You're kiddin' me!

SHRDLU. Every word I speak is the truth, Mr. Zero. I am the foulest, the most sinful of murderers! You only murdered your employer, Mr. Zero. But I — I murdered my mother.

[*He covers his face with his hands and sobs.*]

ZERO [*horrified*]. The hell yer say!

SHRDLU [*sobbing*]. Yes, my mother! — my beloved mother!

ZERO [*suddenly*]. Say, you don't mean to say you're Mr. —

SHRDLU [*nodding*]. Yes.

[*He wipes his eyes, still quivering with emotion.*]

ZERO. I remember readin' about you in the papers.

SHRDLU. Yes, my guilt has been proclaimed to all the world. But that would be a trifle if only I could wash the stain of sin from my soul.

ZERO. I never heard of a guy killin' his mother before. What did you do it for?

SHRDLU. Because I have a sinful heart — there is no other reason.

ZERO. Did she always treat you square and all like that?

SHRDLU. She was a saint — a saint, I tell you. She cared for me and watched over me as only a mother can.

ZERO. You mean to say you didn't have a scrap or nothin'?

SHRDLU. Never a harsh or an unkind word. Nothing except loving care and good advice. From my infancy she devoted herself to guiding me on the right path. She taught me to be thrifty, to be devout, to be unselfish, to shun evil companions and to shut my ears to all the temptations of the flesh — in short, to become a virtuous, respectable, and God-fearing man. [*He groans.*] But it was a hopeless task. At fourteen I began to show evidence of my sinful nature.

ZERO [*breathlessly*]. You didn't kill anybody else, did you?

SHRDLU. No, thank God, there is only one murder on my soul. But I ran away from home.

ZERO. You did!

SHRDLU. Yes. A companion lent me a profane book — the only profane book I have ever read, I'm thankful to say. It was called *Treasure Island*. Have you ever read it?

ZERO. No, I never was much on readin' books.

SHRDLU. It is a wicked book — a lurid tale of adventure. But it kindled in my sinful heart a desire to go to sea. And so I ran away from home.

ZERO. What did you do — get a job as a sailor?

SHRDLU. I never saw the sea — not to the day of my death. Luckily, my mother's loving intuition warned her of my intention and I was sent back home. She welcomed me with open arms. Not an angry word, not a look of reproach. But I could read the mute suffering in her eyes as we prayed together all through the night.

ZERO [*sympathetically*]. Gee, that must 'a' been tough. Gee, the mosquitoes are bad, ain't they?

[*He tries awkwardly to slap at them with his stiff hands.*]

SHRDLU [*absorbed in his narrative*]. I thought that experience had cured me of evil and I began to think about a career. I wanted to go in foreign missions at first, but we couldn't bear the thought of the separation. So we finally decided that I should become a proof-reader.

ZERO. Say, slip me one o' them Camels, will you? I'm gettin' all bit up.

SHRDLU. Certainly.

[*He hands* ZERO *cigarettes and matches.*]

ZERO [*lighting up*]. Go ahead. I'm listenin'.

SHRDLU. By the time I was twenty I had a good job reading proof for a firm that printed catalogues. After a year they promoted me and let me specialize in shoe catalogues.

ZERO. Yeh? That must 'a' been a good job.

SHRDLU. It was a very good job. I was on the shoe catalogues for thirteen years. I'd been on them yet, if I hadn't —

[*He chokes back a sob.*]

ZERO. They oughta put a shot o' citronella in that embalmin'-fluid.

SHRDLU [*he sighs*]. We were so happy together. I had my steady job. And Sundays we would go to morning, afternoon, and evening service. It was an honest and moral mode of life.

SHRDLU. Then came that fatal Sunday. Dr. Amaranth, our minister, was having dinner with us — one of the few pure spirits on earth. When he had finished saying grace, we had our soup. Everything was going along as usual — we were eating our soup and discussing the sermon, just like every other Sunday I could remember. Then came the leg of lamb — [*He breaks off, then resumes in a choking voice.*] I see the whole scene before me so plainly — it never leaves me — Dr. Amaranth at my right, my mother at my left, the leg of lamb on the table in front of me, and the

cuckoo clock on the little shelf between the windows.
[*He stops and wipes his eyes.*]
ZERO. Yeh, but what happened?
SHRDLU. Well, as I started to carve the lamb — Did you ever carve a leg of lamb?
ZERO. No, corned beef was our speed.
SHRDLU. It's very difficult on account of the bone. And when there's gravy in the dish there's danger of spilling it. So Mother always used to hold the dish for me. She leaned forward, just as she always did, and I could see the gold locket around her neck. It had my picture in it and one of my baby curls. Well, I raised my knife to carve the leg of lamb — and instead I cut my mother's throat! [*He sobs.*]
ZERO. You must 'a' been crazy!
SHRDLU [*raising his head, vehemently*]. No! Don't try to justify me. I wasn't crazy. They tried to prove at the trial that I was crazy. But Dr. Amaranth saw the truth! He saw it from the first! He knew that it was my sinful nature — and he told me what was in store for me.
ZERO [*trying to be comforting*]. Well, your troubles are over now.
SHRDLU [*his voice rising*]. Over! Do you think this is the end?
ZERO. Sure. What more can they do to us?
SHRDLU [*his tones growing shriller and shriller*]. Do you think there can ever be any peace for such as we are — murderers, sinners? Don't you know what awaits us — flames, eternal flames!
ZERO [*nervously*]. Keep your shirt on, Buddy — they wouldn't do that to us.
SHRDLU. There's no escape — no escape for us, I tell you. We're doomed! We're doomed to suffer unspeakable torments through all eternity.
[*His voice rises higher and higher.*]
[*A grave opens suddenly and a head appears.*]
THE HEAD. Hey, you birds! Can't you shut up and let a guy sleep?
[ZERO *scrambles painfully to his feet.*]
ZERO [*to* SHRDLU]. Hey, put on the soft pedal.
SHRDLU [*too wrought up to attend*]. It won't be long now! We'll receive our summons soon.
THE HEAD. Are you goin' to beat it or not? [*He calls into the grave.*] Hey, Bill, lend me your head a minute.
[*A moment later his arm appears holding a skull.*]
ZERO [*warningly*]. Look out!
[*He seizes* SHRDLU *and drags him away just as* THE HEAD *throws the skull.*]
THE HEAD [*disgustedly*]. Missed 'em. Damn old tabby cats! I'll get 'em next time. [*A prodigious yawn.*] Ho-hum! Me for the worms!
[THE HEAD *disappears as the curtain falls.*]

SCENE SIX

SCENE: *A pleasant place. A scene of pastoral loveliness. A meadow dotted with fine old trees and carpeted with rich grass and field flowers. In the background are seen a number of tents fashioned of gay-striped silks and beyond gleams a meandering river. Clear air and a fleckless sky. Sweet distant music throughout.*

[*At the rise of the curtain,* SHRDLU *is seen seated under a tree in the foreground in an attitude of deep dejection. His knees are drawn up and his head is buried in his arms. He is dressed as in the preceding scene.*

A few minutes later, ZERO *enters at right. He walks slowly and looks about him with an air of half-suspicious curiosity. He, too, is dressed as in the preceding scene. Suddenly he sees* SHRDLU *seated under the tree. He stands still and looks at him half fearfully. Then, seeing something familiar in him, goes closer.* SHRDLU *is unaware of his presence. At last* ZERO *recognizes him and grins in pleased surprise.*]

ZERO. Well, if it ain't —! [*He claps* SHRDLU *on the shoulder.*] Hello, Buddy!
[SHRDLU *looks up slowly, then, recognizing* ZERO, *he rises gravely and extends his hand courteously.*]

SHRDLU. How do you do, Mr. Zero? I'm very glad to see you again.

ZERO. Same here. I wasn't expectin' to see you, either. [*Looking about.*] This is a kinda nice place. I wouldn't mind restin' here a while.

SHRDLU. You may if you wish.

ZERO. I'm kinda tired. I ain't used to bein' outdoors. I ain't walked so much in years.

SHRDLU. Sit down here, under the tree.

ZERO. Do they let you sit on the grass?

SHRDLU. Oh, yes.

ZERO [*seating himself*]. Boy, this feels good. I'll tell the world my feet are sore. I ain't used to so much walkin'. Say, I wonder would it be all right if I took my shoes off; my feet are tired.

SHRDLU. Yes. Some of the people here go barefoot.

ZERO. Yeh? They sure must be nuts. But I'm goin' t' leave 'em off for a while. So long as it's all right. The grass feels nice and cool. [*He stretches out comfortably.*] Say, this is the life of Riley all right, all right. This sure is a nice place. What do they call this place, anyhow?

SHRDLU. The Elysian Fields.

ZERO. The which?

SHRDLU. The Elysian Fields.

ZERO [*dubiously*]. Oh! Well, it's a nice place, all right.

SHRDLU. They say that this is the most desirable of all places. Only the most favoured remain here.

ZERO. Yeh? Well, that let's me out, I guess. [*Suddenly.*] But what are you doin' here? I thought you'd be burned by now.

SHRDLU [*sadly*]. Mr. Zero, I am the most unhappy of men.

ZERO [*in mild astonishment*]. Why, because you ain't bein' roasted alive?

SHRDLU [*nodding*]. Nothing is turning out as I expected. I saw everything so clearly — the flames, the tortures, an eternity of suffering as the just punishment for my unspeakable crime. And it has all turned out so differently.

ZERO. Well, that's pretty soft for you, ain't it?

SHRDLU [*wailingly*]. No, no, no! It's right and just that I should be punished. I could have endured it stoically. All through those endless ages of indescribable torment I should have exulted in the magnificence of divine justice. But this — this is maddening! What becomes of justice? What becomes of morality? What becomes of right and wrong? It's maddening — simply maddening! Oh, if Dr. Amaranth were only here to advise me!

[*He buries his face and groans.*]

ZERO [*trying to puzzle it out*]. You mean to say they ain't called you for cuttin' your mother's throat?

SHRDLU. No! It's terrible — terrible! I was prepared for anything — anything but this.

ZERO. Well, what did they say to you?

SHRDLU [*looking up*]. Only that I was to come here and remain until I understood.

ZERO. I don't get it. What do they want you to understand?

SHRDLU [*despairingly*]. I don't know — I don't know! If I only had an inkling of what they meant — [*Interrupting him.*] Just listen quietly for a moment; do you hear anything?

[*They are both silent, straining their ears.*]

ZERO [*at length*]. Nope.

SHRDLU. You don't hear any music? Do you?

ZERO. Music? No, I don't hear nothin'.

SHRDLU. The people here say that the music never stops.

ZERO. They're kiddin' you.

SHRDLU. Do you think so?

ZERO. Sure thing. There ain't a sound.

SHRDLU. Perhaps. They're capable of anything. But I haven't told you of the bitterest of my disappointments.

ZERO. Well, spill it. I'm gettin' used to hearin' bad news.

SHRDLU. When I came to this place, my first thought was to find my dear mother. I wanted to ask her forgiveness. And I wanted her to help me to understand.

ZERO. An' she couldn't do it?

SHRDLU [*with a deep groan*]. She's not here! Mr. Zero! Here where only the most favoured dwell, that wisest and purest of spirits is nowhere to be found. I don't understand it.

A WOMAN'S VOICE [*in the distance*]. Mr. Zero! Oh, Mr. Zero!

[ZERO *raises his head and listens attentively.*]

SHRDLU [*going on, unheedingly*]. If you were to see some of the people here — the things they do —

ZERO [*interrupting*]. Wait a minute, will you? I think somebody's callin' me.

THE VOICE [*somewhat nearer*]. Mr. Ze-ro! Oh! Mr. Ze-ro!

ZERO. Who the hell's that now? I wonder if the wife's on my trail already. That would be swell, wouldn't it? An' I figured on her bein' good for another twenty years, anyhow.

THE VOICE [*nearer*]. Mr. Ze-ro! Yoo-hoo!

ZERO. No. That ain't her voice. [*Calling, savagely.*] Yoo-hoo. [*To* SHRDLU.] Ain't that always the way? Just when a guy is takin' life easy an' havin' a good time! [*He rises and looks off left.*] Here she comes, whoever she is. [*In sudden amazement.*] Well, I'll be —! Well, what do you know about that!

[*He stands looking in wonderment, as* DAISY DIANA DOROTHEA DEVORE *enters. She wears a much-beruffled white muslin dress which is a size too small and fifteen years too youthful for her. She is red-faced and breathless.*]

DAISY [*panting*]. Oh! I thought I'd never catch up to you. I've been followin' you for days — callin' an' callin'. Didn't you hear me?

ZERO. Not till just now. You look kinda winded.

DAISY. I sure am. I can't hardly catch my breath.

ZERO. Well, sit down an' take a load off your feet.

[*He leads her to the tree.* DAISY *sees* SHRDLU *for the first time and shrinks back a little.*]

ZERO. It's all right, he's a friend of mine. [*To* SHRDLU.] Buddy, I want you to meet my friend, Miss Devore.

SHRDLU [*rising and extending his hand courteously*]. How do you do, Miss Devore?

DAISY [*self-consciously*]. How do!

ZERO [*to* DAISY]. He's a friend of mine. [*To* SHRDLU.] I guess you don't mind if she sits here a while an' cools off, do you?

SHRDLU. No, no, certainly not.

[*They all seat themselves under the tree.* ZERO *and* DAISY *are a little self-conscious.* SHRDLU *gradually becomes absorbed in his own thoughts.*]

ZERO. I was just takin' a rest myself. I took my shoes off on account of my feet bein' so sore.

DAISY. Yeh, I'm kinda tired, too. [*Looking about.*] Say, ain't it pretty here, though?

ZERO. Yeh, it is at that.

DAISY. What do they call this place?

ZERO. Why — er — let's see. He was tellin' me just a minute ago. The — er — I don't know. Some kind o' fields. I forget now. [*To* SHRDLU.] Say, Buddy, what do they call this place again? [SHRDLU, *absorbed in his thoughts, does not hear him. To* DAISY.] He don't hear me. He's thinkin' again.

DAISY [*sotto voce*]. What's the matter with him?

ZERO. Why, he's the guy that murdered his mother — remember?

DAISY [*interested*]. Oh, yeh! Is that him?

ZERO. Yeh. An' he had it all figgered out how they was goin' t' roast him or somethin'. And now they ain't goin' to do nothin' to him an' it's kinda got his goat.

DAISY [*sympathetically*]. Poor feller!

ZERO. Yeh. He takes it kinda hard.

DAISY. He looks like a nice young feller.

ZERO. Well, you sure are good for sore eyes. I never expected to see you here.

DAISY. I thought maybe you'd be kinda surprised.

ZERO. Surprised is right. I thought you was alive an' kickin'. When did you pass out?

DAISY. Oh, right after you did — a coupla days.

ZERO [*interested*]. Yeh? What happened? Get hit by a truck or somethin'?

THE ADDING MACHINE

DAISY. No. [*Hesitantly.*] You see — it's this way. I blew out the gas.

ZERO [*astonished*]. Go on! What was the big idea?

DAISY [*falteringly*]. Oh, I don't know. You see, I lost my job.

ZERO. I'll bet you're sorry you did it now, ain't you?

DAISY [*with conviction*]. No, I ain't sorry. Not a bit. [*Then hesitantly.*] Say, Mr. Zero, I been thinkin' — [*She stops.*]

ZERO. What?

DAISY [*plucking up courage*]. I been thinkin' it would be kinda nice — if you an' me — if we could kinda talk things over.

ZERO. Yeh. Sure. What do you want to talk about?

DAISY. Well — I don't know — but you and me — we ain't really ever talked things over, have we?

ZERO. No, that's right, we ain't. Well, let's go to it.

DAISY. I was thinkin' if we could be alone — just the two of us, see?

ZERO. Oh, yeh! Yeh, I get you.

[*He turns to* SHRDLU *and coughs loudly.* SHRDLU *does not stir.*]

ZERO [*to* DAISY]. He's dead to the world. [*He turns to* SHRDLU.] Say, Buddy! [*No answer.*] Say, Buddy!

SHRDLU [*looking up with a start*]. Were you speaking to me?

ZERO. Yeh. How'd you guess it? I was thinkin' that maybe you'd like to walk around a little and look for your mother.

SHRDLU [*shaking his head*]. It's no use. I've looked everywhere.

[*He relapses into thought again.*]

ZERO. Maybe over there they might know.

SHRDLU. No, no! I've searched everywhere. She's not here.

[ZERO *and* DAISY *look at each other in despair.*]

ZERO. Listen, old shirt, my friend here and me — see? — we used to work in the same store. An' we got somethings to talk over — business, see? — kinda confidential. So if it ain't askin' too much —

SHRDLU [*springing to his feet*]. Why, certainly! Excuse me!

[*He bows politely to* DAISY *and walks off.* DAISY *and* ZERO *watch him until he has disappeared.*]

ZERO [*with a forced laugh*]. He's a good guy at that.

[*Now that they are alone, both are very self-conscious, and for a time they sit in silence.*]

DAISY [*breaking the silence*]. It sure is pretty here, ain't it?

ZERO. Sure is.

DAISY. Look at the flowers! Ain't they just perfect! Why, you'd think they was artificial, wouldn't you?

ZERO. Yeh, you would.

DAISY. And the smell of them. Like perfume.

ZERO. Yeh.

DAISY. I'm crazy about the country, ain't you?

ZERO. Yeh. It's nice for a change.

DAISY. Them store picnics — remember?

ZERO. You bet. They sure was fun.

DAISY. One time — I guess you don't remember — the two of us — me and you — we sat down on the grass together under a tree — just like we're doin' now.

ZERO. Sure I remember.

DAISY. Go on! I'll bet you don't.

ZERO. I'll bet I do. It was the year the wife didn't go.

DAISY [*her face brightening*]. That's right! I didn't think you'd remember.

ZERO. An' comin' home we sat together in the truck.

DAISY [*eagerly, rather shamefacedly*]. Yeh! There's somethin' I've always wanted to ask you.

ZERO. Well, why didn't you?

DAISY. I don't know. It didn't seem refined. But I'm goin' to ask you now, anyhow.

ZERO. Go ahead. Shoot.

DAISY [*falteringly*]. Well — while we was comin' home — you put your arm up on the bench behind me — and I could feel your knee kinda pressin' against mine. [*She stops.*]

ZERO [*becoming more and more interested*]. Yeh — well — what about it?

DAISY. What I wanted to ask you was — was it just kinda accidental?

ZERO [*with a laugh*]. Sure it was accidental. Accidental on purpose.

DAISY [*eagerly*]. Do you mean it?

ZERO. Sure I mean it. You mean to say you didn't know it?

DAISY. No. I've been wantin' to ask you —

ZERO. Then why did you get sore at me?

DAISY. Sore? I wasn't sore! When was I sore?

ZERO. That night. Sure you was sore. If you wasn't sore, why did you move away?

DAISY. Just to see if you meant it. I thought if you meant it, you'd move up closer. An' then when you took your arm away, I was sure you didn't mean it.

ZERO. An' I thought all the time you was sore. That's why I took my arm away. I thought if I moved up you'd holler and then I'd be in a jam, like you read in the paper all the time about guys gettin' pulled in for annoyin' women.

DAISY. An' I was wishin' you'd put your arm around me — just sittin' there wishin' all the way home.

ZERO. What do you know about that? That sure is hard luck, that is. If I'd 'a' only knew! You know what I felt like doin' — only I didn't have the nerve?

DAISY. What?

ZERO. I felt like kissin' you.

DAISY [*fervently*]. I wanted you to.

ZERO [*astonished*]. You would 'a' let me?

DAISY. I wanted you to! I wanted you to! Oh, why didn't you — why didn't you?

ZERO. I didn't have the nerve. I sure was a dumb-bell.

DAISY. I would 'a' let you all you wanted to. I wouldn't 'a' cared. I know it would 'a' been wrong, but I wouldn't 'a' cared. I wasn't thinkin' about right an' wrong at all. I didn't care — see? I just wanted you to kiss me.

ZERO [*feelingly*]. If I'd only knew. I wanted to do it, I swear I did. But I didn't think you cared nothin' about me.

DAISY [*passionately*]. I never cared nothin' about nobody else.

ZERO. Do you mean it — on the level? You ain't kiddin' me, are you?

DAISY. No, I ain't kiddin'. I mean it. I'm tellin' you the truth. I ain't never had the nerve to tell you before — but now I don't care. It don't make no difference now. I mean it — every word of it.

ZERO [*dejectedly*]. If I'd only knew it.

DAISY. Listen to me. There's somethin' else I want to tell you. I may as well tell you everything now. It don't make no difference now. About my blowin' out the gas — see? Do you know why I done it?

ZERO. Yeh, you told me — on account o' bein' canned.

DAISY. I just told you that. That ain't the real reason. The real reason is on account o' you.

ZERO. You mean to say on account o' me passin' out —?

DAISY. Yeh. That's it. I didn't want to go on livin'. What for? What did I want to go on livin' for? I didn't have nothin' to live for with you gone. I often thought of doin' it before. But I never had the nerve. An' anyhow I didn't want to leave you.

ZERO. An' me bawlin' you out, about readin' too fast an' readin' too slow.

DAISY [*reproachfully*]. Why did you do it?

ZERO. I don't know, I swear I don't. I was always stuck on you. An' while I'd be addin' them figgers, I'd be thinkin' how, if the wife died, you an' me could get married.

DAISY. I used to think o' that, too.

ZERO. An' then, before I knew it, I was bawlin' you out.

DAISY. Them was the times I'd think o' blowin' out the gas. But I never did till you was gone. There wasn't nothin' to live for then. But it wasn't so easy to do, anyhow. I never could stand the smell o' gas. An' all the while I was gettin' ready, you know, stuffin' up all the cracks, the way you read about in the paper — I was thinkin' of you and hopin' that maybe I'd meet you again. An' I made up my mind if I ever did see you, I'd tell you.

ZERO [*taking her hand*]. I'm sure glad you did. I'm sure glad. [*Ruefully.*] But it don't do much good now, does it?

DAISY. No, I guess it don't. [*Summon-

ing courage.] But there's one thing I'm goin' to ask you.

ZERO. What's that?

DAISY [*in a low voice*]. I want you to kiss me.

ZERO. You bet I will!

[*He leans over and kisses her cheek.*]

DAISY. Not like that. I don't mean like that. I mean really kiss me. On the mouth. I ain't never been kissed like that.

[ZERO *puts his arms about her and presses his lips to hers. A long embrace. At last they separate and sit side by side in silence.*]

DAISY [*putting her hands to her cheeks*]. So that's what it's like. I didn't know it could be like that. I didn't know anythin' could be like that.

ZERO [*fondling her hand*]. Your cheeks are red. They're all red. And your eyes are shinin'. I never seen your eyes shinin' like that before.

DAISY [*holding up her hand*]. Listen — do you hear it? Do you hear the music?

ZERO. No, I don't hear nothin'!

DAISY. Yeh — music. Listen an' you'll hear it. [*They are both silent for a moment.*]

ZERO [*excitedly*]. Yeh! I hear it! He said there was music, but I didn't hear it till just now.

DAISY. Ain't it grand?

ZERO. Swell! Say, do you know what?

DAISY. What?

ZERO. It makes me feel like dancin'.

DAISY. Yeh? Me, too.

ZERO [*springing to his feet*]. Come on! Let's dance!

[*He seizes her hands and tries to pull her up*]

DAISY [*resisting laughingly*]. I can't dance. I ain't danced in twenty years.

ZERO. That's nothin'. I ain't, neither. Come on! I feel just like a kid!

[*He pulls her to her feet and seizes her about the waist.*]

DAISY. Wait a minute! Wait till I fix my skirt.

[*She turns back her skirts and pins them above the ankles.* ZERO *seizes her about the waist. They dance clumsily, but with gay abandon.*

DAISY'S *hair becomes loosened and tumbles over her shoulders. She lends herself more and more to the spirit of the dance. But* ZERO *soon begins to tire and dances with less and less zest.*]

ZERO [*stopping at last, panting for breath*]. Wait a minute! I'm all winded.

[*He releases* DAISY, *but before he can turn away, she throws her arms about him and presses her lips to his.*]

ZERO [*freeing himself*]. Wait a minute! Let me get my wind!

[*He limps to the tree and seats himself under it, gasping for breath.* DAISY *looks after him, her spirits rather dampened.*]

ZERO. Whew! I sure am winded! I ain't used to dancin'. [*He takes off his collar and tie and opens the neckband of his shirt.* DAISY *sits under the tree near him, looking at him longingly. But he is busy catching his breath.*] Gee, my heart's goin' a mile a minute.

DAISY. Why don't you lay down an' rest? You could put your head on my lap.

ZERO. That ain't a bad idea.

[*He stretches out, his head in* DAISY'S *lap.*]

DAISY [*fondling his hair*]. It was swell, wasn't it?

ZERO. Yeh. But you gotta be used to it.

DAISY. Just imagine if we could stay here all the time — you an' me together — wouldn't it be swell?

ZERO. Yeh. But there ain't a chance.

DAISY. Won't they let us stay?

ZERO. No. This place is only for the good ones.

DAISY. Well, we ain't so bad, are we?

ZERO. Go on! Me a murderer an' you committin' suicide. Anyway, they wouldn't stand for this — the way we been goin' on.

DAISY. I don't see why.

ZERO. You don't! You know it ain't right. Ain't I got a wife?

DAISY. Not any more you ain't. When you're dead, that ends it. Don't they always say "until death do us part?"

ZERO. Well, maybe you're right about

that, but they wouldn't stand for us here.

DAISY. It would be swell — the two of us together — we could make up for all them years.

ZERO. Yeh, I wish we could.

DAISY. We sure were fools. But I don't care. I've got you now.

[*She kisses his forehead and cheeks and mouth.*]

ZERO. I'm sure crazy about you. I never saw you lookin' so pretty before, with your cheeks all red. An' your hair hangin' down. You got swell hair.

[*He fondles and kisses her hair.*]

DAISY [*ecstatically*]. We got each other now, ain't we?

ZERO. Yeh. I'm crazy about you. Daisy! That's a pretty name. It's a flower, ain't it? Well — that's what you are — just a flower.

DAISY [*happily*]. We can always be together now, can't we?

ZERO. As long as they'll let us. I sure am crazy about you. [*Suddenly he sits upright.*] Watch your step!

DAISY [*alarmed*]. What's the matter?

ZERO [*nervously*]. He's comin' back.

DAISY. Oh, is that all? Well, what about it?

ZERO. You don't want him to see us layin' around like this, do you?

DAISY. I don't care if he does.

ZERO. Well, you oughta care. You don't want him to think you ain't a refined girl, do you? He's an awful moral bird, he is.

DAISY. I don't care nothin' about him. I don't care nothin' about anybody but you.

ZERO. Sure, I know. But we don't want people talkin' about us. You better fix your hair an' pull down your skirts.

[DAISY *complies rather sadly. They are both silent as* SHRDLU *enters.*]

ZERO [*with feigned nonchalance*]. Well, you got back all right, didn't you?

SHRDLU. I hope I haven't returned too soon.

ZERO. No, that's all right. We were just havin' a little talk. You know — about business an' things.

DAISY [*boldly*]. We were wishin' we could stay here all the time.

SHRDLU. You may if you like.

ZERO AND DAISY [*in astonishment*]. What!

SHRDLU. Yes. Any one who likes may remain —

ZERO. But I thought you were tellin' me —

SHRDLU. Just as I told you, only the most favored do remain. But any one may.

ZERO. I don't get it. There's a catch in it somewheres.

DAISY. It don't matter as long as we can stay.

ZERO [*to* SHRDLU]. We were thinkin' about gettin' married, see?

SHRDLU. You may or not, just as you like.

ZERO. You don't mean to say we could stay if we didn't, do you?

SHRDLU. Yes. They don't care.

ZERO. An' there's some here that ain't married?

SHRDLU. Yes.

ZERO [*to* DAISY]. I don't know about this place, at that. They must be kind of a mixed crowd.

DAISY. It don't matter, so long as we got each other.

ZERO. Yeh, I know, but you don't want to mix with people that ain't respectable.

DAISY [*to* SHRDLU]. Can we get married right away? I guess there must be a lot of ministers here, ain't there?

SHRDLU. Not as many as I had hoped to find. The two who seem most beloved are Dean Swift and the Abbé Rabelais. They are both much admired for some indecent tales which they have written.

ZERO [*shocked*]. What! Ministers writin' smutty stories! Say, what kind of a dump is this, anyway?

SHRDLU [*despairingly*]. I don't know. Mr. Zero. All these people here are so strange, so unlike the good people I've known. They seem to think of nothing but enjoyment or of wasting their time in profitless occupations. Some paint pictures from morning until night, or carve blocks of stone. Others write songs or put

words together, day in and day out. Still others do nothing but lie under the trees and look at the sky. There are men who spend all their time reading books and women who think only of adorning themselves. And forever they are telling stories and laughing and singing and drinking and dancing. There are drunkards, thieves, vagabonds, blasphemers, adulterers. There is one —
ZERO. That's enough. I heard enough.
[*He seats himself and begins putting on his shoes.*]
DAISY [*anxiously*]. What are you goin' to do?
ZERO. I'm goin' to beat it, that's what I'm goin' to do.
DAISY. You said you liked it here.
ZERO [*looking at her in amazement*]. Liked it! Say, you don't mean to say you want to stay here, do you, with a lot of rummies an' loafers an' bums?
DAISY. We don't have to bother with them. We can just sit here together an' look at the flowers an' listen to the music.
SHRDLU [*eagerly*]. Music! Did you hear music?
DAISY. Sure. Don't you hear it?
SHRDLU. No, they say it never stops. But I've never heard it.
ZERO [*listening*]. I thought I heard it before, but I don't hear nothin' now. I guess I must 'a' been dreamin'. [*Looking about.*] What's the quickest way out of this place?
DAISY [*pleadingly*]. Won't you stay just a little longer?
ZERO. Didn't yer hear me say I'm goin'? Good-bye, Miss Devore. I'm goin' to beat it.
[*He limps off at the right.* DAISY *follows him slowly.*]
DAISY [*to* SHRDLU]. I won't ever see him again.
SHRDLU. Are you goin' to stay here?
DAISY. It don't make no difference now. Without him I might as well be alive.
[*She goes off right.* SHRDLU *watches her a moment, then sighs, and, seating himself under the tree, buries his head on his arm. Curtain falls.*]

SCENE SEVEN

SCENE: *Before the curtain rises the clicking of an adding machine is heard. The curtain rises upon an office similar in appearance to that in Scene Two, except that there is a door in the back wall through which can be seen a glimpse of the corridor outside. In the middle of the room* ZERO *is seated completely absorbed in the operation of an adding machine. He presses the keys and pulls the lever with mechanical precision. He still wears his full-dress suit, but he has added to it sleeve protectors and a green eye-shade. A strip of white paper-tape flows steadily from the machine as* ZERO *operates. The room is filled with this tape — streamers, festoons, billows of it everywhere. It covers the floor and the furniture, it climbs the walls and chokes the doorways. A few moments later,* LIEUTENANT CHARLES *and* JOE *enter at the left.* LIEUTENANT CHARLES *is middle-aged and inclined to corpulence. He has an air of world-weariness. He is barefooted, wears a Panama hat, and is dressed in bright-red tights which are a very bad fit — too tight is some places, badly wrinkled in others.* JOE *is a youth with a smutty face dressed in dirty blue overalls.*

CHARLES [*after contemplating* ZERO *for a few moments*]. All right, Zero, cease firing.
ZERO [*looking up, surprised*]. Whaddja say?
CHARLES. I said stop punching that machine.
ZERO [*bewildered*]. Stop?
[*He goes on working mechanically.*]
CHARLES [*impatiently*]. Yes. Can't you stop? Here, Joe, give me a hand. He can't stop.
[JOE *and* CHARLES *each take one of* ZERO's *arms and with enormous effort detach him from the machine. He resists passively — mere inertia. Finally they succeed and swing him around on his stool.* CHARLES *and* JOE *mop their foreheads.*]

ZERO [*querulously*]. What's the idea? Can't you lemme alone?

CHARLES [*ignoring the question*]. How long have you been here?

ZERO. Jes' twenty-five years. Three hundred months, ninety-one hundred and thirty-one days, one hundred thirty-six thousand —

CHARLES [*impatiently*]. That'll do! That'll do!

ZERO [*proudly*]. I ain't missed a day, not an hour, not a minute. Look at all I got done.

[*He points to the maze of paper.*]

CHARLES. It's time to quit.

ZERO. Quit? Whaddye mean quit? I ain't goin' to quit!

CHARLES. You've got to.

ZERO. What for? What do I have to quit for?

CHARLES. It's time for you to go back.

ZERO. Go back where? Whaddya talkin' about?

CHARLES. Back to earth, you dub. Where do you think?

ZERO. Aw, go on, Cap, who are you kiddin'?

CHARLES. I'm not kidding anybody. And don't call me Cap. I'm a lieutenant.

ZERO. All right, Lieutenant, all right. But what's this you're tryin' to tell me about goin' back?

CHARLES. Your time's up, I'm telling you. You must be pretty thick. How many times do you want to be told a thing?

ZERO. This is the first time I heard about goin' back. Nobody ever said nothin' to me about it before.

CHARLES. You didn't think you were going to stay here forever, did you?

ZERO. Sure. Why not? I did my bit, didn't I? Forty-five years of it. Twenty-five years in the store. Then the boss canned me and I knocked him cold. I guess you ain't heard about that —

CHARLES [*interrupting*]. I know all about that. But what's that got to do with it?

ZERO. Well, I done my bit, didn't I? That oughta let me out.

CHARLES [*jeeringly*]. So you think you're all through, do you?

ZERO. Sure, I do. I did the best I could while I was there, and then I passed out. And now I'm sittin' pretty here.

CHARLES. You've got a fine idea of the way they run things, you have. Do you think they're going to all of the trouble of making a soul just to use it once?

ZERO. Once is often enough, it seems to me.

CHARLES. It seems to you, does it? Well, who are you? And what do you know about it? Why, man, they use a soul over and over again — over and over until it's worn out.

ZERO. Nobody ever told me.

CHARLES. So you thought you were all through, did you? Well, that's a hot one, that is.

ZERO [*sullenly*]. How was I to know?

CHARLES. Use your brains! Where would we put them all? We're crowded enough as it is. Why, this place is nothing but a kind of repair and service station — a sort of cosmic laundry, you might say. We get the souls in here by the bushelful. Then we get busy and clean them up. And you ought to see some of them. The muck and the slime. Phoo! And as full of holes as a flour-sifter. But we fix them up. We disinfect them and give them a kerosene rub and mend the holes, and back they go — practically as good as new.

ZERO. You mean to say I've been here before — before the last time, I mean?

CHARLES. Been here before! Why, you poor boob — you've been here thousands of times — fifty thousand, at least.

ZERO [*suspiciously*]. How is it I don't remember nothin' about it?

CHARLES. Well — that's partly because you're stupid. But it's mostly because that's the way they fix it. [*Musingly.*] They're funny that way — every now and then they'll do something white like that — when you'd least expect it. I guess economy's at the bottom of it, though. They figure that the souls would get worn out quicker if they remembered.

ZERO. And don't any of 'em remember?

CHARLES. Oh, some do. You see there's different types: there's the type that gets a little better each time it goes back — we just give them a wash and send them right through. Then there's another type — the type that gets a little worse each time. That's where you belong!

ZERO [*offended*]. Me? You mean to say I'm gettin' worse all the time?

CHARLES [*nodding*]. Yes. A little worse each time.

ZERO. Well — what was I when I started? Somethin' big? — A king or somethin'?

CHARLES [*laughing derisively*]. A king! That's a good one! I'll tell you what you were the first time — if you want to know so much — a monkey.

ZERO [*shocked and offended*]. A monkey!

CHARLES [*nodding*]. Yes, sir — just a hairy, chattering, long-tailed monkey.

ZERO. That musta been a long time ago.

CHARLES. Oh, not so long. A million years or so. Seems like yesterday to me.

ZERO. Then look here, whaddya mean by sayin' I'm gettin' worse all the time?

CHARLES. Just what I said. You weren't so bad as a monkey. Of course, you did just what all the other monkeys did, but still it kept you out in the open air. And you weren't women-shy — there was one little red-headed monkey — Well, never mind. Yes, sir, you weren't so bad then. But even in those days there must have been some bigger and brainier monkey that you kow-towed to. The mark of the slave was on you from the start.

ZERO [*sullenly*]. You ain't very particular about what you call people, are you?

CHARLES. You wanted the truth, didn't you? If there ever was a soul in the world that was labelled slave, it's yours. Why, all the bosses and kings that there ever were have left their trademarks on your backside.

ZERO. It ain't fair, if you ask me.

CHARLES [*shrugging his shoulders*]. Don't tell me about it. I don't make the rules. All I know is you've been getting worse — worse each time. Why, even six thousand years ago you weren't so bad. That was the time you were hauling stones for one of those big pyramids in a place they call Africa. Ever hear of the pyramids?

ZERO. Them big pointy things?

CHARLES [*nodding*]. That's it.

ZERO. I seen a picture of them in the movies.

CHARLES. Well, you helped build them. It was a long step down from the happy days in the jungle, but it was a good job — even though you didn't know what you were doing and your back was striped by the foreman's whip. But you've been going down, down. Two thousand years ago you were a Roman galley-slave. You were on one of the triremes that knocked the Carthaginian fleet for a goal. Again the whip. But you had muscles then — chest muscles, back muscles, biceps. [*He feels* ZERO's *arm gingerly and turns away in disgust.*] Phoo! A bunch of mush!

[*He notices that* JOE *has fallen asleep. Walking over, he kicks him in the shin.*]

CHARLES. Wake up, you mutt! Where do you think you are! [*He turns to* ZERO *again.*] And then another thousand years and you were a serf — a lump of clay digging up other lumps of clay. You wore an iron collar then — white ones hadn't been invented yet. Another long step down. But where you dug, potatoes grew and that helped fatten the pigs. Which was something. And now — well, I don't want to rub it in —

ZERO. Rub it in is right! Seems to me I got a pretty healthy kick comin'. I ain't had a square deal! Hard work! That's all I've ever had!

CHARLES [*callously*]. What else were you ever good for?

ZERO. Well, that ain't the point. The point is I'm through! I had enough! Let 'em find somebody else to do the dirty work. I'm sick of bein' the goat! I quit right here and now!

[*He glares about defiantly. There is a thunder-clap and a bright flash of lightning.*]

ZERO [*screaming*]. Ooh! What's that?

[*He clings to* CHARLES.]

CHARLES. It's all right. Nobody's going to hurt you. It's just their way of telling you that they don't like you to talk that way. Pull yourself together and calm down. You can't change the rules — nobody can — they've got it all fixed. It's a rotten system — but what are you going to do about it?

ZERO. Why can't they stop pickin' on me? I'm satisfied here — doin' my day's work. I don't want to go back.

CHARLES. You've got to, I tell you. There's no way out of it.

ZERO. What chance have I got — at my age? Who'll give me a job?

CHARLES. You big boob, you don't think you're going back the way you are, do you?

ZERO. Sure; how then?

CHARLES. Why, you've got to start all over.

ZERO. All over?

CHARLES [nodding]. You'll be a baby again — a bald, red-faced little animal, and then you'll go through it all again. There'll be millions of others like you — all with their mouths open, squalling for food. And then when you get a little older you'll begin to learn things — and you'll learn all the wrong things and learn them all in the wrong way. You'll eat the wrong food and wear the wrong clothes and you'll live in swarming dens where there's no light and no air! You'll learn to be a liar and a bully and a braggart and a coward and a sneak. You'll learn to fear the sunlight and to hate beauty. By that time you'll be ready for school. There they'll tell you the truth about a great many things that you don't give a damn about and they'll tell you lies about all the things you ought to know — and about all the things you want to know they'll tell you nothing at all. When you get through you'll be equipped for your life-work. You'll be ready to take a job.

ZERO [eagerly]. What'll my job be? Another adding machine?

CHARLES. Yes. But not one of these antiquated adding machines. It will be a superb, super-hyper-adding machine, as far from this old piece of junk as you are from God. It will be something to make you sit up and take notice, that adding machine. It will be an adding machine which will be installed in a coal mine and which will record the individual output of each miner. As each miner down in the lower galleries takes up a shovelful of coal, the impact of his shovel will automatically set in motion a graphite pencil in your gallery. The pencil will make a mark in white upon a blackened, sensitized drum. Then your work comes in. With the great toe of your right foot you release a lever which focuses a violet ray on the drum. The ray, playing upon and through the white mark, falls upon a selenium cell which in turn sets the keys of the adding apparatus in motion. In this way the individual output of each miner is recorded without any human effort except the slight pressure of the great toe of your right foot.

ZERO [in breathless, round-eyed wonder]. Say, that'll be some machine, won't it?

CHARLES. Some machine is right. It will be the culmination of human effort — the final triumph of the evolutionary process. For millions of years the nebulous gases swirled in space. For more millions of years the gases cooled and then through inconceivable ages they hardened into rocks. And then came life. Floating green things on the waters that covered the earth. More millions of years and a step upward — an animate organism in the ancient slime. And so on — step by step, down through the ages — a gain here, a gain there — the mollusc, the fish, the reptile, the mammal, man! And all so that you might sit in the gallery of a coal mine and operate the super-hyper-adding machine with the great toe of your right foot!

ZERO. Well, then — I ain't so bad, after all.

CHARLES. You're a failure, Zero, a failure. A waste product. A slave to a contraption of steel and iron. The animal's instincts, but not his strength and skill. The animal's appetites, but not his unashamed indulgence of them. True, you move and eat and digest and excrete and reproduce. But any microscopic organism can do as much. Well — time's up! Back you go — back to your sunless groove — the raw material of slums and wars — the ready prey of the first jingo or demagogue or political adventurer who takes the trouble to play upon your ignorance and credulity and provincialism. You poor, spineless, brainless boob — I'm sorry for you!

ZERO [*falling to his knees*]. Then keep me here! Don't send me back! Let me stay!

CHARLES. Get up. Didn't I tell you I can't do anything for you? Come on, time's up!

ZERO. I can't! I can't! I'm afraid to go through it all again.

CHARLES. You've got to, I tell you. Come on, now!

ZERO. What did you tell me so much for? Couldn't you just let me go, thinkin' everythin' was goin' to be all right?

CHARLES. You wanted to know, didn't you?

ZERO. How did I know what you were goin' to tell me? Now I can't stop thinkin' about it! I can't stop thinkin'! I'll be thinkin' about it all the time.

CHARLES. All right! I'll do the best I can for you. I'll send a girl with you to keep you company.

ZERO. A girl? What for? What good will a girl do me?

CHARLES. She'll help make you forget.

ZERO [*eagerly*]. She will? Where is she?

CHARLES. Wait a minute, I'll call her. [*He calls in a loud voice.*] Oh! Hope! Yoo-hoo! [*He turns his head aside and says in the manner of a ventriloquist imitating a distant feminine voice.*] Ye-es. [*Then in his own voice.*] Come here, will you? There's a fellow who wants you to take him back. [*Ventriloquously again.*] All right. I'll be right over, Charlie dear. [*He turns to* ZERO.] Kind of familiar, isn't she? Charlie dear!

ZERO. What did you say her name is?

CHARLES. Hope. H-o-p-e.

ZERO. Is she good-lookin'?

CHARLES. Is she good-looking! Oh, boy, wait until you see her! She's a blonde with big blue eyes and red lips and little white teeth and —

ZERO. Say, that listens good to me. Will she be long?

CHARLES. She'll be here right away. There she is now! Do you see her?

ZERO. No. Where?

CHARLES. Out in the corridor. No, not there. Over farther. To the right. Don't you see her blue dress? And the sunlight on her hair?

ZERO. Oh, sure! Now I see her! What's the matter with me, anyhow? Say, she's some jane! Oh, you baby vamp!

CHARLES. She'll make you forget your troubles.

ZERO. What troubles are you talkin' about?

CHARLES. Nothing. Go on. Don't keep her waiting.

ZERO. You bet I won't! Oh, Hope! Wait for me! I'll be right with you! I'm on my way!

[*He stumbles out eagerly.* JOE *bursts into uproarious laughter.*]

CHARLES [*eyeing him in surprise and anger*]. What in hell's the matter with you?

JOE [*shaking with laughter*]. Did you get that? He thinks he saw somebody and he's following her! [*He rocks with laughter.*]

CHARLES [*punching him in the jaw*]. Shut your face!

JOE [*nursing his jaw*]. What's the idea? Can't I even laugh when I see something funny?

CHARLES. Funny! You keep your mouth shut or I'll show you something funny. Go on, hustle out of here and get something to clean up this mess with. There's another fellow moving in. Hurry now.

[*He makes a threatening gesture.* JOE *exits hastily.* CHARLES *goes to a chair and seats himself. He looks weary and dispirited.*]

CHARLES [*shaking his head*]. Hell, I'll tell the world this is a lousy job!

[*He takes a flask from his pocket, uncorks it, and slowly drains it.*]

CURTAIN

OLIVER CROMWELL
A PLAY
By JOHN DRINKWATER

COPYRIGHT, 1921, BY HOUGHTON MIFFLIN COMPANY

DRAMATIC RIGHTS IN THE UNITED STATES
CONTROLLED BY WILLIAM HARRIS, JR.

CAUTION

All dramatic rights for John Drinkwater's "Oliver Cromwell" in North America are owned and controlled by William Harris, Jr., Hudson Theatre, New York City. Special notice should be taken that possession of this book without a valid contract for production first having been obtained from Mr. Harris confers no right or license to professionals or amateurs to produce the play publicly or in private for gain or charity. Until further notice performances of this play in North America will be limited to those companies which appear under Mr. Harris's direction, and he absolutely forbids other performances by professionals or amateurs, including "readings," tableaux, and anything of such nature approximating a performance. The play is fully protected by copyright and any violations will be prosecuted.

ACT OF MARCH 4, 1909: SECTION 28

"*That any person who wilfully or for profit shall infringe any copyright secured by this act, or who shall knowingly and wilfully aid or abet such infringement, shall be deemed guilty of a misdemeanor, and upon conviction thereof shall be punished by imprisonment for not exceeding one year, or by a fine of not less than $100 nor more than $1000, or both, in the discretion of the Court.*"

THE CHARACTERS ARE

Mrs. Cromwell, *Oliver's mother*
Elizabeth Cromwell, *his wife*
Bridget Cromwell, *his daughter*
John Hampden
Henry Ireton
Oliver Cromwell
Seth Tanner
Two Agents to the Earl of Bedford
Amos Tanner
A Member of Parliament
The Speaker of the House of Commons
Bassett, *an officer of the House*
The Mayor of Ely
General Fairfax
Colonel Staines
Colonel Pemberton
A Scout
A Surgeon
An Aide
Neal, *Secretary to Charles*
Charles I

Farm labourers — Members of Parliament

OLIVER CROMWELL

SCENE I

CROMWELL'S *house at Ely, about the year 1639. An early summer evening. The window of the room opens on to a smooth lawn, used for bowling, and a garden full of flowers.*

[OLIVER'S *wife,* ELIZABETH CROMWELL, *is sitting at the table, sewing. In a chair by the open window* MRS. CROMWELL, *his mother, is reading. She is eighty years of age.*]

MRS. CROMWELL. Oliver troubles me, persuading everywhere. Restless like this.

ELIZABETH. He says that the time is uneasy, and that we are part of it.

MRS. CROMWELL. There's a man's house. It's enough surely.

ELIZABETH. I know. But Oliver must be doing. You know how when he took the magistracy he would listen to none of us. He knows best.

MRS. CROMWELL. What time is John coming?

ELIZABETH. By nightfall he said. Henry Ireton is coming with him.

MRS. CROMWELL. John Hampden is like that, too. He excites the boy.

ELIZABETH. Yes, but mother, you will do nothing with Oliver by thinking of him as a boy.

MRS. CROMWELL. Of course he's a boy.

ELIZABETH. He's forty.

MRS. CROMWELL. Methuselah.

ELIZABETH. What?

MRS. CROMWELL. I said Methuselah.

ELIZABETH. He says John's the bravest man in England.

MRS. CROMWELL. Just because he won't pay a tax. How if everybody refused to pay taxes? If you don't have taxes, I don't see how you are to have a government. Though I can't see that it governs anybody, except those that don't need it.

ELIZABETH. Oliver says it's a wrong tax, this ship money.

MRS. CROMWELL. There's always something wrong. It keeps men busy, I suppose.

ELIZABETH. But it was brave of John.

MRS. CROMWELL. I know, I know. But why must he come here to-night of all in the year? Oliver's like somebody out of the Bible about to-morrow as it is. This will make him worse. I wish John no harm, but — well, I hope he's got a bad horse.

ELIZABETH. Oliver's mind is made up about the common, whatever happens. John will make no difference.

MRS. CROMWELL. You can't pretend he'll make him more temperate.

ELIZABETH. It's very wrong to take away the common from the people. I think Oliver is right.

MRS. CROMWELL. Of course he's right. But I'm too old. I've seen too many broken heads. He'll be no righter for a broken head.

[BRIDGET CROMWELL, *a girl, comes in. She takes some eggs from her apron and puts them on a dish on a shelf.*]

BRIDGET. Why, grandmother, whose head is to be broken?

MRS. CROMWELL. Your father's is like to be.

BRIDGET. You mean to-morrow?

ELIZABETH. At the meeting, yes.

BRIDGET. But he must do it. Why, the people have fished and kept cattle there longer than any one can remember. Who is an Earl of Bedford to take it away from them? I know I would let my head be broken first.

ELIZABETH. It is said that the King gave leave.

i

BRIDGET. Then the King gave what wasn't his to give.

MRS. CROMWELL. Now, child, don't you encourage your father, too. He's eager enough without that.

BRIDGET. But I must, grandmother. There's too much of this kind of interference everywhere. Father says that Cousin John Hampden says —

MRS. CROMWELL. And that's three of you in one house. And this young Mr. Ireton has ideas, too, I believe.

BRIDGET. Mr. Ireton is twenty-eight.

MRS. CROMWELL. That accounts for it.

BRIDGET. You don't think they just ought to be allowed to take the common away, do you, grandmother?

MRS. CROMWELL. It makes no matter what I think.

BRIDGET. Of course you don't. None of us do. We couldn't.

ELIZABETH. You mustn't tease your grandmother, Bridget.

MRS. CROMWELL. She's a very old lady, and can't speak for herself.

BRIDGET. I meant no ill manners, grandmother.

MRS. CROMWELL. Never mind your manners, child. But don't encourage your father. He doesn't need it. This house is all commotion as it is.

BRIDGET. I can't help it. There's so much going on everywhere. The King doesn't deal fairly by people, I'm sure. Men like father must say it.

ELIZABETH. Have you put the lavender in the rooms?

BRIDGET. No. I'll take it now.

[*She takes a tray from the window and goes out.*]

MRS. CROMWELL. I don't know what will happen. I sometimes think the world isn't worth quarrelling about at all. And yet I'm a silly old woman to talk like that. But Oliver is a brave fellow — and John, all of them. I want them to be brave in peace — that's the way you think at eighty. [*Reading.*] This Mr. Donne is a very good poet, but he's rather hard to understand. I suppose that is being eighty, too. Mr. Herrick is very simple. John Hampden sent me some copies from a friend who knows Mr. Herrick. I like them better than John does.

[*She takes up a manuscript book and reads:*]

Lord, Thou hast given me a cell
  Wherein to dwell;
A little house, whose humble roof
  Is waterproof;
Under the spars of which I lie
  Both soft and dry . . .

But Mr. Shakespeare was best of all, I do believe. A very civil gentleman, too. I spoke to him once — that was forty years ago, the year Oliver was born, I remember. He didn't hold with all this talk against kings.

ELIZABETH. There are kings and kings. Oliver finds no offence in kings — it's in a king.

MRS. CROMWELL. Well, it's all very dangerous, and I'm too old for it. Not but what Oliver's brain is better than mine. But we have to sit still and watch. However [*reading*] —

Lord, 'tis thy plenty-dropping hand
  That sows my land:
All this, and better, dost thou send
  Me for this end:
That I should render for my part
  A thankful heart,
Which, fired with incense, I resign
  As wholly Thine:
But the acceptance — that must be,
  O Lord, by Thee.

Mr. Herrick has chosen a nice name for his book. Hesperides. He has taste as well as understanding.

[*The sound of horsemen arriving is heard.*]

ELIZABETH. That will be John and Mr. Ireton.

[*She looks from the window, puts her work into a box, and goes out.*]

MRS. CROMWELL [*turning her pages*].

Ye have been fresh and green,
  Ye have been filled with flowers,
And ye the walks have been
  Where maids have spent their hours.

Like unthrifts, having spent
  Your stock, and needy grown,
You're left here to lament
  Your poor estates alone.

[ELIZABETH *comes back with* JOHN HAMPDEN, *aged forty-four, and* HENRY IRETON, *twenty-eight. They both shake hands with* MRS. CROMWELL.]

HAMPDEN. How do you do, ma'am?
MRS. CROMWELL. Well, John.
IRETON. Good-evening, ma'am.
MRS. CROMWELL. You're welcome, Master Ireton, I'm sure. If you behave yourself, young man.
IRETON. How may that be, ma'am?
MRS. CROMWELL. No, don't ask me. Only don't you and John come putting more notions into Oliver's head. I'm sure he's got more than he can rightly manage as it is.
HAMPDEN. We were told down there that it's to-morrow that my Lord of Bedford and his like are to claim the common rights.
ELIZABETH. Yes.
IRETON. Mr. Cromwell is to resist, they said.
MRS. CROMWELL. Now, young man, Oliver doesn't need any urging to it. He needs holding back.
HAMPDEN. But that's fine for Oliver. Every man must speak to-day — and do as well, if it comes to it.
MRS. CROMWELL. Yes, but don't be so proud about it, John.
ELIZABETH. I think they should be proud.
MRS. CROMWELL. Remember what Mr. Herbert says —

> A servant with this clause
> Makes drudgerie divine.
> Who sweeps a room, as for thy laws,
> Makes that and th' action fine.

As for thy laws, remember.
HAMPDEN. Surely, we shall remember that always.

[BRIDGET *comes in*.]

BRIDGET. Cousin John.
HAMPDEN. Well, Bridget, my girl.
[*He kisses her.*]
BRIDGET. How do you do, Mr. Ireton?
IRETON [*shaking hands*]. Well, I thank you, mistress.
BRIDGET. Does father know, mother?
ELIZABETH. I've sent down to the field.
MRS. CROMWELL. He'll be here soon enough. I'm sorry the judges were against you, John. I don't know what else you could expect, though. They are the King's judges, I suppose.
HAMPDEN. That's what we dispute, ma'am. The King says that they should serve him. We say that they should serve the laws.
IRETON. It was just when Mr. Hampden was being heard. The law they said was the King's old and loyal servant: that *lex* was not *rex*, but that none could gainsay that *rex* was *lex*.
HAMPDEN. That's what we shall have to decide, and before long, I think.
BRIDGET. Father says that.
MRS. CROMWELL. This house is ready for any kind of revolution, John.
IRETON. But you find it everywhere, ma'am. All along the countryside, in the markets, in the church porches — everywhere.
ELIZABETH. Is the vine doing well this year, John?
HAMPDEN. It's the best year I remember.
ELIZABETH. Ours, too.
BRIDGET. Were you there, Mr. Ireton, when Cousin John's case was tried?
IRETON. Yes.
BRIDGET. It was splendid, wasn't it — although he lost, I mean?
IRETON. It was the note of deliverance.
BRIDGET. I wish I could have been there, Cousin John.
MRS. CROMWELL. Will you give me my shawl, Henry Ireton. [*He does so.*] There's Oliver coming. Now you can all be thunder.
BRIDGET. Now, grandmother, you know you don't think it's just that.
MRS. CROMWELL. So you have hope for me yet, miss?
BRIDGET. Grandmother.

[CROMWELL *comes in. He is in plain country dress. His age is forty.*]

CROMWELL. John — it's good to see you. You're an hour before reckoning.
[*Taking* HAMPDEN'S *hand.*]
HAMPDEN. Yes, Oliver. Is all well?

CROMWELL. Not that — but our courage is well enough. You are very welcome, Henry. [*Taking his hand.*] Was it good travelling.?

IRETON. Not a bad mile on the journey.

BRIDGET. Father, Mr. Ireton heard Cousin John's case tried. Wasn't he lucky?

CROMWELL. Whoever heard that heard history being made, John. It was a great example to set.

HAMPDEN. One works from the spirit, Oliver.

CROMWELL. That's what we must do. You've heard about this affair down here?

HAMPDEN. The common? Yes.

CROMWELL. There's to be no yielding about that.

HAMPDEN. I'm glad of it, Oliver.

MRS. CROMWELL. What will it all come to, John?

CROMWELL. There are times, mother, when we may not count the cost.

MRS. CROMWELL. You're very vexatious sometimes, Oliver.

CROMWELL. But you know I'm right in this, mother.

MRS. CROMWELL. Being right doesn't make you less vexatious.

ELIZABETH. Have they finished in Long Close?

CROMWELL. Yes. They will be here soon.

BRIDGET. They all come up from the field for prayers, Mr. Ireton, at the day's end.

HAMPDEN. Is your hay good, Oliver?

CROMWELL. I haven't much down this year. What there is, is good.

HAMPDEN. We got the floods too late. But it has mended well enough.

BRIDGET. The dancers came for some money, father.

ELIZABETH. Shall I give them something?

CROMWELL. To be sure.

ELIZABETH. How much?

CROMWELL. Oh — a crown or two.

HAMPDEN. Dancers?

CROMWELL. Aye, John. Don't you hold with them?

HAMPDEN. They're no offence, perhaps — but I'm never quite sure.

CROMWELL. Oh, but be sure, John. We must make no mistake about that. They are lovely, the dancers. I'm all for singing and dancing. The Lord is one to sing and dance, I'll be bound.

MRS. CROMWELL. Now you talk sense, Oliver. Mr. Herrick is very clear about that. So was David.

IRETON. Who is Mr. Herrick, ma'am?

MRS. CROMWELL. He's a poet, young man. And he's for being quiet, and not bustling about everywhere. You ought to read him.

IRETON. Do you know Mr. Herrick's work, Mr. Hampden?

HAMPDEN. I've nothing to say against that, though it's not very serious.

MRS. CROMWELL. Don't be silly, Mr. Hampden — if you excuse me for saying so. Mr. Herrick is very serious indeed, only he isn't always telling us of it.

HAMPDEN. Yes: perhaps you're right, ma'am. I prefer George Herbert.

BRIDGET. Yes, I like his book, too, Cousin John.

MRS. CROMWELL. Well, it's no bad judgment to stand for Mr. Herbert. Only I won't have nonsense talked about Mr. Herrick.

ELIZABETH. Are you ready, Oliver? They are coming.

OLIVER. Yes. [*To* HAMPDEN *and* IRETON.] Friends, you are welcome to this house.

[*The labourers from the farm are gathering outside the window. The people in the room form towards them.*]

CROMWELL. Brethren in God, at the end of another day's labour we are met to praise Him from whom are the means to labour and its rewards. As we go about these fields, He is with us. As you deal by me, and I by you, His eye sees us. Nothing good befalls us but it is by His will, no affliction is ours but His loving mercy will hear us. The Lord God walks at our hand. He is here now in our midst. His desires are our freedom, His wrath our tyranny one over another. Be very merciful in all your ways, for mercy is His name. May His counsel be always with our little fellowship. If I should fail towards any man, let him speak. May we be as brothers always, one to another. And may we serve Him to serve whom alone is wisdom. In Jesus Christ's name, Amen. "All people that on earth do dwell." [*They sing:*]

> All people that on earth do dwell,
> Sing to the Lord, with cheerful voice;
> Him serve with fear, his praise forth tell,
> Come ye before Him and rejoice.
>
> The Lord, we know, is God indeed.
> Without our aid He did us make;
> We are his folk, He doth us feed,
> And for his sheep He doth us take.
>
> O enter then his gate with praise,
> Approach with joy his courts unto;
> Praise, laud, and bless his name always,
> For it is seemly so to do.

[*As the men move away, one of them,* SETH TANNER, *comes forward.*]

SETH. As I came up from Long Close I stopped at the ale-house. Two fellows were there from the Earl of Bedford. Talking they were.

CROMWELL. What had they to say?

SETH. It seems they know you are going to stand out for the people to-morrow.

CROMWELL. Well?

SETH. Treason, they call it.

CROMWELL. Treason.

SETH. Seeing that my Lord of Bedford has the King's authority, as it were.

CROMWELL. Thank you, Seth.

SETH. They were coming here, they said. To warn you, and persuade you against it, if it might be.

CROMWELL. Thank you, Seth.

SETH [*to* HAMPDEN]. If I might be so bold, sir?

HAMPDEN. What, my friend?

SETH. That was a brave thing to do, sir, that about the ship money. We common folk know what it means. I'm sure we thank you with all our hearts.

HAMPDEN. I don't know about brave, but I know it is good to be thanked like that.

SETH. Yes, sir. That's all. Good-even, sir; good-even, mistress.

[*He is moving away as two of* BEDFORD'S *agents appear at the window, followed by the other labourers, who have returned with them.*]

FIRST AGENT. Is this Mr. Oliver Cromwell's?

CROMWELL. It is.

MRS. CROMWELL. The door is along there, to the right.

CROMWELL. It's no matter, mother. What do you want?

FIRST AGENT. To see Mr. Cromwell.

CROMWELL. You are speaking to him.

SECOND AGENT. May we come in?

CROMWELL. Why, yes.

[*They do so. The labourers gather round the window again. They follow the coming argument with close personal concern.*]

SECOND AGENT. May we speak with you alone?

CROMWELL. These are all my friends. I have nothing to say that I would not have them hear.

FIRST AGENT. It is discretion for your sake.

CROMWELL. I do not desire your interest. What have you to say?

SECOND AGENT. It is said that you will oppose the proclamation to-morrow.

CROMWELL. Assuredly.

SECOND AGENT. The Earl of Bedford and those with him have not drained these commons for nothing.

CROMWELL. Well?

SECOND AGENT. They have earned the rights to be proclaimed to-morrow.

CROMWELL. By whose will?

FIRST AGENT. By the King's.

CROMWELL. These rights of pasture belong to the people. It is within no man's powers to take them away.

SECOND AGENT. The King decrees it.

CROMWELL. I know not how that may be. I know that these rights are the people's, above any earl or king whatsoever. The King is to defend our rights, not to destroy them.

FIRST AGENT. This is plain treason.

CROMWELL. It is plain sense.

SECOND AGENT. What will you do?

CROMWELL. To-morrow you will proclaim these rights from the people to my

Lord of Bedford. To-morrow I shall tell the people that I alone, if needs be, will oppose it. I will fight it from court to court. I will make these rights my rights — as they are. These people of Ely shall speak through me. They shall pay me a groat a year for each head of cattle they graze, and they shall enjoy every foot of the land as long as I have a word or a pound left for resistance.

SECOND AGENT. You are very arrogant, Mr. Cromwell. There are lessons to be learnt.

CROMWELL. Aye, there are lessons. I do not speak to you, but to your master — to the King himself if it comes to that. You may tell him all that I have said. We folk of Ely will use our own commons, and let the Earl of Bedford keep within his own palings. There are lessons, say you. This is Mr. John Hampden. Will you speak to him of lessons? Mr. Hampden's ship money will be a King's lesson, I tell you.

HAMPDEN. You should tell your masters all that you see and hear. Do not flatter them. Let it be the truth. Say that men talk everywhere, more and more openly. Tell them that you heard John Hampden say that the King's Star Chamber was an abomination, that the King soiled his majesty in treating Mr. Prynne and Mr. Bastwick so. Say that you and your like are reviled by all honest men.

IRETON. And you can say that it is no fear of earls or kings that spared you the whipping you would deserve if you were better than shadows.

BRIDGET. Well said, Mr. Ireton.

[*There is a demonstration of anger from the labourers, but* CROMWELL *checks it.*]

MRS. CROMWELL. Now, Henry Ireton, these gentlemen may be bears, but I won't have you make this room into a bear-pit.

CROMWELL. No, friends, these men say but what they are sent to say. [*To the agents.*] I should not speak to you but in the hope that you will report it to those that should know. I am a plain burgess of this city. I farm a few lands and am known to none. But I have a faith that the people of this country are born to be, under God, a free people. That is the fundamental principle of this English life. If your masters, be they who they may, forget that, then, as you say, there will be lessons to be learnt. Here in Ely it is my part to see that my fellows do not lose their birthright. You shall not find us ignorant nor afraid. I would have no violence; let all be by persuasion and tolerance. But these just liberties must not be touched. Will you ask my Lord of Bedford to reconsider this?

SECOND AGENT. His Lordship will reconsider nothing. The proclamation is to-morrow.

CROMWELL. I have no more to say.

FIRST AGENT. Be you wary, Mr. Cromwell. These arrogances have their penalties. The King's anger is not light.

CROMWELL. You threaten idly. My word is one spoken throughout the land. You can say so.

SECOND AGENT. Mr. Cromwell, we do not —

CROMWELL. My mind is fixed. I think I have made my intention clear. That is all. You may go.

[*There is again a movement against them as they go, followed by the labourers.*]

CROMWELL. Seth.

SETH. Yes, sir.

CROMWELL. Ask your father to stay, will you? We shall want a song after that.

SETH. Yes, sir. [*He calls from the window.*] Father. Master wants you to sing.

[AMOS TANNER *comes back.*]

CROMWELL. Thank you, Amos. Just a minute, will you? When will supper be, wife?

ELIZABETH. In half an hour.

CROMWELL. How would a turn at bowling be, John?

HAMPDEN. Done.

CROMWELL. Henry, you, too?

IRETON. Yes; and, Mr. Cromwell —

CROMWELL. Yes.

IRETON. I don't know how things are going. But I feel that great events are making and that you and Mr. Hampden here may have power to use men. If it should be so, I would be used. That is all.

CROMWELL. John's the man. I'm likely enough to stay the rest of my days in Ely.

IRETON. I don't think so, sir.

CROMWELL. No? Well. A glass of sherry, John — or gin?

HAMPDEN. Sherry, Oliver.

[CROMWELL *pours out the sherry.*]

CROMWELL. Henry?

IRETON. Thank you.

CROMWELL [*giving glasses*]. Amos?

AMOS. I'd liefer have a pot of ale, master, if might be.

CROMWELL. Yes, yes. Bridget, girl.

[BRIDGET *goes.*]

MRS. CROMWELL. Oliver, boy, you were quite right — all that you said to those men, I mean. I don't approve, mind you, but you were quite right.

CROMWELL. Thank you, mother. I knew you would think so.

ELIZABETH. I wonder what will come of it. You never know, once you begin like this.

CROMWELL. You never know, wife.

HAMPDEN. There are lessons to be learnt.

CROMWELL. That's what they said.

[BRIDGET *returns with a foaming pot of ale, which she gives to* AMOS.]

CROMWELL [*drinking*]. To freedom, John. That's good sherry. I respect not such ill reasoners as would keep all wine out of the country lest men should be drunk. Now, Amos. Come along, John, my touch was good last night. I shall beat you.

[*He goes out on to the lawn beyond the window, with* HAMPDEN *and* IRETON. *They are seen passing to and fro, playing bowls.*]

AMOS [*singing*]:

When I shall in the churchyard lie,
  Poor scholar though I be,
The wheat, the barley, and the rye
  Will better wear for me.

For truly have I ploughed and sown,
  And kept my acres clean;
And written on my churchyard stone
  This character be seen:

"His flocks, his barns, his gear he made
  His daily diligence,
Nor counted all his earnings paid
  In pockets full of pence."

[*As he finishes, the bowlers stand listening at the window.*]

THE SCENE CLOSES

SCENE II

The Commons of England in session at Saint Hepburn's Chapel, Westminster, on November 22, 1641. CROMWELL, HAMPDEN, IRETON *among those sitting. We see the east end of the Chapel, with the* SPEAKER. *It is past midnight, and the house is lighted with candles. A member is speaking.*

THE MEMBER. That the grievances set out in this Remonstrance now before you are just is clear. The matter has been debated by us these eight hours, and none has been able to deny the wrongs which are here set forth. It is not well with our state, and correction is needed. Mr. Ireton has very clearly shown us how this is. But we must be wary. The King is the King, a necessary part, as it must seem to us, of the government of this country. [*There are murmurs for and against this; assent in the majority.*] To pass this Remonstrance can be no other than to pass a vote of no confidence in that King. Consider this. Saying so much, how shall you deny to overthrow the crown if need be? And who among you is willing to bear that burden? [*The murmurs grow to conflicting cries.*] I beseech you let us not commit ourselves thus. Nor do not think I am weak in zeal. There are evil counsellors with the King, and they would destroy us. Our liberties must be looked to. But there should be moderation in this act. We should choose some other way. We must defend ourselves, but we must not challenge the King's authority so.

[*He sits down to a confusion of voices, and* HAMPDEN *rises.*]

HAMPDEN. My friend, I think, is deceived. This Remonstrance is not against the King. It is from the people of this country against a policy. We desire no judgment — all we ask is redress. If we assert ourselves as in this instrument, we but put the King in the way of just government. I think the King hardly knows the measure of his wrongs against us, and I say it who have suffered. [*A murmur of assent.*] To speak clearly as is here done will, I think, be to mend his mind towards us. This Remonstrance has been drawn with all care. Not only is its intent free of blame towards the King's majesty and person, but it can, I hope, be read by no fair-minded man in the way that my friend fears. If I thought that, I should consider more closely my support of it. But I have considered with all patience, and it seems to me good.

[*He sits, and again there is a rattle of argument.* CROMWELL *rises.*]

CROMWELL. Sir, this is a day when every man must speak the truth that is in him, or be silent in shame, and for ever. Mr. Hampden is my kinsman, as you know, one who has my best affection. His word has ever been a strength among us, and no man here but knows his valiance in the cause. His has been a long suffering, and his integrity but ripens. But I do not read this occasion as he does, nor, let me say, do I fear it as does our friend who spoke before. That gentleman pleads that this Remonstrance is a vote of want of confidence in the King, such as none of us would willingly pass. Mr. Hampden replies that it is no such vote. I say to you that it is such a vote, and that I would pass it with all my heart. Sir, this country, the spirit of man in this country, has suffered grievances too great to be borne. By whom are they laid upon us? I say it is by the King. Is a man's estate secure to himself? Does not the King pass upon it levies for his own designs? You know that it is so. Is there not ship money? Mr. Hampden can tell you. Is not that the King's affair? Is there not a Star Chamber? Ask Mr. Prynne and those others. These men disliked the King's church — a very dangerous church as it seems to me — and were bold to say so. And for that each was fined five thousand pounds, and had his ears cut off, and is now in prison for life. And does not the Star Chamber belong to the King? Who among you can deny it? And this land is bruised, I tell you, by such infamies. There is no sureness in a man for his purse or his body, or his conscience. The King, — not the head of the state, mark you, expressing the people's will in one authority, — but this man Charles Rex, may use all these as he will. I aim not to overthrow the monarchy. I know its use and fitness in the realm, as well as any. But this can endure no longer. The King is part of the state, but we have a King who has sought to put the state to his private use. The King should have his authority, but it is an authority subject to the laws of the people. This King denies it, and his judges flatter the heresy. You have but one question before you — there is in truth but one raised by this Remonstrance. Is England to be governed by the King or by elected representatives of the people? That is what we have now to decide, not for ourselves alone, but for our children in the generations to come. If the King will profit by a lesson, I with any man will be his loyal and loving subject. But at this moment a lesson must be given. Why else have you appointed my Lord of Essex from Parliament to take command of the armed forces of this country? Did you not fear that the King would use these also against you? You know you did. I say it again, this that is now to be put to you is a vote of want of confidence in the King. I would it were so more expressly.

[*He sits to an angry tumult.* HAMPDEN *rises, and after a time secures order.*]

HAMPDEN. Sir, this question could not be argued to an end if we sat here for a week. Already we have considered it more closely and longer, I think, than any that has ever been before this House. It is morning. Each man has spoken freely from his mind. I move that the question now be put.

THE SPEAKER. The question is, whether this question now be put.

[*There are cries of "Yea," and "No."*]

THE SPEAKER. I think the "Yeas" have it.
[*This is followed by silence in the House.*]
THE SPEAKER. Then the question now before the House is whether this Declaration shall pass.
[*Again there are cries of "Yea" and "No" strongly emphatic on both sides.*]
THE SPEAKER. I think the "Yeas" have it.
[*There are loud and repeated cries of "No."*]
THE SPEAKER. The House will divide. Tellers for the Yeas, Sir John Clotworthy, Mr. Arthur Goodwyn. Tellers for the Noes, Sir Frederick Cornwallis and Mr. Strangwayes. The Yeas to go forth.
[*The House divides, the Yeas, including* CROMWELL, HAMPDEN, *and* IRETON, *leaving the House, the Noes remaining seated. The tellers for the Noes, with their staffs, count their numbers in the House, while the tellers for the Yeas at the door count theirs as they reënter. The pent-up excitement grows as the Yeas resume their seats and the telling draws to a close. The tellers move up to the* SPEAKER *and give in their figures.*]
THE SPEAKER. The Noes, 148. The Yeas, 159. The Yeas have it by eleven.
[*The announcement is received with a loud turmoil of cheering, during which* IRETON *rises.*]
IRETON. Sir, I move that this measure, as passed by this House, be printed and distributed throughout the land.
[*The House breaks out into a wild disturbance. "Yea" shouting against "No," swords being drawn and members hustling each other. The* SPEAKER *and* HAMPDEN *at length pacify them.*]
HAMPDEN. I beg you remember what business you are on. These are grave times, for stout wills, but temperate blood. I beg you, gentlemen.
THE SPEAKER. The question is, whether this Declaration shall be printed and distributed. [*Cries of "Yea" and "No."*]

THE SPEAKER. I think the "Noes" have it.
[*Again there is tumult, during which the* SPEAKER *leaves his chair and the House, and the session breaks up, the members leaving in passionate discussion.* CROMWELL, HAMPDEN, *and* IRETON *stand talking.*]
CROMWELL [*to* HAMPDEN]. It is the beginning.
HAMPDEN. It may mean terror in this land.
CROMWELL. It may. But the country must be delivered. I had thought to live in peace among my Ely acres. I sought none of this. But we must serve. If this Remonstrance had been rejected, I would have sold all I have and have never seen England more. And I know there are many other honest men of this same resolution.
IRETON. The issue is set. We may have to spend all that we have.
CROMWELL. Our goods, our peace, our lives.
HAMPDEN. We must be diligent among the people.
CROMWELL. It is the Lord's will.
IRETON. I can speak for many in Nottinghamshire.
CROMWELL. They will be needed.
HAMPDEN. I can spend one thousand pounds on arms.
CROMWELL. Arms. Yes. If it must be. But God may spare us.
[*There is a sound of argument outside, and* BRIDGET CROMWELL, *persuading an officer of the House to let her enter, comes in with* AMOS TANNER. *They are both from a long journey.*]
BRIDGET [*greeting her father and the others*]. I went to your lodging and learnt that you were still here.
CROMWELL. But what is it, daughter?
BRIDGET. Amos here — we had to come.
CROMWELL. Well?
AMOS. My boy — there, I can't tell.
BRIDGET. Seth — you know he came to London last year.
CROMWELL. Yes.
BRIDGET. It seems he was in a tavern

here one evening, and they were talking about ship money. Seth said it was a bad thing, and he spoke of our Cousin Hampden.

AMOS. He remembered Mr. Hampden when he was at Ely, sir. He always took a great opinion of Mr. Hampden, Seth did.

BRIDGET. He said Cousin John was a great patriot because he wouldn't pay. The King's spies were there. Seth was taken. He got a message sent down to Amos. It was to be a Star Chamber matter.

AMOS. There wasn't a better lad in the shire, sir.

CROMWELL. What has been done?

BRIDGET. We don't know. I brought Amos up at once to find you. I wanted to come alone, but he wouldn't let me.

AMOS. I couldn't stay, sir. They'll not have hurt him surely?

BRIDGET. What will they do? Is it too late? Can't it be stopped?

CROMWELL. Bassett.

[*The officer comes.*]

BASSETT. Yes, sir.

CROMWELL. Have you heard any Star Chamber news these last days?

BASSETT. Nothing out of the way, sir. A few croppings and brandings.

CROMWELL. Any names?

BASSETT. Jollyboy was one. That's an anyhow name for a man, now, isn't it? Lupton there was, too. He was cropped, both ears — said a bishop was a man. That was blasphemous. And a fellow about ship money. That was savage. Tanner his name was.

AMOS. Yes — but not Seth — it wasn't Seth Tanner?

BASSETT. Tanner was all I heard.

AMOS. It wouldn't be Seth.

BRIDGET. What did they do to him?

BASSETT. It's not proper hearing for your sort. But they let him go.

CROMWELL. What was it? The girl has heart enough.

BASSETT. Both thumbs, both ears, the tongue, and a T on the forehead.

AMOS. It wasn't Seth, sir. It couldn't be Seth — not like that. He was the beauty of the four parishes.

BASSETT [*to* CROMWELL]. Was he something to do with you, sir?

CROMWELL. There is a boy, Seth Tanner, we have a care for.

BASSETT. Because I made bold to take him in. He was dazed, as it were — didn't seem to know where to go.

CROMWELL. It was a good man's doing. Where is he?

BASSETT. I live under the walls here, as you might say.

CROMWELL. Could we see him?

BASSETT. Nay — it's no place to take you to. But I'll fetch him if you will. He doesn't sleep.

CROMWELL. Do, then. [BASSETT *goes.*]

AMOS. It's not my Seth, is it, sir? Not his tongue — and a bloody T. They would know how he could sing, and he looked like Gabriel in the books.

HAMPDEN. Shall we go, Oliver?

CROMWELL. No. Let us all see it out.

BRIDGET. Father, it's horrible. They don't do things like that, do they?

AMOS. Dumb — and a bloody T — and the thumbs. It's some other poor lad.

[BASSETT *returns; with him a figure, the hands and ears bound up in rough thick bandages, and on his forehead a burning red T. He looks at them, with reason hardly awake.*]

AMOS [*going to him*]. Seth — Seth, boy.
　　[SETH *moves his lips, but makes no sound. They look at him in horror.*]

BRIDGET. Father — father.

CROMWELL. There — no — no. [*To* BASSETT.] Take him, good fellow. Care for him as you can. Get a surgeon for him. Here's money. No, no, old man.
　　[BASSETT *goes with* SETH.]

AMOS. A bloody T. And dumb. God blast the King!

CROMWELL. Take him to our lodging, daughter. Go with them, Ireton. I'll follow. [BRIDGET, AMOS, *and* IRETON *go.*]

CROMWELL. John, you are my best-beloved friend.

HAMPDEN. I praise myself in that more than in most.

CROMWELL. I call you to witness. That is a symbol. Before God, I will not rest until all that it stands for in this unhappy England is less than the dust. Amen.
HAMPDEN. Amen.
[*A linkman is heard calling in the street.* CROMWELL *and* HAMPDEN *go out.*]

THE SCENE CLOSES

SCENE III

CROMWELL'S *house at Ely. A year later, 1642. It is afternoon in winter.* MRS. CROMWELL *is sitting by the fire, reading. She looks a little more her eighty-odd years than she did in the first scene.*

[*After a few moments* BRIDGET *comes in. She is opening a letter.*]

BRIDGET. Father has written, grandmother. Shall I read it to you?
MRS. CROMWELL. Yes, child.
BRIDGET [*sits by the fire, and reads*].
My dear daughter —
I am lately arrived in London, from Edgehill in the county of Warwickshire, where for the first time our men met the King's army in set dispute. It was late on the Sabbath afternoon, so that, as we lay for the attack, the sound of church bells came to us from three or four places. The King had the better ground, also they exceeded us in numbers, both horse and foot, and in cannon. It is hard to say which way the battle went, the advantage at one time being here, at another there. Their horsemen behaved very well, being commanded by Prince Rupert, a soldier of great courage in the field. Your Cousin Hampden managed a regiment with much honour, and twice or thrice delivered our cause. We were engaged until night stayed us. Some four thousand were slain, their loss, I hear, being the greater. Of the sixty in my own troop, eighteen fell. We had commendation from the general, and indeed I think we did not fail in resolution. But this matter will not be accomplished save we build, as it were, again from the foundation. This is God's service, and all must be given. To which end I am now coming home, to call out all such men as have the love of England in their hearts, and fear God. I shall labour with them. It seems to me that I shall be called to great trust in this, and I will set such example as I can. Expect me as soon as you receive this, for indeed I leave London as soon almost as my letter. Your mother I saw here with her nephew. She loves you as I do. Henry Ireton comes with me — he served very stoutly at Edgehill, and hath a gunshot in the arm. None is like to serve these times better than he. Give my loving duty to your grandmother, which I shall at once deliver myself. God bless you.
Your affectionate Father.
MRS. CROMWELL. You are born into a great story, child. I am old.
BRIDGET. It's wonderful. To stand like that.
MRS. CROMWELL. Not wonder only, girl. There are griefs.
BRIDGET. They are wonderful, too, I think.
MRS. CROMWELL. Youth, you are dear. With an old woman, it's all reckoning. One sees the follies then of this man and that.
BRIDGET. It had to come, grandmother. The King was taking all.
MRS. CROMWELL. It had to come. Men were no wiser than that. To make this of the land! One Cain, as your father says.
BRIDGET. It's as though life were different, suddenly. Do you feel it, grandmother?
MRS. CROMWELL. I know. There are times when wrath comes, and beauty is forgotten. But it must be.
BRIDGET [*from the letter*]. "This is God's service, and all must be given."
MRS. CROMWELL. Yes. Even that.
BRIDGET. But you do think father is right?
MRS. CROMWELL. Yes, child. He could do no other. That's his tribute to necessity. We all pay it. He will pay it greatly. We may be sure of that. [*Horses are heard outside.*] Here they are.
[BRIDGET *goes out to meet* CROMWELL *and* IRETON, *with whom she re-*

turns in a moment. IRETON's *right arm is in a sling.* MRS. CROMWELL *has put her book aside, and is standing. She embraces* OLIVER.]

CROMWELL. Well, mother. Almost before our own tidings, eh?

MRS. CROMWELL. Bless you, son. How d'ye do, Henry Ireton? [*Shaking hands with him.*] Is it Colonel Ireton yet?

IRETON. No, ma'am.

CROMWELL. Soon, mother. He is marked.

BRIDGET. Is the arm —

IRETON. No, nothing.

CROMWELL. The mayor has not come yet?

BRIDGET. No. You expect him?

CROMWELL. Yes. We must work at once. [*A bell rings.*]

BRIDGET. That may be the mayor. I will bring him. [*She goes out.*]

CROMWELL. Elizabeth sends her devotion to you, mother.

MRS. CROMWELL. Thank her, truly. Well, boy, it has begun?

CROMWELL. We must dispute it to the end now.

MRS. CROMWELL. May England prosper by you.

CROMWELL. With God's help, amen.

[BRIDGET *returns with the* MAYOR *of Ely.*]

CROMWELL. Welcome, Mr. Mayor.

THE MAYOR. Your good-day, Captain Cromwell. [*To* MRS. CROMWELL.] Ma'am. [*To* IRETON.] Sir.

CROMWELL. Will you sit?

[*They all sit,* MRS. CROMWELL, BRIDGET, *and* IRETON *by the fire.* CROMWELL *and the* MAYOR *at the table.*]

THE MAYOR. At Edgehill in Warwickshire, I hear?

CROMWELL. Yes.

THE MAYOR. The issue was left uncertain, it is said?

CROMWELL. Of that battle, yes. But I think the issue was there decided, some few of us there learning what must now be done. Those few held firmly at Edgehill, keeping us as far from defeat as we were, though that was little enough. For our troops are most of them old decayed serving-men, and tapsters, and such kind of fellows; and their troops are gentlemen's sons, younger sons and persons of quality. Do you think that the spirits of such base, mean fellows will ever be able to encounter gentlemen, that have honour and courage and resolution in them? We must get men of a spirit that is likely to go on as far as gentlemen will go, or we shall be beaten still. We must raise such men as have the fear of God before them, such men as make some conscience of what they do. We must do this, Mr. Mayor. I never thought to use a sword, but now all must be given that it may be used well. I would have you send a summons to all the people of this town and countryside. Bid them meet two days hence in the market-place at noon. I will tell them of all these things. I will show them how the heart of England is threatened. We must give, we must be diligent in service, we must labour. An army is to be made — we must make it. We have no help but our own hands — by them alone we must save this country. Will you send out this summons?

THE MAYOR [*rising*]. It shall be done, this hour. My service to you.

[*He bows to all and goes.*]

CROMWELL. Nothing is to be spared; the cause must have all. We must be frugal, mother. Daughter, help as you can.

BRIDGET. I will, indeed, father.

MRS. CROMWELL. You commit yourself, boy, beyond turning back in all this.

CROMWELL. It must be so. The choice has been made, and is past.

MRS. CROMWELL. The Lord prosper you. But I am an old woman. Age can but have misgivings.

CROMWELL. We must have none, mother. We have gone to this in prayer, we must establish it in belief. Every yeoman, all the workers in the land, all courtesy and brave reason look to us. What men hereafter shall make of their lives must be between them and God in their own hearts. But to-day it must be given to them, the right to live as they most truly may in the light of their own proper character. No king may be against us. He may lead us, but he may not be against us. Have no misgivings, mother. Faith everywhere, that is our shield.

Mrs. Cromwell [rising]. I will be no hindrance, son.

Cromwell. You are my zeal. I grew to it in you.

Mrs. Cromwell. I must see.
[She goes out.]

Cromwell. How is Seth, Bridget?

Bridget. He mends daily. Amos tends him like a mother.

Cromwell. I must see them. Send to Mistress Hall and Robert. Let us have music this evening. Anthony, too. Let him bring his flute. There's good music here, Henry. [He goes.]

Bridget. Robert Hall sings beautifully.

Ireton. Will you sing, too?

Bridget. I expect so.

Ireton. I once tried to learn the flute. It was no good. I couldn't do it unless I watched my fingers.

Bridget. Was it very terrible at Edgehill?

Ireton. Yes.

Bridget. Were we really beaten?

Ireton. No. A few saved us from that.

Bridget. Were you one?

Ireton. Your father was chief among them.

Bridget. Was he?

Ireton. He will lead armies. Every man will follow him. He never faltered, and there was no misjudgment, ever.

Bridget. Did you keep the horses you had when you left London?

Ireton. Yes, both of us.

Bridget. I was glad to see you then.

Ireton. You know what is coming?

Bridget. Yes. I see it.

Ireton. We shall live with danger now. It may take years. Many of us will not see the end. We are no longer our own.

Bridget. These are the best crusades.

Ireton. To be called, thus. To be led by such a one. I know your father will direct it — he must be the man. He is only a captain to-night, but in a month or two you will see. And we shall be a mighty following. I see them forming, terrible hosts. We must give all, truly. I shall give all, I think. It is little enough. Bridget.

Bridget. Yes.

Ireton. You promised. I might speak again, you said.

Bridget. Yes.

Ireton. Will you wed a man so dedicated?

Bridget. The more for that. Yes, Henry.

Ireton [as they embrace]. May we tell your father now?

Bridget. Yes — if I can but help you to serve.

Ireton. You shape my service. In you shall all the figures of my service dwell. Will he take this kindly?

Bridget. Surely. He loves you, he has said it often. [Cromwell returns.]

Bridget. Father, Henry Ireton has to speak to you.

Cromwell. Eh?

Ireton. Yes, Mr. Cromwell.

Cromwell. Quite so. Mr. Cromwell. That's very interesting now, isn't it?

Ireton. By your leave I would marry Bridget.

Cromwell I dare say. You would be a very foolish young man else. And, what of Bridget's leave?

Bridget. He has that.

Cromwell. I should think so, too. Well?

Ireton. You consent?

Cromwell. I could do nothing more gladly. You have chosen well, both of you. I rejoice for you. But you must wait until this business we have in hand is gathered up a little.

Bridget. Yes, father. It is better so.

Cromwell. Let your mother know of the betrothal. I will write as well.

Bridget. To-night.

Cromwell. Seth asked to see you, Henry.

Ireton. Shall we go?

Bridget. Yes.
[Bridget and Ireton go.]

[Cromwell *lights a candle, gets paper and pen, and sits at the table writing. After a few moments* Mrs. Cromwell *comes in. She carries a large bunch of keys.* CROMWELL *looks up, and continues writing. She unlocks a large wooden chest, and takes some parchment deeds from it. Then she comes to* CROMWELL *at the table.*]

MRS. CROMWELL. Oliver.

CROMWELL. Yes, mother.

MRS. CROMWELL. These are my five Ely houses, and the Huntingdon farmlands. Use them.

CROMWELL. But it's all you have.

MRS. CROMWELL. My needs are few, and I have not many days.

CROMWELL [*rising*]. I will use them, mother, worthily, with God's help.

[*He kisses her.*]

MRS. CROMWELL. Bless you, my son. Bless you always. And may the mercy of God be upon England.

CROMWELL. Upon England — Amen.

[*He places the deeds on the table before him, and resumes his writing.* MRS. CROMWELL *closes the chest, and sits at a spinet, playing.*]

MRS. CROMWELL. Mr. Lawes makes beautiful music, Oliver.

OLIVER. Yes, mother.

[*She plays again for a few moments. Then* BRIDGET *and* IRETON *return.*]

BRIDGET. Amos and Seth want to speak to you, father. The men are coming.

CROMWELL. Yes. [*She beckons them in.*]

CROMWELL. Bridget has news for you, mother.

[BRIDGET *and* IRETON *go to* MRS. CROMWELL.]

AMOS. I meant to speak when you were down there, sir. But I'm a bit slow. There's two things, so to say.

CROMWELL. Yes, Amos.

AMOS. There's to be great wars and spending, I know.

CROMWELL. Yes, Amos.

AMOS. I should like to give the little I've saved. You'll spend it well, sir, I know. It's a matter of two pound. It's not a deal, but it might help by way of an example, as it might be.

[*He offers a small bag of money.*]

CROMWELL. In such measure it shall be taken from all who will give. That is true in spirit, Amos. It shall be used.

[*He places it with the deeds.*]

AMOS. And then if I might speak for Seth.

CROMWELL. Yes, what is it?

AMOS. He's dumb, sir, it's true, but you'll find no better heart nor wits. And he has a fair lot of book-learning now as well, and has come to handle a pen for all his poor hands were treated so. He would be your servant, sir, in the wars.

OLIVER. It's a good offer. Very well, Seth, we'll serve together.

[SETH *acknowledges this, gravely pleased. There are voices outside.*]

BRIDGET. They are coming, father. Are you ready?

CROMWELL. Yes.

[BRIDGET *opens the door on to the stone hall, and the labourers stand at the door and beyond.*]

CROMWELL [*rising*]. My friends, I know not to what labour you will next be called, but we are upon dark and proving days, coming to memorable issues. The tyranny that has worked among us so grievously and long now strikes at our all. We must betake ourselves to defence, or this will be but a rotten realm, fair for no man to live in henceforth. Do not be mistaken. In the way of life out of which has come this menacing destruction upon us is much of beauty, much of nobility, and the light of man's mind. These things it will be for us in season to cherish and preserve. But where these have been is no warrant for authority abused. And authority this day is an abuse against us to the very pitch of wickedness. We are called to stand for the charter of all men's faith, for the charter which is liberty, which is God. Against us are arrayed the ranks of privilege. They are mighty, well used in arms, fearless, and not easily to be turned aside. But we go to battle in the name of God. Let every man consider it. Each one of you is here and now called to service in that name, that hereafter in England a man may call his hearth his own. And now may the love of God inform you. In humble courage let us

go forward, nourishing our strength, sure always in our cause. May God bless us, and teach us the true valiance, and may He spend us according to His will. Amen. The Lord is my Shepherd; I shall not want.
[*Together they sing,* AMOS *leading them.*]
The Lord is my shepherd; I shall not want. He maketh me to lie down in green pastures; he leadeth me beside the still waters.
He restoreth my soul; he leadeth me in the paths of righeousness for his name's sake.
Yea, though I walk through the valley of the shadow of death, I will fear no evil; for thou art with me . . .

THE SCENE CLOSES

SCENE IV

After dawn on July 14, 1645, the day of Naseby.

[GENERAL FAIRFAX, *with* IRETON — *now colonel* — *and two other officers, is holding a council of war in his tent. He is working with a map. During the proceedings sentries pass to and fro.*]

FAIRFAX. Between Mill Hill, and Sulby Hall, there. Broad Moor — yes. You measure their numbers at ten thousand, Staines?

STAINES. Not more than ten, nor less than eight.

FAIRFAX. Four thousand or so of them horse?

STAINES. It is thought so.

FAIRFAX. Yes, yes. We are eleven thousand, eh, Pemberton?

PEMBERTON. Eleven thousand and perhaps three hundred.

FAIRFAX. Naseby will be three quarters — no, half a mile behind us.

IRETON. The right of the field is boggy, and pitted by rabbits. The action is like to move to the left.

FAIRFAX. Yes. There's a high hedge above there below Sulby. It would be useful to us then.

STAINES. It has been marked, and dug almost to the waterside.

FAIRFAX. Good. Skippon and myself with the infantry there and there. Then the cavalry — you have one wing, Ireton, or you must command all, since General Cromwell is not come.

PEMBERTON. Is there any word of him?

FAIRFAX. None.

STAINES. They do not consider us at Westminster.

IRETON. It is disastrous of them to hesitate so. They do not understand.

FAIRFAX. No. I have told them that to-day is to be made the fiercest trial of all, but they do not listen.

PEMBERTON. Where is General Cromwell?

FAIRFAX. None knows. These months he has been up and down the land, exhorting, stirring up opinion, watching the discipline of our new armies, lending his personal authority in bringing men's minds to the cause. But to-day we need him here. He should have been sent. We need him.

IRETON. Urgently. Charles and Rupert are staking all on this.

STAINES. They were never in better tune. It is as though every man were picked.

FAIRFAX. I said this to Westminster.

IRETON. We carry too many callow soldiers against them. Example will be everything. General Cromwell and his chosen troops have that, and experience; none like them.

PEMBERTON. Does the General himself know of our necessity, do you think, sir?

FAIRFAX. There is no tracing him. He almost certainly does not know, or he would have insisted. There are rumours of him from the eastern counties, of some activities with his men, but no more.

IRETON. And the hope of England here in grave peril. Westminster is disgraceful.

STAINES. Your appeal was plain, sir — weighty enough?

FAIRFAX [*taking a paper from the table*]. You may hear for yourself. [*Reading the end of a letter copy.*] "The general esteem and affection which he hath with the officers and soldiers of this whole army, his own personal worth and ability for employment, his great care, diligence, courage, and faithfulness in the services you have already employed him in, with the constant presence and blessing of God that have accompanied him, make us look upon it as the duty we owe to you and the public, to make it our suit."

PEMBERTON. It is shameful of them.

IRETON. It is. But that hope is gone. Do I take the left, sir?

FAIRFAX. You must choose. The horse entirely are your command now.

IRETON. Whalley on the right, and you, Pemberton.

FAIRFAX. What's the hour?

STAINES. Six o'clock, sir.

FAIRFAX. They have had three hours. Let the army sleep till ten if it may be.

STAINES. Yes, sir.

IRETON. Are you satisfied about those footmen on the left, sir?

FAIRFAX. No, not satisfied. But we cannot better it.

PEMBERTON. Rupert is almost certain to see the weakness there.

FAIRFAX. Yes, but there it is. Skippon must cover it as he can. We have spoken of it very exactly.

IRETON. If either wing of our horse breaks, it means certain disaster there, even though Skippon could hold in the centre.

FAIRFAX. That's Cromwell again. And all to satisfy the pride of a few useless members that his self-denying ordinance keeps out of command.

STAINES. Do you think it's that, sir?

FAIRFAX. What else? They are more jealous that he should come to no more honour than that we should succeed. And after all that has been given.

IRETON. The blood.

PEMBERTON. It is abominable.

FAIRFAX. But there — we must not distress ourselves. We have our own loyalty. Keep in touch with Skippon, Staines. If you can push their right foot up towards Sibbertoft there, spare nothing in the doing. Have you all slept, gentlemen?

IRETON AND THE OTHERS. Yes, sir.

FAIRFAX. Since we lack General Cromwell, more depends on you, Ireton, than on any man, perhaps. You will not be wanting, I know.

IRETON. In endeavour at least — and we can die.

[*A scout comes in.*]

FAIRFAX. Yes?

THE SCOUT. Something moves across from the east, sir. It is very faint. It may be haze, or it may be dust.

FAIRFAX. Watch. Come again at once.

[*The scout goes.* FAIRFAX *and the others go to the tent opening, and look out.*]

FAIRFAX. Yes — there. It is moving, isn't it?

IRETON. I think not.

STAINES. Surely.

PEMBERTON. Could it be?

FAIRFAX. No. We should have heard.

IRETON. And yet it seems to be moving.

FAIRFAX. Gentlemen, we must keep counsel with ourselves. This is to waste. Nerves must be unclouded to-day.

[*He returns to his seat, the others with him.*]

FAIRFAX. Finally, if we on the right have to fall back on Mill Hill, bring your horse down on to the Kilmarsh Road Pemberton, if it be any way possible.

PEMBERTON. Yes — there's a ford there, at the fork if we are upstream.

IRETON. I'll speak to Whalley, too.

FAIRFAX. If at last there should be a general retreat, it is to the west of Naseby, remember.

IRETON. Yes. To the west. That there should be that even in the mind!

FAIRFAX. In that case, the baggage is my concern.

[*Outside is heard a low murmur of excitement.*]

FAIRFAX. Staines, will you tell Conway that five hundred of his best men must dispute the Naseby road to the east. And let Mitchell command under him.

STAINES. Yes, sir.

[*The noise outside grows.*]

PEMBERTON. What is it?

FAIRFAX. See.

[PEMBERTON *goes to the tent opening and looks out.*]

PEMBERTON. Our men are watching

something. It is something moving. Horsemen — it must be.

[*The excitement grows and grows.* IRETON *joins* PEMBERTON.]

IRETON. There is something.

FAIRFAX. Gentlemen, let us promise ourselves nothing.

[IRETON *and* PEMBERTON *move into the tent at* FAIRFAX'S *word. As they do so the voices outside break out into a great shout —* "*Ironsides — Ironsides — Ironsides is coming to lead us!*" *The scout comes in, glowing.*]

FAIRFAX [*rising.*] Yes?

THE SCOUT. General Cromwell is riding into the field with his Ironsides, sir, some six hundred strong.

FAIRFAX. Thank God!

[CROMWELL *comes into the tent, fully armed, hot and dusty from the road. The shouting dies away, but outside there is a sound as of new life until the end of the scene.* SETH, OLIVER'S *servant, stands at the tent opening.*]

FAIRFAX. You are welcome; none can say how much.

CROMWELL. A near thing, sir. I only heard from Westminster yesterday at noon.

FAIRFAX. They told us nothing.

CROMWELL. There are many poor creatures at Westminster, sir. Many of them, I doubt not, would have willingly had me kept uninformed of this. But we are in time, and that's all. Henry. Good-morning, gentlemen. How goes it?

FAIRFAX [*taking his seat,* CROMWELL *and the others also at the table*]. The battle is set. Our foot there, Skippon and myself. Colonel Ireton and Whalley are with the horse. They are at your service.

CROMWELL [*at the map*]. Rupert will be there. Langdale, if I mistake not, will be there. That road — is it good?

PEMBERTON. Poor below Mill Hill, sir.

CROMWELL. Then that is the point; it may be decisive there. You take the left, Henry.

IRETON. Yes, sir.

CROMWELL. Let Whalley be on my left here — give him fifteen hundred. I have six hundred. I'll take the right with them myself. Are you on the left, sir?

FAIRFAX. Yes, and the second line.

CROMWELL. Good — can I have two of the best regiments down here behind me?

FAIRFAX. Yes. Staines, let Spilsby see to that.

CROMWELL. Spilsby is good.

STAINES. If I might say it, would you choose him for that, sir? It is a great responsibility, and he has been indiscreet. I thought not to use him to-day.

CROMWELL. Indiscreet?

STAINES. In his utterances, sir. His belief is in some question.

CROMWELL. Surely you are not well advised to turn off one so faithful to the cause, and so able to serve you as this man is. He is indiscreet, you say. It may be so in some things; we all have human infirmities. Sir, the state, in choosing men to serve it, takes no notice of their opinions. If men be willing faithfully to serve it, that satisfies. Let it be Spilsby.

STAINES. Yes, sir.

CROMWELL. Is the army well rested, sir?

FAIRFAX. They are resting now. Till ten o'clock. We moved up at three.

CROMWELL. Three hours for my men. It is enough. The order to advance at eleven?

FAIRFAX. At eleven.

CROMWELL. Is the word for the day chosen?

FAIRFAX. Not yet.

CROMWELL. Let it be, "God our strength." Gentlemen.

[*They all rise, and, bareheaded, together they repeat,* "*God our strength.*"]

THE SCENE CLOSES

SCENE V

The same tent. Night — with torches and candles. An aide stands at the tent opening. The sentries pass to and fro. It is after the action. IRETON, *severely wounded, is on a couch, surgeons attending him.* CROMWELL, *himself battered and with a slight head wound, stands by the couch.*

CROMWELL. It is not mortal. You are sure of that?

THE SURGEON. He is hurt, grievously, but he will live now.

CROMWELL. The danger is gone?

THE SURGEON. Yes. But it will be slow.

IRETON. Whalley — there — in God's name, man. Tell Spilsby to beat down under General Cromwell. There's not a minute to lose. Whalley — that's good — come — no man — left — left — now, once more. God is our strength.

CROMWELL. There, my son. Brave, brave. It is well.

IRETON [*himself*]. How is it — out there?

CROMWELL. They are scattered.

IRETON. Scattered. Write to Bridget.

CROMWELL. Yes — it is done.

IRETON. Read.

CROMWELL [*reading a letter from the table*].

My dearest daughter —

This in all haste. We have fought to-day at Naseby. The field at all points is ours. They are destroyed beyond mending. Henry is hurt, but he is well attended, and the surgeons have no fear. He shall be brought to you by the first means. He has great honour to-day for himself and for us all.

IRETON. He loves you.

[CROMWELL *adds a word to the letter. Then he leaves* IRETON *to the surgeons and speaks to* SETH, *who is at the table.*]

CROMWELL.. Seth, will you write, please.

[*He dictates very quietly, not to disturb* IRETON.]

To the Speaker of the Commons of England, at Westminster.

Sir — This, of which the General advises you, is none other but the hand of God, and to Him alone belongs the glory, wherein none are to share with him. The General served you with all faithfulness and honour; and the best commendation I can give him is, that I dare say he attributes all to God, and would rather perish than assume to himself. Which is an honest and a thriving way; and yet as much for bravery may be given to him, in this action, as to a man. Honest men served you faithfully in this action. Sir, they are trusty; I beseech you, in the name of God, not to discourage them. I wish this action may beget thankfulness and humility in all that are concerned in it. He that ventures his life for the liberty of his country, I wis he trust God for the liberty of his conscience, and you for the liberty he fights for. In this he rests, who is your most humble servant. . . .

From the camp at Naseby field, in Northamptonshire.

[*He signs the letter. Outside in the night the Puritan troops are heard singing the One Hundred and Seventeenth Psalm:* "O praise the Lord, all ye nations: praise him, all ye people. For his merciful kindness is great toward us: and the truth of the Lord endureth for ever. Praise ye the Lord." *They listen:* IRETON *sleeps.*]

CROMWELL. They sing well. [*He looks at a map; then, to the aide.*] Go to General Peyton. Tell him to keep three troops of horse four miles down the Leicester road there. He is not to move them till daybreak. And ask Colonel Reade to let me have his figures as soon as he can.

THE AIDE. Yes, sir. [*He goes.*]

CROMWELL. Finish that other letter, will you? [SETH *writes again.*] I can say this of Naseby. When I saw the enemy draw up and march in gallant order towards us, and we, a company of poor ignorant men to seek how to order our battle, — the General having commanded me to order all the horse, — I could not, riding along about my business, but smile out to God in my praises, in assurance of victory [*the Psalm is heard again*], because God would, by things that are not, bring to naught the things that are. Of which I had great assurance, and God did it.

[*The singing still heard.*]

THE SCENE CLOSES

SCENE VI

An evening in November, 1647. A room in Hampton Court, where CHARLES THE FIRST, *now a prisoner with the army, is lodged.*

[*At a table, writing, is* NEAL, *the King's secretary. He finishes his document, and, going to a bureau, locks it away. He returns to the table, and, taking up an unopened envelope, examines it carefully. As he is doing so* CHARLES *enters from an inner room.*]

CHARLES. From Hamilton?
NEAL. Yes, sire.
CHARLES. Has it been opened?
NEAL. I think not.
[CHARLES *takes the letter, opens and reads it.*]
CHARLES. Good. The commissioners from Scotland are in London. They are prepared to hear from us.
NEAL. Andrews goes to London to-night. He is to be trusted.
CHARLES. Everything begins to move for us again. To-morrow they will miss us here, eh, Neal? In a week we should be at Carisbrooke.
NEAL. Do not be too confident, sire. Things have miscarried before.
CHARLES. But not this time, Neal, believe me. Their House and their army are at odds. I've seen to that. It has gained time, and perplexed their resolution. And now Scotland will strike again, and this time mortally. Yes, the end will be with us, mark me.
NEAL. May Your Majesty reckon truly.
CHARLES. Is Cromwell coming to-night?
NEAL. He said not.
CHARLES. Strangely, the fellow grows on me. But he's a fool, Neal. Brave, but a fool. He sees nothing. Indeed, he's too dull. Ireton too — they are heavy stuff. Clods. Poor country. She needs us again truly. To check such mummers as these — all means are virtuous for that, Neal, eh?
NEAL. Your Majesty knows.

CHARLES. Yes, we need no counsel. You are sure that Cromwell was not coming to-night.
NEAL. That was as he said, sire.
CHARLES. Then let us consider. These Scots. What was it? Did you set it down?
NEAL. Yes, sire.
[*He gets the paper that he put in the bureau, and gives it to* CHARLES.]
CHARLES [*reading it*]. Yes. Write.
[NEAL *does so on a large folio sheet.*]
Clause 1. For the reason that the Scots should invade England. Let the intrigues of Parliament with the army and its leaders — notably Oliver Cromwell — to the peril of the Church and the King, stand to the world in justification. Clause 2. The royal forces in England shall move when and as the Duke of Hamilton directs. Clause 3. The King shall guarantee Presbyterian control in England for three years from this date. But the King shall for himself be at liberty to use his own form of divine service. Clause 4. All opinion and practice of those who call themselves Independents are to be suppressed. To see that this is diligently done may be left to the King's pleasure.... Yes — once we are at Carisbrooke.... Copy that, Neal. I will sign it. Let it go by Andrews to-night.
NEAL. Yes, sire.
CHARLES. Do it now.
[NEAL *proceeds to do so.* CHARLES *moves across to a book-case between the table and the main door. As he stands there, there is a knock at the door.*]
CHARLES. Yes?

[*The door is opened by* CROMWELL, *with whom is* IRETON.]

CHARLES. Mr. Cromwell. We did not expect you.
CROMWELL. No, sir. It is unexpected.
[*As the two men come into the room,* CHARLES *covers* NEAL *from them as he can. The secretary has no time but to conceal his note by placing it under a case of folio papers on the table. As the others approach the*

table, he bows and retires. CHARLES *sits, and motions the others to do the same.* CROMWELL *takes* NEAL'S *place.*]

CROMWELL. We came, sir, to reassure ourselves.

CHARLES. As to what?

CROMWELL. Your Majesty knows that, in treating with you as we have done these months past, we have been subject to suspicions.

CHARLES. I imagined that it might be so. But your character and your reputation, Mr. Cromwell, can ignore these.

CROMWELL. It is suggested that we become courtiers, and susceptible as courtiers are. But that is nothing. Continually we are told that Your Majesty will outwit us.

CHARLES. But that is too fantastic. Between men so open one with another. Our scruples — persuasion — yes, these may take time. We may not always easily understand each other there. But that there should be any question of duplicity between us — it is monstrous. We may disagree, stubbornly, Mr. Cromwell, but we know each the other's thought.

CROMWELL. I believe it. You know nothing of these Scotch agents in London?

CHARLES. Scotch?

IRETON. They arrived yesterday.

CHARLES. Who are they?

CROMWELL. You do not know, sir?

CHARLES. I? Indeed, no.

CROMWELL. I did not suppose it. But already I am beset by warnings. I dismiss them, giving my word in this for your integrity, as it were.

CHARLES. Minds are strained in these days. It is shameless of them to say this.

IRETON. It means so much, you see, sir. Intrigues with Scotland — there are none, we are assured, but if there were it would almost inevitably bring civil war again. The mere shadow of that in men's minds is enough, indeed, to overthrow them. No man can consider the possibility of that without desolation.

CHARLES. No. That is unquestionable.

CROMWELL. And so I was minded to come, and be sure by word of mouth, so to speak. Your Majesty knows how suspicions creep in absence, even of those whom we trust. And I have shown, sir, that I trust you.

CHARLES. We are not insensitive.

IRETON. It is of that trust, truly worn, sir, that we may all yet look for a happy settlement.

CHARLES. It is my hope, devoutly.

CROMWELL. Parliament bends a little to my persuasion. If I could but induce Your Majesty to treat no longer directly with them, but to leave all to me.

CHARLES. It is our Parliament still. We cannot slight them.

CROMWELL. But, sir, you confuse things daily. If the army were no longer intact, it would be another matter. But now it is the army that must be satisfied — in the end there is the real authority. Remember, sir, that these men are not merely soldiers. They are the heart and the conscience of the nation in arms. By their arms they have prevailed, how bloodily Your Majesty knows. They stand now to see that the settlement is not against that conscience that armed them.

CHARLES. But we must consider ourselves. It would be folly to anger the House.

CROMWELL. The House can do nothing without us. And I have considered you, sir. I have persuaded the army that the monarchy is the aptest form of government for this country. It was difficult, but my belief has prevailed. I have even won respect for Your Majesty's person. Do but give us our guarantees, and you will mount a securer throne, I think, than any king has yet held in England.

CHARLES. But Parliament —

IRETON. No, sir. Parliament's demands are not our demands. To give them what they ask will be to lose all opinion in the army. That would be fatal.

CROMWELL. Parliament and the army are at one in asking for constitutional safeguards. All are agreed on that. But after that we are in dispute, irreconcileably. They want a Presbyterian despotism. This land, sir, has had enough of despotism, and we will not exchange one despotism for another. We, the army, demand liberty of opinion. We respect law, we stand, above all, for order and right behaviour, for an observance of the rights of others. But we demand that a man's thought shall be his own, that his faith shall be directed by none. We stand for Bible freedom. And we, sir, are strong enough to make Parliament accept that, but Parliament can never make us accept the tyranny of the Presbyters. We are the new Independents, sir, the Independents of the spirit. We are determined that henceforth in England no man shall suffer for his faith.

CHARLES. I respect these ambitions.

IRETON. Do but let us go to the army with that respect, and not a trooper but will renew your power for you.

CHARLES. A power a little cropped, eh, Mr. Ireton?

CROMWELL. No, sir, enlarged. You have ruled by interest and fear.' You can go back to rule by the affection of a free people. You have the qualities, sir — why waste them?

CHARLES. You persuade well. Honestly, I am sure.

CROMWELL. I could take all. I do not want it. I want to restore your fortune, to give you back a regenerate kingship. Will you take it, sir? It is of love I offer it, love of England, of your great office. And you should adorn that inheritance. Men should be proud to call you King, sir.

IRETON. We have that pride — and we have suffered.

CROMWELL. I can disabuse rumour about Scotland, I can persuade Parliament about the Presbytery, I can convince the army of your good faith as to tolerance, if you will but give me the word. Let us together make Charles Rex the noblest name of Christendom.

CHARLES. How shall I stand with the Episcopacy?

CROMWELL. All tyrannies must go together. We mislike no bishops save that they stand by a tyrannous church. That we will destroy. It is there as I have said. We attack not faiths or opinions, but despotism. Let a man think as he will, but he shall command no other man to think it.

IRETON. We will not persecute even our persecutors. But they shall stay their hands, now and for ever.

CROMWELL. This is just; merciful even. Will you work with us together, sir, to the salvation of our country?

CHARLES. You are very patient.

CROMWELL. To great ends. Why do you deliberate, sir? What invention is needed? All is so plain. And many wish you disaster. If you refuse this, it may be hard to deny them.

CHARLES. We do not fear disaster.

CROMWELL. But I offer you an ascendancy undreamt of. It should be plain.

CHARLES. You offer much, and it should prosper. Or I think so. But I must consider. One has old habits, not easily to be put by. One grows to kingship thus, or thus — the manner does not readily change. But I will consider it.

CROMWELL. Time presses.

CHARLES. Yes, but a day or two. Say three days.

CROMWELL. Three days, then, sir. I brought Your Majesty this. [*He takes a miniature from his pouch.*] It is newly drawn by Mr. Cooper. It is of a young man, Andrew Marvell, of whose verses Your Majesty would think well. He should do much. Cooper has drawn it well — it's very decisive in line, sir?

CHARLES. Yes. A little heavy there in the nostril, perhaps, but good. Yes, very.

CROMWELL. I am told that Van Dyck admires him.

CHARLES. I have heard him say so.

CROMWELL. It's generous of him — the methods are so different.

CHARLES. Van Dyck draws marvellously in sanguine. [*He takes a drawing from the drawer in front of him and places it before* CROMWELL, *on the case of papers.*] That approaches any of the masters, I think.

CROMWELL. Good — yes. And yet Hans Holbein was incomparable — not so assertive — no, copious, and yet as complete, simpler. But — yes, there is great dignity here.

[*He holds up the drawing in front of him, holding it against the folio case for firmness.* CHARLES *makes a movement, but instantly restrains himself.* CROMWELL *is about to replace the drawing and case on the table, when his glance falls on* NEAL'S *paper, which is lying in front of him. He sees nothing, but a second glance arrests all his movement. After a moment he turns to look fixedly at the* King. *There is a silence; then.*]

CROMWELL. What in the name of God is this? [*Striking the paper with his hand.*]

CHARLES. It is private to ourselves.

CROMWELL [*rising*]. To ourselves? For our private pleasure we will destroy this country, and blast the people in it! Read it, Ireton.

[IRETON *takes the paper and rises.*]

CHARLES [*rising*]. These are notes for our own contemplation.

CROMWELL. Here are ten lines of the bitterest damnation that ever came from the mind of treason. [*Taking the paper again.*] The Scots to invade England. The King's arms to be raised again. Presbytery ... Freedom to be destroyed — and diligently, at the King's pleasure. Word blaspheming word as we have spoken. Disastrous man!

IRETON. How far has this gone?

CHARLES. We are not before our judges.

CROMWELL. It will come. This iniquity means we know not what new bitterness of destruction. But know this, Charles Stuart, that, when we draw the sword again, it is the sword of judgment. Out there many call you the man of blood. I have laboured for you, have met them all in persuasion. I had prevailed. It is finished. Blood is upon us again, blood spilled for a perfidious king. The sword that we had put by for ever! My God, how I have feared it! Well, so be it. We go to the field again — but then, prepare you for the reckoning. It shall be to the uttermost.

CHARLES. This argument is ended.

CROMWELL. All arguments are ended.

[*He goes with* IRETON, *taking the paper.*]

THE SCENE CLOSES

SCENE VII

CROMWELL'S *house in London. The morning of January 30, 1649, the day of the King's execution. Outside the window can be seen the grey winter gloom, brightened by fallen snow. The room, in which a fire is burning, is empty, and for a time there is silence. Then from a near street comes the soft sound of muffled drums.*

[BRIDGET *runs in, and goes to the window, opening it. Then she goes back to the door, and calls.*]

BRIDGET. Mother.
    [*She goes back to the window.*]

ELIZABETH [*coming in*]. Yes.

BRIDGET. It is the King. He is passing down to Whitehall.

ELIZABETH. Don't look, child.

BRIDGET. I can see nothing but the pikeheads. The people seem very still. You can hear nothing but the drums.

[*A little later* MRS. CROMWELL *comes in. She goes to a chair by the fire.*]

MRS. CROMWELL. Oliver has just sent from Whitehall for his greatcoat. I've sent Beth with it.

BRIDGET. The King has just passed, grandmother.

ELIZABETH. He has gone into Whitehall.

MRS. CROMWELL. Men will pity him. He had no pity.

BRIDGET. Do you think father is right, grandmother? Saying that it had to be?

MRS. CROMWELL. Yes, I do think so.

ELIZABETH. He betrayed his own people. It was that.

MRS. CROMWELL. There could be no safety or hope while he lived.

BRIDGET. Yes. He betrayed his own people. That's it.

MRS. CROMWELL. Kings must love, too.

ELIZABETH. When your father wanted to give him back his throne, a little simple honesty in the King would have saved all. But he could not come to that.

BRIDGET. The drums have stopped.

MRS. CROMWELL. Is Henry with your father?
BRIDGET. Yes.
MRS. CROMWELL. What is the time?
ELIZABETH. Nearly one o'clock.
BRIDGET. It must be past one.
MRS. CROMWELL. Oliver will be the foremost man in England.
BRIDGET. Henry says he could be king.
ELIZABETH. That he would never be. I know.
MRS. CROMWELL. He will have to guide all.
BRIDGET. Don't you wish it could have been done without this, grandmother?
MRS. CROMWELL. When the world labours in anger, child, you cannot name the hour.
BRIDGET. But Henry thinks it is right, too.
MRS. CROMWELL. If this be wrong, all was wrong.
BRIDGET. Yes. Thank you, grandmother. That is what I wanted. It was necessary.
ELIZABETH. Henry meant to come back before the end, didn't he?
BRIDGET. He said so.
MRS. CROMWELL. It's very cold.
BRIDGET. I think it will snow again.
ELIZABETH. What are the drums beating again for?
BRIDGET. Perhaps — I don't know. Will you have another shawl, grandmother?
MRS. CROMWELL. No, thank you.

[IRETON *comes in.*]

BRIDGET. Has anything happened?
IRETON. Not yet. In a minute or two. At half-past one. It's three minutes yet.
BRIDGET. Is father there?
IRETON. Yes.
ELIZABETH. Not alone?
IRETON. No. Fairfax and Harrison — five of them.
MRS. CROMWELL. The King — very brave, I suppose?
IRETON. Yes. That was inevitable. We are old campaigners.
ELIZABETH. Oliver says that he has been noble since death was certain.
IRETON. Yes.

BRIDGET. If he had but lived so.
IRETON. He made life ignoble. He would have made it ignoble again, and always. He was a king and he despoiled his people. When that is, kings must perish.

[*There is a movement and sound of voices in the streets.* IRETON *opens the window.* ELIZABETH *and* BRIDGET *stand with him.*]

IRETON. Yes. It is done.

[MRS. CROMWELL *slowly moves across to the window and stands with the others.*]

MRS. CROMWELL. Poor, silly king. Oliver will be here directly. Shut the window, Henry.

[IRETON *shuts the window. He,* ELIZABETH, *and* BRIDGET *stand looking out.* MRS. CROMWELL *returns to her seat. All are very still, and there is a long pause. Then, unseen and unheard,* CROMWELL *comes in, moving slowly, his coat and hat still on, his boots carrying snow. He looks at his people, all with their backs to him. He walks across the room, and stands behind his mother, looking into the fire.*]

THE SCENE CLOSES

SCENE VIII

A November night in 1654, *six years later.* MRS. CROMWELL'S *bedroom in Whitehall, where* CROMWELL *is now installed as Protector.*

[MRS. CROMWELL, *now aged ninety, is on her death-bed. Standing beside her is* ELIZABETH, *ministering to her.*]

ELIZABETH. Is that comfortable?
MRS. CROMWELL. Yes, my dear, very comfortable.
ELIZABETH. Bridget is coming now. I must go down to Cheapside. I must see that man there myself.
MRS. CROMWELL. Very well, my dear. Bridget is a good girl. I may be asleep before you come back. Good-night.
ELIZABETH [*kissing her*]. Good-night. [*Softly, at the door.*] Bridget.

BRIDGET [*from the next room*]. Yes, mother.
ELIZABETH. Can you come? I'm going now.
BRIDGET. Yes.

[*She comes in and* ELIZABETH *goes.*]

BRIDGET. Shall I read, grandmother?
MRS. CROMWELL. Yes, just a little. Mr. Milton was reading to me this afternoon. Your father asked him to come. He has begun a very good poem, about Eden and the fall of man. He read me some of it. He writes extremely well. I think I should like to hear something by that young Mr. Marvell. He copies them out for me — you'll find them in that book, there. There's one about a garden. Just two stanzas of it. I have marked them.

BRIDGET [*reading*].

How vainly men themselves amaze
To win the palm, the oak, or bays,
And their incessant labours see
Crown'd from some single herb or tree,
Whose short and narrow-verged shade
Does prudently their toils upbraid;
While all the flowers and trees do close
To weave the garlands of repose.

And then this one?

Meanwhile the mind from pleasure less
Withdraws into its happiness;
The mind, that ocean where each kind
Does straight its own resemblance find;
Yet it creates, transcending these,
Far other worlds, and other seas;
Annihilating all that's made
To a green thought in a green shade.

MRS. CROMWELL. Yes. Far other worlds, and other seas. I wish your father would come. I want to go to sleep, and you never know.

BRIDGET. I think father is coming now.

[CROMWELL *comes in. He wears plain civilian clothes.*]

CROMWELL. Well, mother dear.

[*He kisses her.*]

MRS. CROMWELL. I'm glad you have come, my son. Though you are very busy, I'm sure.

CROMWELL. Is there anything I can do?

MRS. CROMWELL. No, thank you. What date is this?

CROMWELL. The second of November.

MRS. CROMWELL. It's nearly a year since they made you Protector, then.

CROMWELL. Yes. I wonder.

MRS. CROMWELL. You need not, son. You were right. There was none other. And you were right not to take a crown.

CROMWELL. The monarchy will return. I know that.

BRIDGET. Why not always a commonwealth like this, father?

CROMWELL. Hereafter there shall be a true commonwealth. We have done that for England. But there must be a king. There is no one to follow me. I am an interlude, as it were. But henceforth kings will be for the defence of this realm, not to use it. That has been our work. It is so, mother?

MRS. CROMWELL. Truly, I think it. It will be a freer land because you have lived in it, my son. Our name may be forgotten, but it does not matter. You serve faithfully. I am proud.

CROMWELL. You have been my blessed friend.

MRS. CROMWELL. It was kind of Mr. Milton to come this afternoon. I can't remember whether I thanked him as I should like to.

CROMWELL. He likes to come.

MRS. CROMWELL. Be kind to all poets, Oliver. They have been very kind to me. They have the best doctrine.

CROMWELL. That is an aim of mine — to find all men of worth and learning and genius — to give them due employment. The Lord speaks through them, I know. I would have none fail or want under my government.

MRS. CROMWELL. I know that. Bridget, girl, be a stay to your father and your mother. They love you. If you should wed again, may you wed well.

BRIDGET. I will cherish my father's great estate, and I will be humble always.

MRS. CROMWELL. And now, I am tired. Bless you, Oliver, my son. The Lord cause His face to shine upon you, and comfort you in all your adversities, and enable you to do great things for the glory of your most high God, and to be a relief unto His people. My dear son. I leave my heart with you. A good night.

[*They both kiss her.*]

MRS. CROMWELL. Is Amos Tanner here?

BRIDGET. Yes, grandmother.

MRS. CROMWELL. Ask him to sing to me. Very quietly. The song he sang that night at Ely — you remember — when John and Henry were there.

[BRIDGET *goes out.*]

MRS. CROMWELL. You have been a good son.

CROMWELL. Mother, dear.

[BRIDGET *returns with* AMOS. *Very quietly he sings:*]

When I shall in the churchyard lie,
Poor scholar though I be,
The wheat, the barley, and the rye
Will better wear for me.

For truly have I ploughed and sown,
And kept my acres clean;
And written on my churchyard stone
This character be seen;

"His flocks, his barns, his gear he made
His daily diligence,
Nor counted all his earnings paid
In pockets full of pence."

[*While he is singing* MRS. CROMWELL *falls asleep and he goes.*

CROMWELL *stands for a time with* BRIDGET, *watching his mother asleep.*]

CROMWELL. Daughter, we must be loving, one with another. No man is sure of himself, ever. He can but pray for faith.

BRIDGET. Father, you have done all that a man might do. You have delivered England.

CROMWELL. I have said a word for freedom, a poor, confused word. It was all I could reach to. We are frail, with our passions. We are beset. [*He prays at his mother's bedside,* BRIDGET *standing beside him.*] Thou hast made me, though very unworthy, a mean instrument to do the people some good, and Thee service. And many of them have set too high a value upon me, though others wish and would be glad of my death. But, Lord, however Thou dost dispose of me, continue and go on to do good for them. Give them one heart, and mutual love. Teach those who look too much upon Thy instrument to depend more upon Thyself. Pardon such as desire to trample upon the dust of a poor worm, for they are Thy people, too. And pardon the folly of this short prayer, even for Jesus Christ's sake. And give us a good night if it be Thy pleasure.

THE SCENE CLOSES

APPENDIX
I. AUTHORS AND PLAYS
II. NOTES ON THE PRODUCTION OF PLAYS
III. BIBLIOGRAPHIES OF CONTEMPORARY DRAMA AND THEATER
IV. INDEX OF CHARACTERS

APPENDIX

I. AUTHORS AND PLAYS

WHEN numerals are in italics, the reference is to the date of production; when in roman type, to the date of publication. When the year of production and of publication coincide, only one date is given.

STEPHEN PHILLIPS. Born Somertown, near Oxford, 1868. Son of Rev. Stephen Phillips, precentor of Peterborough Cathedral. Educated Stratford and Peterborough Grammar Schools. One year at Queen's College, Cambridge. Joined the dramatic company of his cousin, F. R. Benson. Played small parts for six years in London and provinces. Poet and dramatist. At one time an editor of *Poetry Review*. Died in 1915. PLAYS: Paolo and Francesca, 1900, *1902*; Herod, *1900*, 1901; Ulysses, *1902*; The Sin of David, 1904; Aylmer's Secret, 1905; Nero, *1906*; Faust (with Comyns Carr), *1908*; The Last Heir, 1908; Pietro of Siena, *1910*; The King, 1910, *1912*; Nero's Mother (one act), 1913; The Adversary (one act), 1913; Armageddon, *1915*; Harold, 1916.

HARLEY GRANVILLE-BARKER. Born London, 1877. Made his first appearance on the stage in 1891. With Ben Greet in Shakespearean repertoire, 1895. In 1904 joined J. E. Vedrenne in the management of the Court Theater. One of the important pioneers in the new movement in the theater. In 1909 managed The Duke of York's, Charles Frohman's repertory theater; in 1912 produced a Shakespearean season at the Savoy. Actor, dramatist, and producer. Author (with William Archer) of *Schemes and Estimates for a National Theatre*, 1907; *The Exemplary Theatre*, 1922. Translator and adapter (with Helen Granville-Barker) of several plays by the Spanish dramatist, G. Martinez Sierra. PLAYS: The Weather Hen (with Berte Thomas), 1899; The Marrying of Ann Leete, *1901*, 1909; Prunella (with Laurence Housman), *1904*, 1907; The Voysey Inheritance, *1905*, 1909; Waste, *1907*, 1909; The Madras House, *1910*; Anatol (paraphrase from the Austrian dramatist, Arthur Schnitzler) *1911*; The Harlequinade (with Dion Clayton Calthrop), *1913*, 1918; The Morris Dance (a version of R. L. Stevenson's The Wrong Box), 1916; Deburau *1921* (an English version of Sacha Guitry's play); Rococo, *1911*, Vote by Ballot, *1917*, Farewell to the Theatre (three short plays), 1917; The Secret Life, 1923.

ST. JOHN EMILE CLAVERING HANKIN. Born Southampton, 1860. Educated at Malvern and at Merton College, Oxford. In 1890 began a journalistic career in London. Went to India. Four years at Calcutta as a newspaper writer. Returned to London, 1895. Contributed to *The Times* and to *Punch*. Wrote plays from 1902 until his death, 1909. PLAYS: The Two Mr. Wetherbys, *1903*, 1907; The Return of the Prodigal, *1905*; The Charity that Began at Home, *1906*; The Cassilis Engagement, *1907*; The Last of the De Mullins, *1908*; The Burglar Who Failed (one act), 1908; The Constant Lover (one act), *1912*; Thompson (unfinished: later completed by George Calderon) *1913*, 1924.

ALFRED SUTRO. Born London, 1863. Educated in City of London schools and at Brussels. Began his career as a dramatist in 1896 with an adaptation from the French, in collaboration with the actor-manager Arthur Bourchier. Translated many of the works of Maurice Maeterlinck. PLAYS: The Chili Widow (with Arthur Bourchier; from the French), *1896*; The Cave of Illusion, *1900*; Arethusa, *1903*; The Walls of Jericho, *1904*, 1906; Mollentrave on Women, *1905*; The Perfect Lover, *1905*; The Fascinating Mr. Vanderveldt, *1906*, 1907; The Price of Money, 1906; John Glayde's Honour, *1907*; The Barrier, *1907*; The Builder of Bridges, *1909*; Making a Gentleman, *1909*; The Perplexed Husband, *1911*, 1913; The Fire-Screen, *1912*; The Two Virtues, 1913, *1914*; The Clever Ones, *1914*; Freedom, 1914; Uncle Anyhow, *1918*; The Choice, *1919*; The Laughing Lady, *1922*; The Great Well, *1922*,

1923; Far Above Rubies, *1923*, 1924; Five Little Plays (A Marriage Has Been Arranged, *1904;* The Man on the Kerb, *1908*; The Man in the Stalls, 1911; The Open Door; The Bracelet), 1912; A Maker of Men (one act), *1905*. (Other one-act plays).

HUBERT HENRY DAVIES. Born Woodley, in Cheshire, 1869. Of Welsh descent. Educated at the Grammar School, Manchester. Put into business at the age of seventeen. Parents had a Puritanical objection to the stage. In 1893 came to Chicago. The following year went to San Francisco, where he worked in a shipping office. In 1897 became musical and dramatic critic of *News Letter*, a weekly. Later returned to London to follow the career of a dramatist. Died 1917 in France, following severe work in hospitals. PLAYS: A Dream of Love (one act), *1899*; The Weldons, *1899*; Fifty Years Ago (one act), *1901*; Mrs. Gorringe's Necklace, *1903*, 1910; Cousin Kate, *1903*; Cynthia, *1904*; Captain Drew on Leave, *1905*, 1924; The Mollusc, *1907*, 1914; Lady Epping's Lawsuit, *1908*, 1914; Bevis, *1909*; A Single Man, *1910*, 1914; Doormats, *1912*, 1920; Outcast, *1914*.

ELIZABETH BAKER. Born London. Began her career as a stenographer and private secretary. In 1907 wrote a play for the amateurs of the Croydon Repertory Theater. Was encouraged by her success to continue. PLAYS: Beastly Pride, *1907*; Chains, *1909*, 1910; Miss Tassey (one act), *1910*, 1913; Cupid in Clapham, *1910*; Edith, *1912*; The Price of Thomas Scot, *1913*; Over a Garden Wall, 1915; Miss Robinson, *1918*, 1920; Partnership, 1921.

CHARLES KENYON. Born San Francisco, 1899. Educated at the University of California and at Leland Stanford University. Since 1919 a scenario writer for the Goldwyn Producing Corporation. PLAYS: The Flag Station, *1906*; Kindling, *1911*, 1914; Husband and Wife, 1915; The Claim (with Frank Dare), *1917*.

STANLEY HOUGHTON. Born Ashton-upon-Mersey, Cheshire, 1881, of an old Lancashire family. Educated at the Manchester Grammar School. Entered the cotton business in Manchester, 1897. Contributed frequently to *The Manchester Guardian*, 1907 to 1912. In the latter year he left business to devote himself to a literary and dramatic career. Came to London to write plays for the actor-manager Arthur Bourchier. Died 1913 from an illness contracted while traveling upon the Continent. PLAYS: The Old Testament and the New (one act), 1905; The Dear Departed (one act), *1908*; Independent Means, *1909*, 1911; Marriages in the Making, 1909; The Younger Generation, *1910*; The Master of the House (one act), 1910; Fancy Free (one act), *1911*; Partners (full length version of Fancy Free), 1911; Hindle Wakes, *1912*; Phipps (one act), 1912; Pearls (one act), *1912*; The Perfect Cure, 1913; The Fifth Commandment (one act), 1913; Ginger (one act), *1913*; Trust the People, *1913*; The Hillarys (with Harold Brighouse), *1915*.

KATHERINE GITHA SOWERBY (Mrs. John Kendall). Born Newcastle-on-Tyne. Daughter of John Sowerby, the artist. A writer of short stories and of books for children (with her sister), as well as a dramatist. PLAYS: Rutherford and Son, *1912*; Before Breakfast (one act), *1913*; Jinny (one act), *1914*; A Man and Some Women, *1914*; Sheila, *1917*.

LOUIS KAUFMAN ANSPACHER. Born Cincinnati, Ohio, 1878. Graduated from the College of the City of New York, 1897; A.M., Columbia University, 1899; LL.B., 1902. Studied in the School of Philosophy, Columbia University, 1902–05. Lecturer and dramatist. PLAYS: Tristan and Isolde, 1904; Embarrassment of Riches, 1906; Anne and the Arch Duke John, *1907*; The Woman of Impulse, 1909; The Glass House, 1912; The Washerwoman Duchess, *1913*; Our Children, *1914*; The Unchastened Woman, *1915*, 1916; That Day, *1917*; Madame Cecile, *1918*; The Rape of Belgium (with Max Marcin), 1918; Daddalums, *1919*; The Dancer (with Max Marcin), 1919; All The King's Horses, 1920; The New House, *1921*.

WILLIAM SOMERSET MAUGHAM. Born Paris, 1874. Educated at King's School, Canterbury, and at Heidelberg University. Studied medicine at St. Thomas's Hospital, London. Served as a doctor in France during the war. Novelist and dramatist. PLAYS: Schiffbrüchig (in German), Berlin, 1901; A Man of Honour, *1903*; The Explorer, 1907, *1908*; Lady Frederick, *1907*, 1912; Jack Straw, *1908*, 1912; Mrs. Dot, *1908*, 1912; Penelope, *1909*;

APPENDIX

Smith, *1909*, 1913; The Tenth Man, *1910*, 1913; Grace [Landed Gentry], *1910*, 1913; Loaves and Fishes, *1911*; The Land of Promise, 1913, *1914*; Caroline, *1916*; Our Betters, *1917*, 1923; Love in a Cottage, 1918; Cæsar's Wife, *1919*, 1920; Home and Beauty, *1919* (American title: Too Many Husbands); The Unknown, *1920*; The Circle, *1921*; East of Suez, *1922*; The Camel's Back, *1924*.

EUGENE GLADSTONE O'NEILL. Born New York, 1888. Son of the famous actor, James O'Neill. Studied at Princeton University, 1906–07; Harvard University, 1914–15. Spent two years at sea. An actor in a vaudeville version of Monte Cristo. Reporter on the New London, Connecticut, *Telegraph*. A dramatist since 1914. PLAYS: The Web (one act), 1914; Thirst (one act), 1914, *1916*; Warnings (one act), 1914; Fog (one act), 1914, *1917*; Recklessness (one act), 1914; The Moon of the Caribbees (one act), *1918*, 1919; The Rope (one act), *1918*; Bound East for Cardiff (one act), *1916*, 1919; The Long Voyage Home (one act), *1917*, 1919; In the Zone (one act), *1917*, 1919; 'Ile (one act), *1917*, 1919; Where the Cross is Made (one act), *1918*, 1919; Abortion (one act), *1916*; Before Breakfast (one act), *1916*; The Sniper (one act), *1917*; The Dreamy Kid (one act), *1919;* Beyond the Horizon, *1920*; Chris, *1920*; Exorcism (one act), *1920*; Gold, *1921*; The Emperor Jones, *1920*, 1921; Diff'rent, *1920*, 1921; Anna Christie, *1921*, 1922; The Straw, *1921*; The First Man, *1922*; The Hairy Ape, *1922*; The Fountain (written 1923, unpublished); Welded, *1924*; The Rime of the Ancient Mariner (dramatization of Coleridge's poem), *1924*; Welded, *1924*; All God's Chillun Got Wings, *1924*; Desire Under the Elms, *1924*; S. S. Glencairn, *1925*.

RACHEL CROTHERS. Born Bloomington, Illinois, 1878. Both her parents were doctors. Graduated, 1892, from the Illinois State Normal School. At first a teacher of elocution, later came to New York to study acting. Became interested in writing and producing plays. Has been a dramatist since 1906. PLAYS: The Three of Us, *1906*, 1916; The Coming of Mrs. Patrick, *1907*; Myself Bettina, 1908; A Man's World, *1910*, 1915; Young Wisdom, *1911*; Ourselves, *1912*; The Heart of Paddy-Whack, *1915*; Old Lady 31, *1916*, 1923; Mother Carey's Chickens, *1917*; Once Upon a Time, *1918*; A Little Journey, *1920*, 1923; 39 East, *1920*; He and She, *1920*; Nice People, *1921*; Everyday, *1922*; Mary the Third, *1923*; Expressing Willie, 1924.

OWEN DAVIS. Born 1874. Educated at the University of Tennessee (1888–89) and at Harvard University (1890–93). Has been a dramatist since 1898, during which time he has written or adapted about one hundred plays and fifty melodramas. PLAYS: The Detour, *1921*, 1922; Icebound, *1923*; Lazybones, *1924*.

ELMER L. RICE (Reizenstein). Born New York City, September 28, 1892. He was educated in the public schools and later studied law at the New York Law School, receiving the degree of LL.B. in 1912. He was for a time the director of dramatics at the University Settlement, New York. PLAYS: On Trial, *1914*; Morningside Plays, *1917*; For the Defense, *1919*; Wake up, Jonathan, *1921*; It Is the Law, *1922*; The Adding Machine, *1923*.

JOHN DRINKWATER. Born 1882. For several years in the insurance business at Birmingham. Co-founder with Barry Jackson of The Pilgrim Players, now the Birmingham Repertory Theater. Poet, literary critic, and dramatist. Edited The Plays of St. John Hankin. PLAYS: Cophetua (one act), *1911*; Rebellion, *1914*; Pawns (three one-act plays, The Storm, *1915*, The God of Quiet, *1916*, 1917, X = 0, *1917*); American ed. of Pawns, 1920, contains also Cophetua, *1911*; Abraham Lincoln, *1918*; Mary Stuart, *1921* (revised version), London, *1922*; Oliver Cromwell, *1923*; Robert E. Lee, *1923*.

II. NOTES ON THE PRODUCTION OF PLAYS

PAOLO AND FRANCESCA, by Stephen Phillips, had its first performance at the St. James's Theater, London, March 6, 1902. The part of Paolo was taken by George Alexander; Francesca, by Miss Grace Lane. This production of a modern verse tragedy aroused a literary discussion comparable to that caused by the first performance of Robert Browning's *A Blot in the 'Scutcheon*. The first American performance of Phillips's tragedy was on October 1, 1906, at the New Amsterdam Theater, New York. Mr. H. B. Irving chose this play for his American début. He played Giovanni Malatesta. The Paolo was E. Harcourt Williams, and the Francesca, Dorothea Baird. The play did not arouse as much popular interest in New York, but was nevertheless the subject of much critical comment.

THE VOYSEY INHERITANCE, by Harley Granville-Barker, was first performed at the Court Theater, London, November 7, 1905, under the management of J. E. Vedrenne and Harley Granville-Barker. In the season of 1914 it was revived by Mr. Barker at the Kingsway Theater. The cast for the Court Theater production included A. E. George, as Mr. Voysey; Florence Haydon, as Mrs. Voysey; Dennis Eadie, as Hugh Voysey; Alexandra Carlisle, as Ethel Voysey; O. B. Clarence, as Mr. Booth; and Edmund Gwenn as the Rev. Evan Colpus.

List of Persons, not printed with the play: Mr. Voysey. Mrs. Voysey. Trenchard Voysey, K.C. Honor Voysey. Major Booth Voysey. Mrs. Booth Voysey. Christopher. Edward Voysey. Hugh Voysey. Mrs. Hugh Voysey. Ethel Voysey. Denis Tregoning. Alice Maitland. Mr. Booth. The Rev. Evan Colpus. Peacey. Phœbe. Mary.

THE CASSILIS ENGAGEMENT, by St. John Emile Clavering Hankin, had its first production before the Stage Society at the Imperial Theater, London, on February 10, 1907. The play was produced by Miss Madge McIntosh. The part of Mrs. Cassilis was played by Miss Evelyn Weeden; Mrs. Borridge, by Miss Clare Greet; Ethel Borridge, by Maudi Darrell. Other prominent actors in the cast were Sam Sothern and Florence Haydon. It has had several stock productions in America, notably by the Jewett Players of Boston, Massachusetts, in 1922.

JOHN GLAYDE'S HONOUR, by Alfred Sutro, was produced by George Alexander at the St. James's Theater, London, on March 8, 1907, where it ran for nearly 200 performances. The part of John Glayde was played by George Alexander; Muriel Glayde, by Miss Eva Moore; Trevor Lerode, by Matheson Lang; Christopher Branley, by Norman Forbes; and Michael Shurmur, by Michael Sherbrooke. James K. Hackett produced this play in America, December 23, 1907, when it ran for only two weeks, although the critics praised highly Mr. Hackett's acting in the rôle of John Glayde. Trevor Lerode was played by William Sauter, and Muriel Glayde by Miss Darragh. Beatrice Beckley was Mrs. Rennick.

THE MOLLUSC, by Hubert Henry Davies, was first performed October 15, 1907, at the Criterion Theater, London. The cast was as follows: Tom Kemp, Charles Wyndham; Mr. Baxter, Sam Sothern; Mrs. Baxter, Miss Mary Moore; Miss Roberts, Miss Elaine Innescourt. It was produced in New York, September 1, 1908, at the Garrick Theater. The cast: Tom Kemp, Joseph Coyne; Mr. Baxter, Forrest Robinson; Miss Roberts, Beatrice Forbes-Robinson; Mrs. Baxter, Alexandra Carlisle.

CHAINS, by Elizabeth Baker, was first put on for one performance by the Play Actors at the Court Theater, London, April 18, 1909, and subsequently revived by Charles Frohman for fifteen performances at The Duke of York's Theater, London, May 17, 1910. For the latter, the play was produced by Dion Boucicault. Charles Wilson was played by Dennis Eadie; Percy Massey, by Donald Calthrop; Alfred Massey, by Edmund Gwenn; Fenwick, by Lewis Casson; Lily Wilson, by Hilda Trevelyan; Mrs. Massey, by Sybil Thorndike; and Sybil Frost,

APPENDIX 643

by Dorothy Minto. An adapted version of this play, by Porter Emerson Browne, was produced at New York, on December 6, 1912, at the Criterion Theater. The cast: Ruth Wilson, Olive Wyndham; Richard Wilson, Shelly Hull; Jackson Tennant, Clifford Bruce; Betty Mason, Desmond Kelley; Percy Mason, Edwin Nicander; Charley Mason, Clinton Preston; Morton Lane, Edward Fielding; Sybil Frost, Ruth Boyce; Howard Dunn, Bernard Merifield; P. J. Mason, Robert Fisher; Miranda Mason, Mrs. Thomas Whiffen.
List of Persons, not printed with the play: Charles Wilson, Fred Tennant. Morton Leslie. Percy Massey. Alfred Massey. Walter Foster. Fenwick. Lucy Wilson. Mrs. Massey. Sybil Frost.

KINDLING, by Charles Kenyon, was first produced under the direction of Edward J. Bowes at Daly's Theater, New York, December 3, 1911, with Margaret Illington as the star. She played the rôle of Maggie Schultz. Other members of the cast were: A. Byron Beasley, as Heinrich Schultz; Annie Mack Berlin, as Mrs. Bates; George Probert, as Steve Bates; Helen Tracy, as Mrs. Burke Smith; Anne Meredith, as Alice; Frank Camp, as Rafferty; John Jex, as Mr. Howland; James McCauley, as Donovan; and Albert Kenyon, as Dr. Taylor.

HINDLE WAKES, by Stanley Houghton, was first produced by Miss A. E. F. Horniman's Repertory Company from the Gaiety Theater, Manchester, before the Incorporated Stage Society, at the Aldwych Theater, London, on Sunday, June 16, 1912. On July 16, 1912, the play opened at the Playhouse, London, for a regular run. Later it was transferred to the Court Theater. The play was staged by Lewis Casson, and Miss Horniman's cast was as follows: Mrs. Hawthorn, Ada King; Christopher Hawthorn, Charles Bibby; Fanny Hawthorn, Edyth Goodall; Mrs. Jeffcote, Daisy England; Nathaniel Jeffcote, Herbert Lomas; Alan Jeffcote, J. V. Bryant; Sir Timothy Farrar, Edward Landor; Beatrice Farrar, Sybil Thorndike; Ada, Hilda Davies. The American production was on December 9, 1912, at Maxine Elliott's Theater, New York, with the following cast: Mrs. Hawthorn, Alice O'Dea; Christopher Hawthorn, James C. Taylor; Fanny, Emilie Polini; Mrs. Jeffcote, Alice Chapin; Ada, Kathleen MacPherson; Alan Jeffcote, Roland Young; Sir Anthony Farrar, Charles F. Lloyd; Beatrice Farrar, Dulcie Conry. The play was revived at the Vanderbilt Theater, New York, May 11, 1922, under the title of "Fanny Hawthorn."

RUTHERFORD AND SON, by Katherine Githa Sowerby, was first produced at the Court Theater, London, January 31, 1912. On December 24, 1912, Mr. Winthrop Ames presented the play at The Little Theater, New York. Subsequently this play was translated into nearly all the European languages and has been frequently played upon the Continent. The English actor Norman McKinnel played John Rutherford in the American production.

THE UNCHASTENED WOMAN, by Louis Kaufman Anspacher, had its première at the Thirty-Ninth Street Theater, New York, October 9, 1915, under the management of Oliver Morosco. The cast was as follows: Hubert Knollys, H. Reeves-Smith; Mrs. Murtha, Jennie Lamont; Miss Susan Ambie, Isabel Richards; Caroline Knollys, Emily Stevens; Laurence Sanbury, R. Hassard Short; Hildegarde Sanbury, Christene Norman; Miss Emily Madden, Willette Kershaw; Michael Krellin, Louis Bennison.

THE CIRCLE, by William Somerset Maugham, had its first performance at the Haymarket Theater, London, March 4, 1921. Mr. Ernest Thesiger played the rôle of Clive Champion-Cheney, Miss Lottie Venne that of Lady Catherine, and Miss Fay Compton was the Elizabeth. Among other members of the cast were Holman Clark, Leon Quartermaine, and Allan Aynesworth. This play was first produced in New York by the Selwyns at the Selwyn Theater, September 12, 1921. It ran at this theater for five months, and at the end of that time was transferred to the Fulton Theater, remaining there four weeks. The cast of the American production was as follows: Arnold Champion-Cheney, M.P., Robert Rendel; Footman, Charles L. Sealy; Mrs. Shenstone, Maxine MacDonald; Elizabeth, Estelle Winwood; Edward Luton, John Halliday; Clive Champion-Cheney, Ernest Lawford; Butler, Walter Soderling; Lord Porteous, John Drew; Lady Catherine Champion-Cheney, Mrs. Leslie Carter.

THE HAIRY APE, by Eugene Gladstone O'Neill, was first produced by the Provincetown Players at their theater, The Provincetown Playhouse, 183 Macdougal Street, New York,

March 9, 1922. The cast was as follows: Robert Smith, "Yank," Louis Wolheim; Paddy, Henry O'Neill; Long, Harold West; Mildred Douglas, Mary Blair; Her Aunt, Eleanor Hutchison; Second Engineer, Jack Gude; A Guard, Henry Gottliev; A Secretary, Harold McGee. The stage settings were by Robert Edmond Jones and Cleon Throckmorton.

MARY THE THIRD, by Rachel Crothers, was produced at the Thirty-Ninth Street Theater, New York, February 5. 1923. Louise Huff played the three Marys, 1870, 1897, 1923, and Ben Lyon played the rôles of the three separate lovers. Beatrice Terry played the Mother of Mary the Third.

ICEBOUND, by Owen Davies, was produced by Sam Forrest for the management of Sam H. Harris at the Harris Theater, New York, February 10, 1923. The play was awarded the Pulitzer Prize for the current year. The cast was as follows: Henry Jordan, John Westley; Emma, Lotta Linthicum; Nettie, Boots Wooster; Sadie Fellows, Eva Condon; Orin, Andrew J. Lawlor, Jr.; Ella Jordan, Frances Neilson; Doctor Curtis, Lawrence Eddinger; Jane Crosby, Phyllis Povah; Judge Bradford, Williard Robertson; Ben Jordon, Robert Ames; Hannah, Edna May Oliver; Jim Jay, Charles Henderson.

THE ADDING MACHINE, by Elmer L. Rice, was originally presented by The Theater Guild at the Garrick Theater, New York, March 19, 1923. The direction of the play was by Philip Moeller, the settings and costumes by Lee Simonson, and the incidental music by Deems Taylor. Among the prominent players in the cast were Dudley Digges, as Mr. Zero; Helen Westley, as Mrs. Zero; Margaret Wycherly, as Daisy Diana Dorothea Devore; and Louis Calvert, as Lieutenant Charles. Owing to the popular success of this play, it was later transferred to the larger Comedy Theater, and ran for a total of seventy-two performances.

OLIVER CROMWELL, by John Drinkwater, was first produced by Henry Ainley in the title rôle at His Majesty's Theater, London, May 30, 1923. The run extended until July 30 of the same year when the play was withdrawn. Other members of the cast were: Miss Irene Rooke as Mrs. Cromwell; Miss Mary O'Farrell as Bridget Cromwell; Mr. Harcourt Williams as William Hampden; Mr. Milton Rosmer as Henry Treton; Mr. J. Adrian Byrne as the Speaker of the House of Commons; and Mr. Hayden Coffin as Amos Tanner. It has not yet (1925) had an American production.

III. BIBLIOGRAPHIES OF CONTEMPORARY DRAMA AND THEATER

SPECIAL BIBLIOGRAPHIES

Beegle, M. P., and Crawford, J. R., *Community Drama and Pageantry.* New Haven, 1916.
Brown, F. C., *A Selected List of Essays and Books about the Drama and Theatre.* Drama League of America publications.
Burrill, E. W., *The Modern Drama: A Course of Forty Readings in European and American Drama beginning with Ibsen and continuing to the Present Day.* Columbia University, 1920.
Dramatic Index, The Annual. Boston, 1909 ff.
Foshay, F. E., *Twentieth Century Dramas.* Boston, 1915.
Gamble, W. B., *Development of Scenic Art and Stage Machinery.* Publications of New York Public Library, 1920.
Shay, F., *The Books and Plays of the Little Theatre* (Preface by Pierre Loving.) New York, 1919.

See also files of *The Theatre; The Theater Arts Magazine; The Drama; The London Sketch; The Mask.* Many of the books listed below contain bibliographies.

THEORY AND TECHNIQUE OF DRAMA AND THEATER

Archer, W., *Playmaking; A Manual of Craftmanship.* Boston, 1912. New ed. 1914.
Baker, G. P., *Technique of the Drama.* Boston, 1915.
Bakshy, A., *The Theatre Unbound.* London, 1923.
Belasco, D., *The Theatre Through its Stage Door.* New York, 1919.
Carter, H., *The New Spirit in Drama and Art.* New York, 1913.
Clark, B. H., *European Theories of the Drama.* Cincinnati, 1918.
Columbia University, *Publications of the Dramatic Museum*, 1915 ff.
Craig, E. G., *On the Art of the Theatre.* Chicago, 1911.
    Towards a New Theatre. London, 1913.
    The Theatre — Advancing. Boston, 1919.
    Scene. (With a Foreword and Introductory Poem by John Masefield.) London 1923.
Glover, H., *Drama and Mankind, A Vindication and a Challenge.* London, 1924.
Goldberg, I., *The Drama of Transition, Native and Exotic Playcraft.* Cincinnati, 1922.
Grundy, S., *The Play of the Future.* London, 1914.
Hamilton, C., *The Theory of the Theatre.* New York, 1910.
    Studies in Stagecraft. New York, 1914.
    Problems of the Playwright. New York, 1917.
Hopkins, A., *How's your Second Act?* New York, 1918.
Krows, A. E., *Play Production in America.* New York, 1916.
Latham, M. W., *A Course in Dramatic Composition.* Columbia University, 1921.
MacGowan, K., and Rosse, H., *Masks and Demons.* New York, 1923.
Matthews, J. B., *A Study of the Drama.* Boston, 1910.
    The Principles of Playmaking. New York, 1919.
    Playwrights on Playmaking. New York, 1923.
Montague, C. E., *Dramatic Values.* London, 1911.
Nicoll, A., *An Introduction to Dramatic Theory.* New York, 1924.
Polti, G., *The Thirty-six Dramatic Situations.* (Translated by L. Ray.) Franklin, Ohio, 1921.
Sayler, O. M., edited by, *Max Reinhardt and his Theatre.* New York, 1924.
Vernon, F., *Modern Stage Production.* London, 1923.

AUTHORS AND DRAMATIC MOVEMENTS

Agate, J., *Alarums and Excursions.* London, 1922.
    At Half-past Eight: Essays of the Theatre. London, 1923.
    The Contemporary Theatre, 1923. London, 1924.
Andrews, C., *The Drama of To-day.* Philadelphia, 1913.
Archer, W., *Old Drama and the New.* London, 1923.
Björkman, E., *Voices of To-morrow.* New York, 1913.
Burton, R., *The New American Drama.* New York, 1913.
Chandler, F. W., *Aspects of Modern Drama.* New York, 1914.
Cheney, S., *The New Movement in the Theatre.* New York, 1914.
    The Art Theatre. New York, 1917.
Clark, B. H., *British and American Drama of To-day.* Cincinnati, 1921.
    A Study of the Modern Drama. New York, 1925.
Courtney, W. L., *Old Saws and Modern Instances.* London, 1918.
Darlington, W. A., *Through the Fourth Wall.* London, 1922.
Dickinson, T. H., *The Case of American Drama.* Boston, 1915.
    Contemporary Drama of England. Boston, 1917.
    The Insurgent Theatre. Boston, 1917.
    Dramatists of the New American Theater. New York, 1924.
Dukes, A., *Modern Dramatists.* Chicago, 1912.
    The Youngest Drama, Studies of Fifty Dramatists. London, 1923.
Ervine, St. J., *Some Impressions of My Elders.* New York, 1923.
George, W. L., *Dramatic Actualities.* London, 1914.
Goldman, Emma, *The Social Significance of the Modern Drama.* Boston, 1914.
Hamilton, C., *Conversations on Contemporary Dramatists.* New York, 1924.
Henderson, A., *The Changing Drama.* New York, 1919. (new ed.)
Hornblow, A., *A History of the Theatre in America.* Philadelphia, 1919.
Howe, P. P., *Dramatic Portraits.* New York, 1913.
Huneker, J., *Iconoclasts: A Book of Dramatists.* New York, 1905.
Jameson, S., *Modern Drama in Europe.* London, 1920.
Jeliff, S. E., and Brink, L., *Psychoanalysis and the Drama.* Washington, 1922.
Lewisohn, L., *The Modern Drama: An Essay in Interpretation.* New York, 1915.
    The Drama and the Stage. New York, 1922.
Matthews, B., *A Book About the Theatre.* New York, 1916.
Moderwell, H. K., *The Theatre of To-day.* New York, 1914.
Morgan, A. E., *Tendencies of Modern English Drama.* London, 1924.
Moses, M. J., *The American Dramatist.* Boston, 1917.
Nathan, G. J., *The Critic and the Drama.* New York, 1922.
    The World in False-Face. New York, 1923. (See also earlier volumes by this author.)
Oliver, D. E., *The English Stage.* London, 1912.
Phelps, W. L., *The Twentieth Century Theatre.* New York, 1918.
    Essays on Modern Dramatists. New York, 1919.
Rolland, R., *The People's Theatre.* (Translated by B. H. Clark.) New York, 1918.
Sayler, O. M., *Our American Theatre.* New York, 1923.
Sutton, G., *Some Contemporary Dramatists.* London, 1924.
Vernon, F., *The Twentieth Century Theatre.* (With an introduction by John Drinkwater.) London, 1924.
Walbrook, H. M., *J. M. Barrie and the Theatre.* London, 1922.
Young, S., *The Flower in Drama: A Book of Papers on the Theatre.* 1923.

ORGANIZATION AND THE THEATER

Archer, W., and Granville-Barker, H., *Scheme and Estimates for a National Theatre.* London, 1908.
Barbor, H. R., *The Theatre: An Art and an Industry.* London, 1924.

Burleigh, L., *The Community Theatre in Theory and Practice.* Boston, 1917.
Dean, B., *The Repertory Theatre*, 1911.
Granville-Barker, H., *Foundations of a National Drama.* London, 1912.
    The Exemplary Theatre: A Record and a Criticism. London, 1922.
Grein, J. T., *The Theatre and the World.* London, 1921.
Howe, P. P., *The Repertory Theatre: A Record and a Criticism.* London, 1911.
Jones, H. A., *The Theatre of Ideas.*
MacGowan, K. *The Theatre of To-morrow.* New York, 1921.
MacGowan, K., and Jones, R. E., *Continental Stagecraft.* New York, 1922.
MacKaye, C. D., *The Little Theatre in the United States.* New York, 1917.
MacKaye, P., *The Playhouse and the Play.* New York, 1909.
    The Civic Theatre. New York, 1913.
McCarthy, D., *The Court Theatre, 1904–07.* London, 1907.
Palmer, J., *The Future of the Theatre.* London, 1913.
    The Censor and the Theatres. London, 1913.

IV. INDEX OF CHARACTERS

Ada, maid at Bank Top. *Hindle Wakes.*
Two Agents to the Earl of Bedford. *Oliver Cromwell.*
An Aide. *Oliver Cromwell.*
Alice, Mrs. Burke Smith's niece. *Kindling.*
Miss Susan Ambie. *The Unchastened Woman.*
Angela. A Blind and Aged Servant of the Malatesta. *Paolo and Francesca.*
Aunt. *The Hairy Ape.*

Bassett, an officer of the House. *Oliver Cromwell.*
Mrs. Bates. *Kindling.*
Mr. Baxter. *The Mollusc.*
Mrs. Baxter. *The Mollusc.*
Bobby. *Mary the Third.*
Mr. George Booth. *The Voysey Inheritance.*
Ethel Borridge. *The Cassilis Engagement.*
Mrs. Borridge. *The Cassilis Engagement.*
The Boss. *The Adding Machine.*
Judge Bradford. *Icebound.*
Christopher Branley. *John Glayde's Honour.*

Geoffrey Cassilis. *The Cassilis Engagement.*
Mrs. Cassilis. *The Cassilis Engagement.*
Princess de Castagnary. *John Glayde's Honour.*
Arnold Champion-Cheney, M. P. *The Circle.*
Lady Catherine Champion-Cheney. *The Circle.*
Clive Champion-Cheney. *The Circle.*
Charles I. *Oliver Cromwell.*
Lieutenant Charles. *The Adding Machine.*
Howard Collingham. *John Glayde's Honour.*
Mr. Evan Colpus. *The Voysey Inheritance.*
Corrado, Officer of Paolo's Company. *Paolo and Francesca.*
Costanza, Kinswoman to Francesca. *Paolo and Francesca.*
Bridget Cromwell, Oliver's daughter. *Oliver Cromwell.*
Elizabeth Cromwell, Oliver's Wife. *Oliver Cromwell.*
Mrs. Cromwell, Oliver's Mother. *Oliver Cromwell.*
Oliver Cromwell. *Oliver Cromwell.*
Jane Crosby, a second cousin of the Jordans. *Icebound.*
Doctor Curtis. *Icebound.*

Daisy Diana Dorothea Devore. *The Adding Machine.*

Donovan. *Kindling.*
Dorset, Mrs. Cassilis's maid. *The Cassilis Engagement.*
Mildred Douglas. *The Hairy Ape.*

Elizabeth. *The Circle.*
Emily, wife of Major Booth Voysey. *The Voysey Inheritance.*
Second Engineer. *The Hairy Ape.*

General Fairfax. *Oliver Cromwell.*
Beatrice Farrar, daughter of Sir Timothy Farrar. *Hindle Wakes.*
Sir Timothy Farrar, chairman of the Education Committee at Hindle. *Hindle Wakes.*
Father. *Mary the Third.*
Orin Fellows, son of Sadie Fellows. *Icebound.*
Sadie Fellows, once Sadie Jordan, a widow. *Icebound.*
Fenwick. *Chains.*
Mr. Five. *The Adding Machine.*
Mrs. Five. *The Adding Machine.*
Walter Foster. *Chains.*
Mr. Four. *The Adding Machine.*
Mrs. Four. *The Adding Machine.*
Sybil Frost. *Chains.*

John Glayde. *John Glayde's Honour.*
Muriel Glayde. *John Glayde's Honour.*
Granny. *Mary the Third.*
A Guard. *The Hairy Ape.*

Hal. *Mary the Third.*
John Hampden. *Oliver Cromwell.*
Hannah. *Icebound.*
Christopher Hawthorn, a slasher at Daisy Bank Mill. *Hindle Wakes.*
Fanny Hawthorn, their daughter, a weaver at Daisy Bank Mill. *Hindle Wakes.*
Mrs. Hawthorn, his wife. *Hindle Wakes.*
A Head. *The Adding Machine.*
Mrs. Henderson. *Rutherford and Son.*
Mr. Herries, the Rector. *The Cassilis Engagement.*
Mrs. Herries. *The Cassilis Engagement.*
Mr. Howland, Mrs. Burke Smith's business manager. *Kindling.*

Henry Ireton. *Oliver Cromwell.*
Janet, daughter of John Rutherford. *Rutherford and Son.*

APPENDIX

Jim Jay. *Icebound.*
Alan Jeffcote, son of Nathaniel Jeffcote. *Hindle Wakes.*
Mrs. Jeffcote, wife of Nathaniel Jeffcote. *Hindle Wakes.*
Nathaniel Jeffcote, owner of Daisy Bank Mill. *Hindle Wakes.*
Joe. *The Adding Machine.*
Ben Jordan. *Icebound.*
Ella Jordan, the unmarried sister. *Icebound.*
Emma Jordan, Henry Jordan's wife. *Icebound.*
Henry Jordan. *Icebound.*
Nettie Jordan, Emma Jordan's daughter by a former marriage. *Icebound.*

Tom Kemp. *The Mollusc.*
Caroline Knollys, wife of Hubert Knollys. *The Unchastened Woman.*
Hubert Knollys. *The Unchastened Woman.*
Michael Krellin. *The Unchastened Woman.*

Lady Lerode. *John Glayde's Honour.*
Trevor Lerode. *John Glayde's Honour.*
Morton Leslie. *Chains.*
Lettie. *Mary the Third.*
Long. *The Hairy Ape.*
Dora Longman. *John Glayde's Honour.*
Lucrezia Degl' Onesti, Cousin to Giovanni. *Paolo and Francesca.*
Luigi, Officer of Paolo's Company. *Paolo and Francesca.*
Edward Luton. *The Circle.*
Lynn. *Mary The Third.*

Miss Emily Madden. *The Unchastened Woman.*
Alice Maitland. *The Voysey Inheritance.*
Giovanni Malatesta ("Lo Sciancato"), Tyrant of Rimini. *Paolo and Francesca.*
Lady Larchmont, Mrs. Cassilis's sister. *The Cassilis Engagement.*
Marco, a Soldier. *Paolo and Francesca.*
Martin. *Rutherford and Son.*
Mary, the housemaid. *The Voysey Inheritance.*
Mary the First. *Mary the Third.*
Mary the Second. *Mary the Third.*
Mary the Third. *Mary the Third.*
Maggie Massey. *Chains.*
Mr. Massey. *Chains.*
Mrs. Massey. *Chains.*
Percy Massey. *Chains.*
Max. *Mary the Third.*
The Mayor of Ely. *Oliver Cromwell.*
A Member of Parliament. *Oliver Cromwell.*
Mirra, a Peasant Girl. *Paolo and Francesca.*
Mother. *Mary the Third.*

Mrs. Murtha, a charwoman. *The Unchastened Woman.*
Neal, Secretary to Charles. *Oliver Cromwell.*
Nita, Maid to Francesca. *Paolo and Francesca.*
Nora. *Mary the Third.*

Judy O'Grady. *The Adding Machine.*
Mr. One. *The Adding Machine.*
Mrs. One. *The Adding Machine.*
Lucrezia Degl' Onesti, Cousin to Giovanni. *Paolo and Francesca.*

Paddy. *The Hairy Ape.*
Paolo ("Il Bello"), Brother to Giovanni, and Captain of Mercenaries in the service of Florence. *Paolo and Francesca.*
Peacey, head clerk. *The Voysey Inheritance.*
Colonel Pemberton. *Oliver Cromwell.*
Phœbe, the parlour-maid. *The Voysey Inheritance.*
Policeman. *The Adding Machine.*
Lord Porteous. *The Circle.*
Pulci, a drug-seller. *Paolo and Francesca.*

Rafferty. *Kindling.*
The Countess of Remenham. *The Cassilis Engagement.*
Mrs. Rennick. *John Glayde's Honour.*
Richard. *Mary the Third.*
Richard, son of John Rutherford. *Rutherford and Son.*
Francesca da Rimini, bride of Giovanni, and daughter of Guido da Polenta, Tyrant of Ravenna. *Paolo and Francesca.*
Robert. *Mary the Third.*
Miss Roberts. *The Mollusc.*
Ann Rutherford, sister of John Rutherford. *Rutherford and Son.*
John Rutherford. *Rutherford and Son.*
John Rutherford, son of John Rutherford. *Rutherford and Son.*
Mary Rutherford, young John Rutherford's wife. *Rutherford and Son.*

Hildegarde Sanbury, wife of Lawrence Sanbury. *The Unchastened Woman.*
Lawrence Sanbury. *The Unchastened Woman.*
Heinrich Schultz, husband of Maggie Schultz, a stevedore. *Kindling.*
Maggie Schultz. *Kindling.*
A Scout. *Oliver Cromwell.*
A Secretary of an Organization. *The Hairy Ape.*
Mrs. Shenstone. *The Circle.*
Shrdlu. *The Adding Machine.*
Michael Shurmur. *John Glayde's Honour.*

Mr. Six. *The Adding Machine.*
Mrs. Six. *The Adding Machine.*
Mrs. Burke Smith. *Kindling.*
Robert Smith, "Yank." *The Hairy Ape.*
The Speaker of the House of Commons. *Oliver Cromwell.*
Colonel Staines. *Oliver Cromwell.*
Steve, Mrs. Bates's son. *Kindling.*
A Surgeon. *Oliver Cromwell.*

Amos Tanner. *Oliver Cromwell.*
Seth Tanner. *Oliver Cromwell.*
Dr. Taylor, an interne from a public hospital. *Kindling.*
Fred Tennant. *Chains.*
Tessa, Daughter to Pulci. *Paolo and Francesca.*
Mr. Three. *The Adding Machine.*
Mrs. Three. *The Adding Machine.*
Denis Tregoning. *The Voysey Inheritance.*
Mr. Two. *The Adding Machine.*
Mrs. Two. *The Adding Machine.*

Valentino, Officer of Paolo's Company. *Paolo and Francesca.*
Lady Mabel Venning, Lady Remenham's daughter. *The Cassilis Engagement.*
Beatrice, wife of Hugh Voysey. *The Voysey Inheritance.*
Major Booth Voysey. *The Voysey Inheritance.*
Christopher Voysey, Major Voysey's young son. *The Voysey Inheritance.*
Edward Voysey. *The Voysey Inheritance.*
Ethel Voysey. *The Voysey Inheritance.*
Honor Voysey. *The Voysey Inheritance.*
Hugh Voysey. *The Voysey Inheritance.*
Mr. Voysey. *The Voysey Inheritance.*
Mrs. Voysey. *The Voysey Inheritance.*
Trenchard Voysey. *The Voysey Inheritance.*

Walters. *John Glayde's Honour.*
Major Warrington. *The Cassilis Engagement.*
Watson, Butler at Deynham. *The Cassilis Engagement.*
Charley Wilson. *Chains.*
Lily Wilson. *Chains.*
William. *Mary the Third.*

"Yank," Robert Smith. *The Hairy Ape.*
Young Man. *The Adding Machine.*

Mr. Zero. *The Adding Machine.*
Mrs. Zero. *The Adding Machine.*

www.ingramcontent.com/pod-product-compliance
Lightning Source LLC
Chambersburg PA
CBHW020628230426
43665CB00008B/87